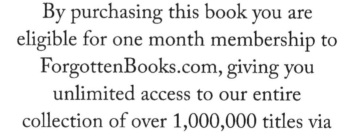

ISBN 978-0-267-53692-4
PIBN 10489396

THE HILL-TOP.
POLAND SPRING.

VOL. I.   SUNDAY MORNING, JULY 8, 1894.   No. 1.

Facts and Fancies at Poland Spring.

THE best of growing young again is that you have previously learned how not to grow old. Sometimes the world swings the other way, and you are willing to declare that to-morrow is week before last. Helpless acquiescence in the esteemed " inevitable " becomes nonsense, when, in new places, you become young again. Then is when days develop longitudinally, and morning hours become full of the peace of ancient days and twilights are long-drawn happiness like the twilights of youth. Given new youth out of that Eternal Fountain that was a wild goose chase by our great, great grandfathers, and now-a-days we would all know how to hold back the hours and keep the crickets from ever again chirruping the autumn.

Years ago, say forty, before any of us (especially the lady readers of THE HILL-TOP) were born, some ancient shepherd of the Rickers lay in the long grasses of the hill and gazed up and saw the clouds, and he swore (legally) that these clouds were pure Poland clouds and that these waters were the only pure Poland waters, and these grasses were full of the dew of youth, and he decreed a pleasure-palace as did Kubla

Khan, and the aforesaid shepherd, it may be believed, tuned his pipes and sang then the first dithyramb to Poland Spring of which we fancy this is the latest stanza, and blessed of men is the fact that all of them are true.

* * * *

I like a hill-top. It is first essential that man be up or down—up on the mount or down by the sea. Give us the grand solemnity of that, or the perfect peace of this. Man was blessed at the sea and transfigured on the mount. On Ricker Hill, daily, is there transformation if not transfiguration. Place your face to the west and love the Lord. Then drink Poland water. Then contemplate Heaven, descended on earth, and listen to the low, sweet communings of Earth and Sky, the droning sounds of Peace and the laughter of happy human souls, and then I should solemnly advise you to drink more Poland water. It will clear your mind of any of the distorted fancies which this conversation with you may engender.

To be didactic is to say that Poland Spring, whose portrait is herewith, is lovelier far than any other spot on earth, in summer. I have fancied this hill a dome rimmed with lakes set in a valley so wide and far-stretching that its sides seem only the canvas for the sky to paint its pictures on. We sit on the veranda at sunset. The winds stir oaks and maples in the groves that are near by and that vitalize the air. The broad verandas, over half a mile in length, are filled with guests. The lights twinkle in the corridors, within, and along the polished floor. The music comes in occasional bursts of melody. The day dies down at our feet, first on the distant lakes, then on the tufted lawn, where the clover blossoms scent the air. The high urns full of flowers become spectral, the fountains are mist-wraiths, and the latest coach tools home with sound of the horn. Night comes placidly at the New England countryside. Here, panoramic displays are, however, the feature. For while night glides up swiftly from the lakes to our feet, it creeps slowly away from the lakes up the long slope on the other side, and dies at last on the mountains of the New Hampshire range,

fading crimson on the crest of Mount Washington.

* * * *

Later the hotel parlors and amusement rooms fill up ; the physical splendor of handsome women dominates the place. You wander about from room to room ; from whist party to whist party ; from table to table ; from corridor to music room ; from group to group. You hear much of the same thing—the happenings of the day, the thousand little incidents of contented people, the good stories that come with good spirits. You are dominated by a placid sense of luxury and comfort and refinement. You wonder whether the world really grows old when you feel more elastic and more youthful each morning and more restful each night.

You wonder how perfect the discipline that maintains, when your wants are supplied so graciously and even are foreseen. If the backlog burns through in the blazing arch of the fireplace, where the cool airs of evening are tempered gratefully, you marvel at the watchfulness that never fails to supply another. Well ! "It is," as they say here, "only what you may expect." Then methinks people's rough edges wear off here. One never gets real cross or real sticky and uncomfortable. Even a high dickey stands up for its rights, and Poland water, judiciously used, will break even a domestic jar. If humanity mellows on the Hill-Top it comes mighty near the transfiguration that we prophesy.

* * * *

The Poland Spring House was erected in 1876, remodeled in 1881, enlarged in 1887 and 1889, and enlarged again to its present size in 1893. It sets 800 feet above the sea and fences in the sky and air instead of fencing it out. It is a noble building as our photographic reproduction shows, and is just in its infancy, provided it escapes the onslaught of the excursionist and the railway, as no doubt it will. Its isolation is perfect—the isolation consistent with a welcome to all good people who come beneath its rooftree. Fancies at Poland stretch far away into the future when all the world will drink its water and be healed. The youth of Poland is still with it and it will never grow old.

Bubbles.

They had flirted, a couple of weeks or so,
    The youth and the maiden shy;
But the time had arrived for him to go
    And he came to say good-bye;
And he said, " Ere we part you will give
        me a kiss ?
    Refuse not, I pray, the boon,
For I should like to remember this
    As a sort of souvenir spoon."

Good morning.

Welcome to " Bonny Poland."

Regular Poland weather.

Who said the seats in Lovers' Lane should be called souvenir spoon-holders?

Rev. Fr. Walsh of the Cathedral, Boston, is drinking the waters.

Did you view the fire-works in Lewiston from the verandas on Wednesday evening?

If you would be a Sandow or a Samson you should play athletic pool. If you don't know the game, George Baker will teach you.

Mr. A. H. Soden, of Boston, and party arrived on Thursday. Mr. Soden is the well-known base-ball magnate of the Hub.

Mr. J. A. Nutter, the popular manager of the Reynolds Hotel, Boston, is at the Poland Spring House for the season.

Jolly Harry Ziegler of Philadelphia and wife arrived on Monday. Mr. Ziegler has made Poland his summer home for a number of seasons.

These breezy mornings are just the time for a jolly crowd to make up a sailing party on the yacht "Emily."

As Driver Doble was coming up from Danville Junction about seven o'clock, Sunday evening, a deer ran out of the woods not a rod ahead of his team. THE HILL-TOP vouches for the truth of this story.

The Amusement Triumvirate, Messrs. Sawyer, Ziegler, and Rogers, have done lots of hustling the past week, and as a result the treasury contains the net sum of $300.00. Have you subscribed yet? If not, do so at once, as the object is a worthy one.

Mr. F. E. Dorsey as whip, tooled the following party of base-ball enthusiasts to Lewiston, Saturday, June 29th, on the new Poland Brake: Mr. and Mrs. Salsbury, Chicago; Miss Helen Stinson of Philadelphia; Miss Borme, of Paris, France; Mrs. Geo. F. Baker, Mrs. Foster, and Mr. Nutter, all of Boston, and Miss DeLima of New York.

On Monday next the new steam launch will be shipped from Boston, where it has just been completed by the Shipman Engine Company. Moonlight parties on the lake will then be in order.

On Saturday afternoon, June 29th, a party composed of Messrs. Barnott of Boston, Taylor of Brooklyn, Anderson of New York, Sawyer of Pittsburg, Morrison of Boston, Barrou of Boston, and Rev. Fr. Walsh of Boston drove to Lewiston to witness the Portland-Lewiston base-ball game.

The champion fisherman on the Hill is Mr. J. B. Sawyer of Pittsburg. Mr. Sawyer is an earnest disciple of Isaak Walton, and brings home numerous fine specimens of the finny tribe. But when it comes to telling fish stories, however, Mr. Sawyer is clearly outclassed by a number of gentlemen whose names THE HILL-TOP forbears mentioning.

Mr. Frank Chaffin makes trips to Lewiston daily. Any orders left at the office will be carefully attended to. THE HILL-TOP would call the attention of its readers to our advertisers, who are the most reliable firms in the twin cities. If you want any goods in their line Mr. Chaffin will get them for you and we guarantee satisfaction.

POLAND SPRING LIVERY

Which is connected with the Poland Spring Hotels is one of the largest and best equipped hotel stables in the country. . . . . .

POLAND SPRING BRAKE

Is a novel of beauty and comfort combined, and a visit to Poland without having enjoyed a ride on the same, is a failure—Bear in mind that we employ none but . . .

EXPERIENCED DRIVERS

Who are acquainted with the roads and the different points of interest.

All parties desiring turnouts, should notify the Clerk at the Office, early to insure accommodation.

POLAND SPRING LIVERY.

H. T. JORDAN,   } Editors.
W. D. FREEMAN, }

PUBLISHED EVERY SUNDAY MORNING DURING THE MONTHS
OF JULY, AUGUST AND SEPTEMBER, IN THE INTERESTS OF

POLAND   SPRING   AND   ITS   VISITORS.

All contributions relative to the guests of Poland Spring will
be thankfully received.
To insure publication, all communications should reach the
editors not later than Thursday preceding day of issue.
Address,
            EDITORS " HILL-TOP,"
                  Poland Spring House,
                        South Poland, Maine.

PRINTED AT JOURNAL OFFICE, LEWISTON.

Sunday, July 8, 1894.

Editorial.

WITH this issue of THE HILL-TOP the
editors enter the field of journalism, with
an illustrated weekly paper, published in
the interests of the Poland Spring Hotels and
their visitors. We realize the responsibility
devolving upon us as editors of the same, but
by dint of hard, faithful, conscientious work, we
hope to overcome all difficulties and present a
bright, clean, newsy, readable publication every
Sunday morning; one that will be worthy of
representing one of the grandest, most magnificent and liberally managed hotel resorts in the
country.

Among the special features of THE HILL-TOP
will be a regular illustrated article on some point
of interest about Ricker Hill, or in the vicinity,
written by the editors or our contributors. All
dances, hops, and germans; boating, fishing,
and riding parties; base-ball games, card parties,
entertainments, etc., will be given full reports,
and in fact everything of interest to the friends
of fair Poland will be given due space.

We ask the co-operation of our friends in contributing to our columns, which will be ever open
to them. We wish THE HILL-TOP to be considered as a medium of information concerning our
guests, so, therefore, we shall always be pleased
to receive short notes for our " Bubble " column.

We would thank those who, by their encouraging words, have aided us in our efforts, and
we trust that we may ever merit their confidence
and friendship.

Our Orchestra.

MUSIC lovers from any of the large cities
will feel well acquainted with our musicians this season. The music is furnished by Kuntz's Orchestra, of Boston.
The leader, Mr. Kuntz, will be pleasantly remembered as the first violinist of the orchestra in '92
by those who had the good fortune to hear his
well-appreciated violin solos.

Mr. Kuntz's organization numbers seven of
the leading musicians of the famous Boston
Symphony Orchestra, and we may congratulate
ourselves on having a small symphony orchestra
of our own. The first concert of the season was
rendered on Wednesday, July 4th, and was well
appreciated. The personnel this season is as
follows : Violins, Daniel Kuntz, Johann Michael ;
'cello, E. Loeffler ; base, E. Golde ; flute, Gus-
tave Krobe ; cornet, H. Burkhardt ; piano,
Max Zach.

The concert programme, Sunday, July 8th,
1894, in Music Hall, at 3.30 P.M., will be as
follows :

1. March from Suite.	Lachner.
2. Overture—Maritana.	Wallace.
3. Lug der Frauen—Lohengrin.	Wagner.
4. Fleur D'Antonne—Gavotte.	G. Marie.
5. Prize Song from Meistersinger.	Wagner.
6. Andante from Surprise Symphony.	Haydn.
7. La Colombe.	Gounod.
8. Swedish Wedding March.	Soedermann.

Coming Events.

Wednesday, July 11th—Base-ball, Poland Spring vs. Saco,
    at 3.30 P.M.
Friday, July 13th, 8 P.M.—Progressive Euchre in Amuse-
    ment Room.
Saturday, July 14, 3.30 P.M.—Base-ball, Poland Spring vs.
    Lisbon Falls.
Saturday, July 14, 8.30 P.M.—Full-Dress Hop, Music Hall.

Mansion House to Poland Spring House, . .	1445 feet.
Mansion House to Spring, ...	2790 "
Poland Spring House to Spring, ...	1066 "
Poland Spring House, North-west Front, . .	275 "
Poland Spring House, South-west Front, . .	340 "
Total length of Piazzas, including Covered Walk	
to end of Annex, ...	1100 "

The Studio.

ONE of the most noticeable of the many improvements since last season is the new photographic studio, which will be ready for occupancy by the middle of the present month. The building is an exceedingly handsome specimen of Queen Anne architecture, situated just beyond the Casino, and connected with it by a broad covered veranda.

Entering we find on the first floor a spacious reception room. The room is well lighted, and will contain a tasty fire-place and mantel. From the reception room we pass into the studio proper. There is not a finer room of its kind in New England. Thirty feet square and twenty-five feet high, it is lighted by a window ten by fourteen feet, and a sky-light fourteen feet by fourteen. Several photographers are in correspondence with the proprietors, and as soon as ready the studio will be occupied by a first-class artist. Adjacent to this room are the requisite dark and finishing rooms.

On this floor also are three dark rooms for the exclusive use of amateur photographers. These are models of their kind, and it is unnecessary to say that the thoughtfulness of the proprietors will be appreciated.

Coming back to our starting point we ascend the broad staircase to the second story. This staircase is a handsome one, by the way, built of birch and finished in the natural color of the wood.

The second floor contains the club-room and four sleeping rooms. The club-room, which is in the south-west corner of the building, is a large apartment, twenty by twenty-seven feet. Finished in hard wood, lighted by a magnificent bay window, and containing a spacious fire-place, it makes a pleasant place for a social game of cards, a comfortable smoke, or an hour's loafing. The whole building is to be lighted by both gas and electricity; contains dressing and toilet rooms; in short, is to be just such a building as the proprietors would be expected to put up. The architect is the popular head carpenter, Mr. Forest Walker.

The Amusement Fund.

DOUBTLESS you have had your attention called to a paper with the above heading which hangs near the news counter. If you are an old sojourner at Poland you understand what it means. If not, it is necessary that you should.

For a number of seasons past the guests on Ricker Hill have enjoyed numerous pleasing entertainments in Music Hall. Those who are partial to out-door sports have been able to witness ball games weekly, in which the home team, a salaried organization by the way, have won glory for themselves and their friends by their skillful work.

All these attractions cost money, but, contrary to the custom of other summer houses, the hat is never passed to obtain funds for their support.

All the expenses have been paid from the treasury of the Amusement Fund, which fund has been made up by voluntary subscriptions from the guests. Last season the amount reached the grand total of $1,200.00. By this money the ball team was supported, and the expenses of the games paid. Every week during the summer there were one or more entertainments, musical, literary, etc., by as good talent as money could procure. Among the organizations here last season may be named the Brown University Glee Club, the Tufts Glee Club, and the Temple Quartette of Boston.

This season a ball team is here which promises to be the strongest hotel nine in the country. Already a number of fine entertainments are booked for Music Hall, and the "triumvirate," Messrs. Sawyer, Ziegler, and Rogers are corresponding with other parties. It is proposed to have a better class of entertainments this year than ever before.

Doubtless you would like to be identified with the cause. If so, you will find Mr. Mullan, of the office force, ready to receive your contribution.

STAGES.

DEPART.

	M. H.	P. S. H.
For Portland and Boston, ...	6.25 A.M.	6.30 A.M.
Lewiston and Farmington, . .	8.25 A.M.	8.30 A.M.
Portland and Boston, ...	9.25 A.M.	9.30 A.M.
Lewiston and Bar Harbor, . .	10.25 A.M.	10.30 A.M.
Lewiston and Bangor, ...	12.45 P.M.	1 P.M.
Portland and Boston, ...	3.25 P.M.	3.30 P.M.

ARRIVE.

	M. H.	P. S. H.
From the West, ...	10.30 A.M.	10.35 A.M.
From the East, ...	1 P.M.	1.05 P.M.
From the West, ...	3.30 P.M.	3.35 P.M.
" " "	7.30 P.M.	7.35 P.M.

MAILS.

CLOSE.

Poland Spring House.	Mansion House.
5.45 A.M.	6 A.M.
8.45 A.M.	9 A.M.
2.45 P.M.	3 P.M.

ARRIVE.

10 A.M.	9.30 A.M.
1.30 P.M.	1 P.M.
4.30 P.M.	4 P.M.
8 P.M.	7.45 P.M.

Guests.

POLAND SPRING HOUSE.

Anderson, Mrs. H. E., Katonah, N. Y.; Anderson, J. M. and wife, Mt. Vernon.

Baker, Geo. F. and wife, Hyannis; Bowker, Mrs. J. H., Brooklyn; Bourne, Geo. T. and wife, Bourne, Miss E., New York; Billings, Mrs. H., Billings, Miss, Cincinnati; Bigelow, W. A., New York; Babcock, Mrs. B., Babcock, Miss C. L., New York; Bishop, Mrs. R. R., Boston; Bailey, Isaac H., Boston; Booth, R. T., New York; Bolster, C. H., Bolster, Mrs. C. H., Bolster, Grace N., Chicago.

Cummings, A. B., Portland; Chipman, Mrs. W. R., Chelsea; Colby, Mrs. M. D., Brooklyn; Coleman, Geo. W. and wife, Boston; Crossett, L. A. and wife, Crossett, Miss Ruth, Boston; Chase, Geo. C. and wife, Chase, Miss New York; Churchill, Miss Lida, Boston; Corbin, C. C. and wife, Webster, Mass.; Caldwell, W. D., Chicago, DeLima, Mrs. D. H., DeLima, Miss, DeLima, Edward, New York; Deleuw, Duncan, Ala.; Dibble, Henry and wife, Chicago; Denny, Wm. G. and wife, Portland; Dickinson, Mrs. N. C., New York; D'Avignon, Mrs. F. L., Boston; DuBois, D. B., Boston.

Edgar, Mrs. F., Edgar, Miss, Montreal.

Foster, Mr. A. S. and wife, Boston; Fish, Miss E. N., Boston.

Goodrich, Mrs. I. H., Boston; Goddard, Wm. and wife, R. I.; Griffin, Benj. and wife, Griffin, Miss, Griffin, Cecil, New York; Gray, Joseph H. and wife, Gray, Miss Bessie, Boston.

Helsey, Randolph and wife, Montreal; Hoffman, Mrs. F. G., New York; Hammond, H. A., Hammond, C. T., Springfield; Hawes, Mrs. R. L., Boston; Helsey, Miss E., Miss Florence, Montreal; Hurlbutt, L. and wife, Brooklyn; Hoagland, Hudson and wife, New York; Huntington, Charles P., N. Y.

Jacoby, Chas. and wife, New York.

Little, Amos R. and wife, Philadelphia; Lang, M. C., Augusta; Morrison, C. E., Boston; Mosher, Mrs. H. A., Mosher, Miss E. H., Mosher, A. G., New York; Maginnis, Mrs. J. H., Maginnis, Mrs. M. J., Maginnis, John H., Maginnis, J. A., New Orleans; McNeal, Miss, New York; Mead, Mrs. J. A., Watertown; Mott, Wm. F., Mott, Mrs. Henry F., Mott, Miss, Tom's River, N. J.; Meinhard, Mrs. H., Meinhard, Miss M., Meinhard, Miss O., New York.

Nuttel, J. A., Boston; Noble, Mrs. Harriet, Portland.

Polhemus, H. D. and wife, Brooklyn; Pomery, Miss A. J., New York; Peterson, Dr. Wm. and wife, Peterson, Miss Florence, Alice and May, New York; Peters, Wm. C., Peters, Ed. D., Boston; Peabody, Charles A. and wife, New York.

Rogers, G. A. and wife, Rogers, Master E., New York; Rogers, Mrs. L. W., Boston; Richardson, Mrs. A. E., Waltham; Rogers, H. A. and wife, Rogers, Allan M., New York; Robinson, Mrs. R. T., West Newton, Mass.

Sawyer, J. B., Pittsburgh; Shipman, Henry and wife, New York; Smith, Mrs. Phineas, Smith, Miss, Smith, Miss Bertha, Smith, Chas. J. and wife, Smith, Nathaniel H., New York; Simms, W. B., New York; Stinson, S. B. and wife, Stinson, Miss Helen, Miss Florence, Stian, Thos. P. and wife, Baltimore; Sherburne, R. and wife, Boston; Salsbury, Warren and wife, Chicago; Shepard, Mrs. T. P., Providence; Skinner, Wm., Miss Katherine, Holyoke; Sweetland, Ralph, Boston; Smith, Mrs. Morgan, New York; Sanbloux, Gust., New York; Soden, A. H., Boston.

Taylor, F. E. and wife, Brooklyn; Tuttle, H. E., New York; Thompson, Mrs. J. B., New York; Tompkins, Mrs. O., Boston; Thomas, Elias and wife, Portland; Travelli, Charles I. and wife, Pittsburgh, Pa.

Weston, W. H. and wife, Boston; Walsh, N. R., Boston; Wescott, Geo. P. and wife, Portland; Wheeler, Mrs. W. H., Boston; Williamson, Mrs. C., Williamson, Richard, Philadelphia; Whitman, Annie S., Somerville, Mass.; Walker, Mrs. G. C., Portland.

Yates, David G., Philadelphia.

Ziegler, Harry D. and wife, Ziegler, Miss O. F., Philadelphia.

MANSION HOUSE.

Adams, Mr. and Mrs. W. S., Marlboro, N. H.; Augustin, Miss M., New Orleans, La.

Bengnor, Mrs. and son, New Orleans, La.; Barrow, J. J., Boston, Mass.; Buck, Mrs. A. E., Atlanta, Ga.

Cassady, Mr. and Mrs. C. D., Philadelphia, Pa.; Collins, Miss Gertrude, New York, N. Y.; Cobb, S. C. and wife, Cushing, Mrs. C. L., Newton-Highlands, Mass.

DeBois, Mr. B. H., New York; Davis, the Misses, Baltimore; DeWint, Mrs. M. E., New York.

Ernst, Mrs. K. M., Brooklyn, N. Y.; Sister Katharine Edith, Providence, R. I.

Filipache, Mr. F. P. and son, Mt. Vernon, N. Y.

Hale, Mr. and Mrs. Edwin, Hale, Miss Stella, Boston, Mass.; Hazen, Mrs. J. W., Cambridge, Mass.

Johns, Mr. Geo., Hazelton, Pa.

Kimball, Mrs., Marlboro, N. H.; Keene, Mr. and Mrs. S. W., Boston, Mass.

Logan, Mrs. W. T., Newton Highlands, Mass.

McFarland, Mr. and Mrs. D., McFarland, Mr., Providence, R. I.

Pierce, the Misses, Boston, Mass.; Pearson, Miss M. G., Newton, Mass.; Pulsifer, Mrs.

Rice, Mr., Rockland, N. Y.

Sturtevant, Miss A. M., Springfield, Mass.; Sanger, Irene, Milton, Mass.

VanZandt, Mr. and Mrs. P. G., Jersey City, N. J.

Woodbury, Myron, Beverly, Mass.; Wood, Mr. and Mrs. Albert, Worcester, Mass.

The other afternoon one of our best-known guests, arriving on the noon train, was very urgent that his trunks be sent away from the station as early as possible. Approaching one of the employees of the railroad he asked him to hurry them up, saying that he must have his baggage so as to dress for dinner. Gazing at the gentleman's immaculate summer suit the native drawled out: "Wal, mister, if I wore as good close as you'd I wouldn't worry about getting my dinner. I should think myself mighty lucky to git a bite with my *old* duds on."

THE HILL-TOP.

POLAND SPRING.

VOL. I.   SUNDAY MORNING, JULY 15, 1894.   No. 2.

Poland Spring in the Past.

A pleasing land of drowsyhed it was,
Of dreams that wave before the half-shut eye;
And of gay castles in the clouds that pass
Forever flushing round a summer sky;
There eke the soft delights, that witchingly
Instill a wanton sweetness through the breast,
And the calm pleasures, always hover'd nigh;
But whate'er smacked of 'noyance or unrest
Was far, far off expell'd from this delicious nest.
        THOMSON.—" The Castle of Indolence."

SUCH a pleasing land is now and has been
for many years the fair hill-side in sunny
Poland, made famous the world around by
the pure and healing flood which pours from the
cleft rock in its wooded side. That it is a castle
of indolence it would perhaps be hardly right to
say; there is too much business on the hill now
for that, but the time is not so far gone by since
the hill-top lay in sleepy quiet from year's end
to year's end, and the occasional visitor found
little to disturb his quiet meditations.

Standing at the present time on the broad
veranda of the palatial hotel, viewing on all sides
the signs of enterprise and thrift, or visiting the
bottling house below the spring and seeing the
busy workmen preparing the water for shipment
to all parts of the world, it is somewhat difficult to

realize that all this is the work of but little more than a quarter of a century. Yet so it is.

Well does the writer remember his first visit to the now-famous spot. It was all of twenty-five years ago, and Poland Spring and Poland Spring water had then but little more than a local reputation. The writer, then a small boy, drove over from Lewiston with a small party for a day's outing in the country. I remember that an important part of the equipment of the party was a number of big jugs to be filled with water and brought home, for at that time all comers were free to take away as much of the water as they desired for their own use.

The Poland Spring House was then a thing undreamed of, or at least if the present proprietors had dreamed of what was to be they had not then dared to even whisper their dreams to themselves. The Mansion House of to-day was the "Old Homestead" then, a big, roomy country tavern, to which already some seekers for health were beginning to come. There were no barreling houses, and only a rough little shed over the spring. The water then flowed from the rock and made its way down the hill-side, unchecked by the hand of man. The grove about the spring was untrimmed, grown up with underbrush, with no seats whereon the weary climber of the hill might rest, while the private way up the hill, over which there is now so much agitation, was then little more than a bridle-path through the woods. The sign at the foot of the hill, "Private Way—Dangerous," then meant something, for a rougher road and a steeper hill was not to be found in a day's journey. But the spring was there, and from that all else has come. Its waters then flowed unchecked from the solid rock, pure, sparkling, and health-giving as they had flowed from the beginning of time, and as they will doubtless continue to flow till time shall be no more.

*　*　*　*　*

The history of the Poland Spring, the wonderful curative powers of its waters, and the manner in which they came to be known is doubtless a familiar story to every summer sojourner on the hill-top. For the benefit of the poor, benighted people who have never visited the place and so are not familiar with it, a slight sketch may not be uninteresting.

History tells us that way back in 1793, Jabez Ricker with his sons, Samuel, Wentworth, and Joseph, moved to this place from Alfred. Four years later, Joseph Ricker opened the first public house, now the Mansion House. He kept it until his death in 1837, and was succeeded by his son, Hiram, who kept it until 1879, since which time the present proprietors, the three lusty sons of Hiram, have been at the helm.

The circumstances connected with the discovery of the medicinal properties of the spring were chiefly accidental. Evidences have been ploughed up from the soil in abundance to prove that the Indians visited the spring long before the advent of the white man. Wentworth Ricker, one of the sons of the original owner, while clearing the land about the spring in 1827, drank freely of the waters, and found that a disease with which he was afflicted was gradually disappearing. He never mistrusted, however, that the water had anything to do with his cure, nor did he to the day of his death.

His son, Hiram, some years later, while suffering from dyspepsia to such an extent that he could not work but only oversee the men at work near the spring, drank frequently from it, and soon found himself improving rapidly. He had faith in the water and kept drinking it until completely cured. Others in the neighborhood came to drink of the water for various troubles, and it attained quite a local celebrity. Sick cattle, also, pastured where they could drink of the water, were cured by it. It was not until 1859 that the water became known outside of the immediate locality. In that year Dr. E. Clark, of Portland, prescribed it with success for kidney troubles, and from that time to the present its use and sale has gradually increased, until to-day there is hardly a country on the globe to which it is not sent.

*　*　*　*　*

If you ask what there is about Poland water to make it different from and better than all other waters, then must the answer be, "that is what no feller can find out." Chemical analysis, it is true, can tell its composition, but that does not tell the story. Other waters there are that show chemical analysis almost identical with it, but they do not have the mystic properties of the Poland. Some say its virtue lies in its absolute purity, but again the chemist says that other waters are equally pure so far as chemical elements are concerned, so this too fails to explain.

But whatever it may be, certain it is that in the crystal depths of the stream which flows from the gneiss and mica schists of the hill-top lurks an element placed there by the benign Creator of all things as a boon to suffering humanity. Moral,—drink Poland water.

William Goddard and wife, Providence, R. I., are here for a month. Mr. Goddard is a large manufacturer of cotton goods in that city.

Mr. A. H. Soden, the Boston Base-Ball Club magnate, who is spending his vacation at the Poland Spring House, is an enthusiastic devotee to bass fishing. Helgamite come nigh, but they must have 'em.

Bubbles.

T₁e "Poland" is a beauty.

T₁e Amusement Fund is g₁owing.

C₁ibbage is t₁e game at t₁e Mansion House.

C₁oquet is fast becoming a ve₁y popula₁ game at Poland.

T₁e bowling alley was occupied Monday by t₁e Mansion House guests.

Mr. & Mrs. Nelson Ba₁tlett, of Boston, we₁e up f₁om Po₁tland, Wednesday, to ₁emain at t₁e la₁ge ₁ouse fo₁ t₁e season.

Mr. C. E. Mo₁₁ison, of Boston, is paying t₁e Poland Sp₁ing House his annual visit. Mr. Mo₁₁ison has his own p₁ivate team wit₁ him, and a ve₁y p₁etty ₁itc₁-up it is, too.

Mr. and Mrs. Lewis A. Gosset, of Boston, accompanied by Miss Rut₁ L. Gosset, a₁e at t₁e la₁ge ₁ouse fo₁ a mont₁. Mr. Gosset is a p₁om-inent boot and s₁oe deale₁ of t₁e Hub.

Mr. and Mrs. Geo₁ge T. Bou₁ne and Miss E. E. Bou₁ne, of New Yo₁k City, a₁e ₁e₁e on t₁ei₁ annual visit. Mr. Bou₁ne is a ₁eti₁ed newspape₁ man, of about fifty yea₁s' expe₁ience.

T₁e eve₁-genial Ha₁₁y Z. celeb₁ated his eig₁ty-sevent₁ bi₁t₁day in Room 146, Wednesday, at ₁ig₁ noon, by a small collation and ₁ef₁es₁ments. About twenty of his many f₁iends gat₁e₁ed to pay t₁ei₁ ₁espects.

Dr. G. E. F₁eeman and wife, of B₁ockton, Mass., a₁e ₁e₁e fo₁ a s₁o₁t stay. T₁e Docto₁ b₁ings wit₁ him one of t₁e ₁andsomest t₁aps seen at Poland fo₁ many yea₁s. T₁e ₁o₁ses a₁e beautiful so₁₁els and a₁e bot₁ able to s₁ow good speed, single o₁ toget₁e₁.

Mr. and Mrs. C. H. Bolste₁, wit₁ t₁ei₁ daug₁te₁, G₁ace N. Bolste₁, of C₁icago, a₁e enjoying t₁e cool b₁eezes of Rieke₁ Hill, domi-ciled in t₁e Poland Sp₁ing House. Mr. Bolste₁ is t₁e manage₁ of t₁e fancy g₁oce₁y depa₁tment of Sp₁ague, Wa₁ne₁ & Co., t₁e la₁gest g₁oce₁y conce₁n in t₁e West.

Miss Kate I₁wing Wheelock, w₁om "Caven-dis₁" styles as t₁e "W₁ist Queen," a₁₁ived at t₁e Poland Sp₁ing House T₁u₁sday, fo₁ a mont₁'s vacation. Miss W₁eelock has t₁e ₁ono₁ of being t₁e only woman playe₁ to be admitted a membe₁ of t₁e Ame₁ican W₁ist League, and of the B₁ooklyn W₁ist Club. She was also t₁e only woman playing in t₁e Annual Cong₁ess last yea₁, in C₁icago. Miss W₁eelock is a c₁a₁m-ing little lady, and has a ₁ost of f₁iends at Poland.

T₁e Amusement Fund is al₁eady swelled to ove₁ $400.

Coming Events.

S₁nday, July 15t₁ — Conce₁t, Music Hall, 3.30 P.M. Song Se₁vice, 8 P.M.

Tuesday, July 17th — Base-ball, Poland Sp₁ing vs. Lew-iston League, 3 P.M. K₁iege₁, t₁e Magician, Music Hall, 8 P.M.

F₁iday, July 20th — P₁og₁essive Euc₁₁e, Amusement Room, 8 P.M.

Satu₁day, July 21 — Base-ball, Poland Sp₁ing vs. Po₁t-land, 3 P.M. Full-D₁ess Hop, Music Hall, 8 P.M.

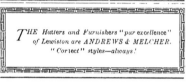

H. T. JORDAN, } EDITORS.
W. D. FREEMAN, }

PUBLISHED EVERY SUNDAY MORNING DURING THE MONTHS
OF JULY, AUGUST AND SEPTEMBER, IN THE INTERESTS OF

POLAND SPRING AND ITS VISITORS.

All contributions relative to the guests of Poland Spring will
be thankfully received.
To insure publication, all communications should reach the
editors not later than Thursday preceding day of issue.
Address,
EDITORS "HILL-TOP,"
Poland Spring House,
South Poland, Maine.

PRINTED AT JOURNAL OFFICE, LEWISTON.

Sunday, July 15, 1894.

Editorial.

WHAT did you think of the first issue of THE
HILL-TOP? Did you send a copy to all
your friends in order that they might enjoy
the reports of some of the pleasures you are
enjoying at Poland?

" Years may come
And years may go,
But I go on forever."

WELL might the bard sing this of " Fair
Poland." Nestled, as it is, amongst the
grandest, most beautiful, and soul-inspir-
ing scenery in all picturesque New England, it
can appropriately be called " Nature's Paradise."
Nature has done much for this famous place, it
is true, but what it has failed to do the enterprising proprietors have supplemented, so at this
day the many claims of Poland Spring have
been echoed and re-echoed around the whole
world. Thousands are loud and voluminous in
their praises of the palatial hostelries which
adorn Ricker Hill, but tens and hundreds of
thousands thank God and Poland Water for their

own lives and the lives of their beloved ones.
The beautiful, sparkling, crystal-like water which
bubbles forth from solid ledges of vast magnitude, at the rate of eight gallons per minute, is
the purest and best beverage on earth, and has
given itself a world-wide fame because of its
many miraculous cures.

Never in the history of the Spring has so
much water been shipped to distant parts as at
present. And the sumptuous hotels which serve
to enhance the beauty of Ricker Hill, are enjoying unprecedented success.

THE editors of THE HILL-TOP feel very much
pleased at the reception the people gave us
on our first issue. The many difficulties
incident to a new publication are not a few, but
we hope to overcome them soon, and present
you every Sunday morning with a paper which
will be a credit to the interests it represents.
With this end in view, kind friends, we further
bespeak the encouragement and patronage which
we trust our efforts may merit.

Music.

Miss DeLima and Miss Bourne, of New
York, are two of the best vocalists at the Poland
Spring House.

The programme for the concert in Music Hall
at 3.30 P.M. Sunday, July 15th, is as follows :

1. Coronation March.		Meyerbeet.
2. Overture—Les Noces de Figaro.		Mozart.
3. { a. Melodrama de Piccolino.		
{ b. Fly Menuet.	E. Gitel and A. Czibulka.	
4. Selection—Lohengrin.		R. Wagner.
5. { a. Sonntagsruhe.		DeWitt.
{ b. Menuet.		Boccherini.
6. Andalouse et Aubade.		Massenet.
7. Selection—Walküre.		Wagner.

Steam Launch.

THAT natty little steam launch, " The
Poland," which will ply the waters of
Upper and Middle Range Lakes this summer, for the pleasure of the guests of the
two houses, has arrived and is being put into
condition for service. The Shipman Engine
Company of Boston are the builders, and a
substantial boat, capable of carrying twenty
passengers, have they furnished us. The length
of " The Poland" over all is thirty feet. The
motive power will be supplied by the use of oil.
The furnishings are all in the natural wood. It
is hoped " The Poland " may be ready for use by
the first of next week.

Base-Ball.

HE base-ball season opened in an exceedingly business-like way on Saturday, July 7th. The home team showed that they are worthy of wearing the Poland uniform, and undoubtedly will prove themselves to be the best nine we have had here.

POLANDS.

	A.B.	B.H.	P.O.	A.	E.
Wakefield,	4	2	0	1	1
Sockelexis,	5	2	0	0	0
Hull,	6	1	11	0	0
Lawson,	5	3	0	14	1
Sykes,	4	1	0	2	0
Mullen,	4	0	0	0	0
Harris,	4	3	11	2	1
Pulsifer,	5	0	2	2	0
Haskell,	5	0	0	0	0
Totals,	47	12	24	21	3

NEW AUBURNS.

	A.B.	B.H.	P.O.	A.	E.
Campbell,	4	2	1	0	0
Pulsifer,	4	0	9	0	1
Slattery,	3	2	4	3	1
Penley,	3	0	2	1	1
Martin,	4	0	1	0	1
Casey,	3	0	6	3	0
Brown,	3	0	2	6	0
Colby,	3	0	2	1	0
Leonard,	3	0	0	0	2
Totals,	30	4	27	14	6

Innings,	1	2	3	4	5	6	7	8	9	
Polands,	3	0	2	0	0	0	3	3	0—11
New Auburns,	0	0	0	0	0	0	0	1	0— 1

Runs made—by Wakefield 3, Sockelexis 2, Hull 1, Lawson 2, Sykes 2, Harris 1, Campbell 1. Earned runs—Polands 5, Auburns 0. Two-base hit—Lawson. Three-base hits—Sockelexis, Sykes. Stolen bases—Wakefield 3, Sockelexis 2, Sykes 1, Harris 2, Campbell 1, Slattery 1, Penley 1. Base on balls—Wakefield 2, Sockelexis 1, Mullen 1, Harris 1, Slattery 1, Penley 2. Struck out—by Lawson 9, by Brown 5. Passed balls—by Casey 4, by Harris 1. Time—1h. 50m. Umpire—Pulsifer.

The game Wednesday with the Sacos was a repetition of Saturday's. Plaisted arrived on Tuesday and was an enigma to the visitors.

The Sacos are a good fielding team and play lively ball, but they are weak in batting, while our boys bat like fiends.

The features of the game Wednesday were the hitting of Lawson and Sockelexis and a remarkable catch by McIlwain. The score:

POLAND SPRING.

	A.B.	B.H.	P.O.	A.	E.
Lawson, m.,	4	2	3	0	0
Sykes, s.s., l.,	5	2	5	2	3
Pulsifer, 3, s.s.,	5	2	1	2	0
Hull, 1.,	4	2	4	0	1
Sockelexis, l., 3,	5	2	1	0	0
Plaisted, p.,	4	1	0	2	2
Harris, c.,	3	2	10	0	1
Haskell 2,	4	2	3	0	2
Holmes, r.,	5	1	0	0	0
Totals,	39	16	27	6	9

SACO.

	A.B.	B.H.	P.O.	A.	E.
Dockerty, l.,	5	1	2	0	0
County, 3,	3	0	3	6	1
Wakefield, 1,	5	1	14	3	0
Murphy, s.,	5	0	0	1	0
Burns, m.,	5	0	1	0	0
Libby, c.,	4	1	1	3	0
Ladd, p.,	5	1	0	3	2
McIlwain, 2,	4	0	4	4	1
Preble, r.,	4	1	2	0	0
Totals,	40	5	27	20	4

Innings,	1	2	3	4	5	6	7	8	9	
Poland Spring,	1	2	3	1	6	0	0	2	0—15
Saco,	0	0	0	0	0	3	1	1	0— 5

Runs made—by Lawson 2, Sykes 2, Pulsifer 3, Hull, Sockelexis 2, Plaisted 2, Harris, Haskell, Holmes. Struck out—by Plaisted 10, by Ladd 2. Earned runs—Poland Spring 6. Two-base hits—Sykes, Pulsifer, Haskell, Preble. Three-base hits—Lawson 2, Ladd. Home run—Sockelexis. Base on balls—by Plaisted, County; by Ladd, Harris and Plaisted. Wild pitches—Plaisted. Passed balls—Harris, Libby 2. Time—2h. 30m. Umpire—Pulsifer.

Progressive Euchre.

HE first progressive euchre party of the season, which came off last Friday evening, was a most successful and enjoyable affair.

At eight o'clock play was commenced with ten tables filled, and continued until ten, when the lucky prize winners were announced. The first prize for the ladies, a handsome linen square, was awarded to Mrs. J. H. Maginnis, of New Orleans. Mrs. Maginnis easily led all her rivals, making thirteen points out of a possible sixteen. Mrs. A. S. Foster, of Boston, won the second prize, a souvenir card-case. Three ladies were tied for this prize, but Mrs. Foster was fortunate enough to turn an ace in cutting, and was, accordingly, given the trophy.

The gentlemen were far behind the ladies in the number of points scored, ten being the highest number. Five had that number of punches on their cards, and accordingly were obliged to cut to settle the matter. Mr. —— Emerson, of Boston, turning an ace, was made the recipient of a handsome and serviceable umbrella, the gentlemen's first prize. Miss —— Grant, of New York, who assumed the character of a gentleman for the nonce, followed with a queen, and was awarded an ash tray. Mr. J. B. Sawyer, of Pittsburg, had a mistaken idea of the game, or else was absent-minded, for he managed to score but three points during the entire evening. That he might be in better condition for the next evening, he was presented a bottle of Poland water, profusely decorated.

Mrs. George F. Baker, of Boston, who made the arrangement for the party, received many congratulations upon its success, and the beauty of the prizes, which were of her selection.

Guests.

POLAND SPRING HOUSE.

Ames, Oakes A.,	North Easton, Mass.
Brinton, Mrs. J. P.,	Philadelphia, Penn.
Brinton, Miss,	Philadelphia, Penn.
Ballington, Prof. L. L.,	Franklin, Mass.
Ballington, Mrs. L. L.,	Franklin, Mass.
Boswoith, C. H.,	North Conway, N. H.
Burton, T. M. and wife,	New York.
Billson, William W.,	Duluth, Mich.
Blight, H. O. and wife,	Cambridge.
Bartlett, Nelson and wife,	Boston.
Bartlett, F. J.,	Boston.
Cassidy, E. E. and wife,	Jersey City.
Carlisle, Mrs. J. T.,	Brooklyn.
Carlisle, Miss,	Brooklyn.
Cook, C. S. and wife,	Portland.
Corby, H. and wife,	Belleville, Col.
Colby, Miss T. M.,	Belleville, Col.
Colby, Miss H. R.,	Belleville, Col.
Colby, Miss A. M.,	Belleville, Col.
Clemens, Cameron,	Boston.
Clemens, Mrs. Cameron,	Boston.
Denny, B. N.,	Northampton.
Diaper, Mrs. J. P.,	Boston.
DeLeuw, M. R. and wife,	New York.
Douglas, Albert and wife,	Chillicothe, O.
Danielson, J. DeFrost,	Providence.
Deape, Miss,	Portland.
Earle, Mrs. W. E.,	Washington.
Eldridge, Mrs. E.,	New York.
Eddy, J. H. and wife,	New Britain, Ct.
Eddy, Miss Bessie M.,	New Britain, Ct.
Freeman, Dr. G. E. and wife,	Brockton.
Fernald, George H.,	Boston.
Fessenden, Mrs. J. D.,	New York.
Fallon, W.,	Lewiston.
Ferland, Mrs. M. C.,	New York.
Fynes, M. Louisa,	Allston.
Fassett, Miss,	Portland, Me.
Graham, William and wife,	Philadelphia.
Graham, Miss,	Philadelphia.
Green, Benjamin and wife,	Brunswick, Me.
Green, George B.,	New York.
Green, Miss Dessie,	New York.
Garm, Joseph A.,	Boston.
Hall, Lewis and wife,	Cambridge.
Harvey, Mrs.,	Cambridge.
Haddock, Miss M. R.	New York.
Huestic, T.,	New York.
Hammond, T. W.,	Worcester, Mass.
Hammond, L. W.,	Worcester, Mass.
Jarvis, R. S.,	Brooklyn.
Jewett, Fred J.,	Marlboro. Mass.
Jones, T. B. and wife,	Chelsea.
Kemble, J. W. and wife,	Philadelphia.
Kemble, Miss Lizzie,	Philadelphia.
Kemble, T. W.,	Philadelphia.
Kemble, Virginia,	Philadelphia.
Kiddel, F. H.,	Boston.
Keith, Mr. and Mrs. B. J.,	Brookline.
Keith, A. Paul,	Brookline.
Licke, Mrs.,	Atlanta.
Lothrop, Cyrus,	North Easton, Mass.
Lovegrove, C. E.,	Northampton.
Lawrence, W. J. and wife,	Brooklyn.
Loring, G. W.,	Boston.
Little, Miss,	Portland.
Murray, Mrs. A.,	Washington.
Morrison, D. J.,	Savannah.
Moulton, Mrs. B. P.,	Rosemont, Pa.
Marston, A. T.,	Boston.

Mackay, Mrs. E. A.,	St. Louis.
Martin, Nelson L.,	Boston.
Moulton, B. C. and wife,	Boston.
McCobb, Mrs.,	Portland.
McCobb, Miss,	Portland.
Ordway, John A.,	Boston.
Phipps, William,	Boston.
Pullen, E. H. and wife,	New York.
Pettus, William H. H.,	St. Louis.
Ray, Joseph G. and wife,	Franklin, Mass.
Ray, Miss Lydia P.,	Franklin, Mass.
Robinson, Mrs.,	Dorchester.
Soden, A. H.,	Boston.
Supplee, Miss,	Philadelphia.
Steigewalt, W. H. and wife,	Philadelphia.
Steigewalt, Miss Mabel,	Philadelphia.
Saltel, A. T. and wife,	Washington.
Small, Miss,	Philadelphia.
Sanborn, Mrs. J. H.,	Haverhill.
Sanborn, Ethel J.,	Haverhill.
Smith, A. A. and wife,	Boston.
Sherlar, Samuel,	New York.
Sherlar, Prentice,	New York.
Sweat, Mr., and wife,	Portland.
Staples, Mr. and Mrs. James,	Bridgeport, Ct.
Townsend, Edwin S.,	New York.
Thayer, Miss H. D.,	Franklin, Mass.
Taylor, W. A.,	Brooklyn.
Taylor, F. R.,	Norway.
Tabor, J. W.,	Portland.
Taylor, Miss,	Worcester, Mass.
Taylor, Forrest,	Worcester, Mass.
Valentine, J. M.,	New York.
Valentine, Miss,	New York.
Wharton, C. W. and wife,	Philadelphia.
Weeks, F. W. and wife,	Brooklyn.
Wentworth, A.,	Boston.
Wingate, C. J.,	Boston.
Wingate, W. H.,	Boston.
Winchester, H. K.,	Santa Barbara, Cal.
Whittemore, C. and wife,	Boston.
Wheelock, Miss Kate I.,	Chicago.

MANSION HOUSE.

Ameiman, Mr. and Mrs. N.,	New York, N. Y.
Andrews, W. W.,	Portland, Me.
Bishop, Mr. C. J.,	Boston, Mass.
Bishop, Misses L. S. and M. J.,	Boston, Mass.
Butler, Mrs. S. T.,	Salem, Mass.
Cobb, Mr. S. C.,	Newton Highlands, Mass.
Cushing, Miss C. L.,	Newton Highlands, Mass.
Dowse, Miss A. F.,	Boston, Mass.
Dana, G. H.,	Boston, Mass.
Dunbar, L.,	Hyde Park, Mass.
Frost, Mr. and Mrs. W. F.,	Boston, Mass.
Gay, Mrs. E. G.,	Boston, Mass.
Gay, Ernest L.,	Boston, Mass.
Hazen, Mr. and Mrs. J. W.,	Cambridge, Mass.
Hoyt, Miss J. C.,	Boston, Mass.
Hatchard, Miss,	Boston, Mass.
Jackson, Miss H. J.,	Boston, Mass.
Jackson, Miss M.,	Boston, Mass.
Low, Miss S.,	Dover, N. H.
Logan, Mrs. W. F.,	Newton Highlands, Mass.
Merrill, Mrs. S. H.,	Salem, Mass.
O'Connor, Mary A.,	Dover, N. H.
Oine, Miss M. E.,	Cambridge, Mass.
Petteplace, Miss,	Providence, R. I.
Petley, P.,	Boston, Mass.
Rice, Mr. and Mrs. Albert,	Rockland, Me.
Schoen, H. and wife and children,	New York, N. Y.
Wheeler, Mrs. W. H.,	Boston, Mass.
Wood, Ira O. and wife.	Boston, Mass.

Vol. I.   SUNDAY MORNING, JULY 22, 1894.   No. 3.

A Summer Shrine.

FROM far and near all over this broad land Poland Spring is hailed as the Mecca of many a summer pilgrimage. Thousands annually lay off the impediments of daily toil, and donning the garb of pleasure-pilgrims, take up their journey to "bonny Poland," the "fairest spot 'neath sun or skies," there to drink deep draughts from the bubbling fountains of health-giving waters, to breathe long breaths of the pure, free air of the hills, and to gaze their full upon the beauty and grandeur of the surrounding landscape.

* * * * *

And such a landscape it is that a painter looking upon its placid lakes in the valleys, its country homes nestling against the hill-sides, surrounded by fields and forests, and far away in the background the outlines of the grand old White Hills fading away into the dim horizon. might find in its ideal loveliness the inspiration for his *chef d'oeuvre*. And even to the ordinary mortal its pleasing variety affords an attractiveness which never ends, a perpetual feast of beauty.

> "But at afternoon or almost eve
> 'Tis better; then the silence glows
> To that degree, you half believe
> It must get rid of what it knows,
> Its bosom does so heave."

* * * * *

The lesser touches with which Nature has adorned the vicinity of Ricker Hill are no less beautiful. The shady drives, the lily pond at the foot of the hill, the groves and forest glens where one may walk at morn or eve and listen to a symphony of bird song; these spots linger lovingly in the memory long after Poland Spring is left behind, and add not a little to the inspiriting restfulness of a sojourn on the Hill.

* * * *

Man cannot find complete enjoyment, however, in feeding the æsthetic sense alone. The cravings of the inner man must be appeased and certain every-day comforts attainable, in order that the manifold beauties of nature be most keenly appreciated. It is needless to say that all these necessaries, together with the luxuries of life, may be found at Poland Spring. The name of the Rickers is everywhere synonymous with whole-hearted hospitality, and no one can come here without realizing that everything he could wish for and many things he would not think of are looked after with the utmost precision and forethought. Here, indeed, may be found a palace of ease and enjoyment.

* * * *

The vicinity of Ricker Hill furnishes many attractions for pleasure parties, and in the stables may always be found the sleekest of well-fed horses, the most comfortable of carriages, and the best-natured and accommodating drivers to take you whithersoever your fancy calls you. Pleasant country roads over sightly hill-tops, through charming valleys and along the shores of

lakes and streams, invite you to an ideal morning drive, and if you wish for more instructive entertainment there are the Shaker village, the Pope kennels, the Sanborn Stock Farm, and many other places of interest within easy reach and always open to your inspection.

* * * * *

In the heat of the day the shady nooks on the veranda and the seats beneath the trees at the spring invite you to sit and read in idle comfort, or, musing, to forget the care and turmoil of the outside world, and to study the harmonies of nature in earth and sky, in hill-top and valley, in tree and flower, till in dreamy imagination life lapses into an idyl of summer, an illusion that ends only with the last sungleam from the gilded dome as you turn from the carriage to cast a lingering, farewell look upon the scene of so many pleasing memories.

Reflections.

THE bright side of life! How bright it is to ourselves and how bright it can be made to others if the best instincts of our nature are emphasized by inclinations having their birth in good-will. Closely allied in force with the principle of life evolved is the lesson taught by that French precept: "*Le plus grand plaisir qu'on peut avoir est ce quel'on donne.*" Finding the greatest pleasure in that which one gives, suggests something beyond mere generosity in its generally accepted sense; it means a forgetfulness of self when thereby good may be done to a friend, kindness in thought, word and action toward our fellow-traveler in life's journey, and affixing the seal of contempt upon a disregard of the obligation to promote the happiness of others whenever possible. *God is Love!* So should be man, made as he is in the image of his Maker.

R. M. F.

Miss Nettie Ricker is receiving lots of congratulations on her handsome souvenir spoons. The design is a most unique one, the handle being a reproduction of the familiar "Moses," while the bowl contains a handsome etching of the Poland Spring House.

Bubbles.

Lovely sunsets.

All aboard for the lake.

"Watch the Professor."

Young men are plentiful.

The farmers have finished haying.

Billiard tables for beds will soon be in order.

The next building to be built will be a chapel.

What's the matter with having a croquet tournament?

Mt. Washington is only forty miles distant on an air line.

The corridors are a favorite lounging place on a warm afternoon.

The Amusement Fund at present amounts to about six hundred dollars.

A boating carnival on the lake would be a nice way of passing one of these moonlight evenings.

The Messrs. Maginnis, of New Orleans, are adepts in that most difficult of all instruments, the mandolin.

Ex-Governor H. M. Plaisted, of Augusta, has arrived at his favorite summer home, the Mansion House.

Captain J. M. Bailey, general agent for the Phœnix Insurance Company of Brooklyn, is here for a short visit.

Mr. R. M. Field, that popular theatrical manager of Boston, is fast becoming a great base-ball enthusiast.

A large number of Lewiston people were over Tuesday to witness their pet team defeat the "Poland Dandies."

With the arrival of B. F. Moulton of Philadelphia the Billiard Room Glee Club has reorganized for the season.

Mr. Charles I. Travelli, that popular lawyer of the Hub, and wife, are at the big house. Mr. Travelli is an expert with the croquet mallet.

Our Philadelphia gentlemen seem to have a mania for large-sized cigars. Quantity as well as quality seem to be combined in their manufacture.

Mr. Kuntz, our popular musical director, is a great devotee to canoeing, and any good day may find him enjoying a quiet spin in his birch-bark canoe.

John T. Dickinson and wife, accompanied by Miss Louise Mattocks of Chicago, are at the large house for a few weeks' stay. Mr. Dickin-

son was the secretary of the World's Columbian Exhibition.

J. P. Bates and wife, of Boston, are here with their private team for the season. Mr. Bates is a member of the firm of Cobb, Bates & Yerxa, grocers, Boston.

David G. Yates, of Philadelphia, is enjoying a much-needed rest at the large house. Mr. Yates is a prominent nurseryman and landscape gardener of the Quaker City.

Mr. and Mrs. C. N. Shaw, of Boston, spent a few days here last week. Mr. Shaw is the junior member of the firm of Page & Shaw, candy manufacturers, Boston.

The Sunday evening songs, which were so popular last season, have not as yet been resumed. With all the musical talent that there is among the guests on Poland Hill these concerts might be made the most enjoyable events of the week.

THE GRIPSACK UMBRELLA

IS THE GREATEST NOVELTY OF ITS KIND EVER INVENTED.

Can be carried in your valise, in your overcoat pocket, or in a lady's shopping bag. **Ask to See It.**

W. B. SPEAR (Night Clerk P, S. H.), AGENT.

POLAND SPRING LIVERY

* Which is connected with the Poland Spring Hotels is one of the largest and best equipped hotel stables in the country. . . . . .

POLAND SPRING BRAKE

* Is a novel of beauty and comfort combined, and a visit to Poland without having enjoyed a ride on the same, is a failure—Bear in mind that we employ none but . . .

EXPERIENCED DRIVERS

* Who are acquainted with the roads and the different points of interest.

All parties desiring turn-outs, should notify the Clerk at the Office, early to insure accommodation.

POLAND SPRING LIVERY.

H. T. JORDAN, } EDITORS.
W. D. FREEMAN, }

PUBLISHED EVERY SUNDAY MORNING DURING THE MONTHS
OF JULY, AUGUST AND SEPTEMBER, IN THE INTERESTS OF

POLAND SPRING AND ITS VISITORS.

All contributions relative to the guests of Poland Spring will
be thankfully received.

To insure publication, all communications should reach the
editors not later than Thursday preceding day of issue.

All parties desiring rates for advertising in the HILL-TOP
should write the editors for same.

The subscription price of the HILL-TOP is $1.00 for the
season, post-paid. Single copies will be mailed at 10c. each.

Address,

EDITORS "HILL-TOP,"

Poland Spring House,

South Poland, Maine.

PRINTED AT JOURNAL OFFICE, LEWISTON.

Sunday, July 22, 1894.

Editorial.

OUR object in publishing the HILL-TOP is
not only to make money but to gain as
much experience in our chosen field of
labor as possible. It is also our object to present a bright, crisp, readable paper worthy of
representing a live hotel firm doing such a class
of business as the Poland Spring Hotels. To
present a live paper, the editors must be live
young men. Now whether we are "live young
men" or not, our modesty won't allow us to say,
but suffice it to say that we are always alive to
the demands of our patrons and friends. Accordingly, the HILL-TOP of this issue has been
enlarged by four pages to accommodate our subscribers and advertisers. Next issue we hope
to enlarge it still more, making sixteen pages
in all.

The HILL-TOP has a bright future before it,
and if hard work and plenty of it will avail anything, our summer's venture will have been a
great success.

The policy which has characterized us so far
will be further maintained, and we hope we may
merit your confidence.

Guests and friends of Poland Spring will
confer us a favor by sending in short notes on
subjects of especial interest to our patrons.

We trust that our efforts will be met with the
same feeling which prompted them, and that we
shall receive your generous support in the future
as in the past.

Announcement.

Commencing Monday, July 23d, carriages
will leave the Poland Spring House daily at
10.30 A.M., connecting at the lake with the
launch Poland. Returning, carriages will leave
the lake at 12.30, reaching the hotels in time
for dinner.

All parties intending to visit the lake for
rowing, bathing, sailing, etc., and wishing seats
in the carriages, should leave their names at the
office by 10 o'clock.

Music.

The programme for the concert in Music Hall
at 3.30 P.M., Sunday, July 22d, is as follows :

1. Vorspiel, 3d Act Meistersinger.		Wagner.
2. Suite L'Arléseenne.		Bizet.
3. { a. Largo.		Handel.
{ b. Intermezzo—Naïla.		Delibes.
4. Selection from Götterdämmerung.		Wagner.
5. Menuet.		Paderewski.
6. The Lost Chord.		Sullivan.
7. Overture—William Tell.		Rossini.

Coming Events.

Sunday, July 22d.—Concert, Music Hall, 3.30 P.M.; Song
Service, 8 P.M.

Tuesday, July 24th.—Base-Ball, Poland Spring vs. Auburn
Y. M. C. A., 3 P.M.; Concert by the Graham Concert
Company, of Boston, Music Hall, 8 P.M.

Friday, July 27th.—Progressive Euchre, Amusement
Room, 8 P.M.

Saturday, July 28th.—Base-Ball, Poland Spring vs. Freeport, 3 P.M.; Full-Dress Hop, 8.15 P.M.

Hours of Meals.

	Week Days.	Sundays.
Breakfast,	7 A.M. to 9 A.M.	8 A.M. to 10 A.M.
Dinner,	1 P.M. to 3 P.M.	1.30 P.M. to 3.30 P.M.
Supper,	6 P.M. to 8 P.M.	6 P.M. to 8 P.M.

Literary.

The One Missing.

BY GEORGE T. BOURNE.

"There were ninety and nine that safely lay
In the shelter of the fold;
But one was out on the hills away,
Far off from the gates of gold."

Are my sheep all here, said the Shepherd's voice,
Not one without the fold;
Not one away on this Winter night,
To perish and die from cold?

There were ninety and nine passed through the gate.
But one who is feeble and old
Has not returned with the evening flock,
But is out in the Winter cold.

Up, up to the hills, search far and wide;
Search near, search low, search high;
I would not one of my Master's sheep
Should stray from the fold and die.

Go find the wanderer e'er the morn;
It must not be lightly told
That even one of my Master's flock
Should perish and die from cold.

When the Master comes in the morning light,
I can say in accents bold,
Safe, Lord, all safe, the count is true,
Each one within the fold.

Jokelets.

In the *spring* a young man's fancy
Lightly turns to thoughts of love.

Poland *Spring?*

In the far East a general told his soldiers that after capturing a city they could have some *elder blow tea.* They saw how the general spelled the order, and they had the LOOT.

A man asked a barber's daughter to marry him. She replied, "poor." Nothing discouraged, he asked again and was accepted, as her refusal was only a *sham poo.*

Tom—"Don't eat that green apple; you can't digest it." Will—"All right, I will take your advice; I don't wish *die gest* now."

Why does a Frenchman eat only one egg for breakfast? Because, to a Frenchman, one egg is always *un oeuf.*

Doctors and chiropodists are alike,—they believe in *mani-cures.*

New arrival: "Begorra, phwat's that?" Park policeman: "Obelisk." New arrival: (to himself): "Oi niver heard of O'Belisk; but judgin' from his grave-stone he must av been hoigh up in Tammany Hall."—*Puck.*

Teacher: "Can you give a sentence illustrating the difference between mind and matter?" Tommy: "Yes, sir; when I don't mind, pretty soon they's suthin' the matter."

Judge Guffy: "What passed between yourself and the complainant?" O'Brien: "I think, sor, a half dozen bricks and a piece of pavin' stone."

Stranger (in country newspaper office): "What's the news?" Office boy: "There ain't any; the editor's away."

Marriage Intentions.

"TIME changes all things." There is more truth embraced in the above line than the average person would behold at a first glance. The latest meaning of the sentence can only be fully understood by careful thought. Often our prejudices, no matter how great they may be, are changed by that little unseen agent of Tempus to a strong desire.

The air at Poland seems to have been infused with those little messengers of Amor, and the result is the announcement of the intended marriage of two of our best known and highly respected guests.—Mr. J. B. Sawyer, of Pittsburg, Pa., and Miss A. M. Sturtevant, of Springfield, Mass.

Mr. Sawyer is a most estimable gentleman, having a host of friends, not only at Poland but also in various parts of the country. He is of a courteous, affable disposition, and in full possession of all the qualities necessary in the making of a true, devoted husband and father. Mr. Sawyer has made Poland his summer home for a number of years, and during that time has identified himself with all that could possibly entertain his fellow-guests. He has had full charge of the collection and distribution of the Amusement Fund for several years, and to him more than to any one man is due our thanks for the pleasure received from the ball games, entertainments, etc.

Miss Sturtevant is a charming little lady, one of those people who have the tact of making friends anywhere and under all circumstances, and a friend once made is always retained. She is an excellent conversationalist, possessed of all those powers of research and entertainment which so few can boast of.

The exact date of the taking of the marriage obligation has not as yet been decided upon, but it will probably be in the early fall.

Congratulations have been in order the past week, and if it is not too late the HILL-TOP wishes to extend its hearty congratulations and well wishes for a happy and prosperous journey through life together.

Base-Ball.

Play ball!

Already have the words which cause the baseball crank to prick up his ears and settle back in his seat for two hours' solid enjoyment, rang out upon the clear air of Ricker Hill.

The game of all games is now well under way, and the joys and sorrows attendant upon watching the alternate victory and defeat of one's home team are being borne.

The nines which have fought for honor upon the Poland diamond in the past have been excel-

lent ones. The team which dons the gray this season will not be one to fall below the standard already attained.

The guests who back the ball team with their financial and vocal support, expect the nine to work. With the men who are under contract we should win a large percentage of the games played. But the nine can feel that if they work, and then lose, they will hear no complaints. Lazy ball playing, however, will not be satisfactory and there will be no place on the team for men who put no life and energy into their play. Dirty ball is out of date now and anything but good, clean work will be frowned upon. Boys, work! hustle! win if you can, but play ball all the time. If the men behind the team have certain things which they may expect from the nine, it is just as true that the nine have reason to expect them to reciprocate. Did you ever notice how much harder the boys play ball when they know

that they have the people with them? Therefore THE HILL-TOP expects that the people who witness the games will give the nine their hearty support. Where a good play is made, cheer. Surely a good hit, a remarkable catch, a well-stolen base is worthy of your applause. Applause costs nothing, but it has won many a game of ball.

There will be two games a week upon the home grounds. All the visiting teams are expected to be gentlemanly ones, and the games will be clean, manly contests for the supremacy of the diamond.

To incite the men to do their best, THE HILL-TOP will offer three prizes, the nature of which will be announced in a later issue. Three prizes will be given : one to the player holding the best batting average at the end of the season ; the second to the man making the most runs ; and the third to the player who holds the highest fielding average.

During the season THE HILL-TOP will have a page devoted to the sport. The scores of all games on the home grounds will be given in detail, and the games arranged for the week commencing with date of issue, notes, etc., will fill up the page.

The ball game of Saturday, July 14th, was the most interesting one played on Ricker Hill for years. Previous games this season have been altogether too one-sided, and the appearance of a team which could make the boys work to win was gladly welcomed.

The Gorhams outfielded our boys, but were unable to find Plaisted's curves when hits meant runs. Lawson and Wakefield led at the bat and also ran bases finely. Sykes put up a nice game at short, accepting nine out of eleven chances, some of which were most difficult ones. Mullen, of the visitors, played finely. The score :

POLAND SPRING.

	A.B.	B.H.	P.O.	A.	E.
Wakefield, 2,	4	3	3	1	0
Lawson, m.,	4	3	1	0	0
Sykes, s.,	3	1	5	4	2
Hull, 1,	4	1	10	0	1
Sockelexis, 1,	3	1	0	1	0
Pulsifer, 3,	4	0	1	2	2
Plaisted, p.,	4	1	0	2	0
Harris, c.,	4	1	7	4	2
Haskell, r.,	4	0	0	0	1
Totals,	34	11	27	14	8

GORHAMS.

	A.B.	B.H.	P.O.	A.	E.
Leavitt, l.,	4	1	0	0	0
Casey, 3,	5	0	5	0	0
Mullen, m.,	4	1	4	2	0
Noyes, 1,	3	1	9	2	0
Chapman, p.,	4	1	0	2	1
Clough, 2,	4	2	4	4	0
Willis, c.,	4	1	3	0	0
Flaherty, r.,	4	1	0	0	0
Lydon, s.,	4	0	2	4	1
Totals,	36	8	27	14	2

Innings,	1	2	3	4	5	6	7	8	9	
Poland Spring,	2	0	3	1	0	0	1	0	0—	7
Gorham,	1	1	2	0	1	0	0	0	0—	5

Runs made—by Wakefield 3, Lawson, Sykes, Pulsifer, Hull, Mullen 2, Noyes, Chapman, Willis. Earned runs—Poland Spring 3, Gorham. Two-base hits—Sykes, Flaherty. Passed balls—Willis. Three-base hits—Wakefield 2, Lawson. Stolen bases—Wakefield 2, Lawson 2, Sockelexis, Pulsifer, Mullen 3. Base on balls—Wakefield, Sockelexis, Leavitt, Mullen, Noyes. Struck out—Hull, Plaisted, Casey 2, Mullen, Chapman, Flaherty 2, Lydon. Double plays—Sykes and Hull, Lydon, Noyes, and Casey. Hit by pitched ball—Sykes. Wild pitch—Chapman. Time—1 hour 50 minutes. Umpire, Pulsifer.

We lost the game on Wednesday. Well, we expected to, and considering the way in which we held the highest-salaried team in the New England league from making a big score we can feel proud of the game.

After our team has worked together more we can make a fine showing with league teams, and the amateur teams which down us will have to hustle. Brown, of New Auburn, who suffered a drubbing at our hands in the first game of the season, started in as twirler for the visitors. He lasted three innings, and then, with the score five to three in our favor, "Willie" Mains took his place. We didn't score again. Now "Willie" has speed, in fact was heated to such an extent from the velocity of the ball as to warp the bats of our youngsters. You can't win games with crooked bats, consequently we didn't win.

The Lewistons hit well, although Plaisted pitched a good game considering the men he was facing. In fielding we excelled, and sharper work could not be asked for. Wakefield at second carried off the honors, while our red man and Powers were good seconds. The score:

LEWISTON.

	A.B.	R.	B.H.	T.B.	P.O.	A.	E.
Bergen, c.,	5	1	2	3	7	0	1
McCormack, 3,	4	1	2	2	6	3	0
Laroque, 2,	4	1	2	2	2	2	0
Polhemus, m.,	4	2	1	3	2	0	1
Shea, l.,	4	1	2	3	7	0	1
Coughlin, l.,	4	1	2	2	1	0	0
Spill, s.,	3	1	2	3	0	0	3
Mains, r., p.,	4	1	1	1	2	1	0
Brown, p.,	0	0	0	0	0	3	1
Stafford, r.,	3	0	0	0	0	0	0
Totals,	35	9	14	19	27	9	7

POLAND SPRINGS.

	A.B.	R.	B.H.	T.B.	P.O.	A.	E.
Wakefield, 2,	4	1	1	2	7	4	0
Lawson, m.,	5	0	1	1	2	0	0
Powers, c.,	5	0	1	2	3	2	0
Plaisted, p.,	4	0	0	0	0	1	0
Sykes, s.,	5	0	1	2	2	1	2
Hull, 1,	4	1	0	0	5	1	0
Sockelexis, l.,	4	1	2	2	3	2	2
Pulsifer, 3,	4	1	2	4	0	0	0
Harris, r.,	4	1	2	3	2	0	0
Totals,	39	5	10	16	24	11	4

Innings,	1	2	3	4	5	6	7	8	9	
Lewiston,	3	0	0	4	1	0	1	0	x—	9
Poland Springs,	0	4	1	0	0	0	0	0	0—	5

Earned runs—Lewiston 6, Poland Springs 2. Two-base hits—Bergen, Shea, Spill, Wakefield, Powers, Sykes, Harris. Three-base hits—Polhemus, Pulsifer. Stolen bases—Wakefield, Pulsifer, Sockelexis. Sacrifice hits—Plaisted. Passed balls—Powers 2. Wild pitch—Plaisted 1. Hit by pitched ball—by Plaisted, Spill. First base on balls—by Plaisted, Brown, McCormack; by Brown, Wakefield, Hull. First base on errors—Lewiston 2, Poland Springs 3. Struck out—by Brown, Sykes; by Mains, Wakefield 2; by Plaisted, Shea. Time—1 hour 50 minutes. Umpire—Orlando J. Hackett.

Powers allows no stealing bases. Did you see how neatly he shut off Coughlin at second and caught Captain Laroque at second?

Mr. Soden says Wakefield is a "dandy."

Sockelexis is the best thrower in New England.

Shea, McCormack, and Stafford want to play here after their season closes. They are a neat trio.

In four games played Lawson has made nine hits with a total of sixteen.

That first catch of Harris's was a beauty.

STAGES.

DEPART.

	M. H.	P. S. H.
For Portland and Boston,	6.25 A.M.	6.30 A.M.
Lewiston and Farmington,	8.25 A.M.	8.30 A.M.
Portland and Boston,	9.25 A.M.	9.30 A.M.
Lewiston and Bar Harbor,	10.25 A.M.	10.30 A.M.
Lewiston and Bangor,	12.45 P.M.	1 P.M.
Portland and Boston,	3.25 P.M.	3.30 P.M.

ARRIVE.

	M. H.	P. S. H.
From the West,	10.30 A.M.	10.35 A.M.
From the East,	1 P.M.	1.05 P.M.
From the West,	3.30 P.M.	3.35 P.M.
" "	7.30 P.M.	7.35 P.M.

MAILS.

CLOSE.

Poland Spring House.	Mansion House.
5.45 A.M.	6 A.M.
8.45 A.M.	9 A.M.
2.45 P.M.	3 P.M.

ARRIVE.

10 A.M.	9.30 A.M.
1.30 P.M.	1 P.M.
4.30 P.M.	4 P.M.
8 P.M.	7.45 P.M.

The Hop.

THE Saturday evening hop of July 14th was by far the most brilliant and dressy affair of the season. Music Hall, the best of its kind in New England, never contained a jollier or prettier party. The smooth, waxen floor, the entrancing strains of Prof. Kuntz's orchestra, and the brilliant lights were all conducive to enjoyment, and the devotee of Terpsichore who could not be happy amidst such pleasant surroundings must indeed have been in a sorry mood. The scene from the corridors was a most beautiful one. The tasty costumes of the young lady dancers, contrasted with the regulation black of their partners, and the more sober shades worn by the matrons, who encircled the room, made a picture well worth the endeavors of a great artist to transfer to the canvas. The dreamy waltzes, the glittering diamonds, and the merry hum of voices all added their charm to the scene, making an evening well worth remembering.

An order of ten dances was enjoyed, one of the prettiest of which was a quadrille danced by the "younger" young ladies. The eight young misses who participated in this figure were perfect dancers and will never want partners when they bloom out into belles.

The HILL-TOP had hoped to give this week a list of the costumes worn, but our society reporter being on the sick list we shall have to postpone it.

Among the many young ladies who were handsomely dressed we noticed: Miss Stinson, of Philadelphia; Miss Maginnis, of New Orleans; Miss Bourne, of New York; Miss Supplee, of Philadelphia; Miss Chase, of New York; Miss Corson, of New York; Miss De Lima, of New York; Miss McNeal, of New York.

Wednesday Drive.

A VERY delightful evening was spent by the "Aristocratic Set" of Poland Spring House on the coaching party to the Wilson House on Wednesday evening. After a very delightful ride a sally was made upon the Wilson House, which surrendered unconditionally to them. Supper was served in the beautiful little dining-room, which was decorated very prettily for the occasion. After supper they adjourned to the piazza. Here they danced to the sweet music furnished by two young ladies stopping at the hotel. Two of the young gentlemen of the party played some very sweet selections on the guitar and banjo. Then games were played until the coach arrived.

The trip home proved the most delightful part of it all, the young gentlemen of the party singing their college songs, and the moonlight streaming into the coach made it a very picturesque scene. The party was chaperoned by Mrs. Maginnis of New Orleans, who contributed much to the charming affair. Those who made up the party were: Miss Helen Stinson and Miss Elsie Supplee, of Philadelphia; Miss Mary Craven, of Salem, N. J.; Miss Gertrude May Chase, of New York, and Miss Maginnis of New Orleans; Mr. Allen Rogers, Jersey City; Mr. Henry P. White, Brockton, Mass.; Mr. Richard Williamson, of Philadelphia; Mr. A. A. Maginnis, Jr., Mr. J. H. Maginnis, of New Orleans.

It is Whispered

That Poland Spring is booming.

That it "often," because it is the finest summer resort in the country.

That we have lots of pretty girls here.

That they are appreciated.

That Messrs. Sawyer and Stinson are not kickers; but,

That they consider one dollar an inch for trout a "leetle high."

That Allen Rogers and party made their ride to the "Wilson" a *howling* success.

That our young lady pool players are "stars."

That the Amusement Fund is increasing.

That it should.

That as a racer the Poland can give the Vigilant points.

That a white yachting cap don't make a man a yachtsman; and

That Lucius is not one of the crew of the Emily.

That our orchestra is "*très bien.*"

That the HILL-TOP is small.

That we know it, but

That it will grow.

That we are satisfied with our ball team.

That Miss DeLima can play nice tennis.

That Miss Maginnis is a good oarswoman.

That her brothers are great favorites with the fair sex.

That Mr. Sawyer's happy smile is good to look upon.

That Miss Wheelock and Mr. Yates are a great pair at whist.

Bubbles.

Judge Charles A. Peabody and wife, of New York City, are domiciled at their favorite summer home for the season.

Mrs. L. W. Rogers, accompanied by Mrs. J. H. Bowker, of Boston, are here for the season. Mrs. Rogers is well known in newspaper circles because of her connection with the *Journal*.

A very natty little lodge for the accommodation of the gate-keeper at the foot of the hill, has been building the past week. It is rather small, but very convenient and comfortable in bad weather.

Dr. Peterson, with his charming wife and family, who have regarded Poland as their summer home for so many years, is here for the season. Mr. Peterson is one of the best-known retired physicians of New York City.

Miss Wheelock and Mr. Yates of Philadelphia are playing a series of games of duplicate whist with Mr. H. A. Rogers of New York and Mr. Spear of Boston. The games are watched by an interested circle of the whist experts.

The amount of business done at the Poland Spring hotels during the month of June, was sixty per cent. better than that done during the same month last year. There are no hotels in the country that are growing more in public favor than these famous hostelries.

Mr. W. H. Bolster of Dorchester, Mass., conducted divine services in Music Hall last Sunday morning. Mr. Bolster is an annual visitor here and is always assured of a large and appreciative audience. Mr. Bolster was accompanied by his two charming daughters.

The "Brackett Cottage," so called, situated at the foot of the hill, near the livery stable, is fast nearing completion, and it is hoped it will be ready for occupancy in a few weeks. The cottage will furnish accommodation for twenty or more of the drivers and stable employees.

The pretty bowling alley adjacent to the billiard hall has been put in readiness for the season's use. The smooth alleys never looked more inviting to the bowling enthusiast than at present. Bowling parties, which were the occasions of so many pleasant afternoons last season, are now in order.

There is not a finer orchestra in the country for its size (seven pieces), than Kuntz Orchestra, which is connected with the Poland Spring House this season. Never before have we had an orchestra which gave better general satisfaction. Every player is a member of the celebrated Symphony Orchestra of Boston.

The Progressive Euchre party of Friday evening was much enjoyed by the small number present. Owing to the non-arrival of some of the to-be players only eight tables were filled. Eight prizes were distributed. Mrs. B. F. Moulton of Philadelphia supervised the picking out of the prizes, which were very tasty.

Mr. H. A. Rogers, the well-known New York club man, reached Poland with his family on July 1st. Mr. Rogers is no stranger to Poland, having been here for a number of seasons. Miss May Rogers, who will be remembered as one of the most popular young ladies here last season, is at present traveling in Europe.

Among the many very strong whist players which we have with us this season, the most prominent are Miss Wheelock of Chicago, whom the celebrated "Cavendish" calls the "Whist Queen"; Mrs. Moulton, of Rosemont, Pa., Mrs. Fessenden of New York, and Mrs. Brigit of Cambridge. Among the gentlemen are: Messrs. Yates of Philadelphia, Rogers of New York, and Spear of the Poland Spring House staff.

The eagerness with which old Polanders return to the broad corridors and shady verandas of the best hotel in the country is well shown in the case of Mr. Fields of the Boston Museum. On Friday evening, June 29th, Mr. Fields and his charming wife arrived in Boston after a pleasant European tour. Saturday morning they left the Hub on the 9.30 A.M. train, and shortly after noon were settled in their summer home.

The "Poland" made her trial trip on Thursday. The run from the wharf to the upper end of the lake and back, a distance of two miles and a half, was made in twenty minutes, and the natty little boat can do much better than that. The boat carried on her initial trip the following ladies and gentlemen: Mr. and Mrs. B. F. Kieth, Boston; Mr. Paul A. Kieth, Brookline; Miss Fym, Brookline; Mr. H. B. Cummings, Boston; Mr. and Mrs. E. P. Ricker, Mr. H. W. Ricker.

Who will be the champion water drinker here this season remains to be seen. There are many who think that the twenty or more glasses which they imbibe daily should entitle them to the honor, but taking into consideration the record made by Mr. George Innis of San Francisco, last season, they are only second raters. Mr. Innis, undoubtedly the champion, made a record of forty glasses in twenty-four hours. This is a large number, but in this record-breaking year it cannot be expected that he will be allowed to wear his proud title long. Doubtless before the season closes some dark horse will make the half-century mark.

Arrivals

POLAND SPRING HOUSE.

Arnold, Dr. E. S. and wife,	Newport, R. I.
Arnold, Miss Jessie,	Newport, R. I.
Andrews, Miss,	Bethel, Me.
Allen, T. P. and wife,	Gardiner.
Blackhurst, Frank,	New York.
Blackhurst, J. T. C.,	New York.
Bass, E. W. and wife,	New York.
Bates, Jacob P. and wife,	Boston.
Bolster, W. H.,	Dorchester, Mass.
Bolster, Miss Gertrude M.,	Dorchester, Mass.
Bolster, Miss Harriet N.,	Dorchester, Mass.
Bacr, Emil,	New York.
Bowling, Thomas H.,	Baltimore.
Brauran, Thomas H.,	Boston.
Burley, Capt. J. W.,	New York.
Cushman, S. T.,	Monson, Mass.
Cushman, Robert H.,	Monson, Mass.
Cushman, Hattie T.,	Monson, Mass.
Craven, Thomas J. and wife,	Salem, N. Y.
Craven, Miss Mary B.,	Salem, N. Y.
Coppenhagen, J. H. and wife,	New York.
Carpenter, F. W. and wife,	Providence, R. I.
Carpenter, Miss Julia,	Providence, R. I.
Carpenter, Miss Hannah,	Providence, R. I.
Carpenter, W. J.,	Katonah, N. Y.
Coburn, N. P. and wife,	Newton, Mass.
Clark, Charles and wife,	St. Louis.
Clark, C. M. L.,	St. Louis.
Crosby, U. C.,	Boston.
Cole, Richard F.,	Brooklyn.
Cotton, John B.,	Washington.
Danielson, Mr. and Mrs. J. W.,	Providence, R. I.
Downing, G. H.,	Boston.
Dewey, Daniel and wife,	Newton.
DeLima, Mrs. Edward,	New York.
Dickinson, Mr. and Mrs. John F.,	Chicago.
Evans, T. W. and wife,	New York.
Embry, Mrs. J. H.,	Washington.
Endicott, Charles,	Canton.
Ellis, C. A. and wife,	Boston.
Flyart, Mabelle K.,	Monson, Mass.
Frissell, H. B.,	Hampton, Va.
Field, Walter,	New York.
Green, Miss M. E.,	New York.
Gale, Mr. and Mrs. Thomas M.,	Washington.
Gale, Miss Olive,	Washington.
Gale, Cyrus,	Northboro, Mass.
Griffin, C. C. and wife,	Haverhill.
Houston, James H.,	Boston.
Houston, Ernest,	Boston.
Hopkins, A. and wife,	Gardiner.
Kent, Henry,	Exeter.
Martin, Mrs.,	Boston.
Martin, Miss,	Boston.

Mitchell, Mr. and Mrs. A. R.,	Newton, Mass.
Mattocks, Miss Louise,	Chicago.
Moulton, B. P.,	Philadelphia.
Oakes, Josiah and wife,	Malden, Mass.
O'Rouke, T. H.,	Boston.
Pike, C. G.,	Portland.
Pike, C. R.,	Calais.
Paul, Fulton and wife,	Hudson, N. Y.
Platt, H. L.,	Lewiston.
Rogers, J. Fred and wife,	Boston.
Rice, John O.,	Portland.
Sanborn, John H.,	Haverhill.
Storey, J. C.,	Boston
Sherwood, Warner,	New York.
Sollenstein, John T.,	New York.
Stellwagen, Mrs. E. J.,	Washington.
Shaw, C. N. and wife,	Boston.
Sterling, F. A. and wife,	Cleveland.
Stark, Charles G. and wife,	Milwaukee.
Willey,	Portland.
White, John S.,	New York.
Weeks, N. E. and wife,	Boston.
Weeks, Master Merton,	Boston.
Wendel, Miss,	New York.
Wendel, Miss J.,	New York.
White, F. E. and wife,	Brockton.
White, Henry P.,	Brockton.
Walsh, Samuel A. and family,	New York.

MANSION HOUSE.

Angell, T. L.,	Lewiston, Me.
Ballantyne, J.,	Lisbon Falls, Me.
Ballantyne, William J.,	Lisbon Falls, Me.
Burbank, O. A.,	Boston, Mass.
Britton, Alice,	Weymouth, Mass.
Cox, Albert S.,	Boston, Mass.
Clapp, Howard and wife,	Boston, Mass.
Brooks, John W.,	Torrington, Conn.
Fales, Charles H. and wife,	Meriden, Conn.
Fales, H. S.,	Meriden, Conn.
Farrell, Carrie,	Boston, Mass.
Greeley, William H.,	Boston, Mass.
Greeley, William H.,	New Gloucester, Me.
Ivers Samuel,	New Bedford, Mass.
Lincoln, H. H.,	Boston, Mass.
Prince, H. L.,	Washington, D. C.
McCulloch, J.,	Montreal.
McCulloch, E. B.,	Montreal.
Plaisted, H. M.,	Bangor.
Peet, Dr. Edw. W.,	New York City.
O'Rouke, T. H.,	Boston, Mass.
Kingsley, E. C. and wife,	Yarmouth.
Moon, M. A.,	Yarmouth.
Lander, Edw.,	Salem, Mass.
Stevens, Miss,	New Gloucester, Me.
Vannar, P. W. and wife,	Philadelphia, Pa.

The Mansion House is a favorite summer home for artists. Mr. Vannar, the famous Philadelphia painter, and Mr. Cox of Boston, are both registered there.

THE HILL-TOP.
POLAND SPRING.

VOL. I.   SUNDAY MORNING, JULY 29, 1894.   No. 4.

CANOEING THE BIG LAKE.

Notches on a Paddle-Blade.

A MAN who asserts that he has tried both "exhilarations" informed us the other day that there wasn't such a great difference between floating on the broad, placid bosom of a summer lake and sailing in a balloon. In one case you seem to be floating between heaven and earth, in the other instance you really are.

It is, furthermore, still an open question which is the more "ticklish," a birch-bark canoe in the hands of a clumsy amateur or a wayward balloon. One day down at Peaks Island a man went up in a balloon and fell out at an elevation of one thousand feet—attached to a parachute, of course. He wasn't injured a particle, but a man who remained on the turf nearly had his spine pounded in with a croquet mallet. You see, it was this way—but that's an entirely different story, we are obliged to confess, and we'll tell it some time when we're talking about balloons. 'Tis the canoe, this time—the airy, fairy birch, the prosaic but more reliable canvas, the joy of flittings over sun-kissed waters,

> The mild delights of the summer nights,
> When o'er the placid lake we flew,
> With the gurgling dip and the silent slip
> Of our fairy boat, the birch canoe.

We'd like to give the rest and have it set to music, but the above is all there is of it, at present. The epic of the birch canoe has never been written and never will be, for the canoe doesn't belong with an epic. It fits well with the lute, the lyric, the twanging harp and the merry triolet. After a long, dreamy, langurous sail in a canoe one goes home feeling as though an epic were all rolled up in one's soul and that if one could but get hold of the end of the roll, it could be pulled out, stanza after stanza, to the astonishment of the world. But alas, no one has yet been able to finger that mystic and elusive end. And then, too, as we said before, the canoe doesn't move to epic measure. There's poetry to it, though, and if ever that trite old saying, "the poetry of motion," takes meaning, it is when some fair maid whispers it as she trails her hand in the limpid stream that laves the canoe's smooth sides. Here is the Elysian of the dainty craft—when it is freighted with love and lovers and swings only in summer waters, beneath soft sunshine or a quiet moon. As you regard its fragile structure then, it seems fit for nothing except to bear dainty maidens on cushioned seats as they listen to the dalliance of lovers. But pshaw! If that is the limit of your experience with canoes, you have never seen this delicate creature of the waters in the pride of its grace, the glory of its being.

Go, sometime. in the season of the rushing spring floods, away up where the turbid Penobscot waters roll and roar through the forests, up above Socattean and silver Brassua. Then watch the docile canoe in the hands of its lord and master, the rough Maine woodsman. Here in these riotous cataracts, in these rapids with

ledges showing like jagged teeth between the angry lips of the parted flood, the stanch steamer, the proud ship, even the mighty cruiser would be wrecked and dashed and torn upon the waiting rocks. No human art could pilot them safely through. But here is the fragile birch in its earliest. its true home, meeting the waters with jaunty buoyancy, dancing like a sprite in the crests of cataracts, fleeing in mock alarm down rolling rapids with the roar of baffled waters echoing behind ; the jagged ledges harm it not, if the eye of the master be steady and the arm be strong.

Yes, the canoe as it dances to summer music on our blue lake at the hill-foot, is a dainty creature, and the flutter of a thought, almost, can swing its nervous prow. Remember, though, that its brother in the far waters to the north is the toiling lumberman's best friend, his faithful steed by day through boiling rapids, his couch by night before the camp-fire's ruddy embers, and his shelter when the tempests and the rains come down.

Our Orchestra.

> "And Music lifted up the listening spirit
> Until it walked exempt from mortal care,
> God-like o'er the clear billows of sweet sound."

TO a regular visitor for ten consecutive years at Poland Springs, no surprise is ever awakened by circumstances giving evidence of that intelligent and liberal enterprise, ever alert in the interest of their guests, that characterizes the management of our delightful summer home on the fairest "hill-top" of this Switzerland of America. But an especial word of commendation is due the generous consideration which procured for us such an organization as that furnishing the music of the present season. The writer is one who knows the worth and standing of Mr. Kuntz's musicians as members of the famous Boston Symphony Orchestra, and bears hearty testimony to the high estimate placed upon their ability by the best musical judges of the "Hub." They are excelled by no organization of the same number in the country, and most assuredly equaled by few.

BOSTONIAN.

Bubbles.

"Love all."

A full house.

The weather is cooler.

Hearts is now the game.

Great mornings for a drive.

The studio is nearly finished.

Jolly parties on the lake this week.

A new croquet ground was laid out Monday.

The "curiosity drawer" is full to overflowing.

Early rising is the rule these beautiful mornings.

Aunt Amelia and her gracious smile are favorite visitors on the hill.

Instead of "barefoot boy with cheek of tan" it is "barefoot girl with hair of brown."

Ex-Governor Plaisted, of Bangor, is enjoying a two weeks' vacation at the Mansion House.

Mr. King, of Quincy, Mass., and his charming daughter were at the big house over Sunday.

Mr. Pike, of Owen, Moore & Co., is on the hill every Friday. You can find him at the store.

Judge A. J. White, wife and daughter, are here for a short stay. Mr. White is a New York police justice.

Dr. Weeks, that celebrated Portland Hospital surgeon, is taking a short respite from duties at his favorite resort.

Miss Hunting, of New York, has been exhibiting an excellent line of fancy linen work during the past week.

"The very garden of the State of Maine," said S. R. Small of Portland as he came out on the veranda Thursday morning.

The Poland brake is in great demand this beautiful weather. Not a day passes but what a gay party of young people enjoy a ride on the same.

When reports have reached us that the thermometers in cities have registered way up in the nineties, we have been enjoying the most refreshing of cool breezes.

Mr. and Mrs. S. R. Small, of Portland, arrived Tuesday for their summer's visit. Mr. Small is an old Poland visitor, coming here for the past ten years or so.

F. Williams, of Boston, has been here the past week in the interest of a large photographing firm. He succeeded in obtaining several fine views of the houses and grounds.

John Anderson, of Portland, accompanied by Mrs. C. F. Matheson and Master Sam A. Matheson, spent Sunday at the large house. Mr. Anderson is the popular manager of the Hotel Ormond, Fla., one of the largest and finest resorts in the South.

The steamboat inspectors visited Poland one day last week and gave the little "Poland" a searching examination. Their verdict was that the pride of the Range Lakes is as staunch and substantially built a steamboat as can be made. The engine is a beauty and sufficiently strong to propel the launch at a good speed.

From July 10th to Sept. 10th, Poland Spring.

H. T. JORDAN, } Editors.
W. D. FREEMAN, }

PUBLISHED EVERY SUNDAY MORNING DURING THE MONTHS
OF JULY, AUGUST AND SEPTEMBER, IN THE INTERESTS OF

POLAND SPRING AND ITS VISITORS.

All contributions relative to the guests of Poland Spring will be thankfully received.

To insure publication, all communications should reach the editors not later than Thursday preceding day of issue.

All parties desiring rates for advertising in the HILL-TOP should write the editors for same.

The subscription price of the HILL-TOP is $1.00 for the season, post-paid. Single copies will be mailed at 10c. each.

Address,

Editors "HILL-TOP,"
Poland Spring House,
South Poland, Maine.

PRINTED AT JOURNAL OFFICE, LEWISTON.

Sunday, July 29, 1894.

Editorial.

THE popularity which the Poland Spring and its famous hotels have been enjoying in past years is ever increasing. Last season a large addition was built to the south-east wing, which, it was thought, would accommodate all our patrons. But even that large amount of guest space does not begin to furnish room for all applicants desiring entertainment. The business done at both houses this season is unprecedented in the history of these famous hostelries. The booking for the remainder of the season is very full, and indications go to show that Poland is enjoying as good as, if not a better season's business than any of the other White Mountain resorts.

THE interest taken by the guests of the houses in our own symphony rehearsals, daily, in Music Hall, is evinced by their large attendance and perfect satisfaction. The class of music furnished is the finest and most select, and the style of rendering is par excellence. It is absolutely necessary that silence should reign supreme during the rendition of the selections, so that the full force each piece is intended to carry should be received. It is, therefore, especially requested by the leader of the orchestra that all conversation and moving about be postponed until the finish of each selection. This, we are sure, will add greatly to the effect of the music.

Announcement.

Commencing Monday, July 23d, carriages will leave the Poland Spring House daily at 10.30 A.M., connecting at the lake with the launch Poland. Returning, carriages will leave the lake at 12.30, reaching the hotels in time for dinner.

All parties intending to visit the lake for rowing, bathing, sailing, etc., and wishing seats in the carriages, should leave their names at the office by 10 o'clock.

The Hop.

SATURDAY evening's hop was what can be characterized as jolly. The evening was delightfully cool, the music was better than ever, and everybody seemed wonderfully good-natured. The attendance was by far the best yet, the dancers being out in force, while the many handsomely dressed matrons and their escorts filled the spectators' seats to overflowing. One of the features of the evening was the Virginia Reel, led by Mr. King of Quincy and Miss Mattocks of Chicago. The Lancers was prettily danced, and the beautiful costumes of the ladies appeared to good advantage. The costumes were all handsome, and it is safe to say that in no summer hotel in the country are the ladies more tastily dressed than here. White was the favorite color on Saturday.

Among the ladies on the floor were noticed Mrs. Dickinson, Chicago; Miss Craven, New York; Miss Carpenter, Boston; Miss DeLima, New York; Miss Mattocks, Chicago; Miss Stinson, Philadelphia; Miss King, Quincy; Miss Maginnis, New Orleans; Miss Eddy, Montreal; Miss Ames, Easton, Mass.; Miss McNeal, New York; Miss Weeks, Portland; Miss Todd, New York; Miss Gray, Boston.

Hours of Meals.

	Week Days.	Sundays.
Breakfast,	7 A.M. to 9 A.M.	8 A.M. to 10 A.M.
Dinner,	1 P.M. to 3 P.M.	1.30 P.M. to 3.30 P.M.
Supper,	6 P.M. to 8 P.M.	6 P.M. to 8 P.M.

Literary.

Jimmy on the "Chute."

I.

Little Jimmy was a scholar,
And his aptitude was such
That his parents and preceptors
Were afraid he'd know too much.
So his grandmama said, "Bless him,
I will take him up to town,
And we'll go to Captain Boynton's,
And they'll water-shoot us down."

CHORUS.

Oh! Jimmy on the "chute," boys;
Won't he have a day?
Going out with grandma—
Granny's getting gay!
Down in half a clap-bang,
Wet from top to toe;
That's the way they "chute" 'em
At the Water Show.

II.

Now, when Jimmy saw the Water-Chute
He laughed until he cried,
Just to see the girls yell out, and grab
The fellows by their side.
And he said to gentle grandma:
"This will suit me to a T,
When I get up there, and have those girls
A grabbing hold of me."

CHORUS.

III.

Then he took his seat with grandma,
And they started off all right;
But a pretty girl beside him screamed,
"You'd better hold on tight!"
They were flying down so fast
That Jimmy's head began to swim;
So he clawed on to that pretty girl,
And she clawed on to him.

CHORUS.

IV.

But the splash was so terrific
That his heart began to quake,
As his grandma turned a somersault
And fell into the lake.
So he held on to the pretty girl
And hugged her tighter still;
For he thought the world was ended,
And he hadn't made his will.

CHORUS.

V.

With a boat-hook poor old grandmama
Was fished up safe and sound;
But the pretty girl and Jimmy
In a close embrace were found.
In the terrible alarm they would
Not hear of letting go;
So they're hugging one another still
For anything I know!

CHORUS.

London. "M."

The Magic Arts of the East.

SOME few years ago as I sat in my bungalow in the far East amid the beautiful and fascinating scenery of the Vale of Cashmere, a spot made memorable and romantic by Tom Moore in his "Lalla Rookh," a man perhaps of sixty years, devoid of clothing save a cloth about his loins, of fine physique and intelligent countenance, appeared at the door and asked if I would give him a rupee to perform some of the famous Hindu tricks of which I had heard so much. I was only too glad and willing to accede, little dreaming of the marvelous and wonderful things in store for me. A few feet in front of the bungalow this Hindu Magi took a rope and threw it in the air where it remained standing and supported by some unseen power; presently a boy of some five or six years, who accompanied this wandering magician, climbed up this rope and disappeared to all appearances, although he appeared again later on the scene. To me this trick was marvelous and more than wonderful; it was incomprehensible, as it bid defiance to all the laws of gravitation and nature. I had purchased a few weeks before a bamboo cane in Manilla in the Philippine Islands. This man of mystery took a piece of thread from a bag which all these itinerant jugglers carry, and in which is their stock in trade—venomous cobras of six to eight feet in length, live hares, etc., and measured the thread exactly of the length of my cane. He cut the thread into small pieces, rolled it into a ball, put it in his mouth and swallowed it, apparently so, as I was within two feet from him. Presently he took a knife and commenced digging into the side of his body with the sharp point, just above his loin cloth, and the blood spurted. He continued until the knife caught the end of the thread and then he asked me to pull it out, which I did, although my hand was covered with blood in this ghastly operation. The thread, when withdrawn, corresponded exactly to the length of my cane, and this Hindu swore by all that was holy that it was the same piece which he had swallowed. Be that as it may it was too mysterious and incomprehensible for me to solve. In a moment or two he said for another rupee he would perform a trick that was the most mysterious of them all. I thought that I had seen the wonder of wonders, in which all the laws of nature had been violated and set at defiance, and told him another rupee was his as soon as this mysterious phenomenon was performed. He took from a box in the bag hereinbefore alluded to, six ordinary orange seeds and a large flower pot, filled the pot with earth taken just a few feet in front of the bungalow, and planted the seeds in the earth. He covered the pot and commenced his Hindu incantations. In eight minutes by my watch there was a tree with several full-grown oranges. He told me to pluck one from the tree, which I did and found it was as sweet as an Havana. I have some of the seeds now at home as a souvenir of this man of mystery. Other tricks these famous jugglers of the far East perform, such as taking a live cobra, one of the most venomous and poisonous, which they handle with the utmost indifference and complacency, and cutting it up into small pieces, taking the pieces and apparently rolling them together and, while doing so, calling on the powers of the unseen to help—and presto change—his snakeship crawls away, raising his head and widening his hoods, which appear on both sides of his head. The basket trick was another mysterious reality. But I had seen enough, and gave the magi his promised rupee and retired to cogitate over and try to fathom what I had seen. But the more I thought, the more bewildering, mysterious, and incomprehensible it was, and so gave it up. It must be remembered that all these above-mentioned feats of juggling were performed within two feet from where I was standing, with no hidden assistance or stage machinery, and that made what I had seen more wonderful and unfathomable.

J. H. C.

Lovers' Lane.

NO well-regulated summer resort would think of existing without a "lovers' lane." It can get along without an orchestra or a tennis court, but a "lovers' lane" never.

The very name itself is an attraction, and I have known of a number of young men who have left a hotel after one day's sojourn on finding that this most useful object was not among the attractions of the place.

But Poland Spring has its "lovers' lane."

Do you know where it is? If you are a young man or maiden you will laugh at the question, especially if you have been here more than twenty-four hours.

Of course you have visited the spring first, but after one evening at the hotel, and having been introduced to all the pretty girls that are here this season, you have investigated the long shady path, and tried the seats that are to be found at intervals, each a sufficient distance from the other.

It is here that the summer girl is supposed to listen to the soft nothings of the summer man. Nothings that sound so pleasant, and that mean so little. Perhaps the heart may beat a little faster, but it is soon forgotten on her part when

he is gone, and she is ready for the next one, while he, some months later, comes across a bit of ribbon or a flower, and wonders where on earth he got that.

"Lovers' lane!" We old people look quietly on and smile, and then closing our eyes we let memory carry us back to another youth and maiden wandering down "lovers' lane" in the long ago.

Perhaps it was no more than a country road, but to us it was paradise.

Happy youth, happy maiden.

But we smile as we look at the companion by our side, and think that it is not the same that wandered with us then, and we know that the ones who walk together down the shady groves of Poland Spring will not be the ones who will walk together down the pathway of life.

Such is fate.

So we look kindly on at the youth and maiden of to-day, careless and happy, and while a pain may tug at our hearts at the thought that we are growing old, we murmur a "God bless them."

And so, friends, when you write to those who are away, about the beauties of Poland, don't forget to add that it has a "lovers' lane."

E. L. J.

The sound of the chime whistle is now heard in the land.

Boating parties are all the rage now since the "Poland" has been put into commission.

As the Tuxedo Quartette was leaving on the coach, Wednesday morning, they sang "Love's Own Sweet Song" in a very pleasing manner, and received a hearty encore.

Orchestra.

The programme for Sunday, July 29th, is as follows:

1. March.	Lachner.
2. Overture—Die Felsenmühle.	Reissiger.
3. Selection—Corolleria Rusheana.	Massoagin.
4. { a. Adagio. { b. Gondoliera—from Puite.	Ries.
Violin Solo—Mr. Kuntz.	
5. Two Hungarian Dances.	Brohm.
6. Fantasia—Martha.	Flotow.
7. Wedding March.	Mendelssohn.

Coming Events.

Sunday, July 29th.—Concert, 3.30 P.M.

Wednesday, August 1st.—Base-Ball, Poland Spring vs. — 3.30 P.M.

Friday, August 3d.—Progressive Euchre, 8 P.M., Amusement Room.

Saturday, August 4th.—Base-Ball, 2.30 P.M., Poland Spring vs. Freeport.—8.15 P.M., Full-Dress Hop.

Base-Ball.

SATURDAY'S base-ball game was a rather unsatisfactory one. The commencement of the game was delayed an hour or more by a heavy shower, and when the men did get to work the grounds and ball were so wet that good ball-tossing was an impossibility. After seven innings of heavy hitting and yellow fielding the game was called in a heavy rain storm, with the score fourteen to ten in favor of the home team. The Murphy Balsams came up loaded for bear, having Grandpa Morse and Dolan of the Portlands as pitchers. The Murphys are old antagonists of ours, and undoubtedly will give us some hot games before the season closes. The score of the game will not appear in print.

* * * *

On Wednesday we tackled the Y. M. C. A. team. There has been a fairy story related that this team went to Rockland once and gave a wonderful exhibition of ball-tossing. Consequently we expected to have a hard tussle to send them home licked. Sad to relate, the team which came over was a far different one from what we expected, and the boys were treated to a nice juicy blueberry pie, with ice-cream and Edam cheese on side. 18 to 3 was the score, and a few more games like it would result in a mighty falling off in the interest in base-ball. Garcelon of Harvard was on third for the visitors and did nicely, though he committed suicide on second twice, his running not being up to Powers's throwing. Slattery, of Bates College, our change pitcher last season, did the twirling for the visitors and was hit hard. "Terry" is a nice boy and can pitch good ball, but the team behind him was enough to beat the best man in the box.

Lawson officiated for us and did elegant work, only four hits being made off his curves. That in Plaisted and Lawson we have the two best pitchers in Maine outside of the League, goes. The score by innings:

Innings	1	2	3	4	5	6	7	8	9	
Poland Springs	2	2	7	0	2	1	2	0	2—18
Y. M. C. A.	0	1	1	0	1	0	0	0	0—3

Hits, Poland Springs 18, Y. M. C. A. 4. Errors, Poland Springs 6, Y. M. C. A. 7. Earned runs, Poland Springs 1, Y. M. C. A. 1. Two-base hits, Wakefield, Powers. Three-base hit, Sockelexis. Home run, Nason. Stolen bases, Lawson, Powers, Sykes 2, Plaisted, Hall, Pulsifer 2, Slattery. Base on balls, by Lawson, Penley, Gerrish, Slattery 2, by Slattery, Wakefield, Lawson, Sykes. Struck out, by Lawson, Nason, Penley, Renney, Merrow, Pulsifer 2, Garcelon, Bumpus 3, by Slattery, Wakefield, Powers, Harris. Double play, Sykes, Hall and Pulsifer. Hit by pitched ball, by Slattery, Pulsifer. Wild pitches, by Lawson 2, by Slattery 4. Passed ball, Gerrish. Umpire, O. J. Hackett. Time, 2h., 30m.

We are too strong for these local teams. On Wednesday a challenge was sent out to any hotel team in New England and soon the battle will be on. The White Mountain teams are good and we shall have some hot work cut out for us.

Concert.

THE amusement committee did themselves proud when they booked Graham's Concert Company for the concert of Tuesday evening. It is safe to say that no company of equal note has ever appeared here and that the work of Mr. Jose and his companions was appreciated. The numerous encores and liberal applause were sufficient proof.

When the Tuxedo Quartette appeared shortly after eight, beautiful Music Hall was crowded to the doors. Their first selection, the "Bridge," caught the audience and they gave a double encore. Master Kimball did nicely with the banjo, his trick playing being exceedingly clever. Mr. Thomas Lewis rendered his baritone solo, the "Venetian Lullaby," in his best style and was obliged to favor with a second number. Mr. Grilley, the reciter, who came next on the programme, is an old favorite here and received a most flattering reception. His first selection, "Tradin' Joe," was especially well appreciated, and in view of happenings during the week came in very "pat." Mr. Grilley was kept relating funny stories until he refused to hold the stage longer.

The next on the programme was a tenor solo, "The Lone Grave," by Mr. R. J. Jose. Mr. Jose's reputation as a singer is world-wide and his solos were up to his usual standard. As encore he gave "Sweet Marie" and "With all her Faults." Miss Hodgen, in her whistling solos, was excellent, her selections from "1492" being exceedingly tuneful. H. W. Frillman sang "The Exile" as he alone can sing it, giving as an encore "The Sexton." Mr. John H. Davis in his solo "Anne o' the banks o' Dee," and Miss Hart, the popular contralto, with the selection "Dear Heart," were both good and well received.

Mr. Graham is to be congratulated on his fine company, and if right receives its reward he will play to large houses.

Mr. and Mrs. J. A. Singer, accompanied by Mr. M. M. Singer, arrived from New York Wednesday evening, to enjoy a few days' sojourn at Poland. Mr. Singer is one of the Singer machine firm.

Chicago and Poland.

ECRETARY DICKINSON of the World's Fair Commission, who, with his wife and her daughter, is at present enjoying the pleasures of Poland, has since his arrival here, written a letter to a prominent official of the Grand Trunk Railway in Chicago, from which he has permitted the HILL-TOP to make the following interesting extracts:

"I am sure that no one ever wrote a letter of thanks with more genuine sincerity than I write this to you for having been so kind and thoughtful, when you understood from me that I was going to Poland Spring, Me., over the Grand Trunk Railway, to suggest that I include in my trip the boat ride down the St. Lawrence River. I accepted your suggestion as I had never before been in Canada and was not familiar with either its rail or water routes. Now that I have made the trip as suggested I wish I could proclaim to all Chicagoans who spend their summers at Eastern and New England resorts in this latitude, the diversified beauties of scenery presented by nature and the varied attractions provided by man along this entire route. We left Chicago via the Grand Trunk at three o'clock last Sunday afternoon, the 15th inst., amidst a sweltering heat, and getting away as fast as possible from all the *striking* effects on the road, we were soon whirling through the rich and variegated farm country of Northern Indiana and Michigan. After passing through a most interesting section of Canada, we reached Cananoque the following afternoon and were soon aboard an excursion boat smoothly gliding through the lovely waters that surround the picturesque Thousand Islands over to Alexandria Bay, where we arrived in time for a good supper at the Crossman House, after which we watched the dancers in the parlors of the hotel and drank in the exquisite scenery of water and island made mellow by a full moonlight. After a cool night's rest and a hearty breakfast we boarded the St. Lawrence River steamer that touches at Alexandria Bay at 7.30 bound for Montreal and due there at 6.30 P.M. If a Chicagoan wants to get a complete rest and at the same time be refreshed and invigorated, let him take this superb river trip and shoot the rapids of the St. Lawrence. If he can't possibly get away from Chicago and would like to experience in miniature the novel sensation of shooting the rapids on a boat, he should go out some evening in the vicinity of Jackson Park and take a ride on the Paul Boynton Chute. It will, however, be but a faint suggestion of the wonderful pleasure of the real trip. It would be like seeing a miniature of the World's Fair for five minutes and afterwards spending a day at the Fair. A memory of the World's Fair and a memory of a trip through the Thousand Islands and down the St. Lawrence would be suitable companion pieces—the one the magnificent handiwork of man, the other the beautiful creation of Nature—both conceived and executed with a prodigality of resources absolutely unlimited.

After the excitement attendant upon shooting the last of the Rapids, the Lachine, and the perpetration of a joke because the Indian pilot failed to come on board just before reaching the Lachine Rapids according to published posters, some one remarking that this was about the last job pool Lo had in this country and the white man was mean enough to cheat him out of that, we soon steamed under the great Victoria Railway Bridge into Montreal, where, after a drive about the city and supper at the Windsor, at 8.40 P.M. we took the Portland Sleeper via the Grand Trunk Railway for Danville Junction, at which place we left the train at 6.30 A.M. An exhilarating drive over the beautiful hills of Maine soon brought us to the famous Poland Spring House, which I visited for the first time last summer at the suggestion of Dr. Z. T. Sowers, one of the best-known physicians in Washington City. He was most earnest in his praise of this ideal place, in the curative properties of the Poland Spring water, and I thought he might be prejudiced in its favor as he claimed there was no place equal to it in all New England. 'I came, I saw, and I concurred' in all the great physician had told me, and I was soon further convinced that the half had not been told and probably never will be in regard to this happy combination of an elegant summer resort and sanitarium, its absolutely healthful location on a charming elevation surrounded by picturesque woodland and lake scenery, with the mountains in the distance, its grand dining-room and sumptuous but home-like table, its large and airy rooms, its long stretch of broad verandas, its manifold attractions both natural and artificial, and its altogether superior management in every detail under the personal control and direction of the three Ricker Brothers whose father was the founder of this splendid property, and who have steadily built up this great resort upon the broadest and most intelligent lines until the place has become so popular that it is upon each recurring summer filled to its utmost capacity.

Nature and the Ricker Brothers have certainly made Poland Spring and its immediate surroundings the happiest dual resort for the seeker after health and the seeker after pleasure that can possibly be found in the United States. From my acquaintance with many Chicagoans I feel satisfied that if they could have their attention called to the trip I have just enjoyed as well as to the attractions to be found at the Poland Spring House as above outlined, they would make the trip and take their summer outing at this ideal place."

Progressive Euchre.

ON Monday evening, the euchre party postponed from the preceding Friday came off in the amusement room. Nine tables were filled by card enthusiasts and a very pleasant evening was passed in handling the picture cards.

At the conclusion the following lucky ones received tasty prizes: First ladies', Mrs Corby; second ladies', Mrs. B. F. Moulton; third ladies', Mrs. Maginnis. First gentlemen's, Mrs. Sanborn of the Mansion House; second gentlemen's, Mr. Worcester, Mansion House; third gentlemen's, Dr. Freeman. Ladies' consolation, Mrs. Frost, Mansion House. Gentlemen's consolation, Mr. Munson.

Bubbles.

Judge E. J. Sherman, of Lawrence, Mass., has arrived and taken his rooms.

Father Clarke, of Boston, is spending his vacation at Poland. He expresses himself as delighted with his choice of resorts.

Elisha Dyer, Adjutant-General of the State of Rhode Island, is among last week's arrivals. Mr. Dyer comes from Providence.

The bath-houses on the beach at Middle Range Lake are used considerably of late, as bathing is being indulged in to a great extent.

Samuel A. Williams and wife, of Boston, are paying Poland their first visit. Mr. Williams is treasurer of the Vassalboro Woolen Mills. Boston.

Hon. Joseph G. Ray and wife, with Miss Lydia P. Ray, are here for the season. Mr. Ray is a large woolen manufacturer, of Franklin, Mass.

Mr. Geo. C. Chase, a prominent tea importer of New York City, who has been stopping at Poland Spring Hotel for some time, left last week for home.

Mrs. J. H. Coppenhagen has been giving an exhibition of fancy goods from the Woman's Exchange, Fifth Avenue, New York City, in the Music Hall, the past week.

Hon. C. E. Morrison, president of the Concord & Montreal Railroad, spent a few days here last week. Mr. Morrison's private turn-out, which he brought with him, was a beauty.

Mr. and Mrs. F. W. Carpenter, Misses Julia and Hannah Carter, and maid, are occupying their old rooms at Poland Spring Hotel. Mr. Carpenter is a large iron and steel manufacturer of Providence, R. I.

William A. Vose and wife, Miss Vose, and Master George A. Vose, of Brookline, Mass., have again hied them to Poland, to sip of the waters of life. Mr. Vose is the well-known piano manufacturer of Boston.

Mr. and Mrs. C. Whittemore of Boston, are stopping at the large house for a few weeks. Mr. Whittemore is much interested in good horse-flesh, having at present a large string of fast ones at Rigby Park. He has a pretty turn-out with him here.

These warm afternoons find the grove and green walk filled with guests, especially the pretty girls. Card parties are often held there during the heat of the day, and together with the swings, hammocks, tents, etc., serve to present a very animated appearance.

E. Lawrence Jenkins, editor of the *Boston Times*, spent Sunday and Monday last at his favorite retreat from all cares. Mr. Jenkins is well known here from his close connection with the Poland Spring Hotel last season, and his friends are recorded in hosts.

I. W. Kemtle and family, together with W. H. Steigervalt and family, left Poland last Monday on a fishing trip through the Rangeley Lake region. They left here for Mount Kineo House, Moosehead Lake. Mr. Kemtle is interested in a large tin-plate manufactory, and Mr. Steigervalt is a prominent shoe manufacturer of the Quaker City.

Ex-Governor Ames and daughter, Miss Susie Ames, of North Easton, Mass., are here enjoying the bracing air and water of the famous Poland Spring. The Governor is loud in his praises of Poland, and especially so of the water, as they have served to strengthen him, not only in muscle but in avoirdupois. He has been here five days and gained five pounds.

Mr. Fulton Paul and wife arrived at the Poland Spring House on Friday for their usual sojourn. Mr. Paul, who claims Hudson, N. Y., as his home, has been a great traveler, having spent the greater part of his life abroad. He has had the honor of representing the United States as Consul at Trinidad, Bermuda Islands; Odessa, Russia, and Consul-General to Roumania. Mr. Paul is a most interesting conversationalist and numbers many friends among the Poland pilgrims.

STAGES.

DEPART.

	M. H.	P. S. H.
For Portland and Boston,	6.25 A.M.	6.30 A.M.
Lewiston and Farmington,	8.25 A.M.	8.30 A.M.
Portland and Boston,	9.25 A.M.	9.30 A.M.
Lewiston and Bar Harbor,	10.25 A.M.	10.30 A.M.
Lewiston and Bangor,	12.45 P.M.	1 P.M.
Portland and Boston,	3.25 P.M.	3.30 P.M.

ARRIVE.

	M. H.	P. S. H.
From the West,	10.30 A.M.	10.35 A.M.
From the East,	1 P.M.	1.05 P.M.
From the West,	3.30 P.M.	3.35 P.M.
" "	7.30 P.M.	7.35 P.M.

MAILS.

CLOSE.

Poland Spring House.	Mansion House.
5.45 A.M.	6 A.M.
8.45 A.M.	9 A.M.
2.45 P.M.	3 P.M.

ARRIVE.

10 A.M.	9.30 A.M.
1.30 P.M.	1 P.M.
4.30 P.M.	4 P.M.
8 P.M.	7.45 P.M.

Arrivals

POLAND SPRING HOUSE.

Anderson, John,	Ormond, Fla.
Allen, Edmund,	Philadelphia.
Allen, Miss L.,	Philadelphia.
Ames, Oliver,	North Easton, Mass.
Ames, Miss Susie,	North Easton, Mass.
Adams, A. H.,	Haverhill.
Adams, Mrs. A. H.,	Haverhill.
Acklaw, W. H.,	Washington.
Bumstead, Horace,	Atlanta, Ga.
Beylle, Mrs.,	Boston.
Bradford, G. H. and wife,	Boston.
Bailey, George H. and wife,	Minneapolis.
Bell, James G. and wife,	Minneapolis.
Buck, Mrs. L. L.,	Brooklyn.
Bladen, James and wife,	Salem.
Bulet, J. H. and wife,	Philadelphia.
Chapman, Mrs. H. L.,	Boston.
Chatman, Mrs. J. W.,	Boston.
Cotton, John B.,	Washington.
Colligan, E.,	New York.
Cole, Miss,	Brooklyn.
Carpenter, Mrs. K. H.,	Brooklyn.
Clark, Van Law and wife,	New York.
Carpenter, W. J.,	Katonah.
Clarke, M.,	Boston.
Childs, Mrs. George W. and maid,	Philadelphia.
Claine, W. N. and wife,	Chicago.
DeLima, Edward,	New York.
Danielson, H. L.,	Providence.
Danielson, J. DeForest,	Providence.
Denning, H. and wife,	Stamford, Conn.
Duzenburgh, J. W.,	New York.
Duzenburgh, Mrs. J. W.,	New York.
Dyer, Elisha,	Providence.
Ely, Mrs. Alfred B.,	Boston.
Ennis, George W.,	Kasto, B. C.
Feltus, Mr. and wife,	Philadelphia.
Ganz, Lewis,	New York.
Gilligan, M.,	Medford.
Grubb, Mrs. H. B. and maid,	Burlington, N. J.
Grubb, Edward B.,	Sheridan, Pa.
Grifford, Mrs. E. and maid,	Jersey City Heights.
Hirsh, Col. and wife,	St. Louis.
Hodge, Dwight and wife,	Franklin.
Hilliard, J. P.,	Boston.
Huntling, K. L.,	Boston.
Haskell, H. S.,	Boston.
Hinckley, Stephen,	Gorham.
Hinckley, Mrs. Stephen,	Gorham.
Higby, Charles and wife,	Salem.
Hartwell, Mrs. M. E.,	Cambridge.
Hill, W. W. and wife,	New York.
Hall, Dr. Thomas and wife,	Boston.
Hill, Dr. and Mrs. Noble H.,	Boston.
Jones, Charles A.,	Boston.
Jenkins, Mr. and Mrs. and child,	Winchester, Mass.
King, T.,	Boston.
King, Miss Jayma,	Boston.
Kisterbock, J. and wife,	Philadelphia.
Longstreet, Mrs. C. A.,	New York.
Matherson, Mrs. C. F.,	New York.
Matherson, Master Sam. A.,	New York.
Mills, Frederick,	Boston.
Miller, R. and wife,	Philadelphia.
O'Cumpagh, E. and wife,	Rochester, N. Y.
Parker, George,	North Easton, Mass.
Patterson, Miss E. P.,	Philadelphia.
Paul, Miss H.,	Newton Centre.

Paige, Mr. and Mrs. F. E.,	Boston.
Reade, R. L.,	New York.
Rodwell, James and wife,	Brooklyn.
Roberts, Miss,	Philadelphia.
Ripley, C. T. and son,	Boston.
Rice, Mrs. M. O.,	Newton Centre.
Sherman, E. J.,	Lawrence.
Simes, S. B. and wife,	Philadelphia.
Spencer, John S. and wife,	New York.
Spring, Mrs. E.,	Portland.
Spring, Miss E.,	Portland.
Sweet, C. M.,	New York.
Smith, Albert W. and wife,	Providence.
Sands, Ledyard,	New York.
Small, S. R. and wife,	Portland.
Singer, I. A. and wife,	New York.
Singer, M. M.,	New York.
Tamer, M.,	Boston.
Todd, Mrs. W. J.,	New York.
Todd, Miss Rita L.,	New York.
Todd, Miss M. Blanch,	New York.
Todd, Jane Rose,	Somerville.
Taimper, Miss,	New York.
True, George W.,	Portland.
Tabor, Joseph W. and wife,	Portland.
Thayer, Emery,	New York.
Van Wyck, H. D.,	Norfolk, Va.
Vose, Williard A. and wife,	Brookline.
Vose, Miss,	Brookline.
Vose, George A.,	Brookline.
Weeks, S. W. and wife,	Portland.
Weeks, Miss,	Portland.
Walker, Thomas J. and wife,	Plymouth, N. H.
White, A. J. and wife,	New York.
White, Miss,	New York.
Williams, F. and wife,	Boston.
Williams, Samuel and wife,	Boston.

MANSION HOUSE.

Bechur, Mrs. A.,	Montreal.
Blake, C. C.,	Portland.
Brown, Mr. and Mrs. F.,	Boston, Mass.
Campbell, Mrs. J.,	Camden, N. J.
Campbell, Miss,	Camden, N. J.
Clark, F. L.,	Gray, Me.
Gilman, D. L.,	Portland, Me.
Goldsmith and child,	Brooklyn, N. Y.
Hay, H. Ludlow,	New York.
Harding, E. B. and wife,	Worcester, Mass.
Jordan, E. C. and wife,	Portland, Me.
Kling. A. H.,	Marion, Ohio.
Kling, Ellen,	Augusta, Me.
Leighton, Ora S.,	Portland.
Middlebrook, F. H. and wife,	Bridgeport, Ct.
Middlebrook, W. B. and wife,	Bridgeport, Ct.
Putnam, Edwin A.,	Worcester.
Raymond, James H.,	Lewiston.
Reed, Mrs. L. S.,	Camden, N. J.
Reed, W. T.,	Camden, N. J.
Smith, R. E.,	Portland.
Thompson, Mr. and Mrs. J. A.,	Boston.
Thompson, J. Gifford,	Boston.
Whyte, Miss,	Montreal.
Whyte, Miss M.,	Montreal.
Wilkinson, Harry C.,	Lewiston.

Mrs. George W. Childs, wife of the late philanthropist and editor of the *Philadelphia Ledger*, is paying Poland an extended visit. Mrs. Childs is accompanied by Miss Patterson as companion.

Vol. I.   SUNDAY MORNING, AUGUST 5, 1894.   No. 5.

On the Poland Brake.

IT was upon an ideal afternoon in July that a merry party of young people left the Poland Spring House on the brake for a drive over the pretty hills and shady woodlands at Poland, including a visit to the celebrated dog kennels of Mr. Pope, a cut of which appears on this page. With that exhilaration of feeling that always accompanies a ride on a brake, the party enjoyed the scenery and landscape on the road to the kennels. Arriving there they were still more delighted with the wonderful exhibit of thoroughbred dogs, embracing all the best breeds of man's faithful friend. It was the unanimous opinion of the party that any one spending the summer at the Poland Spring House and failing to visit Pope's dog kennels had missed a great treat. The party then resumed their seats on the brake and the horses started on a brisk trot towards Gloucester, a beautiful little village situated on the top of a lofty hill, from the summit of which a broad expanse of meadow land is visible. Passing through the village, the party drove through shady roads to the hamlet of Upper Corner, and thence to the old saw-mill, where the young folks alighted to view the beautiful falls below the mill. Each young fellow with his lady-love was held spell-bound by the grand sight which the sparkling water made as it leaped over the rocks and fell into the clear pool beneath. After tearing themselves away from this inspiring spot, they ascended the brake once more and were soon homeward bound over Bald Hill. As the horses pulled up the steep ascent, a glorious scene was soon presented—the setting sun hanging in the heavens like a huge ball of fire, dropped slowly behind Mount Washington. The magnificent sight held the party spell-bound, until the driver, cracking his whip, started the horses down the hill and on through shady woods and picturesque valleys. Arrived at the Poland Spring House tired and hungry, but still confident that one of the most enjoyable ways to spend an afternoon is to take a drive on the Poland brake and visit Pope's dog kennels.

A Jolly Drive.

ON Monday afternoon Miss Mattocks, that most charming of Chicago's fairest daughters, tendered a number of her friends a drive on the Poland brake. The young ladies of the party donned their smartest gowns for the occasion and made a picture most pleasing to the eye. New Gloucester was the objective point and the natives of this secluded hamlet thought that the advance guard of some wandering circus must have struck town. They say that that most popular young man, Mr. A. A. Maginnis of New Orleans, was responsible for that on account of his heroic endeavors to blow the coaching horn. During the returning trip the merry party made the echoes ring with their college songs and the Poland yell.

Home was reached at dusk and Miss Mattocks received the thanks of the party for a most enjoyable afternoon. The following occupied seats: Miss Helen Shuson, Philadelphia; the Misses Todd, New York; Miss Vose, Boston; Miss Mattocks, Chicago; Mr. Allen Rogers, New York; the Messrs. Maginnis, New Orleans; Mr. Vose, Boston; Mr. White, Brockton.

What's the matter with having a coaching parade?

A Pleasant Occasion.

MONDAY evening at ten o'clock, the birthday of Miss Nettie Ricker was celebrated by a most informal little surprise party. The family, with a half-dozen friends, found the birthday cake, at the hour mentioned, waiting to be cut by the young lady in whose honor it was made. The tables were a bower of decoration, small ferns adorned the snowy damask while the larger, graceful green was combined in bouquets with golden-rod and other wild flowers. Pink icing for the cake, raspberry fruit punch with aerated Poland, and a profusion of fragrant pink flowers threw a rosy hue over the table, suggestive of the occasion. Much pleasant chat was exchanged, some pretty gifts received and congratulations warmly extended. The following little verses were written for the evening:

July 30th, 1894.

Midsummer! and a torrid wave
Seems now to sweep about us,
As if the Fairies of the Forge
Were trying hard to rout us!
But what care we for Fahrenheit
When hearts are gaily beating:
When, gathered for a Birthday Fête,
The Birthday Cake we're eating?

We want to wish our hostess fair
Good fortune without limit;
A silver spoon—her very own,
With Moses *profit* in it.
But as her laughing eyes ensnare
A conquered victim neatly,
Let her use wisdom in her choice
And cast her *net* discreetly!

Dear friend, may all prosperity
Attend you now and ever,
And nothing serve this kindly bond
Of loyal hearts to sever!
May future years bring all good gifts
Nor count them in bestowing,
But fill your days with happiness
Brimful and overflowing.

Mrs. Laughlin took great satisfaction in making all the arrangements for the little supper and was much commended for her skill.

J.

Mansion House.

A very pretty walk, which not a few take mornings as a sort of appetizer, is the "One Mile Walk," which starts in just back of the Mansion House and comes out down by the spring. It leads through the prettiest of wooded land, by the quarry and through the well-known and ever-to-be-remembered "Lovers' Lane."

Bubbles.

A Poland chestnut—that the Rickers sell Moses bottles because there is a *prophet* on them.

Mrs. J. S. Diaper, of Canton, Mass., wife of the eminent politician, is here for a short stay.

Mr. O. J. Hackett, of Lewiston, sang before a private party of ladies in Music Hall Wednesday afternoon.

George S. Osgood and wife, of Boston, are occupying one of the best rooms on the second floor of the new part. Mr. Osgood is a prominent musician of the Hub.

Dr. and Mrs. Eugene S. Smith, one of Boston's most celebrated dentists, is enjoying a much-needed vacation from his business at the Poland Spring House.

Three of the base-ball players left Monday last through a refusal to abide by the rules of the club. The players leaving were Plaisted and Lawson, pitchers, and Sykes, fielder.

Whist seems to be the favorite source of amusement for the ladies, and indeed for not a few gentlemen, these fine and sunny afternoons. Progressive euchre is played quite considerably also.

Richard Golden, of "Old Jed Prouty" fame, who registers from that rustic hamlet of Bucksport, Me., was here for a day last week. Mr. Golden made things merry in front of the desk during most of the day.

On the afternoon of July 30th a man fell by the road not far from the Mansion House, in an unconscious condition from fatigue, lack of food, and an attack of heart disease. As he was insensible it was some time before he was discovered, being first seen by the little girl who brings flowers to the hotels. Ice was applied to the head but it was what seemed a long time before the man came to himself. Out of work, he was trying to get to his home in New Brunswick. He was moved to a room, rented by the Rickers, in the Keith cottage, and when able to take it, beef tea and milk were administered to him. The man was self-respecting and had done no soliciting for help. The guests of the Mansion House, under charge of Mr. Robert W. Vonnoh of Philadelphia, raised a tidy little sum to assist the poor man. So near, in these days of hard times in business, do the extremes of comfort and want lie to each other. His full name and address were written on a card in his pocket, with the statement that he was subject to heart disease.

Charles Theodore Russell and wife of Cambridge are here on a short visit. Mr. Russell is the father of ex-Governor William E. Russell of Massachusetts.

The best tennis of the season was played on Monday, between Mr. Singer of New York and Mr. Travelli of Boston. The third and decisive set was won by Mr. Travelli by a score of six games to four. Mr. Singer is a past master of the lawford stroke, but was unfortunate in driving the balls outside the court.

H. T. JORDAN, } EDITORS.
W. D. FREEMAN, }

PUBLISHED EVERY SUNDAY MORNING DURING THE MONTHS
OF JULY, AUGUST AND SEPTEMBER, IN THE INTERESTS OF

POLAND SPRING AND ITS VISITORS.

All contributions relative to the guests of Poland Spring will
be thankfully received.

To insure publication, all communications should reach the
editors not later than Thursday preceding day of issue.

All parties desiring rates for advertising in the HILL-TOP
should write the editors for same.

The subscription price of the HILL-TOP is $1.00 for the
season, post-paid.   Single copies will be mailed at 10c. each.

Address,
EDITORS "HILL-TOP,"
Poland Spring House,
South Poland, Maine.

PRINTED AT JOURNAL OFFICE, LEWISTON.

Sunday, Aug. 5, 1894.

Editorial.

IT is with pleasure that we speak of the reception which the HILL-TOP has been given not only by the guests of the Houses but by the friends of Poland who are unable, on account of business, sickness, or other reasons, to be with us enjoying the multitude of beauties of this well-known resort. We appreciate their many kindnesses shown us, and it has been our earnest endeavor to present them with a publication which should be a credit not only to the editors but also to the interests it represents. The number of contributions handed us have not been so large as we should wish, but we hope as each number is issued, that its pages will contain an increased amount of contributed matter. Remember that our columns are ever open for the discussion of any subject or matter of interest to Polandites. We should be pleased to receive short notices concerning our guests, descriptions of rides, private parties, receptions, etc., and especially so a letter containing your impressions

of Poland and its surroundings. If our friends would contribute more, perhaps the value of THE HILL-TOP would be materially increased.

Ripples.

[Written for the HILL-TOP.]

Our young baby is a real artist—he draws from nature.

Why is the space beneath a dome like the signature on a letter? It is *wrote under.*

The late president of the French, on being asked if he would ride in the tramway, handed simply his card—it read: "Sadi-Carnot."

A lady at a theatre should wear a hoop-skirt—she will be sitting in the "family circle."

Cocoanuts are found in a lot *climb it.*

"A short noise is soon curried." A short course is soon curried.

A log jam is often a *currant* jam.

Tom loved a dry smoke, and his cigar thus ended in a *cigar ate.*

Very dark on the French steamship wharf in New York. The *Gasgogne* out.

Cheap ocean trip—simple *cerate.*

Jones learned more when on a steamer than on land. On the steamer there was always a *tooter.*

He dropped his pocket-book into the material for the new pavement, and, picking it up, remarked, "I like it better in the abstract than in the *concrete.*"

Shakespeare says something about "putting an enemy into his mouth to steal away his brains." When I hear Blobbs talk, I wish some one would put a friend into his brains to steal away his mouth.

The many friends of Mr. F. E. Taylor, of Brooklyn, will be pleased to learn that he has nearly recovered from his recent illness, so much so that a ride of a few miles through some of Poland's prettiest scenery, was given him last Tuesday. We expect to see Mr. Taylor occupying his favorite seat in front of the cashier's desk before many more days have passed.

Mr. Ledyard Sands arrived at the big house on Wednesday of last week, from a two years' tour around the world, during which journey he collected many valuable souvenirs. He is an exceedingly interesting gentleman to talk with and is authority on all questions concerning the history of the "Holy Land," having made an extensive study of that region.

Literary.

The Old Home.

BY GEORGE T. BOURNE.

Tıe falling dooı, tıe time-worn steps,
Tıe beecı tıee dying at tıe gate,
Tıe plasteı dıopping fıom tıe walls,
Are finger-maıks of lost estate.

I know tıat in these gıass-gıown patıs
Ligıt, tiny feet ıave often tıod,
Which now aıe still and ıesting low,
Deep coveıed by tıe daisy sod.

I know the ecıoes never come
To answeı back tıe cıildisı cıy—
Only the biıds tıese ecıoes wake,
In memoıy of the days gone by.

I sit upon tıe time-woın steps
And tıink of days, of yeaıs ago.
I watcı tıe sıadows on the gıass
Tıe sunshine makes in noonday's glow.

And dıeams will come, sad, sad day-dıeams,
Of childıood's ıoıts, of cıildıood's feaıs,
Of bıigıtest smiles, of joyful laugı,
And oft of cıildıood's fleeting tears.

I tuın fıom falling dooı, and sigı,
I leave the moss-gıown stones beıind,
I see the dying beech-tree leaves
Float gently on tıe summeı wind.

And gıass-gıown patıs and tiny feet
Are now tıe dıeams of yesteıday,
Sweet memoıies of a long, long past,
To guide me on life's ebbing way.

Wee Binkelblink.

ADAPTED FROM THE GERMAN FOR THE YOUNG READERS OF THE HILL-TOP.

AMONG many dıops of cıystal-cleaı wateı, foıcing tıeiı way out fıom tıe bosom of Mother Earth tııougı ıock and stone, leaping gladly from daık, cool ıecesses into tıe bıigıt sunsıine, was a ıound, meııy little fellow, Binkelblink by name. Only a dıop of wateı, you may say; yet ıe ıad a mission, a ıistoıy, and moıe ıomantic adventures tıan fall to tlıe lot of most moıtals. You may imagine him as a plump, dimpled little spıite, witı a Cupid-like peısonality and a meııy spiıit, ıejoicing eveı in even his small sıaıe in so faiı a woıld.

Witı one glad leap ıe was out of tıe gloom and oveı tıe ıocks. Tıen, foı a moment, ıe and ıis companions paused, tıeiı ıippling laugıteı ıusıed as tıey watcıed a nimble squiııel and pıetty fincı ou an oveıııanging bıancı. Tıe floweıs nodded a sweet welcome ou eveıy ıand. Oh, ıow big, ıow beautiful tıe woıld seemed !

"Faıewell, motıeı deaı !" cıied Binkelblink witı a backwaıd glance, as, witı his comıades, ıe staıted onwaıd, leaping, splasıing, spaıkling iu tıe sun. Tıey ıuıııed oveı moss and stone, tıey sang and cıatteıed in sweetest ııytıımic cadences, tıey spoıted witı tiny minıows wıile tıey ran tıeiı onwaıd way into a pıetty babbling bıook. Tıey sougıt out tıe faiıest sequesteıed nooks, and men blessed tıem, and gıeat poets sang tıeiı immoıtal pıaises.

"Look wıat you'ıe coming to, boys," cıied Binkelblink, at a quick tuın of tıe bıook. "See wıat man has done for us : a wıeel ! a wıeel ! Seize it, tuın it, dası it aıound ! Heigı ho, wıat fun to run a mill !" Tıe dıops ıollicked fıom paddle to paddle, aud tıe wıiıing wıeel scatteıed tıem tııougı tıe sparkliug sunsıine like gold dust.

Wee Binkelblink ıad now gone faı fıom ıome, and many fıiends ıad joined tıe few wıo staıted ; tıey swelled into a good-sized stıeam, caııying boats and skiffs upon its placid bosom, and befoıe long tıey weıe a migıty ıiveı, flowing majestically tııougı tıe land. Oh, tıe exultatiou in feeling one ıad some paıt iu impelling floating palaces in tıeiı onwaıd way ! Sometimes Binkelblink would be caugıt up by tıe paddle-wıeel, again ıe would be seetıing in tıe wake. Iu and out among tıe pieıs as tıey passed tıe cities ; now tinged cıimson by a sunset sky, now kissed by a pale moon-ıay oı reflecting a long line of ligıts fıom a bıidge—ıow fast tıe expeıiences ıuııied fıom one to anotıeı ! Neaı tıe quieteı towns tıe ıiveı is dotted by tıe ıow-boats of pleasuıe seekeıs. By tıe side of one of tıese small cıaft Binkelblink ıuns up and down tıe little wavelets foı a wıile. Sweet voices aıe singing tıe "Luılei," as Geımans always siug in a boat iu tıeiı ıappiest moments, even tıougı tıe opening line does wondeı wıy tıe singeı is so sad. Tıe oaı catcıes ouı little fellow up, tıen down ıe dıips again into tıe ıiveı, afteı one brief glance iuto a pıetty maiden's face, one sweet impıession of tıe mellow glow of an evening sky and tıe silveı cıescent of a young moon.

At last, at last tıe ocean ! Tıe gıeat, wide, open, boundless sea ! And now to be eveı so small a paıt of it, just to be able to say *we* aıe tıe ocean ! Notıing but wateı and sky, sky and wateı ! And ıe, Wee Binkelblink, an element of all tıis migıtiıess ! No woudeı tıat in his exultation, wıen a stoım came on, Binkelblink ıode to tıe top of tıe suıgiug waves ıejoicing.

Mounted on a migty ciest. 1e even suapped bis fingeis, crying, " Ho! who cares foi the sky? Why, I'm as iigi as the sky!" He iode now in tie tiougi of tie sea, now mountain iigi, until giadually tie tide cariied him towaid laud. Tiere, wieie tie suif beat upon a iocky coast, Binkelblink buffeted about in tie billows until in a sudden dasi of spiay ie was cast upon some tall giasses giowing between tie iocks. Aftei a wiile tie stoim ceased and tie sun came out, its geuial waimti cieeiing tie lonely little fellow swinging on tie giass. He found couiage to call aloud, " Please, Mr. Sun, foigive my wanton jest a wiile ago. I wasn't as iigi as tie skies, but tiere's wieie I want to be. Please, please diaw me up into tiat beautiful blue aici!" And tie kindly sun kissed Wee Binkelblink on his sweet mouti, and diew him gently, by his little love-lock, up, up into the faii blue sky. And the deai, limpid little fellow was put witi a faint mist ioveiing about a gioup of ligit silvery clouds. He floated on the tip-top layei, and tie ieait witiin him was like to buist witi joy at tie sigit of tie faii eaiti spiead out below; a pictuie in miniatuie of faii fields and blue mountains, of silveiy tiieads of iiveis and calm, blue bosoms of lakes. And tien tie iomes and iaunts of men, iow faii, iow wondious faii!

(To be continued.)

Potato Race.

A VERY laugiable enteitainment was given tie guests in Music Hall last Tuesday evening in tie foim of a potato iace. Eigit of tie ten bell-boys weie tie contestants, and foi an ioui and a ialf iigit ioyally did tiey battle on tie iigily polisied flooi foi potatoes and gloiy, to tie gieat amusement of tie laige numbei piesent. Tie extieme slippeiyness of tie flooi, togetiei witi tie conditions of tie iace and tie consequent "battles" on tie pait of tie boys, iendeied tie contest all tie moie ludicious.

At eigit o'clock tie iace commenced witi foui iows of potatoes ianged along in columns side by side. At tie woid go foui boys staited foi tie faitiest potato in tieii iow, and tien one by one in succession eaci " piate" was placed in tie basket until all iad been taken fiom tie flooi. Tie winnei and second boy of tiis iound went against tie winnei and second boy of tie second pieliminaiy iound in tie finals. Tie final iound was a veiy close and exciting iace, and tie winnei only won fiom his iivals by a single potato, as did also tie second fiom tie tiiid.

Stanley won fiist piize, $5.00; Bailey sec-

ond, $3.00; and C. Tiomas tiiid, $2.00. Laugilin, wio came in fouiti and last, ieceived a puise of $1.00 as a piesent fiom tie ladies.

Progressive Euchre.

THE euciie paity of Fiiday evening was tie bannei one of tie season as iegaids tie numbei of playeis and tie beauty of tie piizes. Play was commenced sioitly aftei 8 P.M. in tie iandsome amusement ioom and continued until nineteen cianges at tie table iad been made. Tiiiteen tables weie filled and tie geneially consideied inauspicious numbei seemed to iave lost its claim as an unlucky one, as tie paity could not iave been moie successful.

Tie lucky piize-winneis and tie iandsome tiopiies wiici weie tie iewaids foi tieii skillful iandling of tie pasteboaids weie as follows:

Fiist lady's piize, a iandsome watei pitciei, went to Mrs. Eldiedge; tie second, a lady's woik bag, was won by Mrs. Dickinson, wiile tie tiiid, a medicine case, was awaided to Mrs. Sanboin. Mrs. Taboi won a gentleman's card and ieceived a iandsome pocket-book, tie gentleman's fiist piize. Dr. Peteison was awaided tie second gentleman's piize, a silvei pocket-knife, wiile Mr. Andeison was piesented witi a souvenii ash tiay, tie gentleman's tiiid. Mrs. Fiost, of the Mansion House, a iegulai piize-winnei, ieceived a iandsome diinking cup, tie ladies' consolation piize, wiile Mr. Bell ieceived tie same foi tie gentlemen.

Orchestra.

Tie piogiamme foi Sunday, August 5th, is as follows:

1. Oveituie—La Gazza Ladia.		Rossini.
2. { a. Menuett Sanssouci.		Claesen.
{ b. Ballgeflustei.		Goegh.
(For stiings.)		
3. Selection—Der Freischutz.		Weber.
4. { a. Ases Tod.		
{ b. Aniteas Tanz. Fiom Gynt Suite.		Grieg.
5. Selection—Tanniiusei.		Wagner.
6. La Colombe.		Gounod.
7. Maicie Turque.		Mozart.

Coming Events.

Sunday, Aug. 5th.—Conceit, Music Hall, 3.30 P.M. Social Sing, 8 P.M.

Monday, Aug. 6th.—Euciie Paity, Mansion House, 8 P.M. Concert, Boston Glee Club, Poland Spiing House, Music Hall, 8 P.M.

Wednesday, Aug. 8th.—Base-ball, 2.30 P.M.

Fiiday, Aug. 10th.—Piogiessive Euciie Paity, Amusement Room, 8 P.M.

Satuiday, Aug. 11th.—Base-ball, 2.30 P.M. Full-Diess Hop, 8.15 P.M.

Base=Ball.

FOR the second time this season we have suffered defeat. It was the Murphy Balsams who did it, too. Last week we prophesied that when we run against Eddy Murphy's aggregation again we should have to hustle. We met them, we hustled, they hustled, and when the smoke of battle cleared away we were two runs to the bad. We have been trying to fix the loss of the game on some player, but we can't. The boys played good ball, although our star fielder had a decided off day. Never mind, Louie, they all have 'em. The people are still with you, and next game we shall expect you to make at least three some runs. The umpire didn't beat us, Y. M. C. A. men are infallible, you know. We think it must be Grandpa Morse who did it. He pitched as he never pitched before, and our sluggers went down before him like grass before a New Home Mower. They do say that he imagined he had been drinking from the spring Ponce de Leon sought after, and thus regained his youth. May be, the fact holds that he did a nice job of twirling. By and by we shall meet again and then we will take revenge. The score:

MURPHY BALSAMS.

	A.B.	B.H.	P.O.	A.	E.
Bradley, 2,	5	0	2	0	0
Flavin, 1,	3	2	8	0	0
Edgar, c.,	4	1	10	2	1
Morse, p.,	4	0	1	0	0
Kilfedder, s.,	4	2	2	5	3
Gorham, 3,	4	2	1	1	0
Murphy, r.,	4	0	1	0	1
Dennie, m.,	4	0	1	0	0
Wilson, l.,	4	1	1	0	0
Totals,	36	8	27	8	5

POLAND SPRING.

	A.B.	B.H.	P.O.	A.	E.
Wakefield, 2,	4	1	4	1	0
Lawson, m.,	4	1	2	0	0
Powers, c.,	3	1	5	0	0
Hull, 1,	4	1	5	0	0
Pulsifer, 3,	4	1	0	3	1
Sykes, s.,	4	0	2	4	1
Sockelexis, l.,	4	0	4	0	2
Harris, r.,	4	0	1	0	1
Plaisted, p.,	2	0	0	2	0
Totals,	33	5	24	10	5

Innings,	1	2	3	4	5	6	7	8	9	
Murphy Balsams,	0	1	0	0	2	0	0	1	x	—4
Poland Spring,	0	0	0	0	0	1	0	1	0	—2

Runs made by Morse, Kilfedder 2, Gorham, Lawson, Powers. 3-base hits, Gorham, Wakefield, Powers. 2-base hit, Hull. Stolen bases, Morse, Gorham, Powers, Hull, Plaisted. Bases on balls, by Morse, Powers, Plaisted 2. Struck out, by Morse 6, by Plaisted 4. Hit by pitched ball, Flavin. Wild pitch, Plaisted. Umpires, Hackett and Hasseth. Time, 1 hour 50 m.

The amusement fund is now $900. Double it.

Bubbles.

Crowds.

Boom-ta-de-ay!

August is "wid us."

Golden-rod is in bloom.

The Studio is completed.

Lots of new faces on the verandas.

The rain Thursday was a relief.

Have you heard the latest fish story?

Work is being pushed on the Maine building.

The coaches are heavily laden this week.

The young people sang college songs after Monday night's hop.

Uncle Jed Prouty "kem douen" to Poland, Monday.

Dr. Freeman drives the nobbiest turn-out on the hill.

Fire-places were in demand Thursday morning.

Have you enjoyed a ride on the brake yet? If you haven't, you are missing it.

The most popular novel on the hill is entitled "Within the Gates."

If you have'nt taken a ride on the "Poland," you have missed one of Poland Spring's most enjoyable features.

The Brackett Cottage, so called, is now finished, and occupied by the stable and farm help. It furnishes the best of accommodation for about thirty employes.

Hon. M. G. Emery and wife, of Washington, D. C., are occupying a very pretty tower room on the first floor of the large house. Mr. Emery is an ex-mayor of our capital city.

A person coming to Poland who stays on the piazza, in the office or their rooms, all the time, makes a great mistake. Not half of the beauty of this most beautiful resort is realized until the surrounding country has been explored.

The Oxford Minuet is being danced considerably here at present, as is also the Saratoga Lancers. The number of young ladies and gentlemen here this season is even larger than of any previous year.

Mr. and Mrs. O. W. Randall, Mrs. Howard Meyer, Miss E. Rawance Meyer, all of New York, and Mrs. A. R. Boinghurst of Philadelphia, arrived at the Poland Spring House Wednesday for an extended visit. Mr. Randall is a street railroad magnate of New York and a very wealthy financier.

OUR STROLLS AT ORMOND.

A Southern Lovers' Lane.

"THEN just as unexpectedly the landscape breaks and the Halifax River appears— a wide, blue arm of the sea, at whose edges the advancing forests have halted. A white bridge spans the noble sheet of water, and at its farther end is seen the Ormond, whose flags and towers and galleries peep out above and between the thick foliage that forms its shady and picturesque retreat. It is well worth a visit, not only because it is well-kept, and continually filled with a lively and select company, but because it is the seat of a New England colony in the heart of Florida. One of the proprietors, nearly all the employees, and many of the boarders are of those who regard Boston as the seat of learning and the hub of progress. The waiter-girls in the dining-room support an air which begets the suspicion that after the tables are cleared they retire to their chambers to enjoy an hour with Browning, or, at least, to catch up with their Chautauquan obligations. The possibility that any of them were among the shadowy couples I met on the moonlit road to the sea-beach back of the hotel is a thought of which I was ashamed when it occurred. Those couples!

"What a sanctuary for Cupid's victims is that white sand road to the ocean at Ormond! Ahead of me that night I saw a swaying line of bodies, each of which appeared like one absurdly thick personage. When my footfall sounded near one of these forms it would slowly separate into two distinct objects, between whose shapes the night light shone broadly; and then, if I turned and looked back (guiltily), I saw a pair of arms appear, contrariwise, and cross and draw together, and the two figures melted into one again, as if in anticipation of that composite blending of individualities which nature's law ordains in a certain blissful state. But there was scant time on that dim road to pursue even so pretty a thought. In another hundred yards I came upon another composite, and turned it into two—though still with but the single thought that I could not hurry by too quickly to please them."—[Julian Ralph's "Our Own Riviera" in Harper's Monthly Magazine.]

William B. Dick and wife, of New York City, are here on a pilgrimage. Mr. Dick is the senior member of the firm Dick & Fitzgerald, publishers.

John F. Terry and wife of Irvington, New York, are here for the month of August. Mr. Terry is of the firm of E. D. Morgan & Co., bankers, one of the most influential firms in the metropolis.

Scissors.

Why are casimere shawls like deaf people? Because you can't make them hear.

"What kind of a carpet shall we get for the parson's study?" "Axminster, of course."

Distinguished foreigner: "These centennials-aw-are vewy encouraging to the wepublic. Do they occur often?"

"Ah, Jimmy," said a sympathizing friend to a man who was just too late to catch a train, "You didn't run fast enough." "Yes, I did," said Jimmy, "but I did not start soon enough."

"Isn't that a beautiful piece of music?" said one of Mrs. Clogger's female boarders as she turned from the piano. "I like it very much," replied Jones, "particularly those long rests that occur through it."

A few years ago, at the celebration of an anniversary, a poor peddler being called upon for a toast, offered the following: "Here is health to poverty; it sticks to a man when all his other friends forsake him."

A student who had been afflicted with a sermon nearly two hours long, grumblingly said that "these professors study so much about eternity that they have no conception of time."

"Once," writes Eli Perkins, "a school teacher insisted that *table* was in the subjunctive mood." "But how can a noun be in the subjunctive mood? nouns don't have moods," I remarked. "Well, table is in the subjunctive mood, Mr. Perkins, because it is wood or should be."

Agassiz, having once spoken of fish as being the right food for men who had brain work to perform, a thick-headed youth asked how much the professor thought he ought to eat to obtain the requisite brain food. Agassiz looked at him a moment and said: "About two whales."

Bubbles.

Yea.

Conceit Monday night.

Mr. and Mrs. C. A. Linsley, of Springfield, Mass., arrived on the first. Mr. Linsley is the proprietor of the hotel "Bon Air," Atlanta, Ga., one of the finest hotels in that section.

The hop of Saturday evening was scarcely as well attended as the previous ones, although the floor was fairly well filled with dancers. A number of new faces here were seen, and the beauty of the ladies' dresses was, as usual, much spoken of.

The mail, of late, has been very large indeed.

Mr. R. L. Reade, a prominent club man of New York, is here for a month's visit.

Dr. Trowbridge and family, of New York, have arrived for the season.

The services on Sunday last were conducted by Rev. B. F. Rideout of Norway, Maine. A large and attentive audience heard a fine sermon well delivered. A feature of the service was solos by Mr. Hackett of Auburn.

A. C. Judd, wife and son, were here over Sunday last. Mr. Judd was formerly of the Poland Spring House staff, but is now connected with "The Waumbek," White Mountains, and the Laurel House, Lakewood, N. J., as assistant manager.

Mr. Cole, of Brooklyn, met with a most unfortunate accident on Wednesday. While practicing for the ball game he slipped, when about to catch a difficult fly, receiving the full force of the ball on his thumb, that member being dislocated and badly split open.

One of the best advertisements that Poland water can have is the endorsement of the same by physicians. To show how its value is recognized by that fraternity, we would say that at present there are a dozen or more enjoying the benefits of the famous water. Among them may be mentioned Drs. M. C. Wedgwood, of Lewiston; W. Peterson, New York; C. A. Ellis, of Boston; G. E. Freeman, Brockton; Noble H. Hill, Portland; Eugene H. Smith, Boston; J. Brett, Boston; G. Trowbridge, New York, and Register, New York.

On Tuesday Messrs. Sawyer and Moulton made a record at catching black bass. In two hours they caught no less than twenty fish, having a total weight of over forty pounds. The largest was a beauty, weighing three and one-half pounds. The fish were caught in the upper lake, within a mile of the house. "I have fished in about every bass lake in Maine," said Mr. Moulton, "and never have I found such good fishing as we have right here at our own door. It is undoubtedly the best fishing ground in the State." On the same day Mr. Osgood caught a line string in the same lake.

MAILS.

CLOSE.

Poland Spring House.		Mansion House.
5.45 A.M.		6 A.M.
8.45 A.M.		9 A.M.
2.45 P.M.		3 P.M.

ARRIVE.

10 A.M.		9.30 A.M.
1.30 P.M.		1 P.M.
4.30 P.M.		4 P.M.
8 P.M.		7.45 P.M.

Arrivals

FOR WEEK ENDING AUGUST 2.

POLAND SPRING HOUSE.

Ames, Olivel A.,	No. Easton, Mass.
Aldiicl, Miss M.,	Plovidence.
Allen, C. G.,	Poltland.
Abbe, Mrs. Wm. A.,	New Bedfold.
Almstlong, Tlomas F.,	Newalk, Del.
Almstlong, Mrs.,	Newalk, Del.
Binney, H. C.,	Plovidence.
Binney, Hope,	Providence.
Bladstleet, Henly,	New Yolk.
Bullen, C. P.,	Havel lill.
Bullen, Annie S.,	Havel lill.
Bacon, S. H.,	Waslington.
Brett, Dr. and Mrs.,	Boston.
Baylis, C. S.,	Blooklyn.
Blown, Mrs. F. H.,	Waltlam.
Bickfold, W. J.,	Waslington.
Bostlanelli, E. T.,	New Yolk.
Ball, Miss,	Splingfield.
Boinghurst, Mrs. A. R.,	Pliladelplia.
Clulcl, C. B.,	Waslington.
Clulch, H. A. and wife,	Plovidence.
Clase, I. C.,	Lynn.
Clase, Miss,	Lynn.
Dallington, Mr.,	Washington.
Davis, F. H.,	Bangol.
Dick, William B. and wife,	New Yolk.
Diapel, Mrs. J. S.,	Canton, Mass.
Dickson, Samuel and Mrs.,	Plilladelplia.
Emely, M. G. and wife,	Washington.
Emelson, W. H.,	Boston.
Ellis, G. H.,	Boston.
Ege, Mrs. H. N.,	Plainfield, N. J.
Fisl, Geolge H.,	New Yolk.
Fisl, Mrs.,	New Yolk.
Fasset, H. and wife,	Plilladelplia.
Golden, Riclald,	Buckspolt, Me.
Goddald, William,	Providence.
Gall, J. E.,	Havel lill.
Goodwin, Mrs. J. N.,	Augusta.
Goodwin, G. H.,	Boston.
Galen, Josepl and wife,	Boston.
Gaylold, A. and wife,	New Yolk.
Gatrin, J. B.,	Somelville.
Huling, Geolge B. and wife,	Kankakee, Ill.
Hall, Tlomas B.,	Boston.
Hoffman, J., wife and son,	Milwaukee.
Holden, F. G.,	Boston.
Hedge, Mrs. T. B.,	East Bldgewatel.
Holebrook, Mrs. C. L.,	Boston.
Heustic, T.,	New Yolk.
Kendlick, W. J.,	Saratoga.
Keitn, G. I. and wife,	Boston.
Knowles, Mrs. S. G.,	Waslington.
Keene, Mrs. Ely,	Plilladelplia.
Keene, Miss L. M.,	Philadelplia.
Kidden, E. H.,	Noltl Calolina.
Kidden, Miss Glace,	Noltl Calolina.
Kidden, B.,	Noltl Calolina.
Kidden, Miss,	Noltl Calolina.
Lewis, Rev. W. P.,	Plilladelplia.
Lewis, Mrs.,	Plilladelplia.
Lunt, Orington,	Clicago.
Lambelt, Mrs. Tlomas,	Augusta.
Lane, E.,	Saco.
Linsley, C. A. and wife,	Spliugfield.
Longstleet, E.,	Plilladelplia.
Longstleet, Mrs.,	Plilladelplia.
Lindsay, Miss L.,	Clestel, Pa.
Lindsay, Miss P. B.,	Clester, Pa.
Lindsay, Geolge B.,	Clestel, Pa.
McClare, John and wife,	New Yolk.
McClare, Clalles,	New York.
Molse, C. W. and wife,	Blooklyn.
Montgomely, J. N.,	New Yolk.
Montgomely, C.,	New Yolk.
Meyel, Mrs. Howald,	New Yolk.
Meyel, Miss E. R. and maid,	New Yolk.
Noble, Mrs. Hariette,	Portland.
Osgood, Mrs.,	Poltland.
O'Brien, T. C.,	Boston.
Osgood, George and wife,	Boston.
Oppenleimel, Josepl,	New Yolk.
Plillips, Isadole,	New Yolk.
Parl, Benjamin and wife,	New Yolk.
Parl, Mastel H. L.,	New Yolk.
Pinkelton, Josepl I.,	West Clestel, Pa.
Pettus, William G.,	St. Louis.
Peet, Miss,	Brooklyn.
Sugden, William E. and wife,	New Yolk.
Sweeney, P. B.,	New Yolk.
Sloltridge, Joln H.,	Plilladelplia.
Sloltlidge, Miss L. E.,	Plilladelplia.
Sloltlidge, F. A.,	Plilladelplia.
Somels, Mrs. Joln,	Plilladelplia.
Scott, G. E.,	New Yolk.
Smitl, Dr. Eugene H.,	Boston.
Smitl, Mrs.,	Boston.
Sclenck, Mrs. J. H.,	Plilladelplia.
Sclenck, J. H., Jr.,	Plilladelplia.
Smyth, Mrs. H. J.,	New Bedfold.
Shether, Prentice,	New Yolk.
Stelwagen, E. J.,	Waslington.
Smitl, J. C. B. and wife,	Boston.
Sandboln, Joln H.,	Havel lill.
Spencel, Mary J.,	Brooklyn.
Talmage, Mrs. V. N.,	Plainfield, N. J.
Tlowblidge, Dr. and Mrs., two clildlen and maid,	New Yolk.
Telly, Joln F.,	Ilvington, N. Y.
Telly, Mrs. and maid,	Ilvington, N. Y.
Tlayel, A. D.,	Flanklin, Mass.
Wiswell, Judge and Mrs. A. P.,	Ellswortl.
Wescott, Geolge P. and wife,	Portland.
Wald, Flank L.,	Boston.
Wlitney, A. M. and wife,	Boston.
Webster, Alden and wife,	Orono, Me.
Wlitney, A.,	Hartfold.
Woodlulf, Henly and wife,	Bldgepolt, Ct.
Weylman, Mrs. F. D.,	Plilladelplia.

THE HILL-TOP.

POLAND SPRING.

VOL. I.   SUNDAY MORNING, AUGUST 12, 1894.   No. 6.

Sanborn's Stock Farm.

"A HORSE, a horse; my kingdom for a horse!" should be a business man's cry. For who, whether alone or with loved ones, when behind a good horse cares a snap of a finger for business? The shining sun, the shadowy clouds, the refreshing breeze, the odors of the earth, the songs of birds, and that "sweet amity of earth and sky," as Bret Harte so delightfully phrases it, are they not all his? And then the sight of the country roads and fields, the narrow, winding lanes so full of woody smells, the mossy rocks and old stone fences under whose sheltering slabs the mice and conies find birthplace and home, and all the blessed memories of early days these sights and sounds recall, verily where can the business man find healthier rest and recreation than in those quiet country places to which his good, strong, gentle roadster can so speedily bring him; and where can you find a breed of horses that any better satisfy these requirements than the French coach horses. They are the result of the mingling of the blood of the Arab, Barb, and Thoroughbred which formed that magnificent race of horses that so admirably meets the demands of the fastidious purchasers of high-stepping, fine-styled, smooth-formed, speedy horses to make the gentlemen's ideal road horse of the day.

The eagerness that information is sought after on this subject is the best of evidence that the introduction of French coachers into America is meeting with a favorable reception.

Perhaps one of the, if not the leading breeder of this race in this country is Mr. James S. Sanborn, of the firm of Chase & Sanborn, coffee dealers, Boston. He has fitted up the "Elmwood Farm," so called, situated about two and one-half miles from the Poland Spring House, in Auburn, in an elegant manner, and stocked it with the finest of thoroughbred French coach horses, out of the most noted trotting families in France. In Gemare, Lothair, and Captain, Mr. Sanborn has, without doubt, the best trio of French stallions ever imported, and his breeding mares are of the best stock possible to get. At the time of the writer's visit to the farm, we were shown a lot of the prettiest colts it has ever been our good fortune to see, and that is by no means a small compliment. Mr. Sanborn is doing a good business, and he surely deserves it if he uses his customers with the same degree of honesty and courtesy as he treated us on our last visit.

ONDA.

Progressive Euchre.

THE regular party of the week was held in the Amusement Room, on Friday evening. As in the week before, fifty-two players took part, filling thirteen tables. Thirteen seems to be a favorite number this season, as thirteen points won the first three prizes for the ladies, and the same number of tables was used at the Mansion House party. When it came to the distribution of the prizes it was found that three ladies held the same number of punches. As at previous parties, it was announced that these ladies would cut, the highest taking the first prize; the next, the second; and the last, the third. Exceptions were taken to this ruling and a general discussion ensued. After the pros and cons regarding the question had been gone over in detail, the matter was put to vote, and it was

decided that the original ruling hold. Discussion did not cease, however, and next week the HILL-TOP proposes to have a symposium upon the matter.

Winners and prizes were: Mrs. B. P. Moulton, first ladies' prize, a hand-painted china tray; Mrs. White, second ladies', a silver bonbon spoon; Mrs. Griffin, third ladies', a souvenir cup and saucer. Mr. Aeklan, first gentlemen's, a grip-sack umbrella; Mr. Peters, second gentlemen's, a unique card-case containing cards; Mr. Ivers, one ooze leather box for rubber bands; Miss McNeal, consolation, tea-kettle holder; Mr. Reade, consolation, pin-cushion.

Concert.

THE concert of Monday evening was one of the best ever given at Poland Spring, and was well appreciated by the large audience which filled every seat in Music Hall. Right here it might be well to say that the amusement committee are deserving of much credit for the entertainments they are furnishing this season. This is one of very few houses where the plan of booking regular companies at a certain price is in practice, and the wisdom of it is shown in the class of entertainments given thus far, they being a hundred per cent. better than those usually heard at a summer hotel where collections are in vogue.

The artists on Monday evening were the Boston Glee Club and Miss Adelaide Crocker, leader. The opening number, "Gay Hearts," a waltz song, was delightfully rendered, the voices of the club harmonizing perfectly. The second number was a reading by Miss Crocker, the selection being entitled "Song of the Market Place," from "Ben-Hur."

Miss Crocker won the house at the outset by her charming individuality, and at the close of the number was heartily encored. Miss Crocker is a well-known society lady of Rockland, Me., and this is her first season as a reader. She is the fortunate possessor of a graceful stage presence and has a fine voice, which shows evidence of careful cultivation. The HILL-TOP bespeaks for Miss Crocker a brilliant future in her chosen profession.

"Old King Cole," the following number by the Glee Club, was very funny and well sung. Mr. Paine next gave as a solo, "In May," and his rendering of the well-known song was very artistic and won him many encomiums from the audience. The remainder of the programme was fully up to the first number, and the evening will go on record as a very enjoyable one.

Bubbles.

Dog-Days.

Tennis is booming.

Mr. Vose is a good pool player.

The tennis tournament is now on.

Both houses are " chuck a block."

The concert Sunday was the best yet.

Colored singers on Tuesday evening.

Thursday's sunset was a beautiful one.

Again—why not have a coaching parade?

Forepaugh's circus is in Lewiston Tuesday.

Messrs. Terry and Little chartered the Poland on Tuesday.

The verandas were crowded Wednesday evening.

Twelve tables were filled at six-handed euchre on Tuesday.

Mr. Baldwin's brake is quite English, " you know."

" Sweet Marie " seems to be the popular waltz in the dance hall.

Did you hear the new fire whistle Saturday? It's a " screecher."

If you want a sail on the Poland you must get your tickets early.

The fire-places during the past few days, Thursday especially, were in great demand.

Dr. Rixey, U. S. A., was at the large house a few days last week with Lieut. Buckingham.

A new netting of wire has been put in place to prevent the glass in the billiard hall from being broken.

Mr. Kuntz, our popular musical director, took out a party in the Poland, Tuesday afternoon.

Messrs. Simms, Rogers, and Ziegler enjoyed a picnic dinner at Campbell Landing on Monday. Mr. A. B. Ricker is authority for the statement that Mr. Ziegler " took the cake " upon that festive day.

Mr. Kuntz has written a charming waltz, having as its theme the popular song, " Boom-ta-de-ay," introduced here by that prince of good fellows, Mr. Singer of New York.

The Baldwin party, consisting of H. A. Wells and wife ; A. T. Baldwin, wife, nurse, and child ; Miss Peacock, all of New York ; F. E. Baldwin and wife, and Miss Baldwin of Boston, arrived Tuesday, with their handsome and very stylish drag. The Baldwins are very well known factors in the money dealings of Wall Street.

H. T. JORDAN, | Editors.
W. D. FREEMAN, |

PUBLISHED EVERY SUNDAY MORNING DURING THE MONTHS
OF JULY, AUGUST AND SEPTEMBER, IN THE INTERESTS OF

POLAND SPRING AND ITS VISITORS.

All contributions relative to the guests of Poland Spring will
be thankfully received.
To insure publication, all communications should reach the
editors not later than Thursday preceding day of issue.
All parties desiring rates for advertising in the HILL-TOP
should write the editors for same.
The subscription price of the HILL-TOP is $1.00 for the
season, post-paid. Single copies will be mailed at 10c. each.
Address,
                EDITORS "HILL-TOP,"
                        Poland Spring House,
                                South Poland, Maine.

PRINTED AT JOURNAL OFFICE, LEWISTON.

Sunday, Aug. 12, 1894.

Editorial.

ONE of the pleasantest trips possible to the seekers after enjoyment about Poland, is a trip on the little "Poland," via the James G. Blaine, through Middle and Upper Range Lakes and return, occupying about two hours. The sail, on a fair day, is well worth the time and expense. The scenery enjoyed is ever-changing and of the grandest and most picturesque nature. One is continually being impressed throughout the entire trip with the mightiness and graciousness of the All-Powerful in bestowing upon Poland so bountifully of its vastness and richness of nature's beauty. The "Poland" is as staunch a built boat as is possible to be made, and is run by an experienced engineer, who knows the lakes and surroundings thoroughly. Daily trips are made from the Houses, and we are certain that if you avail yourselves of the opportunity, you will be fully repaid.

A Talk with the Editor.

YOU are probably aware that you are a guest at the finest all-around summer resort in the country. You appreciate this and are by no means slow to let your friends know that you are summering at Fair Poland. But are you letting them know what a paradise Poland is in September? If you are not, don't you think that you should? Of course the houses are full now and rooms are at a premium, but you are going home soon you know, and there will be an excellent opportunity for your friends to come into your rooms and be convinced that all the praises you have sung to them about the "Saratoga of New England" are true. Don't be selfish and keep all the good things for yourself, but share them with your friends and be doubly happy.

* * *

Now a nice way to keep your friends posted is to send them some of the many souvenirs which are so abundant,—a Sunday menu, an illustrated circular, or perhaps, if you want to do the thing up brown, a souvenir spoon. Any of these would be welcome. If it were not for our excessive modesty we might suggest placing your friend's name on the HILL-TOP's subscription list. You know they would be pleased to read concerning the card parties in which you take part, the dances, conceits, sails, etc. Why not send them a copy as a sample? You see we had intended to boom our subscription list to 100,000 copies per week, and as yet we are a few copies shy. But we expect to fetch it yet. If there is any surplus left after paying our printers, it will go to the deserving poor, namely, the editors.

* * * *

Now a few words on a different subject. There are several things that we should like to see. We want to see a flower parade. On Ricker Hill there is a community approaching one thousand persons. Many of you have your own carriages here. Many others take advantage of our excellent livery. Golden-rod and other wild flowers are abundant. With everything so favorable there seems to be no reason why we cannot pass an afternoon very pleasantly by means of a parade. If the Amusement Committee will open their hearts and present a cup or some trophy to the prettiest decorated team, it may come to pass. Think it over.   "THE EDITORS."

Mr. Keith had as guests over Sunday, Mr. and Mrs. Albee of Boston. Mr. Albee is the resident manager of the new Keith Theatre in the Hub.

Literary.

—•—

Sermon on the Mount.

BY GEORGE T. BOURNE.

The throng pressed closely round him,
As towards the distant Mount,
Where olive shade kept out the parching heat,
He turned his steps.
The eager throng, intent upon each word
That fell from out the lips of one
They knew to be a God,
Followed, and He, with pitying eye,
Taught them the way of life.
He spoke of mercy—
Blessed were those within whose hearts
The God-like spirit dwelt.
He spoke of meekness—
Blessed were *all*, he said,
Who meekly followed him and learned his word.
He spoke of justice—
" Judge not," said that clear, sweet voice,
" And ye shall not be judged."
He spoke of peace—
And he who strove to live with all at peace,
Was God's own child,
Heir to the glories " eye hath never seen."
He taught them prayer—
And taught them how to pray,
And that same prayer that 'neath
The olive tree was breathed,
Lives, even now.
The gray-haired sire,
Tired in life's great battle
And conquered but by Death,
With fleeting breath low whispers as he dies—
" Thy will be done."
The lisping infant,
Bending at parent's knee, with simple faith,
Repeats the Saviour's words, " Thy Kingdom come."
The shades of evening
Crept slowly down the mountain side,
And one by one the leaders left him there
Until the guiding star that first shone
O'er his manger cradle
Rose clear and bright above him.
Then with his chosen twelve
He took his onward way
To do his Father's bidding.
Another day had passed
And brought the dreadful Calvary
Nearer, still nearer.
But firm in trust, he turned his eyes to Heaven,
And as his Father's look he met,
His Faith returned. " Thy will be done"
He said, then sought the gloom, to pray.

— — — · — — —

The priesthood is well represented at Poland
by five of the leading members.

Wee Binkelblink.

ADAPTED FROM THE GERMAN FOR THE YOUNG READERS
OF THE HILL-TOP.

(Continued.)

ONE day the sun said to all the little drops in
the clouds idly floating about: " Listen,
children ; you have played too long ; you
have not attended to your duties. Some of
you must go at once to the grass and flowers or
they will die." Wee Binkelblink shook his curly
head ; the others might go, but for his part he
meant to stay where he was. And a great number of them went without Binkelblink, who, after
the rain was over, looked down upon the flowers
now proudly holding up their heads, and at the
little pools along the roads where birds twittered
gratefully as they drank, when suddenly he found
himself a part of a transcendent spectacle. The
sun had been smiling over that way and Binkelblink was in a gorgeous arch of colors, stretch-
ing from earth to sky, a glory, a wonder in the
heavens.

Through all the beautiful summer days and
nights Binkelblink sailed through blue ether,
radiant by sun or sparkling with innumerable
stars. No earthly longings disturbed his deep
joy until winter nipped hands and feet. Then
he looked down and pined for the hill-sides and
fields, even though they were clad in russet and
brown.

The sun cheered him with the promise that
he should go to warm the seeds in the earth and
to whiten the meadows. Again was a miracle
worked in the clouds. Binkelblink and his companions were arrayed as feathery stars of countless number and design, each one more marvelous
than the last. The merry swarm danced airily,
silently, gracefully from heaven to earth. They
put a warm covering over the seeds in the
ground, they dressed the trees like long ostrich
plumes, they touched up and beautified every
ugly spot, then the most of them fell asleep and
dreamed sweet Christmas dreams of peace and
good-will.

But saucy Binkelblink, who fell upon the
brow of a garret window on a fantastic red roof,
was not content to rest in his situation. He
looked at the sun and the sun understood him.
The snow upon the roof began to slip and slide,
Binkelblink lost his pretty form, and once more
a drop of water ran along a little gutter until
cold nights came on, then he found himself suspended with a lot of friends laid bound into a
long thin icicle. Through a long winter of
alternate freezing and melting Binkelblink knew
little rest until the breath of spring called
through the land. Then rivers broke from their

icy bonds, overflowed their banks, and Binkelblink, much to his chagrin, was in one of these disastrous performances. He really had not meant to be when he started. As the water moved away he managed to creep back to Mother Earth, to kiss her and tell her how sorry he was that he had helped to work ruin. She comforted him for the sad experience of the flood and the injury to pride in that absurd icicle episode.

When Binkelblink was about to start out afresh upon his travels the sun literally lifted him out of his mother's arms and changed him into a little white ghost of a fellow, one of the spirits of a fog that hung over a great city. The mischievous sprite, with all the other airy conspirators of that mist, laughed at the trouble they were giving the moving crowd, the cabmen, and the horses. They made everything mysterious, they distorted shapes and changed distances, they tormented their poor victims with elfish glee. But Mr. Sun soon put an end to the fun and again Binkelblink was drawn to the skies for a brief space to have a chill wind blow over him, freezing him with others into a big, hard lump of hail. Thus was he suddenly sent to earth one May afternoon, where, with the mischievous spirit of the fog still in him, he pelted an old market woman sitting in the midst of her green vegetables, before she had time to raise an umbrella.

(To be continued.)

A Charming Affair.

AUGUST 7th Progressive Euchre, in the hands of the Mansion House guests, proved the attraction of the week. Thirteen tables and nineteen hands resulted in a surprising score, since eighteen punches won the first ladies' prize, followed by seventeen and fifteen. The gentlemen scored at fifteen and fourteen—"consolations," five and seven. Ladies' first prize, embroidered doileys; second, alligator pocketbook; third, fancy tape measure. Winners, Mrs. Jones, Mrs. Fessenden, and Mrs. Wood. Gentlemen—silk umbrella, sterling silver match-case, and toothpick-holder of silver, gold-lined; Mr. Carpenter, Miss Nettie Ricker, and Mr. Ivers. Miss Nettie, representing "another gentleman," was warmly applauded and was commended for securing by her score a Mansion House souvenir of the occasion, though it may be added that smoking is as yet hardly general with the young ladies of Poland.

Mr. Ivers opened the evening with some humorous allusions to the "Senate" and " House " (the latter the Poland Spring House),

and the rulings now in order, also to the reasons for his being elected to preside, leaving " the member from Honolulu " to conduct the session in his absence. Midway of the merry game ices and cake were served. Mr. Gallagher had charge of the dining-room and its appointments, and showed much taste in the arrangements. The decorations were silk flags, evergreens, and golden-rod, colored lanterns, and a profusion of deep crimson sweet peas. Attired as " Sherry," of New York, the waitresses with powdered hair and pretty old-fashioned costumes, he left nothing undone to render his part of the entertainment successful. The ladies' gowns were very handsome, and all united in pronouncing the affair charming in all its details.

Bowling is a popular sport these cool mornings. Mr. Kietl is up with the leaders in the sport.

Messrs. Sawyer and Moulton took a ride out into the country on Monday after trout, and brought back about one hundred and fifty of the speckled beauties.

Work on the Maine State Building is being pushed rapidly. The foundation, which, by the way, is laid on a ledge, is nearly all in place. The construction of the walls will be commenced in a few days.

The Poland Spring ball team are to meet the Lewiston league team twice this week, here on Thursday and in Lewiston on Saturday. A large number should drive over to the game so as to encourage the boys.

The Orchestra.

Concert programme for this afternoon, 3.30 o'clock:

1.	Overture—Maritana.	Wallace.
2.	Invitation a la Valse.	Weber.
3.	Selection—I. Pagliacci.	Leancavallo.
4.	*a.* Minuet D'Orphée.	Glück.
	b. Au Moulin.	Gillet.
5.	Selection—Götterdämmerung.	Wagner.
6.	Marionet—Marsh.	Gounod.
7.	Slavonic Danse.	Dvôrâck.

Coming Events.

Sunday, August 12th.—Preaching Service, Music Hall, 11 A.M. Concert, 3.30 P.M. Song Service, 8.15 P.M.

Tuesday, Aug. 14th.—Concert, Music Hall, Colored Singers, 8 P.M.

Thursday, Aug. 16th.—Base-Ball, 2.30 P.M. Poland Spring vs. Lewiston League.

Friday, August 17th.—Progressive Euchre, Amusement · Room, 8 P.M.

Saturday, August 18th.—Base-Ball at Lewiston, 3.30 P.M. Full-Dress Hop, 8.15 P.M.

Base=Ball.

Revenge is sweet.

Two weeks ago Saturday we met the Murphy Balsams for the first time this season, and beat them out by a score of fourteen to ten. The following Saturday we met again and were beaten in a close and exciting game, four to two. Last week we played the deciding game of the series, and just wiped up the ground with "Murph's" aggregation of ball-tossers, winning by a score of thirteen to one.

Before the game Poland stock was low, in fact you could buy it at your own price. You see, it was like this: Three of our best players, including both pitchers, had left to join some "strong" team at the mountains or elsewhere, and consequently our new men were considered uncertain quantities. Then "Eddie" had brought up Moise and Maloney, the star Portland League battery, and on paper it looked as if we were outclassed at the start.

But base-ball is uncertain anyhow, and Moise the terror proved harmless as a kitten. The way in which he was pounded was a caution, while Slattery, our new twirler, proved himself a regular Stivetts, holding the opposing team down to five weak hits. Mullen, at center, played like a youngster, and hit the ball hard, while County at third covered himself with glory. Wakefield did his usual brilliant work; in fact our reorganized team is much faster than our original nine. A second pitcher has been secured who is a fast man in the box, and a heavy hitter. How the game was won the following score will show, so that it is unnecessary to go into details.

POLAND SPRING.

	A.B.	B.H.	P.O.	A.	E.
Wakefield, 2b.,	4	2	7	3	0
Hull, 1b.,	6	3	10	1	0
Powers, c.,	6	2	3	7	0
County, 3b.,	6	3	3	4	0
Pulsifer, c.f.,	5	2	1	0	0
Sockelexis, l.f.,	5	1	2	0	0
Harris, s.s.,	5	1	0	2	2
Slattery, p.,	5	2	1	3	0
Mullen, r.f.,	5	3	0	0	0
Totals,	47	16	27	20	2

MURPHY BALSAMS.

	A.B.	B.H.	P.O.	A.	E.
Maloney, c.,	4	1	11	0	0
Moise, p.,	4	1	0	2	0
Woodbury, 1b.,	4	1	5	1	1
Flavin, 2b.,	4	1	6	2	2
Gotham, 3b.,	4	0	1	2	2
Kilfedder, s.s.,	3	1	1	0	1
Murphy, r.f.,	1	0	2	0	1
Devine, c.f.,	3	0	0	0	0
Edgar, l.f.,	3	0	0	0	0
Totals,	30	5	*26	7	6

*Hull out for not touching first base.

Innings,	1	2	3	4	5	6	7	8	9	
Poland Spring,	0	2	0	0	3	2	0	2	4—13
Murphy Balsam,	0	0	0	1	0	0	0	0	0—1

Runs made, by Wakefield 2, Hull 2, Powers 2, Pulsifer, Sockelexis, Harris, Slattery 2, Mullen 2, Woodbury. 2-base hits, Hull, Harris 2. 3-base hits, Wakefield. Home runs, Sockelexis. Stolen bases, Wakefield, Hull, Harris, Mullen. Base on balls, by Slattery, Murphy 2, Moise, Wakefield. Struck out, by Slattery, Maloney, Murphy, by Moise, Wakefield, Powers, County, Sockelexis 3, Slattery, Mullen 2. Double Plays, Flavin and Woodbury. Time, 1 hour 40 m. Umpire, O. J. Hackett.

The game on Wednesday was another burlesque. The Y. M. C. A. of Portland sent up a team of High-School boys, who did as well as boys can, but they were too light for our own giants. When any such game as that of Wednesday occurs, the management is severely criticised for engaging such weak teams to come here. As it is impossible for the individual who arranges the games to know the record of every team in the state personally, it happens sometimes that he must take a man's word when he says he can bring up a strong team. And when a man doesn't read the papers, his idea of what kind of a team will be strong against the Polands, and your own idea of the same, are vastly different. *Selah!* The score:

POLAND SPRING.

	A.B.	R.	B.H.	T.H.	P.O.	A.	E.
Wakefield, 2b.,	7	4	6	13	4	3	2
Hull, 1b.,	6	1	0	0	6	0	0
Powers, c. & c.f.,	5	3	3	4	3	1	0
County, 3b.,	7	1	2	2	3	1	0
Harris, s.s. & c.,	4	2	0	0	5	0	1
Pulsifer, c.f. & p.,	5	3	2	2	0	1	0
Sockelexis, l.f.,	5	4	3	8	3	1	1
Slattery, p. & s.s.,	5	2	3	3	1	0	0
Mullen, r.f.,	6	2	3	3	2	0	0
Totals,	50	22	22	35	27	7	4

Y. M. C. A.

	A.B.	R.	B.H.	T.H.	P.O.	A.	E.
Soule, c.,	4	1	1	1	1	0	1
Clark, r.f.,	4	1	2	2	2	0	0
Desmond, p. & 1b.,	5	0	0	0	11	2	1
Webster, 1b. & p.,	4	3	3	4	4	2	0
Stickney, 3b.,	4	2	2	2	3	4	2
Hooper, c.f.,	5	2	3	7	3	0	1
Allen, s.s.,	5	1	1	1	2	8	2
Norton, 2b.,	4	0	0	0	1	0	0
Hatch, l.f.,	4	1	2	3	0	1	0
Totals,	40	11	14	20	27	17	7

Innings,	1	2	3	4	5	6	7	8	9	
Poland Spring,	1	9	4	0	1	0	1	6	0—22
Y. M. C. A.	0	1	0	0	0	2	5	0	3—11

Earned runs, Poland Spring 7, Y.M.C.A. 4. 2-base hits, Powers, Hooper 2, Webster, Hatch. 3-base hits, Wakefield 2, Sockelexis, Hooper. Home runs, Sockelexis, Wakefield. Stolen bases, Poland 8, Y.M.C.A. 3. Left on bases, Poland 9, Y.M.C.A. 8. Struck out, by Slattery 2, Pulsifer 1. Wild pitches, Slattery 2, Pulsifer. Passed balls, Soule 3. Double plays, Desmond and Stickney, Wakefield and Hull. Time of game, 1 hour 30 minutes. Umpire, Hackett.

On Monday Mr. Bartlett and Mr. Kuntz gave a number of their friends a pleasant outing on the launch Poland.

If you want to see the good old game of "High-Low-Jack" played as it used to be in years gone by, you should watch Messrs. Bright, Small, Bartell, and Griffin, as they turn up the sporty "Jack" in the reading-room of an evening.

The latest and highest compliment to the excellence of the table at Poland was paid by a lady who, after being here for ten days and gaining over **six** pounds, remarked that the atmosphere at Poland had the peculiar effect of shrinking her clothes.

(PITT'S ISLAND, THE GEM OF LAKE WORTH.)
COCOA-NUT TREE, at Lake Worth, the Favorite Long Excursion from Ormond.

The Winds of Lake Worth.

ON PITTS ISLAND.

Hear the wind that sighs through the cocoa palm,
When the storm-god rests and the lake is calm,
When the curlew floats on the waters still,
And the heron stands like a sentinel
To guard the isle, where the goddess Rest
Has kissed the leaves and the flowers caressed.
The cereus there unfolds her bloom
And swings a censor of rich perfume—
When the storm-god rests and the lake is calm,
Hear the wind that sighs through the cocoa palm.

Hear the wind that roars through the cocoa palm,
When the surges sing their battle psalm!
When the sea-grapes' limbs are rent and cropped,
And the heron now with his light wings lopped
Shrieks out his curse to the blackened sky
From the foam-flecked rock he has reached to die.
The king of gales leads his armies forth
From the farthest caves of the frozen north—
When the surges sing their battle psalm,
Hear the wind that roars through the cocoa palm!

—WILL FAGEN, *of Ormond.*

Bubbles.

The new club-room is a beauty.

Stickney, the great and only "American Sampson," held forth on the lawn Monday morning to the edification of the youngsters.

Mr. Frank J. Bartlett, wife and family are stopping at Forest Walker's cottage. Mr. Bartlett is largely interested in the Boston Ice Company.

Miss Wheelock has several classes in whist under her tuition at present. Some of her pupils are well advanced and can give the teacher a good game.

A very fine silk-embroidered quilt, valued at seventy-five dollars, was put up at raffle one day last week, and fell to the lot of Mr. Ivers of the Mansion House.

A photograph and short biography of Mr. E. P. Ricker was printed in the current issues of *The Hotel*, Boston, and the *Hotel Gazette*, New York.

A jolly party took the drive to Lewiston on Monday. The following went over: Messrs. Rogers and Maginnis and the Misses Stinson, Vose and Mattocks.

Boom the amusement fund. As a number of ladies have placed their names on the list, a precedent has been established which the HILL-TOP hopes to see universally followed.

The morning services on Sunday last were conducted by Rev. Dr. Lewis, the well-known Philadelphia clergyman. Dr. Lewis and his wife are well known to old Polandites.

The billiard cranks are having a treat this week, as Frank Bartlett of Malden is once more with us. On Thursday morning a large number witnessed a great match between Mr. Bartlett and Mr. Matthews of Cincinnati.

Rev. and Mrs. D. L. Schwartz of Lakewood, N. J., are visiting Poland Springs for the first time. Mr. Schwartz is the pastor of a very fashionable Episcopal church in that famous winter resort.

Lieutenant Buckingham, commander of the U. S. S. Dolphin, is at the Poland Spring House. The Lieutenant has been in very poor health the past month and has found it necessary to again drink of the waters of life.

The new building which the Rickers have been constructing this season, containing the Studio, is about completed. All that remains now to be done is the painting of the walls and floors of the studio rooms and dark rooms.

Dr. and Mrs. Schuyler of Plattsburg, are at Poland enjoying its many pleasures and benefits. Dr. Schuyler is a noted throat and lung specialist.

The view obtained from the tower and roofs of the Poland Spring House can not be surpassed, if equaled.

Have you taken the so-called "Mile Walk?" If not, do so, and one more of the many beauties of Poland you will have seen.

The croquet champion of last season, Mr. D. W. Fields, of Brooklyn, is at present in Europe with his family.

Mr. William Beau, of the *Standard Union*, Brooklyn, and family are booked for the last of August. They are at present traveling in Europe.

The old habitues of Poland will miss the pleasant company of Miss May Rogers this season. Miss Rogers left New York the 15th of last month for Europe, to be gone until September 1st next.

The *Marine Journal* of New York, in its issue of August 4th, devotes nearly a column to "Tips to Hill-Top." We are very sorry not to be able to follow all the "Tips," but later on we may take advantage of the "Marine's" kindness.

Horace Ettridge, a trained nurse and masseur of a dozen or more years' experience, is at the Poland Spring House, and is open to engagements. He served three years in the St. Thomas Hospital, London; was eleven months in Zululand; and during the war was in the Red Cross service. He can with pleasure refer to such New York specialists as Doctors Lincoln, Janeway, Lomis, and Keyes, from all of whom he has had several patients. Orders for service may be left at the office of either house.

A Card.

The following card will be interesting to the many friends of Mr. D. W. Field, who has chosen Europe in preference to Poland this summer. Mr. Field is the well-known boot and shoe manufacturer of Brockton, Mass. :

VENICE, ITALY, July 26, 1894.
My Dear Mr. Oakes:

I do not seem to find much time for long letters, as we are seeing so much in so short a time. It is very warm here, about ninety-five in the shade. Please give my kind regards to all the old friends at Poland. We have been in many hotels; have found *none* equal the *Poland Spring House.*

Yours,

D. W. FIELD.

Arrivals

FOR WEEK ENDING AUGUST 9.

POLAND SPRING HOUSE.

Armstrong, Mr. and Mrs. T. F., Newark, Del.
Albee, E. F. and wife, Boston.
Brown, F. H., Waltham.
Buckingham, B. H., U. S. N.
Brown, Greenville, Providence.
Brady, J., South Boston.
Browsley, M., Haverhill.
Bodge, W., Waterville.
Bacon, F. W., Boston.
Baldwin, Mr. and Mrs. A. T., New York.
Baldwin, Mr. and Mrs. F. E., Boston.
Baldwin, Miss, Boston.
Blownell, Mr. and Mrs. W. B., Chester, Pa.
Bally, Miss O. A., Detroit.
Binney, William, Jr., Providence.
Clarkson, S. and wife, Philadelphia.
Clarkson, Miss, Philadelphia.
Clarkson, Miss G. C., Philadelphia.
Conant, Mrs. H., Pawtucket.
Clapp, G., Waltham.
Clocket, Miss A., Rockland.
Cushman, Miss A. L., Cambridge.
Comstock, G. C., New York.
Davol, Ezra, Taunton, Mass.
Davol, Ralph, Taunton, Mass.
Doherty, J. O., Haverhill.
Dutton, Samuel L., Boston.
Edgar, A. B., Montreal.
Edgar, Miss, Montreal.
Edgar, Miss A., Montreal.
Elmes, George W. and wife, New York.
Elmes, Miss, New York.
Fiske, H. A. and wife, Boston.
Gullager, P. D., New York.
Goodwin, Miss, Portland.
Hacket, H. B., Brooklyn.
Hinman, E. and wife, New York.
Holmes, E. and wife, New York.
Holmes, Miss, Detroit.
Hammond, Mrs. George H., Detroit.
Hammond, Miss F. P., Detroit.
Hammond, Miss E. K., Boston.
Hale, E. B., Philadelphia.
Hutchinson, Mrs. J. B., Philadelphia.
Hutchinson, Mrs. J. B., Jr., Baltimore.
Howland, E. and family, Boston.
Hallis, Mrs. E., Melrose.
Hopkins, J. N., Boston.
Ingalls, Mr. and Mrs. J. A., Boston.
Ingraham, Mr. and Mrs. F. A., Brooklyn.
Jewell, J. V., Brooklyn.
Jewell, Miss, Brooklyn.
Jewell, Miss Alice, New York.
Jewett, Mr. and Mrs. N. M., New York.
Jewett, Miss, Philadelphia.
Jenkins, T. F., Philadelphia.
Jenkins, Mrs. T. F., Michigan.
Jennings, W. H., New York.
Knapp, Mrs. E. A., Brooklyn.
Knight, S. B., New York.
Keane, T. J. and wife, New York.
Lawrence, Mr. and Mrs. F. W., Baltimore.
Langdon, Mr. and Mrs. T. P., New York.
Ludington, Mr. and Mrs. B. L.,
Ludington, Marietta B., New York.
Ludington, Helen A., New York.
Mumford, Mr. and Mrs. B. B., Richmond.
Martin, Mr. and Mrs. John T., New York.
Mumford, Mr. and Mrs. A. H., Boston.
Matthews, Mr. and Mrs. George, Cincinnati.
Mollis, L. J., Brooklyn.
McPartland and son, New York.
Millet, E. G., New York.
Pepper, Mr. and Mrs. W. P., Philadelphia.
Pepper, Miss A. M., Philadelphia.
Pepper, Miss N. O., Philadelphia.
Peppel, William P., Jr., Philadelphia.
Peacock, Miss, New York.
Percival, J. H. and wife, New York.
Paul, H. N. and wife, Philadelphia.
Patchen, E. F., Brooklyn.
Patchen, Miss E. A., Brooklyn.
Putnam, E., Boston.
Patchel, George, Leeds.
Rixey, P. M., U. S. N.
Rowe, H. T. and wife, Boston.
Rauh, M., Pittsburgh.
Reynolds, Mrs. S. F., Brooklyn.
Read, F. F., Boston.
Slee, Miss, Baltimore.
Schuyler, Dr. and Mrs., Plattsburg.
Stowell, R. B., Boston.
Shipley, Mrs. C. W., Boston.
Scheeffelin, W. H., New York.
Stearns, R. H. and wife, Boston.
Schwartz, Mr. and Mrs. D. L., Lakewood.
Smith, Miss S. A., Newark.
Towle, E. A., Boston.
Taylor, Mrs. H. S., Baltimore.
Taylor, Miss, Baltimore.
Taylor, Miss Mary, Baltimore.
Tamet, Mrs., Austria.
Whitman, N., New York.
Wells, H. A. and wife, New York.
Walker, Mr. and Mrs. J. N., Brooklyn.
Wood, Mrs. L. P., Brooklyn.
Wood, Clarence D.,

MANSION HOUSE.

Best, Mrs. Rev. E. S., Spencer, Mass.
Bickford, Mrs. L. M., Hyde Park, Mass.
Blanchard, H. C., Cumberland Center, Me.
Clarke, S., Bridgeport, Ct.
Coughlin, Peter and wife, New York, N. Y.
Coughlin, Master Joseph, New York, N. Y.
Drury, C. F. and wife, Boston, Mass.
Dean, A. F. and wife, Portland, Me.
Farrell, Mrs. J. R., Boston, Mass.
Foster, Charles, Portland.
Foster, R. L., Lisbon, Me.
Jordan, E. C., Portland.
Jones, Mrs. W. F., New York.
Jones, Lenora, New York.
Lord, Charles E., Boston.
Monroe, John F. and wife, Philadelphia.
Monroe, Meta, Philadelphia.
McCartney, R. C., Boston.
McCartney, Mrs., Boston.
Millet, E. G., New York.
Todd, Mrs. E. T., Sing Sing, N. Y.
Talbot, A. L., Lewiston.
Tripp, Alex. and wife, Fairhaven, Mass.
Sweet, H. L., Lisbon, Me.
Washburn, Louis F., Sing Sing, N. Y.
Woodman, Mrs. C. C., Fairhaven, Mass.
Woolf, Alfred S. and son, Kansas City, Mo.

WHY
Poland Water Leads Them All.

A 19ᵗʰ Century Triumph

THE POLAND SPRING HOUSE 1893-4

MERIT, POPULARITY, LARGE SALES,

AND THE FACT THAT

POLAND WATER

Was the FIRST SOLVENT AND ELIMINATOR OF URIC ACID
CALCULI from the BLADDER AND KIDNEYS KNOWN TO
THE WORLD; also the ONLY WATER EXHIBITED
(notwithstanding the hundreds competing) at

CHICAGO'S WORLD'S EXPOSITION

To receive a Medal and Diploma for " PURITY AND
GREAT MEDICINAL POWER," prove
conclusively that

POLAND WATER LEADS THE WORLD.

THE ACCOMPANYING ILLUSTRATIONS ARE MOST SUBSTANTIAL AND
CONVINCING PROOF OF THE ABOVE ASSERTIONS.

SPRING HOUSE 1894.

SPRING 1860.

SAPIENTIA DONUM DEI

OFFICES:

BOSTON:	NEW YORK:	PHILADELPHIA:	CHICAGO:
175 Devonshire Street.	3 Park Place.	Avenue 13th and Chestnut St.	Cor. Michigan Ave. and Van Buren St.

HIRAM RICKER & SONS, Proprietors.

VOL. I.   SUNDAY MORNING, AUGUST 19, 1894.   No. 7.

Yachting Party.

NE of the great events of this week was a yachting party given by Mr. and Mrs. Polhemus of Brooklyn. Twenty guests embarked on Friday at 10.30, as merry and light-hearted a party as ever left the Poland House. It was soon discovered, however, that the steam yacht had never before carried over sixteen or eighteen persons, while on this occasion twenty precious souls graced its decks. Some slight misgivings were felt, on account of the many heavy-weights on board, but every one tried to keep up a brave exterior, and for the first half hour all went " merry as a marriage bell." This well-worn expression reminds us that a proposal of marriage was one of the most interesting incidents of the voyage, especially as it was sealed with a good round smack. Hearty applause greeted this most touching demonstration of affection.

Now the first lake was rounded, and we approached the isthmus, or channel, where danger lurked unseen. The whistle was blown to apprize any approaching crafts to clear the way. Every neck was strained over the side of the vessel, some in fear of running aground, others on account of a malady peculiar to the sea, but one which no one was ever known to acknowledge as personal. Intense excitement prevailed ! Some of the brave ones sang songs to cheer the sinking hearts. "A Life on the Ocean Wave," "Rock'd in the Cradle of the Deep," and many other songs equally ancient were wafted from trembling lips. At last we had safely passed under the bridge, and all breathed more freely as we glided out into another lake more beautiful than the first. All on board tried to ignore the fact that our perils were by no means over, as we should be obliged to return by the same narrow, watery path. Each one tried to stimulate the others, though not a flask was produced. Buoyed by the bracing air of old Poland, we made the round of this lake, drinking in the elixir of life (not Poland water) until we again reached the dangerous channel so dreaded by all on board. Like a swan our beautiful vessel glided into this pathway of danger. Suddenly the boat wriggled and pitched ! Ladies paled and sturdy men began to take off their coats ! A grating, ominous sound was heard, way down below the hold of the vessel, and like an electric current, the awful situation was grasped by all. We had run aground ! Yes ! exposed to all the terrors of being dashed to pieces by the mighty waves. Two gentlemen, at the risk of their lives, endeavored to cut loose our only boat, but failed in their perilous undertaking. At this crisis a life-preserver was discovered, and at once a colonel well known alike for his bravery and gallantry, reckless of his own safety, proceeded to envelop one of the ladies not only in this precious life-saving article, but also in his arms. This magnanimous act was met with a round of applause, which, alas ! died out suddenly when it was discovered that his unprotected wife, who was directly behind him, was not the recipient of his just and manly protection. Fortunately at this moment the unparralleled efforts of the seamen and gentlemen were crowned with success, in once more floating the boat. The blowing of the steam whistle fully expressed the joy in every heart. Three cheers were given the lady hostess,

and soon after, we came into port. All felt that our brief encounter with the perils of the deep (or rather the not deep) had only enhanced the pleasures of the trip, as danger is always a piquant sauce to every sort of amusement. It is a significant fact, however, that the distinguished gentleman from Brooklyn who invited the party to this dangerous encounter with wind and waves remained at home, quietly enjoying his peaceful cigar.

ONE OF THE SAVED.

An August Outing.

LATE Tuesday afternoon, a jolly crowd of young people, headed by Miss Florence Vose of the Hub, started in the Poland four-seater to do the Kennels and Wilsons. A perfect day made the excursion a sure success from the start, and as a recent rain laid the dust, a very enjoyable drive resulted. The party, reaching the Kennels, alighted and thoroughly inspected the above, and the juvenile members of the party were especially delighted at the antics of the exponents of the Darwin theory. Some jokes, songs, etc., that came from Messrs. Singer and Rogers kept the party in good spirits, and the excellent alto singing of Miss Blanche Todd was repeatedly applauded. At sunset the party, passing the Wilson House, awoke the echoes of the surrounding hills by giving one ear-splitting Poland yell. "Boom-te-de-ay" was sung with great vigor by all present, and upon reaching home the affair was voted a grand success.

Those present were Miss Stinson, Mattocks, Thomas, Misses Todd, Mr. Vose, Rogers, Singer, Messrs. Maginnis.

TWO OF THE SINGERS.

The Admiral's Revenge.

[From World.]

Quoth Admiral Ting: "It's a very strange thing
    How these confounded Japanese fight;
They sank Chih and Chen and, sad to say, then
    Ching Yuen knocked clean out of sight.

"Hence it won't do for me to venture to sea,
    So I'll not take the blame of that sin;
But a challenge I'll send by the hand of some friend
    For a game which I think I can win.

"Theirs now is the praise, and much racket they raise,
    But 'twill prove quite a different thing
When those blokes from Japan sit down at fan-tan
    And play against Admiral Ting."

Bubbles.

Cupid.

Full moon.

Mixed weather.

Red Astrachans are ripe.

The jolliest week of the season.

Camp-meeting at Empire to-day.

A masquerade is a coming attraction.

The ball game on Saturday was a "corker."

Some great card playing these rainy evenings.

Mayor Gilroy of New York City will be with us soon.

This is the best season Poland Spring ever experienced.

J. Harry Mann of Boston stopped here Monday for the day.

Ex-Mayor True of Portland, is again domiciled here for the season.

People who sit on the veranda all day miss half the delights of Poland.

How is it Allen Rogers always gets the best girl and the front seat?

Ex-Governor J. D. Bedel and wife, of Jersey City, N. J., are here for an extended visit.

Contributions to the HILL-TOP will be paid for at the end of the season (if business is good).

Mr. and Mrs. Zeigler and Miss Zeigler left Thursday, amid a profusion of flowers and shouting.

S. McPartland, a large dry goods dealer of New York, is here for an extended visit, accompanied by his son.

R. J. Kendrick and Geo. L. Connois, of the New York, New Haven & Hartford R. R., have been at the House this week.

Dr. J. H. Schenck, of Philadelphia, arrived Wednesday, as a guest of Mr. and Mrs. John Kisterbock of the same city.

Mr. W. H. Shieftlin of New York City, the largest importer of druggists' supplies in the country, is here for the season.

Lots of interest has been taken by the guests the past week in the actions of Congress, and bulletins have been received regularly.

Jolly Harry Ziegler has left us. At his departure he held a regular reception on the veranda, saying good-by to his many friends.

Two single, one double, one five-seater, and a four-in-hand turn-out, all from the Poland Spring House, were seen at Pope's Kennels at the same time last Tuesday.

H. T. JORDAN, } EDITORS.
W. D. FREEMAN, }

PUBLISHED EVERY SUNDAY MORNING DURING THE MONTHS
OF JULY, AUGUST AND SEPTEMBER, IN THE INTERESTS OF

POLAND SPRING AND ITS VISITORS.

All contributions relative to the guests of Poland Spring will
be thankfully received.

To insure publication, all communications should reach the
editors not later than Thursday preceding day of issue.

All parties desiring rates for advertising in the HILL-TOP
should write the editors for same.

The subscription price of the HILL-TOP is $1.00 for the
season, post-paid. Single copies will be mailed at 10c. each.

Address,

EDITORS "HILL-TOP,"
Poland Spring House,
South Poland, Maine.

PRINTED AT JOURNAL OFFICE, LEWISTON.

Sunday, Aug. 19, 1894.

Editorial.

IF any doubt had heretofore existed as to the
sentiment of the citizens of Poland in regard
to the position the proprietors of Poland
Spring have taken in striving to maintain the
privacy of the Poland Spring grounds and to
defend them from the encroachments of objec-
tionable excursion parties, the result of the town
meeting held on Thursday must effectually remove
it. The efforts which have been made to have
the private road over Poland Hill opened as a
county road are too well known to readers of
the HILL-TOP to require rehearsal at this time.
The town meeting of Thursday was called for
the special purpose of deciding what stand the
town would take in the matter. It was a representative meeting, attended by fully two-thirds
of the voters of the town, and all of them tax-
payers, and by a vote practically unanimous,
there being but one opposing voice, the select-
men were instructed to use all fair and honorable
means to defeat the petition, and to aid the
Rickers in maintaining the privacy of their
grounds. The representative character of the
meeting and the practical unanimity of its action
speaks volumes for the esteem in which the
Messrs. Ricker are held by their townsmen, and
evidences in a most conclusive manner that they
have the sentiment of the local public behind
them in this contest.

Laying of Corner-Stone.

THE foundation of the Maine State Building,
which the enterprising Ricker firm purchased at the close of the World's Fair and
transported to Poland by special train of
twenty cars, is all in, and the corner-stone of the
structure proper was laid on Tuesday afternoon
last. In the receptacle provided for that purpose
were placed souvenirs of all kinds, including
coins bearing the date of the year in which the
Poland Spring House was built and the years in
which additions have been made, printed matter
sent out from the hill, pictures of the proprietors,
a collection of *Lewiston Journals* and a file of
the HILL-TOP, besides many individual cards.
Although no announcement of the event had
been made a large number of the guests were
present and participated in the affair.

Those who visited the Fair remember it as
being one of the prettiest and most substantially
built of any of the State representatives. It is
octagonal in shape, two stories in height, and
built entirely of Maine granite. The first floor
contains four or five large public rooms, while
the next floor is divided into several smaller
rooms, which will probably be utilized in future
seasons as sleeping apartments. The building
will contain a large reading-room and library,
and it is probable that the Poland Spring booth,
which provoked such favorable comment because
of its extreme beauty, will be placed in the
building somewhere.

It is expected that the building will be furnished and ready for occupancy by the middle or
last of September, when it will be appropriately
dedicated.

This will serve as another addition to the
many points of beauty and interest about Poland.

Negotiations are under way at present towards
the giving of a Masquerade Ball to the employees
of the Poland Spring House by the proprietors.
It will probably be held next Thursday evening,
if costumes can be engaged for that evening.

Literary.

"N.—B."

"N" for Nannie and "B" for Ben—
I see them now as I saw them then,
In the bark of the oak tree wed.
She sat waist deep in the clover white,
And the liquid gold of that June sunlight
Shone o'er her sweet young head.

And I stood carving those letters twain,
Which time and tempest have all in vain
Striven to blur and blot.
But they live in the oak tree's dusky grain,
Stamped as their memory on my brain,
Changing but fading not.

Ah, the vows that I vowed that day!
Their broken shafts in my bosom stay,
Wounding it hour by hour.
Could I prove false to one so true?
Dared I be cruel, my love, to you?
Oh, Nannie, my lily flower!

Ere the snow had whitened those letters twain
In the old church porch you hid your pain,
As I and my bride passed by.
Your eye was brave, but your cheek was white—
The cheek that I should have pillowed that night,
Where it never now may lie.

Little Nannie, you are now at rest,
The buttercups glowing above your breast,
Close by the church-yard gate.
And I have learned to rue the day
Gold tempted my steps from love away;
Yet mine is the sadder fate.

I would give the rest of my life to-night
To see you stand in the clover white,
The sun on your locks of gold,—
And carve them now as I carved them then—
"N" for Nannie and "B" for Ben—
In the bark of the oak tree old. —*Anon.*

Possibilities of the Language.

[Boston Transcript.]

"And what has become of Jed Thomas?" asked the little old man with the queer whiskers.

"Jed Thomas," said the other, apparently a clergyman, "has joined the great majority."

"Phew! You don't say so! And Seth Bly, is he living?"

"Mr. Bly passed away about a year ago."

So? But how about old Mrs. Stikton?"

"Mrs. Stikton has solved the great problem."

"Well, it beats all! How they do hang out! And all of 'em up to somethin' oncommon. But it is strange. Hasn't there been any deaths at all down in Seedville since I come away?"

Wee Binkelblink.

ADAPTED FROM THE GERMAN FOR THE YOUNG READERS OF THE HILL-TOP.

(*Concluded.*)

BINKELBLINK soon rolled out of the hard knot into which he and his comrades were tied, and again Mother Earth received him and for a long time hid him deep within her bosom. She worked marvelous changes in him, so that Binkelblink felt very hot and strange. But her parting injunction, as he fell into a boiling spring, was a word of good cheer and encouragement, and he learned that his mission now was the noble one of healing. Already sweet strains of music fell upon his ear, and glasses were dipped down into the spring and people from far and wide were praising these precious drops of water, just as we gaze with gratitude into the crystal depths of our Poland Spring where are, who shall say, how many Wee Binkelblinks?

Binkelblink, always of an adventurous spirit, evaded the glasses dipped down, and slipped through a short pipe to emerge into a hot pool set in a beautiful marble room. Soon came a bather who jumped into the healing waters. What a frolic he gave the drops, and what a frolic they gave him! In the splashing Binkelblink coursing down the man's nose on a toboggan slide, was suddenly shaken off and sent with others through an open window and, oh, what a downfall into a tub of rainwater! Poor, poor Binkelblink! "Alas," he sighed, I know I shall stagnate here. I've never been foul, oh, to come to it now after all my glorious experiences!" He had heard from others of drops boiling in a pot to make potatoes jump, of kitchen sinks and sewers, in fact of all the dark and devious ways where water is forced. But he had also knowledge of how Nature in her wondrous alchemy changes all foulness into absolute purity again, and the little fellow took heart of hope.

Clang-clang, clang-clang, suddenly rang out from the town hall belfry. Hurrying feet and screaming voices announced a fire. The village streets were filled with excited throngs, the quaint buildings were lighted up by a great glare. People rushed by with feather-beds, chests and babies, while pigs, ducks and geese ran squealing and cackling past the tub where Binkelblink reposed. The word was passed that the brook was dry, and so it happened that the village boys put the tub on a cart with many other tubs and barrels, then away to the burning house! Binkelblink's companions shot into the fiery furnace, hissing and steaming in their battle with the flames.

He was sent with many to wet the roof of the railway station and save it from destruction, and well they performed their duty. Binkelblink's pride was once more appeased, and after a few days he found his way into a water tank and was taken up by a steam engine. It delighted him to be a factor in carrying people to their summer vacations; even a little drop of water loves the good things of life.

Our last glimpse of Binkelblink is of that plump little body shot out with the steam, when the valve is opened, shot out and up into the air, to be drawn again to the skies he loves so well. There will be more and more history for him. As he exultingly sang with the brook,
"Men may come and men may go,
But I go on forever,"
so does he indeed share with every atom of matter, working under the Divine Will, in the ever-continuous creation.   I. M. G.

Progressive Euchre.

THE party of Friday evening was the largest and most successful of the season. At eight o'clock seventy-two card devotees sat down to the green-topped tables and for two hours the fight waged fast and furious. At the conclusion of the time allotted for play it was found that the following were entitled to the handsome prizes which Mrs. B. P. Moulton had shown her usual excellent taste in selecting: Mrs. Keene, first ladies'; Mrs. Eldridge, second ladies'; Mrs. Jones, third ladies'; Mrs. Shortridge, fourth ladies'; Mr. Ivers, first gentlemen's; Mr. Carpenter, second gentlemen's; Mr. Peters, third gentlemen's; Mr. Stewart, fourth gentlemen's; Mrs. Maginnis, ladies' consolation; Mr. Sands, gentlemen's consolation.

After the prizes had been distributed, the party adjourned to the dining-hall, where a lunch was partaken of. The whole party were seated at one long table which had been handsomely decorated with ferns, flowers, etc., under the supervision of Mrs. E. P. Ricker, and Mr. Roberts, the popular head waiter. The table was the prettiest ever set in the magnificent hall. After the inner man had been satisfied, a number of speeches were made, Mr. Moulton officiating as chairman. Mr. Sawyer was called upon to respond to the toast of "absent friends," and in reply said that he "plead guilty and threw himself upon the mercy of the court."

To Mr. Sawyer and Mr. Moulton much of the praise for the success of the whole affair was due, and they received many thanks for a most enjoyable evening.

Great Walking.

MR. BYRON P. MOULTON of Philadelphia, accompanied by Miss Catherine Barr of Springfield, Mass., and Miss R. D. Lindsay of Chester, Pa., beat the record for long walks on Monday afternoon. Starting from the hotel they went via the lake up over Oak Hill to the dog kennels, and thence on around by Mr. Pope's stables and house, and back around the lake to the hotel, a distance of from six to seven miles. Mr. Moulton says that Misses Barr and Lindsay are the champion walkers of Poland, and he is good authority.

Wednesday's Launch Party.

ON Wednesday the 8th, a jolly party of young people left the hotel to enjoy a sail on the new steam launch Poland. The party was given by Miss Helen Stinson of the Quaker City to her many friends. The weather being perfect assured the party a success from the start, and aided by the wit of Mr. Singer of New York and the musical selections by Messrs. Maginnis of New Orleans and Mr. Allen Rogers of New York, the morning passed off pleasantly. Among those present were Miss Louise Mattocks of Chicago, Miss Florence Vose of Boston, and the Misses Todd of New York; Mr. Singer of New York and Mr. Vose of Boston; Messrs. Maginnis of New Orleans and Mr. Rogers of New York.   JUDD.

Happy Eleven.

ONE of the merriest parties of the week was a luncheon given on Monday by Miss Theodora P. Trowbridge, of New York, the occasion being her eleventh birthday. At 2 P.M., Miss Trowbridge and her guests sat down to the handsomely decorated table in the large bay window of the dining-hall. The table, with its wealth of flowers and ferns, had as its center-piece a mammoth birthday cake crowned with a coronet of eleven candles.

After a jolly hour at the table, the party adjourned to the Music Hall, where dances and games were in order. Miss Theo is an exceedingly popular young lady among all the guests, and the good wishes she received were numerous and sincere.

The following young ladies made up the party: Misses Theo P. Trowbridge, May Peterson, Rowena Meyer, Olive Gale, Alice Peterson, Julia Trowbridge, Claire Ingalls, Helen Ludington, Florence Peterson, Florence Stinson.

Base=Ball.

Defeated in the Eleventh.

THE CLOSEST GAME OF THE SEASON.

THE home team was defeated last Saturday for the third time this season, by the Atlantics of Portland. The game seemed to be won when four runs were made in the first inning, but the visitors steadied down, and by good fielding, aided by a little good luck, held the Poland Spring boys down to three runs for the remainder of the game. The Atlantics played a strong, up-hill game and succeeded in tieing the score in the sixth, after which neither side could score until the tenth, when the home team scored on Sockalexis's three-base hit and an error by Kilfedder. In the last half, the first two were struck out, but Desmond met one squarely and sent it far into right field, making a circuit of the bases and tieing the score. The Poland Springs went out in order in the eleventh, but the visitors scored on a single and a two-bagger, thus winning a most exciting game. Mullen saved the game in the ninth, catching a long fly from Rafter's bat, which looked to be good for three bases. It was the best play seen here this year. The score:

ATLANTICS.

	A.B.	R.	1B.	T.B.	P.O.	A.	E.
Flavin, 2b.,	5	0	1	1	1	0	1
Kilfedder, s.s.,	6	1	2	3	0	10	2
Gorham, 3b.,	5	1	1	1	2	2	1
Devine, l.f.,	6	0	1	1	5	1	0
Edgar, c.,	3	2	1	1	7	1	3
Rafter, 1b.,	3	1	1	2	14	0	0
Fitzsimmons, r.f.,	5	0	1	1	2	0	0
T. Desmond, c.f.,	4	1	1	1	2	0	1
W. Desmond, p.,	5	2	3	6	0	2	0
Totals,	42	8	12	17	33	16	8

POLAND SPRING.

	A.B.	R.	1B.	T.B.	P.O.	A.	E.
Wakefield, 2b.,	6	2	2	5	2	1	1
Hull, 1b.,	6	1	3	3	9	0	0
Powers, c.,	5	2	2	2	10	2	1
County, 3b.,	5	1	0	0	0	3	1
Harris, s.s.,	5	0	2	4	2	2	0
Pulsifer, c.f.,	5	0	1	2	2	0	0
Sockalexis, l.f.,	4	1	1	3	2	1	0
Slattery, p.,	5	0	0	0	1	2	0
Mullen, r.f.,	5	0	0	0	3	1	0
Totals,	46	7	11	19	*31	13	3

*Winning run made with one man out.

Innings,	1	2	3	4	5	6	7	8	9	10	11
Atlantics,	0	1	2	0	1	2	0	0	0	1	1—8
Poland Sp.,	0	0	4	1	1	0	0	0	1	0—7

Earned runs, Atlantics 2, Polands 2; 2-base hits, Kilfedder, Rafter, Wakefield, Harris 2, Pulsifer; 3-base hits, Wakefield, Sockalexis; home run, W. Desmond; passed balls, Edgar 2; wild pitches, Desmond 1, Slattery 2; base on balls, by Desmond 3, by Slattery 5; hit by pitched ball, by Slattery 1; struck out, by Desmond 7, by Slattery 6. Time, 2 hours 35 minutes.

The game with Lewiston, Thursday, was very unsatisfactory. It is true we were defeated only by a small score, but it might have been larger had the Lewistons wished. It was plainly a case of rattle which lost us the game, seven errors at short telling the story. Burrell, our new twirler, did finely, holding the Lewistons down to nine hits, and with decent support should have won the game easily. Our old invincibles, Wakefield and Hull, played their usual perfect game, while Sockalexis did finely. The score:

LEWISTONS.

	A.B.	R.	1B.	T.B.	P.O.	A.	E.
Grant, c., l.f.,	5	1	1	2	2	0	0
Bergen, c.f., c.,	5	1	3	6	3	1	0
Larocque, 2b.,	3	1	2	3	4	6	2
McCormack, 3b.,	5	1	1	1	0	1	0
Spill, s.s.,	5	0	1	3	3	5	0
Mains, l.f., p.,	4	0	1	1	0	4	0
Leighton, c.f.,	3	1	1	1	1	0	0
McManus, 1b.,	4	1	1	1	14	0	1
Stott, p.,	0	0	0	0	0	1	0
Stafford, r.f.,	4	2	0	0	0	0	0
Totals,	38	8	11	18	27	18	3

POLAND SPRING.

	A.B.	R.	1B.	T.B.	P.O.	A.	E.
Wakefield, 1b.,	3	2	0	0	4	3	0
Hull, 1b.,	5	0	2	2	12	2	0
Burrell, p.,	4	1	0	0	0	1	0
Powers, c.,	3	1	1	2	4	2	1
County, 3b.,	4	1	1	2	1	3	2
Harris, s.s., c.f.,	4	0	1	1	0	2	4
Pulsifer, c.f., s.s.,	5	0	0	0	3	3	3
Sockalexis, l.f.,	4	1	2	3	1	1	0
Mullen, r.f.,	4	0	0	0	1	0	1
Totals,	36	6	7	10	23*	17	11

*Spill out on tapped ball.

SCORE BY INNINGS.

	1	2	3	4	5	6	7	8	9	
Lewistons,	0	0	3	4	0	0	1	0	x—8
Poland Springs,	2	2	0	0	0	2	0	0	0—6

Earned runs, Lewistons 1, Poland Springs 1. 2-base hits, Grant, Bergen, Larocque, Powers, County, Sockalexis. 3-base hits, Bergen, Spill. Base on balls, by Stott 2, by Mains 1, by Burrell 2. Hit by pitched ball, Larocque. Struck out, by Mains 3, by Burrell 1. Time, 2 hours. Umpires, Polhemus and Slattery.

STAGES.

DEPART.

	M. H.	P. S. H.
For Portland and Boston,	6.25 A.M.	6.30 A.M.
Lewiston and Farmington,	8.25 A.M.	8.30 A.M.
Portland and Boston,	9.25 A.M.	9.30 A.M.
Lewiston and Bar Harbor,	10.25 A.M.	10.30 A.M.
Lewiston and Bangor,	12.45 P.M.	1 P.M.
Portland and Boston,	3.25 P.M.	3.30 P.M.

ARRIVE.

	M. H.	P. S. H.
From the West,	10.30 A.M.	10.35 A.M.
From the East,	1 P.M.	1.05 P.M.
From the West,	3.30 P.M.	3.35 P.M.
" " "	7.30 P.M.	7.35 P.M.

Tennis Tournament.

*T*HE HILL-TOP is a very modest little sheet, you know, just large enough to contain such a gist of the local Poland news as, in the minds of its editors, seems best suited to the class of people it caters to. That it knows a good thing when it sees it is certain, while its ability to get up a good entertainment should not be questioned, when the tennis tournament which has been given under its auspices the past week, is considered. It was a great success, of course; that goes without saying.

The attendance throughout the tournament has been large, and, if the enthusiasm manifested by the continual applause counted for anything, the playing was very pleasing. Some of the sets were indeed most exciting, and if a certain young lady did throw her new summer bonnet away up into the air, during the heat of one of the finals, who cares? We dare say many of the fair ones would fain have followed her example had not the influence of older ones near by prevented.

The boys played their hardest to win, and throughout the whole tournament it was very uncertain at all times who would be the victor. But who could help playing their hardest, with such an array of beautiful new summer gowns and bonnets, and such *tremendous* applause that the pretty young ladies, from both houses, who graced the occasion with their presence, gave. It was enough to inspire the soul of a Carthaginian to even greater efforts. The fellows did play fine tennis, and certainly deserved every bit of applause which they received.

The sets between Wood and Parr, and Singer and Pulsifer, in the second round, were hard fought from the time the referee called play until the end of the last game in the third set in each case, when game, set, and match, was announced. In the semi-finals also some good work was done, especially between Singer and Wood, both of whom are fast players. But in the finals the best playing of the tournament was seen. Wakefield is a Bates student, class of '95, and well up in all the athletics usually indulged in by college boys. His specialty, though, is base-ball, which he has played with such success during his college course, and at Poland Spring during his summer vacation, that numerous offers have been tendered him from several professional and semi-professional clubs in this section. But he is no mean tennis player, also. He was runner-up in his college tennis tournament two years ago, and his fellow-students say that he could easily have won the championship this year had he only consented to play. He is a very conscientious worker, and

makes his opponent work for all he is worth. He is very brainy, too, and takes great delight in putting the ball just out of reach. That was the way he won the championship, and the elegant silver and gold cup offered by the HILL-TOP.

Singer, the runner-up in the finals, is the son of I. A. Singer, of Singer machine fame. He has finished his preparation for Yale, and will probably enter this fall. He is an excellent young man, and very popular among his many friends at Poland. He has always been a devotee of tennis and has won several prizes in tournaments in which he has contested. His playing is strong and steady, he never gets rattled, but plays from beginning to end in the same hard, faithful manner. It was though no lack of effort on his part that he suffered defeat. He met a better player.

Everything considered, the tournament was a complete success, and reflects much credit on the officials in charge, and the HILL-TOP, under whose auspices it was given. Below are the results in full :

FIRST ROUND.

Singer beat Harris,	6—1	6—4
Sockalexis beat Gay,	6—4	6—4
Pulsifer beat Vose,	6—2	6—0
Wakefield beat Rogers,	6—2	6—1
Wood beat Williams,	6—4	6—2
Parr beat Maginnis,		Default.
Washburn beat Trowbridge,		Default.

SECOND ROUND.

Gay beat Rogers,		6—2	6—3
Wood beat Parr,	5—7	6—0	6—4
Singer beat Pulsifer,	6—4	7—9	7—5
Sockalexis beat Washburn,		6—2	6—2
Harris beat Williams,	4—6	7—5	6—3
Wakefield beat Vose,		6—1	6—3

THIRD ROUND.

Pulsifer beat Parr,		Default.
Wood beat Sockalexis,	6—2	7—5
Singer beat Gay,	7—5	6—1
Wakefield beat Harris,	6—4	6—4

FOURTH ROUND.

Pulsifer beat Sockalexis,	6—0	6—1
Singer beat Washburn,	6—1	6—2
Wakefield beat Wood,	6—0	6—0

SEMI-FINALS.

Wakefield beat Pulsifer,	6—2	6—3	6—1
Singer beat Wood,	4—6 6—4	6—4	6—1

FINALS.

Wakefield beat Singer,	6—2	6—1	6—2

Capt. G. P. Cotton, Battery H, 1st Artillery, is enjoying his vacation here. Capt. Cotton has command of Governor's Island, and has the honor of being in charge of the battery that fired the first Federal gun during the late war.

On Monday Mrs. Lindsay and Miss Barr, of Springfield, took an eight-mile walk under the guidance of Mr. B. P. Moulton, the well-known Poland guide and ex-president of the Alpean Club.

Bubbles.

He heard them kissing on the sly
And peeked in through the door,
And then he cried in accents high,
"Say, sister, what's the score?"

Mr. J. E. Spencer and his accomplished wife are again with us for the season.

Mr. H. W. Ricker took a flying trip to New York and through the Catskills, the past week.

Miss Vose gave a dinner on Tuesday to the "Sweet Six" and a number of their gentleman friends.

Gov. Greenhalge of Massachusetts, and Gen. Martin of the Boston police investigation, are booked for rooms soon.

This is undoubtedly the banner year with Maine as a summer resort state, and Poland Spring is ahead as usual.

Lucius E. Tuttle, President of the Boston & Maine Railroad, is here enjoying the bracing air and waters of Poland.

R. H. Stearns and wife, of Boston, were here a few days the past week. Mr. Stearns is the great dry goods dealer of the Hub.

Carl Hirsch and wife are stopping here for a month's vacation. Mr. Hirsch is a large manufacturer of railroad supplies in St. Louis.

When on the lakes, or off for a long drive, lunch and hammocks are usually carried, so as to have the benefit of the entire day out.

Three in a buggy seems to be the most enjoyable way of driving among the natives, declares a well-known "Capital City" gentleman.

Mrs. H. C. Swaine, accompanied by her son, are here for an extended visit. Mr. Swaine is a large wholesale and retail dealer in lumber of Newark, N. J.

One of the "sights" which occasions much interest among the "natives" is a popular young "Quaker" taking a five-mile spin in his running tights in the early morning.

B. F. Keith, the Hub theatre man, is the star bicyclist on the hill. Mr. Keith is a great admirer of nature and passes the greater part of his time on his wheel, driving, and on the lakes.

A number of parties did Lewiston and the circus on Tuesday. One party was thoughtful enough to take over a "Poland" lunch, which they enjoyed in the band stand at the city park, surrounded by an awe-stricken circle of visitors from the "rural deestricks."

A very interesting game of whist was played a week ago, Miss Wheelock, the whist queen, and Mr. Yates of Philadelphia playing against Mrs. Moulton of Philadelphia and Mr. Fish of New York. Six games were played, Mrs. Moulton and Mr. Fish winning four games.

Pope's kennels are a great attraction this season and many parties visit them daily. On Tuesday Mr. Pope drove his four-in-hand mule team attached to a nobby coach over to the House. It is a most unique turn-out, and accompanied by a retinue of horseback riders, it made quite a stir.

Mr. Keith has added the bicycle to his list, which he justly claims furnishes more exercise than all the rest put together, especially over the hills and through the sand of the Alpine road. Mr. K. is also gaining some reputation as a sprinter, especially up hills and when passing heavy teams.

Mr. Edward Longstreth and wife, of Philadelphia, are quartered at the Poland Spring House for the season. Mr. Longstreth was formerly a member of the great Baldwin locomotive works of Philadelphia. He and his charming wife are exceedingly well known among the leading philanthropists of the Quaker City.

Mr. Lindsey of Northfield, Mass., with his charming wife and her friend Miss Barr of Springfield, Mass., have been staying at the Spring House for the past two weeks. Mr. Lindsey is the largest owner of the Antlers Hotel at Colorado Springs and also the proprietor of the Bon Air Hotel at Augusta, Ga., one of the very finest watering-place hotels in the United States.

If you want to make a friend of Mr. B., the Boston broker, you should tell him that you have a dog you would like to sell him. You may escape alive, but it would be a ten to one shot that you will not come out unscathed. Why he is so sensitive in regard to canines is due to a joke ad. in the Boston Sunday papers, in which Mr. B. is the "jokee."

Besides the board walks to the spring and Mansion House, and the bewitching wooded paths in many directions, the lawn-tennis and croquet, there is the rowing, sailing, and steam-launch on the lakes, the many magnificent drives, and for the few rainy days, bowling, billiards, and pool, all in the line of healthful exercise, which adds fully fifty per cent. to the enjoyment of the average guest. Mr. and Mrs. B. F. Keith of Brookline and friends are fully alive to the above facts, and including Miss Fynes of Allston, Mr. O'Brien of Brookline, Father Walsh of Boston, and Mr. and Mrs. Dickinson of Chicago, may be found almost daily recreating in one of the above ways.

Arrivals

FOR WEEK ENDING AUGUST 16.

POLAND SPRING HOUSE.

Andrews, Mr. and Mrs. M. H.,	Bangor.
Boardman, Mr. and Mrs. N. S.,	Conn.
Boardman, Mrs. L. A.,	Conn.
Brown, F. H.,	Waltham.
Bawne, W.,	New York.
Bonney, Mrs. A. S.,	Mechanic Falls.
Bostram, Mr. and Mrs. J. B.,	Newark, N. J.
Bostram, Howard P.,	Newark, N. J.
Bedle, Mr. and Mrs. J. D.,	Jersey City.
Bradley, Mr. and Mrs.,	Meriden, Conn.
Borden, Mr. and Mrs. R. B.,	Fall River
Ballett, Mr. and Mrs. A. R.,	Boston.
Bruno, R. M.,	New York.
Buhler, A. W.,	Boston.
Connol, G. L.,	New York.
Cousland, Miss M. M.,	Philadelphia.
Cameron, W. J.,	Boston.
Cummock, Mrs. J. W.,	Springfield.
Colcolan, Mrs. Lake,	Springfield.
Clawson, Mr. and Mrs. J. L.,	Philadelphia.
Clark, Miss E. F.,	Boston.
Child, Mrs. L. M.,	Boston.
Clam, Mrs. E. D.,	Newark, N. J.
Dana, E. and mother,	New York.
Dickinson, Mrs. A. E.,	New York.
DuBois, Mr. and Mrs. L. G.,	Pomfret, Conn.
Dodd, Miss J. Ida,	Newark, N. J.
Dick, Leon St. C.,	White Plains, N. Y.
Frothingham, Miss A.,	Boston.
Findley, Mrs. C. W.,	New York.
Foss, G. E., Jr.,	Methuen, Mass.
Griffin, H. B.,	Haverhill, Mass.
Gunther, F. L.,	New York.
Guider, Mrs. Chas.,	New York.
Guider, Miss J. L.,	New York.
Gleason, Mr. and Mrs. H. P.,	Newark, N. J.
Gage, Mr. and Mrs. Geo. F.,	Huntington, Pa.
Haines, Miss M.,	Boston.
Holbrook, E. F.,	New York.
Hand, J. T.,	Boston.
Holsey, Mr. and Mrs. W. S.,	Philadelphia.
Holmes, E. T.,	New York.
Holmes, Mrs. E. T.,	New York.
Holmes, E. T., Jr.,	New York.
Hunting, K. L.,	Boston.
Haws, Mr. and Mrs. N. S.,	No. Leominster.
Hunt, Otis E.,	Newtonville, Mass.
Hosmer, Mr. and Mrs. E. B.,	Boston.
Johnson, W. S.,	New York.
Johnson, Ella F.,	Boston.
Johnston, Mr. and Mrs. J.,	Lonsdale, R. I.
Johnston, Helen B.,	Lonsdale, R. I.
Kendrick, J. L.,	Boston.
Leadbeater, Miss E. M.,	Philadelphia.
Lawrence, Mrs. L. F.,	Boston.
Lanahan, Mrs. S. J.,	Baltimore.
Lanahan, Wallace,	Baltimore.
Leverick, Mrs. J. F.,	Newark, N. J.
McAndrew, J. J.,	Boston.
Mora, Mrs. E. M.,	New York.
McLeod, J. A.,	Boston.
March, Mr. and Mrs. A. S., Jr.,	New York.
Mann, J. Henry,	Boston.
Martin, Mr. and Mrs. G. H.,	Baltimore.
Newhouse, Mr. and Mrs. F.,	Philadelphia.
Noyes, Dr. J. F.,	Providence.
Osgood, W. S.,	Portland.
Peckham, Alice,	Providence.
Putnam, H.,	New York.
Platt, L. C.,	White Plains, N. Y.
Robinson, L. E.,	Providence.
Robinson, W. G.,	Florida.
Ray, Mrs. G. P.,	Boston.
Ruck, Mr. and Mrs. W. C.,	Philadelphia.
Rice, Mrs. N. W.,	Boston.
Rice, Miss A. T.,	Boston.
Swayne, A. H.,	New York.
Shaw, Mrs. S. E.,	Philadelphia.
Shaw, Miss Isabella,	Philadelphia.
Shoaff, T. B.,	New York.
Sargent, Allston,	Bangor.
Shapleigh, Mrs. A. E.,	Cambridge.
Sneath, Mr. and Mrs. E. H.,	New Haven.
Schenck, J. H.,	Philadelphia.
Stoutenburgh, Mrs. C. V.,	Newark.
Thomas, Mr. and Mrs. Elias,	Portland.
Thomas, Helen B.,	Portland.
Thomas, Elias, Jr.,	Portland.
Thomas, W. W. 2d.,	Portland.
Thorp, J. G.,	Cambridge.
Whitney, G. H.,	Hackettstown, N. J.
Williams, Eben,	Milford, Mass.
Westheimer, A.,	New York.
Williamson, H.,	Philadelphia.
Webster, E. C.,	Orono.
Worthington, Mrs. L. T.,	New York.
Young, S.,	Boston.

Coming Events.

Sunday, August 19th.—Preaching Service, Music Hall, 11 A.M. Concert, 3.30 P.M. Song Service, 8.15 P.M.

Wednesday, August 22d.—Base-Ball, 2.30 P.M.

Thursday, August 23d.—Concert, 8 P.M., Music Hall.

Friday, August 24th.—Progressive Euchre, 8.15 P.M., Amusement Room.

Saturday, August 25th.—Full-Dress Hop, 8.15 P.M.

Concert Programme.

Concert programme for this afternoon, 3.30 o'clock :

1. Overture—"William Tell." Rossini.
2. Andante from Surprise Symphony. Haydn.
3. Selection—"Walkure." Wagner.
4. { a. " Le Crépuscule." Massenet.
   { b. Intermezzo—"Forget me not." Allen Macbeth.
5. First movement from the Unfinished Symphony. Schubert.
6. Fantasia—"Martha." Flotow.

Hours of Meals.

	Week Days.	Sundays.
Breakfast,	7 A.M. to 9 A.M.	8 A.M. to 10 A.M.
Dinner,	1 P.M. to 3 P.M.	1.30 P.M. to 3.30 P.M.
Supper,	6 P.M. to 8 P.M.	6 P.M. to 8 P.M.

WHY
Poland Water Leads Them All.

THE HILL-TOP

POLAND SPRING

VOL. I.   SUNDAY MORNING, AUGUST 26, 1894.   No. 8.

The Lawn Party at Lake View Cottage.

ONE of the most successful social events of the season at Poland Spring was the lawn party given at Walker's cottage on Thursday last. The weather was all that could be desired, and what with the charmingly dressed ladies, the tastefully arranged tables on the lawn, and all the good things set before us to eat, it was indeed a pretty sight to see. The famous Poland Spring House orchestra gave us delightful music on the lawn, and later, dancing was indulged in. The readings by Miss Gahm were highly appreciated. Of the many invited guests not one could say but it was a thoroughly delightful affair.

The following poem was written for the occasion by one of our own guests, who was unable to be present, having left for Texas.

In the quiet town of Poland,
Noted far and noted wide
For the wondrous Poland water
And other good things beside,
On a hill the lake o'erlooking,
Fair to see and famed for cooking,
Stands the Lake View House—a place
Where Mary Walker reigns with grace.

During the season of 'ninety-four
A goodly company—twenty or more—
Were gathered here to escape the din
Of the bustling city and save their tin.
These people I now will tell you about;
In alphabetical order I've sorted them out.

Although the greatest part of their history
Unfortunately is shrouded in mystery
We are still very sure of their names and their ages,
And these you will learn from the following pages.

Of A's there are none, so I start with a B—
And now Mr. and Mrs. Bartlett are the first I see.
At the games of croquet, whist, and letters
You'll look far and wide and not find their betters.
And Mrs. B. thinks she can row a boat,
Some day she won't be ashore or afloat,
The echoes will answer back her cries
As out of the water she struggles to rise.
The steamer comes out and a rope to her lowers,
And she'll row after this with a man at the oars.

The next on the list is Miss Emma Brown;
She hails from Lynn, the great shoe town.
She's fond of boating on the lake,
And at dancing the waltz she takes the cake.

Baker the next—a tall old bach—
If he doesn't hurry and make a match
Will be lost in the shuffle, whirl, and din,
Get badly left or—taken in.

Here's Mrs. Colburn, and her next of kin,
Beatrice, who plays the violin.
They like to ride on Pope's tally-ho,
But must find a mule team a little bit slow.

Mrs. Kuntz is the next I find,
Wife of the musician, both string and wind.
A widow is she from the morn of Monday
Through the week till the eve of Sunday.

From Jacksonville, Florida, comes Mrs. McMurray,
About June first she leaves in a hurry,
For the weather gets hot in that southern clime,
And at the Lake View she has a good time.

Portsmouth, whose praises we will not rehearse,
So often they are sung in prose and in verse,
Sends one of her daughters to join in the band.
I present Mrs. Pickett—yours to command.

In S is Miss Standish—her surname is Lil,
Her home's 'neath the shade of old Bunker Hill.
If her ancestor, Miles, only Lake View had known,
He'd have settled right here and called it his own.

From the rush and roar of busy street,
Tree-covered hill and lake to greet,
Miss Watson comes in early June,
When bees and birds are all in tune.
She likes so well, I have no doubt
September'll find her still about.

A captain there comes who's been over the sea,
A mighty good fellow you will all agree,
Though he is a loser by having no mate,
We thank him for leaving us—Mrs. Wingate.

Our latest arrival is fair Mrs. Wright,
When she reached here the house was filled quite,
Poor Baker was driven outside to a tent,
And Forrest and Mary—none knew where they went.

We have a poet among us too,
Although of her rhymes I have heard but few.
She is very modest, is Mrs. Zach,
And keeps her talent in the dark.
She is also a widow most of the time,
And for the good things I've said owes me a dime.

Fräulein and Randolph both together,
No matter what the wind or weather,
In every word and every tone
Speak in a language quite their own,
While the other children have lots of fun,

From Helen down to the youngest one.
Howard, Nelson, and Margarita
Have been as active as a Jersey mosquiter.
Then there are Edith, Nestor, and Mary Louise,
All very good children, if you please.
And last there are Waldo and sweet Marie,
A joyous band you'll all agree.

Lena, Georgie, Carrie, and Elmer too,
Of comforts from them we've had not a few.
May the girls find good husbands, the man a good wife,
Get rich and be happy the rest of their life.

Although I might have told you more,
From all my wisdom and my lore,
It seems too bad for any sage
To give away a lady's age.
Let this suffice for every one
Although the story's just begun.
Another year I may feel free
To write in full your pedigree.

We cannot better end our rhyme
Than to heartily join in this festive time,
In the following toast to our hostess and host.

May the Walkers' shadows never grow less,
And their broad acres continue to bless
Those lucky ones whose happy lot
Brings them to this enchanted spot.
Long life to Mary and Forrest, too,
May their days be long at fair Lake View.
May peace and plenty long abide,
And happiness smile on every side.

Progressive Euchre.

THE weekly progressive euchre party on Thursday evening was well attended, thirteen tables being filled. Eighteen hands were played, and the following lucky ones received prizes: Miss Keene, first ladies'; Mrs. Eldridge, second ladies'; Mrs. Lamon, third ladies'; Mr. Hale, first gentlemen's; Mr. Raub, second gentlemen's; Mr. Mathews, third gentlemen's; Mr. Adams, consolation; Miss Worthington, consolation.

A Pleasant Definition.
[Portland Times.]

"Jack," said the young girl to her beau, "here's a piece in the paper headed 'Kismet.' What does 'kismet' mean?"

"The word must be pronounced with the 't' silent."

"Why, that would be 'Kiss me!'" said Nettie.

"With the greatest pleasure," replied Jack, and he did.

Guest (morning after arrival) : "Great Scot! I was nearly eaten up by mosquitos last night! And yet you have the face to say upon your circular, 'Not a mosquito upon the place.'" Host: "Yes; but you see, I wrote that circular last winter."—*Portland Times.*

Bubbles.

Mother Goose.

Autumn is due.

Bruno escaped.

Croquet is the game.

Ideal days—bracing days.

General Martin left Thursday.

Tuesday evening was a hot one.

Agricultural fairs are almost due.

The new stable will be a dandy and up to date.

The Mansion House is good for another hundred years.

Not much sleep at the Mansion House on Tuesday evening.

The masqueraders had themselves "cameraed" Saturday morning.

Mr. Fowler, of the Hub Furniture Co., Boston, drives an excellent pair.

The ball team will probably play at Intervale next Wednesday at the coaching parade.

Mr. Stallwagen and his charming wife returned to Washington, Monday.

There are more real sweet girls and genuine good fellows at Poland this summer than ever before.

The "Sweet Six" lost one of their number on Saturday, Miss Vose returning to Boston on that date.

Dr. Eugene Smith, of Boston, gave a sailing party on the Poland to sixteen of his friends on Saturday.

Two of the "belles" here are great sprinters. On Monday evening they did a hundred yards on the verandas in about ten seconds.

Each season surpasses the preceding one in the popularity of Poland. It is rapidly gaining a national reputation as the Carlsbad of America.

The Governor of Massachusetts expressed himself as charmed and delighted with the Poland Spring House and its beautiful surroundings.

Mr. B. F. Keith and party left for Bar Harbor, Sunday. After a week's sojourn by the sea, a coaching trip will be made through the mountains.

Mr. Mullan, the popular room clerk at the big house, has been entertaining his father, Mr. I. B. Mullan, the past week. Mr. Mullan and his wife register from Ontario.

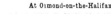
Enjoy the Beautiful Drives Abounding around Ricker Hill.

Utilize the Poland Livery.

No expense has been spared to make this feature so complete and attractive in every detail as to please *every* taste.

Coaching is a most exhilarating pleasure, and in the new

POLAND SPRING

BRAKE

will be found all the delight and comfort capable of being combined in a modern carriage.

Please leave orders for conveyances with Clerk at Office as early as possible.

H. T. JORDAN, } EDITORS.
W. D. FREEMAN, }

PUBLISHED EVERY SUNDAY MORNING DURING THE MONTHS
OF JULY, AUGUST AND SEPTEMBER, IN THE INTERESTS OF

POLAND SPRING AND ITS VISITORS.

All contributions relative to the guests of Poland Spring will
be thankfully received.

To insure publication, all communications should reach the
editors not later than Thursday preceding day of issue.

All parties desiring rates for advertising in the HILL-TOP
should write the editors for same.

The subscription price of the HILL-TOP is $1.00 for the
season, post-paid. Single copies will be mailed at 10c. each.

Address,

EDITORS "HILL-TOP,"
Poland Spring House,
South Poland, Maine.

PRINTED AT JOURNAL OFFICE, LEWISTON.

Sunday, Aug. 26, 1894.

Editorial.

THE majority of men would be more or less
discouraged by such a blow as the proprietors received on Tuesday night. Losing
at one time the majority of their livery horses
and all their harnesses, poles to the carriages,
etc., they were seriously crippled, and it would
be expected that for some days the transportation facilities would suffer. Such was not the
case, however, as with a large number of arrivals
and departures, every stage arrived and departed
on time. On Friday morning the livery was
supplied with horses, harnesses, etc., and in
complete running order. It is evident that the
Rickers spell hustle with a big H, and it is
largely to this fact that they owe their remarkable and deserved success.

Mr. Bartlett had a number of his friends
from Lake View Cottage out for a sail on the
Poland, Saturday morning.

A Card.

Through the columns of the HILL-TOP the
employees of Poland Spring desire to express
their appreciation of the generosity of the Messrs.
Ricker and the Amusement Committee as shown
by Thursday's Masquerade. The party was a
most enjoyable one and will be remembered as
one of the many favors granted by the proprietors
to their employees.

Mother Goose.

THE Mother Goose party of Saturday evening
was the event of the season, and reflected
much credit upon Mrs. B. P. Moulton and
Mrs. Geo. Trowbridge, who supervised the
affair. At 8 o'clock the hall was packed to the
doors, and for an hour hearty applause greeted
the living pictures which were the prettiest ever
seen here. The grand march and dances were
very pretty and much enjoyed. After the dancing the "actors" enjoyed a fine collation in
Music Hall, given by Dr. Trowbridge. As the
HILL-TOP goes to press too early to allow a full
description of the affair it will have to be postponed until next week. Those taking part were:

Miss Jones,	Little Boy Blue.
Mr. Green,	Apple Woman.
Mr. E. E. Denison,	Man of Our Town.
Mr. Thomas,	Piper's Son.
Mr. Singer,	Barber, Barber, Shave a Pig.
Mr. N. Maginnis,	Humpty Dumpty.
Mr. Sweet,	Piper's Son.
Mr. C. H. Dugro, } Mr. B. Stuart, }	Fiddlers for King Cole.
Miss Olive Gale,	Mary, Quite Contrary.
Miss Claire Ingalls, } Mr. Horace Ingalls, }	Went to London to find myself a Wife.
Miss Rowena Meyers,	Little Red Riding-hood.
Miss Theodora Trowbridge, } Miss Julia Trowbridge, }	Lucy Locket and Kitty Fisher.
Miss Helen Luddington,	Little Bo-Peep.
Miss Florence Peterson,	Queen of Clubs.
Miss Alice Peterson,	Queen of Spades.
Miss May Peterson,	Queen of Diamonds.
Miss Jeannette Ricker,	Little Red Riding-hood.
Miss Antonio Dugro,	Old woman, old woman, whither so high?
Miss Marguerite Ricker,	Little Red Riding-hood.
Mrs. Moulton,	Mother Goose.
Mrs. Trowbridge,	Old Woman in Shoe.
Mr. Moulton,	Old King Cole.
Mr. Sawyer,	Simple Simon.
Dr. Trowbridge, } Miss Thomas, }	Where are you going, my pretty maid?
Miss McNeal,	Little Red Riding-hood.
Miss Wheelock,	Queen of Hearts.
Mr. Lake,	King of Hearts.
Mr. W. T. Denison,	Jack of Hearts.
Miss Florence Stinson,	Queen of Hearts.
Miss H. Stinson,	Mary, Quite Contrary.
Mr. H. Maginnis,	The Beggar.
Miss Rita Tod,	Dickory Dickory Dock.
Miss Blanche Tod,	Little Bo-Peep.
Mr. A. Rogers,	Jack.
Miss Mattocks,	Jill.
Miss Carpenter,	Baby.
Baby Ricker,	Flower of the Family.
Miss H. Carpenter,	Little Miss Muffet.
Miss Worthington, } Miss Keen, }	Two Little Girls in Blue.

The Masquerade.

HANDSOME COSTUMES—A JOLLY PARTY.

"On with the dance,
Let joy be unconfined."

"Away with sorrow,
Leave *labor* far behind."

ONCE during the season the employees "own the house," and for the nonce are guests with all the privileges pertaining to the position. This "once" occurred on Thursday evening, when the employees enjoyed the annual masquerade through the generosity of the Rickers and the Amusement Committee. The party was a great success and much enjoyed by both those who were in costume and the guests who were interested lookers-on.

At nine o'clock the spirited strains of a lively march floated out through the windows and the fun commenced. The grand march was led by Floor Director Freeman, and following him came forty couples in every manner of costume. As the long line wound back and forth through the two halls it was greeted with loud applause by the five hundred spectators who were crowded around the rooms and at the windows. The costumes were well chosen and made a brilliant spectacle. After an order of ten dances had been completed the party adjourned to the dining-hall, where Mr. Roberts, assisted by Mrs. Ricker and Miss Nettie Ricker, had two long tables set for one hundred people. The tables were handsomely decorated with flowers and ferns, and were much admired. The inner man having been satisfied a vote of thanks to the proprietors and Amusement Committee was passed amidst loud applause, and the party dispersed after a most enjoyable evening.

The costumes were of such universal excellence that to name the best is no mean task. A costume which received much notice was that of Mr. Gallagher, head waiter at the Mansion House, who dressed as "Aunt Abby" of the "County Fair." Mr. Gallagher acted the part to perfection, and was the recipient of a handsome basket of flowers from his Portland friends. Perhaps the most original costume on the floor was that of Miss May Dunne, who wore a dress made after the latest mode out of HILL-TOPS. The dress represented much labor and was much commented upon. Two original dresses were worn by Miss Annie Hayes and Miss Anne Perry, who wore costumes made from Poland and Ormund labels respectively. Miss Caro Elliott as a flower girl in a pink costume was much admired, and by many was considered the belle

of the evening. A Poland water bottle with Mr. Eugene Buckley on the inside made a hit. Other dancers and costumes were:

W. Donald Freeman.	King Lear.
Wm. Shailer.	New York Cop.
B. G. Gallagher.	"Aunt Abby," of the "County Fair."
F. S. Wakefield.	King Richard III.
Miss Myrtie Woods.	Shakeless.
C. S. VanWell.	Chef.
R. G. Verrill.	Farmer.
Mary McCormack.	School-Girl.
Nellie Corcoran.	Buttercups.
Archie Cole.	Cowboy.
Pearlie Cole.	Uncle Sam.
Delia Scanlon.	School-Girl.
Lizzie Neagle.	Forest Maid.
Maggie Clark.	Fancy costume.
Wm. H. County.	Knight.
Alice Hamilton.	Pink Hungarian.
Nelly Hill.	Daisy.
W. S. Pullen.	Clown.
May Dunne.	Hill-Top.
J. E. Young.	Page.
Mame Connelly.	Spanish Dancing Girl.
Edward W. Buckley.	Poland Water.
Florence H. MacDonald.	Butterfly.
Katie L. Devine.	Dancing Girl.
George Perry.	A Villain.
Annie Crosby.	Gipsey.
Delia Coyne.	Hungarian.
Margaret Munier.	Gipsey.
W. O. Nicholls.	Mexican.
Bessie Rowe.	Fancy Dress.
Howard Laughlin.	Indian Costume.
Edna Rowe.	Fancy Dress.
C. E. Williams.	Song and Dance.
Wm. Crosby.	Skeleton.
Iza Hill.	Spanish Girl.
Nellie Wood.	Night.
Fred Keith.	King Charles II.
Flora McDonald.	Morning.
Anna Hayes.	Poland Water Tags.
Samuel Stewart.	Village Belle.
Caro L. Elliott.	Flower Girl.
Josia Monsey.	Forest Girl.
Julia Marroe.	Irish Peasant Girl.
Mattie Durney.	Hungarian.
Thomas W. Bailey.	George Washington.
Mary Griffin.	Castillian Girl.
Maggie Sullivan.	Flirt.
Maggie O'Neil.	Flirt.
Annie Fitzgerald.	Night.
Nellie Collins.	Jockey.
Charles Thomas.	King George III.
Marcella McDonald.	Pink Hungarian.
Edgar S. Patten.	Turk.
Clara Hamilton.	Indian.
Cassie McDonald.	Spanish Lady.
Mamie Murray.	Daughter of Regiment.
Jennie Scanlon.	Topsy.
Annie Nagle.	Milk-Maid.
C. F. Sockalexis.	Mephistocles.
Katie A. Buckley.	Lady in disguise.
W. E. Davis.	George Washington.
Mary Noonan.	Lady in Blue.
Margaret Marra. } Kate McCarthy. }	Two Little Girls in Blue.

Photographer Seaver has a new lens by which he can take a picture a mile away and have it look as if it were only a hundred feet. He took a picture of the house recently from the lake, and says it would have been perfect had not a young lady on the varanda winked when the plate was exposed.

OUR FIRST FIRE.

Mansion House Stables Burned to the Ground, Cause Unknown.—Loss About $15,000, Partially Insured.

THE first fire of any account that ever visited Poland Hill was that of Tuesday night, when the large livery stable, capable of accommodating about eighty horses, was burned to the ground with much of its contents. How the fire started nobody knows, but conjectures as to its cause are rife.

It was first discovered by one of the stable attaches, named Flannagan, who was about to climb into a cosy phaeton for a nap, when he noticed, just above his head, a small blaze. A moment's thought, and then with a flying leap he left the comfortable carriage to arouse the other drivers, hostlers, and stable men who were in their rooms just above the office.

The wild cry of "Fire! Fire!" awakened them, and almost simultaneously the employees' doors flew open and out rushed the occupants in a hurry. Down stairs they went with a jump and attempted to loosen the horses, and they partly succeeded, but with more than twenty remaining they had to desist from their humane efforts to save their dumb friends and seek safety for themselves. Willing hands hauled out the carriages, and only one, which was on the wash stand and escaped their notice, was left to the mercy of the flames. None of the harnesses or carriage poles, however, were saved.

By this time the barn was a roaring furnace of fire, and over a thousand people were gazing at the sight with wonder. Meanwhile attention was called to the Mansion House, toward which the wind was blowing, and streams of water went pouring over the roofs to protect that famous structure from a possible spark. Men with buckets of water were stationed all over the roofs of the house to be ready in case of necessity. Watchers were also put about all its small out-buildings, the grass just beyond the Mansion House, the woods still further beyond, and a large number were distributed on and about H. W. Ricker's private dwelling, so that every possible chance of a stray spark taking effect was cut off.

The stables were down in about an hour. The chimney fell with a brave shower of sparks. The wind shifted somewhat during the fire and bore somewhat away from the Mansion House. It remained strong, however, and at 10.30 was still scattering the embers. Forty men were on patrol all night and the woods and property were all guarded and searched for fire.

The stables were 125 x 40 feet, with a wing 77 feet long. The wing was the original Wentworth Ricker stable, built in 1825. It was the famous "entertainment for beasts," in the days of stage travel past the Ricker Hill. The new stable was built only a few years ago, and cost complete about $10,000. It was modern in structure and was used wholly for the Rickers' teams and general work horses with a few of the Mansion House livery. The entire lot of poles for double teams was here, and the collection of harnesses was valuable. Mr. H. W. Ricker had to go to Portland, Wednesday, to buy poles and harnesses for work, while teams have been called in from the surrounding county to do the daily traffic. The Rickers have another and more recently built stable near the Poland Spring House. Here are the fancy hitches, the private turn-outs of the guests, the livery of the two houses, and the swell turn-outs that make such an attraction at the Spring. None of these, of course, were disturbed in any way.

The losses included about seventy tons of loose hay, ten tons of baled hay, all the harnesses, two carriages, thirty horses, and the stable. The total loss was estimated by Mr. E. P. Ricker at $15,000. He had an insurance of about one-half. Cyrus Moore, a hostler, lost a gold watch and a check for $50. Others of the help in the stable lost their personal effects. Several had slight injuries.

The Rickers will rebuild upon the same place at once, and will erect a more modern and improved building than even the old one was.

In this fire the efficiency of the fire service was displayed, the available supply being about 40,000 gallons in tanks and the steam pump service from the lake.

How the fire caught is a mystery. No one had been in the hay-loft since 4.30 P.M. Then a man went up to pitch down some hay. The only solution is that some one has disobeyed orders and smoked in the loft. If such is the case, the disobedient made a wild night for Poland Spring and one that will not soon be forgotten.

On Tuesday afternoon the young people gathered in the Music Room, and in a few moments their young voices were heard in bursts of sweetest melody, awakening in many a weary heart memories of by-gone days, as the old, familiar "Vive l' Amour" and "Gay Cavalier" echoed through the hall and corridors. The Glee Club is composed of Miss Blanche and Rita Todd, Helen Stinzen, Allan Rogers, banjo, Harry Maginnis, mandolin, and Arthur Maginnis, guitar.

Base=Ball.

PLAYING ball on the hard "skin" diamond of the Lewiston league grounds, when the ball comes from the bat like a rifle ball, is a vastly different thing from playing the game on the rough grass diamond of the Poland Spring House grounds, as our boys found to their cost when they tackled the New England leaguers on their own stamping-ground last Saturday. As a result they did not make so good a showing against the Lewistons as in the two previous games on the home grounds. "Teddy" Wakefield let two grounders go through him in the first inning and Pulsifer let another through him, the three errors yielding the home team six runs on only two hits. After this the boys did better, but were not in the game for a moment as far as chances for winning it were concerned. Slattery was batted quite freely, while our boys could do but little with "Buck" Sullivan. The score:

LEWISTONS.

	A.B.	R.	1B.	T.B.	P.O.	A.	E.
Polhemus, r.f.,	4	3	3	4	2	0	0
Bergen, c.,	6	2	1	1	5	0	0
Larocque, 2b.,	5	3	2	2	1	3	0
Spill, s.s.,	5	4	3	3	2	3	2
McCormack, 3b.,	5	4	3	4	2	2	1
Leighton, c.f.,	5	1	3	3	2	0	1
Grant, l.f.,	5	0	1	1	3	0	0
Sullivan, p.,	5	0	1	1	0	1	0
McManus, 1b.,	2	0	0	0	10	0	0
Totals,	42	17	17	19	27	9	4

POLAND SPRING.

	A.B.	R.	B.H.	T.B.	P.O.	A.	E.
Wakefield, 2b.,	4	1	0	0	3	4	2
Hull, 1b.,	5	0	1	1	12	0	0
Burrell, c.f., r.f.,	5	0	1	3	0	1	1
Powers, c.,	3	1	1	2	5	2	1
County, 3b.,	4	1	2	3	4	2	1
Harris, r.f., c.f.,	4	1	1	1	2	1	1
Pulsifer, s.s.,	4	0	0	0	0	5	1
Sockalexis, l.f.,	4	0	0	0	1	0	0
Slattery, p.,	4	0	1	1	0	3	0
Totals,	37	4	7	11	27	18	7

SCORE BY INNINGS.

	1	2	3	4	5	6	7	8	9	
Lewistons,	6	3	0	2	1	0	5	0	0—17
Poland Spring,	0	2	0	1	0	0	1	0	0— 4

Earned runs, Lewistons 6, Poland Spring 2. Two-base hits, Polhemus, McCormack, Burrell 2, Powers, County. Stolen bases, Polhemus, Larocque, Spill, Grant, Wakefield. Base on balls, by Sullivan, Wakefield, Powers; by Slattery, Polhemus 2, Larocque, McManus. Struck out, by Sullivan, Wakefield, Hull, Sockalexis, Slattery 2; by Slattery, Sullivan 3, McManus. Double plays, Pulsifer, Wakefield and Hull; County and Wakefield. Hit by pitched balls, by Slattery, Leighton, McManus. Wild pitches, Slattery 2. Time, 1h. 45m. Umpire, J. Lezotte.

About five hundred dollars have been subscribed for the stable men who lost their clothing in the stable fire.

Song of the Wayside Spring.

Weary wanderer, check thy steps,
Come hither and be strong.
Quench thy thirst from my pure depths
And hearken to my song.

Upon my banks rest thou in peace,
Thy throbbing pulse subside!
Cool thou thy fevered brow at will
In the waters, past thee glide.

Into my mirrored eyes look down
And view thine own flushed face,
And see, beyond, the clear blue sky,
And floating clouds that race.

See how my beating heart swells out,
Pouring forth earth's purest blood;
Departing thence in rivulets,
To join the mighty flood.

Drink, wanderer, drink!
Satisfy thy long-felt crave.
'Twill start anew the life in thee,
And make thee young and brave.

Thou hast lingered long upon my brink,
And rested thou must be.
Go thou then upon thy way,
And bear kind thoughts of me.

Be thyself a sacred spring
Whence light and honor flow.
Teach well the world the song I sing:
Drink once again, and go.   NATE TEFFT.

A New English Fish Story.

Mr. Angler: "It sometimes occurs that in trout fishing particularly, all the known arts of the piscator will fail to lure the wary game, and once I remember having to try a very unsportsmanlike recourse."

Mr. Listener: "Yes, what was that?"

Mr. Angler: "I was fishing one day in the Spain Brook, and discovered in an old pool a trout that must have weighed seven pounds. I tempted him first with all the artificial bait at my command, from gray hackle to flamingo flies, shook a button off my flannel shirt into his eye, offered him a strawberry on a hook and a forelock of my red head, flitted all the known brands of worms in front of his suggestive mouth, and wasted all my lunch on him in the way of decoy; and when I was just about to give it up in despair a thought struck me. Acting upon it, I went to a neighboring farm-house, borrowed a two-quart syringe used for the demolition of insect pests, walked back, drew all the water out of the pool, and walked into the exhausted reservoir and picked up my seven-pound trout."

Hours of Meals.

	Week Days.	Sundays.
Breakfast,	7 A.M. to 9 A.M.	8 A.M. to 10 A.M.
Dinner,	1 P.M. to 3 P.M.	1.30 P.M. to 3.30 P.M.
Supper,	6 P.M. to 8 P.M.	6 P.M. to 8 P.M.

THE TALLY-HO ON ORMOND BEACH.

The Tally-Ho on Ormond Beach.

FEW beaches in the world would bear the
weight of a loaded tally-ho coach without
allowing the wheels to sink, but the Ormond
coach has carried twenty-two passengers
on the six-mile drive down the beach to Day-
tona, hardly leaving a wheel mark or hoof print.
The hoofs of the horses clatter on the firm surface as they would upon a concrete pavement.

The Ormond is the only hotel in Florida that
has a tally-ho coach ; indeed Ormond is the only
resort in Florida where coaching could be successful. It is made quite a feature of the Ormond
winter, and the coach and six are often seen
upon the beach even upon moonlight nights.
The six-horse, eleven-passenger wagon is also a
favorite turn-out, while the high-backed, deeply-
upholstered surreys fill the want of those who
require the greatest comfort. The drivers are
experienced drivers from the White Mountains
and Poland Spring. Polanders will be pleased
to find as manager of the stable, Mr. Edwin
Harland, the popular livery man at the Spring.
A number of the employees are from the houses
on Ricker Hill, and the Northern guest is made
to feel at home at the start.

Coming Events.

Sunday, Aug. 26—Preaching Service, Rev. H. W. Bolster,
    11 A.M.   Concert, 3.30 P.M.   Song Service, 8.15 P.M.
Wednesday, Aug. 29—Base-ball, 2.30 P.M.
Thursday, Aug 30—Concert, colored singers, 8 P.M.
Friday, Aug. 31—Progressive Euchre, 8.10 P.M.
Saturday, Sept. 1—Base-ball, 2.30 P.M.   Full Dress Hop,
    8.30 P.M.

Concert Programme

For Sunday, Aug. 26, is arranged as follows :

1.	Marché.	Lachner.
2.	Andante from 1st Symphony.	Beethoven.
3.	Selection—Lohengrin.	Wagner.
4.	Andante.	Gottermann.
	Alto solo.	
	Flirtation.	Freck.
5.	Fantasie—Lij 'etais Roi.	Adam.
6.	Rigandon.	Chaminade.
7.	Overture—Merry Wives of Windsor.	Vicolai.

MAILS.

CLOSE.

Poland Spring House.	Mansion House.
5.45 A.M.	6 A.M.
8.45 A.M.	9 A.M.
2.45 P.M.	3 P.M.

ARRIVE.

10 A.M.	9.30 A.M.
1.30 P.M.	1 P.M.
4.30 P.M.	4 P.M.
8 P.M.	7.45 P.M.

Bubbles.

Variable weather.

Tennis is booming.

Good foot-ball weather.

A week of great events.

Great week for the children.

The bow-wow days are here.

Pleased to have met you, Gov.

The Maine Building is growing fast.

Have your picture "took" by Seaver.

Mr. Keith has a pair of fine chestnuts here.

It took three pails of water to awaken one of the ball players, Friday morning.

No wonder the girls are happy, with men of the six leading colleges to do their bidding.

Mrs. Judge Dugro, of New York, and her son, are guests at the Poland Spring House.

C. French and wife are at the Poland Spring House. Mr. French is an ex-representative to the National House from Connecticut.

The perplexing question now among the "Aristocratic Set" is who is the charming girl addressing notes to one of the young gentlemen in the set and signing herself "E. P. H."

Farmer Moulton, of Philadelphia, finished his haying in the court on Monday. He is exceedingly proud of his skill with the scythe and can cut a fine swath.

President Lucius Tuttle, of the Boston & Maine, and his friends, John C. Paige and E. A. Taft, were the guests of Mr. H. W. Ricker on the launch Poland, on Saturday last.

The Bostonians are the boss bowlers. On a cool morning the alleys are in great demand and some excellent scores are chalked up. Dr. Smith and Messrs. Oakes and Mitchell are the champions.

The two Denison boys from Portland are welcome additions to the younger set. Both the gentlemen, who are Harvard men, are good tennis players and fine dancers, and consequently deservedly popular with the fair sex.

While the excellent livery of the Rickers is being rapidly replaced, there is no better time than this to enjoy a lovely ride on the steam launch. There are no prettier lakes anywhere than the two little gems just at the foot of Ricker Hill.

Captain Cotton, who is a guest here, was sent out by the War Department the year preceding the World's Fair to collect souvenirs and relics from Mexico, the fine collection shown at Chicago being the result of his endeavors. The Captain speaks Spanish like a native.

We have all heard of the "Sweet Singer of Michigan," Ella Wheeler Wilcox, but we are just getting on to the "Sad Singer of New York." He seems to be divosing himself from all amusements lately and seeking consolation from the young lady's best friend.

The morning after the stable fire it was found that all the poles to the carriages had been burned. Some one remarked, however, that, as this was Pole-land, there would be no trouble in getting all the poles needed very quickly, which turned out to be true.

On Sunday last, Mr. E. P. Ricker entertained Governor Greenhalge, President Tuttle, General Martin, Mr. Paige, and Mr. Taft with a drive on the Brake. On the return trip a stop was made at the Elmwood Farm, where the party were the guests of Mr. Sanborn.

Secretary Dickinson, of the World's Fair, who is still with us, says that among other things that Poland water does for suffering humanity, besides curing people of all the ills to which flesh is heir, the constant drinking of it bestows upon a few good people the power of foretelling events; and he adds that that is not because there is a *prophet* on the bottles either.

Mr. Fulton Paul tendered a drive to a number of his friends on Tuesday. The party, which was made up chiefly of New Yorkers, took the New Gloucester drive, filling an eight and a four-seater. The following enjoyed Mr. Paul's courtesy: Mr. Lewis N. Mann, J. A. White, Miss Nahum, Mrs. March, Miss Haddock, New York; Mrs. Talmage, Mrs. Ege, Miss Worthington, Plainfield, N. J.; Capt. Cotton, U. S. N.

Mr. and Mrs. G. H. Martin, of Baltimore, are among the new and popular arrivals at Poland. Mr. Martin is the general representative throughout the South of Mumm's Extra Dry Champagne. Having been here only a few days, he is already convinced that as a steady beverage Poland water discounts any champagne on earth. It cheers but does not inebriate.

Hon. Charles Kern, County Treasurer of Cook County, Illinois, and one of the best-known and popular citizens of Chicago, with his estimable wife, has been spending a few days at the Poland Spring House. They became such enthusiastic converts to the beauties and attractions of Poland that they have decided to spend several weeks here next summer and bring with them several other members of their family.

Arrivals

FOR WEEK ENDING AUGUST 23.

POLAND SPRING HOUSE.

Andetson, Miss Jennie,	New York.
Avctell, A. J.,	Chicago.
Ayel, A. B.,	Boston.
Ayel, Belle,	Boston.
Blown, F. H.,	Waltham.
Baldwin, Miss Bessie,	Boston.
Baldwin, Miss Mabel,	Boston.
Baldwin, Miss Gcttiude,	Boston.
Baldwin, I.,	Elmira.
Blanchaid, Rev. J. W.,	Philadelphia.
Blanchaid, Mrs. J. W.,	Philadelphia.
Bolstel, Mr. and Mrs. W. H.,	Boston.
Bishop, Robelt It.,	Newton, Mass.
Berthune, R. W.,	Boston.
Bickfoid, I. H.,	Boston.
Bickfoid, Mrs. I. H.,	Boston.
Bluudage, Mr. and Mrs. M. T.,	New York.
Blaney, Mr. and Mrs. Geolge A.,	Newton.
Clawfoid, Mr. and Mrs. Geolge,	New York.
Campbell, W. R.,	Boston.
Cummock, J. W.,	Springfield.
Colcotan, Lake,	Springfield.
Camelon, W. J.,	Boston.
Claflin, Mrs. A. B.,	New York.
Clippen, E. G.,	Philadelphia.
Clippen, Mrs. E. G.,	Philadelphia.
Cottin, Mr. and Mrs. C. II.,	New Rochelle, N. Y.
Calpentel, Hannah T.,	Providence.
Denison, E. E.,	Portland.
Denison, W. T.,	Portland.
Dugro, Mrs. P. II., son and daughtel,	New York.
Deuison, J. A.,	Boston.
Delby, Dr. R. H.,	New York.
Delby, Rogel Alden,	New York.
Denny, Mr. and Mrs. Chas. A.,	Leicester.
Davis, Mrs. J. A.,	New York.
Emely, W. G.,	Portland.
Fostel, Mrs. Henly,	Boston.
Fletchel, Mr. and Mrs. T. S.,	New York.
Falouun, Mrs. J. R.,	Waltham.
Ftench, Mr. and Mrs. C.,	Conn.
Fieeman, Miss M. C.,	Cornwall, Pa.
Foote, Mrs. Elastus,	Chicago.
Fianklin, Mrs. James R.,	New York.
Gieenhalge, Gov. Fiedctick,	Lowell.
Gilman, Mr. and Mrs. F. E.,	Montreal.
Gill, Mrs. C. S.,	Boston.
Gaidnet, K. B.,	Boston.
Giay, William R.,	Boston.
Hill, Miss S. B.,	Detroit.
Hitsch, Miss Ruth,	St. Louis.
Hitsch, J. C.,	St. Louis.
Haynes, John C.,	Boston.
Haynes, Mrs. John C.,	Boston.
Haynes, Miss E. M.,	Boston.
Keln, Mr. and Mrs. Chas.,	Chicago.
Keegan, V. E.,	Boston.
Lake, Jas. H.,	Boston.
Law, Geolge,	New York.
Lallabee, Miss S. S.,	Scarboro.
Lockwood, Miss,	Boston.
Lincoln, Mr. and Mrs. C. P.,	Hartford, Ct.

Mellitt, A. A.,	New York.
Mellill, W. W.,	Deering.
Moote, L. H.,	New York.
Mattin, A. P.,	Boston.
Mills, S. C.,	Newburg, N. Y.
Mills, Mrs. S. C.,	Newburg, N. Y.
Mills, Maly D.,	Newburg, N. Y.
Mills, S. McD.,	Newburg, N. Y.
Molle, Mrs. G.,	Chicago.
Mosiel, Mr. and Mrs. M.,	Cincinnati.
Mullan, I. B.,	Fergus, Ont.
Mullan, Mrs. I. B.,	Fergus, Ont.
Macfarlane, Mr, and Mrs. H.,	Sherbrooke, Can.
O'Dwyer, E. F.,	New York.
Pickaid, E. L.,	Boston.
Page, John C.,	Boston.
Rogels, Mrs. Emily,	Boston.
Rusk, Mrs.,	New York.
Richaidson, C. T.,	New York.
Rolin, Mr. and Mrs. H. M.,	Philadelphia.
Rolin, William A.,	Philadelphia.
Sowdon, A. J. C.,	Boston.
Sammons, C. E.,	Boston.
Smith, Miss,	New York.
Staunton, John A.,	Wakefield, Mass.
Simpson, Mrs. A. J.,	Boston.
Shaw, J. Elliot,	Wayne, Pa.
Stuait, W. H., Jr.,	Boston.
Taft, E. A.,	Boston.
Tuttle, Lucius,	Boston.
Thomas, Elias, Jr.,	Portland.
Thomas, W. W.,	Portland.
Tillotson, Mrs. L. G.,	New York.
Taylol, E. W. B.,	Haverhill.
Taylol, Mrs. E. W. B.,	Haverhill.
Taylol, Miss C. B.,	Hartford, Ct.
Tuckel, Mr. and Mrs. Geo. E.,	Ware, Mass.
Tiowbiidge, Mrs. A. II.,	New York.
Viles, A. E.,	
Viles, Mrs. A. E.,	
Waid, M. E.,	St. Louis.
Wentworth, A.,	Boston.
Wallen, Mr. and Mrs. F. S.,	Biddeford.
Witheibee, Mrs. M.,	New York.
Witheibee, Miss,	New York.

MANSION HOUSE.

Batts, Edwaid H.,	Hartford.
Chandlel, Victol C.,	Boston.
Cummings, Geolge W.,	Brookline.
Fallell, John R.,	Boston.
Fowlel, William R.,	Boston.
Fowlel, Clata M.,	Concord.
Fostel, Chaıles,	Portland.
Gilbeıt, F. A.,	Boston.
Gilbeıt, Mrs. F. A., two childıen and nuıse,	Boston.
Gahm, Miss A.,	Boston.
Goodell, Miss Alice,	Worcester.
Ingalls, Molly L.,	Portland.
Kyle, Petel L.,	Portland.
Kingshuıy, W. H. and wife,	Yarmouth.
Kible, E. S.,	Hartford.
Kleisz, Clara V.,	Philadelphia, Pa.
Kuntz, Mrs. D.,	Boston.
Lowell, J. M.,	Boston.
Lowell, Caıtie M.,	Boston.
Lowell, Emma L.,	Boston.
McCartuey, R. C.,	Boston.
Mooı, Miss M. A.,	Yarmouth.
Robinson, James S.,	Boston.
Shurtleff, W. H. and wife,	Portland.
Smith, Milton M. and wife,	New York.
Shine, William and wife,	Portland.
Van Guntel, Maly A.,	Philadelphia.
Wellington, Mrs. Fıed,	Worcester.
Whiting, E.,	New York.

WHY
Poland Spring Leads Them All.

A 19th Century Triumph

THE POLAND SPRING HOUSE 1893-4

MERIT, POPULARITY, LARGE SALES,

AND THE FACT THAT

POLAND WATER

Was the FIRST SOLVENT AND ELIMINATOR OF URIC ACID
CALCULI from the BLADDER AND KIDNEYS KNOWN TO
THE WORLD, also the ONLY WATER EXHIBITED
(notwithstanding the hundreds competing) at

CHICAGO'S WORLD'S EXPOSITION

To receive a Medal and Diploma for "PURITY AND
GREAT MEDICINAL POWER," prove
conclusively that

POLAND WATER LEADS THE WORLD.

THE ACCOMPANYING ILLUSTRATIONS ARE MOST SUBSTANTIAL AND
CONVINCING PROOF OF THE ABOVE ASSERTIONS.

SAPIENTIA DONUM DEI

OFFICES:

BOSTON:	NEW YORK:	PHILADELPHIA:	CHICAGO:
175 Devonshire Street.	3 Park Place.	Avenue 13th and Chestnut St.	Cor. Michigan Ave. and Van Buren St.

HIRAM RICKER & SONS, Proprietors.

Vol. I.   SUNDAY MORNING, SEPTEMBER 2, 1894.   No. 9.

September Days.

"WHAT is so fair as a day in June?" the poet queries, and we would fain agree with him that "then, if ever, come perfect days." But up where the many pilgrims flock to do worship to the "Water God," June holds no monopoly on days when all nature seems striving to convince men that life is worth the living. September is a worthy rival, and is in many respects the most delightful month of all the Poland season. Then is the ideal month for driving. You arise in the morning and inhale the crisp, clear air of early fall, which exhilarates like a draught of sparkling wine, but without the ofttimes undesirable after effects. A walk to the Spring and a glass of water from its crystal depths and you are ready for a hearty breakfast with an appetite which is no more a surprise to your friends than to yourself. By the time you are through the meal you are ready for a ten-mile spin behind a pair of speedy roadsters. Away you go to the crack of the whip and the merry laughter of your party.

The drives are many and widely diversified in character. This morning you go around Sabbath-Day Lake, a cut of which beautiful little sheet of water ornaments our title page. The chill of early autumn has already transformed the green foliage through which you pass into a blazing mass of color. Man has yet to discover the secret of mixing the many colors which Nature has spread on with such a lavish hand. As you bowl merrily along the sprightly chipmunk pauses in its labors of laying by its winter food supply and poses in an attitude of alarm upon the fence rail, until, convinced by your good-natured laughter that he has nothing to fear, he bounds lightly away to continue his interrupted work.

Soon you drive up in the center of the Shaker Village, where you alight from your carriage and enter the emporium of the quaint sect. You had not intended to purchase, but you are open-hearted this morning, and the motherly smile of Aunt Aurelia unlooses your purse-string, so that you carry away numerous souvenirs in the shape of fir pillows warranted to bring balmy sleep and forgetfulness of your troubles of a busy day, candied orange peel, and real maple sugar.

Continuing your drive you come to a little red mill surrounded by a cluster of white farm dwellings. Adjacent is the old school-house, with the stars and stripes floating proudly from the pole in the yard. The merry hum of voices comes out to you through the open windows, and you are carried back to the days when you were a barefooted farmer's son, whose highest ambition was to secure the back seat on the "first day."

As you enter upon the homeward drive around the pond you are at rest with yourself and with mankind, and you enter the open door of the big house a new man—ready to go back to your interrupted business with new courage.

Are you a Nimrod, then you have ample chance to try your skill, and may bring back a heavy bag of the small game so abundant in the adjacent woods. Snipe and partridge are found in large flocks, and you have yourself to blame if you are an unsuccessful sportsman.

In the evening the merry crackle of the flames as they leap from the hearth-log up the broad chimneys gives a most home-like appearance to the office and parlors, and affords every opportunity for a pleasant chat. Surely you who are here in September enjoy many pleasures denied to those who come earlier in the season.

DENNIS.

Bal-Poudré.

ONE of the prettiest parties of this season of pretty parties was the Bal-Poudré of Wednesday evening. Promptly at 8.30 the line of march was taken up through the office to the ball-room, led by Mr. William P. St. John and Mrs. George Trowbridge, the popular New Yorkers. The grand march was a beautiful one and called forth frequent applause from the large audience of spectators. The ladies in their light dresses and with powdered hair were charming, while the gentlemen in their black and white suits appeared to fine advantage. About twenty couples took part in the affair.

The Latin of It.

Boyabus kissabus
Sweet girlorum.
Girlabus likibus,
Wanti somorum.

Fatherus hearibus
Kissum sonorum.
Bootibus kickibus
Out of the dorum.

A Model House.

ON the Gulf-washed shores of Florida, but thirty-four hours from New York, and with luxurious Pullman sleeping-cars running from New York to its very verandas, is situated at Tampa a most wonderful structure of brick and iron, the Tampa Bay Hotel. Built after the Moorish Renaissance, its domes and minarets and crescents rear themselves into the air loftily and impress the new comer on the scene with a sense of littleness. This is the hotel par excellence, the "Modern Wonder of the World." Nor is it in its architecture alone that this palatial hostelry excels, for inside it is a dream of elegance and luxury in its decorations, furnishings, and equipments, while the table is such as to satisfy the most fastidious gourmand and epicure. In front of the hotel, and sloping gently down to the bay, is a garden laid out most artistically and filled with tropical plants gathered from many countries, fruits and flowers, indeed a veritable Eden. On the bay is boating and fishing, while back in the country the most ardent sportsman may satisfy his zeal with the gun. The Tampa Bay Hotel is reached in Pullman sleeping-cars from New York, with absolutely no change, going *via* Pennsylvania Railroad, Atlantic Coast Line and Plant System.

Seaver, the photographer, is the busiest man on the hill.

Bubbles.

September.

A jolly week.

Beautiful days.

The livery is O. K.

The tide is turning.

The leaves are turning.

The ball team has disbanded.

Lots of new faces this month.

The shore resorts are closing.

State Fair at Lewiston this week.

Fine shooting here in September.

The Maine Building is growing fast.

August went out in a blaze of glory.

The progressive euchre party was well attended.

Singer has left us and the "belles" have sad tones.

Rev. W. H. Bolster, of Dorchester, preached an eloquent sermon, Sunday.

Powers, our star catcher, caught for the Intervales at the coaching parade.

Mr. T. M. Gale, the popular Washingtonian, joined his family here on Friday of last week.

General A. C. Barnes of Brooklyn, and wife, have pleasant rooms at the Poland Spring House.

Hon. Fulton Paul and wife returned home Thursday. They will be missed by their many friends.

J. M. Buckley and wife, of New York, are drinking the waters. Mr. Buckley is editor of the *Christian Advocate*, published in New York City.

Mr. William P. St. John and his mother came on from New York, Wednesday. Mr. St. John, who is president of the Mechanics National Bank of that city, is a jolly good fellow and a welcome addition to the dancing set.

The many friends of Mrs. McNeal, of New York, were on hand to bid her adieu when she started for home Thursday. Mrs. McNeal has been here the entire season and has made herself a great favorite by her pleasant manner and fine disposition. She will be missed.

Hon. F. E. and Mrs. Gilman, also Mr. and Mrs. A. D. Nelson from Montreal, Canada, left for home on Saturday, after a stay of a couple of weeks. They expressed themselves as delighted with the place and have taken rooms for next season.

H. T. JORDAN, | EDITORS.
W. D. FREEMAN, |

PUBLISHED EVERY SUNDAY MORNING DURING THE MONTHS
OF JULY, AUGUST AND SEPTEMBER, IN THE INTERESTS OF

POLAND SPRING AND ITS VISITORS.

All contributions relative to the guests of Poland Spring will
be thankfully received.

To insure publication, all communications should reach the
editors not later than Thursday preceding day of issue.

All parties desiring rates for advertising in the HILL-TOP
should write the editors for same.

The subscription price of the HILL-TOP is $1.00 for the
season, post-paid. Single copies will be mailed at 10c. each.

Address,

EDITORS "HILL-TOP,"
Poland Spring House,
South Poland, Maine.

PRINTED AT JOURNAL OFFICE, LEWISTON.

Sunday, Sept. 2, 1894.

Editorial.

THE prosperity of the little HILL-TOP does
not wane, even though the cold and frosty
weather characteristic of fall is fast approaching, and the times endured by thousands
and thousands of our fellow-men are most dis-
couraging. Our circulation is fast, very fast,
increasing. Last week's edition sold like those
proverbial hot cakes, and another lot of two
hundred copies was telegraphed for. These were
sold nearly as soon as they arrived on the Hill,
and not a few more could have been disposed of
had they been ordered. Thus it is that honest
effort is appreciated.

It is probable that but two more editions of
the HILL-TOP will be issued. Our promises have
been more than fulfilled to both our subscribers
and advertisers. In our announcement to the
public we promised the publication of an *eight*-
page illustrated weekly, devoted to the interests
of Ricker Hill," etc. Haven't we followed our
promise? At a considerable additional expense
we enlarged the paper by four pages, without
even hinting to our subscribers of the intended
enlargement. We have always been attentive to
the correct representation of the Ricker interests,
and anything you may have seen in the HILL-
TOP is so.

We trust that in the future as in the past our
efforts will meet with your appreciation and
support.

SEPTEMBER days are upon us, and we
now enter into the enjoyment of the most
delightful part of the whole year. Those
of you who have remained here in former years
during that month remember the many beauties
of nature which are so plentifully laid open
to one's gaze. The trees all assume a faded
appearance, rendering them far more beautiful,
and the fields lose their verdant hue, to reappear
in a new and much prettier dress. The birds then
begin to hie themselves to their winter homes in
the South, and in their last flight, give forth the
most delightful of all their songs. Everything
in fact seems to be inspired with a desire to look
more beautiful, and to appreciate their efforts
you only need to lengthen your stay by a few
weeks.

This season's business at both houses and
the spring has been unprecedented and phenomenal. Every spare cot has been brought into
requisition, and accommodation has been refused
many because of lack of sufficient room.

The fire at the stable was a severe loss to the
proprietors, but their energy and persistency
stood them in good stead, as in the past, and the
business continued as smoothly as if nothing
had happened. The determination and business
ability which is so characteristic of the Ricker
family, is shown more or less prominently in
every department of the great establishments
they control, and has put the fair names of
Poland Spring and Poland Spring House in the
front ranks of successful hotel enterprises.

Coming Events.

Sunday, Sept. 2d.—Preaching Service, 11 A.M. Concert,
3.30 P.M. Song Service, 8.15 P.M.
Tuesday, Sept. 4th.—Concert by Mr. Wallis A. Wallis and
wife of London, 8 P.M.
Friday, Sept. 7th.—Progressive Euchre, 8.10 P.M.
Saturday, Sept. 8th.—Hop, 8.15 P.M.

Told on the Verandas.

AS we sat down on the north-west veranda the moon was just rising into prominence. From the dance hall the strains of a dreamy waltz floated out to us, rising above the merry chatter of voices in the parlors and corridors. There were eight of us in the party, every one an old sojourner at bonny Poland, and, as it happened, our conversation was largely reminiscent of the old days. That night at supper I had noticed the many elegant costumes and the costly jewels worn, and so I ventured the remark that "the ladies know that they must bring their finest plumage to the backwoods of Maine."

"Yes," said Mrs. A—, the wife of one of the Hub's wealthiest sons, "but I remember when it was not so, and for a fact I knew a case where a well-known society lady of the Quaker City had to stay in her room while here because she had an idea that Poland was literally out of the world."

"It was eight years ago, I think,' she continued, "that it happened. At the table next to mine in the dining-hall, I had noticed a lady dressed in black who came regularly at a certain time, ate her meals and then disappeared. As she never remained down stairs to the concerts, took any part in the card parties, or mingled with any of the people stopping at the house, my curiosity was aroused—I am a woman you know—and I made up my mind to find out why she kept so secluded. As good fortune would have it I went into breakfast late one morning and found myself alone at the table with my 'unknown.' After a time I entered into conversation with her, and finally invited her to join me at cards during the afternoon.

"She looked at me a moment and then said, 'I am sorry, but I cannot accept your kind invitation ; doubtless you will wonder why I seem so unsocial and I am going to make a confidant of you. My husband has been sick for some time and this spring his physician advised him to come to Poland Spring. I had, at that time, never heard much concerning the place and my idea of it was rather vague. In fact my idea of Maine was that it consisted solely of forests, and I thought that the only hotel I would find would be some farm-house. Accordingly when we were getting ready to come away I told my maid to put lots of wrappers in my trunk and that I would not need any silks or evening dresses. For traveling I put on this black silk which I am now wearing.

"You may imagine my wonder and chagrin when we drove up to the house. It was just at dusk and the office was crowded. On every hand I saw silks and satins. Instead of coming into the backwoods I found myself thrown among people dressed as for the drawing-room. When I found myself in my room I sat down and enjoyed that luxury of my sex, a good cry. Five hundred miles from home and only one decent dress. My daughters are away at the sea-shore and I cannot send home for anything. We are to stay here two weeks longer. I am so careful of my one dress that I only wear it to meals, putting on a wrapper as soon as I reach my room. You now will understand why I keep to myself.'

"After I had heard her story," concluded Mrs. A—, "I took her to my room and, fortunately, was able to supply her with a dress that she could wear, and so released her from her durance."

After the comments on the foregoing had been made, X, who sees the funny side of life, removed his perfecto from his mouth and took up the story telling.

"I remember," said X, "the first year that the big window was put in the dining-hall. Of course it excited much admiration and was much written about. But there are some people you know who know it all and consequently don't have to read the papers. As it happened, one of these chaps rolled in on the stage one night. He was an art critic from the Hub and his bump of knowledge was rather above the normal size.

"The day after his arrival I met him, and shortly we were discussing Poland. 'A mighty nice house, don't you know,' said he, 'but why in the name of all that is artistic did the Rickers spoil that dining-room by sticking that horrible daub in one end ; a worse landscape I never saw. If I knew the man that perpetrated that piece of work I would go after him with a club.'"

"With difficulty I kept back my mirth, and soon excused myself. The story was too good to keep and soon the whole hotel was laughing at his criticism. Of course he heard the truth soon, and the early coach bore him away to pleasanter fields."

Just then the mantel clock in the parlor chimed the hour of eleven, and our party separated to dream of the "Water God," which rules at the shrine on Ricker Hill.

THE LISTENER.

Mr. W. H. Schefflin, of New York, is the champion sportsman. On Monday and Tuesday, he and Dr. Etridge brought in eleven fine brace of snipe.

MOTHER GOOSE PARTY.

A Merry Party.

IF that good old dame who, history tells us, used to soothe the little Bostonian to sleep by the merry jingles of "Old King Cole" and "Little Bo-Peep" could have been present in Music Hall on Friday evening she would have held up her withered hands in amaze, and ejaculated "Lordy massy, can sich things be?" And the pleasure the motherly old lady would have experienced would not have been greater than that of the immense audience who saw her merry rhymes so faithfully illustrated.

The event of the season was what was advertised, and the event of the events of an eventful season was what the Mother Goose Party really was. Never has a better entertainment been arranged on Ricker Hill, and Mrs. Trowbridge and Mrs. Moulton can not be given too much credit upon the results of their labors.

When the curtains drew back to show the first picture of the evening, the hall was crowded and the verandas outside the windows held an interested overflow. "Mother Goose and her son Jack" was the first tableau, with Mrs. Moulton and Mr. Stuart in the title roles. Mrs. Moulton took off the celebrated lady to perfection, and the picture received a deserved encore. The next picture was the favorite: "The Flower of the Family." Baby Edward in his carriage of green and gold was the hero, and the smiles he distributed to the delighted audience were so genial and happy as to win him a double encore.

Mrs. Trowbridge as the "Old Woman in the Shoe," surrounded by ten little ones, was greeted with hearty applause and made an exceedingly handsome and stately picture.

To the merry sound of the fiddle the curtains opened upon "Old King Cole and His Fiddlers Three." Mr. Moulton, with "his pipe and his bowl," looked supremely happy, while the fiddlers, Messrs. Hay, Thomas, and Dugro, and the page, Master Ingalls, wore an expression of content, as if the servants of a most indulgent sovereign.

Number five, "Went to London to buy myself a wife," was a charming little scene enacted by Claire and Horace Ingalls.

The Misses Trowbridge won the admiration of the audience in the next as "Kitty Fisher and Lucy Locket." Two prettier children than the little brunettes would be hard to find, and they deserved the hearty applause which they received. "Jack and Jill" were next, Mrs. Mattocks and Mr. Rogers taking the parts. Such a Jill will always have many Jacks, and the beautiful young lady well sustained her reputation as the prettiest woman in the house. Mr. Rogers was a most attentive Jack.

Mr. Singer has neglected his calling, for in the next picture, "Barber, barber, shave a pig," he was evidently at home. The picture took and the most popular young man was loudly cheered. The pig was not a property one, as terrific squeals convinced the spectators when the curtains closed. "Where are you going, my pretty maid?" was next, and by many was considered the prettiest picture of the evening. Miss Thomas was a handsome dairy-maid, while Dr. Trowbridge was a most courteous beau of the olden time. The poses were perfect and well sustained.

Miss Wheelock, the popular whist expert, as the Queen of Hearts, with the two handsomest men in the house, Messrs. Lake and Dennison, as her devoted King and Jack, were a nice group and well received.

The last picture was a group of all the characters of the picture, and numerous others in costume. As the curtains parted the orchestra struck up the Mother Goose March, arranged by Prof. Kuntz, and the performers stepped from the gilt frame to the floor, where a complicated march, led by Mother Goose and Jack, was gone through with. After an order of ten dances was danced the party adjourned to the dining-hall, where, at the richly decorated tables, a bountiful collation was enjoyed, given by Dr. Trowbridge. Toasts to another party next year were drank in sparkling Poland, and the merriest evening of the season was at an end.

Music.

TWO excellent concerts have been given in Music Hall this week. The one on Tuesday evening was much enjoyed. Mrs. Jennie King Morrison, the well-known contralto, of Portland, was the star, and won many encomiums for her fine work. Mr. Dennett, the popular treasurer of the Androscoggin Mills, Lewiston, read a number of selections in his own inimitable style and kept the audience in roars of laughter. Mr. Hackett, who conducts the singing at the Sunday services, gave a number of tenor solos most acceptably.

On Thursday evening the Atlanta University Quartette (colored), gave a good programme of their Southern melodies, with several humorous selections. It was very good.

Wallis A. Wallis and his wife, the well-known English singers and readers, are booked for one of their original entertainments on Tuesday evening. A treat is in store for those who appreciate a first-class entertainment.

The new stable will be but one story high.

Seeking the Red Ear.

WEDNESDAY afternoon, the young people embarked in the Blaine and were driven to the beach at Middle Lake, where they enjoyed a real "corn roast" through the courtesy of Dr. Trowbridge. While the fire was being built and arrangements being made for the roast, the party filled numerous rowboats and explored the hidden nooks along the shore. When all was in readiness, the corn was husked in a manner which would have astonished the natives had they been present. But what means these disappointed looks? Alas, a mistake has been made; a red ear is not to be found, and search as they may, the gentlemen cannot find the excuse for osculation. A sadder set of youths it would have been hard to find, but it is said that one ear was finally unearthed which was sufficiently carmine, so that by using a little imagination a *few* of the fair ones were persuaded to *endure* the penalty. The corn was roasted finally and came to the table in first-class condition, although a little smoky. The party ended with a merry war-dance around the fire to the music of familiar songs, the chorus being led by the well-known New York songster, Mr. Allen Rogers. The following were the guests of the popular doctor: Misses Carpenter, Messrs. Dennison, Miss Sudington, Messrs. Maginnis, Miss Palmer, Mr. Rogers, Miss Stinson, Mr. Stuart, Miss Thomas, Dr. and Mrs. Trowbridge, Misses T. and J. Trowbridge, Miss Worthington.

"Brother" Moulton has left us and we miss him. For many years he has been one of the leaders here in all social affairs and has made many friends.

Judge P. H. Dugro arrived Monday last to escort Mrs. Dugro, son and child, home to New York City. Judge Dugro is a prominent judge of the Superior Court of New York, and the largest owner in the Hotel Savoy.

The last edition of the HILL-TOP sold like those proverbial hot cakes. The first edition was not enough to satisfy the great demand, and Monday two hundred additional copies were telegraphed for. These were sold before they arrived on the hill. There is no doubt about the popularity of the HILL-TOP.

Mr. and Mrs. I. A. Singer and son, M. M. Singer, left Poland Wednesday. They will enjoy a few weeks' pleasure trip through the mountains and then take up their abode in the "Plaza," New York City. Mr. Singer, Jr., has made a host of friends during his stay here who will miss him greatly.

Jingles.

Cycling along with a girl at your side,
Is the blissfulest sort of bliss;
But it isn't such fun
When you bump on a stone

puﻉ
puɐl
    ʇno
      pɐǝɥ
        ǝʞɐ!l
          ¡s!ɥʇ

Though in song you are admired,
    Sweet Marie!
We are getting very tired,
    Dear, of thee;
And we wish your poet-swain
Had to wear a ball and chain,
For his song gives us a pain,
    Sweet Marie!

"I'll make you happy, I will," said he,
    His bosom with passion filed.
"Well, maybe you would," responded she,
"But at present you make me tired."

As the stage was rather crowded,
    And the girl most wondrous sweet,
I rose with my politest bow
    And offered her my seat.

Her smile of thanks was charming,
    But I felt my soul demur
When she placed her little doggie
    On the seat I offered her.

She is learning to ride a bicycle,
    So some of her girl friends say;
And those who have seen her attempt to mount
    Say she doesn't get on very well.

"There are no flies on me," she said,
    With vehemence complete;
"I am surprised at this," he said,
    "Because you are so sweet."

A Familiar Response.

He—"You say we have long had a speaking acquaintance; but you'll pardon me for not remembering you."

She—"Why, I am the person you swear at over the telephone every day."

He—"Really? I am delighted to meet you. Shall we take a little stroll?"

She—"Line's busy."

Sunday Concert.

Sunday concert for September 2d:

1.	Wedding Marche.	Mendelssohn.
2.	Overture—Freischutz.	Weber.
3.	Air—Louis XIII.	Ghys.
4.	Selection—Walküre.	Wagner.
5.	Aquarelles.	F. Le Borne.
	Menuet. Danse Villageoise.	
6.	Serenade.	Fittl.
7.	Selection—Faust.	Gounod.

Bubbles.

AN APPROPRIATE KEEPSAKE.

We flirted together a week at the spring,
And strolled on the beach by the light of the moon,
And whispered our love 'neath the old oak trees,
And at parting he gave me a *souvenir spoon*.

Mr. H. A. Dupee of Bridgeport. Ct., is here. Mr. Dupee is proprietor of a large apothecary store in that city.

R. H. L. Townsend of New York has returned, having been unable to find a more comfortable place than Poland.

Mr. W. W. Thomas of Portland is here for an extensive visit. Mr. Thomas, although ninety-one years of age, is as hale and hearty as many of half his years.

Mr. Amos R. Little of Philadelphia is here once more on one of his flying visits. Mr. Little's extensive business interests prevents his remaining longer at a time.

Mrs. Dr. Trowbridge returned to New York Thursday, leaving the popular doctor and the two pretty daughters to longer enjoy the benefits received from Poland water.

Dr. L. G. Hill, of Dover, N. H., and his wife, arrived on Thursday. Dr. Hill enjoys the proud distinction of being the oldest practicing physician in the state.

The ever-genial B. P. Moulton left Poland Tuesday for his home in Rosemont, Pa. Mrs. Moulton will remain for a while to further enjoy the many pleasures of this beautiful spot.

Rockland is reported to have said that they had no use for college players or Indians. There is no doubt whatever of the sincerity of that remark—last Friday's game notwithstanding.

Mr. Ledyard Sands left early Thursday morning in a private team for Bar Harbor to join Mrs. Sands. Mr. Sands is one of the most extensive travelers that has visited us this season.

Mrs. N. St. John and Mr. William P. St. John arrived Wednesday for an extended visit. Mr. St. John is president of the Mercantile National Bank of New York, and a very handsome gentleman.

Our only Michael was called to North Conway Wednesday, to catch Smith of Holy Cross, with the Intervales against Wentworth Hall. That he did honor to the Poland uniform which he wore is certain.

Arrivals

FOR WEEK ENDING AUGUST 30.

POLAND SPRING HOUSE.

Arnold, W. E.,	New York.
Anderson, Mr. and Mrs. Andrew,	South Bend, Ind.
Barker, Miss F. E.,	New York.
Batchelder, Mr. and Mrs. W. R.,	Boston.
Brown, F. H.,	Waltham.
Barclay, C. B.,	New York.
Barnes, A. C.,	Brooklyn.
Barnes, Mrs. A. C.,	Brooklyn.
Batchelder, R. N.,	Washington.
Brown, J. H.,	Boston.
Clark, Mrs. H. H.,	Hartford.
Clark, Miss,	Hartford.
Crambie, Mrs. D. D.,	Kennebunkport.
Cole, Mr. and Mrs. Benjamin E.,	Boston.
Davidson, W. M.,	Jacksonville, Fla.
Dudley, Mr. and Mrs. D. T.,	Haverhill.
Dow, Mr. and Mrs. Fred N.,	Portland.
Dugro, P. H.,	New York.
Dort, O. G. and wife,	Keene, N. H.
Estine, Mrs. A. A.,	Newton, Mass.
Fowler, Mr. and Mrs. G. B.,	Boston.
Fowler, Master Howard,	Boston.
Finlayson, Mr. and Mrs. A.,	Rye Beach, N. H.
Fargo, Mortimer,	New York.
Fetts, L. E. and wife,	Chicago.
Gale, Thomas M.,	Washington.
Godley, Mr. and Mrs. J. F.,	Trenton.
Grey, C. W.,	Chicago.
Hale, Clarence,	Portland.
Hyde, Miss N. O.,	New Haven.
Hess, Robert J.,	Philadelphia.
Harkness, Mr. and Mrs. A.,	Providence.
Hayden, Jessie,	Hartford.
Hunter, William T.,	New York.
Hackett, Mrs. E. J.,	Auburn.
Hackett, Lilla M.,	Auburn.
Hallister, William H.,	New York.
Haynes, John C.,	Boston.
Haynes, James G.,	Boston.
Haynes, Miss Olive E.,	Boston.
Inman, Mr. and Mrs. S. M.,	Atlanta, Ga.
Knille, P. E.,	New York.
Lord, R. W. and wife,	Kennebunk.
Little, Amos R.,	Philadelphia.
Lewis, Mr. and Mrs. Joseph B.,	Allentown, Pa.
Lord, Mr. and Mrs. G. P.,	Elgin, Ill.
Luddington, Miss M.,	New York.
Lane, E.,	Saco.
Molleson, Dean C.,	New York.
Mason, T. F.,	New York.
Morrell, H. K.,	Gardiner.
Morrison, Mrs. J. K.,	Portland.
Moise, Mr. and Mrs. Jacob,	Boston.
Moise, Miss C. R.,	Boston.
Moise, Miss Jessie A.,	Boston.
Musson, G. B.,	New York.
McClannin, Mrs.,	Boston.
Moise, Miss M. M.,	Portland.
Nelson, Mr. and Mrs. A. D.,	Montreal.
Nason, H. B.,	Troy, N. Y.
Nason, Mrs. H. B.,	Troy, N. Y.
Pottle, Miss G. E.,	Westbrook.
Palmer, Miss,	Bridgeport.
Peterson, Mrs. C. L.,	Orange, N. J.
Peterson, Miss Edna,	Orange, N. J.
Peck, Mr. and Mrs. W. H.,	New York.
Quimby, H. C.,	Dover, N. H.

Russell, Charles T., Jr.,	Boston.
Rice, N. W.,	Boston.
Randall, J. F.,	Portland.
Rossiter, Mr. and Mrs. W. W.,	Brooklyn.
Rossiter, William W., Jr.,	Brooklyn.
Stoddard, Mrs. J. H.,	Brooklyn.
Smith, Charles H.,	Providence.
Sandborn, Mr. and Mrs. D. W.,	Boston.
Stoddard, E. B.,	Worcester.
Smith, H. E.,	Worcester.
Sawyer, Mr. and Mrs. George A.,	Cambridge.
St. John, Mrs. N.,	New York.
St. John, William P.,	New York.
Towle, Mr. and Mrs. E. B.,	Hampton Falls, N. H.
Tracy, H. W.,	Detroit.
Thomas, Elias, Jr.,	Portland.
Tiott, George,	Philadelphia.
Townsend, R. H. L.,	New York.
Wheeler, George S.,	Brooklyn.
Wadleigh, P. N. and wife,	Haverhill.
Watson, J. V.,	Philadelphia.
Winslow, Mr. and Mrs. E. B.,	Portland.
Winslow, J. S.,	Portland.
Warren, J. A.,	Cumberland Mills.
Warren, Mortimer,	Cumberland Mills.
Westcott, C. H.,	Kennebunkport.
Watkins, Miss H.,	Clinton, Ia.
White, Mrs. F. A.,	Portsmouth.

MANSION HOUSE.

Adsir, Mrs. F. E.,	New York.
Alcok, R. S.,	New York.
Algue, W. L.,	Washington.
Brown, W. L.,	Washington.
Brown, W. S.,	Lewiston.
Barnes, Mrs. G. W.,	Boston.
Bucknam, J. M.,	Yarmouth.
French, Henry,	Kingston, N. H.
Foster, Charles,	Portland.
Gilbert, F. A.,	Boston.
Gage, Mrs. S. A.,	Rochester, N. Y.
Gage, M. Ruth,	Rochester, N. Y.
Gharzanzi, A. G.,	New York.
Hopkinson, Louise R.,	Boston.
Hackett, E. C.,	Sabbath-day Lake.
Merrill, I. M.,	Sabbath-day Lake.
McHenry, Mrs. Geo. and child,	Boston.
Otis, Alfred W.,	Boston.
Payne, Minnie A.,	Lowell.
Richardson, J. A.,	Liverpool, Eng.
Smith, Hardy and wife,	Wareham, Mass.
Standish, Miss L.,	Boston.
Thatcher, Isabel,	Boston.
Taylor, E.,	New York.
Zach, Mrs. Max,	Boston.

Mrs. Charles Theodore Russell, of 69 Spruce Street, Cambridge, Mass., who left here Thursday, has the finest collection of antique china in the United States. She has been offered as high as $15,000 for her collection, which includes a number of pieces used by the mother of Washington. Mrs. Russell is an authority on china and can tell you anything you may desire to know in regard to it. A visit to her home is an experience to be remembered.

It is whispered that Cupid has been busy again on the hill. Congratulations may soon be in order.

WHY
Poland Spring Leads Them All.

A 19th Century Triumph

THE POLAND SPRING HOUSE 1893-4

MERIT, POPULARITY, LARGE SALES,

AND THE FACT THAT

POLAND WATER

Was the FIRST SOLVENT AND ELIMINATOR OF URIC ACID
CALCULI from the BLADDER AND KIDNEYS KNOWN TO
THE WORLD; also the ONLY WATER EXHIBITED
(notwithstanding the hundreds competing) at

CHICAGO'S WORLD'S EXPOSITION

To receive a Medal and Diploma for "PURITY AND
GREAT MEDICINAL POWER," prove
conclusively that

POLAND WATER LEADS THE WORLD.

THE ACCOMPANYING ILLUSTRATIONS ARE MOST SUBSTANTIAL AND
CONVINCING PROOF OF THE ABOVE ASSERTIONS.

SAPIENTIA DONUM DEI

OFFICES:

BOSTON:	NEW YORK:	PHILADELPHIA:	CHICAGO:
175 Devonshire Street.	3 Park Place.	Chestnut and 13th Streets.	Cor. Michigan Ave. and Randolph St.

HIRAM RICKER & SONS, Proprietors.

Visit Boland's Glove Store,

117 Lisbon Street, LEWISTON.

THE HILL-TOP.

POLAND SPRING.

VOL. I.   SUNDAY MORNING, SEPTEMBER 9, 1894.   No. 10.

Poland Spring

OLAND SPRING is now at its best, and the tourists who rushed into Maine by the thousands early in the season to enjoy invigorating breezes, pure water and ozone laden with the perfume of fir and balsam, although they saw the "Garden of Eden" in all its bloom, did not come here in the most enjoyable season of the year by any means.

They should be here now in these cool and bracing days, and stay until the magnificent panorama is blazing with crimson and gold, and the mountains rising grandly in the midst of it, with not a fleck of cloud to obscure the view. These are the surroundings that will put new life into the jaded pilgrim. And this is the locality to see all these beauties of nature, for never was there a resort more pleasantly located ; and never one, says a cultured traveler (who has made 25 tours of the continent, circumnavigated the globe and visited every noted hotel in the world), which combines so fine a cuisine and service with its luxurious apartments and surroundings ; and never was there a more beautiful time to visit it than now.

The drive from the station at Danville Junction, on the fine drags and coupes, is charming, over the smooth turnpike six miles through the luxuriant foliage—past trees, festooned with swaying branches of the snowy clematis in full bloom, with the graceful, silvery, green, curling plumes, that come like a beautiful afterthought to remain fresh in memory's chamber after the sweetness of the blossom has departed ; past fields radiant with golden-rod, purple and white asters, hedges of elderberry, with their glossy green leaves and bunches of fruit in clustered purple ripeness.

These pleasant afternoons, as the sunlight comes through the brilliant foliage with its wonderful pale green light, in the distance the mountains blue as the sky, throw their shadows on pond and river, the steep sides of which are terraced with all the colors of the rainbow in these cool autumn days.

And when the tourist comes in sight of this elegant hostelry, "a veritable castle on the hill," with its towers, balconies, balustrades and broad verandas, its magnificent lawns, bright with brilliant blossoms, the studio building, the finest in Maine, the "*Maine Building*," purchased from the state and brought here from Chicago, now being set up in its original form of unique architecture, he finds it a fitting termination of the charming drive.

But no sketch can give more than a faint shadowing of the pleasures of a visit to the spring. The freedom from care, the relaxation from bonds which have fettered us to the treadmill of business—the sparkling water, the pure mountain air, every breath of which swells the veins and makes the blood tingle with delight—the wild mountain scenery, awakening new thoughts of grandeur of the creation and the mighty power of God. These combine to render a visit to Poland Spring an epoch in life to be looked forward to and back upon with pleasurable emotions.

The weary pilgrim, coursing over the burning sands of the East, does not hail the sight of an oasis in mid-desert with more joy than the habitues of the spring. Those worn down by cares and trouble, welcome the first glimpse of the sparkling fountain and verdant lawns. To him they promise rest, comfort, health, while to others they tell of pleasures past and joys to come. And no outing is complete till this popular caravansary, which is open till October 15th, is visited.

The Mansion House is open all the year, and here you will find invalids all winter who are here yearly, and who know that the spring bubbles forth its sparkling, health-giving waters just as generously in winter as in summer.

"See Naples and die," was the old-time maxim of the lovers of that beautiful city. But "See Poland Spring and live" seems to meet with more general approval among the distinguished, cultivated and wealthy of this and other countries. Thousands have visited here this season, beside the permanent guests of the hotels, to drink the "nectar of life" from the celebrated fountain, and to enjoy the comforts and elegance of the unrivaled hotels and the endless variety of scenery—the wild beauty that nature has been so exceedingly lavish with at this "Queen of Resorts."

Close by the crystal spring, with its dainty chalet covering it, at the present writing is an encampment of Indians, which carries one back in imagination to the primitive days when the spring was to their ancestors a sacred fount, and they partook of the sparkling water at this, nature's reservoir, 'neath heaven's blue dome, frescoed with colors ever changing and never reproducible, with feelings akin to the invalid of to-day, be he saint or earthworn sinner.

To-day it is cool and bracing. The extensive lawns look beautiful, the groves cool and inviting. The walks to the spring are unusually gay, the boulevards thronged with elegant turnouts. The verandas are the lounging place of ladies and gentlemen in elegant attire. There is a world of faces to see and admire, which, with the classic music that floats out from the hall, makes it a bit of realistic fairy-land.

And, while Newport and Interlaken, Ems and Long Branch, Bar Harbor and other noted resorts have their special charms, for variety in attractions this is their peer.

GEO. H. HAYNES.
Poland Spring, Sept. 2, 1894.

A Delightful Trip.

BUT a few years ago and a trip to Cuba was looked upon as a long and tedious journey. Nowadays, however, with faster trains and more luxurious equipment, and a line of steamers running direct to Havana from Port Tampa, Fla., the trip is performed so quickly and so comfortably that few who go South fail to take it. One gets in a Pullman sleeping-car at Jersey City in the morning, and going via the Pennsylvania Railroad, Atlantic Coast Line and Plant System, is landed on the dock at Port Tampa the next evening, with but one night on the road. Across the dock lies one of the trim steamers of the Plant System (either the Olivette or the Mascotte), and as soon as passengers and mail are aboard, off she goes down the Gulf, along the Florida coast, to Key West, the "Island City." The trip is a most beautiful one, the coast being in sight most of the time. At Key West a stop is made for a few hours, giving passengers a good opportunity to see the sights, and then on across the Gulf Stream to beautiful Havana, which is reached early in the morning just as the sunrise gun is fired from grim Moro Castle, which guards the harbor of Havana. The entire sea trip occupies but 32 hours, and presto! you are in Havana, the city of gaiety and amusement, of quaintness, and of beautiful women.

This is delightfully cool weather—don-cher-know?

Bubbles.

Nice weather.

The people still come.

Great bowling weather.

Every one went to the Fair.

The sun parlors are in great favor.

Mrs. B. P. Moulton has returned to her home in Rosemont, Pa.

The fire-places in Music Hall have all been re-decorated.

A new electric fan has been put up in Music Hall to aid in ventilation.

Our popular tonsorial artist makes an ideal umpire.

Work on the Maine State Building is being pushed as fast as possible.

If you have lost a shawl, a scarf, a fan or a pair of gloves or anything, in fact, just call at the office and look through the curiosity drawer.

We may find out in the course of time from Miss Blanche Todd and Mr. Arthur Maginnis where those delicious apple pies disappeared to on Tuesday returning home from Lewiston.

The lucky seven are to lose three of their number in the persons of Miss Louise Mattocks of Chicago, who left us on Thursday, and the Misses Todd who leave us to-morrow—Monday.

Mr. Romer Gillis, proprietor of that beautiful resort, Passaconaway Inn, York Cliffs, Me., and head clerk at the Ponce de Leon, St. Augustine, Fla., during the winter seasons, is paying his first visit to Poland. He expresses himself as delighted with Poland and compares it with any of the best resorts in the country.

H. T. JORDAN, } Editors.
W. D. FREEMAN, }

PUBLISHED EVERY SUNDAY MORNING DURING THE MONTHS
OF JULY, AUGUST AND SEPTEMBER, IN THE INTERESTS OF

POLAND SPRING AND ITS VISITORS.

All contributions relative to the guests of Poland Spring will
be thankfully received.

To insure publication, all communications should reach the
editors not later than Thursday preceding day of issue.

All parties desiring rates for advertising in the HILL-TOP
should write the editors for same.

The subscription price of the HILL-TOP is $1.00 for the
season, post-paid. Single copies will be mailed at 10c. each.

Address,

EDITORS "HILL-TOP,"
Poland Spring House,
South Poland, Maine.

PRINTED AT JOURNAL OFFICE, LEWISTON.

Sunday, Sept. 9, 1894.

Editorial.

IT is now past the first of September, and the
usual large number of departures incident
to the advent of that most delightful of all
months at Poland, has taken place. But did
you ever know of this famous resort as being
other than in the van with other resort hotels?
We don't think so. Hardly had the coaches
bearing their regretting occupants left the hill,
and the vacated rooms been put in good order,
when the influx of new arrivals commenced, and
has continued throughout the week. Music Hall
contains a new set of devotees to terpsichorean
pleasures, and the favorite retreats in Lovers'
Lane have assumed a changed appearance. The
slippery board walk to the Upper Lake still furnishes toboggan sensations to a more sedate and
quiet few. But the sail on the lakes in the
natty little Poland is more popular than ever,
while the livery connected with the house is
quite unable to supply the demands made upon it.

"A Fair-well Drive."

With a four-in-hand,
On a September morn,
To the cheerful sound of the merry horn;
See, the gay team starts
As we crack the whip,
And off we go for a jolly trip.

BUT, alas! but two miles had been covered
when the host discovered that the "one
thing needful" had been forgotten, and
had to be returned for. Again a start was
made, and this time successfully. The Maine
State Fair, which was the destination, was
reached about twelve o'clock.

The first lunch was promptly served, at which
Mr. Allen Rogers was a prominent figure, creating havoc among the sandwiches and ginger ale.
Several photographs were then taken of the party
on the coach, by our host, Mr. J. H. Maginnis,
after which the party started to "do" the Fair.

The principal buildings being gone through,
tintypes were the order of the day, and turned
out most successfully.

A great variety of musical instruments being
provided by the charming chaperone, Mrs. Maginnis, the party outrivaled the brass band at the
races in the afternoon. The racing in itself was
most interesting, and great excitement prevailed
on top of the brake when a favorite came in first.

Before the return start was made a second
lunch was served, and then amid the cheering of
small boys and the brilliant efforts of A. A.
Maginnis on the horn, the brake rolled gaily from
the grounds. The return trip was made by way
of Minot Corner, and weary laborers were
charmed by the sweet sounds wafted from the
coach. No song was left unsung, and Miss
Blanche Todd particularly distinguished herself.

The brake rolled up in front of the "Big
House" at about quarter of eight, when the
host and hostess were overwhelmed with thanks,
and the affair voted the "great success of the
season." Those present were Mrs. J. H. Maginnis, Miss Rita Todd, Miss Louise Mattocks,
Miss Helen Stinson, Miss Blanche Todd; J. H.
Maginnis, A. A. Maginnis, Jr., and Allen M.
Rogers.

Mr. Charles Rauh, of the firm of Rauh Bros.
& Co., the large wholesale and retail dealers of
men's furnishing goods in Pittsburg, left here
Tuesday. Mr. Rauh, during his extended stay
here, has made a host of friends whose well
wishes for better health follow him. Mr. Rauh
considers Poland Spring as the *ne plus ultra* of
summer resorts.

Bubbles.

Mr. Frank Lincoln, the most famous humorist in the country, is expected here next Tuesday.

Miss Helen Babbidge, of Rockland, Me., has been assigned as operator at this house.

The Maine State Building is growing fast and will be completed by the end of the season.

Powers, our star catcher, is rapidly recovering from his injuries sustained at Rockland.

If any one doubts as to the popularity of whist at Poland, just let him walk through the public rooms any evening.

Miss Josie Laughlin, of the Boston office force, was here over Sunday accompanied by her friend, Miss S. E. Faltz.

Tennis and croquet seem to be the favorite out-door sports, in spite of the cool breezes which we are now enjoying.

William J. Schieffelin, of New York, son of Mr. W. H. Schieffelin, the great wholesale dealer in foreign and domestic drugs, arrived Monday.

Mr. Charles Sias, of the well-known firm of Chase & Sanborn, of Boston, is with us again. Mr. Sias drives a nobby turn-out.

Mr. Seaver, the photographer in charge of the Poland Spring studio, is doing some elegant work now and plenty of it.

Miss Kate Wheelock, the whist teacher, who has been combining business with pleasure here during the past month, returned to her home in Chicago, Tuesday.

Benjamin E. Cole and wife, of Boston, who arrived on the 28th ult., are enjoying the many beautiful rides about Poland, daily, in their handsome victoria.

Secretary Dickinson left us Thursday. Mr. Dickinson and his charming wife won many frends while here and will be much missed by a large circle of acquaintances.

Mr. and Mrs. Charles D. Sias of Boston, accompanied by Mr. and Mrs. W. F. Carleton, arrived Wednesday for an extended stay. Mr. Sias is of the firm of Chase & Sanborn, coffee dealers, Boston, and an old visitor at Poland. Mr. Sias brings his own team and coachman.

Moldauer, the popular first violinist of our last season's orchestra, accompanied by his charming wife, paid his favorite resort a short visit last week. Mr. Moldauer has been playing in the West End Hotel orchestra, Bar Harbor, the past season, and is now enjoying a short vacation before resuming his connection with the Boston Symphony.

Jack is very sad! His Jill left him Thursday and he now is obliged to carry his bucket without the aid of her helping hand.

Miss Maginnis, who has been visiting with friends for a few weeks at Newport and Bar Harbor, returned to Poland Tuesday.

Miss Anderson, our popular telegraph operator, who has considered Poland as her summer home for the past four seasons, was called home last week on account of sickness in her family.

Coming Events.

Sunday, Sept. 9th.—Preaching service, 11 A.M. Concert, 3.30 P.M. Song service, 8.15 P.M.

Tuesday, Sept. 11th.—Frank Lincoln, humorist.

Friday, Sept. 14th.—Progressive Euchre, 8.10 P.M.

Saturday, Sept. 15th.—Hop, 8.15 P.M.

Sunday Concert.

Concert programme for to-day at 3.30 P.M., Music Hall :

1. Coronation March.		Meyerbeer.
2. Overture—Zampa.		Herold.
3. Melodien—	*a.* Herzwunden. *b.* Der Fruhling. (For strings.)	Grieg.
4. Selection—Romeo and Juliet.		Gounod.
5.	*a.* Serenata. *b.* Loin du Bal. (For strings.)	Moszkowski. Gillet.
6. Selection—Tannhäuser.		Wagner.

The Crucial Moment.

Within the hammock's net she swung,
So graceful and so fair!
Her arms about her head were flung,
Lovely beyond compare.

He sat beside her for a while,
Enchanted by her grace,
Till finally a blush and smile
He saw upon her face.

And then he heard her softly say,
First looking all about;
"Now, please, Tom, turn your head away,
I'm going to get out!"

At the Sea-shore.

(From Judge.)

Priscilla (just arrived)—Are there any men here?

Phyllis—Oh, there are a few apologies for men.

Priscilla—Well, if an apology is offered to me I shall accept it.

Stolen.

The Man Who Knows It All.

I love the man who knows it all,
  From East to West, from North to South;
Who knows all things both great and small,
  And tells it with a tireless mouth;
Who holds a listening world in awe,
The while he works his iron jaw!

Ofttimes in evening's holy calm,
  When twilight softens sight and sound,
And zephyr breathes a peaceful psalm,
  This fellow brings his mouth around,
With its long gallop that can tire
The eight-day clock's impatient ire.

His good strong mouth! He wields it well;
He works it just for all it's worth;
Not Samson's jaw-bone famed could tell
  Such mighty deeds upon the earth.
He pulls the throttle open wide,
And works her hard on either side.

Good Lord, from evils fierce and dire,
  Save us each day from fear and woe;
From wreck and flood, from storm and fire,
  From sudden death, from secret foe;
From blighting rain and burning drouth —
And from the man who plays his mouth.

A Mean Trick.

Museum Manager—What's all that disturbance in the lecture hall?

Lecturer—The Aimless Wonder has stolen the Fasting Girl's lunch.

When Woman Votes.

(From Puck.)

Mrs. Franclyn Wilmot—I shall never speak to her again—the mean thing.

Mrs. T. William Franchise—What did she do?

Mrs. Wilmot—She challenged my vote.

She does not heed the cable car,
  Which goes with speed intense;
She cares not for the trolley wire,
  Whose voltage is immense.
The old excursion steamer brings
  No terror to her blow.
But when she's in the country she will run
  across acres of ground and climb barb
  wire fences to escape the affable, though
  inquisitive gaze
Of an aged, docile cow.

Base=Ball.

IN our last issue we announced that our ball team had disbanded. The announcement was somewhat premature as it happened, the team having played four games this week. The step was decided upon as, with our star catcher confined to his room with a fractured rib and our pitchers in the hospital, it seemed impossible to get a team together.

A little hustling was done, however, and a game was played on Saturday last with a picked-up aggregation from Lewiston, whom we defeated in a one-sided game characterized by hard batting. Louis's two home runs in the first inning were the features.

On Monday the team went to Biddeford and were defeated in an exciting game by a score of 7 to 5. The absence of Powers was badly felt, but Gerrish caught well.

On Wednesday, Eddie Murphy came up to take revenge on our youngsters for the numerous defeats he has carried back to the city without a theatre. That he might be sure of victory he brought up the Portland league team in the Balsam's uniforms. It looked like a good thing for the visitors, and they started in to make monkeys of the Polands. Base-ball is uncertain, however, and when the game was called on account of rain we had 19 tallies to the visitors' 16. As the inning was not played out, the score went back to the seventh, leaving it a tie. The game was a corker and the elements added additional excitement to the combat.

On Thursday the boys went to Rockland to play off the tie, each club having won a game. Much to the surprise of the Rocklandites, we beat their pets hands down, winning 12 to 5. The feature was the sharp fielding of our boys.

Not the Right Place.

Salesman—Why don't you try these stockings, ma'am? We warrant them not to crock.

Mrs. Shopleigh—Where were they made?

Salesman—In Philadelphia.

Mrs. Shopleigh—And do you suppose they know anything about fast colors there?

Needed Then.

Nurse—Shall you call again to-day, doctor?

Dr. Druggem—No, I don't think it is necessary. The patient is liable to remain in his present condition for days. But if there is any change for the better, send for me at once.

FEBRUARY ON THE VERANDA OF THE ORMOND.

Florida Winter Weather.

"IN that warmth, wholly apart from any attractions of scene or sport, is the secret of the peopling of Florida by Northerners in the winter months, of the transformation of one of the United States into a pleasure-park and loafing-place during three months of each year. The official records show that during those months the mean temperature varies, in the different parts of the state, between 56° and 70° Fahrenheit. There is not, I am assured, any part of the state which is absolutely exempt from frost, but it is an unfamiliar visitor, and with the general warmth comes a royal proportion of clear days—*a general average of twenty-four fine days in each month* between December and May in all parts of the state. In March the average is about twenty-seven days and in April, twenty-six. [April is to Florida what June is to New England, the loveliest of all the months.] I held the common impression that the state was resorted to as a sanitarium; but when, after several days in Tallahassee and Jacksonville, I had seen but few persons who had the appearance of being victims of any lung disease, I altered my opinion. It was the resort of invalids for many years, it seems, but those who spent their winters there, now go to the so-called piny woods and mountain resorts of Georgia and the Carolinas. Florida has become a resting-place for those who can afford to loaf at the busiest time in the year—the men who have 'made their piles,' or organized their business to run automatically."

Amusements.

THE entertainments since the last HILL-TOP went to press, have been extremely good and reflect much credit upon the Amusement Committee. On Friday evening Prof. H. Russell, the magician, entertained the youngsters, and incidentally, the older ones, by his clever sleight-of-hand. The Professor is very clever and has numerous card tricks which it would be hard to beat. The best part of his entertainment was given in the office after the regular performance.

On Tuesday evening Wallis A. Wallis and wife, of Loudon, gave a humorous entertainment in Music Hall. Mr. and Mrs. Wallis are clever people and their programme was much enjoyed. The "Bells," as recited by Mr. Wallace, was the best of the evening.

The Poland makes two trips a day now.

"Our Girl."

ABOVE we present a picture of the "Hill-Top Girl" in the costume which received so many flattering notices at the masquerade. The dress is made of Hill-Tops and is a marvel of the dress-maker's art. The young lady's name is Miss May Dunne, and you can see by the expression on her countenance that she is rather proud of having worn the most original and tasty costume on the floor, which was wholly of her own designing. The editors are proud of her, and take much pleasure in presenting you with her picture.

The ball team was disbanded last Monday, but as several clubs were so very desirous of again trying conclusions with the Poland "babies," an opportunity was offered by the team being called back.

The son of a prominent hotel proprietor, of New York City, while here a few days ago, became really enamored with a certain young Polandite. The result is that she is the recipient of a photo of that young man, so soon.

The Curiosity Drawer.

EVERY hotel has its bureau of found articles. Not every house can show such a varied collection, however, as the found drawer on the Hill contains. It speaks well for the honesty of the employees. Contents on Thursday evening: Gray shawl, red shawl, two white shawls, black lace shawl, five fans, several pairs of gloves, several packs of cards, one stylographie, toilet soap, handkerchiefs galore, string of beads, three manacles, one moss-agate ring, three cuff buttons, one moonstone pin, one opal pin, one hairpin, cluster brilliants, one monogram pin (G. C.), one pearl pin, two knives, a purse, and other valuables too numerous to mention.

Our Ball Team's Future.

IT may be interesting for our readers to know what the members of our ball team will be doing this winter, so we give the correct information: Captain Powers will probably spend a few weeks at home in Adams, Mass., before resuming his course at Holy Cross College, Worcester, Mass.

Our famous left-fielder, Sockalexis, will be found at Ricker Classical Institute, Houlton, Me., devouring Latin, Greek, and those most delightful of all perplexing studies, mathematics. We are sure he will propound the solution of that world-famous "pons assinorum" just as easily as he pounds the globular horsehide miles beyond the right-fielder.

Our pitchers, Burrill and Slattery, will continue their pleasures at Bates College, by surprising their fair admirers with their dexterity in the passing of the deceitful base-ball.

"Jakey" Wakefield will be at Bates, as will also Pulsifer, who captained Bates's representatives on the diamond last season.

Hull will winter in Ipswich, Mass., where he will work at his trade as a shoe-maker.

"The only" County will lull away the cold winter months in Biddeford, Me., getting into condition for next summer's ball playing.

That illustrious Harris, "than whom there is none other more swift" on turf or clay, and whom the "cranks" have dubbed as "Paderewsky Jo," will cigarette his winter away at masticating apple pie in Haverhill.

Our team this season has been even more strong than last season, and the victories we have won place us beyond doubt as the champion amateur club of the State of Maine.

The Fair at Lewiston the past week has been well patronized by Poland guests.

Arrivals

FOR WEEK ENDING SEPTEMBER 6.

POLAND SPRING HOUSE.

Ames, Mr. and Mrs. E. F.,	Montreal
Adams, Mr. and Mrs. M. F.,	Boston
Blush, Miss H. C.,	New York
Bailey, Mr. and Mrs. C. B,.	Washington
Beal, Mrs.,	Boston
Blood, Mrs. S. L.,	Brooklyn
Budd, Miss,	Edgewater, Ill.
Buck, Mrs. H. T.,	Worcester
Blow, Mrs. E. H. B.,	Fall River
Blow, Miss,	Fall River
Bonaparte, Mr. and Mrs. C. J,.	Baltimore
Benedict, Mrs.,	Albany
Carruth, Mr. and Mrs. John G.,	Philadelphia
Carruth, Miss J. M.,	Philadelphia
Conklin, Mr. and Mrs. John M.,	Philadelphia
Conklin, Miss Maud,	Philadelphia
Coe, Mr. and Mrs. A. L.,	Chicago
Coe, Mrs. C. L.,	Boston
Chase, Mr. and Mrs. C. S.,	Portland
Cocks, Mrs. Charles,	Brooklyn
Cocks, Townsend,	Brooklyn
Clendenier, Mr. and Mrs.,	New York
Chisholm, C. R.,	Montreal
Carleton, Mr. and Mrs. W. F.,	Boston
Dyar, Mr. and Mrs. H. C.,	New York
Dennison, G. E.,	Boston
Drake, Mrs. A. A.,	Westfield, N. J.
Drake, Miss Helen,	Westfield, N. J.
Day, M. C.,	New York
Feetus, R. G,	Philadelphia
Gibson, Miss R.,	Philadelphia
Gould, Miss H. E.,	Boston
Greene, O. P.,	Saco
Gough, Mr. and Mrs. John,	Washington
Guild, Miss M. C.,	Boston
Gun, Mr. and Mrs. E,	Springfield
Gillis, Romel,	York Cliffs
Goodenow, J. H.,	New York
Greene, Benson and wife,	Baltimore
Grenlock, Mr. and Mrs. L. J.,	New York
Hopkins, Mr. and Mrs. G. G.,	Brooklyn
Hetfield, C. R.,	Brooklyn
Holmes, E. T.,	New York
Hood, R. P.,	Longwood
Haydock, Miss S. G.,	Philadelphia
Ivins, Mr. and Mrs. A. B.,	Philadelphia
Johnson, Mr. and Mrs. G. P.,	Cambridge
Keeler, Mrs. J. M.,	San Francisco
Keates, Mr. and Mrs. G. W.,	Boston
Lincoln, Mrs. R. P.,	New York
Lincoln, Miss,	New York
Lewis, Mr. and Mrs.,	New York
Lewis, Miss Amy H.,	New York
Lewis, Jerome G.,	New York
Lasell, Mrs. C. W.,	Whitinsville
Lapham, Mr. and Mrs. B. N.,	Providence
Leonard, Mr. and Mrs. George H.,	Boston
Leonard, Miss,	Boston
Matheson, Mr. and Mrs. Charles,	Providence
Moise, M. M.,	Boston
Moore, Mr. and Mrs. H. M.,	Yonkers, N. Y.
Moore, E. W.,	Yonkers, N. Y.
McManus, Mr. and Mrs. John,	Providence
Maginnis, Miss,	New Orleans
Marshall, Mrs.,	New York
Maxwell, Miss,	New York
Maxwell, Miss R.,	New York
Maxwell, Miss M.,	New York
Merritt, E. P.,	New York
McWilliams, David,	Dwight, Ill.
McMullan, Mr. and Mrs. J. H.,	Portland
McMullan, Miss,	Portland
Marble, Miss E. G.,	Boston
Merrill, Mrs. J. W.,	Manchester, Mass.
Merrill, Mr. and Mrs. J. W.,	Manchester, Mass.
McConike, Mrs. Alonzo,	Troy, N. Y.
McConike, Misses,	Troy, N. Y.
Norris, William,	New York
Norris, Miss,	New York
Peirce, Mr. and Mrs. C. C.,	Brookline
Perkins, Mrs. E. H., Jr.,	New York
Pearce, E. E.,	Brooklyn
Peek, Mr. and Mrs. Samuel W.,	New York
Prall, Miss E. A.,	New York
Parker, Mr. and Mrs. E. E ,	Boston
Parker, Miss C. B.,	Boston
Peirce, Mr. and Mrs. George,	Newport, R. I.
Rogers, Mrs. T. O.,	Boston
Ross, Mr. and Mrs. J.,	Ipswich
Ross, Miss A. W.,	Ipswich
Rogers, Mrs. L. W.,	Boston
Rines, D. F.,	Portland
Rines, R. H.,	Portland
Rittel, Miss Julia C.,	Yonkers, N. Y.
Rhoades, L. F.,	Boston
Rice, Mr. and Mrs. W. E.,	Worcester
Rice, Master A. W.,	Worcester
Richardson, Mr. and Mrs. A.,	Boston
Richardson, Miss M.,	Boston
Sprague, Mrs. G. H.,	Boston
Smith, A. F.,	Chicago
Soniat, Charles T.,	New Orleans
Stephenson, G. H.,	Philadelphia
Stephenson, Miss S. L.,	Philadelphia
Stephenson, Miss Mabel,	Philadelphia
Stein, Miss E. E.,	New York
Sandford, Mr. and Mrs. J. W.,	Plainsville, N. J.
Smith, Mrs.,	Providence
Schieffelin, W. J.,	New York
Skaats, Mrs. S.,	New York
Stuart, W. H., Jr.,	Boston
Seymore, Mr. and Mrs. W. H.,	Brooklyn
Sias, C. D.,	Boston
Squire, Mrs. J. P.,	Boston
Smith, Mrs. B. F.,	New York

Thompson, G. W.,	Philadelphia
Tyler, Miss,	New York
Thomas, Elias, Jr.,	Portland
Taitt, Mrs. C. G.,	Philadelphia
Tabor, Mr. and Mrs. J. W.,	Portland
Tucker, Mr. and Mrs. J. N.,	Boston
Tucker, Miss,	Boston
Ten Broeck, Mrs. N. E.,	New York
Thatcher, M. D. and family,	Pueblo, Col.
Teroy, Mrs. M. C.,	Washington
Underwood, E. P.,	Newark
Weymouth, Mr. and Mrs. G.,	Cambridge
Webb, Mr. and Mrs. F. W.,	New York
Webb, Marie,	New York
Wedgwood, Mr. and Mrs. Geo. S.,	Chicago
Wade, Mrs. R. B.,	New Haven
White, Mr. and Mrs. J. H.,	Brookline, Mass.
Whiting, W.,	Boston
Zach, Mrs. Max,	Boston

MANSION HOUSE.

Adler, Mr. and Mrs. Herman,	New York
Adler, Master Geo. Herman and maid,	New York
Allan, N. S.,	Dennysville
Baines, Mrs. Geo. W.,	Boston
Bassett, Mrs. H. B.,	Providence
Bassett, F. J.,	Providence
Bassett, Miss Lenora,	Providence
Benjamin, Mrs. Eastman,	New York
Benjamin, the Misses,	New York
Benjamin, Harsen R.,	New York
Bucknam, J. M.,	Yarmouth
Cousens, W. T.,	Portland
Childs, E.,	New York
Decoster, V.,	Boston
Dobbin, Horace and wife, nurse and child,	Philadelphia
Eden, M.,	Boston
Forsyth, Mr. and Mrs. Geo. H.,	Boston
Ganes, E. C.,	Waltham
Gilbert, F. A.,	Boston
Gilbert, Mrs. J. F.,	New Haven, Ct.
Gilman, Mrs. Arthur,	Cambridge
Gilman, Miss,	Cambridge
Gilman, Master,	Cambridge
Gibson, Mr. and Mrs. J. W.,	New York
Hall, Chas. W.,	Greene
Hight, Geo. W. and wife,	Boston
Hight, Miss C. L.,	Boston
Hight, Mr. G. W.,	Boston
Hight, Mattie,	Boston
Hight, Miss Susie,	Boston
Hood, R. P.,	Longwood
Hottehoff, Miss,	Cincinnati, Ohio
Keyes, Mrs. Robert,	Baltimore
Keyes, Rebecca,	Baltimore
Keyes, Amelia,	Baltimore
Lawrence, J. J.,	New York
McCartney, R. C.,	Boston
Moulton, Ida,	Greene

Nudd, Miss, .	London
Patten, Mrs. L. E.,	Brooklyn
Perot, Mrs. Elliston,	Philadelphia
Perot, Miss A. L.,	Philadelphia
Plummer, Mrs. Wm. S.,	Philadelphia
Pulver, Lewis and wife,	New York
Reed, J. N.,	Portland
Roberts, Florence E.,	Westbrook
Rockefeller, I. P. and wife,	New York
Richards, Louise,	East Bridgewater
Russell, P. H.,	New York
Sondheim, Pauline,	New York
Sondheim, Mr. and Mrs. H. P.,	New York
Sprague, Mr.,	Greene
Wilkins, W. S.,	Greene

WHY
Poland Spring Leads Them All.

A 19th Century Triumph

THE POLAND SPRING HOUSE 1893-4

MERIT, POPULARITY, LARGE SALES,

AND THE FACT THAT

POLAND WATER

Was the FIRST SOLVENT AND ELIMINATOR OF URIC ACID CALCULI from the BLADDER AND KIDNEYS KNOWN TO THE WORLD; also the ONLY WATER EXHIBITED (notwithstanding the hundreds competing) at

CHICAGO'S WORLD'S EXPOSITION

To receive a Medal and Diploma for "PURITY AND GREAT MEDICINAL POWER," prove conclusively that

POLAND WATER LEADS THE WORLD.

THE ACCOMPANYING ILLUSTRATIONS ARE MOST SUBSTANTIAL AND CONVINCING PROOF OF THE ABOVE ASSERTIONS.

SAPIENTIA DONUM DEI

OFFICES:

BOSTON:	NEW YORK:	PHILADELPHIA:	CHICAGO:
175 Devonshire Street.	3 Park Place.	Chestnut and 13th Streets.	Cor. Michigan Ave. and Randolph St.

HIRAM RICKER & SONS, Proprietors.

THE HILL-TOP
POLAND SPRING

Vol. I. SUNDAY MORNING, SEPTEMBER 16, 1894. No. 11.

Poland Spring.

IN a recent issue of *Once a Week* appears a full page of illustrations of some of the most picturesque places about Poland Spring. It contains a long descriptive article, also, written in a very pleasing and truthful manner, by Lida A. Churchill. We make the following extracts therefrom:

"The Poland Spring House is said to be, with one exception, the grandest and best equipped summer hotel in the United States. It is a veritable castle of liberty and expansion. From the moment one enters its roomy halls and wide passages, care falls from him like a loosened garment, and anxiety becomes a repudiated thing.

"Everywhere are public and private parlors, furnished as only prodigally spent gold and exquisite taste could have furnished them, and in the spacious halls are dome-shaped fire-places warmly colored in terra-cotta, or shining in handsomely contrasted tiles, which, when the keen wind, blowing straight down from the 'White Hills,' or up from the near lakes, chills the air, glow and sparkle with the flames which riot over the resinous, forest-scented logs of the State of pine.

"Everywhere electricity sends out its pure light, brilliantly illuminating the interior of the house, and casting Rembrantesque shadows beneath the stately trees of the grounds.

"The dining-room, about two hundred feet in length and of ample width, is, with its shining floor, gleaming white walls, and exquisite appointments, a royal banqueting hall.

"From the windows and piazzas of this hill-top palace an entrancing view is to be obtained. Plainly in view, their caps sharply piercing the blue of the sky, stand the White Mountains. Below, in the near valley, lie the Range Lakes, a beautiful shrubbery-encircled trio, over whose waters glides the handsome steam launch of the Rickers loaded with happy guests, and dotted with the tiny boats of dreaming lovers and the unweildy craft of alert fishermen. On the hills in another direction noble forest trees whisper together in the always floating breeze; among the valleys, hundreds of feet below, are the Maine homes with the hushed air of peace about them in which their owners so seldom 'find dullness, and afar off, when the atmosphere has that clearness which it often possesses here, one can see from the tower the faint silver sheen and shimmer of the Atlantic, and the lovely Forest City sitting at the entrance to Portland Harbor.

"All the world is here represented. The military Russian, the urbane Frenchman, the practical German, the count of Italy, the heir of some noble house, sit on the wide piazzas conversing like brothers. America is not behindhand in her contributions. The South sends her languorous, handsome daughters and chivalrous sons. New York puts aside its commercial cares and learns fresh joys in this garden of the gods. Cultivated, Ibsenistic Boston removes its spectacles, lets the abstruse volume lie idly on its lap while it laughingly vies with its rival drinkers in disposing of the mysterious elixir of life. Dwellers in the City of the Golden Gate consider a sojourn here worth a trip across the continent, and those whose homes are on the prairies of the world's wheat fields seek this spot in rapturous recognition of the beauty and strength of the hills. The whole atmosphere is surcharged with ozone. One realizes the force of Whittier's words :

'There's iron in our Northern winds,
Our pines are trees of healing.'

"The famous Poland Spring equipages are in constant demand, for the drives about the Spring are exceedingly beautiful. Miles upon miles of shady silence, bethrilled with the songs of birds, the thick trees meeting overhead, the damp, spreading ferns touching the carriage wheels as they pass ; along the white sands of 'Sabbath-Day Pond,' on the shores of which used to gather families from the block-house or guarded log cabin, together with the keen-scented scouts, to pray for protection from their wily foes, and to take heart from each other's counsel and companionship. Out over the bold hills commanding views of the wide stretches of tilled lands, with here and there a lone, straight pine making a sharp silhouette against the sky.

"A favorite halting-place is the near village of the New Gloucester Shakers—a benignant, serene-faced, cordial people, who regard utter chastity as the key to the Kingdom of Heaven, and marriage as a stupendous mistake, and who seem to the harrassed and hurried worldlings who linger for a little within their gates as much a part of another world as their language, with its primitive yea and nea, seems like an alien tongue.

"'Cæsar was Rome and Rome was Cæsar.' Thus are we taught. One might exclaim with equal truth that the Rickers are Poland Spring and Poland Spring is the Rickers, for unto this place, for which Nature has exhausted her resources, and wealth has poured out its treasures as clouds pour out rain, its three proprietors have given a soul. Every inch of its broad domains is under their personal supervision, and each guest is an honored friend to whom the thoughtful attention of his hosts extend.

"Maine has become a recognized Temple of Beauty, in which the summer seeker after that which shall please the eye and delight the heart has set up many gods ; but within her sea-caressed borders, among her hills of grandeur, amid her tales of enchantment, man, however diligent, shall seek in vain for a spot where married Art and Nature have brought forth a fairer offspring than this place where the waters of the deepest earth give healing, and health and pleasure fold about one as surely and tenderly as the evening dusk enfolds the earth of his habitation.

The arches over the grand entrance to the Maine State Building are in place, and the walls are being put up fast. It will be but a few days now when the crew of carpenters will commence their work of putting together the interior of the building. Good work has been done thus far on reconstruction, and when finished it will be one of the best attractions on the hill.

Bubbles.

The new stable has a good start and will be a fine building.

Mr. John C. Haynes, of Boston, joined his wife here Wednesday.

Why not purchase a copy of Vol. I. of THE HILL-TOP to send your friend? You cannot find a better souvenir.

Photographer Seaver took a fine view of Mt. Washington last week, from the veranda, with his new long-distance lens.

Mr. S. S. Pollard, of Boston, a friend of Mr. G. W. Coleman, is enjoying a few days' outing here.

Religious services were held in the main dining-room Sunday evening for the employees, led by Rev. Mr. Blanchard, of Philadelphia.

Mr. and Mrs. C. C. Pierce and Master Pierce are stopping at the big house. Mr. Pierce is one of the leading athletes of the B. A. A. He is a prominent member of the foot-ball team, and is no novice at most of the out-door games. His home is in Brookline.

H. T. JORDAN, | EDITORS.
W. D. FREEMAN, |

PUBLISHED EVERY SUNDAY MORNING DURING THE MONTHS
OF JULY, AUGUST AND SEPTEMBER, IN THE INTERESTS OF

POLAND SPRING AND ITS VISITORS.

All contributions relative to the guests of Poland Spring will
be thankfully received.

To insure publication, all communications should reach the
editors not later than Thursday preceding day of issue.

All parties desiring rates for advertising in the HILL-TOP
should write the editors for same.

The subscription price of the HILL-TOP is $1.00 for the
season, post-paid. Single copies will be mailed at 10c. each.

Address,
EDITORS "HILL-TOP,"
Poland Spring House,
South Poland, Maine.

PRINTED AT JOURNAL OFFICE, LEWISTON.

Sunday, Sept. 16, 1894.

Editorial.

WITH to-day's number is ended the first volume of the HILL-TOP, and our editorial responsibilities, however pleasant or unpleasant they may have been, cease. It has been our purpose to present with each issue a good, clean, readable publication, devoted to the Ricker interests exclusively, and if we have succeeded in our purpose, our object has been attained. Our promises otherwise have been fulfilled to the letter. We found it necessary soon after the first edition to increase the size of the paper by four pages, which we did regardless of the extra expense incurred. We also concluded to issue an additional number, giving our subscribers the benefit thereof rom free of charge. We are much pleased with the reception the HILL-TOP has received from the guests of the house and friends of Poland, and trust we have merited their support. Next season we hope to meet with the same success that has attended us this season. Again thanking you all for your kind words of encouragement and support, we will bid you a kind adieu for the season of '94.

THE question of whether the private way across the Poland Spring property shall be opened as a public county road at the behest of the Portland & Rumford Falls Railroad Company or not will now soon be definitely settled. If the decision is not adverse to the petition and favorable to the Messrs. Ricker it is safe to say that it will be a great surprise to nine out of every ten of those who attended the hearing before the county commissioners at the town house at Poland Corner this week. The weakness of the case for the petitioners as presented at the hearing was certainly a surprise to those present. Of the citizens of Poland who signed the petition some six or eight were called upon to testify in support of it. They were all very positive that public necessity and convenience demanded the opening of the way as a public road, but on cross-examination almost without exception they admitted that they were themselves just as well accommodated by the private way as it now exists as they would be if it were public, and one or two of them were frank enough to admit, when cornered by Judge Savage's skillful questioning, that if the road was to be maintained in future as in the past, it would not be wise to put the town to the expense of buying the road and maintaining it in order that one party, now barred out, might be admitted. Almost without exception the witnesses for the petition from the town of Poland aided the cause of the remonstrants more than they did their own. On the other hand the testimony of the remonstrants was very strong and was very strongly presented by Messrs. Savage and Newell, the attorneys for the remonstrants. On the whole it is a very safe prediction that the prayer of the petitioners for the opening of the way will not be granted.

Isn't that a delightful ride on the little Poland? Haven't enjoyed it? Why, don't let another day pass ere you have availed yourself of the opportunity.

Pleasure and Comfort at Poland Spring.

WHO has not heard of Poland Spring, and who is there who has traveled in search of health and comfort that has not visited it?

Situated a short distance from the coast, upon a high hill with the White Mountains in the foreground, its location is one that cannot be surpassed. Not for grandeur, for if one is looking for the grand in nature he must go among the mountains themselves, but for the beauty of the general view.

First and foremost is the hotel that is kept by the Messrs. Ricker, and which has a name that has no superior in the whole United States. People who have traveled extensively, say they have seen fine hotels and well-kept ones, but never, until they came here, have they seen the perfection of hotel life. What is the use of describing the house and its appointments? Is it not enough to say that everything that goes to make a summer hotel worth living at is found here?

And the pleasures of the place! Are they not all to be found here? Beautiful drives, lovely walks, with the inevitable "lover's lane" that is so inviting and no well regulated resort should be without.

Then there is the music. Poland Spring House has always prided itself upon its orchestra, which has, in seasons past, been of the best, and which knows how to play something besides "Sweet Marie" and "Ta-ra-ra." Concerts twice a day, and in the evening the young people may be seen in the dreamy waltz, as if life had only one object, to be happy. And to them that is its only meaning, for all too soon come the trials and the sober realities of life, so for the present "let us be gay."

There is one thing that is of the most importance, and which draws the most people to the hotel after all, and that is the health-giving water. If it is not exactly the fountain of youth that old Ponce de Leon wandered through the forests of Florida in search of, it is a fountain of health, and many who drink of it find again their youth in the regained health, which is as near as we shall ever get to a real fountain of life or youth.

The writer of this article has just returned from a visit to this famous resort, and found it full of people, many of whom have been there season after season for years, and what can speak louder in its praise, than the fact that the most desirable rooms are engaged a year in advance.

The same employees are to be seen at the same posts, and the guests are greeted not by strange faces, but by those that are familiar, so that it seems like a home-coming.

Mr. Mullan still stands behind the desk, and assures you he is glad to see you, and that he has saved you the most desirable room in the house. Mr. Huggins informs you that your baggage will be sent up at once, and that a package by express is waiting for you, while Harry quietly informs you that your favorite brand of cigars is in stock, and that the ball-team plays next Saturday, at the same time he slips into your hand a prospectus of the new paper just started, called the HILL-TOP. If the face behind the cashier's desk is not the same as last year, you notice it is a familiar one, and are certain that, being a woman, everything will run smoothly, for of course one doesn't care to find fault with a lady.

The smiling postmistress hands you out your letters before you ask for them, and you feel as glad to see her as she is to see you, and after a few words to the telegraph operator, whose bright eyes and rosy cheeks were always a cause of envy to you, you are reminded by Don, that you can have your old bell-boy this year as last.

You go to your room thinking what a pleasure it is indeed, to get back where everybody knows you and is so glad to see you. The thought has hardly left you when there is a knock at the door, and in comes Dennis, the porter, who takes your hand as if you were an old friend, and says he, too, is glad to see you back, and indeed he is.

Oh, it is a rare place to go, if you are an old guest, and if you are a new one, the proprietor, Mr. Edward Ricker, soon makes you feel that you are at home, and assures you that the whole house is yours, or words to that effect. Only don't take this literally, for if there is a place in the country where every one's rights are looked after, it is here, and no guest is allowed to own the house, or to run it.

Of course you expect Julius will give you the same seat and the same table you have always had, and if you are an old guest you will look up the other proprietor, Mr. Al Ricker. He is not seen much in the foreground, but you can feel his presence in all that takes place in the dining-room. Perhaps if you are a personal or old friend of the proprietors you will be allowed to go into the office and greet the young lady that is Mr. Ricker's right hand; but of that I can't say. She is an important part of the machinery of the hotel that does not appear to the public.

—E. L. J.

The ball team was disbanded last Saturday. On Monday the members departed to their respective homes.

Our Cuisine.

IT is a well-known fact that the success of a hotel depends largely upon its cuisine. This applies to a resort house more perhaps than to a city hostelry. The "back of the house," as it is termed in hotel parlance, is often an unknown country to the guests, who know only that the delicious food which they daily enjoy is prepared for them somewhere. The Poland Spring House has long enjoyed a wide reputation for its table, and it is safe to say that at no other hotel, situated so far from the markets, can you find such a cuisine. The man who superintends this department is Mr. A. B. Ricker, who does all the buying, and it is a well-known fact among the marketmen at the Hub, that to show him anything but the best necessitates a loss of time, as he is one of the shrewdest buyers with whom they do business. Mr. Ricker is ably assisted by Mr. W. H. Shailer, who has held the important position of steward for so many years.

The kitchen force numbers eight male and five female cooks under the direction of Mr. J. W. Sparrow, the well-known *chef*. The pastry department is well cared for by Mrs. Cole and Miss Flynn, while Mrs. Walker has charge of the help's kitchen. The dessert room is under the charge of Miss Lizzie Duffy.

The amount of food consumed on a "hungry" day will be a surprise to the majority of the readers of THE HILL-TOP. The following figures are authentic: On one day in August the following food was consumed: 350 lbs. loin beef, 90 lbs. rib beef, 300 lbs. lamb, 200 lbs. duck, 150 lbs. chicken, 75 lbs. turkey, 100 lbs. fowl, 120 dozen eggs, 40 lbs. ham, 50 lbs. corned beef and 200 lbs. beef in the help's department, 16 gallons cream, 80 gallons milk, 205 lbs. fish, 35 lbs. lobster, 3 bushels berries, 18 lbs. coffee, 200 lbs. of sugar, while it took 3 barrels of flour to make the bread and pastry.

Are you surprised that people gain flesh while summering at Poland?

The Poland is in great demand these fine mornings.

Mr. H. T. Jordan, the popular carriage clerk at the Poland Spring House, has been tendered the position of cashier in the "New Raleigh" Hotel, Washington, D. C., and has accepted. Mr. Jordan has occupied his present position for three years, and during that time has won many friends by his faithfulness and gentlemanly conduct. Mr. Jordan is one of the editors of THE HILL-TOP and regular correspondent of the Boston and New York papers.

A Charming Occasion.

WHEN it comes to arranging a pretty party the Mansion House is always in the lead. The last and most enjoyable was a supper on Thursday evening tendered the Misses Nettie and Sadie Ricker by the guests at the Old Homestead. The Misses Ricker are deservedly popular on the hill and number countless friends won by their many kindnesses and courtesies. Wishing to show their appreciation of the many favors received at their hands the Mansion House guests, under the lead of Mrs Sondheim, arranged a little surprise for the young ladies.

Precisely at 10.30 P.M. the Poland Spring orchestra struck up a march, to the martial strain of which the invited guests proceeded to their seats at the handsomely decorated table. Mr. Gallagher, the popular head waiter, had put forth his best efforts in arranging the room and received many congratulations upon the results of his artistic work. The table was set up in the shape of a Maltese cross and was a mass of ferns and goldenrod. Clusters of sunflowers were suspended from the chandeliers while the fire-places were filled with vari-colored autumn leaves. The silken shades of the banquet lamps and candelabra lent a rosy-glow to the scene well adapted to the occasion.

When all were seated, fifty covers having been laid by the way, "Sherry" struck his bell and the pretty waiters filed in with the "bluepoints." The young ladies were in the costume of German frauleins, and well sustained the reputation of the Mansion House for having the most charming girls on the hill.

The various courses having been served to the satisfaction of all present, Mr. Gibson, of New York, proposed a toast to the Misses Ricker in a very witty speech, at the conclusion of which the glasses of sparkling ginger ale were drained amidst good wishes to the young ladies.

Among the ladies present the HILL-TOP representative noted the following: Miss Nettie Ricker, who wore a handsome pink gown; Miss Sadie Ricker, white and blue; Mrs. Soudheim, Mrs. E. P. Ricker, black silk and diamonds; Mrs. Keene; Mrs. Sturtevant, a handsome steel-colored silk; Miss Sondheim, blue and white; Mrs. Vonnah, steel-colored silk; Mrs. Macarthy, black; Mrs. Adler, grey trimmed with black silk and white Spanish lace; Miss Laury, lemon-colored silk; Mrs. Pulsifer, black silk; Mrs. Ernest Black, Mrs. Gibson, black satin; Mrs. Van-Zandt, black lace; Mrs. Taylor, Mrs. H. M. Ricker, Mrs. A. B. Ricker.

Much interest in shown by the guests in the road hearing at Poland Corner.

Maine's Famous Resort.

FOSTER'S *Democrat*. of Dover, N. H., has the following to say editorially in a recent issue about Poland. Editor Foster was here a part of the season and knows whereof he speaks.

The HILL-TOP cannot exaggerate the beauties and merits of Poland Spring nor the mammoth palace on the hill—the Poland Spring House. Anybody so disposed may ransack the continent and he can find no place superior to this. Nature did a great deal for the locality, but what it did not do the Ricker Brothers have done and are doing. Neither money, disposition, nor skill are lacking with them, and the results are becoming more and more apparent as the months and years roll on. What it will be by the time they are through can better be imagined than described. The water there is the purest and best beverage on earth and has given the place a world-wide fame. We have seen as good a bill of fare as the printed one on their table, but when it comes to the cookery and manner of service they " take the cake." The equal we have never seen, and we doubt if it can be found at any other place. All in all it is the cosiest home and at the same time the grandest and finest resort for a summer outing that the Great Republic affords. The visiting company is always the best and the associations the most cheerful, the entertainments the most pleasing and most enjoyable and the pleasure drives the most bracing and inspiring which the landscapes and· scenery of delightful New England can afford. Such, without distortion or exaggeration, is the fairly and properly, though briefly, described character of the Poland Spring resort down in Maine, as we believe everybody who has been there will freely verify.

Kind Words.

EVER since the publication of the first issue of the HILL-TOP congratulatory words have been received by us either through private letters or the columns of our ex-changes. Below we present a few of the clippings. We are pleased to note that our efforts have been sufficiently successful to receive so many and such complimentary words.

Foster's *Democrat* says the following in its editorial columns, under the caption " Exceed-ingly Fine " :

The HILL-TOP is the title of a paper to be published every Sunday morning by H. T. Jordan and W. D. Freeman at Poland Spring, devoted to the interests of that famous resort. The first issue appeared last Sunday, and it promises to fill the bill. The young man Freeman we know well. For a long time he was our Great Falls correspondent and we always found him reliable and true and he has the ability to do things in good shape.

The HILL-TOP is the name of a weekly paper published at the Poland Spring House. Published in the beautiful airy place and under the management of that bright, energetic, popular young man, Mr. H. T. Jordan, it cannot fail of being a very breezy paper. The *Sun* wishes the HILL-TOP good luck, and first of all a good list of subscribers who will all pay in advance.
—*Lewiston Sun.*

Poland Spring, Me., has a weekly newspaper with the unique title of the HILL-TOP. It is published every Sunday morning during the months of July, August, and September in the interests of Poland Spring and its visitors. The editors are Messrs. H. T. Jordan and W. D. Freeman, and they have evolved a unique publication and one that is certain to find much favor in the eyes of all patrons of Poland Spring, whether season or transient.
—*National Hotel Reporter.*

The HILL-TOP is the title of a bright little paper published every Sunday morning at the Poland Spring House, South Poland, Me. The editors are H. T. Jordan and W. Donald Freeman. —*Boston Home Journal.*

The latest comet in the ranks of journalism is the HILL-TOP, published at Poland Spring, Me., in the interests of guests of the famous Poland Spring House. The first issue appeared last Sunday morning. A glance at its attractive columns convinces us that its avowed purpose, " to present a bright, crisp, newsy publication, and one devoted exclusively to the interests of the friends of ' Fair Poland,' " will be fulfilled to the letter.
—*Saratoga News.*

The only addition to the list of vacation papers we know of in Maine this year is the HILL-TOP, hailing from Poland Spring. It is a twelve-page paper, well printed, and filled with local news. It is issued every Sunday morning, and it is a credit to the list of summer-resort journals. —*The Sea Breeze.*

Well Deserved.

IT is with much pleasure that we publish the following card of thanks, handed us by a committee of the guests. THE HILL-TOP editors have an exceedingly warm place in their hearts for Mr. Sawyer, who has been exceedingly kind to them in many ways. We think we voice the general sentiment when we say that the people on Ricker Hill never enjoyed better entertainments than have been offered them this season. To Mr. Sawyer more than to any other one man is the credit due and the thanks are well deserved.

It is our duty and privilege to tender warm thanks to Mr. J. B. Sawyer for the manner in which he has acquitted himself of the charge of the entertainments during the summer. With a fund none too large to satisfy the various tastes of the guests of the House, he has made the most of the means at his disposal, and the task of meeting the wishes of so many with a limited sum is no sinecure. COMMITTEE.

Miss A. M. Sturtevant, who has been enjoying a few weeks' outing at the Mount Kineo House, Moosehead Lake, returned Tuesday.

Poland As It Is.

SOME weeks since, whilst at the famous springs of Homburg, Germany, a friend said to me: "Go home and leave immediately after for the Poland Spring. It will do you more good than Karlsbad, Homburg or Aix les Bains; take my advice and you will be benefited and pleased." So I started for Southampton, took a record-breaker and sailed for my home in New York. Frequently during the trip I heard a quiet voice saying, "Go to Poland Spring," and after I returned the same refrain came back to me.

So, a week ago, I left New York and in eighteen hours after I exclaimed, here I am!

My friend will feel happy when he receives my letter, written this morning, letting him know of the pleasant surprise and the lovely time I am having at his dictation. The writer is somewhat a traveler for one who has just passed his sixty-fifth milestone in life's journey. I have made ninety voyages across the Atlantic and have passed trans-continent between New York and San Francisco eighteen times; have roamed through England, France, Norway, Germany, Italy, Russia, Switzerland, Japan, China, India and Egypt; have sailed upon the Hudson, Ohio, Mississippi, Missouri, St. Lawrence and the Rhine; have enjoyed the beauty of Lakes George, Champlain, Mennagio, Lucerne, Como and the inland sea of Japan; have steamed across the Atlantic, Pacific, Mediterranean, North and Black Seas time and again, but never have I beheld a lovelier scene than, sitting upon the spacious piazza of the Poland House this morning, I cast my glance around. Mountain, lake, valley, forest and stream are within the range of vision—ozone distilled from Heaven's own vault fills my lungs, and water pure and bubbling from the earth quenches my thirst. It is "the fair land of (another) Poland," where we can with health-quickening pulse, look up in the bright sunlight to Nature and to Nature's God and when night comes, sink to rest and sleep like a tired infant on its mother's bosom.

Oh, Haven of Repose! Oh, shelter for the tired! Oh, comfort for the weary! let me abide with you now, and in the coming years let me revisit you in all your loveliness—it is all I ask.

                                    HENRY C. JARRETT.

Prof. A. B. Ivins and wife of Philadelphia arrived on the 4th inst. on their yearly visit to Poland. Prof. Ivins was principal of the Quakers' High School, Philadelphia, for twenty-five years, and has held his present position as superintendent of all their schools in Philadelphia and vicinity for the past twelve years.

Concert Programme

For Sunday, September 16th:

1.	March.	Lachner.
2.	Overture—Maritana.	Wallace.
3.	Andante—Gavotte from Quartette.	Bazzini.
4.	a. Adagio—from Suite.	
	b. Gondoliera—Violin Solo.	Ries.
5.	Molto Lento.	Rubinstein.
6.	Canzonetto—String Quartette.	Victor Herbert.
7.	Intermezzo.	Vailo Delibes.
8.	Serenade.	Tilte.

Bubbles.

Elegant weather!

The people still linger.

Our small symphony orchestra has been broken by the departure of three of the members.

The lights on Mount Washington could be easily seen from the verandas Wednesday evening.

Powers, our star catcher, who was severely injured in the last Rockland-Poland Spring game, is able to leave his room now, although his side is still very lame.

The Right Rev. Bishop Sessums of Louisiana, assisted by the Rev. Mr. Blanchard, of Philadelphia, conducted the Sunday services in Music Hall, last week.

The little "Poland" has done good service thus far this season, but opportunity is still offered you to enjoy that most delightful ride through Middle and Upper Range Lake.

Mr. and Mrs. Jacob Moise, accompanied by Misses C. R. and J. A. Moise, of Boston, left the 10th. Mr. Moise is of the firm of Leopold Moise & Co., large men's furnishers of the Hub.

Hon. Stanley T. Pullen and wife, of Portland, are here for a brief visit. Mr. Pullen is a prominent lawyer and well known in political circles of the State. He was formerly editor of the Portland Press.

Mr. and Mrs. Clark H. Taylor, Jr., Miss Grace Taylor and Miss Doris Taylor and nurse arrived Monday. Mr. Taylor is the business manager of the Boston Globe, and one of the best known successful newspaper men in the Eastern States.

. The Right Reverend Bishop Sessums, of Louisiana, arrived on the 7th inst., accompanied by his charming wife and baby daughter. The Bishop, although a young man comparatively speaking, is known as one of the leading pulpit speakers in the South.

Bubbles.

Mrs. and Miss Brow of Fall River, Mass., are among the recent additions to Poland society.

Mr. and Mrs. A. L. Coe of Chicago are here for an extended visit to the Fountain of Health. Mr. Coe is one of the proprietors of the palatial Auditorium Hotel, same city.

The work sent out from the Poland Spring photograph gallery is comparable with the very best done in the large cities. Mr. Seaver should feel proud of his results.

THE HILL-TOP is not such a "baby" newspaper after all, is it? Hasn't it grown and kept up with the times? Can you show us a better individual hotel paper published than the HILL-TOP?

Mrs. G. W. Coleman and Mrs. Dr. Peterson left the Poland Spring House last Tuesday morning early on a trip through Canada, visiting Montreal and Quebec especially. They are expected back to-morrow.

Mr. P. B. Wade, of St. Louis, is a recent addition to the younger set at the big house. Mr. Wade has just returned from an extended tour in the Orient, where he made a long stop in Turkey, studying the manners and customs of the natives.

The total house count of the Poland Spring House last season was 25,682; the average per day for the whole season, 208. The following cities furnished the number set beside their names: New York, 496; Boston, 510; Philadelphia, 120; Washington, 40; Chicago, 32.

Mrs. M. C. Williamson and son Richard, have returned to their home in Philadelphia. Mrs. W. arrived the first of July intending to remain only a few weeks, but the surroundings were so conducive to good health and enjoyment that they have prolonged their visit by a month or more.

Mr. Eben Jordan, of the famous Jordan-Marsh firm of Boston, was expected to arrive home from Europe on the steamer La Champagne yesterday. John Tukeson, who has been assistant mail clerk here during Mr. Jordan's absence, left Thursday to resume his duties as butler in Mr. Jordan's household.

Professor Albert Harkness, of Brown University, who has made such a name as an authority on all Latin subjects and who is the author of several of our leading Latin text-books, is enjoying the benefits received by imbibing of the famous Poland water, at the Poland Spring House.

Mr. and Mrs. Lincoln Grant, of Berkshire, Mass., are come to the fount of life to imbibe of its health-giving flow.

Walter Raymond and his accomplished wife were here over Sunday. Mr. Raymond is the senior member of the firm of Raymond & Whitcomb, excursionists, Boston, and the proprietor of two of the finest hotels in the West, viz., the Raymond, East Pasadena, Cal., and the Colorado, Glenwood Springs, Col.

One of the most exciting pool matches played on the Hill this season was that on Monday afternoon between Mr. Lincoln Grant of Brookline, Mass., and Mr. Boucher, the assistant barber. The match was for one hundred points, and it was anybody's game until the last ball was pocketed. Mr. Grant won finally by a score of 100 balls to Mr. Boucher's 98.

Amateur photography has taken up the attention of not a few enthusiasts this season. Since the small dark rooms, for the use of the guests, have been finished, an impetus seems to have been given and now it is no uncommon sight to see parties of a half dozen or more starting out through the country, all with cameras in their hands. The views to be had in this vicinity are varied and most beautiful and afford plenty of material to work upon.

Arrivals

FOR WEEK ENDING SEPTEMBER 14.

POLAND SPRING HOUSE.

Allen, Mr. and Mrs. F. E.,	Portland.
Burnhart, Mr. and Mrs. A. E.,	Chicago.
Burnhart, Miss,	Chicago.
Bindel, Wm.,	Boston.
Bergen, Mr. and Mrs. L. L.,	Brooklyn.
Bergen, Miss E. L.,	Brooklyn.
Bonney, A. P.,	Boston.
Bartow, H. T.,	Boston.
Borden, Mr. and Mrs. P. D.,	Fall River, Mass.
Brown, Miss A. P.,	Boston.
Brown, Miss R. W.,	Boston.
Beals, W. B.,	Turner.
Bartley, Francis,	Reading.
Browning, Mr. and Mrs. W. C.,	New York.
Cushing, Miss M. W.,	Newburyport.
Cutler, C. R. and wife,	Boston.
Chadbourne, Jas. H.,	Wilmington, N. C.
Chadbourne, Mrs. Jas. H.,	Wilmington, N. C.
Corey, Mr. and Mrs. H. D.,	Newton, Mass.
Campbell, Wm. A.,	Wilson Springs.
Chandler, Seth,	Lewiston.
Carpenter, F. W.,	Providence.
Cudlipp, G. H.,	New York.
Demmon, Mr. and Mrs. R. E.,	Boston.
Fuller, Mr. and Mrs. C. S.,	Lynn.
Ford, Mr. and Mrs. W. F.,	Boston.
Farrington, C. F.,	Boston.
Grant, Mr. and Mrs. Lincoln,	Berkshire.
Hill, Mr. and Mrs. W. K.,	Portsmouth.
Hill, Master S.,	Portsmouth.
Harwood, Mr. and Mrs. S.,	Newton.
Haynes, J. C.,	Boston.
Heaton, Mr. and Mrs. W. W.,	New York.
Howes, Mrs. F. M.,	Somerville.
Howes, Miss Grace C.,	Somerville.
Hotchkiss, Miss E. S.,	New Haven.
Hotchkiss, Miss S. V.,	New Haven.
Jarrett, H. C.,	New York.
Jordan, E. C.,	Portland.
Keay, C. N.,	Malden, Mass.
Lewis, Miss Clara,	Boston.
Lincoln, Frank,	New York.
Langley, I. C.,	Boston.
Moses, Jno.,	Trenton.
Morse, J. C.,	Boston.
Moat, Mr. and Mrs. W. J.,	Portsmouth.
Moat, C. P.,	Portsmouth.
McGrath, Miss W. B.,	Brooklyn.
Milliken, Mr. and Mrs. W. H.,	Portland.
Nealand, Mr. and Mrs. D. A.,	Boston.
Newell, W. H.,	Lewiston.
Osgood, Mrs. G. L.,	Boston.
Pollard, S. S.,	Boston.
Pullen, S. T. and wife,	Portland.
Pinkham, Mr. and Mrs. C. H.,	Lynn.
Rollins, E. W.,	Boston.
Rollins, Ashton,	Boston.
Raymond, Mr. and Mrs. Walter,	Boston.
Rionda, Mr. and Mrs. M.,	New York.
Rogers, Mr. and Mrs. A. S.,	Salem.
Rogers, Miss R.,	Salem.
Rogers, Miss A. C.,	Salem.
Rogers, Miss T. W.,	Salem.
Squire, Mr. and Mrs. F. F.,	Boston.
Sessums, Rt. Rev. Bishop,	Louisiana.
Sessums, Mrs.,	Louisiana.
Simpson, Mr. and Mrs. G. F.,	Boston.
Sias, Miss Bertha,	Boston.
Sawyer, C. C.,	Portland.
Savage, A. R.,	Auburn.
Said, W. H.,	Chicago.
Staples, G. S.,	Portland.
Taylor, Mr. and Mrs. Chas. H., Jr.,	Boston.
Taylor, Miss Grace,	Boston.
Taylor, Miss Doris,	Boston.
Tooker, Miss A.,	New York.
Taylor, Mr. and Mrs. W. S.,	Philadelphia.
Townsend, Mrs. C. H.,	New Haven.
Wood, Henry,	Philadelphia.
Willes, G. D.,	Trenton.
Weld, B. C.,	Boston.
Wade, R. B.,	St. Louis.
Wing, Geo. C.,	Auburn.
Watson, W. A.,	New York.
Wakefield, Seth D.,	Lewiston.
Ziegler, Mrs. M. E.,	New York.
Ziegler, Miss,	New York.

MANSION HOUSE.

Beacham, R. H. and wife,	Portsmouth, N. H.
Bucknam, J. M.,	Yarmouth.
Dobbins, Horace,	Philadelphia.
Dobbins, Horace,	Philadelphia.
Ferguson, Mrs. R.,	Boston.
Foster, Chas.,	Portland.
Foster, Chas.;	Portland.
Hathorne, F. M.,	West Woolwich.
Hathorne, S. E.,	West Woolwich.
Haskall, Roscoe G.,	North Yarmouth.
Knight, Mrs. E. M.,	Boston.
Knight, Miss,	Boston.
Kelley, Miss M. H.,	Portland.
Lewis, Eva C.,	Portland.
Lewis, Mrs. Fred R.,	Portland.
Miller, Mrs. David,	Yarmouth.
Phillibrick, H. F.,	Watertown, Mass.
Perkins, J. C. and wife,	Portland.
Robinson, Mrs.,	Boston.
Sturtevant, Abbie M.,	Kineo.
Thompson, Mrs. J. A.,	Bath.
Taylor, J. G.,	Tompkinville, S. I.
Vonnah, R. W.,	Philadelphia.
Watson, Miss J.,	New York.
Whitney, P. H. and wife,	Providence.

═ WHY ═
Poland Spring Leads Them All.

A 19th Century Triumph

THE POLAND SPRING HOUSE 1893-4

MERIT, POPULARITY, LARGE SALES,

AND THE FACT THAT

POLAND WATER

Was the FIRST SOLVENT AND ELIMINATOR OF URIC ACID
CALCULI from the BLADDER AND KIDNEYS KNOWN TO
THE WORLD; also the ONLY WATER EXHIBITED
(notwithstanding the hundreds competing) at

CHICAGO'S WORLD'S EXPOSITION

To receive a Medal and Diploma for "PURITY AND
GREAT MEDICINAL POWER," prove
conclusively that

POLAND WATER LEADS THE WORLD.

THE ACCOMPANYING ILLUSTRATIONS ARE MOST SUBSTANTIAL AND
CONVINCING PROOF OF THE ABOVE ASSERTIONS.

SAPIENTIA DONUM DEI

OFFICES:

BOSTON:	NEW YORK:	PHILADELPHIA:	CHICAGO:
175 Devonshire Street.	3 Park Place.	Chestnut and 13th Streets.	Cor. Michigan Ave. and Randolph St.

HIRAM RICKER & SONS, Proprietors.

THE HILL-TOP.
POLAND SPRING

SUNDAY MORNING, JUNE 30, 1895.

The Maine State Building.

THE beginning of the seventh decade of the present century was an epoch-marking period. In 1860 one of the grandest characters in American history appeared suddenly above the horizon, and illumined the world by his brilliancy during its most perilous times.

It was in 1860 the murmurings of the coming great struggle began to reverberate through the land, and it was in this same year that the increasing knowledge of the wonderful properties of the waters of Poland Spring began to crystallize, and make its first appearance in the shape of a covering to protect it from the dust of the air, the leaves of the forest, and the insects and creeping things of the earth.

That Hiram Ricker had for some time foreseen the possibilities of this favored spot, is very fully demonstrated by subsequent events, and by his repeated statements at the time and afterwards.

That his fondest dreams have been realized must indeed be true, for to-day what was formerly a woodland spring, a farm on a hillside, and a set of farm buildings, partly hotel, is now one of the grandest resorts for the health, the comfort, and the pleasure-seeker of the world.

The centennial year of our independence saw the erection of the first hotel upon the crest of the hill, and the Columbian anniversary witnessed the consummation of the plan in the completion of the present structure.

The Columbian Exhibition at Chicago brought

together in one unit, as it were, the consensus of American ideas, in the advancement of Art, Science, Engineering, Literature, Mechanics, and permitted the free exchange of ideas to the great advantage of all, from the most skilled to the most ignorant.

Each state contributed from its store, its best, and aside from the extensive display of its treasures, erected a building as a home, a headquarters for its people who had traveled far to witness the great congress of the world's wealth.

Maine, one of the oldest, and the picket guard of the easternmost border, not to be outdone by its bigger and wealthier brothers in alliance, chiseled and hewed in its quarries and forests, and from its inexhaustible material fashioned a building at once a credit to and the pride of its sons. After this grand exhibition, the question of what should be done with its now historic building came up. It was a much-discussed question until, at length, it was decided to resign its future fate to the care of the Rickers of Poland.

At once the excellent decision met with universal approval. No fitter place could have been selected than crowning the summit of this noble eminence where it could look down upon its forests of pine, its lakes of crystal, its hillsides dotted with the evidences of prosperity; and in the keeping of men, sons of Maine, and sons of sons of Maine, who had already demonstrated their marked ability to build up, and to improve, and not destroy.

The task was a gigantic one; but nineteen days remaining in which to remove the building from the park in Chicago when the labor commenced, with seven more to restore the ground to its original condition.

The railroad track near had already been ordered up, but the Park Commissioners kindly granted an extension of time, and within the allowance, the entire fabric was removed and

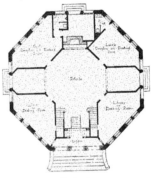

FIRST FLOOR PLAN.
• MAINE · STATE · BUILDING •
Pond · Smith, Ar. .

placed upon the sixteen cars of the Grand Trunk Railway, and safely removed to Poland.

From Chicago to Gorham, the time made by the special train was three days.

The method of removing the building was systematic in the extreme, each course of masonry being designated by letter, and each stone numbered.

Nothing was discarded; every floor-timber and window-frame, even every slate and tile,

ith uni-
d have
of this
n upon
its hill.
sperity;
ive, and
demon-
, and to

nineteen
building
or com-
ground]

It been
kindly
ain the
vel and

whether whole or broken, was loaded upon the train. Forty tons of slate, of the finest quality, were used in its construction. The granite used was furnished by separate firms and quarries, the first course coming from W. A. Roberts and Alfred Goodwin, Biddeford; the second and third from Col. I. S. Bangs, Waterville, the Dodlin Granite Company of Norridgewock; the fourth to the

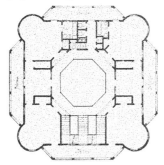

Second · Floor · Plan a
or
· MAINE · STATE · BUILDING ·
· Poland · Spring · Me·

seventh from Hon. E. B. Mallett, Freeport; the eighth to the ninth, Hallowell Granite Co.; the tenth course and half the arch stones, Bodwell Granite Co., Rockland; the eleventh and remainder of arch stones from Hurricane Island Granite Co., Rockland; the granite steps and buttresses from Payson Tucker, Esq., Maine and New Hampshire Granite Co., Portland; the red polished columns and caps from the Maine Red Granite Co., Red Beach, Me.; the black polished columns and caps, the Pleasant River Granite Co., Addison; and the four pieces dark grey granite surmounting the caps of polished columns, were from the Jewell Granite Co., of Bangor.

The building cost the State of Maine $18,000, and as it is now placed stands 87 feet high and is 65 feet in diameter, being octagonal in form.

Outside, the building remains as originally constructed, except four dormer windows between the towers and four skylights where there was formerly but one.

The lower floor partitions have undergone slight changes, as also has the second.

The third floor has been entirely finished, carrying the rotunda one story higher, crowning it with a very elaborate dome light.

Great attention has been paid to fire-proofing, and the insurance inspector pronounced it the nearest fire-proof of any wooden building he ever saw.

There was a very considerable library contained in the building, which was, together with the registers, also voted by the Legislature to the Messrs. Ricker, to be permanently under their charge.

The labor of rebuilding being practically finished, the ceremony of dedication is assigned for Monday, July 1st, and the programme for the same has been very carefully and elaborately planned.

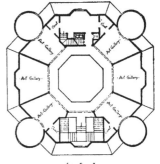

Third · Floor · Plan ·
or·
· MAINE · STATE · BUILDING ·
Poland Spring Me

It includes many noted men among its prominent features, among whom are the Governors of Maine and Massachusetts, and Senators Hale and Frye.

The music will be under the direction of Daniel Kuntz, from the Boston Symphony Orchestra.

Who will be the first golfer on Poland Hill?

Guests visiting Lewiston or Portland will do well to consult the advertising columns, as they represent the best in both places.

Trunk

ade by

was sys-
masonry
e num-

timber
ad tile.

FRANK CARLOS GRiFFiTH, } EDITORS.
NETTiE M. RiCKER,

PUBLISHED EVERY SUNDAY MORNING DURING THE MONTHS
OF JULY, AUGUST AND SEPTEMBER, IN THE INTERESTS OF

POLAND SPRiNG AND ITS ViSiTORS.

All contributions relative to the guests of Poland Spring will
be thankfully received.
To insure publication, all communications should reach the
editors not later than Wednesday preceding day of issue.
All parties desiring rates for advertising in the HILL-TOP
should write the editors for same.
The subscription price of the HILL-TOP is $1.00 for the
season, post-paid. Single copies will be mailed at 10c. each.
Address,
    EDITORS "HiLL-TOP,"
        Poland Spring House,
            South Poland, Maine.

PRINTED AT JOURNAL OFFICE, LEWISTON.

Sunday, June 30, 1895.

Editorial.

TO all the world, greeting. This is to announce our arrival at the first annual mile-
post. We are a year old to-day, but we do
not feel any older; in fact, we hope to enjoy all
the sports of youth just as much this season as
last, and enter with as keen a zest into the
amusements of young or old with an appetite
sharpened by long abstention from Poland water
and Poland air.

We hope the same pleasant faces which
beamed before us last season and looked with
compassion upon our infantile efforts to entertain, will find as much to amuse, and as little to
censure, even if we are getting to be a big boy
now.

Our greeting is to the entire world, and the
expression is advisedly made use of; not that
we see visions of a circulation covering the wilds
of Africa, the steppes of Russia, the jungles of
India, as well as the advanced civilization of
Europe and America, but that we see, not visions,
but the reality of the whole world's representatives coming to Poland, and, as the Mountain
could not go to Mahomet, so Mahomet must perforce come to the Mountain.

The grains of sand could be taken to the
Prophet; the branches of the denuded trees of
Birnam could be carried to Dunsinane, and the
water of Poland transported to the Pyramids,
but for all that, the juggling of terms avails not,
and so the mountain, and the wood, and the
eternal and everlasting fountain remain where
they were placed by the Almighty, and, more
potent than kings, command and are obeyed.

However, seriousness is not our forte, but
rather to cause the lines to tend upward, to bring
the merry twinkle into the eye, when you look
into our face, and to find in us naught that is
disagreeable, cynical, or solemn.

Should we accidentally step upon a tender
spot, accept our apologies in advance, for it will
be useless sending challenges to mortal combat,
as the code duello has been thrown into the waste-
basket, and our income does not permit the employment of a fighting editor.

Now then, one and all, the button has been
pressed, the electric current has flashed along
the wire, the big wheels have revolved, and the
Outing Season of 1895 is a *fin de siecle* fact, so
enjoy it while it lasts and subscribe for THE
HiLL-TOP.

Miss Kate Furbish of Brunswick, Me , has
returned to Poland Spring this season to resume her work on the Flora of this region.
The plants which she procured and mounted
for the Messrs. Ricker in '93, numbering five
hundred and sixty-three specimens, will be on
exhibition at her botanical studio, as soon as it
can be put in readiness for occupying. Miss
Furbish has busied herself for many years in
painting the Flora of the State, and she is
probably the oldest *amateur* botanist in the
field. Her painted specimens number fifteen
hundred, some of which she has with her, and
she will be happy to show them to all guests
who are interested either in botany or water-
colors.

Bubbles.

Dirigo.

Haying.

Do you like butter?

Buttercups and daisies.

The income tax was sat on.

He loves me, he loves me not.

All doubt is ended. Poland is big enough for "Goff." Ili Caddie.

Don't tell secrets near the scales in the office. They will give you a weigh.

Mrs. Morgan L. Smith was in time for the annual opening, as usual. Welcome.

Mr. Charles E. Lord, a former guest, and wife, of Boston, are at the Mansion House.

Mrs. Henry S. Taylor and charming daughters from lovely Baltimore are once more welcomed.

Eleven years is R. M. Field's record. Mrs. Field also could not forego the pleasure, even for a European trip. Wise conclusion.

There's Mr. and Mrs. Sawyer. If I recollect right, last season it was Mr. J. B. Sawyer and Miss Abbie Sturtevant. Congratulations.

Guests will find themselves well repaid in accepting the standing invitation printed elsewhere, of Mr. James S. Sanborn to visit his place.

The HILL-TOP is pleased to see so many familiar faces. There is Mrs. S. S. Hoffman, who has exchanged the Murray Hill for the Poland Hill.

Dr. E. J. Lee, wife and family, the three Misses Lee, and Charles S. Lee from Philadelphia, the hottest city in America in summer, are among the welcome new-comers.

Mrs. William James Todd and Mrs. S. B. Hubbard are faces that are familiar to us as well. The Misses Todd should not be forgotten. We should feel lonely were all the faces new ones.

Through the kindness of Mr. H. A. Spaulding, we received the famous Court Card issued by Tiffany. It was through Mr. Spaulding's remarkable efforts the issuing of such a card was made possible.

It was a flying visit but one which they enjoyed, made by the Hon. J. Don Cameron, the famous senator from Pennsylvania, with his charming wife. They are hoping, however, to return. Let us hope so.

"La Gaiete."

THE first dinner-party of the season at the Poland Spring House was that given to the ladies of "La Gaiete," a club of Lewiston and Auburn young people, on Monday, the 17th.

The dinner was given by the gentlemen of the club and proved to be very swagger.

Covers were laid for 36 and the table was placed in the form of a Maltese cross and artistically decorated with flowers, the whole being arranged by Mr. Wareham. The menus were artistically and elaborately prepared, and the whole affair was very successful on all sides. Come again.

Twin City Literary Union.

AN event long to be remembered by the participants occurred on Tuesday, June 18th, when the Twin City Literary Union, comprising 16 clubs, came over from Lewiston and Auburn and took possession of the Poland Spring House.

There were 263 ladies and gentlemen comprising the party. It was 2 o'clock when they entered the dining-room and sat down to the banquet of good things set before them.

After doing full justice to the viands, speeches were in order, and Mrs. Adeline Small, the president, and Mrs. Charles Cushman, toastmistress, respectively made short addresses.

They were followed by Mrs. J. B. Coyle and Mrs. B. M. Osgood of Portland, Mrs. Oliver Newman and Mrs. W. H. Newell of Lewiston, and Mrs. William Hayes of Auburn.

The flow of eloquence was brought to a close by some very brilliant and graceful language from our own Hon. William P. Frye, who gave the ladies some very sensible and very pertinent advice on the subject of moulding the character and mind of the future man.

The company then adjourned to the Music Hall, where they were entertained with a musicale, of which the following is the brief programme:

Piano Solo. Elizabeth Robinson.
Recitation—"The Little Hero." Mary Raynes Smith.
Song. Florence Stinchfield.
Piano Solo. Lillian Taylor.

Commissioner Roosevelt recently delivered a lecture on Insomnia as an Antidote for Coma, but only six roundsmen thought it attractive enough to attend.

You need a hustling advance agent, Mr. Commissioner.

Geo. Francis Train please write.

A New Cure.

THE remarkable efficacy of Poland water has had a new illustration recently. Mr. H. A. Spaulding came to Poland Spring the 10th of June with his left hand very badly swollen and poisoned by ivy. He started in to drink the water, and incidentally bathed the hand well with it. On the way back from the Spring he sat down on one of the benches, and observed a certain white deposit on the fingers. The feeling appeared also to be a very grateful one, and he returned to the Spring and gave the member a thorough bath in Poland water. This he has repeated during the week, until the swelling has entirely disappeared, and the hand is fast approaching a healthy condition.

In reply to the remark that any pure water would accomplish as much, Mr. Spaulding replies that he knows better for he gave it a thorough trial before using the Poland water.

Here is a visible example of the cleansing properties of this water on the system.

A commonplace life, we say, and we sigh;
  But why should we sigh as we say?
The commonplace sun in the commonplace sky,
  Makes up the commonplace day;
The moon and the stars are commonplace things
  And the flower that blooms, and the bird that sings;
But dark were the world and sad our lot
  If the flowers failed and the sun shone not;
And God who studies each separate soul
  Out of commonplace lives makes his beautiful whole.

Names of Our Several Different Drives and their Round Trip Distance.

	MILES.
Around Middle Lake,	5 1-2
Lower Lake,	7
Sabbath Day Lake,	11
Trip Lake,	13
Lake and Gloucester Shakers,	9 1-2
Lake and Poland Shakers,	7 1-2
Raymond Woods and Shakers,	8
Lower Gloucester,	13
Oak Hill and Lake,	7 1-2
Hotel Wilson and Sturgis Mill,	11
Hotel Wilson and Oak Hill,	14
Upper and Middle Lake,	12
Sabbath Day Lake and Peterson's Woods,	13
New Gloucester and Upper Corner,	12
Harris Hill, Minot Corner, Empire Road,	12
Gray Corner and Gloucester Hill,	22
Black Cat, Tinney Hill, Hotel Wilson,	15
To Mechanic Falls,	13
Lewiston and Auburn,	20
Lake Auburn,	26
Lake Auburn via Lewiston,	30

Why not have a Winter Carnival with an Ice Palace on the lake? For interior decoration Poland water would make a good frieze.

A Poland Tragedy.

See if your name is concealed in this story.

OVER by the village a little smithy stands, in one corner of a field, under the Lee of a great Elm. The brawny workman is as brown and dark as any coal man. He has a daughter whose suitor is, or rather was, a barber by trade, whose father, by name Williams, was a sergeant in the town militia; but Williams' son began as a cook, yet, being fond of a toddy now and then, tried the old Mother Hubbard game of going to the cupboard, too often, thinking that to be tight is but a petty sin.

But at length the blacksmith's pretty daughter caught him, and when he denied the act, she replied, "I saw yer;" and the poor fellow committed suicide and went to that bourne from which no traveller returns.

The young lady soon had plenty more followers, among whom was a tailor and a carpenter. The former found little favor for he was too dictatorial, and soon discovered that to be too curt is to be lost, but the latter, with higher aims, barely saved his bacon by patterning after better models.

One day, returning from a codding trip at Old Orchard, he met the little walker in the road and proposed; and so well he pleaded, he soon placed her affections *hors du combat*, and the troth was plighted, and as a token of the occasion, he presented her with a dainty green leaf.

And so they were married.

The Carafes at the News Stand were made from a design by Miss Nettie M. Ricker, and illustrate first the triangular shape of the Spring, and the trade-mark of Hiram Ricker & Sons. On the three sides respectively are the Poland Spring House, the Mansion House, and the Spring House, and on the top of these appear the head of the ox whose cute first called attention to the Spring. They make a choice souvenir.

Subscriptions may be left at the news stand.

Mr. Hazen B. Goodrich's kindly face is often seen across the green cloth in the billiard room. He is an expert.

Mr. Daniel J. Griffith, his mother and two sisters, from New York, are first-time visitors. Last summer they visited Alaska.

North Attleboro, Mass., has sent most delightful summer companions in the persons of Mrs. H. H. Curtis and her charming daughters, Fannie and Blanche, Mr. T. I. Smith, and Mr. and Mrs. Codding.

Bubbles.

The shirt waist has come to stays.

A fine lot of table girls, Mr. Julius.

Ladies beware of the trick chair in the office.

Bruno is chairman of the reception committee.

The Tiffany Court Card may be seen at the news stand.

Notman of Boston has the studio this year. Here's success.

The tennis court has been laid out and is already in demand.

There are twenty-seven names of guests in the "Poland Tragedy."

The evergreen decorations by Mr. Gallagher have been much admired.

Subscriptions for the HILL-TOP may be left at the news counter. The more the merrier.

We have a charming little story for an early issue, written by William Redmund, the celebrated actor.

Indefatigable energy will paint a house even in a rain. Bad weather has no terrors with a Ricker at the helm.

Mr. William Q. Titus (of the law firm of Titus & Dowling, Mr. B. F. Keith's New York attorneys), is located for the season here with Mrs. Titus. They have been tendered the use of Mr. Keith's horses, which are here awaiting the arrival of Mr. and Mrs. Keith with friends.

The current fad seems to be the vaudeville entertainment. The conventional theatrical show has apparently lost a good portion of its former hold upon the public at large, and its place has been usurped by the lighter and far more welcome variety performance. It is an unquestionable fact that Mr. B. F. Keith, the originator of the delightfully novel idea of a continuous performance, has been the chief factor in this revolution of American theatricals. His new play-house in Boston has been described, not inaptly, as "a nineteenth century palace of vaudeville," while his New York and Philadelphia vaudeville theatres are recognized as the swell theatrical houses of those big cities. In each house, the cream of the variety profession appear weekly, and as the bill is constantly changed, there is a succession of bright, agreeable, and new entertainments.

Tid-Bits.

The Russian Minister of Foreign Affairs expresses surprise that the French Minister of Foreign Affairs had referred to the Russian Minister of Foreign Affairs' Alliance with the French Minister of Foreign Affairs; when the Russian Minister of Foreign Affairs had never had any written alliance with the French Minister of Foreign Affairs. Poor little Japan! Then it was all a bluff? Wow!

Sharpen the snickersnee.

They are talking of employing women on street cars. Calvé and de Lussan have proved themselves good Carmen.

Come, Mme. Modjeska, we haven't any Warsaw or Cracow just now, but what's the matter with *this* Poland, and you may play in our yard all you like.

What a comfortable, cool, and exhilarating sight those light outing suits are, which several of the gentlemen are donning. They take ten years off each man's life.

Cuba is getting very sassy to that little boy over in Spain.

Take one of your size, Cube.

STAGES.

DEPART.

	M. H.	P. S. H.
For Portland and Boston,	6.25 A.M.	6.30 A.M.
Lewiston and Farmington,	8.25 A.M.	8.30 A.M.
Portland and Boston,	9.25 A.M.	9.30 A.M.
Lewiston and Bar Harbor,	10.25 A.M.	10.30 A.M.
Lewiston and Bangor,	12.45 P.M.	1 P.M.
Portland and Boston,	3.25 P.M.	3.30 P.M.

ARRIVE.

	P. S. H.	M. H.
From the West,	10.30 A.M.	10.35 A.M.
From the East,	1.00 P.M.	1.05 P.M.
From the West,	3.30 P.M.	3.35 P.M.
From the West,	7.30 P.M.	7.35 P.M.

MAILS.

CLOSE.

Poland Spring House.	Mansion House.
5.45 A.M.	6 A.M.
8.45 A.M.	9 A.M.
2.45 P.M.	3 P.M.

ARRIVE.

10 A.M.	9.30 A.M.
1.30 P.M.	1 P.M.
4.30 P.M.	4 P.M.
8 P.M.	7.45 P.M.

Hours of Meals.

	Week Days.	Sundays.
Breakfast,	7 A.M. to 9 A.M.	8 A.M. to 10 A.M.
Dinner,	1 P.M. to 2.30 P.M.	1.30 P.M.
Supper,	6 P.M. to 8 P.M.	6 P.M.

Arrivals.

POLAND SPRING HOUSE.

Bourne, George T. and wife,	New York.
Bourne, Miss,	New York.
Barbour, E. D. and wife,	Boston.
Barbour, Mrs. M. E.,	Boston.
Brown, William T.,	Chicago.
Bechstein, F. and wife,	New York.
Bayley, C. H.,	Boston.
Bullingame, Mrs. E. H.,	Providence.
Brown, O.,	Boston.
Bacon, F. W.,	Boston.
Bishop. Mrs. R. R.,	Newton.
Bernet, E. T. and wife,	Milwaukee.
Coleman, G. W. and wife,	Boston.
Cook, Charles Sumner,	Portland.
Coyle, Mrs. J. B.,	Portland.
Cumming, R. L. and wife,	England.
Curtis, Mrs. H. H.,	North Attleboro.
Curtis, Miss Fannie,	North Attleboro.
Curtis, Miss Blanche,	North Attleboro.
Codding, A. and wife,	North Attleboro.
Cameron, J. Don and wife,	Washington.
Colby, Mrs. M. D.,	Brooklyn.
Cumming, M. S.,	Lewiston.
Carpenter, F. W.,	Providence.
Carpenter, Miss Julia,	Providence.
Corning, J.,	New York.
Corning, Miss,	New York.
Crockett, R. W.,	Lewiston.
Driscoll, J. T.,	Boston.
Eames, Edward E. and wife,	New York.
Eames, Miss M. C.,	New York.
Field, R. M. and wife,	Boston.
Fargo, Charles and wife,	Chicago.
Fargo, Miss,	Chicago.
Griffith, Mrs. G.,	New York.
Griffith, Miss M. E.,	New York.
Griffith, Miss S. D.,	New York.
Griffith, Daniel J.,	New York.
Greenleaf, J. A.,	Auburn.
Glidden, Elmer R.,	Boston.
Gunnison, H. F. and wife,	Brooklyn.
Hoffman, Mrs. S. S.,	New York.
Horton, C. B.,	Boston.
Hobart, N. and wife,	New York.
Hubbard, Mrs. S. B.,	Jacksonville.
Hawes, Mrs. S. F.,	Boston.
Hayden, C. F.,	Boston.
Kimball. Mr. and Mrs.,	Lewiston.
Kesmeen, George F.,	Boston.
Keegan, D. W.,	New York.
Little, Mrs. Amos R.,	Philadelphia.
Lee, Dr. E. J. and wife,	Philadelphia.
Lee, Constance G.,	Philadelphia.
Lee, Mildred W.,	Philadelphia.
Lee, Florence F.,	Philadelphia.
Lee, Charles S.,	Philadelphia.
Lindsey, W. M.,	New York.
Mathews, Mrs. E. W.,	Philadelphia.
Mathews, Louis J.,	Philadelphia.
Merrill, J. F. and wife,	Brooklyn.
Marshall, Miss,	York, Me.
Ness, W. T. and wife,	Boston.
Osborn, Charles J.,	New York.
Paul, M. C. and wife,	Philadelphia.
Paul, Miss,	Philadelphia.
Pettee, Mrs. J. A.,	New York.
Peckham, Miss,	Providence.
Patten, William T. and wife,	New York.

Patten, Miss,	New York.
Patten, Miss Grace,	New York.
Rogers, Spencer and wife,	Portland.
Royce, Miss M. C.,	New York.
Ricker, Mr. and Mrs.,	Lewiston.
Read, Robert L.,	Cincinnati.
Rothwell, Mrs. James,	Brookline.
Spaulding, H. A. and wife,	New York.
Spaulding. Miss M.,	New York.
Sawyer, J. D. and wife,	Pittsburgh.
Smith, Mrs. Morgan L.,	New York.
Shipman, Henry and wife,	New York.
Smith, Charles and wife,	Philadelphia.
Sargent, F. W.,	Newton.
Sammons, C. E.,	Boston.
Sutories, Edward and wife,	New York.
Smith, T. I.,	North Attleboro.
Staples, H. M. and wife,	Taunton.
Staples, A. C.,	Taunton.
Slee, Miss,	Baltimore.
Shurtleff, Arthur W., M.D ,	Lewiston.
Titus, William Q. and wife,	New York.
Todd, Mrs. William James,	New York.
Todd, Rita L.,	New York.
Todd, M. Blanche,	New York.
Taylor, Mrs. Henry S.,	Baltimore.
Taylor, Charlotte F.,	Baltimore.
Taylor, Miss,	Baltimore.
Taylor, Miss M. S.,	Baltimore.
Van Ness, Edward and wife,	New York.
Williamson. A. S.,	Chicago.
Walker, William L. and wife,	Taunton.
Williams, Lewis and wife,	Taunton.
Williams, Miss H. S.,	Taunton.
Witham, C. L.,	Lewiston.
Whitman, James H.,	Boston.
Whitman, Allan H.,	Boston.
Walsh, S. H.,	Boston.

MANSION HOUSE.

Arthur, Miss Nathalie,	Detroit.
Arthur, Miss Muriel,	Detroit.
Amermen, N. and wife,	New York.
Brown, H. B.,	London.
Culley, E. J.,	Boston.
De Wint, Mrs. M. E.,	New York.
Dungan, Charles W.,	New York.
Fassett, E. S. and wife,	Portland.
Hayden, Mrs. F. V.,	Philadelphia.
Little, T. Y. and wife,	Portland.
Lord, C. E. and wife,	Boston.
Peters, Miss Sarah L.,	Detroit.
Patten. Mrs. Clara L.,	Brunswick.
Pulsifer, J. R. and wife,	Rochester.
Peet, Mrs. J. B.,	New York.
Ruddick, W. R. and wife,	Boston.
Runlett, Charles E.,	Auburndale.
Thorp, E. G.,	Boston.
Wingate, W. H.,	Boston.

It isn't every person who can lay claim to the distinction of having the State House within their own grounds. We can ; and it is the State House, too. It's a unique distinction. Suppose we have the Legislature meet in the summer time right here.

If the Prince of Wales Came to Poland

H E might pack up his Britannia ware in his Gladstone, and we could give him a yacht race right here that would astonish him, and us. Then if he wanted to follow the hounds, there's Jim and Bruno always ready. For golf, we can lay a course right over Mt. Washington, through Tuckerman's, nature's refrigerator.

There is plenty of sport for his 'ighness if 'e'll only come.

We'll put his picture in the HILL-TOP in advance, and then we'll put in another later, showing the difference, you know, me boy, after drinking our own Poland water. We'll take you to the tower and show you the crowning jewel of New England, Mt. Washington, and present you the freedom of the city in a Moses bottle. You can holler in our rain barrel and have lots of fun.

Vol. II.   SUNDAY MORNING, JULY 7, 1895.   No. 2.

Dedication of Maine State Building.

ALL nature, whose supremely exquisite features had been closely veiled for a week, threw off the misty covering on the morning of the greatest event that Poland ever witnessed.

For days, weeks, nay months, and we had almost said years, the preparation for this grand event had been in progress, and when the *denouement* was almost at hand, the hastening hands and feet hurried to a climax an event long to be remembered by the fortunate participants. The structure was again complete, the welcome guests gathered from far and near, the greatest within our borders, as well as the most humble, and all nature smiled as a benediction upon the completed labors.

The gathering of the clans began on Saturday, June 29th, when the invited guests began to arrive, each train bringing its quota, until the evening, when carriage after carriage came briskly up, and landed its somewhat fog-bedamped human freight beneath the spacious *porte cochere*. Governors, senators, representatives, judges, artists, and men and women whose names are familiar in other walks of life, filled the rotunda of the hotel with a merry chatter.

Supper was disposed of, and all the assembling apartments of the hotel were soon overflowing with the happy throng of visitors. The evening closed with a dance, and the first day's festivities were brought to an end.

Sunday was a day of lowering skies, and threats of impending unpleasantness drifted across the heavens. The day wore on enjoyably notwithstanding; Mr. Kuntz's orchestra furnishing excellent music within doors; and drives around and about the Poland Hill being indulged in by many, seven large teams being placed at their disposal. Among the occupants of these carriages we noted, Gen. A. P. Martin, Gen. Taylor, Congressman Boutelle, Mr. and Mrs. Enneking, Col. Page, and some fifty others.

Monday morning, the first of July, opened and continued superb. The Maine State Building was handsomely decorated by Mr. Chas. Pierce, Mr. Blake, and Mr. Gallagher, a platform for the speakers and the Ricker family being erected at the entrance, and seats placed in the grove in front, which were quickly filled. At 11.20, after a patriotic overture by the band, Judge Symonds of Portland arose and made a felicitous opening address, and then introduced the speakers in turn.

The first was Governor Cleaves, whose stalwart form and ringing enunciation made an excellent impression. His language was forceful, and justly laudatory of the people who had made this ceremony possible.

On behalf of Governor Greenhalge of Massachusetts Judge Advocate General Edgar R. Champlin appeared as his representative, and was listened to with attention and interest. His manner was charming, and his language well chosen.

After a bit of badinage as to who is the senior

Maine State Building, Poland Spring, Me.

Senator of Maine, the Hon. Eugene Hale was introduced. His remarks were replete with witty allusions and good-natured banter, causing the utmost good feeling and amusement among the listeners. He is an easy, fluent speaker, and sprung at once into high favor with those who had never before listened to his voice. Senator Frye followed with one of those charming inimitable addresses which have won him such fame and such distinction. His allusion to his "venerable" colleague caused much merriment, and his mention of Oxford County as the birthplace of so many men of distinction, loud applause.

Congressman Dingley was well known to many of his hearers, and his remarks found willing and appreciative ears. He was followed by Congressman Boutelle, Judge Webb of the U. S. Circuit Court, Judge Whitehouse of the Supreme Court of Maine, the Hon. J. P. Bass of Bangor, and Gen. A. P. Martin, the Police Commissioner of Boston.

The allusions to the Ricker family were most laudatory, and, as all will testify, most heartily deserved. As one listened to these remarks one wondered how that gentle and kindly woman, whose presence here once contributed so much to the success of this enterprise and the happiness and comfort of all about her, and who was the life-long companion of that Hiram Ricker whose name is on every one's lips, would have appreciated the words of eloquence, could she have been here. Yet it was not for Jenette Wheeler Ricker to grace that platform on this occasion in person, but her memory lived in the minds of all who knew her.

In our Maine Senator's exquisitely eloquent speech, his allusion to the cradle of the Washburn family, in Oxford County, was one of those delightful touches of nature which go straight to the heart, but if it might not be considered an impertinence to *attempt* to gild the refined gold of his utterances, he might, had he known, have added that there was *another* cradle in Oxford County, within whose confines was lulled to sleep the baby girl, who was destined to become the mother of these Rickers, so complimented by the speakers for their perseverance, generosity, thrift, and unlimited executive ability, and who have builded a structure unequaled in the history of American progress and American enterprise. All honor to her as a representative American *mother*, a mother to whom the world owes much that is good in it, and much that is great.

The speeches over, an inspection of the building began, and it was soon thronged from bottom to top, and many and loud were the words of praise.

Its furnishings, its art treasures, and air of elegance and comfort were the admiration of all.

It is impossible to enumerate them here, but possibly we may later.

On the exterior are two entablatures, on which are inscribed:

ORIGINAL
STATE BUILDING
ERECTED AND OCCUPIED BY THE
STATE OF MAINE
AT THE
WORLD'S COLUMBIAN EXPOSITION
CHICAGO
1893
REMOVED HERE AND REBUILT
BY
HIRAM RICKER & SONS
1895

Upon the other:

THIS
BUILDING
IS PRESERVED AS A
VALUABLE STATE RELIC
AND
DEDICATED
FOR A
LIBRARY AND ART BUILDING
AND AS A
CENTENNIAL MEMORIAL
OF THE
ORIGINAL SETTLEMENT OF POLAND SPRING FARM
BY THE
RICKER FAMILY

These slabs were presented by Hon. M. P. Frank of Portland, Me.

The arrangement of the flora of Poland, made by Miss Kate Furbish, was very artistic and much admired. The ceremony of dedication being over, a grand banquet was then spread before the guests, of which the following is the menu:

MENU.

Bouillon, a la Royale.
Green Turtle, aux Quenelles.
Radishes.   Olives.
Petit Pates, au Riz de Veau.
Boiled Penobscot River Salmon, aux Petit Pois.
Planked Bluefish, a la Tartare.
Pommes de Terre, aux Œufs.
Sliced Tomatoes.   Cucumbers.
Yorkshire Ham Glace, au Champagne.
Roast Sirloin of Beef, Dish Gravy.
Roast Spring Lamb, Mint Sauce.
Roast Rhode Island Green Goose, Apple Sauce.
Saute de Homard, a la Newburg.
Fricassee of Belgium Hare, a la Chasseur.
Italian Fritters, Sauce Imperiale.
Boiled and Mashed Potatoes.   Butter Beans.

New Squash.   New Cabbage.
New Potatoes, with Cream.   Native Green Peas.
Steamed Rice.
Boned Turkey Truffe, en Aspie.
Frozen Eggnog.
Roast Brant Duck Larded, Bread Sauce.
Water-cress Salad.   Dressed Lettuce.

Steamed English Plum Pudding, Brandy Sauce.
Baked Tapioca Pudding.
Apple Pie.   Blueberry Pie.   Squash Pie.
Strawberry Short-cake, with Whipped Cream.
Sherry Wine Jelly.   Perfection Cake.
French Kisses.   Fruit Cake.   Boston Cream Puffs.
Vanilla Ice-Cream.   Chocolate Layer Cake.
Mixed Nuts.   Raisins.   Figs.
Oranges.   Bananas.   Cherries.
American, Edam, and Roquefort Cheese.
Crackers.
Tea.   Coffee.

The evening was devoted to music and dancing, and the reading of the original poem by
Miss Julia H. May, entitled "Wanderers of
Maine." It was originally written for the Chicago dedication but not used, but re-written, and
read on this occasion by Mrs. Helen Coffin
Beedy, she being introduced by Mr. Griffith of
the HILL-TOP.

The ball, which closed the festivities of this
grand demonstration, was made brilliant by the
exquisite toilettes displayed, and by the presence of a great number of ladies whose gowns
were only exceeded in beauty by their own lovely
faces and forms. Nor should the gentlemen be
omitted from mention, for a finer looking body
of men it is rare to see grace any event. 'Tis
done and 'twas well done.

Among the numerous letters and telegrams
received by the Messrs. Ricker, expressing congratulations, and regrets at inability to attend,
the following telegram from Thomas W. Palmer,
the president of the World's Fair Commission,
is of interest:

DETROIT, MICH.

Mr. E. P. Ricker:

Deeply regret imperative engagements here
prevent acceptance of your kind invitation to
dedication of World's Fair Maine State Building at your beautiful, hospitable, and health-
giving resort. Hope your house is full, as it
always will be if people know what is good for
them.

Kind regards to your family and best wishes
for the success of the occasion on July first.

Yours with great esteem,

T. W. PALMER.

Beauty and Grace.

WHERE so many lovely ladies were present
and so many demands are made for mention on all sides, we can only say that all
were charming, attractive, and elegantly
attired, and deserve and receive the highest compliments of the HILL-TOP.

Mrs. Colonel Moses was charming in a peach-
bloom satin trimmed exquisitely with lace.

Miss Boutelle was daintily attired in white
muslin over pink silk.

Miss Annie Boutelle made a pretty picture in
violet trimmed with valenciennes lace.

Mrs. Amos Little wore black brocade satin,
point lace, and diamonds.

Mrs. Foster, a beautiful silver brocade satin
trimmed with green velvet, point lace, and diamonds.

Miss Bourne wore an exquisite pink Parisian
gown.

Miss Elvina Smith was beautiful in pink silk
with white mousselaine de soie.

Mrs. Colonel Keeler in black moiré and chiffon and diamonds.

Mrs. F. G. Lombard wore yellow satin with
lace and jewels.

Miss Field was becomingly dressed in white
silk.

Mrs. General Martin, black satin with diamonds.

Mrs. George Baker was richly gowned in
black and white silk trimmed with black velvet.

Mrs. R. M. Field was charming in black silk
with diamonds.

Mrs. D. F. Kimball wore pink satin trimmed
exquisitely with lace.

Mrs. Dr. Taggart in black silk with diamonds.

Mrs. B. I. Parker wore a silk gown of yellow and white.

Mrs. William Blake was beautifully gowned
in a violet silk crepe trimmed with yellow velvet.

Mrs. Joseph Sawyer wore pearl brocade with
silver garniture and guimpure lace.

Mrs. Henry Taylor was charming in a grey
crepon with diamonds.

Miss Taylor wore a blue and white silk.

Mrs. Hubbard, red silk with black trimmings.

Mrs. Fessenden, black brocade silk with rich
lace and diamonds.

Miss Brewer was daintily attired in a pink
and white organdie.

Mrs. Wescott wore a combination of black
and gray.

Mrs. Dr. Henry Lee, black silk with diamonds.

Miss Todd looked sweet in pink and Miss
Blanche Todd in a lovely dress of yellow and
white.

Mrs. Winslow was charming in a black satin trimmed with yellow.

Mrs. Twombly, blue silk, rich lace, and diamonds.

Mrs. Wellington wore a combination of yellow and black.

Echoes.

The ladies' costumes are elegant, diversified, and modest.

Miss Dingley's dark beauty is of a most striking character.

Did Massachusetts own Maine, or Maine Massachusetts first?

It must be good moose hunting in that forest Senator Hale alluded to.

Quiet and unassuming were our two Senators, Eugene Hale and William P. Frye.

The souvenir was one of the most elaborate pieces of work ever presented on any occasion.

Shades of James G. Blaine, how Maine would have honored his presence on a day like that.

Talk about the tall Sycamore of the Wabash, our Governor Cleaves is noticeable even among the Pines.

Judge Whitehouse enjoyed the Lancers immensely. Judicial dignity on a genuine, wholesome frolic.

The stately Miss Thomas and the dainty Miss Carpenter were the first ladies upon the floor this season.

Congressman Boutelle is one of the handsomest men in Congress, also in Poland. Hope to see him again.

The Misses Boutelle, daughters of the Congressman, were the second couple at the Saturday evening dance.

Mr. Frye's allusion to the cradle which rocked so many distinguished men, applied to the Washburns of Livermore.

Boston's genial Police Commissioner, General A. P. Martin, was a prominent figure at the dedication, but not in his official capacity, however.

Mr. Van Zandt and "Aunt Martha's" boy had a very successful fishing day, Tuesday, catching several fine bass, the three largest weighing four, three, and two pounds respectively.

A little party Tuesday, consisting of Mr. and Mrs. Ira A. Nay of Boston, Mrs. Oliver Marsh, and Miss Sarah L. Ricker, visited Mrs. Janette (Bolster) Ricker's old homestead at East Rumford. General Bolster bought the farm seventy-five years ago, and the party found everything in good condition. The barn has not been changed and is large enough to contain seventy head of cattle. Mr. A. J. Knight is the present proprietor.

The Oldest Visitor.

IT was to Capt. J. S. Winslow of Portland to whom the Rickers were indebted for the original of the unique, terse, and emphatic circular originally issued by Hiram Ricker, lauding the virtues of Poland water, and modestly stating that board was from $2.50 to $3.50 per week, and which Captain Winslow discovered among a lot of old papers.

It may be added that Captain Winslow, to whom belongs the honor of raising all the flags in the Maine State Building, is undoubtedly entitled to the distinction of being the earliest visitor at the old hotel, present on the occasion of the dedication ceremonies. All honor to the Captain.

The Souvenir.

THE booklet presented by the Rickers was one of remarkable elegance, comprising 89 pages gotten up in the most exquisite manner known to the printer's art, and reflects great credit upon all concerned. Its large number of illustrations comprise a history of progress in themselves, while the record of the Ricker family is one to look back to and admire, where energy and pluck, combined with the sweet and gentle influence of a noble New England woman, have produced a family whose enterprise has builded a palace where but a short time ago was only a wilderness.

May they increase and prosper.

Short contributions, poems with snap, and reports of games, amusements or drives, are welcome. Tell us of your travels.

There are twenty-two varieties of chairs and tete-a-tetes among those elegant furnishings from the Wakefield Rattan Company.

That was a great catch of salmon sent on by Mr. Amos Little—two thirty-pounders and one of forty-five pounds. They were beauties.

The attendants at the news counter are very popular. Good nature, a pleasant word, and a genial smile work wonders.

FRANK CARLOS GRiFFiTH, } EDITORS.
NETTiE M. RiCKER,

PUBLISHED EVERY SUNDAY MORNING DURING THE MONTHS
OF JULY, AUGUST AND SEPTEMBER, IN THE INTERESTS OF

POLAND SPRING AND ITS VISITORS.

All contributions relative to the guests of Poland Spring will
be thankfully received.

To insure publication, all communications should reach the
editors not later than Wednesday preceding day of issue.

All parties desiring rates for advertising in the HILL-TOP
should write the editors for same.

The subscription price of the HILL-TOP is $1.00 for the
season, post-paid. Single copies will be mailed at 10c. each.

Address,

EDITORS "HILL-TOP,"
Poland Spring House,
South Poland, Maine.

PRINTED AT JOURNAL OFFICE, LEWISTON.

Sunday, July 7, 1895.

Editorial.

OUR re-entree into the social whirl has not tended to make us dizzy, notwithstanding the frequency with which our official hat has been doffed to acknowledge the compliments of old friends.

If there is anything in our weekly appearance not exactly to your fancy, remember that that very article may give exceeding delight to others, and that we have a very narrow path to tread, and would rather have a million dollars than give offense.

Don't tempt us, please, for we should not know what to do with the money.

We have no use for a palatial office building as yet, but we are growing, and a large part of our time is devoted to keeping our editorial head down to normal proportions.

We hope to find it necessary, however, to employ a circulation editor soon, so that we may publish one of those enticing weekly tables which glow like the magician's rose-bush and look so decoy-ducky to the unwary advertisers.

The editorial rooms are now in the Maine building, where the staff of editors, sub-editors, and reportorial brigade may be seen at their work.

The fashion editor this week hopes everybody had the finest gown and was the handsomest woman at the "doings;" at all events if it was not so it is not our fault, for the f. e. had *carte blanche* to be as liberal as Santa Claus and lavish silks and jewels without stint.

There was once upon a time a patent medicine labeled "Buy me and I will do you good," and we are not sure but that would be a good head-line for our first page; at all events, try and imagine it is there and that we are endeavoring to live up to that.

These are times when one makes statements, or omits to make statements, which one afterwards regrets, like the medical student who stated that he should administer a teaspoonful of Croton oil as a dose. At the close of the exercises of the day he had realized his error and explained to the professor that he "would like to change that dose." "Too late; the man is dead," was the reply, and that was forcible and emphatic and never to be forgotten.

Send a copy to your friends at home or abroad, and let them see what is going on at Poland. They will appreciate it, be assured.

How did you enjoy the Fourth?

Portland has returned Mrs. J. D. Fessenden to Poland. Unanimously re-elected.

Mr. and Mrs. William S. Blake are among the most charming and interesting guests.

C. H. Bayley, formerly of the *Shoe and Leather Reporter*, is interested in having people enjoy themselves.

Mr. Sawyer went fishing and caught one, two, three, four, five, and they were—thrown back into the water.

The confectionery at the news stand is pure, and manufactured by one of the finest confectioners in New York, who has pushed his way rapidly to the front.

Many complimentary remarks were passed on the carafes, embodying the entire Poland Spring institution, by the visitors. They will grace the table of many of them, combining usefulness with a refinement of taste.

DAN.

By William Redmund.

YOU want me to tell you why we all prize that bear's head! Well, I'll have to go a long way back to tell you that, but being Christmas night I'll try my best. Pass the 'backy, wife, I'll fill my pipe anew. The smoke will help to clear my brain. Those bells ringing out so merrily bring the past back to me as if it were only yesterday, and yet Dan there is twelve years old; and that head had hung just there close upon two years before he was born, so it must be fourteen years ago to-night when I met that bear. I was at the "diggings" over the hills, and bad luck I had, scarcely found enough to buy my food. I had no mate, for no man would work with me. I was a Jonah. So I lived alone in a log hut on the hillside, near an old claim, which had been abandoned as worthless, the owners having dug out the six feet of soil, beneath which no gold was thought to lie.

My little home was not much like this, I can tell you. Just a few logs high, with a hole in the roof, which served for window and chimney. My bed a few branches covered with a heap of dry leaves. I was as low down as a man could be. It was Christmas night! I had my Christmas log, for that cost naught. Through the crevices the wind came in gusts, wafting the sparks from the crackling flames and forcing them upwards amid the smoke in fantastic forms, like so many devils at play, who, when their frolics ended, leaped through the hole in the roof and were lost in space. I lay on the ground watching the wood smouldering on the stone I used for a hearth, and as each gust came and went, so did the log glow white or red with heat.

I remember well it was a long, flat kind of log I had then burning, and on its broad glowing surface I saw faces and scenes of the past. There was the old church, with its massive square ivy-covered tower and its bells sending through the grated windows, upon the night air, a merry Christmas peal. And there the slab that marks my mother's grave,—why, there's Jane's face, how sweet you look with the red glow upon your flaxen hair—I've caught you now—see the mistletoe hanging from the cross-beam—I must have a kiss, your mother did the same when she was young as you—and can you love me, Jane?—Will you always love me?—I believe you, Jane,—and this lock of flaxen hair shall never leave my breast, you'll think of me when I am over the hills. When Christmas comes you'll ne'er kiss another under the mistletoe—Well, not as you kissed me—nay, let not the cloud come over your face, I cannot

see your sweet blue eyes—I'll come back to you, with my pockets full of gold, and the old bells shall send forth a merrier peal than they do now—your mother and your dad shall dance at our wedding—Nay, come not between us, dad, I love her and she loves me, and our love is true and pure—well, no, I have no money now, nor can I more than keep myself, 'tis true,—I would not bring your child to poverty—I love her too dearly for that, and as you say I'll go away, and not see her face again until I can support a wife. O fear me not, I'll keep my word—you need not stamp and storm, old man, you were young once, and no doubt would have lain down your life for Jane's mother, so would I for Jane. You may think we youngsters have no grit, but you will find I've sand enough to keep my word. I'll wed Jane for all you say, if she loves me as I love her—why, yes, my girl, I know you do—don't cry—it may be a year, it may be two, but sure as Christ was born on this blessed day, I'll come back to you, if you are true to me—nay, I want not your ring to remind me of your promise, I have your flaxen hair upon my heart, and till I lose that I'll ne'er cast a doubt on you—Good-bye, Jane—all right, old man, I'm going, and I won't come back for a time, but when I come, I'll come for Jane. Good-bye, Jane, dear—don't put your arms around me so—how heavy your hands feel upon my breast—I'll come back, never fear—why will you hold me so—nay, your arms are like bands of iron—I cannot move—can scarcely breathe—you will kill me—loose your hold, I say—God, the agony—I shall die—

I awoke from this dream. All was dark as pitch. The fire had burned itself out, but I knew that the arms around me were not Jane's, but those of a monstrous bear, who held me tight enough, but thank God one arm was free. I reached my knife, which was in my belt, and quick as thought plunged it up to the hilt into his breast. We struggled awhile, but he slowly relaxed his grip, and finally released me, and made for the door. Well, I got the drop on him as he was departing, giving him two shots from my revolver. I looked out but could see nothing of my departed friend, so locked the door, with my pick and spade, and rolled myself in my blanket. As I slumbered it seemed that the dream was a reality, and the reality only a dream. I was awakened by a voice outside my hut. Yes, it was daylight. The pale gray dawn was peeping through the chinks in the hut's side. My pals were going up the mountain to their separate claims, to woo fortune with pick and spade.

"Hello, Dan, are you dead—open the door," shouted a voice I knew well. It was the voice of Redhead, a nickname the boys had given him, for he looked all the world like a redhead duck. His stomach was large and round. His short legs were set far back. His feet were sprawled and broad. Upon his long neck, which was always thrust forward, set his little head crowned with bright red hair. He couldn't walk, he wobbled. The first time I saw him going up the mountain, I just sat down on a boulder and laughed until my sides ached—but there, I'm forgetting all about the bear. But that Redhead was the funniest fellow you ever set eyes on. Well, he kept shouting, so I opened the door, and there he was with a short pipe between his projecting jaws, adding length to his bill-like mouth. "Going to sleep all day?" he quacked, even his voice had the metallic sound of a duck, and the two or three short laughs or grunts he gave after each speech, completed the aquatic illusion. "Who killed bear?" he quacked. "What bear?" I asked, for I had forgotten all about my caller of last night. "Why, that bear," quacked he, pointing with his little short arm across the path, and sure enough there lay old bruin, in the old abandoned claim. I sprang open my revolver, showing the two empty shells. "Well, I guess they did the job," I said. Redhead laughed and quacked, his big mouth opened wide, as he rubbed his stomach in anticipation of the bear steak he hoped to get. Then he grew solemn and looked at me in doubt, and quacked, "Dan, I suppose I'm in that, good steak there," and he brought his spade down on the bear's haunch. "Course you are, Redhead. You and I be so unlucky with our pick and spade we can't e'en get a pal, so guess you and I will be mates in the bear."

Well, if you had only seen his bill-like mouth open, as he quacked and quacked, "Now, Dan, you be made of the right stuff, you be. Guess we're in luck to-day. Let's skin the bear."

Well, I don't know how it was, but I didn't want any one to touch that bear, so said I'd fix that and bury the carcass too. "Call as you come down and I'll have the steak ready for you." That just pleased him, for he was not fond of work, so he waddled up the mountain path, for all the world like an old drake going to the water. After a snack, and a wash down to the brook (nature's wash-bowl) I took my spade and pick, for I thought I'd just dig a hole for the carcass e'er I skinned it. He was too big a fellow to drag around, so I stuck my spade in the ground just at the bear's nose, and dug down a foot, well, it may be more, when my eyes lighted on something, which made every nerve in my body twitch and leap with joy. Yes, boys, I had struck just as fine a vein of quartz as ever

lay beneath this blessed soil, and I owe it all to that bear's head, for it marked the spot where I found my pile. But as I had told Redhead that he and I were pals in the bear, I considered him pals in the find. When he came for the steak and I showed him the quartz and called him partner, he quacked and quacked until I feared he'd split his red head from his jaws. We didn't sleep much that night, you can bet. Next day we got to work in earnest. The vein panned out even richer than I could have hoped, and we soon made enough to leave the gold fields.

I just made for this village, and a bee line for this house, and there sat old dad in a little garden just as grumpy as ever. Before I could open my mouth, he shouted, "You needn't come in, Dan, I don't want to see you here. My gal is happy and contented, so let her bide." I didn't say a word till I got close up to him, but didn't I feel just proud as I said, "Dad, I've come back. My pockets are full of gold and I've lots more in the bank. I've come to stay, but if you won't have me why then I'll take Jane away." You should have seen the look that came over the old man's face. But I hadn't time to say more, for Jane had heard my voice and was right here in my arms. We were married next day, came home here, and here we've been ever since.

Now you all know why that head hangs over the mantel, and why my wife and I prize it, for that's the nose which pointed out the gold which brought me back to Jane.

𝒯id=ℬits.

Sunshine.

Grand mountain views.

The favorite fish in Hades is said to be fried sole.

Mr. Thomas is welcomed back to his familiar corner.

Dr. and Mrs. W. A. Taggart of Philadelphia are now daily in our midst. May they remain long.

Charles Sumner Cook did some good work for the souvenir, but modestly disclaims any credit.

John J. Enneking, than whom America has no finer artist to-day, and his charming wife, arrived Sunday.

Mr. George T. Bourne was an interesting contributor last season; cannot we prevail upon him this season?

A Grand Achievement.

WHAT Poland Water is to the world so Tiffany & Co. of New York are among the gold and silversmiths—pre-eminent—as the following extract from their superb "Court Card" shows, to which should be added "His Imperial Highness the Emperor of Japan."

Tiffany & Co., Union Square, New York; Avenue de l'Opera, 36 bis, Paris; 5 Argyll Place, W., London; by appointment gold and silversmiths to

Her Most Gracious Majesty the Queen of England.
His Royal Highness the Prince of Wales.
Her Royal Highness the Princess of Wales.
His Royal Highness the Duke of Edinburgh.
Their Imperial Majesties the Emperor and Empress of Russia.
His Imperial Highness the Grand Duke Vladimir.
His Imperial Highness the Grand Duke Alexis.
His Imperial Highness the Grand Duke Paul.
His Imperial Highness the Grand Duke Sergius.
His Imperial Majesty the Emperor of Austria.
His Majesty the King of Prussia.
His Majesty the King of the Belgians.
His Majesty the King of Italy.
His Majesty the King of Denmark.
His Majesty the King of Greece.
His Majesty the King of Spain.
His Majesty the King of Portugal.
The Emperor of Brazil.
The Khedive of Egypt.
H. I. M. the Shah of Persia.
The Gold Medal, "Præmia Digno," from the Emperor of Russia, 1883.
Grand Prix and Legion of Honor, Paris, 1878.

Paintings
IN MAINE STATE BUILDING.

Room G.
"Threatening Weather." Walter L. Dean.
"Looking Off Shore." Water-Color. "
"U. S. Fleet at Hampton Roads."
                                   Water-Color. "
Hayboat. Dordrecht. Water-Color. A. W. Buhler.
Low Tide. " " "
Bass Point. " " "

Room H.
"Daughter of Eve." J. H. Hatfield.
"Springtime." "
"A Student." "
"Vanity."
"Old Bridge Lane."
"Autumn."
"Summer."

Room I.
"Pink and Green."
Chatham Sands.
In Green Mountain State (1).
In Green Mountain State (2).
Garden Path.
"Helping Papa."

Room K.
Still-Life. Nettie M. Ricker.
Road to the Pond. Water-Color. Gallagher.

Room L.
Poppies. J. J. Enneking.
November Twilight. "
Cloudy Day, North Bridgton, Me. "
Spur Pasture, Me., or a New England
                            Hillside. "
Beach and Wreck. "
River and Shore. Nettie M. Ricker.
Spring Morning, Skowhegan, Me. Enneking.
Spring Morning. "
Summer Twilight, Winthrop, Mass. "
Old Mariner. Buhler.
Son of Italy. Gallagher.
Lady and Tea. Caligg.

Room M.
Canton Meadows. Hatfield.
Hauling the Seine. Gallagher.

Balcony.
"Tangled Skein." Hatfield.
The Old Ricker Inn. Wm. J. Bixbee.
The Old Ricker School-house. E. H. Shapleigh.
Landscape. Jenette Bolster Ricker.

After the Fourth.

We put him to bed in his little nightgown,
The most battered youngster there was in the town;
Yet he said, as he opened his only well eye,
"Rah, rah, for the jolly old Fourth of July!"

Two thumbs and eight fingers with lint were tied up,
On his head was a bump like an upside-down cup,
And his smile was distorted, and his nose all awry,
From the rattling and glorious Fourth of July.

We were glad; he had started abroad with the sun,
And all day had lived in the powder and fun;
While the boom of the cannon roared up to the sky,
To salute Young America's Fourth of July.

I said we were glad all the pieces were there,
As we plastered and bound them with tenderest care.
But out of the wreck came the words with a sigh:
"If to-morrow were only the Fourth of July!"

He will glow all together again, never fear,
And be ready to celebrate freedom next year;
Meanwhile all his friends are most thankful there lies
A crackerless twelvemonth 'twixt Fourth of Julys.

We kissed him good-night on his powder-specked face,
We laid his bruised hands softly down in their place,
And he murmured, as sleep closed his one open eye,
"I wish every day was the Fourth of July."

—*Good Roads.*

A Good Shot.

THE fine specimen of a moose's head, hanging in the rotunda of the Maine State Building, is a trophy killed by Mr. W. H. Wingate in the fall of 1894 while on one of his annual hunting and camping trips in the extreme northern part of the State.

In early days moose were very numerous in Maine, but like the buffalo of the West, they were decimated by indiscriminate slaughter for their hides, from which the Indians and early white settlers made their moccasins, mittens, and snow-shoes, until now it is very difficult to get a specimen with a fine set of antlers, and Mr. Wingate is highly pleased at his great success of last fall.

The wisely-protective game laws of Maine are, however, doing much to preserve our wild animals. Deer and caribou have increased wonderfully, while the moose have at least held their own, and have, perhaps, increased somewhat in the past ten years.

Remarkably fine weather prevailed in the fall of 1894, and more game was seen and killed by the sportsmen in the northern part of Maine than for many years.

The trustees of the Boston Public Library have discharged Miss Herring, the foreign correspondent. We thought it against the city ordinances to discharge herring in the swell Back Bay. Perhaps she was only an alewive.

Thistles.

THEY NEVER SPEAK NOW.

He asked the maiden for a kiss—
His love he could not smother:
She said (in fun): " Should you take one,
You'd surely want another."

He shook his head and firmly said:
" I will not ask for two!"
With sweet surprise she murmured: "All
The other fellows do!"
—*Atlanta Constitution.*

Lillian Russell in bloomers. Shades of the
late much-abused Mrs. Bloomer, where art thou?

A creamery in Amherst was recently struck
by lightning. The cream was churned, made
into butter, put up in one-pound " pats,"
stamped and packed in cases all ready for market
—but the lightning didn't do it.

Two policemen in Boston were discharged
lately. The report was said to have been very
loud.

A man in Augusta had his life saved by the
bullet striking his pocket-book. Wonder how
much it struck him for.

A London paper thinks the costume of the
Cornell oarsmen too *décolleté.*

Have they ever been to a Patti concert at the
Royal Albert Hall? My!

The Endeavorers are to hold "sunrise meetings" at 6.30.
Doesn't the sun rise earlier than that in Boston now?

The receiver of the Iron Hall wants $97,500
for his fourteen months' labor in *disbursing.*
He doesn't want much. We should suggest
that he spell it hereafter with a G instead of
an H.

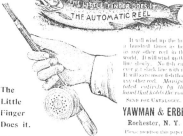

Arrivals.

POLAND SPRING HOUSE.

Alpaugb, Mrs. Ida S.,	Trenton.
Andelson, Mr. and Mrs. A. B.,	Boston.
Amesbuiy, Mr. and Mrs. Geolge D.,	Lewiston.
Adams, Mr. and Mrs. John M.,	Portland.
Allen, Mr. and Mrs. Chailes W.,	Portland.
Andiews, Chailes H.,	Boston.
Andiews, Mrs. Ed. J.,	Boston.
Atwood, Mr. and Mrs. Abiam,	Lewiston.
Abbe, J. T.,	Springfield.
Baikei, Edwaid,	Wakefield.
Blackie, Mr. and Mrs. John,	Boston.
Bigelow, William A.,	New York.
Bakei, Mr. and Mrs. Geo. F.,	Hyannis.
Blake, Mr. and Mrs. Wm. S.,	Boston.
Blake, Doiothy,	Boston.
Boutelle, C. A.,	Bangor.
Boutelle, Miss Giace,	Bangor.
Boutelle, Miss Anne,	Bangor.
Blown, Miss Annq,	New Haven.
Baitlett, Nelson,	Boston.
Biggs, L. P.,	Springfield.
Biggs, Sam. L.,	Boston.
Baiboui, E. D.,	Boston.
Bailey, Isaac H.,	New York.
Bacon, Edwin M.,	Boston.
Bacon, Miss Madeleine L.,	Boston.
Beedy, Mrs. Helen Coffin,	Bangor.
Bouidou, D.,	Boston.
Bass, J. P.,	Bangor.
Bolstei, Mr. and Mrs. J. F.,	Norway.
Bolstei, Mr. and Mrs. H. N.,	South Paris.
Bolstei, Mr. and Mrs. W. D.,	South Paris.
Blake, Gianville,	Auburn.
Biadfoid, Mr. and Mrs J. C.,	Auburn.
Bean, Mr. and Mrs. Geo. W.,	Lewiston.
Biadfoid, Mr. and Mrs. R. C.,	Portland.
Bael, Mrs. Rosa,	Boston.
Bixby, Mr. and Mrs. A. R.,	Skowhegan.
Beals, W. B.,	Turner.
Bacon, D., Jr.,	New York.
Bacon, Mrs. Daniel,	New York.
Bacon, Miss L.,	New York.
Babcock, Mrs. B.,	New York.
Babcock, Miss C. L.,	New York.
Bildgham, Miss,	Providence.
Beckstein, C. D.,	New York.
Bakei, Miss S. P.,	Boston.
Bakei, Chas. T.,	Boston.
Bickfoid, E. F.,	Malden.
Blake, Wm. S.,	Wyoming.
Boyd, Mastei,	Dedham.
Biown, P. S.,	Portland.
Baiton, Geo. D.,	Philadelphia.
Cummings, Mr. and Mrs. A. P.,	New York.
Coles, Col. and Mrs. H. H.,	New York.
Cumuings, A. B.,	Portland.
Claven, Jno. V.,	Salem.
Clark, E. W.,	Portland.
Cleaves, Heniy B.,	Portland.
Cook, Chas. Sumnei,	Portland.
Champlin, Edgai V.,	Cambridge.
Claik, Mr. and Mrs. Eugene L.,	Boston.
Cook, Mr. and Mrs. Chailes,	Portland.
Conant, F. R.,	Auburn.
Conant, Mrs. Lucy W.,	Auburn.
Chandlei, Mr. and Mrs. Seth,	Lewiston.
Conant, Mr. and Mrs. Geoige S.,	Portland.
Cousins, Mr. and Mrs. L. W.,	Portland.
Ciafts, Mrs. W.,	Cambridge.
Colten, Daniel,	Lewiston.
Caiman, Miss Willetta,	Auburn.
Callahan, D. J.,	Lewiston.
Callahan, T. F.,	Lewiston.
Coibin, Mr. and Mrs. C. C.,	Webster.

Dilwoith, Dale,	Salem.
Dingley, Mr. and Mrs. Nelson,	Lewiston.
Dingley, A. G.,	Lewiston.
Dingley, Miss,	Lewiston.
Dean, Mrs.,	Springfield.
Deeiing, Mr. and Mrs. J. W.,	Portland.
Deeiing, Miss,	Portland.
Diew, Mr. and Mrs. F. M.,	Lewiston.
Dana, Dr. and Mrs. Isiael T.,	Portland.
Dow, Fied N.,	Portland.
Dennison, J. A.,	Boston.
DeArgy, Mlle. M. L.,	Brooklyn.
Euneking, Mr. and Mrs. J. J.,	Boston.
Eveiett, Mr. and Mrs. E. F.,	Portland.
Edwaids, C. S.,	Bethel.
Elwell, N. W.,	Boston.
Fiost, Miss Maud,	Norway.
Fletchei, Miss May,	Portland.
Fessenden, Mrs. J. D.,	New York.
Fiye, Hon. and Mrs. William P.,	Lewiston.
Field, Caitie M.,	Boston.
Fostei, Caitie M.,	Boston.
Fostei, Mr. and Mrs. A. S.,	Boston.
Fish, Wm. G.,	Boston.
Fish, Ethel N.,	Boston.
Feinald, Mr. and Mrs. B. M.,	North Poland.
Fianks, Mr. and Mrs. A. C.,	Auburn.
Flint, Mr. and Mrs. D. B.,	Winter Harbor.
Foglei, Helen M.,	Boston.
Gieenleaf, Mr. and Mrs. J. A.,	Auburn.
Goidon, L. C.,	Portland.
Gebhaidt, Mrs.,	Boston.
Goddaid, Mr. and Mrs. Wm.,	Providence.
Giay, Mr. and Mrs. Joseph H.,	Boston.
Gagné, Viiginie,	Lewiston.
Hoiton, C. W.,	New York.
Hamfear, H.,	Boston.
Hathaway, Mr. and Mrs. J. F.,	Somerville.
Haskins, Mr. and Mrs. Chas. E.,	Boston.
Hopkins, R. W.,	Boston.
deHart, Miss Mina,	Portland.
Hale, Eugene,	Ellsworth.
Hale, Claience,	Portland.
Hill, Mr. and Mrs. G. W. R.,	Boston.
Heniy, Mr. and Mrs. John,	Boston.
Hanscom, R. B.,	Lewiston.
Howland, Mrs.,	Lewiston.
Heniy, Thos.,	Boston.
Haiiis, Mr. and Mrs. Nathan W.,	Auburn.
Hutchinson, C. L. and sister,	Portland.
Hale, Mr. and Mrs. Lewis,	Cambridge.
Hovey, Mrs.,	Cambridge.
Haines, D. C.,	Philadelphia.
Haynes, Hoiace,	Bangor.
Haitshoine, Mr. and Mrs. R. B.,	New York.
Haitshoine, Miss,	New York.
Haitshoine, Miss Lydia,	New York.
Haitshoine, Estelle,	New York.
Haitshoine, Douglass,	New York.
Heaton, A. Jr.,	Washington.
Haas, Mr. and Mrs. B.,	New York.
Haas, Floiine,	New York.
Huilbuit, Mr. and Mrs. L.,	Boston.
Holcombe, W. P.,	Boston.
Jewett, Wm. D.,	Paris, France.
Joidan, Eben D.,	Boston.
Jaivis, Haiiiet L.,	Cambridge.
Kuntz, Daniel,	Boston.
Kimball, Mr. and Mrs. D. F.,	Boston.
Keelei, Mr. and Mrs. Geo. A.,	Boston.
Knight, E. W.,	Boston.
King, Mr. and Mrs. Fied G.,	New York.
Kalkoff, G. T.,	Auburn.
Kent, Mr. and Mrs. U. L.,	
Lee, Mrs. Chas. U.,	New York.
Lee, Miss Giace,	New York.

Liscomb, Mr. and Mrs. A. T.,	Portland.
Lacy, Mr. and Mrs. W. N.,	Philadelphia.
Lombard, Mr. and Mrs. F. G.,	Somerville.
Langtry, A. P.,	Springfield.
Leavitt, S. D.,	Eastport.
Lawry, Mr. and Mrs. E. H.,	Rockland.
Lawry, Miss H. S.,	Rockland.
Lawry, Miss Susie,	Rockland.
Libby, John C.,	Portland.
Lee, Stephen,	Lewiston.
Libby, Mrs. G. H.,	Denver.
Loring, Mr. and Mrs. Prentiss,	Portland.
Lincoln, Mr. and Mrs. L. L.,	Rumford Falls.
Larrabee, Mr. and Mrs. Seth L.,	Portland.
Leafe, Miss,	Philadelphia.
Lake, James H.,	Boston.
L'Heurense, W. C.,	Boston.
Murray, Miss A.,	Washington.
Mallet, E. B., Jr.,	Freeport.
Morgan, E.,	Springfield.
Moses, Mr. and Mrs. Geo. W.,	Boston.
Martin, Mr. and Mrs. A. P.,	Boston.
Marion, Mrs. Dr.,	Boston.
Mayo, A. N.,	Springfield.
Mitchell, Mr. and Mrs. James,	Portland.
Milliken, Miss,	Portland.
Marsh, O. A.,	New York.
Merrill, Frank S.,	Boston.
Moore, Dave,	Boston.
Marston, D. W.,	Easton.
Mason, Miss Evelyn,	Auburn.
Mitchell, W. S.,	Portland.
Morgan, Miss A. T.,	New York.
Martin, E. F.,	Boston.
Mandeville, Alf. W.,	New York.
Nealey, A. B. and daughter,	Lewiston.
Newell, Mr. and Mrs. W. H.,	Lewiston.
Neal, Miss,	Lexington.
Nay, Mr. and Mrs. Ira A.,	Boston.
Newhall, Wm. E.,	Philadelphia.
Noble, Miss,	New Orleans.
Osgood, Chas. H.,	Lewiston.
Osgood, H. S.,	Portland.
Osgood, Mrs. W. C.,	Portland.
Osgood, G. N.,	St. Louis.
Osgood, Harold,	St. Louis.
Oakes, Wallace K.,	Auburn.
Pennell, Mr. and Mrs. C. E.,	Brunswick.
Peterson, Dr. and Mrs. W.,	New York.
Pierce, Mr. and Mrs. Geo.,	Newport.
Pierce. Mr. and Mrs. Chas. C.,	Boston.
Page, Col. Cyrus A.,	Boston.
Parker, Mr. and Mrs. B. J.,	Boston.
Porter, Mrs. A. R.,	Boston.
Porter, Mrs. A. H.,	Boston.
Packard, J. A.,	Lewiston.
Pugh, Jennie,	Lewiston.
Penney, C. M.,	Lewiston.
Pulsifer, Abbie,	Auburn.
Pennell, Mr. and Mrs. W. D.,	Lewiston.
Pingree, Mr. and Mrs. R. C.,	Lewiston.
Plummer, Edw.,	Lisbon Falls.
Plummer, H. E.,	Lisbon Falls.
Pratt, Mr. and Mrs. J. S. and daughter,	Auburn.
Pennell, Mr. and Mrs. H. B.,	Portland.
Peck, B.,	Lewiston.
Paine, Mrs.,	Philadelphia.
Paul, E. S.,	Auburn.
Peters, Edw. D.,	Boston.
Quinn, Mr. and Mrs.,	Brooklyn.
Quinn, Miss,	Brooklyn.
Quinn, Miss Ethel Grace,	Brooklyn.
Quinn, Miss Fanny Florence,	Brooklyn.
Rogers, Mr. and Mrs. Spencer,	Portland.
Robinson, Mrs. Elizabeth,	Boston.
Richards, Mr. and Mrs. Fred E.,	Portland.
Rugg, Mrs. Geo.,	Boston.

Robbins, Miss Annie M.,	Boston.
Rogers, Edw. Little.	Boston.
Ricker, Mr. and Mrs. H. H.,	Portland.
Rogers, Miss Bessie,	Portland.
Roeth, Dr. A. Gaston,	Boston.
Ruffner, Bertha,	New York.
Russell, Mr. and Mrs. E. W.,	Lewiston.
Ricker, Mr. and Mrs. Fred B.,	Portland.
Randall, Miss K. M.,	Portland.
Ring, Mr. and Mrs. C. A.,	Portland.
Rich, Edmund L.,	Portland.
Robie, Fred'k and daughter,	Gorham.
Robinson, Mrs. R. T.,	West Newton.
Rowell, Mr. and Mrs. Geo. S.,	Portland.
Rice, Mr. and Mrs. John G,	Portland.
Redfern, Mr. and Mrs. B. S.,	Boston.
Russell, Chas. A.,	Gloucester.
Schmelzel, Geo.,	New York.
Schmelzel, Wm. R.,	New York.
Schmelzel, Miss,	New York.
Smith, Mrs. J. Howard,	San Francisco.
Smith, Miss Edwina D.,	San Francisco.
Stoll, R. P.,	Trenton.
Stoll, Miss Helen,	Trenton.
Seidels, Mr. and Mrs. Geo. M.,	Portland.
Salter, Mr. and Mrs. A. T.,	Washington.
Stearns, Mr. and Mrs. C. S.,	Boston.
Small, Mr. and Mrs. S. R.,	Portland.
Searle, Chas. P.,	Boston.
Smith, Mr. and Mrs. Wm. B.,	Cambridge.
Smith, Mr. and Mrs. Forrest S.,	Boston.
Sanders, H. M.,	Boston.
Smith, J. B.,	Boston.
Spooner, Mrs.,	Portland.
Symonds, Judge J. W.,	Portland.
Sawyer, C. C.,	Auburn.
Stetson, Mr. and Mrs. W. W.,	Lewiston.
Smart, Mr. and Mrs. Wm. T.,	Providence.
Stockbridge, J. C.,	Providence.
Stockbridge, Mrs. A. W.,	Lewiston.
Scruton, J. Y. and daughter,	Lewiston.
Smith, Mr. and Mrs. John B.,	Boston.
Small, Mr. and Mrs. W. L.,	Boston.
Stephenson, H. Walter,	Portland.
Small, Mr. and Mrs. John C.,	New York.
Spitz, Fred'k,	Winchester.
Suter, Mr. and Mrs. John W.,	Boston.
Smith, Mr. and Mrs. A. Otis,	Malden.
Sawyer, H. E.,	
Taylor, Mr. and Mrs. F. E.,	Brooklyn.
Tompkins, Mrs. Orlando,	Boston.
Taggart, Dr. and Mrs. W. A.,	Philadelphia.
Thomas, Mr. and Mrs. Elias,	Portland.
Thomas, Miss Helen B.,	Portland.
Taylor, Mr. and Mrs. G. H.,	Boston.
Taylor, Chas. H.,	Boston.
Twombly, Mr. and Mrs. J. S.,	Brookline.
Tyndale, Mr. and Mrs. J. H.,	Boston.
Taylor, J. N.,	Boston.
Twombly, Miss Lena,	Lewiston.
Tibbetts, Miss Jennie M.,	Pittsburgh.
Travelli, Mr. and Mrs. Chas. I.,	New Orleans.
Trist, Miss,	Portland.
True, F. D.,	
Vantine, Mrs. A. A.,	New York.
Vantine, Miss,	New York.
Wescott, Mr. and Mrs. Geo. P.,	Portland.
Winslow, Mr. and Mrs. J. S.,	Portland.
Winslow, Miss Philena,	Portland.
Winslow, Miss Grace,	Portland.
Winslow, Miss Mabel,	Portland.
Whitehouse, Judge and Mrs. Wm. P.,	Augusta.
Willcomb, Mr. and Mrs. E. S.,	Boston.
Walker, Mr. and Mrs. Thomas J.,	Concord.
Wellington, Mr. and Mrs. Fred W.,	Worcester.
Whitney, Mr. and Mrs. Clarence S.,	Boston.
White, Mr. and Mrs. F. J.,	Boston.
Wright, G. L., Jr.,	Springfield.

Whittum, Miss Blanche, — Lewiston.
Whittum, Miss Florence, — Lewiston.
Witherell, Harvey, — Monmouth.
Witherell, Edith M., — Monmouth.
Webb, Mr. and Mrs. Nathan, — Portland.
Webb, Miss, — Portland.
Wood, Wm., — Portland.
Walsh, Mr. and Mrs. J. A., — Boston.
Wilkinson, Harry C., — Lewiston.
Woodside, Mr. and Mrs. Calvin E., — Portland.
Winslow, Mr. and Mrs. E. B., — Portland.
Walther, Carl, — Montreal.
Walcott, Mrs. J. W., — Dedham.
Wentworth, Anach, — Boston.

MANSION HOUSE.

Bradford, Mr. and Mrs. J. R., — Tallahassee.

Clapp, Alex. H., — Boston.
Culley, M. H., — Boston.

Dudley, John, — New York.

Foster, C., — Portland.

Herrick, Miss I. M., — Brooklyn.

Keene, Mr. and Mrs. S. W., — Boston.

Marsh, Mary J., — Springfield.
Marsh, Robert P., — Springfield.
Marsh, Arthur E., — Springfield.
Marsh, Jane C., — Springfield.
Marsh, Allyn R., — Springfield.
Marsh, Mrs. Oliver, — Springfield.
Morgan, E., — Springfield.
Makepeace, Helen Eva, — Springfield.

Putnam, Delano, — Roxbury.
Putnam, H. W., — Boston.

Raud, Mrs. B. H., — Philadelphia.

Soule, F. W., — Portland.
Smith, H. J., — Boston.
Sabine, Mrs. Alex. F., — Philadelphia.
Staples, Mr. and Mrs. E. P., — Portland.

Vanzandt, Mr. and Mrs. P. G., — New York.
Van Boskerck, Miss E. C., —

Whitney, H. S., — Boston.
Williams, Kate Delano, — Roxbury.
Wentworth, Mr. and Mrs. Otis, — Boston.
Washington, — Philadelphia.

Poland Water Leads Them All.

WHY?

BECAUSE.. It was the FIRST KNOWN SOLVENT OF URIC ACID in the system. . . . .

BECAUSE.. It is the most EFFECTIVE ELIMINATOR of Calculi in the Bladder and Kidneys known to-day. . . . .

BECAUSE.. It was the ONLY water IN NEW ENGLAND to receive ANY AWARD at the World's Columbian Exposition, and the only award of the hundreds exhibited from the WORLD for Purity and Great Medicinal Properties. . . . .

BECAUSE.. The ANNUAL sales exceed the combined sales of all the Saratoga Springs. . . . .

BECAUSE.. Unprecedented as the success of the past has been it is more promising than ever, showing continued increase. . . . .

OFFICES:

BOSTON:	NEW YORK:	PHILADELPHIA:	CHICAGO:
175 Devonshire Street.	3 Park Place.	Corner 13th and Chestnut St.	Cor. Michigan Ave. and Van Buren St.

HIRAM RICKER & SONS, Proprietors.

(INCORPORATED.)

THE HILL-TOP. POLAND SPRING.

VOL. II.   SUNDAY MORNING, JULY 14. 1895.   No. 3.

THE OLD HOMESTEAD,

Not of Josh Whitcomb's Fame, but of Poland Spring's.

RETURN with me, my good readers, to a beautiful morning in August, 1867, and we will stroll in the direction of Shaker Village. Ah! an artist sits sketching at the head of the little lane beyond the Mansion House. Let us pause and ask a few questions; turning to the artist I remark, Your pencil sketch is very good, but what a charming painting that would make. The old house with its gray tints, the great elm trees casting their shadows across the road, and the merry group of people sitting on the lawn. May I ask who they are?

"The gentleman sitting under the tree is a Professor from Chicago. The one at his right is Prof. G. B. Docharty of the College of the City of New York. The other two gentlemen are lawyers, Mr. Benjamin Griffin and Mr. F. J. Palmerton," replies the artist, who was no other than Mr. James Harper of Harper & Brothers of New York.

Are these all the boarders here? I ask.

"No, there are seven of us, Mr. and Mrs. Merriam from Boston and their two little girls. In fact, the house is so crowded that two of our party have to room outside."

How is the table?

"*Good!* No New York *chef* lives that can rival our hostess in her cooking."

Here comes a country lad; may I ask who he is?

The artist, raising his eyes from his work, greets the lad with, "Good morning, Edward," and turning to me replies, "Oldest son of our hostess." Pausing for a minute the lad looks at the picture, then with rake in hand, passes on, little dreaming that the time will come when this sketch will be of intrinsic value to them.

Twenty years passed. Our country lad had pushed out into the great world.

Prosperity smiled, the place grew in popularity and the public requirements demanded a larger circular. Remembering the little sketch that Mr. Harper made, Mr. Ricker went to New York and called upon him.

Mr. Harper had not forgotten and went in search of the sketch-book.

There it was nestling among a hundred others with just two leaves used, the one containing the sketch of the Mansion House and the other, the first house that was ever built over the spring.

It is the only sketch in existence, and let us thank Mr. Harper for his morning's work.

Little did he dream that his sketch would go from north to south and east to west and across the great Atlantic.

And who knows but that in coming years there may be no city on the globe where some one's eyes have not gazed upon this little sketch and read the words, "The Old Homestead."

Last week we published the menu of the Poland Spring House, and now we give that of the Mansion House, which from the time Mr. Harper visited the place to the present has been famous for its excellent table.

MENU.

Soup
Consommè Macedoine
Olives

Fish
Boiled Penobscot Salmon, Sauce Supreme
Sliced Tomatoes

Boiled
Leg of Spring Lamb, Caper Sauce
Pickled Young Onions

Roast
Sirloin of Beef, Dish Gravy
Young Vermont Turkey, Cranberry Sauce
Loin of Veal, Brown Sauce

Vegetables
Boiled New Potatoes   Mashed Potatoes
New Beets   Squash
Bermuda Onions

Entrees
Filet de Bœuf Larded, with Mushrooms
Lamb Chops Breaded, aux Petit Pois
Queen Fritters, Port Wine Sauce

Pastry
English Plum Pudding, Hard and Brandy Sauce
Apple Pie   Lemon Meringue Pie
Banana Ice-Cream
Angel Cake   Macaroons   Walnut Cake
Italian Cream

Water-melon
Nuts   Raisins
American Cheese   Edam Cheese
Bent's Water Crackers
Tea   Coffee

SUNDAY, JULY 7, 1895.

Sunday Services.

Rev. A. J. Patterson, who visited Poland for the first time twenty-five years ago, preached in Music Hall last Sunday. His text was from Ps. viii., 3-5. The eloquent divine was listened to with much attention, and his remarks reached willing and receptive ears.

A Picnic Tea.

Friday afternoon a picnic tea was given on the shore of the middle lake, by Miss Ricker and Miss Jennie Marsh, Mrs. Pulsifer, Miss Makepeace, Mr. Wingate, Miss Mary Marsh. Mr. Allyn Marsh and Mr. Robert and Arthur Marsh were present. The party returned at nine o'clock after a delightful sail on the lake.

PORTLAND, July 10, 1895.

Editors of the Hill-Top :

Dear Summer Journalists,—Write me in these lively columns as one who delights to be a frequenter of your pine groves and Spring House, your Music Hall and new Library, who is an ardent imbiber of your balmy atmosphere and aërated water—a devotee, in short, of America's famous spa!

Neither Maine nor the White Mountains can claim to allure bicyclists by virtue of level roads and continuous macadam, and yet Portland alone has 1,200 wheels in out-of-door gyration and is daily adding to the number.

Is it agreeable to women to learn to ride? Decidedly not.

Do they enjoy the exercise when once acquired? Decidedly they do.

In an ordinary dress which threatens to wind about the wheel at any unguarded moment, you are assisted to your saddle. At once you grasp the handle-bar with a grip entirely rigid. This, naturally, prevents you from steering and so you attempt to steer with your body. Result, disaster! Then you can't keep the pedals. Your feet seem to have left you. You are not quite sure you ever had any.

But bye and bye, lame muscles, black-and-blue decorations and the like honorable scars testify to your perseverance, and you can mount —far more difficult than propelling, once mounted. To be sure, you cannot even scratch your nose or straighten your hat without getting off your steel steed, but—you are arriving! And some fine day sees you, wrench in pocket, confidence in glance, spinning off past green fields, fascinated, bewitched, a creature with new powers and a fresh enchantment.

Many of the costumes are ugly. Better send to Redfern, Hollander, Altman or Stearns, according to your ducats, for it is difficult to get the home-made suit correct and "fit," as our English friends say. It can be done, however. Your correspondent finds a dark blue serge short skirt and Norfolk jacket, black canvas leggins and dark straw hat a not too hideous array. Pointed shoes are pretty but not appropriate; indeed shoes so pointed that they suggest Mephistopheles or an old painting after Giotto, are not even pretty.

There is a curious phenomena in early bicycling. If you fasten your glance upon an object you seem to be drawn to the same by a fatal magnetism, be it a watering trough, a risky hole in the ground or even an acquaintance upon a neighboring wheel. And as your method of saluting these objects or individuals by running into them is scarcely acceptable, beware your

outlook! But ride all the same! Cultivate it next November, fresh from a summer rest!

Poland will be interested in Mr. Anderson's new house, the Mount Pleasant Hotel—not to be confused, by the way, with Pleasant Mountain and its tip-top house, but situated between Crawford's and Fabyans. It is to be a delightful resort. Mr. Anderson asked his old Class of 1872, Portland High School, or they asked him, to a house-warming, or cooling, July 4th, which was very successful in every respect. Poland extends congratulations to Anderson and Price on their bright prospects.

What a feature of vacation it is that the writer of letters and other printed matter may be as desultory as he pleases without insuring censure and may skip from topic to topic like a squirrel in an oak tree bound from bough to bough! which gives me an opening for a disconnected joke. For instance, was your chairman at the Library Dedication asked by one of the speakers, the other day, what he should talk about, and did he receive the reply, "about ten minutes"? No, it was too dignified an occasion and must have occurred at some other gathering I have recently attended!

Were ever feminine fineries so superfluely fine as this summer? Silk petticoats and organdies of dream-like delicacy, big hats and nodding plumes and chiffon parasols! Have you some at Poland? Does the big house piazza blossom like the rose?

But here I am at the end of my paper and not a word about books and summer reading. It must keep for another issue.

Greeting to the HILL-TOP and its readers from one of them,

M. B. J.

"Marimablu."

A delightful little picnic party was held on the island in the Upper lake on Monday. The hitherto nameless little spot of land, so isolated, was on this occasion given its christening by the ladies present, and a very original method was pursued in so doing.

The ladies composing the party were Miss Eames, Miss Bacon, Miss Spaulding, and the Misses Todd. The name given was "Marimablu," embracing the first two letters of their Christian names.

Our rain has almost equaled that of good Queen Bess.

The Lawrence Base-Ball Club has disbanded. Struck out.

FRANK CARLOS GRIFFITH, } EDITORS.
NETTIE M. RICKER,

PUBLISHED EVERY SUNDAY MORNING DURING THE MONTHS
OF JULY, AUGUST AND SEPTEMBER, IN THE INTERESTS OF

POLAND SPRING AND ITS VISITORS.

All contributions relative to the guests of Poland Spring will
be thankfully received.

To insure publication, all communications should reach the
editors not later than Wednesday preceding day of issue.

All parties desiring rates for advertising in the HILL-TOP
should write the editors for same.

The subscription price of the HILL-TOP is $1.00 for the
season, post-paid. Single copies will be mailed at 10c. each.

Address,

EDITORS "HILL-TOP,"
Poland Spring House,
South Poland, Maine.

PRINTED AT JOURNAL OFFICE, LEWISTON.

Sunday, July 14, 1895.

Editorial.

AWAY here in what was so recently the
"wilds" of Maine, what should we care
for the comings and goings of the busy
world, and yet all eagerly seek the daily news of
the toiling and seething masses in the cities far
away.

Go farther back into the woods, seek the
northern lake most remote from rails and high-
way, where you must perforce do without paper,
letter, or telegram for weeks, and you will feel
as if a tremendous weight had been lifted, and
as one might soaring high in a balloon.

Yet here we can still hear the hum of voices,
the tread of hurrying feet as that great army in-
vades and permeates all Boston.

Even here the crafty plans of the leading
spirits of political movements can be watched
and see the tiny web grow to catch the unwary
voter.

The great movements of warlike strife advance and recede, and from the hill-top we note
them all, as if they were in the valley below us.

Oblivious as to results, we drink in the pure
water and pure air, eat of the best in the land,
walk, ride or drive about the cool and shaded
avenues, converse with congenial companions,
and are as happy as it is possible to be. Are we
not?

Why not start that Golf club? It is a
healthful and delightful exercise, not too lively
for a warm day, and sufficiently so for a cool
one. The bicycle is none too much in evidence.

Drink quantities of Poland water, exercise,
and read THE HILL-TOP.

Gen. Martin's Talk.

GEN. A. P. MARTIN gave a very interesting talk in Music Hall at the Poland Spring
House on Friday evening, the 5th. The
General was introduced by Mr. Bailey,
whose remarks were very delightful. His subject was "The Battle of Gettysburg." He entered the war April 19, 1861, four days after the
flag was fired upon, and served in twenty-seven
battles, the famous battle of Gettysburg being
one of them. Gen. Martin began in his charming manner, "It is a pleasure always to gratify
our friends, and thinking that on this beautiful
summer evening that some of you might enjoy
a few remarks on the civil war, I am glad
to give you some of my personal experiences at the battle of Gettysburg,. which reminds me of a story in which a little boy said,
'Papa, were you the only man in the war?'" and
then the General continued, "I was not the only
man in the battle of Gettysburg." He thinks
that Gen. Meade should rank with Grant, Sheri-
dan, and Sherman.

General Martin closed his very interesting
remarks by quoting the following lines from
Thomas Campbell's "Hallowed Ground":

"But strew his ashes to the wind
Whose sword or voice has served mankind,
And is he dead, whose glorious mind
Lifts thine on high?
To live in hearts we leave behind
Is not to die.

"Is't death to fall for Freedom's right?
He's dead alone that lacks her light!
And murder sullies in Heaven's sight
The sword he draws.
What can alone ennoble fight?
A noble cause!

Mrs. Amos R. Little has donated to the Poland Spring Library a very beautiful volume, entitled "The World as We Saw It," written by
herself, and very finely illustrated.

Our Orchestra.

THAT we are favored with excellent music is not to be gainsaid, and no wonder, when we have a selection made from the choicest organizations in America.

Mr. Kuntz, leader, has been a first violinist in the Boston Symphony for fourteen years, ever since the orchestra started. He has played in all the leading quartettes in Boston, and now has a quartette of his own which plays a series of private chamber concerts among the leading society people of Boston. He has also played at the great Wagner Theater in Baireuth, where he became familiar with that great master's most celebrated operas, such as "Parsifal," "Meistersinger," etc.

Mr. O. Kuntz is a brother of D. Kuntz. He has been leader in various theaters in this country with great success. Mr. Loeffler has also been a member of the Symphony Orchestra for twelve years and is known as one of the best cello players of said organization.

Mr. Golde has been in the Symphony Orchestra about seven years. Previous to that he was with the Thomas Orchestra and the American Opera Co.

Mr. Strube, although a first violinist in the Symphony Orchestra, plays flute—in fact he can play almost every instrument and is also known as a composer. His overture, played by the Symphony Orchestra last season in Boston, was a great success, and he was called out several times.

Mr. Merrill is a cornetist well known in Boston, as he played solos when but 12 years old and has since played solo cornet in the leading bands and orchestras in Boston.

Mr. Rose is a cellist in the Boston Symphony Orchestra, and is very often chosen as an accompanist for different soloists. He has also played with the great Baireuth Orchestra in the seasons of 1892-94.

Concert Program.

Kuntz Orchestral Club.

1. March—Coronation. . . . . Meyerbeer.
2. Overture—William Tell. . . . Rossini.
3. Vision of a Dream. . . . . Lumbye.
4. Songs { a. Die Uhr. . . . . Loewe.
        { b. Es war ein alter König. . . Heibsch.
        Mr. D. J. Griffith.
5. Selection—Gioconda. . . . . Ponchielli.
6. Slavonic Dance. . . . . . Dvorack.

A. E. McCarthy, from 1166 Broadway, New York, has supplied the "store" with a fine lot of goods. Step in and see them.

Tid-Bits.

Our list of subscribers constantly grows.

Judge Redman of Ellsworth, Me., was a guest at the Poland Spring House, Monday.

The Maine State Building is now open from 9 A.M. to 9 P.M., week days, and from 10 A.M. to 8.30 P.M., Sundays.

It was a handsome birthday cake and an enjoyable occasion, on the birthday anniversary of Miss Eames on the 6th.

We have had a fine object lesson in haying. The field looked unique and interesting with its haycocks thickly placed all over it.

Mr. J. B. Hutchinson knows where good air can be had, outside the office of the General Superintendent of Transportation of the Pennsylvania Railroad.

All the specimens of the flora of this region in the cases in the Maine Building have been changed, Miss Furbish having replaced them with an entire new set.

The flag which was raised over the Mansion House at the Centennial Celebration of July 1st, still waves gloriously o'er the outer walls of that delightful retreat.

We welcome the return of Mr. Charles Smith, who has been sadly missed during the few days he has been to York Beach with his daughter and grandchild.

The reigning powers in the culinary department at Poland Spring are deserving of much praise. The result of their skill is highly appreciated in the dining-rooms.

This time Mr. Sawyer had better luck, and it was a fine string of bass, seven in number, ranging from two to three and a half pounds, which the party brought home.

C. F. McGahan, M.D., the well-known specialist on throat and lung troubles, who spends the winter at Aiken, S. C., and the summer at Bethlehem, is with us for a while.

Mr. and Mrs. T. S. Quinn and their charming daughter are once more with us. Mr. Quinn is manager of the Export Lumber Co., whose office is in Broad Street, New York.

Three of the most remarkable "cures" by Poland Water are among the recent arrivals. Rev. A. J. Patterson and Joseph H. Gray of Boston, and T. S. Quinn of New York.

Many celebrated French artists, including Millet, Corot and others, were very interesting acquaintances of Mr. Bourne, when he was

collecting for his magnificent private gallery in New York.

Monday a fishing party consisting of Mr. and Mrs. Van Zandt, Mr. and Mrs. Pulsifer, Mr. Wingate, Miss Ricker, and Miss Mary Marsh, spent the day on the middle lake. Miss Ricker caught the only fish of the party, which weighed 2½ pounds.

We had an interesting call from James S. Barrell of Cambridge, on the 6th. Mr. Barrell had not been here in 35 years, when Hiram Ricker took him over to the still unprotected spring in the woods. The house then was as represented in the cut on the first page.

Miss Trist, daughter of the Mr. Trist of New Orleans, who is the "Cavendish" of this country, and Miss Noble, are at the Poland Spring House. They are both fine whist players, and Miss Noble is a teacher of whist and piquet. They have already formed some classes.

Fears for the wheat crop this season having been entertained by many, the HILL-TOP is enabled to give authoritatively, through the kindness of Mr. Charles Faigo, the information which came to him by telegraph, that the wheat crop looks like 80% to 85% of last season, or say 425 to 440 millions.

Mr. Amos R. Little, evidences of whose success as a disciple of Isaak Walton have been already apparent, returned from his Canadian trip on the 6th. Mr. Little is a director of the P. R. R. Mr. David G. Yates has been Mr. Little's companion on his fishing tour among the Canadian waters. Both gentlemen look brown as the traditional berries.

Brute Intelligence.

An illustration of the intelligence of the brute creation was very well illustrated a few days since when a driving party from the Poland Spring House was returning, and on arriving at the lower gate, which was closed, and the gateman not being at once forthcoming, the animal walked deliberately to the obstruction, and with his nose, pushed it by repeated efforts until nearly open before the arrival of the lodge-keeper.

The Magnificent Portrait of Hon. James G. Blaine, hanging over the stairway in the Maine Building, was made by THE SPRAGUE & HATHAWAY Co. of West Somerville, Mass. They also made the enlarged photographs of the World's Fair Views in the same building.

Thistles.

They won't cut ice. Wise saws.

Easiest thing in the world to change still Poland water into effervescent. Have it charged.

Sir John the surgeon puts seige on, when there is a heavy surge on. Regards to Tom Hood.

The Kentucky Populists failed to adopt a plank endorsing woman suffrage. Why not try a shingle?

Cambridge has decided to meet Yale. Will it be comin' through the Rye? Here's to good old Yale, drink it down.

A man jumped into the Chicago river from a height of 110 feet. Wonder his legs were not driven up through his body.

The Cuban insurgents are still doing business at the old stand. Their motto is, "No connection with the firm over the way."

China must yet pay Japan £30,000,000. That would be $150,000,000, or 750,000,000 francs. Consequently a Frenchman would be twenty-five times as rich as an Englishman. *Comprenez vous?*

We can assure our readers that there is no truth in the rumor that the Tsar of Russia is trying to control the output of Poland water. He may have a great bell of Moscow, but we have also a belle of Poland. Who is she? Vote early and often.

'Rastus, you ebber ben ter Poland Spring?

Bet yer life. My folks was dere las' summer. Great mystery down ter der spring house.

Is dat so?

Yas, sah. D'you know dat water comes right up outen de solid rock?

G'long. How's de water gwine ter git frough?

Dar's de mystery, 'Rastus, dar's de mystery.

The Mansion House has a fine lot of new dining-room chairs.

Senator Hale and his family were so infatuated with Poland Spring, like everybody else, they had to return. Accept the compliments of THE HILL-TOP.

Mr. S. Ross Campbell, Mr. Ricker and Mr. Sawyer have interested themselves in having the upper lake stocked with bass, and they most sincerely trust that all the bass taken from there, weighing less than one pound, will be thrown back.

The Value of a Name.

THAT curious anecdote relating to Boston's Police Commissioner, Gen. A. P. Martin, in the June *Munsey*, illustrating the fickleness of fame, is offset by another incident related by the gentleman himself.

One night he was accosted on the street by an Irishman, already a little the worse for liquor, who begged for a quarter to buy food.

"You'll spend it for liquor," said the Commissioner.

"Not a cint of it. It's tired I am, and I want something to eat. Lend me the quarter thin, an' I'll give ye me note."

"Will you really?"

"Sure I will. Give me a pen and paper an' I'll write it now. Phats yer name? Sure I can't write a note unliss I haves yer name."

The General, remembering the incident of the letter, thought to try the man, and replied, "A. P. Martin."

The man's manner changed instantly; he wiped his lips, lifted his cap, and muttering, "I'm sorry I spoke," turned and rushed away as rapidly as if the quarter were at the other end of the street.

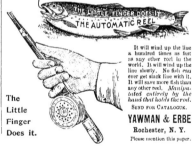

From an Old Bachelor.

[To a salon picture by Bisson, representing a young girl holding a little Love by the wings while she carries others in her hawthorn basket.]

MARCIA B. JORDAN.

Begone, fair maid! I am afraid
I will not hear your song.
For downy wings and such light things
To other days belong!
I, old and gray, what should I say
To May-buds sweet and summerly?
That floating lace about your face
To me is arrant flummery!
Begone, my dear, nor linger here
Where Age would chill the atmosphere!

Off, off, nor wait for harsher fate,
You serve but to deceive.
You set a snare, O maiden fair,
I verily believe.
But take your wares, then, otherwheres
And try your luck with youth,
For he will pay in true love gay
And count it joy forsooth.
Yet 'mid the spells of wedding bells
Spare me a kindly tear,
For I would buy your Cupids shy
Were they not quite so dear!
Off, off, nor linger here!

Wednesday at sunset we were given the unusual sight of a "sun-dog."

The Poland Spring Library is indebted to Mrs. J. D. Fessenden for its first contribution of books.

Hours of Meals.

	Week Days.	Sundays.
Breakfast,	7 A.M. to 9 A.M.	8 A.M. to 10 A.M.
Dinner,	1 P.M. to 2.30 P.M.	1.30 P.M.
Supper,	6 P.M. to 8 P.M.	6 P.M.

Arrivals.

POLAND SPRING HOUSE.

Abbott, Miss Margaret, Auburn.
Adams, Mr. and Mrs. Arthur A., Brookline.
Almy, Mr. and Mrs. W. F., Boston.
Allan, George H., Portland.
Ahern, William, Middleton.

Barbour, E. D., Boston.
Butler, Mrs. Chas. S., Boston.
Butler, Chas. S., Boston.
Burrill, J. W., Lewiston.
Bailey, Isaac H., New York.
Brodil, Wm. F., Boston.
Bailey, Mr. and Mrs. Geo. W., Deering.
Bailey, Miss Georgie, Deering.
Bailey, Miss Mira, Deering.
Boothby, Mrs. F. E., Portland.
Brown, Caleb C., Syracuse.
Ryan, Mrs. C. S., New York.
Blight, Mr. and Mrs. H. O., Cambridge.
Bartlett, Mr. and Mrs. Nelson, Boston.
Bradford, J. C., Auburn.

Carmichael, Geo. A., Providence.
Chase, L. A., Providence.
Cutler, W. F., Boston.
Cushman, Mr. and Mrs. Chas., Auburn.
Colby, Mr. and Mrs. W. W., Portland.
Carmel, W., Lewiston.
Cook, Mr. and Mrs. A. A., Chicago.
Converse, Mr. and Mrs. C. C., Boston.
Craven, Mr. and Mrs. Thomas J., Salem, N. J.
Craven, Miss L. H., Salem, N. J.
Craven, Miss U. B., Salem, N. J.
Craven, Miss Jane F., Salem, N. J.
Candee, Daniel, Syracuse.
Carpenter, F. W., Providence.
Chase, Mr. and Mrs., Auburn.
Chase, Miss, Boston.
Conant, Charles, Auburn.
Coppenhagen, Mr. and Mrs. J. H., New York.
Cheney, Bishop Charles E., Chicago.
Cheney, Mrs., Chicago.
Clancy, William H., Cambridge.

Dingley, Mr. and Mrs. F. L., Auburn.
Dingley, Florence, Auburn.
Dayd, Wm. H., Boston.
Doyle, George B., Cambridge.

Ellis, Mrs. B. F., Boston.
Eddy, Mr. and Mrs. James H., New Britain.
Eddy, Miss Bessie M., New Britain.
Eddy, Chas. B., New York.
Englis, Mrs. John, Brooklyn.
Englis, the Misses, Brooklyn.
Embry, Mrs. J. H., Washington.

Fitzsimmons, Miss M., New York.
Ferrand, Mrs. M. C., New York.
Fitzpatrick, Frank, Cambridge.

Greenleaf, J. A., Auburn.

Hooper, Fred E., Boston.
Hebbinger, Miss C. C., New York.
Hutchinson, Mr. and Mrs. J. B., Philadelphia.
Hill, Edward, New York.
Holmes, C. P., Upper Gloucester.
Hollis, Miss Edith, Hingham.
Hoyt, Mr. and Mrs. Colgate, New York.
Hoyt, Miss, New York.
Hills, Leonard M., Amherst.
Hires, Miss Bessie, Salem, N. J.
Hutchinson, J. B., Jr., Philadelphia.
Holbrook, Miss A., Braintree.
Holbrook, Miss, Braintree.
Hyde, Mrs. James N., Chicago.
Hyde, Charles Cheney, Chicago.

Ivers, Sam. and daughter, New Bedford.
Johnson, Miss, Boston.
Jordan, H. H., Portland.
Jones, Mrs. A., New York.
Jackson, Miss F., Auburn.
Jordan, H. A., Auburn.

Kibbee, H. C., Springfield.
Kibbee, C. A., Springfield.

Little, Amos R., Philadelphia.
Lamphaer, J. E., Providence.
Lewes, J., Jr., Washington.
Lynch, Mr. and Mrs. John, Jr., Washington.
Lewis, Mrs. C. W., Brookline.
Lewis, Miss, Brookline.
Lyster, Mrs. T. G., Colorado.
Libby, Joshua C., Portland.

Martin, A. P., Boston.
Metcalf, Miss, Lewiston.
MacGahan, C. F., Aiken, S. C.
Milliken, Miss, Portland.
Morris, Rev. L. J., Boston.
Morgan, Roger, Springfield.
Moore, Mr. and Mrs. Wm. A. E., Buffalo.
McGill, J. J., Fitchburg.
Mason, Miss A., Auburn.
McGregor, George R. D., New York.
McKeown, J., Lowell.

Nelson, Mrs. M. B., New Berne, N. C.
Newcomb, L. K., Providence.

Ordway, John A., Boston.

Patterson, Rev. A. J., Boston.
Peabody, Mr. and Mrs. Chas. A., New York.
Palmer, Mr. and Mrs. Henry A., Brooklyn.
Perkins, Mrs. Wm. C., Burlington.
Pierce, Mr. and Mrs. Arthur G., New Bedford.
Pingree, R. C., Lewiston.
Pingree, Mrs. Margaret, Lewiston.
Perkins, Mrs. M. A., Mechanic Falls.

Quimby, Mrs. H. C., Saco.

Rogers, Spencer, Portland.
Redman, John B., Ellsworth.
Roecker, W. G., Rhode Island.
Roberts, Mr. and Mrs. J. S., Portland.

Sandford, Mr. and Mrs. J. W., Plainfield.
Searles, Mrs L., Auburn.
Skillings, H. I., Portland.
Shepard, F. O., Salem.
Shethar, Sam., New York.
Shurtleff, Dr. A., Lewiston.
Soule, A. S., Boston.
Sleeper, C. L., Lewiston.
Stetson, Mr. and Mrs. Ed., Lewiston.
Smith, Mrs. F. Percy, Philadelphia.
Smith, Mrs. John B., Lewiston.
Smith, Mrs. S. A., Newark.

Thurston, Mrs. L., New York.
Tabet, Mr. and Mrs. J. W., Portland.
Thorns, S. E., Providence.
Turner, W. L., Providence.
Teale, W. Tracy, Boston.
Turner, Mrs. Ellen, Boston.
Turner, Mrs. John B., Boston.
Turner, Wm. Dall, Boston.
Taft, Dr. R. M., New York.
Tirrell, Mr. and Mrs. Chas. Q., Boston.

Welgwood, Dr. and Mrs. M. C., Lewiston.
Winthrop, Mrs., New York.
White, H. B. G., Chicago.
Webber, Sadie, Boston.
Wadleigh, Mrs. H. W., Watertown, Wis.
Wood, Mr. and Mrs. M. J., New York.
Wilcox, Mrs. D. C., New York.
Wilcox, Miss E., New York.
Wilcox, R. N., New York.

Winn, Mrs. John,   Lewiston.
Whitney, Mr. and Mrs. Geo. E.,   Portland.
Whitney, Mrs. G. M.,   Portland.

Yates, David G.,   Philadelphia.

MANSION HOUSE.

Adams, Mr. and Mrs. S. H.,   Boston.
Ahern, William,   Middleboro.

Butler, H.,   Portland.
Barrows, George D.,   Philadelphia.
Bates, Mr. and Mrs. A. M.,   Brooklyn.

Cordan, F. C.,   Portland.

Dowse, Miss A. F.,   Boston.
Day, Mr. and Mrs. Holman F.,   Auburn.
Donovan, Walter,   Boston.

Freen, J.,   Haverhill.
Freen, Miss K.,   Haverhill.

Griffin, P. T.,   Portland.
Gage, B. W.,   Boston.
Gay, Mrs. E. G.,   Boston.
Gay, Ernest L.,   Boston.

Koch, J.,   Lewiston.
Kilyan, Frank,   Lewiston.
Kelly, Charles F.,   Boston.
Kuntz, Mrs. David,   Boston.

Long, Mr. and Mrs. John D.,   Haverhill.
Long, Miss K. A.,   Haverhill.
Long, Miss W.,   Haverhill.
Leahy, Miss A.,   Haverhill.

Morrill, Mrs.,   Haverhill.
Morrill, Willie,   Haverhill.
McDuffy, Miss,   Haverhill.

Perkins, Mrs. H. Russell,   Newburyport.
Perkins, Miss,   Newburyport.

Reed, J. B.,   Portland.

Schoen, Mr. and Mrs. H.,   New York.

Taylor, Mrs.,   Haverhill.
Teague, H. A.,   Lewiston.

Waite, J. H.,   Templeton.
Woodman, Miss C. Belle,   Springfield.

Poland Water Leads Them All.

WHY?

BECAUSE .. It was the FIRST KNOWN SOLVENT OF URIC ACID in the system. . . . .

BECAUSE .. It is the most EFFECTIVE ELIMINATOR of Calculi in the Bladder and Kidneys known to-day. . . . .

BECAUSE .. It was the ONLY water IN NEW ENGLAND to receive ANY AWARD at the World's Columbian Exposition, and the only award of the hundreds exhibited from the WORLD for Purity and Great Medicinal Properties. . . . .

BECAUSE .. The ANNUAL sales exceed the combined sales of all the Saratoga Springs. . . . . .

BECAUSE .. Unprecedented as the success of the past has been it is more promising than ever, showing continued increase. . . . .

OFFICES:

BOSTON:	NEW YORK:	PHILADELPHIA:	CHICAGO:
175 Devonshire Street.	3 Park Place.	Corner 13th and Chestnut St.	Cor. Michigan Ave. and Van Buren St.

HIRAM RICKER & SONS, Proprietors.
(INCORPORATED.)

THE HILL-TOP.
POLAND SPRING.

Vol. II.   SUNDAY MORNING, JULY 21, 1895.   No. 4.

A Poland Group.

SEVERAL days since, Mr. Ness, of the Notman Photographic Co., was requested to bring his camera around to the Maine State Building and take a picture.

On arriving he found Mr. Spaulding and 29 others covering the steps of the place, and anxiously awaiting some event. The event was the taking in one group, of the thirty people assembled.

With the eye of a true artist, Mr. Ness

arranged his group, Mr. Spaulding offering some valuable suggestions; several of the chairs from the Maine Building being brought into requisition. At length the group was satisfactorily focused, and the button was pressed, with the result shown upon our first page.

The ladies and gentlemen composing the group, beginning at the left of the picture, were:

Miss Nettie Ricker,	South Poland.
Dr. and Mrs. E. J. Lee,	Philadelphia.
The Misses Lee,	Philadelphia.
Col. H. H. Coler,	New York.
Mrs. H. H. Coler,	New York.
Miss Julia Carpenter,	Providence.
Miss Fargo,	Chicago.
Miss Bourne,	New York.
Mrs. H. A. Spaulding,	New York.
Miss Mary Milnor,	Baltimore.
Mrs. J. B. Sawyer,	Pittsburg.
Miss Peckham,	Providence.
Mr. Edward E. Eames,	New York.
Mr. H. A. Spaulding,	New York.
Mr. F. C. Griffith,	Boston.
Mr. Louis J. Mathews,	Philadelphia.
Miss L. Bacon,	New York.
Miss Mary Eames,	New York.
Miss M. Spaulding,	New York.
The Misses Todd,	New York.
Mrs. Chas. Fargo,	Chicago.
Mrs. Geo. T. Bourne,	New York.
Mrs. Milnor,	Baltimore.
Miss Carolyn M. Field,	Boston.
Mr. George T. Bourne,	New York.
Mr. Chas. Fargo,	Chicago.

The groups made this season have been very successful.

Booker T. Washington.

THE name at the top of this article is that of the principal of the Tuskegee Normal and Industrial Institute at Tuskegee, Alabama, for the training of colored youths, and who is himself a colored man. Had we space we should be pleased to enter at greater length upon the subject of his lecture, which was a very excellent presentation of his plea for encouragement in his great work.

He was sufficiently eloquent and convincing in his statements, together with the aid of Mrs. J. W. Walcott, a lady who could personally vouch for the worthy object, to receive as a substantial aid the sum of $256.00. His anecdotes, illustrating the characteristics of the negro, were very clever, one of which refers to an old darkey who stated that, on being sold and sent into Alabama, there were five of them in the lot, himself, his brother, and three mules.

How Royalty Sees the Play.

SHAKESPEARE says, "There's a divinity doth hedge a king," but as royalty attends the play-house in London, there is considerable more than that, in his "hedge-row." The most of the English royal family like the theatre, but the Queen herself never attends any London house, but contrary to the practice of Mahomet, she "commands" the mountain to come to her, and it usually comes, and willingly, too, for it carries a very large advertisement with the journey.

Windsor Castle is the place where Her Majesty witnesses all of the London successes in which she feels any interest. These performances are given gratis, the manager sustaining all the expense consequent upon the journey, and the closing of his theatre for a night, but he benefits to the extent of the "thanks of the Queen" and a trifling souvenir, as well as calling the attention of the public to his production more forcibly; yet, as Her Majesty seldom "commands" the presence of anything which is not already a pronounced hit, it is questionable whether the "royal command" is advantageous in a pecuniary sense or not.

Her "command" can be ignored, if the commanded wishes, and without any very serious consequences, as her royal displeasure carries no punishment with it.

Now when the Prince of Wales and any of his family or friends, wish to attend the theatre, a regular system is pursued. In London, there are several places where theatre tickets can be procured, similar to the theatre ticket offices in the chief American hotels; these places are called "libraries." Mitchell's is one of the principal of these. These "libraries" issue their own tickets, but notify the theatre of each ticket sold.

There is a gentleman attendant upon the Prince, at all of his visits to the London amusement places. This gentleman is notified that His Royal Highness and such other notables, naming all, wish to attend the performance at, well, we will say the St. James's Theatre, on a certain night. Mr. Sutton (we will call this functionary) goes out to Mitchell's. "The Prince and Princess of Wales, the Duke and Duchess of York, and the Duke of Fife and the Princess Louise, will attend the St. James's Theatre on —— evening next." That is all that is necessary there. Mitchell's notifies the theatre and the Royal Box is marked off to Mitchell's for that evening. The evening arrives, and at the theatre certain routine preparations have been made, viz.: An awning has been stretched from the theatre to the curb, and a carpet covers the sidewalk. These lead to the Royal Entrance, a private entrance devoted exclusively to notable visitors. This leads to a private staircase, and a corridor in the rear of the Balcony Tier. Two ordinary private boxes on that tier have been let into one, by removing a temporary partition. A beautiful bouquet has been placed in the box, for each of the ladies who constitute the party, and if possible the taste of each has been studied, in the selection of these flowers. Satin programs have been printed and placed in the box, just enough for the party, and they are sufficiently fond of both flowers and programs to never leave one or either, on departing from the theatre.

At the end of the passage-way, at the front of the theatre, is a private room for the Prince and the gentlemen of his party. This apartment is tastefully and neatly gotten up, and is provided with cigars, cigarettes, brandy and soda, Scotch whiskey, etc., and to this room he generally repairs between acts, while the ladies remain in the box have the observed of all observers.

A half hour before "curtain time" Mr. Sutton appears, and is found to be a most affable and genial gentleman. He goes over the entire preparation, and finds every detail attended to, and remains to conduct the royal party to the box on arrival, and later on perhaps disappears.

The Prince is a good listener, and is much liked by all theatrical people, and the Princess as well is most lovable and considerate. They are always welcome at all theatres. Do they pay for their box? Most assuredly, and at an advanced price. The amount is sent to Mitchell's in settlement, and the theatre is not only the richer for the box rent, but by the increased patronage which the visits entail, for of course the management have made the intended visit known in advance through the press.

At the St. James's there is an opening from the foyer into the side passage, and when the boxes are occupied by royalty the portiere is kept close drawn and an important officer of the house stands there between acts to prevent improper intrusion. On one occasion, stationing myself there, the portiere was thrown aside, and I threw myself in the opening just as the Prince was approaching through the passage. Grasping the gentleman firmly by the arm I endeavored to hold him back until the Prince had passed, but he being a much larger and more powerful man, thrust me aside. At that moment His Royal Highness, observing that there was some movement in that direction, glanced at the intruder, recognized him, and

each extended the arm, resulting in a cordial handshake and a hearty "how do you do?"

I subsided, but who the gentleman was, whether a Prince, Duke or Earl, I never discovered. This was my first encounter with royalty.

B. B.

THE name of Buffalo Bill is one to conjure with, and it conjured a very considerable number of our otherwise staid and exemplary young people to the metropolis of Androscoggin County last Tuesday.

This party of fifteen, from the Mansion (made with hands), traveled in state, with a doughnut and a bit of cheese in their wallets, besides other more elaborate concoctions from the famous larder of the aforementioned hostelry, and, so great was the fascination of the Hon. B. B., that all idea of train was obliterated from the collection of fifteen brains, and when they gathered at the river,—no, the station, not the police station, but the *Gare du Rue du Butes,* they were "already too late in season" as the Hungarian said, and there was nothing but a cattle train and a Flying something-or-other later. It was decided to hitch the car on to the cow's tails, and hang on as far as the junction and then let go, which was successfully accomplished, the long-suffering kine giving a kick of satisfaction when the boarders ahoy loosened their grip, and the "special freight" glided swiftly on its way.

By the aid of a crowbar the palace car was sidetracked, and the usual method of return to the Spring was adopted.

It was a jolly time, and as it is a long time between Buffalo Bills, no regrets were indulged in, but all admit that had it not been for the firmness of the caudal appendages of the bovine passengers, they would have been in the consomme,—the jolly fifteen, not the ox tails.

Come again, Bison William.

A Good Example.

ON a recent visit to the Shaker village, Mr. Spaulding became so interested in the exercises of the children in the school-house, that it occurred to him to stimulate their ambition to excel, by offering two prizes for excellence. The designs are very neat and elegant and are in the shape of badges, one a laurel wreath and star supported by a pin and chain, and the second a scroll with neat design above. These are to be executed by Spaulding & Co., Chicago and Paris.

FRANK CARLOS GRiFFiTH, }
NETTIE M. RiCKER, } Editors.

PUBLISHED EVERY SUNDAY MORNING DURING THE MONTHS
OF JULY, AUGUST AND SEPTEMBER, IN THE INTERESTS OF

POLAND SPRING AND ITS VISITORS.

All contributions relative to the guests of Poland Spring will
be thankfully received.

To insure publication, all communications should reach the
editors not later than Wednesday preceding day of issue.

All parties desiring rates for advertising in the HILL-TOP
should write the editors for same.

The subscription price of the HILL-TOP is $1.00 for the
season, post-paid. Single copies will be mailed at 10c. each.

Address,

EDITORS "HILL-TOP,"
Poland Spring House,
South Poland, Maine.

PRINTED AT JOURNAL OFFICE, LEWISTON.

Sunday, July 21, 1895.

Editorial.

THE *genus* Editorial belongs to the amphibious order of animals, and adapts itself with ease to any element, climate, situation or previous condition of servitude. It contracts or elongates in sharpest rivalry to the leech, which will escape through a pin-hole, or present the appearance of a rock of Gibraltar, impervious and impregnable.

It vomits forth fire, or swallows itself with perfect ease; will roar with sufficient horse-power to dwarf the capacity of Niagara Falls, or coo so gently that "nothing lives 'twixt it and silence."

Its brain is that of the mammoth, its capacity, that of the tun of Heidleberg, and its strength that of the trip-hammer of Krupp, and yet no one fears this monster, and every one seeks its society.

The "Thunderer" of John Bull and the HILL-TOP of Poland are the mammoth and the pigmy, and on this occasion the "Editorial"

will crawl into its shell, and give way to far more interesting material, only to emerge on another occasion, when news is scarce but talk is cheap.

Last Sunday's Concert.

THE program for last Sunday's concert was a most excellent one, and beautifully rendered by the orchestra, especially fine being the rendition of Lumbye's "Visions of a Dream." Such a dream must have been exceedingly delightful to have inspired the composer, and such a rendering was fully worthy of its theme.

Mr. D. J. Griffith, one of the guests of the hotel, volunteered a song in German, entitled "Die Uhr," and was a most delightful surprise. His voice is full, rich, and of exquisite quality, and the reception his efforts received was most hearty and deserved. He was honored with a double encore, giving Schubert's "Wanderers Nacht Lied," followed by "Es war ein alter Konig," by Heitsch.

Concert Program.

SUNDAY, JULY 21, 3.30 P.M.
Kuntz Orchestral Club.

1. Marche—La Reine de Saba. . . . . Gounod.
2. Overture—Zampa. . . . . . Herold.
3. { *a.* Elegie. } . . . . . . S. Strube.
   { *b.* Serenade. }
            For Strings.
4. Selection—Walküre. . . . . . Wagner.
5. Lässer Wonnetraum. . . . Meyer Felmund.
6. Ungarische Rhapsodie. . . . . . Liszt.

Drink, Pretty Creature.

THOSE wishing to take away with them a useful souvenir of Poland Spring, and one which will recall daily the loveliest spot upon which a hotel is placed in America, should not fail to possess themselves of one of those very artistic carafes, so excellently embodying the special features of this favored spot.

The price at which they have been placed ($1.50) is extremely reasonable, and their intrinsic value, together with their serviceable quality and pleasant associations, should cause them to be rapidly disposed of.

Sister Aurelia's "Wedding" Present.

A VERY pleasant surprise, on Wednesday evening, was the present given to that sweet and gentle Shaker, Sister Aurelia, by Mr. H. A. Spaulding, consisting of a very elegant case of silver—forks and spoons. It was a very kindly and thoughtful act.

The Cacoethe Scribendi.

If all the trees in all the woods were men,
And each and every blade of grass a pen;
If every leaf on every shrub and tree
Turned to a sheet of foolscap, every sea
Were changed to ink, and all earth's living tribes
Had nothing else to do but act as scribes;
And for ten thousand ages, day and night,
The human race should write, and write, and write
Till all the pens and paper were used up,
And each great inkstand were an empty cup,
Still would the scribblers cluster round its brink,
Call for more pens, more paper, and more ink.

The Indians.

ALL who have seen the souvenir will doubtless recall the picture of the famished and thirsty red man drinking from the spring over in the woods. To-day, if one takes the trouble to penetrate into the shade, off a little to the right of the Spring House, he will find the end of the nineteenth century red man, devoid of yellow ochre, feathers and bear's teeth, but presenting the cast of features, the black straight hair, and penetrating eye of his progenitor.

Look well at him; converse with him, and you will quickly discover the progress the aborigine has made in a century.

Well spoken, courteous, polite, graceful, tall, manly, vigorous and interesting, Newell Neptune sits in his tent, and makes the bows and arrows, or stands behind his display of baskets and tells you of his work.

Examine the neat construction, inhale the fragrance of the sweet grasses, and imagine this stalwart descendant of the savage, drinking from the same spring his forefathers drank from, and we think all will admit it is an object lesson in the possibilities of human progress and development.

The tent of the peaceful visitor from Oldtown is well worth a visit.

Botanical.

THE finest list of plants quoted at the Maine Botanical Association formed at Portland last week, was exhibited from Poland Spring. Anemone cylindrica, new to the State, created much surprise. Miss Furbish finds the flora of Poland very rich in *rare* plants.

Mr. James Staples and wife, of Bridgeport, Conn., accompanied by Mrs. George Richardson, are registered for a two weeks' visit. Mr. Staples was here last year, and like nearly everyone else who visits Poland, has repeated his visit.

Tid=Bits.

Blackberries.

The Fakir lifted well.

The magazines are tabled.

Croquet still has its devotees.

More paintings for the Art Gallery.

Base-Ball. Bell Boys. Buffalo Bill.

113 was a big run on the billiard table.

The Indians are trundling their war whoops.

The Editors of THE HILL-TOP do *not* sing.

Collectors of paintings will do well to inspect those of Mr. Enneking and Mr. Hatfield.

What parts of a carriage does this place remind one of? Send replies to the HILL-TOP.

Three very welcome old friends are Messrs. Oakes, Hammond, and Mitchell, all former visitors.

It was a flying visit, that of ex-Governor Long of Massachusetts. *But*, he is coming again.

Mr. Bartlett, Mr. Ivers, Mr. Travelli, Mr. Boynton, are the champion croquet players at Poland Spring.

Thirty-two guests from the Poland Spring House went to see Buffalo Bill. P. S. H. furnished a lunch.

Mr. S. Boileau, of Easton, Pennsylvania, the well-known banker, is at the Poland Spring House, with his wife.

Dr. Wood, a prominent physician of Worcester, Mass., and Mrs. Wood are spending a few weeks at Poland Spring.

J. P. Bates, of the well-known house of Cobb, Bates & Yerxa, probably the largest grocery and tea house in America, is registered.

Dr. Warren F. Gay, son of the celebrated Dr. George H. Gay of Beacon Street, Boston, arrived at Poland Spring, Monday.

Miss Marguerite Ricker and Miss Janette Ricker have returned from Portland, where they have been visiting Mrs. Folsom for a week.

On the register are the names of five people with their three initials the same. One E. E. E., one A. A. A., one L. L. L., and two C. C. C's.

D. D. Coombs of Auburn, has recently graced the corridors of the Poland Spring House. He has placed one of his best works in the Art Gallery.

Mr. and Mrs. Harry D. Zeigler and Miss C. F. Zeigler, of Philadelphia, who for many years have annually visited Poland, were welcomed by their many friends, on their arrival a few days since.

When you return home, think of the books you can spare from your library which might interest others, and send them to the Maine State Building.

Charming Miss McNeil of New York, niece of Mrs. Morgan Smith, is a guest at the Poland Spring House. Miss McNeil has a beautiful soprano voice.

The Souvenir Carafes, designed by Miss Nettie M. Ricker, have recently been placed upon the tables at the Mansion House, and are much commended.

Mrs. J. Don Cameron has returned from Washington, and is welcomed by Mrs. Colgate Hoyt, as well as by all who met this charming lady on her former visit.

Mr. and Mrs. J. Sinclair Armstrong and family and Miss Tweddle, of New York, are making their first visit at Poland, and express themselves as much pleased with the place.

Mr. Sawyer and Mr. Goodrich went fishing Wednesday. They caught one fish weighing four pounds. One man caught the fish and the other pulled it in. Which was which?

Mr. and Mrs. George H. Conley of Boston are at the Mansion House. Mr. Conley is supervisor of the Boston public schools, and a member of the Massachusetts State Board of Education.

Have you made the tour of the lakes yet, on the "Poland"? The Scottish lakes, Ben Lomond and the Trosachs "cut no ice" in comparison. What, warder, ho! Let the portcullis fall.

Monday, three of our orchestra, Messrs. Kuntz, Golde and Strube swam the Hellespont— no, it was the middle lake, from shore to shore, but there was no Hero to meet these Leanders. Alack and alas!

Rev. B. S. Rideout of Norway, Maine, preached in Music Hall last Sunday. His text was Phil. iv., 22. A collection was taken for the purchase of an organ for his church in Norway. Thirty-five dollars and five cents was contributed.

Mr. and Mrs. S. H. G. Stewart, of New York, were among last week's arrivals. Mr. Stewart is well known in Wall Street. His business interests prevented his remaining long, and after seeing Mrs. Stewart comfortably located, he returned to New York; but his many friends here hope to see him return for a longer sojourn in the near future.

The Doll that Owned a Little Girl.

There was a big wax dolly once
  Who owned a little girl,
With lovely eyes that opened wide
  And golden hair in curl.

At first by her delightful toy
  The dolly set great store,
But presently she let her drop
  Head downward on the floor.

She left her sitting all alone,
  Neglected and forlorn;
Her hair had not been combed for days;
  Her pretty frock was torn.

And shortly after that—they say
  Dolls are a thoughtless race—
The empty-headed thing forgot
  To wash her plaything's face.

The dolly's mother said, "If that
  Is how you treat poor Pearl,
It's very clear you don't deserve
  To have a little girl."

Two Fakirs.

On Monday afternoon two traveling Fakirs, after the manner so common in England, appeared upon the lawn, resplendent in green tights and spangles, and gave a very good exhibition of their skill in feats of strength, balancing, and contortion acts. The balancing of ten common heavy wooden chairs was very cleverly done, as also were those with the heavy cartwheel and the plough. His companion performed some very good feats of contortion, and from appearances they were very well rewarded.

"Noirtier."

The above is the name of a dog. Not a "truly" dog, nor a dog made of Athens, but a dog made of Persian lamb. It is a black dog, with the whitest of paws and tip of tail, and is the result of the laborious efforts of an old lady who makes them for foot rests. Look in at the "store" and ask the young lady to show Noirtier, the prize dog, and you will be highly pleased at the life-like reproduction.

Mr. and Mrs. E. S. Converse of Boston, are welcome guests. Mr. Converse is a gentleman of the most progressive and liberal spirit, and his magnificent gift of a park at Middlesex Fells is a great boon.

The Magnificent Portrait of Hon. James G. Blaine, hanging over the stairway in the Maine Building, was made by THE SPRAGUE & HATHAWAY Co. of West Somerville, Mass. They also made the enlarged photograph of the World's Fair Views in the same building.

Base-Ball.

THE two attempts of Saturday and Monday last, on the diamond, were not quite so brilliant as that gem, but in one case the "purest water" was from the clouds, and in the other the annunciator called "time" on the Bell Boys in the fourth inning, to the tune of 7 to 9 or 11 or 12 as variously reported, in favor of the B. B's. Front!

The Exchange Bank of Milton, Ill., has been robbed of its *entire* contents. The robbers did not even leave a draft of air, or a check on their movements. The cashier will not state how much money he left there the night before for the burglars to take, but it is shrewdly suspected there was as much as a dollar and eighty-eight cents.

"I Shall Not Pass Again."

The bread that bringeth strength I want to give,
The water pure that bids the thirsty live;
I want to help the fainting day by day,
I'm sure I shall not pass again this way.

I want to give good measure running o'er,
And into angry hearts I want to pour
The answer soft that turneth wrath away,
I'm sure I shall not pass again this way.

I want to give to others hope and faith;
I want to do all that the Master saith;
I want to live aright from day to day,
I'm sure I shall not pass again this way.

We have among us Col. W. N. Coler, who was in the Mexican war, also the war of the Rebellion, and an intimate friend of President Lincoln and General Grant, and who is now one of the prominent bankers of New York and Chicago.

Another new book presented to the Library by the author, is entitled "Pushing to the Front," by Orison Swett Marden. Published by Houghton, Mifflin & Co. It contains sketches of many great men, and is fully illustrated with portraits. A very fascinating work.

N. B. Trist of New Orleans is the originator of the "American Leads," and Miss Trist, his charming daughter, who has been a guest at the Poland Spring House for some time, is meeting with excellent success, in conjunction with Miss Noble, in teaching this popular game.

The Buffalo Bill show reckons its patronage by the mile. In Hartford they claim sixteen miles of people. These were not General Miles but statute miles.

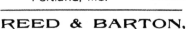

Arrivals.

POLAND SPRING HOUSE.

Atwood, W. P.,	Auburn.
Armstrong, Mr. and Mrs. Johnstone,	New York.
Akers, Geo. J.,	Chicago.
Anderson, E. J.,	Boston.
Bradford, Miss Grace,	Auburn.
Boileau, Mr. and Mrs. S.,	Easton, Pa.
Burnham, Mr. and Mrs. C. H.,	Boston.
Byrne, Mr. and Mrs. Wm. A.,	Boston.
Bates, Mr. and Mrs. Jacob P.,	Boston.
Bedford, Mr. and Mrs. T. H.,	New York.
Bacon, F. W.,	Boston.
Barbour, E. D.,	Boston.
Booth, Mrs. W. V.,	Chicago.
Bailey, Dr. Geo. H.,	Deering.
Boynton, Mr. and Mrs. W. W.,	Cleveland.
Buck, Mrs. C. E.,	Richmond.
Buck, Miss Ella,	Richmond.
Bell, Mr. and Mrs. James F.,	Minneapolis.
Brown, Lydia M.,	New York.
Curtis, Mrs.,	Portland.
Cowles, Mrs. E. P.,	Rye, N. Y.
Chandler, Mrs. Z .,	Detroit.
Converse, Mr. and Mrs. E. S.,	Boston.
Coombs, D. D.,	Auburn.
Cozens, Miss,	Philadelphia.
Chase, Capt. Amos A.,	Cumberland Mills.
Chase, Master Frank A.,	Chicago.
Chandler, Wm. A.,	Providence.
Chase, Miss,	Philadelphia.
Colburn, Bert S.,	Toledo.
Crowell, Nathan,	Boston.
Cameron, Mrs. J. D.,	Washington.
Clapp, Mrs. G. W.,	Cambridge.
Colburn, Mr. and Mrs. A. T.,	Toledo.
Colburn, Charlotte,	Toledo.
Callahan, W. E.,	Lewiston.
Clark, Henry N.,	Boston.
Clifford, Miss M. A.,	Newton.
Duval, Mrs. A.,	New York.
Dunn, D. F.,	Worcester.
Davis, Mr. and Mrs. Albert F., and daughter,	Providence.
Dwight, Henry Butler,	New York.
Drew, F. L.,	Boston.
Drew, Geo. A.,	Lewiston.
Doremus, G. H.,	Jersey City.
Dotger, Mr. and Mrs. A. J.,	So. Orange, N. J.
Dow, Mr. and Mrs. F. P.,	Epsom.
Dresser, Mrs. A. G.,	Boston.
Dresser, Horatio W.,	Boston.
Ely, Mrs.,	New York.
Eames, Stewart W.,	New York.
French, C. H.,	Chicago.
Fenn, A. H.,	Jefferson.
Fowler, Nehemiah,	Newburgh.
Fillebrown, C. B.,	Boston.
Fallon, Wm. B.,	Lewiston.
Fillebrown, Louise J.,	Newton.
Frye, Mr. and Mrs. J. C.,	Boston.
Griffin, C. C.,	Haverhill.
Gregg, Mrs. Joshua,	Philadelphia.
Gregg, Miss,	Philadelphia.
Gregg, J. Howard,	Philadelphia.
Hale, Mrs. Eugene,	Ellsworth.
Hale, Chandler,	Ellsworth.
Hammond, T. W.,	Worcester.
Hammond, B. T.,	Worcester.
Holmes, Mr. and Mrs. E.,	New York.
Hayden, C. F.,	Lewiston.
Holmes, Chas. F.,	New Gloucester.
Howland, Florence D.,	Boston.
Holbrooke, Miss,	Boston.

Hall, A. C.,	New York.
Hack, F.,	New York.
Hall, Mrs. W. H.,	New York.
Hubley, Mr. and Mrs. J. M.,	Chelsea.
Hibbard, C. P.,	Lisbon, N. H.
Jordan, E. L.,	Auburn.
Johnson, Maude,	Salem.
Jordan, H. I.,	Auburn.
Joly, Mrs. C. C.,	Philadelphia.
Joly, Miss,	Philadelphia.
Kilbourne, Hattie F.,	E. Hampton.
King, Welham J.,	St. Louis.
Keegan, D. W.,	New York.
Kimball, the Misses,	Brookline.
Kimball, Miss M. F.,	Boston.
Locke, Lara,	Salem.
Loring, Mrs. L. W.,	Boston.
Moulton, Mrs. Byron P.,	Rosemont.
Mantel, G. B.,	Superior.
Moore, Ethel,	New York.
Mullin, J. C.,	Salem.
McGregor, Geo. R. D.,	Boston.
Mitchell, Mr. and Mrs. A. R.,	Newton.
Mason, James,	New York.
McNeil, Miss,	New York.
Moulton, Mr. and Mrs. B. C.,	Boston.
Main, Mrs C. H.,	Jackson.
Mitchell, E. C.,	N. Y. Journal.
Nolan, A. Eugene,	Fitchburg.
Nevens, Mr. and Mrs. W. H.,	Lewiston.
Nichols, Geo. C.,	Boston.
Osgood, Mr. and Mrs. H. P.,	Portland.
Oakes, Mr. and Mrs. Josiah,	Malden.
Osborn, Mrs. E. T.,	Peabody.
Plummer, E.,	Lisbon Falls.
Pope, Lara,	Boston.
Phillips, Fred S.,	Providence.
Peeples, T. R.,	Savannah.
Palmer, Mr. and Mrs. A. W.,	Boston.
Perkins, Mr. and Mrs. S. M.,	Brooklyn.
Perkins, Harold H.,	Brooklyn.
Pearson, Lewis B., Jr.,	New York.
Pierce, Mr. and Mrs. Moses,	Norwich.
Rines, Mr. and Mrs. A. S.,	Portland.
Ring, Frances G.,	Gardiner.
Rees, Mr. and Mrs. W. D.,	Cleveland.
Rice, Mr. and Mrs. Richard W.,	Springfield.
Richardson, Mrs. Geo.,	Bridgeport.
Redfern, Mr. and Mrs. B. S.,	Boston.
Rogers, Mr. and Mrs. J. Fred,	Boston.
Robb, Thos.,	Philadelphia.
Richardson, Jas. H.,	Boston.
Rideout, Mr. and Mrs. B. S.,	Norway.
Rose, Hanson Wheeler,	Pittsburgh.
Richaldson, Mr. and Mrs. A. P.,	Chicago.
Richardson, A. Howard,	Chicago.
Raymond, Mrs. S. B.,	Chicago.
Rydel, H. M.,	Boston.
Rines. R. H.,	Boston.
Ruggles, E. O.,	Boston.
Russell, Miss,	Portland.
Stewart, Mr. and Mrs. S. H. Gardyne,	New York.
Stratton, Mr. and Mrs. J. D.,	Springfield.
Staples, Mr. and Mrs. James,	Bridgeport.
Souther, Mary.	Boston.
Southard, Louise,	New York.
Speer, Wm. H., Jr.,	Jersey City.
Sherman, Howard,	New York.
Sweetland, Mrs. S. A.,	Boston.
Sanborn, F. B.,	Lisbon, N. H.
Tweddle, Miss,	New York.
Townsend, R. H. L,	New York.
Tabot, Mr. and Mrs. J. W.,	Portland.
Thorp, E. G.,	Boston.
Thayer, Belle,	Boston.
Townsend, Edwin S.,	New York.
Tamar, N.,	Damascus.

Tatum, Miss,   Brooklyn.
Vose, Julien W.,   Boston.
Weeks, Mr. and Mrs. N. E.,   Longwood.
Weeks, Master Norton,   Longwood.
White, Mr. and Mrs. W. L.,   Taunton.
White, Mr. and Mrs. J. Stuart,   New York.
Wilkins, H. M.,   Mobile.
Wescott, Dr. Geo. F.,   Portland.
Williams, Mrs. T.,   Richmond.
Williams, Miss,   Richmond.
Williams, T. C., Jr.,   Richmond.
Wallace, Thos. H.,   Lewiston.
Williams, C. B.,   Corning.
Young, Mr. and Mrs. Henry W.,   Lewiston.
Zeigler, Mr. and Mrs. Harry,   Philadelphia.
Zeigler, Miss C. F.,   Philadelphia.

MANSION HOUSE.

Burgess, Miss J. A.,   Boston.
Bumstead, Horace,   Atlanta.
Brown, Mrs. A. C.,   Boston.
Chandler, P. L.,   Westbrook.
Campbell, Mary,   Camden, N. J.
Conley, Mr. and Mrs. Geo. H.,   Boston.
Coes, Mr. and Mrs. John H.,   Worcester.
Coes, Mary M.,   Worcester.
Chandler, Paul L.,   Westbrook.
Duffee, Miss,   Haverhill.
Elliott, Mrs. F. J.,   Philadelphia.
Eastman, Miss J.,   Boston.
Foster, C.,   Portland.
Gay, Warren F.,   Boston.
Heffernan, Jas.,   New York.
Heffernan, Mrs.,   Brooklyn.
Heffernan, Catharine P.,   Brooklyn.
Howe, G. M.,   Lewiston.
Long, John D.,   Hingham.
Long, Chas. S.,   Boston.
Long, Miss Katie,   Haverhill.
McLean, A. B.,   Boston.
Mylick, Rev. and Mrs. N. L.,   Sing Sing.
Read, Mrs. L. S.,   Camden, N. J.
Read, Wm. T.,   Camden, N. J.
Ricker, Alice B.,   Falmouth.
Sullivan, Miss A.,   Lewiston.
Sullivan, Miss L.,   Lewiston.
Sullivan, T. J.,   Lewiston.
Samson, E. P.,   Lewiston.
Steinmetz, S. J.,   Philadelphia.
Sweetser, Edwin C.,   Philadelphia.
Thurston, Jessie L.,   Portland.
Wood, Mr. and Mrs. Albert,   Worcester.
Wood, Emily C.,   Worcester.
Wood, Mr. and Mrs. Samuel,   Northboro.

VOL. II.   SUNDAY MORNING, JULY 28, 1895.   No. 5.

An Inexhaustible Subject.

AS THE wearied and almost exhausted employee said on retiring to take an afternoon forty winks, "don't call me for anything short of fire and E. P. Ricker."

So it would seem to many that the theme of the Poland Spring House had become exhausted, but yet it rises readily to the call of the public to present new phases, and interest new readers.

Have you ever realized that the room you occupy may have been in the past the resting place of men great in Art, in Literature, or in Politics? Governors, senators, professors, congressmen, artists, generals, or descendants of royalty?

Yet such is the fact, and even before this grand establishment was built, William Hunt, the great artist, sat upon a rock, upon its site, and watched the sunsets, which he said were equal to anything in Italy for their magnificence.

James Harper also came, years ago, and made his modest little sketch, which has traveled to the uttermost parts of the earth. James G. Blaine, the pride and boast of Maine, has often found rest and comfort in the house on the hill.

Among the governors of this and other states we may instance a few such as Governors Robie, Bodwell, Plaisted, Burleigh, and the present Chief Executive of Maine, Governor Cleaves.

Of other states, Governors Rice, Long, and

Butler, of Massachusetts, besides many from other states.

Art has been represented also in this modern paradise by Robert Vonnoh, the head instructor in the Academy of Design in Philadelphia, and not only well known in America, but in Europe as well.

Among the numerous great universities represented, Harvard has sent its Instructor of Music, Professor Paine, and its Instructor of Elocution, Professor Hayes.

F. W. Palmer, the President of the World's Fair Commission, has praised its elegance and comfort; while the great arena of politics has had its ranks represented by many of its eloquent sons, none, however, more welcome than such familiar names as Senator Frye, of our neighboring city; Senator Hale, from the far eastern border; Congressman Dingley, again one of our neighbors, and Boutelle from the centre of the State; Gen. A. P. Martin, born near the place, and a man risen to prominence; Senator J. Don Cameron, Pennsylvania's favorite son, and son of a famous cabinet officer under Lincoln.

Another cabinet officer has graced its halls as well, Wayne MacVeigh; and an eloquent man from the capital of Indiana, John Griffith, found shelter here during the second Harrison campaign.

Royalty even has not been unrepresented, for a direct descendant of the great Napoleon, Charles Napoleon Bonaparte, has been happier here than he would have been on the throne of France.

Fred Douglass, the great negro—but why multiply names, for to continue a list which embraces thousands would be but a tedious task.

In private life the names of men and women, no less great, might be added *ad nauseum*, and so we will let it rest at this brief mention, and only add, that once a guest, always a guest, once welcomed, always welcomed, until the growth of its reputation has become dear to every frequenter of its corridors, verandas, and its shady walks.

Translation Wanted.

WE have been allowed to read a letter of a Japanese, written in English, in which he refers to the "Pigtailed Government," and also quaintly says: "Our people never always asks about the expense of time against the one to present (free of charge) but I suppose that your country has, on the contrary, a costume to fix it beforehand. I astonished very much at it having read your letter."

One Effect of Poland Water.

Have you ever been to Poland ?
Have you stayed a season there?
And partaken of its comforts
And the water pure and rare?
Have you met the host and hostess ?
Had the welcome of a guest?
Seen how many things are thought of
For one's pleasure and one's rest?
Well, if you've never done so,
A word will now suffice
To bring you quickly hither
To this hotel so nice.
The train to "Danville Junction '
Is the one in every case,
And a carriage there to meet you
Will be waiting in its place.
It will take you onward, upward
To the "Hill-Top," where you'll meet
The genial E. P. Ricker,
As he stands his guests to greet.
He will give you a warm welcome,
Have you shown to your fine room;
He will make you feel such comfort
You won't wish to go home soon
As at first you thought you ought to,
And, in fact, you *said* you *would*;
But, after dining once here,
To remain you really should.   —ANON.

The Flowering Fern.

THE *Osmunda regalis* (or flowering fern), which was so kindly exhibited by an English woman during her stay here as identical with the "royal fern of England," is also a *native* of America. It grows abundantly in our swamps and wet woods. The fertile stem is very attractive. A specimen of the fern can be seen at the Herbarium in the Maine State Building.

Botanical.

THE few guests who are interested in Nature's garden here will be pleased to know that Mrs. B. F. Redfern of Boston has collected *Desmodium paniculatum* and *D. Dillenii* this week at West Poland. Both plants belong to the Pulse Family. Their home must be quite *locale* in Maine, as Miss Furbish in her work of "Nineteen Summers" had not seen them, though she has traveled extensively in localities widely separated, and for seven years in succession made 1,000 miles per season on foot. She expresses herself as being greatly pleased with the "find," and is happy to add the name of Redfern to her painted flora and herbarium, as well as to add two plants over this signature to the Poland Spring Collection of Plants.

A Drinking Song.

Should in Nubia I be stationed,
In an office governmental,
I mean to distance the giraffe
By means experimental.
For water there is scarcer
Than hens' teeth by quite a half;
So the " purest water " I shall take
From a Poland Spring Carafe.
For I don't propose to die of thirst,
And I don't propose to sicken;
But as I drink shall gaze on scenes
Which make the pulses quicken.
The inner man will be refreshed;
The eye will find relief;
And as I quaff from the carafe,
Shall drown all cares and grief.

Mrs. Bailey's Lectures.

Mrs. John Bailey gave a series of lesson lectures at the Poland Spring House on the mornings of July 23, 24, and 25, at 11 o'clock. Her subjects were : Tuesday, July 23d, " Harmony of the Body" (how to sit, stand, and walk) ; Wednesday, July 24th, " Voice in Speaking" (tones and words—their value in expression) ; Thursday, July 25th, " Dress" (suggestions upon beauty and improvement in dress).

Mrs. Bailey remains until the middle of August. Her charge for private lessons is $5.00 and, in a class of twenty, $15.00 for ten lessons.

Maine State Building.

The reading-room in the rotunda of the Maine State Building has already become a favorite place for those who seek the advantages of the best periodicals, and cool and quiet nooks.

If parents will kindly request their children to observe quiet, it will conduce to the comfort of readers.

The work of cataloging has been necessarily delayed, but is now progressing as rapidly as possible.

The list of periodicals now includes the Art Amateur, Arena, Atlantic Monthly, McClure's, Youth's Companion, Ladies' Home Journal, Century, Frank Leslie's, Harper's Monthly, Weekly, and Bazaar, London Illustrated News, Judge, Munsey's, North American Review, Puck, St. Nicholas, Life, Review of Reviews, London Graphic, Scribner's, Home Journal, Pathfinder Guide.

The paintings are now being hung in the Art Gallery.

Several very fine paintings by Adelaide Palmer have been received, and are very excellent works, well worth attention.

A Generous Gift.

Gen. Augustus P. Martin, who was one of the speakers at the dedicatory exercises of the Maine State Building, has presented to the Library one hundred and thirty-eight volumes of standard books as follows :

Waverly Novels,	24 volumes.
Thackeray,	10 "
George Eliot,	12 "
Bartlett's Familiar Quotations,	1 "
Dickens,	15
Victor Hugo,	12
Bulwer,	13
Charles Kingsley,	6
Kipling,	6
Oliver Wendell Holmes,	13
James Russell Lowell,	12
Hawthorne,	13
Roget's Thesaurus,	1 "

This is a noble beginning for what will undoubtedly result in very large additions to the Library in the immediate future. All honor to Gen. Martin for his splendid gift.

Fire at White Oak Hill.

Those who were up late on Monday night witnessed a sight well worth seeing. It was the destruction by fire of all the farm buildings of John Hanscom on White Oak Hill. The illumination was very brilliant, and even the crackling of the wood was plainly audible. Our own Forrest Walker, head carpenter at Poland Spring, was one of the five men present at the fire, and assisted in saving the piano and furniture.

Moral : sit up late if you would see fires at their best.

Krieger.

Such is the name of that little bit of humanity who claims to "set all nature's laws aside." Quite a contract for a wee little man, especially when he guarantees to keep you "in one continuous smile," broken only by "one hundred laughs."

One must take this to mean that the serious attempts at legerdemain are provocative of mirth as well. Be that as it may, the Lilliputian Russian juggled some thirty to forty dollars from the pockets of the well-to-do, who will be none the poorer, and the absentee from the domain of the Tzar will be that much nearer the day of his retirement.

Rev. Thomas F. Butler of Lewiston held mass on Sunday last, at 6 A.M., which was very well attended.

FRANK CARLOS GRIFFITH, } EDITORS.
NETTIE M. RICKER, }

PUBLISHED EVERY SUNDAY MORNING DURING THE MONTHS
OF JULY, AUGUST AND SEPTEMBER, IN THE INTERESTS OF

POLAND SPRING AND ITS VISITORS.

All contributions relative to the guests of Poland Spring will
be thankfully received.
To insure publication, all communications should reach the
editors not later than Wednesday preceding day of issue.
All parties desiring rates for advertising in the HILL-TOP
should write the editors for same.
The subscription price of the HILL-TOP is $1.00 for the
season, post-paid. Single copies will be mailed at 10c. each.
Address,

EDITORS "HILL-TOP,"
Poland Spring House,
South Poland, Maine.

PRINTED AT JOURNAL OFFICE, LEWISTON.

Sunday, July 28, 1895.

Editorial.

IT is a desirable feature that all good things
should grow, and that the bad should "dwin-
dle, peak and pine," to use the language of
Micawber, and we feel already that there are
people who are kind enough to consider THE
HILL-TOP one of the former.

Look at the grand building in which our spacious offices and editorial rooms are located, and
then wonder if you can at our success. One can
draw in inspiration at the pores from such surroundings. A noble edifice, books, magazines,
works of art, and, not to be outdone by our older
competitors, we have grown to the dignity of a
roll-top desk, in place of the table we began on.

It will be well for you to watch us and see us
grow, for very soon we expect the tops of our
boots to appear, unless precautions are taken to
keep our costume in keeping with our dimensions.

We have felt the genial influence of encouragement, the past week, in receiving calls from
persons interested, who have contributed a number of articles which grace our columns this
week, and we hope the work, once begun, will
be carried on to the last. When you have something which you realize is interesting, don't keep
it all to yourself, for that is selfish, and selfishness is a plant not native to Ricker Hill, and not
classified in our Botany. No, let it be spread
broadcast, for in the columns of our Poland
journal it will be relished by a thousand readers.

We are now approaching the height of the
season, and what more appropriate place to view
its features than from THE HILL-TOP?

Mr. Sawyer.

ALL who have met Mr. J. B. Sawyer are
interested to learn tidings of him during his
serious illness. He is a man universally beloved,
and all who have the pleasure of his acquaintance will regret, as we do, his present trouble.

The latest report, as we go to press, is very
hopeful, he being reported by Dr. Wedgwood
as in an improved condition and able to take
nourishment. This will be glad tidings to all,
and we can only express the wish uppermost in
everyone's mind, that the improvement may continue, and he may be blessed with a speedy
recovery.

Concert Program.

SUNDAY, JULY 28TH, AT 3.30 P.M.

Kuntz Orchestral Club.

1. Overture—Rosamunde.   .   .   .   .   . Schubert.
2. Selection—Oberon.   .   .   .   .   .   . Weber.
3. { *a.* Andalouse. }   .   .   .   .   . Massenet.
   { *b.* Aubade.   }
         Air de Ballet.
4. Unfinished Symphony.   .   .   .   . Schubert.
         First Movement.
5. { *a.* Serenata.   .   .   .   .   . Moskowski.
   { *b.* Intermezzo.   .   .   .   .   . Macbeth.
         For Strings.
6. Marche from Leonora Symphony.   .   .   . Raff.

Last Sunday's concert was one of excellence,
and great interest is shown in them by the guests
who appreciate good music.

It is much to be regretted that the testimonial
to Mr. Kuntz came too late in the week to receive
attention to-day, but we shall endeavor to do so
in the next issue.

The Reading-Room of the Maine State Building is indebted to Morris, Phillips & Co. for a
copy of the *New York Home Journal*, to be
regularly found on the table. It is the standard
society paper of America.

Bits of Conversation on the Verandah.

"YES, we have two children, and we think the world of them. They're simply priceless treasures. Why, do you know—" "What'll you take for them?" "Oh, I don't know, perhaps four dollars for the biggest and two and a half for the smallest. You see land in that vicinity is worth more a foot—"

"Foot, I didn't see anything surprising about her foot, except the heel, and that was long enough in all conscience."

"It had puffed sleeves, and took four yards of silk for each one—"

"Mercy, what a record. He used to drink as much whisky in a day, but thirty glasses of Poland water, that's—"

"Out of sight, well I should say so. It might be worse though, for a mile in 2.16 ain't to be sneezed at. She'll make music for them when—"

"These organ pipes are all the rage now for dress skirts. I hope the Princess somebody or other will—"

"Come to Poland by all means every year. It'll do you the world of good; it has me. Now look at me—"

"You're a sight. Go up stairs and brush yourself. Your coat looks as if you had had—"

"Bright's disease in two volumes. It's a standard work. It's the best thing on the subject since—"

"McGinty or Sweet Marie or something of that sort. It's played out anyway. I'm looking for something new and startling. I'll give a hundred dollars for a—"

"Divorce, yes, she's after one now. For heaven's sake don't say anything to make her change her mind; I want her to get it, and then perhaps I can—"

"Sleep nights—? Bet your life, like a top. The air here is great, it makes a new man of you. Have a cigar. Where in this wide world—"

"Did you get that hat in Paris? Its a beaut, ain't it, sis? Makes you look like a Marguerite, with those 'he loves me' whatevers, all around—"

"And that's why the creditors couldn't touch them, understand! Diamonds all over them too."

The Magnificent Portrait of Hon. James G. Blaine, hanging over the stairway in the Maine Building, was made by THE SPRAGUE & HATH-AWAY Co. of West Somerville, Mass. They also made the enlarged photograph of the World's Fair Views in the same building.

Tid-Bits.

Dog-days.

Compliments to the new moon.

Mr. Matthews was taken for Louis Napoleon—by a Kodak.

Mr. and Mrs. David Slade, well known in Chelsea, arrived Monday.

The "Pole and Springs" is what it readily reminds one of. Who spoke?

Two new ferns added to the flora of Poland,—Mr. and Mrs. B. S. Redfern.

Miss Bacon is a devoted tennis player, and the tennis players seem devoted to her.

The young set are glad to welcome back Miss Florence Vose and Mr. George Vose from the Hub.

Lost.—Miss Fargo on Friday morning, July 19th. Large reward offered for her speedy return.

Hinds' Honey and Almond Cream can now be had at the News Counter. There is nothing superior for the complexion.

Among recent departing guests, Mr. H. A. Spaulding will be sadly missed by the HILL-TOP, for he has shown great interest in its success.

A visitor to the Maine Building remarked that they had two of those "table d'hote chairs" in the round-house.

Say, Endeavorers, how about holding your next convention at Poland Spring? We can handle 50,000, give us time, C. E.

Mrs. W. H. Linberg and Miss A. M. Crozer of Trenton, N. J., on their way from Bar Harbor, were interested visitors to the Maine Building.

Mrs. Ole Bull and daughter, Mrs. Vaughn, have found Poland Spring a delightful place, like everybody else. Poland Spring returns the compliment.

J. H. Hatfield, whose paintings are so much admired in the Art Gallery, made a flying visit, and left on a sketching tour among the White Mountains.

Miss Bourne's very artistic and clever sketches on the souvenir cards at Miss Spaulding's dinner party were unique and very much admired.

The library is indebted to Mr. N. E. Weeks of the Railway Publishing Co. for a contribution of the Pathfinder Railway Guide, which will be found constantly on the table, and much appreciated.

If Senator Hale could not come himself, we are very pleased to welcome Eugene Hale, Jr., who rejoined Mrs. Hale late last week.

Mr. Charles Smith and his family will be much missed during August, while at the Crawford House, but fortunately they are to return in September.

J. J. Van Alen, recently United States Minister to Italy, arrived too late to get into the last HILL-TOP, but we are pleased to record his presence, even a week late.

Rev. H. L. Myrick, rector of All Saints Church, Briar Cliff, Sing Sing, preached in the parlor of the Mansion House, Sunday evening. His text was from Gen. IV., 3.

Rev. Edwin C. Sweetser, a Universalist clergyman from Philadelphia, preached in Music Hall, Poland Spring House, at eleven o'clock, July 21st. His text was St. John, IV., 7, 10.

Mr. and Mrs. Wm. M. Keepers of Newark, N. J., made a short stay on their way from Bar Harbor to the White Mountains. They were much interested in the Maine Building.

> 'Tis only a turn of the wrist
> In playing the game known as whist,
> But if you would beat,
> 'Tis really a treat,
> To watch the game played by Miss Trist.

On the eve of her departure for Loon Lake, Miss Marguerite Spaulding gave a little party to eleven of her friends at the Poland Spring House. The round table in the North Tower was beautifully decorated for the occasion.

Mr. T. R. Peeples, of Savannah, Ga., after a pleasant sojourn of a week among us, left last Tuesday, weighing eight and one-half pounds more than he did when he came to "The Poland." He is the young man who drank fifty glasses of Poland water in a single day and improved so much by its use. He left home with the intention of going to Nova Scotia, but on seeing a "Moses" bottle at Portland, decided to spend his vacation here. He takes a couple of these bottles home with him as a souvenir.

The Book of the Fair.

Mr. E. F. Delano, agent of the Bancroft Publishing Company of Chicago, publishers of the beautiful edition of the World's Fair Books in the Maine State Building, made a brief call recently. He will return in about two weeks, and in the meantime, those contemplating a purchase of the works can examine those in the library, where any information will be given. He reports the expensive editions as almost exhausted.

A Question of Pedigree.

From Harper's Round Table.

"Now who is that?" asked a dignified hen;
"That chicken in white and gray?
She's very well dressed, but from whence did she come?
And her family, who are they?"

"She can never move in our set, my dear,"
Said the old hen's friend to her later;
"I've just found out—you'll be shocked to hear—
She was hatched in an incubator."

Hidden Treasures.

The following story contains a large number of the names of jewels and minerals. The first person sending in a correct list of the names will receive a season's subscription to "THE HILL-TOP."

I AM in Mexico, that land of jewels, truly named, if turquoise skies and sapphire streams can make it so. My host has a native wife, fat, indolent, so pale and listless one might think her always asleep but for her continual consumption of cigarettes and chocolate. She uses little sponge cakes (dry as a dining-car bun) cleverly to dip up this beverage, and to see her eat it, thick with sugar, nettles me! She shows an ephemeral delight in yards of chambery, lawn or linen, and a work-basket sits beside her; but she uses this utensil very seldom. The twins, Zaidee and Xavier, she utterly neglects; and the husband is looking old and disappointed. The children appear loving and generous; they succor all beggars, stray dogs and cats. Eyes of jet, marble white skins, and golden curls, make them very beautiful; but if they approach this unnatural mother with caresses, it is, "Thou givest me an agony, Xavier," or "Go to Pa, Zaidee. Why rub your hot hands on me?" Yesterday they went up the mountain hunting wild hyacinths, and staid late. In the light of the moon, stones glittered like jewels, and in search of supposed treasures they wandered far. Rough cactus tore their hands and brought blood, stones bruised their little feet, and finally, by accident, they clambered through the thicket and discovered a gate which led into their own premises. They reached home at midnight, finding the father wild with anxiety and the mother asleep. When roused she called Zaidee an animal, a chit, even a cat; and asked, "How came thy starched skirt so limp, Xavier?" and fell asleep again. Such indifference so aggravates me. I find I am on dangerous ground here, and deaf as are the father and children, I am on the eve of departure.

The Endeavorers have not only endeavored, but appear to have accomplished.

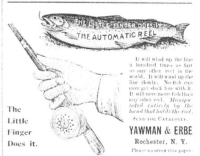

Thistles.

Stage held up—Sir Henry Irving did it.

Tom Reed never wears a silk hat. Cæsar didn't.

Haying may be called one of the features of the land-scrape.

The Yost Typewriter Company is in a receiver's hands. Dot vas yost as we expected.

Paper bags are going up. The trust has blown in them.

An eight-year-old miss in South Boston fell from the roof to the pavement, a distance of sixty-five feet, and was picked up uninjured.

A man fell off a trolley car in New Haven, two feet, and sustained serious injuries.

All hands up to the roof and jump off. Elevator. Going up please.

The drouth has been broken in Michigan. It was smashed, broken, annihilated and utterly and entirely demoralized here.

We can utilize the discharged men of the West End street railway right here as electric light poles. They should make good non-conductors.

A North Adams man found his wife and money missing one day last week, and a note saying it would be useless to try to find her. She had probably gone to Boston.

A man left Pine Point for Old Orchard with one hundred dollars in his pocket, and never returned. He said he was going to get shaved. He probably did.

MR. N. Q. POPE, president of the Lewiston & Auburn Electric Railway, and formerly owner of White Oak Farm at Poland, was married at Knightville, Me., Thursday, to Miss Jennie B. Barnes of Knightville, a school teacher at that place for several years. Mr. Pope, as is well known, makes his home winters in Brooklyn, N. Y. He is reported to be a multi-millionaire, and has been well known in these cities for some time. His former wife was a native of Poland, her death having occurred about a year ago. Mr. Pope has given up his country home at Poland. He and Mrs. Pope will travel for a time, returning to make their home in Brooklyn. —*Lewiston Journal.*

Arrivals.

POLAND SPRING HOUSE.

Angell, Mary F.,	Lewiston.
Angell, Prof. T. L.,	Lewiston.
Abbott, Madelaine,	Providence.
Abbott, Anne,	Providence.
Abbott, Caroline,	Providence.
Austin, Mr. and Mrs. J. W.,	Boston.
Andrews, Mr. and Mrs. H. E.,	Lewiston.
Andrews, Gertrude,	Lewiston.
Alvord, Mrs. A. Z.,	Newton.
Anthony, Mrs. D. U.,	Fall River.
Adams, Mr. and Mrs. A. H.,	Haverhill.
Billings, Mr. and Mrs. A.,	New York.
Bull, Mrs. Ole,	Cambridge.
Bailey, Mrs. John,	New York.
Bathori, E. D.,	Boston.
Beylle, Mrs.,	Philadelphia.
Butler, Thomas F.,	Lewiston.
Beale, Mr. and Mrs. H. P.,	Lowell.
Brett, Dr. and Mrs. George,	Boston.
Branch, Charles J.,	Minneapolis.
Burnett, John W.,	Brooklyn.
Bartlett, Mr. and Mrs. A. G.,	Boston.
Bacon, R. A.,	Graysville, Ga.
Bogert, Theo. P.,	Providence.
Curtis, Mrs.,	Portland.
Carlsmith, Lilian,	Boston.
Cahl, Sophie,	Boston.
Cushman, Mr. and Mrs. Ara,	Auburn.
Chase, Mr. and Mrs. C. S.,	Portland.
Chase, Miss,	Portland.
Clay, A. G.,	Brunswick.
Carter, Mrs. A. M.,	Anburn.
Crozer, Mrs. A. M.,	Trenton.
Carr, F. W.,	Bangor.
Clark, Mr. and Mrs. H. P.,	Boston.
Clark, Miss Mary,	Boston.
Cooper, Mr. and Mrs. J. G.,	Boston.
Chase, Miss,	Lynn.
Cammann, Mr. and Mrs. H. H.,	New York.
Cuttan, Jas. J.,	Boston.
Clark, Mr. and Mrs. J. T.,	New York.
Doyle, P. M.,	Lewiston.
Dingley, Miss,	Lewiston.
Danforth, E. F.,	Skowhegan.
Davol, Mr. and Mrs. Joseph,	Providence.
Delano, E. F.,	Chicago.
Danielson, A. Lockwood,	Providence.
Endicott, Charles,	Canton.
Englis, John,	Brooklyn.
Evans, Mr. and Mrs. T. W.,	New York.
Etheridge, Mr. and Mrs. Francis,	Chicago.
Ellard, G. W.,	Lewiston.
Fraser, Mr. and Mrs. D. R.,	Chicago.
Fisher, J. W.,	Brunswick.
Fairbanks, Mrs. S.,	Springfield.
Fettus, Mr. and Mrs. R. G.,	Philadelphia.
Freeman, Eben Winthrop,	Portland.
Griffin, Mr. and Mrs. C. C.,	Haverhill.
Gutmann, W. U.,	Lewiston.
Gotham, Mrs. S. K.,	New Rochelle.
Goodwin, Mr. and Mrs. J. B.,	South Sudbury.
Goodwin, Mr. and Mrs. C. W.,	Kennebunk.
Gould, Mr. and Mrs. C. I. T.,	Baltimore.
Gould, Miss,	Boston.
Gutmann, Mr. and Mrs. F.,	Lewiston.
Gutmann, Miss,	Lewiston.
Greenleaf, J. A,	Auburn.
Hall, Lewis 2d,	Niagara Falls.
Hayden, Rev. and Mrs. C. A.,	Augusta.
Higgins, Mr. and Mrs. I. C.	Elizabeth.
Hale, Eugene,	Ellsworth.
Hale, Eugene, Jr.,	Ellsworth.
Hoagland, Mr. and Mrs. Hudson,	New York.

Hartshorne, R. B.,	New York.
Hatfield, J. H.,	Canton Junction.
Hasbrouck, Lewis B.,	New York.
Hoyt, Colgate,	New York.
Hayes, Mr. and Mrs. W.,	Auburn.
Hill, Charles Stanton,	Anburn.
Harvey, Mr. and Mrs. Henry W.,	Providence.
Hall, Ernest W.,	Boston.
Holton, B. W.,	New York.
Jennings, Mr. and Mrs. P. R.,	New York.
Kugel, Dudley H.,	Niagara Falls.
Kreiger, L.,	New York.
Keeper, Mr. and Mrs. Wm. M.,	New York.
Kimball, George C.,	Springfield.
Lambert, Mr. and Mrs. C.,	New York.
Lincoln, C. H.,	Millbury.
Lough, Walter E.,	Toronto.
Livermore, C. D.,	Portland.
Linburg, Mrs. W. H.,	Trenton.
Leech, John B.,	New York.
Lee, Stephen,	Lewiston.
Lord, Mrs. E. C.,	New York.
Moulton, Byron P.,	Rosemont.
Metcalf, Mr. and Mrs. S. O.,	Providence.
Morrison, C. E.,	Boston.
Maddock, Mrs. Thomas,	New York.
Moore, Rev. J. J. Joyce,	Philadelphia.
Mitchell, E. C.,	N. Y. Journal.
McGillicuddy, D. J.,	Lewiston.
Nelson, Mrs. H. B.,	Portland.
Osgood, W. C.,	Portland.
Osgood, H. S.,	Portland.
Platt, G. W.,	Lonsdale.
Prince, C. J.,	Boston.
Peavey, F. L.,	Lowell.
Puffer, F. A.,	Lowell.
Palmer, Mr. and Mrs. L.,	Brooklyn.
Palmer, Lily C.,	Brooklyn.
Purnell, Mr. and Mrs. L. B.,	Baltimore.
Plummer, E.	Lisbon Falls.
Rich, Mrs. T. H.,	Lewiston.
Roberts, Miss,	Philadelphia.
Redpath, Mr. and Mrs. N. H.,	Boston.
Redpath, Miss Loretta,	Boston.
Redpath, Chesleigh A.,	Boston.
Rogers, Mr. and Mrs. Spencer,	Portland.
Rogers, Miss Mildred,	Portland.
Smith, Mrs. Wesley,	Old Orchard.
Stearns, Mrs.,	Hyde Park.
Shapleigh, Mrs. A. E.,	Cambridge.
Stockbridge, Miss,	Providence.
Sanford, Mr. and Mrs. H. B.,	Bridgeport.
Sanford, Miss,	Bridgeport.
Sanford, Miss B.,	Bridgeport.
Scoville, Wm. H.,	Stamford.
Shaw, Mr. and Mrs. H. E.,	Lowell.
Stanwood, J. R.,	Brunswick.
Staples, Arthur G.,	Lewiston.
Slade, Mr. and Mrs. David,	Chelsea.
Smith, Mr. and Mrs. Albert W.,	Providence.
Sloat, T. S.,	New York.
Schuyler, Mr. and Mrs.,	Plattsburg.
Shaw, Mrs. E. F.,	Lisbon Falls.
Sweet, Mr. and Mrs. Leprilete,	Providence.
Stewart, Donald M.,	Montreal.
Stinson, John,	San Francisco.
Small, Mr. and Mrs. S. R.,	Portland.
Sullivan, Jas.,	Manchester.
Spencer, Mrs. M. J.,	Brooklyn.
Thornton, Mr. and Mrs. David,	Brooklyn.
Thornton, May,	Brooklyn.
Thornton, C. C. G.,	Boston.
Tenney, Geo. F.,	Brunswick.
Taminosian,	Antioch, Syria.
Tatam, Mr. and Mrs. Geo. H.,	Boston.
Taylor, Forrest W.,	Worcester.
Taylor, Miss Emma S.,	Worcester.
Van Alen, J. J.,	Newport.

MR. CHARLES SMITH is greatly missed by a large circle of young ladies, both for his cheery greetings and also for his dainty attentions in the way of bouquets for each and all.

PROF. L. WATER gave an entertainment of magic, slight of hand, mind reading, ventriloquism, etc., in the Music Hall, Wednesday evening, which suggests the query, also uppermost in the magician's mind, "Was he better than the last one?"

Poland Water Leads Them All.

 WHY?

BECAUSE.. It was the FIRST KNOWN SOLVENT OF URIC ACID in the system. . . . .

BECAUSE.. It is the most EFFECTIVE ELIMINATOR of Calculi in the Bladder and Kidneys known to-day. . . . .

BECAUSE.. It was the ONLY water IN NEW ENGLAND to receive ANY AWARD at the World's Columbian Exposition, and the only award of the hundreds exhibited from the WORLD for Purity and Great Medicinal Properties. . . . .

BECAUSE.. The ANNUAL sales exceed the combined sales of all the Saratoga Springs. . . . .

BECAUSE.. Unprecedented as the success of the past has been it is more promising than ever, showing continued increase. . . . .

OFFICES:

BOSTON:	NEW YORK:	PHILADELPHIA:	CHICAGO:
175 Devonshire Street.	3 Park Place.	Corner 13th and Chestnut St.	Cor. Michigan Ave. and Randolph St.

HIRAM RICKER & SONS, Proprietors.

(INCORPORATED.)

THE HILL-TOP

POLAND SPRING

VOL. II.   SUNDAY MORNING, AUGUST 4, 1895.   No. 6.

What You Eat.

WE propose to give to-day some idea of the effect of Poland water and Poland air on the appetite; to bring to your attention a few facts illustrating what it is to run the works behind the scenes, and for to-day, as you sit down to your breakfast, to enable you to more fully comprehend the magnitude of an institution like this, with its limitless accommodations, and its inexhaustible larder.

Is it easy for you to realize that you are eating 8,400 eggs in a single week? That those eggs, placed end to end, would reach one-third of a mile, solid? Do you know that you are devouring a ton of sirloin steak in the same time? No wonder you grow well and strong. You also ate, in one healthy week, twenty-seven whole lambs and the backs of sixty more. What did you do with the remainder of the sixty? A whole big flock of Mary's pets. Baah!

Think of six hundred chickens, and what a pretty sight they must have been all together. You ate them, in a week, too, and that's not all

THE STEAM TABLE.

the winged creation your ravenous appetite demanded, for 250 pounds of the choicest turkey, 400 pounds of fowl, and—wait a bit, 400 pounds of duck. Quack, quack! Fact. Could prove it, too, if old Bill Jones was alive.

To take a dive beneath the cooling waters of the earth and produce the records of your havoc among the finny tribe, there are recorded against you for seven days, 300 lbs. of salmon, 140 lbs. of blue-fish, 110 lbs. of mackerel, 170 lbs. of halibut, 300 lbs. of cod, and 75 lbs. of trout, or in all 1095 lbs. of fish for the second course are missed from the waters of the seas and lakes. You have much to answer for. What a lot of good fishing.

Now we come to the innocent little bossy-calf, 160 lbs. of him having been served as veal, while 200 lbs. of bacon and 250 lbs. of ham have gone the same way in the same length of time.

The slaughter is now ended, so far as the above-mentioned articles are concerned, and for your side-dishes, what do you say to the utter annihilation of 25 bushels of potatoes, 800 lbs. of squash, 15 bushels of peas, and 8 of beans? Don't believe it, possibly? Can show the figures. But, bless you, that is only a few of the necessary articles to satisfy a real Poland appetite.

Even the butter alone which you put on your bread ought to satisfy any reasonable person for a year, but 400 lbs. are spread upon your rolls, and 500 lbs. more go into the composition of your food in the compass of a single week.

Can you lift a barrel of flour? We opine not. Very well; fourteen barrels are the weekly allowance, and you can reckon that up for the season, and see what it costs to feed you.

Your berries and fruit are picked from the bushes and trees to the amount of 25 bushels of berries, 10 boxes of oranges, the same amount of bananas, and 20 bushels of peaches. It is a healthy and growing family.

Of course you must drink, and notwithstanding the fact of your drinking as much Poland water as you do, yet 150 lbs. of coffee disappear in a week, 40 lbs. of tea, and with all this, 441 quarts of delicious cream; but, wait a bit, *2,000 quarts of milk*, my dear sir or madam. Think of the number of cows working over time this season, and the milk-maids' merry "Coo-bos, coo-bos" at the pasture bars.

One item more this time and we have done. You think you are sweet enough, and perhaps you are; at all events if 2,500 lbs. of sugar in a week can make you so, doubtless honey is acid to you.

If you survive all this, and much more left unmentioned, you will live, and live to grow old and gray. Let us hope you may, but that you may always feel young enough to come regularly to Poland Spring. You are welcome to eat, drink, and be merry, and even if it were double the amount the welcome is the same. Five miles from a railroad, and up hill, but everything gets here, just the same.

We present two views of the Kitchen this week, the work of the Notman Photographic Co. and the Suffolk Engraving Co. of Boston.

A Merry Birthday.

ON THE evening of Tuesday, July 30th, a very jolly party of friends sat down to a supper given in honor of Miss Nettie M. Ricker's birthday, at the Mansion House. It was an entire surprise her friends had prepared for her, and Mr. Gallagher had placed the tables in " T " shape and very beautifully decorated its entire ample proportions. The birthday cake was placed before Miss Ricker, and proved to be fully as delicious as it looked.

Mrs. Jordan read an original poem which we give entire, it being of unusual excellence and interest. It was nearly twelve o'clock before the friends dispersed, wishing Miss Ricker all the usual nice things possible on such occasions.

TO NETTIE M. RICKER.

BY MARCIA B. JORDAN.

Another year is counted off
  On Time's unerring finger;
The century is almost done!
  We fain would sigh and linger,—
For all the 1800s have
  been faithful friends and true,
And 1900 seems to us
  Preposterously new.
But, all the same, we're moving fast,
  We're just a little older
Than when we drank together last
  In shrub, or something colder,
A health to one who, since that time,
  Has furnished us for toasting,
A crystal jug, a clear carafe,
  That well sets off the boasting
Which christens Poland's water as
  The fairest in our land,
And claims a sparkle quite unknown
  To any other brand.

To drink a health then first of all,
  With tumbler and carafe;
A health that rallies with it
  The merry smile and laugh;
A health to Nettie Ricker,
  Our hostess of to-night—
May happiness surround her,
  And all things glad and bright
Salute the year is advancing,
  And bring, perhaps—who knows—
That Fairy Prince,—a handsome man,
  To share her joys and woes.

This isn't a Centennial—
  We're not so old as that;
It's not a Maine State Building—
  Speeches eloquent and pat;
It's not a trip to Europe
  (Although we own it fine);
It's just a birthday party
  To the youngest of the line—
The original Ricker baby,
  Who must be very sweet
To have her friends so love her
  And lay tributes at her feet.

But why not special honors,
  When the very latest fad,
A new profession welcomes her
  To paper, ink, and pad?
And lures her from the valley,
  Where contented home folks stay,
To the Hill-Top and Excelsior
  And visions far away.
We feel a swelling fortune
  Does not await our two;
But they show us as good journalists
  How much enterprise can do;
And if the Hill-Top's coffers are
  Not crowded over much,
Its editors may realize
  They've helped to keep in touch

The guests who visit Poland
  (Who from east and west are whirled
To this attractive center)
  With each other and the world.

We may not be so dignified
  As some great meetings are,
But we're going to have Welsh rarebit,
  Which we think is jollier far;
And beer and ginger ale and cake,
  And my! how good they sound,
Let's have our ginger ale at once,
  And pass the brakers round;
Or while we wait the moments
  That Miss Sadie needs to stir
The cayenne, mustard, cream, and egg
  Let's keep an eye on her;
But call for recitation, for violin, or song;
  Time-honored ways at festivals,
Of wafting hours along.
  Once more, our hostess' health, dear friends,
Unanimously passed:
  May every following birthday
Be happier than the last.

MANSION HOUSE,
  July 30, 1895,

Another Grand Gift.

The Poland Spring Library is rapidly assuming the dignity of metropolitan proportions, and is bursting its bonds with the rapidity of a growing boy in buttons. Mrs. H. O. Bright of Cambridge, Mass., the oldest regular visitor to Poland Spring, has donated to the library a very excellent list of standard and popular works and reference books, as the following will show. The thanks of all are due to Mrs. Bright for all will benefit by her excellent example.

Those already received are as follows:

Lippincott's Gazetteer,	1	volume.
Geo. Meredith,	3	"
Emerson's Essays,	2	"
Count Tolstoi,	3	"
Macaulay's Essays and Poems,	3	"
Golden Treasury of Songs,	1	"
Fisk's " The Idea of God,"	1	"
Thomas Carlyle,	2	
" How to Know the Wild Flowers,"	1	"
Aguilar's " The Days of Bruce,"	1	"
Lamb's " Elia and Eliana,"	1	"
" Uncle Remus,"	1	
" Pride and Prejudice,"	1	
Blackmore's " Lorna Doone,"	1	"
Charlotte Bronte,	1	"
Scottish Chiefs,	1	
Thoughts of Marcus Aurelius,	1	"
Francis Parkman's Works,	12	"
Imbert de St. Amand,	19	"
" Clawford,"	1	
Fisk's " Destiny of Man,"	1	
	58	

There are some seventeen more volumes yet to come, chiefly juvenile works.

The Magnificent Portrait of Hon. James G. Blaine, hanging over the stairway in the Maine Building, was made by THE SPRAGUE & HATHAWAY CO. of West Somerville, Mass. They also made the enlarged photograph of the World's Fair Views in the same building.

FRANK CARLOS GRiFFiTH,   } EDITORS.
NETTiE M. RiCKER,   }

PUBLISHED EVERY SUNDAY MORNING DURING THE MONTHS OF JULY, AUGUST AND SEPTEMBER, IN THE INTERESTS OF

POLAND SPRiNG AND ITS ViSiTORS.

All contributions relative to the guests of Poland Spring will be thankfully received.

To insure publication, all communications should reach the editors not later than Wednesday preceding day of issue.

All parties desiring rates for advertising in the HiLL-TOP should write the editors for same.

The subscription price of the HiLL-TOP is $1.00 for the season, post-paid. Single copies will be mailed at 10c. each.

Address,

EDITORS "HiLL-TOP,"
Poland Spring House,
South Poland, Maine.

PRINTED AT JOURNAL OFFICE, LEWISTON.

Sunday, August 4, 1895.

Editorial.

H AS the idea ever occurred to any of our friends that Poland Spring succeeds without any one of those seemingly indispensable adjuncts of a summer resort, called "natural curiosities?"

We have no such thing as a cave, and what place can possibly succeed without a cave? We have no "devil's den," which every supposed well-ordered country place has, and sometimes several, just to show the capabilities of Dame Nature in that direction. Again, we have no "silver cascade" or "bridal veil falls" or any other imaginary effect or defect of that sort. No "pulpit rock" or "balancing boulder" or "sunset rock" or "profile rock" or any other freak of nature.

We ought to have a hermit, and we have seriously thought of sending to Philadelphia for one of theirs, and paying him a handsome salary from the profits of the HiLL-TOP just to give us something sensational to write about. He could give us a blood-curdling story of his escape from an infuriated rabbit, now and then, and how he was criss-crossed in love once upon a time, and how he swore to become a pirate, but changed his mind and became a liar instead, which paid him much better and with not half the danger.

No, we are obliged to succeed without them, but *some* day we *do* propose to have a sea-serpent, and when you see *our* sea-serpent cavorting and ricocheting through the Middle Range Pond at the rate of a hundred knots an hour, as we shall stipulate shall be his guaranteed speed, you will have your curiosity in the serpent line fully gratified. Watch the bulletins for his arrival.

The Shakers.

The HiLL-TOP extends its thanks to the Shakers for a very handsome bouquet, and the Library is the richer by a copy of "A Concise History of the United Society of Believers, called Shakers," by Charles Edson Robinson, also a gift from that society.

The Studio.

Drop into the Studio and see some of the very superior work done by the Notman Photographic Co. All this work, as will be readily seen, is of a class entirely above the ordinary, and their group pictures, are such that when reproduced for printing, as has been seen and can be seen in this issue, are almost as perfect specimens as the original photographs. Mr. Ness of the Notman Photographic Co., located here, is to be complimented for the excellence of his work.

Farewell to Miss Bacon.

It was a very charming little dinner party, that of Miss Bacon's, on Saturday evening, July 27th, given to her friends before her departure on Monday.

Everything was very tastefully arranged, the table being daintily arranged with lovely flowers, and the cards neatly decorated with exquisitely painted forget-me-nots.

Those participating were the Misses Fargo, Eames, Hartshorne, Bourne, Peterson, and the Misses Todd. The gentlemen were Messrs. Brown, Wilcox, Gregg, Bacon, Eames, and Vose.

It is to be regretted the photograph was not taken as was intended.

Concert and Tableaux.

ON Friday evening of July 26th we were favored with one of the finest affairs of the season in Music Hall. It consisted of vocal and instrumental music and tableaux, the latter designed and arranged by the Misses McNeel and Royce, and, considering the very short time they had to complete their labors, the results were quite remarkable and reflect great credit upon them both.

Mr. Kuntz's Orchestra distinguished itself, under his able leadership, and the music was well chosen and delightful.

Mr. Gallagher should be praised for his artistic labors in the way of decorations and "stage effects," which include the arrangement of Chinese lanterns, Persian rugs, ferns, etc.

The stage and proscenium arch was the work of Mr. Forrest Walker, who directed that portion of the work most effectively.

Mr. D. J. Griffith was heard once more, and his rendering of "Die Uhr" by Loewe, and "The Two Grenadiers" by Schumann, gave additional evidence of his musical abilities as a singer of high quality.

The tableaux, which were represented by young ladies and gentlemen of the hotel, were capital and were very highly satisfactory, and those in Part First illustrated Richard Harding Davis's story of "The Princess Aline."

TABLEAU I.
"Then Carlton opened the paper and propped it up against a carafe and continued his critical survey of the Princess Aline."

Carlton. . . . . . . Mr. McNeel.

TABLEAU II.
H. R. H. the Princess Aline of Hohenwald.

Miss Eames.

TABLEAU III.
"Mrs. Downs and her niece, with Carlton, stood together, leaning with their backs to the steamer rail."

Mrs. Downs. . . . . Miss Bourne.
Miss Morris. . . . . Miss Hartshorne.

TABLEAU IV.
"Carlton turned in his chair and found he was within two feet of the girl who had been called Aline."

TABLEAU V.
"If that was any other girl, thought Carlton, I would go up and speak to her."

TABLEAU VI.
"'I had forgotten the Princess Aline,' said Carlton, 'I cannot let you go now, I love you so.'"

TABLEAU VII.
"The Princess Aline saw Carlton kiss Miss Morris lightly on the cheek. She folded the pieces of paper together and tore them slowly into tiny fragments and threw them into the street below."

The tableaux included in Part Second were:

I. A Story Told by a Sleeve.
    Mr. Eames, Mr. Brown, Miss Hartshorne.
II. Tillby. . . . . . . Miss Bacon.
III. A Bachelor's Dream.

The latter was especially noteworthy, and represented the passing by the window, while the bachelor slept, of a gypsy girl (Miss Blanche Todd), a nun (Miss Bourne), a farmer's daughter (Miss Todd), girl on bicycle (Miss Fargo), "A Summer Girl" (Miss Vantine), "A Horsey Girl" (Miss Eames), a bride (Miss Estelle Hartshorne), and it is needless to add that this climax of loveliness brought the sleeper to his waking senses.

The final tableau was called "Poland Water," and embraced the entire company of ladies and gentlemen—Happy Poland Water.

The two ladies, Miss McNeel and Miss Royce, labored most assiduously, and too much credit cannot be given them for the success of their efforts, which were artistic and excellent. Perhaps they will favor us with another illustration of their gifts in this direction.

Answers to Hidden Treasures.

TURQUOISE, sapphire, opal, carbuncle, garnet, emerald, beryl, silver, gold, pearl, coral, catseye, jet, marble, onyx, topaz, ruby, hyacinth, moonstone, bloodstone, amber, agate, malachite, amethyst, diamond, and tin,—26.

We Said So.

THEY are going, not like the traditional wild-fire, but like the engine to the fire, for they are to hold water, and how beautifully it sparkles, seen through the windows of the Poland Spring House as it stands upon the table, and guarded by that grand old ox at the top.

Get a carafe, and when you cannot come to Poland you can look into the Spring House and see the water inside in its triangular receptacle.

Taminosian.

MR. EZEKIEL TAMINOSIAN of Antioch, Syria, preached in Music Hall, Sunday. He read the XI. chapter of Acts, and also from the Psalms. Mr. Taminosian has founded a non-sectarian Christian school for boys and girls at Antioch, which was opened in September, 1892. Since then seventy boys and girls have enjoyed a common-school education. This school is sustained through Mr. Taminosian's efforts, who lectures in churches of all Protestant denominations. The subject of his lecture is "An Hour in Historic Syria, Ancient and Modern." In the evening Mr. Taminosian gave an entertainment consisting of Syrian school, Syrian courtship, Syrian wedding, Mohammedan prayers, songs, etc. A collection was taken and $76.17 was realized.

Tid=Bits.

More books.

Canteloupe.

Peaches and cream.

Roll on, silver moon.

All the flags up, Wednesday.

Don't hurry, there is a good moon.

Now you know how 'tis done in Syria.

Have you seen "The Promised Land?"

The Danvilles did up the B. B.s to the tune of 14 to 0 on Wednesday.

Did you ever hear it rain harder than it did last week, Saturday night?

The birch logs blazed for the first time in the Maine State Building on Wednesday.

The old original hundred-year-old barn has been painted, and looks as fine as new.

Mr. and Mrs. Redfern passed a very enjoyable day with the Cushmans in Auburn on Wednesday.

Mr. and Mrs. H. O. Bright are the senior guests of the Poland Spring House, having been here every season from the start.

Rev. Wm. Henry Bolster of Boston, cousin of the late Mrs. Hiram Ricker, will preach in Music Hall to-day at the usual hour.

John I. Pinkerton, the well-known lawyer of Westchester, and former partner of Wayne MacVeigh, is a welcome guest. He is an old frequenter of the place.

If you are not an expert, and desire to be an expert at whist, Miss Trist is a teacher of the art, for it is an art, and a subtle one at that. So play whist with Miss Trist.

A son has been born to the wife of Mr. Elmer Bright, son of Mr. and Mrs. H. O. Bright. A telegram from the happy father states the "mother and father are doing well."

Mr. Sawyer has shown slow but steady improvement during the week, and hope for his ultimate recovery rises with each succeeding day. May he "live long and prosper," is the wish of the HILL-TOP.

Mrs. Robinson of Boston, who, as Miss Lizzie Putnam, had many warm friends in Portland a few years ago, is spending some weeks at the Poland Spring House. She will be glad to receive massage patients. Mrs. Robinson is accomplished in her profession and is a lady of such agreeable qualities that it is a pleasure to speak a cordial word in her behalf.

Tid-Bits.

Mr. and Mrs. George Williamson Smith are among the arrivals too late for the last HILL-TOP. Mr. Smith is the President of Trinity College, of Hartford.

Another Connecticut man who arrived the same day was Mr. C. T. Hempstead, the well-known General Passenger Agent of the N. Y., N. H. & H. R. R. He was accompanied by Mrs. Hempstead.

Mr. and Mrs. C. H. Hackett and Miss Grace Hackett are with us on their first visit to Poland Spring. Mr. Hackett is the head of the well-known firm of Messrs. Hackett, Carhart & Co., of New York City, and is a devoted visitor to the beautiful "Lake Mohonk." We hope he will find Poland and its water all he can desire, and that another season will find him booked for a longer stay.

Still They Come.

Mrs. Amos Little, whose excellent work in "The World as We Saw It," has already been acknowledged, has sent five more books to the library. It was a very thoughtful and kind act, and the books, which are all popular, will certainly find appreciative readers.

The books mentioned are:

Beside the Bonnie Brier Bush,	Ian MacLaren.
The Three Graces,	The Duchess.
A Roman Singer,	F. Marion Crawford.
A Tale of a Lonely Parish,	F. Marion Crawford.
The Dolly Dialogues,	Anthony Hope.
A Couple Magazines.	

Pungent.

At sweet sixteen, and when alone,
She loved to tease her chaperone.
But when to three-and-twenty grown,
She loves to tease a *chap, her own.*

"See," said the jolting Arabella to her regular caller, "You have torn a leaf from my music book." "That's so," he sweetly answered, "but as this is a *court-in'* session, we will have it bound over to *keep the piece.*"

He kept a heavy walking-stick always in the hat stand, and called it his modern novelist. "Why?" asked a friend. "*Hall caine,*" he answered, "See?" "Oh!"

The new spiritualistic cigar—"Medium, dark rappers."

FOR THE HILL-TOP, BY A READER.

It is reported that the mayor of Marlboro will serve his term out. What was the sentence?

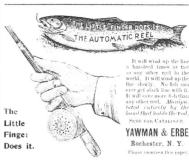

Concert Program.

SUNDAY, AUGUST 4TH, AT 3.30 P.M.

Kuntz Orchestral Club.

1. Marche Militaire. . . . . . Schubert.
2. Overture—La Gazza Ladra. . . . Rossini.
   Serenade. . . . . Tilte.
   Selection—Gotterdammerung. . . Wagner.
3. { *a.* Cradle Song. . . . . Latam.
   { *b.* Serenade. . . . . . Pierne.
                For Strings.
6. Andante from First Symphony. . . Beethoven.
7. Selection—Martha. . . . . Flotow.

The Only One.

As far as can be ascertained, the Messrs. Ricker are in possession of the only collection of "wild flowers" ever on exhibition at any hotel in the world. Another evidence of their desire to suit all tastes and make their palatial estate as perfect as possible.

Physical Culture.

Mrs. John Bailey gave one of her interesting talks at the Mansion House on Monday morning, and interested a large number of guests in the subject of her discourse. There is very much advantage to be gained by following the true rules of physical training, and Mrs. Bailey appears to be meeting with much success.

Try It.

FILL in the blanks in the following lines, using a word in the place of the first blank which can be transposed to fill in all the others, without adding to or taking from it one letter, the word to contain six letters.

A —— sat in his —— gray,
Watching the moonbeams —— play,
Who —— the weak —— the strong?
The —— of great battles to him does belong.
  John Barleycorn my king.

A boy in Williamstown coughed up a nickel. Report fails to state what it was for; probably an idea struck him—for five.

A Portland clergyman entered a newspaper office there and in some mysterious manner lost a portion of one foot. He undoubtedly attempted to kick the editor. The moral is obvious.

If you wish to see the cunningest little animal on Ricker Hill, see the little colt, born last Monday, at the stable. The "Baker Mare," also the mother of Poland Boy, is quite proud of her offspring, but the sire, Lothair, is at Sanborn's and has not yet been heard from on the subject.

Arrivals.

POLAND SPRING HOUSE.

Atwood, Mr. and Mrs. Abram,	Lewiston.
Bill, Mr. and Mrs. Frederic A.,	Springfield.
Bolster, William H.,	Boston.
Barrett, Cecil,	Newport.
Birns, Mrs. M. A.,	Lawrence.
Birns, Miss,	Lawrence.
Birns, George,	Lawrence.
Birns, Master Gus.,	Lawrence.
Batcheller, Alfred,	Boston.
Bechstein, Mr. and Mrs. A. C.,	New York.
Baxter, Mrs. Mary A.,	Deering.
Baxter, W. E.,	Deering.
Barbour, E. D.,	Boston.
Bitler, Thos. F.,	Lewiston.
Bullock, Mrs. A. G.,	Worcester.
Bullock, A. H.,	Worcester.
Bergen, Mrs. Jas. C.,	New York.
Carpenter, F. W.,	Providence.
Carpenter, Miss Hannah,	Providence.
Curtis, Ronald E.,	New York.
Curtis, Mrs.,	Portland.
Craig, P. J.,	West Quincy.
Callahan, Clara G.,	Lewiston.
Coombs, D. D.,	Auburn.
Chauncy, Elihu,	New York.
Chedister, O. H.,	Newark.
Cullen, Miss,	Washington.
Dayton, Miss,	Trenton.
Drake, Mr. and Mrs. Albert A.,	Westfield, N. J.
Drake, Miss Helen,	Westfield, N. J.
Douglass, Mr. and Mrs. A. E.,	New York.
Dow, W. N.,	Exeter.
Day, Mr. and Mrs. John W.,	Gloucester.
Dinton, Mrs. Wm. C.,	New York.
Dyer, Mr. and Mrs. D. P.,	Providence.
Ege, Mrs. H. N.,	Plainfield.
Embry, James H.,	Washington.
Field, Mr. and Mrs. D. W.,	Brockton.
Forster, C.,	Portland.
Fowler, Mrs. N.,	Newburgh.
Fowler, Miss Margaret,	Newburgh.
Fowler, Albert M.,	Newburgh.
Fassett, Mr. and Mrs. Horace,	Philadelphia.
Gondran, Mr. and Mrs. A. L.,	New York.
Greer, Geo. B.,	New York.
Greer, Miss,	New York.
Greer, Louis M.,	New York.
Gross, E. W.,	Auburn.
Girney, Mrs. Ruth B.,	Lewiston.
Glynn, F. J.,	Atlanta.
Gadsden, R. W.,	Atlanta.
Gilman, Mr. and Mrs. F. E.,	Montreal.
Getchell, Lucy B.,	Exeter.
Hackett, Mr. and Mrs. C. H.,	New York.
Hackett, Miss,	New York.
Hempstead, Mr. and Mrs. C. F.,	Glenbank, Conn.
Hatch, Mr. and Mrs. E. R.,	Newtonville.
Harlow, Mr. and Mrs. B. W.,	Rockland.
Haskell, Mr. and Mrs. N. P.,	New Gloucester.
Holmes, Mrs. G. F.,	New Gloucester.
Holmes, Chas. P.,	New Gloucester.
Holbrook, Mrs. C. L.,	Boston.
Hack, F.,	New York.
Hall, Mrs. W. H.,	New York.
Hopkins, Mr. and Mrs. Benj.,	Philadelphia.
Horner, Mr. and Mrs. E. B.,	Boston.
Hale, Frederic,	Ellsworth.
Ingraham, Mrs. F. A.,	Boston.
Kahn, L.,	New York.
Kahn, Mrs. R.,	New York.
Kahn, Mrs. F. L.,	New York.
Keen, Mrs. Eli,	Philadelphia.
Kilgore, Frank,	Lewiston.
Kingsbury, May,	Franklin.
Longstregth, Mr. and Mrs. Edw.,	Philadelphia.
Lambert, Miss Cora W.	Brockton.
Lynch, Mr. and Mrs. W. R.,	
Lewis, Rev. Dr. and Mrs. W. P.,	Philadelphia.
Lloyd, Wm. H.,	Boston.
Lynde, Mr. and Mrs. John F.,	Machias.
Leech, Mrs. J. P.,	New York.
Leech, Miss Belle,	New York.
Leech, Miss Edith,	New York.
Leech, Miss Josephine,	New York.
Leech, Miss Florence,	New York.
Leech, Miss May,	New York.
Leech, J. B.,	New York.
Leech, J. E.,	New York.
Landry, Leonie,	Bradford, Me.
Low, Miss J. N.,	New York.
Low, Miss L. H.,	New York.
Markham, E. Z.,	Springfield.
McQueston, Geo. E.,	Boston.
McGillicuddy, J. P,	Lewiston.
Martin, G. A.,	Franklin.
McGregor, Mr. and Mrs. A.,	Boston.
Masterton, Mr. and Mrs. W. E.,	New York.
Mills, Mr. and Mrs. S. C.,	Newburgh.
Mills, S. McD.,	Newburgh.
Mills, Mary D.,	Newburgh.
Osgood, H. S.,	Portland.
O'Rourke, J. H.,	Boston.
Pearson, W. C.,	Newark.
Porter, Jos. D.,	Atlanta.
Porter, Geo. F.,	Atlanta.
Pinkerton, John I.,	Westchester.
Peet, Miss,	Brooklyn.
Peabody, Mrs. J.,	Danvers.
Prescott, Mrs. W. G.,	Pepperell.
Ricker. H. H.,	Portland.
Richardson, W.,	Boston.
Riffner, Bertha,	Brooklyn.
Riblet, Mrs. Edward J.,	Erie.
Riblet, Mabel Thayer,	Erie.
Rogers, Mrs. J. C.,	Boston.
Scott, Geo. E.,	New York.
Sawyer, L. N.,	Chicago.
Stewart, S. H. Gardyne,	New York.
Smith, Mr. and Mrs. Geo. Williamson,	Hartford.
Safford, Mr. and Mrs. Nathaniel M.,	Milton.
Stephenson, H. W.,	Boston.
Somers, Mrs. J.,	Philadelphia.
Sorja, Mr. and Mrs. C. M.,	New Orleans.
Soria, Annie C.,	New Orleans.
Tabor, J. W.,	Portland.
True, Geo. W.,	Portland.
Trowbridge, Mrs. G.,	New York.
Trowbridge, Miss Theodora,	New York.
Trowbridge, Miss Julia,	New York.
Torbett, Jas. H.,	Atlanta.
Thayer, O. C.,	Erie.
Terry, Mr. and Mrs. John T.,	Irvington.
Talmage, Mrs. V. N.,	Plainfield.
Trimper, Miss,	New York.
Thomson, Mr. and Mrs. Eugene,	New York.
Underwood, J. T.,	Brooklyn.
Underwood, Miss,	Brooklyn.
Voorhees, Mr. and Mrs. P. V.,	Camden.
Voorhees, Master J. Dayton,	Camden.
Valentine, Mr. and Mrs. W. B.,	London.
Weeks, N. E.,	Boston.
Waldron, C. W.,	Vassalboro.
White, Mrs. F. M.,	Boston.
Whittemore, Mr. and Mrs. S. D.,	Boston.
Webster, Edgar H.,	Atlanta.
Warner, Mrs. Chas.,	Troy.
Warner, Miss C. S.,	Troy.
Warner, Miss M. V.,	Troy.
Winslow, Miss M. A.,	Troy.

Warner, E., Troy.
Walker, Mr. and Mrs. J. Albert, Portsmouth.
Walker, Miss, Portsmouth.
Woodruff, Mr. and Mrs. Henry C., Bridgeport.

MANSION HOUSE.

Andrews, Miss P. N., Paris Hill.
Chase, Bernard A., Auburn.
Dewey, D. R., North Adams.
Forster, Charles, Portland.
Goodhue, Mrs. Geo. C., Salem.
Goodhue, Geo. H., Salem.
Gardiner, Nellie R., Providence.
Gardiner, C. P., Providence.
Highson, Mr. and Mrs. F. and two daughters, New York.
Hammond, Mrs. E. M., Boston.
Johnson, Mr. and Mrs. F., New York.
Lincoln, L. L., Rumford Falls.
deLissa, Mrs. M. S., New York.
O'Neill, M. E., Danville.
O'Neill, J. J., Coaticook, P. Q.
Perley, Putman, Boston.
Staples, E. P., Portland.
Small, W. W., Rumford Falls.
Simmons, Mrs. F., New York.
Schlegermilch, Mrs. and daughter, Boston.
VanBeill, Mrs. E. S., New York.
Webster, Miss E. B., Boston.
West, J. W., Boston.
Weed, G. A., Auburn.
Williams, Mrs. Geo. W., Salem.
Wood, W. H., Boston.

Elroy C. Davis, the man with the voice in the Union Station, Boston, sued for $10,000, and settled for $225. Cash in the hand better than judgment in the bush.

A recent journal has the following epitaph:

> "Beneath these stones
> Repose the bones
> Of Theodosius Grimm;
> He took his beer
> From year to year
> And then the bier took him!"

GENARE, 134.

Poland Water Leads Them All.

◎═══ WHY ? ═══◎

BECAUSE .. It was the FIRST KNOWN SOLVENT OF URIC ACID in the system.   .   .   .   .

BECAUSE .. It is the most EFFECTIVE ELIMINATOR of Calculi in the Bladder and Kidneys known to-day.   .   .   .   .

BECAUSE .. It was the ONLY water IN NEW ENGLAND to receive ANY AWARD at the World's Columbian Exposition, and the only award of the hundreds exhibited from the WORLD for Purity and Great Medicinal Properties.   .   .   .   .

BECAUSE .. The ANNUAL sales exceed the combined sales of all the Saratoga Springs.   .   .   .   .   .

BECAUSE .. Unprecedented as the success of the past has been it is more promising than ever, showing continued increase.   .   .   .   .

OFFICES:

BOSTON:	NEW YORK:	PHILADELPHIA:	CHICAGO:
175 Devonshire Street.	3 Park Place.	Corner 13th and Chestnut St.	Cor. Michigan Ave. and Randolph St.

HIRAM RICKER & SONS, Proprietors.
(INCORPORATED.)

Vol. II.   SUNDAY MORNING, AUGUST 11, 1895.   No. 7.

Poland Facts.

WE told you a little story about food, last week, and it was our purpose to show in that article simply what was consumed at the Poland Spring House by the guests thereof; but we find on examination that the subject has not been half exhausted, and it appears that we may be able to increase the interest of those who make Poland their summer home, if we continue the theme further, and show then how many people it takes to keep the machine in motion, to provide for their comfort, and to add to last week's figures those of the other two establishments under the direction of the famous Ricker Brothers of Poland Hill, the Mansion House and the Brackett, which latter is entirely devoted to employees.

In the first place, then, we will explain that at the Poland Spring House your wants are supplied at the table, after being seated by 2 head waiters, by 75 table-girls in neat, white dresses, who bring to you the result of the labors of 14 cooks and 2 butchers, who are aided by 16 women and 4 men.

You sleep in rooms which 18 chamber-maids keep tidy, and you press the button and receive replies from 13 bell-boys, but, bless you, not that unlucky number all at once.

You wish to send your parcel to the laundry, where 21 girls attack it and return it clean.

It requires 3 porters to handle your baggage, it is so heavy, and 3 horse-keepers direct the efforts of the numerous girls upstairs.

At night you sleep, but 6 watchmen keep guard within and without, so you can sleep in comfort.

The rooms must be lighted and the machinery kept in running order, and that takes 6 engineers to look after it.

Last, but far from least, for here is the head and the clerical labor of competent directing power; in the office are 10 people looking after your wants.

Now we will go down to the Mansion House and take a peep in and we find it requires 5 people in the office, 3 cooks, and 5 assistants in the kitchen, 9 girls in the dining-room, under the charge of a head waiter, 3 bell-boys to answer your calls, 3 laundresses, and 2 chamber-maids.

About the grounds we find 5 gardeners caring for the grass and flowers; at the bottling and spring house are 20 men; picking peas, digging potatoes and in such like labors are 11 farmers; at the gates and at Danville Junction, 2 each.

Now a little further on down the road is the Brackett House, where four employees look after the requirements there, they not requiring bell-boys and such luxuries, for bell-boys, you know, come under the head of luxuries.

But we must pass the stable on the way, where 23 men attend to the equine department there, and if we continue to the stable on the hill we will find 6 more. Horses must be shod, and water sometimes barreled, so 2 blacksmiths and 2 coopers attend to these departments.

Something new is constantly wanted, and the old is getting out of repair, so 12 carpenters are constantly employed, and before we close this portion of our article we must remember that the Poland Spring House help must be cared for in their own building, where 10 more people are kept busy.

At other points not enumerated are at least 7 more people not classified here, making in the aggregate 330 people, all of whom must eat, as well as the five hundred and more guests.

Now we will add to the list of supplies given last week, the amount it requires for the Mansion House and the help, and as these latter are pu-

DINING ROOM.

chased in bulk by the same buyer, and then properly distributed we will give them together in the following table, for one week:

	P. S. H.	M. H.	TOTAL.
Eggs,	8,400	1,680	10,080
Beef,	2,000 lbs.	846 lbs.	2,846
Whole Lambs,	27	7	34
Backs,	60	7	67
Chicken,	1,500 lbs.	313½ lbs.	1,813½
Turkey,	250 lbs.	45 lbs.	295
Fowl,	400 lbs.	108½ lbs.	508½
Salmon,	300 lbs.	50 lbs.	350
Blue-fish,	140 lbs.	40 lbs.	180
Mackerel,	110 lbs.	35 lbs.	145
Halibut,	170 lbs.	60 lbs.	230
Cod,	300 lbs.	50 lbs.	350
Veal,	160 lbs.	185½ lbs.	345½
Bacon,	200 lbs.	25 lbs.	225
Ham,	250 lbs.	90 lbs.	340
Potatoes,	63 bu.	18 bu.	81
Squash,	800 lbs.	150 lbs.	950
Peas,	15 bu.	19 bu.	34
Beans.	8 bu.	15 bu.	23
Butter,	900 lbs.	125 lbs.	1,025
Flour,	14 bbls.	5 bbls.	19
Berries,	25 bu.	4 bu.	29
Peaches,	20 bu.	3 bu.	23
Oranges,	10 boxes.	2 boxes.	12
Coffee.	150 lbs.	60 lbs.	210
Tea,	40 lbs.	15 lbs.	65
Cream,	441 qts.	100 qts.	541
Milk,	2,000 qts.	500 qts.	2,500
Sugar,	2,500 lbs.	400 lbs.	2,900

Last week our statement of 25 bushels of potatoes should have been 25 barrels.

This department of the Poland Spring interests is looked after by Mr. A. B. Ricker, and all must admit it is one of tremendous importance and surrounded by many difficulties, so far from a railroad.

Just another item before closing and that relates to the dining-room, which is 181 feet in length, and seats 430 people, as now seated, at 60 tables, seating 6, 8, 10, 12, and 14 people respectively.

The large glass at the end of the dining-room is 8 feet high and 14 feet wide.

Now have your breakfast and drink a cup of coffee.

THERE is a very rare geological formation at the "White Farm" (formerly known as the Hill Farm), Naples, Me., fifteen miles from Poland Spring. This formation is known as "Carpet Rock," is sixty feet long by twenty wide, and exhibits fifteen stripes of black and white rock; each stripe a foot wide, continuing the same breadth in both the white and. black stripes throughout the extent of the so-called carpet. A growth of curiously-patterned lichens makes the pattern of the carpet. This curious stone has never been photographed or heard of outside of Naples.

Mrs. Griffin, Mrs. Small, and Mrs. Nichols were the happy winners at a pleasant little game of six-handed euchre at a recent meeting.

The Cotillion.

THE Cotillion on the 2d came too late of course for last week's edition, and if not too late for the "Fair" we will say that it was participated in by a very brilliant and attractive throng of Poland's *élite*.

Mr. McNeel led the Cotillion, and others upon the floor were the Misses Gregg, Leech, McNeel, Hartshorne, Lillian Hartshorne, Vose, Thornton, Helen Drake, Edith Talcott, Trowbridge, Julia Trowbridge, and the Misses Peterson.

Among the gentlemen were the Messrs. Greer, Brown, Eanes, Vose, Batchelder, Leech, and Mr. Elder Leech.

Mrs. Trowbridge contributed the favors, and presided at the favor table, which were bows and arrows (cupids) tied with ribbons (instead of golden chains) and bells, rattles, and flowers.

At 10.30 a supper was served, which was provided by the gentlemen, and the first Cotillion of the season passed into history as an enjoyable event.

The First Ones.

MR. BENJAMIN GRIFFIN of New York, now a guest, whose welcome is as large as the hearts of the proprietors, was one of the gentlemen mentioned by Mr. James Harper as a guest in 1867, at the time he made his historic sketch, reproduced in No. 3 of the HILL-TOP.

Mrs. M. E. Hildreth, who is a very welcome guest at the Poland Spring House, is one of the earliest visitors to Poland Spring. Twenty-one years ago she came here and then Mr. Ricker used to remark that he believed a hotel on the top of the hill would pay. It does. At that time Mr. and Mrs. Hildreth and two children drove here with a span of English thoroughbreds, one of which was named Stridaway, who had won several races. Whenever driven to the spring, he would neigh and whinny until given a drink from a pail filled with Poland water, even if he had but a few moments before a completely satisfied his thirst at the old barn from the clear brook water. There it is again. Instinct, you know.

The first picture sold from the Art Gallery in the Maine Building is that of D. D. Coombs, and called "In Green Pastures." It is a painting which has been greatly admired by many, and the purchaser, Mr. Geo. F. Parker of Philadelphia, is to be congratulated on the acquisition of so admirable a composition. The purchase was made Monday, August 5th.

The first book taken out of the Poland Spring Library was "The Caxtons," No. 30, by Mr. A. T. Salter of Room 23, Poland Spring House, at 10.55 A.M., Monday, August 5th.

A Mansion House Group.

IN grouping a number of people there are several difficulties to be overcome, and that Mr. Ness, the resident artist for the Notman Photographic Co., does so admirably is not to be denied.

The group we present in this number was taken in front of the Mansion House recently, and is admirable in every respect.

The persons represented in it, beginning at the left of the picture with the back row, are:

George H. Conley,	Boston.
Miss M. E. Barbour,	Boston.
Emily C. Wood,	Worcester.
William T. Read,	Camden, N. J.
Mr. Badger,	Boston.
Miss Washington,	Philadelphia.
Miss A. F. Dowse,	Boston.
Mrs. Alex F. Sabine,	Philadelphia.
Mrs. Badger,	Boston.
Ernest Peterson.	
N. Amerman,	New York.

In the second row were:

Mrs. George H. Conley,	Boston.
Mrs. D. Kintz,	Boston.
Mrs. J. C. Crombie,	Lawrence.
Mrs. Oliver Marsh,	Springfield.
Mrs. E. C. Jordan,	Portland.
Mrs. E. G. Gay,	Boston.
Mr. J. H. Danforth.	Boston.
Mrs. Jessie L. Thurston,	Portland.
Mrs. N. Amerman,	New York.
Rev. Edwin C. Sweetser,	Philadelphia.

In the third row were:

Mr. Talbot.	
Mrs. J. R. Pulsifer,	Rochester.
Baby Pulsifer,	Rochester.
Mr. Perley.	Boston.
Mr. F. C. Jackson,	New York.
Mrs. F. C. Jackson,	New York.
Miss C. Belle Woodman,	Springfield.
Mrs. L. S. Read,	Camden, N. J.
Miss Mary Minor.	Baltimore.
S. W. Keene,	Boston.
J. C. Crombie,	Lawrence.

In the fourth or front row were:

Mrs. E. P. Staples,	Portland.

Mrs. Milnor,   Baltimore.
Mrs. P. G. Vanzandt,   Jersey City.
Robert Marsh,   Springfield.
Marguerite Thurston,   Portland.
Marguerite Ricker,   South Poland.
Master Conley,   Boston.
Mary Campbell,   Camden, N. J.
Miss Jane C. Marsh,   Springfield.
Miss Nettie Ricker,   South Poland.

Here are forty-two souls in a single group, every one of which is clear and distinct. The reproduction is the work of the Suffolk Engraving Co. of Boston, and needs no other words of praise.

Capt. W. H. Daily.

THE announcement comes to us that on the evening of Tuesday, August 13th, in Music Hall, Capt. William H. Daily, the world-famous life-saver and swimmer, will give a talk on his remarkable experiences in saving life.

The great gold medal, voted to him by special act of Congress for saving thirty-six lives, is an indication of the value of his services to humanity.

Harper's Weekly, in speaking of him, said he had taught more people to swim than any other man in the world, and the *Cincinnati Commercial Gazette* remarked that he had "saved more people from drowning than any other man."

He is an athlete in appearance, and as modest as he is powerful. He also bears the reputation of having taught more ladies and children to swim than any man in the world.

Foremost among his pupils, who are now in the cast, he counts Mrs. Herman Oelrichs of Newport, and her sister, Miss Virginia Fair, the family of Hon. Hall McAllister of San Francisco, family of Governor Tuttle of Arizona, family of Hon. Judge McKinstry, Mrs. Senator Stuart, family of Hon. R. C. Harrison, family of Banker Harrington of Napa, family of Hon. C. O'Connor, and in general all the leading people of the Pacific Coast have been his pupils. The California ladies who *do not* swim are the exceptions to the general rule.

Mrs. Herman Oelrichs, Newport, has kindly permitted Captain Daily to refer to her as to his ability and character as a teacher of ladies and girls.

On Wednesday morning, August 14th, Captain Daily will give an exhibition at the pond in the vicinity of the bath houses, of which the following is the

PROGRAMME OF NATATION.

1. DIVING.
2. FLOATING.—On back; on side; on breast, and upright; motionless.
3. SWIMMING.—Breast stroke; side stroke; with feet alone; with hands alone; feet foremost; on back; racing stroke.

SAVING FROM DROWNING.—Illustrating method of swimming with a person, and resuscitation.

Captain Daily will allow his feet to be firmly tied together, his hands tied behind his back, and in that condition will jump into the water and swim ashore.

A Useful Article.

MRS. OLIVER MARSH'S cooking utensil, which is advertised in this number, has been most kindly received by the public. Her demonstration at Jordan & Marsh's, the 11th and 12th of June, was a great success.

Mrs. Marsh's invention has received the endorsement of many prominent women, among the number Mrs. Mary A. Livermore.

Progressive Euchre.

AT the Poland Spring House the first progressive euchre party of the season was given Friday evening, August 2d. Mrs. Snall and Mrs. Jackson, having won an equal number of games, cut for the first prize, a sofa pillow, and Mrs. Jackson won. Mrs. Snall received the second prize, a glove case. Mrs. Embry and Miss Grace Hackett cut for the third prize, a picture frame, Miss Hackett being successful. Mrs. Spencer became the happy possessor of a Poland Spring carafe. Among the gentlemen, the successful players were Hon. F. E. Gilman, a silver tray; Major Stephen C. Talbot, who received a Poland Spring orange spoon; and Mr. Hackett, a cigar case.

Boston.
Boston.
Lawrence
Springfield.
Portland
Boston
Boston.
Portland
New York
Philadelphia

Rochester
Rochester
Boston
New York
New York
Springfield
Camden, N. J
Baltimore
Boston.
Lawrence

on where?
Portland

FRANK CARLOS GRIFFITH, } EDITORS.
NETTIE M. RICKER, }

PUBLISHED EVERY SUNDAY MORNING DURING THE MONTHS
OF JULY, AUGUST AND SEPTEMBER, IN THE INTERESTS OF

POLAND SPRING AND ITS VISITORS.

All contributions relative to the guests of Poland Spring will
be thankfully received.

To insure publication, all communications should reach the
editors not later than Wednesday preceding day of issue.

All parties desiring rates for advertising in the HILL-TOP
should write the editors for same.

The subscription price of the HILL-TOP is $1.00 for the
season, post-paid. Single copies will be mailed at 10c. each.

Address,
EDITORS "HILL-TOP,"
Poland Spring House,
South Poland, Maine.

PRINTED AT JOURNAL OFFICE, LEWISTON.

Sunday, August 11, 1895.

Editorial.

A VILLAGE of a thousand souls down here
in Maine is quite a town, and allowing five
souls to each habitation it makes a town of
two hundred houses.

It would have a bank, one, two or perhaps
three churches, several stores, a town house and
a hall, one or two hotels, two schools, a lock-up,
and a church fight.

Here we have from nine hundred to a thousand people, no tows, no lock-up, but every
other peaceful requirement of a city, including a
public library and art gallery.

It becomes quite a metropolitan center when
you come to think of it, without any policeman,
or rings, even from bells, although our belles
have numerous rings, and our books are not in
the running brooks.

We could carry this subject on interminably
but that our columns are required for more important matter, and to-day are forced to enlarge

again to sixteen pages to satisfy this craving of
the public for mental food.

It is a pleasure to know that it is desired, as
well as to realize that we have an abundance of
material this week which is of more or less
interest to our readers.

We are ever ready with pen, pencil, paste-
pot and shears.

Crystal Purity.

To the pure all things are pure, hence the
most impure may imagine themselves pure when
they gaze into the pure crystal of the Poland
Spring Carafe, and witness the purity of its
contents; and become purer for the vision and
the thought.

They are unique, artistic, and useful, and,
for once, get away from the everlasting squatty,
bulging, round receptacle we have hitherto seen
upon the table.

This Carafe carries a history with it, besides
being extremely ornamental.

The Winding Horn.

"CAN anyone wind the horn?" "Wall, by
gosh," said a country visitor standing by,
"Ef anybody can wind that great long
tin horn, I sh'd like t' see 'em dew it."
Tally-ho! Tally-ho!
They're off. No!
"What's the matter?"
"I've forgotten my scarf-pin, and I shall
take cold without it; wait a minute."
"Well," remarked the rosy-checked flower-
girl, "that feller must be stuck unit with that
girl, coz he buys flowers for her every day.
Ain't she handsome?"
"Sing us a German student song, Mr.
Griffith, and we'll all join in the chorus."
"Of *chorus* I will."
"Oh! O—h! Hit him!"
"Now we have the scarf-pin, let them go,"
and away goes one of the merriest crowds imagin-
able, on the Poland Brake.

Mr. Eames naturally feels proud of such a
party, for the ride is in his honor. The precious
freight includes the Misses Woodford, Eames,
and the Misses Hartshorne, and Messrs. McNeel,
Vose, Griffith, and Eames, eight light-hearted
and merry mortals.

Of course it was a pleasant ride, over hill
and through valley, by lake and stream; how
could it be otherwise.

May they repeat it often and with as much
success.

Our War Article.

BY GEN. D. MORRELL I. ZATION.

HAVING solicited every conceivable magazine in Delaware, as well as Canada and the United States, and the Kingdoms of Ireland and Great Britain, to be allowed to relate the true state of affairs at the battle of Blue Creek, I have at length succeeded in inducing (by persistent effort) THE HILL-TOP to publish—hold on, I did not mean to give away the whole business in that way,

Perhaps I had better begin again.

The attention of Congress having been called to my gigantic failure in the campaign of Jincks Mill, I was suddenly promoted from my grade of general to that of corporal, which was much more advantageous, as the shoulder straps were replaced with a stripe on the arm, which enabled me to get about the field much more lively and reconnoitre the defences in the rear of our camp much more effectively than if I had worn my straps as formerly. Besides I had not the bother of a horse, which was an inestimable boon, as my former milk-blue charger had devoted, in his hungry phrenzy, four of my best reports of victories won by me, thus depriving the knowledge of them ever reaching the halls of Congress.

But regarding the battle of Blue Creek, I distinctly fail to remember whether the day was hot or cold, but if memory be not at fault it was muddy overhead.

I had ordered up my reserves from a cow pasture, where he had been milking a dilapidated looking kine, and placed my pickets on the fence, expecting the next day to be the most bloody and sanguinary of the entire war; nor was I mistaken, for it proved the most hotly-contested fight in the history of modern warfare, so my orderly said, and he was there all the time, so he reported to me when he found me three days after, twenty miles north of the spot.

My detachment consisted, if I am not in error, of four thou——; no, it was four men; no, I am wrong again; it was miles, not men, and I was determined to bring on the conflict on the approach of daylight, unless the enemy had formed the same plan and should attack just ahead of my appointed hour, in which case, of course, I should retreat in as masterly a manner as possible, and cross the creek and burn the magnificent bridge which spanned the angry waters, and which was built at an expense of not less than—mpty-two dollars in Confederate bonds.

My position, selected with great caution, was flanked in front by an *abatis* of corn husks gathered from far-off fields, and directly on my right wing was the river, or it may have been a mountain, I can't exactly recall which it was, but reference to a map of the region will establish which. At all events, if it was a river it was deep, and if it was a mountain it was no hill, you may be certain.

It was by the sides of this mountain I intended to charge the enemy if he waited for me, but as events proved he had decided to cross the river and force the fighting, which was terrific, or rather would have been.

The river, being frozen at the time, would have made a natural bridge, and I had placed dynamite conveniently to blow up the mountain if the enemy attempted to cross in his boats, or to place a pontoon. Luckily for me, however, my left wing rested on the extreme summit of a ravine which divided the country right here.

My commissary department was well supplied, as I had sent out a foraging party the day before, who had returned with a can of baked beans, and had driven before him a cow frame with milk aboard.

But to return to the battle proper. Having made my disposition satisfactorily, I began to speculate on the probability of the enemy's actions.

In this I resemble General Sherman, who admits he has the same fear I always enjoyed, viz., what the enemy was likely to do, whereas General Grant never bothered himself about anyone's plans but his own.

I think that Grant was wrong. He may have been very lucky in winning every battle he fought, but it takes genuine skill to get out of the way of a victorious foe.

It is for this very reason that I claim a certain superiority over Grant. My plans were always well laid, and the enemy invariably laid them out just as I planned he might if I had not reckoned on his making plans at all.

The battle of Blue Creek was one of this kind of battles where superior numbers and disciplined troops overwhelmed an inferior opponent.

By midnight (to return directly to the subject of the engagement proper once more) I might have been seen still up and excessively nervous. I could not sit still on the edge of the shingle I had placed edgewise for a seat, and paced the ground with my loose boot heels rattling and jingling merrily.

A bray of one of our mules might be heard occasionally, which reminded me that it might prove a clue to our whereabouts if the enemy were approaching within forty miles. I was too much alarmed, I should say preoccupied, to go out and muzzle the mule, and so let him bray.

One o'clock, two o'clock, three o'clock came, when I distinctly heard a sound as of an enemy approaching. I could not tell in my nich-wrought-up condition whether it was a rifle shot, a cannon, a mortar, or a man whistling. I am sure it was a sound.

I know, or I had read somewhere, that sharp-shooters placed in ambush in rifle-pits carefully erected in tree tops, could pick off an advancing enemy, provided the enemy were not too numerous and there were sharp-shooters and tree tops enough.

In consequence of this I had wished I had more sharp-shooters, but man proposes and the enemy disposes,—the man, and so it was with me.

At the instant I heard the noise, I blew out the half inch of candle in my tent and, grasping my sword, valorously rushed forth into the night.

I had said the night before that I knew the enemy would attack before me; it would be just like him, and consequently I was not prepared.

I remember now, I had only one boot on at the time. However, with blanched face and set, quivering lips, I cried under my breath, "forward," and having previously laid out my line of march, I struck boldly for the back country, due north, reckoning from the long-handled dipper, which was partly visible.

Undaunted by obstacles, I continued my headlong march toward the enemy, by the way of the north pole, for I knew it was only a question of time when I should be able to come up and attack him in the rear.

Twenty miles seems a long distance, but when twisting the above plan it is very short, and by noon the next day I was certain the sanguinary conflict must be over, and I rested.

This was certainly the hardest-fought battle of the entire war, at least so my orderly reported when we met next.

Had I not been so ably seconded I might have lost the battle, but I believe in giving honor where honor is due, and it is on this principle I lay claim to so much, as the survivor of that campaign.

But to return to the battle itself,—I firmly believe to-day that if the mountain had been a river, or the river had been a mountain, I should not be here to relate the circumstances as they really were. You may hear from me again.

The Magnificent Portrait of Hon. James G. Blaine, hanging over the stairway in the Maine Building, was made by THE SPRAGUE & HATHAWAY Co. of West Somerville, Mass. They also made the enlarged photograph of the World's Fair Views in the same building.

Alaska.

Col. C. H. French gave his lecture on Alaska on Thursday evening, in the Music Room, to an overflowing house. His lecture was interesting and well delivered, and his views especially fine, the colored views unusually so. He received $50.31.

The Salmagundi.

TUESDAY evening witnessed the Salmagundi and it is reported by an eye witness on the roof that it was great sport, and from so lofty a view-point it was high-ly successful.

Then this it was; six tables were arranged with flowers of a different description, and the tally cards were tied with ribbon to correspond with the colors of the flowers.

At one table the game of Euchre was in progress, at the next, Hearts, and so on, including Parchesi, Slap-Jack, Verbarium (?), and Thread the Needle.

Did you ever see a man thread a needle? No? Well, our reporter on the roof could see the eye from there, but the nearest gentleman failed to connect the thread with the bar of steel, and great was the mirth thereupon.

There were prizes, and they were won by Miss Green, first; Miss Hartshorne, second; and the third by Miss——, ny, we nearly told, and we mustn't.

The gentlemen who took away valuable souvenirs were Mr. Hartshorne, first; Mr. Gregg, second; and the third again, to Mr. ——; yes, to Mr. Blank, and it was a case of catch it for him.

Now the prizes are secrets, and the reporter on the roof cannot divulge them, but it is shrewdly suspected the "U cur" prize was a dog, the "Haits" was a doe, "Pa-cheesey" was a Dutch one, or it may have been a German-favor; the "Slap-Jack was a frying-pan, the "Verbarium" a pocket dictionary, and the "Thread and Needle" was a camel.

Now don't take our word for it, for our reporter was too far away to discern accurately, possibly, but can ask one of these ladies, Mrs. Trowbridge, Miss Eames, the Misses Carpenter, the Misses Todd, the Misses Hartshorne, the Misses Leech, Miss Greer, Miss McNeel, Miss Royce, Miss Gregg, Miss Vose, or Miss Thornton, all of whom were present, or Mr. Griffith, the Messrs. Leech, Hartshorne, Gregg, McNeel, Wilcox, Vose, Brown, or Greer, and *possibly* they may.

One of the ladies was very appropriately presented with some chewing gum, for her jaws were distinctly seen to move rapidly soon after. Selah!

Complimentary Art Talks.

A SERIES of three talks on the "History of Art" were given in the rotunda of Maine State Building by Miss Carolyn M. Field, August 5, 7, and 9, at 10 A.M.

August 5th: subject. "Ancient and Classic Art"; 5000 B.C to 70 A.D; Architecture, Painting, and Sculpture in Egypt, Assyria, Asia Minor, Greece, and Italy.

August 7th: subject, "Early Christian Art"; 70 A.D. to 10th Century; Catacombs, Basilica Church Art in Ravenna, Art in Byzantium, Mosaic Painting.

August 9th: subject, "Romanesque and Gothic Architecture"; 10th Century to 13th Century; in Italy, France, Germany, Spain, and England.

In following this outline, Miss Field endeavored to bring out the points which characterize the growth in art, from the crude work of the Egyptians and Assyrians, up to the perfect structure and ornamentation of the Late Gothic Cathedral. She showed how subservient to and dependent upon architecture has always been painting and sculpture. She pointed out in what ways the grand plan and methods of lighting places of worship developed, from the ancient cave-like mosques and temples of Cairo, the Greek Parthenon and Roman Pantheon, through the Christian Basilica churches in Ravenna and the mosque of St. Sophia, Byzantium; the Romanesque churches of San Marco, Venice; the Palatine Chapel, Sicily; Sainte Chapelle, Paris; Sistine Chapel, Rome; the Pisa Cathedral and Baptistry, to the beautifully-decorated Gothic cathedrals of Notre Dame, Paris, and Amiens.

Miss Field's grasp of her subject was firm and kept well in hand. She carried her audience with her and held their attention from beginning to end.

Her talks were illustrated by means of photographs of ancient art relics now in existence or crumbling into decay.

The attendance was excellent and the rotunda of the Maine State Building proved an admirable location for talks of this or a kindred nature.

It would seem to be a pleasing idea to have a series of similar talks continued in this place so recently dedicated to literary and art purposes.

Miss Field is to be congratulated upon her success, which was emphatic.

She was presented with a very fine basket of flowers by the gentlemen, and several bouquets.

Miss Virginia Fair is pronounced the best swimmer at Newport. She is a pupil of Captain Daily.

The Answer.

Here is the solution to last week's puzzling rhyme:

A sutler sat in his ulster gray,
Watching the moonbeams luster play,
Who lurest the weak rulest the strong?
The result of great battles to him does belong.

John Barleycorn my king.

Paintings.

ARE you a connoisseur of paintings? If so, it is to be supposed you have examined those in the Maine State Building. The best artists in America, those taking the highest rank, are there represented.

Where will you find more exquisite effects than in those of Enneking? There are several examples of his style there, which are superb.

Note Hatfield's beautiful touches of Nature in his child paintings; they stand right out from the canvass; there is atmosphere and delicacy of feeling in them.

Waltman's portraits are excellent, and should find appreciation from art lovers.

Miss Palmer's flower pieces are among the best examples of that class of painting, and would be admired in any gallery in America or elsewhere.

Then there are splendid examples of Dean's, Sears Gallagher's, and Buhler's art, and two delicate little bits by Kay, "The Mouse-Trap" and "Me and Fido," which are full of life.

There is also a hound's head, called "Penelope," which can scarcely be excelled short of Landseer, and painted by that excellent French artist, Robert Forcade.

A new marine by Halsall has been added recently and is a gem. It should find many admirers, and undoubtedly will.

A gentleman capable of judging remarked recently that the collection now in the Maine Building is really an unusual and remarkable one, and that it would be difficult to duplicate it in merit.

This is an exceptional year for the purchase of paintings, and probably there has been no time for many years, nor will there be again soon, when pictures are to be had at such reasonable prices.

Mr. Coombs' picture of landscape and cows, so recently sold, is but one instance of what can be done by people of good judgment in the selection of paintings, and if true lovers of art will look about in the Art Gallery, they will find there a great variety of subjects and schools, and excellent examples of each with which to beautify their homes.

Mr. Coombs has added another fine cattle piece, equally as good as the one disposed of.

Mrs. Bailey.

PHYSICAL culture, voice, dress, and kindred subjects have been ably discussed by Mrs. Bailey during the week to her usual interested hearers.

She has a very happy faculty of expression and agrees with Sir Henry Irving that the ungainly method of hand-shaking, practiced by some of late, is awkward, inelegant, and not to be advised.

"Whisht."

A noble name, and a noble game
Is the noble game of whist,
But Miss Noble's game is far from tame;
And if we might be permitted to add, so is
also the game played by Miss Trist.

Both these young ladies have taught successfully the intricacies of the game to many here and if their ideas, which are a standard, are followed, you need never be beaten at whist by a non-professional.

Concert Program.

SUNDAY, AUGUST 11TH, AT 3.30 P.M.

Kuntz Orchestral Club.

1. Xorsprel—Third Act of Meistersinger. . Wager.
2. Selection—Der Freischutz. . . . . Weber.
3. { a. Menuett Orpheus. . . . . . Sluch.
   { b. Valse from Suite. . . . . Volkmanna.
4. Andante from Surprise Symphony.
5. { a. Ases Death.
   { b. Anitras Danse.
6. Selection—Faust. From Peer Gynt Suite. . Greig.
   . . . . . Gounod.

Mr. Oakes and Mr. Field are thinning out the fish in the Range Lakes. They recently spent a day at the sport and caught only one, whose combined weight was eight ounces.

Tid=Bits.

Blake rides galore.

Don't fail to see Captain Daily.

Saved forty lives, just think of it!

What a lovely lot of young ladies!

Magnificent pink sky, Monday eve.

Mr. Sawyer is reported by Dr. Wedgwood as improving daily and getting along finely. All are rejoicing.

Mrs. DeWitt Smith from Boston, now one of our guests, is the wife of the DeWitt Smith who held a foreign office under President Lincoln.

The menus which were used at the Poland Spring House last Sunday were painted by Miss Stevens, who has a young ladies' boarding-school in the town of Gloucester.

Boston sends no more welcome guests each season than Mr. B. C. Moulton and his charming wife. May they add many more seasons here to their already lengthening list.

Not everyone who leaves for a few days, returns to find that the ladies have decorated his table with ferns and sweet peas, as was the case with Mr. Nelson Bartlett recently.

It has been remarked by those competent to judge, that the large portrait of Colonel Coler, now hanging in the office, is the best piece of work ever produced. It is by the Notman Photographic Co.

Mr. Nathan Crowell of Boston, a recent visitor, writes to a friend that he has been to Europe twice, and across the continent several times, but has never seen a spot more beautiful, or a hotel better kept than the Poland Spring.

A party consisting of Mr. and Mrs. Benjamin Griffin, Miss Griffin, and Mr. Cecil Griffin, Mrs. George W. Crossman, Miss Stichler, Mr. James Talcott, Mrs. Talcott, Miss Grace Talcott, and Miss Edith Talcott had a delightful trip on the steam yacht, "The Poland," Monday morning.

Rev. William Henry Bolster of Boston preached in Music Hall last Sunday, and was favored with the largest congregation of the season. His remarks were eloquent and impressive, and found a ready response in the hearts of his hearers. His text was Hebrews IV., 11.

THE HILL-TOP's compliments to Master Johnny Chamberlain, whose consideration for the Editors thereof prompted him to grace our table in the Maine State Building with an immaculate bunch of sweet peas. When Johnny goes marching home again, may it be with a light and merry heart, and a pocket heavy with silver.

The Key Fund.

Through the instrumentality of Mrs. Coppenhagen, the *New York Mail and Express* fund for Miss Key, the granddaughter of the composer of the "Star Spangled Banner," is likely to be considerably increased. At present it amounts to about $50.00.

The Brake.

"COME on, there's always room for one more." "Yes, indeed, you're a light-weight; you can ride in the basket, you know."

"No, thank you; try it yourself."

With light banter and merry laughter they were off, and the one for whom there was no seat aboard waved her kerchief and joined as heartily in the merriment.

The Brake, with the party of Mansion House guests, which included Mrs. Elliot, Mrs. Sabine, Mrs. Jordan, and the Misses Barbour and Campbell, and Messrs. Danforth, Goodrich, Gay, and Read, started on its delightful summer-day trip.

It was a thoroughly enjoyable occasion, and the trip around Sabbathday Lake and home through the pine woods was one to be remembered.

"Did they have a yell, this staid and sober party?"

Indeed they did, and this it was:

"Chi-he! chi-ha! chi-ha-ha-ha! Poland, Poland! rah, rah, rah!

"Yell! yell! Everybody yell! Mansion! Mansion! well, well, well!"

Where can lovelier families of young ladies be found than those of the Hartshornes, Todds, O'Briens, Leechs, Talcotts, Carpenters, and Trowbridges, not to mention a score or more of young ladies who are the only daughters of the family?

Of the many delightful guests at the Poland Spring House this season, none have carried with them in departing warmer friendships than the genial Col. Coler and his charming wife, to whom *au revoir* was said last week. When they again visit Poland they are sure of a most cordial welcome.

On Monday last a very pleasant occasion was the picnic supper from the Mansion House on Middle Lake, and participated in by Mrs. Badger, Mrs. Kuntz, the Misses Campbell, Mary Marsh, Sarah Ricker, Gardner, Schlegermilch, Leonard, and Hale, and Messrs. Goodrich, Reed, Gay, and Dr. Dewey. Corn was roasted, but as the sun was low the picnickers were not, but were as cool as a professional stump speaker.

Arrivals.

POLAND SPRING HOUSE.

Allen, Miss F. L.,	Pawtucket.
Allen, Mr. and Mrs. Geo. O.,	Scituate.
Austin, Mr. and Mrs. C. M.,	Westfield.
Alden, Mrs. G. A.,	Waterville.
Alden, Mrs. S. F.,	Clinton, Ia.
Allen, Mrs. G. Frank,	Fall River.
Andrews, Mrs. F. E.,	Boston.
Brooks, Mr. and Mrs. W. B., Jr.,	Boston.
Brooks, Miss Alice,	Boston.
Boland, Miss,	Portland.
Barbour, E. D.,	Boston.
Buckley, W. F.,	New York.
Banks, J. W.,	Portland.
Briggs, Mr. and Mrs. F. H.,	Auburn.
Buchanan, Mrs. and son,	Syracuse.
Berry, Mr. and Mrs. J. F.,	Boston.
Bixbee, Wm. F.,	Montreal.
Bradstreet, Mrs. F. T.,	Gardiner.
Bradstreet, Miss Laura,	Gardiner.
Brayton, Mrs. David A.,	Fall River.
Brayton, Elizabeth H.,	Fall River.
Brayton, Dana D.,	Fall River.
Briggs, G. L.,	Portland.
Backinston, Mrs. D. B.,	Geneva.
Bolster, Mrs. C. H. and daughter,	Chicago.
Bonny, Adeline L.,	Portland.
Borden, Mrs. P. H.,	Portland.
Conway, Mrs. J. D.,	Somerville.
Conway, Miss,	Somerville.
Conway, Harry A.,	Somerville.
Curtis, Mrs. Clara,	Portland.
Crowell, Geo.,	Bangor.
Cooper, Geo.,	Pawtucket.
Codman, James M.,	Brookline.
Cushen, Mr. and Mrs. W. B.,	Melrden.
Cutting, Miss P. W.,	Boston.
Coombs, D. D.,	Auburn.
Callahan, Eugene A.,	Lewiston.
Crossman, Mrs. Geo. W.,	New York.
Crossman, Miss,	New York.
Crossman, Herman,	New York.
Curtis, Mrs. C. L.,	Portland.
Dexter, Mrs. W. W.,	Pawtucket.
Davidge, Mr. and Mrs. James,	Binghamton.
Davidge, Mr. and Mrs. S. B.,	Newark Valley.
Dearborn, D. F.,	Chicago.
Dibble, Miss Sara F.,	Westfield.
Dillon, John,	Montreal.
Dillon, Miss,	Montreal.
Elsworth, C. B.,	Irvington.
Egbert, Miss E.,	New York.
Ewell, Geo. A.,	New York.
Floyd-Jones, Edward H.,	New York.
Fish, Mr. and Mrs. Geo. H.,	New York.
Farr, F. D.,	Boston.
Feek, Mr. and Mrs. A. J.,	Syracuse.
French, C. H.,	Chicago.
Gilbert, Louis,	Boston.
Griffin, Mr. and Mrs. Benj.,	New York.
Griffin, Miss,	New York.
Griffin, Cecil,	New York.
Gray, Thomas,	Fitchburg.
Gray, Mrs. A. H.,	New York.
Goodrich, Hazen B.,	Haverhill.
Hale, Chandler,	Ellsworth.
Hale, Mr. and Mrs. John C.,	Cleveland.
Hale, Edwin B.,	Boston.
Haskell, Mrs. L. B.,	New Bedford.
Haskell, Miss H.,	New Bedford.
Haynes, Geo. H.,	Portland.
Haitshorne, H. M.,	New York.
Hellyar, Wm. H.,	Boston.
Holmes, Mr. and Mrs. E. T.,	New York.
Holmes, E. T., Jr.,	New York.
Holmes, Mildred,	New York.
Harvey, Mr. and Mrs. Huxley,	Wilmington.
Hebbard, Mr. and Mrs. A.,	New York.
Howard, J. C.,	Lewiston.
Hoyt, Colgate,	New York.
Hubbard, Mrs. E. G.,	New York.
Hutchinson, A. J.,	Brunswick.
Haskell, C. C.,	Portland.
Hartshorne, Edwin C.,	New York.
Hill, Mr. and Mrs. A. E.,	Somerville.
Hunt, Otis E.,	Newtonville.
Hildreth, Mrs. M. E.,	Boston.
Hildreth, Miss Alma,	Boston.
Ingalls, Joseph A.,	Boston.
Knight, Mr. and Mrs. T. Morris,	Philadelphia.
Kelsey, Mrs. E.,	Freeport.
Kalkoff, F.,	New York.
Kessler, Wm. L.,	Philadelphia.
Knapp, Mrs. E. A.,	New York.
Lawler, Mr. and Mrs. John,	Portland.
Lawler, Wm.,	Portland.
Lawler, Alice,	Portland.
Lord, Mr. and Mrs. Henry G.,	Brookline.
Layng, Mr. and Mrs. F. S.,	Philadelphia.
Lambert, Mrs. Thos.,	Augusta.
Lambert, Catholina,	New York.
Locke, Miss Mary L.,	Fall River.
Lord, Mr. and Mrs., E. A.,	Rosemont, Pa.
Lord, Miss,	Rosemont, Pa.
Little, Amos R.,	Philadelphia.
Langdon, Mr. and Mrs. Thos. P.,	Baltimore.
Martin, Mr. and Mrs. John T.,	U. S. Army.
Meredith, Mrs. J. K.,	Boston.
MacGregor, Geo. R. D.,	Portland.
Mason, Miss,	Auburn.
Mountford, Mrs. M. E.,	Portland.
Maxwell, Mrs. H. E.,	Auburn.
Milliken, Mrs. H. P.,	Augusta.
Meany, Mr. and Mrs. Edw. P.,	New Jersey.
Meany, Edw. B.,	New Jersey.
Mowel, Mrs. C. B.,	New York.
Mendellson, A.,	Lewiston.
Nichols, Mrs. W. M.,	Haverhill.
Nealey, A. B.,	Lewiston.
Neal, Victor,	Gardiner.
Nash, Mrs. C. J.,	Lewiston.
O'Connor, Mrs.,	New York.
O'Brien, Mrs. L.,	New York.
O'Brien, Miss K.,	New York.
O'Brien, Miss M.,	New York.
O'Brien, Miss A. R.,	New York.
O'Brien, Miss A. L.,	New York.
O'Brien, Miss G.,	New York.
O'Brien, Master F. X.,	New York.
Osgood, H. S.,	Portland.
Paul, Dr. James,	Philadelphia.
Paul, Miss C. W.,	Philadelphia.
Paul, Miss M. W.,	Philadelphia.
Prall, Miss E. A.,	New York.
Peten, H. O.,	New York.
Paul, Mr. and Mrs. Henry N.,	Philadelphia.
Peters, Mr. and Mrs. B. F.,	Washington.
Parker, Mr. and Mrs. S. F.,	Philadelphia.
Parsons, Mrs. B. W.,	Providence.
Palmer, Lowell M.,	Brooklyn.
Packard, Bessie,	Brockton.
Parrich, Mrs. J. Scott,	Richmond.
Randall, C. A.,	Brunswick.
Reade, John L.,	Lewiston.
Rouse, Henry C.,	Cleveland.
Russell, Dr. and Mrs. E. W.,	Lewiston.
Schlemper, John G.,	Brooklyn.
Skaats, Mrs. S.,	New York.
Starbird, F. L.,	South Paris.
Smith, Mrs. Meredith,	Boston.
Smith, Mr. and Mrs. John B.,	Lewiston.
Slade, Mrs. C. N.,	Fall River.
Spencer, Mr. and Mrs. James E.,	New York.

Stickney, Miss,   New York.
Swayne, Alfred H.,   New York.
Sprague, P. W.,   Boston.
Stockbridge, Mr. and Mrs. J. C.,   Providence.
Stetson, H. L.,   DesMoines.
Stetson, Mrs. W. W.,   Auburn.
Sawyer, L. N.,   Chicago.
Small, Mr. and Mrs. H. C.,   Portland.
Swain, Mr. and Mrs. H. C.,   New York.
TenBroeck, Mrs. N. E.,   New York.
Talcott, Mr. and Mrs. James,   New York.
Talcott, Miss Grace,   New York.
Talcott, Edith C.,   New York.
Taggart, Mr. and Mrs. R. M.,   New York.
Tibbetts, H. S.,   Lewiston.
Towle, M. F.,   Boston.
Towle, Myra M.,   Lewiston.
Towle, B. Frye,   Lewiston.
Trowbridge, Dr. Geo.,   New York.
Turner, John,   Boston.
Vincent, W. S.,   Boston.
Wyeth, Mr. and Mrs. F. H.,   Philadelphia.
Woodford, Mrs. Stewart L.,   Brooklyn.
Woodford, Miss,   Brooklyn.
Warren, Mr. and Mrs. J. E.,   Portland.
Winch, Jos. R.,   Brookline.
Winch, Mr. and Mrs. Geo. Fred,   Brookline.
Webber, S. B.,   Brunswick.
Windram, Mr. and Mrs. W. T.,   Boston.
Williams, Miss Jessa,   Hartford.
Wardwell, F. W.,   Portland.
Whitman, G. L.,   Portland.
Wheeler, Mrs. T. H.,   New York.
Wheeler, Miss J. E.,   New York.
Williams, Miss E. C.,   Portland.
Wing, Mr. and Mrs. Henry T.,   Brooklyn.

MANSION HOUSE.

Arrington, Benj. F.,   Lynn.
Blackett, J. B.,   Portland.
Barton, Walter,   Hyde Park.
Fogg, Mr. and Mrs. Geo. E.,   Greene, Me.
Goodhue, Geo. C.,   Salem.
Goodhue, L. H.,   Salem.
Gilbert, Mr. and Mrs. F. A.,   Boston.
Gilbert, Florence A.,   Boston.
Gilbert, Master Lester F.,   Boston.
Gilbert, Ruth,   Boston.
Haight, Chas. N.,   Yonkers.
Hill, Mr. and Mrs. Henry,   Minneapolis.
Hill, Miss,   Minneapolis.
Hill, A. E.,   Minneapolis.
Hawthou, J. W.,   Keokuk.
Hawthon, F. M.,   Keokuk.
Jordan, E. C.,   Portland.
Johnstone, M. M.,   Keokuk.
Keene, Mr. and Mrs. S. W.,   Boston.
McRonald, F. S.,   Portland.
Maloon, Mrs.,   Brockton.
Martin, G. A.,   Franklin, Me.
McInnis, Mrs.,   Rangeley.
McCarthy, Mrs. R. C.,   Boston.
Paine, Mr. and Mrs. S. B.,   Greenfield.
Wilson, Helen F.,   New York.
Wood, Mr. and Mrs. Wm. F.,   Providence.
Wilbur, Eva J.,   Providence.
Williams, Geo. W.,   Salem.

Vol. II. SUNDAY MORNING, AUGUST 18, 1895. No. 8.

Equine Poland.

HAVING given some facts which have been of more or less interest on the subject of people and food, we propose briefly to mention, this week, a subject dear to the heart of many—the horse.

Our illustration this week embraces nine private carriages, with their elegantly caparisoned horses. There are thirty-four private horses kept at the stable by guests at this time, with every variety of vehicle, nine of which are here represented, with fourteen horses.

In the picture, on the left, will be seen F. W. Carpenter's, with a single horse; next comes A. R. Mitchell's, with two; then Joshua P. Bates' span, by the side of which is Dr. Geo. Brett's single animal and top buggy.

The central span with driver, in the foreground, is that of J. Albert Walker, while just behind, but a little advanced, is the pair of Charles Trevelli. Beyond that again, and a little in advance of it, is visible the top buggy of H. O. Bright. E. Holmes is the possessor of the handsome pair on the extreme right, while just beyond and a trifle advanced, may be seen that of Col. Joseph A. Ingalls. These, with two lively teams modestly in the background, comprise a portion of our private equipages.

Other guests who have their own horses and carriages, but not represented here, are D. J. Griffith, who keeps five; Nelson Bartlett, two; A. R. Mitchell, two; J. W. Tabor, one; D. W. Field, two; Mrs. L. B. Haskell, two; J. R. Winch, two; Mrs. Milliken, two, and Dr. Wedgwood, one.

Is it to be marvelled at that the roads for miles around present such an animated appearance on every fair day? And where can pleasanter drives be found, or better roads, in the country?

For those who depend upon the livery for their pleasures in this way, the stable near the Mansion House is well equipped, with excellent carriage horses and every variety of vehicle. This department, as well as the water, is under the immediate charge of Mr. Hiram Ricker, and it is probably superfluous to add, it receives the same careful attention the other features of Poland Hill are blessed with.

Careful drivers make riding safe and agreeable, and guests are sure of safe animals and sound conveyances.

"Wait for the wagon and we'll all take a ride."

The Magnificent Portrait of Hon. James G. Blaine, hanging over the stairway in the Maine Building, was made by THE SPRAGUE & HATHAWAY Co. of West Somerville, Mass. They also made the enlarged photograph of the World's Fair Views in the same building.

A Real Hero.

IN the same quiet way in which he has performed scores of heroic and daring deeds, Capt. Wm. H. Daily came to Poland Spring, gave his very interesting talk on the subject of swimming, and incidents connected with his life-saving experience, and departed. Not, however, without scoring a triumph in the way of creating an interest in himself and his labors.

His exhibition at the lake was lessened in interest by the shallow nature of the waters there, but he drew at least two hundred interested spectators a long way from the hotel, and gave the place the appearance of a holiday. All, old and young, took a great interest, and the examination of his medal, presented by Congress for his heroism in saving lives, was accompanied by remarks of the most complimentary nature.

We understand that could he form a class of fourteen, he would return and they might have the advantage of being taught by one of the world's most famous swimmers and life-savers.

Miss Trowbridge's Birthday.

ONE of the prettiest events of the season was Miss Theodora Trowbridge's birthday party Monday afternoon. It was her twelfth birthday, and twelve of her young friends sat at the table, which was beautifully decorated with ferns and flowers. Among the bright faces were Julia Trowbridge, Clara Ingalls, Estelle Hartshorne, Florence Peterson, Alice Peterson, and May Peterson, Helen Drake, Annie Soria, Horace Ingalls, Douglass Hortshorne, and Ronald Curtis. The birthday cake contained a ring, a thimble, and a coin. The finder of the ring was Florence Peterson; of the thimble, Estelle Hartshorne; and of the coin, Julia Trowbridge.

At each plate was a bunch of sweet peas and a dish of candy. After dinner they all marched into the music-room and had dancing and games.

Corn Roast.

FRIDAY afternoon, August 9th, a jolly party, consisting of Dr. and Mrs. Trowbridge, Miss Eames, Miss Royce, Miss Carpenter, the Misses Hartshorne, the Misses Todd, Miss Woodford, Miss Leech, Miss Julia Trowbridge, and Miss Theodora Trowbridge, Mr. Green, Mr. McNeel, the Messrs. Leech, the Messrs. Hartshorne, Mr. Wilcox, Douglass Hartshorne, and Roland Curtis gathered on the shore of the middle lake to have a corn roast. While the corn was roasting some of the party went sailing and rowing.

Poland Guests.

THINKING it might be of interest to many to have a list of all the guests now in the Poland Spring House we give, this week, a complete list taken after breakfast on Tuesday, August 13th, which will be found to be accurate.

In addition to the names given, many of the guests have small children whose names do not appear, which also applies to a considerable number of maids, valets, and coachmen.

Allen, Mr. & Mrs. Geo. O.
Adams, Mrs. A. H.
Andrews, Mrs.
Andrews, Chas. N.
Backeustose, Mrs. D. B.
Bigelow, W. A.
Blight, Mr. and Mrs. H. O.
Balbout, Mrs. E. D.
Balbout, Miss M. E.
Baylis, C. T.
Bolster, Mr. and Mrs. W. H.
Bolster, Mrs. C. H.
Bolster, Miss.
Beech, Mrs. J. M.
Bael, Mrs. Rosa.
Bates, Mr. and Mrs. Jacob E.
Bartlett, Mr. & Mrs. Nelson.
Babcock, Mrs. B.
Babcock, Miss C. L.
Brett, Dr. and Mrs. Geo.
Burns, Mrs. M. A.
Burns, Miss.
Burns, Geo. and Gus.
Birks, Mrs. F.
Bacon, F. W.
Boynton, Mr. & Mrs. W. W.
Benedict, Mrs. T. H.
Brown, C. C.
Bradley, Moses.
Buckley, W. F.
Beylle, Mrs.
Cappenhagen, Mr. & Mrs. J. H.
Coleman, Mr. & Mrs. Geo. W.
Carpenter, F. W.
Carpenter, Julia.
Carpenter, Hannah.
Curtis, Ronald E.
Corbin, Mr. and Mrs. C. C.
Crossman, Herman.
Crossman, Mrs. G. W.
Crossman, Miss.
Coombs, D. D.
Candee, Daniel.
Diggins, Mr. and Mrs. D. H.
Diggins, Mr. and Mrs. D. H.
David, Dr. C. A. and son.
Daily, W. H.
Dunton, Mrs. W. C.
Douglass, Mr. and Mrs. A. E.
Dearborn, D. F.
Dillon, Miss.
Dotger, Mr. and Mrs. A. J.
Drake, Mr. and Mrs. A. A.
Drake, Miss Helen.
Dayton, Miss.
Donnelly, J. G.
Embry, Mr. and Mrs. J. H.
Elliott, Mr. and Mrs. A. S.
Elliott, Miss J. L.
Ege, Mrs. H. N.
Evans, Mr. and Mrs. T. W.
Engliss, Miss.
Eames, Miss M. C.
Eddy, James H.
Felters, Mrs. R. G.
Flannely, Mr. and Mrs. J. L. and family.
Findley, Mr. & Mrs. J. L. V.

Findley, Miss May V. L.
Field, Mr. and Mrs. D. W.
Flye, Mr. and Mrs. J. C.
Fessenden, Mrs. J. D.
Ferrand, Mrs. W. C.
Fish, Mr. and Mrs. Geo. H.
Fitzsimmons, Miss M.
Fassett, Mr. & Mrs. Horace.
Gilman, Mr. and Mrs. J. D.
Glines, Mr. & Mrs. Arthur N.
Griffin, Mr. and Mrs. Benj.
Griffin, Miss.
Griffin, Cecil.
Griffith, Mrs. Geo.
Griffith, Miss S. D.
Griffith, Miss M. E.
Griffith, Daniel J.
Gondron, Mr. and Mrs. A. L.
Griffin, Mr. and Mrs. C. C.
Gilman, Mr. and Mrs. F. E.
Greel, Louis M.
Greel, Geo. B.
Greel, Miss.
Heacox, Mrs. H. A.
Haynie, Henry.
Hoaglund, Mr. & Mrs. Hudson
Hubbard, Mrs. S. B.
Hoyt, Mrs. Colgate.
Hoyt, Miss.
Hildreth, Mrs. M. E.
Hildreth, Miss Alma.
Hurlburt, Mr. and Mrs. L.
Hartshorne, Miss.
Hartshorne, Mrs. R. B.
Hartshorne, Estelle.
Hartshorne, Lydia.
Hartshorne, Douglass.
Hale, Edwin B.
Holmes, Mr. and Mrs. E. T. and two children.
Hoffman, Mrs. F. S.
Huntington, J. C.
Holmes, Mr. and Mrs. E.
Hosmer, Mr. and Mrs. E. B.
Hunt, Otis E.
Horner, Miss.
Harvey, Mr. & Mrs. Huxley.
Harris, Mrs. J. W. and two children.
Hebbard, Mr. and Mrs. A.
Hutchings, Miss R. S.
Harriot, Mr. & Mrs. T. Catman.
Haskell, Mrs. L. B.
Haskell, Miss N.
Haslehurst, Mrs. J. W.
Harriot, Miss F.
Holbrook, Mrs. C. L.
Ingalls, Mr. and Mrs. J. A., son and daughter.
Ivers, Samuel.
Ivers, Miss.
Joly, Mrs. C. C. & daughters
Knight, Mr. & Mrs. T. Morris
Kessler, W. T.
Keene, Mrs. Eli.
Knapp, Mrs. E. A.
Little, Mrs. Amos R.
Lewis, Rev. and Mrs. W. P.

Little, Mr. and Mrs. A.
Lombard, Mr. & Mrs. W. A.
Longstreth, Mr. and Mrs. E.
Lambert, Miss C.
Lambard, Mrs. Thos.
Layng, Mr. and Mrs. F. S.
Langdon, Mr. and Mrs. T. P.
Leech, Mr. and Mrs. J. B.
Leech, Miss Belle.
Leech, Miss Edith.
Leech, Josephine.
Leech, Florence.
Leech, May.
Meany, Mr. and Mrs. E. P.
Meany, Edw. B.
Murray, Mrs. A.
Merrill, W. W.
Merrill, Mr. and Mrs. J. F.
Maginnis, A. H.
Maginnis, J. H.
Mitchell, Mr. and Mrs. A. R.
Meredith, Mrs. J. H.
McNeel, Mrs.
Milliken, Mrs. H. P.
Moulton, Mr. and Mrs. B. P.
McCoy, Mrs. J. F.
McGill, J. J.
McGregor, Mr. & Mrs. A. J.
McGowan, Wm. Knight.
Maginnis, Mrs. J. H.
Maginnis, Miss J. H.
Mills, S. McD.
Mills, May D.
Mills, Mr. and Mrs. S. C.
McCall, M. J.
Nichols, Mrs. W. M.
Noble, Miss.
Nussbaum, E.
Oakes, Mr. and Mrs. Josiah.
Osgood, Mrs. H. S.
Ordway, John A.
O'Brien, Mrs. L.
O'Brien, Miss K.
O'Brien, Miss M.
O'Brien, Miss A. R.
O'Brien, Miss A. L.
O'Brien, Miss G.
O'Brien, Master F. X.
Palmer, Mrs. L. M.
Palmer, Miss.
Palmer, Mr. and Mrs. H. W. and two children.
Pinkerton, John I.
Paul, J. Rodman.
Paul, Mr. and Mrs. Fulton.
Paul, Mr. & Mrs. Henry N.
Paul, Miss C. W.
Paul, Miss M. W.
Paul, Dr. James.
Prael, Miss E. A.
Peters, E. D.
Pettee, Mrs. J. A.
Peterson, Dr. and Mrs. W.
Peterson, the Misses.
Peet, Miss.
Parrish, Mrs. J. S.
Perkins, Mrs. W. C.
Roberts, Miss.
Royce, Miss M. C.
Redfern, Mr. and Mrs. B. F.
Robinson, Mrs. Elizabeth.
Robinson, Mr. and Mrs. J.
Rose, Geo.
Sisler, Mr. and Mrs. J. D.
Salter, Mr. and Mrs. A. T.
Small, Mr. and Mrs. S. R.
Skaats, Mrs. S.
Spencer, Mrs. M. J.
Sawyer, Mr. and Mrs. J. B.
Sotia, Mr. and Mrs. C. M.
Sotia, Miss Annie E.
Smith, Mr. and Mrs. E. P.

Sanford, Mr. and Mrs. J. W.
Shipman, Mr. & Mrs. Henry.
Smith, Mrs. Meredith.
Smith, Mrs. Morgan L.
Smith, Mr. and Mrs. George Williamson.
Somers, Mrs. J.
Snowden, Mr. and Mrs. A. Lowden.
Stechler, Miss.
Slee, Miss.
Shethar, Samuel.
Smith, Mr. and Mrs. W. B.
Spencer, Mr. and Mrs. J. E.
Swayne, Mr. and Mrs. H. C. and child.
Spooner, Edw. S.
Schuyler, Dr. and Mrs.
TenBroeck, Miss N. E.
Todd, Mrs. Wm. James.
Todd, Miss Rita L.
Todd, Miss M. Blanche.
Talmage, Mrs. V. N.
Taylor, Mr. and Mrs. F. E.
Tompkins, Mrs. O.
Trowbridge, Dr. & Mrs. Geo.
Trowbridge, the Misses.
Tatum, Miss.
Terry, Mr. and Mrs. John S.
Tabor, Mr. and Mrs. J. W.
Thornton, Miss May.
Thornton, Mr. & Mrs. David
Taylor, Mrs. Henry S.
Taylor, Miss.
Taylor, Miss Charlotte F.
Tolley, Mr. and daughter.
Tolley, Mr. and Mrs. Alexis.
Trimper, Miss.
Taggart, Dr. and Mrs. W. H.
Taylor, Mrs. E.
Taylor, Miss M. T.
Trist, Miss.
Taggart, Mr. and Mrs. R. M.
Travelli, Mr. and Mrs. C. I.
Talcott, Mr. and Mrs. Jas. and family.
Townsend, Mr. & Mrs. J. A.
True, Geo. W.
Underwood, Miss.
Valentine, Mr. & Mrs. W. B.
Voorhees, Mr. & Mrs. P. V.
voorhees, J. D.
Vose, Mr. and Mrs. Willard.
Vose, Miss.
Vose, Geo. A.
Williams, Miss Jessie.
Warner, Mrs. Chas.
Warner, Miss C. A.
Warner, Miss M. V.
Williams, Mr. & Mrs. F. H.
Williams, Miss L. A.
Winslow, Miss M. A.
Willoughby, Miss.
Whitman, Anna S.
Wedgwood, Dr. & Mrs. M. C.
Woodruff, Mr. & Mrs. H. C.
Winch, Mr. & Mrs. Geo. F.
White, J. Stewart.
White, Mrs. J. S.
Winch, Joseph R.
Wyeth, Mr. and Mrs. F. H.
Wilcox, N. H.
Wilcox, D. C.
Wilcox, Miss E.
Woodford, Mrs. S. L.
Woodford, Miss.
Webster, Mr. & Mrs. Geo. H.
Webster, Miss May.
Webster, Miss Kate C.
Wing, Mr. & Mrs. Henry T.
Zeigler, Mr. & Mrs. Harry.
Zeigler, Miss C. F.

FRANK CARLOS GRIFFITH, } EDITORS.
NETTiE M. RICKER,

PUBLISHED EVERY SUNDAY MORNING DURING THE MONTHS
OF JULY, AUGUST AND SEPTEMBER, IN THE INTERESTS OF

POLAND SPRING AND ITS VISITORS.

All contributions relative to the guests of Poland Spring will
be thankfully received.

To insure publication, all communications should reach the
editors not later than Wednesday preceding day of issue.

All parties desiring rates for advertising in the HILL-TOP
should write the editors for same.

The subscription price of the HILL-TOP is $1.00 for the
season, post-paid. Single copies will be mailed at 10c. each.

Address,

EDITORS "HILL-TOP,"
Poland Spring House,
South Poland, Maine.

PRINTED AT JOURNAL OFFICE, LEWISTON.

Sunday, August 18, 1895.

Editorial.

IT is probably patent to all that this is the
height of the summer season, but for some
time it will be difficult to say just when the
Matterhorn peak of business is reached, for it
has kept, and is likely to keep, at about a certain
barometric level, which, while at a dizzy height,
is yet a Mexican-like plateau of even altitude
and comfortable prosperity.

This is Business.

THE patronage at the Poland Spring House,
thus far this season, has broken the record
of all previous seasons, the daily house
count each day at the Poland Spring House
having been for the last ten days between four
and five hundred guests, without a vacant room
a single night, which without a doubt can not be
said of any other house in America.

The average for July was larger by twenty-
eight daily than July of '94, and thirty-one daily
in August this far, with a tendency to still further increase.

The Mansion "Progressive."

THE first progressive euchre party of the season at the Mansion House was held on
Thursday evening, and proved a notable
event. Mr. Gallagher, who had grown suddenly grey in the service, had handsomely decorated the dining-room with evergreens, Chinese
lanterns, and bunting, and sixty people sat down
to the game, at the fifteen tables provided.

The result of this highly successful affair was
as follows : Ladies' first prize, a beautiful center-
piece of fancy work, to Mrs. C. M. Soria. Second prize, a silver tea strainer, to Mrs. Small.
The third, silver scissors, to Mary Marsh, and
the fourth, a picture frame, to Miss Gilbert.

The gentlemen's first prize, a silk umbrella,
to Mr. George H. Fish. Second, a cane, to Mr.
Adams. The third, a Poland Spring carafe, to
Mr. Hill, and the fourth, a pen-wiper, to Mr.
Moulton.

The second ladies' prize the number of punches
was 11, and nine ladies cut for it. Three ladies
cut kings, and the one who won the prize had to
cut a second time, and cut an ace. A supper was
served during the evening.

Botanical.

THE lady familiarly called "Aunt Martha"
made a contribution to the Poland Spring flora
last week, by finding *Desmodium nudiflorum* or
"Tick-Trefoil." And little George Ricker, in-
heriting his father's *love* of wild flowers, expressed a wish to get a flower, and gathered, as
the result, a plant in fruit, which Thomas Hill,
D.D., late President of Harvard University,
eulogizes this :

"Thrice welcome, earliest flower of Spring!
Thy praise, but *not* thy *name*, I'll sing.
Ungrateful men have christened thee
With names unkind, *unsavory*;
Because when they, with wanton tread,
Their crushing heel set on thy head,
Thou dost resent so foul a wrong,
They give thee names unfit for song.
Vain is their *spite* while thus my verse
Thy praise and merit shall rehearse,
And oft as woodland memories bring
The pleasant thoughts of early spring,
Welcome among them all to me
Thy face *without a name shall be.*"

What personage mentioned in the Bible whose
name is not given, died a death that none of us
can ever die and whose shroud is in every one's
house?

A Lynn highwayman demanded money of a
Salem man. Bad beginning. When he refused,
as of course he was obliged to, a bullet was sent
through his hat. When we pass through Lynn
again without money, we shall wear our hat on
the end of a long stick.

Tid=Bits.

What's trumps?

Tuesday was rainy.

Progressive euchre.

The "Blaine" in great demand.

All aboard for the tour of the lakes.

Mr. Sawyer is reported as still improving. So glad.

We are pleased to extend the freedom of the city to Mr. and Mrs. H. A. Wells of New York.

We regret the departure of Mr. and Mrs. Bates, and Mr. and Mrs. Smith, who left August 15th.

The Library is indebted to Mrs. J. P. Bates for "The Story of Bessie Castrell," by Mrs. Humphrey Ward.

It is undoubtedly true that no orchestra of its size, in America, is superior to the one now at the Poland Spring House.

A mid-August guest is Mr. James V. Watson, president of the Consolidated Bank of Philadelphia. May he linger long.

Among the prominent arrivals of the season from Boston we are pleased to add the name of Mayor Curtis to the long list.

Walk down through the "farm" in front of the Hotel, if you wish to see where a great deal of the food product comes from.

Among hotel men Mr. A. B. Darling, of the Fifth Avenue Hotel, New York, is a prominent figure, as he is among our latest visitors.

The prettiest *flower girl* of the season was Mrs. E. P. Ricker, who sold the Shakers' flowers Wednesday evening. She had a large sale.

Mr. Henry A. Hildreth of Boston, who is president of the National Manufacturing Co. of Worcester, has joined his mother and sister.

Mr. O. H. Taylor, who has favored Poland with a visit, is the General Passenger Agent of the Fall River line, and located in New York.

Gen. A. Loudon Snowden, formerly Comptroller of the Mint, and later Minister to Greece under President Harrison, is one of our guests, with Mrs. Snowden.

O. M. Hanscomb, Boston's Police Inspector, made a short visit the latter part of last week. We have no police of our own, so we are pleased to borrow Boston's chiefs.

Have you accepted Mr. James S. Sanborn's invitation, published in another column, and examined his fine lot of horses? If not you have missed a very interesting experience.

If we could play croquet as well as young Mr. Ingalls, it would almost reconcile us to hazard the numerous quarrels it entails, in playing. We were always unlucky at croquet.

A welcome guest is Henry Haynie, one of the most noted and best of newspaper correspondents, who for many years has been the Paris correspondent of the Boston *Herald* and other papers.

If we cannot have the Hon. J. H. Manley, of Augusta, the long-time friend of James G. Blaine, his attractive daughter is none the less welcome. She is the guest of Mrs. Lombard of Augusta.

Do not fail to remember that if you require massage treatment that Mrs. Robinson, *née* Lizzie Putnam, is at the Poland Spring House, and is accounted skilled, beside being a lady of agreeable and pleasant manners.

A. C. Kendall, General Passenger Agent of the Old Colony System of the N. Y., N. H. & H. R. R., is a recent and welcome addition to the Poland Spring House family, together with Mrs. Kendall and their two lovely children.

If you enjoy a pleasant walk, the one to the lower lake, which starts in just below the bottling house, is in many respects the best. It has very recently been put in excellent condition. The terminus at the lake is a lovely spot.

A charming party, consisting of Mr. and Mrs. O. H. Taylor, Mr. and Mrs. A. C. Kendall, Miss Kendall and Master Charles Kendall, were recently the guests of Mr. and Mrs. E. P. Ricker on a brake-ride through the Gloucester woods, and over to Mr. Sanborn's fancy stock farm.

A very agreeable word comes from those two young ladies, Miss Trist and Miss Noble, that they are meeting with excellent success in teaching the intricacies of whist. It is a great game, and to be expert at it is a consummation devoutly to be wished.

An item, unfortunately omitted last week, for which THE HILL-TOP'S apologies are offered, relates to a friendly card struggle between the following "girls" —*Miss* Francis E. Gilman, Miss Tatum, and Mrs. J. Stuart White, and these gentlemen—Messrs. C. H. Hackett, E. T. Holmes, and J. Stuart White, which resulted in a signal victory for the "girls," the score standing 316 to 138 points. Bravo, girls.

Progressive Euchre.

PROGRESSIVE Euchre party, Friday evening, August 9th, at the Poland Spring House. First ladies' prize went to Mrs. Jackson, the happy winner of the first prize the week previous. It was a photograph case. Mrs. Perkins won the second prize, a beautiful porcelain photograph case. The dainty pink silk and lace pin-cushion went to Miss Pail. Miss Mary Marsh won the fourth prize, an engagement book. Mr. Boynton is to be congratulated upon winning the first gentlemen's prize, a Moses orange spoon. Mr. Keen won a Poland Spring carafe. The third prize went to Hon. F. E. Gilman, who was successful in winning a prize last week. It was a case for newspaper clippings (don't forget clippings from the HILL-TOP). Miss Wilcox took the part of a gentleman at the game, and won the fourth prize, a pug dog.

The Poland.

It is always a happy and delightful party which boards or "unboards," as the little fellow said, the *Poland*, and this applied to Thursday's party of eleven, which was made up by Helen Drake, Annie Soria, Florence, May and Alice Peterson, Theodora and Julia Trowbridge, Claire Ingalls, and Estelle and Douglass Hartshorne.

This most interesting party made the tour of the "great lakes" under the chaperonage of Dr. Peterson.

Do Not Forget.

Do you drink Poland water?

Do you have it in your home?

A very large proportion of the Poland Spring guests will answer "guilty" to the above. Then all the guilty ones should place upon their tables a carafe which will remind them of the place the water comes from, the rock-riven crystal fountain of health, pure and eternal. Keep it in your memory to take one home with you.

When you require anything either in Lewiston or Portland read our advertisements, for each house represented will be found reliable and the best in their line.

(Mt.) Pleasant tidings float to us of a most successful summer at Messrs. Anderson and Price's new White Mountain Hotel. A fine cuisine, excellent livery, and delightful orchestra are making this resort a favorite, and the House wears a charming aspect of gaiety and prosperous conditions. The location, between Crawford's and Fabyan's, is unexcelled in beauty. Many Portland parties visit the House, and former guests of the Ormond also seek out its attractions, coming from distant parts of the States.

Concert Program.

Special Notice.

THE "Women's Educational and Industrial Union" of Boston, will open a sale of fancy articles, at the Poland Spring Hotel, Tuesday, August 22d. There will be offered the very rare opportunity of obtaining a few pieces of exquisite hand-made antique Swiss lace, which were brought to this country three months ago by Viscountess Vidart, to be sold for benevolent purposes. These laces were wrought by Viscountess Vidart's grandmother, while her husband, a noted surgeon, was serving under Napoleon.

Two More Brake Rides.

THURSDAY, August 9th, two more of those very exuberant, gay, and joyous parties of health seekers, climbed to the top of the brake and took a bird's-eye view of the surrounding country, through its shaded country roads, and over its lovely hills.

One was from the Poland Spring House, and included Mrs. Trowbridge, the Misses Haitshorne and Miss Eames, and the Messrs. Trowbridge, McNeel, and Leech.

The other, from the Mansion House, was enjoyed by Mrs Badger and the Misses Barbour, Campbell, and Marsh, and the Messrs. Goodrich, Dewey, Gay, and Read. The latter party drove to Tenny Hill.

Caricature and Ventriloquism.

MR. R. H. MOHR came on Wednesday and gave one of his excellent entertainments of caricature and ventriloquism, and gave great pleasure to a large audience.

He is very clever at both these arts, and has added one more delightful evening to our season of entertainment.

Poetic Italy.

MARCIA B. JORDAN.

From Orvieto our departures were;
Weary the travelers, full of *Baedeker*,
A jolting train, eleven by the watch, and cold!
A hand put back the curtain, and behold,
Venus and Jupiter conjoined—a heavenly pair—
As if two golden hearts beat in the air!
I heard our artist say—he of aesthetic touch,
In whom our faith was almost over-much,
"The night, 'worthy of note,' 'double starred,'"—
a groan!
The guide-book fiend had claimed us for his own.

Sunday Services.

ONE of the finest sermons delivered this season was that of Rev. George Williamson Smith, of Hartford, President of Trinity College, in Music Hall, Sunday morning, August 11th. His text was taken from the 6th Chapter of St. John, the 10th verse.

In the evening Rev. W. P. Lewis, of Philadelphia, delivered a very fine address to the employees and guests as well, in the Dining Room. There was a large attendance.

Brake Ride.

TUESDAY, Miss Barbour gave a brake ride to her Mansion House friends. The jolly party consisted of Mrs. Badger, Miss Campbell, Miss Mary Marsh, Mr. Goodrich, Dr. Dewey, Mr. Ernest Gay, and Mr. William Read. They made the circuit of Trip Lake and visited the old cemetery. During the thunder storm they took shelter in an old barn, where they fed the calves on candy and apples. And the calves still live.

The Notman Photographic Co., through their artistic representative, Mr. Ness, continue to make this season a remarkable one in the respect of magnificent work. It would be difficult to find anything superior anywhere *in the world.*

Four former and ever welcome guests are found in Mr. J. F. Godley, Mr. and Mrs. H. P. Gleason, and J. H. Lake. May they long continue to come.

Two agreeable additions to the circle of ladies at the Poland Spring House are made by the arrival of Mrs. W. B. Frothingham and Miss Frothingham of Boston.

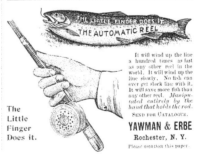

Arrivals.

POLAND SPRING HOUSE.

Adams, A. H.,	Haverhill.
Ames, Geo. E.,	Richmond, Me.
Appleton. Daniel Fuller,	New York.
Baker, Miss F. L.,	Boston.
Benedict, Mrs. T. H.,	New York.
Bradley, Moses,	Haverhill.
Brady, Mr. and Mrs. Daniel M.,	New York.
Byram, Mr. and Mrs. Geo. L.,	Dorchester.
Blaisdell, Mrs. L. H.,	Dorchester.
Byram, Howard,	Dorchester.
Baylis, C. S.,	New York.
Bolster, Mrs. W. H.,	Boston.
Beech, Mrs. H.,	Boston.
Carroll, Mrs. L. A.,	Bay Shore, L. I.
Clark, Mr. and Mrs. Mortimer,	Toronto.
Clark, Abbie A.,	Worcester.
Conway, J. D.,	Somerville.
Coombs, W. C.,	Lisbon Falls.
Carpenter, Dr. Frank,	New York.
Cubert, Grace,	New York.
Craven, J. Stuart,	Salem, N. J.
Diggins. Mr. and Mrs. D. F.,	Cochillac, Mich.
Drew, Nathaniel J.,	Cambridge.
Donnelly, J. A.,	Natick.
David, Dr. C. A,,	Chicago.
David, Master V. C.,	Chicago.
Daily, Capt. Wm. H.,	San Francisco.
Dexter, Mr. and Mrs. W. H.,	Worcester.
Durgin, Violet V.,	Lisbon.
Douglas, Mrs. Charles,	Boston.
Eaton, Mrs. W. S.,	Portland.
Emerson, W. H.,	Cambridge.
Emerson, Marguerite E.,	Cambridge.
Elliott, Mr. and Mrs. A. S.,	Wilmington.
Elliott, Miss Jessie L.,	Wilmington.
Elder, Mr. and Mrs. C. R.,	Malden.
Fairbrother, J. M.,	Pawtucket.
Frothingham, Mrs. W. B.,	Boston.
Frothingham, Miss Marion,	Boston.
Fernald, Mr. and Mrs. B. M.,	West Poland.
Fessel. Miss,	New Broughton, L. I.
Fogg, Ollie R.,	New Gloucester.
Flannery, Mr. and Mrs. J. L.,	Chicago.
Flannery, J. L., Jr.,	Chicago.
Flannery, Florence,	Chicago.
Findlay, Mr. and Mrs. John D. L,	Baltimore.
Findlay, Miss May D. L.,	Baltimore.
Frothingham, W. O.,	South Paris.
Fogg, G. R.,	Skowhegan.
Ferguson, C. A.,	Boston.
Fisher, Claudine,	Lewiston.
Gilman, Mr. and Mrs. J. D.,	Boston.
Glines, Mr. and Mrs. Arthur W.,	Somerville.
Green, Mr. and Mrs. W. H.,	Raymond Spring House.
Haynes, Winnie R.,	Portland.
Holliday, Mr. and Mrs. W. J.,	Indianapolis.
Haslehurst, Mrs. J. W.,	New York.
Hanscomb, O. M.,	Boston.
Hayford, J. H.,	Boston.
Harris, Mrs. J. W.,	Galveston.
Hutchings, Miss R. S.,	Galveston.
Harrington, J. C.,	Lynn.
Harriot, Mrs. S. Catman,	New York.
Harriot, Florence,	New York.
Harriot, S. Catman,	New York.
Heacox, Mrs. H. A.,	Morris, N. J.
Haynie, Henry,	Paris, France.
Howe. Mr. and Mrs. Freeland,	Norway.
Hildreth, H. A.,	Boston.
Johnson, Charles H.,	Boston.
Johnson, Miss M. E. R.,	Boston.
Johnstone, Mr. and Mrs. E. M.,	Brooklyn.

Jordan, Mr. and Mrs. Eben,	Danville Junction.
Jordan, Mr. and Mrs. Chandler,	Danville Junction.
Jordan, Master Clifford,	Danville Junction.
Kendall, Mr. and Mrs. A. C.,	Boston.
Kendall, Alice F.,	Boston.
Kendall, Master C. P. F.,	Boston.
Kelley, Stillman F.,	Cambridge.
Kilgore, Frank,	Lewiston.
Lockitt, Miss F. E.,	Brooklyn.
Lockitt, W.,	Brooklyn.
Lockitt, Mr. and Mrs. Clement,	Brooklyn.
Lowell, Mr. and Mrs. P. G.,	Lewiston.
Laughton, William,	Cambridge.
Lombard, Mr. and Mrs. Wm. A.,	New York.
Lloyd, Mr. and Mrs. J. G.,	Boston.
Little, Mr. and Mrs. A.,	New York.
Mallory, Mrs. H. G.,	New York.
Milliken, Mrs. H. P.,	Augusta.
Manley, Miss Sydney,	Augusta.
McCoy, Mrs. John F.,	New York.
Merrill, W. W.,	Deering.
McGowan, T. P.,	Portland.
Maxwell, Gilbert,	Richmond.
Maginnis, A. A., Jr.,	New Orleans.
Maginnis, Jno. H.,	New Orleans.
MacNaughton, Flora W.,	Brooklyn.
MacNaughton, Dr. George,	Brooklyn.
McCall, M. J.,	Salem.
McGowan, Wm. Knight,	New York.
Maginnis, Mrs. J. H.,	New Orleans.
Maginnis, Miss,	New Orleans.
Mayo, Mr. and Mrs. A. N.,	Springfield.
Mayo, Miss,	Springfield.
Mayo, Miss Ada,	Springfield.
Mohr, R. H.,	Boston.
Newbaum, E.,	Boston.
Nollinrake, J.,	Sanford.
Osgood, H. S.,	Portland.
Pond, Mr. and Mrs. Fulton,	Hudson, N. Y.
Palmer, Henry U.,	Brooklyn.
Pake, Elsie,	Auburn.
Paul, J. Rodman,	Philadelphia.
Potter, Mrs. F.,	Raymond Spring House.
Peters, Mrs. Winfield,	Baltimore.
Peters, Miss Gilvin,	Baltimore.
Peters, J. Girvin,	Baltimore.
Ruggles, E. O.,	Boston.
Reech, Mr. and Mrs. W. C.,	Philadelphia.
Riker, S. S.,	New York.
Riker, John L.,	New York.
Richardson, Mr. and Mrs. A.,	Boston.
Richardson, Miss,	Boston.
Richardson, Marion A.,	Boston.
Rose, George,	New York.
Rhodes, Carrie E.,	Springfield.
Sisler, Mr. and Mrs. J. D.,	Wilmington.
Sisler, Madeline,	Wilmington.
Snowden, Mr. and Mrs. A. Loudon,	Philadelphia.
Stedman, Lizzie,	New Orleans.
Smith, Mr. and Mrs. Elijah P.,	New York.
Spooner, Edward,	New York.
Shaw, Mrs. Geo. C.,	Portland.
Sullivan, Mr. and Mrs. J. T.,	Meriden.
Sawyer, Fred L.,	Boston.
Stockman, Daisy,	Bangor.
Scott, Mr. and Mrs. W. G.,	Redmond, Ind.
Shortridge, John H.,	Philadelphia.
Shortridge, Miss F. A.,	Philadelphia.
Shivers, Mrs. S. J.,	Philadelphia.
Shivers, Miss Anna W.,	Philadelphia.
Suen, Mr. and Mrs. J. S.,	Boston.
Thayer, Mr. and Mrs. Geo. L.,	Jersey City.
Taylor, Mr. and Mrs. O. H.,	Boston.
Tolley, Mr. and Mrs. Alexis,	Boston.
Tolley, Mrs. F. H. and daughter,	New York.
Taylor, Mrs. E.,	Bay Ridge.
Townsend, Mr. and Mrs. J. A.,	Brooklyn.
Underwood, Jno. T.,	

Miss Susan B. Anthony has been obliged to cancel her engagements. Didn't know Susan was engaged.

Poland Water Leads Them All.

⊛══ **WHY?** ══⊛

BECAUSE.. It was the FIRST KNOWN SOLVENT OF URIC ACID in the system.   .   .   .   .

BECAUSE.. It is the most EFFECTIVE ELIMINATOR of Calculi in the Bladder and Kidneys known to-day.   .   .   .   .

BECAUSE.. It was the ONLY water IN NEW ENGLAND to receive ANY AWARD at the World's Columbian Exposition, and the only award of the hundreds exhibited from the WORLD for Purity and Great Medicinal Properties.   .   .   .   .

BECAUSE.. The ANNUAL sales exceed the combined sales of all the Saratoga Springs.   .   .   .   .   .

BECAUSE.. Unprecedented as the success of the past has been it is more promising than ever, showing continued increase.   .   .   .   .

OFFICES:

VOL. II.   SUNDAY MORNING, AUGUST 25, 1895.   No. 9.

Aquatic Poland.

WATER is one of the greatest features of Poland, but the water we refer to to-day is not the clear and crystal-like liquid taken internally. No, it is that upon which we sail or in which we swim.

Our view to-day represents a portion of the middle lake, but not on a holiday as its gay appearance might indicate, but on the occasion of the appearance of that famous life-saver, Captain William H. Daily, who gave his exhibition there at that time.

It shows that Poland Spring is not restricted to land amusements, but has boats in plenty and bathing places most delightful.

There is a yacht, for those fond of that delightful sport, and for the lone timid a small steam yacht, upon which a tour of these lakes is charming.

Even the Suez Canal is here in miniature, cut by the enterprise of the Rickers, which shows you what we should do at Nicaragua, and you can imagine a lilliputian city of Alexandria at the entrance, and the low regions of the Nile in close proximity.

Now if they would only place a diminutive Sphinx, and a pyramid or two in its neighborhood, a visit to Egypt would be useless waste of time.

Will some kind traveller send us an obelisk and a mummy or two, to add to our collection?

Progressive Euchre.

AS usual, the progressive euchre party at the Poland Spring House Friday evening proved a great success. Miss Carey possessor of the ladies' first prize, a beautiful shell comb. Mrs. Elliott won the ladies' second prize, a hand-painted box. The third prize, a fan, went to Mrs. Griffin. Mrs. Mills won the fourth prize, a pen-wiper. Several ladies took the part of gentlemen and carried off the prizes. Miss Jessie Elliott won the first prize, which was a Poland Spring etched spoon. Mrs. Frisby gained the second prize, a handsome penholder. The third prize, a Poland Spring carafe, went to Mrs. Spencer, and Mr. Read won the consolation prize, a receptacle for cigars. Mr. Read is to be congratulated.

The International Cyclopædia.

A. J. BAKER FLINT, M.D., of Boston, has most generously donated to the Poland Spring Library a complete new set of the International Cyclopædia of the latest edition, and bound in leather. It is a very valuable acquisition to the library, and doubtless will be highly appreciated. The thanks of the reading public will surely be extended most heartily to Dr. Flint.

As for THE HILL-TOP, should an irate subscriber call the editors, accidents, we shall be able to analyze his meaning correctly and take no mistake in the tone of our challenge. We wish to err on the right side always.

Nellie.

BY WILLIAM REDMUND,

Author of "Herminie," "Cuchillo," "Life's Storm," "Sis," "Bob," etc.

IN one of the beautiful valleys of the Connecticut State lays a small village, with its little white houses dotted here and there along the street. Its inhabitants number scarcely five hundred. About half-way up the street stands the village smithy, with its owner, a man of muscle, wielding his ponderous hammer as if it were a feather; on the right stands an old farm-house, its grounds divided from the road by a massive stone wall, which age and neglect have let run to decay. On the top of this wall are some fearless children playing with a great boulder, which is loose and serves then in the place of a rocking-horse. How they laugh and shout, and yet death may be so near, for should the stone roll from the wall, it would surely deal death to some of the little ones.

The next house but one is a quaint little cot, all covered with ivy. From the porch and large casement window droops in graceful curves the sweet-smelling jasmine. As the needle is attracted to the pole, so one's eyes are turned to the casement, from whence cometh the perfume which delights our senses. We pause beneath the wide-spreading branches that overshadow the sidewalk, for at the casement is a face, only a little face, the face of a child; the little hand with its dimpled knuckles waves back the jasmine and the face peers out into the sunlight. The wooing breeze wafts the flossy hair back from the temples, the dark blue liquid eyes gaze up to heaven, as if in supplication to spend one more day on earth, in which to gladden the sight of mortals with glimpses of a heavenly being. And yet it is only little Nellie, the blacksmith's child, who has opened the casement for her mother.

"Come, mother dear, and sit here; see how brightly the sun is shining and how merrily the birds sing, and the bees—how they hum, how gay and beautiful all looks, and yet, my own dear mother is sad, so sad. The roses have gone from your cheeks, and the tears are in your eyes; you are a naughty mother, you are always crying now. Can not little Nellie make her mother happy, and make her smile just once? Smile, mother dear, just to please your Nellie."

"Listen, child, can you not hear another sound upon the air, besides the singing of the birds and the humming of the bees, now listen, there, and now again, do you not hear it, child?"

Nellie clasped her tiny hands, and laughing cried: "Oh yes, I can hear my father ham-her-ing at the forge—dong, dong, dong, dong. Why don't father come home to his little Nellie every night, and dance her on his knee, and kiss her and play horse; I see him now only when I sleep, in at the forge, and then he sends me home; sometimes he will talk, but not often, he says he is too busy."

"Nellie, my child, when he returns to us the roses will come back to my cheeks and my tears will cease to flow."

And the child pondered on the words, "When father comes back he'll bring the roses to mother's cheeks, and her tears will cease to flow." When upon the pillow the little golden head was laid to rest, and Morpheus claimed the fragile frame for a time, the coral lips still moved. With loving care the mother bent over her child to hear the lisping words go up to heaven : "Please, Mr. God, send father home with roses for mother's cheeks."

The mother went and slept, and slept, and wept the night away, and in her slumbers dreamed that her little Nellie, with smiles upon her face, her golden hair floating in the breeze, flew from out the casement up to heaven, and with a cry she awoke, looked around. It was only the morning's first ray of the sun, that came through the casement and spread its lustre over the child lying in the cot. Nellie had not fled to heaven, but heaven had sent (upon the golden sunbeam) a message to the child. The child awoke, and throwing her soft warm arms around her mother's neck, said : "The roses will soon come back to mamma's cheeks now."

That afternoon, while the mother was busy with her household duties, Nellie crept down the street, crossed the road to the blacksmith's shop, and running in, she cried : "Father, dear, Nellie has come to see you."

The man stopped in his work as if a shot had pierced his heart, his arm uplifted, hammer in hand, high in the air it stayed. It was not a shot that had pierced his heart, but the voice of his only child. Laying the hammer upon the anvil, he took the child in his arms, and kissed her fondly. "And what brings my little daughter to see me to-day?"

"I want you to come home and kiss mother as you used to do."

With a start he put the child down ; seizing the tongs, he drew a red-hot shoe from the forge and plied the hammer with such force and rapidity that from the anvil flew a fountain of burning sparks. A cry from the child made him pause ; he turned to see that one of the sparks had settled on her dress, from which a flame now shot. Quick as the lightning flash, the great bronzed hand had crushed the life out of the

flame. Nellie sprang to her father's breast, where she was fondly and tenderly held. "Oh, Nellie, child, you are so dear to me, I wish you could understand, but you are too young to know why I do not come home."

"I know that my poor mother is very unhappy and does cry so."

"Oh, she cries, does she?" grunted the blacksmith.

"Yes, she wants you to come home and make us all happy, and I am sure you will, now your little Nellie has come for you," and in her sweet coaxing way she slid her little fat hand into her father's coarse and horny fist, which closed upon it as tenderly as a woman's.

"For mother should not cry, now should she? She is so good, you know she is."

"I know she wants her own way in everything, and I want mine, and our ways are different, and that's just what's the matter."

Little Nellie crept upon her father's knee, and with a puzzled look exclaimed : "Why, father dear, is not mother's way, your way, and your way mother's? I heard you read one Sunday out of the great book that lays upon the parlor table, you know the one I mean?"

"Yes, the Bible."

"Yes, the Bible. Well, one Sunday, or a long time ago, I heard you read that husband and wife are one. I don't understand it, but if you and mother are one how can you have two ways, or two thoughts?"

The blacksmith knew not what answer to make the child, and like many a man of his class when perplexed, he lit his pipe and smoked and thought. But still the little maid was clasped in his. The great mystery that has not yet been fathomed was at work ; yes, the child's determined mind was swaying the great muscular man, who turned to her and said : "Nellie, I'll come home ; run along and tell your mother I am coming."

The child said not a word, kissed her father and ran on her way, and as she went she cried in joyous tones, "I have got the roses for mother's cheeks." On the way home Nellie stopped a minute to see the boys playing with the great boulder on the old stone wall.

The blacksmith went to the well, drew some water, washed the soot from his hands and face, and standing at the open door he reads his pipe. "Guess I'll smoke a pipe as I stroll up to the house ; I don't want her to think I'm over anxious to make it up, and if she—"

He did not finish the sentence, for a little boy with face as pale as death ran up to him and shouted, "Come quick, Nellie is under the boulder and we can't get her out." The man and boy lay to the decayed wall and there lay little Nellie, beneath the huge boulder that had rolled from the wall. In a second the muscular form was bent; with Herculean strength the boulder was seized and thrown aside; but Nellie lay as one dead, the life's stream issuing from her mouth; her senses had fled.

"Go, some of you, and bring Dr. Thornton, quick." Lifting the child tenderly in his arms, he bore her towards their home, but was yet half way by the sorrowing mother, who had heard the news. She took the child from him and laid her in her cot. The father or mother did not speak, but they clasped hands and a look in their eyes told more than a volume of words. The doctor came and examined the motionless form that lay in the cot. The verdict, what was it? The mother and father, still clinging together, dared not ask. The kind old doctor's face told the sad news, and the mother cried, "She will die." "Yes, internal hemorrhage. I cannot save her."

At those words that great, strong man reeled like a drunkard; the mother knelt by the cotside and covered the little hand with kisses, and then a silence, more eloquent than words, for it revealed to the soul the presence of death. At last came a weak little voice from the cot: "Do not cry for me, mother; I have brought father home. The roses will soon bloom on your cheeks again."

"But am I to lose my little Nellie?"

"No, mother dear, I shall ever be near father and you."

The doctor passed out of the room, and laying his hand kindly upon the man's shoulder, said: "I am sorry, very sorry. I can feel for you; I have lost a child; but you must remember that she died just as she was born, and is spared the misery of this world. I loved that child; she always made me think of an angel, that might be sent to earth to accomplish some task."

With tears in his eyes the doctor went his way. The blacksmith seemed to understand that his child had fulfilled her task on earth and was about to return to heaven. He rejoined his wife, and by the cotside they watched the light away. As the day broke, Nellie regained consciousness, and held out a little trembling hand to both. The mother took one, the father the other, and Nellie smiled on both a sweet, sad, heavenly smile, that never once left her face.

"Please, father, open the casement—wide. Thank you, that is so nice. Give me your hand again, so. Father dear, mother's ways and your ways are one, now, are they not?"

"Yes, child, and always shall be."

"Kiss me, father, and dear mother, kiss me, too; I have no pain, I am so happy, for we three are one now."

"No, dear child, that can never be."

"Yes, mother dear, the big book says that man and wife are one, and I am but—"

The little head drooped, the morning's glorious sunbeam came through the open casement, and on its golden rays bore the soul of Nellie to its heavenly home. The father clasped the wife to his breast and cried: "The child was right, we three are one, man and wife, reunited by the memory of our child."

Upon the hill-side you will find among the white slabs that mark the many homes of earth, a small cross, bearing the following words:

Sacred to the Memory of Our Angel Child
Nellie.
Having Fulfilled Her Mission Returned
September 10, 1890.

The White Mountain Parade.

IN the Coaching Parade, August 20th, at the White Mountains, one of the finest features of the parade was the so-called "Poland" wagon, furnished by the Mt. Pleasant House, and modeled after the great four-seated Poland wagon made for this place.

It was drawn by six magnificent chestnuts, and carried fifteen persons, beside the driver, as follows: Andy Lord and Lambert Whitney, of Newton; L. R. Parker and Miss Russell, of Hartford; Paul Gould, Miss Jordan, Miss Carey, Miss Webb, Miss Hunt, and Miss Edmunds, of Portland; S. Butler Smith, of Toronto; Arthur Howard, of Chicago; and L. H. Bingham, of Orlord, Fla. The trumpeters were Sergeant Dyer of the Portland Cadets, and Sergeant Norton of the Portland High School Cadets.

The Humorist.

Mr. Charles Williams gave a monologue entertainment on Wednesday evening in the Music Hall, consisting of dialect and character sketches, embracing both humor and pathos. He was rather more successful in the latter than in dialect selections, although he showed versatility, cleverness, and skill in all.

The Magnificent Portrait of Hon. James G. Blaine, hanging over the stairway in the Maine Building, was made by THE SPRAGUE & HATHAWAY Co. of West Somerville, Mass. They also made the enlarged photograph of the World's Fair Views in the same building.

Poland Guests.

WE give a list to-day of all the guests in the Poland Spring House, Thursday, August 22d, at 1 P.M.

In addition to the names given, many of the guests have small children whose names do not appear, which also applies to a considerable number of maids, valets, and coachmen.

Ayers, Mrs. Thos. W.
Ayers, Florence Newman.
Abell, Mrs. Geo. L.
Butterfield, Wm.
Bedell, Mr. and Mrs. B. W.
Barry, Miss Madeline.
Butterfield, Gertrude.
Brady, Mr. and Mrs. D. M.
Bloom, Helen Godley.
Barry, Ella M.
Backenstose, Mrs. D. B.
Bigelow, W. A.
Bright, Mr. and Mrs. H. O.
Barbour, Mrs. E. D.
Bartlett, Mr. & Mrs. Nelson.
Babcock, Mrs. B.
Babcock, Miss C. L.
Bacon, F. W.
Benedict, Mrs. T. H.
Bradley, Moses.
Buckley, W. F.
Beylle, Mrs.
Cook, Miss A. B.
Clark, Mary M.
Coppenhagen, Mr. & Mrs. J. H.
Coleman, Mr.& Mrs. Geo.W.
Carpenter, F. W.
Carpenter, Julia.
Carpenter, Hannah.
Corbin, Mr. and Mrs. C. C.
Coombs, D. D.
Dill, Mr. and Mrs. L.
DeForrest, Mr. & Mrs. A.W.
Dizer, Mrs. S. C.
Darling, Mr. and Mrs. A. B.
Doran, Miss.
Decatur, H. E.
David, Dr. C. A. and son.
Dunton, Mrs. W. C.
Drake, Mr. and Mrs. A. A.
Drake, Miss Helen.
Dayton, Miss.
Early, F. J.
Embry, Mr. and Mrs. J. H.
Ege, Mrs. H. N.
Englis, Miss.
Eames, Miss M. C.
Frothingham, Mrs. V. B.
Frothingham, Marian.
Finlay, Mr. and Mrs. Mark.
Eddy, James H.
Feltus, Mrs. R. G.
Findley, Mr. & Mrs. J. L. V.
Findley, Miss May V. L.
Field, Mr. and Mrs. D. W.
Fessenden, Mrs. J. D.
Ferrand, Mrs. W. C.
Fish, Mr. and Mrs. Geo. H.
Fitzsimmons, Miss M.
Fassett, Mr. & Mrs. Horace.
Gleason, Mr. and Mrs. H. P.
Godley, Mr. and Mrs. J. F.
Goldsmith, Mrs. S. and daughter.
Griffith, Mrs. Geo.
Griffith, Miss S. D.
Griffith, Miss M. E.
Griffith, Daniel J.
Gondron, Mr. and Mrs. A. L.
Griffin, Mr. and Mrs. C. C.

Greer, Louis M.
Greer, Geo. B.
Greer, Miss.
Harris, John F.
Harris, Ami.
Hildreth, H. A.
Heacox, Mrs. H. A.
Haynie, Henry.
Hoagland, Mr. & Mrs. Hudson
Hubbard, Mrs. S. B.
Hoyt, Mrs. Colgate.
Hoyt, Miss.
Hildreth, Mrs. M. E.
Hildreth, Miss Alma.
Hurlburt, Mr. and Mrs. L.
Hartshorne, Miss.
Hartshorne, Mrs. R. B.
Hartshorne, Estelle.
Hartshorne, Lydia.
Hartshorne, Douglass.
Hale, Edwin B.
Holmes, Mr. and Mrs. E. T. and two children.
Hoffman, Mrs. F. S.
Holmes, Mr. and Mrs. E.
Horner, Miss.
Haskell, Mrs. L. B.
Haskell, Miss N.
Haslehurst, Mrs. J. W.
Holbrook, Mrs. C. L.
Ingalls, Mr. and Mrs. J. A., son and daughter.
Jewell, Mrs. Leyman.
Kenyon, Mrs. E. C.
Keene, Mrs. Eli.
Knapp, Mrs. E. A.
Leyman, Pauline.
Lewis, A. L.
Lake, Jas. H.
Little, Mrs. Amos R.
Lewis, Rev. and Mrs. W. P.
Little, Mr. and Mrs. A.
Longstreth. Mr. and Mrs. E.
Lambert, Miss C.
Lombard, Mrs. Thos.
Layng, Mr. and Mrs. F. S.
Leech, Mr. and Mrs. J. B.
Leech, Miss Belle.
Leech, Miss Edith.
Leech, Josephine.
Leech, Florence.
Leech, May.
Merrill, Mary.
McKnight, Mr. & Mrs. Chas.
McKnight, Harriet.
Mayo, Mr. and Mrs. A. N.
Mayo, Miss.
Moore, Joseph, Jr.
McConvil, Mrs. C.
Markham, E. F.
Morgan, Mr. and Mrs. A. O.
Meany, Miss E. P.
Meany, Edw. B.
Murray, Mrs. A.
Merrill, Mr. and Mrs. J. F.
Maginnis, A. H.
Maginnis, J. H.
Mitchell, Mr. and Mrs. A. R.
Meredith, Mrs. J. H.
McNeel, Miss.

Milliken, Mrs. H. P.
Moulton, Mr. and Mrs. B. P.
McCoy, Mrs. J. F.
McGill, J. J.
McGowan, Wm. Knight.
Maginnis, Mrs. J. H.
Maginnis, Miss.
Newman, Miss S. M.
Noble, Miss.
Nussbaum, E.
Otis, Mr. and Mrs. W.
Oakes, Mr. and Mrs. Josiah.
Osgood, Mrs. H. S.
Pratt, Albert J.
Palmer, Mrs. L. M.
Palmer, Miss.
Palmer, Mr. and Mrs. H. W. and two children.
Paul, Mr. and Mrs. Fulton.
Prall, Miss E. A.
Peters, E. D.
Pettee, Mrs. J. A.
Peterson, Dr. and Mrs. W.
Peterson, the Misses.
Parrish, Mrs. J. S.
Perkins, Mrs. W. C.
Richardson, Marian A.
Richardson, Mr. and Mrs. A.
Richardson, Miss.
Ricker, S. S.
Randell, Mr. and Mrs. A. H.
Roberts, Miss.
Royce, Miss M. C.
Robinson, Mrs. Elizabeth.
Rose, Geo.
Sears, Mrs. L. B.
Shortridge, John H.
Shortridge, Miss L. E.
Shortridge, Miss F. A.
Sears, Chas. B.
Scott, Mr. and Mrs. W. G.
Shaw, Mr. and Mrs. B.
Stormes, Mrs. A. D.
Shaw, Mrs. John W.
Samson, Ella B.
Sprunt, Mr. and Mrs. Jas.
Salter, Mr. and Mrs. A. T.
Small, Mr. and Mrs. S. R.
Skaats, Mrs. S.
Sawyer, Mr. and Mrs. J. D.
Soria, Mr. and Mrs. C. M.
Soria, Miss Annie E.
Sanford, Mr. and Mrs. J. W.
Shipman, Mr. & Mrs. Henry.
Smith, Mrs. Meredith.
Smith, Mrs. Morgan L.
Somers, Mrs. J.
Snowdon, Mr. and Mrs. A. Lowden.
Slee, Miss.
Shethar, Samuel.
Spencer, Mr. and Mrs. J. E.

Spooner, Edw. S.
Thayer, Mr. and Mrs. Geo. L.
Thomas, Mr. and Mrs. E.
Thomas, Miss.
Titus, Mr. and Mrs. W. Q.
TenBroeck, Miss N. E.
Todd, Mrs. Wm. James.
Todd, Miss Rita L.
Todd, Miss M. Blanche.
Talmage, Mrs. V. N.
Taylor, Mr. and Mrs. F. E.
Tompkins, Mrs. O.
Trowbridge, Dr. & Mrs. Geo.
Trowbridge, the Misses.
Tatum, Miss.
Taylor, Mrs. Henry S.
Taylor, Miss.
Taylor, Miss Charlotte F.
Trimper, Miss.
Taggart, Dr. and Mrs. W. H.
Taylor, Mrs. E.
Taylor, Miss M. T.
Trist, Miss.
True, Geo. W.
Varick, Mr. and Mrs. J. Leonard.
Valentine, Mr. & Mrs. W. B.
Voorhees, Mr. & Mrs. P. V.
Voorhees, J. D.
Vose, Mr. and Mrs. Willard.
Vose, Miss.
Vose, Geo. A.
Wales, Mr. and Mrs. John.
Winn, Mr. and Mrs. John S.
Watson, Jas. V.
Williams, Mr. & Mrs. F. H.
Wells, Mr. and Mrs. H. A.
Wellington, Mrs. Henry.
Wellington, Nellie L.
Williams, Miss Jessie.
Warner, Mrs. Chas.
Warner, Miss C. A.
Warner, Miss M. V.
Williams, Mr. & Mrs. F. H.
Williams, Miss L. A.
Willoughby, Miss.
Whitman, Anna S.
Wedgwood, Dr. & Mrs. M. C.
Woodruff, Mr. & Mrs. H. C.
Winch, Mr. & Mrs. Geo. F.
White, J. Stewart.
White, Mrs. J. S.
Winch, Joseph R.
Wyeth, Mr. and Mrs. F. H.
Woodford, Mrs. S. L.
Woodford, Miss.
Webster, Mr. & Mrs. Geo. H.
Webster, Miss May.
Webster, Miss Kate C.
Zeigler, Mr. & Mrs. Harry.
Zeigler, Miss C. F.

Another Birthday.

SUNDAY evening, Robert Marsh had a few of his friends take supper with him at the Mansion House, to celebrate his fourteenth birthday. Among the bright faces were Horace Ingalls, Douglas Hartshorne, Ronald Curtis, Dayton Voorhees, George Goodhue, Augustus Bull, Lester Gilbert, and Arthur Marsh. The birthday cake, which was made by the cook at the Mansion House, was delicious, and the table was adorned with bunches of sweet peas.

FRANK CARLOS GRIFFITH, } EDITORS.
NETTIE M. RICKER,

PUBLISHED EVERY SUNDAY MORNING DURING THE MONTHS
OF JULY, AUGUST AND SEPTEMBER, IN THE INTERESTS OF

POLAND SPRING AND ITS VISITORS.

All contributions relative to the guests of Poland Spring will
be thankfully received.

To insure publication, all communications should reach the
editors not later than Wednesday preceding day of issue.

All parties desiring rates for advertising in the HILL-TOP
should write the editors for same.

The subscription price of the HILL-TOP is $1.00 for the
season, post-paid. Single copies will be mailed at 10c. each.

Address,
    EDITORS "HILL-TOP,"
        Poland Spring House,
            South Poland, Maine.

PRINTED AT JOURNAL OFFICE, LEWISTON.

Sunday, August 25, 1895.

Editorial.

AGAIN we are obliged to enlarge, and as we claim the "largest circulation" of Poland Hill, and larger than the *combined circulation* of all our esteemed contemporaries in the same metropolitan district, we expect some day to arrive at the supreme distinction of issuing a colored supplement.

It will be observed that we are somewhat elevated in our ideas this week, which comes doubtless from the gigantic strides we have made in circulation, of late, which is the inflating element, to lift the balloon of hope to cloud-like realms. If the gentle and patient public continue to invest their dimes as generously as of late, it will all be returned to them in buoyancy of spirits through the columns of THE HILL-TOP.

The hotels are full, and it is to be hoped the coffers of the generous triumvirate who preside over the destinies of Poland Hill, may overflow, and require a new set of coffers to supply the demand. They will never be iron-bound, like

the bucket, of song, for the proprietors are too generous for that, and are too desirous of being able to get their hands in quickly and easily, in order to disburse, as soon as earned, and to add to the attractions of this favored spot.

Nature has done much, but nature cannot do everything, but when a combination of Nature and Ricker is formed it is a firm all-powerful.

A New Arrival.

IT is always a pleasure to announce events which give pleasure to others, and if you will look across the middle lake to the southwest, at the yellow cottage of Forrest and Mary Walker, you can almost see the happy faces of the father and mother, for—it is a boy, and an eight-pound boy, at that.

Many have been the happy and contented summer boarders within that cottage of "Lakeview," and very much are we all indebted to the skill of Mr. Walker, on Poland Hill, for he it was who superintended the removal and re-erection of the Maine State Building, the erection of the new stable and of many of the new features about us. May the sun continue to shine on the Walker family and their happy home.

The Cooking Utensil.

MRS. OLIVER MARSH gave an exhibition of her cooking utensils in the office of the Poland Spring House at 2 P.M. Friday, August 16th. The radiator, covered with a table-cloth and sweet peas, served as a table. The dishes, which are advertised elsewhere in this paper, were filled with doughnuts, fish-balls, and chicken croquettes. She was successful in disposing of a number of her very useful inventions.

Miss Claire Ingalls assisted Mrs. Marsh in selling cooking recipes for the Day Nursery in Springfield, Mass., and her winning manner and interested effort was rewarded by a sale of twenty-two at ten cents each.

Infantile Eloquence.

THAT most charming scion of the house of Ricker, E. P., Jr., 21 months old, was recently left in charge of his aunt Sadie, while his mother was away in Boston.

On her return he greeted his mama with "Mama,—boat,—Hadie,—sleep,—bed,—go," intimating very eloquently that she was to go again and leave him with his much admired aunt.

The Mid-Summer Hop.

THE Saturday night hop of August 17, was one of the most successful of the season. All of the ladies were charming, attractive, and elegantly attired, and with the light, airy costumes of the young ladies who danced, made a pretty picture long to be remembered. Among the beautiful dresses were noticed Mrs. Hildreth in a steel brocade Parisian gown and elegant jewels.

Miss Manley looked sweet in a white satin.

Miss Gilbert made a pretty picture in blue satin with pearl trimmings.

Miss Hildreth wore an exquisite pink satin Parisian gown trimmed with lace, and a beautiful pearl necklace.

Mrs. Amos Little was charming in a black satin, point lace, and choice jewels.

Mrs. Henry S. Taylor, in grey crepon and diamonds.

Miss Lombard was daintily attired in white muslin.

Miss Carpenter, in pink chiffon over pink satin.

Mrs. Gilbert wore black brocade satin, point lace, and diamonds.

Miss Thomas, in white mousseline de soie.

Mrs. Ingalls was beautifully gowned in a pink silk with lace bodice and jet trimmings.

Miss Todd, in red crepon.

Miss Frothingham with Swiss muslin over red silk.

Mrs. Darling wore pearl brocade satin, rich lace, and diamonds.

Mrs. Salter wore blue satin and lace trimmings.

Miss Maginnis was daintily attired in a black and white organdie trimmed with lace.

Mrs. Hibbard wore a combination of red and black.

Mrs. Morgan Smith, black silk and diamonds.

Miss Drake looked lovely in yellow.

Miss Taylor, pink brocade satin.

Mrs. Osgood wore a beautiful combination of pearl satin, black lace, and old rose.

Mrs. Holmes, a moire heliotrope, black trimmings, and diamonds.

Mrs. Peterson, a light green and black silk with green velvet trimmings.

Mrs. Coleman, lavender silk.

Mrs. Trowbridge, grey silk, chiffon, and diamonds.

Mrs. White, cream crepon.

Mrs. Taggart, black satin with diamonds.

Mrs. Coppenhagen, steel satin trimmed with light green velvet.

Mrs. Wedgwood, black satin with silver garniture.

Mrs. Dan Field, light grey brocade with pink trimmings.

Mrs. Griffin, a combination of black and light green satin with beautiful lace.

Mrs. Mitchell, black silk with heliotrope and diamonds.

Mrs. Brett, green silk and jet trimmings.

Mrs. Hoagland was elegantly attired in a brocade silk with magnificent jewels.

Mrs. Thomas was charming in a black crepon trimmed with lavender.

Miss Vose was becomingly dressed in a yellow muslin.

Astronomical.

A PICTURESQUE figure, characteristically Yankee, plain in manner, dress, and speech; uneducated, unrefined, yet dominated by a single idea, and that idea in opposition to every advanced theory, every scientific investigation, every intelligent result,—rose to confront an audience on Monday evening, which nearly filled the Music Hall.

Mr. Edwin B. Hale of Boston volunteered to introduce the speaker, Mr. Joseph Holden, which he did gravely, seriously, and gracefully.

Mr. Holden, in endeavoring to prove the earth flat, and non-revolving, placed himself among those enthusiasts of history who had risen in opposition to accepted theories, and will, in his own estimation, be classed with Columbus, Galileo, John Brown, Garrison, and scores of men who either died for a forlorn hope or in the firm belief in its truth.

This ardent resurrectionist of a theory many centuries mummified, bearing seventy-five weighty years upon his shoulders, was a study in character, and to those who looked beneath the surface, presented a figure, unique, enthusiastic, and self-deceived.

Another Gift.

THROUGH the instrumentality of the Hon. William P. Frye, the United States Census Bureau has contributed to the Poland Spring Library a complete set of the Census Report of 1890 in seven large volumes.

The interest shown in the success of the library is truly gratifying, and if it continues, in a few years it will become one of great value. Let the good work go on.

For a place where politics cuts so small a figure, there is a great deal of "wire-pulling" and "pipe-laying" since the new electric plant and water main was started.

Kings and Queens.

*T*HERE has been much interest manifested in whist at the Poland Spring House this summer, and a number of fine whist players.

Some notable games have been played in the men's smoking-room and one can rarely pass the card-rooms without seeing the devotees crowding the tables. Scientific whist is gaining ground steadily. Miss Trist and Miss Noble's classes are full, and many of the guests will leave the house at the end of the season feeling that they are better whist players than when they came.

Two games of compass whist we think deserve especial mention. In July there was a tournament in Mrs. Byron P. Moulton's room, the contestants being Miss Trist, Miss McNeal, Mrs. Charles Travelli, Mr. Frank W. Carpenter, against Mrs. Moulton, Mr. David G. Yates, Mrs. William Goddard, Miss Noble. Twenty hands of compass whist were played, with a gain of ten points for Mrs. Moulton, Mr. Yates, Mrs. Goddard, and Miss Noble.

Last week another tournament was played in the same room between Miss Trist, Mr. Carpenter, Miss McNeal, and Mr. George H. Fish, against Mrs. Moulton, Dr. Otis E. Hunt, Mrs. Eugene Hale, and Miss Noble, twenty hands again being played, the four last named gaining ten points.

Several minor games have been enjoyed, one of duplicate whist between Mrs. J. D. Fessenden and Miss Noble, against Miss Trist and Mrs. Moulton, with a heavy gain in favor of the two first-named women; and another this last week by Miss McNeal and Mr. Fish, against Mrs. Moulton and Dr. Hunt; score, eight in favor of Miss McNeal and Mr. Fish.

We have lost seven of our good whist players recently. Mr. and Mrs. Travelli, Mr. and Mrs. Jacob Bates, Mr. and Mrs. E. B. Thomas, and notably Dr. Otis S. Hunt. But other games are played as well, and much interest centers in seven and six-hand euchre, and almost every night parties of six and seven steal away to some quiet (?) spot to indulge in their favorite amusement.

Several parties worthy of especial notice have been given respectively by Mesdames Coppenhagen, Taggart, Moulton, Perkins, and Misses Noble and Trist. Mrs. John C. Frye gave a farewell party to Mesdames Lombard, Soria, Moulton, and Misses McNeal and Trist. Mrs. Frye's score was the largest; Mrs. Moulton second; and Mrs. Frye, being hostess, gracefully gave the prize to second highest, Mrs. Soria getting the other.

On Thursday, Aug. 15, fourteen women gathered in Mrs. Moulton's room in honor of Mrs. Perkins' birthday. Two tables of seven-hand euchre were played, Miss McNeal and Mrs. Coppenhagen winning head prizes, and Mrs. Lombard and Mrs. Osgood the consolations. Mrs. Perkins was the recipient of many good wishes and pretty presents. The room was daintily decorated with flowers, and the evening was all too short. Mesdames N. S. Taylor, Lombard, Trowbridge, Little, Fessenden, Osgood, Coppenhagen, Taggart, Moulton, Frye, Perkins, Misses Trist, Noble, and McNeal were present.

The Sentinel.

BY GEORGE T. BOURNE.

The march was o'er—the toilsome march,
Through forest dark and tangled wild.
Each soldier sought his couch of leaves,
And slumbered like a wearied child.
The swift Potomac coursed along
Beside them, like a silver thread,
And, mingled with its rushing tide,
Came echoes of the sentry's tread.

The watch-fires out—no tell-tale light
Must point the foe to where they lay,
While thus they slept beneath the trees,
And dreamed the starry night away.
In hours like these of hurried rest,
In whom to trust they knew full well;
They slept in peace beneath the care
Of tried and trusted sentinel.

And he, with careful, steady step,
Walked to and fro among the trees,
With eager ear to catch each sound
That reached him, coming with the breeze.
The rustling branches, sighing winds,
Each dying leaf that slowly fell,
Were heard, and not a sound escaped
The watchful, trusted sentinel.

But ere the dawn, the tramp of men,
The battle shout, the quick alarms—
Then hand to hand in conflict stood
The true and tried with strengthened arms.
That morn Potomac's stream flashed red,
Through rocky banks and shadowed dell,
And foremost, noblest in the fray,
Died he, the trusted sentinel.

KUNTZ'S ORCHESTRAL CLUB,
OF BOSTON.

MR. D. KUNTZ, }	
MR. A. KUNTZ, }	Violins.
MR. E. LOEFFLER,	'Cello.
MR. E. GOLDE,	Bass.
MR. G. STRUBE,	Flute.
MR. CARL MERRILL,	Cornet.
MR. EDWARD ROSE,	Piano.

Concert Program.

SUNDAY, AUGUST 25TH, AT 3.30 P.M.

I. Overture—Maritana. . . . . . . Wallace.
II. Pavane. . . . . Louis Ganne.
III. Selection—Les Huguenots. . . Meyerbeer.
IV. Nocturino. . . . . Doppler.
For Violin, Flute, 'Cello, and Piano.
V. *a.* { Grossmütterchen. . . . . . . Langler.
   b. { Au Moulin. . . . . Gillet.
For strings.
VI. Selection—Cavalleria Rusticana. . . Mascagni.

Brake Rides.

THAT youthful and distinguished gentleman, Mayor Curtis of Boston, enjoyed the beauties of Poland and of the Gloucester woods, as well as the exhibition of blooded horses at Sanborn's, on the only full day he could spare from his labors.

He was accompanied by Mr. A. T. Foster, Mr. Benjamin Pope, Mr. James D. Tanner, and Mr. Frank F. Woods.

The same party of gentlemen were favored similarly on Monday morning at 6.30 in the crisp, clear air, to Danville Junction, on their return to Boston.

It is to be hoped they may return and enjoy the beauties of this favored spot, at greater leisure, some day.

Monday last the brake was again in demand, for the pleasurable and healthful entertainment of Miss Englis, and Mr. and Mrs. Palmer and family, whose enjoyment of the occasion was undoubtedly as great as that of the many scores who have indulged in this favorite pastime of the season.

On Black Cat.

THURSDAY a party of delighted picnickers ascended the tortuous steeps of the giant "Black Cat," and enjoyed the view and a lunch. These bold and fearless Appalachianswere, Miss Hildreth, Miss Lombard, Mr. Hildreth, Mr. Sears, Miss Campbell, Miss Gilbert, Miss Mary Marsh, Mr. Leonard, Mr. Gay, Mr. Read, Mr. Marsh, Mr. Hosley, Lester Gilbert, and George Goodhue. They took three boats and a canoe and started from Mr. Hale's landing. The large rock on the top of "Black Cat" served as a table, and the lunch was served at one o'clock. The girls are good climbers, and the lunch was served "a la box."

Inspiration.

"In high or low land, there's none like Poland," as the poet sings, and if he had seen our carafe, there is no knowing to what flights of eloquence he might have been inspired.

There is inspiration in Poland water, and why not in its crystal receptacle? Place one on your table, fill it with Poland water, and see what delightful reminiscences it will conjure up. Try it when you get home.

A Poland potato, weighing three and a half pounds, attracts attention on the counter.

Tid-Bits.

Full.

Fuller.

Fullest ever known.

Is it flat or round?

Look out and not fall off.

The answer: Lot's wife.

Mass was held in Music Hall, Sunday morning, August 18th.

A ball need not necessarily be round, brother Holden. How about last night's?

The "Key" Fund was closed Saturday, August 17th, the total amount contributed being $100.00.

Our illustration this week has been sent by an admiring newspaper man, for use in a Paris, France, journal.

The Rev. Fathers J. G. Donnelly, M. J. McCall, and J. C. Huntington, are stopping at the Poland Spring House.

Mr. Goodrich, Mr. Harvey, and Mr. Elliott made a fishing trip Tuesday, and caught over one hundred and thirty trout.

The Herbarium is an object of much interest to many, and Miss Furbish's indefatigable labors have provided a rare treat for the student in botany.

Rev. Dr. W. P. Lewis, of Philadelphia, preached in Music Hall, Poland Spring House, Sunday, August 18th. His text was from St. James, 1st chapter, 27th verse.

What more welcome guests than Mr. and Mrs. E. Thomas, of Portland, and their handsome daughter? The height of the season is none too busy to welcome them.

Miss Robinson is still at the Poland Spring House, and where her services are required, as a massage artiste she will be found fully accomplished, and a pleasant and agreeable companion for the invalid.

If you wish to purchase a really beautiful painting, the price of nearly all in the Art Gallery can be given by the Librarian. Also, any one wishing to purchase a set of those artistic books of the World's Fair, can leave their order at the same place.

Our illustration this week is a superb one, and plainly shows it was the work of artistic photographers. It is but another illustration of how we are favored this season by having such an admirable equipment as the Notman Photographic Co. have provided.

An appetizing Welsh rarebit was the attraction Tuesday evening in the private dining-room, made by the fair hands of Mrs. Trowbridge. The fortunate partakers of it were: Misses Hartshorne, Miss Royce, the Misses Carpenter, the Messrs. Leech, Mr. Green, Dr. and Mrs. Trowbridge, and Miss Thomas.

Fifty-four years ago Mr. A. B. Darling of the Fifth Avenue Hotel, New York, and Mr. A. Richardson were partners in the Ocean House, at Newport. One day last week they suddenly found themselves occupants of adjoining rooms here. What a queer old fellow is Father Time, and what pranks he plays.

Two very much regretted departures on Wednesday, were Mr. and Mrs. Redfern of Boston, who have been delightful and delighted guests. Mrs. Redfern has made valuable additions to Miss Furbish's grand collection in the Maine Building, and both take with them the best wishes of THE HILL-TOP.

The Small Cotillion.

THE above was given Thursday evening, and want of space prevents a lengthy notice this week. Mrs. Trowbridge presided at the favor table as before. The favors were rattles, pink and blue, badges, flowers, and favored flowers.

Mr. Leech led with Miss Thomas, then Dr. Trowbridge and Miss Hartshorne, Mr. Green and Miss Theodora Trowbridge, Mr. J. Leech and Miss L. Hartshorne, Mr. Sears and Miss Gilbert, Mr. Meany and Miss E. Leech, Mr. Vose and Miss A. Soria, Miss H. Drake and Miss M. Leech, Mr. Platt and Miss Richardson, Miss Todd and Miss Carpenter.

Some noticeable gowns were those of Miss Carpenter, white muslin and blue ribbon.

Miss Todd, in green silk.

Miss Gilbert, in white muslin, pink ribbon.

Miss Hartshorne, white muslin over blue silk.

Miss Leech, steel.

Miss Leech, white.

Miss Richardson, combination of yellow and black.

Miss Thomas, in pink silk and mull.

Miss Soria, in pink silk.

Miss Drake, in pink.

Miss Trowbridge, gray and pink.

Miss Hartshorne, in white muslin over pink.

Mrs. Trowbridge wore white crepon silk, with violets.

Paintings in the Maine State Building.

ROOM A.

1. "Daughter of Eve." J. H. Hatfield.
2. "Threatening Weather." Water-Color.
Walter L. Dean.
3. "Looking Off Shore." "
4. "U. S. Fleet at Hampton Roads." "
5. Hayboat. Dordrecht. Water-Color. A. W. Buhler.
6. Low Tide. "
7. Bass Point. " Seais Gallaghei.
8. "Monarch of the Glen." Colani.
55. Grand Manan. L. A. Pulsifer.
56. Cape Cod Shore. W. F. Halsall.

ROOM B.

9. "Springtime." J. H. Hatfield.
10. "A Student." "
11. In My Garden. "
12. "Vanity." "
13. "Old Bridge Lane." "
14. "Autumn." "
15. "Summer." "

ROOM C.

16. "Pink and Green." "
17. Chatham Sands. "
18. In Green Mountain State (1). "
19. In Green Mountain State (2). "
20. Garden Path. "
21. "The Masquerader." H. F. Waltman.

ROOM D.

22. "Helping Papa." Hatfield.
23. Portrait of R. P. Hughes. Waltman.
24. Still-Life. Nettie M. Ricker.
25. Road to the Pond. Water-Color. Gallagher.
27. "The Mouse-Trap." Kay.
28. "Me and Fido." "

ROOM E.

29. Poppies. J. J. Enneking.
30. November Twilight. "
31. Cloudy Day, North Bridgton, Me. "
32. Spur Pasture, Me., or a New England Hillside. "
33. Beach and Wreck. "
34. River and Shore. Nettie M. Ricker.
35. Spring Morning, Skowhegan, Me. Enneking.
36. Spring Morning. "
37. Summer Twilight, Winthrop, Mass. "
39. Son of Italy. Gallagher.
40. A Cup of Tea. Caliga.

ROOM F.

41. Canton Meadows. Hatfield.
42. Hauling the Seine. Gallagher.
43. The Pool. Francais.
44. Horse-Chestnut Blossoms. Adelaide Palmer.
45. Mountain Laurel. "
46. Memet Roses. "
47. Pears and Grapes. "
49. Roses. "

BALCONY AND STAIRWAY.

50. "Tangled Skein." Hatfield.
51. The Old Ricker Inn. Wm. J. Bixbee.
52. The Old Ricker School-house. E. H. Shapleigh.
53. "Penelope." (Hound.) Robert Forcade.
54. Britain Peasant Woman. C. W. Hawkins.

ROTUNDA.

A Morning Ride from Poland Spring House.
Scott Leighton.
Presidential Range from Poland Spring House.
S. P. Hodgsdon.

Miss Ricker's Drive.

Miss Ricker gave a drive to Black Cat, Tuesday afternoon. The party consisted of Mrs. Badger, Miss Campbell, Miss Marsh, Miss Mary Marsh, Miss Nettie Ricker, Dr. Dewey, Mr. Ernest Gay, Mr. Walter Hosley, Mr. Read, Mr. Lewis, and Mr. Allyn Marsh. Upon their return Mrs. Oliver Marsh and Mr. Goodrich joined the party, and all took supper at the Poland Spring House. The table was artistically decorated with golden-rod, by Mr. Wareham.

Lost.

A gentleman, arriving here about the 10th of June, brought with him an old lame back. It has been lost somewhere on Mr. Ricker's grounds. Don't know when nor where. If found the finder will please return to Maine State Building and have locked up in a case where no one else can get it. Need not take any pains to find original owner for he don't want it,—will have no further use for it.

Thistles.

The iron moulders of Lynn have struck. We hope the iron was hot.

"What's Jim agoin to do when he leaves college?" "Well, if he's got eddication enough he'll teach school, but if he haint I reckon he'll edit a newspaper."

A family near Williamsport, Pa., sought shelter under a tree, and the parents were struck by lightning, and the two children were severely shocked. Naturally.

Laidlaw got nothing by the first trial; $25,000 on the second; nothing again on the third, and $40,000 on the fourth. Better settle, Mr. Sage, before it gets up to a clean $100,000. That's sage counsel.

Arrivals.

POLAND SPRING HOUSE.

Abbott, Leon M.,	Boston.
Abbott, Florence T.,	Boston.
Ayers, Mrs. Thomas W.,	Philadelphia.
Ayers, Florence Newman,	Philadelphia.
Abell, Mrs. Geo. L.,	Boston.
Battelle, Miss M. A.,	Portland.
Briggs, Mr. and Mrs. B. F.,	Auburn.
Balboui, E. D.,	Boston.
Bosworth, Arthur S.,	Portland.
Bank, C. E.,	Richmond.
Bright, E. H.,	Boston.
Baxter, Miss A. A.,	Boston.
Bedell, Mr. and Mrs. B. W.,	New York.
Bates, Mrs. E. C.,	Westboro.
Beal, John V.,	Boston.
Barry, Madeline,	Brookline.
Berry, Mr. and Mrs. Melvin,	Milwaukee.
Belyea. Miss L. M.,	Boston.
Butterfield, Wm.,	Center Harbor.
Butterfield, Gertrude,	Center Harbor.
Bennet, Everett G.,	Portland.
Brooks, Herbert H.,	Boston.
Benton, Mr. and Mrs. J. B.,	Cambridge.
Bloom, Helen Godley,	Trenton.
Barry, Miss Ella M.,	Brooklyn.
Bolster, W. W.,	Auburn.
Bolster, Mattie F.,	Auburn.
Bell, Mr. and Mrs. Samuel,	Montreal.
Cushman, Mr. and Mrs. Ara,	Auburn.
Carpenter, F. W.,	Providence.
Curtis, Mrs.,	Portland.
Chase, Miss A.,	Auburn.
Curtis, E. U.,	Boston.
Cook, Mr. and Mrs. S. W.,	Lewiston.
Cushman, Mrs. C. L.,	Auburn.
Coombs, D. D.,	Auburn.
Casey, Mrs. J. Oscar,	Hartford.
Cooke, Miss A. B.,	Brooklyn.
Cushman, S. F.,	Monson.
Cushman, T. L.,	Monson.
Clark, Mary M.,	Boston.
Choate, Mrs. Rufus,	Washington.
Curtis, Mrs. C. L.,	Portland.
Darling, Mr. and Mrs. A. B.,	New York.
Doran, Miss,	New York.
Drinkwater, Bessie M.,	Boston.
DeForrest, Mr. and Mrs. A. W.,	New Haven.
Dill, Mr. and Mrs. L.,	Baltimore.
Dizer, Mrs. S. C.,	Boston.
Decatur, H. E.,	Boston.
Early, F. J. and niece,	New York.
Eddy, Mr. and Mrs. Geo. M.,	Brooklyn.
Foster, A. S.,	Boston.
Freeman, Mrs. Mary F.,	Boston.
Frost, W. G.,	Lewiston.
Fuller, Mrs. H.,	Auburn.
Fuller, Miss M.,	Auburn.
Finlay, Mr. and Mrs. Mark,	Brooklyn.
Frost, L.,	Haverhill.
Godley, Mr. and Mrs. J. F.,	Trenton.
Greeley, W. H.,	Boston.
Gleason, Mr. and Mrs. H. P.,	Newark.
Goldsmith, Simon and family,	Boston.
Guttmann, Mr. and Mrs. F.,	Lewiston.
Guttmann, Miss,	Lewiston.
Gutmann, Walter U.,	Lewiston.
Graham, Mrs. A. B.,	San Francisco.
Hartshorn, R. B.,	New York.
Hill, Edward,	New York.
Hill, Miss Naomi,	New York.
Howard, Mrs.,	Milwaukee.
Harris, John F.,	Marblehead.
Harris, Ami A.,	Marblehead.
Harris, J. Frank, Jr.,	Marblehead.
Hendrie, J. A.,	Boston.
Hildreth, Miss H. A.,	Auburn.
Harris, Mrs. A. J.,	Auburn.
Jewel, Mrs. Lyman,	Hartford.
Kenyon, Mrs. E. C.,	New York.
Lake, James H.,	Boston.
Lewis, Mr. and Mrs. C. S.,	Boston.
Lane, E.,	Saco.
Lara, A. S.,	Virginia.
Lara, S. B.,	Virginia.
Lockwood, Mrs. F. H.,	Englewood.
Leyman, Miss Caroline,	Hartford.
Lewis, A. L.,	New York.
Lapham, Mr. and Mrs. Benj. N.,	Providence.
McKnight, Dr. Chas. S.,	Saratoga Springs.
McKnight, Miss Harriet,	Saratoga Springs.
Marston, J. A.,	Portland.
Merrill, Mary,	Metcalf.
Moore, Joseph, Jr.,	Philadelphia.
Mason, Clint,	Salem.
McConville, Mrs. C.,	Brooklyn.
Markham, E. F.,	Springfield.
Morgan, Mr. and Mrs. A. O.,	Boston.
Nussbaum, Mrs. E.,	Boston.
Newman, Miss S. M.,	Philadelphia.
Osgood, H. S.,	Portland.
Otis, Mr. and Mrs.,	Brooklyn.
Pierson, Mrs. E.,	Sing Sing.
Pierson, Master,	Sing Sing.
Pettingill, Mrs. D.,	Auburn.
Pettingill, Mrs. F. W.,	New York.
Pettingill, H. S.,	New York.
Pettingill, C. H.,	New York.
Porter, Mrs. A. D.,	Plainfield.
Patten, Stanley S.,	Portland.
Pope, Benj.,	Boston.
Platt, Albert J.,	Boston.
Parsons, Miss A. B.,	New York.
Reehle, Mr. and Mrs. Frank A.,	Philadelphia.
Root, Fred L.,	Lewiston.
Rich, J. M.,	New York.
Ricker, John S.,	Milwaukee.
Ricker, Ralph J.,	Milwaukee.
Roberts, N. J.,	Waterville.
Rideout, Elmer E.,	Boston.
Rideout, Grace L.,	Boston.
Rideout, O. L.,	Boston.
Ruggles, Mr. and Mrs. F. H.,	Worcester.
Randell, Mr. and Mrs. A. H.,	Navesink.
Rosener, Mrs. H.,	New York.
Rodenbough, J. S.,	Easton.
Reed, Miss O. S.,	Pittsburg.
Snow, Rev. and Mrs. J. C.,	Haverhill.
Shaw, Mr. and Mrs. B.,	Boston.
Stetson, W. W.,	Auburn.
Sturges, G. H.,	Boston.
Smith, Cora,	Auburn.
Smith, Marion,	Auburn.
Shirley, A. L.,	E. Bridgewater.
Stain, Carrie,	Granville, O.
Samson, Ella B.,	Boston.
Sears, Mrs. Leona B.,	Brooklyn.
Sears, Chas. B.,	Brooklyn.
Snowden, C. Randolph,	Philadelphia.
Splunt, Mr. and Mrs. James,	Wilmington.
Stormes, Mrs. S. D.,	
Shaw, Mrs. John W.,	New York.
True, Mrs. J. H.,	Portland.
Tolman, Miss A. L.,	Boston.
Totley, F. H.,	Boston.
True, J. H.,	Portland.

Titus, Mr. and Mrs. Wm. Q.,	New York.
Thomas, Mr. and Mrs. E.,	Portland.
Thomas, Miss H. B.,	Portland.
Thomas, Elias, Jr.,	Portland.
Thomas, M. W.,	Portland.
True, Sam. A.,	Portland.
Tannel, James D.,	Portland.
True, Mr. and Mrs. W. P.,	Maiden.
Tannott, Mrs. R. H.,	Brockton.
Thomas, L. A. and son,	Pittsburg.
Varick, Mr. and Mrs. I. Leonard,	New York.
Van Pelt, Geo. H.,	Chicago.
Webster, Alden,	Orono.
Wiedesheim, Mrs. W. A.,	Philadelphia.
Wilson, Miss M. S.,	South Paris.
Whitney, A.,	Hartford.
Walter, R. M.,	New York.
Walter, Miss,	New York.
Woods, Frank F.,	Boston.
Wood, A. E.,	New York.
Williams, Chas.,	Boston.
Winch, Mrs. C. M.,	Westboro.
Wales, Mr. and Mrs. John,	Brookline.
Wilson, Mr. and Mrs. Jas. S.,	Boston.
Wellington, Mrs. Henry,	Brooklyn.
Wellington, Miss Nellie L.,	Brooklyn.
Wescott, Dr. Geo. F.,	Portland.
Yiesley, Geo. C.,	Hudson, N. Y.

MANSION HOUSE.

Arkush, Amelia,	New York.
Arkush, Rebecca,	New York.
Aigue, W. L.,	Washington.
Brown, H. R.,	London.
Carter, Mr. and Mrs. H. C.,	Auburn.
Clark, Mr. and Mrs. C. N.,	Boston.
Chandler, P. L.,	Westbrook.
Gilbert, F. A.,	Boston.
Haynes, Phineas,	Haverhill.
Hamerschlag, Miss,	New York.
Hackett, E. C.,	Sabbath Day Lake.
Leonard, L. L.,	Oakland.
Libby, Mrs. F. M.,	Portland.
Merrill, T. M.,	Sabbath Day Lake.
Otis, A. W.,	Boston.
Perkins, Miss A. F.,	Salem.
Perkins, Miss A. D.,	Salem.
Richardson, J. A.,	Liverpool.
Severus, Mrs. J. H.,	London.
Thompson, Mr. and Mrs. E.,	West Falmouth.
Wilbur, Mr. and Mrs. G. A.,	Syracuse.
Williams, Chas.,	Boston.
Whiting, E.,	New York.

Poland Water Leads Them All.

⊛══ **WHY** ? ══⊛

BECAUSE .. It was the FIRST KNOWN SOLVENT OF URIC ACID in the system. . . . .

BECAUSE .. It is the most EFFECTIVE ELIMINATOR of Calculi in the Bladder and Kidneys known to-day. . . . .

BECAUSE .. It was the ONLY water IN NEW ENGLAND to receive ANY AWARD at the World's Columbian Exposition, and the only award of the hundreds exhibited from the WORLD for Purity and Great Medicinal Properties. . . . .

BECAUSE .. The ANNUAL sales exceed the combined sales of all the Saratoga Springs. . . . . .

BECAUSE .. Unprecedented as the success of the past has been it is more promising than ever, showing continued increase. . . . . . .

OFFICES:

VOL. II. SUNDAY MORNING, SEPTEMBER 1, 1895. No. 10.

THE BOTTLING HOUSE IN WINTER.

Poland in Winter.

HAVE you ever pictured to yourself the beauty of Poland Spring in winter? Perhaps you think the cold is almost unendurable and the roads impassable. If so you are mistaken, for even when the thermometer condescends to come down to the level of human beings, you would scarcely credit it without consulting its figures for yourself.

Poland in winter is delightful; the air is crisp and clear, and the distant mountains stand out in bold relief.

You rise, and take a brisk walk on the piazza of the cozy, home-like Mansion House, and have a fine appetite for breakfast. You take a walk, over to the Spring perhaps, and drink from the great stone reservoir in the bottling house, watch the bottles with their masks on, and return ready for a sleigh ride over the slippery roads.

Possibly you jump upon one of the ice teams and go down to the lake, and watch the process of cutting ice, with all its geometrical exactness and systematic rapidity. Men on the ice with scrapers, ploughs, and picks. How rapidly they are hauled up the long shute, and deposited in the house, where a gang of men are placing them in position. It is all very instructive when you have plenty of time on your hands.

Get a sled, just for fun, and coast down the long hill; it is worth the effort of dragging it back. Pile on the big logs in the fire-place, and see how cheerful the office looks. Books and games for the long evenings, and when the moon is full, off for a moonlight sleigh ride, when it is as light as day almost, and the country for miles around is plainly visible.

There is skating, and ice-boating, and the hauling of hay and wood, and—plenty of diversion and lots of comfort, real, solid comfort. What with an excellent table, nice warm rooms, and a big bottle of Poland water always at your door, who says "Poland Spring in winter" with a shiver? It is a mistake, for it is exhilarating, health-giving, and delightful.

The Bal Masque.

THE most important social event of the season was the Bal Masque of last Saturday night, most successfully managed by Mrs. Geo. Trowbridge, who, in an effective costume as Martha Washington, opened the ball by leading the intricate march with Mr. W. H. Strait in his court costume.

They were followed by Mr. Louis Greer as a rather lively nun, and Dr. Geo. Trowbridge in an extremely becoming Continental costume with knee-breeches, ruffled shirt, etc.

The young ladies were costumed as follows: Miss Lydia Hartshorne in a *chic* gown, as "Fi Fi."

Miss Estelle Hartshorne in an exquisite costume, as a French peasant.

Miss Carpenter in pink tarleton and roses, as "*Printemps.*"

Miss Hannah Carpenter in a becoming Spanish costume, as "Perreult de la Grene."

Miss McNeel in a charming empire gown, as a sixteenth century girl.

Miss Gilbert in a gorgeous costume, as Anne Boleyn.

Miss Josephine Leech made a fascinating Carmen.

Miss Edith Leech appeared as a gay gypsy.

Miss Mary Leech was a dainty wood-nymph.

Miss Todd had an extremely clever costume, as a twentieth century girl.

Miss Blanche Todd was a picturesque daughter of Italy.

Miss Thomas, in an artistic costume, was a fair Alsacienne.

Miss Frothingham, in a becoming evening gown, represented "Miss Nobody of Nowhere."

Miss Annie Sorin was sweetly patriotic, in a French flag.

Miss Helen Drake, as the fair Maid Miller.

Miss Maginnis was stunning as Ermine.

Miss Lyman looked very sweet as a Swiss peasant.

Miss Wilson, in a smart gown, was a "Maiden up to Date."

Miss Theodora Trowbridge, as a modest little red-cross nurse.

Miss Julia Trowbridge, as a bewitching little Italienne.

Miss Vose, as a typical summer girl with her engagement finger full of rings.

Miss Peterson as a lovely little flower girl.

The gentlemen, who dressed alike in the Continental style, were as follows: Mr. J. Leech, Mr. E. Leech, Mr. Rose, Mr. Sears, Mr. Vose, Mr. Meany, Mr. Pratt, Mr. Gay, Mr. H. Maginnis, and Master Gilbert.

After the march all unmasked and danced until time for supper, which was kindly given by the Messrs. Ricker, to whom many thanks are due for their entertainment.

It was announced at the table that the Notman Photograph Company invited all the participants in the ball to have their pictures taken and to receive one finished copy free of charge, a most generous offer which was appreciated by all.

Altogether the bal masque was a great success, and many thanks are due Mrs. Trowbridge for her untiring energy in behalf of the guests of the Poland Spring House.

For such a display of wealth it is surprising the Knights Templar should announce everything "*in hoc.*"

The Employees' Ball.

PERHAPS you have been to masquerade balls before, and perhaps you have not, but in any case all will admit that those who contribute to your comfort while at Poland Spring know something about masquerading, and not only having a good time themselves but contributing to the entertainment of others.

Through the generosity of the Ricker brothers, who contributed all the expenses of costumes and supper, and of the guests who furnished the prizes, the affair of Wednesday became a notable success.

Mr. B. J. Gallagher had been to Boston and secured many of the costumes and had, beside, attended to its organization, and succeeded admirably.

Most of the ladies' dresses were designed and made here, and through the untiring efforts of Mrs. E. P. Ricker and Miss Nettie Ricker the ladies would have been a credit to any bal masque in Christendom.

The grand march began at 9 o'clock, which was followed by dancing until 11.30, when a supper was served in the dining-room for the entire party. Those in the march and the costumes were:

Dora Steele,	Bride.
Bessie Rowe,	Queen Louise.
Belle Towle,	Baby.
Annie Bennett,	Little Miss Muffet.
Della Glancy,	Rainbow.
Mary Cross,	Golden-Rod.
Jennie Hartley,	Maid of Erin.
Norah Sullivan,	Washerwoman.
Edith Glidden,	Priscilla.
Mamie Glancy,	Japanese.
Grace Hartley,	Japanese.
Florence Tripp,	Swiss Girl.
Katherine Murphy,	Pine Cone.
Josephine Susep,	Indian Girl.
Marie McKenna,	Tambourine.
Edna Rowe,	Variety.
Bertha Boothby,	Snow Flake.
Hattie Cole,	Buttercup.
Clara Hamilton,	Orphan.
Alice Cole,	America.
Bertha Jordan,	The Hill-Top.
Mettie Jordan,	School-girl.
Nettie Folsom,	Artist.
Marie Saunders,	Gypsy.
Angie Silver,	Indian Princess.
Mary Ingraham,	Summer Girl.
Annie Coyne,	Court Costume.
Janette Fletcher,	Italian Peasant.
Mary Hevius,	Pea-nut Girl.
Hannah Hayes,	Nurse.
Sadie Merrill,	Little Bo-Peep.
Annie McCarthy,	Poland Water.
Hattie Wade,	Topsy.
Josephine Streeter,	Ferns and Sweet Peas.
Carrie Hubbard,	Flower Girl.
Annie Donahue,	Pop-Corn Girl.
Linda Chase,	Sunflower.
Clara Morrell,	Chocolate Girl.
Della Coyne,	Apple Woman.
Cora Saunders,	Spanish Girl.
Annie Mullen,	Old Lady.
Helen McGee,	Goddess of Liberty.
Flora Murphy,	Milkmaid.
Marjorie Hatch,	Red Riding-Hood.
Mary Murphy,	Cards.
Mary Gordon,	Empire Costume.
Mollie Ridge,	Night.
Katie McCarthy,	Large Sleeves.
Ellen McQuade,	Bootblack.
Alice McCarthy,	Jockey.
Maggie O'Neil,	Daughter of the Regiment.
Theresa Perry,	Morning.
Katie McCormack,	Scotch Girl.
Maria Sawyer,	Chambermaid.
Nellie Corcoran,	Butterfly.
H. J. Gallagher,	King of Hungary.
A. L. Frank,	Irish Jockey.
L. A. Lothrop,	King George.
Hector McKey,	Clown.
W. S. Pullen,	Scotch.
L. F. Berry,	Indian.
H. N. Nason,	Duke of Norfolk.
Ira Hubbard,	Mexican.
F. N. Carpenter,	Uncle Sam.
Archie Cole,	Don Cæsar.
Arthur Peterson,	Clown.
Frank Murphy,	Duke of Buckingham.
Horace H. Bird,	Jockey.
Daniel Shea,	Coxey's Army.
Daniel Ford,	Coxey's Army.
Harry McCann,	Song and Dance.
Wm. Ford,	Mephistopheles.
G. A. Pulsifer,	Engineer.
Arthur Wilson,	Corsican.
Melvin Ano,	Earl of Leicester.
Charles Berry,	Don Salluste.
Ernest Peterson,	Clown.
Walter Cookson,	Chinaman.
Fred Keetle,	Richard III.
J. E. Sawyer,	Charles II.
	Sir Walter Raleigh.

The prizes given were, first, for the handsomest dressed ladies, two prizes, awarded as follows: First, to Dora Steele, as the "Bride," some Dresden figures; second to Bertha Boothby, as "Snowflake," a cup and saucer.

Two special prizes were then given, one to Katherine Murphy, as "Pine Cone," a match box, and the other to Mary Murphy, as "Cards," a pin-cushion.

Next, to the handsomest dressed gentlemen, two prizes. First, to Mr. B. J. Gallagher, as the King of Hungary, a silver pencil; second, to L. F. Berry, as the Indian, a picture frame.

The second set of prizes was awarded for the best comic characters, and were distributed as follows: First, to Hattie Wade, as Topsy, a candlestick; second, to Norah Sullivan, as the washerwoman, a pin-cushion.

The gentlemen to receive prizes in this class were the two members of Coxey's Army, Daniel Shea and Daniel Ford, the prizes being a horse-shoe frame and a paper weight.

The prizes were distributed by Mrs. J. H. Coppenhagen, and the judges were Hon. A. Lowden Snowden, Mr. F. W. Carpenter, Mr. P. Van Voorhees, Mrs. Snowden, Mrs. Keene, Miss Campbell, and Miss Dayton.

Miss E. Byrne gave much aid and valuable assistance in the matter of dresses, and Miss

Hannah Hayes made the very unique dress composed of labels and constituting the "Poland Water" dress.

To Mr. Wareham much credit is due for his very artistic decoration of the dining-table, and THE HILL-TOP extends its hearty congratulations to Miss Bertha Jordan for the very elegant dress made up entirely of copies of this paper, including the parasol, and for the very creditable manner in which she impersonated the character. It may be some satisfaction to her to know that of the special prizes given, it was an even thing in the minds of the judges, between "THE HILL-TOP" and "Poland Water," the latter won the draw, the prize being a work-basket.

The prizes were contributed by Mrs. Coppenhagen, Mrs. and Miss Burns, Mr. Carpenter, Mrs. Meredith, Miss Warner, and Mr. Longstreth.

It has passed into history as the most successful employees' ball ever given at Poland Spring, and has given pleasure to many whose pleasures are none too numerous.

Spoony.

ARE you a collector of souvenir spoons? If so, doubtless you have often seen so-called "souvenir" spoons about which there was absolutely nothing representative or indicative of the locality they claim to "solve."

The "Moses" spoon is very decidedly a souvenir spoon, emblematic of Poland Spring and reminiscent of the place, teeming with reminders of your pleasant walks and drives, your good dinners, and inspires Poland Water. They have always been in great demand.

The Hampton Quartette.

THE Hampton students from the Hampton Normal Agricultural Institute, gave one of their very interesting entertainments of song on Monday evening last in the Music Hall.

There were also addresses made by Dr. H. B. Frissell, the principal of the school, and by Mr. G. E. Stephens, a colored man.

A stereopticon was used very effectively during the evening, and the amount contributed for the enterprise was $70.87.

The Magnificent Portrait of Hon. James G. Blaine, hanging over the stairway in the Maine Building, was made by THE SPRAGUE & HATHAWAY Co. of West Somerville, Mass. They also made the enlarged photograph of the World's Fair Views in the same building.

Hearts and Diamonds.

PEOPLE come and people go. The season is waning, and the place that now knows us will soon know us no more — until another summer — but cards are as much an attraction as ever. Last week an enjoyable game of compass whist was played in Mrs. Moulton's room, between Miss Noble, Miss McNeel, Mrs. Moulton and Mr. Mayo, against Mrs. Richardson, Mr. Fish, Mrs. Perkins and Mr. Ziegler, in which the four last-named persons scored seventeen points. On Tuesday evening Mrs. Moulton and Miss Noble played ten hands of duplicate whist against Miss McNeel and Mr. Fish, with a gain of three points in favor of Miss Noble and Mrs. Moulton. Last Thursday evening twenty hands of compass whist were played by Miss Trist, Mrs. Scott, Mrs. Perkins, and Mr. Fish against Miss Noble, Miss McNeel, Mrs. Richardson and Mrs. Moulton, with a gain of one point in favor of the four last named.

On Saturday Miss Trist took her departure after a very successful summer. She and Miss Noble have made many friends during their stay, and it is with regret we say good-bye to them, although we are not called upon to say it to Miss Noble yet, as she is to remain another week. Monday night Mrs. Fessenden gave an enjoyable seven-hand euchre party to Mesdames Lombard, Osgood, Taggart, Perkins, Moulton, and Messrs. Goodrich and Talbot. Mrs. Perkins won first prize, a dainty thermometer; Colonel Talbot carrying away the consolation, a handsome paper-knife.

Progressive Euchre.

PROGRESSIVE euchre still has its votaries, and the game of Friday evening, August 23d, showed no lessening in interest. The result of the contest was as follows:

First ladies' prize, a beautiful China bon-bon box, to Mrs. Charles Warner.

Second ladies' prize, a Dresden powder box, to Miss Mary Marsh.

Third ladies' prize, a lovely embroidered case for embroidery silk, to Miss Newton.

The consolation prize, a Delf bell, to Miss Campbell.

The gentlemen's first prize, an art portfolio, to Mrs. Ziegler, who played as a gentleman.

The second, a collar box, to Mr. Ernest Gay.

The third, a photograph frame, to Mrs. Small, and the fourth, or consolation prize, went to Miss E. Taylor, who, as well as Mrs. Small, played as a gentleman.

Poland Guests.

WE give a list to-day of all the guests in the Poland Spring House, Thursday, August 29th, at 1 P.M.

In addition to the names given, many of the guests have small children whose names do not appear, which also applies to a considerable number of maids, valets, and coachmen.

Barnes, Miss Madeline.
Butterfield, Gertrude.
Brady, Mr. and Mrs. D. M.
Bloom, Helen Godley.
Barry, Ella M.
Backenstose, Mrs. D. B.
Bigelow, W. A.
Blight, Mr. and Mrs. H. O.
Barbour, Mrs. E. D.
Bartlett, Mr. & Mrs. Nelson.
Babcock, Mrs. B.
Babcock, Miss C. L.
Bacon, F. W.
Beylle, Mrs.
Brown, Mr. and Mrs. J. F.
Bull. Miss E. B.
Bunning, Miss G. B.
Bradstreet, Henry.
Bishop, J. O.
Bishop, Miss.
Bishop, F. W.
Bernheime, A. L.
Cooke, Miss A. B.
Coppenhagen, Mr. & Mrs. J. H.
Coleman, Mr. & Mrs. Geo. W.
Carpenter, F. W.
Carpenter, Julia.
Carpenter, Hannah.
Corbin, Mr. and Mrs. C. C.
Cole, Mr. and Mrs. B. E.
Corning, John J.
Colfax, Mrs. A. E.
Colfax, Miss.
Colfax, Miss Natalie.
Curran, Mrs. S. C.
Curran. A. D.
Champlin, Mrs. E. R.
Campbell, Dr. and Mrs. B. F.
Campbell, Miss G.
Campbell, Miss B. S.
Cary, Miss V.
DeForrest, Mr. & Mrs. A. W.
Dizer, Mrs. S. C.
Darling, Mr. and Mrs. A. B.
Dunton, Mrs. W. C.
Drake, Mr. and Mrs. A. A.
Drake, Miss Helen.
Embry, Mr. and Mrs. J. H.
Ege, Mrs. H. N.
Eames, Miss M. C.
Frothingham, Mrs. V. B.
Frothingham, Marian.
Eddy, James H.
Eames, Miss.
Feltus, Mrs. R. G.
Findley, Mr. & Mrs. J. L. V.
Findley, Miss May V. L.
Field, Mr. and Mrs. D. W.
Fessenden, Mrs. J. D.
Ferrand, Mrs. W. C.
Fish, Mr. and Mrs. Geo. H.
Fitzsimmons, Miss M.
Fassett, Mr. & Mrs. Horace.
Forbes. Miss.
Furbish, Miss Alice.
Griffith, Mrs. Geo.
Griffith, Miss S. D.
Griffith, Miss M. E.
Griffith, Daniel J.
Griffin, Mr. and Mrs. C. C.

Greer, Louis M.
Greer, Geo. B.
Greer, Miss.
Goodwin, Mrs. J. N.
Harris, John F.
Harris, Ann.
Hoagland, Mr. & Mrs. Hudson
Hubbard, Mrs. S. B.
Hildreth, Mrs. M. E.
Hildreth, Miss Alma.
Hurlburt, Mr. and Mrs. L.
Hoffman, Mrs. F. S.
Holmes, Mr. and Mrs. E.
Haslehurst, Mrs. J. W.
Holbrook, Mrs. C. L.
How, Charles.
Haynes, Mr. and Mrs. J. C.
Haynes, E. Margaret.
Haney, Mr. and Mrs. E. J.
Haney, Jenny C.
Ingalls, Mr. and Mrs. J. A.,
son and daughter.
Jewell, Mrs. Lyman.
Keene, Mrs. Eli.
Knapp, Mrs. E. A.
Lyman, Pauline.
Lewis, A. L.
Lake, Jas. H.
Little, Mrs. Amos R.
Lewis, Rev. and Mrs. W. P.
Little, Mr. and Mrs. A.
Lambert, Mrs. Eli.
Lombard, Mrs. Thos.
Leech, Mr. and Mrs. J. B.
Leech, Miss Belle.
Leech, Miss Edith.
Leech, Josephine.
Leech, Florence.
Leech, May.
Lapham, Mr. and Mrs. B. N.
Lattabee, E. F.
Markham, E. F.
Murray, Mrs. A.
Merrill, Mr. and Mrs. J. F.
Maginnis, A. H.
Maginnis, J. H.
Mitchell, Mr. and Mrs. A. R.
Meredith, Mrs. J. H.
McNeel, Miss.
Morse, Mr. and Mrs. R. M.
Morse, Miss A. G.
Murray, M.
Murray, Miss.
Morrison, A.
Morrison, L. N.
Moser, A. G.
Morrison, Mrs. E.
Moser, Miss H. A.
Moser, Miss E. H.
Miller, Charles S.
Moulton, Mrs. B. P.
Milliken, Mrs. H. P.
McCoy, Mrs. J. F.
Maginnis, Mrs. J. H.
Maginnis, Miss.
Noble, Miss.
Nussbaum, Mr. and Mrs. E.
Otis, Mr. and Mrs. W.
Oakes, Mr. and Mrs. Josiah.
Osgood, Mrs. H. S.

Palmer, Mrs. H. U. and two children.
Paul, Mr. and Mrs. Fulton.
Prall, Mrs. E. A.
Peters, E. D.
Pettee, Mrs. J. A.
Peterson, Dr. and Mrs. W.
Peterson, the Misses.
Parrish, Mr. and Mrs. J. S.
Perkins, Mrs. W. C.
Paine, Mrs. J. S.
Richardson, Marian A.
Richardson, Mr. and Mrs. A.
Richardson, Miss.
Riker. S. S.
Roberts, Miss.
Royce, Miss E. A.
Robinson, Mrs. Elizabeth.
Rose, Geo.
Sears, Mrs. L. B.
Shortridge, John H.
Shortridge, Miss L. E.
Shortridge, Miss F. A.
Sears, Chas. B.
Sprunt, Mr. and Mrs. Jas.
Salter, Mr. and Mrs. A. T.
Small, Mr. and Mrs. S. R.
Skaats, Mrs. S.
Sawyer, Mr. and Mrs. J. B.
Sotia, Mr. and Mrs. C. M.
Sotia, Miss Annie E.
Sanford, Mr. and Mrs. J. W.
Shipman, Mr. & Mrs. Henry.
Smith, Mrs. Meredith.
Smith, Mrs. Morgan L.
Somers, Mrs. J.
Slee, Miss.
Shethar, Samuel.
Spencer, Mr. and Mrs. J. E.
Starr, Dr. and Mrs. Louis.
Simpson, Mrs. A. J.

Stuart, W. H., Jr.
Thayer, Mr. and Mrs. Geo. L.
Titus, Mr. and Mrs. W. Q.
Ten Broeck, Miss N. E.
Todd, Mrs. Wm. James.
Todd, Miss Rita L.
Todd, Miss M. Blanche.
Talmage, Mrs. v. N.
Taylor, Mr. and Mrs. F. E.
Tompkins, Mrs. O.
Trowbridge, Dr. & Mrs. Geo.
Trowbridge, the Misses.
Tatum, Miss.
Taylor, Mrs. Henry S.
Taylor, Miss.
Taylor, Miss Charlotte F.
Trimper, Miss.
Taggart, Dr. and Mrs. W. H.
Taylor, Mrs. E.
Taylor, Miss M. T.
Trist, Miss.
True, Geo. W.
Tucker, Grace.
Townsend, R. H. L.
Terry, Mrs. A. J.
Thomson, Mr. and Mrs. E.
voorhees, Mr. & Mrs. P. V.
voorhees, J. D.
Wales, Mr. and Mrs. John.
Williams, Mr. & Mrs. F. H.
Wellington, Mrs. Henry.
Wellington, Nellie L.
Williams, Miss Jessie.
Warner, Mrs. Chas.
Warner, Miss C. A.
Warner, Miss M. V.
Whitman, Anna S.
Wedgwood, Dr. & Mrs. M. C.
Woodruff, Mr. & Mrs. H. C.
White, Mrs. J. S.

Names of Our Several Different Drives and their Round Trip Distance.

	MILES.
Around Middle Lake,	5 1-2
Lower Lake,	7
Sabbath Day Lake,	11
Trip Lake,	13
Lake and Gloucester Shakers,	9 1-2
Lake and Poland Shakers,	7 1-2
Raymond Woods and Shakers,	8
Lower Gloucester,	13
Oak Hill and Lake,	7 1-2
Hotel Wilson and Sturgis Mill,	11
Hotel Wilson and Oak Hill,	14
Upper and Middle Lake,	12
Sabbath Day Lake and Peterson's Woods,	13
New Gloucester and Upper Corner,	12
Harris Hill, Minot Corner, Empire Road,	12
Gray Corner and Gloucester Hill,	22
Black Cat, Tinney Hill, Hotel Wilson,	15
To Mechanic Falls,	13
Lewiston and Auburn,	20
Lake Auburn,	26
Lake Auburn via Lewiston,	30

MAILS.

CLOSE.

Poland Spring House.	Mansion House.
5.45 A.M.	6 A.M.
8.45 A.M.	9 A.M.
2.45 P.M.	3 P.M.

ARRIVE.

10 A.M.	9.30 A.M.
1.30 P.M.	1 P.M.
4.30 P.M.	4 P.M.
8 P.M.	7.45 P.M.

FRANK CARLOS GRiFFiTH, } EDITORS.
NETTiE M. RiCKER,

PUBLISHED EVERY SUNDAY MORNING DURING THE MONTHS
OF JULY, AUGUST AND SEPTEMBER, IN THE INTERESTS OF

POLAND SPRING AND ITS VISITORS.

All contributions relative to the guests of Poland Spring will
be thankfully received.
To insure publication, all communications should reach the
editors not later than Wednesday preceding day of issue.
All parties desiring rates for advertising in the HILL-TOP
should write the editors for same.
The subscription price of the HILL-TOP is $1.00 for the
season, post-paid. Single copies will be mailed at 10c. each.
Address,
EDITORS "HILL-TOP,"
Poland Spring House,
South Poland, Maine.

PRINTED AT JOURNAL OFFICE, LEWISTON.

Sunday, September 1, 1895.

Editorial.

IT has been a week of hurly-burly, bustle and
excitement, what with the departure of those
who flee with the last days of summer, and
the coming of those who wish to enjoy the beautiful month of September and the glorious Indian
Summer; taken together with the gayety of the
guests' ball, and the preparation for and occurrence of the grand bal masque of the employees,
it has been a busy season.

With this week we arrive at the tenth number
of our existence, which was intended to be the
limit, but so much kindly interest has been
shown in our success, that we shall continue to
chronicle events on Poland Hill for yet another
week.

The most beautiful season of the year is yet
to come, with its days of sunshine without the
uncomfortable heat of summer and its humidity,
but instead, clear air, and rare mountain views.

What nights to sleep; the harvest moon; the
fresh fruit of autumn; the strolls in comfort;
no mosquitoes; no flies.

What a prospect! Remain and enjoy it, even
if you do not have THE HILL-TOP all the time.
We shall come again, and so will you doubtless,
and we shall often meet, and exchange a smile
of pleasure.

The Library.

OUR guests have been generous in contributions during the past week, foremost among
them being Mr. Nelson Bartlett, with a
very fine new edition of Webster's International Dictionary, a much-needed volume.

Mr. and Mrs. F. J. Bartlett have also placed
upon the shelves that valuable contribution to
the war literature, entitled " Battles and Leaders
of the Civil War," published in four volumes by
the Century Company.

Mr. Henry P. Sondheim provides the readers
with a beautiful work, in " The Picturesque St.
Lawrence River," with elegant illustrations, maps,
etc. The thanks of all are due to these generous
guests who have placed such well-selected material at their disposal.

A nice addition to the library is acknowledged
by the receipt of five volumes from Mrs. Frank-
lin E. Taylor, who sends " The Ebb-Tide," by
Robert Louis Stevenson; " The Story of Law-
rence Garthe," by Ellen Olney Kirke; " The
Dolly Dialogues " and " A Change of Air," by
Anthony Hope, and " A Suburban Pastoral," by
Henry A. Beers.

KUNTZ'S ORCHESTRAL CLUB,
OF BOSTON.

MR. D. KUNTZ, } MR. A. KUNTZ, }	Violins.
MR. E. LOEFFLER,	'Cello.
MR. E. GOLDE,	Bass.
MR. G. STRUBE,	Flute.
MR. CARL MERRILL,	Cornet.
MR. EDWARD ROSE,	Piano.

Concert Program.

SUNDAY, SEPTEMBER 1ST, AT 3.30 P.M.

I. Marche.	Lachner.
II. Overture—Cavallerie legére.	Suppé.
III. Serenade.	Tittl.
IV. Selection—Si j'élais Roi.	Adam.
V. Marionet Funeral March.	Gounod.
VI. Preislied, from Meistersinger.	Wagner.
VII. Selection—Mignon.	Thomas.

Tid=Bits.

She was lovely.

Bal masques galore.

Who was the prettiest?

What a pretty picture it was.

The season is just beginning to be glorious.

August this year has 31 days and 20,000 knights.

In Miss Washington we are honored by the presence of a relative of the immortal George.

Miss Robinson continues in her good work in rejuvenating the weary human frame, for as a massage artist her services are in demand.

Another good angler is Mr. John Wales, who landed in three days forty-five pickerel, some of which were seen upon the radiator in the office.

Tuesday, the steamer Poland took a party invited by Mrs. F. S. Hoffman for a tour of the lakes, through the canal, and back past the lost city of Atlantis.

A Brake ride of Wednesday was enjoyed by Mr. and Mrs. J. L. Varick, Mrs. Holbrook, Mrs. Haslehurst, Mr. and Mrs. A. L. Gondrou, and Mr. and Mrs. E. T. Holmes.

Mr. and Mrs. Bartlett found their table handsomely decorated with asters and ferns on their return from Boston, Wednesday, the work of Mrs. Griffin and Mrs. Small.

Dr. J. H. Hodson, one of our New York guests, is a great collector of etchings, and expressed much admiration at some in the portfolios of the World's Fair views in the Library.

Rev. H. C. Woodruff of Bridgeport, Conn., favored the guests with a very fine address in Music Hall, on Sunday morning last. His text was taken from the 6th chapter of St. Paul's epistle to the Romans, 17th verse.

Mr. Vauzandt has been fishing,—where he went, and who went with him,—well, never mind, but the guests of the Mansion House enjoyed the fruits of their catch Sunday morning at breakfast, fifty-two fine bass.

Do not let the time pass too quickly to visit the Notman Studio and sit for Mr. Ness to "take you," for you may regret it when too late. The exhibition of their work, wherever placed, will commend it to a critical judgment.

Rise early, as our 84-year-old guest, Frederick Wood of Providence, did recently; take the walk to the Spring, take a drink of Poland water, return, and *beat* at croquet as he did, all before breakfast. He has been here fifteen seasons and knows how 'tis done.

Miss Alice Furbish, who is by the way an expert oarsman, is favoring Poland Spring with a visit, as the guest of her aunt, Miss Kate Furbish, to whom we owe so much for our beautiful botanical exhibit. On Tuesday, both were out on the lake at 7 A.M. More early risers.

The Poland Spring Farm produces much that is common, but sometimes an uncommon vegetable, as the "Kolie Rabbi," a favorite vegetable with the Germans, which has been exhibited on the counter, proves. It is cooked the same as a cabbage, but is of a more delicate flavor.

Mrs. H. W. Ricker, Miss Marguerite Ricker, Hiram, Jr., and Charles, are spending two weeks at the Ocean Bluff House, Kennebunkport, Maine. It is to be hoped the change of scene, while it may be of benefit to them, may make them even more than ever appreciative of the beauties of Poland Spring.

Mr. Harry M. Jordan, a well-known face in the office of the Poland Spring House last season, and the originator of THE HILL-TOP, is a guest this week. The present editors extend a most cordial welcome to Mr. Jordan, and trust he will find that the little sheet has not degenerated under his successors.

The Brake has been in demand again for the pleasurable diversion of Mr. and Mrs. D. W. Field, Miss Lumbert, Mr. and Mrs. J. Scott Parrish, Mrs. M. E. Hildreth, Miss Alma Hildreth, and Mr. H. A. Hildreth. These eight delighted sojourners here, took the drive on Monday last, returning refreshed and happy.

Tourists to the White Mountains will do well to remember that the new Mount Pleasant House is the starting point for the summit of Mount Washington All the Boston & Maine trains have their terminus here, and the through trains from Boston and New York start from and arrive at the Mount Pleasant House. The station of the Maine Central Railroad is directly at the rear of the house, connected by a covered passage-way. This is the line which runs through the Crawford Notch. For the month of September the managers of the Mount Pleasant House, Messrs. Anderson & Price, will offer special prices to all tourists, and will keep the house open until early in October, as long as the fast express trains are running.

The Spartan Mother.

BY GEORGE T. BOURNE.

My boy came home from battle fields,
Where blood, like rivers, coursed along.
"We met the foe, we conquered all,"
This was the glory of his song.
His bright eye shone when telling o'er
The conflicts passed, the victories won,
And on my knees I thanked my God
That He had brought me back my son.

But soon again came war's alarm,
The foe returned with stronger might.
My boy once more went joyous forth,
Once more to battle for the right.
I gave him up, as once before,
And bade him in this darker hour
To make his home the tented field,
Nor leave it in the foeman's power.

Borne on the winds and to my ears
There came the news of deadly strife.
No word from him—ah! then I knew
My boy would come no more in life.
Still on my knees I thanked my God,
And will until my latest breath,
That my brave boy, though lost to me,
Had sought and died a noble death.

NEW YORK, October 22, 1861.

Something to Talk About.

A PLAIN woman, well and tastefully dressed,
becomes at once more attractive, and oftentimes
positively fascinating ; so it is with water. Put
ordinary drinking water into a Poland Spring
carafe, and it at once becomes more agreeable,
not only to the eye but apparently to the palate.
If, however, you fill it with Poland water, *then* it
is positively a feast to the eye.

A choice of a carafe for your table is all-
important, and, with one of these, it is a subject
for conversation as well, and can be dwelt upon
at length at table when the conversation flags.
Try it.

The Monologue Artiste.

Miss Adelaide Westcott gave a monologue
entertainment in the Music Hall, Wednesday
evening, giving character sketches, and announced for the benefit of the New York Flower
Mission. The programme was as follows :

Overture.
1. " Just Out,"   By Chas. Barnard.
2. " Little Girl" (in costume).
3. Old Woman (in costume).
4. Song, by John W. Hutchinson (volunteered).
5. Selected.

"Don't" for Men.

DON'T wiggle the tidy off the back of the chair and sit on it. It is preferable by far to pull it off before you sit down, and throw it under your feet.

Don't refuse to button your wife's boots. You may easily take revenge by yanking off a dozen or two of buttons in the operation, and she will soon forget to ask you. This is called diplomacy.

Don't prevaricate about the off-colored long hair on your shoulder. Own up promptly that it blew on there in the horse-car. This will disarm her. Women are very credulous.

Don't retain the half of the evening paper with the latest news, every time. One time in twenty will be a fair average to let your wife have it first. Arrange it so that her night will come on a holiday, when there are no evening papers. This tends to promote concord.

Don't mention anything about lock-jaw if you step on a few nails, pins, or hair-pins, now and then. It may quicken your wife's perceptions, and she may increase the allowance, if you do.

Don't inquire with the air of a millionaire, where that fifty cents you gave her last month, has gone to. She may tell you, and then you will wish you hadn't said anything.

Don't object to giving your wife fifty dollars in advance of Christmas. She may be intending to surprise you with a silk handkerchief, purchased at the time of "a big drive."

Don't hold the umbrella entirely over yourself, and let the drippings fall on your wife. Remember, her hat cost you fifteen dollars, and your own only five. As a rule, rain the cheapest.

Don't hold the umbrella entirely over any other lady you may be with. Recollect, your hat cost you five dollars, and hers cost you nothing. Discriminate. Discriminate.

Don't be over-demonstrative. If you step on a lady's foot in a horse-car, don't grab up her foot like a grief-stricken Sioux squaw, and hug and caress it. The best etiquette is to know when to defy the rules of etiquette.

Don't wipe your feet on the dress of the lady opposite in the car. Why not ask her civilly for the loan of her mouchoir? Besides, what is your wife's fur trimming for? Be a gentleman, always; don't forget that.

Paintings in the Maine State Building.

Room A.

1. "Daughter of Eve." J. H. Hatfield.
2. "Threatening Weather." Water-Color.
   Walter L. Dean.
3. "Looking Off Shore." "
4. "U. S. Fleet at Hampton Roads." "
5. Hayboat. Dordrecht. Water-Color. A. W. Buhler.
6. Low Tide. " "
7. Bass Point. " Seals Gallagher.
8. "Monarch of the Glen." Colaun.
55. Grand Manan. L. A. Pulsifer.
56. Cape Cod Shore. W. F. Halsall.

Room B.

9. "Springtime." J. H. Hatfield.
10. "A Student." "
11. In My Garden. "
12. "Vanity." "
13. "Old Bridge Lane." "
14. "Autumn." "
15. "Summer." "

Room C.

16. "Pink and Green." "
17. Chatham Sands. "
18. In Green Mountain State (1). "
19. In Green Mountain State (2). "
20. Garden Path. "
21. "The Masquerader." H. F. Waltman.

Room D.

22. "Helping Papa." Hatfield.
23. Portrait of R. P. Hughes. Waltman.
24. Still-Life. Nettie M. Ricker.
25. Road to the Pond. Water-Color. Gallagher.
27. "The Mouse-Trap." Kay.
28. "Me and Fido." "

Room E.

29. Poppies. J. J. Enneking.
30. November Twilight. "
31. Cloudy Day, North Bridgton, Me. "
32. Spur Pasture, Me., or a New England
    Hillside. "
33. Beach and Wreck. "
34. River and Shore. Nettie M. Ricker.
35. Spring Morning, Skowhegan, Me. Enneking.
36. Spring Morning. "
37. Summer Twilight, Winthrop, Mass. "
39. Son of Italy. Gallagher.
40. A Cup of Tea. Caliga.

Room F.

41. Canton Meadows. Hatfield.
42. Hauling the Seine. Gallagher.
43. The Pool. Francais.
44. Horse-Chestnut Blossoms. Adelaide Palmer.
45. Mountain Laurel. "
46. Mermet Roses. "
47. Pears and Grapes. "
49. Roses. "

BALCONY AND STAIRWAY.

50. "Tangled Skein." Hatfield.
51. The Old Ricker Inn. Wm. J. Bixbee.
52. The Old Ricker School-house. E. H. Shapleigh.
53. "Penelope." (Hound.) Robert Forcade.
54. Brittain Peasant Woman. C. W. Hawkins.

ROTUNDA.

A Morning Ride from Poland Spring House.
Scott Leighton.
Presidential Range from Poland Spring House.
S. P. Hodgsdon.

Art Criticism.

A T the Rudolphson Gallery there are some fine works of genuine art. There is one picture by Scrathz, after Gravelle, representing a thimble and a barrel stave. The combination is a happy one. The chiari oscura is perfect, and the mauve color blends with the crimson lake, causing a perfect ebullition of warmth and glow, discernable at a great distance. It is one of those art subjects to which distance not only lends but gives enchantment. The edge of the stave is of the proper thickness, but if possible the bung-hole in it might be the thirty-second part of an inch more contracted, without detracting from its beauty. The perfection of the outline is elaborate in the extreme, and the Rembrandt shade in the bung-hole is exquisitely managed. The legend of the Thimble and Stave is a fit subject for elaborate illustration.

The Old Tune.

From out a windless realm it flowed,
　Fragrant and sweet as balm of rose;
Upon its breast soft sunlight glowed,
　And still it glides where the jasmine blows.

An old, sweet tune of other days!
　Full of the tints of the autumn time;
Scents of russets and August haze,
　Gathered and fell like thoughts in rhyme.

May never again that once loved tune
　Fail in my heart as a stream that flows!
Let it run as it will, like a vine in June,
　Fragrant and sweet as the summer rose.

　　　　　—*Eugene Field, in Chicago Record.*

The British Vice-Consul from Wilmington, N. C., Mr. James Sprunt, is honoring Poland Spring with a visit. All nations hear of Poland Spring.

THE NEW MOUNT PLEASANT HOUSE.

The centre of tourist travel in the White Mountains. On the White Mountain Plateau the Mount Pleasant House is situated, overlooking the plain of the Ammonoosuc 1,700 feet above sea level, and commanding the finest of all the views of the great **PRESIDENTIAL RANGE**, the grandest panoramic mountain view east of the Rocky Mountains. Purest of Water from the Mount Pleasant Spring. Purest Air of the White Mountain Plateau, and one of the Most Luxurious Hotels in New England.

Arrivals.

POLAND SPRING HOUSE.

Adams, A. A.	New York.
Avers, O. H.	Boston.
Allen, Miss H. R.	Standish.
Abbott, R. S.	Hampton.
Blowning, Mrs. A. B.	New York.
Berquer, I. B.	Newport.
Barboui, E. D.	Boston.
Bradstreet, Henry	New York.
Blown, Mrs. P. H.	Portland.
Blown, Miss	Portland.
Berryman, Mrs. Edgal	Sherbrooke.
Berryman, Miss Lizzie	Sherbrooke.
Benson. C. C.	Lewiston.
Belg. Mr. and Mrs. Jos. L.	East Orange, N. J.
Bernheime, Adolph L.	Maplewood.
Blaineid. Geo. C.	Brooklyn.
Bartlett, Mr. and Mrs. Thos. M.	Brooklyn.
Buck, Anna	Lewiston.
Buit, Edith B.	Philadelphia.
Bowers, W. C.	Brooklyn.
Bartlett, Mr. and Mrs. Nelson	Boston.
Benedict. Mr. and Mrs. F. L.	Portsmouth.
Blown, Mr. and Mrs. J. S.	Denver.
Bishop, Miss J.	Auburndale.
Bishop, J. O.	Auburndale.
Bishop, T. W.	Auburndale.
Bushnell. Mr. and Mrs. F. C.	New Haven.
Bushnell, Miss	New Haven.
Cornish, Mrs. D. E.	Lewiston.
Champlin. Mrs. E. R.	Cambridge.
Cole, Mr. and Mrs. B. E.	Boston.
Caty, Miss V.	New York.
Coarsen, D. F.	Portland.
Conley, E. W.	Portland.
Cullan, Mrs. S. C.	Philadelphia.
Cullan, A. S.	Boston.
Calvelt, Wm. W.	Washington.
Campbell, Irene	
Corning. John J.	New York.
Champlin, Augustus	Portland.
Cummings. E. B.	Portland.
Clarance. E. O.	Providence.
Curtis, Mrs. C. L.	Portland.
Colfax, Mrs. A. E.	New York.
Colfax, Miss	New York.
Colfax, Miss Natalie	New York.
Campbell, Dr. and Mrs. B. F.	Boston.
Campbell, Glace	Boston.
Campbell, Blanche S.	Boston.
Child, Mr. and Mrs. L. M.	Boston.
Dingley, Mr. and Mrs. F. L.	Auburn.
Dingley, Blanche	Chicago.
Dingley, Anna L.	Chicago.
Dingley, B. H.	Chicago.
Dingley, Miss	Auburn.
Dolan, Mrs. Hugh F.	Hampton.
Daggs, W. H.	Lewiston.
Dinty, Mr. and Mrs. A. A.	New York.
Eames, Miss	West Philadelphia.
Eibel, Miss	West Philadelphia.
Eibel, Miss R.	Springfield.
Emoly, Mr. and Mrs. P. P.	Springfield.
Emoly, Miss C. J.	Brunswick.
Fulbish, M. Alice	Hampton.
Fussell, Rev. H. B.	Brooklyn.
Forbes, Mrs.	Lewiston.
Fallon, Rev. Wm. F.	Mechanic Falls.
Gammon. Mr. and Mrs. G. A.	Hampton.
Gleason, F. D.	Augusta.
Gaidner, Mrs. J. N.	New York.
Hoyt, Colgate	Kansas.
Hone, Chas.	

Hartshorne, R. B.	New York.
Hodson, Dr. J. F. P.	New York.
Harris, J. Flank, Jr.	Marblehead.
Hesse, P.	Lewiston.
Haynes, Mr. and Mrs. John C.	Boston.
Haynes, Miss E. Margaret	Boston.
Haney, Mr. and Mrs. E. J.	New York.
Haney, Jenny C.	New York.
Hancy, Mrs. A. J.	New York.
Hatch, W. L.	New York.
Hutchins, John W.	Lynn.
Jackson, Mr. and Mrs. B. M.	Providence.
Jordau, H. F.	Washington.
Jordan, H. A.	Auburn.
Johnson, H. D. and son	South Bend.
Kelley, John G.	Lewiston.
Keeler, N. E.	Cincinnati.
Lunt, W. F.	New York.
Lunt, Alex D.	Washington.
Leary, Mrs. J.	
Larrabee, E. F.	Baltimore.
Little, Amos R.	Philadelphia.
Lee, Alice	Westport.
Macy, Mr. and Mrs. A. W.	New Bedford.
Mosel, Mrs. H. A.	New York.
Mosel, Miss E. H.	New York.
Mosel, A. G.	New York.
Marston, Chas. S.	Portland.
Matthews, W. S. B.	Chicago.
Mutch, N. A.	Lewiston.
Murray, N.	Baltimore.
Murray, Mrs.	Paterson.
Miller, Chas. S.	Brooklyn.
Mowel, Mrs. E. S.	Brooklyn.
Morrison, Mrs. E.	New York.
Morrison, A. M.	New York.
Morrison, L. N.	New York.
Moise, W. H.	Boston.
Morse, Alice G.	Boston.
Newell, W. H.	Lewiston.
Nelson, Richard	New York.
Osgood, H. T.	Portland.
Peterson, J. W.	Portland.
Parrish, J. Scott	Richmond.
Paine, Mrs. J. S.	Cambridge.
Pressey, Mrs. C. G.	Concord.
Pratt, Mr. and Mrs.	Boston.
Pentze, Fanny	Baltimore.
Patterson, Kate	Baltimore.
Rix, W. H.	Hampton.
Reed, Mr. and Mrs. W. F.	Lewiston.
Somerville, Miss	Springfield.
Stuart, W. H., Jr.	Boston.
Staples, Arthur G.	Auburn.
Small, Chas. W.	Portland.
Stephens, Geo. E.	Hampton.
Simpson, A. J.	Boston.
Stall, Dr. and Mrs. Louis	Philadelphia.
Swain, H. C.	New York.
Thomas, Elias, Jr.	Portland.
True, Mr. and Mrs. F. D.	Portland.
Tuckerman, Mr. and Mrs. Alfred	New York.
Tucker, Glace	Boston.
Townsend, R. H. L.	New York.
Underhill, Mr. and Mrs. W. H.	East Orange, N. J.
Waterhouse, W. P.	Portland.
Wolf, H. A.	Boston.
Williams, E. E.	Boston.
Wainwright, J. H.	Hampton.
Willett, Mrs. May G.	South Paris.
Wetherbee, F. A.	Boston.
Wallace, Rev. Thos. H.	Lewiston.
Webster, Mr. and Mrs. W. C.	Coaticook.
Westcott, Adelaide	New York.

MANSION HOUSE.

Baines, F. W.	Boston.
Bourdon, J. S.	Augusta.
Cook, M. A.	New York.
Dunham, Mrs. E. S.	Boston.
Dunham, Florence L.	Boston.
Durkee, Mr. and Mrs. Joseph H.	Jacksonville.
Greene, S. W.	Brookline.
Gahn, Mrs. J.	Boston.
Hayden, Mrs. F. V.	Philadelphia.
Hayes, H. M.	Portland.
Johnson, Mr. and Mrs. S. H.	Philadelphia.
Johnson, E. W.	Philadelphia.
Johnson, Mrs. Emery S.	Salem.
Judd, E. W.	Orono.
Kempe, K.	New York.
Lord, Mrs. Frederick H.	Lynn.
McCarthy, R. C.	Boston.
Myshall, Frank	Portland.
Myshall, Joseph	Portland.
Millett, Mrs. F. L.	South Paris.
Pressey, Mrs. C. G.	Concord, N. H.
Parsons, Mr. and Mrs. Robert B.	Flushing.
Parsons, Miss	Flushing.
Parsons, William B.	Flushing.
Ross, Charles	Portland.
Rouget, S. V. N.	Brooklyn.
Robbins, Chandler	Boston.
Small, C. W.	Portland.
Sauger, Mrs. L.	New York.
Sauger, C. A.	New York.
Sauger, L.	New York.
Towle, N. S., Jr.	Auburn.
Todd, Mr. and Mrs. E. L.	Sing Sing.
Thompson, Mr. and Mrs. Geo. F.	New Gloucester.
Thompson, Edward C.	New Gloucester.
Whitney, Mr. and Mrs. H. L.	Boston.
Whitney, Albert	Hebron.
Wheeler, Marie H.	Boston.
Wilcox, Regina	Baltimore.

Poland Water Leads Them All.

WHY?

BECAUSE.. It was the FIRST KNOWN SOLVENT OF URIC ACID in the system.   .   .   .   .

BECAUSE.. It is the most EFFECTIVE ELIMINATOR of Calculi in the Bladder and Kidneys known to-day.   .   .   .   .

BECAUSE.. It was the ONLY water IN NEW ENGLAND to receive ANY AWARD at the World's Columbian Exposition, and the only award of the hundreds exhibited from the WORLD for Purity and Great Medicinal Properties.   .   .   .   .

BECAUSE.. The ANNUAL sales exceed the combined sales of all the Saratoga Springs.   .   .   .   .   .

BECAUSE.. Unprecedented as the success of the past has been it is more promising than ever, showing continued increase.   .   .   .   .

OFFICES:

BOSTON:	NEW YORK:	PHILADELPHIA:	CHICAGO:
175 Devonshire Street.	3 Park Place.	Corner 13th and Chestnut St.	Cor. Michigan Ave. and Randolph St.

HIRAM RICKER & SONS, Proprietors.
(INCORPORATED.)

Vol. II.   SUNDAY MORNING, SEPTEMBER 8, 1895.   No. 11.

Poland Water.

THE principal and primal feature about Poland is its water, for without that you never would have been brought face to face with all these grand evidences of the enterprise, good judgment, and mental capacity of the three brothers who control the destinies of Poland Spring.

The spring was here, but they have turned it into a fountain of health and a mountain of wealth, of which you reap the benefit as well as they.

Behold, on all sides, the result of liberal and skillful uses of the proceeds of that noiseless little triangular bit of water under the trees. See what it has done, is doing, and imagine what is yet to come. Look upon the representations of the future Spring and Bottling House, and you can but admire its architectural beauty, and wish to enter it when it is completed.

Let us step into the present one, and take a look about, and make a few inquiries.

Ah, yes, tanks of water and lots of floating bottles jostling each other, and we learn that these two tanks are the soaking tanks for every bottle before using, with a capacity of 2,000 bottles each. In these tanks the bottles soak twelve hours in a strong solution of soda ash, before washing.

In the next tank they are thoroughly washed in clean hot water before going through the third process of cleansing, which is the machine process, by which a stream of hot water is forced into the bottle, at the same time a revolving brush opens on the inside, making 1,900 revolutions a minute.

Nor is this sufficient, for they are next subjected to a steam bath and rinsed with clean hot water heated to 212 degrees Fahrenheit.

The fifth and last handling is to place them on racks, nose down, and send to the filling room.

The water from the spring is conveyed into a large stone tank, and the bottles filled directly from this as it flows from the spring. They are corked as filled and conveyed to the labelling room, where each bottle is carefully inspected, and if the least speck is detected, it is discarded, emptied, and the bottle goes back through the same process again. If found perfect, it is labelled, the signature seal placed over the cork, the bottle wiped and placed in its case.

A case contains 24 half-gallon bottles, 50 quart bottles, or 100 pint bottles as the case may be.

Charged water is held in a silver-plated fountain, passing into it as it is charged, and from which it is drawn to the bottles and corked, passing on to the next man to be wired.

Those having the position of filling charged bottles wear a wire mask, as the bottles are often burst, the breakage alone, here and in transit, amounting to about $1,500 annually.

Of Poland water about 5,000 barrels, aside from other receptacles, are shipped annually, and the use of barrels has been curtailed of late and more shipped either in bottles or carboys; of the latter, which hold 12 to 15 gallons, some 200 to 300 weekly are shipped.

The corks used in the bottles and carboys are bought through a New York house, and are imported direct from Spain especially for Poland Spring; the trade-mark is burned into each cork.

To transport this immense amount of water, which goes to the uttermost parts of the earth, four four-horse teams are constantly in this service alone, often making two trips daily; and on the rail, four to five carloads are weekly started on their journey. Six months in the year a double gang of men are employed, running night and day in the Bottling House.

FUTURE SPRING AND BOTTLING HOUSES.

Ask Archie Cole, the very polite and genial superintendent, and he will tell you that you drink 60 family cases, of 6 gallons each, daily at the two hotels, so that it appears that you are drinking 360 gallons of Poland water daily, and it does you good.

All the half-gallon bottles come from Craven Bros., Camden, N. J.

The new building will be built of stone, iron, and brick, and the motive power and light will all be supplied by electric motors.

The structure, which will occupy the same site as the present one, will be used exclusively for bottling, all the washing and packing to be done in another building 200 feet away.

The visitor to Poland Spring two years hence will find a marvelous advancement made, not only in this feature, but in others as well.

The water department is looked after by Mr. Hiram W. Ricker, which, together with the stable, gives him sufficient employment to prevent his being accused of idleness. Idleness is something not tolerated on Poland Hill, and the example of industry, thrift, and liberality has excellent exponents in the Ricker family.

Poland Brake, First Prize.

MAINE STATE FAIR.

Many notable teams were in line, but none attracted more attention than the Poland Spring hitch and its six bay horses, with the Cheerup Club on top. The decorations were in yellow, purple, and green, a canopy lifting over the top, and every horse floating yellow and white from his breastplate. The harnesses were of the finest, the reins were white, and Charles Nevens, the distinguished veteran Poland whip, handled the ribbons. The doors of the coach had been boxed in so that the material could be affixed, but on the wheels it was tied in with ribbons. Satin ribbons in broad bands floated in streamers. The design was artistic and fetching, and the white dresses of the young ladies, combined with the dark suits and high hats of the young men, made a most complete and beautiful picture. The entire turnout was a thing of life and color, and it won the beautiful special prize given by Col. C. H. Osgood of Lewiston, and the banner for coaches given by the Fair.

Col. Osgood himself presented the prizes, and it will be extended to Mr. Ricker at Poland Spring at a supper given there this evening by Mr. Ricker.

The cup is a beautiful thing, some ten inches high, inscribed, "The Osgood Loving Cup, presented for best four-horse coach at Maine State Fair floral parade, September 4, 1895."

The Cheerup Club that rode on the Poland coach were Mrs. W. O. Foss, Miss Elizabeth Peables of Auburn, Miss Bonney and Miss Henrietta D. Rice of Portland, Mr. Geo. R. D. McGregor, Mr. H. J. Jordan, Mr. Charles W. Conant, and Dr. A. W. Shurtleff.

—Lewiston Journal.

The Brake was decorated under the direction of Miss J. G. Gray, of the Dennison Manufacturing Company of Boston, by the Misses Julia Mullaly, Lottie Abbott, and Katharine Murphy from the Poland Spring House, to whom much credit is due for their artistic labors.

Mr. J. J. Van Alen once more leaves gay Newport for the quiet loveliness of Poland Hill. A very good exchange.

FRANK CARLOS GRIFFITH, } EDITORS.
NETTIE M. RICKER,

PUBLISHED EVERY SUNDAY MORNING DURING THE MONTHS
OF JULY, AUGUST AND SEPTEMBER, IN THE INTERESTS OF

POLAND SPRING AND ITS VISITORS.

All contributions relative to the guests of Poland Spring will
be thankfully received.

To insure publication, all communications should reach the
editors not later than Wednesday preceding day of issue.

All parties desiring rates for advertising in the HILL-TOP
should write the editors for same.

The subscription price of the HILL-TOP is $1.00 for the
season, post-paid. Single copies will be mailed at 10c. each.

Address,

EDITORS "HILL-TOP,"

Poland Spring House,

South Poland, Maine.

PRINTED AT JOURNAL OFFICE, LEWISTON.

Sunday, September 8, 1895.

Editorial.

THE end of all things must come, and so it
is with THE HILL-TOP, for, after having
labored eleven weeks to give the chronicle
and brief abstract of the comings and goings,
the sayings and doings, in and about this grand
establishment, the time comes when to say farewell is, like Romeo's, a sweet sorrow.

We have not only been tolerated, but have
even caught words of praise, and, as dear old
Josh Whitcomb puts it, "I lived longer than I
thought I should."

For our success we have many to thank. We
thank you, our subscribers and readers, for your
interest and generous investment of your dollars
and dimes.

To the Messrs. Ricker for their generous
encouragement, and their more tangible and substantial assistance in many ways, we are deeply
indebted. We have also been placed under obligations to various contributors who have shown
a kindly interest in our success; and to our
advertisers,—well, a government appropriation
would have been the only suitable substitute for
them. We only trust we have been as useful to
them as they have to us.

A very hearty word of praise must be given
the Notman Photographic Company, who have
furnished us such superior material wherewith to
illustrate the familiar scenes about us, for they
have been far above the average and not to be
excelled.

In conjunction with this work, we must not
forget the Suffolk Engraving Company of Boston,
who have made so many of our magnificent
plates. They have been exceptionally good, and
have called forth the favorable comments of
hosts of good judges.

Even the superior work of these two artistic
co-laborers in the art of illustration might have
come to naught had it not been for the excellent
work performed in the Job Printing Office of the
Lewiston Journal, for they are largely responsible for the neat, correct, and, may we add,
elegant appearance of our little sheet. Their
skill, good taste, promptness, excellent composition, and superior press-work have enabled us
to feel quite at home on the news counter beside
the far more pretentious publications.

A word of thanks must be given to Mr. Frank
Chaffin, who is not exactly the courier of the
Czar, but is certainly the courier of Poland, and
to whom has been intrusted the duty of weekly
bringing us from Lewiston, and promptly and
unfailingly depositing us in the office of the
editors.

To all, our thanks, and to all, adieu, not
au revoir, and let us hope to meet again in the
first summer month of '96; and this ends the
second volume of THE HILL-TOP.

Poland Guests.

WE give a list to-day of all the guests in the Poland Spring House, Thursday, September 5th, at 4 P.M.

In addition to the names given, many of the guests have small children whose names do not appear, which also applies to a considerable number of maids, valets, and coachmen.

Adams, Mr. and Mrs. C. H.
Bonaparte, Mr. & Mrs. C. J.
Blake, Mr. and Mrs. Wm. S.
Brown, Jos. A.
Brown, Miss B. G.
Benedict, Mr. & Mrs. F. L.
Budd, the Misses.
Baldwin, W. H.
Baldwin, Miss S. A.
Binder, Wm.
Bagley, S. K.
Barbour, Miss.
Butterfield, Gertrude.
Blight, Mr. and Mrs. H. O.
Barbour, Mrs. E. D.
Bartlett, Mr. & Mrs. Nelson.
Bacon, F. W.
Beylle, Mrs.
Bishop, T. W.
Butterfield, Mr. & Mrs. A. B.
Carleton, Miss E. B.
Carroll, E. A.
Carroll, Mrs. E. M.
Clark, Mrs. E. E.
Colfax, Mrs. A. E.
Colfax, the Misses.
Converse, Mrs. F. S.
Coppenhagen, Mr. & Mrs. J. H.
Coleman, Mr. & Mrs. Geo. W.
Carpenter, F. W.
Carpenter, Julia.
Carpenter, Hannah.
Corbin, Mr. and Mrs. C. C.
Cole, Mr. and Mrs. B. E.
Colfax, Mrs. A. E.
Colfax, Miss.
Colfax, Miss Natalie.
Curran, Mrs. S. C.
Curran. A. D.
Dill, Mrs. J. B.
Douglas, Mrs. Albert, Jr.
Dwyer, Mr. and Mrs. F. P.
DeForrest, Mr. & Mrs. A. W.
Dizer, Mrs. S. C.
Dunton, Mrs. W. C.
Drake, Mr. and Mrs. A. A.
Drake, Miss Helen.
Embry, Mrs. J. H.
Ege, Mrs. H. N.
Eames, Miss M. C.
Eames, Miss.
Feitus, Mrs. R. G.
Fessenden, Mrs. J. D.
Fitzsimmons, Miss M.
Fassett, Mr. & Mrs. Horace.
Furbish, Miss.
Gray, Mr. and Mrs. J. H.
Griffith, Mrs. Geo.
Griffith, Miss S. D.
Griffith, Miss M. E.
Griffith, Daniel J.
Griffin, Mr. and Mrs. C. C.
Harris, R. B.
Hansed, Mrs. S. F.
Haydock, Miss S. G.
Harwood, Mr. and Mrs. N.
Haley, Mrs. C. J.
Haley, Chas. G.
Harris, John F.
Harris, Ann.
Hubbard, Mrs. S. B.

Hildreth, Mrs. M. E.
Hildreth, Miss Alma.
Hurlbutt, Mr. and Mrs. L.
Hoffman, Mrs. F. S.
Haynes, Mr. and Mrs. J. C.
Haynes, E. Margaret.
Jackson, Dr. W. H.
Jacoby, Mr. and Mrs. C.
Kennard, Mr. and Mrs. J.
Kennard, Dr. H. D.
Knapp, Mrs. E. A.
Lee, Dr. E. J. and family.
Lockwood, Mrs. R.
Lockwood, Miss R. N.
Leonard, Miss G.
Leonard, Miss G. H.
Larrabee, E. F.
Leonard, Mr. and Mrs. J. F.
Leonard, Miss.
Lyman, Pauline.
Lapham, Mr. and Mrs. B. N.
Larrabee, E. F.
Matthews, L. J.
Matthews, Mrs. E. W.
Merrill, Mrs. J. W.
Malcomson, A. S.
Morrill, Mr. and Mrs. A. K.
Mills, Mrs. H. F.
Mills, Mountford.
Marsh, Oliver.
McMillan, Mr. & Mrs. J. H.
McMillan, Miss.
Miller, Mr. & Mrs. Lewis E.
Miller, Miss.
Markham, E. F.
Murray, Mrs. A.
Merrill, Mr. and Mrs. J. F.
Maginnis, S. H.
Maginnis, J. H.
Mitchell, Mr. and Mrs. A. R.
Miller, Charles S.
Moulton, Mrs. B. P.
Maginnis, Mrs. J. H.
Maginnis, Miss.
Noble, Miss.
Oakes, Mr. and Mrs. Josiah.
Palmer, Mrs. A. W.
Palmer, Mrs. H. U. and two children.
Prall, Miss E. A.
Pettee, Mrs. J. A.
Peterson, Dr. and Mrs. W.
Peterson, the Misses.
Perkins, Mrs. W. C.
Ross, Mr. and Mrs. J.
Ross, Miss A. W.
Rogers, Mrs. Geo. B.
Rosengarten, J. G.
Rosengarten, Miss.
Richardson, Marian A.
Richardson, Mr. and Mrs. A.
Richardson, Miss.
Riker, S. S.
Royce, Miss M. C.
Rose, Geo.
Salter, Miss.
Smith, Mrs. Morgan L.
Smith, Mrs. Chas.
Schmidt, the Misses.
Stokes, Miss C. P.
Staunton, J. A.

Seals, Mrs. L. B.
Shortridge, John H.
Shortridge, Miss L. E.
Shortridge, Miss F. A.
Seals, Chas. B.
Salter, Mr. and Mrs. A. T.
Skaats, Mrs. S.
Sawyer, Mr. and Mrs. J. B.
Sotia, Mr. and Mrs. C. M.
Sotia, Miss Annie E.
Sanford, Mr. and Mrs. J. W.
Slee, Miss.
Spencer, Mr. and Mrs. J. E.
Simpson, Mrs. A. J.
Thayer, Mr. and Mrs. F. A.
Trowbridge, Miss C. H.
Trowbridge, Mrs. F. R.
Trott, Geo.
Thayer, Mr. and Mrs. Geo. L.
Titus, Mr. and Mrs. W. Q.
TenBroeck, Miss N. E.
Todd, Mrs. Wm. James.
Todd, Miss Rita L.
Todd, Miss M. Blanche.

Talmage, Mrs. V. N.
Taylor, Mr. and Mrs. F. E.
Tompkins, Mrs. O.
Taylor, Mrs. Henry S.
Taylor, Miss.
Taylor, Miss Charlotte F.
Taggart, Dr. and Mrs. W. H.
Taylor, Miss M. T.
Thomson, Mr. and Mrs. E.
Voorhees, Mr. & Mrs. P. V.
Voorhees, J. D.
Warner, E.
Weymouth, Mr. & Mrs. Geo.
Watson, Mr. and Mrs. Geo.
West, John.
Wade, Mrs. R. B.
Wells, B. F.
Wellington, Mrs. Henry.
Wellington, Nellie L.
Warner, Mrs. Chas.
Warner, Miss C. A.
Warner, Miss M. V.
Whitman, Anna S.
Wedgwood, Mr. & Mrs. M. C.

Concert Program.

SUNDAY, SEPTEMBER 8TH, AT 3.30 P.M.

I.   Overture—Rosamunde.   .   .   .   Schubert.
II. Andante—From Surprise Symphony.   .   Haydn.
III. Selection—Robert Le Diable.   .   .   Meyerbeer.
IV. { a. Andante.   .   .   .   .   .   Gottermann.
     { b. Gavotte. .   .   .   .   .   .   Popper.
                              'Cello Solo.
V.   { a. Serenade.   .   .   .   .   .   Pierne.
     { b. Intermezzo.   .   .   .   .   .   Macbeth.
VI. Selection—Tannhauser.   .   .   .   .   Wagner.

THE IDEAL ROAD HORSE.

GENARE, 134.

ELMWOOD FARM, - South Poland.

The Home of the Ideal Road Horse of America.

I most cordially invite every visitor at Poland Spring to call upon me at my Summer home (distance only 5 miles from the Hotel). You will be made very welcome, whether intending to purchase a horse or not. It is my pleasure to show, and I am still it will be yours to see, a race of horses standing 16 hands, weighing about 1100 pounds, standard colors, handsome and stylish, good dispositions and fearless, with courage, endurance, and action that allow them to road 12 miles an hour, and trot as fast as you want to ride on the road. The ideal horse for the brougham and victoria, for the four-in-hand, the tandem, and the dog cart. Our exercising and training hours are from 3 to 4.30 daily, which is the only time we can show you these horses in harness, bringing out their fine finish and grandeur.

JAMES S. SANBORN, Proprietor.

Book Title Party.

A UNIQUE, fascinating, and highly interesting "Book Title Party" was given recently in Mrs. E. L. Todd's room at the Mansion. Each one of the ladies present, Mrs. Sabine, Mrs. Richardson, Miss Sidford, Miss Spencer, the Misses Hughson, Mrs. Amerman, and Miss Washington was furnished with pencil and paper, and guessed the books represented by the mystic emblems.

Progressive Euchre.

The progressive euchre party at the Poland Spring House, Friday evening, was a great success. Mrs. Keene won the first prize, a hand-painted china plate; Mrs. Soria, the second ladies' prize, a leather bag. The third prize, a card case, went to Mrs. Griffin. Mr. Aigue won the gentlemen's first prize, a Poland Spring spoon. Mrs. Eddy and Miss Williams cut for the second gentlemen's prize, and Mrs. Eddy was successful in winning a laundry sachet. The third prize, a magazine cover, went to Mrs. Coppenhagen.

Maine State Fair.

Excelsior Grange, No. 5, of South Poland, was represented by Mr. and Mrs. J. E. Sawyer, Mr. and Mrs. M. C. Davis, Mr. and Mrs. R. B. Estes, Mr. and Mrs. A. F. Chapman, and Mrs. Scannell, who occupied one of the three-seated Poland wagons. The carriage was decorated by Mr. Gallagher and the Misses Sadie and Nettie Ricker, and was used to represent the floral exhibit of the Grange. It was highly complimented, and many thanks extended to the Messrs. Ricker for the use of the carriage.

A Game of Six-Handed Euchre.

Friday evening of last week one peeping into Mrs. Franklin Taylor's room would have seen a pleasant game of six-handed euchre in progress, and would have beheld, beside herself, her daughter, Mrs. Douglass, for whom a special carriage had been sent to the station, that she might be in time to be beaten at the game; also Mrs. Bright, Mrs. Ingalls, Mrs. Todd, and Colonel Ingalls.

As in previous years, Mrs. Bright, Mrs. Taylor, and Mrs. Ingalls were the winners against Mrs. Douglass, Mrs. Todd, and Colonel Ingalls.

A recent contributor to the Poland Spring library and a regular visitor here, Mr. Henry P. Sondheim, together with Mrs. Sondheim and their daughter Pauline, arrived Saturday. Others in their party were Mrs. Gibson, Mr. and Mrs. Adler, and Master George Adler.

𝒯𝒾𝒹-𝓑𝒾𝓉𝓈.

Last Sunday's issue required an extra edition.

Mr. and Mrs. William S. Blake are more welcome return visitors.

Religious services were held Sunday last in Music Hall by Rev. F. W. Bishop, of Auburndale, Mass., at 11 A.M. His text was from the 2d chapter of Titus, 10th verse.

We are honored once more by the presence of Mr. and Mrs. Charles J. Bonaparte, of Baltimore, in our midst. May they continue long to favor Poland Spring with their visits.

Friday a picnic was given in honor of Miss Alice Furbish. The party rowed through the middle and upper lakes, and Miss Furbish received many compliments for her skillful oarsmanship.

A singular coincidence is the presence here at the same time of a Bonaparte, a Wellington, and a Washington, the first and last named being descendants of their respective famous families.

A delightful picnic took place recently at the pumping station, lower lake. The party included Mr. and Mrs. Van Zandt, Mr. and Mrs. Bowker, Mr. and Mrs. McCartney, Mrs. Jackson, Mrs. Eva Wilber, Mrs. Wood, Mrs. Taylor, Mrs. Hubbard, Mr. and Mrs. Wilbur, Dottie Wilbur, Aurora Gurley, and Helen Gurley. The day was perfect and all had a pleasant time.

On Thursday a game of croquet was played by Miss Noble and Mrs. Todd, against Miss Royce and Miss Brown. The famous green ball of Mrs. Todd's won the game, and on returning to her room, she was surprised to find a box sent to her from Colonel Ingalls, enclosing the gift of a very pretty miniature green ball and mallet.

September is the great month to visit the White Mountains. The new Mt. Pleasant House will remain open until October 1st or 7th, and Messrs. Anderson and Price, the managers, are offering special rates for tourists and others until the season closes. The house is heated by steam throughout, and has open fire-places in all the parlors and large rooms. Through trains, with parlor cars, run direct to the door of the house, via the Boston and Maine or Maine Central Railroads.

The Magnificent Portrait of Hon. James G. Blaine, hanging over the stairway in the Maine Building, was made by THE SPRAGUE & HATHAWAY Co. of West Somerville, Mass. They also made the enlarged photograph of the World's Fair Views in the same building.

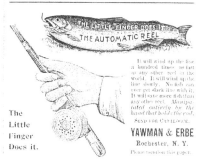

The Last Call.

This is the last opportunity to mention carafe to you, so take one more look at its artistic proportions, its excellent design and finish, and note the various features of Poland it typifies, and then.—buy it. It will grace your table, and be a delight to the eye, and be a welcome relief from the stereotyped article commonly seen.

A Senator's Gift.

During the week just passed Senator William P. Frye has sent to the library one hundred and twenty-seven volumes of valuable government works, which will be of great interest to visitors to the Maine State Building, and no more appropriate place could have been selected for their safe keeping. Many thanks to the very thoughtful and considerate Senator from Maine.

THE NEW MOUNT PLEASANT HOUSE
In the Heart of the White Mountains.

Arrivals.

POLAND SPRING HOUSE.

Alvard, Henry E.	Washington.
Ayling, Chas F.	Boston.
Ambrose, James E.	Lewiston.
Andrews, Charles	Lewiston.
Adams, Mr. and Mrs. C. H.	New Bedford.
Adams, Miss	New Bedford.
Blaineid, Mr. and Mrs. Albion Hale	Augusta.
Blaisdell, Mr. and Mrs. F. H.	Lynn.
Bayley, S. K.	Boston.
Butterfield, Mr. and Mrs. A. B.	Boston.
Blake, Mr. and Mrs. William S.	Boston.
Bradley, Mr. and Mrs. Geo. L.	Pomfret.
Bradford, Grace L.	Auburn.
Burrows, Jno. C.	Chicago.
Brown, Joseph A.	Boston.
Brown, Miss B. S.	Boston.
Binder, William	Boston.
Bradbury, Mrs. F. T.	Boston.
Butler, Mr. and Mrs. F. S.	Richmond.
Budd, Miss	Chicago.
Budd, Miss Blanche	Chicago.
Bonaparte, Mr. and Mrs. Charles J.	Baltimore.
Baldwin, W. H.	Baltimore.
Baldwin, Sallie R.	Baltimore.
Bird, Mrs. S. T.	Boston.
Bailey, Mr. and Mrs. Charles J.	Boston.
Bonney, Adeline	Portland.
Bailey, Mrs.	Winthrop.
Bradford, Grace L.	Auburn.
Barbour, Miss M. E.	Boston.
Bryant, Mrs. E. P.	Boston.
Baldwin, Mr. and Mrs. N. A.	New Haven.
Capen, Mr. and Mrs. S. B.	Boston.
Capen, Mary W.	Boston.
Carlisle. Mrs. M. E.	Portland.
Clark, Mrs. Edward E.	Boston.
Carleton, Edith B.	Brookline.
Crocker, Mr. and Mrs. C. F., Jr.	Fitchburg.
Chilton, Miss	Philadelphia.
Carroll, Mrs. E. M.	Boston.
Carroll, E. H.	Boston.
Cushing, Mr. and Mrs. Thomas	Montreal.
Chase, Miss H. M.	Haverhill.
Craig, Mr. and Mrs. J. W.	Portland.
Converse, Mr. and Mrs. F. S.	Chestnut Hill.
Crosby, Miss	New York.
Conant, Charles L.	Lewiston.
Caisse, Rev. L. J.	Lewiston.
Dwight, Mrs. J. W.	Dryden.
Dwight, Miss	Dryden.
Douglas, Mrs. Albert, Jr.	Chillicothe.
Dodson, Mr. and Mrs. R. B.	New York.
Douglas, C. F.	Portland.
Dade, Mrs. L. H.	Philadelphia.
Dodge, Mrs. A. R.	Jacksonville.
Dwyer, Mr. and Mrs. F. P.	New York.
Dill, Mrs. J. B.	East Orange.
Dwinell, J. C.	Boston.
Drake, Mrs. Nathan	Boston.
Duer, Miss Caroline J.	New Haven.
Duel, Sarah	New Haven.
Ehrlich, Miss E.	Newark.
Finch, Adelaide V.	Lewiston.
Fellows, C. H.	Haverhill.
Foss, Mrs. W. O.	Auburn.
Gray, Miss J. G.	Boston.
Gray, Mr. and Mrs. J. H.	Boston.
Guptill, Mr. and Mrs. George H.	Portland.
Gleason, Patrice	Boston.
Goodwin, W. H.	New York.
Harris, J. Frank, Jr.	Marblehead.
Haggaty, D. W.	Kingston.
Herndon, Richard	Boston.

Henderson, Miss	Philadelphia.
Henderson, Gertrude	Philadelphia.
Humphrey, Edith G.	Yarmouth.
Hildreth, Mr. and Mrs. H. A.	Auburn.
Hildreth, Mrs. C. W.	Westford.
Hildreth, Miss E. F.	Lowell.
Hildreth, Miss	New York.
Hildreth, H. W.	Cambridge.
Haydock, Miss S. G.	Philadelphia.
Haley, Mrs. C. J.	Cambridge.
Haley, Charles G.	Cambridge.
Hansell, Mrs. S. F.	Philadelphia.
Hilliard, J. C.	Boston.
Hubbard, Mrs. L. M.	Boston.
Hunt, W. B.	Boston.
Harris, R. B.	Marblehead.
Harwood, Mr. and Mrs. N.	Leominster.
Hovey, Mrs. C. E.	
Hardenbergh, Miss	New York.
Hotchkiss, Miss E. S.	New Haven.
Hotchkiss, S. V.	New Haven.
Jacoby, Mr. and Mrs. Charles	Los Angeles.
Jackson, Dr. W. H.	Boston.
Judge, Mr. and Mrs. James W.	Portland.
Jordan, E. L.	Auburn.
Jordan, Harry J.	Lewiston.
Jordan, E. L.	Auburn.
Johnson, Mr. and Mrs. J.	Winona, Wis.
Kellogg, Mr. and Mrs. William L.	New Bedford.
Kilborn, J. E.	Portland.
Kennard, Mr. and Mrs.	Somerville.
Kennard, Dr. H. D.	Somerville.
Kimball, Robert R.	Boston.
Lyon, Mrs. A. S.	Lowell.
Littleton, W. E.	Philadelphia.
Lockwood, Mr. and Mrs. Rhodes	Boston.
Lockwood, Miss R. N.	Boston.
Lewis, L. B.	Boston.
Lord, Mr. and Mrs. Hartly	Kennebunk.
Lord, Kate M.	Kennebunk.
Leonard, Mrs. H.	Boston.
Leonard, Gwendolin	Boston.
Lee, Mrs. Luther M.	Boston.
Lee, Dr. E. J. and four children	Philadelphia.
Liscomb, Mr. and Mrs. J. F.	Portland.
Liscomb, Mary	Portland.
Malcomson, Alfred S.	New York.
Morton. George D.	Boston.
Mann, G. G.	Boston.
Martin, Jessie	Jacksonville.
Merrill, J. L.	Auburn.
McAllaster, J. G.	Manchester.
Miller, Mr. and Mrs. A. Q.	Auburn.
Mosly, Mr. and Mrs. Herbert	London.
Mills, Mrs. H. F.	Boston.
Mills, Mountford	Springfield.
Marsh, Oliver	Brooklyn.
Meeker, Mrs. A.	Brooklyn.
Meeker, Miss	Brooklyn.
Meeker, Miss T.	Portland.
McMillan, Mr. and Mrs. J. H.	Portland.
McMillan, Miss	Boston.
Merrill, Mrs. J. Warren	Philadelphia.
Matthews, Mr. and Mrs. E. W.	Philadelphia.
Matthews, L. I.	Lewiston.
McGregor, Geo. R. D.	Gardiner.
Morrill, Mr. and Mrs. H. K.	Cincinnati.
Miller, Mr. and Mrs. Louis E.	Cincinnati.
Miller, Mary	Boston.
Matheson, S., Jr.	
Newton, John F., Jr.	Boston.
Osgood, H. S.	Portland.
Osgood, Mr. and Mrs. Charles H.	Lewiston.
Osborn, Mrs. John	Boston.
Page, Mr. and Mrs. Kilby	Boston.
Page, Annie D.	Boston.
Parker, Mrs. Clara Webster	Yonkers.
Parkman, Mr. and Mrs. H. G.	Portland.
Plummer, P. M.	Portland.
Patten, Stanley S.	Portland.

Pitkin, Mr. and Mrs. A. J. — Schenectady.
Pyatt, Mr. and Mrs. R. — New York.
Parker, Mrs. J. A. — Terre Haute.
Parker, Miss — Terre Haute.
Pierce, Lewis — Portland.
Peirce, Mrs. R. B. F. — Indianapolis.
Palmer, Mrs. A. H. — East Orange.
Peables, Elizabeth — Auburn.
Pray, G. H. — Lewiston.

Root, Mr. and Mrs. G. R. — Indianapolis.
Roberts, George I. — New York.
Roberts, Marcia A. — Boston.
Rankin, Mr. and Mrs. E. S. — Kalamazoo.
Ross, Mr. and Mrs. J. — Ipswich.
Ross, Miss A. W. — Ipswich.
Ricker, H. H. — Portland.
Rosengarten, Miss — Philadelphia.
Rosengarten, L. G. — Philadelphia.
Rice, Henrietta D. — Portland.
Rogers, Mrs. George Bliss — New Haven.
Ring, Lucretia — Gardiner.
Riker, Chas. L. — New York.
Rich, Wm. D. — Boston.

Sargent, Mr. and Mrs. W. E. — Hebron.
Sanders, Mr. and Mrs. H. J. — Louisiana.
Stokes, Miss — Jackson.
Stokes, Miss Caroline P. — Jackson.
Schuyler, Mrs. — Jackson.
Sanders, H. M. — Boston.
Staunton, John A. — New York.
Stout, Mr. and Mrs. George E. — Boston.
Salter, Miss — Brookline.
Stearns, James P. — Boston.
Stearns, Miss — Maiden.
Stout, Ada B. — Maiden.
Smith, Mr. and Mrs. E. L. — Auburn.
Small, Dr. and Mrs. W. B. — Lewiston.
Smith, Gardiner — Brooklyn.
Spencer, Mrs. — Brooklyn.
Spencer, Miss — Tarrytown.
Stockham, Mrs. G. T. — New York.
Smith, Mrs. Charles — Philadelphia.
Sayre, Mr. and Mrs. E. H. — Brooklyn.
Schmidt, Miss — Philadelphia.
Schmidt, Miss D. M. — Philadelphia.
Shurtleff, Dr. Arthur W. — Lewiston.
Summerbell, Rev. M. — Lewiston.
Snelling, W. — Roxbury.
Stimson, M. W. — Los Angeles.

Thompson, George F. — New Gloucester.
Towle, Mrs. H. H. — Portland.
Tiott, George — Philadelphia.
Thayer, Mr. and Mrs. F. A. — New York.
Thorne, W. K. — New York.
Thompson, Mrs. W. C. — New York.
Thurston, Mr. and Mrs. H. E. — Mechanic Falls.
Trowbridge, Mrs. S. R. — New Haven.
Trowbridge, Miss C. H. — New Haven.
Tyler, Geo. L. — Gardiner.
Townshend, Mrs. C. H. — New Haven.

Vaughan, Mr. and Mrs. S. E. — Boston.
Vandervoort, the Misses — New York.
Vau Alen, J. J. — Newport.

Weir, Mrs. E. E. — Haverhill.
Wills, B. F. — Belfast.
Witherell, O. D. — Boston.
Worth, Herbert — Brooklyn.
Williams, Mr. and Mrs. J. N. — Boston.
Williams, S. W. — Orange.
Williams, E. C. — Maiden.
Warren, Mr. and Mrs. Jno. C. — Terre Haute.
Wiggin, Mr. and Mrs. H. D. — Medford.
Warner, E. — Troy.
White, George R. — Boston.
Watson, Mr. and Mrs. George — Philadelphia.
Weymouth, Mr. and Mrs. George — Cambridge.
Wade, Mrs. R. B. — New Haven.
West, John — Springfield.
Willett, Mrs. J. K.

MANSION HOUSE.

Bray, Miss M. C. — Salem.
Bagley, Miss — Boston.
Curtis, Mrs. L. J. — Yarmouth.
Ellis, Mrs. Wm. Lee — Macon.
Gilman, Mrs. Arthur — New York.
Gilman, Miss — New York.
Gibson, Mrs. Joseph W. — New York.
Groh, Mr. and Mrs. M. J. — New York.
Hammond, L. H. — Manchester.
Hayes, H. Miller — Portland.
Kimball, the Misses — Brookline.
Keane, Mrs. A. C. — New York.
Keane, Pauline — New York.
Lord, C. F. — Brookline.
Lord, Mrs. Frank N. — Boston.
Lord, N. A. — Oxford.
McLaw, Mrs. M. L. — Macon.
McCrea, Mr. and Mrs. A. L. — New York.
Odler, Howard — New York.
Sondheim, Mr. and Mrs. H. P. — New York.
Sondheim, Pauline — New York.
Skillings, H. I. — Westboro.
Sedgwick. E. — Philadelphia.
Searles, Mr. and Mrs. G. W. — Chelsea.
Smillie, Geo. H. — New York.
Wallace, the Misses — Chicago.
Waldron, C. W. — No. Vassalboro.
Waltman, H. F. — New York.
Whitney, A. G. — Brookline.

Poland Water Leads Them All.

WHY?

BECAUSE.. It was the FIRST KNOWN SOLVENT OF URIC ACID in the system. . . . .

BECAUSE.. It is the most EFFECTIVE ELIMINATOR of Calculi in the Bladder and Kidneys known to-day. . . . .

BECAUSE.. It was the ONLY water IN NEW ENGLAND to receive ANY AWARD at the World's Columbian Exposition, and the only · award of the hundreds exhibited from the WORLD for Purity and Great Medicinal Properties. . . . .

BECAUSE.. The ANNUAL sales exceed the combined sales of all the Saratoga Springs. . . . . .

BECAUSE.. Unprecedented as the success of the past has been it is more promising than ever, showing continued increase. . . . .

OFFICES:

BOSTON:	NEW YORK:	PHILADELPHIA:	CHICAGO:
175 Devonshire Street.	3 Park Place.	Corner 13th and Chestnut St.	Cor. Michigan Ave. and Randolph St.

HIRAM RICKER & SONS, Proprietors.
(INCORPORATED.)

The Hill-Top

POLAND SPRINGS   SO. POLAND, ME.

HARRY C. WILKINSON

THE HILL·TOP

VOL. III.　　　　SUNDAY MORNING, JULY 5, 1896.　　　　No. 1.

The Art Exhibition.

THE Art Gallery is located on the third floor of the Maine State Building, which is divided into six alcoves well lighted by natural light by day and electric in the evening.　A brief sketch of the artists and their works of this year will give a complete idea of the value of this exhibition.　It is well worth the attention of all lovers of art.

Mr. Ed. H. Barnard presents four admirable

works, each being gems in their own way. His "Looking Over the Oaks" is a remarkably fine picture, which will be quickly appreciated. This picture took second prize at the recent Jordan Exhibition in Boston.

William H. Beard is famous the world over as a humanizer of the brute creation in his own cleverly satirical way. He is an exhibitor in the European and American galleries and a member of the National Academy. He has four unframed canvases, fully up to his reputation.

An excellent water-color is the work of William J. Bixbee, representing the original Wentworth Ricker Inn, which in time developed into the Mansion House. This is a very successful work, made from an old sketch.

Walter M. Brackett has three fish pictures which probably cannot be excelled. He is pre-eminently the fish painter, and his work has the stamp of universal favor. His canvases hang in the queen's apartments at Windsor Palace.

A. Loring Brackett is a son of the celebrated trout and salmon artist, and inherits to a large extent his father's talent. His pictures represent game, but of the feathered kind.

Caliga has two pictures in the gallery. One a life-size figure, called "Purity," and the other a small one of delicate coloring, entitled "The Toilet." The larger one is a most ambitious and successful work, and the other admirably calculated to adorn any home.

One of the oldest artists in America, Champney, is known at home and abroad, and his work takes high rank. "A Dessert" is the title of his only picture here, and is in his best style.

Churchill's work is admirable. For splendid effect in light and shade one will seldom find a finer specimen than his "Lamplight." It is an exquisite picture.

Mr. D. D. Coombs is to the manor born, being a Maine man, and an excellent painter of the pastoral. His cattle live and move in green pastures, so naturally does he treat his subjects.

Walter L. Dean, although a young man, has won high honors as an artist, and ranks among the foremost of the marine artists of the day. His three pictures are admirable in color, and true to nature.

Enneking takes a leading position in the world of art. His fame is wide-spread, and his work recognized as worthy of his fame. Attention is called to his "Mt. Washington," which enables one to feel the grandeur of his beautifully rendered subject, and to almost breathe the atmosphere of the breezy summit.

Forcade is a French artist, whose head of a four-year-old hound, called "Penelope," is of the highest order of merit.

Francais, a member of the Legion of Honor, was an artist of high renown during his long life. He was a pupil of Corot, and his little gem called "The Pool" shows the touch of the master.

Abbott Graves is represented by a single picture. His "Load of Poppies" adorns the rotunda, and was his work for the World's Fair. It is a grand result in flower painting.

In Halsall's work we have some of the finest effects. The water is "wet," and one seems almost to hear the roar of the sea. Halsall's marines are standard; one of his large canvases being in the Capitol at Washington.

Hatfield is an artist constantly winning new honors, and fast commanding the attention of the lovers of art. His work is rapidly placing him on an eminence which any artist may be proud of attaining. His "After the Bath" is exquisite in coloring, and admirable in effect.

An admirable work is that of C. W. Hawkins, called "Britain Peasant Woman." It is worthy the old masters.

Hayden has placed three of his most excellent pictures here, one called "Bass River" being a remarkably excellent example of his art. It is well worthy of the highest praise.

Henwood, who contributes quite a number of his paintings, was a pupil of Schenck, and his several works will each attract attention for their excellence. "Ere Awaiting Nightfall" will be found an unusually attractive picture.

There are seven of Helen Knowlton's very interesting small pictures in the gallery. Miss Knowlton is not only a very clever artist, but a writer of rare excellence on art subjects.

Walter F. Lansil is a rich colorist. A Maine man by birth, his genius reflects credit upon his State. His paintings are warm, rich, soft, and delicate in touch, and a constant delight. A beautiful example may be seen in his "Sunset, Harbour of Venice."

Major's work, whether in portraiture, flowers, or landscape, is in all respects excellent. Note his "Lily Pond" and "Estelle," both very superior pictures, distinctive in style and perfect in detail.

Burr Nichols has an exquisite little gem in a "Country Road." Although unframed, it would command attention at any time.

Adelaide Palmer covers one wall with her exquisite flower and fruit pictures. The flower pieces seem to exhale a fragrance, while the fruit would almost appear to render any other unnecessary in a dining-room. Her "Chrysanthemums and Palms" was at the World's Fair.

Paxton's style is peculiarly his own, in the expressions of light and shade, and very unusual effects are produced by him, his pictures taking high rank at all art exhibitions.

Miss Nettie M. Ricker shows an attractive little picture of still-life, quiet in its pretensions but effective, and true in its drawing and coloring. Miss Ricker was a pupil of Abbott Graves.

Schenck is world-famous, and noted as one of the greatest sheep painters of this age. One large and magnificent canvas and two smaller ones are to be seen, and will at once command attention for their true artistic worth.

Shapleigh is represented by a picture of local interest, it being the old red school-house on Ricker Hill. It is a thoroughly excellent work.

E. C. Tarbell has two only of his pictures here, but these are very pleasing and artistic to a degree. We could well wish we might have had more of this superior artist's work.

Nellie Thompson's water-colors are carefully and correctly drawn, and rich in color. Her style is pleasing, and meets with instant approval. She is an artist of rare attainments.

Tompkins' "Hemlocks" is a bit of nature chipped right out of the forest. Its subject renders it of high color, while its effects are startling in their naturalness and rugged beauty.

Triscott easily takes high rank as a water-color artist, five very superior works of his being shown. Whatever subject he treats comes from his brush a charming conception and an admirable result.

Our illustration shows one side only of the gallery, but gives a very excellent idea of its extent. A very complete catalogue is in preparation and will be given free, while the prices of the pictures can be had on application to the librarian.

Space will not permit further mention this week, but the late additions will be noticed next week.

A Photographic Exhibition.

THERE are many visitors to Poland Springs who are interested in photography, and who as amateurs are more or less expert in the art.

It is intended to do everything possible to encourage the development of that talent, and with such a wealth of subjects for fine pictures, on every hand, in the way of wood, lake, and mountain scenery; interesting architectural features of interior and exterior; charming groups; elaborate turnouts, etc., very excellent results should be obtained.

To this end it is proposed to hold, in August, an exhibition of amateur photographic work, in the Art Gallery of the Maine State Building, and to offer some elegant prizes for the best work contributed, two classes being allowed,—adjustable focus and fixed focus.

This will enable all the small cameras of the Kodak, Quad, Hawkeye, and Detective class, a fair field, as against the larger and more expensive ones. It will afford a very interesting recreation, and it is desired that all who take views, of whatever nature, will contribute to make this a success, whether or not they consider themselves sufficiently expert, or well enough equipped to win one of the prizes.

Dark rooms are at the service of the guests in the studio building, and every facility will be afforded them in their favorite amusement.

Progressive Euchre.

AN enjoyable progressive euchre party was given in the amusement room of the Poland Spring House, June 26th. The party consisted of Mr. and Mrs. Baggaley, Mr. Lucas, Mrs. R. M. Field, Mrs. Coleman, Mrs. Stinson, Miss Helen Stinson, Miss Goldthwait, Miss Thomas, Miss Bourne, Mrs. J. B. Sawyer, Mrs. George Baker, Miss Howe, Miss Failes, Mr. Maginnis, and Miss Carpenter. Miss Florence Stinson very kindly kept tally. The greatest number of moves was 13. There were four prizes. The first, a cup and saucer, went to Mrs. J. B. Sawyer. Second, ivory tablet, silver mounting, was won by Miss Bourne. Third, silver glove-buttoner, to Miss Carpenter. Fourth, box of candy, to Miss Howe.

Our Menu.

DURING the season of 1896 THE HILL-TOP will publish each week some recipe. It is intended to give the recipe for a full menu during the summer. Our last edition will contain the menu made out, as it would go into the dining-hall of the Poland Spring House, we having given the recipe for each article on the menu.

RECIPE NO. 1.

Consommé à la Royale.

The first foundation of a soup. The stock prepared for a "Consommé Soup."

Take fifty pounds of beef bones and four beef shins. Cut them up so as to allow the marrow to cook out. Place them in a stock pot, add a garnish of vegetables, such as new carrots, new turnips, a small bunch of parsley, and *never use but one onion.* The vegetables are to be cut fine. To this add spices according to taste. Cover with cold water and cook gently all day. Strain off at night and set away to cool until morning. Then skim off the fat. The next morning take this stock and continue the preparation by the following recipe:

Consommé and clear soup is made by preparing a soup as to strength and flavoring complete, and generally without any thickening ingredients. After removing the fat from the soup stock prepared the night before, strain it through cheesecloth, always into a *copper kettle.* To this add chopped lean raw beef and sliced vegetables and spices. Mix this well with a *wooden paddle* and set on a quick fire and let it come to a boil. After this remove it to one side and let it simmer slowly three hours. Then it will strain clear and transparent through a jelly bag or a fine cloth.

We are now ready for Consommé à la Royale. This is a clear, light-brown soup, containing *egg custard.* This garnish is made by mixing a very little broth with some eggs, as if for an omelet. Take five yolks and one whole egg. Cook it in a buttered earthen mould, set into a copper sauce pan of boiling water. If subjected to too much heat and rapid boiling, the contents become spongy and cannot be cut as desired. Therefore it should cook slowly. When done, the custard is turned out on to a napkin and cooled, and then cut diamond-wise and a few of these pieces served with each order.

The changes of color are made in the custard by use of yolks of eggs for yellow, whites of eggs for white. For red, color the *white custard* with *beet juice,* and for green, color it with spinach or parsley juice.

Fifty pounds of beef and twenty pounds of shins will prepare stock for consommé soup for one hundred people.

NOTE.—The Consommé à la Royale, which THE HILL-TOP has given the recipe for, will be served this noon at the Poland Spring House and Mansion House.

RECIPE NO. 2.

Purée de Volaille à la Reine.

Prepare a good strong stock from fowl. Remove fat and strain into soup kettle. Add pounded chicken and rice. Set on a hot fire until it comes to a boil, and then set it one side and let it cook slowly for two hours. Remove from fire and add cream and butter mixed well, and pass through a purée sieve. Then add sherry wine, yolks of eggs, *roux* and season to taste.

To prepare *roux* for white soup: Put butter into a sauce-pan; add flour until it becomes thick. Draw off one gallon of the strong stock made from the fowl. Mix butter, flour, and stock slowly together, and beat with a wire whip until it becomes smooth and creamy. Then it is ready to thicken the soup.

Sixty pounds of fowl will make stock for a Purée de Volaille à la Reine for one hundred people.

The Raymond Excursion.

THE following ladies and gentlemen arrived Tuesday, to remain over Sunday. They comprise a delightful party of Raymond pleasure seekers: Mrs. Z. B. Dana, Mrs. D. W. Foster, Miss H. W. Foster, Miss S. E. Foster, Mrs. Samuel Harrington, and Mr. and Mrs. J. P. C. Marshall, of Boston; Miss Alia Somes and Geo. H. Somes, of Brookline; Mrs. Lizzie A. Bowker and Miss Anna L. Kendall, of Worcester; Miss Alice S. Barton of Newton; Mr. and Mrs. Jas. Edwards of Quincy; Mrs. Geo. M. Haskell, and Mr. and Mrs. John T. Tillinghast, of New Bedford; Mr. and Mrs. Richard T. Howes of Cambridgeport; Mrs. O. E. Lewis and Miss Nellie Lewis, of Winthrop; Mr. and Mrs. Geo. H. Morrill of Norwood; Miss Anna H. Parsons, and Mrs. A. M. Parsons, of Falkington, Pa.; Mrs. Frank Patch of Lynn; and all under the special guidance of Mr. Geo. H. Cross of Boston.

Mr. and Mrs. D. H. Sweetser, Mrs. H. F. Tapley, Mr. and Mrs. C. O. Floyd, Mrs. A. L. Floyd, Miss Mary Townsend, and Miss Mary L. Floyd, had a delightful ride on the brake, through the Gloucester woods and around Sabbath-day Lake.

Poland Springs Library.

THE following is a list of the books contributed to the library since the close of last season, making the present number 1,160 volumes.

FROM MRS. EDWARD E. CLARK.

Whispering Pine Series, by Elijah Kellogg,	6 vols.
Margery, by Georg Ebers,	2 vols.
An Egyptian Princess, by Georg Ebers,	2 vols.
Uarda, by Georg Ebers,	2 vols.
Homo Sum, by Georg Ebers,	1 vol.
The Bride of the Nile, by Georg Ebers,	2 vols.
Joshua, by Georg Ebers,	1 vol.
Jimmy Boy, by Sophie May,	1 vol.
Wee Lucy, by Sophie May,	1 vol.
Brother Against Brother, by Oliver Optic,	1 vol.
In the Saddle, by Oliver Optic,	1 vol.
Two Years on the Alabama, by Arthur Sinclair,	1 vol.
voyage in a Paper Canoe, by N. H. Bishop,	1 vol.
The Winning of the West, by Theodore Roosevelt,	3 vols.
Watch-Fires of '76, by Samuel Adams Drake,	1 vol.
Standish of Standish, by Jane G. Austin,	1 vol.
Betty Alden, by Jane G. Austin,	1 vol.
A Nameless Nobleman, by Jane G. Austin,	1 vol.
Life, Letters, and Journals of George Ticknor,	2 vols.
Hypatia, by Charles Kingsley,	2 vols.
Three Heroines of New England Romance, by Harriet Prescott Spofford,	1 vol.
Dissolving Views in the History of Judaism, by Rabbi Solomon Schindler,	1 vol.
On the Lake of Lucerne, by Beatrice Whitby,	1 vol.
Sheridan's Comedies, Ed. by Brander Matthews,	1 vol.
A Collection of Letters of Thackeray,	1 vol.
Personal Memoirs of U. S. Grant,	2 vols.
Appleton's Journal,	10 vols.
Galaxy,	12 vols.
	—
	62 vols.

FROM MRS. W. PETERSON.

Half-Hours with Best Authors, by Knight,	6 vols.
Self-Help; Character; Duty; Thrift, by Smiles,	4 vols.
George Eliot's Works,	8 vols.
Broken Chords, by Mrs. George McClellan,	1 vol.
Boots and Saddles, by James H. Stevenson,	1 vol.
Napoleon III., by Pierre de Lano,	1 vol.
Grandpa's Darlings, by Pansy,	1 vol.
Carrots, by Mrs. Molesworth,	1 vol.
Once Upon a Time,	1 vol.
Elsie, series by Martha Finley,	21 vols.
	—
	45 vols.

FROM HON. WILLIAM P. FRYE.

Government Works,	29 vols.

FROM MRS. ORLANDO TOMPKINS.

Bradley's Atlas of the World,	1 vol.
Lippincott's Biographical Dictionary,	1 vol.
Longfellow's Complete Works,	11 vols.
	—
	13 vols.

FROM GEORGE B. GREER.

Popular Science Monthly,	32 vols.

FROM ROBERT S. GARDINER.

Japan as We Saw It,	1 vol.

FROM MRS. AMOS R. LITTLE.

A Lady of Quality,	1 vol.

FROM MR. R. M. FIELD.

Charles Reade's Works,	16 vols.
W. D. Howells's Works,	5 vols.
F. Marion Crawford's Works,	6 vols.
Bourrienne's Memoirs of Napoleon,	4 vols.
	—
	31 vols.

FROM MRS. HENRY F. TAPLEY.

The Stickit Minister, by Crockett,	1 vol.

FROM GEN. AUGUSTUS P. MARTIN.

Official Records of the War of the Rebellion,	100 vols.
And a great number of maps.	

A Lesson in Geography.

MARCIA D. JORDAN.

"A lesson in geography,
    With all the states to bound!"
My boys grew sober in a trice,
    And shook their heads and frowned,—
And this was in the nursery,
    Where only smiles are found.

Then suddenly up jumped Boy Blue,—
    Youngest of all is he,—
And stood erect beside my chair.
    "Mamma," he said, "bound me!"
And all the other lads looked up
    With faces full of glee.

I gravely touched his curly head:
    "North by a little pate
That's mixed in mental 'rithmetic
    And can't get fractions straight,
That never knows what time it is,
    Nor where are books or slate.

"South by two feet—two restless feet—
    That never tire of play,
Yet always gladly run abroad
    (Although a holiday)
On others' errands willingly
    In most obliging way.

"East by a pocket stuffed and crammed
    With, O so many things!
With tops and toys and bits of wood,
    And pennies, knives, and strings,
And by a little fist that lacks
    The glow that water brings.

"West by the same; and well explored
    The pocket by the fist;
The capital, two rosy lips
    All ready to be kissed.
And, darling, now I've bounded you,
    Your class may be dismissed."

[CONTRIBUTED.]

PROFESSOR of Psychology (trying to illustrate a coincidence)—Now, Mr. P., suppose you were to shake dice and threw five aces. What would you think of that?

P.—Why, Professor, I shouldn't think much about that.

Prof.—Ah! Your usual amount of thought! Well, suppose you should again throw five aces?

P.—Nothing so very strange in that.

Prof.—But if you should throw five aces a third time?

P.—Well, in that case, I should think the dice were loaded.

(Professor gives up in despair).

FRANK CARLOS GRIFFITH, } EDITORS.
NETTIE M. RICKER,

PUBLISHED EVERY SUNDAY MORNING DURING THE MONTHS
OF JULY, AUGUST, AND SEPTEMBER, IN THE INTERESTS OF

POLAND SPRINGS AND ITS VISITORS.

All contributions relative to the guests of Poland Springs
will be thankfully received.

To insure publication, all communications should reach the
editors not later than Wednesday preceding day of issue.

All parties desiring rates for advertising in the HILL-TOP
should write the editors for same.

The subscription price of the HILL-TOP is $1.00 for the
season, post-paid. Single copies will be mailed at 10c. each.

Address,
        EDITORS "HILL-TOP,"
            Poland Spring House,
                South Poland, Maine.

PRINTED AT JOURNAL OFFICE, LEWISTON.

Sunday, July 5, 1896.

Editorial.

THE story of the communistic tramp who wished all the money of the country called in and equally divided, and on being told that it would speedily return to the coffers of the thrifty, the economical, or the crafty; without being disturbed in the least by this possibility, said he would have it "all called in again," and another division made,—leads us to the reflection as to what has become of our regular division daily of the hours.

Each day all the time is "called in" and each one is given an equal share. Some squander it recklessly, while others husband it to advantage, but whether wasted or made profitable it is all "called in again" and a new trial given us.

Look at us to-day. We are vain enough to believe that we look better, weigh more, and present an improved appearance for the daily distribution. We have a new overcoat of artistic design, whereas last season we had none; our title may be read clearer; our advertising columns have become plethoric; our readers are more numerous; our surroundings present even more attractions than ever; the environments pertaining to Art and Literature are vastly enhanced; success perches upon our banner, and we are not going to shake the staff.

All this comes from the encouragement of the previous year, so it remains for you to make a good use of your daily share of the "called in" moments, by aiding THE HILL-TOP with your favor, your encouragement, and your smile.

Why Not?

[CONTRIBUTED.]

SMALL Boy (who has strayed into the barber shop, to guest who has complained of having to be shaved every day)—What would you do if you had whiskers way down on your vest?

Guest—Young man, I'd go into the Poland Water business.

Mexican Drawn Work.

A LADY living in Texas, on the Mexican border, sends to Mrs. Hiram W. Ricker a large variety of this material of the finest and most superior quality in the art of needle-work. This is the *genuine*, and of great beauty. Mrs. Ricker will be pleased to show the work to all interested, at their cottage, and to dispose of the same at very reasonable rates.

Mr. and Mrs. Coleman were early comers and met with hearty greetings.

Mr. and Mrs. R. M. Field are as regular as the seasons. May they long continue to favor the fair land of Poland.

Mr. and Mrs. L. Hurlbut were so delighted with their surroundings a year ago, we are highly favored by their early return.

THE HILL-TOP's compliments to Mr. and Mrs. Bourne and Miss Bourne, and hopes they may yet add many years to their number at Poland Springs.

It was a fine catch of black bass, made by Miss Florence Stinson and Mr. S. B. Stinson, from the upper lake. There were six of them, weighing 2¼ lbs. each,—and they were gone but two hours.

Three salmon, the largest weighing about 40 lbs., were caught in the Moisie river in Canada, by Mr. Amos R. Little, and forwarded with his compliments to the hotels. The largest was handsomely displayed by the *chef*, Mr. Sparrow, upon the radiator, garnished elaborately with vegetable roses, lettuce, lemons, frills and other fancy devices.

Our Fourth of July.

OUR entire force of lightning reporters, stenographers, editors, linotypes, and octuple perfecting presses, would have been set at work yesterday, in order to give a full report of the celebration of the great and glorious Fourth, only that event would insist upon coming in on Saturday this year, and hence our entire force were powerless to accomplish this feat.

In honor of the occasion, it was recommended to have all the bells ring out the incoming of the day, but various reasons conspired to prevent its accomplishment, much to our regret, and we know it will be a sad loss to the enjoyment of the sleeping guests, who have been accustomed to this pastime.

In the first place, a few of the younger guests objected to the early disturbance of the ozone in this clangourous manner, doubtless preferring the more sonorous fish-horn in theirs, or the sanguinary colored cracker.

Next it was argued that too emphatic clanging of the metal might place another cracked specimen of the Bell of Liberty upon an already overstocked market, and in time prove a dangerous rival to the genuine all-wool, copper-bottom, yard-wide, Philadelphia article, and in deference to the guests from that portion of Pennsylvania, it was deemed not quite business-like, or hospitable.

Another objection arose, inasmuch as it might serve to loosen the tongues, so that curfew could not ring to-night; and consider for one moment the havoc a few loose tongues could create, if once set at Liberty. We should be sorry for Liberty. Perhaps the most satisfactory reason of all was—that, in short, we have no bells to ring. If that reason had been advanced first, our space writer would not have made so much money on this article.

In concluding this vivid and graphic description of our Poland Hill celebration, we wish to say, that it has been the boast of our rival contemporaries that they have been able to give the critique of a dramatic or musical performance written hazardously in advance, of a performance which later failed to materialize, and as we have accomplished the unheard-of feat of writing up this monster celebration, and having the entire paper printed hours before the day arrives, our mental dread now is that the second advent theory *may* eventuate first, and the great and glorious not arrive on schedule time, which would leave us,—well, feeling anything but elated by our perspiring haste.

It is reported that General Weyler is watching closely every act of General Lee in Cuba. In fact Weyler is on the lee watch.

General Martin's War Library.

It may not be generally known that the government some years ago began the collection and publication of every report, telegram, letter, or order relating to the late war between the states, gathered from both sides, these to be complete and authentic, without comment of any kind.

These valuable records were to be accompanied by plates of maps, illustrating every phase of the great battles, as well as the minor skirmishes.

This work is nearly completed, and is now to the 101st volume, with 35 portfolios of maps.

Gen. A. P. Martin, of Boston, has generously contributed his entire set of this great work to the Library, where it will be most highly appreciated. It is an invaluable work, and the thanks of all interested ones are due to the General for his kindness.

Children's Column.

"Not a thing that we do, nor a word that we say,
Should injure another in jest or in play."

Anecdote of Meissonier.

AN interesting story is told about the famous French artist, Meissonier, and a noted physician living at Versailles.

Meissonier had a little black dog that he was very fond of. He was the pet of his studio and always with his master. One day while Meissonier had him out for a bit of fresh air, a carriage accidentally drove over him and broke his leg. Meissonier called a cab, hurried to a telegraph office, and sent a telegram to his friend, the physician at Versailles. It read: "Come at once. I am in trouble. Bring medicine and instruments."

The physician received the telegram and hastened to Paris, fearing that Meissonier was very ill. He went at once to his studio and found him sitting with a pillow in his lap and the dog stretched upon it. He set the dog's leg, bandaged it, and after chatting with his dear friend, returned home.

Now this physician was building a beautiful chateau at Versailles. When nearly completed he sent a telegram to Meissonier. It read: "Come at once. I am in trouble. Bring paint and brushes."

The very next train found Meissonier, with his little black dog, paint box and brushes, comfortably seated and bound for Versailles. When he arrived at his friend's the physician smiled and said, "There is a door and I wish you to paint a picture on it."

Meissonier painted the picture, and to-day the door is of more value than the whole house.

Five Little Chickens.

Said the first little chicken
With a queer little squirm,
"Oh, I wish I could find
A fat little worm!"

Said the next little chicken
With an odd little shrug,
"Oh, I wish I could find
A fat little bug!"

Said the third little chicken
With a sharp little squeal,
"Oh, I wish I could find
Some nice yellow meal!"

Said the fourth little chicken
With a small sigh of grief,
"Oh, I wish I could find
A green little leaf!"

Said the fifth little chicken
With a faint little moan,
"Oh, I wish I could find
A wee gravel stone!"

"Now, see here," said the mother,
From the green garden patch,
"If you want any breakfast
You just come and scratch."

Our advertisers in Lewiston and Portland are the best in their respective business, and may be relied upon.

The removal of the stone wall between the grove and the Mansion House will be a loss to the weary stroller, on an evening walk.

Hinds' Honey and Almond Cream at the news stand, or it will be sent by mail. It has a national reputation, and has made a fortune for its inventor.

A very elegant catalogue of the pictures in the Maine State Building is in preparation, and has only been delayed on account of the non-arrival of important works. The work is now in progress and will soon be completed.

Benjamin Champney.

THIS artist is represented in the Poland Springs Gallery this year by a still-life picture, called "A Dessert," which is an admirable work, and one which would be an excellent adornment to any dining-room.

Mr. Champney was born in New Ipswich, N. H., November 20, 1817, and in early life was a lithographer. In 1841 he went to Paris, and studied the art of the masters, exhibiting in the Salons of '44 and of '45, remaining abroad five years. He also made subsequent visits to Europe. He was one of the incorporators of the Boston Art Club.

Mr. Champney's work is of a high order, and is recognized as such in all the principal art exhibitions. During each summer he has a studio at North Conway, while in the winter he may be found in Boston. His earlier work was devoted largely to White Mountain scenery, but of late years he has paid more attention to the subject of flowers and fruit, in which he has been very successful.

Some new books have been received, which will receive notice in the next issue.

Thistles.

A rural swain in announcing his approaching nuptials in the town paper, wrote as follows: "Friends and relatives of the family are invited to attend. Kindly omit rice, as it disagrees with the bride."

A pair of lovers were struck by lightning, while kissing, in Tibbetts brook lane. The man was instantly killed, while the woman was only stunned. Does this indicate that the woman can stand the most kissing or the most lightning?

Debs says that strikes are useless, and Debs ought to know. He seems to have been a great success as a failure at that exercise.

On account of famine in China, rice is selling at 8 to 9 cents a pound and scarce; while girls are a drug in the market, and selling at from $3 to $30 apiece. Probably the $3 article is not China, only plain ordinary every-day crockery, possibly "seconds" at that.

The Spanish authorities think the claims of Americans for damages in Cuba are excessive. Probably due to in-cuba-tion.

Tid=Bits.

Fizz-Boom.

Good morning.

Subscribe now.

Delighted, I'm sure.

Welcome to old friends.

It is a pleasure to add new ones.

Which is it at the Spring, he or his brother?

Mr. Maginnis's pleasant features are again observed. Good.

Mr. and Mrs. Zeigler found a hearty welcome awaiting them, on their return.

Mr. and Mrs. Sawyer have been summered and wintered. They stood the test.

Mrs. Pettee is staunch in her loyalty to Poland Springs. She is here when THE HILL-TOP sleeps.

Mr. and Mrs. Thomas of Portland made a brief visit, but they will return, we are happy to say.

. Mrs. M. B. Hoffman has entered upon her eighth season. May it yet reach many times eight.

Mrs. Amos R. Little early seeks relief from the heat of Philadelphia. No one more welcome than she.

Many most interesting and charming guests left with June. THE HILL-TOP'S best wishes go with them.

E. B. Mallet, Jr., of Freeport, has presented the two magnificent century plants which grace the north lawn.

It is pleasant to see pleasant faces, and so the Carpenters of Providence are welcome friends to THE HILL-TOP.

The departure of many interesting guests, who were here during June, is to be regretted. May they all come again.

Mr. and Mrs. Henwood have made many friends during their stay. Mrs. Henwood's medallions are much admired.

Now is the time to subscribe. One dollar for the season, and the paper mailed free of postage to any address in the United States.

Mrs. S. B. Hubbard finds Jacksonville delightful in winter, but Poland finds Mrs. Hubbard equally charming in summer.

The thoroughly charming family, the Stinsons of Philadelphia, missed Poland last year, and Poland mourned; but to-day they are thrice welcome.

Miss Helen Thomas, of Portland, has joined Mr. and Mrs. Thomas, and adds another to the group of remarkably fine-looking young ladies here this summer.

Mrs. Orlando Tompkins returns to the health-giving atmosphere of Poland. May it give her added years of health and happiness.

Get all your Huyler's candies and whist prizes at the news stand. You are sure to get the best, as well as prompt and polite attention.

We are requested to ask that the visitors to the Maine State Building kindly converse in low tones, so that readers be not disturbed.

It is pleasant to greet old friends like Mr. and Mrs. Salter. Mr. Salter has the distinguished honor of having taken out the first book ever taken from the library.

Mrs J. Reed Whipple, of Boston, arrived early in the week. Mr. Whipple is the well-known proprietor of the Parker House, Young's Hotel, and the new Hotel Touraine.

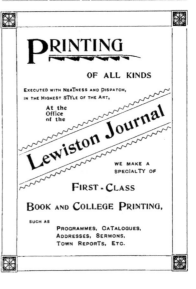

Arrivals.

POLAND SPRING HOUSE.

JUNE 1 TO JULY 1, 1896.

Allen, Miss	Tamworth.
Andrews, Ruth	Bethel.
Armstrong, Geo. D.	Lewiston.
Armstrong, B. W.	Lewiston.
Armstrong, E. D.	Lewiston.
Boothbay, W. A. R.	Waterville.
Bosworth, Mr. and Mrs. J. S.	New York.
Boothbay, Mr. and Mrs. F. E.	Portland.
Bernard, Mr. and Mrs. Albert	Boston.
Blakey, J. M.	Boston.
Blake, Mrs. E. H.	Bangor.
Brown, Mr. and Mrs. Leroy S.	Cambridge.
Brewster, Mr. and Mrs. Benj.	Jamaica Plains.
Baker, Mr. and Mrs. Geo. F.	Hyannis.
Briggs, Mrs. F. H.	Auburn.
Bowers, E. T.	Lewiston.
Bourne, Mr. and Mrs. Geo. T.	New York.
Bourne, Miss	New York.
Brown, Mrs. Wm. T.	New York.
Barker, W. P.	Boston.
Bichot, Mr. and Mrs. H. P.	Quebec.
Burke, Mrs. Wm. A.	Lowell.
Baldwin, T. W.	Orange, N. J.
Bigelow, Wm. A.	New York.
Brown, Freeman M.	N. Bridgton.
Baggaly, Mr. and Mrs. Ralph	Pittsburg.
Bolster, Mr. and Mrs. C. H.	Chicago.
Bolster, Grace N.	Chicago.
Bailey, Geo. H.	Portland.
Bailey, Mrs. Chas.	Portland.
Bonney, C. W.	Lewiston.
Baker, Mrs. H. M.	New York.
Baker, Miss C. V.	New York.
Cleaves, Henry B.	Portland.
Coleman, Mr. and Mrs. Geo. W.	Boston.
Clark, E. W.	Portland.
Culver, Andrew R.	Brooklyn.
Cushman, Mrs. C. L.	Auburn.
Chester, W. R.	Brookline.
Carpenter, Mr. and Mrs. F. W.	Providence.
Carpenter, Miss Hannah	Providence.
Campbell, Mr. and Mrs. E. P.	New York.
Crowell, Geo. G.	Philadelphia.
Clark, Mr. and Mrs. J. T.	Lewiston.
Clark, Arthur W.	Deering.
Chapman, E. E.	Boston.
Cox, E. W.	Portland.
Carpenter, Miss	Crawford House.
Cox, Mr. and Mrs. Henry P.	Portland.
Cutler, Geo. T.	Boston.
Condon, J. W.	Lewiston.
Caldwell, Mr. and Mrs. J. C.	New York.
Chillis, Mrs. M. J.	Portland.
Caldwell, E. A.	Boston.
Carlile, Mr. and Mrs. W. B.	New York.
Carr, Mr. and Mrs. Geo. W.	Providence.
Dana, Mr. and Mrs. Geo. S.	Boston.
Depew, Mr. and Mrs. E. D.	New York.
Dreyfus, Mr. and Mrs. Jacob	Boston.
Declow, Mrs. R. S.	Boston.
Dickson, W. J.	Salem.
Dennett, L. D.	Saco.
Dingley, Edith	Lewiston.
Dingley, Florence	Auburn.
Dingley, Anna L.	Auburn.
Driscoll, Rev. J. T.	Boston.
Driscoll, Francis	Albany.
Decker, Grace B.	Rumford Falls.
Daily, Carl	York, Pa.
Doran, D.	New York.
Douglass, Mrs. Albert, Jr.	New York.

Eddy, Jesse L. and family	New York.
Ewing, Miss	New York.
Emerson, Chas. A.	Charleston.
Field, Mr. and Mrs. R. M.	Boston.
Fenn, A. H.	Waterbury.
Fisk, Alex. G.	Boston.
Frost, W. P.	Lewiston.
Faile, Miss A. L.	New York.
Faile, Thos. H.	New York.
Farwell, E.	Boston.
Faguy, P.	Quebec.
French, G. H.	No. Attleboro.
French, J. M.	Boston.
Furme, L. Marie D.	Westfield, Mass.
Farmer, J. P.	Sioux Rapids.
French, Geo. B.	Boston.
Fletcher, Miss	Boston.
Griffith, Daniel J.	New York.
Glavin, Mr. and Mrs. W. L.	Boston.
Goldthwait, John	Boston.
Goldthwait, Miss E. B.	Boston.
Gardiner, Mr. and Mrs. Robert S.	Boston.
Gardiner, Miss	Boston.
Giraud, Joseph	New York.
Gagnon, C. O.	Quebec.
Griffin, C. C.	Haverhill.
Hunt, Mr. and Mrs. Horace	New York.
Hilbron, Mrs.	New York.
Hobart, Mrs. F. A.	So. Braintree.
Hinckley, Mrs. Daniel	Bangor.
Harvey, Mrs. Frederic	Bangor.
Hall, E. B.	Boston.
Hubbard, Mrs. S. B.	Jacksonville.
Hallow, Mrs. J. M.	Woburn.
Howe, L. B.	Rochester, N. Y.
Hurlburt, Mr. and Mrs. L.	Brooklyn.
Howe, Mrs. Henry C.	Lowell.
Howe, Miss	Lowell.
Hall, Blakeley	New York.
Hoffman, Mrs. M. B.	New York.
Henwood, Mr. and Mrs. F. D.	Boston.
Hyneman, Bernard	Boston.
Howard, Mrs. C. G.	Brooklyn.
Halle, Mr. and Mrs. M.	Cleveland.
Halle, E. S.	Cleveland.
Hough, C. T.	Boston.
Hersey, E. C.	Portland.
Howe, Rev. G. M.	Lewiston.
Haynes, Geo. H.	Portland.
Howe, Mr. and Mrs. J. F.	Auburn.
Henderson, Mr. and Mrs. J. B.	Washington.
Henderson, J. B., Jr.	Washington.
Harrington, John M.	Lewiston.
Harris, A. H.	Montreal.
Hollinshead, H. B.	Montreal.
Hazen, Mr. and Mrs. J. W.	Boston.
James, Mrs. Julien	Washington.
James, Miss	Cincinnati.
Kinney, Wm. C.	New York.
Kendall, Dr. and Mrs. W. G.	Boston.
Kuntz, John, M.D.	Washington.
Knapp, Geo. W.	Worcester.
Koon, Mr. and Mrs. M. B.	Minneapolis.
King, Mrs. F. H.	Portland.
Leighton, Scott	Boston.
Livermore, A. S.	Boston.
Lucas, John	Philadelphia.
Lucas, John T.	Philadelphia.
Little, Mrs. Amos R.	Philadelphia.
Lane, Eustace	Saco.
Laird, Jas. D.	San Francisco.
Lawrence, S. M.	New York.
Ludlum, David S.	New York.
Loomis, Miss H. N.	Boston.
Loomis, Miss M. L.	Boston.
Leicty, Mr. and Mrs. J. S.	Brookline.
Little, Bessie	New York.
Lewis, C. A.	Freeport.

New Orleans.	Rice, Miss S. V.	Boston.
New Orleans.	Rust, Mr. and Mrs. Wm. A.	Boston.
New Orleans.	Roche, Thos.	Boston.
New Orleans.	Roth, Samuel D.	Boston.
New Orleans.	Richardson, Mrs. Frank T.	Boston.
New Orleans.	Rappard, R. R.	Savannah.
New Orleans.	Ridlon, Mr. and Mrs. C. H.	Portland.
Chicago.	Robinson, Mr. and Mrs. J. F.	Lewiston.
Beverly Farms.	Robinson, Miss	Lewiston.
New York.	Rollins, Mr. and Mrs. H. G.	Portland.
Brooklyn.	Rice, John O.	Portland.
New York.	Sawyer, Mr. and Mrs. J. B.	Dover.
Washington.	Stokes, Miss	New York.
Washington.	Stokes, Caroline Phelps	New York.
Boston.	Sanborn, Mr. and Mrs. D. W.	Boston.
Boston.	Shepherd, Mr. and Mrs. H. S.	Rockport.
Hyannis.	Shurtleff, Mrs. E. M.	Lewiston.
Pittsburg.	Stinson, Mr. and Mrs. S. B.	Philadelphia.
Buffalo.	Stinson, Miss Helen B.	Philadelphia.
New York.	Stinson, Miss Florence S.	Philadelphia.
New York.	Staples, Mrs. A. G.	Lewiston.
Boston.	Seaver, Chandler	W. Newton.
Auburn.	Swett, E. A.	Portland.
New York.	Scott, Mrs. R. B.	Washington.
Portland.	Scott, W. O. U.	Washington.
Chicago.	Small, Dr. W. B.	Lewiston.
Boston.	Scott, Mr. and Mrs. W. M.	Boston.
Portland.	Strauss, Benj.	Boston.
New York.	Sawyer, C. H.	Saco.
Freeport.	Saxton, Rufus, U. S. A.	Washington.
Portland.	Strawbridge, J. C.	Philadelphia.
New Orleans.	Soule, Mrs. Wm. H.	Portland.
Kentucky.	Soule, Mrs. Howard	Portland.
Boston.	Shaw, Mr. and Mrs. Thos. P.	Portland.
Boston.	Sargent, Wm. W.	Worcester.
Portland.	Stevenson, Mr. and Mrs. David	Portland.
New Orleans.	Saxton, Mrs. Rufus	Washington.
Brookline.	Sloan, A. T.	Salem.
Boston.	Swift, Dr. and Mrs. E. P.	Pleasantville, N. Y.
Washington.	Smart, Mrs. Emely	Portland.
	Salter, Mr. and Mrs. A. S.	Washington.
Boston.	Savage, Mr. and Mrs. S. H.	Boston.
Portland.		
	Treat, Mr. and Mrs. H. W.	Chicago.
Yarmouth.	Tracy, W. A.	Boston.
Yarmouth.	Tidd, Miss Alice S.	Woburn.
Providence.	Talbot, A. L.	Lewiston.
Providence.	True, P. A.	Portland.
	Tabor, J. W.	Portland.
New York.	Thomas, Mr. and Mrs. Elias	Portland.
Saco.	Tompkins, Mrs. Orlando	Boston.
Providence.	Thomas, Miss Helen	Portland.
Portland.	Thomas, E., Jr.	Portland.
Lisbon Falls.	Turnbull, Miss M. A.	Minneapolis.
Salem.	Turnbull, Miss Rose	Minneapolis.
New York.	Thomas, Mr. and Mrs. Frank R.	Boston.
New York.	Taylor, Mr. and Mrs. F. E.	Brooklyn.
New York.		
Boston.	Verrill, Mr. and Mrs. A. E.	Auburn.
Bangor.	Voorhees, Mr. and Mrs. John H.	Brooklyn.
Portland.	Voorhees, Miss Jessie	Brooklyn.
Lewiston.		
Lewiston.	Winslow, Mr. and Mrs. E. B.	Portland.
Lewiston.	Willis, Mr. and Mrs. Geo. D.	Boston.
Lewiston.	Williams, Mr. and Mrs. Fred	Somerville.
Lewiston.	Winslow, J. S.	Portland.
Brooklyn.	Wedgwood, Dr. M. C.	Lewiston.
Bath.	Wolfenden, J. W.	No. Attleboro.
New York.	Williams, Geo. W.	Salem.
New York.	Wyman, J. H.	New York.
Brooklyn.	Williams, Miss L. E.	New York.
Boston.	Weiner, E. A.	Lebanon, Pa.
	Weiner, Mrs. Geo. R.	Lebanon, Pa.
Portland.	Wescott, Dr. Geo. F.	Portland.
Portland.	West, Gen. and Mrs.	Boston.
Lewiston.	Wescott, Mr. and Mrs. Geo. P.	Portland.
Boston.	Whitmore, Winslow	Portland.
Franklin, Mass.	Winslow, Howard	Portland.
Franklin, Mass.	Welch, Jas. A.	Lewiston.
Boston.	Walker, Mr. and Mrs. Chas. T.	Lewiston.
Boston.	Wallace, Rev. Thos. H.	Lewiston.

Woodbury, Mr. and Mrs. John P. Boston.
Whipple, Mrs. J. Reed Boston.
Ziegler, Mr. and Mrs. Harry D. Philadelphia.
Ziegler, Miss C. F. Philadelphia.

MANSION HOUSE.
JUNE 1 TO JULY 2.

Barbour, E. D. Boston.
Burrows, Mr. and Mrs. Wm. H. Malden.
Calkin, Geo. F. St. John, N. B.
Carter, John W. Portland.
Cousens, Mr. and Mrs. L. M. Portland.
Cousens, W. T. Portland.
Cousens, L. A. Portland.
Clapp, A. W. Lynn.
Caldwell, Mr. and Mrs. J. C. New York.
Daly, Miss M. F. Chelsea.
Dewey, D. R. No. Adams.
Eastman, Mr. and Mrs. Geo. W. Malden.
Foster, C. Portland.
Hovey, Mrs. James Chelsea.
Kimball, T. F. Boston.
Lyman, Mr. and Mrs. H. D. New York.
Marsh, Robert P. Springfield.
Plaisted, H. M. Bangor.
Stevens, Mrs. F. E. New York.
Sweetser, Mr. and Mrs. D. H. Lynn.
Stearns, Wm. F. Boston.
Stearns, Mrs. Boston.
Turner, Mrs. John B. Boston.
Townsend, Mary A. Lynn.
Tapley, Mr. and Mrs. Henry F. Lynn.
Thurston, Mrs. Geo. F. Portland.
Thurston, Margaret G. Portland.
Thurston, Theodore K. Portland.
Thurston, Clara A. Portland.
Vivian, May New York.
Williams, Geo. H. New York.

Martin Borque and Sadie O'Brien were very indignant, because their "wedding bells could not ring out," he having a duplicate wife and an abundance of children living. Shocking. What are we drifting "at?"

A distinguished arrival from Italy attracted much attention. Paderewski could hardly have excited more. Music is highly appreciated here, and this son of Naples was an expert organist. He was attended by his valet, Sig. A. Simian, a sometime resident of Africa, and an expert kopper katcher.

A man experienced in the care of invalids; an extensive traveller, not only all over this country, but frequently in Europe; gentle, intelligent, well-read, and conversant with people and places, desires an opportunity to accompany an elderly invalid gentleman or lady in the capacity of companion. He can be highly recommended. Information may be had from the Librarian, Maine State Building.

THE NEW MOUNT PLEASANT HOUSE,

In the Heart of the White Mountains.

Through Parlor Cars from New York, Boston, and Portland, also from Burlington, Montreal, and Quebec.

The Hotel faces the Grandest Display of Mountain Peaks in America east of the Rocky Mountains. It is lighted throughout by electricity, thoroughly heated by steam, and has an abundance of private and public baths. Its orchestra is made up largely from the Boston Symphony Orchestra. Its table is unsurpassed. Absolutely pure water from an artesian well, 400 feet in solid rock.

IT IS THE NEAREST HOTEL TO MT. WASHINGTON, AND THE TRAIN FOR THE SUMMIT STARTS FROM A STATION ON THE HOTEL GROUNDS.

All Trains, Maine Central Railroad, from Portland to Burlington, Montreal, Quebec, and Lake Champlain stop at the platform close to the House.

Leave Portland 8.45 A.M., arrive Mt. Pleasant House, 12.45 P.M. O
  "   "   1.25 P.M.,   "   "   "   "   5.05 P.M. O
  "   "   8.15 P.M.,   "   "   "   "   11.25 P.M. O

POST, TELEGRAPH, AND TICKET OFFICE IN THE HOTEL.

ANDERSON & PRICE, of the Hotel Ormond of Florida, Managers.

Address by wire or mail, "Mount Pleasant House, N. H."

JOHN O. RICE,

PROFESSIONAL ACCOUNTANT AND AUDITOR

Expert Examinations made for Banks, Corporations, Estates, or Mercantile Houses, and general accountant work solicited. P. O. Box 1,639.

Office, Room 4, Centennial Building, 93 Exchange Street, PORTLAND, ME.

References: H. Ricker & Sons, Poland Springs; First National Bank, Portland, Me.

PRINCE'S EXPRESS CO.

For all Points in the West and South.

Freight FROM New York, Philadelphia, Baltimore, and Washington, D. C., should be forwarded via United States Express Co. Boston Office, 34 and 35 Court Square, 105 Arch Street, and 77 Kingston Street. Portland Office, 103 Exchange Street.

Courteous Attention, Low Rates, and Quick Despatch.

PREBLE HOUSE,

Adjoining Longfellow's Home,

J. C. WHITE.   PORTLAND, ME.

H. M. SANDERS & CO.,

Hardware, Paints, Oils, AND Varnishes.

Carpenters' and Machinists' Tools.

A full assortment of CUTLERY.

THEATRICAL STAGE HARDWARE.   27 Eliot St., BOSTON.

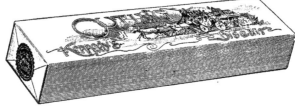

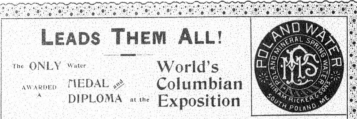

The Hill-Top

POLAND SPRINGS, SO. POLAND, ME.

HARRY C. WILKINSON

THE HILL · TOP ·

Vol. III.   SUNDAY MORNING, JULY 12, 1896.   No. 2.

Highways and By-ways.

I T is generally the case that at summer resorts the drives are confined to those in one or two directions only, either controlled by tumbling streams between rugged gorges, or confined to a single drive by towering peaks, along a narrow valley.

We present this week a bit of roadway, looking down and across from Ricker Hill as one passes down toward the lake.

The drives are of a most diversified nature, combining lake, wood, village, hill, and valley scenery, and with roads which invite one to try either the horse, the carriage, or the wheel, with the result of adding greatly to the many attractions of this favored spot.

A good short drive may be had by descending the hill in front of the hotel, and following around the middle lake, past the pleasant home of the Walkers, and back between the middle and upper lake, crossing the "Suez Canal"; or by starting on the Lewiston road, and then bearing to the left by Poland Corner, and so back again.

There is a lovely drive past the Mansion House, over the hill by the deserted village of the Poland Shakers, with its towering stone house, to Sabbath-day Lake. This will take one, also, to the Gloucester Shakers and their saw-mill, through pleasant woods, and giving delightful glimpses from gentle slopes now and then of attractive farming lands with well-kept houses.

White Oak Hill is directly across the middle lake, and a delightful drive may be had over and beyond that, past the Pope Kennels, with its dogs and other animals, which may be seen on certain days.

Another nice drive takes in the Raymond Woods, with its logging camps, and the Shakers, either going or coming. In fact, any way one turns, the return may be made by some other road than the one taken in going, which generally adds to the attractiveness of an outing.

Should one wish more frequented paths, past the pretty villages and farms, the roads leading to Gray or Gloucester are pleasant and attractive.

The Hotel Wilson site was a well-selected one, and is attractive to many, which may be reached by taking the road past the Mansion House to North Raymond. This is only about five miles, and it may be made by passing around the middle lake, either going or coming.

Bicyclers may favor the road to and through Peterson's Woods, which is well adapted to the wheel, and is pleasant and refreshing in its shade.

Sanborn's Stock Farm is one of the attractions of Poland which no one should neglect. It is on the Lewiston road, and all are welcome. By referring to Mr. Sanborn's card in another column they will find his cordial invitation to all, and, after viewing his establishment, one may diverge a little on the return trip and take in Empire Road and Minot Corner, returning by Poland Corner, not forgetting to make another call at the Creamery at the latter pretty village.

For a longer drive the one to Gray Corner and Gloucester Hill is a delightful one. It takes one over the Portland stage road to Gray Corner, where in the coaching days horses were changed on the trip from Portland, and then the journey resumed until the old Ricker Inn was reached and a good old-fashioned dinner was had, such an one as could only be had there, and eaten with a relish. At Gray Corner is the Pennell Institute, founded by Mr. Henry Pennell.

For a delightful picnic trip the one to the top of Black Cat is a most satisfactory one. One may

drive nearly to the top and leave their team at a farmer's and pursue the remainder on foot, or a single team can reach the summit. Here there is a large flat rock, used as a table, and the pleasures of out-of-door eating may be enjoyed to the fullest extent.

From the top of Tinney Hill seven lakes can be seen, and on clear days Portland Harbor is visible. There are several roads leading to and from these places.

Another lengthy drive will take one through Poland Corner to Mechanic Falls, a very pleasant New England village, and so on to Hebron Academy. An interesting feature there is Sturtevant Hall, given by the late Benjamin Sturtevant of Jamaica Plains, who was born in Maine.

Other drives may be had to Lewiston and Auburn and Lake Auburn, where there are excellent stores, great mills, and some fine residences, besides presenting much that is picturesque in the way of rock formation. These places are well worth visiting, but take a HILL-TOP with you that you may know where to do your shopping to the best advantage.

At the offices of the Poland Spring House and Mansion House one will be given a list of the drives around Poland, with a map showing all the roads and villages.

On the grounds are numerous pleasant walks, a particularly attractive one leading from near the bottling house to the lower lake, the terminus at the lake being very delightful.

Names of Our Several Different Drives and their Distance.

		MILES.
Around Middle Lake,	. . . . .	5 1-2
Lower Lake,	. . . . .	7
Sabbath-day Lake,	. . . . .	11
Trip Lake,	. . . . .	13
Lake and Gloucester Shakers,	. .	9 1-2
Lake and Poland Shakers,	. .	7 1-2
Raymond Woods and Shakers,	. .	8
Lower Gloucester,	. . . . .	13
Oak Hill and Lake,	. . . .	7 1-2
Hotel Wilson and Sturgis Mill,	.	11
Hotel Wilson and Oak Hill,	. . .	14
Upper and Middle Lake,	. . . .	12
Sabbath-day Lake and Peterson's Woods,	13
New Gloucester and Upper Corner,	.	12
Harris Hill, Minot Corner, Empire Road,	12
Gray Corner and Gloucester Hill,	.	22
Black Cat, Tinney Hill, Hotel Wilson,	15
To Mechanic Falls,	. . . . .	13
Lewiston and Auburn,	. . . . .	20
Lake Auburn,	. . . . . .	26
Lake Auburn via Lewiston,	. . . .	30

The Art Gallery.

DURING the week just passed, the Art Gallery has been visited by a very large number of people, and has received the unreserved praise of all. It is pronounced superior in all respects, and the evening lighting, now complete, is charming. One will make no mistake in the selection of a painting from this collection, as almost without exception they are by artists of recognized rank and even world-wide fame.

A. W. Buhler has within a few days added five of his exquisite water colors to the gallery, "A Wreck on the Bar" being the most notable. This and two others of exceptional merit will be found directly at the head of the stairway.

A landscape by Fligtoff will attract attention for its rugged strength and the amount of detail in its composition. It has already received high praise. Its subject is the upper lake, Poland Springs.

Sears Gallagher, who has but recently returned from Europe, sends five water colors, fresh from his studio. Three of them are English and French subjects, while "Mt. Washington in October," with its corn stacks and pumpkins, is of undoubted home production. All of them are very superior pictures.

Grace Henwood favors us with three fine canvases of French scenes, and two Algerian; also a frame of excellent medallion portraits. Mrs. Henwood's work is sure to find appreciative admirers, as it deserves. The "Salon Carré-Louvre" will be recognized by many for its faithfulness.

Leo Mielziner is represented by several small pictures, which will be found in Alcove D. A head, called "Una Vechia," is a remarkably strong and well-executed example, while "A Cavalier" and "Roses" are sure to attract attention and admiration.

Jacob Wagner's five pictures are positive gems; his "East Gloucester" is warm, rich, and marvelously true to nature; and they are sure to receive an amount of attention which is justly their due.

It is believed that the Art Gallery is now complete, and with the new lighting completed, the evening will be a far more attractive time to visit it than the day time. Do not fail to visit it and enjoy all its beauties, remembering that the price of any one of the paintings may be had on application to the librarian. The catalogue is in a very forward state, and before another week it is expected that it will be received from New York.

As one enters the Art Gallery now, they will be greeted by the gentle, sweet and refined features of Janette W. Ricker, whose portrait has but recently been placed there. This kindly New England mother will add a welcome to all visitors, as she did while living, and her likeness is appropriately placed at the entrance of a gallery of art, of which she was very fond.

One Furlong Makes Many Miles.

GENERALLY speaking it takes three miles to make one furlong, and it will be remembered that in the case of the Chicago strike General Miles had the strikers where the wool was short, while this is strictly a case of fur-long, we may say, General Furlong.

General Furlong, now a guest at the Poland Spring House, has just returned from his seventh tour around the world, which is a wonderful record. On his recent trip he stopped over a minute or two at Moscow to witness the coronation of the Czar, which occupied several hours of his autocratic majesty's time, causing our esteemed guest to miss several trains to Poland (Springs).

Being in a rather cold climate it is to be presumed that our friend's name was needed to keep him warm, but whether or not he wore it like the old Indian in the legend with the "warm side, fur side, outside," or the reverse, it is fair to suppose that, like the "B'ar," he knew which side out to wear his skin.

General Furlong is to be congratulated on being located in a Poland which is not under the government of his Imperial Majesty.

Bourne's Happy Returns.

SHAKESPEARE remarked some little merry trifle, about there being no return from the bourne he referred to, but on Monday last, July 5th, Mr. Charles Griswold Bourne had the pleasure of experiencing the twenty-first return of his natal hour, in which he rather discounts the respected William, with all due respect.

There was supper, and there was euchre, lovely women, and naturally fashionable and courtly gentlemen, elegant gowns, a hop, and all that sort of thing you know, together with twenty-one flaming and typical candles.

Mr. Bourne is now a man, in years, as he was before in size, if feet count, and he has six of them, not on his extremities, dear no, but altitudinous feet, and he carries them gracefully and well.

As to the supper, Mr. Bourne was honored by the presence of Mr. and Mrs. George T. Bourne and Miss Bourne, Mr. and Mrs. Baggaley, the Misses Stinson, Carpenter, Chipman, Howe, and Faile, and Messrs. Maginnis and Olney. With such companions one's digestion ought to be admirably aided.

This was followed by euchre, the friendly contestants being Mesdames Maginnis, Stinson, and Field, Mr. and Mrs. Baker, Mr. and Mrs. Rose, and Miss Goldthwaite. Some one naturally won, and in winning, we are able to name the winners, with marvelous aftersight. Therefore we will say that the first prize, a pair of silver nail scissors, went to Mrs. Baker; the second, a Limoges cup and saucer, was won by Miss Howe; the third, Delft inkstand, went to Miss Chipman; and the fourth, a blue match stand, to Mr. Baker.

The gowns on this occasion were elegant and becoming in all respects, but we might instance Mrs. Baggaley's black velvet Louis XVI. body with white lace; Miss Stinson's dainty green summer gown (presumably dimity), ribbon and lace; Miss Helen Stinson's pink gown; and Miss Chipman in white, with diamond wings in her hair. Miss Howe was also in pink; Miss Faile in white, with violets; Mrs. Rose, a charming body of lace, long sleeves, *décolleté*, with smart heliotrope bows and diamonds on corsage. Mrs. Maginnis wore black and pale blue, very tasteful; Mrs. Baker, black; Mrs. Stinson, pale grey; Miss Goldthwaite in green; and Mrs. Field was charmingly gowned, with jewels.

And so they were—oh no—we wish Mr. Bourne many happy returns of the day.

THE many friends of Miss May Rogers and Miss Lucy P. Newhall are glad to welcome them again to Poland. Miss Rogers spent the last two summers in Europe. Both ladies ride the wheel gracefully.

Our Menu.

RECIPE NO. 3.

Lobster à la Newbury en Caises.

OPEN 15 pounds of fresh boiled lobsters and clean them. Cut in one-inch squares. Place them in a sauté pan with 10 ounces of butter, salt and cayenne pepper to taste. Also two medium-sized truffles sliced. Cook twenty minutes, then add one-half pint of Madeira or good Sherry wine, and set it back on hot fire and allow it to reduce one-half. Then take two quarts of rich country cream and allow it to come to a boiling point. Whip in 20 egg yolks and cook until it comes to a rich yellow cream. Put lobster and sauce together and serve hot in caises.

This serves to fifty people.

RECIPE NO. 4.

White Sponge Cake.

Whites of 20 eggs beaten stiff; 1 1-2 pounds of powdered sugar; 10 ounces of flour; 2 teaspoonfuls of cream tartar sifted in. Flavor with orange and almond to taste.

Serves to fifty people.

New Books Received.

MRS. PETTEE.—4 vols.

Thirty Select Sermons, by Rev. E. C. Bill.
Prisoner of Zenda, by Anthony Hope.
Change of Air, by Anthony Hope.
The Play Actress, by Crockett.

MRS. L. HURLBURT.—1 vol.

Peter Ibbetson, by George du Maurier.

HON. HENRY B. CLEAVES.—1 vol.

Constitutional Convention of Maine, 1819-1820.

GEN. A. P. MARTIN.—3 vols.

Dedication of the Martin School-House.
Inaugural Address of Mayor Martin.
250th Anniversary Settlement of Boston.

Mr. Disraeli.

[Boston Home Journal.]

ONE good story is about the courtship of Mr. Disraeli, as he then was, and Mrs. Wyndham Lewis. That lady was living near Cardiff, when through the window she saw Mr. Disraeli approaching, and ordered the servant to say she was not at home. When the servant descended to the hall, Mr. Disraeli was hanging his light overcoat on a peg. "Mrs. Lewis, sir, is not at home," said the flurried maid. "I did not ask for Mrs. Lewis," was the calm, statesmanlike reply. "But I don't know when she will be back," urged the maid. "Neither do I," philosophically replied he; "but I am going to wait till she does come back, so make me some tea." He did wait, he got his tea, and he married the widow.

Children's Column.

The Fright of Forty-Five Elephants at a Single Rat.

LAST winter a party of scientific and newspaper men visited Barnum and Bailey's circus headquarters in Bridgeport, to ascertain whether an elephant was in terror of a rat or not.

The following story was given by a New York newspaper.

The visitors left this city on a special car at 9 o'clock, and at Bridgeport were joined by Professors O. C. Marsh and D. C. Eaton of Yale and Mayor Clark, Dr. Downs, Dr. Porter, and L. M. Rich of Bridgeport. In the New York party were Prof. H. F. Osborne of Columbia College and Dr. Wortman of the Museum of Natural History. The chief interest centered in the elephant and rat experiment. Thirty-five elephants, of whom half a dozen were little fellows, were gathered in the large enclosure, double chained by order of Mr. J. A. Bailey, who personally conducted the visitors after they reached the headquarters. In spite of his reputation as a tractable and reliable animal, the elephant is more feared by circus men than any other member of the menagerie. He is liable to sudden fits of rage or panic, and on these occasions is about as manageable as a runaway locomotive and has equal powers of destruction.

The visitors didn't know this, but Jeff Callan and a number of other experienced circus men there understood it well, and stood lined up near the door ready to control a hasty exit of all the visitors in case any of the giants broke away. The rat, on account of which all these precautions were taken, was a particularly insignificant specimen, and looked unhappy by reason of a long string tied to its tail. One of the circus men tossed it out among the elephants and the performance began. First to catch sight, or perhaps it was scent of it, was one of the small elephants. He threw his trunk in the air, trumpeting shrill and loud. This was the alarm. Instantly a swaying motion went through the elephant ranks. Some screamed, others plunged, and others doubled their feet down under them, probably to keep the rat out of the crevices in them. Hindu mahouts say that the elephant fear of the rat is a dread that the rodent will crawl

into his feet. Plainly the fear was there. It was not confined to the elephants either. The rat was just as scared as they. Its shrill squeaks as it dodged about among the ponderous feet made the big fellows still more frightened.

Finally all the elephants began plunging, and at that Professor Marsh performed a feat that would doubtless have edified his classes had they been there to see. A pile of big bales of hay stood near him. An agile leap carried him to a foothold upon the first tier and he squirmed up the rest of the way with the grace and ease of a chipmunk ascending a tree. A number of newspaper men went after him. Professor Marsh perched himself near the edge and looked down at the elephants.

"Self-preservation is the first law of nature," he remarked. "I can observe in a more scientific frame of mind from here."

Presently the rat, having found a corner, stayed quiet until it was hauled back by the string. The attendant tossed it upon the back of Bad Hattie, a particularly bad-tempered elephant. Hattie did everything but turn somersaults in her efforts to dislodge her rider, but the rat clung, while she bucked, flapped her skin, shook, plunged, and rubbed against the wall, shrieking with fear all the time. Finally one of the other elephants came to her rescue and swept the rodent off with his trunk. Then there were more lively times, but finally a big fellow backed down upon the enemy and put a foot upon it, destroying it.

May a little bundle of dainty lace
When opened reveal a tiny face;
May two little fists, so soft and white,
And two little eyes that open so bright,
A dear little mouth, a sweet little chin,
And a cute little nose tell what is within!
May a dear little voice soon learn to say
"Mamma" and "Papa," and prattle all day;
May two dear little feet soon trot about,
Get into mischief and put you to rout.
'Tis a heartfelt wish that you have from me,
That you may the dawn of motherhood see.
—LOUISE PRICE LOW.

There may be ten thousand lies; there can be but one truth.

Two Flags.

HON. FRED ATWOOD of Winterport, Maine, has contributed two souvenirs of the Maine State Building to that interesting building. These are the two flags, one American and the other English, which were used at the original dedication of the building in Chicago, and which floated from the head of the engine on the return trip of the Executive Council. Thanks are extended to Mr. Atwood for his thoughtful kindness, and it is to be hoped they may forever twine in peace and harmony.

FRANK CARLOS GRIFFITH, } EDITORS.
NETTIE M. RICKER,

PUBLISHED EVERY SUNDAY MORNING DURING THE MONTHS
OF JULY, AUGUST, AND SEPTEMBER, IN THE INTERESTS OF

POLAND SPRINGS AND ITS VISITORS.

All contributions relative to the guests of Poland Springs
will be thankfully received.

To insure publication, all communications should reach the
editors not later than Wednesday preceding day of issue.

All parties desiring rates for advertising in the HILL-TOP
should write the editors for same.

The subscription price of the HILL-TOP is $1.00 for the
season, post-paid. Single copies will be mailed at 10c. each.

Address,
      EDITORS "HILL-TOP,"
            Poland Spring House,
                  South Poland, Maine.

PRINTED AT JOURNAL OFFICE, LEWISTON.

Sunday, July 12, 1896.

Editorial.

HOW pleasant it is to welcome returning
guests ; to see the same faces turning again
towards the scenes which they have learned
to love, and witness the delight invariably stamped
upon their features as they are greeted on alight-
ing at the door.

Not every place can number among its visitors
so many old friends, friends who have made the
new hotel, as well as the old, their summer abode
with delightful constancy for these many, many
years.

Such is the growth of this attachment that it
amounts almost to a friendly rivalry, and the fact
that this is the fifth, seventh, tenth, and even
twentieth season here, is like the decorations worn
to commemorate the winning of honors, customary
in foreign lands.

It is the invisible cross of the legion, and
legions are gradually winning it, and wearing it
proudly.

That an establishment (we came near saying,
purely commercial in its nature) which has added

to its original attractions provided so lavishly by
nature, so much that the hand of the artist and
artisan alone can furnish, can so firmly cement and
retain this affection, is a compliment which is
doubtless deeply felt, and as the years roll on and
the numbers of these " societaires " increase, they
will form an " old guard " proud of the distinction,
won without scars and worn with great pride.

Edward H. Barnard.

MR. BARNARD was born in Belmont, Mass.,
July 10, 1855. He began to study drawing
seriously at Massachusetts Institute Technology, taking a two years course in architecture under Prof. W. R. Ware and M. Letaing
winning prize offered by the Society of Architects.
After a year spent in an architect's office he entered
the studio of John B. Johnston, Boston, remaining there and under his immediate instruction until
the opening of the school of drawing and painting
at the Museum of Fine Arts in that city. After
four years of study there, the summer's work guided
by Mr. Johnston, he took a position offered him as
figure designer for a well-known stained glass firm.

In 1886 he went to Paris, studying in the
drawing schools there under Boulanger and Lefebre,
and Raphael Collin for three years, exhibiting
portraits in the Salons of 1888 and 1889, and a
figure composition entitled, "Un Paise-Temp en
Moyen Age," at the International Exposition, now
owned by Mrs. Corliss of Providence, R. I.

Returning to Boston in the summer of that
year he became interested in landscape, to which
he has devoted the greater part of his time since.
He has received several commissions for portraits,
however, and among them Dr. Walcott, President
of Horticultural Society of Boston, Rev. S. B.
Stewart of Lynn, William Underwood and R. V.
Fletcher of Belmont. He exhibits in all the
important exhibitions, American Society of Artists,
New York ; Philadelphia Academy, Chicago Art
Institute, etc., etc. Received medals from Massachusetts Charitable Mechanics Association for
portrait and landscape, and Jordan second prize
for landscape, 1895. Is a member of the Boston
Art Club.

Mr. Barnard is represented in the Art Gallery
by four of his very successful works, among them
being "Looking Over the Oaks," which took
second prize at the recent Jordan Exhibition in
Boston.

His other pictures here are " Sunlight and
Mist, Morning on Fisher's Island," " A Quiet
Morning," and " Looking Up the Valley." All
Mr. Barnard's pictures will be found in Alcove A.

Tid-Bits.

Haying.

Pink sunsets.

Gold, Politics and Silver.

Enough paper or copper is not bad.

All croquet lovers are glad to welcome Mr. Ivers.

Mr. and Mrs. H. A. Rogers of New York arrive this week.

Col. Stephen C. Talbot will spend the summer again at Poland Springs.

Judge James M. Barker of Pittsfield, Mass., is at the Poland Spring House.

Mrs. D. K. Phillips of Phillips Beach, Swampscott, is a guest at Poland Springs.

Dr. Pray and family of Boston are at the Lake View Cottage for the summer.

All England is crazy over the discovery in the slums of East London of a boy poet of great promise.

The many friends of Mr. B. J. Gallagher will be glad to know that he has won the bicycle at the Mansion House.

Mr. and Mrs. S. W. Keene of Boston are at the Mansion House. This is their seventh season at Poland. Welcome.

Mr. and Mrs. Baggaley, guests at the Poland Spring House, are fond of sailing and horseback riding. They ride well.

Mr. and Mrs. Rose (Miss Maginnis) are at the Poland Spring House. In pleasant weather they may be seen driving a pair of fine horses.

Miss Washington, a descendant of the Washington family, is a guest at the Mansion House. Miss Washington comes early and remains late.

Mr. and Mrs. H. O. Bright of Cambridge, Mass., arrived Wednesday morning, they having driven from Portland. A cordial welcome awaited them.

Austin and Chester Palmer, aged respectively twelve and eight years, celebrated the 4th of July by sending up eight balloons and setting off "big fire crackers."

Mr. and Mrs. Nelson Bartlett have begun a new and pleasant year at their favorite resort, where they are also extreme favorites. They are among the very earliest patrons.

All lovers of music are glad Miss Georgie Pray will spend the summer at Lake View Cottage. We hope she will favor us with some of her playing. She is a noted 'celloist.

The Hour of Prayer.

BY GEORGE T. BOURNE.

It was the houi of piayei.
The shades of evening fell o'er eaith and sea
With holy calm—and natuie was at iest.
The leaves weie still—the zephyi's bieath
Had won them to a gentle sleep,
And the cleai lake, with scaice a iipple
Winding o'er its face,
Reflected in its miiioied depths
The fiist biight stai of evening.
It was the houi of piayei.
No vespei bell awoke the echoes soft
Fiom out the wood-ciowned hill,
Beneath whose shade the temple walls
Stood foith in giant shape.—
The temple gates weie opened wide,
That all the hastening thiong might entei in,
And bow to God, in piayei.
Within the temple gloom, in all his powei of piide,
Reclined the Phaiisee,
And lifting up his voice that all might heai,
He utteied one by one his oft-iepeated piayeis,
And thanked the King of Kings
That he was bettei fai than all who knelt beside him.
His piayei at end, with stately mien
And haughty biow he passed fiom out the temple;
His jeweled hand held close his iobe of iich aiiay,
Lest contact with the kueeling Publican
Should diin its puiity.
And he, thus so despised,
Had bowed his face upon the temple flooi,
Afiaid to lift his eyes,—he gazed upon the altai fiies
And theie he muimured foith a piayei,
The nevei-dying woids: "Be meiciful to me, oh God,
I am a sinnei."
The temple gates weie closed.
The last, slow lingeiing supplicant
Had sought his home,
And Heaven's Recoiding Angel
Had enteied in the Book of Life
The piayeis that ieached Jehovah's ears.
The high-boin Phaiisee, he that piayed and scoined
  humanity,
Was left in sin's enthiallment still,
While he who ciied for meicy, found his piayei was
  answeied,
And in his heait dwelt sweet contentment,
For he was paidoned—justified.

Brake Ride.

Mi. and Mrs. Thomas, Mi. and Mrs. Somes, Mi. and Mrs. Howes, Miss Goldthwaite, and Mi. Geoige B. Fiench visited the Shakeis; diove thiough Peteison's woods, uppei and lowei Gloucestei, and Gloucestei woods, a distance of sixteen miles. A pleasantei iide was nevei taken on the biake.

Massage.

Mrs. E. J. Robinson, whom many of the guests will favoiably iecollect, aiiived on Fiiday and is piepaied to iesume tieatment of all who need her seivices. Mrs. Robinson is a lady of laige experience, skilled in the art, and pleasant manneied. Massage is of acknowledged efficacy, and a veiy effective method of ievivifying the system when fatigued, and of iestoiing one to full musculai activity and stiength.

Prestidigitation.

Prof. G. H. Pray, a jugglei, gave a pleasing exhibition of his skill in the art, in the Music Hall, July 2d, too late for the pievious issue. Piofessoi Piay is the fiist enteitainei of the season, and found an inteiested audience befoie him.

Stereopticon.

Col. C. H. French followed close upon the fiist enteitainment, and gave his illustiated desciiption of Alaska, befoie a laige and well-pleased audience, on the evening of July 3d. His views are veiy fine.

Rev. H. E. Dunnack fiom the Empiie pieached in Music Hall, Sunday, July 5th. His discouise was excellent and the hall was well filled.

A man expeiienced in the caie of invalids; an extensive tiavellei, not only all ovei this countiy, but fiequently in Euiope; gentle, intelligent, well-iead, and conveisant with people and places, desiies an oppoitunity to accompany an eldeily invalid gentleman or lady in the capacity of companion. He can be highly iecommended. Infoimation may be had fiom the Libiaiian, Maine State Building.

Guests at Poland Spring House.

JULY 7, 1896.

Mr. and Mrs. Geo. T. Bourne	New York.
Miss Bourne	New York
Mr. Griswold Bourne	New York.
Mr. and Mrs. Geo. F. Baker	Hyannis, Mass.
Mrs. Wm. S. Brown	New York.
Mr. and Mrs. Ralph Baggaley	Pittsburg.
Mr. Wm. A. Bigelow	New York.
Mr. and Mrs. Amos Barnes	Boston.
Mrs. B. Babcock	New York.
Miss Babcock	New York.
Rev. Dr. Baxter	Boston.
Miss S. P. Baker	Boston.
Mr. Chas. T. Baker	Boston.
Mr. Isaac H. Bailey	New York.
Miss L. Belyea	Boston.
Miss S. E. Brody	Boston.
Judge Jas. M. Barker	Pittsfield.
Mr. and Mrs. Jacob P. Bates	Boston.
Rev. F. A. Brogan	Boston.
Rev. T. E. Brannan	Boston.
Mr. and Mrs. Geo. W. Coleman	Boston.
Mr. Andrew K. Culver	Brooklyn.
Mr. and Mrs. F. W. Carpenter	Providence.
Miss Hannah Carpenter	Providence.
Mr. A. W. Clark	Deering.
Mr. and Mrs. Geo. W. Carr	Providence.
Mr. and Mrs. C. C. Corbin	Webster, Mass.
Miss Mabel Chipman	Boston.
Mrs. A. A. Conner	New York.
Miss T, E. Cameron	Boston.
The Misses DePeyster	New York.
Mrs. Albert Douglass	New York.
Mrs. M. E. Dexter	Brooklyn.
Miss Dexter	Brooklyn.
Mrs. N. C. Dickerson	New York.
Mr. and Mrs. R. M. Field	Boston.
Miss A. L. Faile	New York.
Mr. Thos. H. Faile	New York.
Miss Fletcher	Boston.
Mr. Geo. B. French	Boston.
Mrs. J. D. Fessenden	New York.
Gen. Chas. E. Furlong	New York.
Mr. John Goldthwaite	Boston.
Miss E. B. Goldthwaite	Boston.
Mrs. G. F. Gregory	Brooklyn.
Miss Gregory	Brooklyn.
Mrs. M. R. Goodwin	Boston.
Miss Goodwin	Boston.
Mrs. L. M. Gale	Washington.
Miss Olive Gale	Washington.
Mr. and Mrs. Alfred A. Glasier	Boston.
Mr. and Mrs. Horace Hunt	New York.
Mrs. S. B. Hubbard	Jacksonville, Fla.
Mr. and Mrs. L. Hurlburt	Brooklyn.
Mrs. M. B. Hoffman	New York.
Mr. and Mrs. L. D. Henwood	Boston.
Mr. Nat Huggins	New York.
Mr. and Mrs. J. W. Hazen	Boston.
Mr. and Mrs. S. Haas	New York.
Miss Flottie Haas	New York.
Mr. Emil Herz	Trenton.
Mr. and Mrs. Hudson Hoagland	New York.
Mr. W. J. Holden	Boston.
Mr. and Mrs. L. Hall	Cambridge.
Miss M. R. Haddock and maid	New York.
Mr. Samuel Ivers	New Bedford.
Miss Ella F. Ivers	New Bedford.
Mrs. Julian James	Washington.
Mr. and Mrs. M. B. Koon	Minneapolis.
Mr. John Lucas	Philadelphia.
Mrs. Amos R. Little	Philadelphia.
Miss H. N. Loomis	Boston.
Miss M. L. Loomis	Boston.
Mr. and Mrs. B. Lemann and family	New Orleans.
Mrs. O. E. Lewis	Winthrop, Mass.
Miss Nellie Lewis	Winthrop, Mass.
Miss Leland	New York.
Mr. and Mrs. Wm. R. Lynch	Brooklyn.
Mr. and Mrs. T. B. M. Mason	Washington.
Mrs. T. B. Myers	Washington.
Mr. and Mrs. C. E. Morrison	Boston.
Mrs. Jno. H. Maginnis	New Orleans.
Mr. Jno. H. Maginnis	New Orleans.
Mr. R. I. McClure	Chicago.
Mrs. A. Murray	Washington.
Miss A. G. Miller	Brooklyn.
Dr. and Mrs. Ira L. Moore	Boston.
Mr. Stephen W. Marston	Boston.
Gen. A. P. Martin	Boston.
Mrs. Newbegin	Portland.
Mr. and Mrs. W. T. Ness	Boston.
Miss Lucy P. Newhall	Philadelphia.
Mr. and Mrs. Frank F. Olney	Providence.
Mr. Elam W. Olney	Providence.
Mr. John A. Ordway	Boston.
Mrs. J. A. Pettee	New York.
Mr. and Mrs. W. S. Patten	New York.
Miss Patten	New York.
Miss Grace Patten	New York.
Mrs. Pattison	Boston.
Judge and Mrs. Chas. A. Peabody	New York.
Mr. and Mrs. Henry M. Palmer	Brooklyn.
Masters Austin and Chester Palmer	Brooklyn.
Mrs. M. E. Parsons	Boston.
Mrs. E. D. Peters	Boston.
Mrs. H. D. Polhemus	Brooklyn.
Miss A. J. Pomeroy	New York.
Mr. Joseph G. Ray	Franklin, Mass.
Miss L. P. Ray	Franklin, Mass.
Mr. and Mrs. Geo. Rose	New Orleans
Mr. and Mrs. H. A. Rogers	New York.
Miss May Rogers	New York.
Mrs. S. B. Stinson	Washington.
Miss Stinson	Washington.
Miss Florence Stinson.	Washington.
Gen. and Mrs. Rufus Saxton	Washington.
Miss Alia Somes	Brookline, Mass.
Mr. Geo. H. Somes	Brookline, Mass.
Mr. and Mrs. A. T. Salter	Washington.
Mr. and Mrs. A. W. Smith	Providence.
Mr. and Mrs. Irving T. Smith and family	Boston.
Mrs. Orlando Tompkins	Boston.
Mr. and Mrs. Frank R. Thomas	Boston.
Mr. and Mrs. F. E. Taylor	Brooklyn.
Mr. and Mrs. J. W. Tabor	Portland.
Dr. J. M. Thompson	Boston.
Mr. and Mrs. John H. Voorhees	Brooklyn.
Miss Jessie Voorhees	Brooklyn.
Mr. and Mrs. W. B. Valentine	London, Eng.
Mr. and Mrs. John P. Woodbury	Boston.
Mrs. J. Reed Whipple	Boston.
Dr. M. C. Wedgwood	Lewiston.
Mr. and Mrs. J. R. Winters	New York.
Mr. A. Wentworth	Boston.
Miss Waldo	Salem.
Mr. and Mrs. H. D. Ziegler	Philadelphia.
Miss C. F. Ziegler	Philadelphia.

Musical Programme.

SUNDAY EVENING, JULY 12, 1896.

1. Sanctus—From St. Cecilia.   Gounod.
2. Overture—Poet and Peasant.   Suppé.
3. Lost Chord.   Sullivan.

Mr. Pierre Müller.

4. Selection—From Oberon.   Weber.
5. Lucretia Borgia.

Mr. A. Brooke.

6. Grand Selection from Faust.   Gounod.

A case of Poland Water was shipped this week to Chief Justice Fuller at Sorrento, at his request. It will be seen that he is still loyal to Maine.

Thistles.

AT NIGHT.

O lots of men are homeless,
And we can plainly see
That many more are home less
Than they really ought to be.

The cart-wheel silver dollar so looms up at Chicago that the tariff, at present, is out of sight.

HAD A VARIETY.
[From Judge.]

Flowery Fields—" Kind lady, end yer help an honest man dat's got a sick wife and ten small children starvin' ter death?"

Mrs. Goodman—" Why are they starving? Can't you get work?

Flowery Fields—" 'Tain't dat, mum. Terday's deir regular starvin' day; termorrer I'll hev 'em down wid de measles, an' next day I'll hev 'em dead an' no money ter bury 'em. I gives my customers variety, mum."

ACTUAL FIGURES.
[New York Recorder.]

The young man smote his forehead.

"Why, father," he cried earnestly, "she's worth her weight in gold."

The old man laid his hand impressively on the young man's knee.

"That may be," he said, carefully, "but even in that case you will bear in mind she wouldn't foot up above thirty-five or forty thousand dollars."

WORTH THE TROUBLE.
[From Life.]

"Miss Swift is learning to ride a wheel, she tells me."

"But she rode one last year. Why does she have to learn again?"

"Another fellow is teaching her."

WHERE THE MIRACLE CAME IN.
[Washington Times.]

"Well, Uncle Rasbury, how did you like the sermon?"

"It war a pow'ful sermon, Marse John."

"What was it about?"

"It war 'bout de mir'cle ob seven thousand loaves and five thousand fishes bein' fed to de twelve 'postles."

"Seven thousand loaves and five thousand fishes being fed to the Apostles; but where does the miracle come in?"

Uncle Rasbury scratched his head a few moments meditatively, then he replied:

"Well, Marse John, de mir'cle, 'cordin' to my perception ob de circumstances, is dat dey all didn't bust."

AN OKLAHOMA WEDDING.
[From Judge.]

Rev. Mr. Harps (solemnly)—" Do you take this woman for better or for worse?"

Tarantula Jack (peevishly)—" How kin I tell? I hain't known her but a week."

The following is one of the most expressive Fourth of July poems, for its size, ever written :

Boys,
Noise!

Chulalongkon, king of Siam, is now on a vacation at ten million a year. Most of us would be willing to go on a vacation for half that.

An East Machias young lady recently made a picture of two boys on a bicycle. She was much surprised, on developing the negative, to find a splendid likeness of a full-grown buck deer, which had ventured into the open unnoticed by all save the camera.

This ought to encourage the snap-shot artists who intend to exhibit specimens of their ability in the coming August exhibition of amateur photographic work, to be held in the Maine State Building. While there are no buck deer in this neighborhood, yet another species of dear is sometimes found in Lovers' Lane, which might make an exceedingly interesting picture. The small cameras of the Kodak type will, of course, have an advantage over the larger and adjustable focus type in pursuing this kind of game, but with the wealth of landscapes, groups, etc., the latter would not be left behind in the contest for the prizes.

It is intended to encourage amateur work on the Hill in every way possible, and guests will find dark rooms for their use in the studio building, where every facility will be afforded them.

The noted artist, Mr. August Franzen of Stockholm, Sweden, is spending the summer at Poland Springs. Mr. Franzen's work is well known in this country. His portrait of Mr. Eugene Field, which was exhibited in Chicago last winter, was greatly admired.

Arrivals.

POLAND SPRING HOUSE.

JULY 2 TO JULY 9, 1896.

Adams, Mr. and Mrs. C. H.	Jamaica Plain.
Allen, Mrs. W. C. and son	Mechanic Falls.
Anderson, Mr. and Mrs. A.	Camden.
Bailey, George H.	Deering.
Bailey, J. H.	New York.
Bourne, Griswold	New York.
Blackett, Mr. and Mrs. Dexter	Brighton, Mass.
Blackett, Herbert D.	Brighton, Mass.
Baker, Chas. T.	Boston.
Baker, Miss S. P.	Boston.
Baxter, Rev. Dr.	Boston.
Babcock, Mrs. B.	New York.
Babcock, Miss C. L.	New York.
Barnes, Mr. and Mrs. Amos	Boston.
Belyea, L.	Boston.
Boody, Miss S. E.	Boston.
Barker, James M.	Pittsfield.
Bates, Mr. and Mrs. Jacob P.	Boston.
Brogan, F. A.	Boston.
Brannan, T. E.	Boston.
Bright, Mr. and Mrs. H. O.	Cambridge.
Bartlett, Mr. and Mrs. Nelson	Boston.
Bossange, E. R.	New York.
Colvin, H. J.	Somerville.
Cowles, Mr. and Mrs. E. B.	Boston.
Connel, G. L.	New York.
Connel, Mrs. A. A.	New York.
Chaffee, A. B.	Montreal.
Chipman, Miss Mabel	Boston.
Colbin, Mr. and Mrs. C. C.	Webster, Mass.
Crocker, Mr. and Mrs. U. H.	Boston.
Closson, D. B.	Boston.
Closson, Miss Hope	Boston.
Call, Mr. and Mrs. Geo. W.	Providence.
Carlisle, Mr. and Mrs. W. B.	Carlisle.
Cameron, Miss T. E.	Boston.
Dexter, Mrs. M. E.	Brooklny.
Dexter, Miss	Brooklyn.
Douglas, Mrs. A., Jr.	New York.
De Peyster, Misses	New York.
Deering, J. M.	Saco.
Dickerson, Mrs. N. C.	New York.
Fessenden, Mrs. J. D.	New York.
French, C. H.	Chicago.
Furlong, Chas. E.	New York.
Gregory, G. F.	Brooklyn.
Gregory, Miss	Brooklyn.
Gray, Wm. R.	Boston.
Goodwin, Mrs. and Miss	Boston.
Gleason, James S.	Boston.
Gale, Mrs. L. M.	Washington.
Gale, Miss Olive	Washington.
Glasier, Alfred A. and wife	Boston.
Herz, Emil	Trenton, N. J.
Hoagland, Mr. and Mrs. H.	
Hutchinson, A. S.	Lynn.
Howe, H. C.	Lowell.
Holden, N. J.	Boston.
Hall, Mr. and Mrs. L.	Cambridge.
Haddock, Miss	New York.
Hood, Mr. and Mrs. C. H.	Somerville.
Hillman, Mr. and Mrs. S. I.	Cincinnati.
Ivers, Mr. and Mrs. Samuel	New Bedford.
Jordan, N. J.	Lewiston.
Jenkins, Mr. and Mrs. F. L.	Brooklyn.
King, Mrs. F. H.	Portland.

Libby, S. B.	Auburn.
Libby, Edith F.	Auburn.
Lewis, O. E.	Boston.
Leavitt, Mr. and Mrs. John	Newton, Mass.
Leavitt, Miss	Newton, Mass.
Littlefield, Miss	Melrose, Mass.
Lambert, Mrs Mary	Brooklyn.
Lambert, Miss	Brooklyn.
Miller, Miss A. G.	Brooklyn.
Milliken, Mr. and Mrs. W. H.	Portland.
Moore, Mr. and Mrs. Dr. Ira L.	Boston.
McCartney, R. C.	Boston.
McKenna, J.	Boston.
Morrill, Mr. and Mrs. J. A.	Auburn.
Marston, Stephen W.	Boston.
Martin, Gen. A. P.	Boston.
Mallouf, Mrs. H. G.	New York.
Mallouf, H.	New York.
Murray, Mr. and Mrs. Harvey	Portland.
Morrill, Mrs. Chas. T.	Mechanic Falls.
Morrill, Miss Helen	Mechanic Falls.
Mackenzie, M.	Lewiston.
Mackey, Mrs.	St. Louis.
Ness, Mr. and Mrs. W. T.	Boston.
Nichols, Mr. and Mrs. L. B.	Cambridge.
Nichols, Miss Alice	Cambridge.
Nichols, Miss Florence	Cambridge.
Newhall, Miss L. P.	Philadelphia.
Ordway, John A.	Boston.
Percy, A.	Portland.
Paige, John C.	Boston.
Peters, Edw. D.	Boston.
Polhemus, Mrs. H. D.	Brooklyn.
Pomeroy, Miss A. J.	New York.
Pray, G. H.	Lewiston.
Peck, Mr. and Mrs. B.	Lewiston.
Robinson, A. E.	Oxford.
Rickel, H. H.	Portland.
Rose, Mr. and Mrs. Leo	New Orleans.
Roberts, H. R.	Pittsburg.
Rich, Edward L.	Portland.
Rogers, Mr. and Mrs. H. A.	New York.
Rogers, Miss May	New York.
Rogers, Mr. and Mrs. J. Fred	Boston.
Smith, Mr. and Mrs. Irving T.	Brooklyn.
Savage, Mrs. A. R.	Auburn.
Savage, Miss May	Auburn.
Smith, Mr. and Mrs. Albert W.	Providence.
Slack, F. W., Jr.	Hillsdale, Mich.
Smith, Mr. and Mrs. Chester Ballou	Woonsocket.
Talbot, Mr. and Mrs. J. W.	Portland.
Tillinghast, Mr. and Mrs. C. M.	Boston.
Thompson, Dr. J. M.	Boston.
Valentine, Mr. and Mrs. W. B.	London, Eng.
Winters, Mr. and Mrs. J. R.	New York.
Woodbury, Mr. and Mrs. John	Lynn, Mass.
Wentworth, A.	Boston.
Whitman, Miss A. S.	Somerville, Mass.
Waldo, Miss	Salem.
Wescott, Mr. and Mrs. G. F.	Portland.

MANSION HOUSE.

JUNE 1 TO JULY 9.

Alger, L. W. and wife	W. Stewartstown, N. H.
Angel, Thos. L.	Lewiston.
Angel, R. J.	Providence.
Blackwell, C. F. and wife	Boston.
Balbour, Mrs. E. D.	Boston.
Balbour, Miss M. E.	Boston.
Balbour, Mr. E. D.	Boston.
Burrows, W. H. and wife	Malden.
Bradford, E. F.	Mechanic Falls.
Bradbury, Clara E.	Lewiston.
Buck, G. S.	New York.

Conover, Mrs. J. C.	New York.
Conover, Miss Alice	New York.
Calkin, Geo. F.	St. John.
Carter, John W.	Portland.
Cousens, L. M. and wife	Portland.
Cousens, W. T.	Portland.
Cousens, L. A.	Portland.
Chandler, N. L.	Portland.
Cutts, O. F.	North Anson.
Crawshaw, J. M.	Auburn.
Clapp, A. W.	Lynn.
Caldwell, J. C.	New York.
Chase, John B.	Bellows Falls.
Campbell, C. A.	Boston.
Chase, John D.	Bellows Falls.
Campbell, C. A.	Boston.
Cummings, Stephen A.	Boston.
Danforth, J. H.	Boston.
Daley, Miss M. F.	Chelsea.
Dewey, Dr. D. R.	North Adams.
Decker, Miss G. B.	Rumford Falls.
Dunn, A. A.	Portland.
Eddy, Chas. E.	Newton.
Ernst, Mrs. K. M.	Brooklyn.
Floyd, Mr. and Mrs. C. O.	Lynn.
Floyd, Miss	Lynn.
Floyd, Mrs. A. L.	Boston.
Foster, Chas.	Portland.
Farine, L. Marie D.	Westfield, Mass.
Fleming, Miss M. E.	New York.
Franzen, August	Stockholm, Sweden.
Floyd, A. Leander	Boston.
Goodwin, Mr. and Mrs. F. A.	New York.
Greely, Wm. H.	New Gloucester.
Greely, W. H.	Boston.
Greene, S. W.	Brookline.
Goodwin, F. A.	New York.
Goodwin, Mrs. F. A.	New York.
Hovey, Mrs. Jas.	Chelsea.
Houghton, Arthur J.	Boston.
Icarus, R. B.	New York.
Jordan, Mr. E. C.	Portland.
Jordan, Mrs. E. C.	Portland.
Johnson, S. W.	Portland.
Jordan, R. H.	Portland.
Keene, Mr. and Mrs. S. W.	Boston.
Knight, G. L.	Portland.
Kuntz, Mrs. Daniel	Boston.
Kimball, T. F.	Boston.
Keene, T. W. and wife	Boston.
Lyman, H. D. and wife	New York.
McDowell, F. W.	Portland.
Marston, Charles L.	Yarmouth.
Morse, W. W.	Boston.
Morse, Mrs. W. W., Jr.	Boston.
McDowell, Miss	Portland.
Marston, F. E.	Boston.
Morrell, C. O.	Lewiston.
Mason, L. S.	Belfast.
Mason, C. A. and wife	Philadelphia.
Marsh, Robert P.	Springfield.
Mason, Mr. and Mrs. Chas. A.	Philadelphia.
Millet, F. A.	Mechanic Falls.
Neal, Jas.	Portland.
Norton, W. H. and wife	Portland.
Parsons, Miss	Kennebunk.
Plaisted, H. M.	Bangor.
Peet, Mrs. J. B.	New York.
Phillips, Mrs. D. K.	Swampscott.
Poole, Mr. and Mrs. D. J.	Merrimac.
Ross, Miss	Gorham.
Rowell, Eugene	Auburn.
Runyon, Mrs. E. L.	Lewiston.

Stebbins, Miss	New York.
Stebbins, Miss E. A.	New York.
Swain, William N.	Dorchester.
Swain, Eva M.	Dorchester.
Swain, Eliza S.	Boston.
Sullivan, Mrs. John	Savannah.
Sullivan, Miss R.	Savannah.
Stevens, Mrs. F. E.	New York.
Sweetser, D. H. and wife	Lynn.
Stearnes, W. F.	Boston.
Stearnes, Mrs.	Boston.
Small, A. H.	Portland.
Safford, W. F.	Portland.
Simmons, Rose M.	Auburn.
Staples, Mr. and Mrs. E. P.	Portland.
Soule, W. H. and wife	Portland.
Small, C. W.	Portland.
Sawyer, R. F.	Portland.
Stone, Mrs. Chas.	Springfield.
Tobe, Edw. W.	Newton.
Townsend, Miss M. A.	Lynn.
Tapley, Henry F. and wife	Lynn.
Turner, Mrs. J. B.	Boston.
Thurston, Mrs. J. B. and maid	Portland.
Thurston, Margaret G.	Portland.
Thurston, Theo. K.	Portland.
Thurston, Clara A.	Portland.
Talbot, Stephen C.	Brooklyn.
Underhill, Mr. and Mrs. J.	New York.
Underhill, Miss	New York.
Vivian, Miss May	New York.
De Wint, Mrs. M. E.	New York.
Wingate, W. H.	Boston.
Williams, Geo. H.	New York.
Williams, Miss Ada	New York.
Washington, Miss	Philadelphia.
Wiley, Theo. C.	Boston.
Warren, F. E.	Portland.

Mexican Drawn Work.

A LADY living in Texas, on the Mexican border, sends to Mrs. Hiram W. Ricker a large variety of this material of the finest and most superior quality in the art of needle-work. This is the *genuine*, and of great beauty. Mrs. Ricker will be pleased to show the work to all interested, at their cottage, and to dispose of the same at very reasonable rates.

MESSRS. ANDERSON & PRICE, the managers of the new Mount Pleasant House at the White Mountains, won "golden opinions from all sorts of people" for the perfect manner in which they entertained their guests last season. The house itself is perfectly equipped in everything that appertains to a first-class hotel. The cuisine is something to be remembered with delight, but beyond all these matters is the fact that Messrs. Anderson & Price are gentlemen of taste and culture, and know how to cater to the wants of those who have been accustomed to good living and good service. These gentlemen conduct the Hotel Ormond, at Ormond, Volusia County, Florida, one of the most delightful places in the South.

IT is pleasant to see Miss Campbell, who is a universal favorite, again at the Mansion House.

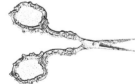

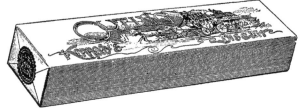

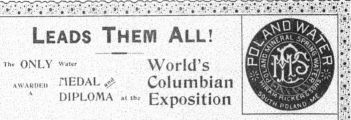

The Hill-Top

POLAND SPRINGS, SO. POLAND, ME.

THE HILL·TOP

VOL. III.   SUNDAY MORNING. JULY 19, 1896.   No. 3.

The Shakers of Sabbath-day Lake.

IF you are in need of experiencing a sense of perfect peacefulness and calm repose, you should take a trip over to the Shaker settlement, but a few miles from here.

As one enters the house, in which is the post-office, reception room, and store, a feeling of perfect tranquility at once takes possession of you, and you involuntarily exclaim, "What ease, what mind and body's rest is here!"

The pleasant faces that one meets are cheerful, smiling, contented ones, and they seem to be at peace with all the world, and conscious that such things as strife, bustle, and competitive jostling of one another, has either never entered here, or has been long since banished forever.

Many men of fame have sought a few moments' rest within the walls, such as Blaine, Butler, Frye, and many more, and doubtless turned from the place with a sigh of regret, that they must again face the howling tempest of the political or business cyclone.

The Shakers are familiar personages to the guests at Poland

Springs, they making many visits here during the season, bringing with them a great variety of their goods which their industrious and deft fingers have fashioned during the winter months, when out-of-door occupation is at its minimum. These they display, and the proceeds of their sales go into the general coffers of the community. They raise great quantities of flowers, especially sweet peas, of which they have a thousand feet under cultivation at the present time.

Industry is one of their ruling characteristics, and each hour of their waking moments finds some work accomplished or in progress.

One of the best-known faces to be seen there, as well as at the Poland Spring House, is undoubtedly that of Sister Aurelia, who has been identified with the place from infancy. Her sweet and kindly face seems to give assurance of all that is hospitable and gentle in the human composition, and looks out from the simple bonnet or cap, beaming with absolute good nature.

It was the mother of sister Aurelia who secured to the women of Maine the right to hold their property, through the medium of a dream, the petition for which she beheld before her, and on awakening wrote it down verbatim, and it was sent in to the legislature of this state, acted upon without revision, was passed, and became the law.

She, as well as the other believers, are very fond of good books, Sister Aurelia being especially so of Lew Wallace's writings.

We present her portrait this week, which shows the dress long identified with the sect, and this particular dress was presented to her and made by Mrs. Benjamin Sturtevant of Jamaica Plain, Mass., and worn by Sister Aurelia for the first time at the dedication of the Maine State Building, upon which occasion she was presented to all the principal speakers.

Guests at Poland Springs, as well as all others, will find welcome at all times should they stop at the door, and will find it one of the most interesting spots imaginable to visit.

It is to be regretted that want of space prevents our presenting a more extended description of them, at this time; but they are pleased at all times to inform any one who genuinely desires enlightenment, concerning themselves, their surroundings, and their belief.

The Poland Steam Launch.

A PARTY from the Mansion House took the steam launch Tuesday and went through the canal into the upper lake. The party consisted of Mr. W. H. Burrows, and Mrs. Burrows, Miss Flemming, Dr. and Mrs. Mason, Mrs. Turner, Mrs. Underhill, Miss Underhill, Mrs. Ernst, Mr. and Mrs. Soule, and Mr. Green.

EDWARD H. BARNARD.

The Art Exhibition.

IT was our intention to have presented the above likeness of Mr. Edward H. Barnard last week, but it failed to arrive in time, so we present it here.

During the week five very excellent pictures by William F. Stecher have been added, and they will be found most attractive. The gallery should be visited in the evening now, as the lighting is a great improvement over daylight. Numerous small easels add also to the favorable position of many of the works, and taken altogether, no brighter, more artistic or attractive spot can be found upon the hill.

Pictures are always desirable and add much to the adornment of a home, and good opportunities should never be missed to secure them.

Musical Programme.

SUNDAY EVENING, JULY 19, 1896.

1. Priest's March.   Mendelssohn.
2. Overture—William Tell.   Rossini.
3. Benedictus.   Mackenzie.
4. First movement from B Minor Symphony. Schubert.
5. *a.* Notturno—F sharp.   Chopin.
   b. Gavotte.   Bach-Saint Saens.
                        Mr. Edmund Kuntz.
6. Romanza.   Goltermann.
                        Mr. E. Loeffler.
7. Selection—Mignon.   Thomas.

Children's Column.

" More tender than the tenderest flower of earth is the flower of heaven,—Love."

Royal Disobedience.

An amusing anecdote is told of Princess Royal, now Empress Frederick. When a child the queen had some difficulty in keeping her in order.

On one occasion, when Dr. Brown was staying at Windsor in attendance on Prince Albert, the little princesses, hearing their father call him " Brown," used the same form of speech to him also.

The queen at once corrected them for it; all obeyed her except the Princess Royal, who was threatened with " bed " if she did it again.

The next day when Dr. Brown came down to breakfast the little princess got up and said : " Good morning, Brown ! " Then, seeing her mother looking at her, she continued : " And good night, Brown, for I'm going to bed ! " And she walked resolutely away to her punishment.

Book-Plates.

Dr. John P. Woodbury has presented to the library two very elaborate book-plates, designed by him and used in his very large private library, at his residence in Lynn. One is especially unique, and embraces in the design many volumes which he has enlarged and made exceedingly valuable from his added illustrations. Dr. Woodbury's library embraces some ten thousand volumes. His son is the secretary of the Metropolitan Park Commission of Massachusetts and a most cultured and genial gentleman.

At the Ex-Librarian Society's (London, England) exhibit in May, Dr. Thompson's book-plate was considered as peculiarly unique and original, and nothing more artistic or appropriate has been seen among the book-plates of professional men.

The Doctor found little opposition to his admission into the Grolier Club, New York, last May, when his book-plate first came out. He has presented a very fine proof of his book-plate to the library in the Maine State Building.

Gettysburg.

Gen. A. P. Martin repeated his successful talk of last year on the battle of Gettysburg, he having since re-written a considerable portion of it. He related an incident, characteristic of President Lincoln, in which he wrote to Hooker : " If you find Lee coming to the north of the Rappahannock, I would by no means cross to the south of it. . . . In one word, I would not take any risk of being entangled upon the river, like an ox jumped half over a fence, liable to be torn by dogs front and rear, without a fair chance to gore one way or kick the other."

General Martin is thoroughly familiar with his subject and was listened to with great attention.

Mexican Drawn Work.

A lady living in Texas, on the Mexican border, sends to Mrs. Hiram W. Ricker a large variety of this material of the finest and most superior quality in the art of needle-work. This is the *genuine*, and of great beauty. Mrs. Ricker will be pleased to show the work to all interested, at their cottage, and to dispose of the same at very reasonable rates.

FRANK CARLOS GRIFFITH, } EDITORS.
NETTIE M. RICKER,

PUBLISHED EVERY SUNDAY MORNING DURING THE MONTHS
OF JULY, AUGUST, AND SEPTEMBER, IN THE INTERESTS OF

POLAND SPRINGS AND ITS VISITORS.

All contributions relative to the guests of Poland Springs
will be thankfully received.

To insure publication, all communications should reach the
editors not later than Wednesday preceding day of issue.

All parties desiring rates for advertising in the HILL-TOP
should write the editors for same.

The subscription price of the HILL-TOP is $1.00 for the
season, post-paid. Single copies will be mailed at 10c. each.

Address,
        EDITORS "HILL-TOP,"
            Poland Spring House,
                South Poland, Maine.

PRINTED AT JOURNAL OFFICE, LEWISTON.

Sunday, July 19, 1896.

Editorial.

THOSE here this calm Sabbath morning, who were present on that memorable morning July 1, 1895, will doubtless remember the words of the Hon. William P. Frye, when he began his address, to the effect that his colleague who had preceded him "has spiked all my guns, has driven me to the pulpit, and I am now going to preach." I do not know what better I can do than to follow him a bit further:

"What is success? It is not alone to occupy high position by the favor of your fellow-citizens. It is not alone to be at the head of one of the great professions. It is not alone to be conspicuous in literature, or science, or art. The farmer, in any community, who produces the most from a given number of acres, who raises the best blooded stock, who brings to agriculture the best knowledge and science, who is a model to his neighbors, is a successful man. The blacksmith in your village, at the head of his profession, who brings all the necessary brains and science to his work, who understands thoroughly the anatomy of the foot of the animal he is to clothe with the iron shoe, is a successful man. Your most skilled artisan, whoever he may be, is a successful man. A great

man, in other words, is that man who stands at or near the head of any profession, or business, or occupation in which he is seeking a livelihood."

No words which we could add to these eloquent utterances would be of interest, and we will not occupy more space by attempting it.

W. W. Churchill.

IN visiting the Art Gallery, the attention of all is certain to be attracted to two very excellent pictures; one called "Lamplight" in Alcove A, and the other "The Mirror," in C. They will explain themselves; and are delightful in their treatment, pleasing in their subjects, and will always find ready admirers.

These were the work of Churchill, a Boston-born artist, still only about thirty-six years of age, but whose work has found favor in the Paris Salon, where he studied for four years in the Atelier Bonnat. He has also exhibited in all the principal American exhibitions, including the World's Fair.

Churchill's work is always satisfactory and artistic, and is to be found in the galleries of the critical in art.

Dr. and Mrs. Ira L. Moore are making their first visit to Poland Springs, and of course find it delightful. They reside permanently at the Parker House in Boston.

Valentines.

BY MARCIA B. JORDAN.

Fluttering wings and
Blinded eyes
    And an old-time arrow and bow!
What are these weapons
To meet a world
    Where every one wants to know!
Where science is life
And method is life
    And systems flourish, heigho!

Two carmine lips and
A beating heart
    And wealth but in caresses!
What is the chance
To win a glance
When Clotilde wears Worth dresses?
When millions make,
And love's laid low,
And poor little Cupid is snubbed, heigho!

'Tis true, we own!
Yet why bemoan
    Since Cupid frowns at law?
No bicycle suits,
Nor feminine votes,
    Can silence *him* with awe!
And even the coming woman smiles
At the fair little god's illogical wiles!

. . . .

Friend, be glad with me one dream
    Continues spite of all dissection;
One little lord still holds his sway
    And counts on absolute subjection;
One pair of wings remains unfurled,
One sweet enchantment rules the world!
"Dear little Love, warm beats thy heart,
And keen as ever flies thy dart!"

Progressive Euchre.

THE first large progressive euchre party of the season took place Friday evening, July 10th, at the Poland Spring House. Mrs. Bates won the first ladies' prize, a beautiful piece of Mexican drawn work. The second prize went to Mrs. Keene, a Dresden tray and nail polisher. Mrs. Maginnis won the third prize, a Wedgwood jewel box. The fourth prize, a Delft dariner, went to Miss Voorhees. Mr. George F. Baker won the first gentlemen's prize, a silver calendar; Mr. Morrison, the second prize, silver whist counters; Mr. Cooke, the third prize, cut cordial glass in a mosaic case; Mr. Rose, the fourth prize, a Delft candlestick.

Poland Water is now used on the tables of one of the great ocean steamship lines.

Mr. Griswold Bourne gave a very delightful sailing party on board the yacht Emily. At first a sudden shower threatened to break up the trip, but owing perhaps to the smiling faces and sunny eyes of the Misses Newhall, Bourne, Gregory, and Stinson, and Mr. and Mrs. Baggaley, not to mention those of Messrs. Olney, Maginnis, and Bourne, the clouds melted away, and a good breeze gave them a very pleasant two hours' spin.

Our Menu.

RECIPE NO. 5.

Planked Blue-fish au Madeira.

TAKE five good-sized blue-fish, clean and remove the backbone. Lay in a large pan with pepper, salt, sweet oil, juice of four lemons. Then set away for one hour until it is seasoned. After this, place the fish upon a two-inch plank four feet square, with butter and vegetables cut up fine.

Place the plank in a pan with two inches of cold water, and cook before the fire until done.

Sauce Madeira.

Take one gallon of Espagnole and add juice of three lemons, and fine herbs, pepper, salt, and wine-glass of Madeira. Let it come to a boil and strain off and serve with the fish.

Potatoes à la Brabanconne.

Take two gallons of mashed potatoes; add one quart of cream, salt, pepper, nutmeg to taste; add parboiled onion, parsley, and cheese chopped fine, and mix thoroughly. Place in a shallow pan and have the top of the potatoes perfectly smooth. Then garnish with butter, cracker crumbs, cheese, pepper, salt, and a very little butter over all. Place in the oven and brown. Remove and cut in diamond shape and serve with the fish.

RECIPE NO. 6.

Fried Fillet of Northern White-fish, Sauce D'Uxelles.

Clean and take the fillets from ten good-sized white-fish. Then take the fillets and slice into small, thin portions. Lay them on a large pan, add pepper, salt, and lemon juice to taste. Allow them to remain one hour in a cool place. Then bread and flatten them out with a wooden paddle, to get the shape of the fillets. Fry in hot, deep fat.

Sauce D'Uxelles.

Take one gallon of rich chicken stock; add ruex until it becomes the right thickness. Finish by beating in five yolks of eggs, the juice of two lemons, mace, pepper and salt to taste. Then add chopped parsley, mushrooms, shalots, and fresh estragon.

A man experienced in the care of invalids; an extensive traveller, not only all over this country, but frequently in Europe; gentle, intelligent, well-read, and conversant with people and places, desires an opportunity to accompany an elderly invalid gentleman or lady in the capacity of companion. He can be highly recommended. Information may be had from the Librarian, Maine State Building.

A Fishing Party.

It is a most interesting story, that of Mr. Amos R. Little and his friend David G. Yates, respecting their fishing trip to the Moisic, which empties into the Gulf of St. Lawrence, 350 miles below Quebec. Their camp is eighteen miles up the Moisic, and there were six gentlemen in the party. They caught 441 salmon, whose combined weight was 8,950 pounds. These were all caught in the pools opposite the camp.

It required fifteen men, guides, servants, and cooks to do the work, each gentleman having two guides, which left a chef, boy, and servant's cook beside.

Robbins, the English auctioneer, in advertising an estate for sale, said its only drawbacks were "the litter of the rose leaves and the noise of the nightingales." Thus a friend, speaking to us of the famous new Mt. Pleasant House in the White Mountains, said its only out was that the table was so excellent that he was at times in danger of dyspepsia. This hotel has not only the advantage of being new, clean, and fresh, and situated in the most charming section of the "Switzerland of America," but it is thoroughly equipped with capital and brains, as well as the ordinary requisites of an hotel. Its owners and managers know what the comforts and luxuries of living are, and furnish them right up to that line which separates excellence from ostentation. The Mt. Pleasant is managed by Messrs. Anderson & Price.

Guests at Poland Spring House.

JULY 15, 1896.

Mr. and Mrs. A. Anderson	Camden, N. J.
Mr. and Mrs. Geo. T. Bourne	New York.
Miss Bourne	New York.
Mr. Griswold Bourne	New York.
Mr. and Mrs. Geo. F. Baker	Hyannis, Mass.
Mrs. Wm. S. Brown	New York.
Mr. and Mrs. Ralph Baggaley	Pittsburg.
Mr. Wm. A. Bigelow	New York.
Mr. and Mrs. Amos Barnes	Boston.
Mrs. B. Babcock	New York.
Miss Babcock	New York.
Rev. Dr. Baxter	Boston.
Miss S. P. Baker	Boston.
Mr. Chas. T. Baker	Boston.
Miss L. Belyea	Boston.
Miss S. E. Brody	Boston.
Mr. and Mrs. Jacob P. Bates	Boston.
Mr. and Mrs. H. O. Blight	Cambridge.
Mr. and Mrs. Nelson Bartlett	Boston.
Mr. E. R. Bossange	New York.
Mrs. H. W. Briggs	Newport.
Master E. N. Briggs	Newport.
Mr. and Mrs. C. A. Browning	Boston.
Mr. E. N. Briggs	Saginaw, Mich.
Mr. E. C. Babb	Minneapolis.
Mr. and Mrs. Geo. W. Coleman	Boston.
Mr. Andrew K. Culver	Brooklyn.
Mr. and Mrs. F. W. Carpenter	Providence.
Miss Hannah Carpenter	Providence.
Mr. A. W. Clark	Deering.
Mr. and Mrs. C. C. Corbin	Webster, Mass.
Mrs. A. A. Connel	New York.
Mr. and Mrs. Thomas J. Craven	Salem, N. J.
Miss L. H. Craven	Salem, N. J.
Miss Mary B. Craven	Salem, N. J.
Miss Jane Y. Craven	Salem, N. J.
W. H. Chappall	Chicago.
Miss Chappall	Chicago.
Miss R. B. Cabeen	Bristol, Pa.
Mr. and Mrs. H. D. Carroll	Springfield.
The Misses DePeyster	New York.
Mrs. Albert Douglass	New York.
Mrs. M. E. Dexter	Brooklyn.
Miss Dexter	Brooklyn.
Mrs. N. C. Dickerson	New York.
Mrs. D. L. Dudley	Haverhill, Mass.
Mr. and Mrs. R. M. Field	Boston.
Mr. and Mrs. James H. Eddy	New Britain, Conn.
Miss Bessie M. Eddy	New Britain, Conn.
Mr. Charles Endicott	Canton, Mass.
Miss A. L. Faile	New York.
Mr. Thos. H. Faile	New York.
Miss Fletcher	Boston.
Mr. Geo. B. French	Boston.
Mrs. J. D. Fessenden	New York.
Gen. Chas. E. Furlong	New York.
Mr. John Goldthwaite	Boston.
Miss E. B. Goldthwaite	Boston.
Mrs. G. F. Gregory	Brooklyn.
Miss Gregory	Brooklyn.
Mrs. M. K. Goodwin	Boston.
Miss Goodwin	Boston.
Mrs. L. M. Gale	Washington.
Miss Olive Gale	Washington.
Mr. and Mrs. Alfred A. Glasier	Boston.
Mr. and Mrs. C. C. Griffin	Haverhill, Mass.
Mr. and Mrs. Horace Hunt	New York.
Mrs. S. B. Hubbard	Jacksonville, Fla.
Mr. and Mrs. L. Hurlburt	Brooklyn.
Mrs. M. B. Hoffman	New York.
Mr. and Mrs. L. D. Henwood	Boston.
Mr. Nat Huggins	New York.
Mr. and Mrs. J. W. Hazen	Boston.
Mr. and Mrs. S. Haas	New York.
Miss Florrie Haas	New York.
Mr. Emil Herz	Trenton.
Mr. and Mrs. Hudson Hoagland	New York.
Mr. W. J. Holden	Boston.
Mr. and Mrs. L. Hall	Cambridge.
Miss M. R. Haddock	New York.
Miss E. M. Haines	New Brighton.
Mr. and Mrs. J. B. Hutchinson	Philadelphia.
Mr. J. B. Hutchinson, Jr.	Philadelphia.
Mr. Samuel Ivers	New Bedford.
Miss Ella F. Ivers	New Bedford.
Mrs. Julian James	Washington.
Mr. John Lucas	Philadelphia.
Mr. and Mrs. Amos R. Little	Philadelphia.
Miss H. N. Loomis	Boston.
Miss M. L. Loomis	Boston.
Mr. and Mrs. B. Lemann and family	New Orleans.
Miss Leland	New York.
Mr. and Mrs. Wm. R. Lynch	Brooklyn.
Mrs. Mary Lambert	Brooklyn.
Miss Lambert	Brooklyn.
Mr. Francis L. Leland	New York.
Mr. and Mrs. T. B. M. Mason	Washington.
Mrs. T. B. Myers	Washington.
Mrs. Jno. H. Maginnis	New Orleans.
Mr. Jno. H. Maginnis	New Orleans.
Mrs. A. Murray	Washington.
Miss A. G. Miller	Brooklyn.
Dr. and Mrs. Ira L. Moore	Boston.
Mrs. Chas. E. Morrill	Portland.
Miss Helen Morrill	Portland.
Mrs. McKay	St. Louis.
Mrs. J. T. Montgomery	Philadelphia.
Mrs. B. P. Moulton	Rosemont, Pa.
Mr. and Mrs. A. R. Mitchell	Newtonville.
Mrs. Christine Marburg	Baltimore.
The Misses Marburg	Baltimore.
Mr. C. L. Marburg	Baltimore.
Mrs. Newbegin	Portland.
Mr. and Mrs. W. T. Ness	Boston.
Miss Lucy P. Newhall	Philadelphia.
Mr. and Mrs. Frank F. Olney	Providence.
Mr. Elam W. Olney	Providence.
Mr. John A. Ordway	Boston.
Mrs. J. A. Pettee	New York.
Judge and Mrs. Chas. A. Peabody	New York.
Mrs. Henry U. Palmer	Brooklyn.
Masters Austin and Chester Palmer	Brooklyn.
Mrs. M. E. Parsons	Boston.
Mrs. E. D. Peters	Boston.
Mrs. H. D. Polhemus	Brooklyn.
Miss A. J. Pomeroy	Brooklyn.
Mr. and Mrs. E. W. Pratt	Boston.
Miss Emily Pratt	Boston.
Mr. Joseph G. Ray	Franklin, Mass.
Miss L. F. Ray	Franklin, Mass.
Mr. and Mrs. H. A. Rogers	New York.
Miss May Rogers	New York.
Mr. and Mrs. J. Fred Rogers	Boston.
Mrs. G. H. Richardson	Bridgeport.
Mr. E. J. Robinson	Boston.
Mr. and Mrs. A. S. Rines	Portland.
Mr. and Mrs. S. B. Stinson	Washington.
Miss Stinson	Washington.
Miss Florence Stinson	Washington.
Mr. and Mrs. A. T. Salter	Washington.
Mr. and Mrs. A. W. Smith	Providence.
Mr. and Mrs. Irving T. Smith and family	Boston.
Mr. and Mrs. James Staples	Bridgeport.
Mr. and Mrs. Joseph W. Sandford	Plainfield, N. J.
Mr. E. S. Stinson	Hopedale, Mass.
Mrs. Orlando Tompkins	Boston.
Mr. and Mrs. Frank R. Thomas	Boston.
Mr. and Mrs. F. E. Taylor	Brooklyn.
Dr. J. M. Thompson	Boston.
Miss E. R. Tilden	New Brighton.
Mr. and Mrs. John H. Voorhees	Brooklyn.
Miss Jessie Voorhees	Brooklyn.
Mr. and Mrs. W B. Valentine	London, Eng.
Mr. and Mrs. John P. Woodbury	Boston.
Mrs. J. Reed Whipple	Boston.
Dr. M. C. Wedgwood and Mrs. Wedgwood	Lewiston.
Mr. and Mrs. J. R. Winters	New York.
Mr. A. Wentworth	Boston.
Miss Waldo	Salem.
Mr. F. K. Wharton	Philadelphia.
Miss Whitney	New York.
Mr. and Mrs. C. T. White	Boston.
Mr. David G. Yates	Philadelphia.
Mr. and Mrs. H. D. Ziegler	Philadelphia.
Miss G. F. Ziegler	Philadelphia.

Tid-Bits.

Pond lilies.

1,208 volumes in the Library.

Pictures were never to be purchased for less than at present.

Why is a barbed-wire fence like a barn? Because it keeps the Cattle Inn.

Have you observed the bird's nest in the electric light globe on the north piazza?

The friends of Mr. and Mrs. Richard T. Howes of Cambridge regret much their early departure.

Mr. and Mrs. H. M. Sanders of Boston are at the Poland Spring House. Mr. Sanders is a brother of Mrs. A. B. Ricker.

The Indians are now encamped at the Spring. It may be pleasant to visit them, and procure some of their pretty things, during the week days.

The ladies at the Mansion House are having a series of progressive whist parties. Miss Campbell made the highest number of points on Wednesday evening, which was 57.

Prof. William E. Sargent and Mrs. Sargent, Dr. and Mrs. Crane, of Hebron, Maine, and Professor and Mrs. Brainard of Augusta, spent Tuesday at the Poland Spring House.

The night-blooming cereus from Mrs. Hiram W. Ricker's conservatory, which was exhibited at the Poland Spring House, Saturday evening, was greatly admired. It had three blossoms.

Mrs. Robinson may be found at the Poland Spring House now by those desirous of the services of a masseuse. She will be found skilled and satisfactory in her art, which is recognized as a most beneficial one.

Hon. and Mrs. Charles Emory Smith are guests at the Poland Spring House. Mr. Smith, who is the editor of the Philadelphia *Press*, was our minister to St. Petersburg during President Harrison's administration. Mr. Smith is a friend and supporter of Mr. McKinley.

It having been proposed that an Amateur Photographic Exhibition be held in the Maine State Building in August, if there are any here who would like to participate in such a friendly contest of their artistic labors, they may communicate with the Librarian to that effect.

Mrs. Baggaley gave a delightful drive to White Oak Hill, around the middle lake and to the Gloucester Shakers. The party included the Misses Carver, Miss Stinson, Miss Newhall, Miss Bourne, Miss Gregory, Miss Faile, Mr. Maginnis, Mr. Griswold Bourne, Mr. Olney, and Mr. and Mrs. Baggaley.

The Tuskegee Normal and Industrial Institute had $119 added to its funds through the eloquent appeal of Mr. Booker T. Washington, who addressed the guests on Thursday evening. It would have been pleasant to have been able to state that it was a much larger sum, as the Institute is pronounced most worthy by people qualified to judge.

Arrivals.

POLAND SPRING HOUSE.
JULY 9 TO JULY 16, 1896.

Atwood, Abiam	Auburn.
Atwood, S. C.	Auburn.
Atwood, Fred S.	Auburn.
Archibald, Edgar	Hyde Park.
Allen, C. R.	Brooklyn.
Allen, R. G.	Brooklyn.
Atkins, Mrs. Morris Fletcher	Montpelier.
Adams, Albert J.	New York.
Anderson, Mr. and Mrs. A.	Camden, N. J.
Aldrich, Mrs. Frank R.	Detroit.
Allen, Frances L.	Brunswick.
Briggs, Mrs. H. W.	Newport.
Briggs, E. N.	Newport.
Babb, E. B.	Minneapolis.
Bonney, Arthur P.	Boston.
Browning, Mr. and Mrs. C. A.	Boston.
Benson, C. C.	Lewiston.
Bean, Mr. and Mrs. I. S.	Portland.
Blaineid, Mr. and Mrs. A. H.	Augusta.
Brayton, Mr. and Mrs. Dana D.	Fall River.
Bartley, E. H., M.D.	Brooklyn.
Browning, William, M.D.	Brooklyn.
Craven, Mr. and Mrs. Thomas J.	Salem, N. J.
Craven, Miss L. H.	Salem, N. J.
Craven, Miss Mary B.	Salem, N. J.
Craven, Miss Jane T.	Salem, N. J.
Conant, H. W.	Auburn.
Corsa, O. H.	New York.
Chappall, William H.	Chicago.
Chappall, Miss	Chicago.
Crowley, Mrs. J. H.	Lewiston.
Crane, Mr. and Mrs. R. R.	Hebron.
Cabeen, Miss K. B.	Bristol, Pa.
Carroll, Mr. and Mrs. H. D.	Springfield.
Curtis, Mrs. D. D.	Medfield.
Curtis, Miss Daisy	Medfield.
Campbell, G. H.	Lawrence.
Chandler, Mrs. Z.	Detroit.
Calloway, Thos. J.	Tuskegee, Ala.
Cotterell, Mr. and Mrs. G. H.	New York.
Dudley, Mrs. D. T.	Haverhill.
Dwyer, Rev. T. A.	Hyde Park.
DeLong, F. E.	Philadelphia.
Esterly, Harriet B.	Columbiana, O.
Eddy, Mr. and Mrs. James H.	New Britain.
Eddy, Bessie M.	New Britain.
Endicott, Charles	Canton.
Field, Mr. and Mrs. D. N.	Brockton.
Fischer, Mr. and Mrs. C. S.	New York.
Fischer, Miss Hattie P.	New York.
Fischer, A. H.	New York.
Griffin, Mr. and Mrs. C. C.	Haverhill.
Goodrich, H. L.	Haverhill.
Harris, Miss E. M.	New Brighton, N. J.
Hutchinson, Mr. and Mrs. J. B.	Philadelphia.
Hutchinson, J. B., Jr.	Philadelphia.
Hearmes, Mrs. Elgin A.	Detroit.
Holmes, Mr. and Mrs. E.	New York.
Josephs, Mrs. Samuel	Philadelphia.
Josephs, Harry S.	Philadelphia.
Kidder, F. H.	Boston.
Lord, C. K.	Baltimore.
Lowell, Miss	Auburn.
Little, J. R.	Lewiston.
Leland, Francis L.	New York.
Lovejoy, G. W.	Portland.
Little, Amos R.	Philadelphia.
Lambert, Cora W.	Brockton.
Lynch, William Richard	Brooklyn.
Montgomery, Mrs. J. T.	Philadelphia.
Marston, Mrs. F. R.	Philadelphia.
Munroe, Mrs. C. A.	Boston.
Morrill, Charles S.	Portland.

McSkimmon, Miss Mary	Brookline.
Moulton, Mrs. B. P.	Rosemont, Pa.
Mitchell, Mr. and Mrs. A. R.	Newtonville.
McCully, Jessie R.	New York.
Marburg, Mrs. Christine	Baltimore.
Marburg, C. L.	Baltimore.
Mitchell, Charles R.	Lewiston.
McIntire, Miss May	Lewiston.
Norton, Miss E. F.	Portland.
Oakes, Mr. and Mrs. Wallace K.	Auburn.
Oakes, Miss Methyl	Auburn.
Oakes, Herbert H.	Auburn.
Oakes, Mr. and Mrs. Josiah	Malden.
Plummer, Mr. and Mrs. Edward	Lisbon Falls.
Platt, Mr. and Mrs. E. W.	Boston.
Platt, Miss Emily F.	Boston.
Pope, N. Q.	Boston.
Rice, Samuel S.	Cambridge.
Richardson, Mrs. G. B.	Bridgeport.
Robinson, Mrs. E. J.	Boston.
Rowe, Mrs.	Woburn.
Rich, E. H.	Boston.
Rines, Mr. and Mrs. A. S.	Portland.
Rogers, Ethel W.	Boston.
Ruggles, E. O.	Boston.
Staples, Mr. and Mrs. James	Bridgeport.
Sandford, Mr. and Mrs. Joseph W.	Plainfield, N. J.
Sutor, Mr. and Mrs. John W.	Boston.
Stinson, S. B.	Philadelphia.
Sammons, Charles E.	Boston.
Stimpson, E. S.	Hopedale, Mass.
Smiley, Mr. and Mrs. William H.	Haverhill.
Safford, Agnes M.	Portland.
Sargent, Mr. and Mrs. W. E.	Hebron.
Stearns, Mr. and Mrs. R. H.	Boston.
Steelwagen, Mr. and Mrs. Edward J.	Washington.
Sperb, William	New York.
Smith, Mr. and Mrs. Charles Emory	Philadelphia.
Smith, Mr. and Mrs. W. M.	New York.
Scott, G. E.	New York.
Thomas, W. M.	New York.
Tyler, Daniel	Boston.
Tilden, Miss E. R.	New Brighton, N. J.
Taggart, Col. G. I.	Savannah, Ga.
Taggart, Jno. P.	Savannah, Ga.
Van Santvoord, A.	New York.
Van Santvoord, Miss	New York.
White, Mr. and Mrs. J. Stuart	New York.
Whitney, Miss	New York.
White, Mr. and Mrs. Charles T.	Boston.
Washington, Booker T.	Tuskegee, Ala.
Yates, David G.	Philadelphia.
Yeomans, Mr. and Mrs. A. H.	Boston.

MANSION HOUSE.
JULY 9 TO 16.

Amerman, Mr. and Mrs. N.	New York.
Ayers, Mrs. W. M.	Oakland.
Campbell, Mary	Camden, N. J.
Chandler, P. L.	Westbrook.
Cook, Mr. and Mrs. Charles	Portland.
Chapman, Alice G.	Milwaukee.
Chapman, Cecile	Bethel.
Chapman, Christie	Bethel.
Coes, Mr. and Mrs. John A.	Worcester.
Coes, Miss M. M.	Worcester.
Marks, Mr. and Mrs. S. C.	Montgomery, Ala.
Marks, Ethel	Montgomery, Ala.
Patton, L. F.	Mechanic Falls.
Read, Miss L. S.	Camden, N. J.
Read, William T.	Camden, N. J.
Sabine, Mr. and Mrs. A. F.	Philadelphia.
Thomas, Mr. and Mrs. E. A.	Milford.
Vedder, O. F.	Portland.
Wood, Mr. and Mrs. Albert	Worcester.
Wood, Miss E. C.	Worcester.

THE NEW MOUNT PLEASANT HOUSE,

In the Heart of the White Mountains.

Through Parlor Cars from New York, Boston, and Portland, also from Burlington, Montreal, and Quebec.

The Hotel faces the Grandest Display of Mountain Peaks in America east of the Rocky Mountains. It is lighted throughout by electricity, thoroughly heated by steam, and has an abundance of private and public baths. Its orchestra is made up largely from the Boston Symphony Orchestra. Its table is unsurpassed. Absolutely pure water from an artesian well, 409 feet in solid rock.

IT IS THE NEAREST HOTEL TO MT. WASHINGTON, AND THE TRAIN FOR THE SUMMIT STARTS FROM A STATION ON THE HOTEL GROUNDS.

All Trains, Maine Central Railroad, from Portland to Burlington, Montreal, Quebec, and Lake Champlain stop at the platform close to the House.

Leave Portland 8.45 A.M., arrive Mt. Pleasant House, 12.21 P.M.	
" " 1.25 P.M., " " " " 5.05 P.M.	
" " 3.20 P.M., " " " " 7.20 P.M.	POST, TELEGRAPH, AND TICKET OFFICE IN THE HOTEL.
" " 8.45 P.M., " " " " 11.47 P.M.	

ANDERSON & PRICE, of the Hotel Ormond of Florida, Managers.

Address by wire or mail, "Mount Pleasant House, N. H."

JOHN O. RICE,

PROFESSIONAL ACCOUNTANT AND AUDITOR

Expert Examinations made for Banks, Corporations, Estates, or Mercantile Houses, and general accountant work solicited. P. O. Box 1.639.

Office, Room 4, Centennial Building, 93 Exchange Street, PORTLAND, ME.

References: II. Ricker & Sons, Poland Springs; First National Bank, Portland, Me.

PRINCE'S EXPRESS CO.

For all Points in the West and South.

Freight FROM New York, Philadelphia, Baltimore, and Washington, D. C., should be forwarded via United States Express Co. Boston Office, 34 and 35 Court Square, 105 Arch Street, and 77 Kingston Street. Portland Office, 103 Exchange Street.

Courteous Attention, Low Rates, and Quick Despatch.

PREBLE HOUSE,

Adjoining Longfellow's Home,

J. C. WHITE. —— PORTLAND, ME.

H. M. SANDERS & CO.,

Hardware, Paints, Oils, and Varnishes.

Carpenters' and Machinists' Tools.

A full assortment of CUTLERY.

THEATRICAL STAGE HARDWARE. 27 Eliot St., BOSTON.

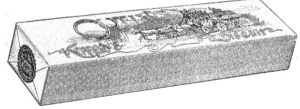

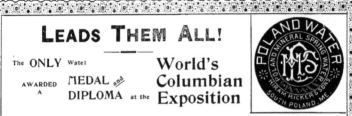

The Hill-Top

POLAND SPRINGS, SO. POLAND, ME.

HARRY C. WILKINSON.

VOL. III.   SUNDAY MORNING, JULY 26, 1896.   No. 4.

The Reading-Room.

AS one enters under the low but exquisitely designed stone arches, crossing the Roman pavement, which carries the name "Maine State Building," and enters that structure, the first impression is one of surprise that so stupendous an enterprise should have been undertaken, in removing this building from a spot a thousand miles away.

In entering the spacious rotunda one feels that the air is purer, cooler, and fresher than in the usual "Reading-Room," so called, and the comfortable rattan furniture invites occupancy.

It broadens as one enters, opening out into two side wings, and on looking upward, it is observed that the great dome light which spans its entire width, and lights its every corner, is three stories above, thus affording a free circulation of air and a constant changing of the atmosphere.

Pleasant nooks wherein to lounge and read in comfort are found on every hand, while the central table is strewn with the current periodical literature of the day.

On each hand, as one enters, is a staircase, symmetrical in design, which join in their ascent to the upper stories, while upon the opposite side of this octagonal apartment is a grand and architecturally handsome fire-place. Between two fluted columns, and sunk within a spacious recess, is the high, wide, and roomy mantel, with the coat of arms of Maine carved within the center, while beneath is the tiling which so pleasingly surrounds the fire-place proper, with its massive andirons which rest upon the hospitable hearth.

The head of a monarch moose surmounts the whole of this feature of the apartment, as if he had but just thrust it through a paper hoop, and was petrified with surprise at the result. Again, and appropriately as well, is seen the American Eagle, a splendid specimen of our National Bird of Freedom, proudly and fearlessly perched above his head, to scan the features of each new arrival. The Moose is typical of Maine ; the Eagle, of the Nation.

> " Then from his mansion in the sun
>   She called her Eagle bearer down;
> And placed within his mighty hand
>   The emblem of her chosen land."

These are the words of Drake in his beautiful poem, and here we have, floating proudly over all, the banner he so eloquently praised.

Placed at convenient points the eye is pleased with the view of jardinieres filled with the wild field flowers, as well as the cultivated palm, rubber or other plants, while upon the walls are placed the permanent reproductions of the ever-memorable scenes of the World's Columbian Exhibition, of which this building was a part, and as it has proved, and will prove, a permanent and everlasting portion, devoted to the advancement and the perpetuation of Art and Literature. It is probably safe to say that no hotel enterprise in the wide world possesses such a structure devoted to such purposes.

As time progresses, and its walls become thicker encrusted with the counterfeit presentments of Maine's illustrious sons, and its nooks and alcoves afford resting-places for their historic souvenirs, this charming, grand, and restful place will become,

Reading-Room, Maine State Building.

like the two loved spots of Avon and Ayr, the Mecca of the sons of Maine.

The view we have presented on the second page is selected because it presents more clearly the detail, in one view, than were its lovely features hidden, as at most times, by its numerous occupants.

Within its library, opening directly off, may be found its shelves crowded with books, the gifts of its most generous guests, and behind the glass of its herbarium, also an adjunct, can be scanned the exquisitely-prepared specimens of the flora of Poland, over 600 in number, the work of Miss Kate Furbish, itself a labor of love.

Stepping into an alcove one finds the names of many visitors to this historic edifice already inscribed upon the register, while upon inquiry it is found that the original registers used at the greatest fair ever known are here and carefully preserved.

Works preserving the salient features of the fair, in picture and in prose, are to be seen in generous variety, while on every hand are quiet, interested readers of the standard and current literature of the age.

LIST OF PERIODICALS.

Arena.	Ladies' Home Journal.
Atlantic Monthly.	Life.
Black Cat.	Lippincott's Magazine.
Cassell's Magazine of Art.	Mc'Clure's Magazine.
Century.	Munsey's Magazine.
Cosmopolitan.	North American Review.
Figaro Illustre.	New England Magazine.
London Graphic.	Puck.
Harper's Monthly.	St. Nicholas.
Harper's Weekly.	Scribner's.
Harper's Bazaar.	Strand Magazine.
Illustrated American.	Scientific American.
Illustrated London News.	Whist.
Judge.	Youth's Companion.
Leslie's Weekly.	

Mansion House Whist.

TUESDAY evening, July 21st, the guests of the Mansion House gave an impromptu progressive whist party and easily found players enough to fill six tables. At the conclusion, to the surprise of all, a few appropriate prizes were bestowed upon the victors, Mr. and Mrs. Keene; and the vanquished ones, Mrs. Soule and Mrs. Ernst, were duly consoled,—the former received balm for all bruises resulting from her evening's struggle with bad cards, and the latter was granted a trip abroad in the *Poland*, with limited leave of absence.

After the awards, the chairs and tables were removed, and an informal, but very merry dance, finished the evening.

When the Tide Comes In.

BY A. HURLBURT.

Ah, this world in rapturous joy exults,
When the flashing spray comes dancing in
With the first bright beam and breath of day—
How gay my heart when the tide comes in !

And the splendid sun rides on and on,
Over trackless seas which seek the shore,
Till the sunset gilds high-crested waves
Which move as gods when the tide comes in.

Then a frowning night enshrouds the earth,
And the restless breakers surge and moan;
But the night shall pass, the seas shall chant:
" Oh, life is full when the tide comes in."

Though the waves recede, and souls shall yearn
For the joys they knew which ebbed and fled,
Let them watch with brave and steadfast hearts,
New bliss is theirs when the tide comes in.

Picnic Party.

[Contributed.]

THE exceeding hot weather of Wednesday filled the hearts of the young people of the Mansion House with picnic longings, which were gratified by the hospitable invitation of Miss Campbell, of Camden, N.J., and her cousin, Mr. Read, who made up a party of twenty-one members, as follows : Mrs. Lewis, Miss Townsend, Miss Marsh, Mr. Lewis, Mrs. Jordan, Miss Hall, Miss Ricker, Miss Nettie Ricker, Mr. Read, Mr. Franzèn, Mrs. Kuntz, Miss Barbour, Miss Campbell, Miss Sullivan, Mr. D. Kuntz, Mr. Edmund Kuntz, Mr. Dudley Lewis, Mr. Robert Marsh, Mr. Arthur Marsh, Miss Thurston, Miss Conover.

"The little party set sail," as the United States histories have it, for the further side of the Middle Lake, and re-discovered America in pine needles, green groves, and the fairest of water-caressed shores. Story-telling, laughter, and light chat occupied the hours, till something more substantial, in the shape of hot coffee, lemonade, sandwiches, and various dainties, were unpacked from the hampers.

A disposition, seconded by the appearance of a full moon, to divide the party into relays, showed itself, arrivals appearing from the boat-house, or the lower wharf, as the case might be, so that the last group added a bona-fide sail to the rowing parties and prolonged the early into the late evening. Cordial thanks were extended to host and hostess, and one more charming occasion was recorded in the minds of the merry-making guests.

SHE COULD TRAIN HIM.

[From Tid-Bits.]

He—"You are the first girl I ever loved."
She—"Never mind. Some don't like beginners, but I'm not at all particular."

Children's Column.

Children are the anchors that hold a mother to life.

LITTLE HARRY, who was about to be placed on the retired list for the night, without the company of his mamma, inquired: "Ain't you going to hear my prayer?"

"No, Harry, you have been so naughty, I am afraid it is useless."

"But, mamma, I've got a new prayer."

"Well, what is it?"

"Dod bless papa and mamma, and help Harry to be a dood boy. An' get all your angels to help you, cos it's going to be a putty tough job. I dess that 'll fix it."

Grandma's Ginger Cakes.

[From the San Francisco Post.]

Come, my dears, and I will show you
  How I make my ginger cakes,
How I mix the dough together,
  And how long the baking takes.

With a quart of good molasses
  Mix a pound of sugar sweet,
Add a pound of lard and butter,
  Half of each is my receipt.

Ounces two of powdered ginger,
  With a pinch of salt or two—
Mix one egg—with flour stiffen,
  Roll out thin and you are through.

How to keep them when they're finished?
  When they're baked and nicely browned?
Well, good strong lock and key, dears,
  Is the best thing that I've found.

THE following story is told of Mr. Herkomer, the well-known English artist: Once on "show day" two of Mr. Herkomer's lady friends called upon him. One brought with her some sketches made by a young man, in whose career she was much interested, and in whose talent she firmly believed. She wished for Mr. Herkomer's opinion. After closely scrutinizing the drawings, he assured her that in his estimation the sketch did not show any sign of talent, and spoke most disparagingly of the future of the youth. Furthermore, he advised his lady friend to influence the young man to adopt some other profession. To the great mortification of Mr. Herkomer, his friend proved to him that he, in his youth, made the sketches and presented her with them.

Our Menu.

RECIPE No. 7.

Boiled Fowl, with Pork, au Vin Blanc.

SELECT 25 nice fat fowl and clean. Boil three hours. Take the stock that the fowl have been boiled in and reduce to one gallon.

Make a rich Beckamel sauce; add chopped mushrooms, one clove of garlic, ground mace, salt to taste, and juice of two lemons. Finish with two egg yolks, beaten in thoroughly.

RECIPE No. 8.

Pop-Over.

One cup of flour, one cup of milk, one teaspoon of butter, one teaspoon of sugar, one saltspoon salt, one egg. Beat the egg thoroughly, add milk to the beaten egg, stir gradually into dry materials, add butter, melted. Beat rapidly for five or ten minutes with an egg-beater. Bake in a hot oven in hot iron-clads from 20 to 30 minutes.

RECIPE No. 9.

Bavarian Cream.

One quart of cream, whipped stiff, one cup of sugar, yolks of three eggs, one ounce of gelatine, dissolved in a little water. Flavor with wine or vanilla. Beat all together, stir in the gelatine, and set away to cool. Serve with cream.

Cyclist Column.

THE world having divided itself into three classes, the makers of bicycles, the sellers, and the riders, it makes it necessary that we should pay some attention to what the world appears to be unanimously interested in, so we start in modestly with some slight allusions to the wheel.

B. H. E.

" Gazes with a timid glance
  On the cyclist's swift advance.
  Wonders—Shall she take the chance !
  Trips half way across the street;
  Stops, turns back in time to meet,
  Raging, baffled cyclist fleet.
  Cyclist in the gutter tossed,
  Maiden learning to her cost:
  She who hesitates is lost."

A party of bicyclists took a spin of thirteen miles down past the Shaker's saw-mill, Sabbath-day Lake, and through the Gloucester woods. The party intended to go three miles, but lost their way. They were gone two hours and had a most delightful time. The road through the Gloucester woods they pronounced very good.

The drizzling, sizzling sprinkler,
  While bad enough, we find,
Can't sadden man so much as can
  The roaring, pouring kind.

Punctures are hole-y terrors.

Look on the bright side, but ride on the shady side.

Perpendicular riders· are prettier than horizontal ones.

A soft answer turneth away wrath, but a rough road stirreth up anger.

Ride for rest. Don't try to see how far, but how pleasantly you can go.

The average young lady never hears of a transaction involving an engagement ring without wishing she had a finger in it.

Every town that expects summer visitors should dress up its highways; and a town that does not dress up its highways should expect no one to visit it.

To PRESERVE NICKEL.

There are many compounds advertised (and most of them good) for preserving the bright surface of nickel-plated work. In the absence of anything specially prepared for the purpose take any oil that is suitable for lubricating the bearings and rub the bright work thoroughly with it. If the machine is to be left standing for a few days, leave the oil on until you are ready to use it; then rub the surface vigorously with a dry cloth.

TOURISTS TO CANADA.

You cannot enter your wheels without presenting the proper membership ticket. Temporary certificates cannot be accepted, as it would be possible for a tourist to enter one wheel on the certificate and another on his membership ticket.

Wolfe Island is not a port of entry. The only customs official there is a Preventive Officer who is frequently absent. Wheelmen must not attempt to enter Canada at this point.

[From the L. A. W. Bulletin.]
CYCLING PROVERBS.

The following proverbs are taken from the catalogue issued by the Revere Cycle Co., Boston :

New cycles ride easy.

Small choice in poor bicycles.

Live and learn (to ride a wheel).

Never too old to learn (to ride).

Faint heart never won a record.

Bicycles don't laugh at tacksmiths.

To a rickety wheel all roads are bad.

You can't ride your wheel and lend it too.

The proof of a bicycle is in the riding.

A reckless rider makes a fat church-yard.

No wheel so poor as not to have its rider.

Experience is the best spoke in your wheel.

Mount in haste and mend your bones at leisure.

A mile in the morning is worth two in the evening.

Beware of the fore part of a cheap horse, the hind part of a cheap mule, and all parts of a cheap bicycle.

Progressive Euchre.

ONE of the most enjoyable progressive euchre parties of the season took place at the Poland Spring House, Friday evening, July 17th. There were fourteen tables. Mrs. Yeoman made the highest number of moves, fifteen, and won the first ladies' prize, a beautiful hand-painted plate. The second prize, also a plate, went to Mrs. Griffin. The third prize, six exquisite doilies, were won by Mrs. Lambert. Mrs. Ernst won the fourth prize, an address book.

Miss Barbour won the first gentleman's prize, a brush broom with a silver handle. The second, a silver shoe horn, went to Mr. Bates. Mr. Yeoman won the third prize, whist counters; Mr. French, the fourth prize, a silk handkerchief.

A man experienced in the care of invalids; an extensive traveller, not only all over this country, but frequently in Europe; gentle, intelligent, well-read, and conversant with people and places, desires an opportunity to accompany an elderly invalid gentleman or lady in the capacity of companion. He can be highly recommended. Information may be had from the Librarian, Maine State Building.

FRANK CARLOS GRIFFITH, } EDITORS.
NETTIE M. RICKER,

PUBLISHED EVERY SUNDAY MORNING DURING THE MONTHS
OF JULY, AUGUST, AND SEPTEMBER, IN THE INTERESTS OF

POLAND SPRINGS AND ITS VISITORS.

All contributions relative to the guests of Poland Springs
will be thankfully received.

To insure publication, all communications should reach the
editors not later than Wednesday preceding day of issue.

All parties desiring rates for advertising in the HILL-TOP
should write the editors for same.

The subscription price of the HILL-TOP is $1.00 for the
season, post-paid. Single copies will be mailed at 10c. each.

Address,

EDITORS "HILL-TOP,"
Poland Spring House,
South Poland, Maine.

PRINTED AT JOURNAL OFFICE, LEWISTON.

Sunday, July 26, 1896.

Editorial.

A LADY recently advanced, within our hearing,
the very pretty theory, that as infants first
learn through the medium of sight, before
they can speak or even understand any language,
smiling and happy faces should be ever about and
over them. This even might have its drawbacks,
for who knows but another humorous poet might
be the result, and many of us remember what
Holmes said about that. For fear all do not, we
quote his own words:

"I wrote some lines once on a time
    In wondrous merry mood,
And thought as usual men would say
    They were exceeding good.

"They were so queer, so very queer,
    I laughed as I would die;
Albeit in the general way,
    A sober man am I.

"I called my servant, and he came;
    How kind it was of him
To mind a slender man like me,
    He of the mighty limb.

"'These to the printer,' I exclaimed,
    And in my humorous way,
I added (as a trifling jest),
    "There'll be the d—l to pay.""

"He took the paper, and I watched,
    And saw him peep within;
At the first line he read, his face
    Was all upon a grin.

"He read the next; the grin grew broad,
    And shot from ear to ear;
He read the third; a chuckling noise
    I now began to hear.

"The fourth; he broke into a roar;
    The fifth; his waistband split;
The sixth; he burst five buttons off,
    And tumbled in a fit.

"Ten days and nights, with sleepless eye,
    I watched that wretched man,
And since, I never dare to write
    As funny as I can."

Our Cows.

A VERY important and agreeable announcement
is made by George H. Bailey, the State Veterinary
Surgeon, to the following effect:

POLAND SPRINGS, July 23, 1896.

This is to certify that the above ninety-one
cows that furnish milk and cream to the Poland
Spring and Mansion House have been tested with
tuberculin, and proved to be free from all species
of disease.

GEO. H. BAILEY,
State Veterinary Surgeon.

This followed a list of the cows, and is self-
explanatory.

A Private Party.

MRS. MAGINNIS's private parlor was the scene
of a pleasant ten o'clock supper party, Thursday
evening.

The table was artistically decorated with a
center-piece of variegated flowers and ferns, and
here and there vases of sweet peas. The souvenirs
for the young ladies were Shaker baskets and
bunches of sweet peas tied with white satin ribbon.

The gentlemen were favored with flower pen-
wipers, dainty work of the Shakers, representing
carnations. The party comprised the following:
Miss Gregory, Miss Stinson and Miss Florence
Stinson, Miss Carpenter, Miss Rogers, Miss New-
hall, Miss Bonine, Miss Vose, Miss Gale, Mr.
Vose, Mr. Eddy, Mr. Olney, Mr. Bell, Mr.
Bossange, and Mr. Maginnis.

Musical Programme.

SUNDAY EVENING, AT 8.15, JULY 26, 1896.

1. March.		Lachner.
2. Adagio—From Sonata Pathetique.		Beethoven.
3. Romanza—Non e'ver.		Mattei-Müller.
	Mr. P. Müller.	
4. Selection—Lohengrin.		Wagner.
5. Parane Favorite.		Gabriel Marie.
6. Nocturno.		Doppler.
	For Flute, Violin, 'Cello, and Piano.	
7. Ungarische Rhapsodie.		Liszt.

Walter L. Dean.

ing selection, the "Bay of Naples," and an "August Twilight."

All of Dean's work is of the highest order, and finds the utmost favor with the critical, at the same time possessing the merit of pleasing the eye of all.

This excellent artist, still a young man, was born in Lowell, Mass., although he did not remain there long before his parents removed to Boston, which is yet his home.

Passing through the Institute of Technology, the Normal Art School, and studying under several teachers subsequent to those experiences, he held a sale of his works and with the profits started across the water. His first experience there was acquired during seven months in Brittany, and then study in Paris under Boulanger and Lefebvre, and this in turn followed by the tour of Italy, Venice, Capri, Holland, and England.

He is a member of the Art Club, the Paint and Clay, and the Boston Water-Color Society. Mr. Dean is an exhibitor in all the principal galleries of the United States, has received the silver medal of the Massachusetts Mechanics' Charitable Association in 1887, and the highest award in 1895.

His works have been purchased and now hang in the Boston Art Club and the art and library buildings of other cities.

In Alcove A of the Poland Springs Art Gallery are three of Dean's excellent works, the larger one representing "Gloucester Harbor," a most charm-

Tid=Bits.

Haying.

Midsummer.

New settees in the grove.

New rocking-chairs for the office of the Mansion House.

Mr. and Mrs. E. Holmes arrived Thursday at the Poland Spring House.

Mr. and Mrs. J. Stuart White are guests at the Poland Spring House.

Mr. and Mrs. Edward J. Stellwagen, from Washington, D.C., are at the Poland Spring House.

Mrs. J. Pennington Mellor and daughter, from Biarritz, are at the Poland Spring House.

Mr. and Mrs. Augustus Richardson and Miss Richardson, of Boston, are here for another season.

A beautiful silver tray, selected by Mrs. E. P. Ricker, graces the counter where the Poland Water is served.

Mr. and Mrs. Willard A. Vose of Brookline, Mass., are once more with us; also Miss Vose and George A. Vose.

The barn in front of the Mansion House has been moved, and a beautiful lawn will be made where the barn stood.

A fine record at bowling was made, this week, between Mr. Oakes and Mr. Sanders. Mr. Sanders, 279 ; Mr. Oakes, 277.

Five pickerel, weighing 2 lbs. each, were caught in the lower lake by Mr. Oakes, Mr. Dan Field, and Mr. Sanders.

Everything is free to guests, in the Maine State Building. Twelve hundred books, the Art Gallery, and a well-stocked Reading-Room.

Stroll down and see the Indian encampment by the spring. A pleasant chat and lots of pretty things to see will well repay a visit.

Adelaide Palmer, the artist, made a brief call the middle of the week. She will return the coming week for a longer stay, it is hoped.

The Poland Spring carafe and the souvenir spoons are excellent articles to procure as pleasant reminders of a quiet, peaceful, and enjoyable summer.

A letter just received says : " I have an *asbestus mind* for sale ; are you interested in that line?" We should say we—but there, that would be too—but no matter.

Mr. Robert Vonnoh, the artist, is spending the summer at Poland Springs. Mr. Vonnoh is one of the strongest painters in the United States, especially on portraiture.

Gen. Martin writes that he has since discovered that the Lincoln letter he referred to in his lecture is not only in Blaine's book, but in the war records, Vol. 27, Part I, Page 31, given in full.

Mr. August Franzen of New York has contributed five pictures to the Art Gallery. The portrait of Gudrun Torpadie, a noted Swedish singer, makes a very important addition to the collection.

If you have time to visit Portland, you will find it a very fine city.

"Often in thought I wander down
The pleasant streets of the dear old town"

was what Longfellow said of it, and his residence will be found next door to the Preble House. THE HILL-TOP will be a safe guide to its stores, which are very excellent. There is much of interest to see there.

Mexican Drawn Work.

A LADY living in Texas, on the Mexican border, sends to Mrs. Hiram W. Ricker a large variety of this material of the finest and most superior quality in the art of needle-work. This is the *genuine*, and of great beauty. Mrs. Ricker will be pleased to show the work to all interested, at their cottage, and to dispose of the same at very reasonable rates.

In a Cathedral.

BY GRISWOLD BOURNE.

The coolness slowly, softly coming down,
The grandeur of the solemn pillars grey,
The sunlight striking on the Saviour's crown
And on His face upturned to the day.

The colored windows glinting thro' the mist
That always hangs within these churches old,
And silence reigning, yet the voice of Christ
My soul can hear 'midst melodies untold.

My footsteps ring upon the aisle of stone
As walking towards the altar tall and grim,
Upon its steps of marble, all alone
I kneel and tell my sorrow unto Him.

New Books Received.

FROM N. Q. POPE.

Blaine and Logan Campaign.	1 vol.
History of Italy.	1 vol.
In the Levant.	1 vol.
Dickens's Child's History of England.	1 vol.
Tennyson's Poems.	2 vols.
American Scenery.	2 vols.
Speeches, Wit, Wisdom, and Eloquence, by R. G. Ingersoll.	1 vol.
Marvel of Nations.	1 vol.
Smith's Anatomy.	1 vol.
Fourteen Weeks in Chemistry.	1 vol.
Elements of Astronomy.	1 vol.
Fourteen Weeks in Geology.	1 vol.
Physiology and Health.	1 vol.
The Translator.	1 vol.
English into French.	1 vol.
Here and Beyond.	1 vol.
Works of Josephus.	1 vol.
The Bible—1809.	1 vol.
	20 vols.

FROM GEORGE T. BOURNE.

McKinley's Masterpieces.	1 vol.
Vashti and Esther.	1 vol.
A Member of Tattersalls.	1 vol.
A Family Failing.	1 vol.
Nada the Lily.	1 vol.
Only a Commoner.	1 vol.
Tales of Mean Streets.	1 vol.
Constance.	1 vol.
	8 vols.

FROM R. M. FIELD.

The Day of their Wedding, by W. D. Howells.	1 vol.

FROM CHARLES A. MAISON.

Fraukley, by Henry Greville. (In the original French.)	1 vol.

General Martin relates that during the war he was returning home, and stated to a gentleman who had engaged him in conversation that he was going to surprise his wife. This caused a reply as to the selfishness of such a proceeding; as the greatest enjoyment in life is in anticipation, he should have shared the news with her. It presented a new view of the matter, and he telegraphed at the next station, with most agreeable results. Every action in life should be studied to eliminate selfishness, for even where it is not suspected it often lurks.

Guests at Poland Spring House.

JULY 22, 1896.

Mr. and Mrs. A. Anderson	Camden, N. J.
Mr. and Mrs. Geo. T. Bourne	New York.
Miss Bourne	New York.
Mr. Griswold Bourne	New York.
Mr. and Mrs. Geo. F. Baker	Hyannis, Mass.
Mrs. Wm. S. Brown	New York.
Mr. and Mrs. Ralph Baggaley	Pittsburg.
Mr. Wm. A. Bigelow	New York.
Mrs. B. Babcock	New York.
Miss Babcock	New York.
Rev. Dr. Baxter	Boston.
Miss S. P. Baker	Boston.
Mr. Chas. T. Baker	Boston.
Miss L. Delyea	Boston.
Miss S. E. Brody	Boston.
Mr. and Mrs. Jacob P. Bates	Boston.
Mr. and Mrs. H. O. Bright	Cambridge.
Mr. and Mrs. Nelson Bartlett	Boston.
Mr. E. R. Bossange	New York.
Mr. E. N. Briggs	Saginaw, Mich.
Mr. and Mrs. Wm. Berri	Brooklyn.
Walter Berri	Brooklyn.
Herbert Berri	Brooklyn.
Mrs. Beylle	Philadelphia.
Mr. and Mrs. Jas. S. Bell	Minneapolis.
Mr. Jas. F. Bell	Minneapolis.
Mr. and Mrs. Geo. W. Coleman	Boston.
Mr. Andrew K. Culver	Brooklyn.
Mr. and Mrs. F. W. Carpenter	Providence.
Miss Hannah Carpenter	Providence.
Miss Julia Carpenter	Providence.
Mr. and Mrs. C. C. Corbin	Webster, Mass.
Mrs. A. A. Connel	New York.
Mr. and Mrs. Thomas J. Craven	Salem, N. J.
Miss L. H. Craven	Salem, N. J.
Miss May B. Craven	Salem, N. J.
Miss Jane Y. Craven	Salem, N. J.
W. H. Chappall	Chicago.
Miss Chappall	Chicago.
Miss R. B. Cabeen	Bristol, Pa.
Mrs. Z. Chandler	Detroit, Mich.
Mr. and Mrs. W. N. Craine	Chicago.
Mrs. C. S. Chase	Portland.
Miss Chase	Portland.
Mrs. A. W. Colton	Toledo, O.
Miss Colton	Toledo, O.
John J. Corning	New York.
The Misses DePeyster	New York.
Mrs. Albert Douglass	New York.
Mrs. M. E. Dexter	Brooklyn.
Miss Dexter	Brooklyn.
Mrs. N. C. Dickerson	New York.
Mrs. D. L. Dudley	Haverhill, Mass.
Rev. T. A. Dwyer	Hyde Park, Mass.
B. Wood Davis	New York.
Mr. and Mrs. James H. Eddy	New Britain, Conn.
Miss Bessie M. Eddy	New Britain, Conn.
Mr. Charles Endicott	Canton, Mass.
Mr. Chas. B. Eddy	Brooklyn, N. Y.
Mr. and Mrs. Thomas W. Evans	New York.
Mr. and Mrs. R. M. Field	Boston.
Miss A. L. Faile	New York.
Mr. Thos. H. Faile	New York.
Miss Fletcher	Boston.
Mr. Geo. B. French	Boston.
Mrs. J. D. Fessenden	New York.
Gen. Chas. E. Furlong	New York.
Mr. and Mrs. D. H. Field	Brockton, Mass.
Miss Fischer	New York.
Mr. and Mrs. C. S. Fischer	New York.
Mrs. M. C. Furand	New York.
Mrs. R. G. Feltus	Philadelphia.
Miss C. O. French	Canton.
Mr. and Mrs. W. H. Fernekees	Boston.
Mr. John Goldthwaite	Boston.
Miss E. B. Goldthwaite	Boston.
Mrs. G. F. Gregory	Brooklyn.
Miss Gregory	Brooklyn.
Mrs. M. R. Goodwin	Boston.
Miss Goodwin	Boston.
Mrs. L. M. Gale	Washington.
Miss Olive Gale	Washington.
Mr. and Mrs. C. C. Griffin	Haverhill, Mass.
Mrs. J. R. Gibney	New York.
Mr. and Mrs. Horace Hunt	New York.
Mrs. S. B. Hubbard	Jacksonville, Fla.
Mr. and Mrs. L. Hurlburt	Brooklyn.
Mrs. M. B. Hoffman	New York.
Mr. and Mrs. L. D. Henwood	Boston.
Mr. and Mrs. J. W. Hazen	Boston.
Mr. and Mrs. S. Haas	New York.
Miss Florrie Haas	New York.
Mr. and Mrs. Hudson Hoagland	New York.
Miss M. R. Haddock	New York.
Miss E. M. Harris	New Brighton.
Mr. and Mrs. J. B. Hutchinson	Philadelphia.
Mr. J. B. Hutchinson, Jr.	Philadelphia.
Mr. and Mrs. E. Holmes	New York.
Mr. Samuel Ivers	New Bedford.
Miss Ella F. Ivers	New Bedford.
Miss Jacoby	New York.
Mrs. Julian James	Washington.
Mr. John Lucas	Philadelphia.
Mr. and Mrs. Amos R. Little	Philadelphia.
Mr. and Mrs. B. Lemann and family	New Orleans.
Mrs. Wm. R. Lynch	Brooklyn.
Mrs. Mary Lambert	Brooklyn.
Miss Lambert	Brooklyn.
Miss Cora W. Lumbert	Brookton.
Mrs. B. L. Luddington	New York.
Miss Luddington	New York.
Miss Helen Luddington	New York.
Miss Lottie B. Lowry	Rockland, Me.
Mr. and Mrs. T. B. M. Mason	Washington.
Mrs. T. B. Myers	Washington.
Mrs. Jno. H. Maginnis	New Orleans.
Mr. Jno. H. Maginnis	New Orleans.
Mrs. A. Mully	Washington.
Miss A. G. Miller	Brooklyn.
Dr. and Mrs. Ira L. Moore	Boston.
Mrs. McKay	St. Louis.
Mrs. J. T. Montgomery	Philadelphia.
Mrs. B. P. Moulton	Rosemont, Pa.
Mr. and Mrs. A. R. Mitchell	Newtonville.
Mrs. Christine Marburg	Baltimore.
The Misses Marburg	Baltimore.
Mr. and Mrs. John T. Martin	New York.
Mrs. P. C. Meek	Worcester.
Mrs. Newbegin	Portland.
Mr. and Mrs. W. T. Ness	Boston.
Miss Lucy P. Newhall	Philadelphia.
Mr. and Mrs. Frank F. Olney	Providence.
Mr. Elam W. Olney	Providence.
Mr. John A. Ordway	Boston.
Mr. and Mrs. Josiah Oakes	Malden, Mass.
Miss Cora Pardee	Hartford, Conn.
Miss Sarah Pardee	Hartford, Conn.
Miss Susan S. Piper	Worcester.
Mrs. J. A. Pettee	New York.
Judge and Mrs. Chas. A. Peabody	New York.
Mrs. Henry U. Palmer	Brooklyn.
Masters Austin and Chester Palmer	Brooklyn.
Mrs. M. E. Parsons	Boston.
Mrs. E. D. Peters	Boston.
Mrs. H. D. Polhemus	Brooklyn.
Miss A. J. Pomeroy	New York.
Mr. and Mrs. E. W. Platt	Boston.
Miss Emily Platt	Boston.
Mr. Joseph G. Ray	Franklin, Mass.
Miss L. P. Ray	Franklin, Mass.
Mr. and Mrs. H. A. Rogers	New York.
Miss May Rogers	New York.
Mr. and Mrs. J. Fred Rogers	Boston.
Mrs. G. H. Richardson	Bridgeport.
Mrs. E. J. Robinson	Boston.
Mr. and Mrs. A. S. Rines	Portland.

Miss Roberts — Philadelphia.
Moses W. Richardson — Boston.
Mr. and Mrs. S. B. Stinson — Washington.
Miss Stinson — Washington.
Miss Florence Stinson — Washington.
Mr. and Mrs. A. T. Salter — Washington.
Mr. and Mrs. Irving T. Smith and family — Boston.
Mr. and Mrs. James Staples — Bridgeport.
Mr. and Mrs. Joseph W. Sandford — Plainfield, N. J.
Mr. and Mrs. E. J. Stellwagen — Washington.
Mr. and Mrs. R. H. Stearns — Boston.
Mr. and Mrs. Chas. Emory Smith — Philadelphia.
Mr. and Mrs. H. M. Sanders — Boston.
Mr. Samuel Shethar — New York.
Mrs. Charles Sinnickson, — Philadelphia.
Mr. and Mrs. Thomas Sinnickson, Jr. — Salem, N. J.
Miss Alice Sinnickson — Salem. N. J.
Mrs. Orlando Tompkins — Boston.
Mr. and Mrs. Frank R. Thomas — Boston.
Mr. and Mrs. F. E. Taylor — Brooklyn.
Miss E. R. Tilden — New Brighton.
Col. G. I. Taggart — Savannah, Ga.
John P. Taggart — Savannah, Ga.
Mr. and Mrs. David Thornton — Brooklyn.
Giraud F. Thomson — New York.
Mr. and Mrs. W. A. Vose — Brookline.
Mr. Geo. A. Vose — Brookline.
Miss Vose — Brookline.
Miss John H. Voorhees — Brooklyn.
Miss Jessie Voorhees — Brooklyn.
Mr. and Mrs. W. B. Valentine — London, Eng.
Mr. and Mrs. John P. Woodbury — Boston.
Mrs. J. Reed Whipple — Boston.
Dr. M. C. Wedgwood and Mrs. Wedgwood — Lewiston.
Mr. A. Wentworth — Boston.
Miss Waldo — Salem.
Mr. F. R. Wholton — Philadelphia.
Miss Whitney — New York.
Mr and Mrs. W. S. Wymond — Louisville, Ky.
Miss Wymond — Louisville, Ky.
Mr. and Mrs. J. Stuart White — New York.
Mr. and Mrs. W. W. Washburn — Galesburg, Ill.
David G. Yates — Philadelphia.
Mr. and Mrs. A. H. Yeomans — Boston.
Mr. David G. Yates — Philadelphia.
Mr. and Mrs. H. D. Ziegler — Philadelphia.
Miss C. F. Ziegler — Philadelphia.

Mary's Unoriginal Sheeplet.

[Minneapolis Journal.]

Mary had a little lamb,
His ways showed cause for blame,
For everything the old sheep did
This lamb did just the same.

He never seemed to grasp the law
Of progress in the race,
Whatever this lamb's pa had done
For him had set the pace.

His pa had lived and died a sheep,
Without a sense of loss;
So Mary's lamb walked in his ways,
And ended with mint sauce.

Explained.

[Cleveland Plain Dealer.]

Bings—That new typewriter girl is a corker on spelling and synonyms. She seems to be thoroughly well grounded in English.

Wiggins—Yes, she is. Her mother told me that when she was little they always had her sit at the table on a Webster's dictionary.

Last Sunday's Services.

REV. B. S. RIDEOUT, of Norway, Me., preached in Music Hall, Sunday. His text was from the 6th chapter of Galatians, 2d verse: "Bear ye one another's burdens, and so fulfill the law of Christ." A collection was taken and $19.52 was given.

Following His Directions.

[Detroit Free Press.]

SHE was very young for the responsibilities of housekeeping (as every woman is who has not been married long), and he was doing his best to give her good advice about how to economize and systematize her affairs. And (as most young husbands do) he was constantly casting discredit on his own fitness to advise by making applications to borrow back, for his personal expenses down town, money which he had given for her domestic use.

"I have only a little money, dear," she protested, "barely enough to market with."

"But I thought I handed you quite a little sum for an emergency some time ago. This is an emergency, you know. You wouldn't want a man to go without his lunch and a cigar, would you?"

"I don't know what money you mean!"

"Why I gave it to you only last week and told you there was something for a rainy day."

"O! Why, dear, I used that the same afternoon."

"What for?"

"For a rainy day."

"I guess you must have misunderstood me."

"Maybe I did. But I certainly got a lovely mackintosh; and it was a real bargain too."

An Interesting Meeting.

[Somerville Journal.]

Dr. Portman—I understand that you young ladies have organized a debating society. What do you talk about?

Ethel—Well, the subject at the last meeting was: "Which is the more to blame in the present difficulty, Spain or Venezuela?" but we really spent most of the time talking about Dolly Daring's new bicycle costume.

She Had Been There.

[Clips.]

Mrs. Nuovo Reesh—She called me a barmaid, and I flew at her and pulled her hair.

Mrs. Toplofty—O, how terrible! Still, even that did not justify you in fighting her.

Mrs. Nuovo Reesh—Yes, but if you had ever been a barmaid you would understand how mad it made me.

Thistles.

ITS POSSIBILITIES.

[From the Chicago Tribune.]

The lawyer—"I have just been reading about the latest experiments with the X-ray. By George, it's wonderful! I wish it could be used in courts of justice. Think what the effect might be if a judge could turn it on a witness and learn whether he is telling the truth or not."

The professor — "Yes, but think what the effect would be if the jury could turn it on the lawyers."

[From Lexington (Ky.) Herald.]

A tramp asking for food at the door of a certain good deacon residing near one of the country thoroughfares was given a loaf of bread by the master of the house, with the rather inhospitable remark that "the Bible says that if any man will not work, neither should he eat." Looking down at the gift with a shade of disgust, the tramp quickly responded: "Yes, and does it not also say that man cannot live by bread alone?" It is but truth to add that he received a generous slice of country ham as a reward for his quick-witedness.

[contributed.]

A new story: Two girls are sitting on a hotel piazza reading, when one inquires the name of her companion's book.

"The Man Without a Country,"—such a sad story.

"Humph, not half so sad as the country without a man."

A chiropodist advertizes that he has removed corns from nearly all the crowned heads of Europe.

The Studio.

THE NOTMAN PHOTOGRAPHIC CO. are again represented at Poland Springs by Mr. Ness, whose work is the equal of any photographer extant. They will be pleased at any time to receive the guests and show them some fine examples of their work.

Massage.

IF you are weary in mind or body, or feel a loss of vitality and strength, there is nothing so restful and refreshing as a treatment administered by one who has the strength to give and the skill to properly apply it.

Mrs. Robinson, now at the Poland Spring House, is very successful, and should be consulted under all such circumstances.

THE NEW MOUNT PLEASANT HOUSE faces the great "Presidential Range" of the White Mountains, the mighty peaks, although five miles distant, appearing to be within an easy twenty minutes' walk. There is no view of any mountain range east of the Rocky Mountains equal to this great mountain panorama as seen across the plateau from the little steppe upon which is built the Mount Pleasant House. The Ammonoosuc is one of the finest trout streams in the mountains. It heads on Mt. Washington, and in about a seven-mile run from the base flows by the door of the Mount Pleasant House. Mount Pleasant Brook and Black Brook are tributaries of importance—at least from a fisherman's standpoint. The latter is the one upon which are Gibbs's Falls and is the feeder for Lake Carolyn, upon the Mount Pleasant House estate and to which there is a pleasant walk along the bank of the Ammonoosuc. Lovely wood paths wind about the slope of Mount Stickney just back of the hotel. Mount Stickney is a part of the Rosebrook Range, which separates the valley of the Ammonoosuc from the valley of the Zealand River, and to its summit is being constructed a fine carriage road, and it is expected that many will visit this section of the mountains to make the ascent and gain the great view practically just added to the attractions of the White Mountains. The Mount Pleasant House will cater for early and long season business, making rates to favor the early arrivals. It will make a specialty of entertaining travelers and tourists coming to the White Mountains to make the ascent of Washington, as it is the nearest house to the mountain, and the trains on the Mt. Washington Railway leave from a station on the grounds to make the ascent, and it is the first hotel reached on the descent. From their own windows guests can see Mt. Washington from base to summit, and can decide in the morning whether to prepare for the ascent or await a more favorable day. The Mount Pleasant House is the terminus in the White Mountains of the Connecticut River Line from New York, and of the Boston & Maine Line from Boston, both of which roads run all their White Mountain trains to the hotel station, and it has a platform landing close to the house for passengers from Boston and Portsmouth by the Boston & Maine and Maine Central Railroads; from Burlington, on Lake Champlain, by Central Vermont Railway; and from Mt. Desert, Poland Springs, and Portland by the Maine Central Railroad. Thus, by its accessibility from the outside, having through parlor cars to its very doors from New York, New Haven, Hartford, Springfield, Boston, Montreal, Burlington, and Portland, and the ease with which it is reached from all the neighboring resorts, it is a most desirable tourist center.

Arrivals.

POLAND SPRING HOUSE.

JULY 16 TO JULY 23, 1896.

Archibald, E. S.	Hyde Park.
Aldrich, C. E. and son	Boston.
Armstrong, Jas. C.	New York.
Allen, W. C.	Portland.
Andrews, Mr. and Mrs. H. E.	Lewiston.
Bartlett, Mr. and Mrs. Frank	New York.
Berri, Mr. and Mrs. Wm.	Brooklyn.
Berri, Walter	Brooklyn.
Berri, Herbert	Brooklyn.
Beyile, Mrs.	Philadelphia.
Brewster, Mr. and Mrs. H. L.	Rochester.
Bell, Mr. and Mrs. James S.	Minneapolis.
Bell, James T.	Minneapolis.
Burrill, John W.	Auburn.
Bonney, Percival	Portland.
Bonney, A. L.	Portland.
Crane, Mr. and Mrs. W. N.	Chicago.
Carpenter, Mrs. F. W.	Providence.
Carpenter, Julia S.	Providence.
Chamberlain, Miss Lora	Norwich.
Chase, Mr. and Mrs. C. S.	Portland.
Chase, Miss	Portland.
Carter, Mrs.	Norway.
Carter, Miss	Norway.
Carter, Emma	Norway.
Cushman, Mr. and Mrs. Chas. L.	Auburn.
Colton, Mrs. A. W.	Toledo.
Colton, Miss	Toledo.
Curtis, Fred L.	Lynn.
Carpenter, Harriet T.	Providence.
Corning, John J.	New York.
Davis, Albert L.	Portland.
Dwyer, Rev. F. A.	Hyde Park.
Davis, B. Wood	New York.
Eddy, Chas. B.	Brooklyn
Eames, Thos. W.	New York.
Edgerly, Peter	Boston.
Ferrand, Mrs. M. C.	New York.
Farrell, Wm. J.	New York.
Feltus, Mr. and Mrs. R. G.	Philadelphia.
Filley, Mr. and Mrs. H. G.	Waterbury.
French, C. O.	Canton.
Fernckees, Mr. and Mrs. Wm. H.	Boston.
Gleason, T. F.	St. Paul.
Gilbert, Mr. and Mrs. F. A.	Boston.
Goodrich, H. L.	Haverhill.
Gibney, Mrs. J. R.	New York.
Gae, C. R.	Boston.
Gustin, D. F.	Westbrook.
Herden, R.	Portland.
Howe, Geo. R.	Norway.
Hatch, Mrs.	Lewiston.
Holmes. C. P.	New Gloucester.
Hartwell, Mrs. W. W.	Plattsburgh.
Havens, W. Burkis,	Tom's River, N. J.
Hersey, A. L.	Oxford
Hersey, Mrs. C. L.	Oxford.
Hersey, Heloise E.	Boston.
Hamblett, Mrs. S. F.	Boston.
Hoxie, Mr. and Mrs. John R.	Chicago.
Hoxie, Miss Anna	Chicago.
Jones, Chas. W.	Boston.
Kendrick, C. E.	Boothbay.
Ludington, Mrs. B. L.	New York.
Ludington, Miss	New York.
Ludington, Miss Helen	New York.
Lightfoot, Mr. and Mrs. T. M.	Philadelphia.
Lawry, Miss Lottie E.	Rockland.
Lucas, Wm. H.	Philadelphia
Martin, Mr. and Mrs. John T.	New York.
Milne, J. S.	Philadelphia.
Mulligan, Mrs. Col. Jas. A.	Chicago.

Morrill, Chas. S.	Portland.
May, Mrs.	Lewiston.
Maxey, H. C.	New York.
Meek, Mrs. P. C.	Worcester.
McGuire, Elizabeth M.	Rochester.
Mitchell, Mr. and Mrs. J. K.	Galesburg, Ill.
Mellor, Mrs. J. Pennington	Biarritz.
Mellor, Miss	Biarritz.
Newman, Mr. and Mrs. A. H.	Boston.
O'Leary, W. C.	Lakewood, N. J.
Oliver, Mr. and Mrs. Stephen H.	Jersey City.
Pope, M.	Danvers.
Peck, B.	Lewiston.
Peck, Summer S.	Lewiston.
Peck, Miss Hazel H.	Lewiston.
Pike, A. L. F.	Norway.
Pardee, Miss Cora	Hartford.
Pardee, Miss Sara	Hartford.
Piper, Susan S.	Worcester.
Palmer, Adelaide	Boston.
Phelan, C. C.	Westbrook.
Pettus, Wm. H. H.	St. Louis.
Pettus, J. Harold	St. Louis.
Roberts, Miss	Philadelphia.
Root, Mr. and Mrs. Samuel	Waterbury.
Richardson, M. W.	Boston.
Rideout, Rev. B. S.	Norway.
Robertson, A. R.	Somerville.
Richardson, Mr. and Mrs. Augustus	Boston.
Richardson, Miss	Boston.
Robinson, Mr. and Mrs. C. A.	Auburn.
Sanders, Mr. and Mrs. H. M.	Boston.
Smith, Mrs. J. B.	Lewiston.
Stethar, Prentice	New York.
Stethar, Samuel	New York.
Shaw, Edna	New York.
Sinnickson, Mrs. Charles	Philadelphia.
Sinnickson, Mr. and Mrs. Thomas	Salem, N. J.
Sinnickson, Miss Alice M.	Salem, N. J.
Stickney, W. H.	Boston.
Schuyler, Mrs. C. C.	Plattsburgh.
Sewall, A. W.	Boston.
Thornton, Mr. and Mrs. David	Brooklyn.
Tarr, E. W.	Boston.
Thomson, Girard F.	New York.
Tyler, F. B.	Brookline.
Tyler, Mrs. G. C.	Brookline.
Thornton, C. C. G.	Boston.
Vose, Mr. and Mrs. Willard A.	Brookline.
Vose, Miss	Brookline.
Vose, George A.	Brookline.
Vedder, O. F.	Portland.
Whitgreave, Mr. and Mrs. C. T.	Chicago.
Weferling, J. H. F.	Portland.
White, L. G.	Boston.
Washburn, Mr. and Mrs. W. W.	Galesburg, Ill.
Wisner, Mr. and Mrs. H. S.	Brooklyn.
Wood, Miss Mattie J.	Lewiston.

MANSION HOUSE.

JULY 16 TO 23.

Barbour, E. D.	Boston.
Cooke, Mr. and Mrs. W. H.	Norristown, Pa.
Eastman, C. W.	Milford.
Forster, C.	Portland.
Hammond, D. A.	Boston.
Hooker, Ralph	Springfield.
Jackson, Mr. and Mrs. F. C.	New York.
Jordan, Mrs. E. C.	Portland.
Lewis, E. M. S.	Springfield.
Lewis, Dudley P.	Springfield.
Lewis, Elisha P.	Springfield.
Lincoln, Edmund,	Milford.
Marsh, Arthur	Springfield.
Marsh, Jane C.	Springfield.
McCoy, J. F.	New York.
Townsend, Emily A.	New Haven.
Thomas, Miss	Flushing.
Thomas, Miss C. K.	Flushing.

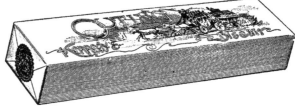

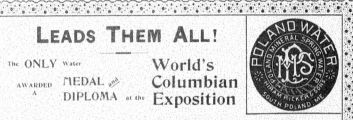

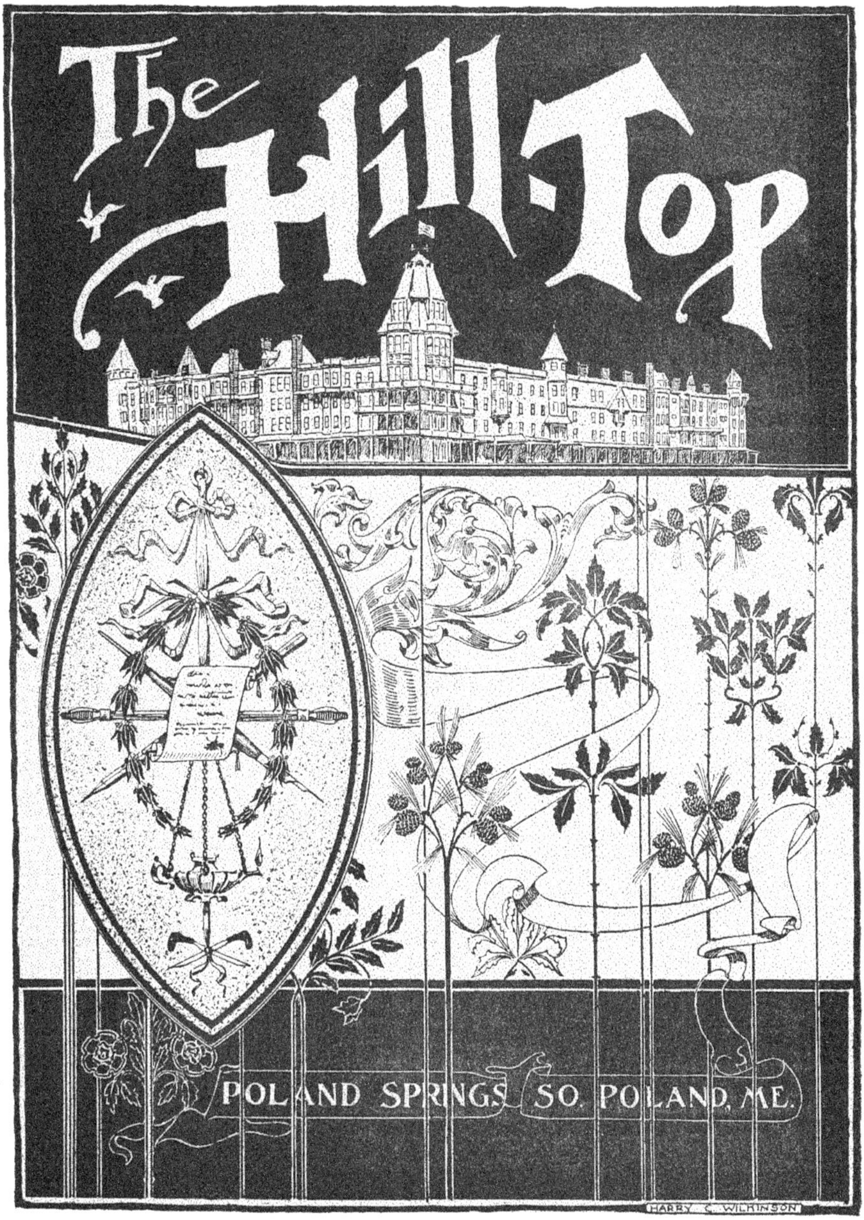
The Hill-Top
POLAND SPRINGS SO. POLAND, ME.
HARRY C. WILKINSON

VOL. III.　　　SUNDAY MORNING, AUGUST 2, 1896.　　　No. 5.

The Green Bottle.

OUR illustration this week shows a new feature, this season, inasmuch as a considerable projection into the office has been removed to provide for this much appreciated improvement.

It is the Poland water counter, where nature's pure and healthful drink is freely dispensed to all comers.

One cannot have too much Poland water, and to have it fresh and cool from the spring, in freshly-filled bottles every day, without the exertion of a walk to the spring house, is a boon to many who otherwise might imbibe less of its health-giving properties than their system required.

The little goddess who presides over the Poland Fountain of Health, shown in the picture, is Harriet Mabel Cole, of the Class of '97 of Hebron Academy, and accounted a bright student. She pours into your glass from one hundred to a hundred and twenty-five two-quart bottles a day, and nearly as many more one-quart bottles of the natural water, with about an equal number of one-quart bottles of aerated. This is a warm day's work, and while the latter is "charged," you will never find it in your bill.

Poland water is a name almost as well known to-day as that of the State from which it springs, and the little fissures in this rock-ribbed hill pour forth a stream "of liquid living pearl" which finds its way across the continent of America and over the great salt seas, upon the tables of every crowded steamer upon which you sail, and to the continent of Europe and the arid sands of Egypt; until this crystal stream is found sparkling upon the tables of the rich, and bringing health and happiness to all athirst.

This is a boast which not even the Mississippi or the majestic Amazon can equal with the volume of their mighty waters combined, for the limit of Poland's silver stream is not known in its extent, while the measure of those giant rivers is reckoned to a fraction of their bemuddled length.

And all this comes from beneath the roof of that little spring house on the hill-side, and the happiness it brings to thousands is immeasurable as well.

Our illustration also gives a glimpse of other things: the beginning of the ascent to the second story, the fire-place beyond, and then the telegraph office, so gracefully attended for several years by Miss Anderson, and finally the news counter with its souvenirs and postal facilities, admirably cared for by Miss Byrne and Mr. Abbey.

Now, in a glass of Poland water is "your good health and your families', and may they all live long and prosper."

The Standard Dictionary.

This valuable and complete work in two volumes, bound in full Russia, has just been received at the library, as the gift of Mr. Geo. G. Crowell.

It is not only remarkable as a dictionary, but its colored plates, which are quite numerous, are of unusual beauty of execution. It is one of the most valuable single contributions ever made to this already fine collection of books.

Sea-Sonable.

When you feel a yearning desire for an exhilarating ocean voyage, and a sniff of the breezes from off the raging main, with a bit of shuffle board, on a side track, just jump aboard the "Blaine" some fine morning, and in a few minutes you will find yourself at the Poland Docks, with the steamer awaiting your arrival. Step on board, and you will soon realize that you are embarked upon one of the greyhounds of the deep.

Presently the great hawsers, which bound "The Poland" to the pier, are cast loose, falling with a mighty splash upon the surface of the waters, and the throbbing engines are set in motion, and away you go upon your voyage.

Now you begin to realize the benefit of sea air, and you inflate your lungs and stretch your legs, perhaps, if you do not kick some one on the opposite side of the steamer; and start for a walk around the deck. This exercise, which takes about the sixteenth part of a minute, gives you a raging appetite, and you begin to listen for eight bells, which fail to arrive, there being but one on board, and that seated by your side of course.

On, on you go, across the deep blue sea, through the "Suez Canal" and into the "Red Sea" beyond; across that, and then comes the return trip, until, when the good ship Poland is again at her moorings, and the customs officer is ready to grab your watch, you make a dash for the "Blaine," and are in splendid condition to enjoy a good dinner at the hotel, when you arrive beneath the spacious porte-cochère. Try it and see.

The lover of trout fishing should not fail to visit the New Mt. Pleasant House, as the streams in the vicinity are well stocked. The "Base Brook" rises at the foot of Mt. Washington, near the starting point of the Mt. Washington Railway, and empties into the Ammonoosuc River. A good day's work on this stream is from near its rise to Twin Farm, two miles; another from the Twin Farm to Upper Ammonoosuc Falls; and another from the Falls to the Mt. Pleasant House, two and a half miles. From Mt. Pleasant to the Lower Ammonoosuc Falls is a good day's fishing. The Crawford Brook begins its course just back of the Crawford House, the cascade stream which forms Gibbs' Falls uniting with the outlet of Ammonoosuc Lake in its make-up. The stream runs towards Mt. Pleasant and finally joins the waters of the Ammonoosuc River. It may be fished for about four miles; but, if properly worked, not more than two miles of its waters can be covered in any one trip. It is fished very largely, but always with good results, by the experienced angler.

Afternoon Progressive Euchre.

At 3 P.M. Wednesday, forty-eight ladies from the Poland Spring House gathered in the amusement room for progressive euchre. The room was beautifully decorated by Mrs. E. P. Ricker. One mantel-piece was banked with sweet peas and ferns, while the other was a symphony of orange and green. Pink and white asters formed the center-piece, where two charming young ladies, Miss Florence Stinson and Miss Olive Gale, "kept time."

Mrs. Maginnis and Mrs. Griffin showed exquisite taste in their selection of prizes. There were six prizes. The ladies were divided, half wearing the "white ribbon" and half the "green ribbon." Nineteen games were played. The highest number of moves, fifteen, was made by Mrs. Hunt.

Prizes for the Green Ribbon: Mrs. Hunt won a lovely hand-painted cracker-jar; Mrs. Eugene Hale, a beautiful plate; Mrs. Vose, an exquisite fan. Prizes for the White Ribbon: Mrs. Griffin won the first prize, a daintily hand-painted tray; Mrs. Moulton, a lovely pitcher; Mrs. Rogers, a white alligator card-case with silver mountings.

The ladies played two hours, and it was one of the most enjoyable occasions of the season.

White Mountain "Freezers."

THEY WERE COLD DAYS FOR THE CRAWFORDS.

The Mt. Pleasant House team in the White Mountains has been having an unbroken chain of victories. They have thus far played three games with the following results:

At Crawford House, July 18th:

SCORE BY INNINGS.

	1	2	3	4	5	6	7	8	9	Total
Mt. Pleasant House,	2	0	1	4	3	3	0	3	—	16
Crawford House,	1	0	0	0	0	1	0	0	1	3

Mt. Pleasant House catcher—Nichols; pitcher—Bird. Crawford catcher—Lapham; pitcher—A. Fitzgerald.

At Crawford House, July 22d:

SCORE BY INNINGS.

	1	2	3	4	5	6	7	8	9	Total
Mt. Pleasant House,	0	0	1	1	3	1	7	0	—	13
Crawford House,	0	0	0	1	3	0	5	1	0	10

Mt. Pleasant House catcher—Nichols; pitcher—Bird. Crawford catcher—Aldrich; pitcher—Libby (of Bowdoin).

At Fabyán House, July 28th:

SCORE BY INNINGS.

	1	2	3	4	5	6	7	8	9	Total
Mt. Pleasant House,	0	0	3	2	0	0	1	0	—	6
Fabyan House,	0	1	1	0	0	3	0	0	0	5

Mt. Pleasant House catcher—Smith; pitcher—Nichols. Fabyan House catcher—Aldrich; pitcher—Scribner.

Yesterday they played with the Maplewood nine at Maplewood, N. H.

Cynthia.

[Kansas City Journal.]

Tip-toes Cynthia
Down the beach,
For her lips
The glad waves reach.

Yet they feel not
Love's emotion,
Though they say
That "love's an ocean."

If some fairy
Could but change me,
From this human
Life estrange me,

When she comes,
So runs my notion—
I'd give worlds
To be the ocean.

On a coral
Throne I'd place her;
Gently should
My waves embrace her,

Till in love's
Enchanted blisses,
I should drown her
With my kisses!

Whist at the Mansion House.

Progressive whist at the Mansion House, Thursday, July 23d. The first ladies' prize, a sterling silver button-hook, went to Miss Conover. Mrs. Cooke won the first gentlemen's prize, a Poland souvenir pen-wiper.

Mr. Cooke gained the consolation prize for the gentlemen, and Mrs. Thomas was presented with a bunch of sweet peas.

Mrs. Keene and Miss Campbell made the guests of "The Old Homestead" happy, in getting up a progressive whist party, Monday evening.

There were nine tables, the guests played for two hours, and the largest number of points made was sixty.

Miss Campbell won the first prize, a Mexican center-piece, and Miss Sarah Ricker the second prize, a Mexican handkerchief.

The first gentlemen's prize, a cigar tray, went to Mr. Cooke.

After the prizes were distributed, the guests gathered in the parlors and Mrs. Cooke kindly played the Virginia Reel for them, and a jolly Virginia Reel it was. The guests pronounced it the "best whist party" and the "best dance" of the season.

Gowns.

Mrs. Harriet Newbegin, one of the best dress-makers in this state, has been spending a few weeks at the Poland Spring House.

Mrs. Newbegin's work has been much admired. She will open a dress-maker's establishment this coming autumn, in Portland, Maine.

Children's Column.

"A little seeing saves much looking; a little speaking saves much talking."

Wedding in Lilliput.

ONE of the most noted weddings of the season took place in the "oak grove," Poland Springs. The bride, little Janette Ricker, was beautifully attired in a pink and green gingham. Her veil was exquisite, a white apron, fastened with choice ferns. Master Arthur Leman was the groom.

The maid of honor, Miss Marion Ricker, sister to the bride, wore a white lawn with blue ribbons. The bridesmaid, Miss Harriet Fisher, was charming in a pink gingham. Jacob Leman was best man and little E. P. Ricker, Jr., acted as page. He looked sweet in a white blouse and brown kilts. Marie, the nurse girl, was the clergyman, and little James Ricker furnished the music.

A well-known caterer furnished the refreshments, consisting of peaches, pears, cookies, plums, nuts, and candy. The tent was artistically decorated with ferns and grasses.

The bride, amid a shower of grass, was driven away in little George Ricker's express cart, drawn by Albert Rosenhein and Chester Palmer.

Her "wedding journey" was a trip around the grove. Returning to the tent, she and her husband went to housekeeping.

A kind lady said to the groom: "My dear, don't you think it was a little unkind not inviting me to the wedding?"

He looked down in a thoughtful manner for a minute, and then replied: "Well, I'll tell you; owing to the scarcity of refreshments, we were obliged to limit the number of guests."

Blue Bell Wood.

[Selected by "Marguerite."]

Three little maidens,
  Merry and good;
They're off for a ramble
  In Blue Bell wood.
Not one is afraid
  Too far to roam;
For Mona and Leo
  Both know the way home.

A Mortifying Mistake.

[New York Evening Post.]

I studied my tables over and over, and backward and forward too;
But I couldn't remember six times nine, and I didn't know what to do
Till sister told me to play with my doll and not to bother my head.
"If you call her 'fifty-four' for a while, you'll learn it by heart," she said.

So I took my favorite, Mary Ann (though I thought 'twas a dreadful shame
To give such a perfectly lovely child such a perfectly horrid name),
And I called her my dear little "Fifty-four" a hundred times, till I knew
The answer of six times nine as well as the answer of two times two.

Next day Ella Wigglesworth, who always acts so proud,(liz bet)
Said "Six times nine is fifty-two," and I nearly laughed aloud!
But I wished I hadn't when teacher said, "Now, Dorothy, tell if you can,"
For I thought of my doll, and—sakes alive!—I answered "Mary Ann."

The following story was related by Mr. Enneking:

I was sketching in Switzerland. After enjoying the glorious scene for a short time, I chose my subject, and went to work with a will to transfer it to canvas. In a few hours, when the sketch was about finished, the effect changed, clouds covering the mountains. In hope that the clouds would soon lift again, I took my sketch book and went up a little way, on a hill-side, to take a hasty outline of another view. I was scarcely twenty minutes about it, and then returned to my easel and oil-sketch, which I had left standing below. But you can imagine my surprise and consternation to find my sketch completely rubbed out, and on examining it, it seemed as though a large brush had been used to accomplish the ruin.

My brushes were strewn in all directions, and my palette was almost all cleaned of paint. I looked in all directions, but could not discover any living thing. I was completely dumbfounded. After I had descended about half a mile I came across a flock of goats with the most brilliant whiskers, and faces well tattooed with all the colors of the rainbow. They eyed me as innocently as though they were my best friends, and had not been up in the clearing, raising Ned.

The Atlanta University Quartette gave an enjoyable entertainment in the Music Hall, Poland Spring House, Tuesday evening. They played upon the mandolin, guitar, and banjo, and sang darkey melodies. The sum raised by their collection was $47.23. From Poland Springs they went to Rockland.

Cyclist Column.

Diamond Run—around Snake Hill.
Time, 9.40–10.20 A.M.
Miles—5.25.
Wind—Strong.
Weather—Fair.
Roads—Good and fair hills.
Temperature—73.

Spring Hill Run—Around Ricker Hill.
Time—30 minutes.
Miles—4.
Wind—Moderate.
Weather—Cloudy.
Road—Bad and hilly.
Temperature—75.

A GODDESS OF GIRLS.
[Susie M. Best in the New Bohemian.]

Brief-skirted and slender,
   She mounts for a ride;
Six gallants attend her—
Brief-skirted and slender,
She claims the surrender
   Of all at her side.
Brief-skirted and slender,
   She mounts for a ride.

O, radiant creature;
   She wheels and she whirls,
Till no one can reach her—
O, radiant creature;
In figure and feature
   She's goddess of girls—
O, radiant creature;
   She wheels and she whirls.

There's no use denying
   She's captured my heart;
There's no use denying
She did it by trying
   The bicycle art.
There's no use denying
   She's captured my heart.

I'll ask her to marry
   Without more ado;
No longer I'll tarry—
I'll ask her to marry
And try in a hurry
   A wheel built for two—
I'll ask her to marry
   Without more ado.

"Better to wear out than to rust out" a bicycle.
They call it the road-bed because the tired
wheels go there.

Mr. B. J. Gallagher is receiving congratulations on his success in winning the bicycle,
Wednesday evening, July 29th.

Mr. Plumb, the night clerk at the Poland Spring
House, is very successful in teaching the guests to
ride the wheel. Mr. Plumb is an expert rider.

HOW THE SAVING IS EFFECTED.
[From the Indianapolis Journal.]

Walker—Your claim that you save from 60
cents to $1 car fare every day is simply ridiculous.
You never averaged more than two car rides a
day.

Wheeler—My dear boy, you don't understand.
Every time I go out on my wheel—and that comes
to ten to twenty times—I just imagine that I would
have taken a car.

Sunday Services.

Mass was held at the Poland Spring House
last Sunday by Rev. John M. Harrington of
Lewiston, Me.

At 11 o'clock Rev. T. A. Dwyer preached in
Music Hall, Poland Spring House. His text was
Romans, chap. 15, verse 13.

Sunday morning, at the Mansion House, Mr.
Alexander F. Sabine of Philadelphia read the Episcopal service.

Sunday evening, in the dining-hall at the
Poland Spring House, Rev. T. A. Dwyer gave a
lecture. The subject was "The Moral Lesson of
the Hour-Glass."

FRANK CARLOS GRIFFITH, } Editors.
NETTIE M. RICKER,

PUBLISHED EVERY SUNDAY MORNING DURING THE MONTHS
OF JULY, AUGUST, AND SEPTEMBER, IN THE INTERESTS OF
POLAND SPRINGS AND ITS VISITORS.

All contributions relative to the guests of Poland Springs
will be thankfully received.

To insure publication, all communications should reach the
editors not later than Wednesday preceding day of issue.

All parties desiring rates for advertising in the HILL-TOP
should write the editors for same.

The subscription price of the HILL-TOP is $1.00 for the
season, post-paid. Single copies will be mailed at 10c. each.

Address,
EDITORS "HILL-TOP,"
Poland Spring House,
South Poland, Maine.

PRINTED AT JOURNAL OFFICE, LEWISTON.

Sunday, August 2, 1896.

Editorial.

THE love of Art is instilled by Nature. One
of the earliest evidences of the exercise of the
functions of the infantile mind is its appreciation of Art. When the child cries, the production
of a picture book, be the work never so badly
executed, will generally still the little troubled
bosom, and peace will reign. As it grows older,
it takes better pictures to divert its attention from
its woes.

The workman who constructs the complicated
loom is a mechanic, and possibly greatly skilled,
but to the child mind, the man who works in front
of the completed machine, and is apparently engaged
in laying in the colors, and fashioning the intricate
pattern, is far more interesting to him. He is,
however, but a part of the machine which the
artisan and the artist have planned. The artisan
has conceived and constructed the mechanism, and
the artist has skillfully and artistically drawn the
pattern, with its delicacy of color and intricacy of
design.

Art is constantly advancing. Glance at the
pages of an early magazine and at those of the
present day. Methods have been changed, which
places the average far higher than it was. Exceptional examples of greater skill in the past may
easily be cited, but in the multitude of illustrations
to-day, there is a greater satisfaction.

In Painting, we find the average more
interested in Art, and in the artistic decoration of
the home; where once the cheap and inartistic
chromo served to adorn the wall, the work of the
recognized artist is only satisfactory to accomplish
this, which shows advancement at the fountain
head, for it is the appreciation and encouragement
of Art which makes the Artist.

What is true Art? It is difficult to explain.
The picture we admire most may or may not
answer its requirements. It may be photographic,
or it may be impression; it may be of soft and
delicate treatment, or heavy and strong in color.
The tree may be an oak, or it may be a linden;
it may be a pine, or it may be a poplar; but it is
still a tree, and it is Nature, true Nature.

So it is with Art. Art is not "cabined, cribbed,
confined," but broad, and covers the world with its
skilled accomplishments. Nature and Art. Art
and Nature. Life companions. Forever hand in
hand.

New Books.

FROM MISS E. M. HARRIS.

Won by Waiting, by Edna Lyall.	1 vol.

FROM MRS. AMOS R. LITTLE.

The Honorable Peter Stirling, by Paul Leicester Ford.	1 vol.
Sultan to Sultan.	1 vol.
The Seats of the Mighty.	1 vol.
A Daughter of the Tenements.	1 vol.

FROM MRS. M. E. PARSONS.

The New Rector, by Stanley J. Weyman.	1 vol.
Memoirs of a Physician, by A. Dumas.	1 vol.

FROM GEORGE G. CROWELL.

The Standard Dictionary.	2 vols.

FROM N. Q. POPE.

Hume's History of England.	3 vols.
Middleton's Cicero.	3 vols.
Memoirs of the Life of Anna Jameson.	1 vol.
Mickie's Lusiad.	2 vols.
Hours with the Evangelists.	2 vols.
Cyclopædia of American Literature.	2 vols.
Hand-Book of Universal Geography.	1 vol.
The Print Collector.	1 vol.
	15 vols.

FROM MRS. J. C. CONOVER.

When a Man's Single, by J. M. Barrie.	1 vol.
A Daughter of the King.	1 vol.

John J. Enneking.

THIS most excellent artist was born at Minster, Ohio, in 1841. His first lessons in drawing were received at St. Mary's College, Cincinnati. After passing through various experiences, including service in the Union army, in which he enlisted at the beginning of the war, he went to Europe in 1872, and in Paris was a pupil of Bonnet for two years, after which he studied landscape under Daubigny. He also studied at Munich.

Mr. Enneking had the distinguished honor of being selected as a member of the Jury on Fine Arts at the World's Columbian Exposition, and has received four gold and three silver medals at the Massachusetts Charitable Mechanics' Exhibition; cash prize at the Jordan Exhibition of '95, and other marked indications of approval of his work elsewhere. His pictures are owned by the Boston Museum of Fine Arts and the Boston Art Club, and are to be found in many other public and private collections.

Mr. Enneking possesses the instincts of the true artist, and his work bears the analysis of the most skilled critic. Is it possible, to look at his picture of "Mt. Washington," in Alcove E of the Art Gallery, and not feel the grandeur of the subject, or to breathe in the cooling atmosphere from about its summit? By the side of this is hung one of his best examples, of "Twilight," with its rich, mellow glow, so true to nature and so perfect in its art.

A third and quite different style is a "Sheep Pasture," equally good, and a picture pleasing in its subject and perfect in its treatment.

No one can make a mistake in the selection of a work from the brush of this famous artist. Any one visiting his studio at 174 Tremont Street, Boston, will find a welcome, and leave there with an added admiration for the art of painting and the genius of the artist.

Tid-Bits.

Golf.

Thundering weather.

Showers are plentiful.

"Strings are out of fashion."

Barnum's at Lewiston, August 6th.

Mrs. Eugene Hale, wife of the Maine Senator, arrived on Monday.

We are pleased to welcome Mr. James H. Lake, of Boston, again to Poland.

E. B. Mallett, Jr., of Freeport, may add some invaluable works to the library, shortly.

Adelaide Palmer has returned, and will give us some more good work from her brush.

The Lippincotts of Philadelphia have taken one of the beautiful suites in the Maine State Building.

Samuel J. Elder of Winchester, was an interested visitor to the Maine State Building, recently.

The illustrated article on the Reading-Room last week, doubled the attendance at that place last Sunday.

Our thanks to Master Johnnie Chamberlain for a fine bunch of sweet peas, which made the library quite fragrant.

The Boston Home Journal finds THE HILL-TOP "a very readable paper." We return the compliment with interest. You're another.

Col. G. I. Taggart of Savannah was Chief Commissary of the 13th Army Corps, in the Vicksburg campaign, and on General Grant's staff.

Massage treatment is very artistically administered by Mrs Robinson, who is at the Poland Spring House, and prepared at all times to receive patients.

Miss Campbell of Camden, N. J., is the champion whist player at the Mansion House. She has won the highest number this season in progressive whist; 60 points.

Our compliments to the Boston Globe for a very generous mention of THE HILL-TOP. To receive the distinction of favorable notice from so prominent a metropolitan daily is very gratifying.

A Poland lady of distinguished literary ability, famous for her definitions, was missing Sunday for several hours, and caused her family extreme anxiety. A couple of hours past dinner time, a pale-cheeked group of friends set out in search of her, and after scouring woods and fields, entered the library of the Maine State Building, and there, deeply immersed in Webster's Unabridged, was found the literary lady, studying definitions in H.

Miss Minnie R. Haynes of Portland gave an exhibition of painted china at the Poland Spring House, Monday, July 27th. She received many compliments for her work and was successful in selling it.

The thanks of THE HILL-TOP are extended to the sisterhood of the Shakers, for a very handsome bouquet, which has adorned the table of the Reading-Room for several days the past week.

All who have had the pleasure of listening to Mr. Julius's Sunday evening services bear testimony to the excellence of his discourses. Mr. Julius's friends are limited only by the capacity of the house.

We were pleased to receive a call from Samuel S. Miles, a Boston artist and the art editor of the Boston Globe, on Thursday last. Mr. Miles expressed great gratification at the excellence of the Art Gallery.

"I consider your Honey and Almond Cream the best cream I have ever used for the complexion."—Camille D'Arville. This of course refers to Hinds' Honey and Almond Cream. It may be had at the news counter.

Miss Rogers gave a delightful brake ride over Bald Hill, Gloucester woods, and Sabbath-day Lake. The party included Mr. and Mrs. Baggaley, Miss Newhall, Miss Pratt, Miss Stinson, Miss Luddington, Miss Rogers, and Mr. Olney.

An informal dinner party, in honor of Miss Jane C. Maish's birthday, was given at the Poland Spring House, Monday, July 27th. Miss Maish is a Vassar girl, class of '98. Among her Springfield friends were Mrs. Lewis, Miss Townsend, Mr. Lewis, Mr. Dudley Lewis, and Mr. Ralph Hooper. There were also present her cousin, Miss Mattie Bolster of Auburn, Me., and Master Robert and Arthur Maish, the Misses Ricker, and little Janette Ricker.

Fan Fearnaught is the name of a bay horse owned by a gentleman spending the summer at Poland Springs. One warm day this gentleman started for a horseback ride around the middle lake. Reaching the lake, the water looked so tempting that he thought he would give his horse a drink. Walking the horse several feet into the lake, he loosened the check rein, and while the horse drank, the gentleman enjoyed the beautiful scenery. The horse liked the water so well that he thought he would take a bath, and down on "all fours" he went, the gentleman still on his back. The rider lived to tell the story, and the horse loves the water of the middle lake.

Our Menu.

The roasts for one dinner at Poland:
160 lbs of sirloin of beef.
180 lbs. of young duckling.
125 lbs. of spring lamb.

RECIPE No. 10.

Baked Chicken Pie, New England Style.

Take 130 lbs. of fresh country chickens. Clean and dress them the same as for a roast. Then cut through the joints so as not to fracture the bones and remove all the meat, leaving the backs, necks, and wings for stock. Put these in a stock pot and boil three hours. Put the chicken meat in a copper kettle and cook until it is done. Then strain off the stock and skim off all the fat and add roux until it becomes a rich, smooth cream. Beat in 12 egg yolks, add pepper, salt, and mace to taste, and the juice of 6 lemons. Take a large baking sheet and line with puff crust. Place the chicken in the pan and pour the sauce over all. Cover with a rich puff paste and bake one-half hour, then cut in diamond shapes and serve.

RECIPE No. 11.

Haricot of Mutton a l'Anglaise.

Select 10 legs of fat mutton and cut them up into large dice shapes. Put this in a copper sauce pan with carrots, turnips, onions, cut in fancy shapes. Put on range and cook three hours. Then add one dozen good-sized tomatoes cut in dice shapes. Add two gallons of rich Espagnole sauce and season to taste and serve hot.

This will serve 360 people.

Progressive Euchre.

One of the pleasantest evenings of the week is when the guests of Poland Springs gather in the amusement room for progressive euchre.

Mrs. Maginnis showed excellent taste in her selection of the prizes for last Friday week's party. Miss Marburg was the happy winner of the first ladies' prize, an exquisite center-piece with doilies. Mrs. Yoeman won the second ladies' prize, a Dresden sugar and cream set. Six Mexican doilies went to Mrs. Keene. The fourth prize, also a Mexican doilie, was won by Mrs. Dudley. Mrs. Palmer won the first gentlemen's prize, a silver shoe horn and a button-hook; Mrs. Hurlburt the second prize, a silver key ring with a chain. Mr. Pratt won a clock for the third prize, and the fourth went to Miss Ziegler,—court plaster in a silver case.

Eighteen moves were made. The highest number for the ladies was fourteen and the highest number for the gentlemen, fifteen.

Guests at Poland Spring House.

JULY 29, 1896.

F. Aston and daughter	New York.
J. Munn Andrews and wife	Lowell.
Mr. and Mrs. Ralph Baggaley	Pittsburg.
Mr. Wm. A. Bigelow	New York.
Mrs. B. Babcock	New York.
Miss Babcock	New York.
Miss S. P. Baker	Boston.
Mr. Chas. T. Baker	Boston.
Miss L. Belyea	Boston.
Mr. and Mrs. Jacob P. Bates	Boston.
Mr. and Mrs. H. O. Bright	Cambridge.
Mr. and Mrs. Nelson Bartlett	Boston.
Mr. E. R. Bossange	New York.
Mr. E. N. Briggs	Saginaw, Mich.
Mr. and Mrs. Wm. Berri	Brooklyn.
Walter Berri	Brooklyn.
Herbert Berri	Brooklyn.
Mrs. Beylle	Philadelphia.
Mr. and Mrs. Jas. S. Bell	Minneapolis.
Mr. Jas. F. Bell	Minneapolis.
Miss Alice P. Chase	Lynn.
Geo. B. Clark	New York.
Mr. and Mrs. Geo. W. Coleman	Boston.
Mr. Andrew K. Culver	Brooklyn.
Mr. and Mrs. F. W. Carpenter	Providence.
Miss Hanna Carpenter	Providence.
Miss Julia Carpenter	Providence.
Mr. and Mrs. C. C. Corbin	Webster, Mass.
Mr. and Mrs. Thomas J. Craven	Salem, N. J.
Miss L. H. Craven	Salem, N. J.
Miss Mary B. Craven	Salem, N. J.
Miss Jane Y. Craven	Salem, N. J.
W. H. Chappall	Chicago.
Miss Chappall	Chicago.
Mrs. Z. Crandler	Detroit, Mich.
Mr. and Mrs. W. N. Craine	Chicago.
Mrs. A. W. Colton	Toledo, O.
Miss Colton	Toledo, O.
John J. Corning	New York.
Mrs. Albert Douglass	New York.
Mrs. M. E. Dexter	Brooklyn.
Miss Dexter	Brooklyn.
Mrs. N. C. Dickerson	New York.
Rev. T. A. Dwyer	Hyde Park, Mass.
Miss Englis	Brooklyn.
Miss A. B. Englis	Brooklyn.
Mr. and Mrs. James H. Eddy	New Britain, Conn.
Miss Bessie M. Eddy	New Britain, Conn.
Mr. Charles Endicott	Canton, Mass.
Mr. Chas. B. Eddy	Brooklyn, N. Y.
Mr. and Mrs. Thomas W. Evans	New York.
Mr. and Mrs. R. M. Field	Boston.
Miss Fletcher	Boston.
Mr. Geo. B. French	Boston.
Mrs. J. D. Fessenden	New York.
Gen. Chas. E. Furlong	New York.
Mr. and Mrs. D. H. Field	Brockton, Mass.
Miss Fischer	New York.
Mr. and Mrs. C. S. Fischer	New York.
Mrs. M. C. Furand	New York.
Mrs. R. G. Feltus	Philadelphia.
Miss C. O. French	Canton.
Mr. John Goldthwaite	Boston.
Miss E. B. Goldthwaite	Boston.
Mrs. G. F. Gregory	Brooklyn.
Miss Gregory	Brooklyn.
Mrs. M. R. Goodwin	Boston.
Miss Goodwin	Boston.
Mrs. L. M. Gale	Washington.
Miss Olive Gale	Washington.
Mr. and Mrs. C. C. Griffin	Haverhill, Mass.
Mrs. J. R. Gibney	New York.
Mrs. W. W. Hartwell	Plattsburgh, N. Y.
Mr. and Mrs. John R. Hoxie	Chicago.
Miss Anna Hoxie	Chicago.
Mr. and Mrs. E. B. Hall	Boston.
Mrs. Eugene Hale	Ellsworth, Me.

Mr. and Mrs. Horace Hunt	New York.
Mrs. S. B. Hubbard	Jacksonville, Fla.
Mr. and Mrs. L. Hurlburt	Brooklyn.
Mrs. M. B. Hoffman	New York.
Mr. and Mrs. L. D. Henwood	Boston.
Mr. and Mrs. J. W. Hazen	Boston.
Mr. and Mrs. S. Haas	New York.
Miss Flohie Haas	New York.
Mr. and Mrs. Hudson Hoagland	New York.
Miss E. M. Harris	New Brighton.
Mr. and Mrs. E. Holmes	New York.
Mr. Samuel Ivers	New Bedford.
Miss Ella F. Ivers	New Bedford.
Mrs. Samuel Joseph	Philadelphia.
Harry S. Joseph	Philadelphia.
Miss Jacoby	New York.
Mrs. Julian James	Washington.
T. King	Quincy.
Miss King	Quincy.
James D. Laird	San Francisco.
Mr. and Mrs. Chas. Lippincott	Philadelphia.
Mr. and Mrs. F. H. Lippincott	Philadelphia.
Miss Lucille Lippincott	Philadelphia.
Mr. and Mrs. Amos R. Little	Philadelphia.
Mr. and Mrs. B. Lemaun and family	New Orleans.
Mrs. Wm. R. Lynch	Brooklyn.
Miss Cora W. Lumbert	Brockton.
Mrs. B. L. Luddington	New York.
Miss Luddington	New York.
Miss Helen Luddington	New York.
Miss Lottie E. Lowry	Rockland, Me.
Byron P. Moulton	Philadelphia.
Mrs. C. J. McDermott	Brooklyn.
Mr. and Mrs. T. B. M. Mason	Washington.
Mrs. T. B. Myers	Washington.
Mrs. Jno. H. Maginnis	New Orleans.
Mr. Jno. H. Maginnis	New Orleans.
Mrs. A. Murry	Washington.
Miss A. G. Miller	Brooklyn.
Dr. and Mrs. Ira L. Moore	Boston.
Mrs. McKay	St. Louis.
Mrs. J. T. Montgomery	Philadelphia.
Mrs. B. P. Moulton	Rosemont, Pa.
Mr. and Mrs. A. R. Mitchell	Newtonville.
Mrs. Christine Marburg	Baltimore.
The Misses Marburg	Baltimore.
Mr. and Mrs. John T. Martin	New York.
Mrs. A. H. Newman	Boston.
Mr. and Mrs. Dan C. Nugent and family	St. Louis.
Mr. and Mrs. W. I. Ness	Boston.
Miss Lucy P. Newhall	Philadelphia.
Mr. and Mrs. Frank F. Olney	Providence.
Mrs. H. S. Osgood	Portland.
Mr. Elam W. Olney	Providence.
Mr. John W. Ordway	Boston.
Mr. and Mrs. Josiah Oakes	Malden, Mass.
Mrs. Pattison	Boston.
Miss Cora Pardee	Hartford, Conn.
Miss Sarah Pardee	Hartford, Conn.
Miss Susan S. Piper	Worcester.
Mrs. J. A. Pettee	New York.
Mrs. Henry U. Palmer	Brooklyn.
Masters Austin and Chester Palmer	Brooklyn.
Mrs. M. E. Parsons	Boston.
Mrs. E. D. Peters	Boston.
Miss A. J. Pomeroy	New York.
Mr. and Mrs. Augustus Richardson	Boston.
Miss Richardson	Boston.
Allen M. Rogers	New York.
Thomas A. Robinson	Philadelphia.
W. T. Robinson	Philadelphia.
Mr. and Mrs. H. A. Rogers	New York.
Miss May Rogers	New York.
Mrs. J. Fred Rogers	Boston.
Mrs. G. H. Richardson	Bridgeport.
Mrs. E. J. Robinson	Boston.
Mr. and Mrs. A. S. Rines	Portland.
Miss Roberts	Philadelphia.
Moses W. Robinson	Boston.
Dr. and Mrs. C. C. Schuyler	Plattsburgh, N. Y.
Mr. and Mrs. Chas. G. Stark	Milwaukee.

The Preacher, the Dam, and the Fish.

[From the Amateur Sportsman.]

Those who have fished at the Upper, Middle or Lower Dam at the Rangeleys, will enjoy the following: "You must be on your good behavior this evening, George, for the minister is to take dinner with us," said a Jonesville lady to her worser half, as he got home from his office. "What have you for dinner?" he queried.

"Well, I know he is fond of fish, so I bought quite a string of small river fish, and several larger ones from the dam."

"I'm not much at doing the honors when we have a minister at the table," said George, "but I guess we can get through with it all right."

Half an hour later, they were seated at the table, and a blessing had been asked by the minister. A little nervously, the head of the family began dishing out the vegetables, and, turning to the guest, said: "Will you have some of the little river fish, or would you prefer some of the dam big fish?" He knew he had blundered, and cold beads of perspiration started out on his forehead.

"I mean," trying to repair the error, "will you have some of the dam river fish, or some of the big fish?"

Worse and more of it. His daughter slyly pulled his coat-tail, to bring him to his senses.

"That is, would you like some of the river fish, or some of the other dam fish?" The deep carnation spreading over the good lady's face, didn't mend matters a bit, and with a gasp he plunged in once more. "Ahem! Which of the dam fish do you prefer, any way?"

Size of the Sun.

TO JOURNEY ACROSS IT BY TRAIN WOULD TAKE TWO YEARS AND A HALF.

The sun, provided we measure only the disk seen with smoked glass, is 866,000 miles in diameter, i. e., 108 earths could be comfortably ranged side by side across the disk. To cover the surface would require many thousands. To fill the interior we should need 1,300,000. On a smaller scale we might represent the sun by a ball two feet in diameter and the earth by a good-sized grain of shot.

Let the sun be hollowed out, then place the earth at its center, and let the moon revolve about it at its real distance of 240,000 miles. There would yet remain nearly 200,000 miles of space between the moon's orbit and the inclosing shell of the sun.

Indeed, to journey from one side of the sun to the other, through the center, would take one of our swift express trains nearly two years and a half.

So vast a globe must be heavy. Since its density is only one-quarter that of the earth, it only weighs as much as 332,000 earths or 2,000,000,-000,000,000 of tons.

The attraction of gravity on its surface would cause a man whose weight was 150 pounds to weigh two tons.—*Ladies' Home Journal.*

A wheel should always be thoroughly tired, but its rider should never be so.

A man experienced in the care of invalids; an extensive traveller, not only all over this country, but frequently in Europe; gentle, intelligent, well-read, and conversant with people and places, desires an opportunity to accompany an elderly invalid gentleman or lady in the capacity of companion. He can be highly recommended. Information may be had from the Librarian, Maine State Building.

Golf.

And now we have golf, and the air will be thick with remarks about "brassy niblicks," "putters," "lofters," "bunkers," "the one off two," and the like technical terms, and there will be interesting games to follow, with goodly exercise, and hearty appetites resultant.

Mr. A. H. Fenn, under whose supervision the links have been laid out, informs THE HILL-TOP that the course is 1 3-4 miles around, and that the ground is all that could be desired for the game. It has its natural hazards, like fences, roads, etc., and will be found in every way admirable. The starting point is near the grove at the south-west front of the hotel, and the end is opposite the north-west front. "Address the Ball."

The first record made on the links was 47, made by Mr. Fenn, Thursday, July 30th, which he lowered to 45 on Friday.

A Prince's Birthday.

Thursday, Master James Prince of Portland had a birthday picnic at Peaks Island, Portland Harbor.

The following assisted in testing the birthday cake, which was surrounded by six candles: The Ricker children, cousins to master Prince; Edith Walker, Mr. Dudley Lewis, Robert Marsh, also a cousin; Mrs. A. B. Ricker, Mrs. Sanders, Miss Pray, Miss Lawey, Mrs. H. W. Ricker, Mrs. Brickett, Miss Ricker, Miss Redrick, Mrs. Prince and Janie, made up the party. The children had a jolly time riding the merry-go-rounds and watching the waves come in.

Musical Programme.

SUNDAY EVENING, AT 8.15, AUGUST 2, 1896.

1. Zug der Frauen—From Lohengrin.   Wagner.
2. Prize Song—From Meistersinger.   Wagner.
       Violin Solo—Mr. D. Kuntz.
3. Selection—From Hänsel and Gretel.   Humperdinck.
4. Piano Solo.
       Mr. Edmund Kuntz.
5. Minuet—From Orpheus.   Gluck.
       Flute Obligato—Mr. Brooke.
6. Selection—Martha.   Flotow.

Mexican Drawn Work.

A lady living in Texas, on the Mexican border, sends to Mrs. Hiram W. Ricker a large variety of this material of the finest and most superior quality in the art of needle-work. This is the *genuine*, and of great beauty. Mrs. Ricker will be pleased to show the work to all interested, at their cottage, and to dispose of the same at very reasonable rates.

Thistles.

It's hard to keep a kiss a secret. It's sure to pass from mouth to mouth.

Two artists were sitting on the piazza of the Mansion House, watching the cloud effects and gazing at the noon. During the intermission of the progressive whist party a lady stepped out on the piazza, looked around, and merely said: "Gentlemen, you will have pneumonia."

[From Harper's Weekly.]
He: He who courts and runs away
       May live to court another day.
She: But—he who courts and does not wed
       May find himself in court instead.

I wonder if "Prince Ananias" on Friday's programme was originally intended for the "lyre."

The origin of "Everything is lovely and the goose hangs high" is asked by a subscriber. Will some one please answer?

[From the Lewiston Journal.]
"I wish," said the Democratic donkey as he sidled up to the Republican elephant, "that you'd read what there is on my new silver collar so that I'd know to whom I belong and for what I'm braying."

[Contributed.]
"Oh, would some power the giftie gie us
To see oursel's as others see us."
But how much better if, by spells,
Others could see us as we see oursel's.

Arrivals.

POLAND SPRING HOUSE.
JULY 24 TO JULY 31, 1896.

Ashton, F. and daughter	New York.
Andrews, Mr. and Mrs. J. Munn	Lowell.
Armstrong, Helen S.	Lewiston.
Albis, D. Hurlbuit	Springfield.
Ayer, Mrs. Eli	Scranton.
Bailey, Mrs. C. B.	Washington.
Bennet, E. G.	Portland.
Bailey, Chas. B.	Washington.
Barker, C. O.	Lewiston.
Barker, Mrs. R. H.	Lewiston.
Brown, A. H.	Atlanta.
Brownell, Mr. and Mrs. W. F.	Brookline.
Breed, Mr. and Mrs. J. W.	Lynn.
Chase, Mabel	Portland.
Chase, Chas. S.	Portland.
Carpenter, F. W.	Providence.
Chase, Alice P.	Lynn.
Clark, Geo. B.	New York.
DuBois, L. M.	Poughkeepsie.
Davis, Miss Della	Lewiston.
Dove, H. C.	New York.
Elder, Samuel J.	Winchester.
Englis, Miss	Brooklyn.
Englis, Miss A. B.	Brooklyn.
Fischer, Mr. and Mrs. Bernardo F.	New York.
Fischer, Frederic G.	New York.
Fenn, A. H.	Boston.
Fogg, Mrs. E. F.	Boston.
Gadsden, Robt. W.	Atlanta.
Gaze, Dr. and Mrs. D. S.	Newark.
Goodrich, H. L.	Haverhill.
Gray, Samuel M.	Providence.
Hawley, Mrs. William Dean	Syracuse.
Harkness, Mr. and Mrs. William	Brooklyn.
Hubbard, S. B.	Jacksonville.
Hochdorfer, Mr. and Mrs. R.	Springfield, O.
Hayman, Miss Grace	Milwaukee.
Hayman, Miss Mary	Milwaukee.
Hartington, John M.	Lewiston.
Hall, Mr. and Mrs. E. B.	Boston.
Haynes, M. R.	Portland.
Hale, Mrs. Eugene	Ellsworth.
Hutchins, Mrs. H. H.	Boston.
Haigh, Chas. A.	Boston.
Haigh, Chas.	Boston.
Holmes, Mrs. Israel	Waterbury.
Holmes, M. C., M.D.	New York.
Howell, Miss	Baltimore.
Hyatt, Miss	Baltimore.
Hunt, Otis E.	Newtonville.
Irvine, Robt.	Galveston.
Jaastad, A. W.	Boston.
Jaynes, Mr. and Mrs. C. P.	°Boston.
Johnson, Jas. W.	Atlanta.
Jordan, H. I.	Auburn.
King, T.	Quincy, Ill.
King, Miss Zayma	Quincy, Ill.
Layton, Mr. and Mrs. Fred	Milwaukee.
Lougee, Miss M. H.	Minneapolis.
Lougee, Miss Helen	Minneapolis.
Lake, James H.	Boston.
Lippincott, Mr. and Mrs. Chas.	Philadelphia.
Lippincott, Mr. and Mrs. F. H.	Philadelphia.
Lippincott, Lucille	Philadelphia.
Linnell, Miss S. D.	Galveston.
Lindsey, W. B.	Carlisle, Pa.
McIntire, B. O.	Carlisle, Pa.
Miles, Samuel S.	Boston.
Melcher, J. R.	Brooklyn.
Moulton, Byron P.	Philadelphia.
McDermott, Mrs. Chas. J.	Brooklyn.
Mallett, E. B., Jr.	Freeport.
Maddox, Mr. and Mrs. I. H.	New York.
North, Mr. and Mrs. John H.	Boston.
Nugent, Mr. and Mrs. Dan. C.	St. Louis.
Osgood, Mr. and Mrs. H. S.	Portland.
Orr, Everett	New York.
Palmer, Adelaide	Boston.
Pierce, Miss Laura F.	Boston.
Pierce, Chas. F.	Boston.
Pulington, Mr. and Mrs. F. O.	Mechanic Falls.
Pollock, Mr. and Mrs. James	Philadelphia.
Pollock, Miss Lillian M.	Philadelphia.
Perram, Ernest A.	Newport News, Va.
Pingree, Mr. and Mrs. R. C.	Lewiston.
Packard, Mrs. F. H.	Lewiston.
Packard, C. F.	Lewiston.
Richardson, Miss Marion A.	Boston.
Rogers, Allen M.	New York.
Robinson, Thos. A.	Philadelphia.
Robinson, W. T.	Philadelphia.
Russell, Mr. and Mrs. E. H.	Lewiston.
Ryder, C. M.	Boston.
Sherman, Mr. and Mrs. G. A.	Fall River.
Sherman, Miss Carrie H.	Fall River.
Sherman, Marion	Wollaston.
Sherman, Geo. W.	Cambridge.
Sawyer, Alice Clara	Randolph, Vt.
Snow, Mr. and Mrs. C. W.	Newton.
Snow, Miss Alice N.	Newton.
Stark, Mr. and Mrs. Chas. G.	Milwaukee.
Smith, Miss Stella M.	Providence.
Sweatt, Mr. and Mrs. W. H.	City Mills, Mass.
Schuyler, D.	Plattsburgh.
Stetson, Mr. and Mrs. G. B.	Lewiston.
Smith, Mr. and Mrs. John B.	Lewiston.
Smith, Philip L.	Cambridge.
Smith, Mrs. J. Edwin	Worcester.
Schoen, Mr. and Mrs. Chas. T.	Philadelphia.
Souther, Mrs. G. E.	Boston.
Souther, Master Geo. A.	Boston.
Thornton, David	Brooklyn.
Tafton, Mr. and Mrs. G. B.	Lewiston.
Tafton, N. H.	Lewiston.
Thompson, Geo. F.	Lewiston.
Thorndike, Mr. and Mrs. Albert A.	Braintree.
Towns, Geo. A.	Atlanta.
Taylor, Mrs. Warren S.	Hartford.
Underwood, Miss H.	Brooklyn.
Walsh, J. A.	Lewiston.
Waitt, Dr. J. E.	Boston.
Watts, Mr. and Mrs. Samuel	Boston.
Wilson, Mr. and Mrs. John	New York.
Whitney, H. L.	Boston.
Whitgreave, C. T.	Chicago.
Walsh, L. S.	Boston.
Warden, R. C.	New York.
Wright, Mrs. N. M.	St. Louis.
Woods, Mr. and Mrs. Henry F.	Boston.
Woodman, W. I.	St. Augustine.

MANSION HOUSE.
JULY 23 TO 30, 1896.

Broughton, H. E.	Chicago.
Jordan, E. C.	Portland.
Moise, W. A.	Chicago.
Staples, E. P.	Portland.
Vanzandt, Mr. and Mrs. P. G.	New York.

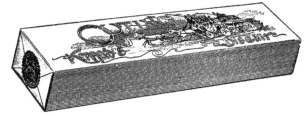

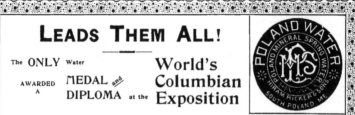

The Hill-Top

POLAND SPRINGS, SO. POLAND, ME.

HARRY C. WILKINSON

THE HILL-TOP.

VOL. III. SUNDAY MORNING, AUGUST 9, 1896. No. 6.

A Poland Saw Mill.

HAVE you ever visited a saw mill; one of
the regular down-east kind, which look as
if they had been taking a tramp about the
country, looking for a good location, and "when
found, made a note of," as our friend Capt'n Ed'ard

Cuttle would say; and then and there settled down
in a quiet, shady nook, ready to disturb the peace
at any moment?

That is the kind of a saw mill this saw mill is.
It found a lovely spot in the woods, right by the
shore of the lake, and the woodsman's axe did not

spare the trees, but cried havoc and let slip the sharpened steel, until the great piles of slabs and sawdust indicate a very profitable use of the time.

Get a team at the stable and drive there in a half hour or less, going down the hill and around the west side of the middle lake, until you arrive almost at the upper lake, and then diverging a little, where great piles of boards are visible, you will see a rocky road, which leads, not to Dublin, but down to the mill.

It is a bit rough, but we got there all right, and you can, although if you are on a wheel we should advise dismounting just at this point.

Although not a large mill, yet it is very interesting to watch the rapidity and exactness of its operations. The logs are hauled up the run from the lake, and rolled on to the carriage, where they are "dogged," which holds them fast in their place, as it moves rapidly toward the great circular saw. As the saw passes through it, the slab is instantly sawed into short "lengths" and cast aside, by which time a newly sawed board has arrived, which is grasped by another man and the uneven edge quickly sawed from it, and the board in its perfect form, with square and regular edges, is thrown upon the pile. As fast as these accumulate they are loaded upon a team and hauled to the yard and stacked.

Everything in this impromptu mill works like clock-work, from the drawing of the wet log from the water to the disposal of the sawdust in a heap, well out of the way.

Seven men are employed at the work, and at the camp, which is close at hand, is a comely and modest appearing maid of all work, who cooks the food, that feeds the men, that run the mill, that saws the logs, that once were trees, that cast the shade, upon the shore, of the upper lake of Poland. And the lass was a pleasant lass to look at; and the men were good, healthy, robust, representative men of Maine, whom it is a pleasure to know, for they have honest faces and a firm, hearty grip of the hand. Here they stay, month in and month out, caring little for the outside world and the frivolities of life, with no desire to know who is the winner of the Derby or the 'Varsity race at Henley; or whether pointed shoes or square toes are the only wear; neither are they at all disturbed if the crease in their trousers has not been ironed for a week. They are quite happy in their isolation, less than three miles from one of the most famous summer resorts in the world, and the old straw hat which cost nine cents two years ago is just as serviceable, and far more comfortable, than a silk hat, a derby, or a sombrero, which cost a hundred times as much.

Our illustration was made from a photograph taken by Mr. Ness of the Notman Photographic Company, and like all their work, it is admirable.

The return trip can be made by crossing the "Suez Canal" and coming back between the two lakes, and around the foot of Shaker Hill, past the Mansion House.

The saw mill may be plainly seen from the steamer Poland, when in the upper lake, but a trip to the spot on shore will be found enjoyable.

The proprietor, Mr. O. C. Stinchfield, is seated at the right of the picture in the group, with head uncovered.

Do not all be prompted with the desire to become saw millers, because there appears to be money, health, and pleasure in it, for if it were to become the fad, what then would become of the hatters and the tailors?

Salmagundi Party.

Notwithstanding the many attractions offered on the part of the magician at the Poland Spring House, Thursday evening, July 30th, much interest was taken by the young people in the Salmagundi Party, which took place in the amusement room.

Eight tables were arranged for Bagatelle, Letters, Whistling, Slap Jack, Ribbon Bowling, Zoölogy, and a game of Hearts.

Miss Carpenter and Miss Stinson did the scoring, and the following took part in the game: Mrs. Baggaley, Mrs. McDermott, the Misses Chase, Luddington, Rogers, King, Newhall, Stella Smith, Englis, Richardson, Smith, Lippincot, Eddy, Dexter, Gale, Stinson, Pierce, and Messrs. Baggaley, Carpenter, Rogers, Olney, Clark, Lippincott, Lewis, Smith, Pierce, Berri. Miss Newhall took the first prize and Miss Luddington and Miss Stella Smith received the second and third prizes. The gentlemen's first prize went to Mr. Pierce, and Mr. Clark and Miss Richardson second and third.

After the awarding of the prizes, the party was invited to the dining-room, by Mr. and Miss Carpenter, where refreshments were served. The tables were placed lengthwise in the large dining-room, and were beautifully decorated with flowers. The evening's pleasure ended with a toast and health to Miss Carpenter, by Mr. Rogers.

Mexican Drawn Work.

A lady living in Texas, on the Mexican border, sends to Mrs. Hiram W. Ricker a large variety of this material of the finest and most superior quality in the art of needle-work. This is the genuine, and of great beauty. Mrs. Ricker will be pleased to show the work to all interested, at their cottage, and to dispose of the same at very reasonable rates.

Congratulations.

The Mansion House dining-room was the scene of an agreeable surprise on the evening of July 31st, when at 10.30 a party of about thirty relatives and friends gathered about Miss Nettie Ricker, to congratulate her on her arrival at another milestone in life's journey.

Miss Ricker was entirely taken by surprise, the actual birthday having passed by with the previous day, without any demonstrations, so when ushered into the very handsomely decorated dining-hall, surrounded by troops of friends, it was wholly unexpected.

During the time occupied by Miss Sadie Ricker in concocting a most delicious Welsh rarebit, others were employed in marking and cutting out silhouettes of various ladies and gentlemen present, and placing them against a black background upon the wall. This and the pleasant chat filled in the time agreeably, until the feast was ready, when all were seated and the banquet proceeded. The birthday cake was partaken of, and the round of merry conversation continued, until twelve o'clock, when the party dispersed, after congratulating Miss Ricker, and wishing her many happy returns of the day.

The Art Gallery.

Visit the Art Gallery in the evening. It is open until 9 P.M., and is very brilliantly lighted, the pictures being seen to better advantage then than by natural light.

Mr. August Franzen has added nine pictures, which may be seen in "D" and "E," and Adelaide Palmer has placed a canvas of cherries and a landscape in "B" and "C." All of these pictures are worthy of attention.

The exhibition is very strong in water-colors, and particular attention is called to those by Buhler, Gallagher, Stecher, Thompson, and Triscott, all of which are fine examples.

Buhler's "Bit of Dordrecht," Gallagher's "Mt. Washington, October," and Stecher's "In His Den," all at the head of the stairway at the entrance to the gallery, are very strong and interesting, and can scarcely fail to find admirers. Then in Alcove "B," Nellie Thompson's "Summer" and "Winter" are two very companionable young ladies; while Triscott's "Mamana Island" is a grand work, which no one should miss seeing. It is in Alcove "F."

Remember that the catalogues, which are illustrated with portraits of the artists, are free, and you are requested to mail them to your friends who may be interested in art. Any one at a distance, who receives THE HILL-TOP, can have one mailed free of charge by sending address.

All the pictures are for sale, and prices will be found to be never more reasonable.

Brake Rides.

On July 30th, a party from the Mansion House, consisting of Miss Barbour, Miss Conover, Miss Sullivan, Miss Jane Marsh, Mr. Franzen, Mr. Read, Mr. Lewis, and Mr. Dudley Lewis, went on the brake to Shaker Village, around Sabbath-day Lake, Upper Gloucester, over Bald Hill, past Elmwood Farm, where they saw one of Mr. Sanborn's fine horses. Returning, they passed through the lower gates, over the Spring Hill to the Mansion House. The cheers when they reached home, assured us that they had a good time.

Mr. and Mrs. Baggaley gave a brake ride over Tenny Hill and through the Raymond woods. The party consisted of Miss Rogers, Miss Newhall, Miss Stinson, Miss Lippincott, Mr. Clark, Mr. Olney, and Mr. Rogers.

Saturday afternoon, August 1st, Miss Luddington gave a brake ride over Oak Hill and around the middle lake. The party included Miss Lippincott, Miss Carpenter, Miss Newhall, Mr. Fessenden, Mr. Clark, Mr. Olney, and Mr. Rogers.

A Blueberry Party.

Monday, a party of five from Poland Springs went to gather blueberries. Two people picked forty-five cupfuls of the berries, and in all there were ten quarts gathered. One of the gentlemen, whom we will call Mr. Sun-flower, did not work but rested under the shade of an apple tree. The party rebelled, and for fear he would not have any of the berries, he threw his cane across his shoulder and to this attached the ten-quart pail, heavy with its contents, and walked home, a distance of a mile.

Sunday Services.

Rev. T. A. Dwyer preached at 11 o'clock Sunday in Music Hall. His text was from St. John, chapter 15, verse 12: "This is my commandment, that ye love one another, as I have loved you." A collection was taken of $12.

In the evening he gave a lecture in the dining-hall. The subject was "A Summer Ramble in Jerusalem, the Holy City." The lecture was well attended.

Lecture.

A very interesting talk on the cathedrals of Europe was given on Monday evening last by Rev. T. A. Dwyer in the Music Hall. He took his audience with him to Rheims, Cologne, St. Peter's, Notre Dame, Westminster, and other noted places, and his word-painting of these world-famous structures was much enjoyed by all who had the pleasure of hearing him.

Children's Column.

"Love can make the humblest life the most sweet."

The Origin of "Creme Renverse au Caramel," Our Recipe for the Poland Springs Menu.

A Russian Count came home very tired one day and said to his *chef:* "Prepare me a sweet entrée as soon as possible." The *chef* was beside himself for a few minutes, but remembering some caramels that he had, melted them and put them into moulds and poured a rich custard over it, then served it to the Count and called it "Crême Renversé au Caramel." The Count liked it so well that it became a favorite dish with him.

Little Janette Ricker has returned from Boston, where she has been spending a week with her uncle, Mr. Sanders.

Mr. and Mrs. Ricker were making a visit to the Art Gallery recently, accompanied by little Edward, who made a tour on his own account. Presently a joyous shout was heard, and, on hastening to learn the cause, the little fellow was found before Hatfield's picture of "After the Bath," and in great glee over the life-like representation of the two children.

Little Miss Mildred Holmes and Master E. T. Holmes, Jr., are registered at the Poland Spring House.

Master Clay Swain is also a guest at the Poland Spring House.

In a large rattan basket at the Mansion House are two little kittens, three weeks old. They are exactly alike, with deep blue eyes, and their color is buff, striped with a bit of white. One is a little smarter than the other, as he is constantly getting out of the basket, while the other looks with longing eyes, and cries. They drink milk, and one gets in on all-fours, much to the disgust of the young ladies to whom they belong. Will some child who reads THE HILL-TOP name our kittens?

Little Edward H. Pulsifer, of Rochester, N. Y., arrived at the Mansion House Friday.

A little girl in Sherman, Me., pointing to a cow's horns, asked what they were. On being told, she exclaimed: "How do she blow it?"

My Blessing.

A blessing was sent from heaven
 Into my life one day.
It came a God-given sunbeam
 Lighting my world with its ray.
It entered my holy of holies,
 And I know that it will be
A joy in the lives of others,
 As well as a joy to me.

My blessing lies here beside me,
 Nestling close and warm;
A wee hand clasping my finger,
 A tiny head on my arm.
Ah! marvellous gift from heaven—
 The Scripture's priceless pearl,
This blessing lives, and will love me,
 My own little baby girl.
 —E. D. C.

Not in the Ark.
[From the Pittsburg Bulletin.]

Mr. Reynolds is a bright and well-preserved old gentleman, but to his little granddaughter Mabel he seems very old, indeed. She had been sitting on his knee, and looking at him seriously for a long time one day, when she asked, suddenly: "Grandpa, were you in the Ark?"

Why, no, my dear," gasped the astonished grandparent.

Mabel's eyes grew large and round with astonishment.

"Then, grandpa," she asked, "why weren't you drowned?"

Sure Enough.
[From Puck.]

"Lucy, I've half a mind to spank you! Why is it you never want a drink of water until after I have turned out the gas?"

"I don't know, mamma. Why is it you allers turn out the gas jus' 'fore I want a drink o' water?"

Fred Sweetland of Rockland, Me., tells a rat story which can't be beaten, and every word of it is truth, says the *Star* of that city. Tuesday afternoon, when he got home, his son's wife was sitting on the doorstep mourning the loss of ten little chickens, which she believed to have been carried off by a rat. When her husband came home he found the rat's hole in the yard, dug into it a piece, and then fired into it with a revolver. Upon opening the hole he found that he had blown a big rat to pieces. He also found seven of the chickens.

Cyclist Column.

MODERN VERSION.
[From Judge.]

If a body meet a body
Bungling on a wheel,
If a body bump a body,
Need a body squeal?

Mother's slipper was the original tanned'em.

There are ten bicycles at the Mansion House.

There are thirty bicycles at the Poland Spring House.

Eighty Connecticut towns are building macadam highways.

Mr. D. Kuntz and Mr. August Franzen have become expert riders on the wheel.

A party of three took their bicycles and rode to Gray, a distance of ten miles, for a dance. They had a jolly time and returned at two o'clock in the morning.

F. N. Summersides and N. H. Cobb of Gorham, Me., stopped over a few hours for recreation at the Poland Spring House, Monday, August 3d. They are making a tour of the state on their wheels. Owing to the bad roads they are unable to travel more than sixty miles per day.

BICYCLE-BELL DRINKING CUPS.

A New York member writes that while wheeling with a lady companion, recently, they came to a spring where there was no cup to drink with, when the happy thought of using the bicycle bell for that purpose occurred to him. It was quickly removed from the bar and served the purpose admirably, and he wishes to convey this hint to other wheelmen in similar straits.

AGAINST COAST DEFENSES.
[From the Washington Star.]

"It is perfectly fascinating," Maud exclaimed, "to read about the proceedings of Congress."

"I suppose it is interesting," Mamie answered with a sigh. "But it's rather hard to understand."

"Yes. But that's where the enjoyment comes. You find out so many things. I never realized until a short time ago how greatly we are in need of coast defenses."

"I don't think we need them at all," Mamie replied, with emphasis.

"Why, of course we do."

"I know better. A brake is only in the way. If you come to a hill so steep you are afraid to coast it with one foot on the front tire, the only thing to do is to get off your bicycle and walk."

And Maud admitted that this was a view of the subject that had not been presented to her.

Progressive Euchre.

Friday evening, July 31st, was cool and delightful for playing progressive euchre. The first ladies' prize, an exquisite hand-painted tea caddy, was won by Mrs. E. C. Jordan. The second prize, a beautiful painted plate, went to Miss Colton. The third to Miss Nettie Ricker, a silver-mounted blotter. The fourth prize to Miss Ricker, a book for newspaper cuttings.

The gentlemen's first prize, silver whist counters, was won by Mr. Ivers. The second prize, a silver pen-knife, went to Col. Talbott. Miss Dickinson won the third prize, a card-case, and Mrs. E. P. Ricker the fourth, a silver paper-cutter. Eighteen games were played and thirteen was the highest number of moves made.

Picnic on the Lower Lake.

Miss Craven, Miss Mary Craven, Miss Jane Craven, Miss Sinnickson, Miss Vose, Miss Gregory, Mr. Bossange, Mr. Maginnis, Mr. Bell, and Mr. Vose, had a delightful picnic on the lower lake.

They took their mandolins and cameras with them, and were successful in getting some very good pictures; while the sweet strains of music gave a charm to the whole affair.

FRANK CARLOS GRiFFiTH, } EDITORS.
NETTiE M. RiCKER,

PUBLISHED EVERY SUNDAY MORNING DURING THE MONTHS
OF JULY, AUGUST, AND SEPTEMBER, IN THE INTERESTS OF
POLAND SPRINGS AND ITS VISITORS.

All contributions relative to the guests of Poland Springs
will be thankfully received.

To insure publication, all communications should reach the
editors not later than Wednesday preceding day of issue.

All parties desiring rates for advertising in the HILL-TOP
should write the editors for same.

The subscription price of the HILL-TOP is $1.00 for the
season, post-paid. Single copies will be mailed at 10c. each.

Address,

EDITORS "HILL-TOP,"
Poland Spring House,
South Poland, Maine.

PRINTED AT JOURNAL OFFICE. LEWISTON.

Sunday, August 9, 1896.

Editorial.

PERHAPS some of our friends would like our views on the political situation, or possibly on the Roentgen rays, or silver, gold, or on paper. Unfortunately our special photographer is not able *as yet*, to take our views on these subjects, but we hope for better things.

At the present time our views on politics would resemble a pile of jack-straws, immediately after they have been dropped from the hand, in an inextricable jumble, which would require an experienced crook, with steady nerves, to untangle.

In the matter of currency, we find on emptying the various receptacles which our " Herring " contains, that the pile of cash heaped mountains high on our editorial table, which has not been shipped to Europe to satisfy the insatiate demand of the gold-bugs, or barons, of Threadneedle Street or the Rue de la Paix, contains gold, plugged silver, soiled and new silver certificates, Canadian silver, copper, nickel, nitrate of silver, a few silver threads among our gold, and numerous cheeks upon our career.

Such are the rewards of journalism. Our immediate fear is, however, that others will become so envious of our sudden rise to wealth as the result of our journalistic career, that they will rush in where angels fear to tread, for it is said they *do* give the editorial rooms a wide berth ; but we console ourselves with the reflection that our altitude is scarcely high enough for them, and beside, they are not addicted to pedestrianism, anyway.

We hope, however, that our photographer will get his Roentgen-ray machine in order speedily, for we have contracted for some half-tone plates, showing a remarkable photograph of the contents of our editorial wallet ; of the metallic substance in the brain of McKinley and Bryan, and of the profane expressions of disgust in the brain of the typical donkey, when he finds out where he is " at."

Our views on paper in the meantime have been a great success, and whether it be a grand and gorgeous interior, or of a saw mill, they are always very superior results.

Musical Programme.

SUNDAY EVENING, AUGUST 9, 1896, 8.15 P.M.

1. Cujus Animum, from Stabat Mater.   Rossini.
2. { *a.* Le Cygne.   Saint-Saëns.
   { *b.* Mazurka.   Poppei.
            Cello Solo, Mr. E. Loeffler.
3. Songs. { Ave Maria.   Schubert.
          { Untube.
            Mrs. S. B. Shoninger.
4. { Cradle Song.   Latan.
   { Intermezzo—Forget-me-not.   Macbeth.
5. Piano Solos.
            Mr. Edmund Kuntz.
6. Selection from Rigoletto.   Verdi.

Junior Republic.

A very interesting entertainment was given by the young men of the Junior Republic Association, in Music Hall, Thursday evening, August 6th, consisting of musical features, and talks on the Junior Republic. The collection for the same amounted to $69.85.

Fish.

The best string of fish to be brought into the Mansion House this season was caught by Mr. Van Zandt and Mr. Read in the middle and upper lakes, Wednesday, August 5th. The gentlemen took a lunch and were gone all day, but fished only three hours. Fifteen black bass were caught and five were brought home. Four weighed three pounds each.

Mr. August Franzen,

whose portrait we present to-day, was born on
Bieika Faim, in the Province of Ostei-Gotland,
Sweden, Febiuaiy 4, 1863. He can haidly remember the time when he did not diaw or paint.
As a child at school he diew the designs on the
blackboaid for the othei childien to copy. At the
age of thiiteen he painted in watei-colois veiy
successfully. Showing this gieat love for art, his
fathei placed him undei the instruction of Dagnon-
Bouveret, one of the famous and most successful
of Fiench aitists.

Ten yeais ago Mi. Fianzen was called to this
countiy to paint on the Cyclorama of the Battle of
Gettysbuig. So gieat was his success that he
iemained two yeais. Retuining to Fiance, he
spent foui yeais theie—two yeais at Giez and
two yeais in Paiis, wheie he studied at the Académie Juliau. Among the noted people whom he
has painted in this countiy aie Eugene Field and
Mi. Eihaidt, collectoi of the poit of New Yoik.
Last wintei he painted an impoitant gioup of six
poitiaits of one family, Mi. Chauncey J. Blaii's
of Chicago.

When one looks at the poitiaits of his fathei
and the noted Swedish singei, Gudiun Torpadie,
in Alcove E of the Art Galleiy, one iealizes that
Mi. Fiauzen is paiticulaily stiong in his delinea-
tion of chaiactei. His coloiing is usually somewhat in the minoi key, and his tone is always
distinguished. Mi. Fianzen seeks the impiession
of human chaiactei, a biauch of art in which he
is intensely inteiested, putting his whole heait
and soul into it. Technically his woik has gieat
naiveté.

He is a membei of the Society of Ameiican
Aitists, and also of the Playeis' Club in New
Yoik. He won a medal at the Columbian Exhibition, wheie he had two paintings. He will
spend the wintei in Chicago, having seveial commissions theie.

Mr. Fiauzen piizes his Ameiican citizenship,
and Ameiica can well be pioud that she has added
to her iauks so stiong an aitist.

POLAND SPRINGS LIVERY

Which is connected with the Poland
Springs Hotels is one of the largest
and best equipped hotel stables in
the country.

POLAND SPRINGS BRAKE

Is a marvel of beauty and comfort
combined, and a visit to Poland without having enjoyed a iide on the
same, is a failure—Beai in mind that
we employ none but

EXPERIENCED DRIVERS

Who are acquainted with the roads
and the different points of interest.

All paities desiiing tuin-outs, should notify the Cleik
at the Office eaily to insuie accommodation.

POLAND SPRINGS LIVERY.

Tid-Bits.

"Full up."

Kite-flying.

Sun-flowers.

Catalogues ready.

Did you go to Barnum s?

Two deer seen in Peterson woods.

W. T. Maginnis of New Orleans is an arrival of a week ago.

Miss Gregory left Poland Springs, Saturday morning, much regretted.

Miss Florence I. Fuller of Springfield, Mass., is a guest at the Mansion House.

The catalogues of the Art Gallery are free. Take one with you as a souvenir.

Chandler Hale and Frederick Hale, sons of Senator Hale, have joined Mrs. Hale.

Judge A. P. Wiswell of Ellsworth, Maine, has been spending a few days at Poland Springs.

F. E. Gilman, M.P., of Montreal, and Mrs. Gilman, are guests at the Poland Spring House.

Rev. W. P. Lewis and Mrs. Lewis of Philadelphia arrived Saturday at the Poland Spring House.

Mr. King and Mr. Moulton furnish the following record at golf: Mr. King, 70, and Mr. Moulton, 81.

To new guests we will say that the books in the library can be taken to the hotel to read. There is no charge of any kind.

Mr. S. B. Hubbard has rejoined Mrs. Hubbard at the Poland Spring House. Mr. Hubbard is always a most agreeable guest.

Mrs. John R. Pulsifer of Rochester, N. Y., and Miss Mary Marsh of Springfield, Mass., arrived Friday at the Mansion House.

Miss Palmer is putting into her picture a pond lily 5 1-2 inches in diameter, the actual measurement of one brought her from the pond.

Kennedy's biscuit are world-famous, and they take every conceivable form and are calculated to gratify any taste, and form of entertainment.

Mr. Frank N. Nay, a well-known Boston lawyer, is spending a few days at the Poland Spring House on his way to Rangeley Lakes.

Mr. John I. Pinkerton of West Chester, Pa., is a guest at the Poland Spring House. Mr. Pinkerton has spent a great many seasons at Poland.

One has only to mention the name of Tiffany to guarantee excellence in everything. Read their advertisement each week and see what they have to offer.

James D. Fessenden of New York recently arrived, and in company with Mrs. Fessenden, his mother, was an interested visitor to the Maine Building.

Mrs. J. Olcott Rhines of New York, arrived at the Poland Spring House, Monday. Her welcome was most hearty and her many friends were delighted to see her so much improved in health.

The many friends of Miss Craven, Miss Mary Craven, Miss Jane Craven, and Miss Siunickson, regret their departure on Friday morning. The young ladies were very popular at Poland Springs.

The Poland Spring House has been so full recently that telegrams were sent to Danville to stop new arrivals who had not previously made engagements for rooms. How is this for hard times?

The many friends of Mrs. B. F. Sturtevant of Jamaica Plain, were glad to welcome her Tuesday evening. She and her granddaughter, Miss Ruth Kellen, are guests at the Poland Spring House.

D. I. Reynolds & Son's weekly change of novelties should attract the interest of each and every one. Every article mentioned is useful and ornamental. Send for their "Summer Suggestions." It is free.

Saturday afternoon a ride on the "Poland" was given in honor of the Misses Lougee. The young gentlemen took their cameras, and were fortunate in getting several good views of the middle lake.

Mrs. E. P. Ricker wishes, through the columns of the HILL-TOP, to thank the ladies of the afternoon progressive euchre party, for their loving attention to her in the gift of an exquisite bureau cover and work basket.

If you should at any time feel the need of massage treatment, you are reminded that Mrs. E. J. Robinson is a skillful masseuse, and can be found at all times at the Poland Spring House. Her card is in another column.

The little Miss Lucy Sone, the daughter of the gardener, whose "divinely tall" and willowy form is known to all the guests, is very successful in disposing of her flowers. The nasturtiums and sweet peas are noticeably fresh and pretty.

Our very excellent illustration on the first page this week is by the Notman Photographic Co. We are pleased to acknowledge that probably no publication in America has the advantage of better photographic work than has the HILL-TOP.

Miss Wheelock, the whist queen, is stopping at the Poland Spring House. She has been spending some time at Bar Harbor since leaving her home in Chicago in the early part of the summer. Miss Wheelock is the best whist teacher in this country.

Mr. H. K. Morrell of Gardiner, Me., has presented to the library fifty-two volumes which will be found ready for delivery. Mr. Morrell was for many years editor and proprietor of the Gardiner *Home Journal*, and is a director of the Gardiner Public Library.

Mr. George G. Crowell, who presented the very fine edition of the Standard Dictionary, is the President of the Insurance Company of the State of Pennsylvania. These volumes have already proved of great value and have been the means of settling several disputed points.

We have had the pleasure of examining a very nice collection of sea mosses, made by Mr. Wareham, the second head-waiter of the Poland Spring House. The specimens are twenty-three in number, and very delicate and handsome. They were collected on the Pacific coast, and may be seen in the Herbarium of the Maine State Building.

Mrs. Frederick Henwood, whose miniatures are on exhibition at the Maine State Building, is the grand-niece of the late Sir George Hayter, the well-known portrait painter of London, Eng. Among his most celebrated pictures is the "Coronation of Queen Victoria," which is at Windsor Castle, with many of his other portraits of the royal family.

Dinner Party.

Thursday night, July 30th, a delightful dinner party was given on the eve of the departure of the Misses Craven. The table was artistically decorated with sweet peas and ferns. Mr. and Mrs. Smith chaperoned the party. Miss Craven, Miss Mary Craven, Miss Jane Craven, Miss Sinnickson, Miss Vose, Miss Gregory, Mr. Bossauge, Mr. Maginnis, Mr. Bell, and Mr. Vose composed the party. After the dinner, they went to the music hall, where they danced until nearly eleven o'clock. It was one of the most enjoyable evenings of the season.

Mrs. Elizabeth Robinson,

POLAND SPRING HOUSE.

Pupil of the Posse Gymnasium, Boston.
Swedish Movements and Massage. Room 319.

Guests at Poland Spring House

AUGUST 5, 1896.

Mr. and Mrs. G. O. Allen	Scituate, Mass.
Mr. and Mrs. H. W. Allen	Troy, Ohio.
Mr. W. H. Arnold	New York.
Miss Amy T. Arnold	New York.
Mrs. Jas. Boyd	Harrisburg.
Dr. and Mrs. Geo. Brett	Boston.
Mr. and Mrs. F. H. Browne	Waltham.
Mr. and Mrs. N. A. Baldwin	New Haven.
Mr. and Mrs. W. W. Boynton	Cleveland.
Mr. M. Bradley	Haverhill.
Mr. F. L. Benedict	Portsmouth.
Mr. and Mrs. Ralph Baggaley	Pittsburg.
Mr. Wm. A. Bigelow	New York.
Mrs. B. Babcock	New York.
Miss Babcock	New York.
Miss L. Belyea	Boston.
Mr. and Mrs. Jacob P. Bates	Boston.
Mr. and Mrs. H. O. Bright	Cambridge.
Mr. and Mrs. Nelson Bartlett	Boston.
Mr. E. R. Bossange	New York.
Mr. E. N. Briggs	Saginaw, Mich.
Mr. and Mrs. Wm. Berri	Brooklyn.
Walter Berri	Brooklyn.
Herbert Berri	Brooklyn.
Mrs. Beylie	Philadelphia.
Mrs. Agnes S. Curtis	New York.
Mr. and Mrs. Geo. W. Coleman	Boston.
Mr. Andrew K. Culver	Brooklyn.
Mr. and Mrs. F. W. Carpenter	Providence.
Miss Hannah Carpenter	Providence.
Miss Julia Carpenter	Providence.
Mr. and Mrs. C. C. Corbin	Webster, Mass.
W. H. Chappall	Chicago.
Miss Chappall	Chicago.
Mrs. Z. Chandler	Detroit, Mich.
Mr. and Mrs. Robt. Dorian	Philadelphia.
Mrs. Wm. C. Dunton	New York.
Miss C. S. Duer	New Haven.
Mrs. Albert Douglass	New York.
Mrs. M. E. Dexter	Brooklyn.
Miss Dexter	Brooklyn.
Mrs. N. C. Dickerson	New York.
Rev. T. A. Dwyer	Hyde Park, Mass.
Mrs. Wm. Engel	Bangor.
Miss Engel	Bangor.
Rev. T. J. Earley	New York.
Miss Englis	Brooklyn.
Miss A. B. Englis	Brooklyn.
Mr. and Mrs. James H. Eddy	New Britain, Conn.
Miss Bessie M. Eddy	New Britain, Conn.
Mr. Chas. B. Eddy	Brooklyn, N. Y.
Mr. and Mrs. Thomas W. Evans	Lock Haven.
Mrs. C. G. Furst	Lock Haven.
Mr. and Mrs. R. M. Field	Boston.
Miss Fletcher	Boston.
Mr. Geo. B. French	Boston.
Mrs. J. D. Fessenden	New York.
Gen. Chas. E. Furlong	New York.
Mr. and Mrs. D. H. Field	Brockton, Mass.
Miss Fischer	New York.
Mr. and Mrs. C. S. Fischer	New York.
Mrs. M. C. Feland	New York.
Mrs. R. G. Feltus	Philadelphia.
Miss C. O. French	Canton.
Mr. and Mrs. A. L. Gourdan	New York.
Mr. and Mrs. F. E. Gilman	Montreal.
Mr. M. F. Greene	Milford.
Master Fred Gude	New York.
Mr. John Goldthwaite	Boston.
Miss E. B. Goldthwaite	Boston.
Mrs. G. F. Gregory	Brooklyn.
Miss Gregory	Brooklyn.
Mrs. M. R. Goodwin	Boston.
Miss Goodwin	Boston.
Mrs. L. M. Gale	Washington.
Miss Olive Gale	Washington.
Mr. and Mrs. C. C. Griffin	Haverhill, Mass.

Mrs. J. R. Gibney	New York.
Miss Howell	Baltimore.
Miss Hyatt	Baltimore.
Dr. Otis E. Hunt	Newtonville.
Mrs. Wm. D. Hawley	Syracuse.
Mr. S. B. Hubbard	Jacksonville.
Mrs. W. W. Hartwell	Plattsburgh, N. Y.
Mr. and Mrs. John R. Hoxie	Chicago.
Miss Anna Hoxie	Chicago.
Mrs. Eugene Hale	Ellsworth, Me.
Mr. and Mrs. Horace Hunt	New York.
Mrs. S. B. Hubbard	Jacksonville, Fla.
Mr. and Mrs. L. Hurlburt	Brooklyn.
Mrs. M. B. Hoffman	New York.
Mr. and Mrs. L. D. Henwood	Boston.
Mr. and Mrs. Hudson Hoagland	New York.
Mr. and Mrs. E. Holmes	New York.
Mr. Samuel Ivers	New Bedford.
Miss Ella F. Ivers	New Bedford.
Miss Jacoby	New York.
Mrs. Julian James	Washington.
Mrs. A. E. Kittredge	New York.
Miss Ruth Kellen	Marion, Mass.
Miss Bessie Lippincott	Philadelphia.
Rev. and Mrs. W. P. Lewis	Philadelphia.
Mrs. B. C. Lake	New Haven.
Miss Leland	New York.
Mr. and Mrs. Malcolm Lloyd	Philadelphia.
Miss Lloyd	Philadelphia.
James D. Laird	San Francisco.
Mr. and Mrs. Chas. Lippincott	Philadelphia.
Mr. and Mrs. F. H. Lippincott	Philadelphia.
Miss Lucille Lippincott	Philadelphia.
Mrs. Amos R. Little	Philadelphia.
Mr. and Mrs. B. Lemann and family	New Orleans.
Miss Cora W. Lumbert	Brockton.
Mr. and Mrs. J. S. Martin	New York.
J. S. Martin, Jr.	New York.
Mr. A. N. Mayo	Springfield.
Byron P. Moulton	Philadelphia.
Mr. and Mrs. T. B. M. Mason	Washington.
Mrs. T. B. Myers	Washington.
Mrs. Jno. H. Maginnis	New Orleans.
Mr. Jno. H. Maginnis	New Orleans.
Mrs. A. Mully	Washington.
Miss A. G. Miller	Brooklyn.
Dr. and Mrs. Ira L. Moore	Boston.
Mrs. J. T. Montgomery	Philadelphia.
Mrs. B. P. Moulton	Rosemont, Pa.
Mr. and Mrs. A. R. Mitchell	Newtonville.
Mrs. Christine Marburg	Baltimore.
The Misses Marburg	Baltimore.
Mr. and Mrs. John T. Martin	New York.
F. N. Nay	Boston.
Mr. and Mrs. J. L. Nason	Boston.
Miss Nason	Boston.
Mr. and Mrs. Dan C. Nugent and family	St. Louis.
Mr. and Mrs. W. T. Ness	Boston.
Miss Lucy P. Newhall	Philadelphia.
Mr. and Mrs. Frank F. Olney	Providence.
Mrs. H. S. Osgood	Portland.
Mr. Elam W. Olney	Providence.
Mr. John A. Ordway	Boston.
Mr. and Mrs. Josiah Oakes	Malden, Mass.
Mr. and Mrs. H. N. Paul	Philadelphia.
Mr. John I. Pinkerton	West Chester, Pa.
Miss E. A. Prall	New York.
Mr. and Mrs. Platt	Portland.
Mr. and Mrs. J. H. Pearson	Chicago.
Mr. and Mrs. C. W. Purinton	Topsham.
Miss Octavia Purinton	West Bowdoin.
Mrs. Pattison	Boston.
Mrs. J. A. Pettee	New York.
Mrs. Henry U. Palmer	Brooklyn.
Masters Austin and Chester Palmer	Brooklyn.
Mrs. M. E. Parsons	Boston.
Mr. E. D. Peters	Boston.
Miss A. J. Pomeroy	New York.
Miss Marion Richardson	Boston.
Mrs. Runyon	Plainfield, N. J.
Mrs. J. O. Rhines	New York.
Mr. and Mrs. E. H. Randolph	Louisiana.

Mr. and Mrs. Augustus Richardson	Boston.
Miss Richardson	Boston.
Allen M. Rogers	New York.
Thomas A. Robinson	Philadelphia.
W. T. Robinson	Philadelphia.
Mr. and Mrs. H. A. Rogers	New York.
Miss May Rogers	New York.
Mrs. E. J. Robinson	Boston.
Mr. and Mrs. A. S. Rines	Portland.
Miss Roberts	Philadelphia.
Moses W. Richardson	Boston.
Mr. and Mrs. S. B. Shopinger	New Haven, Ct.
Dr. and Mrs. E. H. Smith	Boston.
Mr. and Mrs. H. C. Twain and son	New York.
Mr. and Mrs. J. D. Sisler	Wilmington.
Miss Madeline Sisler	Wilmington.
Mr. and Mrs. J. E. Spenser	New York.
Mr. and Mrs. S. R. Small	Portland.
Mrs. S. Skaats	New York.
Miss Ella Smith	Boston.
Miss Slade	New York.
Mrs. Mary J. Spencer	Brooklyn.
Mrs. B. F. Sturtevant	Boston.
Dr. and Mrs. C. C. Schuyler	Plattsburgh, N. Y.
Mr. and Mrs. Chas. G. Stark	Milwaukee.
Mrs. S. B. Stinson	Philadelphia.
Miss Stinson	Philadelphia.
Miss Florence Stinson	Philadelphia.
Mr. and Mrs. A. T. Salter	Washington.
Mr. and Mrs. Joseph W. Sandford	Plainfield, N. J.
Mr. and Mrs. E. J. Stellwagen	Washington.
Mr. Samuel Shethar	New York.
Miss Tillotson	New Haven.
Miss N. E. Ten Broeck	New York.
Mrs. Orlando Tompkins	Boston.
Mrs. Frank R. Thomas	Boston.
Mr. and Mrs. F. E. Taylor	Brooklyn.
Mr. and Mrs. David Thornton	Brooklyn.
Miss H. Underwood	Brooklyn.
Mr. and Mrs. Peter Van Voorhees	Camden, N. J.
J. D. Van Voorhees	Camden, N. J.
Mr. and Mrs. W. A. Vose	Brookline.
Mr. Geo. A. Vose	Brookline.
Miss Vose	Brookline.
Mrs. John H. Voorhees	Brooklyn.
Miss Jessie Voorhees	Brooklyn.
Mr. and Mrs. W. B. Valentine	London, Eng.
Mr. and Mrs. Samuel Watts	Boston.
Mr. and Mrs. John Wilson	New York.
Miss P. W. Willets	So. Amboy, N. J.
Mr. and Mrs. A. H. Wellman	Malden, Mass.
Mrs. Chas. Warner	Troy, N. Y.
Miss C. A. Warner	Troy, N. Y.
Miss M. V. Warner	Troy, N. Y.
Miss M. A. Winslow	Troy, N. Y.
Mr. E. M. Warner	Troy, N. Y.
Mrs. H. W. Wadleigh	Boston.
Mr. and Mrs. F. H. Wyeth	Philadelphia.
Miss Kate Wheelock	Chicago.
Miss Jennie Williams	Topsham.
Mrs. N. M. Wright	St. Louis.
Mr. and Mrs. John P. Woodbury	Boston.
Mrs. J. Reed Whipple	Boston.
Dr. M. C. Wedgwood and Mrs. Wedgwood	Lewiston.
Mr. A. Wentworth	Boston.
Mr. F. R. Wharton	Philadelphia.
Mr. and Mrs. W. S. Wymond	Louisville, Ky.
Miss Wymond	Louisville, Ky.
Mr. and Mrs. J. Stuart White	New York.
Mr. David G. Yates	Philadelphia.
Mr. and Mrs. H. D. Ziegler	Philadelphia.
Miss C. F. Ziegler	Philadelphia.

You can have your cards written very prettily by Mr. Lockhead at the Mansion House. Samples will be shown and orders received at the news stand of the Poland Spring House. Prices will be very reasonable.

New Books.

FROM MRS. J. P. BATES.

His Honour and a Lady, by Mrs. Everard Cotes.

FROM H. K. MORRELL.

Michael Strogoff.
Victory.
Wych Hazel.
Saratoga.
Woodburn Grange.
Mapleton.
Agnes de Mansfelt.
Harry Lorrequer.
Scottish Chiefs.
The Lost Love.
Central Idea of Christianity.
Spain and the Spaniards.
Report State Assessors 1894.
Report State Industrial and Labor Bureau 1894.
Artesian Wells Investigation 1890.
Adjutant General's Report of Maine 1863.
Ike Partington and his Friends.
Merry's Book of Prose and Poetry.
Merry's Book of Travel and Adventure.
The Pitcher of Cool Water.
The McAllisters.
Rachael Noble's Experience.
Our Parish.
Life of Charles Sumner.
Life of U. S. Grant.
Life of P. T. Barnum.
Life of Abraham Lincoln.
Life of Rutherford B. Hayes.
Life of Rev. John W. de la Flechere.
Life of Seymour and Blair.
Life of Richard Williams.
History of Kennebec County.
The Fishermen's Memorial and Record Book.
The Soldier's Story.
Lives of the Popes.
Picturesque Gardiner.
Path of Life.
Domestic Life.
Olmstead's Astronomy.
Temperance Anecdotes.
Our Wasted Resources.
Davies Legendie.
Hand Book of Games.
The True Woman.
Battle of the Bush.
The Grape Culturist.
The Basis of the Temperance Reform.
Socialistic, Communistic, Mutualistic, etc.
National Temperance Orator.
The Triangular Society.
The Art Idea.
Alcohol, its Nature and Effects.   52 volumes.

FROM MRS. J. B. SAWYER.

Westward Ho, by Charles Kingsley.
Adventures of Captain Horn, by Frank R. Stockton.

The Mount Pleasant House at the White Mountains will cater for long season business, making special rates for the fall. It will make a specialty of entertaining travellers and tourists coming to the White Mountains to make the ascent of Mt. Washington, as it is the nearest house to the mountain, and the trains on the Mt. Washington Railway leave from a station on the grounds to make the ascent, and it is the first hotel reached on the descent. From their own windows guests can see Mt. Washington from base to summit, and can decide in the morning whether to prepare for the ascent or await a more favorable day.

Arrivals.

POLAND SPRING HOUSE.

JULY 31 TO AUG. 7, 1896.

Adams, Mr. and Mrs. A. H.	Haverhill.
Atwood, Horace	Hampden, Me.
Allen, Mr. and Mrs. Fred E.	Portland.
Allen, Miss Marjorie	Portland.
Allen, Mr. and Mrs. Geo.	Scituate.
Allen, Mr. and Mrs. H. W.	Troy, O.
Arnold, W, H.	New York.
Arnold, Miss A. T.	New York.
Bailey, I. A.	Portland.
Boyd, Mrs. Jas.	Harrisburg.
Brett, Dr. and Mrs. Geo. O.	Boston.
Browne, Mr. and Mrs. Frank H.	Waltham.
Baldwin, Mr. and Mrs. N. A.	New Haven.
Boynton, Mr. and Mrs. W. W.	Cleveland.
Beelin, Mrs. D. S.	New York.
Bradley, M.	Haverhill.
Brett, Mr. and Mrs. M. W.	New York.
Benedict, F. L.	Portsmouth.
Butler, John A.	Boston.
Cammack, Mr. and Mrs. John	Washington.
Cammack, J. Edmund	Washington.
Coleman, Amelia	New York.
Costello, C. P.	Portland.
Curtis, Mrs. Cyrus S.	New York.
Curtis, Mr. and Mrs. W. M.	Freeport.
Curtis, Mr. and Mrs. J. D.	Haverhill.
Clymer, Mrs. J. F.	Troy.
Clark, Mrs. M.	Danville.
Darrian, Mr. and Mrs. Robert	Philadelphia.
Dizer, Mr. and Mrs. T. C.	Boston.
Dunton, Mrs. Wm. C.	New York.
Diel, Miss Caroline Stydam	New Haven.
Day, H. A.	Danville.
Engel, Mr. and Mrs. Wm.	Bangor.
Engel, Miss	Bangor.
Edgar, Wm. S.	South Orange.
Earley, T. J.	New York.
Fessenden, James D.	New York.
Frost, Mrs. C. G.	Lock Haven.
Fassett, Mrs. F. H.	Portland.
Field, Chas. H.	Belfast.
Goodrich, Hazen B.	Haverhill.
Goodrich, Hazen L.	Haverhill.
Gordian, Mr. and Mrs. A. L.	New York.
Gilman, Mr. and Mrs. F. E.	Montreal.
Green, M. F.	Milford.
Gade, Fred	New York.
Hersey, Heloise E.	Boston.
Holmes, Mr. and Mrs. E. T.	New York.
Holmes, Master E. T., Jr.	New York.
Holmes, Mildred	Boston.
Holbrook, Mrs. C. L.	Boston.
Howard, Mr. and Mrs.	Boston.
Hayden, Dr. and Mrs. W. R.	Bedford Springs, Mass.
Hale, Chandler	Ellsworth.
Hale, Frederick	Ellsworth.
Hicks, Mrs. H. E.	New York.
Hunt, Chas. F.	New York.
Hunt, E. Lawrence	New York.
Horner, Miss	Philadelphia.
Jeffries, Mr. and Mrs. James	Louisiana.
Keating, Mrs. P.	Buffalo.
Kellen, Miss Ruth	Marion, Mass.
Kittredge, Mrs. Abbott E.	New York.
Kinney, E. B., Jr.	New York.
Lewis, Rev. and Mrs. W. P.	Philadelphia.
Lippincott, Miss Bessie	Philadelphia.
Lindsay, Thos. Bond	Boston.
Lord, Mr. and Mrs. E. A.	Boston.
Lake, Mrs. B. C.	New Haven.
Larrabee, Seth L.	Portland.
Leland, Miss	New York.
Lawrence, Mrs. J. D.	New York.
Lloyd, Mr. and Mrs. Malcolm	Philadelphia.
Little, J. R.	Lewiston.
Mehle, Allen	New Orleans.
Maginnis, W. T.	New Orleans.
Martin, Mr. and Mrs. John S.	New York.
Martin, J. S., Jr.	New York.
Millett, Asa	Lancaster.
Miller, Dr. A. H.	Lewiston.
Mayo, A. N.	Springfield.
Mason, Miss	Syracuse.
Moore, Joseph, Jr.	Philadelphia.
Merrill, Mrs. J. Warren	Boston.
Merrill, Miss	Boston.
Morrison, Bergh	New York.
Nealey, A. B.	Lewiston.
Nay, Frank N.	Boston.
Nason, Mr. and Mrs. J. L.	Boston.
Nason, Miss	Boston.
Osgood, H. S.	Portland.
O'Neil, J. P.	Boston.
Pain, Mr. and Mrs. H. N.	Philadelphia.
Putnam, Alice	Boston.
Pinkerton, Jno. I.	West Chester.
Prall, Miss E. A.	New York.
Pratt, Mr. and Mrs.	Portland.
Pearson, Mr. and Mrs. J. H.	Chicago.
Pemberton, Mr. and Mrs. C. W.	Topsham.
Pemberton, Octavia	W. Bowdoin.
Poillon, Mr. and Mrs. J. O.	New York.
Roninger, Mr. and Mrs. S. B.	New Haven.
Runyon, Mr. and Mrs. A. M.	Plainfield, N. J.
Rice, John O.	Portland.
Riggs, Mr. and Mrs. Henry B.	New York.
Rhines, Mrs I. Olcott	New York.
Randolph, Mr. and Mrs. E. H.	Louisiana.
Robinson, Mr. and Mrs. C. A.	Auburn.
Staples, Chas., Jr	Portland.
Swain, Mr. and Mrs. H. C.	New York.
Swain, Master H. C.	New York.
Sisler, Mr. and Mrs. J. D.	Wilmington, Del.
Sisler, Miss Madeline	Wilmington, Del.
Spencer, Mr. and Mrs. Jas. E.	New York.
Small, Mr. and Mrs. S. R.	Portland.
Skaats, Mrs. S.	New York.
Smith, Miss Ella	Boston.
Smith, Dr. and Mrs. Eugene H.	Boston.
Slade, Miss	New York.
Sweet, Mrs. W. A.	Syracuse.
Spencer, Mrs. Mary J.	Brooklyn.
Scannell, J. M.	Lewiston.
Sturtevant, Mrs. B. F.	Jamaica Plain.
Smith, Miss Ada M.	New York.
Spofford, Mr. and Mrs. C. A.	New York.
Shell, R. Montgomery	New York.
Tatum, Miss	Brooklyn.
Tillotson, Miss	New Haven.
Thom, Chas. B.	New Orleans.
Ten Broeck, Mrs. N. E.	New York.
Underhill, Miss S. H.	New York.
Vandenburgh, Dr. and Mrs. J. T.	New York.
Van Voorhees, Mr. and Mrs. Peter	Camden, N. J.
Van Voorhees, Master J. Dayton	Camden, N. J.
Walton, Mrs. C.	Trenton.
Wilson, Mr. and Mrs. E. W.	Pekin, Ill.
Wood, Beverly R.	New York.
Willits, Miss Katie P.	South Amboy, N. J.
Wellman, Mr. and Mrs. A. H.	Malden.
Wilson, Mrs. S. T.	Plainfield, N. J.
Wilson, E. T.	Plainfield, N. J.
Warner, Mrs. Chas.	Troy.
Warner, Miss C. A.	Troy.
Warner, Miss M. V.	Troy.
Winslow, Miss M. A.	Troy.
Warner, E.	Troy.

MANSION HOUSE.

July 31 to Aug. 7, 1896.

Our Menu.

Recipe No. 11.

Crême Renversé au Caramel.

To prepare the caramel, take five pounds of sugar, one-fourth pound of butter, and place them in a copper sauce-pan. Then place on a slow fire until the caramel is done boiling. When the sugar stops boiling and begins to brown, then remove and put one tablespoonful into small molds and set away until cold and hard like candy.

Then take five quarts of milk, and add twenty-five eggs, two pounds of sugar, and vanilla to taste. Finish by filling the molds, and place in large baking-pan, with one gallon of water in the bottom of the pan, so as to form a slight steam. Place in the oven and cook until done. Serve bottom side up, as the caramel forms a sauce when hot and runs over all. This will serve 400 people.

Recipe No. 13.

Brown Fricassee of Chicken.

Select three good-sized chickens, clean and cut off the wings, legs, and remove the breast meat. Parboil this until it is nearly done. Remove from the water and fry in a pan with butter. Brown both sides of the chicken. Then take the pan the chicken has been fried in and fill it with the stock the chicken has been boiled in. Add to this flour thickening, salt, and pepper to taste. Pour this over the fried chicken and serve. This recipe is for a family of twelve.

Recipe No. 14.

Taylor Cake.

One and one-half cups of sugar, one-half cup of butter, one cup of sour milk, two eggs, two and three-fourths cups of flour, one teaspoon soda, one cup of chopped raisins, and all kinds of spice to taste.

Recipe No. 15.

Blueberry Cottage Pudding.

Two cups of pastry flour, one-half cup of sugar, one-half cup of butter, one teaspoon of soda, two of cream of tartar, one egg, milk enough to make a thick batter, one cup of blueberries.

Dinner Party.

Wednesday, August 5th, Mr. Olney gave a dinner to a party of his friends at the Poland Spring House. The table was beautifully decorated with flowers, and the ladies were each supplied with a bunch of roses, while the gentlemen found a dainty boutonniere by each plate.

Covers were laid for twelve people, which included Mrs. Baggaley, the Misses Rogers, Newhall, Stinson, Carpenter, and Lippincott, and Messrs. Baggaley, Maginnis, Bossange, Martin, and Rogers. The service was especially complimented, the dinner being prepared and served faultlessly.

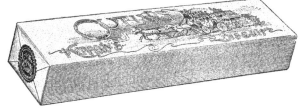

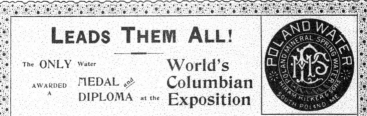

The Hill-Top

POLAND SPRINGS, SO. POLAND, ME.

THE HILL-TOPS

VOL. III.　　　SUNDAY MORNING, AUGUST 16, 1896.　　　No. 7.

Elmwood Farm.

ABOUT three miles from the Poland Spring House, a bit off the Lewiston road, is an old New England farm of some three hundred acres and called "Elmwood Farm," and with some reason, for in front of the farm-house are four stately elms which tower far above the hospitable roof. Several intermediate buildings fill in the space between the house proper, with its large, central chimney, and the great stable, upon whose lofty front is placed the inscription "Elmwood Farm, 1887," which date was that of the year following the one upon which the present proprietor, Mr. James S. Sanborn, purchased the place.

The low, one-storied building, which partially shows in our illustration, was the original homestead erected by the Pulsifers, five generations ago, three generations of the family having occupied the premises previous to its purchase by Mr. Sanborn, who has added much to the structural appearance of the place, he transforming it into a stock farm for the breeding of horses of a superior class, quite a number of which are shown in our cut, perhaps the most noteworthy being the famous stallion, Gemare, in the foreground on the left, and Lothaire, a magnificent animal, with glossy hide which glistens like the finest silk, upon the right, beyond which is Kenilworth; while in the background are two beautiful breed mares, Flora G. and Sadie W.

Mr. Sanborn, who is a member of the famous firm of Chase & Sanborn, the coffee dealers, is cordial in his treatment of visitors, and extends the invitation to all who feel interested in beautiful specimens of horseflesh to call any day except Sunday, at 10 A.M. or 3 P.M. and inspect his stock.

Our illustration is from a photograph, taken only last week especially for THE HILL-TOP by the Notman Photographic Co. Copies of the original photograph can be had at the studio.

Poland on the Rangeleys.
[Contributed.]

On August 5th a merry party of thirteen left the Poland Spring House to make a trip of the Rangeley Lakes. They went to Poland Corner, where a special car was awaiting them which took them, by way of Rumford Falls, to Bemis, where they were to spend the night. Bemis is a camp at the southern end of Lake Mooseluckmeguntic. The party stayed there over night, and next morning, by special boat, they went up the lake to Upper Dam. This place was made the butt of many jokes. One of the party caught a large trout here, which was carried on with them that afternoon to Rangeley, where they stayed over night, and the fish was cooked there and eaten for supper that evening, every one getting a small piece. The next morning the party started back for Poland, where they arrived along towards evening, tired out, but in very good spirits. The guests at the hotel can get some idea of the fun the party enjoyed when they hear them refer to such things as "fricasseed liver," "dynamite," "upper dams," "squash, apple, and blueberry pies," thinking of interesting incidents which happened to members of the party. Everybody had lots of fun from start to finish. And we want to go again.

WALTER BERRI.

Cyclist Column.

THREE OF A KIND.

They pushed their tandem wheel along
  At a rate they thought was clever;
They fairly flew, and the sun scorched, too,
  And tanned 'em worse than ever.

Join the L. A. W.

Mr. H. W. Lathan of East Orange, N. J., and Mr. F. H. Hayward of Cambridge, Mass., rode on their bicycles from Portland to Willow Brook Farm, Oxford, Tuesday, August 11th. They stopped at the Mansion House for dinner. Owing to the excessive heat, a punctured tire, and bad roads a portion of the distance, the young men were four hours between Portland and Poland Springs.

Although Tuesday, August 11th, was very rainy, Mr. Edgar R. Dow of Portland rode from that city to Poland Springs on his wheel.

One hundred and ninety-two members of Philadelphia Century Club made the century run from Newark, N. J., each member coming in to Philadelphia on the club on Broad Street on time.

BY WAY OF ENCOURAGEMENT.

A member of "Philadelphia Century Club" rode the century run from Newark, N. J., to Philadelphia, over hill and dale, rough roads and all, without using handle bars. This was the first of July, 1896.

STERN LIGHTS FOR BICYCLES.

It is suggested that a bicycle light should show from the rear, and that it be located so that the form of the rider will not obscure it. This is to prevent the scorchers from running over those who ride for pleasure.

Master Henry I. McCord, 2d, rides the wheel well.

[From The Four Hundred, American Journal of Society and Travel.]

The bicycle is in evidence at Niagara Falls as furiously as everywhere else, and many a modern visitor sees the grand panorama from a wheel. The fine streets and park roadways make wheeling very easy and delightful there. A half-dozen stores have opened with wheels for rent, and are doing the lively business of the resort. The electric cars and the bicycles have about exterminated the once autocratic and gormandizing carriage bandit.

Love and War.

"PAPA, can nothing be done?"

"Nothing but wait."

"How much longer, dear papa?"

"Not long, my child, not long," was the reply of General Weston, with a sigh, which meant more than he intended his daughter to divine.

This conversation took place within the enclosure of a military post in a far western state during an uprising of those wards of the nation, the Apaches, who had taken it upon themselves to annihilate our sixty-five million of inhabitants, and to restore this fair land to its rightful owners.

The savages had laid siege to the post, and were leisurely starving out the gallant little band of Uncle Sam's boys.

"Will no brave man hazard the chance of getting through the Indian lines, and carrying word to Colonel Raines at Red Gulch?" ventured Miss Weston.

"No, it would be simply rushing upon his death. There are at least a thousand redskins in the vicinity, and he could not escape. I was in hopes this gale of wind which is blowing night cause them to seek shelter for a time in the foot-hills, but it only forces them to lie flat upon the ground where they were," sadly replied the General.

"But papa, you are a man, and a man of skill and experience; can not your mind devise some means of rescue?"

"My child, do you think I would stand idly here if it were so? Come, let us walk about a bit. Look; do you see how calmly that Englishman lays there on the ground, watching his kites, in the midst of such danger?"

"Do I see him, yes indeed, the poltroon. To think that I had even for a moment considered a proposition of marriage from such an idle fellow; a man who can waste his time flying kites, when he might handle a musket."

"Ah, beg pardon, Miss Weston," said the object of their remarks, rising languidly. "Isn't it extraordinary, directly I get five flyers in tandem, along comes this seventy-mile breeze, and they pull like a draught horse? Feel the cord, Miss Weston, do."

"Extraordinary, yes. Extraordinary that you can play with a kite, instead of shooting savages."

"But my dear Miss—"

"Don't dear me, if you please."

"I beg your pardon—but every man to his trade. Now I should only waste powder, don't you know?" I couldn't hit a savage three feet away. You see, General," appealing to the father, "I have got on my largest flyer, an eight-footer, and it only weighs seventeen ounces. That is the lowest one. There are four above that, smaller—"

"The last can of biscuit opened, General," reported an officer to his superior, at this moment, "and the last pound of dried beef is in sight."

"Sh," said the commander. "Alicia, you had better retire a while, within the quarters. I will join you there presently."

"No, papa, let me share all your troubles, and know the worst."

"Well, General," resumed the officer, "unless word is gotten to Colonel Raines, at Red Gulch, within a few hours, we are as good as dead, every mother's son of us."

"Dear me, is it as bad as that?" drawled our English friend, Professor Carstover.

"Bad as that!" indignantly exclaimed Miss Weston. Oh, you make me—tired, there. Here we are with only a hundred and fifty men, and on their last biscuit and ounce of beef, with not over three rounds of ammunition left, and you coolly ask, 'Is it as bad as that?'"

"Where is this Dead Dog—I beg pardon, Red Dog—I mean Red Gulch, eh, General?" the Professor inquired calmly, not appearing to notice Miss Weston's sarcasm.

"Dead east."

"Yaas, thank you. Now the wind is blowing a gale straight out of the west—er—now, er—if a cannon were fired, wouldn't they hear the sound, don't you think?"

This absurd proposition caused all three of his listeners to fall into a hearty fit of laughter, which provoked all the other men within hearing to suddenly gaze in wonder at them and gradually approach.

"Hear it, did you say, Professor?" at length inquired General Weston, when he could control himself sufficiently. "Why, man alive, it is sixty miles from here."

"Oh, as much as that. What's the nature of the country between?"

"Same as this, clear rolling prairie, with two rivers."

"How wide?"

"One about a thousand feet, and the other about fifty, but deep."

"Dear me, very unfortunate, isn't it now, General?" persisted the imperturbable Professor.

"What is?"

"So many rivers, you know."

"Rivers would not interfere with the sound; it's the distance."

"Well, really now, General, if a man were to get past the savages, he couldn't get across the rivers before they would have his scalp now, could he now?"

"No, it's worse than a forlorn hope, and besides, every decent horse we had has been already captured by the enemy. There is nothing to be done but to wait, and hope that Colonel Raines will send a party to investigate our condition."

"I say, General," pursued the Professor leisurely, as he laid his hand on his kite cord, which was securely fastened to a stake, "just feel that pull; isn't that exciting?"

"Very, most as exciting as catching a runner," drily replied the General as he turned to go.

"B-by the way, General, what's the distance, did you say?"

"Sixty miles."

"Dead east?"

"Dead east."

"Extraordinary, and the wind's dead west, you know," mused the Professor, slowly removing his coat and folding it carefully and placing it on the ground.

"I fail to see anything extraordinary in that," replied the General seriously.

"Oh, it's marvelous, I assure you," went on the Professor, again feeling the kite cord, and casting his eyes upward, along the fiercely tugging line. "And where are the Indians now, General?"

"Nearly all have retired to the little grove, just north-west of here. Come, Alicia."

"W-wait a moment, General. If a man had a horse, a swift horse, a very swift horse, how soon could he get there?"

"Well, rivers and all, say six to eight hours, if the horse lived."

The Professor began coolly emptying his pockets, and placed his revolver, ammunition, watch, money, keys, and other valuables, in a pocket handkerchief, which he threw upon his coat.

"Miss Weston, if a fellow could bring relief, he—he'd deserve some little kind word from you, wouldn't he now?"

"He would, indeed; but what do you mean, Mr. Carstover?"

"Well, not much, Miss Weston, only I'm going to be that man."

"Impossible, you couldn't—"

"Wait and see. I've got a horse, and he's a winner. Many a man has ridden him, and he has been praised and abused, and gotten his owner into no end of controversy. Talk about your Arabian steeds; they ain't in it with mine, for he's the fastest horse that ever covered sage brush. They call it a hobby, but wait; by daylight to-morrow you will see the United States Cavalry enter these gates in triumph, or the hobby horse and I will ride to the devil."

"How will you accomplish such a seemingly impossible feat?" The Professor had hold of the cord, exerting all his strength till in his tandem of kites, when suddenly he drew his knife across the line, and with a run and a spring he bounded clear of the stockade, which was fifteen feet high, and touched the earth fully a hundred feet away, when with another spring he cleared at least two

hundred feet, and in a few moments more was a mere speck in the distance.

To say that all who were left behind gazed in silence at each other for several moments in surprise, but feebly conveys the amazement of the General and his friends, while the surprise of the savages was even more complete, for they had no sooner realized the means of the escape than he was beyond pursuit, even of the swiftest horse.

"A hero, but who would have thought it?" at length exclaimed the commander.

Miss Weston was too overcome to utter a syllable, and the General directing that the property of the Professor be carefully taken to his (the General's) office, led his daughter back to his quarters.

Hope now buoyed up every one of the beleaguered troop, and they awaited patiently the result of the Professor's "flying trip."

Professor Carstover knew exactly the lifting power of his "tandem" in a gale of this proportion, while his college athletic training served him well in such an emergency as this.

He bounded over the prairie, in leaps of fifty, a hundred, and two hundred feet at a spring, and on arriving at the small river referred to by the General he easily cleared it, and more, at one leap. There was no stopping to breathe, or for refreshments on this express, and at the second stream, which was very wide, he simply flung himself into the water, and let his "sails" take him across, which they quickly did.

One hour and fifty-six minutes after he left the astounded group in the besieged fort, he made the leap of the stockade at Red Gulch, landing in the midst of a similar group of officers, at that government post.

"Whoa, gee, gee!" he cried, pulling hard on the cord. "Lend me a hand, one of you, please. Thank you. Good evening, gentlemen. How d'ye do? Very glad to see you. Sergeant, please tie my horse somewhere, will you, that's a good fellow. Thank you. Ah, Surgeon, will you kindly attend to my hand; I think it—needs—you—" and the brave fellow fell in a dead swoon into the arms of one of the astonished officers.

. . . .

As morning dawned the next day, shots were heard in lively succession near General Weston's post, and soon after, at the bugle's blast, three hundred United States Cavalry came clattering within the enclosure, having killed or dispersed the entire band of Apaches.

Professor Carstover was among them, with a hand bandaged, but beaming with joy at his success.

"Miss Weston, I say, what is the matter with kite flying, is it all right?"

"Right, yes, you're an angel."

"Not quite—I came near being one; but I'll
marry one if you'll permit me."

"The General issues all permits here; but if
you get the permit, we shall neither of us require
wings, it appears, so long as you can fly kites."

Poland Paragraphs.

[Continued.]

ONE ON THE PROPRIETOR.

While at Benis one of our party, after sawing
at his steak for a few minutes, looked up at the
waiter and asked him if he could bring him a
sharper knife. He did not know that the waiter
was the proprietor.

GREAT WALKERS AT POLAND.

Last Sunday morning Jack Martin and George
Vose, guests of the Poland Spring House, had the
courage to take a long walk in the hot sun. They
started at 9.30 o'clock and walked to the Shakers
and then around Middle Lake, making the tour of
about nine miles in two hours and thirty minutes.

Although Monday was one of the hottest days
of the summer, Mr. Moulton had the pluck to take
a tramp through the woods for about four miles.

GOLF.

Golf has proved a great attraction, so much so
that some of the guests have risen at six in the
morning in order to play while the day is coolest.

Mr. Walter Berri has been round the course
in 78; Mr. Bossange in 80; Mr. George Vose
in 76.

POOL.

Mr. Allen Rogers and Mr. Harry Maginnis
find the pool table very useful.

Mr. Bates and Mr. Vose play their usual fifty-
point game every morning.

Brake Ride and Dinner Party.

Monday afternoon, August 10th, Mr. and Mrs.
Dan Field of Brockton, Mass., gave a brake ride in
honor of Mr. and Mrs. George Hutchinson of
West Newton, Mass. The party included Mr. and
Mrs. Hazzard Lippincott, Miss Ivers, and Miss
Lambert. They had a most delightful drive around
Tripp Lake and home by way of Poland Corner.

Upon their return Mr. and Mrs. Lippincott
gave an eight o'clock dinner in honor of Mr. and
Mrs. Hutchinson. The table was spread in the
large bay window of the Poland Spring House,
and was artistically decorated with roses. The
center piece was especially pretty, being composed
of Catherine Mermet roses, while from underneath
the maiden-hair ferns scattered here and there,
a Marechal Niel bud peeped out. Each lady had a
bouquet of the choice flowers, and the gentlemen
boutonnieres.

Progressive Euchre.

FRIDAY EVENING, AUGUST 7.

Although Friday evening was warm, a large
number of guests gathered in the amusement
room to play progressive euchre. The room was
prettily decorated, and the center-piece on the table
where Mr. Chandler kept time was especially
lovely, being composed of ferns and pink and white
asters. There were fourteen tables, and sixteen
games were played. Thirteen was the highest
number won for the ladies' prize and fourteen for
the gentlemen's.

Mrs. Warner was the happy winner of the first
ladies' prize, an exquisite cup and saucer. Mrs.
Moulton won the second prize, a beautiful plaque.
The third prize, a silver polisher, went to Miss
Voorhees, and Mrs. Maginnis won the fourth prize,
an address book.

Miss Englis won the first gentlemen's prize, a
brush mounted with ebony and silver; Mrs. Ziegler, the second prize, silver button-hook and nail-
file. The third went to Mrs. Nugent, a silver-
mounted comb, and the fourth prize, a silver
knife, went to Miss Englis.

The prizes were beautiful and the two hours
passed quickly.

FRANK CARLOS GRIFFITH, } EDITORS.
NETTIE M. RICKER,

PUBLISHED EVERY SUNDAY MORNING DURING THE MONTHS
OF JULY, AUGUST, AND SEPTEMBER, IN THE INTERESTS OF

POLAND SPRINGS AND ITS VISITORS.

All contributions relative to the guests of Poland Springs
will be thankfully received.

To insure publication, all communications should reach the
editors not later than Wednesday preceding day of issue.

All parties desiring rates for advertising in the HILL-TOP
should write the editors for same.

The subscription price of the HILL-TOP is $1.00 for the
season, post-paid. Single copies will be mailed at 10c. each.

Address,
    EDITORS "HILL-TOP,"
        Poland Spring House,
            South Poland, Maine.

PRINTED AT JOURNAL OFFICE, LEWISTON.

Sunday, August 16, 1896.

Editorial.

POLAND SPRINGS is now in the enjoyment
of its greatest success. Its spacious halls
and corridors are thronged with a joyous
crowd; every seat in the immense dining-hall is
in demand, and as for sleeping accommodations,
there are no vacancies, every corner of every building being utilized. Such is the undying fame of
this beautiful resort. So much space is taken by
our "storiette" this week that we beg to be excused
from inflicting any further personal remarks upon
our friends at this time.

New Books.

The Heart of Life, by W. H. Mallock.

FROM MRS. AMOS R. LITTLE.

Kokoro, by Lafcadio Hearn.
Next Door, by Clara Louise Burnham.
When Valmond Came to Pontiac, by Gilbert Parker.
The House, by Eugene Field.
Beside the Bonnie Brier Bush, by Ian Maclaren.

FROM WILLIAM N. SWAIN.

Proceedings Supreme Council Royal Arcanum,   3 vols.
Proceedings Grand Council Royal Arcanum,   2 vols.

FROM MRS. J. B. SAWYER.

The Dolly Dialogues, by Anthony Hope.
Gold Elsie, by E. Marlitt.

Musical Programme.

SUNDAY EVENING, AUGUST 16, 1896, 8.15 P.M.

1.	Sanctus from St. Cecilia Mass.	Gounod.
2.	Flute Solo—Romanza.	Oitnei.
	Mr. A. Brooke.	
3.	Selection—Oberon.	Weber.
4.	Piano Solo.	
	Mr. Edmund Kuntz.	
5.	Andante from First Symphony.	Beethoven.
6.	Violin Solo—Adagio.	Ries.
	Vivace.	
	Mr. D. Kuntz.	
7.	Selection from Lohengrin.	Wagner.

A Cool Cashier.

Mr. Archie S. Hibbard, cashier of the Southern Savings and Trust Bank, Jacksonville, Fla.,
who is well known to a great many Poland guests,
was quite recently the hero in a dastardly attempt
to rob that bank by a business man named Walter
L. Chamberlain. A demand for $5,000 was made
with a threat if refused, and it was not only refused, but the would-be robber shot, notwithstanding his throwing of vitriol at Cashier Hibbard,
who barely escaped a terrible disfigurement. Chamberlain was mortally wounded and Cashier Hibbard
is receiving the congratulations of his friends on
his escape, and their compliments for his heroic
action.

To-night, at the New Mount Pleasant House
in the White Mountains, there will be a grand
concert by the combination of Mr. Wiley P.
Swift's two fine orchestras, the Mount Pleasant
House orchestra and the Maplewood orchestra,
composed of the following artists: Mount Pleasant
House—Miss Jessie Mabelle Downer of "Boston
Rivals," piano; Mr. Felix Winternitz, soloist in
"Boston Rivals," and W. A. Canon of Reeves's
Band, Providence, violins; Mr. Carl Hennann,
Jr., of New York, 'cello; Mr. Charles T. Howe
of Columbus, O., flute; Mr. W. B. Mayberry,
Boston, cornet; Mr. F. H. Coolidge, Boston,
clarinet. Maplewood—Wiley P. Swift, Boston,
leader; Karlo Ondricek, Boston Symphony Or-
chestra, and Charles Becker, Maplewood Orchestra,
violins; George Sauer, Boston Symphony Or-
chestra, viola; E. T. Mingels, Boston Symphony
Orchestra, 'cello; Max Kuntz, Boston Symphony
Orchestra, bass; Walter M. Johnson, Maplewood
Orchestra, flute; E. G. Blanchard, Maplewood
Orchestra, cornet; F. H. Goddard, Maplewood
Orchestra, trombone.

The orchestra will be assisted by Madame
Marian Van Duyn, contralto, of New York. The
concert will undoubtedly be the finest ever given
in the White Mountains, and the beautiful music
hall of the Mount Pleasant House is worthy of
the event.

Abbott Graves.

The above-named artist was born in Weymouth, Mass., the son of James Griswold Graves, his mother's maiden name being Eliza Nichols Fuller of Hingham, a direct descendant of Dr. Samuel Fuller, the first physician of the Plymouth Colony.

He has made several European trips, the one of 1887 being for three years, when he studied under Cormon and exhibited in the Paris Salon.

Mr. Graves has won several medals, which bear the dates of 1877, 1890, and two of 1892. He is a graduate of the Institute of Technology School of Design, is chairman of the Executive Committee of the Paint and Clay Club, is a member of the Society of Boston Water-Color Painters, and a member of the Boston Art Students' Association.

Mr. Graves has delightful studios in the Studio Building, Boston, and formerly was especially noted as a painter of flower pieces, but more recently is even better known as an artist in figures.

He is represented in the Poland Springs Art Gallery by a single canvas, but that is a very large one and hangs to the left of the great fire-place in the rotunda, and is a particularly noticeable feature as one enters the building. It is called "A Land of Poppies," and was exhibited at the World's Columbian Exposition. He was also an exhibitor at the Paris Exposition of 1889.

Some of Mr. Graves's best-known works are "A Labor of Love," "Making Things Shine," and "The Other Side." Although still a young man, Abbott Graves has already made a name for himself, and his work is hung in many places of note.

Children's Column.

"Boys flying kites haul in their white-winged birds;
You can't do that way when you're flying voids."
— *Will Carleton.*

A married lady relates that sometime away back in 1865, when she was a very little girl, whom we will call Elizabeth, because that is not her name, was stealing away to play with her big brother, and as she was dressed in her best "bib and tucker" at the time, her clothes were much tumbled and soiled, which she carefully hid away from the gaze of a very strict aunt who was "acting mamma" to the little orphan.

It appears that this happened on the morning of the day peace was declared, and later in the day the auntie was to take the children to the village to the " doings" in honor of that event.

Great was her dismay on discovering the condition of little Elizabeth's "Sunday-go-to-meeting" attire, and serious was the frown which portended trouble for the little truant, but finally she remarked in a tone which would sell for a dollar a hundred-weight to a cold storage house: "Elizabeth Ann, if it were not that to-day peace was declared, I would *warm you well.*" And hence Elizabeth always remembers the day when peace was declared.

The Little White Lamb.

Green are the pastures of Sleepy Land,
 Fresh are the fields and fair;
Wide are the ways to its Wonder fold—
 And my little lamb is there.

Blue are the skies of Sleepy Land;
 Clear are the brooks and bright;
With a shepherd dream to the Slumber Gate
 Went my little lamb last night.

O tall dream-shepherd, I pray you, hear!
 Fair though you pasture be;
Let down the bars and bring once more
 My little white lamb to me.

Miss Natalie March and Miss Dorothy March are guests at the Poland Spring House. They arrived Saturday, August 8th.

Miss Margerite Ricker is spending the week in Augusta visiting her cousins, Dr. and Mrs. Brickett.

Master Horace B. Ingalls and Miss Claire Ingalls registered at the Poland Spring House, Saturday, August 8th.

The names of Dot and Ditto have been suggested by Miss Margerite Ricker, and Frisky and Jaco by Miss Maud M. Colony, for the Mansion House kittens. They have accordingly been christened Dot and Frisky.

Children's Croquet Tournament.

[Contributed.]

TUESDAY afternoon, August 11th, there took place a very enjoyable croquet tournament for children in the grove at the Poland Spring House.

It was started by Messrs. Monte Lemann and Eben Judd, who, after meeting with many difficulties, finally succeeded. The entries were divided into two classes, owing to the fact that the smaller children could not compete with the larger ones. Each person who entered was taxed five cents, in order that some prizes might be bought.

The spot selected for the tournament was surrounded with trees and was therefore quite cool. Mr. George French kindly officiated as umpire, and there was quite a large number of spectators, consisting of the maids, people playing cards, and those reading. The prizes, which were bought by a committee appointed for the purpose, were very pretty indeed.

The championship prize, which was won by Mr. Eben Judd, was a book-mark with the picture of the hotel engraved upon it. The ladies' prize was awarded to Miss Jeannette Ricker. It was a bottle of cologne, in a celluloid basket lined with satin.

Then the little ones began playing, and the first prize was won by Master Casey Nugent, who received a Poland Spring Souvenir. Master Albert Rosenheim captured the second prize, which was a bag of gum drops.

It had been originally intended to play partners, also, but owing to the lateness of the hour the idea was abandoned. We wish to express our thanks to Mrs. A. B. Ricker for her kindness in allowing us the use of her croquet set, and also for the refreshments she served after the tournament. Also we wish to thank Mrs. Griffith for her kind suggestions. As I remarked before, after the tournament every one repaired to Mrs. Ricker's, where the refreshments this time were, owing to her generosity, unlimited. MONTE LEMANN.

A star-gazing party at the Mansion House counted forty falling stars Monday evening. Some were very brilliant.

Tid-Bits.

Hot?

It *has* been hot.

Full, fuller, fullest.

New tennis court at the Mansion House.

Bathing in the middle lake has become very popular.

Rev. E. C. Smith of Boston, is a guest at Poland Springs.

Mr. and Mrs. A. S. Marsh, Jr., of New York, are guests at the Poland Spring House.

Mrs. Edwin L. Todd of Sing Sing, New York, is a guest at the Mansion House.

The sweet little flower girl, alluded to last week, should have been called Lucy Thorne.

Mr. and Mrs. G. P. Wescott of Portland arrived at Poland Springs, Friday, August 7th.

A. S. Hanson, General Passenger Agent of the Boston and Albany Railroad, was a recent guest.

Mrs. W. M. McCord and Master Henry I. McCord, 2d, of New York, are at Poland Springs.

Massage is the thing. Try it if nervous or fatigued. Mrs. E. J. Robinson's card is in another column.

Mr. Charles R. Eddy, a well-known lawyer of Brooklyn, N. Y., has been spending a few days at the Poland Spring House.

August 8th Mr. A. R. Mitchell made a fine record at bowling, 254; Mr. King another good record, 217; and J. Oakes, 273, August 13th.

Col. J. A. Ingalls and Mrs. Ingalls received a hearty welcome at Poland Springs, Saturday, August 8th. They have spent many seasons at the Poland Spring House.

Miss J. E. Wales of Cambridge, Mass., is a guest at the Mansion House. Miss Wales has not visited Poland for thirteen years, and she finds many changes that are delightful.

Saturday, August 8th, Professor W. E. Sargent and Mrs. Sargent of Hebron, Me., Captain and Mrs. Scribner of New York, and Mr. Merrow, New York, were entertained at the Poland Spring House by Mrs. Benjamin F. Sturtevant of Jamaica Plain, Mass.

Capt. William H. Dailey, the famous life-saver, who has been very successful teaching the art of swimming at Cottage City this summer, recently had a fall from his bicycle, breaking his arm. It was most unfortunate, happening as it did in the middle of the season. Guests of last summer will remember his very interesting talk on life-saving here at that time.

Guests at Poland Spring House

AUGUST 12, 1896.

Mr. and Mrs. A. H. Adams	Haverhill.
Mr. and Mrs. M. W. Brett	New York.
Rev. J. A. Butler	Boston.
Mrs. C. A. Barratoni	New York.
Miss Beatrice Barratoni	New York.
Mrs. L. Beard	Brooklyn.
Mr. and Mrs. H. S. Beard	Brooklyn.
Mr. Henry Bayley	Boston.
Mr. Joseph A. Brown	Boston.
Miss Belle G. Brown	Boston.
Mr. and Mrs. E. H. Brown	Fall River, Mass.
Mrs. Jas. Boyd	Harrisburg.
Dr. and Mrs. Geo. Brett	Boston.
Mr. and Mrs. F. H. Browne	Waltham.
Mr. and Mrs. N. A. Baldwin	New Haven.
Mr. and Mrs. W. W. Boynton	Cleveland.
Mr. M. Bradley	Haverhill.
Mr. Wm. A. Bigelow	New York.
Mrs. B. Babcock	New York.
Miss Babcock	New York.
Miss L. Belyea	Boston.
Mr. and Mrs. Jacob P. Bates	Boston.
Mr. and Mrs. H. O. Bright	Cambridge.
Mr. and Mrs. Nelson Bartlett	Boston.
Mr. E. N. Briggs	Saginaw, Mich.
Mr. and Mrs. Wm. Berri	Brooklyn.
Walter Berri	Brooklyn.
Herbert Berri	Brooklyn.
Mrs. Beylle	Philadelphia.
H. L. Cabell	Richmond, Va.
Mr. and Mrs. G. C. Currier	New York.
Miss Causland	Philadelphia.
Mrs. Agnes S. Curtis	New York.
Mr. and Mrs. Geo. W. Coleman	Boston.
Mr. Andrew R. Culver	Brooklyn.
Mr. and Mrs. F. W. Carpenter	Providence.
Miss Julia Carpenter	Providence.
Mr. and Mrs. C. C. Corbin	Webster, Mass.
W. H. Chappall	Chicago.
Miss Chappall	Chicago.
Mrs. Z. Chandler	Detroit, Mich.
Mr. E. W. Ditmars	New York.
Mr. and Mrs. Robt. Dornan	Philadelphia.
Mrs. Wm. C. Denton	New York.
Miss C. S. Diet	New Haven.
Mrs. Albert Douglass	New York.
Mrs. M. E. Dexter	Brooklyn.
Miss Dexter	Brooklyn.
Mrs. N. C. Dickelson	New York.
Mrs. Wm. Engel	Bangor.
Miss Engel	Bangor.
Rev. T. J. Earley	New York.
Miss Englis	Brooklyn.
Miss A. B. Englis	Brooklyn.
Mr. and Mrs. James H. Eddy	New Britain, Conn.
Miss Bessie M. Eddy	New Britain, Conn.
Mr. Chas. B. Eddy	Brooklyn, N. Y.
Mr. and Mrs. Thomas W. Evans	New York.
Mrs. C. G. First	Lock Haven.
Mr. and Mrs. R. M. Field	Boston.
Miss Fletcher	Boston.
Mr. Geo. B. French	Boston.
Mrs. J. D. Fessenden	New York.
Gen. Chas. E. Furlong	New York.
Mr. and Mrs. D. H. Field	Brockton, Mass.
Miss Fischer	New York.
Mr. and Mrs. C. S. Fischer	New York.
Mrs. M. C. Ferand	New York.
Mrs. R. G. Feltus	Philadelphia.
Mr. and Mrs. E. W. Greene	Newtonville.
Mr. and Mrs. A. L. Goudian	New York.
Mr. and Mrs. F. E. Gilman	Montreal.
Mr. M. F. Greene	Milford.
Mr. John Goldthwaite	Boston.
Miss E. B. Goldthwaite	Boston.
Mrs. M. R. Goodwin	Boston.
Miss Goodwin	Boston.

Mrs. L. M. Gale	Washington.
Miss Olive Gale	Washington.
Mr. and Mrs. C. C. Griffin	Haverhill, Mass.
Miss Howell	Baltimore.
Miss Hyatt	Baltimore.
Mr. S. B. Hubbard	Jacksonville.
Mrs. W. W. Hartwell	Plattsburgh, N. Y.
Mr. and Mrs. John R. Hoxie	Chicago.
Miss Anna Hoxie	Chicago.
Mr. and Mrs. Horace Hunt	New York.
Mrs. S. B. Hubbard	Jacksonville, Fla.
Mr. and Mrs. L. Hulburt	Brooklyn.
Mrs. M. B. Hoffman	New York.
Mr. and Mrs. F. D. Henwood	Boston.
Mr. and Mrs. Hudson Hoagland	New York.
Mr. and Mrs. E. Holmes	New York.
Col. Joseph A. Ingalls and family	Boston.
Mr. Samuel Ives	New Bedford.
Miss Ella F. Ives	New Bedford.
Gov. and Mrs. Jas. Jeffries	Louisiana.
Miss Jacoby	New York.
Mrs. Julian James	Washington.
J. J. Kennedy	New Brighton.
Miss Ruth Kellen	Marion, Mass.
Miss Leadbrater	Philadelphia.
Miss Bessie Lippincott	Philadelphia.
Rev. and Mrs. W. P. Lewis	Philadelphia.
Mrs. B. C. Lake	New Haven.
Miss Leland	New York.
Mr. and Mrs. Malcolm Lloyd	Philadelphia.
Miss Lloyd	Philadelphia.
James D. Laird	San Francisco.
Mr. and Mrs. Chas. Lippincott	Philadelphia.
Mr. and Mrs. F. H. Lippincott	Philadelphia.
Miss Lucille Lippincott	Philadelphia.
Mr. and Mrs. Amos R. Little	Philadelphia.
Mr. and Mrs. B. Lemann and family	New Orleans.
Miss Cora W. Lumbert	Brockton.
Joseph R. Moore. Jr.	Philadelphia.
Mrs. J. W. Merrill	Boston.
Miss Merrill	Boston.
Mr. and Mrs. A. S. March, Jr., and family	New York.
Miss C. McGrath	Boston.
Mrs. Paul F. Meher	Washington.
Henry P. Morrison	New Brighton.
Mr. and Mrs. J. S. Martin	New York.
J. S. Martin, Jr.	New York.
Mr. A. N. Mayo	Springfield.
Byron P. Moulton	Philadelphia.
Mr. and Mrs. T. B. M. Mason	Washington.
Mrs. T. B. Myers	Washington.
Mrs. Jno. H. Maginnis	New Orleans.
Mr. Jno. H. Maginnis	New Orleans.
Mrs. A. Mully	Washington.
Miss A. G. Miller	Brooklyn.
Dr. and Mrs. Ira L. Moore	Boston.
Mrs. J. T. Montgomery	Philadelphia.
Mrs. B. P. Moulton	Rosemont, Pa.
Mr. and Mrs. A. R. Mitchell	Newtonville.
Mrs. Christine Marburg	Baltimore.
The Misses Marburg	Baltimore.
Mr. and Mrs. John T. Martin	New York.
Rev. J. P. O'Nell	Boston.
Mr. and Mrs. J. L. Nason	Boston.
Miss Nason	Boston.
Mr. and Mrs. Dan C. Nugent and family	St. Louis.
Mr. and Mrs. W. T. Ness	Boston.
Miss Lucy P. Newhall	Philadelphia.
Mrs. H. S. Osgood	Portland.
Mr. John A. Ordway	Boston.
Mr. and Mrs. Josiah Oakes	Malden, Mass.
Mr. and Mrs. J. O. Poillon	New York.
Lovell Palmer	Brooklyn.
Dr. Morton Prinnell	New York.
Mr. and Mrs. H. O. Perley	New York.
Mr. and Mrs. H. N. Parl	Philadelphia.
Mr. John I. Pinkerton	West Chester, Pa.
Miss E. A. Prall	New York.
Mr. and Mrs. Pratt	Portland.
Mr. and Mrs. J. H. Pearson	Chicago.
Mrs. Pattison	Boston.
Mrs. J. A. Pettee	New York.

Mr. and Mrs. Henry U. Palmer	Brooklyn.
Masters Austin and Chester Palmer	Brooklyn.
Mrs. M. E. Parsons	Boston.
Mr. E. D. Peters	Boston.
Miss A. J. Pomeroy	New York.
S. S. Riker	New York.
Miss Marion Richardson	Boston.
Mrs. Runyon	Plainfield, N. J.
Mrs. J. O. Rhines	New York.
Mr. and Mrs. E. H. Randolph	Louisiana.
Mr. and Mrs. Augustus Richardson	Boston.
Miss Richardson	Boston.
Allen M. Rogers	New York.
Mr. and Mrs. H. A. Rogers	New York.
Miss May Rogers	New York.
Mrs. E. J. Robinson	Boston.
Mr. and Mrs. A. S. Rines	Portland.
Miss Roberts	Philadelphia.
Moses W. Richardson	Boston.
Miss Ada M. Smith	New York.
Rev. and Mrs. W. E. C. Smith	Boston.
Rev. J. J. Shaw	Chelmsford, Mass.
Mrs. E. H. Shethar	New York.
Mr. and Mrs. C. A. Shafer	Washington.
Mr. and Mrs. S. B. Shoninger	New Haven, Ct.
Dr. and Mrs. E. H. Smith	Boston.
Mr. and Mrs. H. C. Swain and son	New York.
Mr. and Mrs. J. E. Spenser	New York.
Mr. and Mrs. S. R. Small	Portland.
Mrs. S. Skaats	New York.
Miss Ella Smith	Boston.
Miss Slade	New York.
Mrs. Mary J. Spencer	Boston.
Mrs. B. F. Sturtevant	Plattsburgh, N. Y.
Dr. and Mrs. C. C. Schuyler	Milwaukee.
Mr. and Mrs. Chas. G. Stark	Philadelphia.
Mrs. S. B. Stinson	Philadelphia.
Miss Stinson	Philadelphia.
Miss Florence Stinson	Washington.
Mr. and Mrs. A. T. Salter	Plainfield, N. J.
Mr. and Mrs. Joseph W. Sandford	Washington.
Mr. and Mrs. E. J. Stellvagen	New York.
Miss Tattin	Brooklyn.
Mr. and Mrs. J. B. Toppan	Glen Cove, N. Y.
Miss Tillotson	New Haven.
Miss N. E. Ten Broeck	New York.
Mrs. Orlando Tompkins	Boston.
Mrs. Frank R. Thomas	Boston.
Mr. and Mrs. F. E. Taylor	Brooklyn.
Mr. and Mrs. David Thornton	Brooklyn.
Miss H. Underwood	Brooklyn.
Mr. and Mrs. Peter Van Voorhees	Camden, N. J.
J. D. Van Voorhees	Camden, N. J.
Mr. and Mrs. W. A. Vose	Brookline.
Mr. Geo. A. Vose	Brookline.
Miss Vose	Brookline.
Mrs. John H. Voorhees	Brooklyn.
Miss Jessie Voorhees	Brooklyn.
Mr. and Mrs. W. B. Valentine	London, Eng.
Mrs. C. Walton	Trenton, N. J.
Mr. and Mrs. Washington	Doylestown, Pa.
Miss Washington	Doylestown, Pa.
Mr. and Mrs. G. P. Wescott	Portland.
J. V. Watson	Philadelphia.
Mr. and Mrs. D. Welch	Boston.
Mrs. G. N. Wilson	Washington.
Rev. L. S. Walsh	Boston.
Mr. and Mrs. F. H. Williams	Boston.
Miss Lizzie A. Williams	Boston.
Mr. and Mrs. John Wilson	New York.
Miss P. W. Willets	So. Amboy, N. J.
Mrs. Chas. Warner	Troy, N. Y.
Miss C. A. Warner	Troy, N. Y.
Miss M. V. Warner	Troy, N. Y.
Miss M. A. Winslow	Troy, N. Y.
Mr. E. M. Warner	Troy, N. Y.
Mrs. H. W. Wadleigh	Boston.
Mr. and Mrs. F. H. Wyeth	Philadelphia.
Miss Kate Wheelock	Chicago.
Mr. and Mrs. John P. Woodbury	Boston.
Mrs. J. Reed Whipple	Boston.

Dr. M. C. Wedgwood and Mrs. Wedgwood	Lewiston.
Mr. A. Wentworth	Boston.
Mr. F. R. Wharton	Philadelphia.
Mr. and Mrs. W. S. Wymond	Louisville, Ky.
Miss Wymond	Louisville, Ky.
Mr. and Mrs. J. Strait White	New York.
Mr. David G. Yates	Philadelphia.
Mr. and Mrs. H. D. Ziegler	Philadelphia.
Miss C. F. Ziegler	Philadelphia.

Tid-Bits.

Mr. Samuel C. Keene of Boston has been spending a few days at the Mansion House. He left Tuesday morning much regretted.

All interested in the money question will find the "Report of the Proceedings of the International Monetary Conference," now in the Library, of great value.

The many friends of Mr. and Mrs. Hutchingson, at Poland Springs, regret their departure on Tuesday, August 11th. Mr. Hutchingson is of the firm of Hutchingson & Co., Boston, Mass.

Saturday, August 8th, the following guests from the Poland Spring House had a delightful brake ride: Mrs. Dorman, Mrs. Stinson, Miss Rogers, Miss Newhall, Miss Lippincott, Miss Stinson, Miss Olive Gale, and Miss Florence Stinson.

In the same quiet manner in which she came, Adelaide Palmer departed on Monday last. Her stay in Poland gave gratification to many, because of her gentle refinement, and simple, modest demeanor. The work which she began here will doubtless be seen later in a finished state.

Friday night, August 7th, the jolly party that had been visiting Rangeley Lakes returned to the Poland Spring House. The party included Mr. and Mrs. Berri, Mr. and Mrs. Thornton, Mr. and Mrs. Dan Field, Miss Lambert, Miss Ivers, Mr. Moulton, Mr. Oakes, Mr. Walter Berri, and Mr. Bert Berri.

Thursday morning, August 13th, Mr. Greenlee, Mr. Van Zandt, and Mr. Patro, from the Mansion House, went blueberrying. They were gone two hours and picked sixteen quarts. The blueberries were very large, one measuring one and a quarter inches in circumference. The guests were favored with a generous supply of the berries.

An Episcopal clergyman's wife living in southern Texas sends to Mrs. Hiram Ricker a large quantity of Mexican drawn work. Mrs. Ricker will be glad to show it to all who will call at her cottage. It is charity work and the prices are very reasonable.

Arrivals.

POLAND SPRING HOUSE.

FROM AUG. 7 TO AUG. 14, 1896.

Abbott, T. S.	Hampton, Va.
Allen, Dr. Harrison	Philadelphia.
Atterbury, Mr. and Mrs. Henry	New York.
Avely, Emma	Boston.
Bailey, Mrs. C. H.	Portland.
Bates, Dr. and Mrs. H. E.	New York.
Baratoui, Mrs. C. A.	New York.
Baratoui, Miss Beatrice	New York.
Bayley, S. K.	Boston.
Beals, J. G.	Boston.
Beede, J. W.	Auburn.
Beede, Abby M.	Auburn.
Beede, Helen R.	Auburn.
Biker, Henry	Providence.
Beede, O. F.	Portland.
Beggs, Mr. and Mrs. William	Woburn.
Bennet, H. K.	Knightville, Me.
Bolster, Mrs. S. A.	Boston.
Bolster, Mr. and Mrs. W. H.	Boston.
Brown, B. B.	Auburn.
Breed, Mrs. L.	Brooklyn.
Breed, Mr. and Mrs. H. S.	Brooklyn.
Brown, Joseph A.	Boston.
Brown, Miss Belle G.	Boston.
Brown, Mr. and Mrs. E. H. B.	Fall River.
Cabell, S. V. L.	Richmond, Va.
Cardary, Mrs. S. E.	Athol, Mass.
Causland, Miss	Philadelphia.
Clark, Mr. and Mrs. J. Y.	Lewiston.
Currier, Mr. and Mrs. G. C.	New York.
Cushman, S. F.	Monson.
Cushman, Miss Hattie F.	Monson.
Cushman, Edw. F.	Monson.
Daggs, W. H.	Hampton, Va.
Darling, Mrs. J. R.	New York.
Dean, the Misses	New York.
Dinnars, E. W.	New York.
Doe, H. A.	Danville.
Eastman, Mr. and Mrs. John C. R.	New York.
Eddy, Charles R.	Brooklyn.
Fisher, Mrs. E.	Portland.
Fisher, Emma A.	Boston.
Fizzell, H. B.	Hampton, Va.
Frothingham, F. G.	Boston.
de Gamo, Charles H.	Media, Pa.
Gilbert, Mrs. Frank	Troy.
Goodrich, H. L.	Haverhill.
Griffin, N. B.	Haverhill.
Greene, Mr. and Mrs. E. W.	Newtonville.
Glove, Mrs. E. M.	Orange, Mass.
Grinnell, Dr. Morton	New York.
Hale, E. B.	Boston.
Hanson, A. S.	Boston.
Harms, Miss Anna	Boston.
Harris, Nathan W.	Auburn.
Harris, Mrs. H. A.	Auburn.
Harris, Miss Nellie E.	Auburn.
Hertzog, Wm. F.	Cape Town, So. Africa.
Hitchinson, Mr. and Mrs. George	Boston.
Ingalls, Joseph A.	Boston.
Ingalls, Mrs. J. A.	Boston.
Ingalls, Horace B.	Boston.
Ingalls, Miss Claire	Boston.
Kenney, John J.	New Brighton.
Laws, Alfred	Brockton.
Laws, Frank A.	Boston.
Leland, Francis L.	New York.
Leadbeater, Miss	Philadelphia.
Little, Amos R.	Philadelphia.
Mackenzie, M.	Lewiston.
Mann, Mrs. T. S.	Orange, Mass.
Mahet, Mrs. Paul F.	Washington.
Mallouf, Mrs. H. G.	New York.
Match, Mr. and Mrs. A. S., Jr.	New York.
Match, Miss Natalie	New York.
Match, Dorothy	New York.
McGrath, Miss C.	Boston.
Merriam, Mr. and Mrs. A. G.	Springfield.
Merroy, Frank S.	New York.
Mottison, Henry P.	New Brighton.
Needham, J. W.	New York.
Osgood, H. S.	Portland.
Palmer, Henry U.	Brooklyn.
Palmer, L. M.	Brooklyn.
Peters, William T.	Boston.
Peters, Mrs. Chas.	Portland.
Peirce, A. F.	Lewiston.
Petley, Dr. and Mrs. H. O.	
Ring, Mrs. F. G.	Portland.
Riker, S. S.	New York.
Roots, Mrs. Logan H.	Little Rock, Ark.
Roots, Miss I.	Little Rock, Ark.
Ricks, S. G.	Hampton, Va.
Rich, M. C.	Portland.
Richards, Mrs. M. E.	New York.
Ruggles, E. O.	Boston.
Scribner, Mr. and Mrs. D. A.	New York.
Shafer, Mr. and Mrs. C. A.	Washington.
Shay, John J.	North Chelmsford.
Shannon, Miss E.	Portland
Shethar, Mr. and Mrs. E. H.	New York.
Sink, E.	New York.
Small, S. R.	Portland.
Smith, Rev. and Mrs. W. E. C.	Boston.
Smith, Mr. and Mrs. E. P.	New York.
Stabler, Roy	Hampton, Va.
Stetson, Mrs C. W.	Boston.
Stetson, U. S.	Boston.
Stetson, Miss Ruth M.	Boston.
Stinson, S. B.	Philadelphia.
Taylor, Mr. and Mrs. W. E.	Hebron.
Toppan, Mr. and Mrs. J. B. Coles	Glen Cove, N. Y.
Wainwright, J. H.	Hampton, Va.
Walsh, L. S.	Boston.
Walter, E. B.	Boston.
Washington, Mr. and Mrs. L. P.	Doylesboro, Pa.
Washington, Miss	Doylesboro, Pa.
Watson, James V.	Philadelphia.
Wescott, Mr. and Mrs. George P.	Portland.
Welsh, Mr. and Mrs. D.	Boston.
Wilson, G. H.	Washington.
Wheelock, Mr. and Mrs. H. M.	Boston.
Williams, Mr. and Mrs. F. H.	Boston.
Williams, Miss Lizzie A.	Boston.
Wolcott, W. A.	Hartford.

MANSION HOUSE.

AUGUST 7 TO 14, 1896.

Dow, Edgar R.	Portland.
Evans, W. S.	Boston.
Hayward, F. H.	Cambridge.
Hall, J. Elmer	Worcester.
Keene, Samuel C.	Boston.
Latham, H. W.	East Orange, N. J.
McCord, Mrs. W. M.	New York.
McCord, Henry D., 2d	New York.
Potter, Mr. and Mrs. Benj.	Portland.
Quimby, Mr. and Mrs. J. Murray	Boston.
Reiss, J.	St. Louis.
Rose, Mr. and Mrs. W. E.	Greene.
Stevens, W. W.	Boston.
Todd, Mrs. Edwin L.	Sing Sing.
Wales, Miss J. E.	Cambridge.

Our Menu.

RECIPE No. 16.

Boned Turkey.

Prepare force meat as follows : Chop fine, separately, two pounds of white meat of turkey and the same of fresh fat pork. Put it in a mortar and pound vigorously for ten minutes and add salt, white pepper, nutmeg to taste, and four yolks of eggs, one glass of Sherry wine, and pound again in the mortar. Then put it in a mixing basin. Cut in long square shreds about one-fourth inch thick, one-half each of fat pork, red beef tongue, ham and lean veal or pork tenderloin.

Singe lightly the fine dry picked turkey and cut off the wings and legs and then bone carefully.

Lay the turkey open, the inside uppermost, on a large napkin. Transfer sliced pieces from the breast. Where it is too thin, place the pieces cut from the breast onto the places, such as the second joints and neck. Then sprinkle with salt and pepper, and add the layer force meat on the center almost an inch thick, and seven inches wide and ten long. Then a layer of pork and beef tongue, veal, and slices of truffles and mushrooms, arranging then neatly, then another layer of force meat, and so on until all has been used. Finish the force meat with thin slices of fat pork on top. Bring up the sides together, sew the back from end to end. Then roll tightly in a napkin and fasten both ends firmly. Put in an old deep copper pan (or Braisiére), add two sliced onions, two carrots, then pork and veal trimmings. Next the boned turkey, a bunch of parsley, pepper corns, two leeks, one head of celery, two blades of mace, and finally the broken carcass of the turkey.

Add six quarts of boiling broth, one tablespoonful of salt; cover and let simmer gently for three hours on the range. Then remove and drain dry. When cool enough to handle remove the napkin carefully and press the water out. Then spread the napkin on the table and turn the turkey in it. Then roll and tie firmly again, place it in a hollow dish, with fat from the broth. Put a flat dish and heavy weight on top, and leave it over night in a cool place. Strain and free the broth of every bit of fat. There ought to be about three quarts of broth. Add one gill of Sherry wine, the same of tarragon vinegar, also add six ounces of isinglass. Clarify in the usual way with four beaten eggs. Strain through a jelly bag, add one-half cup of brandy, and set away to cool. When ready to serve take the turkey out of the napkin, remove the strings, and trim both ends. Then cut in slices and place on cold platters or dishes with jelly cut in little dice squares.

Hampton Students.

An enjoyable entertainment was given by the Hampton Quartette in Music Hall, Tuesday evening, August 11th. After the singing of darkey melodies, Dr. H. B. Frizzell made a few remarks, telling of the work Hampton Institute was accomplishing, and then introduced Mr. J. S. Abbott, who is a graduate of Hampton. Mr. Abbott spoke for the colored people; then Mr. Omahah told of the good work that was being done among his people, "the Indians." Mr. Daggs was the last speaker and gave a description of the schools in the south for colored people. A collection was taken and $54.53 was raised.

Sunday Services.

AUGUST 9TH.

Rev. T. J. Earley of New York held mass in Music Hall.

Rev. Julius Gassauer held his usual service in the dining-hall, which was well attended.

On account of illness, Rev. N. P. Lewis of Philadelphia did not preach as intended.

A man experienced in the care of invalids; an extensive traveller, not only all over this country, but frequently in Europe; gentle, intelligent, well-read, and conversant with people and places, desires an opportunity to accompany an elderly invalid gentleman or lady in the capacity of companion. He can be highly recommended. Information may be had from the Librarian, Maine State Building.

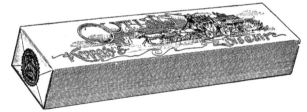

The Hill-Top

POLAND SPRINGS, SO. POLAND, ME.

HARRY C. WILKINSON

THE HILL·TOP

VOL. III.   SUNDAY MORNING, AUGUST 23, 1896.   No. 8.

Behind the Scenes.

WHEN one looks about in a large dining-room like the one in the Poland Spring House, with its length of 181 feet and its 60 tables, and realizes that 430 people sit and dine together at one time on this Sunday in August, the question of supply and demand is one which often presents itself.

Think for one moment what it requires to satisfy the cravings of so many hundred appetites as are congregated on Ricker Hill. The hotel is full, the Mansion House is full, and there are hundreds of employees also requiring food. How many beeves and lambs must be slaughtered when it takes 2,850 pounds of beef and 2,250 pounds of lamb to "go around" on Ricker Hill in one week?

The winged fowl of the air, although not high flyers, are called upon to supply 2,650 pounds of their precious meat, and this alone from chicken, turkey, and fowl, not including other game. Ten thousand eggs find their way to the tables in one week without a guide, and between 1,200 and 1,300 pounds of fish of various kinds get along swimmingly in their endeavors to please a much diversified taste for brain food.

The solids are not all disposed of yet, for the bossy calf and the "cured" parts of the pig are yet to be heard from, hence veal, bacon, and ham are in evidence to the extent of 862 pounds in a span of seven consecutive days, 83 bushels of potatoes accompanying them.

A few of the other vegetable products, like squash, 900 pounds; peas, 24 bushels; beans, 11 bushels; green corn, 3,000 ears; dandelion greens, 28 bushels (the two latter at the Poland Spring House alone), are worth consideration.

Nineteen barrels of flour must be made into bread and other articles of food, requiring the accompaniment of 1,080 pounds of butter to make it palatable.

Fruit becomes a necessity as well, which if piled in one room for one week's consumption, would require a large apartment, for 28 bushels of berries, 21 bushels of peaches, and 10 boxes of oranges are required on the hill, and, beside this, 14 boxes of pears, 10 bunches of bananas, 40 huge water-melons, and 21 barrels of canteloupes are consumed at the Poland Spring House tables alone.

We all know that Poland water is drunk to an enormous extent, but 200 pounds of coffee, 55 pounds of tea, and 553 quarts of cream are used in a single week.

If milk appears large, it is very insignificant when we realize that 2,700 quarts of milk are used in addition to this, and *one and a half* tons of sugar are mixed with your food.

This great department of a great hotel is under the immediate and personal direction of Mr. A. B. Ricker, and all will cheerfully testify that it is admirably managed and supplied. The general, however, must have good officers in order to succeed, and in this case he is ably seconded by Mr. Dockham the steward and Mr. Sparrow the *chef*, two excellent and reliable assistants. The result of their careful supervision of the culinary department is seen on every tray, and all the articles which we have enumerated, and many more,

depend upon the skill of the best meat cooks, pastry cooks, and bakers which can be brought together.

So much for "behind the scenes," where superiority is far more appreciated than in any department of life's hasty journey. "The way to a man's heart is through his stomach," and in this case it is paved with delicious morsels.

Our illustration is again the work of the Notman Photographic Co., who are *par excellence* the artists of the close of the nineteenth century.

Drive to Oxford.

A party of guests from the Poland Spring House, August 18th, went to Oxford to a small hotel which has been opened this summer, to take dinner. The hotel is kept by Mrs. Keith of Boston, and will accommodate about fifty guests. The party included Mr. and Mrs. Bartlett, Mrs. and Miss Hildreth, Mrs. Bates, Mr. and Mrs. Lippincott, Miss Eddy, Mr. and Mrs. D. W. Field, Miss Lambert, Dr. and Mrs. Smith, Mrs. Frank Brown, Mrs. Marburg, the Misses Marburg, Mrs. Small, and Mrs. Spencer. The party had a delightful time, and the hail and thunder storm while returning only added to the pleasure of the day.

The drive to the little hotel at Oxford has become so popular that a party from the Poland Spring House went over for a 7.30 supper, Wednesday, August 19th. The party included Mrs. Edwin Holmes, Mrs. Wilson, Mrs. Maginnis, Mr. and Mrs. White, Mr. and Mrs. Gilman, Mr. and Mrs. E. T. Holmes, Mr. Lake, Miss Carrie Warner, Miss Tatun, Miss Simpson, Mr. Hale, Mrs. Mohr, Mr. and Mrs. Gordion, Mrs. Holbrook, Mr. and Mrs. March, Mr. McClellan, and Mr. Richardson. The beautiful scenery going over and the moonlight drive home added to the charm of the occasion.

Fish.

FISHING THROUGH A THUNDER STORM.

August 18th, Miss Greenlee, Miss Sullivan, and Mr. Read, from the Mansion House, went fishing on the lower lake. They were hardly seated in the boat when the clouds began angry, and in a few minutes it began to thunder and lighten. The young ladies were not the least frightened, but pulled out their rods and lines and went to fishing. They were gone two hours and caught fifteen perch.

———

Mr. Van Zandt, Mr. Campbell, Mr. Wanpole, and Mr. Read went fishing in the Upper Lake, August 13th. They were gone four hours and fished two hours, and returned with eleven black bass, one weighing three and one-half pounds.

Cyclist Column.

August 16th, Messrs. L. P. Noble, C. C. Ross and A. L. Boothbay of Portland rode on their wheels from that city to the Mansion House in two hours and thirty minutes. One of the young men was unfortunate and broke the front wheel to his bicycle half a mile from Poland Springs. Through the kindness of Mr. B. J. Gallagher, who loaned him the front wheel to his bicycle, the young man was enabled to return with the party to Portland.

Master Eben Judd rides the wheel splendidly.

A-WHEELING.
[From the New York Times.]

Have you never felt the fever of the thrilling, whirling
wheel,
Of the guiding and resisting of the shining cranks of
steel?
Never felt your senses reel
In the glamour and the gladness of the misty morning
sky,
As the white road rushes toward you, as the dew-bathed
banks slip by,
And the larks are soaring high?

Never known the boundless buoyance of the billowy,
breezy hills,
Of the pine scents all around you and the running, rip-
pling rills,
Chasing memory of life's ills—
Dashing, flashing through the sunshine, by the windy
wold and plain,
The distant blue heights lifting onward, upward to the
strain
Of the whirling wheel's refrain?

Fled from prison, like a prisoner, sped the turning, spin-
ning wheel,
Changed the city's stir and struggling, jar, and vexing
none can heal,
For the peace the fields reveal,
And with spirit separate, straining above the town's low
reach,
Found a tender satisfaction, which the steadfast summits
teach—
In their silence—fullest speech.

Never known the wistful wandering back, in pleasurable
pain,
Met the kine, from milking sauntering to pastures sweet
again,
Straggling up the wide-margined lane?
You have never felt the gladness, nor the glory of the
dream
That exalts, and tired eyes linger still on sunset, mead, and
stream?
Haste, then! Taste that bliss supreme.

Maud Murray.

Thursday evening, Miss Murray gave a reading in the Music Hall before a large and well-pleased audience. Miss Murray is a young lady of fine personal appearance, and created a favorable impression. Her greatest success appeared to be in character or dialect sketches, although her serious selections were well chosen and finely rendered.

A Poland Incident.

Mrs. Bright relates the following anecdote which readers of THE HILL-TOP will find entertaining:

"Eighteen summers ago," she says, "the second of my coming to Poland, the house was small and strangers were easily recognized. We noticed an attractive lady who, for several weeks, had come regularly to the table and then vanished to her room. We wondered at the strangeness of it.

"After a Sunday evening service, in which an interesting sermon was preached by the Oak Hill clergyman—who told us, I remember, that his salary of $350 he eked out by work in neighboring hay-fields—this lady, whose seat had been next mine, introduced herself to me, and said she would like to explain what must be considered her singular custom of always sitting in her own room.

"She had been ordered to Poland Springs for her husband's health, and had made no inquiries about the place, supposing it in the heart of the pine woods, with few conveniences. In the packing of her trunks she desired her daughter to fill them with sheets, candles, and for her wearing apparel—wrappers. Her usual gowns and jewels she felt would be quite out of place. They arrived well supplied with all which a country inn night lack.

"The stage stopped before a hotel with plenty of people dressed in something beside wrappers, and she was told that she was at the Poland Spring House. Her heart sank; visions of sheets and wrappers, illuminated by candles, danced before her bewildered mind. What a contrast was the tavern of her dreams to the hotel of her senses.

"So, you see, she concluded, nothing remained for her but to seclude herself and her wrappers, and carefully to preserve her traveling gown to appear in at table, for her Philadelphia house was closed."

Sunday Service.

Rev. W. E. C. Smith of Boston preached in Music Hall, Sunday, August 16th. His text was Matthew, chapter 6, 22-23 verses. A collection was taken, the sum being $31.35.

One of the pleasantries of the Mount Pleasant House, N. H., is a little card envelope for the reception of postage stamps and court plaster; the first to stick to letters, the last to stick to friends. But, really, is it the way to make friends to suggest that they may be cut and need to be emplastered? However, some chunks of Andersonian wisdom scattered over the envelope should be sufficient to remove such an unkind thought.

An Ab-original Tale,

Displaying some Indian-uity.

BY A SAVAGE.

Down in the eastern part of Maine
  Lived a Penobscot brave;
He was the pride of all his tribe,
  Who named him "Happy Dave;"
Though of a barbarous race, yet he
  Was never known to shave.

Now David, in his youth, was not
  In ignorance kept dark;
He soon could read and write as well
  As any parish clerk;
And yet his teacher said he would
  Be sure to make his mark.

He loved the gentle "Weeping Cloud,"
  Who lived across the river;
His hand and home, and all he had,
  He was resolved to give her.
When Cupid's dart had pierced his heart,
  Of course 'twas in a quiver.

He met her in a field of corn,
  In early autumn days:
And when he first declared his love
  She was all in a maize;
She hurried quickly home, because
  She wasn't used to stays.

Unto his quiet wigwam then
  With happy steps they went;
He thinking on the morrow's chase,
  And she on love in tent;
And when he bowed to welcome her,
  She saw her beau was bent.

[To be continued.]

Drag Rides.

Saturday morning, August 15th, a jolly party took a drive on the English drag which was purchased a few months ago by the Messrs. Ricker. The party included Mrs. J. H. Maginnis, Mr. and Mrs. E. T. Holmes, Mr. and Mrs. J. Stuart White, Mr. and Mrs. A. L. Gondran, Mrs. A. S. March, Mrs. C. L. Holbrook, Mrs. Paul F. Mohr, Miss Tatum, Mr. James H. Lake, Mr. E. B. Hale. The party went around Sabbath-day Lake and through the Peterson Woods.

The English drag has become so popular that parties have it in the forenoon and afternoon. Saturday afternoon, August 15th, the party consisted of Mr. and Mrs. J. O. Poillon, Mr. and Mrs. H. S. Beard, Miss H. Underwood, Miss Bessie M. Eddy, Miss Wymond, Miss Dexter, Miss Englis, Miss A. B. Englis, Mr. John Englis, and Miss H. L. Cabell. Around Sabbath-day Lake and through Peterson Woods is always delightful, and so this was the drive taken.

Monday, August 17th, a party, composed of the following, Mr. and Mrs. H. A. Rogers, Mr. and Mrs. F. O. Rhines, Mr. and Mrs. H. D. Ziegler, Mr. and Mrs. Robert Dornan, Mrs. Dickerson, Mr. and Mrs. Berri, Mr. and Mrs. Stinson, took a drive on the English drag, making the same trip.

Our Menu.

RECIPE No. 17.

Cream Crullers.

Two cups cream, 1 1-2 cups sugar, 2 teaspoons baking powder, 2 eggs, salt. Mix in flour to a soft dough; cut in desired shapes; fry in very hot fat.

RECIPE No. 18.

Crust for a Lemon Pie.

One cup flour, 1-4 teaspoon salt, 3 tablespoons lard, a speck of soda. Mix with cold water. Roll out and cover plates.

RECIPE No. 19.

English Plum Pudding.

One cup molasses, one cup sugar, one cup suet chopped fine, one cup milk, one teaspoonful soda, cloves, cassia, one-half nutmeg, two eggs, three and one-half cups flour, one cup raisins, one cup currants. Steam four hours.

Brandy Sauce for Plum Pudding.

One cup sugar; beat very light with three yolks of eggs. Whites of five eggs beaten stiff. Stir into the yolks lightly. Flavor with brandy.

RECIPE No. 20.

Mountain Dew Pudding.

Take one loaf of stale bread and cut off the crust and soak it in milk so as to make it soft. Then to this add the yolks of ten eggs, two cups of sugar, salt; flavor with lemon; one-half cup of butter. Steam one hour. After this bake it in the oven one-half hour.

RECIPE No. 21.

Sea Foam Sauce.

Two cups of sugar, one-half cup of water, and boil until it threads. Into this beat the whites of five eggs and pour on to it, and flavor with vanilla.

Progressive Euchre.

Friday evening, August 14th, an enjoyable progressive euchre party took place at the Poland Spring House.

The prizes were beautiful. Mrs. Williams won the first ladies' prize, a cut-glass powder-box; Miss Wyman the second prize, a painted bonbon dish; Miss Currier the third prize, a Mexican handkerchief; Miss Campbell the fourth, a silver knife. The first gentlemen's prize went to Mr. Gilman, a picture; Mr. DeWint won the second prize, a silver-mounted hat brush; Mrs. Jackson the third prize, a silver nail polisher; Mr. Lake the fourth prize, a silver button-hook.

Brake Rides.

A brake ride was given by Mr. and Mrs. Daniel C. Nugent, Thursday, August 13th, in honor of the birthday of Rev. T. J. Earley, pastor of St. Peter's Church, New Brighton, S. I. The other guests were Rev. Father Walsh of St. John's Seminary, Boston; Father Shaw of Lowell, Mass.; Rev. John A. Butler of Brookline, Mass.; Father O'Neill of Conway, N. H.; and Miss Louise Nugent.

A most enjoyable time is reported, and the party returned with a high appreciation of the scenery round and about Poland Springs.

August 18th, Miss Florence Stinson celebrated her sixteenth birthday by taking a brake ride to Gray. Miss Stinson and Miss Lippincott chaperoned the party, which included Miss Olive Gale, Miss Anna Lloyd, Messrs. Horace Ingalls, Walter Berri, and Bert Berri. Miss Florence Stinson was the recipient of many beautiful gifts.

Wednesday, August 19th, the following party enjoyed a brake ride: Miss Stinson, Miss Rogers, Miss Newhall, Miss Lippincott, Miss Florence Stinson, Mr. Moore, Mr. A. Rogers, Mr. Horace Ingalls.

Thursday morning, August 20th, an enjoyable brake ride was taken by the following party: Mrs. Thomas, Miss Mason, Miss Brown, Miss Goldthwait, Miss Chappelle, Miss Pecker, Mr. French.

The orchestra of the Poland Spring House, accompanied by Mrs. Daniel Kuntz, had a delightful ride on the brake around Tripp Lake, August 20th.

The Art Gallery.

This grand feature of Poland Springs grows in interest daily, and well it may, for a finer exhibition of paintings it would be difficult to bring together under similar circumstances.

Any one who has not visited it should not fail to do so, not only by day, but in the evening when it is brilliantly lighted.

It would be a trying task to select any one artist's name for mention when all are excellent, but of the one hundred and forty-eight paintings there presented, each one is admirable, and should find a place in the home of a lover of art.

See Lansil's Venetian scenes; Henwood's Algerian and other excellent works; Hayden's very delightful landscapes; Hatfield's home life; Enneking's grand strong masterpieces; Dean's bright and fresh marines, and Churchill's beautiful effects, beside a score more of equally fine examples of art.

The catalogues are free, and contain portraits of many of the artists, and the gallery is open from 9 A.M. to 9 P.M., week days, and on Sundays from 10 A.M. to 8.30 P.M.

Dance at the Mansion House.

Miss Campbell gave an informal dance Tuesday evening, August 18th, to the guests of the Mansion House. The tables in the dining-room were moved one side and Miss Byrne from the Poland Spring House furnished the music. Pretty waitresses served lemonade, and the guests pronounced it one of the jolliest occasions of the season.

One thing that added to the pleasure of the evening was the arrival, from the Treasury Department, Washington, of the medals won by Mr. August Franzen at the Columbian Exposition. Mr. Franzen is to be congratulated upon his success, and he can well be proud of the medals.

Indians.

In the shade of the forest, down where the red man was the first to slake his thirst, you will find to-day the descendants of that great race, the first owners of the land. Extend your walk from the spring a little and call at their tents, examine their handiwork, and talk with the Indian of the close of the nineteenth century. It will tell you, and he will tell you of his days and nights when on the still hunt for moose and caribou in the northern part of the state in the great wilderness. Take with you some souvenir of your visit and the Indian will be pleased and so will you.

FRANK CARLOS GRIFFITH, } Editors.
NETTIE M. RICKER. }

PUBLISHED EVERY SUNDAY MORNING DURING THE MONTHS OF JULY, AUGUST, AND SEPTEMBER, IN THE INTERESTS OF

POLAND SPRINGS AND ITS VISITORS.

All contributions relative to the guests of Poland Springs will be thankfully received.

To insure publication, all communications should reach the editors not later than Wednesday preceding day of issue.

All parties desiring rates for advertising in the Hill-Top should write the editors for same.

The subscription price of the Hill-Top is $1.00 for the season, post-paid. Single copies will be mailed at 10c. each.

Address,

EDITORS "HILL-TOP,"
Poland Spring House,
South Poland, Maine.

PRINTED AT JOURNAL OFFICE, LEWISTON.

Sunday, August 23, 1896.

Editorial.

TO be successful in this life one must not only keep up with the procession, but it is well to lead the band. We cannot all be leaders, of course, not of the same procession, but lead a smaller one, and make that one grow. Force the fighting for advancement, and not be forced into it, for "it is good fighting anywhere along the line," as the general replied to an anxious officer.

Right here is a great and successful enterprise, which has grown and existed upon merit, and would doubtless continue to increase upon the same basis, but to lead, one must be progressive, liberal, and enterprising; hence a great and superb structure is erected and dedicated to the purposes of art and literature, and all as the adjunct of a hotel. The result of this is an added interest in the place, a pleasant as well as an educational pastime, and other resorts of a similar nature must add similar attractions or fall behind in the parade.

A few years ago, a card placed in a street car, printed in type, or an advertisement in a magazine, printed in like characters, was all that was thought to be necessary, until the artist was joined in matrimonial bonds to business, and we began to see alluring results.

The picturesque, the attractive, the unique, was spread before our gaze, until type, pure and simple, was abandoned entirely, and the back pages of a great magazine, and the frieze of a street car, are evidences of the great struggle of business art to attract the eye of the purchaser.

It is not always possible to tell just what particular feature, or what especial advertisement brings its return, yet good judgment must be exercised in methods and mediums.

Art has become a necessity to business, and it is seen even in the elaborate arrangement of the window display of a show window; so in all enterprises which cater to the comfort and pleasure of the public, the one who leads is the one who succeeds.

Musical Programme.

SUNDAY EVENING, AUGUST 23, 1896, 8.15.

1. Overture—Semiramide. Rossini.
2. Nazareth. Gounod.
3. First Movement from Symphony (B Minor). Schubert.
4. Cello Solo—(a) Herbstblume. Poppel.
   (b) Gavotte.
   Mr. E. Loeffler.
5. Doux Sommeil. G. Marie.
6. Piano Solo.
   Mr. Edmund Kuntz.
7. Selection from Freischutz. Weber.

Music.

The musical programme of August 16th was one of the finest given this season. The solos by Mr. Kuntz and Mr. Brooks were remarkably full of feeling, and their faultless execution gave the audience the keenest musical enjoyment. Truly Mr. Edmund Kuntz can be congratulated upon reaching such results so young. His deeply felt productions never fail to arouse sympathy. The morning concerts are, as somebody said, "little musical gems."

A man experienced in the care of invalids; an extensive traveller, not only all over this country, but frequently in Europe; gentle, intelligent, well-read, and conversant with people and places, desires an opportunity to accompany an elderly invalid gentleman or lady in the capacity of companion. He can be highly recommended. Information may be had from the Librarian, Maine State Building.

William F. Halsall.

Mr. Halsall is an artist of whom it is said, "He never attempts to depict a scene without making careful studies on the spot, whether the place be the top of Mt. Washington in the dead of winter, or the Roaring Forties of the fickle North Atlantic." The United States government was the purchaser of his "First Fight Between Ironclads," and it may now be seen in the Capitol at Washington. The *New England Magazine* further says of Mr. Halsall: "If one is under the impression that Halsall is nothing more than a literal realist, that is to say, an artist without much imagination, one has but to look at his painting of a Boston pilot-boat, plunging down into the trough of a mighty sea, off soundings at dawn, amidst the huge grayish green waves, which are just catching the first rays of the wintry sun on their foaming crests, and one will be undeceived on this point; for it is evident that he knows and feels the wild poetry of the ocean, and there is a strain of the old Norse sailor's blood in his veins."

We have three of Halsall's pictures in the Poland Springs Art Gallery this season, all marines, and in Alcove "D." Visitors to the gallery will do well to note them, for they are strong and characteristic. Halsall is one of the foremost marine painters of the day.

An Episcopal clergyman's wife living in southern Texas sends to Mrs. Hiram Ricker a large quantity of Mexican drawn work. Mrs. Ricker will be glad to show it to all who will call at her cottage. It is charity work and the prices are very reasonable.

Children's Column.

A cheerful face is every man's debt to the world.

A Treasure of a Cat.

[From Boston Herald.]

In Paris, years ago, a young girl named Cosette lived in a shabby attic, with her old uncle, a rag-picker. He gave every evidence of being very poor, and the two had many a hardship to endure and often experienced cold and hunger.

Cosette at length went out to service in the household of a trades-man in another part of the city. She still retained a warm affection for her old uncle, and every week would bring him a part of her wages. The rest she carefully saved, and, before many years, she had a sum laid by, though it was small. She became engaged to be married to a baker, and was very happy.

But while she was planning what wedding clothes she should buy with the money she had saved, word came that her uncle, the ragpicker, had died suddenly, alone in his garret.

Cosette hastened to the place, and finding there none to care for the body or give it burial, she had it done at her own cost, expending in this way nearly all her little hoard.

When her lover, the baker, heard what she had done, he was furious at the loss of her dowry, and refused to marry her. Her employer also was displeased and discharged her.

Sadly Cosette found her way again to the desolate attic, where she wept bitter tears. But she soon took heart again, and determined to seek another situation.

She took a survey of the room, to see if her uncle had left anything of use, but there was nothing, save a large, stuffed cat, of which they had been very fond.

Cosette reached up and lifted this carefully down from its dusty shelf. It seemed very heavy. As she was moving it part of the hide broke away, and a shower of gold pieces fell to the floor.

Her uncle had been a miser, and for years had secretly hidden his earnings in this strange receptacle, where he knew they would be safe, as no one would ever think of treasure being concealed there.

Cosette could scarcely believe her good fortune.

When the gold was counted there was a full thousand louis d'or, equal to about $4,000, and this made her wholly independent. She had no longer need of a situation. It was not long before she married—not the faithless baker, now, but his employer. And she found through her life abundant reason to be glad that her devotion to her old uncle had been so richly rewarded.

Master Henry McCord, 2d, celebrated his eighth birthday last Saturday, from 5 to 6 o'clock, in the Mansion House parlor. Five young masters and one miss had a merry time playing games, in which some of the older ones participated. Then came supper on the veranda. The table was artistically decorated with ferns and pink sweetpeas. The birthday cake, surrounded by eight candles, was a thing of beauty, even if the candles persisted in blowing out as fast as lighted, but, alas! not a joy forever, for it soon disappeared with the other good things. After supper more games ended a very pleasant birthday party.

Many very happy returns, Master Henry.

An Interesting Letter.

The following extract is from a letter from the wife of Rev. A. J. Patterson, D.D., of Boston, and is self-explanatory:

"In Mr. Morrell's contribution of books to your library, I see 'Victory.' Is it my 'Victory,' a story of the war—a prize story? If so, will you write on the fly leaf, my name? When the book took the first prize, and was published in 1866, I was foolish enough to think it best unsigned, but I made a mistake. It has been out of print for years. There is some talk of a new edition. The plates have been saved. If I should die, they would doubtless publish that and my poems anew. We have a fashion of waiting until our friends are dead before we let them know that we care for them or their work."

JANE LIPPITT PATTERSON.

New Books.

The Deemster, by Hall Caine.

    FROM MRS. W. F. WOOD.

The World Between Them, by Bertha M. Clay.

    FROM MISS T. ROSENHEIM.

A Woman Intervenes, by Robert Barr.

    FROM EVERETT N. HUGGINS.

The American Hoyle, by "Trumps."

    FROM ALBERT T. SALTER.

Oliver Wendell Holmes.—Life and Letters. By John T. Moise, Jr.

Life of James McCosh, by William M. Sloane.

Tid-Bits.

We are very sorry to lose Mr. and Mrs. R. M. Field.

Mr. James H. Lake of Boston is at Poland Springs.

The Maine State Building opens at 10 A.M., Sundays.

Mrs. John I. Pinkerton has joined Mr. Pinkerton here.

Rev. W. H. Bolster and Mrs. Bolster are agreeable additions to our list of guests.

Mrs. S. A. Bolster, wife of Judge Bolster, of Boston, is a recent and welcome arrival.

The Bournes are at Somerset Inn, Bernardsville, N. J., and having a delightful time.

The scientific possibilities embodied in the story in last week's HILL-TOP, entitled "Love and War," are facts, and procured from reliable sources.

When guests come from so great a distance as Cape Town, South Africa, as Mr. Wm. F. Hertzog has, it is an indication of the extent of the fame of Poland Springs.

Mr. and Mrs. Wiener of Philadelphia (formerly Miss Bessie Elliott) are receiving congratulations. It is a dear baby girl. Mrs. Wiener has many friends at Poland Springs.

Thursday and Friday, August 13th and 14th, Miss Wheelock, the whist queen, gave an interesting lecture in one of her pupils' rooms at the Poland Spring House. By means of stereopticon views Miss Wheelock is able to teach a much larger class. She illustrates both the rules and the full hands. This idea is wholly original, and she gives her first lecture this autumn in Indianapolis.

Monday morning, August 17th, a party consisting of four started to walk to the lower lake. When a short distance from the hotel they noticed a falling meteor. As it passed through the air it looked like a ball of silver, followed by a long trail of smoke. One of the party looked at his watch, and it was 10 o'clock. As nearly as the party can locate it, it fell between the hotel and the lower lake.

A dinner was given August 17th at the Poland Spring House, in honor of Mr. August Franzen's departure. The table was spread in the large bay window, and was decorated with the colors of Sweden, yellow, blue, and red. The party included Mrs. Turner, Mrs. Van Zandt, Mrs. Vonnoh, Mrs. Kuntz, Mrs. Henwood, Miss Campbell, Miss Poor, and Miss Nettie Ricker; Mr. Franzen, Mr. Van Zandt, Mr. Vonnoh, Mr. Henwood, Mr. D. Kuntz, and Mr. Edmund Kuntz.

Guests at Poland Spring House

AUGUST 20, 1896.

Mrs. C. A. Barratoni	New York.
Miss Beatrice Barratoni	New York.
Mrs. L. Beard	Brooklyn.
Mr. and Mrs. H. S. Beard	Brooklyn.
Mr. Henry Bayley	Boston.
Mr. Joseph A. Brown	Boston.
Miss Belle G. Brown	Boston.
Mr. and Mrs. E. H. Brown	Fall River, Mass.
Mrs. Jas. Boyd	Harrisburg.
Dr. and Mrs. Geo. Brett	Boston.
Mr. and Mrs. F. H. Browne	Waltham.
Mr. and Mrs. N. A. Baldwin	New Haven.
Mr. M. Bradley	Haverhill.
Mr. Wm. A. Bigelow	New York.
Mrs. B. Babcock	New York.
Miss Babcock	New York.
Miss L. Belyea	Boston.
Mrs. Jacob P. Bates	Boston.
Mr. and Mrs. H. O. Bright	Cambridge.
Mr. and Mrs. Nelson Bartlett	Boston.
Mr. E. N. Briggs	Saginaw, Mich.
Mr. and Mrs. Wm. Bell	Brooklyn.
Walter Bell	Brooklyn.
Herbert Bell	Brooklyn.
Mrs. Beylle	Philadelphia.
H. L. Cabell	Richmond, Va.
Mr. and Mrs. G. C. Currier	New York.
Miss Lora Chamberlain	Norwich, Ct.
Miss Causland	Philadelphia.
Mrs. Agnes S. Curtis	New York.
Mr. and Mrs. Geo. W. Coleman	Boston.
Mr. Andrew R. Culver	Brooklyn.
Mr. and Mrs. F. W. Carpenter	Providence.
Miss Julia Carpenter	Providence.
Mr. and Mrs. C. C. Corbin	Webster, Mass.
W. H. Chappall	Chicago.
Miss Chappall	Chicago.
Mrs. Z. Chandler	Detroit, Mich.
Mr. and Mrs. Robt. Dornan	Philadelphia.
Mrs. Wm. C. Druton	New York.
Miss C. S. Dier	New Haven.
Mrs. Albert Douglass	New York.
Mrs. N. C. Dickerson	New York.
Miss C. A. Dier	New Haven.
Mrs. J. R. Darling	New York.
Mrs. Wm. Engel	Bangor.
Miss Engel	Bangor.
Miss Euglis	Brooklyn.
Miss A. B. Englis	Brooklyn.
Mr. and Mrs. James H. Eddy	New Britain, Conn.
Miss Bessie M. Eddy	New Britain, Conn.
Mrs. C. G. First	Lock Haven.
Miss Fletcher	Boston.
Mr. Geo. B. French	Boston.
Mrs. J. D. Fessenden	New York.
Gen. Chas. E. Furlong	New York.
Mr. and Mrs. D. H. Field	Brockton, Mass.
Miss Fischer	New York.
Mr. and Mrs. C. S. Fischer	New York.
Mrs. M. C. Feraud	New York.
Mrs. R. G. Feltis	Philadelphia.
Mr. F. G. Frothingham	Boston.
Miss Laura A. Farnham	Boston.
Mr. and Mrs. J. C. Frye	Boston.
Mr. and Mrs. A. L. Gondran	New York.
Mr. and Mrs. F. E. Gilman	Montreal.
Mr. John Goldthwaite	Boston.
Miss E. B. Goldthwaite	Boston.
Mrs. L. M. Gale	Washington.
Miss Olive Gale	Washington.
Mrs. F. A. Gilbert	Brookline.
Miss Gilbert	Brookline.
Miss Ruth Gilbert	Brookline.
Mr. Lester Gilbert	Brookline
Miss Howell	Baltimore.
Miss Hyatt	Baltimore.
Mr. and Mrs. S. B. Hibbard	Jacksonville.
Mrs. W. W. Hartwell	Plattsburgh, N. Y.
Mr. and Mrs. John R. Hoxie	Chicago.
Miss Anna Hoxie	Chicago.
Mr. and Mrs. Horace Hunt	New York.
Mr. and Mrs. L. Hulburt	Brooklyn.
Mrs. M. B. Hoffman	New York.
Mr. and Mrs. Hudson Hoagland	New York.
Mr. and Mrs. E. Holmes	New York.
Mr. and Mrs. E. T. Holmes and family	New York.
Miss Horner	Philadelphia.
Miss Anna Havens	Boston.
Mrs. W. D. Hawley	Syracuse.
Mrs. M. E. Hildreth	Boston.
Miss Alma Hildreth	Boston.
Mr. A. S. Hanson	Boston.
Mr. and Mrs. A. Harkness	Providence.
Mr. and Mrs. Sam. Henderson, Jr., and family	New Orleans.
Col. Joseph A. Ingalls and family	Boston.
Gov. and Mrs. Jas. Jeffries	Louisiana.
Miss Jacoby	New York.
Mrs. Julian James	Washington.
J. J. Kennedy	New Brighton.
Mrs. E. A. Knapp	New York.
Miss Leadbeater	Philadelphia.
Miss Bessie Lippincott	Philadelphia.
Rev. and Mrs. W. P. Lewis	Philadelphia.
Mrs. B. C. Lake	New Haven.
Miss Leland	New York.
Mr. and Mrs. Malcolm Lloyd	Philadelphia.
Miss Lloyd	Philadelphia.
James D. Laird	San Francisco.
Mr. and Mrs. Chas. Lippincott	Philadelphia.
Mr. and Mrs. F. H. Lippincott	Philadelphia.
Miss Lucille Lippincott	Philadelphia.
Mr. and Mrs. Amos R. Little	Philadelphia.
Mr. and Mrs. B. Lemann and family	New Orleans.
Miss Cora W. Lumbert	Brockton.
Mr. James H. Lake	Boston.
Mr. J. Wilson Leakin	Baltimore.
Mr. and Mrs. Thomas P. Langdon	Baltimore.
Mr. and Mrs. B. N. Lapham	Providence.
Mrs. J. W. Merrill	Boston.
Miss Merrill	Boston.
Mr. and Mrs. A. S. March, Jr., and family	New York.
Miss C. McGrath	Boston.
Mr. C. T. McGrath	Boston.
Mr. A. D. McClellan	Boston.
Mrs. Paul F. Meher	Washington.
Henry P. Morrison	New Brighton.
Mr. and Mrs. J. S. Martin	New York.
Mr. A. N. Mayo	Springfield.
Byron P. Moulton	Philadelphia.
Mr. and Mrs. T. B. M. Mason	Washington.
Mrs. T. B. Myers	Washington.
Mrs. Jno. H. Maginnis	New Orleans.
Mr. Jno. H. Maginnis	New Orleans.
Mrs. A. Murry	Washington.
Miss A. G. Miller	Brooklyn.
Dr. and Mrs. Ira L. Moore	Philadelphia.
Mrs. J. T. Montgomery	Rosemont, Pa.
Mrs. B. P. Moulton	Newtonville.
Mr. and Mrs. A. R. Mitchell	Baltimore.
Mrs. Christine Marburg	Baltimore.
The Misses Marburg	Baltimore.
Mr. and Mrs. John T. Martin	New York.
Mr. and Mrs. J. L. Nason	Boston.
Miss Nason	Boston.
Mr. and Mrs. Dan C. Nugent and family	St. Louis.
Mr. and Mrs. W. T. Ness	Boston.
Miss Lucy P. Newhall	Philadelphia.
Mrs. H. S. Osgood	Portland.
Mr. John A. Ordway	Boston.
Mr. and Mrs. Josiah Oakes	Malden, Mass.
Mr. and Mrs. J. O. Poillon	New York.
Lovell Palmer	Brooklyn.
Mr. and Mrs. John I. Pinkerton	West Chester, Pa.
Miss E. A. Prall	New York.
Mrs. J. A. Pettee	New York.

Miss Anne J. Pecker	Boston.
Miss Mary L. Pecker	Boston.
Mr. and Mrs. Fulton Paul	Hudson, N. Y.
Mr. and Mrs. Henry U. Palmer	Brooklyn.
Masters Austin and Chester Palmer	Brooklyn.
Mrs. M. E. Parsons	Boston.
Mr. E. D. Peters	Boston.
Miss A. J. Pomeroy	New York.
S. S. Riker	New York.
Miss Marion Richardson	Boston.
Mrs. Runyon	Plainfield, N. J.
Mrs. J. O. Rhines	New York.
Mr. and Mrs. E. H. Randolph	Louisiana.
Mr. and Mrs. Augustus Richardson	Boston.
Miss Richardson	Boston.
Allen M. Rogers	New York.
Mr. and Mrs. H. A. Rogers	New York.
Miss May Rogers	New York.
Mrs. E. J. Robinson	Boston.
Miss Roberts	Philadelphia.
Moses W. Richardson	Boston.
Mrs. M. E. Richards	New York.
Mr. and Mrs. F. H. Raymond	Somerville.
Mr. J. Olcutt Rhines	New York.
Mr. C. W. Rice	Boston.
Mr. and Mrs. Edward C. Rice	New York.
Rev. and Mrs. W. E. C. Smith	Boston.
Dr. and Mrs. E. H. Smith	Boston.
Mr. and Mrs. H. C. Swain and son	New York.
Mr. and Mrs. J. E. Spenser	New York.
Mr. and Mrs. S. R. Small	Portland.
Mrs. S. Skaats	New York.
Miss Slade	New York.
Mrs. Mary J. Spencer	Brooklyn.
Dr. and Mrs. C. C. Schuyler	Plattsburgh, N. Y.
Miss Stinson	Philadelphia.
Miss Florence Stinson	Philadelphia.
Mr. and Mrs. A. T. Salter	Washington.
Mr. and Mrs. Joseph W. Sandford	Plainfield, N. J.
Mr. Samuel Shethar	New York.
Mr. and Mrs. J. B. Sawyer	Dover, N. H.
Mr. and Mrs. S. B. Stinson	Philadelphia.
Mr. and Mrs. E. P. Smith	New York.
Mrs. G. W. Simpson	Brooklyn.
Miss B. C. Simpson	Brooklyn.
Miss Mabel Simpson	Brooklyn.
Mrs. J. Edwin Smith	Worcester.
Mrs. A. D. Stormes	
Miss J. C. Stevens	Bangor.
Miss Tattin	Brooklyn.
Miss Tillotson	New Haven.
Miss N. E. Ten Broeck	New York.
Mrs. Orlando Tompkins	Boston.
Mrs. Frank R. Thomas	Boston.
Mr. and Mrs. F. E. Taylor	Brooklyn.
Miss A. L. Tolman	Boston.
Mr. John H. Voorhees	Brooklyn.
Mr. and Mrs. Peter Van Voorhees	Camden, N. J.
J. D. Van Voorhees	Camden, N. J.
Mr. and Mrs. W. A. Vose	Brookline.
Mr. Geo. A. Vose	Brookline.
Miss Vose	Brookline.
Mrs. John H. Voorhees	Brooklyn.
Miss Jessie Voorhees	Brooklyn.
Mr. and Mrs. G. P. Wescott	Portland.
J. V. Watson	Philadelphia.
Mr. and Mrs. D. Welch	Boston.
Mrs. G. N. Wilson	Washington.
Mr. and Mrs. F. H. Williams	Boston.
Miss Lizzie A. Williams	Boston.
Mr. and Mrs. John Wilson	New York.
Miss P. W. Willets	So. Amboy, N. J.
Mrs. Chas. Warner	Troy, N. Y.
Miss C. A. Warner	Troy, N. Y.
Miss M. V. Warner	Troy, N. Y.
Miss M. A. Winslow	Troy, N. Y.
Mr. and Mrs. F. H. Wyeth	Philadelphia.
Mr. and Mrs. John P. Woodbury	Boston.
Mrs. J. Reed Whipple	Boston.
Dr. M. C. Wedgwood and Mrs. Wedgwood	Lewiston.
Mr. A. Wentworth	Boston.
Mr. F. R. Wharton	Philadelphia.
Mr. and Mrs. W. S. Wymond	Louisville, Ky.
Miss Wymond	Louisville, Ky.
Mr. and Mrs. J. Stuart White	New York.
Mrs. L. P. Worthington	Doylestown, Pa.
Miss Worthington	Doylestown, Pa.
Mr. N. Whitman	New York.

Tid-Bits.

Mr. and Mrs. F. H. Raymond of Somerville, Mass., are at the Poland Spring House.

Hon. F. E. Gilman walked around the middle lake last Monday in three and a half hours.

The ant-hills on the road around the lower lake from Poland Corner are something wonderful.

Mr. Henry C. Byrne of Roxbury, spent Tuesday, August 18th, at the Poland Spring House.

Mrs. F. A. Gilbert, Miss Gilbert, Master Gilbert, and Miss Ruth H. Gilbert, are guests at the Poland Spring House.

Mr. and Mrs. Ziegler and Miss Ziegler, who have been spending the summer at Poland Springs, returned to their home in Philadelphia, August 19th.

One hundred and sixty-one books out on one day last week. This shows the interest in the library, and not an exceptional day either. Only one book to each person also.

The well-known oculist, Dr. Myles Standish, and Mrs. Standish, have been spending some time at Poland Springs. Their departure Wednesday, August 19th, is much regretted.

The celebrated artist, Mr. Frederick D. Henwood, and Mrs. Henwood, returned to Boston, August 19th. Mr. Henwood made several fine paintings while at Poland Springs.

Miss Barbour of the Mansion House left Thursday, August 13th, for Digby, N. S., where she will spend a few weeks visiting friends. Miss Barbour is very popular at Poland Springs, and her departure is much regretted.

For one month, ending August 19th, 2,044 books were exchanged in the library, 1,022 being given out and a like number returned, making an average of 66 books exchanged daily. The smallest number returned was 16 and the highest 51.

Mr. Robert Marsh celebrated his birthday, August 18th, by an informal supper given at the Mansion House. The party included Mr and Mrs. Greenlees, Mrs. Pulsifer, Miss Fuller, Miss Ricker, Miss Marsh, Miss Mary Marsh, Mr. Daton Voorhees, Mr. Lester Gilbert, Master Arthur Marsh. The birthday cake, which was made by Miss Nellie Corcoran, was delicious.

Arrivals.

POLAND SPRING HOUSE.

FROM AUG. 14 TO AUG. 21, 1896.

Allen, Addison	New York.
Allen, Miss F. L.	Brunswick.
Brooks, W. A., Jr.	Boston.
Bradbury, Mrs. Lydia W.	Avon, N. Y.
Bradbury, M.	Auburn.
Bickley, W. F.	New York.
Biever, N.	New York.
Byrne, H. C.	Boston.
Boyd, Mrs. James	Harrisburg.
Bradshaw, Mr. and Mrs. A. M.	Lakewood.
Brown, F. H.	Waltham.
Brown, Miss	Brooklyn.
Butterick, E.	Brooklyn.
Butterick, Miss M. E.	Brooklyn.
Callahan, W. E.	Lewiston.
Callahan, Frank L.	Lewiston.
Cooper, Geo.	Pawtucket.
Colby, W. W.	Portland.
Colby, Mrs.	Portland.
Clark, A. N.	Peabody.
Cony, W. T.	Boston.
Cushman, Mrs. Chas. L.	Auburn.
Chafin, Mr. and Mrs. Geo. R.	Charlestown.
Chafin, Miss	Charlestown.
Davis, A. L.	Portland.
Daniel, Miss Marie B.	Cambridge.
Dizer, Mrs. S. C.	Boston.
Davis, Mrs. Simon	Boston.
Dingley, Mr. and Mrs. F. L.	Lewiston.
Davis, Mrs. Westmoreland	New York.
Emery, Geo. B.	Gorham.
Espenscheid, N. Jr.	Brooklyn.
Espenscheid, Miss	Brooklyn.
Eaton, Mrs. C. D.	Somerville.
Eaton, Miss Lucy	Somerville.
Elton, Eleanor F.	Boston.
Elton, Herbert C.	Boston.
Englis, John	Brooklyn.
Foster, Mr. and Mrs. Wm. H.	Somerville.
Farnham, Miss Latta A.	Boston.
Flaherty, Jas. V.	New London.
Frye, Mr. and Mrs. J. C.	Boston.
Frost, Mrs. C. G.	Lock Haven, Pa.
Fowler, Mr. and Mrs. Harry S.	Brooklyn.
Gilbert, Mrs. F. A.	Brookline.
Gilbert, Miss Florence A.	Brookline.
Gilbert, Lester F.	Brookline.
Gilbert, Ruth H.	Brookline.
Goodwin, Mr. and Mrs. M.	New York.
Gregory, Mrs. Geo.	Brooklyn.
Gregory, Miss	Brooklyn.
Godfrey, Mr. and Mrs. Geo. F.	Bangor.
Grace, Miss	Freeport.
Gilbert, Mr. and Mrs. A.	Plainfield, N. J.
Hawley, Mrs. W. D.	Syracuse.
Hildreth, Mrs. M. E.	Boston.
Hildreth, Miss Alma	Boston.
Hildreth, Mr. and Mrs. C. F.	Boston.
Hildreth, Mrs. J. W.	Boston.
Hildreth, Miss May	Boston.
Hansill, S. M.	Cleveland.
Henderson, W. B.	Boston.
Hayes, Helen A.	Malone, N. Y.
Holden, E. F.	Syracuse.
Halljan, Joseph	Cambridge.
Hughes, Mr. and Mrs. Matt S.	Minneapolis.
Hanson, A. S.	Boston.
Heighe, Mr. and Mrs. John M.	Baltimore.
Henderson, Mr. and Mrs. Sam.	New Orleans.
Hunt, Mrs. Lee B.	Gray.
Harkness, Mr. and Mrs. S.	Providence.
Iselin, Mrs. W. S.	
Inman, Mrs. W. H.	New York.
Inman, Miss W. L.	New York.
Jordan, Mr. and Mrs. H. H.	Boston.
Kelsey, Mrs. E.	Freeport.
Knapp, Mrs. E. A.	New York.
Leonard, T. F.	Lawrence.
Lasher, Mr. and Mrs. Geo. F.	Philadelphia.
Lewis, Geo.	So. Berwick.
Lane, Mrs. C. E.	Freeport.
Lapham, Mr. and Mrs. B. N.	Providence.
Lake, James H.	Boston.
Loring, R.	Boston.
Leakin, J. Wilson	Baltimore.
Langdon, Mr. and Mrs. Thos. P.	Baltimore.
Murray, Maud	Boston.
Morrell, Miss Nina K.	Avon, N. Y.
Moore, Mr. and Mrs. James E.	Boston.
McClellan, A. D.	Boston.
Mason, Mr. and Mrs. Fletcher S.	Providence.
Mason, Miss	Providence.
Merrill, W. W.	Deering.
Munson, G. B.	New York.
McCartney, R. C.	Boston.
Mayer, Miss Beatrice	Peaks Island.
McGrath, C. T.	Boston.
Newell, Mrs.	Auburn.
Osgood, H. S.	Portland.
Overstolz, Miss	St. Louis.
Perry, G. T.	Boston.
Pecker, Miss Anne J.	Boston.
Pecker, Miss Mary L.	Boston.
Parker, Mrs. M. A.	Philadelphia.
Pinkerton, Mrs. John I.	West Chester, Pa.
Parker, Mrs. H. K.	Somerville.
Parker, Miss A. E.	Somerville.
Pulsifer, Mr. and Mrs. Jas. A.	Auburn.
Paul, Mr. and Mrs. Fulton	Hudson, N. Y.
Raymond, Mr. and Mrs. F. H.	Somerville.
Rhines, J. O.	New York.
Rice, C. W.	Boston.
Rice, Mr. and Mrs. Edward C.	New York.
Ricker, Mr. and Mrs. J. S.	Portland.
Reade, John L.	Lewiston.
Randolph, Miss	Plainfield, N. J.
Scannell, J. M.	Lewiston.
Sandford, Joseph W.	Plainfield, N. J.
Simpson, J. C.	Brooklyn.
Stevens, Josephine C.	Bangor.
Shorttidge, John H.	Philadelphia.
Shorttidge, Miss L. E.	Philadelphia.
Shorttidge, Miss F. A.	Philadelphia.
Schaul, Mr. and Mrs. H. H.	Atlanta.
Sawyer, Mr. and Mrs. Edw.	Newton.
Stockbridge, A. L.	Lewiston.
Stockbridge, Edith	Lewiston.
Stockbridge, Helen	Washington.
Stockbridge, Margaret	Washington.
Smith, C. K.	Philadelphia.
Sealy, Mrs. Frank L.	Newark.
Simpson, Mrs. G. W.	Brooklyn.
Simpson, Miss B. C.	Brooklyn.
Simpson, Miss Mabel	Brooklyn.
Small, S. R.	Portland.
Sanborn, Robert E.	Boston.
Smith, Mrs. J. Edwin	Worcester.
Stormes, Mrs. A. D.	
Shethar, E. H.	New York.
Stedman, Miss Georgie M.	Denver.
Stewart, W. W.	St. Louis.
Scheffer, Mrs.	Peaks Island.
Standish, Mr. and Mrs. Myles	Boston.
Taylor, F. R.	
Townsend, Miss M. E.	Wellesley.
Thurnauer, Mrs.	Peaks Island.

Tolman, Miss A. La l ia	Boston.
Voorhees, J. H.	Brooklyn.
Vinton, W. N.	Gray.
Wall, Frances H.	New York.
Whitman, N.	New York.
Wilcox, Miss Annie M.	Boston.
Welch, Daisy E.	Boston.
Washbt in, Miss Katherine B.	Avon, N. Y.
Waid, Mrs. Warren	Brookline.
Waid, Miss Minnie	Brookline.
Yuex, M. A.	New York.

MANSION HOUSE.
AUGUST 14 TO 21, 1896.

Blell, Mr. and Mrs. H. A.	Lawrence.
Crane, Gertrude A.	Portland.
Keene, Samuel C.	Boston.
Morrison, D. J.	Savannah.
Marsh, Mr. and Mrs. C. C.	New York.
Otis, Alfred W.	Boston.
Riggles, Chas. R.	Chicago.
Riggles, Chas. F.	Chicago.
Rice, C. W.	Boston.
Todd, Ed v in L.	Sing Sing.
Viale, J. F.	Denver.
Woodall, A.	Liverpool.

The many friends of Mr. Atgist Franzen regret his departure on Atgist 20th.

Mrs. M. E. Hildreth and Miss Alma Hildreth of Boston, received a warm welcome tpon their arrival at the Poland Spring Hotse, Friday, Atgist 14th.

The menus that were used at the Poland Spring Hotse, Atgist 16th, were painted by Miss Florence Miner of Chicopee, Mass. Miss Miner has studied at the Normal Art School in Boston, and recently *Life* has accepted one of her sketches. The menus were much admired.

Miss Ada M. Smith entertained a few of her friends in Music Hall, Monday afternoon, Atgist 17th, by playing an Etude by Moszkowsky, and selections by Raff and Liszt. Miss Smith is a brilliant pianiste, her technique is well developed, and she is a young lady of great promise. She has studied with Alexander Lambert, a teacher in New York College of Music, New York City.

Mr. Van Grass at player-meeting said : "Brethren, this is a hard world to live in and few leave it alive."

THE THREE GRACES.

Teacher—Johnny, what are the three graces?
Johnny—Breakfast, dinner, and supper.

Loving a grass widow is the pleasantest kind of a hay fever.

The girl who is dazzled by her beau's diamonds is stone blind to his faults.

A colored pastor in Texas, demanding his salary, is reported to have said, " Brudren, I can't preach heah and boa'd in heb'n."

No AMATEUR WANTED.
[From the Detroit Free Press.]

She—Are you sure I am the first woman you ever loved?
He—I swear it.
She—Then you may go. After you have obtained some experience come to me again.

A LITTLE QUEER.
[From the Chicago Inter-Ocean.]

An observing official of the Chicago, Milwaukee & St. Paul road has made a note of some funny signs and advertisements that have come to his notice. The following are taken as the best in the collection :

Animal sale now on. Don't go anywhere else to be cheated. Come in here.

A lady wants to sell her piano, as she is going abroad in a strong iron frame.

Furnished apartments suitable for gentlemen with folding doors.

Wanted—A room by two gentlemen about thirty-six feet long and twenty feet broad.

For sale—A piano-forte, the property of a musician with carved legs.

A boy wanted who can open oysters with reference.

Bulldog for sale ; will eat anything ; very fond of children.

Wanted—An organist, and a boy to blow the same.

Wanted—A boy to be partly outside and partly behind the counter.

To be disposed of, a small phaeton, the property of a gentleman with movable headpiece as good as new.

THE NEW MOUNT PLEASANT HOUSE,

In the Heart of the White Mountains.

Through Parlor Cars from New York, Boston, and Portland, also from Burlington, Montreal, and Quebec.

The Hotel faces the Grandest Display of Mountain Peaks in America east of the Rocky Mountains. It is lighted throughout by electricity, thoroughly heated by steam, and has an abundance of private and public baths. Its orchestra is made up largely from the Boston Symphony Orchestra. Its table is unsurpassed. Absolutely pure water from an artesian well, 400 feet in solid rock.

IT IS THE NEAREST HOTEL TO MT. WASHINGTON, AND THE TRAIN FOR THE SUMMIT STARTS FROM A STATION ON THE HOTEL GROUNDS.

All Trains, Maine Central Railroad, from Portland to Burlington, Montreal, Quebec, and Lake Champlain stop at the platform close to the House.

Leave Portland 8.45 A.M., arrive Mt. Pleasant House, 12.21 P.M.
"   "   1.25 P.M.,   "   "   "   "   5.05 P.M.
"   "   3.20 P.M.,   "   "   "   "   7.20 P.M.
"   "   8.45 P.M.,   "   "   "   "   11.47 P.M.

POST, TELEGRAPH, AND TICKET OFFICE
IN THE HOTEL.

ANDERSON & PRICE, of the Hotel Ormond of Florida, Managers.

Address by wire or mail, "Mount Pleasant House, N. H."

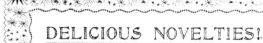

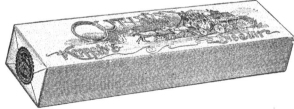

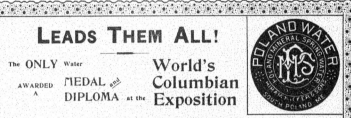

The Hill-Top

POLAND SPRINGS, SO. POLAND, ME.

HARRY C. WILKINSON

THE HILL-TOP

Vol. III.　　SUNDAY MORNING, AUGUST 30, 1896.　　No. 9.

Our Young Folks.

I T is always charming to see children enjoying themselves at healthful recreation, and at this beautiful resort they are favored with a lovely play-ground, shaded by tall pines, and yet in close proximity to the hotel.

This season the children have risen to the occasion and provided considerable entertainment, not only for themselves but for their elders who have witnessed their frolics and read with interest of their games.

On two occasions recently their clever proceedings have been found to be of more than ordinary interest, and have been gladly chronicled in the Hill-Top, and in the second of these, the croquet tournament, Mr. Ness made an excellent photograph of the entire group, clustered about the tent, on the play-ground, and a report of the game was given in No. 7 of the Hill-Top.

We give herewith the names of the children represented in the group, beginning at the left:

Margaret G. Thurston, Ruth Kellen, Edward H. Pulsifer, Beatrice Barratoni, Henry McCord, Miriam Lemann, Claire Ingalls, Edward P. Ricker, Jr., Monte Lemann, Ray Lemann, Chester Palmer, Marion Ricker, Mildred Holmes, Theodore K. Thurston, Arthur Lemann, Janet Ricker, Eben Judd, Austin Palmer, E. T. Holmes, Jr., Jamie Ricker, Dick Voorhees, Lucille Lippincott, Jacob Lemann, Robert Marsh, Clay Swain, Arthur Marsh, Casey Nugent, Morgan Nugent, George Alvin Ricker, Albert Rosenheim, Dorothy Marsh, Harriet Fischer, Natalie Marsh.

The Difference.

[Contributed.]

Knowledge of the scriptures is more to be desired than riches, and those are indeed blessed who, out of the abundance of their worldly life, can fit to each happening of worldly life a pearl from the Book of Books.

Two there are who summer with us—related only by ties of kindred wit—habitually partners in the enlivening game of six-handed euchre; she a lovely westerner; he from the opposite shore of our country. When the score runs in their favor, both vie in biblical quotations expressive of their own fortune and commiserating the poor skill of their opponents. But, alas! When the scene changes and their despised adversaries are for a space upon the winning side, we say it with grief, nothing of the consolation with which their fertile book abounds occurs to this crest-fallen pair. They play their cards, their faces downcast, their tongues for once at rest.

May they not, perchance, glean from this dispassionate comment a useful hint?

J. O. B.

Drag Ride.

Monday, August 24th, Mr. Moses W. Richardson of Boston gave a very enjoyable drag ride to Gloucester. The day was perfect, and the party left the hotel about ten o'clock. It included Mr. and Mrs. White, Mr. and Mrs. Gourdan, Mr. and Mrs. Vose, Mrs. Holbrook, Mrs. March, Miss Warner, Miss Williams, Mr. Lake, Mr. Corbin, and Mr. McClellan. It was one of the pleasantest drag rides of the season.

Progressive Euchre.

August 20th, Mr. and Mrs. Wescott gave a delightful progressive euchre party in honor of Mr. and Mrs. Raymond.

There were four tables, and the party included Mr. and Mrs. Little, Mr. and Mrs. Moulton, Mr. and Mrs. Stinson, Mrs. Maginnis, Mrs. Corbin, Mrs. Coleman, Mrs. Hoffman, Mrs. Pettee, Mrs. Richardson, Mrs. Bates, Mrs. J. B. Sawyer, and Mr. Lake.

The prizes were beautiful. Mrs. Stinson won the first ladies' prize, an exquisite center-piece; Mrs. Moulton, the second prize, a pair of scissors with oxidized silver mountings. The third prize went to Mrs. Maginnis, a gold spoon. Mr. Moulton won the first gentlemen's prize, a paper-cutter; Mr. Stinson the second, a silver knife; Mr. Lake the third prize, a pen-holder.

At 10.30 the party went to the dining-room, where they found a table artistically decorated with ferns and flowers. Each lady had a large bunch of sweet peas with mignonette; and the gentlemen, sprays of sweet peas. It was one of the most enjoyable occasions of the season.

Friday, August 21st, the guests of the Poland Spring House gathered in the amusement room for progressive euchre. There were fourteen tables. Eighteen moves were made, and the highest number gained by the ladies was twelve; by the gentlemen, fourteen. Mrs. March won the first ladies' prize, a beautiful plate; Mrs. Maginnis the second, cut-glass vinaigrette; Miss Shorridge the third prize, a mirror with gold mountings; Mrs. Keene the fourth, a pin-cushion. Mr. Williams won the first gentlemen's prize, a brush with silver mountings; Miss Bessie Simpson the second prize, a cork-screw; Colonel Talbott the third, a beautiful picture; and the fourth went to Mr. McClellan, an address book.

Picnic, Fishing, and a Ride on the Steam Launch.

Monday, August 24th, Mr. and Mrs. Ross Campbell gave a picnic at their boat-house and a fishing trip through the Upper Lake. The party included Mr. and Mrs. Van Zandt, Mrs. Martha Pulsifer, Miss Frames, Miss Fuller, Miss Mary Marsh, Mr. Read, and Mr. Harry Wampole.

Seventeen fish were caught, and Mrs. Martha Pulsifer caught the largest one, weighing two pounds.

In the evening Mr. and Mrs. Campbell gave the party a moonlight ride on their steam launch. Mrs. Read and Master Albert Wampole joined the party. Upon their return a late lunch was served at Mr. and Mrs. Campbell's home.

Golf.

Entries Handicap Golf Tournament, Poland Springs, August 20, 1896.

NAME.	HANDICAP.	1st Round.	Net.	2d Round.	Net.	Average.
C. C. Schuyler	35	88	53	90	55	54
H. Belli	28	85	57	80	52	54½
H. B. Ingalls	12	72	60	65	53	56½
H. S. Beald	32	99	67	84	52	59½
S. B. Stinson	20	73	53	87	67	60
D. C. Nugent	30	91	61	89	59	60
B. P. Moulton	22	88	66	78	56	61
H. N. Palmer	22	94	72	78	56	64
F. H. Lippincott	10	84	74	72	62	68
Walter Belli	5	86	81	61	56	68½
J. H. Maginnis	15	84	69	84	69	69
J. J. McLaughlin	14	90	76	77	63	69½
George A. Vose	Scratch		71		73	72
A. M. Rogers	40	116	76	108	68	72
M. Palmer	13	86	73	87	74	73½
D. W. Field	13	85	72	(Withdrawn.)		
William Belli	20	77	57	(Withdrawn.)		

Dr. Schuyler announced that he would offer the prize he had won (a golf bag and three balls) for competition by the following players. The gentlemen will play in pairs, the highest score man in each pair withdrawing after the first round of nine holes; play to begin at 9.30 sharp, Monday morning, August 24th. The game was accordingly played at that time, with the following score:

PLAYERS.	First Round.	Second Round.
George A. Vose	61	
H. B. Ingalls	70	63
S. B. Stinson	80	
Walter Belli	56	81
Withdrawn.		
Withdrawn.		
H. N. Palmer	73	79
J. J. McLaughlin	77	
Belt Belli	70	83
H. S. Beald	71	
H. B. Ingalls—Winner.		

Handicap Scratch Golf Tournament, Tuesday, August 25th, 3 P.M.

		1st Round.	2d Round.	Total
1st, H. B. Ingalls	Scratch	62	64	126
2d, G. A. Vose	"	71	61	132
3d, W. Belli	"	67	71	138
4th, J. J. McLaughlin	"	78	70	148

Winner—H. B. Ingalls. Prize, one golf ball.

Golf has taken a great hold upon the guests, and is one of the fixed features of the season.

A two-round handicap golf was played on Wednesday, August 26th, the prizes being offered by Mr. S. B. Stinson, handicaps being based upon the records of August 21st. The following was the result:

Players.	Handicaps.	1st Round.	2d Round.	Average Totals.
H. B. Ingalls	Scratch	64	56	60
George A. Vose	3	65–62	63–60	61
Walter Belli	5	70–65	73–68	66½
S. B. Stinson	11	76–65	85–74	69½
Bert Belli	14	81–67	73–59	63
J. H. Maginnis	15	72–57	74–59	58
L. M. Palmer	18	71–53	86–68	60½
Dr. Schuyler	20	81–61	87–67	64
H. S. Beald	23	86–63	77–54	58½
A. M. Rogers	43	102–59	101–58	58½

Winner—1st, J. H. Maginnis.

Tie { 2d, H. S. Beald.
{ 3d, A. M. Rogers.

Our Menu.

RECIPE NO. 21.

Lemon Meringue.

Twenty-four lemons, three dozen eggs (separate the yolks from the white and save the white for frosting), eight pounds of sugar, one and one-half cups of flour. Mix half of the sugar with the yolks of the eggs and the other half of the sugar with the juice of the lemons. With one quart of boiling milk mix the yolks and sugar. After this mix the sugar and lemon juice and the eggs and sugar all together. Make a frosting and cover over this. Make the pie crust the same as you make the upper crust of an ordinary pie. This recipe will make twelve pies.

RECIPE No. 22.

Orange Jelly.

Eight ounces of gelatine, five quarts of water, one dozen oranges (grated outside and the juice), one-half dozen lemons (grated outside and the juice), four pounds of sugar.

RECIPE No. 23.

Spice Cake.

Four cups of sugar, eight eggs, two cups of butter, two cups of milk, six cups of flour, two dessert-spoonfuls of cream of tarter and one of soda. Flavor with cloves, nutmegs, and cassia.

Frosting for Spice Cake.

Whites of four eggs, two cups of granulated sugar. Flavor with cassia.

Sunday Service.

Rev. William H. Bolster of Dorchester, Mass., preached an excellent sermon in Music Hall, August 23d. His text was taken from II. Corinthians, chapter 4, verse 18: "While we look not at the things which are seen, but at the things which are not seen: for the things which are seen are temporal; but the things which are not seen are eternal." The hall was well filled, as it always is when the Rev. Mr. Bolster preaches.

Picnic.

August 25th, Miss Ricker gave a picnic to a few of her friends at the Mansion House. The party took "The Blaine" and went to Dry Mills, a distance of 7½ miles. It included Mrs. Read, Mrs. Rawson, Mrs. Pulsifer, Mrs. Kuntz, Miss Campbell, Miss Rogers, Miss Fuller, Miss Mary Marsh, Miss Margaret Thurston, Mr. Keene, Mr. De Wint, Mr. Wampole, Mr. Edmund Kuntz, Mr. Read, Mr. Dayton Voorhees, Mr. Robert Marsh, and Arthur Marsh. The party returned at six o'clock after a pleasant outing.

Recollections of My First Visit to Poland Springs.

Rev. T. A. Dwyer.

"BEAUTIFUL! beautiful!" This is the ejaculation that is voiced by the stranger who, for the first time, wends his way along the hilly road that leads from Danville Junction to Poland Springs. The encircling mountains make him feel that he is now within a fortification where all the busy noises of the world are shut out, and where the bustle and hum of business life cannot penetrate. "This is rest—complete rest!" he says to himself as he takes another look at the girdling landscape, made vocal by the songs of sweet-singing-birds.

But now, as his advancement on the journey changes the scene, he catches a faint glimpse of a majestic palace, as it were, crowning one of the hills like the princely home of some great potentate. Clearer and clearer it becomes, and with the increasing clearness is seen the symmetry of its lines, its angles, and turrets. If he asks what the meaning of such a structure, so far away from the busy city and the haunts of men, the answer to his question will depend largely upon the person of whom he asks it. Some farmer lad might simply tell him that it is the Poland Spring Hotel. But if he should ask one of the guests, whom perchance he meets strolling about the grounds,—some grateful guest, bubbling over with happiness for the boon of fully-restored health,—he might receive a reply something like this: "That palatial building, sir, is a monument to the integrity and zeal of the Ricker Brothers." The reply evokes another question from the curious stranger: "Who are the Ricker Brothers?" The guest, if well acquainted with the worthy gentlemen, might give a satisfactory answer even to this question; might tell the eager inquirer how that name, Ricker, has in its tone the ring of ancient lineage; how it had its birth among the hills and plains of old Saxony, and was once claimed by many a noble knight, who bore with the name the family motto written on his breastplate: "Sapientia Donum Dei"— "Wisdom is the Gift of God"—worthy motto of a worthy family.

The guest might continue to relate, as the stranger becomes interested, that in later years, when the old-time chivalry of Europe passed away, and the members of loyal Saxon families became a scattered people, two brothers, George and Maturin Ricker, came to our shores about the middle of the seventeenth century and settled at Dover, N. H. From these brothers sprung the Rickers of Poland Springs.

Now the story is told. The stranger enters and sees that the interior of the great building is worthy of the beauty of its exterior, and he abides a while to rest and recuperate. The genial spirit that exists among the guests, making them like one great family, tells him to feel "at home."

There is a charm about the place that seems indescribable. Days come and go and the guest never wearies of the same faces or the same scenes. Of all dreamy delights that of viewing the peaks of the surrounding hills of Poland, all bathed in the soft glows of a golden sunset, is to the lover of nature, surely, one of the greatest. I remember, particularly, such a glorious scene which I beheld with delight one evening during my stay at the hotel. Not only were the hill-tops radiant with the splendor, but a lake in one of the vales was flushed with the reddened light. I should have liked it to last for hours; it was the sort of scene in which one could most readily forget his own existence and feel melted into the general life of God's creation. The words which the genial Irish poet, Tom Moore, so fittingly wrote of the Vale of Avoca could be applied as well to Poland Springs:

"In that Eden of the West
Angels fold their wings to rest."

Or those other lines of his:

"Angels often wandering there
Doubt if Eden were more fair."

Ineffable, too, are the influences of hospitality that bless the place and give it the warmth of the "home sanctuary." You need not be more than a week in the house before the idea of a hotel recedes entirely from your mind, and the great structure becomes transformed by your feelings into a reflection of the generous, kind hearts of the Ricker Brothers, who are untiring in their efforts to please their guests. That their efforts meet with a responsive gratitude is proven by the fact that the guests return year after year and never weary or grow tired. Their summer home seems annually to hold out some new fascination for them.

As an evidence of the place the Ricker Brothers and their hotel hold in the hearts of the representative people of our country, let me quote here two letters I received from two of my clerical brothers, who are well known throughout New England not only as distinguished scholars and preachers, but as men of influence and high social standing. Both the letters were received by me during my stay at Poland Springs. I quote them because I feel they will be of interest to all the guests of the hotel. The first is from Rev. A. J. Patterson, D.D.

Isles of Shoals, August 1, 1896.

Dear Bro. Dwyer:

I am glad you have found a home at the best summer place in the world! Remember me with a great deal of regard to my good, kind friends, the Ricker Brothers. Drink of the water each day, and remember, that if my life for the past twenty years has been of any worth to the world, it is, under God, through the healing virtues of that spring.

With sincere respect and affection, I am very truly yours,

A. J. PATTERSON.

The second is from Rev. Almon Gunnison, D.D., pastor of the First Universalist Church, Worcester, Mass. :

WORCESTER, August 4, 1896.

Dear Bro. Dwyer:

I am very glad to learn that you are at Poland Springs. A few years ago I was there with my family spending I think six weeks. I had a severe kidney trouble, and had grave doubts of my recovery. The Ricker Brothers were very kind to me. I wrote several articles about the Spring, and have sent, I cannot tell how many, people there. It is one of the most delightful spots in the world, and the Spring is the fountain of perpetual youth that the old Spaniard sought for. Give my kindest regards to Mr. Ricker.

Yours with affectionate esteem,

ALMON GUNNISON.

These words are few, but they will always express much to the reader who knows anything of the character of the men who utter them. They are instances of the thousands of people all over the land who have found health and happiness at Poland Springs, and who lift their voices to-day to call the names of Ricker and Poland blessed.

Lecture and Sunday-School.

Professor Greer of Boston lectured in Music Hall, August 26th, on Mark Twain's "Innocents Abroad." A collection was taken of $5.25, which Professor Greer kindly gave to the Hillside Sunday-school.

This Sunday-school was organized January 5, 1896, by Miss Sarah Ricker, Miss Pamela Leonard, and Miss Grace Hall, for the benefit of the children at Poland Springs. It opened with nineteen scholars, and closed June 28th, with twenty-seven. A little library was formed and forty books donated by kind friends. There are four teachers, and the school will re-open on September 20th.

Dinner Party.

August 23d, Mr. and Mrs. Van Zandt, of the Mansion House, gave a dinner party in honor of Mr. and Mrs. Ross Campbell. The table was artistically decorated by Mr. B. J. Gallagher with Early Dawn sweet peas and choice ferns. The party included Miss Frames, Miss Mary Marsh, Miss Fuller, Mr. Read, and Mr. Harry Wampole.

Cyclist Column.

A CYCLER'S EPITAPH.

[L. A. W.]

A burning sun,
A century run,
And then iced drinks galore;
A sudden chill,
A doctor's bill,
And life's brief spin was o'er.

Join the L. A. W.

We want good roads—bicycle roads.

A good wheel is a splendid servant, a kind friend, and a pleasant companion.

If the road is kept good in front of every one's house, it will be good in front of everybody's house.

THE FLIGHT OF ROMANCE.

[New York Sun.]

I used to know a quiet lane
Where lovers oft would stray
And whisper tender vows of love
When twilight closed the day.

No more this shady, cool retreat
Is sought by couples shy,
Since every novice in the town
Goes there his wheel to try.

FRANK CARLOS GRiFFiTH, } EDITORS.
NETTiE M. RiCKER,

PUBLISHED EVERY SUNDAY MORNING DURING THE MONTHS
OF JULY, AUGUST, AND SEPTEMBER, IN THE INTERESTS OF

POLAND SPRiNGS AND iTS ViSiTORS.

All contributions relative to the guests of Poland Springs
will be thankfully received.

To insure publication, all communications should reach the
editors not later than Wednesday preceding day of issue.

All parties desiring rates for advertising in the HILL-TOP
should write the editors for same.

The subscription price of the HILL-TOP is $1.00 for the
season, post-paid. Single copies will be mailed at 10c. each.

Address,

"EDITORS HILL-TOP,"
Poland Spring House,
South Poland, Maine.

PRINTED AT JOURNAL OFFICE, LEWISTON.

Sunday, August 30, 1896.

Editorial.

THIS is the last Sunday of the summer
months, and every out-of-door pursuit may
now be indulged in freely without the accompaniment of the pests of the air which a warmer
season entails.

Mosquitoes have presented their bills for the
last time and will now fold up their tents and
migrate southward. The mighty and ubiquitous
fly is enjoying his final buzz with the guests,
making appointments for another season, doubtless, before taking to his place of concealment,
from which it is to be hoped he may not be able
to find his way out.

Now golf, fish, hunt, play tennis to your
heart's content; ride, drive, walk, and enjoy your
spin on the "bike," and realize that the beauties
of nature are seen to perfection in the lovely
month of September and from the hill-top at
Poland Springs.

The nights will be charmingly cool and comfortable and the evenings afford full enjoyment
for the friendly games or the tripping of the light
fantastic toe; and when that is done sleep will
woo you to a calm and refreshing repose.

What is lovelier than the country in autumn,
when the fruit and grain is ripening and the
harvest is being gathered in? The lingering
harvest moon makes the night brilliant with its
light, and what more delightful than a drag ride
at such a time, with the moon for an arc lamp
and the sound of the horn echoing among the hills?

Even if there were to be a cool or a rainy day,
the big open fire-places will glow with a cheerful
warmth and all will be merry as a marriage bell.

Stay through the autumn.

Musical Programme.

SUNDAY EVENING, AUGUST 30, 1896, 8.15.

1. Overture—Zampa.		Herold.
2. Violin Solo—Romanza.		Svendson.
Mazurka.		Wienieawski.
Mr. Daniel Kuntz.		
3. Selection from Don Giovanni.		Mozart.
4. Flute Solo—Andante and Rondo (from Concerto).		Popp.
Mr. A. Brooke.		
5. Piano Solo.		
Mr. Edmund Kuntz.		
6. Selection from Martha.		Flotow.

White Mountain Coaching Parade.

Mount Pleasant House brake; colors, dark
and light green; six black horses, gold-mounted
harness; driver, Ned Howland. Party: Dr. and
Mrs. Blake White, Mrs. Marion Van Duyn, Miss
Pepin, New York; Mrs. K. H. Carpenter, Miss
Cole, Miss Foster, Brooklyn; Mr. S. Delbert, Jr.,
Miss Delbert, Mr. W. P. Newhall, Miss Anna P.
Newhall, Philadelphia; Miss Guild, Boston; Miss
Helen M. Potter, Providence.

Open "Poland wagon"; colors, dark and light
green; six bay horses, gold-mounted harnesses;
driver, Clarke Allen. Party: Miss Helen Guild,
Miss Elizabeth Leavitt, Boston; Miss Florence
Russell, Hartford, Conn.; Miss Ethel Carney,
Miss Alice Clarke, Miss Annie L. Edmands, Miss
Helen Hunt, Miss H. L. Harris, Portland; Miss
Alice Ashley, Norwood, N. Y.; Miss Edith
Tilghman, Miss Abbie White, Miss Mattie White,
New York; Miss Helen F. Condon, Brooklyn.

Eight-passenger surrey; medley of college
flags; four chestnut horses; gold-mounted harness;
driver, Charlie Porter. Party: Mr. Louis Emmes,
Mr. Ernest Emmes, Mr. W. J. Ross, Mr. Howard
Ives, Mr. O. M. Harris, Boston; Mr. Arthur
Boyd, Mr. W. B. Boyd, New Brunswick, N. J.;
Mr. H. Fuguet, Philadelphia.

Helen M. Knowlton.

This lady is a daughter of the late Hon. J. S. C. Knowlton of Worcester, Mass. Trained in early life as a journalist, she studied art as a recreation. A pupil of William Morris Hunt, she compiled two volumes of his "Talks on Art," and also published a hand-book, "Hints to Pupils in Drawing and Painting."

She has long been a teacher of art in Boston, studying for a while with Frank Duveneck. Her work embraces chiefly portraits and landscapes, and she has exhibited in Boston, New York, Philadelphia, and Chicago.

Miss Knowlton's works in the Poland Spring Gallery are seven in number and are 71 to 77 inclusive. She is an artist of very excellent attainments, and her works find favor in all galleries. "Willows" and "August Morning" are two of her best works here.

Miss Knowlton is considered one of our best teachers of art, and her studio, 17 Harcourt Building, Boston, is a delightful place to visit.

An Episcopal clergyman's wife living in southern Texas sends to Mrs. Hiram Ricker a large quantity of Mexican drawn work. Mrs. Ricker will be glad to show it to all who will call at her cottage. It is charity work and the prices are very reasonable.

Children's Column.

Happiness is not in 'what we take, but what we give.

Two Mothers in Lincoln Park Zoo.

EACH HAS TWINS TO CARE FOR. ONE IS A LEOP-
ARDESS, THE OTHER A MOUNTAIN LIONESS.

[From the Chicago Tribune.]

There are two mothers at Lincoln Park, and each has twins to care for. The mothers are neighbors, but their natures are antipodal. One is a leopardess and the other is a mountain lioness. There is not a trace of difference in the action of their cubs. They play all day long, run rough shod over their mothers, and do not always pull their claws within the velvet when they slap each other with their paws.

The leopard mother's conduct is that of constant protest. Her ears are always back, her teeth are ever showing, and her growl is ceaseless. She will sit on her haunches while both cubs run up her body, as a jumper runs up a springboard, to leap from her head to catch the leaves which have found their way into the top of the cage from an overhanging bough. The youngsters invariably fall back square upon their mother's back, sorely testing the strength of her spine. She will allow this rough play for half an hour, never for an instant ceasing her snarling. When the cubs turn attention to the maternal tail for a plaything, she lies down and growls at the spectators.

Occasionally the mother, with ears still back and a savage light in her eyes, will completely encircle the neck of one of her offspring with her great jaws, but she never closes down hard. She appears to think : "If I did my duty by you I would end the misery of captivity for you, but maternal love is too strong."

The mountain lioness in the next cage takes the rough usage of her offspring with a meekness of expression which is the more striking by its forcible contrast with the countenance of her neighbor. Her ears are bitten, her tail pulled, and her sides scratched by her young, and she returns the ill usage with a caress. The lioness has the characteristic hatred of the cat family for water, yet smilingly she lies quiet while the cubs, one on either side of the drinking place, dash the water from the pan with their paws until her hide is soaked with the flying shower. The operation is precisely similar to that in which boys indulge when in swimming.

The mountain lioness regards the throngs of humanity which daily press against the railing with a look in which lurks no malice. For this mother was born in captivity.

Miss Marie Henderson of New Orleans is a guest at the Mansion House.

Miss Marguerite Ricker has returned from Augusta, where she has been visiting for a few weeks.

Miss Maud M. Colomy and Miss Effie A. Colomy are visiting friends in Boston. They left by steamer, August 25th, and will return in two weeks.

Monday, August 24th, a golf tournament took place between the following : Masters Dayton Voorhees, Eben Judd, Lester Gilbert, Robert Marsh, and Austin Palmer. Robert Marsh won the first prize, a golf stick ; he made 111 strokes. Eben Judd won the second prize, two golf balls ; he made 113 strokes. Lester Gilbert won the third prize, a golf ball ; he made 127 strokes.

Mr. and Mrs. J. H. Connois of Lynn, Mass., are guests at the Mansion House.

Edward G. Wyckoff, vice-president of the Wyckoff, Seamans & Benedict Co., manufacturers of the Remington Typewriter, is a guest at the Poland Spring House.

Miss Katherine Ricker, the well-known contralto singer of Boston, is here for a few days. Her coming is always anticipated with much pleasure, she being a great personal favorite, and her vocal efforts afford the greatest enjoyment to all.

New Books.

FROM JUDGE HORATIO ROGERS.

Mary Dyer of Rhode Island, the Quaker Martyr that was Hanged on Boston Common; by Horatio Rogers.

FROM J. DAYTON VAN VOORHEES.

Trooper Ross and Signal Butte; by Capt. Charles King, U. S. A.
The Thirsty Sword, by Robert Leighton.

FROM MRS. R. G. FELTUS.

Thelma; by Marie Corelli.

FROM JOHN C. PAIGE.

Celebrated Crimes; by Alexandre Dumas. 3 vols.
Adam Johnstone's Son; by F. Marion Crawford.
The Master Mosaic Workers; by George Sand.
This Goodly Frame, the Earth; by Francis Tiffany.
A Voyage to Vikingland; by Thomas Sedgwick Steele.
Kokoro; by Lafcadio Hearn.
Venezuela; by William Eleroy Curtis.
Our English Cousins; by Richard Harding Davis.
Red Men and White; by Owen Wister.
The Old Settler, The Squire, and Little Peleg; by Ed. Mott.
Oliver Wendell Holmes, Life and Letters; by John T. Morse, Jr. 2 vols.
Josephine, Empress of the French; by Frederick A. Ober.
Personal Recollections of Joan of Arc; by Mark Twain.
Pushing to the Front; by Orison Swett Marden.
Rome; by Emile Zola. 2 vols.
Jacques Damour; by Emile Zola.
Pierre and His People; by Gilbert Parker.
When Valmond Came to Pontiac; by Gilbert Parker.
The Trespasser; by Gilbert Parker.
Mrs. Gerald; by Marie Louise Pool.
Against Human Nature; by Marie Louise Pool.
Briseis; by William Black.
Highland Cousins; by William Black.
A Connecticut Yankee in King Arthur's Court; by Mark Twain.
King Noanett; by F. J. Stinson.
A Lady of Quality; by Frances Hodgson Burnett.
As the Wind Blows; by Eleanor Merton.
A Humble Enterprise; by Ada Cambridge.
The Picture of Las Cruces; by Christian Reid.
The Mystery of Witch Face Mountain; by Charles Egbert Craddock.
Samantha in Europe; by Marietta Holley.
Centuries Apart; by Edward T. Bouve.
When Love is Done; by Ethel Davis.
Black Diamonds; by Maurus Jokai.
The Crimson Sign; by S. R. Keightley.
Tom Grogan; by F. Hopkinson Smith.
The Red Cockade; by Stanley J. Weyman.
Bunch Grass Stories; by Mrs. Lindon W. Bates.
Doctor Warrick's Daughters; by Rebecca Harding Davis.
The Damnation of Theron Ware; by Harold Frederic.
The Village Watch-Tower; by Kate Douglas Wiggin.
Zoraida; by William C. Queux.
An Army Wife; by Capt. Charles King, U. S. A.
A Daughter of the Tenements; by Edward W. Townsend.
Time's Revenges; by David Christie Murray.
Cinderella, and Other Stories; by Richard Harding Davis.
The Honour of Savelli; by S. Levett Yeats.
From One Generation to Another; by Henry Seton Merriman.
My Fire Opal; by Sarah Warner Brooks.
A House-Boat on the Styx; by John Kendrick Bangs.
Madelon; by Mary E. Wilkins.
A Singular Life; by Elizabeth Stuart Phelps.
The Under Side of Things; by Lillian Bell.
A House of Cards; by Alice S. Wolf.
The Gypsy Christ; by William Sharp.
The Ebb Tide; by Robert Louis Stevenson.
Amos Judd; by J. A. Mitchell.

FROM MRS. M. E. HILDRETH.

A Singular Life; by Elizabeth Stuart Phelps.
The Gates Ajar; by Elizabeth Stuart Phelps.
Beyond the Gates; by Elizabeth Stuart Phelps.

FROM MRS. S. W. KRENK.

The True Christian Religion; by Emanuel Swedenborg. 3 vols.
Heaven and Hell; by Emanuel Swedenborg. 1 vol.

FROM JOHN P. WOODBURY.

Buddhism in Translations; by Henry Clarke Warren.

FROM ?

Cinderella, and other Stories; by Richard Harding Davis.

Mr. and Mrs. J. A. Townsend of Bay Ridge, N. Y., are spending a few weeks with us here.

Guests at Poland Spring House

AUGUST 26, 1896.

Leroy H. Anderson	Princeton, N. J.
Mrs. L. Beard	Brooklyn.
Mr. and Mrs. H. S. Beard	Brooklyn.
Mr. Joseph A. Brown	Boston.
Miss Belle G. Brown	Boston.
Dr. and Mrs. Geo. Brett	Boston.
Mr. and Mrs. F. H. Browne	Waltham.
Mr. and Mrs. N. A. Baldwin	New Haven.
Mr. Wm. A. Bigelow	New York.
Mrs. B. Babcock	New York.
Miss Babcock	New York.
Mrs. Jacob P. Bates	Boston.
Mr. and Mrs. H. O. Bright	Cambridge.
Mr. and Mrs. Nelson Bartlett	Boston.
Mr. E. N. Briggs	Saginaw, Mich.
Mrs. Wm. Berri	Brooklyn.
Walter Berri	Brooklyn.
Herbert Berri	Brooklyn.
Mrs. Beylle	Philadelphia.
W. F. Buckley	New York.
W. H. Bolster	Boston.
Mr. and Mrs. A. Charles Barclay	Philadelphia.
Mrs. J. F. Beckwith	Savannah.
Miss Madeline Barnes	Brookline, Mass.
Mr. and Mrs. P. H. Bathydt	New York.
Mrs. B. L. Burt	Taunton, Mass.
Mr. and Mrs. G. C. Currier	New York.
Miss Lora Chamberlain	Norwich, Ct.
Mrs. Agnes S. Curtis	New York.
Mr. and Mrs. Geo. W. Coleman	Boston.
Mr. Andrew R. Culver	Brooklyn.
Mr. and Mrs. F. W. Carpenter	Providence.
Miss Julia Carpenter	Providence.
Mr. and Mrs. C. C. Corbin	Webster, Mass.
W. H. Chappall	Chicago.
Miss Chappall	Chicago.
Mrs. Z. Chandler	Detroit, Mich.
Mrs. B. B. Claxton	Philadelphia.
George F. Curtis	Boston.
Miss F. H. Curtis	Boston.
Mr. and Mrs. Robt. Dornan	Philadelphia.
Mrs. Wm. C. Dunton	New York.
Miss C. S. Duer	New Haven.
Mrs. N. C. Dickerson	New York.
Mrs. J. R. Darling	New York.
Mrs. S. C. Dizer	Boston.
Mrs. W. Davis	New York.
Mr. and Mrs. Andrew J. Dotger	South Orange, N. J.
Mr. and Mrs. James H. Eddy	New Britain, Conn.
Miss Bessie M. Eddy	New Britain, Conn.
Miss Fletcher	Boston.
Mrs. J. D. Fessenden	New York.
Gen. Chas. E. Furlong	New York.
Mr. and Mrs. D. H. Field	Brockton, Mass.
Mrs. M. C. Ferand	New York.
Mrs. R. G. Feltus	Philadelphia.
Miss Laura A. Farnham	Boston.
Mr. and Mrs. F. C. Frye	Boston.
Annie L. Fall	Boston.
Mrs. J. R. Farnham	Waltham.
Mrs. Louis R. Fox	Philadelphia.
Mrs. Fenton	Baltimore.
Miss Jean B. Fenton	Baltimore.
Mr. and Mrs. A. L. Gondran	New York.
Mr. John Goldthwaite	Boston.
Miss E. B. Goldthwaite	Boston.
Mrs. L. M. Gale	Washington.
Miss Olive Gale	Washington.
Mrs. F. A. Gilbert	Brookline.
Miss Gilbert	Brookline.
Miss Ruth Gilbert	Brookline.
Mr. Lester Gilbert	Brookline.
Mrs. A. Gilbert	Plainfield, N. J.
Mrs. George F. Gregory	Brooklyn.
Dr. Morton Grinnell	New York.
Mr. and Mrs. T. Gilman	Montreal.
Miss Gordon	Lakewood, N. J.
C. B. Gordon	Lakewood, N. J.
Thomas M. Gale	Washington, D. C.
Mr. and Mrs. J. F. Godley	Trenton, N. J.
Miss Gregory	Brooklyn.
Miss Howell	Baltimore.
Miss Hyatt	Baltimore.
Mr. and Mrs. S. B. Hubbard	Jacksonville.
Mrs. W. W. Hartwell	Plattsburgh, N. Y.
Mr. and Mrs. John R. Hoxie	Chicago.
Miss Anna Hoxie	Chicago.
Mr. and Mrs. Horace Hunt	New York.
Mr. and Mrs. L. Hurlburt	Brooklyn.
Mrs. M. B. Hoffman	New York.
Mr. and Mrs. Hudson Hoagland	New York.
Mr. and Mrs. E. Holmes	New York.
Mr. and Mrs. E. T. Holmes and family	New York.
Miss Hornel	Philadelphia.
Miss Anna Havens	Boston.
Mrs. M. E. Hildreth	Boston.
Miss Alma Hildreth	Boston.
Mr. and Mrs. A. Harkness	Providence.
Wilford L. Hooper	Boston.
Col. Joseph A. Ingalls and family	Boston.
Mrs. W. H. Inman	New York.
Miss W. L. Inman	New York.
Mrs. Julian James	Washington.
Dr. E. N. Judd	Greenwich, Ct.
J. J. Kennedy	New Brighton.
Mrs. E. A. Knapp	New York.
Mr. and Mrs. W. W. Kimball	Chicago.
Miss S. S. Kimball	Bar Harbor.
Miss Bessie Lippincott	Philadelphia.
Rev. and Mrs. W. P. Lewis	Philadelphia.
Mrs. B. C. Lake	New Haven.
Miss Leland	New York.
James D. Laird	San Francisco.
Mr. and Mrs. Amos R. Little	Philadelphia.
Mr. and Mrs. B. Lemann and family	New Orleans.
Miss Cora W. Lumbert	Brockton.
Mr. James H. Lake	Boston.
Mr. J. Wilson Leakin	Baltimore.
Mr. and Mrs. Thomas P. Langdon	Baltimore.
Mr. and Mrs. B. N. Lapham	Providence.
Mr. and Mrs. E. H. Linley	St. Louis.
Mrs. J. W. Merrill	Boston.
Miss Merrill	Boston.
Mr. A. D. McClellan	Washington.
Mrs. Paul F. Mehel	New Brighton.
Henry P. Morrison	New York.
Mr. and Mrs. J. S. Martin	New York.
Byron P. Moulton	Philadelphia.
Mr. and Mrs. T. B. M. Mason	Washington.
Mrs. T. B. Myers	Washington.
Mrs. Jno. H. Maginnis	New Orleans.
Mr. Jno. H. Maginnis	New Orleans.
Mrs. A. Murry	Washington.
Miss A. G. Miller	Brooklyn.
Dr. and Mrs. Ira L. Moore	Boston.
Mrs. J. T. Montgomery	Philadelphia.
Mrs. B. P. Moulton	Rosemont, Pa.
Mr. and Mrs. A. R. Mitchell	Newtonville.
Mrs. Christine Marburg	Baltimore.
The Misses Marburg	Baltimore.
Mr. and Mrs. John T. Martin	New York.
E. B. Mead	Greenwich, Ct.
Mr. and Mrs. J. L. Nason	Boston.
Miss Nason	Boston.
Mr. and Mrs. W. T. Ness	Boston.
Miss Lucy P. Newhall	Philadelphia.
Harry L. Nason	Boston.
Mrs. H. S. Osgood	Portland.
Mr. and Mrs. Josiah Oakes	Malden, Mass.
J. P. Orr	Cincinnati.
Lowell Palmer	Brooklyn.
Miss E. A. Prall	New York.
Mrs. J. A. Pettee	New York.
Miss Anne J. Pecker	Boston.
Miss Mary L. Pecker	Boston.
Mr. and Mrs. Fulton Paul	Hudson, N. Y.
Mr. and Mrs. Henry U. Palmer	Brooklyn.
Masters Austin and Chester Palmer	Brooklyn.

Mrs. M. E. Parsons	Boston.
Miss A. J. Pomeroy	New York.
W. H. Peterson	Boston.
S. S. Riker	New York.
Miss Marion Richardson	Boston.
Mrs. Runyon	Plainfield, N. J.
Mrs. J. O. Rhines	New York.
Mr. and Mrs. Augustus Richardson	Boston.
Miss Richardson	Boston.
Allen M. Rogers	New York.
Mr. and Mrs. H. A. Rogers	New York.
Miss May Rogers	New York.
Mrs. E. J. Robinson	Boston.
Miss Roberts	Philadelphia.
Moses W. Richardson	Boston.
Mrs. M. E. Richards	New York.
Mr. J. Olcutt Rhines	New York.
Miss Randolph	Plainfield, N. J.
Miss Emma Rods	Philadelphia.
D. T. Rines	Portland.
R. H. Rines	Boston.
Mr. and Mrs. James	Randell, N. Y.
Miss K. M. Ricket	Falmouth.
Rev. and Mrs. W. E. C. Smith	Boston.
Dr. and Mrs. E. H. Smith	Boston.
Mr. and Mrs. H. C. Swain and son	New York.
Mr. and Mrs. J. E. Spenser	New York.
Mr. and Mrs. S. R. Small	Portland.
Mrs. S. Skaats	New York.
Miss Slade	New York.
Mrs. Mary J. Spencer	Brooklyn.
Dr. and Mrs. C. C. Schuyler	Plattsburgh, N. Y.
Miss Stinson	Philadelphia.
Miss Florence Stinson	Philadelphia.
Mr. and Mrs. A. T. Salter	Washington.
Mr. and Mrs. Joseph W. Sandford	Plainfield, N. J.
Mr. Samuel Shethar	New York.
Mr. and Mrs. J. B. Sawyer	Dover, N. H.
Mr. and Mrs. S. B. Stinson	Philadelphia.
Mr. and Mrs. E. P. Smith	New York.
Mrs. G. W. Simpson	Brooklyn.
Miss B. C. Simpson	Brooklyn.
Miss Mabel Simpson	Brooklyn.
Mrs. A. D. Stoines	Worcester.
Mrs. J. Edwin Swift	Philadelphia.
John H. Shottidge	Philadelphia.
Miss L. E. Shottidge	Philadelphia.
Miss F. A. Shottidge	Atlanta.
Mr. and Mrs. H. H. Schaul	Boston.
Mr. and Mrs. C. N. Shaw	Philadelphia.
Mr. and Mrs. C. A. Sparks	Philadelphia.
Miss Sparks	Philadelphia.
Mr. and Mrs. A. Loudon Snowden	Cleveland.
Mr. and Mrs. F. A. Sterling	Montreal.
Miss Smith	New York.
E. H. Shethar	New Haven.
Miss Tillotson	New York.
Miss N. E. Ten Brorck	Boston.
Mrs. Orlando Tompkins	Brooklyn.
Mr. and Mrs. F. E. Taylor	Worcester.
Mr. and Mrs. R. F. Taylor	Worcester.
Miss Emma S. Taylor	Worcester.
Miss Matie L. Taylor	Bay Ridge, N. J.
Mr. and Mrs. J. A. Townsend	Taunton, Mass.
Mrs. A. H. Tetlow	Brooklyn.
Mr. John H. Voorhees	Camden, N. J.
Mr. and Mrs. Peter Van Voorhees	Camden, N. J.
J. D. Van Voorhees	Brookline.
Mr. and Mrs. W. A. Vose	Brookline.
Mr. Geo. A. Vose	Brookline.
Miss Vose	Brooklyn.
Mrs. John H. Voorhees	Brooklyn.
Miss Jessie Voorhees	Washington.
Mrs. G. N. Wilson	Boston.
Mr. and Mrs. F. H. Williams	Boston.
Miss Lizzie A. Williams	So. Amboy, N. J.
Miss R. W. Willets	Troy, N. Y.
Mrs. Chas. Warner	Troy, N. Y.
Miss C. A. Warner	Troy, N. Y.
Miss M. V. Warner	Troy, N. Y.
Miss M. A. Winslow	Philadelphia.
Mr. and Mrs. F. H. Wyeth	

Mr. and Mrs. John P. Woodbury	Boston.
Mrs. J. Reed Whipple	Boston.
Dr. M. C. Wedgwood and Mrs. Wedgwood	Lewiston.
Mr. A. Wentworth	Boston.
Mr. F. R. Wharton	Philadelphia.
Mr. and Mrs. W. S. Wymond	Louisville, Ky.
Miss Wymond	Louisville, Ky.
Mr. and Mrs. J. Stuart White	New York.
Mrs. L. P. Worthington	Doylestown, Pa.
Miss Worthington	Doylestown, Pa.
Mr. N. Whitman	New York.
Mr. and Mrs. E. F. Watkins	Chicago.
Ira W. Wood	Trenton, N. J.
Mrs. S. H. Weeks	Cortland, N. Y.
Miss Weeks	Cortland, N. Y.
Mr. and Mrs. A. R. Wright and son,	Philadelphia.
Mr. and Mrs. John Wales	Brookline.
Miss Watson	Montreal.

An Ab-Original Tale.

BY A SAVAGE.

[Continued.]

One morning David started out
  With arrows and with bow,
And Weeping Cloud upon his hunt
  Resolved with him to go.
Said she, " If there's no other game
  You'll have your deal, you know."

But she got lost as on they sped
  Through field and wood and dale,
She was not looking for a storm,
  And did not heat his hail:
She could not find her lover till
  He was upon her trail.

But suddenly behind a tree
  He drew his bow with care,
And straightway with unerring aim
  His arrow cleaved the air!
He did not hit a rabbit, but
  He shot his lady's hair.

A lass! he cried, is all my joy
  To end in woe like this!
But soon he found she was not hurt;
  She smiled to meet his kiss.
" I'm safe enough, my dear," she said,
  But 'twas an arrow miss.

And he resolved that she should be
  His own, come woe or weal;
That soon before the altar they
  Their vows of love should seal.
Oh, happy time, he thought, when she
  Would share his Indian meal.

Their dream of love was soon dispelled,
  Alas! by war's alarms;
For David joined the volunteers
  From factories, shops, and farms,
And Weeping Cloud was left, although
  Accustomed to bare arms.

She saw her lover, as the troop
  Went marching through the street,
And the applause of thousands made
  Her heart with gladness beat;
She knew that his small arms would soon
  Accomplish some great feat.

And day by day our hero grew
  In all the soldier graces;
He shunned the company of those
  Who went to naughty places!
Who drank the sutler's whiskey till
  It made them have wry faces.

[To be continued.]

Arrivals.

POLAND SPRING HOUSE.
FROM AUG. 21 TO AUG. 28, 1896.

Anderson, Mr. and Mrs. Leroy H.	Princeton, N. J.
Arnold, Mrs. E. W.	New York.
Arnold, A.	New York.
Bartlett, Mr. and Mrs. Thomas M.	Brooklyn.
Brown, Mrs. Leyman D.	Brooklyn.
Brown, Dr. Lucy Hall	Brooklyn.
Brown, R. G.	Brooklyn.
Browne, F. H.	Waltham.
Bolster, W. H.	Boston.
Boyle, E. J.	Boston.
Boyle, T. F.	Boston.
Barclay, Mr. and Mrs. A. Charles	Philadelphia.
Beckwith, Mrs. I. F.	Savannah.
Bathydt, Mr. and Mrs. P. H.	New York.
Barnes, Miss Madeline	Brookline.
Claxton, Mrs. R. B.	Philadelphia.
Chamberlain, Mr. and Mrs. R. E.	Auburn.
Clark, Mr. and Mrs. L. C.	Detroit.
Clapp, Miss L. H.	Boston.
Curtis, George S.	Boston.
Curtis, Miss F. H.	Boston.
Cram, Miss A.	New York.
Dotger, Mr. and Mrs. A. J.	South Orange, N. J.
Dingley, Mrs.	Lewiston.
Dunham, Florence L.	Boston.
Dunham, Mrs. E. S.	Boston.
Engel, William	Bangor.
Flatley, J. F.	Boston.
Fall, Annie L.	Boston.
Fischer, Bernardo F.	New York.
Fischer, Dr. Charles S., Jr.	New York.
French, C. H.	Chicago.
Farnham, Mrs. J. R.	Waltham.
Fox, Mrs. Louis R.	Philadelphia.
Fenton, Mrs.	Baltimore.
Fenton, Miss Jean B.	Baltimore.
Grinnell, Dr. Morton	New York.
Gilmour, Mr. and Mrs. T.	Toronto.
Galaian, C. E.	Hartford.
Gale, Thomas M.	Washington.
Godley, Mr. and Mrs. J. F.	Trenton.
Harrington, Mrs. John M.	Lewiston.
Hudson, Mrs. C. H.	Lynn.
Hill, W. L.	Boston.
Hooper, Wilford Lawrence	Boston.
Hinckley, G. W.	Boston.
Hill, Mrs.	Lawrence.
Hill, Miss	Lawrence.
Hanscom, O. M.	Boston.
Hersey, Mrs. A. L.	Oxford.
Hersey, Heloise E.	Oxford.
Jones, Leslie E.	Bangor.
Judd, Dr. E. N.	Greenwich, R. I.
Jordan, Miss	Lakewood, N. J.
Jordan, C. B.	Boston.
Kimball, Mr. and Mrs. W. W.	Chicago.
Kimball, Miss S. S.	Bar Harbor.
Kelsey, Mrs. S. B.	Portland.
Leonard, Oliver B.	Plainfield, N. J.
Leonard, Elizabeth Marsh	Plainfield, N. J.
Long, C. P.	Wilkesbarre.
Linley, Mr. and Mrs. E. H.	St. Louis.
Lord, Mrs. Frederick H.	Lynn.
Lewis, Robert	Boston.
Martin, Miss S.	Somerville.
Munroe, Mr. and Mrs. W. N.	Auburn.
Middleton, Mr. and Mrs. Samuel W.	Philadelphia.
Millet, A. Q.	Auburn.
Mead. E. B.	Greenwich, R. I.
Maybury, Dr. and Mrs. William J.	Saco.
Mack, Mr. and Mrs. Thomas	Boston.
Nash, Mrs. C. J.	Lewiston.
Nason, Harry L.	Boston.
Nichols, Miss C. A.	Lynn.
Osgood, H. S.	Portland.
Orr, J. P.	Cincinnati.
Pollard, Miss H. W.	Lowell.
Penley, Ferd.	Auburn.
Peterson, W. H.	Boston.
Plummer, Mrs. H. S.	Portland.
Robertson, Miss	Brooklyn.
Reynolds, J. A.	Cambridgeport.
Rose, Mr. and Mrs. George	New Orleans.
Rods, Miss Emma	Philadelphia.
Rines, D. T.	Portland.
Rines, R. H.	Portland.
Ricker, Miss K. M.	Falmouth.
Small, S. R.	Portland.
Stevens, Samuel	Bangor.
Shaw, Mr. and Mrs. C. N.	Boston.
Staples, E. E.	Boston.
Sparks, Mr. and Mrs. C. A.	Philadelphia.
Sparks, Miss Amelia	Philadelphia.
Swett, Mrs. G. L.	Portland.
Sallet, Miss	Philadelphia.
Snowden, Mr. and Mrs. A. Louden	Philadelphia.
Sax, Miss	New York.
Sterling, Mr. and Mrs. F. A.	Cleveland.
Staples, Mr. and Mrs. Arthur G.	Lewiston.
Smith, Miss	Montreal.
Tuttle, N. D.	Croton on Hudson, N. Y.
Tuttle, Miss	Croton on Hudson, N. Y.
Taylor, Miss Emma S.	Worcester.
Taylor, Mr. and Mrs. R. F.	Worcester.
Taylor, Miss Marie Q.	Worcester.
Townsend, Mr. and Mrs. J. A.	Bay Ridge, N. Y.
Van Tassel, Mr. and Mrs. E. D.	Boston.
Watkins, Mr. and Mrs. E. T.	Chicago.
Wood, Ira W.	Trenton.
Wood, William P.	Trenton.
Wood, Miss Ellen P.	Trenton.
Weeks, Dr. and Mrs. S. H.	Portland.
Weeks, Miss	Portland.
Watson, Mr. and Mrs. M. B.	Auburn.
Wright, Mr. and Mrs. A. R.	Philadelphia.
Wales, Mr. and Mrs. John	Brookline.
Walker, Mrs. H. M. L.	Philadelphia.
Walker, Miss A. M. E.	Philadelphia.
Wolf, Mr. and Mrs. Benjamin	Philadelphia.
Wyckoff, Mr. and Mrs. E. G.	Ithaca.
Ward, Mr. and Mrs. F. L.	Boston.
Watson, Miss	Montreal.
Zanoni	Montreal.

MANSION HOUSE.
AUGUST 21 TO 28, 1896.

Forster, Charles	Portland.
Hayes, H. W.	Portland.
Henderson, Mr. and Mrs. Sam, Jr.	New Orleans.
Jones, Leslie E.	Bangor.
Page, J. E.	Jamaica Plain.
Pulsifer, John R.	Rochester.
Runyon, R.	Boston.

Croquet.

The Rev. William H. Bolster and Mr. Dan. Field have played seven games of croquet against Mr. Holmes, Jr., and Mr. Williams. Mr. Field and Mr. Bolster have won five out of the seven. The games have been very close and very enjoyable.

Tid-Bits.

Great business.

Oysters can be E10 2sday.

Come again next summer.

HILL-TOP boomed last week.

The last rose of summer to-morrow.

1,291 volumes in the library, August 24th.

Big offers are numerous now
  To the beauty at sweet sixteen;
Big golfers with faces sun-burned
  Find ease in Hinds' Honey and Cream.

Mr. and Mrs. W. W. Kimball of Chicago are recent arrivals.

Mr. and Mrs. E. T. Watkins of Chicago are lately registered.

Mr. Thomas M. Gale of Washington, D. C., is a welcome guest.

Dr. Morton Grinnell was a guest of Mr. and Mrs. N. A. Baldwin.

Mr. John R. Pulsifer of Rochester, N. Y., is at the Mansion House.

Mr. O. M. Hanscom of Boston spent August 26th at the Poland Spring House.

Mr. and Mrs. A. Charles Barclay of Philadelphia are at the Poland Spring House.

Mr. and Mrs. George Rose of New Orleans have been spending a few days with Mrs. Maginnis.

Dr. and Mrs. Weeks and Miss Weeks of Portland have been at Poland Springs for a few days.

Mr. and Mrs. Samuel Henderson, Jr., of New Orleans, are spending a few weeks at Poland Springs.

Mrs. John B. Turner's departure from Poland Springs, August 26th, is much regretted by her many friends.

The departure of the Lippincotts on Monday is much regretted. Young Mr. Lippincott was an earnest golfer.

August 24th, Mr. H. C. Swain scored 225, and on the same day Mr. E. H. Smith scored 213—highest numbers this week.

Gen. A. Loudon Snowden and Mrs. Snowden of Philadelphia and Mrs. Fox of Chicago are guests at the Poland Spring House.

The Notman Photographic Company will welcome all guests to their studio, and the specimens of their work there shown are the best known in the art of photography.

The following party—Mr. and Mrs. S. B. Stinson, Mrs. Polhemus, Mr. and Mrs. Robert Dornan, Miss Miller, and Miss Slade—took a brake ride to Oxford, August 25th.

Mrs. Robinson, who is now in her second season here, is accounted very skilled and successful as a masseuse. Guests in need of her services will find her card in another column.

Judge Horatio Rogers, Associate Justice of the Superior Court of Rhode Island, who is stopping at the Mansion House, has presented a work of his, called "Mary Dyer," to the library.

By invitation, Mrs. Griffith passed Tuesday afternoon at the Shakers, and had a most enjoyable time. She was the recipient of many kindly favors and made to feel the full extent of their boundless hospitality and friendly interest.

The one-hour pencil sketch made by Mr. Robert Vonnoh of Miss Greenlees has been much admired. Mr. Vonnoh is so well known in this country that anything from his brush or pencil is of great value. Miss Greenlees is charming, with clear-cut features, and the likeness is excellent.

Mr. Henry U. Palmer of Brooklyn has purchased Adelaide Palmer's fine painting of "Raspberries," No. 98 in the catalogue of the Art Gallery. This picture has received a very great amount of most favorable comment since it has been here. We congratulate both the purchaser and the artist.

The following party—Mr. and Mrs. Voorhees, Miss Voorhees, Mr. and Mrs. Van Zandt, Mrs. Conner, Mr. and Mrs. Keene—took a drive to Oxford, August 25th. It was a typical Poland day, clear and cool. The drive over was delightful, as there was no dust. The little hotel they found neat and very attractive, and Mrs. Keith served them with a good dinner.

Dinner at Oxford.

Mr. and Mrs. Gilbert, Miss Gilbert, Mr. Lester Gilbert, and Miss Freda Gilbert took a drive to Oxford, August 25th, and had dinner at the Oxford Spring Hotel.

THE NEW MOUNT PLEASANT HOUSE,

In the Heart of the White Mountains.

Through Parlor Cars from New York, Boston, and Portland, also from Burlington, Montreal, and Quebec.

The Hotel faces the Grandest Display of Mountain Peaks in America east of the Rocky Mountains. It is lighted throughout by electricity, thoroughly heated by steam, and has an abundance of private and public baths. Its orchestra is made up largely from the Boston Symphony Orchestra. Its table is unsurpassed. Absolutely pure water from an artesian well, 409 feet in solid rock.

IT IS THE NEAREST HOTEL TO MT. WASHINGTON, AND THE TRAIN FOR THE SUMMIT STARTS FROM A STATION ON THE HOTEL GROUNDS.

All Trains, Maine Central Railroad, from Portland to Burlington, Montreal, Quebec, and Lake Champlain stop at the platform close to the House.

Leave Portland 8.45 A.M., arrive Mt. Pleasant House, 12.21 P.M.	O
" " 1.25 P.M., " " " " 5.03 P.M.	O
" " 3.20 P.M., " " " " 7.20 P.M.	O
" " 8.45 P.M., " " " " 11.47 P.M.	O

POST, TELEGRAPH, AND TICKET OFFICE IN THE HOTEL.

ANDERSON & PRICE, of the Hotel Ormond of Florida, Managers.

Address by Wire or mail, "Mount Pleasant House, N. H."

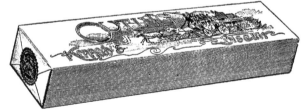

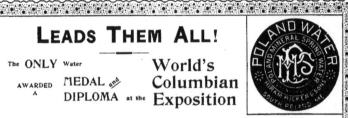
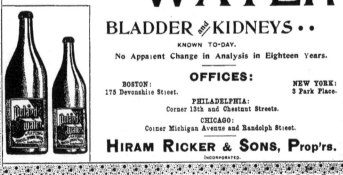

The Hill Top

POLAND SPRINGS, SO. POLAND, ME.

HARRY C. WILKINSON

THE HILL-TOP

VOL. III.   SUNDAY MORNING, SEPTEMBER 13, 1896.   No. 11.

Poland Springs Library.

WHAT is the Poland Springs Library, what was its origin and its purpose?" These are questions frequently asked, no doubt; and perhaps a little explanation here may be of service.

When the Maine State World's Fair Building was re-erected at Poland Springs it was intended to become a Library and Art Building for the convenience of the guests of the Poland Springs Hotels, and a room on the first floor, opening off the Rotunda or Reading-Room, was given over to the

Library, and supplied with a large book-case and such other appurtenances as were thought necessary. .With the building came 175 books which had been donated to the World's Fair Commission, and by them transferred to the new owners. These books, together with 97 volumes contributed by Mrs. J. D. Fessenden, constituted the nucleus of the Library, on the day of the dedication of the building, July 1, 1895, amounting to a little less than three hundred volumes.

Presently other interested guests took up the subject, and occasional books were given, General Augustus P. Martin's gift of 138 standard authors, and Mrs. H. O. Bright's of 75 similar valuable works, being among the number; until at the close of the season, October 15, 1895, there were 854 volumes in the cases, another large case having been added.

During the winter which intervened, and the present season up to September 5th, the contributions of books have raised the number of volumes to 1,412, classified very nearly as follows: Standard, 265; Light Fiction, 233; Historical, 60; Travel, 27; Juvenile, 103; Poetical, 57; Biographical, 57; Bound Magazines, 73; Miscellaneous, 70; Religious, 70; Reference, 31; Public Documents, etc., 358.

There is no printed catalogue, as yet, but the books are conveniently shelved, and when a selection is made a blank form is filled out, the book and slip dated, and no other ceremony required; the guests taking the books to the hotels for a period of seven days if desired. When the library has a much larger growth, a longer period will be granted, but until then it is obviously unfair to permit one person to monopolize a desirable volume for a longer time where the season for reading is so short to many.

All books presented, bear upon the cover a slip stating that fact with the name of the donor, also another with the very few and simple regulations; it being preferred to place every one upon their honor rather than trouble them with rigid rules; and to their credit be it said that up to this time not a volume has been lost or shown any signs of willful abuse. There is no deposit required; there are no fees for the use of books, and no fines, should a book be retained over time.

The Library is open week days from 9 A.M. to 9 P.M., and on Sundays from 10 A.M. to 8.30 P.M. During the period covering July 20th to August 19th inclusive, 1,022 books were taken out, and a like number returned during that time; the smallest number of daily transfers being 32 and the highest 102, which latter was increased on the day following the placing of Mr. John C. Paige's gifts upon the shelves, to 74 taken out and nearly as many returns.

Only one book is permitted to one person, for obvious reasons, considering the size of the Library, and the highest number of books out of the Library on any one day was 161.

Nearly all the books have been gifts of interested guests, only 38 volumes bearing no name as the donor; many of those, however, having been given, but for reasons of their own the donors were not willing for their names to appear.

Below we give a complete list of the contributors to the Library and the amount of their gifts:

Mrs. Herman Adler	1
Mrs. H. O. Bright	75
Mr. Nelson Bartlett	1
Mr. and Mrs. F. J. Bartlett	4
Mrs. J. P. Bates	2
Mrs. Joseph S. Bosworth	3
Mr. George T. Bourne	8
Mr. Edmund S. Clark	1
Mrs. George W. Coleman	1
Mr. M. V. B. Chase	1
Mrs. Edward E. Clark	62
Hon. Henry B. Cleaves	1
Mr. George G. Crowell	2
Mrs. J. C. Conover	1
Mr. George Barker Clarke	1
Mr. William Dickey	17
Mrs. Horace Fassett	4
Mrs. J. D. Fessenden	97
Mrs. A. J. Baker Flint, M.D.	15
Mrs. George H. Fish	1
Mr. R. M. Field	32
Hon. William P. Frye	205
Mrs. R. G. Feltus	1
Mr. Curtis Guild	3
Mr. Robert S. Gardiner	1
Mr. George B. Greel	32
Mrs. L. B. Haskell	51
Mrs. L. Hurlburt	1
Miss E. M. Harris	1
Mr. Everett N. Huggins	3
Mrs. M. E. Hildreth	1
Mrs. John R. Hoxie	4
Dr. Bushrod W. James, A.M., M.D.	1
Mrs. Julian James	4
Mrs. S. W. Keene	6
Mrs. Amos R. Little	16
Mrs. E. J. Lee	2
Dr. E. J. Lee	1
Gen. Augustus P. Martin	241
Hon. H. K. Morrill	53
Mr. Charles A. Mason	1
Mrs. W. Peterson	48
Miss E. A. Prall	2
Mr. Albert W. Paine	2
Mrs. J. A. Pettee	4
Mr. N. Q. Pope	35
Mrs. M. E. Parsons	2
Mr. John C. Paige	61
Miss L. P. Ray	3
Miss T. Rosenheim	3
Judge Horatio Rogers	1
Mr. Allen Merrill Rogers	1
State of Maine	175
Mr. Henry P. Sondheim	1
Mrs. Henry P. Sondheim	2
Shakers of Sabbath-day Lake	1
Mrs. J. B. Sawyer	7
Miss Helen J. Sanborn	1
Miss C. Phelps Stokes	1
Mrs. Morgan Smith	10
Mr. William N. Swain	5
Mr. Albert T. Salter	3
Mrs. Franklin E. Taylor	6
Mrs. Orlando Tompkins	13
Mrs. Henry F. Tapley	1

Mr. J. Dayton Van Voorhees 5
Mr. I. A. Whitcomb 21
Dr. Milton C. Wedgwood 1
Mrs. W. F. Wood 1
Mr. John P. Woodbury 1

This shows 38 ladies as contributors against 31 gentlemen, and the number in volumes to the ladies' credit is 458, while that to the gentlemen aggregates 781.

Our illustration is from a photograph made by the Notman Photograph Co., and is one of the many excellent negatives which they have furnished THE HILL-TOP with during the season.

New Books.

A Gentleman of France; by Stanley J. Weyman.
Unchaperoned; by Helen Riemensnyder.

FROM MISS M. G. DEXTER.
His Honor and a Lady; by Mrs. Everard Cotes.

FROM MISS M. E. FLEMING.
A Lady of Quality; by Frances Hodgson Burnett.
Vashti and Esther.
An Unsatisfactory Lover; by "The Duchess."
Aldath; by Marie Corelli.
Checked Through; by Richard Henry Large.

FROM MRS. JULIAN JAMES.
With Fire and Sword; by Henryk Sienkiewicz.
The Deluge (2 volumes); by "   "
Pan Michael; by "   "

FROM MRS. CRAIGE LIPPINCOTT.
The Madonna of a Day; by L. Dougall.
Jill; by L. T. Meade.
The Story of a Clergyman's Daughter; by W. Heimburg.
The Woodlanders; by Thomas Hardy.

FROM MISS E. A. PRALL.
Saracinesca; by F. Marion Crawford.
Sant' Ilario; by F. Marion Crawford.
Thelma; by Marie Corelli.

FROM MRS. N. E. TEN BROECK.
All Sorts and Conditions of Men; by Walter Besant.
The Black Tulip; by Alexandre Dumas.

FROM MRS. FRANKLIN E. TAYLOR.
Weir of Hermiston; by Robert Louis Stevenson.
The Damnation of Theron Ware; by Harold Frederic.

The Art Gallery.

One last word about pictures. Here you have an art exhibition the equal of any given at your Art Clubs or National Academies, so far as the general average of excellence is concerned, with many names of world-wide fame; others of national fame; and many of great local fame, but whose works are receiving attention and who will become famous. In most instances the works are of a very high order of merit, and in all are excellent.

For the same reasons which apply to nearly everything, the works of artists can be purchased at more reasonable prices now than ever before; but with a return of prosperity these works will rise in price, and it will cost more to adorn the home then than now.

This gallery with its wealth of pictures of all kinds is free, at all times, and the illustrated catalogues are free as well, hence there is no excuse for a neglect in visiting it, it being open from 9 A.M. to 9 P.M. on week days, and from 10 A.M. to 8.30 P.M. on Sundays. In the evening the electric light displays the pictures to better advantage, but at all times they are well worth a visit.

The very excellent painting of "Pond Lilies," by Adelaide Palmer, which was begun at Poland Springs and finished at Piermont, N. H., has been hung in Alcove B. Every lover of art should see it.

Menu.

SOUPS.
Consommé à la Royale.   Puree de Volaille à la Reine.
Olives.   Sliced Cucumbers.
Lobster à la Newburg en Caises.

FISH.
Fried Fillet of Northern White-fish, Sauce d'Uxelles.
Planked Blue-fish, au Madeira.
Sliced Tomatoes.   Potatoes à la Brabanconne.

BOILED.
Boiled Fowl with Pork, au Vin Blanc.
Home-made Pickles.   Chow-Chow.

ROAST.
Sirloin of Beef, Dish Gravy.   Spring Lamb, Brown Sauce.
Rhode Island Buckling.   Orange Marmalade.

ENTREES.
Baked Chicken Pie, New England Style.
Haricot of Mutton a l'Anglaise.
Crême Renversé au Caramel.

VEGETABLES.
Boiled and Mashed Potatoes.   Boiled Sweet Potatoes.
New Squash.   Dandelion Greens.
Native Sweet Corn.   Shelled Beans.   Green Peas.
Buttered Beets.   Stewed Tomatoes.   Steamed Rice.

Roman Punch.
Young Squab on Toast.
Salad à la Russe.
Plain Lettuce.   Dressed Lettuce.
Boned Turkey, Truffled en Aspic.
Pate de Foie Gras.

DESSERT.
English Plum Pudding, Brandy Sauce.
Mountain Dew Pudding, Sea Foam Sauce.
Apple Pie.   Mince Pie.   Vanilla Cream Pie.
Orange Jelly with Whipped Cream.
Lemon Meringue.   Charlotte Russe.
Spice Cake.   White Sponge Cake.   Assorted Cake.
Cup Custard.   Spice Drops.
Philadelphia Ice-Cream.

Apples.   Peaches.   Water-melon.   Bananas.   Pears.
Nuts.   American and Edam Cheese.   Raisins.
Boston Water Saltines and Assorted Crackers.
Tea.   Coffee.

The recipes for all of the above-named dishes have been given during the season of THE HILL-TOP.

Tid=Bits.

Mr. R. G. Feltus of Philadelphia arrived this week.

Mr. Oakes made a fine record in the bowling alley—260.

Mr. C. E. Cameron of Toledo, Ohio, arrived this week.

Mrs. Eugene Hale is spending a few days at Poland Springs.

Mr. and Mrs. Joel Goldthwait of Boston arrived September 3d.

Col. and Mrs. Andrews are at the Poland Spring House.

Dr. Gordon of Portland is a guest at the Poland Spring House.

Dr. William Argyle Watson of New York arrived this week.

Mr. Theodore F. Cogswell of Ipswich is at Poland Springs.

Mrs. Ashe of San Francisco arrived Saturday, September 5th.

Poland Water can be had at 104 Newgate Street, London, E. C.

Col. and Mrs. Ingalls took their departure Saturday, September 5th.

Mrs. A. Hurlburt of Utica, N. Y., is a guest at the Mansion House.

Have you bought a picture? You will never have a better opportunity.

Mr. and Mrs. H. H. Schaul of Atlanta, Ga., are at the Mansion House.

Dr. and Mrs. Daniel McFarlan of Washington, D. C., are at Poland Springs.

Mr. and Mrs. M. F. Atwood of New York are at the Poland Spring House.

Mr. E. D. Barbour of Boston is spending a few days at Poland Springs.

Mr. Thomas Roache of the Western Union is at the Poland Spring House.

Mrs. Robert B. Wade and Miss Trumbull are at the Poland Spring House.

Mr. and Mrs. C. G. Mitchell of Cincinnati are at the Poland Spring House.

Mr. W. H. Chappell and Miss Chappell left Poland Springs, September 8th.

Mr. and Mrs. Joseph B. Ames of Brookline, Mass., are at the Mansion House.

Mr. D. C. Dawson of St. John, New Brunswick, is a guest at Poland Springs.

The best photograph of the Maine State Building was taken by Miss Goldthwait.

Mrs. Barker and Miss Barker of Bridgewater, Mass., are visiting Poland Springs.

Mrs. M. E. Zeigler and Miss Zeigler of New York are at the Poland Spring House.

Mrs. DeWint, who has spent the summer at the Mansion House, left September 8th.

Mr. and Mrs. Herman Adler and Mrs. Joseph Gibson are guests at the Mansion House.

Mr. and Mrs. Harold M. Sewall of Bath, Maine, are at the Poland Spring House.

Mr. L. G. Reynolds and Mr. D. L. Reynolds spent Sunday at the Poland Spring House.

Mr. and Mrs. J. H. Rhodes and Miss Rhodes of New York are at the Poland Spring House.

While walking through one of the woody paths, a beautiful large gray squirrel put in an appearance.

Mr. and Mrs. C. L. Reynolds and Miss Reynolds of Toledo, Ohio, are guests at Poland Springs.

The Lakeside Press of Portland, Maine, have made the half-tone plates for our first-page illustrations.

Mr. and Mrs. Nelson Bartlett have returned to Boston. They have spent the summer at Poland Springs.

Mrs. Trowbridge, Miss Trowbridge, and Mrs. Rogers, of New Haven, arrived Friday, September 4th.

Mr. Chandler Hale and Mr. Eugene Hale, Jr., have been visiting their mother at the Poland Spring House.

Mr. and Mrs. Van Zandt of New Jersey, who have spent the summer at the Mansion House, left Thursday.

Mr. and Mrs. Corbin, who have spent the summer at the Poland Spring House, left Tuesday, September 8th.

Mrs. C. H. Townshend and Miss S. V. Hotchkiss of New Haven are spending a few days at Poland Springs.

Mr. Culver left, Tuesday, for Moosehead Lake, where he will spend a few days, returning later to Poland Springs.

Mr. and Mrs. W. H. Moorehouse of Chicago, and Mrs. J. R. Parker of Minneapolis, arrived Saturday, September 5th.

Mrs. Warner and Mrs. Dunton and the Misses Warner, who have spent the season at Poland Springs, left Tuesday morning.

Mr. and Mrs. Gale and Miss Gale took their departure Tuesday, September 8th. They have spent some time at Poland Springs.

Mr. and Mrs. R. H. Beacham of Portsmouth, N. H., are at the Mansion House. They are seen driving a beautiful pair of bay horses.

Cyclist Column.

Join the L. A. W.

Marjorie—"Uncle Daniel, why is a bicycle like sweet milk?" Uncle Daniel—"Dunno, 'less it's because it makes the calves grow."

It's a poor wheel that won't carry both ways.

There's many a slip 'neath hub and hip on a wet asphalt.

WHEELING COSTUMES ON SHIP,

WITH SOME OBSERVATIONS ON CYCLING ABROAD.

There has been talk from time to time of laying out a bicycle path on the big transatlantic steamers, so that wheelmen would not need to forego their favorite amusement while on shipboard. However, nothing has come of this yet; but on a recent voyage of a well-known liner at least half the young men among the passengers wore bicycle suits. The last day of the trip, when the trunks and other luggage were brought up from the hold, there was a brave display of bicycles—bicycles in straw cases, bicycles in wooden boxes, bicycles without any wrappings at all, except perhaps of newspaper around the handle bars. The principal topic of conversation everywhere is the wheel, and travelers expect to and do meet it everywhere, yet one must own to a little shock of surprise when a row of bicycles is seen propped up against the fine old weather-beaten walls of Westminster Abbey, or in the courtyard of the palace at Versailles.

There are bicycles everywhere in Europe. The fever has spread even into conservative Holland, and there one sees the stolid Dutchman, pipe in his mouth, slowly and seriously wending his way over the hard and beautifully shaded roads out to the House in the Wood. All the roads here are fine, and almost without a break there stretches a hard level road from Paris to The Hague, which is visible from the railroad.

In going from one country to another one sees the characteristics of the people more displayed in their cycling. In Paris you see riders everywhere, most of them going rapidly and talking the while. Perhaps riding among the women is not quite so universal abroad as it is in New York. Parisian women, however, have gone at riding with a will, and adopted wheelwomen's dress reform with a vengeance. They wear something between a bloomer and knickerbocker costume, entirely innocent of skirts, and if occasion requires walking or riding in a boat or tram for a while, they do so with perfect equanimity, judging that their costumes will betray their occupation or pastime, as they certainly do.

You cross the Channel and are set down in London, bewildered, perhaps, by the multitude of "'buses" and hansom cabs that pounce down upon you. You notice that wheelwomen are more scarce here than in Paris, but, true to the old-time English conservatism, the costumes worn are eminently what they should be, or rather, for the sake of safety, perhaps they are what they should not be. The skirts are walking length, and the women, by their slow and graceful riding and the becomingness of their costumes, really surpass American women, from the point of view of looks at least; perhaps Americans have found the happy medium in combining looks with safety.

Chap—"Why don't you get married, old man? Can't you afford it?" Snap—"Oh, yes, I can afford to get married all right, but I haven't money enough for an engagement."

A little girl of our acquaintance has an older brother who uses a great deal of slang. One morning in school the teacher asked the pupils for a definition of "chilly." "I know what chilly is, teacher. It is when you meet some one that goes past you like this, and says, 'Good morning' right ugly to you and goes right on. That's 'chilly.'" She knew the slang definition well.

FRANK CARLOS GRIFFITH, } EDITORS.
NETTiE M. RiCKER, }

PUBLISHED EVERY SUNDAY MORNING DURING THE MONTHS
OF JULY, AUGUST, AND SEPTEMBER, IN THE INTERESTS OF

POLAND SPRINGS AND ITS VISITORS.

All contributions relative to the guests of Poland Springs
will be thankfully received.

To insure publication, all communications should reach the
editors not later than Wednesday preceding day of issue.

All parties desiring rates for advertising in the HILL-TOP
should write the editors for same.

The subscription price of the HILL-TOP is $1.00 for the
season, post-paid. Single copies will be mailed at 10c. each.

Address,
"EDITORS HILL-TOP,"
Poland Spring House,
South Poland, Maine.

PRINTED AT JOURNAL OFFICE, LEWISTON.

Sunday, September 13, 1896.

Editorial.

WITH the present number this volume of the HILL-TOP will have run its course, and cease, not to exist, but to be visible, until a winter's snows shall have come and gone, when it will emerge from its place of concealment and be ready for another campaign.

It is hoped that no event of interest to our readers has escaped the careful chronicler, and that in the relation of the happenings on Poland Hill we have made truthful record, as it has at all times been our desire.

We are pleased, however, to admit exceptional success in certain directions, among which has been the generous confidence of our advertisers, who have filled our advertising columns; the unusual number of our subscribers, and the largely increased sales; all of which indicate the favorable tendency toward our little sheet on its annual appearance.

To all these we extend our thanks, and to those interested guests who have assisted in supplying our columns with their contributions from time to time.

We also wish to remember with thanks the ones who have been earnest in their various capacities in getting the paper into the hands of the guests, from the compositor, the press-man, and the driver of the express, to the enterprising people at the news stands, each and all of whom have labored hard and interestedly in the cause.

Among our chief features we number our illustrations, and we are under special obligations to the two companies which are responsible for them, from the first photograph to the finished plate, and to all others who have in any way aided our efforts to please.

We have met many pleasant faces whom we part with regretfully, but trust all have found Poland Springs so agreeable that many more meetings may be had on the hill-top.

Musical Programme.

SUNDAY, SEPTEMBER 13, 1896, 8.15 P.M.

Cujus Auimum—Stabat Mater.—Rossini.
Selection—Tannhauser.—Wagner.
1. Violin Solo—Prize Song from Meistersinger.—Wagner.
4. { a. Doux Sommeil.—Marie.
{ b. Minuet.—Voccherine.
Piano Solo.   Mr. Edmund Kuntz.
8. Selection—Martha.

Music.

Those who have attended the concerts this season have listened to a very fine orchestra. Mr. Daniel Kuntz is the leader, and nearly all of his men are from the Boston Symphony.

Mr. Edmund Kuntz, whose solo playing has given so much pleasure, has studied four years with Leschetitzky. Mr. August Kuntz is a member of Damrosch Orchestra.

Mr. Brooke's flute solo and Mr. Loeffler's 'cello have been much enjoyed. Mr. Miller is considered one of the best, if not the best, cornetists of this country. Mr. Golde is recognized as an exceptionally fine player on the bass-viol, and Mr. McLaughlin graduated from the New England Conservatory this year with very high honors.

With Mr. Kuntz as a leader and such strong men to assist him, one is not surprised to hear the guests remark: "Poland Springs has the finest music of any summer resort."

An Episcopal clergyman's wife living in southern Texas sends to Mrs. Hiram Ricker a large quantity of Mexican drawn work. Mrs. Ricker will be glad to show it to all who will call at her cottage. It is charity work and the prices are very reasonable.

Wilbur Henry Lansil.

This celebrated cattle painter is a native of Bangor, Maine, but of French descent. He moved to Boston in 1872, where he entered mercantile life, after a few years of which he withdrew and went abroad, studying art in France and Holland, devoting his time exclusively to cattle painting, also visiting Belgium, Germany, and Italy. Returning home he established his studio in Dorchester, where for several years he kept a fine herd of cattle to study from.

His paintings are owned principally in and about Boston. Among his best-known works are: "Early Spring-time," owned by Mrs. Henry Howard Dresser of Boston; "Early Morning," owned by Mrs. C. U. Thomas, Boston; "Sundown on the Coast," "Repose Near the Sea," and "Hillside Pasture," owned by L. S. Conant, Brookline; "Stable Interior," in the collection of Mrs. B. F. Sturtevant, Jamaica Plain; "Resting Near the Sea-Coast," owned by J. L. Grandin, Boston; "The Return of the Herd," owned by W. B. Kimball, Bradford, Mass.; "On the Sea-Coast," owned by B. C. Clark, Boston; and many others.

Mr. Lansil is a member of the Boston Art Club, and has his studio in Studio Building, 110 Tremont Street, Boston.

Two of Mr. Lansil's superb works are to be seen here in Alcove E, numbers 82 and 83, being heads only, but both are admirable in their treatment and very superior examples of their class.

Parent—"Who is the laziest boy in your class, Johnny?" Johnny—"I dunno." "I should think you would know. When all the others are industriously writing or studying their lessons, who is he that sits idly in his seat and watches the rest, instead of working himself?" "The teacher."

Tommie is fond of using big words and of expressing his opinion on all family matters. He was apprised recently that it was his sister Grace's thirtieth birthday. He rose to the occasion. "Well, Grace," he said, "if any one had said you were twenty-five I wouldn't have thought it strange, but that you are thirty, surprises me. You're so vigorous!"

Children's Column.

Gratitude is the music of the heart when its chords are moved by kindness.

Kaiser Wilhelm brings up his sons with Spartan severity. Only one hour and a half play time each day.

In the Spartan up-bringing of his children the kaiser rivals his ancestor, Friedrich Wilhelm of Prussia. According to Klausman's "Leben im Deutschen Kaiserhause," the life of the royal children at Berlin is not sweetened by hours of inactivity.

In their years of infancy the kaisirin ministers to almost all their wants, spends a good part of the day with them, and enters into all their amusements. When the princes arrive at the age of nine, things are changed, and it is all work.

They are then allowed about an hour and a half out of their waking hours to themselves; all the rest of their day is spent in study and physical training. Even in holiday time their tutors accompany them to superintend their studies. Here, for example, is an ordinary day's work for the Crown Prince and his two brothers:

In summer the happy dreams of childhood are disturbed at six o'clock, in winter at seven. Breakfast, consisting of one cup of tea and a roll, is served at 7.30. From 8 till 9.30 they are hard at work at lessons, to help the digestion, after which they are supplied with a second Fruhstuck of bread, with water tinged with red wine.

Immediately afterwards they start on their books again, but mental exercise is mixed with physical, and an hour is spent in gymnastics and horse-exercise, which lasts till 1.15. Thereupon they accompany to dinner the military and civil governors of the castle, and, following this, they have a brief breathing time to themselves.

But the happy moments soon flee away, and again they have to be at their exercises—this time science and music, till six o'clock. Then supper is served, and by eight o'clock they are all snug in bed.

In sport and other manly exercises they are proficient, and can ride as well without a saddle as most people can with. Their military education is also pushed to the utmost, and, that they should understand the principles of war thoroughly, a miniature fortress has been built for them of solid masonry; the walls are nine feet high, and in revolving towers the beleagured have the opportunity of repelling hostilities by means of miniature Krupp guns and all the latest implements of modern warfare.

A part of their education is also devoted to the gentler arts of peace. In the royal gardens each child has a plot of ground, and each is his own gardener and is responsible to headquarters for the maintenance of the said plot. After a riding lesson, too, they are not allowed to throw the reins of the ponies to a groom and then walk off. Every prince has to take his pony to its stall, unsaddle it, and put everything in its proper place before leaving.

Miss Claire Ingalls has returned to Boston.

Master George Adler of New York is a guest at Poland Springs.

"Mamma, what is classical music?" "Oh, don't you know? It's the kind that you have to like whether you like it or not."

An Ab-Original Tale.

BY A SAVAGE.

[Concluded.]

And David to his daily toil
    With cheerful heart did go;
The rising sun saw him employed
    With plow, or spade, or hoe;
His happy wife would follow him—
    She loved to see him sow.

A quiet and a peaceful home
    You may be sure was theirs;
And Weeping Cloud was happy, raised
    Above so many cares.
She was a second Flora; they
    Lived up two flights of stairs.

Their joys and cares are multiplied
    As pass the years so fleet.
A sister in a nest of boys
    Now makes their bliss complete.
Nor do they think more lasses would
    Make their home life more sweet.

In their suburban, quiet home,
    The factory bell they hear,
And noise of the machines upon
    The morning air so clear.
Of course 'tis a familiar sound
    To every Indian ear.

For all their peace and happiness
    They bless their lucky stars;
Rejoicing that no bitter strife
    Their life domestic mars;
That they are not two martyrs, to
    Be kept in family jars.

Madame Van Duyn.

This very excellent artiste gave a concert on Tuesday evening in the Music Hall, assisted by Kuntz's orchestra and Miss Jessie M. Downer, accompanist.

Madame Van Duyn may be complimented at once upon her success, possessing a voice of rare excellence, clear, full, and rich in tone, and possessing a personality at all times pleasing and full of grace. She received numerous encores, and was recognized as a contralto of superior attainments.

The following is the programme in full :

Overture—Semiramide.—Rossini.   Orchestra.
Songs { L'esclave.—Lalo.
       { Aime moi.—Bemberg.
How Sweet to Dream.—Pizzi.
       (Flute obligato—Mr. A. Brooke.)
Songs { The Night Has a Thousand Eyes.
       { Love Me if I Live—Love Me if I Die.—A. Foote.
Selection—Freischutz.—Weber.   Orchestra.
Mon cœur s'ouvre à la voix.—Saint-Saens.
Alla Stella Confidente.—Robaudi.
       ('Cello Obligato—Mr. E. Loeffler.)
March.—Lachner.   Orchestra.

Miss Katherine Ricker sang several selections at Thursday morning's concert. Her singing of "The Lost Chord" showed the rich quality of her voice, and the guests were loud in their applause. She responded to an encore.

Guests at Poland Spring House

SEPTEMBER 2- 1896.

Mr. and Mrs. C. H. Andrews	Boston.
Mary L. Allen	Augusta.
Mr. and Mrs. M. T. Atwood	New York.
Miss Atwood	New York.
Mr. and Mrs. A. B. Butterfield	Boston.
Miss Barstow	Boston.
Mrs. H. Batterman	Brooklyn.
Miss A. H. Batterman	Brooklyn.
H. E. Barnard	San Antonio.
Mr. and Mrs. C. J. Bonaparte	Baltimore.
Mrs. A. E. Buchanan	Elizabeth, N. J.
Mr. Joseph A. Brown	Boston.
Miss Belle G. Brown	Boston.
Mr. and Mrs. N. A. Baldwin	New Haven.
Mr. and Mrs. H. O. Bright	Cambridge.
Mrs. J. F. Beckwith	Savannah.
Mr. and Mrs. P. H. Bathydt	New York.
Miss Bishop	Connecticut.
Mr. and Mrs. H. A. Budd	Boston.
Mrs. M. E. Barker	Bridgewater.
Miss Barker	Bridgewater.
Mr. and Mrs. J. D. Bedle	Jersey City.
Mr. and Mrs. W. G. Burnsted	Jersey City.
H. W. Briggs	Newport, R. I.
Miss Mabelle Carroll	Boston.
Miss Clark	Boston.
Miss E. M. Chandler	Boston.
A. E. Carroll	Boston.
Mr. and Mrs. W. A. Castle	Springfield.
Mrs. E. M. Carroll	Boston.
E. A. Carroll	Boston.
Mrs. Edw. E. Clark	Boston.
Miss Florence Cregle	New York.
Mrs. W. R. Clarkson	New York.
Mr. and Mrs. G. C. Currier	New York.
Mrs. Agnes S. Curtis	New York.
Mr. and Mrs. Geo. W. Coleman	Boston.
Mr. Andrew R. Culver	Brooklyn.
Mr. and Mrs. F. W. Carpenter	Providence.
Miss Julia Carpenter	Providence.
Mrs. Z. Chandler	Detroit, Mich.
Mrs. B. B. Claxton	Philadelphia.
George F. Curtis	Boston.
Miss F. H. Curtis	Boston.
Mr. and Mrs. Westmoreland Davis	New York.
Miss C. S. Duer	New Haven.
Mr. and Mrs. Andrew J. Dotger	South Orange, N. J.
Miss Jessie M. Downer	Boston.
Mr. and Mrs. E. D. Dickerman	Chicago.
Miss D. C. Fitch	New Haven.
Miss E. T. Fitch	New Haven.
Miss Fletcher	Boston.
Mrs. J. D. Fessenden	New York.
Mrs. R. G. Feltus	Philadelphia.
Annie L. Fall	Boston.
Mrs. J. R. Farnham	Waltham.
Mrs. C. E. Fisher	Roxbury.
Mr. and Mrs. Joel Goldthwait	Boston.
Mr. and Mrs. Jos. H. Gray	Boston.
S. E. Gordon	Portland.
A. Gilbert	Plainfield, N. J.
Miss Gardiner	Brookline.
Miss Ada T. Griswold	Columbus, Wis.
Miss Edith M. Griswold	Columbus, Wis.
J. H. Goodenow	New York.
Mrs. M. M. Gross	Chicago.
Mr. John Goldthwaite	Boston.
Miss E. B. Goldthwaite	Boston.
Mrs. A. Gilbert	Plainfield, N. J.
Mrs. George F. Gregory	Brooklyn.
Mr. and Mrs. T. Gilman	Toronto.
Mr. and Mrs. J. F. Godley	Trenton, N. J.
Miss Gregory	Brooklyn.
Mr. and Mrs. J. C. Haynes	Boston.
Miss E. Margaret Haynes	Boston.
Henry A. Hildreth	Boston.
Mrs. F. A. Harter	Brooklyn.
Miss Isabel Harter	Brooklyn.

Mr. and Mrs. I. K. Hamilton	Chicago.
Miss I. G. Haydock	Philadelphia.
Mrs. S. B. Hubbard	Jacksonville.
Mrs. W. W. Hartwell	Plattsburgh, N. Y.
Mr. and Mrs. Horace Hunt	New York.
Mrs. M. B. Hoffman	New York.
Miss Anna Havens	Boston.
Mrs. M. E. Hildreth	Boston.
Miss Alma Hildreth	Boston.
Miss Hubert	Montreal.
Mr. and Mrs. W. W. Heroy	New York.
Miss S. V. Hotchkiss	New Haven.
Mrs. H. McI. Harding	New York.
Miss Marion Harding	New York.
Mrs. W. H. Inman	New York.
Miss W. L. Inman	New York.
Mr. and Mrs. J. C. Kittredge	Brookline.
Misses Kittredge	Brookline.
Mr. and Mrs. Thos. Lewis and family	New York.
Mrs. Victor F. Lawson	Chicago.
Mrs. LaBan	New York.
Miss May Lord	New Jersey.
Mr. Walter A. LaBan	New York.
Mrs. B. C. Lake	New Haven.
Miss Leland	New York.
James D. Laird	San Francisco.
Mr. and Mrs. B. N. Lapham	Providence.
Mrs. G. H. Leonard	Boston.
Miss Leonard	Boston.
Mrs. Prentiss Loring	Portland.
Mrs. P. I. Loring	Portland.
Mr. and Mrs. Wm. Lambert	New York.
Mr. and Mrs. Thomas Mack	Boston.
Mr. and Mrs. T. B. M. Mason	Washington.
Mrs. Jno. H. Maginnis	New Orleans.
Mr. Jno. H. Maginnis	New Orleans.
Mrs. A. Mully	Washington.
Mrs. J. T. Montgomery	Philadelphia.
Mrs. Christine Marburg	Baltimore.
The Misses Marburg	Baltimore.
Mr. and Mrs. John T. Martin	New York.
Miss M. R. Manley	New York.
Mr. and Mrs. W. H. Morehouse	Chicago.
Mr. and Mrs. C. G. Mitchell	Cincinnati.
Mrs. C. H. Meir	Philadelphia.
Mr. and Mrs. W. T. Ness	Boston.
Mr. and Mrs. Josiah Oakes	Malden, Mass.
Thomas Peckham	Newport R. I.
Miss L. Paig	New York.
Miss S. Paig	New York.
Miss E. A. Prall	New York.
Mrs. J. A. Pettee	New York.
Mrs. Henry U. Palmer	Brooklyn.
Masters Austin and Chester Palmer	Brooklyn.
Mrs. J. A. Parker	Minneapolis.
Mrs. Geo. J. Putnam	Brookline.
S. S. Pollard	Boston.
Mrs. J. W. Phillip	Boston.
Mrs. E. G. Powers	Boston.
Frank K. Priest	Boston.
S. S. Riker	New York.
Miss Marion Richardson	Boston.
Mr. and Mrs. Augustus Richardson	Boston.
Miss Richardson	Boston.
Mrs. E. J. Robinson	Boston.
Miss Randolph	Plainfield, N. J.
Mr. and Mrs. Wm. J. Riker	New York.
Mr. and Mrs. Geo. Bliss Rogers	New York.
Mr. and Mrs. C. L. Reynolds	Toledo.
Miss Reynolds	Toledo.
Mr. and Mrs. Chas. E. Riley	Newton.
Miss Mabel L. Riley	Newton.
Mrs. J. H. Rhoades	New York.
Miss Rhoades	New York.
Miss Katherine M. Ricket	Falmouth.
Mr. and Mrs. Edw. Russell	Brookline.
Miss C. A. Richards	Boston.
Miss A. L. Richards	Boston.
Mr. and Mrs. E. A. Strong	Boston.
Mrs. S. Skaats	New York.
Dr. and Mrs. C. C. Schuyler	Plattsburgh, N. Y.
Mr. and Mrs. A. T. Salter	Washington.

Mr. and Mrs. Joseph W. Sandford	Plainfield, N. J.
Mr. and Mrs. J. B. Sawyer	Dover, N. H.
Mrs. G. W. Simpson	Brooklyn.
Miss B. C. Simpson	Brooklyn.
Miss Mabel Simpson	Brooklyn.
John H. Shortridge	Philadelphia.
Miss L. E. Shortridge	Philadelphia.
Miss F. A. Shortridge	Philadelphia.
Mr. and Mrs. C. N. Shaw	Boston.
Miss J. S. Sands	New York.
H. Hayden Sands	New York.
Mr. and Mrs. John J. Sutton	Rye, N. Y.
Mr. and Mrs. S. Scholl and family	New York.
George Trott	Philadelphia.
Mr. and Mrs. E. G. Thurber	New York.
Miss Tillotson	New Haven.
Miss N. E. Ten Broeck	New Haven.
Mrs. Orlando Tompkins	Boston.
Mr. and Mrs. F. E. Taylor	Brooklyn.
Mrs. Thos. R. Trowbridge	New Haven.
Miss Carolyn H. Trowbridge	New Haven.
Miss Trumbull	New Haven.
Miss C. H. Townshend	New Haven.
G. P. Tenney	Boston.
Mr. and Mrs. A. L. Thorne	New York.
Mr. and Mrs. John B. Taylor	Brooklyn.
D. B. Vickery	Haverhill.
Mrs. Marian Van Duyn	New York.
Mrs. A. Van Wagener	Auburndale, Mass.
Miss Ida B. Van Wagener	Auburndale, Mass.
Mr. and Mrs. Henry C. Weston	Boston.
Mrs. J. Reed Whipple	Boston.
Dr. M. C. Wedgwood and Mrs. Wedgwood	Lewiston.
Mr. F. R. Wharton	Philadelphia.
Mr. and Mrs. W. S. Wymond	Louisville, Ky.
Miss Wymond	Louisville, Ky.
Mr. N. Whitman	New York.
Mr. and Mrs. E. F. Watkins	Chicago.
Wm. Argyle Watson	New York.
Mrs. Robt. B Wade	New York.
Mr. and Mrs. Jos. H. White	Brookline.
Mrs. M. E. Ziegler	New York.
Miss Ziegler	New York.

Progressive Euchre.

The usual progressive euchre party took place Friday evening, September 4th. Mrs. LaBau and Miss Brown showed excellent taste in selecting the prizes. There were eleven tables and seventeen games were played. The highest number of moves made was eleven. Mrs. Jackson won the first ladies' prize, a silver plate; Colonel Talbot the first gentlemen's prize, a corkscrew, silver-mounted. Colonel Talbot and Mrs. Jackson entered the game as partners. When the game was over they were at the same table as partners. Each had the same number of points, and each cut for the first prize. Miss Dexter gained the second ladies' prize, a silver shoe horn; the third went to Miss Wyman, a silver tape measure; and Miss Richardson won the fourth prize, a silver seal. Mrs. Wales gained the second gentlemen's prize, a silver nail file; Miss Campbell the third, a paper cutter; and Mrs. H. W. Ricker a pen-wiper.

An irate female seeks admittance to the editor's sanctum. "But I tell you, madam," protests the clerk, "that the editor is too busy to talk to any one to-day." "Never mind; you let me in. I'll do the talking."

Thistles.

———•———

Jonah was the first man who really got right in the swim.

The artist (exhibiting sketch)—"It is the best thing I ever did." The critic (sympathetically)—"Oh, well, you musn't let that discourage you."

"My task in life," said the pastor, complacently, "consists in saving young men." "Ah!" replied the maiden, with a soulful longing, "save a good one for me, won't you?"—*Life.*

What vessel is it that no woman objects to embark in? Answer—A courtship.

Why is a clergyman's horse like a king? Answer—Because he is guided by a minister.

Lothario—"I came to ask the hand of your daughter in marriage. I have been hourly intoxicated with her charms." Old Bertrand—"Say, young fellow, what do you think marriage is—a gold cure?"—*New York Journal.*

Cure for Love.—Take 12 ounces of dislike, 1 pound of resolution, 2 grains of common sense, 2 ounces of experience, a large sprig of time, and 3 quarts of cooling water of consideration. Set them over the gentle fire of love, sweeten it with the sugar of forgetfulness, skim it over with the spoon of melancholy, put it in the bottom of your heart, cork it with the cork of clear conscience and let it remain and find ease, and be restored to your sense again. The things can be had of the apothecary, next door to reason, on Prudent street, in the village of contentment, for 10 cents' worth of determination.

Few summer resorts in the White Mountains are so well provided with beautiful drives as Twin Mountain, Dame Nature having richly endowed her in that respect. Starting from the Twin Mountain House one may drive in every direction and yet find a new charm, a new attraction in each drive. For short trips, that to the Fabyan or the new Mount Pleasant House, with its superb view of the Presidential Range and the minor peaks that surround the entire valley appeals most strongly to the lover of nature, while the drive over Cherry Mountain to Jefferson and back is also very delightful, the view in all directions being magnificent. The drive to Bethlehem is one of infinite variety and constantly changing phases of scenery, and one that will well repay he who undertakes it. Want of space forbids a more detailed mention of the different points of interest, but among those not mentioned above are Crawford House, Willey House, Mount Willard, Profile House, Lancaster, Littleton, and Whitefield.

Arrivals.

POLAND SPRING HOUSE.

SEPTEMBER 4 TO 11, 1896.

Allen, Mr. and Mrs. J. H.	Boston.
Andrews, Mr. and Mrs. C. H.	Boston.
Ashe, Mrs.	San Francisco.
Allen, Mary L.	Augusta.
Bubier, Mr. and Mrs. F. L.	Lynn.
Bishop, Miss	Connecticut.
Budd, Mr. and Mrs. H. A.	New York.
Barker, Mrs. M. E.	Bridgewater.
Barker, Miss M. E.	Bridgewater.
Bubier, T. S.	Lynn.
Bedle, Mr. and Mrs. J. D.	Jersey City.
Bumstead, Mr. and Mrs. Wm. G.	Jersey City.
Bancroft, Mrs. Samuel, Jr.	Wilmington, Del.
Bancroft, Miss E. R.	Wilmington, Del.
Belford, S. W.	Denver.
Briggs, H. W.	Newport.
Brown, Mrs. F. M.	Auburn.
Brooks, Mrs. G. H.	Boston.
Britt, E. H.	San Francisco.
Bearce, H. M.	Hebron.
Clark, Miss	Boston.
Chandler, Miss E. M.	Boston.
Cameron, C. E.	Toledo.
Cogswell, Theodore F.	Ipswich.
Cogswell, Mrs.	Ipswich.
Currier, Mr. and Mrs. Chas. L.	Boston.
Cannell, Mr. and Mrs. Joseph H.	Everett.
Clifford, Mrs. J. D.	Lewiston.
Clifford, Miss Katharine	Boston.
Carroll, A. E.	Boston.
Chamberlain, James A.	Boston.
Cole, E. L.	Mexico, Mex.
Dupee, Mr. and Mrs. Wm. R.	Boston.
Dawson, D. C.	St. John, N. B.
Dans, Miss Jennie	Milford, Del.
Dans, Miss May	Milford, Del.
Dourell, Miss Jessie Mabelle	Boston.
Dickerman, Mr. and Mrs. E. D.	Chicago.
Dodge, Mr. and Mrs. John E.	Boston.
Dunlop, G. F.	Washington.
Fish, W. G.	Boston.
Feltus, R. S.	Philadelphia.
Fisher, Miss C. E.	Roxbury, Mass.
Forsyth, J. D.	Popham Beach.
Gorman, Miss	Pittston, Pa.
Gordon, S. C.	Portland.
Gardner, Mrs. O. W.	Caribou.
Gilbert, A.	Plainfield, N. J.
Givernand, Joseph L.	Gloster, N. J.
Gurney, Sanford K.	Boston.
Gilson, H. C.	Portland.
Gleason, Dr. and Mrs. W. T.	Newburgh.
Gardner, Miss	Brookline.
Hersey, Mr. and Mrs. W. W.	New York.
Hale, Chandler	Ellsworth.
Hale, Eugene, Jr.	Ellsworth.
Hotchkiss, Miss S. V.	New Haven.
Hackett, O. J.	Boston.
Hunter, D. W.	New York.
Harding, Mrs. H. McI.	New York.
Harding, Miss Marion	New York.
Hutchins, H. Wesley	Auburn.
Haynes, John C.	Boston.
Ivins, Mr. and Mrs. A. B.	Philadelphia.
Kittredge, Mr. and Mrs. J. C.	Brookline.
Kittredge, Miss Estelle	Brookline.
Kittredge, Miss Clarissa	Brookline.
Kennedy, Miss K. L.	New York.
Kent, Miss K. A.	Norwich.
Leavitt, Mr. and Mrs. F. L.	Auburn.
Lesser, Mr. and Mrs. J. Mona	Boston.
Loring, Prentiss	Portland.
Lambert, Mr. and Mrs. Wm.	New York.
Loring, P. S.	Portland.
Moorhouse, Mr. and Mrs. W. H.	Chicago.
Mitchell, Mr. and Mrs. C. G.	Cincinnati.
Megguire, Mrs. A. H.	Portland.
Manning, John B.	New York.
Manning, Katherine	New York.
Manning, Mary G.	New York.
Morton, Thomas	Raymond.
Mein, Mrs. C. H.	Philadelphia.
Mackellar, Mrs. W. B.	Philadelphia.
McMichael, Mr. and Mrs. Chas. B.	Philadelphia.
McMichael, Miss Carol	Philadelphia.
McMichael, Charles Prevost	Philadelphia.
Pollard, Mr. and Mrs. A. T.	Philadelphia.
Patterson, Mr. and Mrs. W. W.	Scranton.
Payson, Walter G.	Boston.
Parker, Mrs. J. S.	Minneapolis.
Puvel, Dr. and Mrs. M.	New York.
Putnam, Mrs. Geo. J.	Brookline.
Pollard, S. S.	Boston.
Page, Mr. and Mrs. George R.	Auburn.
Phillip, Mrs. J. W.	Boston.
Platt, Miss A. R.	Boston.
Priest, Frank K.	Boston.
Powers, Mrs. E. G.	Boston.
Packard, Gertrude	Auburn.
Pollister, Blanche	Auburn.
Platt, Miss A. H.	New York.
Platt, Miss E. H.	New York.
Richards, Miss	Scranton.
Rogers, Mrs. Geo. Bliss	New Haven.
Reynolds, Mr. and Mrs. C. L.	Toledo.
Reynolds, Miss	Toledo.
Reynolds, Master L. G.	Toledo.
Reynolds, Master D. L.	Toledo.
Ridlon, C. H.	Portland.
Roche, Wm.	Boston.
Riley, Mr. and Mrs. Chas. E.	Newton.
Riley, Miss Mabel L.	Newton.
Rhodes, Mr. and Mrs. J. Harmon	New York.
Rhodes, Miss	New York.
Ricker, Mr. and Mrs. Wm. I.	New York.
Ricker, Katharine M.	Falmouth.
Russell, Mr. and Mrs. Edw.	Brookline.
Richards, Mrs. C. A.	Boston.
Richards, Miss A. L.	Boston.
Rigol, D. M.	Baltimore.
Sanders, Mr. and Mrs. H. M.	Boston.
Sewall, Mr. and Mrs. Harold M.	Bath.
Shibley, John A.	Providence.
Sampson, O. H.	Boston.
Sanderson, J. Murray	Newark.
Sands, Miss J. S.	New York.
Sands, H. Hayden	New York.
Scholl, Mr. and Mrs. S.	New York.
Spaulding, Mrs. S. M.	Wilmington, Del.
Stearns, Mr. and Mrs. E. L.	Bangor.
Sutton, Mr. and Mrs. John J.	Rye, N. Y.
Sayles, Mr. and Mrs. John B.	Brooklyn.
Sutherland, Mr. and Mrs. I. G.	Lynn.
Savage, Mrs. A. R.	Auburn.
Savage, Miss	Auburn.
Stetson, Mrs. J. H.	Lewiston.
Stetson, Mrs. G. B.	Lewiston.
Stetson, Mr. John	Boston.
Sherman, Mr. and Mrs. H. H.	Boston.
Swett, Mrs. L. J.	Brookline.
Smyser, Mrs. C. F.	Brookline.
Smyser, J. S.	Brookline.
Trowbridge, Mrs. Thos. R.	New Haven.
Trowbridge, Miss Carolyn H.	New Haven.
Tuck, E. W.	Boston.
Trumbull, Miss	New Haven.
Townshend, Mrs. C. H.	New Haven.
Thorne, Mr. and Mrs. A. L.	New York.
Tenney, G. P.	Boston.

Van Duyn, Marian	New York.
Vye, Miss Amy J.	Boston.
Vye, Miss Elizabeth J.	Auburn.
VanDoren, Miss	York, Pa.
Wharton, Miss	Portland.
Watson, Wm. Argyle	New York.
Wade, Mrs. Robert B.	New York.
White, Mr. and Mrs. Joseph H.	Brookline.
Wilson, F. C.	Portland.
Wessen, Alfred J.	Auburn.
Warner, A. H.	Salem.
Walsh, J. A.	Lewiston.
Wright, Miss H. H.	Utica.
Whelen, Mrs. Wm. N.	Philadelphia.
Whelen, Mrs. A. E.	Philadelphia.
Webster, E. C.	Orono.
Warren, Mrs. C. H.	New York.
Zeigler, Mrs. M. E.	New York.
Zeigler, Miss	New York.
Little Sara	Denver.
Little Master Frankie	Denver.

MANSION HOUSE.

SEPTEMBER 4 TO 11, 1896.

Beacham, Mr. and Mrs. R. H.	Portsmouth.
Barbour, E. D.	Boston.
Holbrook, Mr. and Mrs. C. L.	Newton.
Leonard, L. L.	Oakland.
Schaul, Mr. and Mrs. H. H.	Atlanta.
Wentworth, Mr. and Mrs. H. W.	New Bedford.

Tid-Bits.

Mr. and Mrs. J. R. Peterson of Portland and Elizabeth Hallowell of Westbrook stopped on their way north, on a bicycling tour.

Mr. Robert Vonnoh is painting a portrait of Mr. Edmund Kuntz. The portrait will be exhibited in Boston this coming winter.

Mrs. O. W. Gardner of Caribou, Maine, has been visiting her daughter, Miss Margaret Gardner, at the Poland Spring House.

"The New Bethesda," by Mrs. Patterson, will be recognized as located at Poland Springs. It is especially interesting to all visitors here.

Mr. and Mrs. Read, Mrs. Keene, and Miss Campbell, took their departure Thursday. They have spent the summer at Poland Springs.

Monday, September 7th, Mr. Campbell, Mr. Beacham, Mr. Van Zandt, and Mr. Read, caught 127 brook trout and brought home eighty of them.

Rev. Dr. Pullman of Lynn lectured in Music Hall, Wednesday evening, September 9th, on "The Moral Capital of the World." The lecture was excellent.

Mrs. Robinson, the Masseuse, is at the Poland Spring House, where she has continued two seasons with the greatest success. Her card may be found in another column.

The Notman Photographic Company have furnished all the photographs for our illustrations this season, and the work of Mr. Ness, their operator here, has been of a very superior character.

Miss Whitman, who has been very successful as a manicurist during the past two seasons here, is still at the Poland Spring House. Her services as chiropodist as well are highly valued by many.

Mr. L. L. Leonard of Oakland, Maine, spent Monday and Tuesday at Poland Springs. Mr. Leonard, who is a graduate of Trinity College, contributed two poems to the HILL-TOP this season.

Professor L. Water gave an entertainment in Music Hall, Friday evening, September 5th, in sleight-of-hand, mind-reading, and ventriloquism. Mr. Water was very clever, and the hall was well filled.

The guests who have followed the publication of the "Menu" from week to week, and the editors of the HILL-TOP as well, are indebted for the recipes given to Mr. Sparrow the chef, and Mrs. Cole the head pastry-cook, for their very kind contributions.

Miss Brown's singing, Wednesday morning, September 9th, was much enjoyed. She has a high soprano voice, which is very sweet and of a bird-like quality. Miss Brown has studied with Madam Lucca in Vienna, and Madam Marchesi. She was well received and responded to an encore, "The Last Rose of Summer."

Needle-Work in Mexico.

A person walking along the narrow sidewalks of the historic old city of Matamoras, in Mexico, will see through the grated bars girls and women bent nearly double with frames in their laps and needles working. They are engaged in the intricate and delicate work of making perfilado, or drawn needle-work. Matamoras is the principal city in Mexico where perfilado is manufactured. Thousands of dollars' worth of this work is exported annually to the United States. Some of it is very expensive, one year being required to make a single piece.

There is a duty of 50 per cent. imposed by the United States on this class of manufactures. For a long time perfilado was made an industrial feature of the public schools; every girl learned to make it. In this way the art was acquired, and others in the family were taught, until nearly every girl and woman in Matamoras could either perform the work or assist in its manufacture. It is hard, difficult work, from which the earnings are very small, frequently amounting to less than fifteen cents a day.

THE NEW MOUNT PLEASANT HOUSE,

In the Heart of the White Mountains.

Through Parlor Cars from New York, Boston, and Portland, also from Burlington, Montreal, and Quebec.

The Hotel faces the Grandest Display of Mountain Peaks in America east of the Rocky Mountains. It is lighted throughout by electricity, thoroughly heated by steam, and has an abundance of private and public baths. Its orchestra is made up largely from the Boston Symphony Orchestra. Its table is unsurpassed. Absolutely pure water from an artesian well, 409 feet in solid rock.

IT IS THE NEAREST HOTEL TO MT. WASHINGTON, AND THE TRAIN FOR THE SUMMIT STARTS FROM A STATION ON THE HOTEL GROUNDS.

All Trains, Maine Central Railroad, from Portland to Burlington, Montreal, Quebec, and Lake Champlain stop at the platform close to the House.

Leave Portland 8.45 A.M., arrive Mt. Pleasant House, 12.21 P.M.	
" " 1.25 P.M., " " " " 5.05 P.M.	POST, TELEGRAPH, AND TICKET OFFICE
" " 3.20 P.M., " " " " 7.20 P.M.	IN THE HOTEL.
" " 8.45 P.M., " " " " 11.47 P.M.	

ANDERSON & PRICE, of the Hotel Ormond of Florida, Managers.

Address by wire or mail, "Mount Pleasant House, N. H."

JOHN O. RICE,

PROFESSIONAL ACCOUNTANT AND AUDITOR

Expert Examinations made for Banks, Corporations, Estates, or Mercantile Houses, and general accountant work solicited. P. O. Box 1,639.

Office, Room 4, Centennial Building, 93 Exchange Street, PORTLAND, ME.

References: H. Ricker & Sons, Poland Springs; First National Bank, Portland, Me.

PRINCE'S EXPRESS CO.

For all Points in the West and South.

Freight FROM New York, Philadelphia, Baltimore, and Washington, D. C., should be forwarded via United States Express Co. Boston Office, 34 and 35 Court Square, 105 Arch Street, and 77 Kingston Street. Portland Office, 103 Exchange Street.

Courteous Attention, Low Rates, and Quick Despatch.

PREBLE HOUSE,

Adjoining Longfellow's Home,

J. C. WHITE. ———— PORTLAND, ME.

H. M. SANDERS & CO.,

Hardware, Paints, Oils, and Varnishes.

Carpenters' and Machinists' Tools.

A full assortment of CUTLERY.

THEATRICAL STAGE HARDWARE. 27 Eliot St., BOSTON.

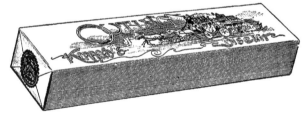

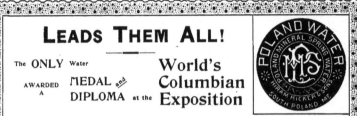

The Hill-Top

POLAND SPRINGS, SO. POLAND, ME.

HARRY C. WILKINSON

Vol. III.   SUNDAY MORNING, SEPTEMBER 6, 1896.   No. 10.

The Mansion House.

ONE hundred and two years ago, two men stopped one morning at a little farm-house, with one chimney and no hearth, and asked for food. The occupant of the house, with his large family of six girls, had but taken possession of the place the night before, and cooked food was "rare," but the family soon had a meal prepared, to the satisfaction of the travellers, and they departed satisfied.

This was the very beginning of inn-keeping on Ricker Hill, and Jabez Ricker was the landlord, and the house stood near the site of the present Mansion House.

Wentworth Ricker, son of Jabez, was a pushing, energetic man, and before the year 1795 was at an end, a "tavern" was built, which, one hundred years ago, was two stories high, with nine windows and a door in the front, and from whose square and unpretentious form arose two chimneys. Behind the house was a small "L," and in front, at the corner, soon after was the sign which indicated its hospitable character, and bearing the name "Wentworth Ricker, 1797."

If those two travelers could revisit the "glimpses of the moon" they would scarcely recognize the spot where Jabez Ricker's daughters found it a matter requiring some calculation to prepare a breakfast for two.

Wentworth Ricker did teaming during the war of 1812, and from the money he received he built a big barn, which still stands down near the rear of the new stable, although it has been twice moved from its original location.

We find, in 1859, the original "tavern" just about the same, but with a more extensive "L;" but in 1875 the business requirements had already caused the alteration in the roof which remains the same in appearance to this day.

It was in 1834 that Hiram Ricker took active charge of the affairs, then only twenty-five years of age, and continued the management for thirty-five years, when he in turn relinquished it to his eldest son, Edward P., then only twenty-two years old. This was in 1869. In 1883-4 the old Mansion House was enlarged to its present size, giving it about sixty-six rooms, with accommodations for one hundred guests.

Now here was a roadside inn, erected by sturdy pioneers, whose attention was directed to inn-keeping, probably, by the needs of two travelers, who later on were succeeded by other hungry men, on their way from Portland.

It occurred, doubtless, to Jabez Ricker and his son Wentworth, that more money was to be had from that employment of their talents than tilling the soil, but they little thought of the inexhaustible mine of wealth running away from the top of their farm, and which was eventually to cause the extension of the business until six hundred guests would sleep at once under their roofs on Ricker Hill, and the name would go forth to the uttermost parts of the earth.

The north-west corner of the Mansion House to-day is the Wentworth Ricker Inn of a hundred years ago, and the old tree, which stands within the close embrace of the piazza, grew without restraint beyond the confines of the structure.

Here is an object lesson in enterprise, which any man who possesses seemingly as little as Jabez Ricker possessed in his hill-side farm, should take to heart; thrift, perseverance, good judgment, and generous methods, may and will bring about great results from small beginnings. His six daughters assisted at the getting of the first travellers' breakfast, and now it requires nearly three hundred and fifty assistants to the three general directors, to run an establishment, upon a wooded hill, ten miles from any considerable town.

Progressive Euchre.

Friday, August 28th, the guests gathered in the amusement hall for progressive euchre. The hall was prettily decorated by Mrs. Sherman, with asters and ferns.

There were sixteen games played, and the highest number of points gained by the ladies was twelve. The first ladies' prize went to Miss Chapell, a beautiful plate; the second to Miss Voorhees, a cut-glass vaseline jar; the third to Mrs. Vose, a cut-glass vinaigrette; the fourth to Mrs. Mac, a silver tape needle.

Col. Talbot won the first gentleman's prize, a hair brush, silver-mounted; Mrs. Wales the second, a silver knife; Mrs. Dickenson the third, hand-glass, gold-mounted; Mr. DeWint the fourth, a paper-weight.

Golf.

Saturday, August 29th, Mr. D. W. Field offered as prizes choice of a pair of tennis, bicycle, or golf shoes to winner in each of the following classes:

1st class. Open to those having made a score of 70 and under.

2d class. Open to those having made a score of 90 and not less than 71.

3d class. Open to all ladies and those whose previous score is not less than 91.

Play began at 3.30 P.M.

Horace B. Ingalls, winner of 1st class; score, 58.

James J. McLaughlin, Jr., winner of 2d class; score, 74.

L. F. Gilbert, winner of 3d class; score, 82.

The *Commercial Bulletin* says of the New Mount Pleasant House, White Mountains: "This house is a perfect revelation to old habities of the White Mountains, with its splendid rooms, which can be had *en suite* or with bath-room, its admirable management and superior cuisine. We are in receipt of the 'dinner bill' of the house, which, for variety and excellence, challenges comparison with the best New York or Boston hotels."

The Employees' Ball.

AGAIN it is our most agreeable task to chronicle the events of the employees' masquerade ball, which occurred on the evening of Monday, August 31st, which annual event was the climax of a summer's festivities. It is always an affair looked forward to with much pleasure by the participants, and a most friendly rivalry exists in the devising of unique and tasteful costumes, the preparation for it being long previous in contemplation.

In this instance the ladies are to be congratulated on the exceedingly neat, original, and elaborate costumes worn by them, and when it is said that all were made here it will be understood that some skill and much labor has been devoted to the work.

The Music Hall and Amusement Room were both thrown open to the revellers, and at nine o'clock the grand march of maskers began, which was led by Mr. B. J. Gallagher in a superb costume, as "Prince Florizelle," and Miss Pearl Gardner as "Golden Star."

There were eighty ladies and forty gentlemen in the march, among whom were noticeable Miss Mary Ingraham as the "Goddess of Liberty," draped with the stars and stripes; Miss Galvin,

uniquely attired in a dress composed of Poland Water labels; and it may be said here that of the several paper dresses, all were artistic and beautiful, as also was a very odd costume worn by Miss Maggie O'Neil, representing the "Bates Mill," and made up of all the different colored cottons manufactured by that corporation.

These are not selected because of any marked superiority, but are mentioned as indicating the diverse nature of the entire assemblage.

Other ladies in the party and their various costumes were:

Miss Corbett,	Maine, Pine Tree State.
" Collier,	The Ormond.
" Catherine Murphy,	The Hill-Top.
" Leavett,	Lewiston Journal.
" Granvill,	Mount Pleasant House Tags.
" Hartley,	Lewiston Daily Sun.
Mrs. Maria Sawyer,	Poland caps or seals.
Miss Nellie Corcoran,	Pink chrysanthemum.
" Danally,	Chinaman.
" Alice McCarthy,	Snow-ball.
" Tosney,	Highland Lassie.
" Tewksbury,	Topsy.
" Mullay,	Pop-Corn Girl.
" Addie Moore,	Red Riding-hood.
" Addie Wood,	Greek costume.
" O'Malley,	Tambourine Girl.
" Delia Glancy,	Night.
" McCormick,	Morning.
" Stephenson,	Quakeress.
" Hackett,	Bluebell.
" Butler,	Street Waif.
" Doughty,	School Girl.
" Totten,	Organ-grinder.
" Waddell,	Violet.
" Levine,	Lady in Red.
" Mildred Wentworth,	Card Girl.
" Tierney,	Sweet Peas.
" Clapperson,	Buttercup.
" Mayse,	Queen of Hearts.
" Fahey,	Japanese.
" Crowley,	Japanese.
" Bristow,	French Dancing Girl.
" Lund,	Fern Girl.
" Goldrick,	Irish wash-woman.
" McWalter,	Aunt Samanthy.
" Hoyt,	Artist.
" Sheehen,	Looking Backward.
" McDonald,	Looking Backward.
" Donohue,	Symphony of the Rose.
" Winslow,	Milkmaid.
" Stephens,	Rainbow.
Mrs. Harper,	Irish Apple Woman.
Miss Cullinan,	Bootblack.
" Darcy,	Beggar.
" Harris,	Beggar.
" Tierney,	Lady in Yellow.
" Minahan,	Violet.
" Smith,	Clothes-Pin Girl.
" Riley,	Swiss Girl.
" Coyne,	Fern Girl.
" Wilson,	Sweet Pea Girl.
" Pickle,	Orphan.
" McLane,	Orphan.
" Merrill,	Summer Girl.
" Longeley,	Spanish Lady.
" Connors,	Poppy.
" Edwards,	Evening Star.
" McKenna,	Mistress Mary.
" Boothbay,	Lady in Pink.
" Kate Galvin,	Maud Muller.
" Buckley,	Cobweb Sweeper.
" Stowell,	Dewdrop.
" Winslow,	Butterfly.
" Lund,	Ferns and Sweet Peas.
" Hill,	Coming Woman.

The costumes for the gentlemen were all selected in Boston, and were elegant and artistic.

The following is the list of the gentlemen so far as we were able to procure it:

Joe Thompson,	Hungarian King.
H. Head,	Bull Fighter.
C. Harris,	Cowboy.
P. Cook,	Up-to-date Jockey.
B. Chipman,	Bluebeard.
E. Hallow,	Dancing Bear.
L. Small,	Hamlet.
M. Lunt,	Mexican.
C. McCann,	Knockabout Clown.
A. Wilson,	Prince Carnival.
W. Harrigan,	Page.
H. Bird,	Charles II.
P. Murphy,	Matador.
F. Carpenter,	Indian.
G. Hamilton,	Turk.
E. Noyes,	The Dago.
I. Hubbard,	The Duke.
W. Shaylor,	Clown.
H. Dockham,	G. Washington.
P. Cole,	Large Mexican.
Ira Hubbard,	Don Jose.
J. Chipman,	Silver Prince.
A. Cole,	Pierrot.
P. Lowe,	Garnet Armor.
E. Sawyer,	Don Cæsar.
T. Davis,	Mephistopheles.
J. Chamberlin,	Romeo.
E. Polley,	Irish Jockey.
H. Skillins,	Darky Sport.
M. Mills,	The Highlander.
H. Thurlow,	Uncle Sam.
N. Lochhead,	Prince of Wales.
C. Chipman,	School-Boy.
S. Wilbur Rowe,	Mexican Cowboy.
James Stone,	Hungarian King.
G. A. Sawyer,	King of Sandwich Islands.

Such is the list of the merry crowd of maskers who took active part and at 11.30 sat down to the generous repast provided for them by Hiram Ricker & Sons, as also were all the expenses attendant upon the festival.

The success of the annual masque was very largely due to the interested and indefatigable efforts of Mrs. E. P. Ricker and Miss Nettie Ricker, who very earnestly labored for its successful accomplishment, in which they were greatly aided by Miss Leonard, Miss Byrne, and Miss Danahy.

The hall was artistically decorated by Mr. Gallagher in his usual tasteful manner, while Mr. Wareham very successfully attended to the elaborate embellishment of the tables and dining-room.

It appears to be conceded that it was even more successful than that of any previous event of the kind, which reflects great credit upon all concerned. The whole affair passed off smoothly, and by one o'clock was entirely a thing of the past.

The thanks of the editors are due Miss Catherine Murphy for her appropriate realization of "THE HILL-TOP," the dress being made entirely from the covers of this paper, an illustration of which heads this article.

Our Menu.

RECIPE No. 24.

Strawberry Short-Cake.

One quart of flour, one cup of washed butter, two large spoonfuls of baking powder wet with milk enough so as to roll it out one-half inch thick. Cut it in halves. Butter one half and put the other half on top, and cut through this with a cutter. Bake twenty minutes.

Prepare strawberries with sugar. Put one quart of cream on the ice and whip until it is stiff. Serve all together.

RECIPE No. 25.

Charlotte Russe.

One cup of yolks, one cup of sugar, one cup of flour, one tablespoonful of water. Beat eggs, sugar, and water together until light. One small teaspoonful of baking powder. Bake in thin sheets on paper, and cut in strips to serve in the molds.

Filling for Charlotte Russe.

One quart of cream whipped stiff, and one-half ounce of gelatine dissolved in water. Sweeten the cream, and flavor with vanilla.

RECIPE No. 26.

Philadelphia Ice-Cream.

One quart of cream, one and one-half cups of sugar. Flavor with vanilla. Freeze. This will serve fifteen people.

RECIPE No. 27.

Chocolate Frosting.

Whites of four eggs, one cup of granulated sugar. Beat the eggs stiff, and beat in sugar. Flavor with vanilla. Put a small piece of chocolate in the oven with a piece of butter. After it is melted, beat it into the whites of the eggs.

Zanoni.

Prof. Zanoni gave one of the most enjoyable entertainments of the season, in the Music Hall, Friday evening, August 28th. The hall was crowded.

Prof. Zanoni is unquestionably the greatest mind reader of the nineteenth century. The *London Times* says of him: "Zanoni is the most marvelous expositor of psychological transmission that the world has ever seen." The guests were so much interested in him that he remained and gave another entertainment Saturday evening in the amusement room.

Children's Column.

In heaven's scales a great heart weighs more than a big brain.

Down South, a charming young lady took it upon herself to try and educate the little darky children, and was doing very well, when one day one of the pickaninnies, who had been made a pet about the house, asked for some "bread and 'lasses." Whereupon his mistress took it upon herself to correct him. "You should not say 'lasses, but molasses." This was evidently slightly puzzling, for with a moment's hesitation he said, "How can I say mo-lasses, when I haint had none yet?"

During the progress of the great fire in Boston, years ago, a certain family living in the outskirts of the city were up all night, except the little ones, who were sleeping quietly through it all, until about three o'clock, when the youngest of the family, a little girl of three, awoke; and, astonished at seeing the lights burning and every one up and dressed, inquired the cause.

"There is a great fire in the city," was the reply.

She pondered for a moment, and then said: "Why don't papa put his foot on it?"

New Books.

FROM MRS. S. W. KEENE.
Mrs. Romney; by Rosa Nouchette Carey.
Drawn Blank; by Mrs. Robert Jocelyn.

FROM ALLEN MERRILL ROGERS.
A Rogue's Daughter; by Adeline Sergeant.

FROM GEORGE BARKER CLARK.
Flotsam; by Henry Seton Merriman.

FROM MISS T. ROSENHEIM.
A Change of Air; by Anthony Hope.
At the Green Dragon; by Beatrice Harraden.

FROM MRS. FRANKLIN E. TAYLOR.
Adam Johnstone's Son; by F. Marion Crawford.

FROM MRS. JOHN R. HOXIE.
Tale of Two Cities; by Charles Dickens.
A Study in Scarlet; by A. Conan Doyle.
The Old, Old Story; by Rosa Nouchette Carey.
Romance of the New Bethesda; by Jane Lippitt Patterson.

Rondel.

In vain we cry, "Our love's not dying,
The sweet love, dear, we knew of yore."
We feel, the while in sadness sighing,
'Twill soon have passed forevermore.

Naught hath the future, dear, in store
Save hate, all tenderness defying.
In vain we cry, "Our love's not dying,
The old sweet love we knew of yore."

'Tis better, dear, we part, not trying
To nurse the love we can't restore,
But live in memory once more
Those days with sweet love beautifying.
In vain we cry, "Our love's not dying,
The old sweet love we knew of yore."

Musical Programme.

SUNDAY, SEPTEMBER 6, 1896, AT 8.15 P.M.

1. Marche Hongrois. Berlioz.
2. Cornet Solo—Romanza Non e'vel.—Mattei-Müller. Mr. P. Millet.
3. First Movement from Symphony in B Minor.—Schubert.
4. { a. Etude Reverie.—Müller.
    { b. Grossmutterchen.—Lange.
5. Piano Solo. Mr. Edmund Kuntz.
6. Selection—Si j'etais Roi.—Adam.

FRANK CARLOS GRIFFITH, } EDITORS.
NETTIE M. RICKER,

PUBLISHED EVERY SUNDAY MORNING DURING THE MONTHS
OF JULY, AUGUST, AND SEPTEMBER, IN THE INTERESTS OF

POLAND SPRINGS AND ITS VISITORS.

All contributions relative to the guests of Poland Springs
will be thankfully received.

To insure publication, all communications should reach the
editors not later than Wednesday preceding day of issue.

All parties desiring rates for advertising in the HILL-TOP
should write the editors for same.

The subscription price of the HILL-TOP is $1.00 for the
season, post-paid. Single copies will be mailed at 10c. each.

Address,

"EDITORS HILL-TOP,"
Poland Spring House,
South Poland, Maine.

PRINTED AT JOURNAL OFFICE, LEWISTON.

Sunday, September 6, 1896.

Editorial.

WITH this number we present our weekly
display of the happenings on Ricker Hill,
to very largely a new audience, and our
vitascopic journal reminds all new-comers that with
each succeeding week, from the first of July annually, THE HILL-TOP has faithfully chronicled the
comings and goings of the multitude of visitors at
this busy place, and will live its allotted span of
life, and retire to its winter slumbers after one
more week of a busy life.

By perusing the edition of '96 one will get as
comprehensive an idea of Poland life as it would
be possible to give in a complete illustrated guide-
book, and will form a nice souvenir of a visit to
Poland Springs.

The white mantle which covers the hill-tops in
Poland in winter, will spread itself over the HILL-
TOP of summer and hide its green cover, it is to
be hoped with charity for its shortcomings, and
preserve its slumbering life for another campaign
in '97.

Tid-Bits.

Miss M. B. Whitney of Boston is visiting
Poland Springs.

Dr. and Mrs. Ring of New Haven, are at the
Poland Spring House.

Mrs. A. M. Cunningham of Washington
arrived September 1st.

Mr. and Mrs. C. J. Bonaparte of Baltimore
are guests at Poland Springs.

Miss Allison and Miss M. Allison of Germantown, Pa., are at the Mansion House.

The pencil sketch made by Mr. Robert Vonnoh
of Mr. Daniel Kuntz is excellent.

Mr. John Reed Whipple is visiting his mother,
Mrs. Whipple, at the Poland Spring House.

Mr. and Mrs. F. W. Rice of Chicago are at the
Poland Spring House. Mr. Rice is editor of the
National Hotel Reporter.

Henry M. Heath of Augusta, one of Maine's
state senators, has been an interested visitor,
accompanied by Mrs. Heath.

Mr. J. D. Price of the Ormond, Florida, and
also of the Mount Pleasant House, witnessed the
employees' ball, Monday evening.

Mr. and Mrs. T. J. Evans, Mr. and Mrs. T.
D. Thayer, and Miss Jennie F. Thayer, of East
Weymouth, Mass., arrived September 2d and
occupied one of the Maine State suites.

Poland Springs extended a hearty welcome to
Governor Cleaves on his return, September 2d.
His delightful powers as a speaker were exempli-
fied fully at Poland Corner, that evening, when
clever and pointed story after story kept his audience in the best of humor.

Mrs. Edwin Todd entertained her friends,
August 26th, in her room with an interesting
game. It was this: pictures of different authors
were placed around the room. Under each picture
the title of one or two of his works was written
or a quotation from them. Each person was asked
to guess the name of the author.

At the concert, Saturday morning, August
29th, Miss Katherine Ricker sang an Italian aria
and a group of three songs by d'Hartelot, Cham-
inade, and Schubert. Miss Ricker has a very
rich and full contralto voice, which she has under
perfect control. Her musical ability is well developed, and she is a young lady of great promise.
The orchestra rendered a selection from "Tannhäuser" and Beethoven's "Adagio from Sonata
Pathetique." The concert was very fine, as it
always is.

Walter F. Lansil.

This celebrated marine painter is a native of Bangor, Me., but is of French descent, and came to Boston in 1870, opening his first studio in the Studio Building, where he still is located.

Mr. Lansil was one of the Jury of Awards for the Dominion of Canada at the Fine Arts Exhibition at St. John, N. B., in 1883, and the next year went to Europe and entered Julian's Studio in Paris, subsequently visiting Holland, Belgium, Germany, and Italy, devoting considerable time to painting in Venice, since which time he has made Venetian subjects a specialty.

The following are some of his works: "Fisherman Becalmed," owned by Smith College, Northampton, Mass.; "In Vineyard Sound," owned by Wellesley College; "Trawlers Making Port and Midnight Arrival," owned by Adams House, Boston; "Dutch River Craft," owned by Boston Art Club; "Veteran of the Heroic Fleet," owned by Massachusetts Charitable Mechanics Association; "Engagement Between the Enterprise and Boxer, 1813," bought by the State of Massachusetts and placed on board the nautical training ship, Enterprise; "Nantasket Beach," owned by ex-Secretary Vilas of the Interior Department. His pictures may be found in the private collections of ex-Governor Oliver Ames of Massachusetts; Hon. Frank M. Ames; Mrs. General Lander of Salem; Hon. John Quincy Adams, Hon. Jona-

than A. Lane, Boston; Capt. George H. Perkins, U. S. N.; Commander John F. Merry, U. S. N.; Col. Albert A. Pope, Boston, etc.

He is a member of the Boston Art Club, having been on the Board of Management in 1880, 1881, 1887, 1888, and 1889; was President of Unity Art Club, 1892-1893; and received medals in 1878, 1881, and 1884.

The Poland Springs Art Gallery has four of his magnificent Venetian paintings on exhibition at the present time, all in Alcove E and numbered 78 to 81. Lansil's work is sufficiently beautiful to be its own recommendation.

Cyclist Column.

> "The scorcher is a man of speed
> Upon his steed of steel,
> But an X-ray of him looks quite like
> A barrel-hoop on a wheel."

FOR A BICYCLE TRIP.
[New York Times.]

The Bicycle Book has come to take its place with the various gift blank books that thoughtful caterers to the public taste provide. It is a diary for a trip on the wheel, suitably bound and inscribed. It has blank spaces for the record of events, the autographs of chance acquaintances who may prove interesting, and photographs of bits of scenery that one may wish to secure with that *vade-mecum* of every bicycle journey—a camera. The book is not practical, but ministers to the sentiment of the trip, and such impedimenta as road maps and other material aids to wheeling are not for its dainty and ornamental leaves.

PUTS THE WHEEL ON RUNNERS.
New Device for Cycling on Ice Put on the Market.

A device has been made which will enable the bicycle enthusiast to ride upon ice. After removing the front wheel of the bicycle a runner like that of a skate is attached. The rear wheel is provided with spurs, and is held slightly above the surface of the ice by a runner attached to the rear axle. The standard of this runner is capable of being adjusted in length by a screw so the grip of the spurs on the ice may be regulated. The inventor claims that great speed may be attained, and no slipping is encountered.

WHEELING FOR SPITE.
[New York Telegram.]

A few days ago a young lady, almost gasping for breath, entered the riding school of a local bicycle establishment and said she wanted to learn to ride. "Can I learn this evening?"

"I don't know," said the obliging clerk, "but there's the school and teacher, if you desire to make an effort."

"I must learn," she said. "I don't see why you can't teach me. I'm a sufferer from heart trouble, but then I guess that won't make any difference."

She was soon in charge of the best teacher in the school, and although taken good care of she got the usual number of knocks and falls. But the young lady was determined, and she assured the teacher that she did not mind a little rough experience.

Before departing she told one of the ladies, confidentially, that she and her sweetheart were on the " outs." He did not want her to ride a wheel, and because of their strained relations she had concluded that she would learn. All she wanted was to ride past his house, where he could see her, and then she would be happy.

She returned the second day and then mastered the machine. Now she has no use for the wheel, for she and the young man are no longer on the " outs."

KISMET.
[Somerville Journal.]

He watched her riding down the street,
　So fleet!
Propelled by dainty, twinkling feet,
　Petite;
Her cycling suit was trim and neat,
　Complete;
A prettier girl you'd seldom meet—
　Or never.

She looked at him—the shyest glance,
　Askance;
Took in his quiet elegance,
　Perchance;
Then how his laughing eyes did dance!
　For chance
Upset her, ending her romance
　Forever!

An Ab-Original Tale.

BY A SAVAGE.

[Continued.]

At last the hour of battle came,
  That hour so still and solemn,
And David thought upon the foe
  And hoped that they might maul 'em.
"I'll have my bullet in," said he,
  "Upon the leaded column."

He took the letters from his love
  And read them o'er and o'er;
He smiled at her endearing term:
  "The flower of all the corps!"
I ought to be," he said, "if I
  Had only ten drills more."

She wrote to him of many thoughts
  Her tenderness would utter;
And not a pang of jealousy
  Her loving heart did flutter;
She knew that he, a soldier bred,
  Would not have any but her.

And David served until he joined
  The victor's joyous shout;
They clove the ranks of sinner men,
  And put them to a rout;
The enemy were peppered well
  When he was mustard out.

The war was o'er; the purpose gained
  For which the soldiers rose;
And in the early spring they turned
  Their backs upon their foes;
Although the lilacs were put out
  They hadn't come to blows.

And now, on the return of peace,
  Our lovers' hearts were gay;
Their marriage was accomplished in
  The good old-fashioned way;
And they had many stable joys
  Upon their bridal day.

Matterhorn.

Miss Annie S. Peck delivered her lecture, illustrated by very excellent views, on her ascent of the Matterhorn, on Thursday evening, in the Music Hall. It was very well attended, and gave much satisfaction.

When the mail brought this letter for me
My joy I could hardly restrain,
For I thought it was written by Maud
In her usual *light, airy* vein.

I opened the seal, but, alas!
Its contents weren't what I supposed;
Yet I'll own they were *airy* and *light*—
'Twas my gas bill I found there enclosed.

An Episcopal clergyman's wife living in southern Texas sends to Mrs. Hiram Ricker a large quantity of Mexican drawn work. Mrs. Ricker will be glad to show it to all who will call at her cottage. It is charity work and the prices are very reasonable.

Guests at Poland Spring House

SEPTEMBER 2, 1896.

Mr. and Mrs. M. T. Atwood	New York.
Miss Atwood	New York.
Mrs. W. H. Baines	Boston.
Miss Rose P. Brown	Brookline.
C. W. Blodgett	Boston.
Mr. and Mrs. A. B. Butterfield	Boston.
Miss Barstow	Boston.
Mrs. H. Batterman	Brooklyn.
Miss A. H. Batterman	Brooklyn.
H. L. Batterman	Brooklyn.
H. E. Barnard	San Antonio.
Mr. and Mrs. C. J. Bonaparte	Baltimore.
Miss M. E. Bertrams	Hyde Park.
Mrs. A. E. Buchanan	Elizabeth, N. J.
Mr. and Mrs. Wm. H. Brown	New York.
Mr. and Mrs. A. de Barry	New York.
Miss de Barry	New York.
Miss Anita de Barry	New York.
T. M. Brumby	New York.
Mr. Joseph A. Brown	Boston.
Miss Belle G. Brown	Boston.
Mr. and Mrs. N. A. Baldwin	New Haven.
Mr. Wm. A. Bigelow	New York.
Mr. and Mrs. H. O. Blight	Cambridge.
Mrs. Beyrle	Philadelphia.
Mrs. J. F. Beckwith	Savannah.
Miss Madeline Baines	Brookline, Mass.
Mr. and Mrs. P. H. Bathydt	New York.
Mr. and Mrs. W. A. Castle	Springfield.
Mrs. E. M. Carroll	Boston.
E. A. Carroll	Boston.
Mrs. Edw. E. Clark	Boston.
Miss Florence Cregle	New York.
Mrs. W. R. Clarkson	New York.
Gov. Henry B. Cleaves	Portland.
Mr. and Mrs. G. C. Currier	New York.
Mrs. Agnes S. Curtis	New York.
Mr. and Mrs. Geo. W. Coleman	Boston.
Mr. Andrew R. Culver	Brooklyn.
Mr. and Mrs. F. W. Carpenter	Providence.
Miss Julia Carpenter	Providence.
Mr. and Mrs. C. C. Corbin	Webster, Mass.
W. H. Chappell	Chicago.
Miss Chappell	Chicago.
Mrs. Z. Chandler	Detroit, Mich.
Mrs. B. B. Claxton	Philadelphia.
George F. Curtis	Boston.
Miss F. H. Curtis	Boston.
Mr. and Mrs. Westmoreland Davis	New York.
Miss Durkee	Philadelphia.
Mrs. Wm. C. Dunton	New York.
Miss C. S. Duel	New Haven.
Mr. and Mrs. Andrew J. Dotger	South Orange, N. J.
Mr. and Mrs. T. J. Evans	East Weymouth, Mass.
Miss D. C. Fitch	New Haven.
Miss E. T. Fitch	New Haven
Miss Fletcher	Boston.
Mrs. J. D. Fessenden	New York.
Mrs. R. G. Feltus	Philadelphia.
Annie L. Fall	Boston.
Mrs. J. R. Farnham	Waltham.
Miss Ada T. Griswold	Columbus, Wis.
Miss Edith M. Griswold	Columbus, Wis.
J. H. Goodenow	New York.
Franklin N. Gregory	Brooklyn.
Mrs. M. M. Gross	Chicago.
Mr. John Goldthwaite	Boston.
Miss E. B. Goldthwaite	Boston.
Mrs. L. M. Gale	Washington.
Miss Olive Gale	Washington.
Mrs. A. Gilbert	Plainfield, N. J.
Mrs. George F. Gregory	Brooklyn.
Mr. and Mrs. T. Gilman	Montreal.
Thomas M. Gale	Washington, D. C.
Mr. and Mrs. J. F. Godley	Trenton, N. J.
Miss Gregory	Brooklyn.
Mr. and Mrs. J. C. Haynes	Boston.
Miss E. Margaret Haynes	Boston.
Henry A. Hildreth	Boston.
Mrs. F. A. Harter	Brooklyn.
Miss Isabel Harter	Brooklyn.
Mr. and Mrs. I. K. Hamilton	Chicago.
Miss I. G. Haydock	Philadelphia.
Mrs. T. B. Hellner	Elizabeth, N. J.
Mr. and Mrs. H. M. Heath	Augusta.
Mr. and Mrs. F. D. Hatfield	New York.
Mrs. S. B. Hubbard	Jacksonville.
Mrs. W. W. Hartwell	Plattsburgh, N. Y.
Mr. and Mrs. John R. Hoxie	Chicago.
Miss Anna Hoxie	Chicago.
Mr. and Mrs. Horace Hunt	New York.
Mrs. M. B. Hoffman	New York.
Mr. and Mrs. Hudson Hoagland	New York.
Mr. and Mrs. E. Holmes	New York.
Miss Horner	Philadelphia.
Miss Anna Havens	Boston.
Mrs. M. E. Hildreth	Boston.
Miss Alma Hildreth	Boston.
Col. Joseph A. Ingalls and family	Boston.
Mrs. W. H. Inman	New York.
Miss W. L. Inman	New York.
Chas. L. Johnson	New York.
Fred C. Johnson	New York.
Miss Johnson	Connecticut.
Mr. and Mrs. J. Oswald Jimenis and family	New York.
Mrs. Julian James	Washington.
Mrs. E. A. Knapp	New York.
Mrs. Craige Lippincott	Philadelphia.
Miss Constance Lippincott	Philadelphia.
Miss Lippincott	Philadelphia.
Mr. and Mrs. Thos. Lewis and family	New York.
Mrs. Victor F. Lawson	Chicago.
Mrs. LaBan	New York.
Miss May Lord	New Jersey.
Mr. Walter A. LaBan	New York.
Rev. and Mrs. W. P. Lewis	Philadelphia.
Mrs. B. C. Lake	New Haven.
Miss Leland	New York.
James D. Laird	San Francisco.
Mr. and Mrs. Thomas P. Langdon	Baltimore.
Mr. and Mrs. B. N. Lapham	Providence.
Mr. and Mrs. E. H. Linley	St. Louis.
Mr. and Mrs. Thomas Mack	Boston.
Mrs. V. McLean	New York.
Miss V. McLean	New York.
Miss H. G. McLean	New York.
Mrs. J. W. Merrill	Boston.
Miss Merrill	Boston.
Henry P. Morrison	New Brighton.
Mr. and Mrs. T. B. M. Mason	Washington.
Mrs. T. B. Myers	Washington.
Mrs. Jno. H. Maginnis	New Orleans.
Mr. Jno. H. Maginnis	New Orleans.
Mrs. A. Mully	Washington.
Mrs. J. T. Montgomery	Philadelphia.
Mrs. Christine Marburg	Baltimore.
The Misses Marburg	Baltimore.
Mr. and Mrs. John T. Martin	New York.
Mr. and Mrs. W. T. Ness	Boston.
Mr. and Mrs. H. S. Osgood	Portland.
Mr. and Mrs. Josiah Oakes	Malden, Mass.
Thomas Peckham	Newport R. I.
Miss L. Paig	New York.
Miss S. Paig	New York.
Miss E. A. Prall	New York.
Mrs. J. A. Pettee	New York.
Mrs. Henry U. Palmer	Brooklyn.
Masters Austin and Chester Palmer	Brooklyn.
Mrs. M. E. Parsons	Boston.
Miss A. J. Pomeroy	New York.
W. H. Peterson	Boston.
S. S. Riker	New York.
Dr. and Mrs. Ring	New Haven.
Miss Marion Richardson	Boston.
Mrs. Runyon	Plainfield, N. J.
Mr. and Mrs. Augustus Richardson	Boston.
Miss Richardson	Boston.
Mrs. E. J. Robinson	Boston.
Miss Roberts	Philadelphia.

Mrs. M. E. Richards	New York.
Miss Randolph	Plainfield, N. J.
D. T. Rines	Portland.
Mr. and Mrs. E. A. Strong	Boston.
Mrs. W. M. Snow	Brookline.
H. O. Seixas	New Orleans.
Mrs. T. P. Shepard	Providence.
Mrs. John H. Silsbee	Boston.
Mr. and Mrs. S. R. Small	Portland.
Mrs. S. Skaats	New York.
Miss Slade	New York.
Dr. and Mrs. C. C. Schuyler	Plattsburgh, N. Y.
Mr. and Mrs. A. T. Salter	Washington.
Mr. and Mrs. Joseph W. Sandford	Plainfield, N. J.
Mr. and Mrs. J. B. Sawyer	Dover, N. H.
Mr. and Mrs. E. P. Smith	New York.
Mrs. G. W. Simpson	Brooklyn.
Miss B. C. Simpson	Brooklyn.
Miss Mabel Simpson	Brooklyn.
Mrs. A. D. Stormes	
John H. Shortridge	Philadelphia.
Miss L. E. Shortridge	Philadelphia.
Miss F. A. Shortridge	Philadelphia.
Mr. and Mrs. H. H. Schaul	Atlanta.
Mr. and Mrs. C. N. Shaw	Boston.
Miss Sparks	Philadelphia.
Mr. and Mrs. A. Loudon Snowden	Philadelphia.
Miss Smith	Montreal.
George Trott	Philadelphia.
F. Tompkins	Newport, R. I.
Mr. and Mrs. E. G. Thurber	New York.
Mr. and Mrs. F. D. Thayer	East Weymouth, Mass.
Miss Jennie F. Thayer	East Weymouth, Mass.
Mr. and Mrs. J. P. Talliaferro	Jacksonville, Fla.
Miss J. P. Talliaferro	Jacksonville, Fla.
Miss Anna V. Talliaferro	Jacksonville, Fla.
Miss Tillotson	New Haven.
Miss N. E. Ten Broeck	New York.
Mrs. Orlando Tompkins	Boston.
Mr. and Mrs. F. E. Taylor	Brooklyn.
D. B. Vickery	Haverhill.
Mrs. A. Van Wagener	Auburndale, Mass.
Miss Ida B. Van Wagener	Auburndale, Mass.
Mr. and Mrs. Peter Van Voorhees	Camden, N. J.
J. D. Van Voorhees	Camden, N. J.
Miss Wray	Southampton.
Miss J. Wray	Southampton.
Mr. E. Warner	Troy, N. Y.
Miss M. B. Whitney	Boston.
Mr. John Reed Whipple	Boston.
Mr. and Mrs. Henry C. Weston	Boston.
Mrs. Chas. Warner	Troy, N. Y.
Miss C. A. Warner	Troy, N. Y.
Miss M. V. Warner	Troy, N. Y.
Miss M. A. Winslow	Troy, N. Y.
Mrs. J. Reed Whipple	Boston.
Dr. M. C. Wedgwood and Mrs. Wedgwood	Lewiston.
Mr. F. R. Wharton	Philadelphia.
Mr. and Mrs. W. S. Wymond	Louisville, Ky.
Miss Wymond	Louisville, Ky.
Mrs. L. P. Worthington	Doylestown, Pa.
Miss Worthington	Doylestown, Pa.
Mr. N. Whitman	New York.
Mr. and Mrs. E. F. Watkins	Chicago.
Mr. and Mrs. A. R. Wright and son	Philadelphia.
Mr. and Mrs. John Wales	Brookline.

Sunday Service.

Rev. H. B. Smith of Troy, N. Y., preached in Music Hall, Sunday, August 30th. His text was Job, chapter 12, verse 8. The hall was well filled and the sermon was excellent.

Mrs. Edward E. Clark of Boston is a guest at the Poland Spring House. Mrs. Clark has been a large contributor to the library.

Household Hints.

[Boston Herald.]

It does not take long for a pair of boots that are worn constantly to get so shabby that frequent blacking seems powerless to restore their freshness. Then is the time to cut off all the old buttons and put on a set of bright new ones.

Grease stains on cloth may often be removed with magnesia. The stained place is first dampened; then the magnesia is moistened and vigorously rubbed on the stain. It must be allowed to dry thoroughly. Then the powder can be easily shaken off.

Many housewives, from a desire for neatness, have their coal wet or dampened before laying it in the cellar. This is a practice full of danger, as wet coal throws off poisonous gases, which injure the health of the people breathing them. These gases cannot be kept from penetrating through the house.

Ink may be taken out of paper in the following way if the stain is not too old: Take a teaspoonful of chlorinated lime and pour just enough water over it to cover it. Take a piece of old linen and moisten it with this mixture, and do not rub, but pat the stain, and it will slowly disappear. If one application does not remove the stain let the paper dry and then apply again.

Baking dishes that become burned in the oven, and plates and platters that become blackened with the food scorched upon them, should not go through the tedious process of scraping. Simply put a little water and ashes in the dish and let it become warm, and the burnt and discolored portions may be easily cleaned without injuring the dish.

Women who wish their families to be fed on the most nourishing and healthful food will do well to discourage the eating of potatoes in the morning, and to provide in their place a well and thoroughly cooked cereal, with cream or rich milk. Boiled rice or hominy may be profitably exchanged for potatoes at dinner at least three or four times a week, and it is a most admirable food with meat, and easily digested.

To stain wood to look like ebony, take a solution of sulphate of iron, and wash the wood over twice. When the wood becomes dry apply two or three coats of a strong decoction of logwood. Wipe the wood dry and polish with a flannel wet in linseed oil.

A man experienced in the care of invalids; an extensive traveller, not only all over this country, but frequently in Europe; gentle, intelligent, well-read, and conversant with people and places, desires an opportunity to accompany an elderly invalid gentleman or lady in the capacity of companion. He can be highly recommended. Information may be had from the Librarian, Maine State Building.

Arrivals.

POLAND SPRING HOUSE.

FROM AUG. 28 TO SEP. 4, 1896.

Atwood, Mr. and Mrs. Tascus	Auburn.
Atwood, Mr. and Mrs. M. F.	New York.
Atwood, Miss	New York.
Abbott, Mrs. L. F.	Boston.
Bradley, Mr. and Mrs. H.	Boston.
Brown, Mr. and Mrs. H. J.	Portland.
Brown, Miss Rose P.	Brookline.
Bates, Jacob P.	Boston.
Baines, Mrs. W. H.	Boston.
Blanchard, C. G.	Boston.
Blanchard, Mrs. E. O.	Boston.
Browne, F. H.	Waltham.
Batton, Miss Clara	Massillon, O.
Blodgett, C. W.	Boston.
Blackman, G. E.	Boston.
Burt, Mrs. B. L.	Taunton.
Butterfield, Mr. and Mrs. A. B.	Boston.
Barstow, Miss	Boston.
Batterman, Mrs. H.	Brooklyn.
Batterman, Miss A. H.	Brooklyn.
Batterman, H. L.	Brooklyn.
Baldwin, N. A. 2d	Brooklyn.
Bernard, H. E.	San Antonio.
Bonaparte, Mr. and Mrs. C. J.	Baltimore.
Buttams, Miss M. E.	Hyde Park.
Buchanan, Mrs. A. E.	Elizabeth, N. J.
Brown, Mr. and Mrs. Wm. H.	New York.
Breemby, T. M.	New York.
deBarry, Mr. and Mrs. A.	New York.
deBarry, Miss	New York.
deBarry, Miss Anita	New York.
Bickford, Miss Tavie	Norway.
Chandler, C. P.	New Gloucester.
Chase, Miss Mary E.	Philadelphia.
Clayson, Mrs.	Jersey City.
Callahan, J. H.	Lewiston.
Crosby, Miss Maude	Auburn.
Conant, Charles	Auburn.
Clark, Mrs. Charles P.	New Haven.
Clark, Miss	New Haven.
Cluet, A. E.	Quebec.
Clarkson, Mrs. W. R.	New York.
Cleaves, Henry B.	Portland.
Carter, Miss Ethel	Norway.
Carroll, Miss Mabelle	Boston.
Carson, Miss	Connecticut.
Clough, Mr. and Mrs. J. A.	Chicago.
Cobb, Mr. and Mrs. A. R.	Portland.
Castle, Mr. and Mrs. W. A.	Springfield.
Carroll, Mrs. E. M.	Boston.
Clark, Mrs. Edward E.	Boston.
Carroll, E. A.	Boston.
Dexter, Mr. and Mrs. C. W.	Auburn.
Durkee, Miss	Philadelphia.
Davis, Mrs. Lombard	New York.
Elliot, Mr. and Mrs. G. C.	St. Louis.
Elliot, Mr. and Mrs. G. C., Jr.	St. Louis.
Evans, Mr. and Mrs. T. J.	E. Weymouth.
Engle, Miss Florence	New York.
Endicott, Wm. F.	Haverhill.
Falconer, Wm. L.	Saco.
Farnum, Paul	Philadelphia.
Fulton, Mr. and Mrs. E. M.	New York.
Flye, C. M.	Boston.
Fitch, Miss D. C.	New Haven.
Fitch, Miss E. T.	New Haven.
Greer, Misses J. W. and M. L.	Doylestown, Pa.
Gutmann, Mr. and Mrs. F.	Lewiston.
Grays, E. W.	Auburn.

Ganger, A. E.	Mechanic Falls.
Gammon, Mr. and Mrs. E. O.	Mechanic Falls.
Griswold, Miss Ada T.	Columbus, Wis.
Griswold, Miss Edith M.	Columbus, Wis.
Griffin, Mrs. Delia M.	New Gloucester.
Gilbert, J. H.	Brooklyn.
Golden, Miss A. E.	New York.
Gregory, Franklin N.	Brooklyn.
Gross, Mrs. M. M.	Chicago.
Gilchrest, Miss Ethel	Thomaston.
Goodhue, Mr. and Mrs. A. P.	Salem.
Goldthwait, Mr. and Mrs. J.	Boston.
Gray, Mr. and Mrs. Jos. H.	Boston.
Goodenow, J. H.	New York.
Hoffman, F. S.	Schenectady.
Herbert, Mr. and Mrs. Albert	Boston.
Hildreth, Henry A.	Boston.
Haynes, Mr. and Mrs. John C.	Boston.
Haynes, Miss E. Margaret	Boston.
Hungerford, Mr. and Mrs. R. S.	Watertown.
Hungerford, Miss Ida R.	Watertown.
Harter, Mrs. F. A.	Brooklyn.
Harter, Miss Isabel	Brooklyn.
Haydock, Miss S. G.	Philadelphia.
Hellmer, Mrs. F. B.	Elizabeth, N. J.
Heath, Mr. and Mrs. H. M.	Augusta.
Hatfield, Mr. and Mrs. Frank D.	New York.
Harris, Mrs. A.	New York.
Harris, Henry S.	New York.
Harris, Rosalie T.	New York.
Herbert, P. S.	Norway.
Howe, Geo. R.	Ellsworth.
Hale, Mrs. Eugene	Montreal.
Hubut, Miss	Chicago.
Hamilton, Mrs. I. K.	
Jimenis, Mr. and Mrs. J. Oswald	New York.
Jordan, Miss Harriet	Auburn.
Jellison, Mr. and Mrs. Z.	Brooklyn.
Johnson, Charles T.	New York.
Johnson, Fred C.	New York.
Johnson, Miss	Connecticut.
Jackson, R. E.	Hot Springs, Ark.
Lippincott, Mrs. Craige	Philadelphia.
Lippincott, Miss Constance	Philadelphia.
Lippincott, Miss	Philadelphia.
Lawton, A. F.	Lewiston.
Lincoln, M. E.	Boston.
Lord, Hartley L.	Saco.
Lathrop, Mrs. A. G.	Lewiston.
Lawson, Mrs. Victor F.	Chicago.
LaBau, Mrs.	New York.
LaBau, Walter A.	New York.
Lord, Miss Mary	New Jersey.
Little, Mr. and Mrs. Francis H.	Boston.
Lewis, Mr. and Mrs. Thos.	New York.
Leonard, Mrs. Geo. H.	Boston.
Leonard, Miss	Boston.
Loring, Mrs. Prentis	Portland.
Loring, Mrs. Philip Quincy	Portland.
Mackenzie, M.	Lewiston.
McDonnell, Mrs. D. D.	Minneapolis.
McCracker, J. E.	New York.
Manley, W. R.	New York.
Mohr, R. H.	Boston.
Maltby, Mrs. W. L.	Montreal.
Maltby, Miss Emma	Montreal.
McLean, Mrs. V.	New York.
McLean, Miss V.	New York.
McLean, Miss H. G.	New York.
Nealey, A. B.	Lewiston.
Osgood, H. S.	Portland.
Osgood, W. C.	Portland.
Page, Mr. and Mrs. Kilby	Boston.
Pattee, Stanley S.	Portland.
Pullman, Mr. and Mrs. J. M.	Lynn.
Pullman, Mr. and Mrs. Fred A.	Lynn.
Packer, Charles	Newport.

Pendleton, Dr. and Mrs. L. W.	Portland.
Pendleton, Miss	Portland.
Pendleton, Dana	Portland.
Pendleton, Mr. and Mrs. Edward W.	Detroit.
Price, J. D.	Ormond, Fla.
Pitcher, Mr. and Mrs. F. W.	New York.
Peck, Miss A. S.	
Phinney, Miss Edith	Boston.
Peckham, Thos. P.	Newport.
Paig, Miss L.	New York.
Paig, Miss S.	New York.
Rose, Rev. and Mrs. Henry R.	Auburn.
Reed, Horace	Whitman.
Rice, Mr. and Mrs. F. W.	Chicago.
Ricker, H. H.	Portland.
Randall, Mr. and Mrs. James W.	New York.
Rogers, Mr. and Mrs. B.	Boston.
Ross, Mr. and Mrs. J.	Ipswich.
Ross, Miss A. W.	Ipswich.
Ring, Dr. and Mrs.	New Haven.
Rice, John O.	Portland.
Ramsdell, Mrs. G. W.	
Ruddick, Miss M.	
Shepard, Mrs. T. P.	Providence.
Shethar, E. H.	New York.
Strong, Mr. and Mrs. Edward A.	Boston.
Shoemaker, C. J.	Wilkesbarre.
Silsbee, Mrs. John H.	Boston.
Smith, Miss Heloise	Bath.
Simpson, Mrs. Myra	Boston.
Snow, Mrs. W. M.	Brookline.
Smith, Mr. and Mrs. H. B.	Troy.
Slack, F. W., Jr.	Hillsdale, Mich.
Seals, E. B.	Boston.
Scudder, Mrs. T. H.	Newton Center.
Tompkins, F.	Newport.
Thomas, C.	Lewiston.
Thurber, Mr. and Mrs. E. G.	New York.
Thayer, Mr. and Mrs. T. D.	E. Weymouth, Mass.
Thayer, Miss Jennie T.	E. Weymouth, Mass.
Taliaferro, Mr. and Mrs. Jas. P.	Jacksonville.
Taliaferro, Miss J. P.	Jacksonville.
Taliaferro, Miss Anna V.	Jacksonville.
Tetlow, Mrs. A. H.	Taunton.
Thornton, Miss R. E.	Boston.
Tirue, Samuel A.	Portland.
Tirott, George	Philadelphia.
Taylor, James R.	Brooklyn.
Urquhart, D.	Lewiston.
Vickery, D. B.	Haverhill.
Valentine, Benj. Eyre and daughter	Brooklyn.
Van Wagenen, Mrs.	Auburndale.
Van Wagenen, Miss Ida B.	Auburndale.
Wray, Miss	Southampton, L. I.
Wray, Miss J.	Southampton, L. I.
Warner, E.	Troy.
Whitney, Miss M. B.	Boston.
Whipple, John Reed	Boston.
Weston, Mr. and Mrs. Henry C.	Boston.
Weymouth, Mr. and Mrs. Geo.	Cambridge.
Weymouth, Miss Grace C.	Cambridge.
Webster, Miss Mary	Lowell.
Walker, Miss Susan M.	Fryeburg.
Wheelock, Miss A. D.	Auburn.
Wheelock, Warren	Auburn.
Wood, K. L.	Natick.
White, Miss Alice	Auburn.
Watkins, Dr. W. W.	Lewiston.
Yeaton, Mrs. John	Boston.

MANSION HOUSE.
AUGUST 28 TO SEPT. 4, 1896.

Allison, Miss	Germantown, Pa.
Allison, Miss M.	Germantown, Pa.
Ames, Mr. and Mrs. Joseph B.	Brookline.
Adler, Mr. and Mrs. Herman	New York.
Adler, Master G. H.	New York.

Barbour, M. E.	Digby, N. S.
Cunningham, A. M.	Washington.
Gibson, Mrs. Joseph W.	New York.
Hayes, H. W.	Portland.
Hume, Harrison	Robbinston.
Hurlburt, Mrs. A.	Utica.
Kenrick, Mrs. John	So. Orleans, Mass.
McFarlan, Mr. and Mrs. Daniel	Washington.
Neal, Mrs. T. A.	Boston.
Neal, Miss	Boston.
Shoemaker, C. J.	Wilkesbarre.
Thompson, Mr. and Mrs. F. H.	Portland.
Thompson, F. M.	Portland.

Tid-Bits.

Mr. and Mrs. A. B. Butterfield of Boston, arrived September 1st.

Mr. and Mrs. W. A. Castle of Springfield, Mass., are at Poland Springs.

Mrs. Wood has found 256 four-leaf clovers this season between the Poland Spring House and Mansion House.

August 28th, Mrs. Thurston, Miss Campbell, Miss Margaret Thurston, and Theodore Thurston drove to Oxford and had dinner.

Although not verdant, the HILL-TOP girl was very green; and yet we had always flattered ourselves that the HILL-TOP was read.

August 29th, the following party took a brake ride: Mrs. L. Beard, Mrs. Gregory, Mr. and Mrs. Page, Mr. and Mrs. H. S. Beard, and the Misses Richardson.

Saturday afternoon the following party—Mrs. Hildreth, Mrs. Bates, Mrs. Dan Fields, Miss Hildreth, Miss Gilbert, Miss Katherine Ricker, Miss Eddy, Miss Lumbert, Miss Wymond, Rev. W. H. Bolster, Mr. Oakes, Mr. Dan Field, and Mr. Bolster—took a drag ride around Sabbathday Lake.

Monday, August 31st, Mr. Barhydt found, in the grove near the Maine State Building, a fungus growth of a single night which measured thirty inches long and twenty-one inches wide. The color is a delicate salmon, with all the shades of an exquisite shell. In some parts of it the form is like a lily, while in others it is a perfect four-leaf clover. It is now on exhibition at the Maine State Building.

Lost.

A lace shawl, the early part of the week. The finder will confer a favor by leaving it at the office of the Poland Spring House.

THE NEW MOUNT PLEASANT HOUSE,

In the Heart of the White Mountains.

Through Parlor Cars from New York, Boston, and Portland, also from Burlington, Montreal, and Quebec.

The Hotel faces the Grandest Display of Mountain Peaks in America east of the Rocky Mountains. It is lighted throughout by electricity, thoroughly heated by steam, and has an abundance of private and public baths. Its orchestra is made up largely from the Boston Symphony Orchestra. Its table is unsurpassed. Absolutely pure water from an artesian well, 409 feet in solid rock.

IT IS THE NEAREST HOTEL TO MT. WASHINGTON, AND THE TRAIN FOR THE SUMMIT STARTS FROM A STATION ON THE HOTEL GROUNDS.

All Trains, Maine Central Railroad, from Portland to Burlington, Montreal, Quebec, and Lake Champlain stop at the platform close to the House.

Leave Portland 8.45 A.M., arrive Mt. Pleasant House, 12.21 P.M. O
"   "   1.25 P.M.,   "   "   "   "   5.05 P.M. O
"   "   3.20 P.M.,   "   "   "   "   7.20 P.M. O
"   "   8.45 P.M.,   "   "   "   "   11.47 P.M. O

POST, TELEGRAPH, AND TICKET OFFICE
IN THE HOTEL.

ANDERSON & PRICE, of the Hotel Ormond of Florida, Managers.

Address by wire or mail, "Mount Pleasant House, N. H."

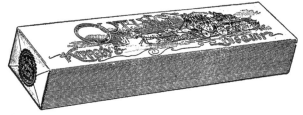

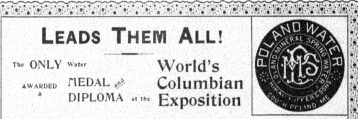

The Hill-Top

POLAND SPRINGS, SO. POLAND, ME.

HARRY C. WILKINSON

THE HILL-TOP

VOL. IV.   SUNDAY MORNING, JULY 4, 1897.   No. 1.

Ever Young and Fair.

AS Boston is one of those cities which is perpetually in the act of being dug up for the purpose of making improvements, it has come to be a common saying, that it "will be a fine city when it is finished."

The city which is comprised within the precincts of Poland Springdom always has the appearance of being finished, and yet the eagle eyes which watch over its destinies do not sleep in winter, for then it is, an army of men march in and take possession, with the result that nothing ever grows old, gets grey and bald in turn, but metaphorically imbibes the life-giving Poland Water, and comes out each summer rejuvenated, and with a fine complexion.

The Poland Spring House presents as new an appearance as the day it was built, as a result of the labors of the painters, and comes out of its several months' sleep as bright as a new gold piece from the mint, and all its connections glisten with the same freshness. Nothing is neglected; the sanguinary towers, the kitchen, the "quarters," the annex, the studio, and so on *ad infinitum*, all glow alike, with a smile, which says, "My dress is as good as yours and cut off the same piece," yet the smartest of the set gives the retort courteous that she had a Paris dress-maker.

One of the most important features among the changes concerns the Music Hall, and so important and elaborate is this work that we feel justified in leaving a description of its details to another issue, together with an illustration.

The next most important work in connection with the subject of decoration, has been accomplished in the Maine State Building, which has been entirely gone over. The inside finish is of cypress and quartered oak; the decorator has here most happily met the harmony with tints of soft,

woody colors, which harmonize with smoky blues
and olive tints mixed with gold. On the ceiling
of the main staircase, leading from the rotunda,
the Ricker coat of arms is to be placed. Directly
opposite is the coat of arms of the State of Maine,
in carved oak. The library and reading-rooms
suggest quiet and retirement in the treatment of
walls and ceilings, and from art gallery to lower
floor the colors seem most appropriate.

A new hot-water heating system has been
introduced into the building, and hereafter cool
September or October days will be shorn of their
terrors.

The elegant new conservatory, located near the
Maine State Building, we will leave to a future
article; also we will briefly allude to the new
driveway and bicycle path, which makes a graceful curve in front of the south façade of the
Poland Spring House, and greatly improves the
grade and the adjacent lawn.

Passing to the Mansion House, the original
beginnings of things in the history of the Ricker
occupation of the hill, the old jackknife has a new
blade, and the new blade has a new handle,
inasmuch as the trail of the artist and artisan is
over all there as well. New floors, new decorative effects—the dining-room being especially
improved in appearance—and new plumbing and
sanitary requirements, are some of the more
noticeable features. Truly, the Genius which
presides over Poland Spring has not slumbered,
and the reward of its enterprise should be, and
will be, overflowing coffers.

Mrs. Whipple's Contributions.

Among the valuable additions to the Library
this season, the fifty volumes forwarded by Mrs.
J. Reed Whipple will be found of great interest in
adding to its shelves a well selected list of standard
works, a full list of which is given in another column. The Shakespeare, Carlyle, and Burroughs,
are all splendid acquisitions, and Mrs. Whipple is
to be thanked for her interest and generosity.

Sunday-School Picnic.

The Hill-Side Sunday-School had its annual
picnic Saturday, June 27th. There were forty
children present, and fifty-one partook of the
luncheon which was served under the pines at the
pumping station. Mr. H. W. Ricker kindly sent
the James G. Blaine for them and gave them a
ride home. The day was perfect, and the children
had a jolly good time. Dame Rumor says that
the older members of the party played tag, much
to the delight of the children. One little girl said:
"Miss Sadie, I thought I had a good time last
year at the picnic, but this is the best of all."

June Days.

WHEN lovely June came to Poland this year,
she melted into tears and wept many, many
days. She had been hypnotized by capricious
May, who sulked all through her reign, and
in passing, touched the coming queen. June was
not herself. The trees, the grass, the very atmosphere, were saturated with the tokens of her sorrow.
Occasionally a glowing smile would promise coming
gladness, when suddenly, in torrents and floods,
her grief overcame her fair promises.

People come long distances for Poland water.
They believe in it—they love it, and feel that they
can never have enough of it; and yet with the
inconsistency of dear human nature, when they
could have oceans of it, they objected—rebelled—
mutinied. Poland Spring water is a joy forever;
but Poland rain-water, after a reasonable cruise,
is a monumental nuisance! But as these loyal,
tariff-agitated states all received the same remarkable baptism, the faithful pilgrim to the Mecca of
the Pine Tree State, pocketed his moistened hopes,
his vial of wrath, and yearned for sunstroke
weather.

After forty days the spell was broken by a
wonderful sunset, like the inside of a sea-shell in
its exquisite tinting. June wept no more. Splendid
sunshine, pure tonic air, soft soughing music in
the trees. announce the real June, the joyous June
of other days. Proud, sturdy robins dash over the
lawns in bold disregard of humankind. Fresh
breezes bow the daisy faces toward us as we pass.
Sometimes passing clouds cast their long, poetic
shadows, for the moment, over the dreamy blue
mountains. These are signs of the times, and
among the many joys of beautiful Poland. Jean
Paul Richter says, "Under a dull sky, I want the
quill of a goose to write; under a clear sky, I long
for the pinions of an eagle to fly." The dull,
dripping skies are past, and now, in spirit, we
mount into the enchanting summer skies.

A. HURLBURT.

A Suggestion.

If the owners of forests, quarries, and mines of
Maine, would send small but suitable specimens
of the products of their land, we might establish a
permanent exhibition of Maine woods and minerals
here in the Maine State Building, and thus enable
the visitor from other states and counties to
become more familiar with our interests, and the
natural wealth of the state.

Thousands of people annually visit this building, and if the specimens were of suitable size,
and one side polished, of those specimens which
are intended to receive such, it would become an
interesting feature. Pass the word along.

Mr. Hartshorne's Gift.

MR. R. B. HARTSHORNE placed with the librarian ten dollars to be expended for books. Two books purchased with a portion of that fund are:

American Genealogical Index. Fourth revised edition, and latest. Albany, 1895.

This is an alphabetically arranged work of 22,000 references, which shows at a glance whether the genealogy or pedigree of any family, or any portion thereof, has been printed in any volume of genealogy, history, biography, magazine, town or county history, centennial anniversary celebration, society transaction, proceeding, report or periodical. But few persons have an adequate knowledge of the amount of genealogical material to be found in such volumes, from the fact that anything like a full collection of works in those departments can only be found in large cities, and in the hands of a few private parties; and without consulting them it is often an impossibility to prepare a family history, or of learning anything very definite of any particular family. With the assistance furnished by this volume, no difficulty will be experienced in collecting needed information by any one interested in such investigations. It also affords instruction to the general reader who may not know whether the history of his native country, town or village has been written and published.

Handy-Book of Literary Curiosities. By William S. Walsh.

A collection of the bric-à-brac of literature, literary forgeries, hoaxes, jests, enigmas, conundrums, paradoxes, etc., exploited; proverbs, sayings, slang phrases, and familiar lines correlated and traced to their source; plagiarisms, analogies, and coincidences detected; the whole forming a complete encyclopædia of all that is most amusing and entertaining in the ana of the past and present, and an indispensable reference-book of curious, quaint, and out-of-the-way information that has never before been collected in book-form.

Both these works will be found to be of exceeding interest and value, and undoubtedly much sought after.

Genealogy.

An interest, which has grown remarkably of recent years, is in the direction of research into the family history. Societies of various kinds have been formed, and to be without a Genealogical Chart is to be an isolated being. It is a pastime which not only has great advantages, but which becomes positively fascinating, and has far better arguments in its favor than the fad of collecting stamps, coins, or china. By all means get a chart at once and try it, if you have not already.

Cyclist Column.

A bicycle track is being built at Poland Spring, which will be over three miles when completed.

Messrs. W. E. Burrows and Charles B. Doten, of the L. A. W., made a fine run from Portland to Poland Spring, June 27th. The time was two hours and fifteen minutes.

Mr. Louis Hill came on his wheel from Gray and took dinner at the Mansion House, June 27th.

The following wheelmen, Messrs. E. E. Elliott, J. E. Smith, R. G. Brooks, F. W. Richardson, D. S. Elliott, and E. Pettee, left Portland at 6.30 A.M. Sunday, and dined at the Mansion House. On account of a strong wind they did not make very good time. Mr. Elliott broke his saddle, but was able to repair it, and so returned with the party.

Messrs. George D. Knight, F. E. Warren, R. F. Sawyer, J. W. Bank, members of the Athletic Club in Portland, made a good run from Portland, June 27th. They dined at the Poland Spring House.

Miss Edith Walker is often seen on her wheel between Lake Side Cottage and Poland Spring. She rides well.

Mr. Wyckoff's Generosity.

Last season Poland Spring had the pleasure of entertaining Mr. Edward G. Wyckoff, of the well-known establishment of Wyckoff, Seamans & Benedict, and as a result of his visit, eighty-three choice volumes of elegant and much desired works have been added to our rapidly increasing Library. A full list of them may be found in the list of new books. The guests will fully appreciate the value of his gift, when works of this nature are desired. Mr. Wyckoff may consider that Poland Spring is under deep obligations to him for his liberality.

The Art Exhibition.

JUST a few words about pictures and painters. If you are an admirer of this class of art and come to Poland Spring for rest and to "take your ease in your inn," a visit to the Gallery of Art, instituted by the proprietors of this resort, will prove a source of pleasure and a mental feast, only equalled by the feast of other good things here provided.

One will find, on visiting this summer's exhibition, a variety of subjects ably dealt with, and all classes of painting.

On entering the gallery, the principal picture which confronts you is the "Monarch of the Field," by Miss Frances B. Townsend, a painter of animals, of great strength and fidelity to nature. This picture impresses one at once with the power of the artist and the ability she possesses to place upon the canvas a work which places her at once in the front rank of the animal painters of the day.

On turning to the right, the next most fascinating and remarkable production is from the brush of Eva D. Cowdery, who has reproduced, with a touch that is almost inspiration, a young miss, whom she calls "The Bridesmaid." No one who looks upon this picture will fail to return to it, and find each time new beauties to admire in its rich yet delicate treatment.

Another work, this time a water-color, but full of the richness of color more commonly associated with oil, is a group of great birches, which are to be seen in alcove F. This, again, is the work of a lady, Agnes Leavitt, and it will unquestionably become one of the features of this exhibition.

These are not the only superb works, contributed by the ladies, for there are many more, but among the examples of the sterner sex, Walker's "Salting the Sheep," in alcove C, will arrest the attention of all who appreciate true artistic feeling, for it is a subject treated with skill, and full of the rich, mellow light which gives a pleasing and restful effect. It is a superb picture.

Portrait painting is at its best in this exhibition, far surpassing that of any previous one. Wagner shows four of his oil pastels; a remarkably good one of a gentleman, two young ladies, and another, which, from its attitude and quality, he terms "Reverie." This latter is one of a soft, delicate tone, and will interest any one who appreciates excellence in portraiture.

Henwoods's central figure of Mrs. Ulman is a most successful picture. Few portrait painters of the present day succeed better than this artist has in this particular work. It constantly receives the warmest praise from visitors, and is universally pronounced a work of superior merit.

Gallison furnishes some of his landscapes, one particularly large one in "F," and a delightful picture of a hill-side village in "B." His treatment of his subject is of the "heroic" kind, and the thought of the artist is as clearly set forth on the canvas as life itself, and finely and skillfully portrayed. In the landscape, the fresh air of the hills seems to sweep through it and give it freshness and reality.

One wishing to purchase pictures will certainly find something here to admire; for a better or a more pleasing collection of its size has seldom been gotten together anywhere. The gallery contains one hundred and thirty paintings, and not a poor one among them.

Miss "Fly Rod."

MISS CORNELIA T. CROSBY, better known among the angler fraternity as "Fly Rod," spent Friday and Saturday at the Poland Spring House. Miss "Fly Rod" is the most expert woman fly caster in the world. She is a Maine woman, and is proud of it. Her home is at Phillips. I said to her, "Maine has given much to the world in the way of politics, music, and literature, to say nothing of the smaller things of life, has it not?" She said, "I had rather have been born in Maine than any country in the world. I love its woods and lakes."

Miss "Fly Rod" is as fond of shooting as she is of fishing, and is considered a fine shot.

"Do women make good anglers?" I asked. "Life in the woods broadens women and makes them more companionable to men, and when they love fishing I think they are more enthusiastic over it and better anglers than men."

It is not an uncommon thing for Miss "Fly Rod" to catch one hundred trout a day, with a fly, and return them to the water.

Saturday morning, the Messrs. Ricker enjoyed for their breakfast a handsome five-pound speckled beauty, fresh from the Rangeleys, which Miss "Fly Rod" brought with her. Mr. T. L. Page, who has charge of the Senate Café, Washington, and is now proprietor of the Mooselucmeguntic House at the Rangeleys, caught the trout in the rain the morning Miss "Fly Rod" started.

Fishing Party.

Mr. and Mrs. J. B. Sawyer with their friends, Mrs. Leeds and Mr. Lippincott, had a delightful time Monday, June 29th, fishing in Middle and Upper lakes. They were gone all day, and had their luncheon on the island in the Upper Lake. They caught twenty-three bass, each weighing over a pound, and several weighed three pounds.

Children's Column.

Small service is true service while it lasts;
Of friends however humble, scorn not one.
The daisy, by the shadow that it casts,
Protects the lingering dew-drops from the sun.
—Wordsworth.

Echoes from a Sunday-School Picnic.

Charlie—"Say, Jim, have you had a good time?"

Jim — "I guess so; I've eaten thirteen sand-wiches, five dishes of ice-cream, one slice of cake, one banana, and drank seven glasses of water."

Charlie—"Well! some one will have to give you an *epidemic*."

A little boy and girl were standing together, when the boy's papa passed with a lady. "Say, Jack, I didn't know your papa had a sister."

"Why, that isn't his sister," responded Jack, "that is his step-wife."

Morning and Evening.

[From Harper's Weekly.]

The husk of the darkness slips away;
Out of the dusk blooms the flower of day.

And the sweetest thing in the world to me
Is the chattel of children full of glee,
The patter of feet on the nursery floor,
The rap of elves at my chamber door;
All the little ones wide awake,
I face the world for the children's sake.

In the gathering dusk the day-flower shuts;
Wearily plodding in year-long ruts
I seek my home; as I turn the key
The chattel of children welcomes me.

Never was music half so sweet
As the merry rush of the little feet;
I hear the sound of a blithe uproar
As I turn the key in my dear home door;
With hurry and flurry the little band
Fall on me, storm me, seize my hand,
And then the soft, warm cloak of the dusk
Wraps the day in a circling husk.
The stars come out, the day is done,
Sleep gathers my babies, every one;
And what do I care for the world's hard fight,
I am safe with my own till the morning light.

Miss Helen Paddock, Master Eugene Paddock, little Anna Marguerite, and Arthur Paddock of New York, are spending a few weeks at Poland Spring.

Little Dexter Henry Marsh of Springfield, Mass., is at the Mansion House.

Miss Ethel Campbell and Gladys Campbell are at the Mansion House.

A Natural Question.

[From Puck.]

Little Clarence—"Pa?"

Mr. Callipers—"Eh?"

Little Clarence—"Pa, does a woman preacher kiss the bride or the groom after marrying 'em?"

The Mount Pleasant House.

Special attention will be given this season to golf, the golf links of the Mount Pleasant House being exceptionally well laid out. A popular college man has been engaged to take charge of the sport. The managers of the Crawford House and the Mount Pleasant House are considering the work of building a good bicycle path between the two houses, the route to be through the woods, and following the course of Black Brook, which is the outlet of Ammonoosuc Lake, back of the Crawford House. The orchestra at the Mount Pleasant House this season is to have an additional piece, making eight in all. Mr. Felix Winternitz returns as soloist and director. The house opens July 3d.

Tid-Bits.

"Let Independence be our boast,
Ever mindful what it cost."

S–t Boom !

Robins and squirrels !

Col. S. C. Talbot of Brooklyn is with us.

Mr. and Mrs. George F. Baker are with us.

Mrs. A. Gracie is at the Poland Spring House.

Mr. and Mrs. Edward Strong of Boston are here.

Mr. W. Ballantyne of Boston is at the Mansion House.

Mr. and Mrs. J. B. Sawyer of Dover are with us.

Mr. and Mrs. P. W. Wildey of New York are here.

Mr. and Mrs. John P. Woodbury, Boston, are with us again.

Mrs. M. E. Parson of Boston is at the Poland Spring House.

Mrs. M. E. de Wint of New York is at the Mansion House.

Mrs. S. B. Hubbard of Jacksonville, Fla., is with us once more.

Mrs. J. A. Hartshorne of New York arrived Friday, June 25th.

Mr. Andrew R. Culver of Brooklyn is at the Poland Spring House.

Mrs. Amos R. Little of Philadelphia has returned for the season.

Miss Edith King, Calais, Me., is spending a few days at Poland Spring.

Mr. and Mrs. O. I. Kimball of Newton Center, Mass., are with us.

Mrs. Thomas Howard of Brooklyn is registered at the Mansion House.

Mr. and Mrs. N. Amerman of New York have returned for the season.

Mr. James H. Danforth of Boston is spending the summer at Poland Spring.

Mr. and Mrs. J. R. Bradford of Tallahassee, Fla., are at the Mansion House.

Miss Peterson, Misses Alice and May Peterson, are spending the summer at Poland.

Mr. and Mrs. Benjamin Brewster of Jamaica Plain, are at the Poland Spring House.

Mr. and Mrs. Wilmon Whilldin of Cape May, N. J., are at the Poland Spring House.

Mrs. J. Reed Whipple of Boston is spending the summer at the Poland Spring House.

Mr. Eben C. Webster of Orono, Me., has been spending a few days at Poland Spring.

Mrs. T. C. Conover and Miss Alice N. Conover of New York, have returned for the season.

Mr. and Mrs. J. Rosenheim and Miss Tessie Rosenheim, Savannah, Ga., are at Poland Spring.

Mrs. F. T. Hoffman arrived June 3d. Mrs. Hoffman comes early, and remains until the house closes.

Mrs. W. G. Wilson and Master M. Wilson of New York are registered at the Poland Spring House.

Mr. and Mrs. Carpenter, F. W. and Miss Carpenter of Providence, R. I., have returned for the season.

Mr. and Mrs. S. Ross Campbell of Philadelphia, have returned to their summer home in Poland.

Mr. and Mrs. J. W. Hazen of Boston have been spending the month of June at the Poland Spring House.

Mr. and Mrs. William S. Patten, Miss Patten, and Miss Grace Patten of New York, are at Poland Spring.

Mrs. Cyrus S. Curtis of New York, and Mrs. B. C. Lake of New Haven, are registered at the Poland Spring House.

The many friends of Mrs. W. H. Emery and Miss Emery of Newton, Mass., regret their departure Tuesday, June 29th.

Lieutenant Commander Buckingham and Mrs. Buckingham of Washington, are spending the summer at Poland Spring.

Mr. and Mrs. S. P. Leeds and Mr. J. H. Lippincott, of Haddon Hall, Atlantic City, are at the Poland Spring House.

Mr. and Mrs. Columbus Iselin, and Miss Adrienne Iselin of New York, have been spending two weeks at the Poland Spring House.

Mrs. Louis Pettee of New York is the first guest to register. She is as fond of the winters at Poland as summers, having spent four here.

Miss M. Estes of Boston registered at the Poland Spring House. Miss Estes's friends regret that she could not spend more than a day at Poland.

The many friends of Mrs. N. Huggins of New York are glad to see her at Poland Spring. Mrs. Huggins has just returned from a trip to the Holy Land.

Mr. Godfrey Phelps Koop of New York is on a fishing trip to the Rangeley Lakes. Mr. and Mrs. E. P. Ricker were the recipients of two fine trout weighing three and one-half pounds each, which Mr. Koop caught.

French Dishes Anglicized.

A l'Anglaise implies that the dish is roast or boiled in the plainest manner.

A l'Italienne implies that the dish is made of, or garnished with, savory macaroni, or paste of that kind, or with ravioli, or is made savory with Parma cheese.

A la Française is, curiously enough, a surname which is applied to the least typical preparations, and is generally made to denote some peculiarities favored in the ancient provinces; thus:

A la Périgord is applied to dishes flavored with or consisting of truffles, from the circumstance that these mushrooms grow in that province.

A la Normande indicates that apples enter into the composition of the dish in some shape or other.

A la Parisienne is applied to dishes which are generally luxuriously prepared and overladen with expensive garnishes.

A la jardinière signifies a typical collection of cooked vegetables given in soups, ragoûts, and removes.

A la printanière implies a typical collection of cooked early vegetables, but has, contrary to origin, a somewhat wider application than the foregoing.

A la macédoine is also applied to typical collections of green vegetables, mostly in white sauce; it includes collections of ripe fruit imbedded in jellies.

A la maître d'hôtel generally signifies a dish prepared by a substantial but homely, modest sort of cooking.

A la Crécy is similarly connected with carrots, particularly in the form of purée.

A l'Allemande is a surname given to dishes to which French cooks have applied German provincial peculiarities of preparation. The most frequent application is to a dish with a garnish of sauerkraut, as given with pork or partridges or pheasants; also prunes stewed in wine, to German sweet sauce for venison, or to quenelles of potatoes.

A la Polonaise is applied to every effort to introduce red beetroot or red cabbage, their juice, color, and taste, into various dishes, of which Polish ragoût, or Borsch, is the type.

A l'Irlandaise is applied to dishes which contain potatoes in some form.

A l'Espagnole is not applied to any typical dish, but to any preparation made savory with the brown typical sauce bearing that surname.

—*Spirit of Cookery.*

Mr. and Mrs. D. T. Lufkin of Sacramento, California, have been spending a few weeks at the Poland Spring House. They were married in Hartford, Conn., in June, and came here on their wedding journey. Mrs. Lufkin was formerly a resident of South Poland.

Recipes.

ASPARAGUS OMELET.

Take yolks of five eggs and the whites of three, beaten very light; add two tablespoonfuls of salt and a pinch of pepper. Chop fine the heads of one dozen stalks of asparagus; dip into the batter; fry and serve hot.

STUFFED EGGS.

Boil the eggs for twenty minutes, then plunge into cold water and remove the shells. When cool, cut carefully in two and remove the yolks. Cut a bit off the end of the egg so it will stand, and place each half on a lettuce leaf. When all the eggs are done, mash the yolks with one tablespoonful of soft (not melted) butter, one tablespoonful of finely-chopped celery, one teaspoonful of chopped capers or pickles, one teaspoonful of chopped olives, one teaspoonful of chopped parsley, and one-half teaspoonful of grated onion; add salt and pepper to taste. Form this into round balls, about the size of the yolk of one egg, and drop them into the cavity in the whites.

Mr. and Mrs. R. B. Hartshorne of New York, Miss Hartshorne, Miss Lydia, and Miss Estelle, and Master Douglas Hartshorne, are guests at Poland Spring.

FRANK CARLOS GRIFFITH. } EDITORS.
NETTIE M. RICKER, }

PUBLISHED EVERY SUNDAY MORNING DURING THE MONTHS
OF JULY, AUGUST, AND SEPTEMBER, IN THE INTERESTS OF

POLAND SPRING AND ITS VISITORS.

All contributions relative to the guests of Poland Spring
will be thankfully received.

To insure publication, all communications should reach the
editors not later than Wednesday preceding day of issue.

All parties desiring rates for advertising in the HILL-TOP
should write the editors for same.

The subscription price of the HILL-TOP is $1.00 for the
season, post-paid. Single copies will be mailed at 10c. each.

Address,

EDITORS "HILL-TOP,"
Poland Spring House,
South Poland, Maine.

PRINTED AT JOURNAL OFFICE, LEWISTON.

Sunday, July 4, 1897.

Editorial.

A PERFECTLY dazzling array of pleasant
faces is before us on this double anniversary
to-day. We reach the third celebration of
our coming into life, and put on added dignity upon
entering our fourth year. Again, this is the day
on which the greatest republic on earth was born,
and while we are not inclined to emulate the frog
in the fable, who aspired to equal the ox in size,
we are getting on in years, and dimensious as well.

Pleasant faces indeed. Many of them are
familiar to the HILL-TOP, and others look upon
its features for the first time, but it is to be hoped
that the chance acquaintance may ripen into an
attachment which shall continue many years, and
that the scenes we know, may know us yet many
and many a day.

Old friends, welcome, not to Elsinore, but to
Poland, again. Another year has been added to
our lives since we said good-bye in the autumn,
and many have been the days of sunshine in your
lives, we hope; and, sad to relate, many have been
the days of clouds for us all; damp clouds, moist
clouds; damp with a wetness that nothing can

transcend; clouds which have been saturated with
a seeming perpetual and everlasting super-satura-
tion, and which were pressed between the heavens
and the earth with the result of dampening all
between. Be that as it may, the whirligig of time
keeps on and on in an unceasing round, and brings
joys as well as sorrows, pleasures as well as pain.

As a nation, think of the marvelous advancement since the '76 of the eighteenth century, and, as
a great resort for the children of the nation, consider
the progress on this hill-top since the '76 of the
present century. Poland Spring is to-day so
fixed in the affections of the people that its fame is as
far-reaching as the waters of its spring are ever carried; and then on and on, until the line ends
again at the very place where it began.

Good morning, and once more welcome; and
remember these lines of Kingsley:

The world goes up, and the world goes down,
And the sunshine follows the rain;
And yesterday's sneer, and yesterday's frown,
Can never come again.

Musical Programme.

SUNDAY, JULY 4, 1897.

1. Marsch de Nuit.	. . . . .	Gottschalk.
2. Berceuse and Serenade.	. . .	Godard.
3. Selection—Tannhäuser.	. . .	Wagner.
4. Adagio from Sonata Pathétique.	. .	Beethoven.
5. Gavott de l'Enfant.	. . . .	Marie.
6. Spring Song.	. . . . .	Mendelssohn.
7. Cujus Animum, from Stabat Mater.	. .	Rossini.

r. Daniel Kuntz }		
r. August Kuntz }	. . . . .	Violins.
r. Arthur Brooke	. . . . .	Flute.
r. Adolf Cannes	. . . . .	Cornet.
Erich Loeffler	. . . . .	'Cello.
Mr. Emil Golde	. . . . .	Bass.
Mr. Carl Hauser	. . . . .	Piano.

Compliment to a Boston Artist.

In a letter received from Mr. H. Davis, an
American student at Juglaris studio, he states
that at the recent art exhibition of the "Society
to Encourage and Protect Young Artists," held in
Turin, Italy, there was exhibited a landscape by
H. H. Gallison of Boston. The critic of the
Gazetta del Popolo of Turin says that "while
excessively simple, it is of great strength of color,
composed of but three tints—a yellow tone which
represents the plane, a blue the hills of the background, and white the sky. It is a strong and
grand study from nature." Mr. Gallison's painting attracted the attention of King Humbert, who
asked about Mr. Gallison and American art.

Mr. Gallison has two fine examples of his work
in the Poland Spring Art Gallery.

New Books

Added to the Library subsequent to the last announcement in the HILL-TOP, September 13, 1896 :

FROM MISS A. H. PLATT.

Romola; by George Eliot.

FROM MISS E. B. GOLDTHWAIT.

The Deemster; by Hall Caine.
The Reproach of Annesley; by Maxwell Gray.

NO NAME.

The Story of Dan; by M. E. Francis.
An Army Wife; by Capt. Charles King, U. S. A.
Phra the Phœnician; by Edwin Lester Arnold.

FROM MRS. J. P. MURPHY.

Science and Prayer; by W. W. Kinsley.

FROM JOHN P. WOODBURY.

The Philosophy of P. P. Quimby; by Annetta Gertrude Dresser.
The Power of Silence; by Horatio W. Dresser.

FROM MRS. CHARLES FULLER.

The World Beautiful; by Lillian Whitney.

FROM HOWARD SCHOLLE.

Cleopatra; by H. Rider Haggard.

FROM MRS. F. H. THOMPSON.

The Scarlet Letter; by Nathaniel Hawthorne.
The Vicar of Wakefield; by Oliver Goldsmith.

FROM JOHN C. PAIGE.

Secret Court Memoirs—Edition de Grand Luxe.   6 vols.

FROM MISS M. A. BAYLEY.

Desperate Remedies; by Thomas Hardy.

FROM H. D. LYMAN.

Order of Creation; by Gladstone, Huxley, Müller, etc.
Proceedings of "The Proteus" Court of Inquiry.

FROM MRS. H. D. LYMAN.

Letters and Social Aims; by Ralph Waldo Emerson.

FROM MISS M. A. BAYLEY.

Old Ma'mselle's Secret; by E. Marlitt.

FROM MRS. JOHN C. Haynes.

Frivolous Cupid; by Anthony Hope.
The Bondman; by Hall Caine.
The Romance of a Transport; by W. Clark Russell.
'Lisbeth Wilson; by Eliza Nelson Blair.

FROM GEN. A. P. MARTIN.

The American Soldier in the Civil War.
Campaigns in Virginia, 1861–2; by Theodore F. Dwight.
Virginia Campaign of 1862; by Theodore F. Dwight.
Some Federal and Confederate Commanders; by Theodore F. Dwight.
The Peninsular Campaign of 1862.
The Virginia Campaign of 1862.
The Army of Virginia; by George H. Gordon.
History of the Civil War; by the Comte de Paris. 4 vols.
Reminiscences of the Blue and Gray; by Frazer Kirkland.
Memorial of Frederic T. Greenhalge.
Memorial of the 250th Celebration of the Settlement of Boston.
Our Journey Around the World; by Rev. Francis E. Clark, D.D.
Giants of the Republic.
Uncle Sam's Story World.
War of the Rebellion (continued).   3 vols.
Soldier in the Civil War.   2 vols.

FROM GRIFFITH AND RICKER.

Bound HILL-TOPS, 1894, 1895, 1896.   3 vols.

FROM MRS. THEODORUS B. M. MASON.

A Costly Freak; by Maxwell Gray.
L'Abbe Constantin; by Ludovic Halevy.
Forging the Fetters; by Mrs. Alexander.
The Romance of a Transport; by W. Clark Russell.
The Head of the Firm; by Mrs. J. H. Riddell.

FROM MARY F. BISHOP.

Philip Vernon; by S. Weir Mitchell.
When All the Woods are Green; by S. Weir Mitchell.
A Magnificent Young Man; by John Strange Winter.
The Old, Old Story; by Rosa Nouchette Carey.

FROM MRS. J. B. SAWYER.

A Flash of Summer; by Mrs. W. K. Clifford.
Mrs. Romney; by Rosa Nouchette Carey.
The Owl's Nest; by E. Marlitt.

FROM EDWARD G. WYCKOFF.

The Chronicles of Barsetshire; Trollope.	13 vols.
Tennyson's Poetical Works.	10 "
Bancroft's History of the United States.	6 "
Novels of the Brontës.	12 "
Rhode's History of the United States.	3 "
Lafayette in the American Revolution.	"
Phineas Finn.	"
Phineas Redux.	2 "
Clarence; by Bret Harte.	1 vol.
Protégé of Jack Hamlins; by Bret Harte.	1 "
Col. Starbottle's Client; by Bret Harte.	1 "
A First Family of Tasajara; by Bret Harte.	1 "
In a Hollow of the Hills; by Bret Harte.	1 "
A Knight of the White Cross; by G. A. Henty.	1 "
When London Burned; by G. A. Henty.	1 "
Bonnie Prince Charlie; by G. A. Henty.	1 "
True to the Old Flag; by G. A. Henty.	1 "
The Tiger of Mysore; by G. A. Henty.	1 "
In Greek Waters; by G. A. Henty.	1 "
Through Russian Snows; by G. A. Henty.	1 "
His Vanished Star; by Charles Egbert Craddock.	1 "
The Phantoms of the Foot-Bridge; by Charles Egbert Craddock.	1 "
Where the Battle was Fought; by Charles Egbert Craddock.	1 "
In the Stranger People's Country; by Charles Egbert Craddock.	1 "
The Prophet of the Great Smoky Mountain; by Charles Egbert Craddock.	1 "
History of the United States; by John Fiske.	1 "
Civil Government in the United States; by John Fiske.	1 "
Pudd'nhead Wilson; by Mark Twain.	1 "
Charles O'Malley; by Charles Lever.	1 "
Sub-Coelum; by A. P. Russell.	1 "
In a Club Corner; by A. P. Russell.	1 "
Sawson's Art Criticism; by G. W. Samson, D.D.	1 "
The Realm of Nature; by H. R. Mill.	1 "
Letters of Celia Thaxter.	1 "
The Making of the Ohio Valley States; by S. A. Drake.	1 "
Cousin Anthony and I; by E. S. Martin.	1 "
Literary Landmarks of London; by L. Hutton.	1 "
Brown Studies; by G. H. Hepworth.	1 "
Essays in Miniature; by Agnes Repplier.	1 "
	83 vols.

FROM HON. WILLIAM P. FRYE.

Government Works.	29 Vols.

FROM HON. EUGENE HALE.

Government Works.	9 vols.

FROM F. W. RICE.

Kirkman's Primitive Carriers.	1 vol.

FROM HIRAM RICKER & SONS.

Macaulay's History of England.	5 vols.
Life of Albert Sidney Johnston.	

FROM MRS. W. PETERSON.

The Stickit Minister.

FROM MRS. A. HURLBURT.

Great Humorists.
Idle Thoughts of an Idle Fellow; by Jerome.
The Snow Image; by Hawthorne.

FROM MRS. J. REED WHIPPLE.

Shakespeare.	12 vols.
Works of John Burroughs.	9 "
Life and Works of Robert Burns.	4 "
Carlyle's Complete Works.	20 "
Goldsmith's Works.	4 "
Quo Vadis; by Henryk Sienkiewicz.	1 vol.
	50 vols.

FROM MRS. AMOS R. LITTLE.

A House-Boat on the Styx; by J. K. Bangs.
The Murder of Delicia; by Marie Corelli.
Peter Ibbetson; Du Maurier.
Philadelphia's Better Self.

FROM DOUGLAS R. HARTSHORNE.

Beric the Briton; by G. A. Henty.

FROM FRANK CURTIS.

The Finding of the Gentian; by Alice Wellington Rollins.
Little Page Fern; by Alice Wellington Rollins.
Unfamiliar Quotations; by Alice Wellington Rollins.
Aphorisms for the Year; by Alice Wellington Rollins.

FROM THE SPRAGUE & HATHAWAY CO.

Photo Souvenirs, 26th Triennial Conclave.

FROM MR. R. B. HARTSHORNE.

Index to American Genealogies.
Handy-Book of Literary Curiosities.

FROM MRS. HERMAN ADLER.

Popular Tales, Vols. 1 and 3; by Maria Edgeworth.
Tales of Fashionable Life, Vols. 1, 3, 4, 5, 6; by
Maria Edgeworth.   7 vols.

An Official Visit.

Between Monday and Wednesday, Poland has been inspected by the Maine State Board of Health. To mitigate the rigors of official visiting, the members brought their wives, who could view the kitchens, from the ice-cream freezers to the "jumbo" washing machine, while physicians, chemists, and engineers did the more formal portion of the investigation. The party was made up as follows : Lewiston, Dr. and Mrs. Wedgwood and Mrs. Shurtleff; Portland, Dr. and Mrs. Smith, Mr. and Mrs. F. C. Jordan; Augusta, Dr. and Mrs. Young; Bangor, Dr. and Mrs. Woodcock; Brunswick, Professor and Mrs. Robinson; Whitefield, Dr. Smith and Miss Sargent; Auburn, Dr. and Mrs. Oakes. Fine weather added to Poland's charms, and it is very certain that the officers of the Board carried away delightful impressions of the health, exquisite cleanliness, and fine appointments of this peerless summer resort.

M. B. J.

Mr. and Mrs. E. H. Paddock of New York left Wednesday, June 30th. Mr. and Mrs. Paddock are much interested in the Hill-Side Sunday-school, and they will be missed by their many friends at Poland.

Our Fourth of July Visitors.

Raymond & Whitcomb, those excellent providers of outings for those who seek a change of scene and air, have shown the way to Poland Spring to another of their delightful and delighted parties. This time it comprises Mr. and Mrs. Chas. D. Mather, Mrs. L. B. Dane, Mrs. A. M. Clement, Miss Edith C. Clement, Mrs. Frank Ridlon and Wm. B. Jones, Mr. and Mrs. Chas. M. Tillinghast, and Mrs. Josephine E. Henry of Boston ; Mrs. John Utley and Mrs. Gertrude Goodie of Brookline ; Mrs John Woodbury, Miss Laura Woodbury, Miss Alice H. Dodge, and Miss Patch of Hamilton, Mass.; Mrs. Wm. J. Crowley of Woburn ; Mrs. Alden B. Richardson of Lowell ; and Mr. and Mrs. Clinton Bacon of North Cambridge.

Golf.

We have not much to say about golf this week, because we have had so much to say about rain, and then again, the grass has not been cut, and one cannot play golf in high grass, can they, now? This is a game the ladies should enjoy, for they can still have their afternoon Tee, although it may not be without grounds. It is a very ancient game, we are told, and we cannot recall seeing the first one the promoter sprung upon us, but if memory serves us right, Robert, the Bruce, holed out at fifty-five, with Macbeth a close second, who remarked to Macduff, that Bob won because he was'nt "holed enough," or words to that effect. Robert got there in fourteen rounds, and it has been a great thing for the plaid manufacturers, who have had a revival only revivaled, I mean rivaled, by one or two of brother Moody's.

Mr. F. D. Ellis of Portland and Miss S. D. Ellis of Boston, are at the Mansion House.

Rear Admiral Carpenter and Mrs. Carpenter of Portsmouth, N. H., are at Poland Spring.

Tid=Bits.

Hello!

You're looking well!

Have you subscribed?

Genealogy is the great fad.

In our fourth year and growing.

Tame squirrel at the Spring House.

Mrs. A. Hurlburt of Utica, N. Y., is with us.

Miss Edith N. Hastings is at the Mansion House.

Miss Kimball of Brookline is at the Mansion House.

Have you seen the tame squirrel down by the Spring?

Mr. and Mrs. James Swan of Chicago are with us.

From the Mansion House to the Spring is 2,790 feet.

What is your favorite painting in this season's exhibition?

Mrs. M. E. Bacon of Boston is at the Mansion House.

Mr. and Mrs. Frank R. Thomas are welcome returning guests.

Mr. Robert T. Lee and Miss Lee, Westport, Conn., are with us.

You can have it "Blake" or "Break," and still enjoy your ride.

Wagner's, Cowdery's, and Henwood's portraits are exceptionally fine.

Mr. D. W. Keegan of New York is at the Poland Spring House.

Mr. L. T. Thornton of St. Louis is registered at the Poland Spring House.

Mrs. J. B. Turner of Boston is spending the summer at the Mansion House.

Mr. W. E. Hadley and Miss Hadley of San Diego, Cal., are at Poland Spring.

Mrs. Sarah E. Stickert and Miss Mary A. Witham are at the Mansion House.

From July 20 to October 15, 1896, there were 2,683 books taken from the library.

Mrs. L. J. Tingley and Mrs. H. A. Bridell of Philadelphia, are at Poland Spring.

Mr. and Mrs. C. H. Child and Miss Child of Providence, R. I., are at Poland Spring.

If you do not find a picture to suit you in this year's exhibition, it will be remarkable.

Miss Helen Lawry and Mr. G. A. Lawry of Rockland, are at the Poland Spring House.

Mrs. Z. Chandler leaves Detroit for the calm retreat on Poland Hill.

Mr. and Mrs. John C. Black and Mr. Lawrence Black of Chicago are at the Poland Spring House.

Mr. and Mrs. George Rose of New Orleans are receiving congratulations. It is a beautiful boy baby.

If you do not like "cometer" you can still say "cometist," and if that does not suit, try "comist."

On the eve of going to press we are pleased to note the arrival of Mr. and Mrs. A. T. Salter of Washington.

Poland Spring hopes to "retain" Justice Brown and Mrs. Brown of Washington for a lengthy period.

Just carefully look through our advertisements. If you require anything they have, they are all to be recommended.

Squiblets.

Truth and dust, though crushed to earth, will rise again.

A gentleman put his head in at the door of one of the public rooms and inquired, "Where is Mr. Golf?" "Out on the Fens," was the ready reply.

Mme. Nordica is to receive $50,000 for forty conceits, "and found." They could "find us" promptly on every occasion on a similar contract.

G. Washington was a great success as the father of his country, and as a non-liar, but his pie has received much adverse criticism.

When Thanksgiving comes we shall have more respect for Turkey, for he not only waded into boiling Greece without damaging his drumsticks, but proceeded to lick it, without injury to his esophagus either. Great Crete-ure the Turk.

We have had much fish, but the biggest one has fully sustained his reputation. Break away.

The favorite song in June, was, "Rain, rain, go away, come again s'm'other day."

HAPPY THOUGHT.
[New York Tribune.]

Assistant Editor—"There's nothing to fill the seventh column, sir."

Editor—"Tell the foreman to set a lot of type at random, and we'll call it a Scotch dialect story."

THE CHRONIC BACHELOR.
[From the Indianapolis Journal.]

The Giddy Young Thing—"What is that proverb about there being no marrying in heaven?"

The Chronic Bachelor—"Fools rush in where angels fear to tread."

ABSENT–MINDED.
[From the Fliegende Blaetter.]

Professor—"Delighted to meet you again after so many years, miss."

Elderly Lady—"No longer miss, professor, I am married."

Professor—"Married? Well, well, who would have thought that."

EXPERT ON THE OTHER THING.
[From Pearson's.]

Mrs. Shears (in jeweler's shop buying diamonds)—"I wish my husband were here."

Jeweler—"Is he an authority on diamonds?"

Mrs. Shears—"Not exactly; he is an editor, and he knows paste when he sees it."

Tid=Bits.

Mrs. A. Murray of Washington prefers Poland to the Capitol in summer. ·

Mr. George B. French of Boston is again seen about the Poland Spring House.

Professor W. E. Sargent of Hebron Academy spent Tuesday, July 1st, at Poland Spring.

Mrs. Orlando Tompkins arrived on Thursday evening. No one is more welcome than she.

Who says we have no fishing, after Mr. S. H. Howe has landed a 2 1-2 pound land-locked salmon from the Middle Lake?

The new Steinway Baby Grand in the Music Hall, is an elegant instrument. It will be of great advantage with the orchestral music.

Not to be outdone by their elders, Masters Hartshorne and Wilson have been bass fishing with good results, inasmuch as they are said to have returned with a good half dozen.

The many friends of Dr. and Mrs. Peterson are delighted to see them again at Poland Spring. Last season is the first they have missed for nine years, having spent the summer in Europe.

Arrivals.

POLAND SPRING HOUSE.

FROM JUNE 1 TO JULY 1, 1897.

Aymar, Miss	New York
Aymar, Johnson	New York
Allen, Mr. and Mrs. Charles W.	Portland
Allen, Neal W.	Portland
Aiken, W. F.	Portland
Andrews, Ruth	Bethel
Adams, F. H.	Dorchester
Atwood, Abram	Auburn
Atwood, Tillie M.	Auburn
Brewster, Mr. and Mrs. Benjamin	Jamaica Plains
Blight, Emily	Wellesley Hills
Bond, Mr. and Mrs. Joseph	Chicago
Baker, Mr. and Mrs. George F.	Hyannis
Boothby, Mr. and Mrs. F. E.	Portland
Boothby, W. A.	Waterville
Bergen, Mr. and Mrs. George P.	Freeport, N. Y.
Buttling, Mrs. William J.	Brooklyn
Babcock, Mr. and Mrs. E. H.	Brooklyn
Bailey, B. M.	Brooklyn
Buckingham, Mr. and Mrs. B. H.	Washington
Barney, Rachel	Melrose
Benson, C. C.	Lewiston
Bryer, Mrs. James M.	Newport
Brown, Mrs. William S.	New York
Briggs, L. P.	Springfield
Barnes, J. W.	Portland
Bradford, J. C.	Auburn
Blake, Granville	Auburn
Blandford, Mrs. W. C.	Brooklyn
Blandford, Miss	Brooklyn
Blandford, Miss Ada	Brooklyn
Brown, Judge and Mrs. H. B.	Washington
Brown, Miss S. M. Harman	New York
Brown, Jessie	Boston
Bacon, Mr. and Mrs. Clinton	No. Cambridge
Baxter, James J.	Boston
Chandler, Mrs. Z.	Detroit
Conant, Miss Carrie A.	Auburn
Conant, Mrs. Lucy W.	Auburn
Conant, Mr. and Mrs. A. H.	Auburn
Curtis, Mrs. Cyrus S.	New York
Cross, Mr. and Mrs.	W. Newton
Culver, Andrew R.	Brooklyn
Cranley, James W.	Brooklyn
Cleary, Peter	Brooklyn
Colby, Mrs. Samuel F.	Brooklyn
Corey, Chester	Boston
Child, Mr. and Mrs. C. H.	Providence
Child, Miss	Providence
Carpenter, Mr. and Mrs. F. W.	Providence
Carpenter, Miss Hannah	Providence
Crosby, Miss Cornelia T.	Phillips, Me.
Clowell, George S.	Philadelphia
Clark, L. M.	Portland
Conant, F. R.	Auburn
Conant, C. L.	Auburn
Craig, R. A.	New York
Crawley, Mrs. William I.	Woburn
Clement, Mrs. A. M.	Boston
Clement, Miss Edith C.	Boston
Davenport, Mrs. F. H.	Boston
Davenport, Brewster	Boston
Danforth, James	Boston
Denton, Mr. and Mrs. H.	Brooklyn
Denton, H., Jr.	Brooklyn
Denton, E. J.	Brooklyn
Dennis, Mr. and Mrs. C. S.	Melrose
Dennis, Lulie S.	Melrose
Dennis, Mildred	Melrose
Delatour, Mrs. J.	Brooklyn
Delatour, Miss M.	Brooklyn
Dyer, Edwin L.	Portland
Dane, Mrs. Z. B.	Boston
Dodge, Miss Alice H.	Hamilton, Mass.
Emery, Miss	Portland
Ellis, Miss C. B.	Chicago
Estes, Miss C.	Boston
Edwards, Miss	New York
Elkens, R. G.	Boston
Evans, H.	Bradford
Fraser, W. C.	Brooklyn
Fernekees, Mr. and Mrs. William H.	Boston
Flint, Mr. and Mrs. John C.	Salem
Faile, Thos. H.	New York
French, George B.	Boston
Gragg, Mrs. Oliver	Boston
Gragg, Miss Mary C.	Boston
Goodenow, J. H.	New York
Gunnison, Mr. and Mrs. H. F.	Brooklyn
Grampp, N. J.	Brooklyn
Guild, Miss Marianna C.	Boston
Gracie, Mrs. A.	New York
Goodwin, Mrs. Daniel	Chicago
Goodie, Mrs. Gertrude	Brookline
Hazen, Mr. and Mrs. J. W.	Boston
Hoffman, Mrs. F. T.	New York
Hartshorne, Mr. and Mrs. R. B.	New York
Hartshorne, Miss	New York
Hartshorne, Lydia R.	New York
Hartshorne, Estelle	New York
Hartshorne, Douglas	New York
Howe, Mr. and Mrs. S. H.	Marlboro
Harwood, Miss	Bowdoinham
Ball, Mr. and Mrs. Lewis	Cambridge
Humphrey, Mrs.	Cambridge
Hubbard, Mrs. S. B.	Jacksonville
Huggins, Mrs. N.	New York
Heenan, Frank C.	Brooklyn
Hudson, Mrs. A.	New Rochelle
Hawes, Mrs. R. L.	Boston
Hoy, Mrs. James	Washington
Hoy, Miss E. W.	Washington
Hoy, Miss M. L.	Washington
Hartshorne, Mrs. J. A.	New York
Henry, Mrs. Josephine E.	Brighton
Hawkes, J. R.	Boston
Iselin, Mr. and Mrs. Columbus	New York
Iselin, Miss Adrienne	New York
Johnson, Mr. and Mrs. Bradish	New York
Jordan, Mr. and Mrs. E. C.	Portland
Jones, William B.	Boston
Knight, G. D.	Portland
Kursheedt, M. A.	New York
Kimball, Mr. and Mrs. W. A.	Portland
Kenna, Mr. and Mrs. Thos.	Brooklyn
King, Mr. and Mrs. William A.	Brooklyn
Kuntz, Daniel	Boston
Keenan, Mr. and Mrs. James	Boston
Kilbourne, J. W.	Portland
Kalkhoff, G. F.	New York
Kimball, Mr. and Mrs. O. I.	Newton Centre
Kingsbury, Miss May	Brooklyn
Kiegan, D. W.	New York
King, Miss Edith	Calais
King, Fred	Portland
Lane, Miss Sadie	Marlboro
Luke, Mrs. B. C.	New Haven
Little, Mrs. Amos R.	Philadelphia
Little, F. C.	Chicago
Leman, P. A.	Brooklyn
Littlefield, Abbie	Melrose
Lufkin, Mr. and Mrs. D. T.	Sacramento
Leeds, Mr. and Mrs. S. P.	Atlantic City
Lippincott, J. H.	Atlantic City
Lawry, G. A.	Rockland
Lawry, Helen	Rockland
Love, Mr. and Mrs. Jno. W.	New York
Leland, Miss	New York
Morrison, Miss E.	New York
Morrison, L. J.	New York
Mathewson, Mr. and Mrs. F. M.	Providence
Mack, Mr. and Mrs. John C.	Chicago
Mack, Lawrence W.	Chicago
Martin, Gen. and Mrs. A. P.	Boston

Mann, Mr. and Mrs. Jonathan H.	Boston
Mann, Katy Maud	Cambridge
McKenny, Archibald J.	Brooklyn
McKenny, Alexander	Brooklyn
Mc Sherly, Mrs.	Brooklyn
Mc Sherly, Miss M.	Brooklyn
Marble, Mr. and Mrs. Jerome	Worcester
Marble, Miss Nella	Worcester
Mac Murray, Mrs. J. C.	Worcester
Montgomery, Mrs. T. J.	Philadelphia
Marsh, Mrs. Charles	Boston
Melcher, Arthur S.	Auburn
Merrall, William J.	New York
Merrall, W. H.	New York
Marsh, Charles R.	Boston
Mc Clellan, W. B.	Boston
Mallouf, Mr. and Mrs. H. G.	New York
Mallouf, Nazzeem	New York
Mathel, Mr. and Mrs. Charles D.	Boston
Murray, Mrs. A.	Washington
Niles, Mrs. S. R.	Boston
Nelson, Andrew L.	New York
Newhall, J. Walter	Melrose
Nealey, Col. A. B.	Lewiston
Oak, Mrs. J. P.	Skowhegan
Overman, A. H.	Springfield
Osgood, Mr. and Mrs. H. S.	Portland
Oakes, Mr. and Mrs. Wallace K.	Auburn
Peterson, Dr. and Mrs. W.	New York
Peterson, Florence	New York
Peterson, Alice	New York
Peterson, May	New York
Paine, J. B.	Buffalo
Patten, Mr. and Mrs. William S.	New York
Patten, Miss	New York
Patten, Miss Grace	New York
Paine, Mr. and Mrs. L. L.	Bangor
Paine, L. G.	Portland
Powers, Minta S.	Boston
Parsons, Mrs. M. E.	Skowhegan
Patch, Miss	Hamilton, Mass.
Rogers, Mr. and Mrs. A.	Portland
Robinson, A. E.	Oxford
Rich, Miss	Auburn
Richardson, Mr. and Mrs.	St. Louis
Rich, Edmund L.	Portland
Rosenheim, Mr. and Mrs. Jos.	Savannah
Rosenheim, Miss Tessie	Savannah
Ruffner, Bertha	New York
Robinson, Mr. and Mrs. Franklin C.	Brunswick
Richardson, Mrs. Alden B.	Lowell
Ridlon, Mrs. Frank	Dorchester
Robinson, Mr. and Mrs. F. C.	Brunswick
Stinger, Kate	New York
Stevens, Mr. and Mrs. O. H.	Marlboro
Stevens, Herbert	Marlboro
Stevens, Master Louis	Marlboro
Sparrow, Mrs. H. F.	Cambridge
Sawyer, Mr. and Mrs. J. B.	Dover
Saunders, Mr. and Mrs. H. M.	Boston
Swan, J. Wesley	Norway
Story, Mrs. Fred E.	Freeport, N. Y.
Seaman, Mr. and Mrs. L. W.	Brooklyn
Seaman, Master	Brooklyn
Seitz, L. F.	Brooklyn
Strong, Mr. and Mrs. Edward A.	Boston
Swan, Mr. and Mrs. James	Chicago
Sears, Mr. and Mrs. L. B.	Brookline
Swift, Mrs. W. J.	Marlboro
Sullivant, A.	New York
Stuart, J. G.	New York
Seaman, Mr. and Mrs. S. W.	New Orleans
Scott, Mr. and Mrs. W. M.	Boston
Solomon, A.	Chicago
Swift, H. M.	Marlboro
Savage, Henry	Boston
Small, C. R.	Portland
Sawyer, R. T.	Portland
Shurtleff, Mrs. E. M.	Lewiston
Savage, Samuel H.	Boston

Smith, Mr. and Mrs. Charles D.	Portland
Smith, A. R. G.	Whitefield
Smith, Mr. and Mrs. Charles D.	Portland
Steer, Mr. and Mrs. C. E.	Brookline
Salter, Mr. and Mrs. A. T.	Washington
Taft, Mrs. E. A.	Boston
Thornton, L. N.	St. Louis
Tabor, Mr. and Mrs. J. W.	Portland
Talbot, C. M.	Portland
Twombly, Mr. and Mrs. J. S.	Boston
Tillinghast, Mr. and Mrs. Charles M.	Brighton
Thomas, Mr. and Mrs. Frank R.	Boston
Tompkins, Mrs. Orlando	Boston
Utley, Mrs. John	Brookline
Voorhees, Judah B.	Brooklyn
Voorhees, Anson A.	Brooklyn
Wilson, Mrs. W. G.	New York
Wilson, Master M.	New York
Worthington, Mr. and Mrs. C. E.	Wellesley Hills
Worthington, Miss Gertrude M.	Wellesley Hills
Worthington, Isabel	Wellesley Hills
Warner, A. F.	Boston
Wood, Mrs. Walter G.	Philadelphia
Weaver, Mrs. J. G.	Newport
Ward, Mr. and Mrs. George	New York
Wood, Mrs. Ambrose	Staten Island
Wedgwood, M. C.	Lewiston
Whipple, Mrs. J. Reed	Boston
Wildey, Mr. and Mrs. P. W.	New York
Whitney, Mrs. M. E.	Boston
Wood, Mrs. C. V.	Boston
White, F. L.	Summit, N. J.
Wallace, A. B.	Springfield
Walker, Fred	Portland
Wheelden, Mr. and Mrs. W.	Cape May
Webster, Eben C.	Orono
Whitman, Mr. and Mrs. James H.	Boston
Woodbury, Mr. and Mrs. J. P.	Boston
Warren, T. E.	Portland
Warren, E. M.	Boston
White, Miss May	Auburn
Woodcock, Mr. and Mrs. Galen G.	Bangor
Whitney, H. L.	Boston
Williams, A. S.	Portland
Woodbury, Mrs. John	Hamilton, Mass.
Woodbury, Miss Laura	Hamilton, Mass.
Young, Mr. and Mrs. A. G.	Augusta

MANSION HOUSE.

JUNE 3 TO JUNE 10, 1897.

Amerman, Mr. and Mrs. N.	New York
Ballantyne, W.	Boston
Bradford, Mr. and Mrs. J. R.	Tallahassee
Bailey, Mrs. C. C.	Portland
Brooks, R. G.	Portland
Burrowes, W. E.	Portland
Conover, Mrs. J. C.	New York
Conover, Miss Alice V.	New York
Clitz, R.	Boston
Cousens, Mr. and Mrs. L. M.	Portland
Cousens, L. A.	Portland
Carpenter, Rear Admiral and Mrs.	Portsmouth
Doten, Charles B.	Portland
Elliot, E. E.	Portland
Elliot, D. S.	Portland
Forster, C.	Portland
Fisher, O. M.	Boston
Gorham, R. H.	Boston
Hastings, Miss Edith N.	Cambridge
Hurlburt, Mrs. A.	Utica
Hadley, W. E.	San Diego
Harward, Mrs. Thos.	Brooklyn
Kimball, Miss	Brookline
Libby, A. J.	Gardiner
Longstreth, Mrs. Morris	Philadelphia

Lucas, Mr. and Mrs. J. S.	Brooklyn
Lew, Mr. and Mrs. Robert T.	Westport, Ct.
McPherson, George W.	Boston
Moll, Edw.	Boston
Marsh, Mrs Oliver	Springfield
Marsh, Robert P.	Springfield
Nason, Mr. and Mrs. Fred E.	Boston
Pettingill, Mrs.	Portland
Pettingill, G. S.	Portland
Pettee, E. C.	Portland
Ryder, Capt. G.	Chelsea
Rice, Mr. and Mrs. John O.	Portland
Rice, Miss S. C.	New York
Richardson, F. W.	Portland
Stockman, Frank M.	Portland
Smith, J. G.	Portland
Stuart, Mrs. J. R.	Roxbury
Thurston, Miss M. R.	Boston
Turner, Mrs. J. B.	Boston
Turner, Mr. and Mrs. H.	Boston
deWint, Mrs. M. E.	New York
Bacon, Mrs. M. E.	Boston
Bridels, Mrs. H. A.	Philadelphia
Brigham, Robert B.	Boston
Brigham, Miss E. L.	Boston
Ellis, F. D.	Portland
Emery, Mrs. W. H.	Newton
Eddy, Charles E.	Newton
Eddy, Miss Caroline	Newton
Koop, G. P.	New York
Paddock, Mr. and Mrs. E. H.	New York
Tingley, Mrs. L. J.	Philadelphia
Talbot, Col. S. C.	Brooklyn

Brake Ride.

Mrs. J. W. Hazen of Boston gave an enjoyable brake ride July 1st. The party consisted of Mrs. Patten, Mrs. Swan, Mrs. Hubbard, Mrs. Parsons, Mrs. Judd, Miss Patten, and Miss Grace Patten. The party drove through Peterson's Woods, and upon their return had their pictures taken on the brake.

Lost.

Mr. Frank E. Curtis, while climbing the cliffs at Little Sebago Lake, Sunday, June 27th, lost his gold watch and chain. A reward has been offered, and any one finding it will please return it to the HILL-TOP.

"What's De Score?"

Several years ago Dr. Joseph Burnet had an English clergyman visiting him at his summer home in Southboro. While discussing college games the stranger wanted to see the American game of base-ball. The Doctor took him to the South-End Arena next day, to witness a famous game, and when leaving the rear of the stand to catch the train, a ragged, bare-footed boy, of small size, accosted the Doctor, saying: "What's de score?" Doctor—"I think, my lad, it's 2 to 5." "Who's at de bat?" rejoined the boy.

J. J.

The · New · Mount · Pleasant · House,

In the Heart of the White Mountains.

Through Parlor Cars from New York, Boston, and Portland, also from Burlington, Montreal, and Quebec.

IT STANDS AT THE HEAD.

Unrivalled in Popularity!
Unsurpassed in Location!
Unapproached in Patronage!

THE

POLAND ✳ SPRING ✳ HOUSE

IS A SUPERB ILLUSTRATION OF

⚬ ⚬ SUCCESS ⚬ ⚬ ⚬

EMBRACING AS IT DOES

ALL THE DESIRABLE FEATURES

EXPECTED IN THIS

The Leading Resort of America,

WHILE THE

MAINE STATE BUILDING

WITH ITS

SUPERB ART FEATURES

IS UNEQUALLED BY ANY SIMILAR ENTERPRISE

IN THE WORLD.

⚬ ⚬ ⚬

HIRAM RICKER & SONS (Incorporated),

PROPRIETORS.

MAINE STATE BUILDING.

The Hill Top

POLAND SPRINGS, SO. POLAND, ME.

HARRY C. WILKINSON

Did you know that the majority of the large portraits hanging in the Maine Building were made
by The Sprague & Hathaway Company of Somerville, Mass.? The World's Fair pictures were
also made by the same company.

VOL. IV.   SUNDAY MORNING, JULY 11, 1897.   No. 2.

The Music Hall.

WE gave but the briefest intimation last week of the importance of the work in the Music Room, finding that to do half justice to this feature of the Poland Spring House would require more space than we had at our disposal.

In this grand *salon* the daily orchestral concerts are given by a superior selection of musicians, under the leadership of Mr. Daniel Kuntz and chiefly from the famous Boston Symphony Orchestra.

Here it is the best works of Beethoven, Wagner, Mozart, Rossini, Bach, and all the great composers are daily listened to through the season, while the evenings are given over principally to the devotees of Strauss and all the caterers to the light fantastic. Other entertainments of a light and pleasing nature are also frequently given in this place.

It has been newly provided with a beautiful selection of rattan chairs in great variety, which harmonize completely with the new decorations, of which we will endeavor to give a description.

As you step inside, the impression of eternal youthfulness impresses you, and, when ushered into the Music Hall, a positive return to the delicate tints of babyhood is recognized with astonishment and joy. New light is shed upon this delicately ornate apartment by means of two large windows let into the south side, overtopped with specially designed and appropriate stained glass windows, lighting this charming spot with a new brilliancy. All is light, soft, delicate; and the paneled ceiling rests as easy over all as the downy counterpane on the slumbering babe. It is composed of eighteen panels, about twelve feet square, the beams dividing these being done in old ivory, and the surface of the plastering finish done in fine pebbly stipple.

The designs are laid out in *papier-maché*. In the center of each panel is a large circle of a delicate tint of Nile green, surrounded by a small figure of Italian Rennaissance design, with smaller circles of a soft shade of Pompeian red, with wreaths of laurel and knots and ribbons in white and gold, colonial style, outside of which is a quiet tint of olive, very restful to the eye. On the face of the beams the laurel branch, knot, and ribbons are also repeated in fine relief in white and gold.

The mouldings and smaller members are of pale straw color, the knees or brackets supporting beams are faced with acanthus leaves in relief in white and gold on ground of soft Pompeian red; the frieze is of a high grade of embossed paper in designs of leaves and blossoms of the *Convolvulus* or *Morning Glory*, conventionalized with Rennaissance scroll at base, finished in a deeper shade of old ivory. The side walls are of a tone of warm buff, with bands of soft salmon color, dado a soft tone of olive with band of deeper shade; wood work and mantels are old ivory glossed, the whole effect being a happy combination, and most harmonious and artistic blending of soft, delicate tints. The coloring and gilding is the most successful effort of Mr. William Thresher of Boston, and the *papier-maché* work is that of Mr. Charles Emmel, also of Boston, the whole labor being the happy culmination of artistic designing.

The writing and smoking rooms adjoining are treated in the same manner, the latter being much improved by the addition of a large bay-window, let into the piazza on the north side, and lighted by an ornamental sky-light.

Art Sketches.

AMONG the artists represented in the Exhibition this year it may be of interest to learn something of some of them. Hayden is a native of Plymouth, Mass., and studied his art under such masters as Boulanger, Lefebvre, and Raphael Colin. He was an exhibitor in the Salon and the Exposition of 1889, receiving honorable mention. The Boston Art Club purchased one of his pictures in 1891, and in 1895 he received the grand prize of $1,500 at the Jordan Exhibition, Boston, for his "Turkey Pasture," which now hangs in the Boston Museum of Fine Arts; also received silver medal at the Atlanta Exposition.

Marcus Waterman, an artist of very high rank, was born in Providence, R. I., and he is generally conceded to be one of the finest colorists in America. His work is always prized in the best exhibitions, and his representations of Eastern and Algerian subjects are among the best by any American artist.

Closson is another native of New England, having been born in Vermont. He studied abroad and received honorable mention from the Paris Salon for engraving, and later on a medal. The Massachusetts Charitable Mechanics Association has awarded him bronze and silver medals, gold medal, and diploma. He has been awarded medals at the Paris Exposition of 1889 and at the World's Columbian Exposition of 1893, and the grand diploma of honor at the Graphic Art Exhibition in Vienna.

Hardwick came to the United States from Nova Scotia, and has painted with the leading Dutch painters. His water colors are much prized, and one has been purchased by the Boston Art Club.

Miss Cowdery was born in Richmond, Me., and first studied at the old Lowell Institute in Boston, the Art Students' League, New York, and finally at Munich and Paris. Her work is strikingly interesting, and her figures are placed upon the canvas with great strength and truth.

Sid Brackett is a native of Newton, Mass., and has always painted animals, being best known by his kittens and puppies. He was a pupil of John B. Johnston, Frederick P. Vinton, and the Boston Art Museum. He is a member of the Boston Art Club, the Sons of the American Revolution, on the record of six ancestors, and of the Colonial Wars Society.

There is scarcely a picture in the gallery this season but is the work of an artist who has won high recognition, and no mistake can be made in the selection of any work from their brush.

We had day fire-works the Fourth of July, and the "old lady" was the greatest success of all.

A Western Woman's Trip Up the Hudson with the New England Woman's Press Association.

BEING one of the "wild and wooly contingent" annexed to the N. E. W. P. A. in their recent outing up the Hudson, and the very wildest and wooliest, if distance west counts, I am perhaps the best able of them all to descant upon the joys of nature in the effete East as compared with her charms in the West.

To a westerner, unused to anything but the "beastly glare of modern civilization" on the one hand, and the trackless wastes of southern California sage brush on the other, the beauties of New England and New York scenery come as a revelation.

"Oh," I said to myself as I gazed at the shifting panorama of stream and grove and hill and dale and picturesque stone walls and well-sweeps on the journey by rail to New London—"Oh, that the deluded Californian, secure in his illusion that the one spot on earth is around him, could be here. What are his little irrigated dots, his much-vaunted orange trees, set in bleak, bare, ploughed fields, to this restful verdure; his attenuated, muddy sloughs—miscalled rivers—disappearing ever and anon in the yellow sand, to these limpid streams bordered on either side by plumy ferns knee deep; his flowers, almost totally devoid of fragrance, to these dewy blossoms filling the air for miles about with their sweetness? Nothing! And as for his climate, there is more of the elixir of life to the square inch in the ozonic air of New England than in several atmospheres floating about on the Pacific!"

On board the City of Lowell at New London and off for New York "as the birds fly." What a glamour over all connected with ship life—at least such ship life as we now see! How clean and burnished is everything! How the music rises and swells as we skim over the sound! And how one's appetite increases and what marvellous capacities are developed for stowing away the good things the gods have provided in the shape of savory and appetizing viands! Almost with sorrow we reach New York. But there is the trip up the Hudson still to come. That consoles us.

"Up the Hudson!" A vista of idyllic loveliness and vanished delight cannot but open with these words to those who have ever taken the trip, while palisades, highlands, white houses with "christmas trees" around them, and palatial mansions pass by in a shifting panorama.

Past Tarrytown and Sleepy Hollow, those historic and belegended spots made familiar and dear to us by benign old Diederick Knickerbocker, we went; on by beautiful estates interspersed by picturesque peaks and falls; past Treason Hill, the meeting place of Arnold and Andre, to West Point, where we were saluted vigorously by a little group of cadets; thence to Newburgh, Washington's headquarters during some of the most trying months of the Revolution, and on to the great bridge at Poughkeepsie, where we faced about and returned. Then a repetition of the loveliness which could never grow old, and New York Harbor again, with a parting, glorious vision of the sun slowly sinking behind the palisades.

For the courtesy of Mr. W. R. Babcock, General Passenger Agent of the New England Railroad Company, and the indefatigable efforts of Mrs. Mary Sargent Hopkins, editor of *The Wheelwoman*, to whom the association is indebted for making the arrangements for the outing, there can be nothing but the heartiest words of thanks and appreciation, and memories of them must ever be linked with thoughts of the sail up the Hudson on the beautiful City of Lowell.

ELEANOR ROOT.

31 EAST NEWTON STREET, BOSTON, MASS.

Mount Pleasant Orchestra.

An unusually fine combination has been effected for this season's orchestra at the Mount Pleasant House, White Mountains. The personnel is as follows: Soloist and Director, Felix Winternitz, the well-known violin virtuoso, of Boston; Violin, W. H. Capron, of Reeves Band, Providence, R. I.; Viola and Piano Accompanist, William Howard, of Philharmonic Orchestra, Boston; 'Cello and Trombone (the latter used in two-steps), Charles Behr, Boston Festival Orchestra; Bass, O. L. Southland, Boston Festival Orchestra; Flute, Max Guetter, Reeves Band; Clarinet, Fred S. Coolidge, Boston; Cornet, William B. Mayberry, Boston.

Golf.

WHAT game has sprung into popularity so suddenly as golf? There is no doubt but what there are more people playing golf the present season than any other outdoor game in this country. The game was little known this side of the water five years ago.

It owes its rise to popularity to the good exercise it gives the middle-aged business man that sadly needed it. It became popular with him, as the exercise was moderate and all that was required.

Again, it became a natural outlet for many men whom business cares made it impossible for them to keep up a training that is called for in other games, such as lawn-tennis, cricket, baseball, etc., but he can gain all the exercise needed from the game of golf, and pleasure as well.

It also makes a splendid game for the summer visitors who are away for recreation or pleasure, as they get both at the same time.

The writer has played most of the outdoor games, and thinks golf the most fascinating game of them all. There is so much to interest one in the lie of the ball and what can be done with it. Then we have the record of the links always to play against, also your own record and the record of each hole. I do not know of any one that has taken up the game and given it up again because he did not like it. There is not a doubt but the game is here to stay and will always be played in this country hereafter, and will be more popular as it is better known.

The past year has seen thousands of new links started all over the country; all of them cannot be called good, in fact a very small percentage are really good from a golfer's point of view. The laying out of the links should be studied thoroughly and the hazards and bunkers should be arranged in their proper places, so that a good stroke should never be punished. It is a great mistake among some golfers that the links should be made very hard and sporty, as it is called.

There is as much danger in having too many bunkers as not enough; on the other hand, it should not be made too easy. There should be as much variety in the lay of the land, also the distances between the holes, as possible. The length of the holes should range from 125 to 550 yards, and shorter or longer holes I would not advise. To keep the links in good condition, as has been fully demonstrated, there is nothing better than sheep, as they keep the grass down close and their feet improve the lies very much.

The writer has only been playing since February, 1895, but has played over most of the best links in the east. It is difficult to compare their relative merits, but among the best links are the Myopia at Wenham, Mass.; Knollwood at White Plains, N. Y.; St. Andrews, Yonkers, N. Y.; Meadowbrook, Long Island; Essex County, Manchester, Mass.; Shinnecock, Southampton, L. I.; Lenox, Lenox, Mass.; Brookline Country Club at Boston, Mass.; Newport, Newport, R. I.; Lakewood, Lakewood, N. J.; Ardsley, Ardsley, N. Y.; Palmetto Golf Club, Aiken, S. C. The Myopia and Palmetto are the best links, in my judgment, of the above mentioned, although the others have their strong features.

The Palmetto links at Aiken, S. C., are the first that were started in the South, and are by far the best winter links we have in this country. A great many of the best players of the North spend their winters there, where they can enjoy the game and keep in good practice, having an advantage over the players that cannot play during the winter months. Aiken is to America what Pau, France, is to the golfers abroad—a place where the prominent golfers go for their winter sport. Last season there was not a day all winter but what golf could be played with comfort.

In regard to players who have learned the game in this country, there is much that could be said. While we cannot yet compete with the older players of Great Britain, we are making rapid progress, and hope in the near future to be able to compete with them on an equal footing. The progress of the players in this country has been varied. In 1895 there was not as much difference shown as the past season has developed, and the play has been of a much higher class. Many of the players who were last year among the best have not improved their play this season, and have found themselves left behind by those that have continued to improve, and no doubt this will be the experience this year. It will not be surprising if some of the younger players that have shown such good form this spring are not among the leaders this fall.

The competition for the championship of the United States this year, which will be held in September at Chicago, will undoubtedly show the rapid development of the game, and a larger number and stronger players will compete for the honor, and in my judgment there will be many surprises for the older players, who have been carrying everything before them in the past.

A. H. FENN.

Fishing.

Monday, July 5th, Mr. Sawyer, Mr. Love, and Mr. Strong went fishing in the Middle Lake. They caught 12 bass, weighing 18 pounds.

Messrs. Archie Cole and Martin Davis were successful in catching 17 trout in the Gloucester brook, each weighing over a pound.

Children's Column.

"Manners must adorn knowledge and smooth its way through the world."

Two Car Loads of Clothes.

THESE THE GERMAN EMPEROR TAKES WITH HIM
ON HIS TRAVELS.

The German emperor has twelve valets, charged with keeping the imperial wardrobe, valued at $500,000. Every uniform bears precious decorations. The uniforms of all the regiments of the German army, with their helmets, caps, shakos, rifles, swords, and sabres, are shut up in immense cupboards. The uniforms of the imperial German navy are arranged in the same way. Next to these come the uniforms of the Saxons, Bavarians, Hessians, and others.

Separated in other large cupboards are the Austrian, Russian, Swedish, English, and Italian uniforms, all ready to accompany the kaiser on his journeys, or to be used on the occasion of princely visits.

Finally, must be mentioned his hunting and shooting costumes, his court dresses, his yachting and lawn-tennis uniforms, and his private dresses. When the emperor travels, his uniforms and costumes fill two or three carriages.

His majesty is very fond of jewelry and curios. He wears half a dozen rings, a large watch and chain, and a bracelet on his right arm.
—*London Globe.*

Sunday-school teacher—"I wonder how many of my little scholars remember the name of the queen who visited Solomon."

George—"I do! I do! teacher."

Teacher—"What was her name?"

George —"Queen of Diamonds."

IN THE UPPER BERTH.

A little four-year-old occupied an upper berth in a sleeping-car. Awaking once in the middle of the night, says the *Youth's Companion*, his mother asked him if he knew where he was. "'Tourse I do," he replied. "I'm in the top drawer."

OLDEST FLAG.

The oldest national flag in the world is that of Denmark, which has been in use since the year 1219.

Master Lawrence Black of Chicago is at the Poland Spring House.

Miss Ruth Blackford of Brooklyn, N. Y., is at Poland Spring.

Little Sidney Ross of Richmond, Va., is with us.

Little Elaine Putnam and Master Endicott Putnam arrived at the Poland Spring House, Tuesday, July 6th.

Tid-Bits.

Have we had a "heated term?"

Mr. F. H. Green of Boston, is at Poland Spring.

Mr. W. Hester of Brooklyn, is at the Poland Spring House.

Miss Washington of Philadelphia, has returned for the season.

Mrs. J. R. Stuart, Roxbury, Mass., is at the Mansion House.

Mr. George T. Duncan and Mrs. Duncan of Portland, are here.

Mr. and Mrs. E. B. Cowles of Brookline, Mass., are with us.

Mrs. Mary T. Hoeffner of Boston, is at the Poland Spring House.

Mr. and Mrs. F. E. Taylor of Brooklyn, arrived Tuesday, July 6th.

Mr. H. E. Barnard of San Antonio, Texas, is at the Poland Spring House.

Mrs. J. M. Comstock, Cambridge, Mass., is at the Poland Spring House.

Mr. David Rines of Portland, and Mr. R. H. Rines of Boston, are with us.

Mr. William H. Scoville of Stamford, Conn., is registered at the Poland Spring House.

Arioch Wentworth is a welcome addition to the already large numbers of old friends at Poland.

Miss Jean W. Cox and Miss T. C. Williams of Haddenfield, N. Y., are at the Mansion House.

Mr. and Mrs. Amos Barnes are again among those whom Poland Spring is pleased to entertain.

Miss Evelyn Purdy of New York, and Miss Nonie Ryer of Hartsdale, New York, are at Poland Spring.

Mr. and Mrs. W. H. Fernekees, Miss Beatrice, Miss Elsa, Master Louis and William Fernekees, Jr., are at Poland Spring.

Mr. Samuel Ivers and Miss Ivers of New Bedford, have returned for the season. Mr. Ivers plays a fine game of croquet.

Francis Wiggin, editor of the *Industrial Journal*, Bangor, renewed old associations with the Maine State Building on the 7th.

Mr. Nat Huggins is spending a few days at the Poland Spring House. Mr. Huggins is a pupil at Sedgwick Institute, Great Barrington, Mass.

Mr. and Mrs. Nelson Bartlett were among the ever-welcome guests, of the middle of the week, who make Poland Spring annually their summer home.

Mr. and Mrs. George L. Osgood of Boston, have sought relief from the city's heat on Poland Hill.

Our thanks to the Shakers for a very handsome bouquet, which has graced the editorial table of late.

Mr. H. H. Ricker, Mr. E. J. Everett, and Master Everett of Portland, spent July 3d at Poland Spring.

Elegant remarque proof etchings of Closson's painting "Saxon" in Alcove A, can be purchased in the Library.

The many friends of Mr. and Mrs. H. O. Bright were glad to welcome them Wednesday morning, July 7th.

Mr. and Mrs. H. L. Piatt, Dr. E. W. Russell and Mrs. Russell, of Lewiston, dined at the Poland Spring House, Sunday.

Mr. and Mrs. C. C. Corbin, Webster, Mass., have returned for the season. Mr. and Mrs. Corbin come early and remain late.

Mr. and Mrs. Joseph H. White of Brookline, and their daughter, Mrs. George J. Putnam, are at the Poland Spring House.

Mr. J. H. Whittemore, President of the Naugatuck Malleable Iron Co., and Mr. H. H. Peck, a well-known resident of Waterbury, Conn., are at the Poland Spring House.

Mr. and Mrs. L. I. Carson of Malden, Mass., are at the Mansion House. This is Mr. and Mrs. Carson's first visit to Poland, and they are delighted with the beauties of the place.

Eugene E. Partridge, the Vice-President of the North American Insurance Co. of Boston, made a brief call on Sunday last. He has just celebrated his fiftieth birthday, and received many presents and congratulations.

Mr. William R. Gray, who has been attracted to Poland again, with Mrs. Gray, is of the new firm of the John C. Paige Co. He reports Mr. Paige as having had a high regard for Poland Spring, and especially interested in the library.

The old apple trees near the Mansion House stables, which were set out in 1800 by Wentworth Ricker, grandfather of the Messrs. Ricker, were removed July 1st. The trunk of one of the trees was hollow, and was filled in for a foot with exquisite mushrooms.

Mrs. Campbell and her daughter, Miss Mary Campbell of Camden, N. J., are spending the summer in California. Miss Campbell, who is very popular at the Mansion House, is greatly missed this season. Mr. Samuel Keene of Boston, announced his engagement to Miss Campbell this winter. A Poland romance.

Cyclist Column.

BEN BOLT UP TO DATE.

Oh, don't you remember sweet Alice, Ben Bolt,
Sweet Alice, whose hair was so brown,
Who wept with delight when you gave her a smile,
And trembled in fear at your frown.

A few years have changed sweet Alice, Ben Bolt,
She now has a wheel of her own,
And arrayed in blue bloomers that fit her too soon,
Sweet Alice goes scorching alone.

WHAT DID HE SAY HIMSELF?

The clergyman—"I had no idea profanity was
so prevalent till I began to ride a bicycle."

His wife—"Do you hear much of it on the
road?"

The clergyman—"Why, nearly every one I run
into swears frightfully."—*Odds and Ends.*

Miss Mazie Harrigan is receiving congratulations on her winning a bicycle. She rides well.

Master Webster Judd is at Poland Spring, and
he rides the wheel splendidly.

Mr. Warren Davenport and his sons, Messrs.
W. W. and Allen Davenport of Boston, came on
their wheels from that city, and spent the night of
July 7th at the Mansion House. They left early
the next morning for Paris, Maine. Mr. Warren
Davenport is a well-known music teacher of
Boston.

Guests at Poland Spring House,
WEDNESDAY, JULY 7, 1897.

Buckingham, Mr. and Mrs.
B. W.
Brown, Mr. and Mrs. H. B.
Brown, Mrs. W. S.
Bright, Mr. and Mrs. H. O.
Baker, Miss F. P.
Baker, Charles T.
Bartlett, Mr. & Mrs. Nelson
Brown, Miss L. M. Harman
Brown, Miss Jessie
Baxter, James J.
Baker, Mr. and Mrs. Geo. F.
Brewster, Mr. and Mrs. Benj.
Barnes, Mr. and Mrs. Amos
Black, Mrs. John C.
Black, Lawrence W.
Blackford, Mrs. W. E.
Blackford, Miss
Blackford, Miss Ada
Barnard, H. E.
Cummings, Miss
Child, Mr. and Mrs. C. H.
Child, Miss
Carpenter, Mr. & Mrs. F. W.
Carpenter, Miss Hannah
Curtis, Mrs. Cyrus S.
Chandler, Mrs. Z.
Corbin, Mr. and Mrs. C. C.
Clewley, Mrs. William J.
Converse, Mr. and Mrs. C. C.
Culver, Andrew R.
Danforth, James H.
Ives, Samuel
Ives, Miss
Lake, Mrs. B. C.
Little, Mr. and Mrs. Amos R.
Love, Mr. and Mrs. John W.
Leland, Miss
Mallouf, Mr. and Mrs. and
family
Murray, Mrs. A.
Montgomery, Mrs. J. T.
Maclennan, Miss
Ordway, John A.
Osgood, Mr. and Mrs. Geo. L.
Peters, Mrs. A.
Peters, Edwin D.
Peterson, Dr. and Mrs. W.
Peterson, Miss Florence
Peterson, Miss Alice
Peterson, Miss May
Parsons, Mrs. M. E.
Putnam, Mrs. George J. and
family
Ridlon, Mrs. Frank
Richardson, Mrs. Alden B.
Robinson, Mrs. P. T.
Rines, David T.
Rines, R. H.
Rosenheim, Mr. & Mrs. Jos.
Rosenheim, Miss Tessie
Savage, Mr. and Mrs. Henry
Savage, Samuel H.
Strong, Mr. & Mrs. Edwin A.

Evans, H.
Ellis, Miss C. B.
Faile, Thomas H.
French, George B.
Fernekees, Mr. and Mrs.
William H.
Fernekees, Miss Beatrice
Fernekees, Miss Elsa
Fernekees, Master Louis
Fernekees, Master Wm., Jr.
Green, F. H.
Gracie, Mrs. A.
Goldenberg, S.
Goldenberg, Mary
Gale, Mrs. L. M.
Gale, Miss Olive
Goodwin, Mrs. Daniel
Huggins, Mrs. N.
Huggins, Miss
Hastel, W.
Hubbard, Mrs. S. B.
Hobart, Mrs. M. E.
Hoffman, Mrs. F. T.
Hoeffner, Mrs. Mary T.
Salter, Mr. and Mrs. A. T.
Sawyer, Mr. and Mrs. J. B.
Swan, Mr. and Mrs. James
Taylor, Mr. and Mrs. F. E.
Thomas, Mr. & Mrs. Frank R.
Tompkins, Mrs. Orlando
Trevelli, Mr. & Mrs. Chas. I.
Thornton, L. N.
Wood, Mrs. Walter G.
Wood, Mrs. Ambrose
Wentworth, Alloch
White, Mr. & Mrs. James H.
Whitman, Anna S.
Woodbury, Mr. & Mrs. J. P.
Whilldin, Mr. and Mrs.
Wilmon
Wiggin, Francis
Wescott, Mr. & Mrs. Geo. P.
Walker, Mrs. C. T.
Whipple, Mrs. J. Reed
Wharton, Mrs. F. R.
Wilson, Mrs. W. G.
Wilson, Master M.
Yates, David G.

FRANK CARLOS GRIFFITH, } EDITORS.
NETTIE M. RICKER,   }

PUBLISHED EVERY SUNDAY MORNING DURING THE MONTHS
OF JULY, AUGUST, AND SEPTEMBER, IN THE INTERESTS OF

POLAND SPRING AND ITS VISITORS.

All contributions relative to the guests of Poland Spring
will be thankfully received.

To insure publication, all communications should reach the
editors not later than Wednesday preceding day of issue.

All parties desiring rates for advertising in the HILL-TOP
should write the editors for same.

The subscription price of the HILL-TOP is $1.00 for the
season, post-paid.   Single copies will be mailed at 10c. each.

Address,
EDITORS "HILL-TOP,"
· Poland Spring House,
South Poland, Maine.

PRINTED AT JOURNAL OFFICE, LEWISTON.

Sunday, July 11, 1897.

Editorial.

THERE was recently a Fourth of July. Did
any one hear *of* it? Certainly no one heard
it. By the way, though, our Fourth fell upon
the fifth this year, which was somewhat curious,
come to think of it.

In reading the reports of the reports on that
day, it becomes the duty of an up-to-date, end-of-
the-century, local paper to chronicle the celebration
programme of the Poland Fourth.

The day opened with a brilliant illumination,
only equaled in rare localities in Italy, by the
rising of the sun, and a more brilliant (and inex-
pensive) illumination was never sprung upon a
waiting multitude.

Suddenly the stillness was annihilated by the
simultaneous and deafening peal of every church
bell upon the hill.   Even our tame whip-poor-will
was awed into silence (thank goodness), and as
the day wore on and out at the knees the enthusiasm waxed warm, almost to fever heat, as salvo
after salvo of Kennedy's crackers were fired in the
neighborhood of the bakery.

The music of a hundred military bands in
bright uniforms with polished brass ornaments
might have been heard (the band, not the ornaments) as they passed in rapid succession, had
they been here, and the interest of the populace
reached its height as the orator of the day tried to
recall the words of the "Star-Spangled Banner,"
which, unfortunately, Peary had the manuscript
of in his Tuxedo pocket up along toward New-
foundland, and cabling was out of the question.

The grand regatta on Poland Loch was an
object of interest to those of our citizens who were
there, and, contrary to the expectation of all, the
'varsity parlor match was awarded to the winners,
who have loving cups to burn, having been sent a
catalogue of samples by a manufacturer of these
useless articles.

Thunders of silence rent the air as Poland Boy
won the Poland Derby (hat), which was one of
the day's features.   He won it by a neck, and that
is where he got his speed, so one young America
said under his breath, having succeeded in crawl-
ing beneath it before venturing the remark.

Did we have tie-works?   Well,—but never
mind,—we have said enough to make Greater
New York ashamed of its own provincialism now,
and will only say in conclusion that Poland had a
Fourth which was the delight of all, and may we
have many happy returns of the day.

Musical Programme.

SUNDAY, JULY 11, 1897.

1. Coronation March	. . .	Kretschmar.
2. Overture—Semiramide	. . .	Rossini.
3. Nocturno	. . .	Anderson.
Flute Solo—Mr. A. Brooke.		
4. { Love Song	. . .	Jonas.
{ Fly Minuett	. . .	Czibulka.
For Strings.		
5. Selections—Mignon	. . .	Thomas.
6. Sanctus	. . . . .	Gounod.

A Welcome Visitor.

One of our most interesting visitors has been
Mr. John L. Stoddard, the well-known lecturer.
His stay was exceedingly brief, stopping only a
few hours, but in that time his conductor, Mr. F.
E. Boothby, took him to the principal points of
interest, including, of course, the Maine State
Building, in which the world-wide traveller was
much interested, as a unique and valuable adjunct
of this great resort.   This was Mr. Stoddard's
first visit to Poland Spring, but it is easy to sur-
mise that it will not be the last.

𝒯id-𝒷its.

Hot.

Minerals.

Raspberries.

Hand-organs.

Read the advertisements.

Miss S. P. Baker is at Poland Spring.

Mrs. K. M. Ernst of Brooklyn, is with us.

Mr. J. F. McCoy, Kingfield, Maine, is here.

Mr. John A. Ordway of Boston, arrived July 5th.

Miss Anna S. Whitman has returned for the season.

New-comers will find lots of good books at the library.

Mr. A. T. Milliken of Roxbury, Mass., arrived July 4th.

Miss Cummings of New York is at the Poland Spring House.

Mr. Edward D. Peters of Boston, has returned for the season.

Mrs. Samuel H. Savage of Boston, is at Poland Spring.

A catalogue for the Art Exhibition is in the printer's hands.

Mr. and Mrs. C. L. Riddle, Boston, are at the Mansion House.

Mr. and Mrs. E. S. Williams of Malden, Mass., are with us.

Mrs. M. E. Hobart, Brooklyn, N. Y., is at the Poland Spring House.

Mr. and Mrs. W. T. Ness of Boston, have returned for the season.

Mrs. R. T. Robinson of Newton, Mass., is at the Poland Spring House.

Mr. and Mrs. J. F. Gallagher, Dover, N. H., are at the Mansion House.

Mr. Charles T. Travelli and Mrs. Travelli of Pittsburg, Pa., are with us.

. Mr. Charles T. Baker of Boston, is registered at the Poland Spring House.

Mr. C. C. Converse and Mrs. Converse of Boston, are at the Poland Spring House.

A welcome which is annually extended, is that to Mr. Amos R. Little, who has just returned.

Mr. S. J. Shaw and Mrs. Shaw of Boston, are spending the season at the Mansion House.

The many friends of Mrs. T. M. Gale and Miss Olive Gale of Washington, D. C., are glad to welcome them again.

An Episcopal clergyman's wife living in southern Texas sends to Mrs. Hiram Ricker a large quantity of Mexican drawn work. Mrs. Ricker will be glad to show it to all who will call at her cottage. It is charity work, and the prices are very reasonable.

Recipes.

LEG OF MUTTON A LA CIPOLATA.

Procure a leg of mutton about eight pounds, trim it and three parts roast it, then place it in a tin with some onions, carrots, and celery, cut into slices; add a quart of stock, some seasoning, and a glass of vinegar; cover the mutton with buttered paper, and bake one hour in a hot oven, occasionally turning it in the liquor; when cooked, strain off the gravy into a stewpan, thicken it with a little roux, add a little soy and a glass of sherry; let boil one minute; place the leg of mutton on a very hot dish, pour the sauce round, serve very hot.

ROLLED BEEF.

Take four pounds of the thinnest part of the flank, spread on a board, and with a thin knife shave off the inside skin. Dust over with salt and pepper. Prepare one pint of bread crumbs, one-half cup of cold water, half a teaspoonful of sage, one-half teaspoonful of thyme, one-third teaspoonful of pepper, one spoonful of salt; mix well and add one well-beaten egg. Spread this evenly over the meat. Roll, and tie with twine. Flour and butter a pudding bag; put the rolled beef into it, and place in a stew-pan with just enough water to cover; cook four hours; remove, place on a hot dish, and serve with tomato sauce.

BREAD OMELET.

One cup bread crumbs, one tablespoon parsley, one-half chopped onion, one egg, salt and pepper; soften crumbs in milk, add the other ingredients. Butter a frying pan and pour in the mixture; cover and cook five minutes, then uncover and brown. Serve with gravy.

Mineral Exhibit.

A very complete and interesting exhibition of minerals is being arranged in the Maine State Building at the time our paper is being made up this week, and next week we expect to give a more general description of its features.

We wish to say, however, that it is probable that when the stranger to Maine's wealth looks upon these specimens, he will be astonished at their beauty and value.

The collection also includes specimens from other states and countries, which in many instances are of rare excellence.

The Photographic Studio is now open for the season, under the management of the Notman Photographic Company of Boston. A cordial invitation is extended to all to visit the Studio and inspect samples of their specialties in Carbon and Repoussé productions.

The Maine Building in Chicago.

The State Building was opened May 1st and continued so to visitors until the close of the Fair, November 1, 1893.

During the progress of the Fair, the public were admitted daily, from 8 A.M. to 6 P.M., Sundays excepted, when only Maine visitors were admitted. Ten thousand two hundred fifty residents of Maine registered as visitors at the State Building. Six thousand one hundred natives of Maine, but residing in other states, registered at the Maine building also.

Visitors from every state and territory of the Union and many of the foreign countries placed their names on these volumes, which may be seen by applying to the Librarian.

Rain.

There is one peculiarity about rain which is possessed by many other things, and that is, that it is generally wet. There are other wet goods, which are not taken externally like rain, but are more effective in their immediate results. Rain is made for external application, but incessant application of rain sometimes causes permeation.

All kinds of application do not result in permeation. We once knew a man who made the most persistent application to the President for a post-office, but he never permeated the department he sought to.

We know Rain. We have been close companions of late, and have spent days together. He is like some pictures, much better at a distance, and then familiarity is apt to breed a contempt which is unpleasant, and especially where one's presence is forced upon you, as it were, without invitation. The disposition of the chap is to drop in on you unceremoniously, and the eccentricities of the creature are such that he prefers windows to doors, and still more strange, sky-lights are his favorite. Rain has a perfect mania for sky-lights, and will invariably enter that way in preference to any other.

His predilections are demoralizing in their tendency, and he shows no desire to begin at the bottom and work up, but invariably falls from whatever lofty eminence he may reach by force of circumstances.

Victoria's reign has lasted sixty years, but that's different. As a permeator, however, she has been an Amazonian success, for her reign has had its effects around the world.

This year Rain has been like the mother-in-law visits, comes twice a year and stays six months each time.

Mr. F. R. Wharton of Philadelphia, is with us.

Arrivals.

POLAND SPRING HOUSE.

FROM JULY 2 TO 8, 1897.

Beals, Gardner	Boston
Boothby, Mr. and Mrs. F. E.	Portland
Baker, Miss S. P.	Boston
Baker, Charles T.	Boston
Barnard, H. E.	San Antonio, Texas
Bright, Mr. and Mrs. H. O.	Cambridge
Bartlett, Mr. and Mrs. Nelson	Boston
Barnes, Mr. and Mrs. Amos	
Barhydt, Mr. and Mrs. P. H.	New York
Black, Mrs. Jno. C.	Chicago
Bates, Mr. and Mrs. Jacob P.	Boston
Converse, Mr. and Mrs. C. C.	Boston
Corbin, Mr. and Mrs. C. C.	Webster, Mass.
Cotterson, Charles	Red Bank, N. J.
Cummings, Miss	New York
Cowles, Mr. and Mrs. E. B.	Brookline
Comstock, Mrs. J. M.	Cambridge
Cummings, Charles P.	Boston
Clark, Mrs. S. H.	Boston
Clark, Miss E. L.	Boston
Clark, George H.	Portland
Chadbourne, Mr. and Mrs. E. R.	Lewiston
Countiss, Mrs. R. H.	Chicago
Countiss, Miss Claribel	Chicago
Duncan, Mr. and Mrs. George L.	Portland
Dunham, R. C.	Boston
Everett, E. S.	Portland
Fernekees, Mr. and Mrs. William H.	Boston
Fernekees, Miss Beatrice	Boston
Fernekees, Miss Elsa	Boston
Gray, Mr. and Mrs. William R.	Boston
Gale, Mrs. T. M.	Washington
Gale, Miss Olive	Washington
Griffith, Mrs. F. C.	Boston
Greene, F. H.	Boston
Green, Mrs. Aug. W.	Chicago
Green, Miss Grace	Chicago
Hobart, Mrs. M. E.	Brooklyn
Herald, C. G.	Conway, N. H.
Huggins, Nat.	New York
Hubbard, Mr. and Mrs. Thos. H.	New York
Hubbard, Miss G. E.	New York
Hubbard, Miss A. W.	New York
Hester, W.	Brooklyn
Hoeffner, Mrs. Mary T.	Boston
Holton, Mr. and Mrs. H. S.	New York
Ives, Samuel	New Bedford
Ives, Miss	New Bedford
Little, Amos R.	Philadelphia
Milliken, A. T.	Roxbury, Mass.
Maclenan, Miss	Brooklyn
M'Clellan, Mr. and Mrs. C. H.	Lakewood
Morgan, Jas. L.	Brooklyn
Ness, Mr. and Mrs. W. T.	Boston
Ordway, John A.	Boston
Osgood, Mr. and Mrs. George L.	Boston
Peters, Edw. D.	Boston
Purdy, Evelyn	New York
Patridge, E. E.	Boston
Pratt, Mr. and Mrs. H. L.	Lewiston
Putnam, Mrs. George J.	Brookline
Robinson, Mrs. R. T.	Newton
Rickel, H. H.	Portland
Ryel, Nonie	Hartsdale, N. Y.
Rines, David T.	Portland
Rines, R. H.	Boston
Ray, Joseph G.	Franklin, Mass.
Ray, Miss	Franklin, Mass.
Savage, Mrs. Samuel H.	Boston
Stoddard, John L.	Boston
Safford, Miss M. A.	Portland
Smith, Miss V. B.	Portland
Scoville, William H.	Stamford
Sexton, Mrs. George Hobart	New York
Sexton, William Lord	New York
Talmage, Mrs. M. R.	St. Louis
Talmage, William Scott	St. Louis
Taylor, Mr and Mrs. F. E.	Brooklyn
Trevelli, Mr. and Mrs. Charles I.	Pittsburg
True, Samuel A.	Portland
White, Mr. and Mrs. Jos. H.	Brookline
Whitman, Anna S.	Somerville
Wharton, F. R.	Philadelphia
Wescott, Mr. and Mrs. George P.	Portland
Walker, Mrs. C. T.	Boston
Wentworth, Arioch	Boston
Wiggin, Francis	Bangor
Yates, David G.	Philadelphia

MANSION HOUSE.

Baxter, Mrs. Mary A.	Portland
Cox, Miss Jean W.	Haddenfield, N. J.
Carson, Mr. and Mrs. L. J.	Malden
Davenport, Warren	Boston
Davenport, W. W.	Boston
Davenport, Allen	Boston
Ernst, Mrs. K. M.	Brooklyn
Elmore, Samuel D.	Boston
Gallagher, Mr. and Mrs. J. F.	Dover
Gardner, Mrs. Florence N.	Portland
Greene, S. W.	Brookline
Keene, Mr. and Mrs. S. W.	Boston
deLissa, Mrs. M. S.	New York
McCoy, J. F.	E. Orange, N. J.
Riddle, Mr. and Mrs. C. L.	Boston
Read, Mrs. L. S.	Camden, N. J.
Read, William T.	Camden, N. J.
Shaw, Mr. and Mrs. S. J.	Boston
Stoty, O. H.	Boston
Van Bell, Mrs. E. S.	New York
Williams, Miss T. C.	Haddenfield, N. J.
Washington, Miss R.	Philadelphia
Williams, Mr. and Mrs. E. S.	Malden

The Store.

We note with pleasure the return of Mrs. Mallouf, and the re-opening of the store. Her goods, chiefly oriental, are very interesting and valuable, and form a perfect bazaar in the small space afforded for their display.

Mr. Mallouf this year accompanies her, and we also welcome the return of their two sons, fresh from the Rugby Military Academy.

UNEDUCATED.

[From Judge.]

Aunt—"Well, Ethel, how do you like your new little brother?"

Ethel (aged four)—"I don't like him at all. He can't even speak English."

Hinds' Honey and Almond Cream may be had at the news stand.

Tid=Bits.

Quiet is requested.

306 books taken out, June 14th to 30th.

Mrs. J. C. Black of Chicago, is at the Poland Spring House.

Mr. and Mrs. George Wescott of Portland, have returned.

Mrs. C. T. Walker of Boston, is at the Poland Spring House.

Mr. and Mrs. P. H. Barhydt of New York, have returned.

Mr. Joseph G. Ray and Miss Ray of Franklin, Mass., are with us.

Mrs. George Hobart Sexton and Mr. William Lord Sexton of New York, are with us.

Rev. C. H. McClellan and Mrs. McClellan of Lakewood, N. J., are at Poland Spring House.

Three of the celebrated Henty juvenile books have been purchased from the funds left with us by Mr. R. B. Hartshorne.

Mr. and Mrs. S. W. Keene arrived July 3d. Mr. and Mrs. Keene always spend July and August at the Mansion House.

Mr. and Mrs. Thomas A. Hubbard, Miss S. E. Hubbard, and Miss A. W. Hubbard of New York, are at the Poland Spring House.

Mr. David G. Yates shares with Mr. Little his pleasures and discomforts on their fishing trips, and finds a hospitable welcome at Poland later on.

On the register of July 2d may be seen two signatures, one following the other, each with three initials, and one letter alone serving for the six initials.

A jolly party, composed of twenty-three of the employees from the Poland Spring House, took the James G. Blaine, July 5th, and went to Dry Mills for a dance.

New Books.

From Lieutenant-Commander B. H. Buckingham. Register of the Navy, 1897.

From Miss Lydia Hartshorne. Out of India; Rudyard Kipling.

From R. B. Hartshorne. Held Fast for England; by G. A. Henty. With Lee in Virginia; by G. A. Henty. With Wolfe in Canada; by G. A. Henty.

From John C. Paige. Secret Court Memoirs, Edition de Grande Luxe. 4 vols.

The · New · Mount · Pleasant · House,

In the Heart of the White Mountains.

Through Parlor Cars from New York, Boston, and Portland, also from Burlington, Montreal, and Quebec.

A COMPETENT GREENS-KEEPER

WILL HAVE CHARGE OF THE GOLF LINKS.

The Hotel faces the Grandest Display of Mountain Peaks in America east of the Rocky Mountains. It is lighted throughout by electricity, thoroughly heated by steam, and has an abundance of private and public baths. Its orchestra is made up largely from the Boston Symphony Orchestra. Its table is unsurpassed. Absolutely pure water from an artesian well, 400 feet in solid rock.

Water Bottles Filled from Birch-Rock Spring on the Mountain Side.

IT IS THE NEAREST HOTEL TO MT. WASHINGTON, AND THE TRAIN FOR THE SUMMIT STARTS FROM A STATION ON THE HOTEL GROUNDS.

All Trains, Maine Central Railroad, from Portland to Burlington, Montreal, Quebec, and Lake Champlain, stop at the platform close to the House.

Leave Portland 8.45 A.M.,	arrive Mt. Pleasant House,	12.21 P.M.
" " 1.25 P.M.,	" " "	5.05 P.M.
" " 3.20 P.M.,	" " "	7.20 P.M.
" " 8.45 P.M.,	" " "	11.47 P.M.

Post, Telegraph, and Ticket Office in the Hotel.

ANDERSON & PRICE, of the Hotel Ormond of Florida, Managers.

☞ Address by wire or mail, "Mount Pleasant House, N. H."

IT STANDS AT THE HEAD.

Unrivalled in Popularity!
Unsurpassed in Location!
Unapproached in Patronage!

THE

POLAND * SPRING * HOUSE

IS A SUPERB ILLUSTRATION OF

◦ ◦ ◦ SUCCESS ◦ ◦ ◦

EMBRACING AS IT DOES

ALL THE DESIRABLE FEATURES

EXPECTED IN THIS

The Leading Resort of America,

WHILE THE

MAINE STATE BUILDING

WITH ITS

SUPERB ART FEATURES

IS UNEQUALLED BY ANY SIMILAR ENTERPRISE

IN THE WORLD.

◦◦

HIRAM RICKER & SONS (Incorporated),

PROPRIETORS.

MAINE STATE BUILDING.

The Hill-Top

POLAND SPRINGS, SO. POLAND, ME.

Did you know that the majority of the large portraits hanging in the Maine Building were made
by THE SPRAGUE & HATHAWAY COMPANY of Somerville, Mass.? The World's Fair pictures were
also made by the same company.

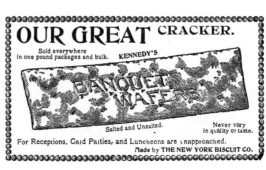

THE HILL TOPs

VOL. IV. SUNDAY MORNING, JULY 18, 1897. No. 3.

The Conservatoiy.

ANOTHER important new featuie which has been added to the myriad already at Poland Spring, is the Conservatory, which was begun in November and finished in January, and which, although completed so far as it goes, does not yet comprise all that it is intended it ultimately shall.

At the present time it is a long, evenly-built structure, built so with the idea of adding at the end a high octagonal palm house, which will add greatly to its beauty and usefulness.

It is 113 feet long and 20 feet wide, affording

2,260 square feet of floor space, and divided into three sections: first the potting room, next the flowering plants, and then the roses and carnations.

Ten thousand is the number of pots used in the building, which is heated by a system of hot water heating, the invention of T. W. Weathered's Sons, who were also the constructors of the building.

The frame is of iron, and it has patent gutters and conductors, to carry off the water, to prevent freezing, and also has the best system of ventilation possible, all those on the side in each section and at the top as well, being opened or closed from one point.

Underneath the building is the boiler room, where there are sixteen coils of two-inch pipe.

The partitions between the sections are of glass, and the entire building contains 2,628 distinct pieces of glass, used in its composition. Our illustration shows a portion of the middle section. The grounds immediately adjoining are laid out, next the drive-way, as a lawn with eight beds of flowers, one representing a huge Poland Water bottle, done in Alternanthera, with the letters of "Poland Water" in Sempervivum.

Next the lawn comes the bed of a hundred dahlias, immediately behind which are the hot-beds, fifty feet long, covered with glass. There are three of these, and two others seventy-five feet long. Following along the side of the wall of the Conservatory is a bed of flowers, the entire length of the building, and in fact the whole adjoining space is devoted to flowering plants, excepting a portion of the glass-covered hot-beds, which contain early vegetables, melons, etc.

On a hot day, a Turkish bath may easily be indulged in, for on the hottest of them the mercury reaches 132° in the interior.

The building, as well as the ornamental gardening of Poland Spring, is under the charge of Mr. Charles Thorne, who is now in his second season here, but the result of whose skill may be seen on all sides.

Thus it may be seen there is likely to be no lack of flowers the present season, and Poland Hill will blossom as the rose.

Notes on Bayreuth.

JUST now many pilgrims are journeying toward the operatic paradise of the world, for the three cycles of July and August, beginning July 20th. Everybody who is musical is deeply interested in Bayreuth, the home of Wagner operas. Poland Spring is most fortunate in having for director of the summer orchestra, a musician who not only is first-violin in the Boston Symphony Orchestra, but who also has been first-violin at Bayreuth. The subscriber had the pleasure of hearing Mr. Kuntz in the summer of 1891 in "Tristan and Isolde," "Tannhäuser," and "Parsifal." In the latter opera, he was one of several who were elevated unseen above the stage in the first and third acts, to guide the sopranos and tenors, who sing alternately. The overture to "Tannhäuser," as interpreted here, vividly suggests the same composition as rendered at the Wagner Opera House. To have played in the orchestra at Bayreuth establishes the standing and reputation of a musician, and thereafter he is in demand in the best orchestras of Europe, including Vienna. Musical temperament, fine poetic feeling, and perfect technique, distinguish the interpretations of the leader, while the men who compose the summer orchestra, also from the Boston Symphony, are all delightful artists.

This year "Der Ring des Nibelungen," which comprises the operas "Rheingold," "Walküre," "Siegfried," "Gotterdämmerung," is to be presented with eight representations of "Parsifal," which is the crown of all Wagner operas. It is a revelation of indescribable beauty. It leaves one in a rapture. The solemn, mystical ceremonials are thrilling and impressive. The orchestra seems like an inspired soul in its utterance. One cannot realize instruments. Music seems to evolve in the air. Wagner considered "Parsifal" his best production.

During the presentation of the operas one listens spell-bound. Such silence one never experiences elsewhere in an audience. It is called the "Bayreuth silence." No one stirs, whispers, coughs, or breathes, apparently. Fans, programmes, and hats are prohibited. At the beginning of each act lights are turned down until the auditorium is almost in darkness, people drop into their seats, and profound silence reigns. To one who is distressed by the fussy audience such stillness is blissful. If an audience suffers from aggravating noises, how intolerable they must be to the musicians, with their finely attuned nerves and intensified sense of hearing.

The unique opera house, at the edge of a forest, is a colossal red-brick structure, extraordinary in form, and without decoration. It seats 1,800 persons, including the royal gallery. The seats are in an amphitheatre form, and every one is good. Entrance is made to the auditorium from numerous doors at the sides. There are no aisles. The orchestra is out of sight, twelve feet below the front of the stage. There is no prompter. The enormous stage is deeper than the auditorium, the wings extending either side farther than the width of the stage, across the entire length of the building. Underneath the stage is a large chanber, used in every opera. The apparatus for electric lighting is very extensive. Miles of ropes and pulleys, scenes, and stage properties, suggest operations. From floor to roof, over arches, and in various directions, thousands of colored glasses are strung before electric lights ready for instant use. Dressing rooms are large and in exquisite order. One long, secluded room is filled with broad ribbons or sashes, decorated with gilt and color, bearing distinguished names from artists to kings, some from America, which were sent with flowers for the funeral of Richard Wagner. There are at least several hundred, beside dried wreaths, pictures, and other souvenirs.

During the progress of an opera no one is allowed to enter or leave the auditorium. Between the acts people go out and stroll in the groves or dine at the restaurant. The operas begin at four o'clock and end at ten. The intervals between acts are often an hour in length. It is very romantic to wander through the gardens, the open meadows, and even in the woods. One fancies it another phase of the opera, with all the brilliant throng in gay costumes, chatting in many languages. The setting sun adds another element of beauty, and the odor of new-mown hay, the haymakers, and an early noon, all conspire to promote the dream. The audience is recalled by bugles, giving short strains, thrice repeated, from the opera of the day.

The management consists of a syndicate, of whom Madame Wagner is one. She is present at every rehearsal and is severely critical of every gesture and tone of the singers. She is always in the front row with her son and daughters at every opera given.

Wagner's tomb is in a small clearing in the wood, close to the house. The trees come very near, leaving only room enough to walk around the mound, which is very large and high, covered at the sides with English ivy. A massive flat stone of granite covers the top. It is heaped with flowers and plants from friends and strangers. Pictures and busts of Wagner are everywhere to be seen in Bayreuth. A beautiful vine-covered walk through the lawn leads to the Wagner mansion, where Madame Wagner still resides. Pictures from opera scenes, one of "Woton," and German inscriptions decorate the front of the house.

Liszt, whom Madame Wagner strongly resembles, rests in the cemetery, in a pretty chapel. It is filled with flowers and other memorials. Two doves are over his head. At the entrance, in an arch, are the words, "I know that my Redeemer liveth."

A. HURLBURT.

Renfrew, Quebec, for Furs. Remember.

Welsh Rabbit.

It is not our intention to explain the concoction of this delectable dish, but to explain the error into which the public have been led by etymologists who saw no meaning in the above spelling, but imagined they did in that of "rare-bit."

Welsh rabbit was the name given derisively to the article in question, the same as we call the codfish a "Cape Cod turkey," or in England, a sheep's head, stewed with onions, is often termed a "Digby chicken," or potatoes, "Irish apricots."

The fondness of the Welsh for toasted cheese brought about this term, and it finds its synonym in many languages.

Mount Pleasant.

The Mount Pleasant House, on the slope of Mount Stickney, and about half a mile from the Fabyan House, is the nearest house to Mount Washington of the hotels in this district. It is the perfection of hotel development, and under the management of Anderson & Price, of the Ormond, Ormond, Florida, has gained a wide reputation. It is luxurious without ostentation, and is an example of the highest ideal of hotel construction and management.

The cottage, for college men, was a feature last summer, and nearly all the rooms are engaged this season.

The tennis courts and bowling alleys are models, while a trout pond, a short walk from the house, affords a delightful chance for canoeing. The walks and drives are varied and attractive, the views magnificent, while the social life of the house is of the most charming character.

Mr. E. B. Winslow and Mrs. Winslow of Portland, Mr. D. W. Sanborn and Mrs. Sanborn, were welcome guests at the Poland Spring House, July 10th. Mr. Sanborn is General Superintendent of the Boston & Maine Railroad.

Art Notes.

THE Poland Spring Exhibition this season is especially strong in the work of the female artists. Among the most notable of these is Agnes Leavitt, whose "Birches" are quite famous. She is a native of Boston, and has studied and worked in that city almost exclusively. She is a pupil of Enneking, Hardwick, and Sandham of Boston, and is an exhibitor in many of the principal exhibitions.

Grace Woodbridge Geer was also born in Boston, and received her art education there, under such excellent masters as Robert Vonnoh, S. P. Rolt Triscott, Tarbell, Tompkins and others, and exhibits in the principal galleries.

Notice her admirable picture of an old New England homestead in alcove F, and the "Iris," in D. She paints in oil or water, and the beautiful head of Katherine, in B, is an excellent work.

F. M. Fenety has some work in alcove E, of which he may well be proud. Mr. Fenety was born in England, and studied constantly with his brother, A. C. Fenety, the portrait painter. His work has been shown at the National Academy, New York, Philadelphia Academy, and Boston Art Club with success. His beautiful flower pieces, in alcove E, are superb illustrations of his style.

George Harvey was also born in England, at Torquay, Devonshire, and a student of the Royal Academy, London. His work has been exhibited there, and his last one was purchased by the Secretary of the Art Union as a prize for one of the subscribers. He came to Nova Scotia later, and became an associate of the Royal Canadian Academy; was a director of the Victoria School of Art. His large central picture in E, called "Evening," is very rich in color and lovely in effect. Another of his typical English scenes is a cottage, in A.

Stuart came from near Bangor, Maine, and later, found his way to the Pacific coast, where for eight years he made his home among the mountains, Alaska, Washington, and Oregon being his favorite spots. He has been a mountain climber, and has hunted with the Indians, finally returning to Chicago, where his studio now is.

We have three exquisite pictures from his brush, one of "Sunset on Mt. Shasta," with a rich glow upon the snow-covered peak seldom attained by any artist. Another small but excellent picture is of a "Dreamy Day, Napa Valley, Cal.," both in alcove E, while in B is a fine picture of "California Peaches."

The catalogue is now expected any day, and it will be found to contain many works of rare merit. These pictures are for sale, and as all the works are from artists of excellent standing in the art world, and in many instances winners of the highest rewards, purchases may be made with the assurance of their excellence.

Mr. George Burrette Waldo, the artist, is spending the summer with his father and mother at the Mansion House. Mr. Waldo is from New York. He was born in Danielson, Conn., and studied at the Academy of Design and the Art Students' League in New York. He then became a pupil at the Académie Julian, studying under M. Jean Paul Laurens and M. Benjamin Constant. Mr. Waldo took honors at Julian's and exhibited in the Salon de Champ de Mars. He has painted a portrait of Madame Helena Modjeska, which has met with great success and is now owned by the Players' Club in New York. Madame Modjeska and her friends are much pleased with the portrait, and it is most fitting that it should remain permanently at the Players' Club. Mr. Waldo has four pictures in the Maine State Building. The portrait of the young woman was hung in the Salon in 1894. "The Mother" was exhibited in New York this spring. He has a fine sense of color and a delicate feeling for tone. He draws well, is essentially a painter, and is a young man of great promise.

The MacNabs.

Among the Scottish clans, the head of each who is the chief, is further distinguished by the apellation "The," as "The Macgregor," "The MacLaren." When The MacNab came to America years ago on a visit, while in Canada he called upon a relative MacNab, who aspired to the same designation. The former left his card bearing his rightful title, "The MacNab." When the call was returned, his relative left his own card bearing the legend—"The Other MacNab."

The MacNabs are celebrated for their independence, away back to the flood. When Noah started out in the ark, the father of his race, the old, original MacNab, refused to join Noah's party, declaring his intention of going on the voyage alone, in his own boat. There is, in Edinburgh, a picture of the great waters, with the ark of exaggerated dimensions, sailing away in the background, and in the near foreground is a tiny row-boat, with the ancient progenitor, sitting erect, head in the air, rowing with all his existence.

Certified to by one of the MacNabs, now enjoying Poland Spring.

Massage.

It may be of interest to some to know that Mrs. E. J. Robinson, the very excellent Masseuse, who has annually visited Poland, is again at the Poland Spring House.

There is nothing more beneficial, in scores of instances, than a thorough massage treatment, and Mrs. Robinson is a graduate of the celebrated Posse Gymnasium, and bears a high reputation.

Children's Column.

"A blessed companion is a book—a book that, fitly chosen, is a life-long friend."
—*Douglas Jerrold.*

A little boy was taken by his papa to see the newly arrived twin brothers. The little fellow knew that on several occasions when a family of kittens had appeared, all but one of them had been drowned. "Papa," said he, upon viewing the new brothers, "which one are you going to keep?"

Sunday-school teacher: "Now, Mildred, you can recite your verse." Mildred—"A soft answer turneth the way round."

The Wail of the Cat Mummy.

[BY S. B. GRIGGS, from the Independent.]

Oh, I was a little Egyptian cat,
And I lived in King Pharoah's house, I did!
The rats and the mice I would chase with delight,
I often caught birds (which I know wasn't right),
And whenever I could I would steal out at night
To miaou on the top of a pyramid.

But one day I was greedy, and ate a whole crane,
So I had a bad fit, and I died, I did.
Then they hurried to make me this beautiful case
(It covers me all, just excepting my face),
And they laid me away in a quiet little place,
On a shelf right inside of the pyramid.

And there I have lain for these thousands of years,
And I hoped I was hidden forever, I did.
But they hunted me out, and they brought me away!
Oh, isn't it horrid that I have to stay
In the dusty museum here, day after day,
When I want to go back to my pyramid!

His First Fish.

Little Hiram Ricker, Jr., was very happy Thursday morning, July 15th, when he caught a black bass in the Middle Lake weighing one pound. His little cousin, Winthrop Nay, was with him. He, also, caught a black bass, and as he had almost landed him the line broke and away went hook and fish.

Master Chester Palmer of Brooklyn, N. Y., is at the Poland Spring House.

Miss Beatrice Fernekees, Master Louis Fernekees, and Willie Fernekees are at the Poland Spring House.

The Art Store.

Mrs. Mallouf has a wonderful display of useful and fancy articles. Art Embroidery is made a feature, and all the fancy stitches of all countries are shown and taught. Oriental goods are to be seen in great profusion.

Fishing.

On Saturday, July 10th, Mr. S. Ross Campbell and Mr. William Read caught several black bass in the Upper Lake. Each weighed over a pound, and two weighed three pounds.

Tid-Bits.

Exit paint.

Middle of summer.

Mexican filigree at the Art Store.

Lots of good things in Lewiston stores.

Mr. E. C. Hersey of Portland, is with us.

Mr. Isaac H. Bailey of New York, is with us.

Mr. Jacob P. Bates and Mrs. Bates of Boston, are here.

Preston's simple remedies are to be had at the News Stand.

How about your genealogical chart, have you gotten one yet?

Several old trees have lately been removed from the grove.

Mrs. Daniel Kuntz of Boston, arrived Saturday, July 10th.

Mrs. M. S. deLissa and Mrs. E. S. Van Beil of New York, are with us.

Mr. Austin Palmer of Brooklyn, N. Y., is at the Poland Spring House.

Personal knowledge warrants Curtis & Spindell, Lynn, for elastic stockings.

Mr. and Mrs. Joseph W. Sandford, Plainfield, N. J., are at Poland Spring.

Mr. James S. Staples and Mrs. Staples of Bridgeport, Conn., are here.

Mr. Archibald C. V. Wills of Philadelphia, is at the Poland Spring House.

Mr. and Mrs. Charles H. Utley of Brookline, are at the Poland Spring House.

Mr. S. W. Greene of Brookline, Mass., is registered at the Mansion House.

Mr. A. R. Mitchell and Mrs. Mitchell of Newtonville, Mass., arrived July 12th.

Master Andrew Dodd and James Dodd, Salem, Mass., are at the Poland Spring House.

Mr. Floyd McGown of San Antonio, Texas, is registered at the.Poland Spring House.

Mrs. H. E. Barnard, wife of Judge Barnard of San Antonio, Texas, arrived July 10th.

Before visiting Portland, study the HILL-TOP advertisements. It is as good as a directory.

Mrs. Mary A. Baxter and Mrs. Florence Gardner of Portland, are at the Mansion House.

Mrs. L. S, Read and her son, Mr. William T. Read of Camden, N. J., have returned for the season.

Mrs. J. H. Worthington of Germantown, Pa., and Miss G. Collins of New York, are at the Mansion House.

J. M. Winfield, M.D., of Brooklyn, has been spending a few days at the Poland Spring House. He left July 10th.

Mr. and Mrs. George M. Nay and Master Winthrop S. Nay of Boston, are visiting Mr. and Mrs. H. W. Ricker.

Mr. John H. Maginnis of New Orleans and his friend, Mr. Edward H. Holland of Scranton, Pa., arrived July 9th.

Miss Stella M. Smith, Miss Florence M. Smith, and Mr. W. P. Comstock of Providence, R. I., are at Poland Spring.

Despite the warm weather of last week, the average temperature at the New Mount Pleasant House, White Mountains, was barely above 70°.

Mr. Amos R. Little and Mr. David G. Yates caught 23 black bass in the Upper Lake, Wednesday, the largest weighing 3 1-2 pounds. This beats the record.

Miss Anna Whitman is now at the Poland Spring House, being an annual visitor for the season. She is an expert manicurist, and her services may be had at any time.

Mr. and Mrs. F. J. Simmons, Miss Edith Simmons, and Mr. Harry Simmons of Detroit, are visiting Mr. and Mrs. S. Ross Campbell, at their summer home in Poland.

Among the welcome guests, Saturday, July 10th, were Mr. George L. Connor, General Passenger Agent of the N. Y., N. H. & H. R. R., and his mother, Mrs. A. A. Connor of New York.

Mr. and Mrs. F. W. Stone, Miss Marion Stone, Miss Catherine Stone, Miss Mary G. Leonard, Miss Elizabeth G. Leonard, and Mr. C. A. Stone of Boston, spent Saturday and Sunday, July 10th and 11th, at the Poland Spring House. They were driving from Boston to Shelburne, N. H., on their brake.

Mr. and Mrs. S. Ross Campbell gave a delightful ride on their naphtha launch, Friday evening, July 9th. The party included Mr. and Mrs. Gallagher, Mrs. Conover, Mrs. Read, Miss Conover, Miss Sarah Ricker, Mr. Keene, and Mr. Read. They went through the canal into the Upper Lake, and twice around the Middle Lake.

Among the welcome guests, July 9th, were Mr. and Mrs. Louis Alman. Mr. Alman is well known in the world of photographic art, New York, having spent over thirty years there. They now make their home in Turin, Italy. This is Mrs. Alman's first visit to Poland, and she is charmed with the beauties of the place. Looking from the veranda of the Poland Spring House, she said: "You have Italy in Maine, and I believe my husband came all the way, just for a glass of Poland Water."

Tid-Bits.

Mr. and Mrs. C. A. Kidder of Boston are at Poland Spring.

Mr. and Mrs. C. C. Griffin of Haverhill, Mass., are with us.

Mr. Josiah Oakes and Mrs. Oakes of Malden, Mass., have returned for the season.

Mr. H. D. Carroll and Mrs. Carroll of Springfield, Mass., are at the Poland Spring House.

The Indians are again encamped down by the Spring. Go down and see them.

Mr. and Mrs. W. B. Fay, Southboro, Mass., are at the Poland Spring House.

The Indians are upon us. Let us bury the hatchet and smoke the pipe of peace.

If we had three hundred per cent. increase we should have three big hotels on Ricker Hill.

Among the welcome guests July 13th, were Mr. and Mrs. S. S. Waldo of Danielson, Conn.

Mr. and Mrs. James H. Eddy and Miss Bessie Eddy of New Britain, Conn., arrived July 12th.

Mr. E. O. Ruggles, who is representing the Boston & Maine Railroad, is at the Poland Spring House.

Miss Mary L. Spear gave a very enjoyable reading in the Music Room on the evening of Thursday last.

The house count at the Mt. Pleasant for the past week has averaged three hundred per cent. increase over last year, and "the golf fiends are thickening on the plains." Fore!

The stained glass windows in the newly-decorated Music Room were from Redding, Baird & Co. They were from designs by Mr. Thresher, whose ideas were most artistically carried out.

Mr. Frank Curtis has recovered his watch. It was hanging in a similar place to that in which the fond mamma told her charming daughter to hang her clothes, when preparing for a swim, but "not go near the water."

Among the welcome guests July 15th were Mr. Alex. S. Thweatt, Eastern Passenger Agent of the Southern Railway, Piedmont Air Line, and Mr. George C. Daniels, Traveling Passenger Agent of the same line.

The *Cape Ann Journal of Society*, a neat, new, bright paper, says of the HILL-TOP: "It is bright and newsy, and contains a number of well-written articles on current topics. . . . . Taken all in all, the HILL-TOP is one of the brightest little papers, covering society, in resortdom."

Mr. and Mrs. W. F. McPherson, Miss Roach, Mr. Stephen Roach, and Mr. Belden Roach arrived at Poland Spring July 10th. Mrs. McPherson and Miss Roach are daughters of Mr. John Roach, one of the greatest ship-builders in the United States. Mr. Roach built all of the magnificent Fall River boats.

Excuse Our Blushes.

"Bud Brier," in "Under the Rose" of the *Boston Daily Globe*, says:

"My cheerful young friend, the HILL-TOP, comes forth smiling, for the season of '97. And the HILL-TOP is not so much of a youngster, either. It entered upon its fourth year, July 4th, and the birth of the HILL-TOP, and the birth of the republic, were both becomingly celebrated. Long live the republic!—and may the HILL-TOP live as long!"

WHITE MOUNTAINS.

FRANK CARLOS GRIFFITH. | EDITORS.
NETTIE M. RICKER, |

PUBLISHED EVERY SUNDAY MORNING DURING THE MONTHS OF JULY, AUGUST, AND SEPTEMBER, IN THE INTERESTS OF

POLAND SPRING AND ITS VISITORS.

All contributions relative to the guests of Poland Spring will be thankfully received.

To insure publication, all communications should reach the editors not later than Wednesday preceding day of issue.

All parties desiring rates for advertising in the HILL-TOP should write the editors for same.

The subscription price of the HILL-TOP is $1.00 for the season, post-paid. Single copies will be mailed at 10c. each.

Address,

EDITORS "HILL-TOP,"
Poland Spring House,
South Poland, Maine.

PRINTED AT JOURNAL OFFICE, LEWISTON.

Sunday, July 18, 1897.

Editorial.

DID it ever occur to you what *great* things *little* things are? A drop of ink is a little thing as compared with a glass of milk, and how opposite in every feature.

The milk is good, and in the drop of ink may be the signature to a death warrant. Drop the latter globule into the former snowy liquid, and the former is ruined and the latter lost.

A mouse may annoy an elephant into a frenzy; a pin may let life out at any one of a thousand vulnerable places; a harsh word will deprive the pleasures of a life, of their sweetness; a kind, appreciative one, will smooth the roughest journey.

It is the little things of life which make our lives great, or make them failures.

"Many a mickle makes a muckle" is a familiar Scotch saying, and the pennies make the pound; while the crowns of kings are composed of many jewels.

We may escape a great danger, and be destroyed utterly by the most trivial circumstance.

A cat falls from the top of the Washington monument 500 feet to the ground, unhurt, and is killed the next minute by a wheelbarrow, in crossing the street.

A soldier passes unscathed through a terrible battle, with an hundred thousand men taking deadly aim, and falls the victim of a tiny grape seed.

Look out for the little things in life, and the great ones will take care of themselves. Lay each separate stone well, and the entire structure is solid. Choose each word well, and mark where it falls, and the result. If the words are good, the result will be good; but if bad, only bad things will spring from the seed.

Musical Programme.

SUNDAY, JULY 18, 1897.

1. March from Athalia. . . . . Mendelssohn.
2. Overture—Mirella. . . . . Gounod.
3. Cello Solo— { a. Sarabande. . . . Corelli.
   { b. Murmuring Breezes. . Jensen.
4. Minuett from Orpheus. . . . . Glück.
5. Selection—Tannhäuser. . . . Wagner.
6. Largo—Hallelujah Chorus. . . . Handel.

Mr. Sanborn's House-warming.

It was a delightful occasion which caused the assemblage of so many of Mr. and Mrs. J. S. Sanborn's friends to give them a house-warming on Wednesday last, despite the unfavorable weather. The house is charming, and delightfully situated, and their myriads of friends wish them all happiness. The presentation of one of Mr. Coombs's fine paintings was one of the events, and with so many old friends, a bountiful collation, and delightful music, the new house-was "warmed" to a fever heat. May they enjoy many years of happiness beneath its roof.

New Books.

FROM MISS L. P. RAY.

John Ward, Preacher; by Margaret Deland.
Taquisara; by F. Marion Crawford. 2 vols.
On the Face of the Waters; by Flora Annie Steel.
Marie Bashkirtseff's Journal.
A War-Time Wooing; by Capt. Charles King.
The £1,000,000 note; by Mark Twain.
Trilby, the Fairy of Argyle; by Charles Nodier.

Mr. Fenety will exhibit some of his very fine flower pieces in the hotel, Monday. His work should attract all interested in art and the artistic decorations of the home.

An Episcopal clergyman's wife living in southern Texas sends to Mrs. Hiram Ricker a large quantity of Mexican drawn work. Mrs. Ricker will be glad to show it to all who will call at her cottage. It is charity work, and the prices are very reasonable.

Recipes.

FRICASSEE CHICKEN.

Cut chicken in pieces for serving; cover with boiling water, adding one teaspoon salt and a little pepper. Simmer until tender; take the chicken out of the liquor and dredge with flour and brown in hot butter. Strain the liquor and remove fat, and thicken with flour.

HAMBURGH STEAK.

Pound a slice of round steak enough to break the fibre. Fry two or three onions, minced fine, in butter till slightly browned. Spread the onions over the meat, fold the ends of the meat together, and pound again, to keep the onions in the middle. Broil two or three minutes. Spread with salt and pepper.

WHEAT MUFFINS.

One egg, one cup milk, three tablespoons melted butter, two cups flour, two tablespoons sugar, one-fourth teaspoon salt, one teaspoon cream tartar, one-half teaspoon soda. Bake in ironclads, small tin cups, or in one sheet.

Golf.

The record for the six holes which they are now using (as the other three are not in condition for playing on) was lowered by Mr. Fenn, who made them in twenty-seven strokes.

The links will be completed by the first of the week. The young ladies at the hotel are as enthusiastic over the game as the men. On pleasant days the links are well filled.

The Minerals.

THE collection now exhibited in the Maine Building has been designed to show fine examples of the showy minerals of the state, with minerals of distant parts of the world that are remarkable for beauty, perfection, rarity, or novelty. The cut tourmalines, beryls, and topazes, Maine gems that rival the diamond in beauty and brilliance, will doubtless be viewed with surprise by those who see these choice products of the state for the first time. Besides these, are numerous Maine specimens—like the gems, attractive souvenirs—suitable for the cabinet, the mantel or the centre-table. The crystals and masses of tourmaline of variegated colors from Mount Mica, and the cinnamon garnets from Phippsburg, may be mentioned in particular.

Of the minerals from out of the state, many might astonish even residents at the localities. The groups of sulphur crystals from Sicily are some of the finest of Dr. Foote's stock, and his stock of sulphurs is said to excel any other in Europe or America. The native gold, silver, and copper will interest many. Native terrestrial iron, singular as it seems, is one of the rare minerals, and these specimens are from the mass brought from Greenland and described by Baron Nordenskjold. The meteoric iron from Cañon Diablo, Arizona, is remarkable as being the first meteoric iron in which diamonds—minute, of course—have been discovered.

The magnificent slab of polished and etched meteoric iron from the Sacramento Mountains has an extraordinary history. In 1876 Mr. M. Bartlett of Florence, Arizona, saw a meteor pass across the heavens in a southerly direction and fall with a report like a cannon, and a long and fruitless search was instituted for the stone. At last it was learned that a shepherd had found a mass of native iron partly buried in a limestone hill in Eddy County, New Mexico. Here a search party found the iron, a single mass weighing about 500 pounds, and from the evidence at hand appearing to be undoubtedly the same Mr. Bartlett had seen in the heavens long before, and after much labor succeeded in dragging it six miles to a road. The polished sections, when etched with nitric acid, show the crossed lines known as "Widmanstatten figures"—due to the crystalline structure of meteoric iron—in a perfection seldom equaled. These figures are so strikingly marked, in fact, that an etched section of the iron was used as a printing block to illustrate the original account of the meteorite, which was published by Mr. W. M. Foote in the *American Journal of Science* of last January, and they distinguish this meteorite as one of the finest and rarest known.

There are many beautiful specimens of pyrite—iron and copper—from Pennsylvania, Italy, and the island of Elba; halite from California in groups of cubes and in elongated transparent crystals; and choice crystals and groups of fluorite from England. The assortment of quartz from the famous locality of Hot Springs, Ark., is especially fine; and there are excellent specimens of the unrivaled little crystals from Herkimer County, N. Y. Other forms of quartz—moss-agate, amethyst, carnelian, cairngorm stone, jasper, jasperized wood, etc., are shown in good variety.

The opalized wood from Idaho is the finest petrifaction ever discovered, not only the grain, bark, and heart of the wood being preserved, but even the minutest detail of cellular structure being perfectly distinguishable. The precious opal in the matrix is very attractive, while few minerals are more showy in the cabinet than the green semi-opal of Washington.

No hematites equal in beauty those of Elba and England, of which choice specimens have been obtained. The rutilated quartz, or "*flèches d'amour*," from Brazil, is of remarkable quality, and seldom fails to excite exclamations of surprise and wonder on first sight. The calcites from Australia, England, Mexico, Arizona, and Missouri present many and exquisite forms.

Other especially notable specimens include those of selenite from Sicily and Utah, sidenite from France, smithsonite from New Mexico, azurite and malachite from Arizona, amazon stone from Colorado, sunstone from Norway, labradorite from Labrador, pectolite from New Jersey, vanadinite from New Mexico and Arizona, rubellite and colemanite from California, chabazite from Oregon, anglesite and phasgenite from Sardinia, barite and satin spar from England, turquois from New Mexico, and many that space will not permit us to mention.

From California also there are several new minerals—discoveries of the last two or three years; and Australia is represented by a variety of rare minerals.

There are no uninteresting specimens, for all have been selected carefully for some attractive quality, such as beauty, rarity or novelty. The aim has been to please all, whether mineralogically inclined or not. Guests wishing to purchase gems or other specimens can do so at any time, but, if convenient, should call at the Maine Building on Thursday, as on that day of each week the exhibitor is expected to be at Poland.

Mr. J. Jay Watson gave a violin recital in the Music Room on Tuesday evening. Mr. Watson claims to be the only pupil of Ole Bull.

ELMWOOD FARM

OF FRENCH COACHERS

IMPORTED STALLIONS

GEMARE, 134. LOTHAIR, 979. TELMAQUE, 515.

3 Miles from Poland Spring, Maine,

the Home of the Ideal Coach and Road Horse of America. Half-Bred French Coach Carriage Horses for Sale.
Also, Young Registered French Coach Stallions. Size, Intelligence, Courage, Endurance, and Conformation Instilled.
STOCK SHOWN DAILY.

J. S. SANBORN.

Arrivals.

POLAND SPRING HOUSE.

FROM JULY 9 TO 15, 1897.

Anderson, Grace	Portland
Alman, Mr. and Mrs. Louis	New York
Armstrong, E. S.	Lewiston
Ambrose, J. H.	Orono
Bailey, Isaac H.	New York
Barnes, Mary Y.	Toledo
Barnard, Mrs. H. E.	San Antonio, Tex.
Barroll, Mr. and Mrs. B. C., Jr.	New York
Barroll, Miss	New York
Chase, Mr. and Mrs. Homer N.	Auburn
Culver, H. H.	Taunton
Cheetham, Thos.	Lewiston
Cook, Mrs. A.	New York
Collins, Mrs. James A.	Cincinnati
Collins, Alpheus	Cincinnati
Conroy, J. H.	New York
Colby, Mrs. William W.	Portland
Carroll, Mr. and Mrs. H. D.	Springfield
Cox, Mr. and Mrs. Henry P.	Portland
Connor, George L.	New York
Connor, Mrs. A. A.	New York
Comstock, H. P.	Providence
Capen, Carol B.	Boston
Capen, H. S.	Boston
Curtis, George	Auburn
Chaplin, A. M.	Lewiston
Claxton, Mrs. B. B.	Philadelphia
Devlin, P. J.	Chatauqay, N. Y.
Daniels, George C.	Boston
Davis, Ruth	Lynn
Davis, Edith	Lynn
Dodd, A. W.	Salem
Dodd, A. W., Jr.	Salem
Dodd, James	Salem
Eddy, Mr. and Mrs. Jas. H.	New Britain, Conn.
Eddy, Miss Bessie M.	New Britain, Conn.
Fay, Mr. and Mrs. W. B.	Southboro
Fenety, F. M.	Boston
Fellows, Fowler	Providence
Goshorn, Miss	Cincinnati
Griffin, Mr. and Mrs. C. C.	Haverhill
Gilmore, Mrs. G.	Providence
Gay, F. H.	Chicago
Hall, Mr. and Mrs. Lewis	Cambridge
Howell, Mr. and Mrs. A. J.	New York
Hall, Mrs. William H.	New York
Hall, William H., Jr.	New York
Huck, Frederick	New York
Holland, Edw. W.	Scranton
Hartz, Mr. and Mrs. John J.	Boston
Helsey, C. C.	Portland
Howland, Florence D.	Boston
Hyde, George E., Jr.	Boston
Hayes, Miss N. L.	Auburn
Hall, Mrs. E. J.	Auburn
Ireson, Mrs. S. E.	Boston
Jones, Mr. and Mrs. C. B.	Sheboygan, Wis.
Jordan, Mrs. Howard	New Gloucester
Jaggar, Mrs. S. E.	Burlington, Ia.
Jennison, S. S.	New York
Kern, Mr. and Mrs. G. I.	Boston
Kennurth, Mr. and Mrs. William	Philadelphia
King, David James	New York
Kibbee, Mrs. H. C.	Springfield
Kibbee, C. A.	Springfield
Kidder, Mr. and Mrs. C. A.	Boston
Kilby, Mrs.	Boston
Leonard, Miss Mary G.	Boston
Leonard, Miss Elizabeth G.	Boston

Maginnis, John H.	New Orleans
McGown, Floyd	San Antonio, Tex.
McPherson, Mr. and Mrs. William F.	New York
Mallin, Jack C.	Boston
Mason, Miss	Auburn
Mitchell, Mr. and Mrs. A. R.	Newtonville
Nathan, S.	New York
Newhall, Dr. and Mrs. Herbert W.	Lynn
Oakes, Mr. and Mrs. Josiah	Malden
Olney, Mr. and Mrs. Frank F.	Providence
Olney, Elam Ward	Providence
Oviatt, Angeline W.	Rochester
Palmer, Mr. and Mrs. Henry U.	Brooklyn
Pope, Laura S.	Boston
Pumphrey, F. R.	Boston
Pearson, Mr. and Mrs. J. C.	Boston
Ripley, Mr. and Mrs. William A.	Newark
Robinson, Mrs. E. J.	Boston
Roach, Miss	New York
Roach, Stephen G.	New York
Roach, Belden	New York
Roberts, Mr. and Mrs. E. Gerry	Red Bank, N. J.
Ruggles, E. O.	Boston
Richard, Mrs. L. P.	Boston
Speare, Mary L.	Newton
Staples, Mr. and Mrs. James	Bridgeport
Sexton, William Lord	New York
Sanborn, Mr. and Mrs. D. W.	Boston
Sandford, Mr. and Mrs. Joseph W.	Plainfield, N. J.
Stone, Mr. and Mrs. F. W.	Boston
Stone, Miss Marion	Boston
Stone, Miss Catharine	Boston
Stone, Mr. C. A.	Boston
Smith, Miss Stella M.	Providence
Smith, Miss Florence M.	Providence
Sturges, Mr. and Mrs. J. I.	New Gloucester
Sturges, Mr. and Mrs. Alfred	Portland
Sturges, Miss Ethel	Brooklyn
Stellwagen, Mr. and Mrs. Edw. J.	Washington
Sturtevant, Mr. and Mrs. H. L.	Malden
Sturtevant, Lewis D.	Malden
Speer, Mr. and Mrs. W. H.	Jersey City
Speer, Harold	Jersey City
Speer, Miss Cassie	Jersey City
Tucker, W. A.	New Bedford
Thweatt, Alex. S.	Boston
Thaw, Mr. and Mrs. Benj.	Pittsburg
Utley, Mr. and Mrs. Charles H.	Brookline
Walkin, Mr. and Mrs. E. T.	Chicago
Watson, Prof. and Mrs. J. Jay	Boston
Walsh, Mr. and Mrs. J.	Brooklyn
Winfield, J. M., M.D.	Brooklyn
Winslow, Mr. and Mrs. E. B.	Portland
Wells, Archibald C. V.	Philadelphia
Wessen, Alfred J.	Auburn
Yeomans, Mr. and Mrs. A. H.	Brookline
Young, Mrs. C. F.	Morristown, N. J.

MANSION HOUSE.

Ambrose, Mr. and Mrs. F. M.	New York
Babcock, D. B.	New York
Collins, Miss G.	New York
Cook, M. D.	Denver
Coes, Mr. and Mrs. John H.	Worcester
Coes, Miss Mary M.	Worcester
Kuntz, Mrs. Daniel	Boston
Kienbusch, Mrs. O. G. v.	New York
Merritt, W. C.	Boston
Rivas, Jose de	New York
Thomas, W. E.	Boston
Worthington, Mrs. J. H.	Germantown, Pa.
Waldo, Mr. and Mrs. S. S.	Danielsonville, Ct.
Waldo, George B.	New York
Wood, Mr. and Mrs. Albert	Worcester
Wood, Miss E. C.	Worcester

Tid-Bits.

Didn't we have a storm, though?

Mount Mica specimens are placed.

Mr. W. C. Merritt of Boston, is at the Mansion House.

Mr. N. D. Cook of Denver, Colo., arrived July 12th.

Mr. and Mrs. F. M. Ambrose of New York, are at the Mansion House.

Mr. R. C. Dunham of Boston, is registered at the Poland Spring House.

Mr. and Mrs. Henry U. Palmer of Brooklyn, have returned for the season.

Mr. and Mrs. Frank F. Olney and Mr. Elam Ward Olney of Providence, R. I., are with us.

If you require elastic stockings or things of that nature, read Curtis & Spindell's advertisement on the last cover.

Mrs. A. W. Green, Miss Grace Green, Mrs. R. H. Countiss, Miss Claribel Countiss of Chicago, are at Poland Spring.

We have much pleasure in greeting Mr. F. M. Fenety, two of whose exquisite flower pictures we have in the Art Gallery.

Mr. Henry S. Wampole and Master Albert Wampole, Philadelphia, are guests of Mr. and Mrs. S. Ross Campbell.

Are you a Colonial Dame, a Son or a Daughter of the Revolution? Send for a chart, if you want fascinating and useful occupation.

Fine catch of thirteen black bass the early part of the week, by Mr. George L. Osgood. The largest one weighed 3 1-4 pounds, and the whole 31 pounds.

Mrs. Gay and Miss Anna Dowse of Boston, are spending a few weeks at Franconia, N. H. Mrs. Gay and Miss Dowse have many friends at Poland Spring.

THE ALPS OF NEW ENGLAND.

New Mount Pleasant House

WHITE MOUNTAINS.

The Hill Top

POLAND SPRINGS, SO. POLAND, ME.

HARRY C. WILKINSON

THE HILL-TOP

Vol. IV.   SUNDAY MORNING, JULY 25, 1897.   No. 1.

Biiefly Put—Golf.

GOLF is a game, while not of great antiquity as coi)ared with the age of Sethi the First of Egy)t, or Rameses the Second, yet its beginning runs back into the Scotch mists wiici befog the Lochs and Bons of Norti Britain previous to the time of Jaies the Sixti of Sentland and First of England.

He it was who popularized the links tiere, and, as he had nothing else to do, except to be the son of Mary, Queen of Scots, wiici left much tiie on his hands, ie took u) the gaie. Now, tiis iust iave been subsequent to 1566, for tiat was the year he was born, and he could not possibly have commenced so soon.

The game, be it said, has no connection with Odd Fellowship, Sausages, or the Detective Industry, despite the links, but is a serious thing.

James followed Elizabeth, who did not play golf, but was otherwise popular, but James kept at golf and became unpopular, and it was not until a few weeks ago the game was revived, having been in a comatose condition several centuries or so. Charles I. tried to resuscitate the game, and was playing a game of foursomes with Buckingham when news of a semi-weekly rebellion in Ireland was brought to him on a salver. He was so wroth at this he threw down his stick and rushed into Holyrood Palace with much agitation and Buckingham. The palace is still standing. We have seen it, and observed the husj place where Charley entered.

It takes its name from Kolf, a Dutch name for the kind of club used, and is good exercise without being lively.

Bad plays sometimes result in bad words, and a London player relates that a gentleman agreed to put a stone into his pocket every time he used a naughty word. When once around, his pockets were observed to bulge alarmingly. "These stones," taking them out of his top outside pocket, "are for 'curse it.' These, right-hand side pocket, are for some favorite strong expressions of mine. These, left-hand side pocket, are words unsuited to ears polite. Now, gentlemen, go outside, and you will see a man with a wheelbarrow full of stones, which stand for interjections loud and deep."

Now, joking aside, we have a golf course of nine holes, over the Poland Links, which are constantly played over by Mr. A. H. Fenn, who holds the Southern championship, and is a winner of some thirty-four trophies. He has placed on exhibition, in the billiard room, a number of these trophies, which, however, are only a few, which have been won from the best players in America. One of the largest cups he has here was taken in the open championship of the South last winter, for which a number of the best players of the North came to compete.

One of the handsomest trophies ever put up in this country is being played for in Lenox. Last fall it was played for for the first time, and won by Mr. Fenn. It must be won twice, however, to retain it, and Mr. Fenn expects to play for it again this fall. There is also a handsome gold medal which goes with the cup.

Another of the handsomest cups he has on exhibition was won at Knollwood, N. Y., last spring. The last cup won by Mr. Fenn was at the Myopia Hunt Club, at which all the best players of the East competed. There were eighty-three entities and he had to allow strokes, as a handicap, to all.

A number of Poland's fair sex have become enamored with the game, and some are progressing rapidly. Mrs. Putnam of Brookline, Miss Grace Green of Chicago, Miss Brown of New York, Miss Rosenheim of Savannah, the Misses Blackford of Brooklyn, the Misses Peterson of New York, and others are frequently on the green.

Among the gentlemen are some expert players, notably, Mr. Trevelli of Pittsburg, Messrs. Olney and Comstock of Providence, Mr. Maginnis of New Orleans, Mr. Howell of New York. There are many more who are upon the reels of these gentlemen, and Mr. Putnam of Brookline, and Mr. Corbin of Webster, Mass., are in training for honors.

Monday last an interesting foursome was played by Mr. Fenn and Mrs. Putnam against Mr. Trevelli and Mr. Putnam, the former winning by one hole up.

Our illustration represents Mr. A. H. Fenn about to play, with some of the interested bystanders watching his methods. Mr. Ness, of the Notman Photographic Company, has succeeded admirably, as is the custom with this excellent house.

Perhaps You Did Not Know

That the celebrated Tichborne claimant is still alive, and living in the suburbs of London.

That Napoleon III was the first European to use a dining-car.

That Glasgow levies no taxes, paying all its expenses out of the income derived from its ownership of public works.

That the British possessions in America are 250,000 square miles more than those of the United States.

That white cats are generally deaf.

That women average nearly two inches taller than thirty years ago.

That during the reign of Queen Victoria we have had seventeen Presidents.

That the greatest length of England and Scotland is 608 miles.

That Patti never sings for less than 800 guineas; about $4,200.

That Victoria has sixty pianos in three of her official residences.

That the longest drive on record at cricket, was 157 yards.

A supper was given by Mr. and Mrs. S. Ross Campbell at the Poland Spring House, Saturday, July 17th, in honor of Mr. and Mrs. Simons. Other guests were Miss Edith Simons, Miss Alice Conover, Mr. Harry Simons, Mr. William Read, Mr. Harry Wampole.

Tid=Bits.

See the sea 1oss.

Fortunate Fenety.

Mr. W. W. Fuller and Mrs. Fuller are at Poland Spring.

Miss Alden of Los Angeles, Cal., is at the Poland Spring House.

Rev. Thomas F. Braman of Boston, is at the Poland Spring House.

Mr. and Mrs. C. H. Duhme of Cincinnati arrived here July 20th.

Mrs. H. V. Meeks of Buena Vista, N. J., is at the Poland Spring House.

Mr. and Mrs. David Thornton are registered at the Poland Spring House.

Mr. and Mrs. J. M. Johnston of Brooklyn, N. Y., are at Poland Spring.

Mr. DeForest Danielson of Boston made a flying trip to Poland last week.

Mrs. O. G. v. Kienbusch and Miss Kienbusch of New York, are at Poland Spring.

Mr. H. W. Longe and Mrs. Longe of Wilmington, Del., are at the Poland Spring House.

Mr. Augustus Rafelye and Mrs. Rafelye of Newtown, Queens County, N. Y., are at Poland.

Mr. F. L. Castner was very successful, Tuesday, in his first game of golf. He made the round in 68 strokes.

Some very fine specimens of sea moss, arranged by Mr. Marchal, have been placed on exhibition in one of the cases in the Maine State Building.

Mr. Little and Mr. Yates, Thursday afternoon caught 12 black bass, several weighing over three pounds. The largest one weighed 3 1-2 pounds.

Miss M. C. Chamberlain, daughter of Rev. Dr. Chamberlain of Bahia, Brazil, is visiting Poland Spring with her aunt, Miss J. C. Sherman of Montclair, N. J.

Wardwell Brothers, proprietors of the Lincoln House, Swampscott, are also proprietors of a very nice lunch place on Washington Street, Boston, run on the same plan as Thompson's Spa.

The cut of the apple blossom, which was plucked here the 20th, was made by the Lakeside Press, Portland, from a remarkably successful photograph by the Notman Photographic Co.

Among the arrivals at the Poland Spring House from Brooklyn, N. Y., July 20th, were Mr. and Mrs. John Englis, Miss Janet Englis, Miss Anna Englis, Miss Bell Englis, Mrs. William F. Englis.

The New Mount Pleasant House, White Mountains, is the terminus of all Boston & Maine trains in the White Mountains, through parlor and sleeping cars and coaches leaving the door of the house.

Col. C. H. French gave his annual lecture on Thursday evening, this time the subject being "India," with considerable of "Alaska" added, in deference to the present great interest in the subject.

Wednesday evening 125 pounds of broiled live lobster were served at the Poland Spring House. One lobster which the chef took such pride in, weighed six pounds and was exhibited to the guests in the office.

A successful fishing party came from the Upper Lake on Monday afternoon, July 19th. A string of twelve fine black bass was exhibited to friends. The largest, weighing four pounds, was caught by Miss Edith Simmons.

Mr. Fenety made a number of sales from his very excellent pictures, Mrs. Sawyer, Mrs. Palmer, Mrs. Mitchell, and several others, securing pictures which are sure to be a constant source of pleasure to themselves and the visitors to their homes.

A quartette from the Atlanta University gave a benefit concert in the Music Hall on Tuesday evening. The hall was well filled, and the sum of $73.48 was raised for the University, $20 of which was given by a gentleman at the Poland Spring House.

The first number of the *Coös County Tourist* comes to us, and it is edited by Amy L. Phillips, whose work appears to have been cleverly done. We wish to compliment the accomplished editress upon the neat, bright, and newsy appearance of her paper.

Although an inland resort, Poland Spring is as much noted as any sea-side resort for its line fish. It is not entirely confined to the sea, but serves a large amount of bass, trout, landlocked salmon and other fish, taken from the lakes and brooks in the vicinity.

This morning, as we go to press, "an egg was laid on our desk," as the country editor said, by Johnny Chamberlain. The egg was the product of a robin, but Johnny found it upon the board walk. If robins do not know any better than to mislay their eggs that way they must expect to get into the newspapers.

Mr. and Mrs. T. D. Elsbree of Valley Falls, R. I., arrived at the Mansion House, July 21st. Their first visit to Poland Spring was in 1879. Not having been here since that year, they find the Poland of to-day so much improved from the earlier times that the only unchanged part is Poland Water, *which never changes.*

A Perilous Experience.

AMONG the numerous features of interest to the Poland guest, that of mountain climbing is not of the least importance. Wishing to become eligible to membership in the Appalachian Club, and add another button for week days to our lapel, we put ourselves in training for several minutes lately, and with a party of a few, started across country, past the picturesque Pologne Tarn, to the base of Mont Chat Noir, or, as it is termed by the peasant, "Black Cat."

Having provided ourselves with each a flask of "eau de vie," bearing the inscription, "I need thee every three-quarters of an hour," and a long rope, to connect us, and prevent being precipitated into the depths below; and a flask; and a new pair of thick, solid, heavily-nailed shoes, which our guide said we must have, his father being a shoe-maker; and a flask; and a trusty alpenstock with a sharp steel joint; and a flask,—we proceeded to adjust our rope,—and flasks, and enter upon the perilous journey which lay before us.

Some faint-hearted ones there were among us, but we were brave, and planted our foot, which resulted in the most rapid raising of corn we ever witnessed. The soil at the base of the Mont is very rich, but stingy, and we proceeded on our way.

After a fatiguing effort, which consumed several minutes, as well as some e-d-v, we halted for lunch, gazing fearfully upward at what was left of the before us. Presently the guide uttered a whoop, which was the signal for the ascent, and tightening our pocket-books and belts, we proceeded to do so.

Our route now lay along a narrow shelf of porphyritic rock, scarcely ten feet in width, down one side of which descended the abyss, fully six inches wide and two feet to the bottom below, where it belongs. Dizziness attacked one of our party as he realized the result of a misstep, and we again sat down to recover. The overhanging perpendicular cliff on the other side towered above us to the height of at least three feet, and we leaned affectionately against it, and gazed far out upon the placid waters of the lovely tarn below.

On, on, we presently pursued our way again, thrusting our steel-shod pikes into the glacier, or perhaps we should say "glass mere," for the remains of shattered bottles of the *Eau de Pologne* were numerous along the shady stubble. Frantically we grasped at trees at the last straw, which fringed the narrow *arête*, and when the noonday sun had "toled in," over the summit, our party of hardy Matterhorners were fearlessly attacking their stations astride the sharp summit of le Mont Chat Noir, at the fearful altitude of 400 feet above the level of Sabbath-Day Lake Harbor, at low tide.

Having carefully consulted our chronometers, cyclometers, pedometers, and gasometers, we found we had consumed exactly 29 3-4 minutes and our e-d-v, in the perilous ascent. Having several hours to spare, we spent them in social recreation, then counting our wheels, returned by the way of White Oak Hill and the Dog Kennels, in 42 1-2 minutes, better and wiser men.

Picturesque Maine.

If you want to hear all about the interesting features of Maine, and see beautiful reproductions of its scenic and picturesque localities, you can do so on the evening of Tuesday, August 5th, in the Music Hall, when Mr. Edward C. Swett will be present. Mr. Swett has the personal endorsement of both our Senators, all our National Representatives to Congress, and many others of note.

Of Mr. Swett's lecture the *Boston Globe* says: "For an hour and a half Maine's best social orator talked on 'Picturesque Maine,' and showed one hundred and twenty-five lime-light pictures to illustrate what he said. Some of these pictures could only have been obtained by getting into the heart of the lumbering regions and game preserves. It was a whole evening's pleasure just to see them. Mr. Swett's talk on Maine takes in all the interesting landscape features of the state—its mountains, woods, stones, homes, and hotels."

THE NEWEST THING IN TABLE ETIQUETTE.

Here is what children call a "really, truly story" from Boston. A lady was engaging a servant for a small family where the duties of chambermaid and waitress are combined. The preliminary questions having been satisfactorily answered, she was proceeding to speak of the work in detail, when the would-be help interrupted with "Would you expect me to wait on the table, ma'am, or do you do your own reaching?"

Children's Column.

Music wastes away from the soul the dust of every-day life.—*Auerbach.*

Skip and Trip.

Upon your arrival at Poland and as you are welcomed by friends, the question asked is, "Have you seen the squirrel at the spring?" The animals of interest are two small chipmunks, or perhaps better known as ground squirrels. At the commencement of the year they were running wild in the woods; but through simple kindness the writer has won their confidence. Skip, the older of the two, has afforded much pleasure to the children as well as to the other guests, who have seen him come running in answer to his name and dive down into the coat pocket in search of nuts for his winter's store. He has many tricks; one among them is to thrust out of any one's hand with his little nose, Brazils or nuts which he does not approve, as a hint to offer no more of that kind.

Trip, who is a much later visitor at the spring, will only take his rations from the hand; but before long it is hoped that his courage will equal that of the other. Jealousy, that characteristic which is so frequently seen in human beings, reigns beyond a doubt in the nature of these lower representatives of the animal kingdom. When Skip is around, Trip betakes himself into the woods for shelter.

We trust that they may become better friends and continue to visit us during the season.

E. T.

A SNOW-BALL TREE.

Snow forts and winter sports
In December.
Balls in fight flew left and right,
We remember!
But in July the sorcerer Sun
Waves his wand—a magic one
Round this very tree, and lo!
Petaled snow-balls softly blow!
What do they say, these boys of ours,
To winter snow-balls made of flowers?
—MARCIA B. JORDAN.

Master Winthrop S. Nay caught two black bass in the Middle Lake, Saturday morning, July 16th. Each list weighed two pounds.

Attention, Wheelmen.

Raymond & Whitcomb announce a special tour to Philadelphia to include the League Meet, August 4th to 7th, going one way and returning another, for $45.00, which includes six days at the Continental Hotel, Philadelphia. Leave Boston July 31st and returning August 11th.

An Episcopal clergyman's wife living in southern Texas sends to Mrs. Hiram Ricker a large quantity of Mexican drawn work. Mrs. Ricker will be glad to show it to all who will call at her cottage. It is charity work, and the prices are very reasonable.

Tid-Bits.

Haying.

Filling full.

1,732 nooks.

Black flies or midges. Never!

Mr. J. W. Tabor of Portland is here.

Poland is proud to entertain so many lovely young ladies.

Mr. J. M. Wood of Chicago is at the Poland Spring House.

Mr. A. S. Rines and wife are again enjoying Poland Spring.

Mrs. T. P. Shaw and Master Thomas Shaw are enjoying Poland.

Miss Delphine Hubert of Montreal, Canada, is at the Poland Spring House.

Mr. and Mrs. George Mathews of Cincinnati, are again at Poland Spring.

Mr. and Mrs. David Boyd of Baltimore, Md., arrived at Poland, July 20th.

Mr. and Mrs. J. W. Danielson of Providence are at the Poland Spring House.

Mr. and Mrs. L. Newman of Toledo, Ohio, have arrived at Poland Spring.

Mrs. M. A. Goodwin of Washington, D. C., is at the Poland Spring House.

Dr. George H. Bailey, with Miss Bailey, are among recent arrivals at Poland.

Dr. and Mrs. George B. Lyons of Germantown, Pa., are at Poland Spring.

Mr. and Mrs. R. Gair of Brooklyn, and son, have recently come to Poland Spring.

Mrs. E. M. Carroll, M.D., and Miss Mabelle Carroll of Boston, have arrived at Poland.

Mr. Benjamin E. Cole and Mrs. Cole of Boston are stopping at the Poland Spring House.

Mr. Cyrus Gale of Northboro, Mass., is a welcome guest at the Poland Spring House.

Among the arrivals from Middleboro, Mass., are Mr. G. W. Copeland and Miss Mary L. Dorrance.

Mr. J. B. Field, the manager of the Academy of Music, Chelsea, enjoyed Poland's beauties for a day, on Wednesday.

Mr. and Mrs. S. T. Wellman, with Masters Hadley and Fred Wellman, are stopping at the Poland Spring House.

Little Miss Hall gave a pleasing solo dance, to the delight of her young friends, in the Music Hall on Tuesday afternoon.

Mrs. E. C. Jordan of Portland, Me., is again welcomed at the Mansion House by her many friends.

Among the guests who are registered from Plainfield, N. J., are Mr. and Mrs. A. Gilbert and Miss A. F. Randolph.

Mr. and Mrs. C. M. Soria and their daughter Miss Annie Soria of New Orleans, have returned to Poland for the season.

The Poland Spring House is entertaining Mr. D. E. Snow of Newton, Mass., and his daughter, Miss Snow, and Helen Snow.

As a manicurist and chiropodist, Miss Whitman, at the Poland Spring House, has had the patronage of the guests for several years.

Mr. Ira Allen Nay, Jr., leader of the Bergman Orchestra of Boston, was at the Mansion House for a few days this week.

The best score yet made among the guests in golf was accomplished by Mr. Travelli, who covered the nine holes in 61 strokes.

Mr. and Mrs. Augustus Richardson, Miss Richardson, and Miss M. A. Richardson are among the welcome guests at Poland Spring.

From Worcester, Mass., are the welcome guests—Dr. and Mrs. Albert Wood, Miss Wood, Mr. and Mrs. John H. Coes, and Miss Coes.

Visitors to Atlantic City at any time throughout the year, will find Haddon Hall one of those superior, comfortable, hospitable inns which it is a delight to visit.

On Saturday, July 17th, Mr. Campbell and Mr. Simmons caught several black bass while fishing on the Upper Lake. The largest fish, weighing three pounds, was landed by Mr. Simmons.

The new steamer of the Maine Steamship Company, which has recently been put into service between New York and Portland, is named after the president of the company, Mr. John Englis.

Swampscott has an excellent beach, and is near Lynn, and Lynn is near Boston. Shoes are made in Lynn. Comfort is to be had in Swampscott, at the Lincoln House. Wardwell Bros. will send you a circular.

A party of four men from the Mansion House caught nine black bass on Tuesday. The largest was a three-pounder. It is rumored that the two younger men out-fished their seniors—in the size of their catch.

Massage has proved a great relief to those worn down with fatigue, or whose nerves are unstrung from any cause, and the best of it all is, there is no medicine to take. Mrs. Robinson, now at the Poland Spring House, is to be highly recommended.

Minerals.

Our mineral exhibit has attracted a vast deal of attention of late. Any one, whether skilled in gems or not, cannot fail to appreciate their beauty, and in fact several specimens have been already purchased for cabinet display. There are tourmalines, beryls, and topazes from this old Pine Tree State, which are of exceptional beauty; then there are crystals of various kinds, cinnamon garnets, and turquoise; petrified wood, opalized wood, hematites, and scores of valuable and interesting specimens, beside a wonderful section of a meteorite.

Mr. Chadbourne will be at the Maine State Building, Thursdays of each week, and give full information and prices, while at other times the Librarian will be pleased to do so.

Progressive Euchre.

Friday evening, July 16th, a progressive euchre party was given at the Mansion House, in honor of Mr. and Mrs. Simmons.

The first ladies' prize, a vinaigrette, was won by Mrs. Simmons; the second prize, a silver button hook, went to Miss Hastings; the third prize, a silver spoon, to Miss Wood.

The gentleman's first prize, a china smoking set, was taken by Mr. Read; the second, a match box, was won by Mr. Simmons; and Mr. Green gained the third prize, a cushion.

Fish.

Mr. George Osgood caught seven black bass, July 21st, weighing fifteen pounds. The largest weighed over three pounds.

Wednesday, July 21st, Mr. F. J. Simmons and Mr. Harry Wampole caught nine black bass in the Upper Lake. They weighed 31 3-4 lbs.

July 22d, Mr. Simmons, Mr. Read. and Mr. Wampole caught twelve black bass in the Upper Lake. The party was on the fishing ground at six o'clock and fished two hours. Seven weighed over three pounds.

An Ocean Experience.

A recent guest relates that on one of the Portland steamers, she asked one of the attendants to get her state-room changed, which he did, and removed her luggage, she being alone, for which service she gave him a dime.

He was profuse in his thanks, and wanted to know if there was nothing else he could do. She replied that there was not.

" K'yant I bring you some ice water? " When he brought it, he continued: " I'se gwine ter be on watch ter night, an' ef youse nerviss, ring de bell fer me."

Every now and then during the night she was awakened by, " Miss. is you sick?" or " Miss, is you nerviss?" and she thanked her lucky stars she had'nt given him a quarter.

The Art Store.

Mexican drawn work, Bagdad curtains, Persian Rugs, Bureau Covers. and everything else that is beautiful and difficult to make, such as gold dress trimmings, jackets and belts, are to be had here in great profusion.

MUCH TROUBLE.

Mrs. Musicus—" Did you have much trouble in learning to sing so beautifully?"

Miss Frankly — " Yes, especially with the neighbors."—*Standard.*

SHE NEVER TOUCHED IT.

" How did the vase get broken, Mary? "

" It fell off the pedestal, ma'am."

" How did you upset the pedestal? "

" Oi niver touched it. The chair bunked into it, ma'am."

" And didn't you push the chair? "

" Oi did not, ma'am. It was the table done that. All Oi did was to push the sofy up agin the table, an' Lord knows Oi can't see phot's a-goin' to happen that far off! "—*Harper's Bazar.*

FRANK CARLOS GRIFFITH, } EDITORS.
NETTIE M. RICKER, }

PUBLISHED EVERY SUNDAY MORNING DURING THE MONTHS
OF JULY, AUGUST, AND SEPTEMBER, IN THE INTERESTS OF

POLAND SPRING AND ITS VISITORS.

All contributions relative to the guests of Poland Spring
will be thankfully received.

To insure publication, all communications should reach the
editors not later than Wednesday preceding day of issue.

All parties desiring rates for advertising in the HILL-TOP
should write the editors for same.

The subscription price of the HILL-TOP is $1.00 for the
season, post-paid. Single copies will be mailed at 10c. each.

Address,

EDITORS "HILL-TOP,"
Poland Spring House,
South Poland, Maine.

PRINTED AT JOURNAL OFFICE, LEWISTON.

Sunday, July 25, 1897.

Editorial.

IT IS well to keep the mind from running in
narrow grooves. Do all possible to broaden
the ideas, study other phases of a subject than
from your own standpoint.

A picture which might be utterly condemned,
if bigotry ruled, and position unaltered, might
prove a revelation from another point of view, or
under another light. A statue must be criticised
from all points, and in all parts, and a critic would
be a fool who condemned or praised from only one
point.

A bright youth refuses to read a book written
about the rebellion, from the Southern point of
view, because he has had loyal ideas instilled into
him, which is good; but let him read or hear what
the other man has to say for himself, from his
environment and training, and he will see that had
he been thrown into the same surroundings he
might have done the same.

In illustration of this point, a gentleman who
loyally upheld the honor of the nation was once
asked if he would come and hear Wendell Phillips
speak. On replying that he would not, and being
asked his reasons, he gave them to this effect:
That he considered him just as responsible for our
troubles in '61 to '65 as the Southern fire-eaters
who shouted as loudly on the other side, and not
so honest or courageous, for they went in and
fought, while he did not.

"Very well, now," replied his friend, "we
will waive that view of it for a moment. Wendell
Phillips is a great orator, as great an orator
doubtless as Demosthenes or any man who ever
lived. Suppose now a case. Suppose you were
to meet a man to-day who lived in the time of
Demosthenes, and who knew of his oratorical
powers, and of his greatness, and walked the same
streets with him day after day, but who held a
poor opinion of his motives or acts, and would not
go to hear him, what would you think of him?"

"I'd think he was a d—d fool. Come, let's go
and hear Phillips."

Musical Programme.

SUNDAY, JULY 25, 1897.

1. Processional March from Lohengrin	.	Wagner.
2. Overture—Rosamunde	. . .	Schubert.
3. Violin Solo { (a) Dream	. .	Wagner.
{ (b) Mazurka .	. .	Wieniawski.
4. Pavane	. . . .	Ganne.
5. Serenade for Flute and 'Cello .	. .	Tittl.
6. Selection—Martha	. . . .	Flotow.

Cows, Milk, Cream, Butter.

The following document would appear to need
only an introduction to be able to explain itself:

OFFICIAL HEALTH CERTIFICATE.

This certificate is given after a careful inspection of Messrs. Hiram Ricker & Sons' ninety cows,
by the State Cattle Commissioners, and is an assurance that said cattle are in a healthy condition.

None genuine unless signed by one of the Commissioners.

J. M. DEERING,
F. O. BEAL,
DR. G. H. BAILEY, D.V.S.

(Signed)   GEO. H. BAILEY, V.

New Books.

FROM EBEN WEBSTER JUDD.
With Cochrane the Dauntless ; by G. A. Henty.

FROM MISS L. P. RAY.
The Martian; by George DuMaurier.
The Pursuit of the House-Boat; by John Kendrick Bangs.

FROM HON. WILLIAM P. FRYE.
Commercial Relations of the United States.
Department of State. 2 vols.

FROM MRS. AMOS R. LITTLE.
The Country of the Pointed Firs; by Sarah Orne Jewett.

The Waumbek.

"The White Mountain Range is so much grander when seen from Jefferson than from any other point where the whole of it is displayed, and yet is set at such a distance as to show the richest hues with which, as one feature of the landscape, it can be clothed, that we must award to this village the supremacy in the one element of mountain majesty."

That is what Starr King said, and it is true to-day, as all visitors to the Waumbek will attest.

Sunday Services.

Divine service was held in the Music Hall of the Poland Spring House on Sunday, July 18th, at 11 A.M. Rev. G. I. Keirn of the First Universalist Church of Charlestown, Mass., preached from the text found in the 16th chapter of John : "I have overcome the world." The service was well attended.

The Reverend Father J. M. Harrington of Lewiston held mass in the Poland Spring House, Sunday, July 18th.

Mr. S. T. Wellman, president of the Wellman-Seaver Engineering Company of Cleveland, Ohio, knows a good thing when he sees it, and has selected from the mineral exhibition several fine specimens of tourmaline, hematite, and meteorite.

Owl's Head Hotel is beautifully situated near the lower end of Lake Memphremagog, which lies 900 feet above the sea, partly in Vermont and partly in Canada. The mountain and lake scenery is said to be superb. Their advertisement is to be found in another column.

Apple Blossoms in Mid-July.
[For the Hill-Top.]

The sun sets slowly at Poland Spring
  And touches the fields with a lingering glow;
Lighting the slopes from east to west,
  Eager to come and loath to go.

The lakes at Poland hold lustered depths
  And ripple contentedly over their banks;
Fond of the shallows and rocky shores
  And scarlet lilies in settled tanks.

Queen of all seasons, bereft by none!
  Nature plays Poland a trick or two sly;
Here is her latest to puzzle the wise,
  Apple blossoms in mid-July!

Pink and puckered, fragrant and fresh,
  They seem to nod at the passer-by
And toss a challenge from bough to bough,
  Apple blossoms in mid-July!

                  M. B. J.

Art Notes.

THE Art Gallery is on the top floor of the Maine State Building, reached by two easy flights of stairs with midway landings. The entire upper floor is divided into six alcoves, and devoted entirely to the pictures by prominent artists. There are chairs in each alcove, which will be found convenient for elderly people who may desire the rest.

The catalogue is expected any day and will be freely distributed. If you see any picture which appeals to you, inquire its price, and you will doubtless become its possessor very shortly.

Notice the work of Ross Turner at the head of the stairway. Mr. Turner was born in Westport, Essex County, N. Y., and studied art abroad, and is Vice-President of the Boston Art Club, beside being a member of the Boston Art Students' Association; American Water Color Society, New York; Water Color Club, Boston, etc. His specialty is marines, and he paints in both oil and water. His work is highly prized in all exhibitions.

Henry Orne Ryder, whose impressive picture of "Storm Clouds, Franconia Notch," graces a prominent position in Alcove D, was a pupil of Boulanger, Lefebvre, and Pelouse, of Paris, and his work has been exhibited at the Paris Salon of 1889, 1890, and 1891, also the Berlin International Exhibition of 1890, the World's Columbian Exposition, Chicago, the Boston Art Club, National Academy, and all the noted exhibitions, where pictures are carefully selected.

In Alcove A, and again in Alcoves C and F, are some excellent works by William J. Bixbee The picture called "After a Blow" received special distinction at a recent Art Club Exhibition in Boston, where it received, with nine others, the highest number of votes for excellence. Mr. Bixbee was born in Manchester, N. H., and is a pupil of that excellent artist, S. P. Rolt Triscott, also of Tomasso Juglaris, and is a member of the Boston Art Club and Secretary of the Boston Society of Water Color Painters. Mr. Bixbee's picture of the old Ricker Inn is a very faithful and interesting work.

Miss Martha A. S. Shannon has a very fine flower picture in Alcove B. The subject is "Chrysanthemums," and it is a picture full of warmth and color. Miss Shannon studied at the Cooper Union, New York, and was also a pupil of Fenety's, whose superb work Poland guests are familiar with. Her work has been exhibited at the Massachusetts Charitable Mechanics' Association, and at the Jordan Exhibition and elsewhere.

In Alcoves C and E are several examples of modern style of painting much in vogue at the present day. They are by George L. Noyes, who studied four years in Paris, under Courtois, Rixens, Blanc, and Delance, and his work was exhibited at the Paris Salon, Boston Art Club, Society of American Artists, New York, and other exhibitions. Mr. Noyes's Venetian and Algerian pictures are thoroughly characteristic representations, and find many admirers.

ELMWOOD FARM

OF FRENCH COACHERS

IMPORTED STALLIONS

GEMARE, 134. LOTHAIR, 979. TELMAQUE, 515.

3 Miles from Poland Spring, Maine,

the Home of the Ideal Coach and Road Horse of America. Half-Bred French Coach Carriage Horses for Sale. Also, Young Registered French Coach Stallions. Size, Intelligence, Courage, Endurance, and Conformation Instilled.

STOCK SHOWN DAILY.

J. S. SANBORN.

Arrivals.

POLAND SPRING HOUSE.
FROM JULY 16 TO 22, 1897.

Alden, Miss	Los Angeles, Cal.
Boothby, Mrs. Samuel	Portland
Biggs, Mrs. F. H.	Auburn
Biggs, Mrs. B. F.	Auburn
Bolles, Mr. and Mrs. E. C.	New York
Bolles, Miss Margaret	New York
Barker, Edw.	Wakefield
Bailey, George H.	Deering
Buckley, William F.	New York
Billings, George W.	Cleveland
Billings, Miss	Cleveland
Brown, Mr. and Mrs. Louis M.	Paris, Me.
Boyd, Mr. and Mrs. David	Baltimore
Braman, Thos. F.	Boston
Butt, Mrs. Alvin C.	New York
Coe, Ward	New Haven
Choate, Mr. and Mrs. S. A.	Boston
Carpenter, Mrs. F. W.	Providence
Copeland, Mrs. G. W.	Middleboro
Chadbourne, Mr. and Mrs. E. R.	Lewiston
Cony, M. R.	New York
Cornish, Mrs. A. D.	Lewiston
Cornish, Miss	Lewiston
Cole, Mr. and Mrs. Benj. E.	Boston
Chase, Mrs. M. H.	New York
Carpenter, F. W.	Providence
Carroll, Mrs. E. M.	Boston
Carroll, Miss Mabelle	Boston
Caton, L. P.	Brunswick
Danielson, J. D.	Boston
Diapeau, George	Brunswick
Diapeau, Frank	Brunswick
Diapel, Mr. and Mrs. James Pickering	Boston
Dorrance, Miss Mary L.	Middleboro
Duhme, Mr. and Mrs. C. H.	Cincinnati
Dolan, Miss	New York
Deering, J. W.	Portland
Englis, Mr. and Mrs. John	Brooklyn
Englis, Mrs. Janet	Brooklyn
Englis, Miss Anna Bell	Brooklyn
Englis, Mrs. Will F.	Brooklyn
Earley, T. J.	New York
Elwell, Mrs. E. H.	Deering
Elwell, Dr. and Mrs.	Togus
Eaton, Mrs. B. F.	Skowhegan
Eddy, Charles B.	New York
Frost, Miss Maud	Norway
Flaherty, Morgan J.	Lewiston
Francis, Mr. and Mrs. C. S.	Troy
Fuller, Mr. and Mrs. W. W.	New York
Fernekees, William H.	Boston
Field, James B.	Chelsea
Fuller, S. K.	Brooklyn
French, C. H.	Chicago
Goodwin, G. H.	Boston
Goodwin, Mrs. M. A.	Washington
Gadsden, Robt. W.	Atlanta
Gilbert, Mr. and Mrs. A.	Plainfield, N. J.
Gale, Cyrus	Northboro, Mass.
Gail, Mr. and Mrs. R.	Brooklyn
Hatheway, Mr. and Mrs. H. J.	Houlton
Harrington, John M.	Lewiston
Hunt, Mr. and Mrs. Arthur K.	Portland
Hubert, Miss Delphine	Montreal
Heckscher, Mrs. Austin S.	Philadelphia
Holton, H. H.	Providence
Hatwell, E. T.	Rockland, Mass.
Innes, Mrs. George, Jr.	Paris, France
Johnston, Mrs. J. M.	Brooklyn
Kimball, Mrs. J. W.	Paris
Kitz, Miss S. Edith	Reading, Pa.
Kitz, John F.	Reading, Pa.
Kershaw, Mrs. A. M.	Quincy, Mass.
Kinsley, Mrs. H. M.	New York
Lander, Mr. and Mrs. E. H.	New York
Lyon, Dr. and Mrs. George B.	Germantown, Pa.
Little, Mr. and Mrs. G. W.	New Haven
Little, Miss	New Haven
Lodge, Mr. and Mrs. H. M.	Wilmington
Matthews, Mr. and Mrs. Geo.	Cincinnati
Meeks, Mrs. H. V.	Buena Vista, N. J.
Mitchell, Mr. and Mrs. Chas. G.	Cincinnati
Mortimer, Mrs. W. G.	New York
Mullen, Miss	New York
Mitchell, H. W.	New York
Mereyman, Miss A. F.	Brunswick
Myers, Mrs. Wm. H.	Reading, Pa.
Morse, A. G.	New York
Newman, Mr. and Mrs. L.	Toledo
Newell, Mrs. W. H.	Lewiston
Nias, Miss	Chicago
Oskamp, Wm.	Cincinnati
Oskamp, Master W. Herbert	Cincinnati
Porter, Mrs Florence	Caribou
Putnam, George J.	Brookline
Pierce, A. F.	Lewiston
Parrie, Miss E. H.	Portland
Pierce, Miss	Boston
Parish, J. H.	New Haven
Parish, Miss Eunice W.	New Haven
Peck, Mr. and Mrs. B.	Lewiston
Peck, Miss Georgie E.	Chelsea
Peck, Lewis L.	Lewiston
Peck, Sumner S.	Lewiston
Peck, Frank G.	Lewiston
Peck, Miss Hazel H.	Lewiston
Palmer, Lowell M., Jr.	Brooklyn
Rines, Mr. and Mrs. A. S.	Portland
Richardson, Mr. and Mrs. Augustus	Boston
Richardson, Miss	Boston
Richardson, Miss M. A.	Boston
Randolph, Miss A. F.	Plainfield, N. J.
Rafelye, Mr. and Mrs. Augustus	Newtown, N. Y.
Richardson, Moses W.	Boston
Snow, D. E.	Newton
Snow, Miss Nellie B.	Newton
Snow, Miss Helen H.	Newton
Shaw, Mrs. T. P.	Portland
Shaw, Master Thos.	Portland
Stringer, Miss Mary	New York
Sammons, Mr. and Mrs. C. E.	Boston
Sammons, Miss	Boston
Shaw, T. P.	Portland
Swett, Edw. C.	Portland
Smith, W.	Salem
Simon, E. L.	Atlanta
Sengstacke, A.	Atlanta
Soria, Mr. and Mrs. C. M.	New Orleans
Soria, Miss Annie E.	New Orleans
Towns, George A.	Atlanta
Tabor, J. W.	Portland
Thornton, Mr. and Mrs. David	Brooklyn
Tucker, Winfield	New York
Tucker, Miss	New York
Tucker, Miss A.	New York
Underwood, Miss H.	Brooklyn
Witt, Mr. and Mrs. George H.	Boston
Wellman, Mr and Mrs. G. T.	Cleveland
Wellman, Master H.	Cleveland
Wellman, Master Fred	Cleveland
Wood, J. M.	Chicago
Williams, Mr. and Mrs. Francis	Sheboygan
Walsh, James A.	Lewiston
Wheeler, Mrs. Albert	Lowell
Wheeler, Miss Marietta	Lowell
Woods, Mr. and Mrs. Henry F.	Boston.
Young, S. L	Auburn

MANSION HOUSE.

Chamberlain, Miss M. C.	Bahia, Brazil
Deering, Henry	Portland
Elsbree, Mr. and Mrs. T. D.	Valley Falls, R. I.
Jordan, Mrs. E. C.	Portland
Lappin, Mr. and Mrs. N.	Portland
Marsh, Arthur	Springfield
Nay, J. A., Jr.	Boston
Noyes, Mrs. G. F.	Portland
Sherman, Miss J. C.	Montclair, N. J.
Taylor, Mr. and Mrs. H. A.	No. Bridgton
Turner, R. H.	Portland

Master Arthur Marsh of Springfield, Mass., is at the Mansion House.

On Wednesday, July 21st, a party from Lewiston drove to the Poland Spring House, where they dined. The number included Mr. and Mrs. B. Peck, Miss Georgie E. Peck, Miss Hazel N. Peck, Mr. James B. Field, Mr. Lewis L. Peck, Mr. Samuel S. Peck, and Mr. Frank G. Peck.

The hop on Saturday night, July 17th, was one of the most successful of the season. The ladies were handsomely gowned. The hall was not too crowded, and the weather was cool. Besides the onlookers in the hall, a good number of guests took advantage of the seats on the veranda, where they enjoyed the sight through the new plate-glass windows.

On Thursday evening, July 15th, a delightful Launch Party was given by Mr. and Mrs. S. Ross Campbell. The guests included Mr. and Mrs. Simmons, Mr. and Mrs. Gallagher, Miss Edith Simmons, Mr. Harry Simmons, Mr William Read, Mr. Harry Wampole, and Master Albert Wampole. On their return to their cottage, Mrs. Campbell served lunch. A most enjoyable time is reported.

THE ALPS OF NEW ENGLAND.

New Mount Pleasant House

WHITE MOUNTAINS.

OPEN FOR   The bracing air. pure water, immunity from hay-fever, sumptuous furnishings, and magnificent scenery
make it the ideal place to spend the summer. **The Table is Famed for Its Dainty Elegance.** The fine
THE SEASON.   drives, walks, tennis courts, golf links, base-ball grounds, and bowling alleys provide opportunities for
recreation.

THROUGH PARLOR CARS FROM PORTLAND TO THE HOTEL GROUNDS.

Nearest point to Mt. Washington.
All trains start from the grounds.

ANDERSON & PRICE, Managers,

Winter Hotel, The Ormond, Ormond, Florida.

Mount Pleasant House, N. H.

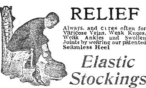

IT STANDS AT THE HEAD.

Unrivalled in Popularity!
Unsurpassed in Location!
Unapproached in Patronage!

THE

POLAND * SPRING * HOUSE

IS A SUPERB ILLUSTRATION OF

o o o SUCCESS o o o

EMBRACING AS IT DOES

ALL THE DESIRABLE FEATURES

EXPECTED IN THIS

The Leading Resort of America,

WHILE THE

MAINE STATE BUILDING

WITH ITS

SUPERB ART FEATURES

IS UNEQUALLED BY ANY SIMILAR ENTERPRISE

IN THE WORLD.

o o o

HIRAM RICKER & SONS (Incorporated),

PROPRIETORS.

MAINE STATE BUILDING.

The Hill-Top

POLAND SPRINGS, SO. POLAND, ME.

HARRY C. WILKINSON

Vol. IV.   SUNDAY MORNING, AUGUST 1, 1897.   No. 5.

Some of Our Friends.

WE are afforded the opportunity, this week, of presenting a few of Poland's guests as a frontispiece to our paper. All guests at this hospitable resort are valued, but as we cannot present them all together, we must be content to do so occasionally by small parties.

This week we have in the group, commencing at the left, Mr. Thornton of Brooklyn, Mr. Olney, Jr., and Mr. Olney, Sr., of Providence, Miss Tessie Rosenheim and Mr. Rosenheim of Savannah, Mr. Comstock and Miss Florence Smith of Providence, Mr. Ray of Franklin, Mass., Mrs. Olney of Providence, Mrs. Swan of Chicago, Mrs.

Blackford, Mrs. Johnston, and Mrs. Thornton of Brooklyn, Miss Stella Smith of Providence, and Miss Ada Blackford of Brooklyn.

We hope to present another group before the season is over, and where there is so vast a number of guests as at Poland Spring we may be able to do so.

Summer on the East Side.

IT was a bachelor's fate, when he drove from the Cunard pier to the paternal dwelling, to find the house closed and the sleepy servant giving reluctant consent even to a night's lodging. It was the fate which unexpected homecoming in July merits, and consequently accepted in a Platonic spirit. .

Business ties made it necessary to remain in town for the month, and where to live meantime without burying within the dismal recesses of the Club, became the question.

A note from a friend at the University Settlement seemed to offer a suggestion quite unique and novel in its promise. The tailors were on a strike, and help was needed in their difficulty. Instead of writing my reply I went in person and there took up my abode.

The Settlement guest-chamber is a little hall bed-room on the third floor front of a tenement house across the way. A narrow bedstead, a small wash-stand, and a portable bath that slips beneath the bed, constitute the furnishings.

Here I resided during the four weeks of July, and when the weeks were ended wished more time at my command, so thrilling was the life, so full of meaning and of tangible result for every thought and effort.

The University Settlement is an anchor of hope for the thousands of toilers in the tenth ward of New York. From it emanates the subtle forces that make for the amelioration of evil conditions, and the constant inspiration toward higher ideals. There the tailors came for counsel, and found a mediating power which secured an arbitration of the difficulties and a favorable settlement. I came to know the leaders of the strike, and found then men of strength and fortitude, that put to shame our own superficiality and selfishness. Living on bread and tea, these men, their wives and children, fought week after week in order to secure their rights, and at last were victors.

But life in the tenth ward is not altogether tragic. The swarms of children in the clubs, the library, and the bank (four thousand every week) were given, as far as possible, the vantage of picnics and vacations in the country. Too little money was available for the benefit of all, but four hundred and more children were taken to country

homes for a two weeks' outing. Several times I went on steamboat rides when a thousand mothers and their babies were given a day of sunshine and ocean breeze. It made me long for the wishing cap, and fleets of boats, with oceans of milk and lemonade to satisfy the longings of those women and children sweltering in the prisons of the " white slaves" of New York.

Here in the mountains, with the restfulness, the beauty of scenery, and the social life making mere living a luxury, I ofttimes recall the joy of four-year-old Tommy, who frequently piped up to my window, ",Say, knock me down a cent! I'm thirsty, see?" Of course I went down to witness the transformation of the cent into that poisonous-looking "Violetine" soda. His brother sent me a note one day. He was ill with fever and eleven years old. He enclosed ten cents, saved from the sale of papers, and offered to give it me if I would loan him 'Grimm's fairy tales until he should recover.

The experience of the summer was well worth the while, and the insight gained into the purposefulness of the Settlement has made me an enthusiast.

Five of the brightest men in the city college are products of the Settlement boys' club, and upon just such boys, saved from craft and given a new bent, the salvation to good citizenship of the immigrant population of the city rests.

RICHARD CAREW.

The Perfect Woman.
[From the New York Tribune.]

The perfect woman, physically, says an artist in this city, should measure 5 feet 5 inches in height and should weigh 128 pounds.

The extended arms, from the tip of the middle finger to the tip of the middle finger, should measure the exact height of the body—5 feet 5 inches.

The diameter of the chest should be one-fifth of the height, the foot one-seventh, and the hand one-tenth.

From the thigh to the ground should be the same length as from the thigh to the top of the head, and the knee should come exactly midway between the heel and the thigh.

The distance from the elbow to the middle of the chest should be the same as from the elbow to the middle finger, and the length of the foot should measure the same as the distance from the lower point of the chin to the top of the head.

The waist measure should be 24 inches; bust measure, if taken under the arms, 34 inches; if measured over them, 43 inches.

The wrist should measure 6 inches, upper arm 13 inches, thigh 25 inches, calf of leg 14½ inches.

Maine Gems.

MAINE'S choicest production, next to Poland water, is its tourmalines. These were first discovered in 1820, the year Maine became a state. Elijah L. Hamlin, an elder brother of Vice-President Hamlin, was returning with Ezekiel Holmes from a mineralogical trip, when the former was attracted to a gleam of light at a tree's root, and picked up a beautiful green crystal. Since then the locality—Mount Mica in Paris—has become everywhere famous for its rare tourmalines. These are among the finest in the world, the other principal localities producing transparent crystals being Siberia, Brazil, and Ceylon. The ledge at Mount Mica has been systematically mined, with some interruptions, since 1881, when the operations of the Mount Mica Company began.

The tourmaline is essentially a borosilicate of aluminum, colored by varying proportions of lithium, manganese, iron, and other elements, and it is in several respects the most wonderful of all minerals. It probably excels all other minerals in the marvellous range of its tints, embracing every hue perceptible to the senses. All shades have been found at Mount Mica except the rare pigeon-blood tint of some Siberian and Brazilian specimens. Some of the colors have distinguishing names, the colorless variety being called achroite, while the red or pink is rubellite, the blue is indicolite, and the green is sometimes known as the Brazilian emerald and the black as schorl. The tourmaline is also remarkable for its electric excitability; and for its dichroism, or property of showing a different color when the light passes through it lengthwise from that seen across the crystal. A crystal viewed through the side, for instance, may be a transparent green, but either opaque or yellowish-green when viewed through the end of the prism, and gems from the same crystal vary in color according to the manner of cutting.

It is estimated that about a hundred crystals have been found at Mount Mica that would be considered remarkable specimens of the mineral, while the smaller crystals have numbered several thousand. A large part of these crystals, large and small, have been absorbed by the Hamlin cabinet, by far the finest collection of tourmalines in the world, which has lately passed into the possession of Harvard University.

One of the most magnificent tourmaline specimens known, now in the British Museum, is a group of pink crystals that came from the mysterious locality of Burmah, unknown to foreigners, and was presented in 1795 to Colonel Symes, British ambassador, by the King of Burmah. It is about a foot across, and has been valued at 1,000 pounds sterling. A touching incident told in Dr. Hamlin's intensely interesting "History of Mount Mica" was the destruction, while mining operations for mica were being carried on, of a specimen that must have surpassed in beauty this one from Burmah, and that would have been one of the rarest mineral treasures of the world if it could have been secured uninjured. Examination of the debris showed that nine distinct transparent tourmalines had been deposited upon a matrix of white quartz about eight inches square and five inches deep. One of the transparent crystals was two inches in diameter and more than two inches in height, changing from pink at the base to a delicate and gorgeous carmine at the summit; another was three-fourths of an inch in diameter and more than three inches long, of the purest grass-green color; a third was of unknown length, more than an inch in diameter, of a clear blue-green in the center, which was overlaid by four thin layers—in turn colorless, pink, colorless, and sea-green; and the other crystals were of white and green, or white passing to a very light blue. A single crystal found on another occasion would have been the finest known if it had not been somewhat shattered by blasting. It is of light blue, shading into dark blue and deep blue-black, is nine inches long, and if it had not been broken, would have furnished several hundred carats of fine stones. It is now in the State Museum at Albany, New York.

Choice examples of the tourmaline are shown in the Maine Building at Poland Spring. The cut gems include one of a fine pink color, and several beautiful green ones of about one to four carats in size. The cabinet specimens give a good idea of the occurrence of the crystals. They show also the minerals with which the tourmalines are usually associated in Nature's marvellous laboratory at Paris, and some of these specimens are among the best of their kind that have been found.

The other rare and brilliant Maine gems of the Poland collection are exquisite yellow and colorless beryls, colorless topaz from Stoneham, and deep-colored amethyst from Stowe. From these gems and the other beautiful minerals, purchasers will have no difficulty in selecting pleasing specimens for personal or home decoration or for the cabinet.

The Art Store.

Mexican Drawn Work, in all its wondrous intricacy and beauty, may be found at Mrs. Mallouf's. Her Art Needle Work, with its unlimited variety of stitches of all styles and nations, is displayed in abundance, as well as taught.

Mrs. F. K. Piper of Boston is at the Mansion House.

Art Notes.

SEARS GALLAGHER, who has been an annual and valued contributor to the Poland Spring Art Exhibition, was a pupil of Benjamin Constant and Jean Paul Laurens in Paris, and also of Tomasso Juglaris in Boston. His work has found favor at the Salon des Champs Elyssee in 1896, and he has been represented at the American Water Color Society, Boston Art Club, and the Philadelphia Art Club. Mr. Gallagher paints in water colors, and four of his very excellent pictures are in Alcove F.

A. W. Buhler is also well known at the Poland Spring Exhibitions. He was originally a decorator, after which he did illustrative work for several New York and Boston publishing houses. Higher ambition led him to Europe, where he put in two years' hard study in Paris under Benjamin Constant, Jules Lefebvre, and Paul Delance. Mr. Buhler also made sketching tours in Holland, and his Dutch pictures are among the most highly prized of his works. Two Dutch scenes and one in France will be found at the head of the stairs and in Alcove F.

Edward H. Barnard has won much distinction as an artist, his work having been exhibited and had honors bestowed upon it in many exhibitions of note. He studied in Paris under Boulanger, Lefebvre, and Collin, and has exhibited at the Paris Salon two seasons, and at the Paris Exposition of 1889; also the World's Fair, Chicago. He has received medals for portraits and landscape, and was the recipient of the second Jordan prize, 1895. Mr. Barnard paints in the impressionist style, and his works show rare skill and true artistic feeling. Four of his works are exhibited here this season.

Benjamin Champney was one of the founders of the Boston Art Club, and his flower pictures are well known at all the principal exhibitions. He was educated in Europe and has exhibited at the Salon. In Alcove B are two of his pleasing pictures, one being of violets and the other roses.

The Exhibition comprises some hundred and thirty very superior works, and is free to all, the building being open week days from 9 A.M. to 9 P.M., and on Sundays from 10 A.M. to 8.30 P.M.

Progressive Euchre.

Friday evening, July 23d, an enjoyable progressive euchre party was given in the amusement room at the Poland Spring House. There were thirteen tables. Eighteen games were played, and the highest number of points gained by the ladies was thirteen and the same number for the gentlemen.

The first ladies' prize, a handsomely-decorated china tray, was won by Miss Goshorn. Mrs. Keene gained the second prize, a china bon-bon dish. The third, a doily, went to Miss Kutz; and Mrs. Wood won the fourth, a silver book-mark.

The first gentlemen's prize, a silver corkscrew, went to Mr. Carpenter. Mr. Mathews won the second, a picture frame, decorated with violets. Mrs. Meeks gained the third, a silver pencil. Mrs. Roach won the fourth, a stamp-holder.

Mrs. Griffin displayed excellent taste in selecting the prizes.

The Waumbek.

A variety of delightful drives and walks form an especial attraction of the place. The roads, which stretch away on every hand, are in excellent condition, and afford direct communication with the interesting localities in the vicinity. No place among these mountains is more favored in this particular than Jefferson, and the superiority of its drives to those offered by other resorts in this section of the country is admitted by all who have once visited the place. Especially charming for long drives are those to the Crawford House, sixteen miles, and to Bethlehem, eighteen miles.

Oh!

If one paints the sky grey and the grass brown, it is from the good old school; if one paints the sky blue and the grass green, then he is a realist; if one paints the sky green and the grass blue, then he is an impressionist; if one paints the sky yellow and the grass violet, then he is a colorist; if one paints the sky black and the grass red, then he has decorative talent.

Translated from "*Das Echo,*" Berlin.

To the enthusiastic golfer, male or female, Hinds' Honey and Almond Cream is a very pleasant article to apply to the face and hands after a day afield.

Children's Column.

Let not a day pass, if possible. without having
heard some fine music, read a noble poem, or seen
a beautiful picture.   —*Goethe.*

Out of Tune.

A little girl, not long ago,
    Sat sulking by the fire.
Outside, the world was white with snow;
The playful winds began to blow,
    The pearly drifts grew higher.

"What ails my little girl?" said one
    Who saw her sober face.
"I'm tired," said she, "the bright old sun
Has lost his way, or else has gone
    To light some other place.

"For days and days I have not seen
    A single bit of shine!
I want to see the grass glow green,
With yellow buttercups between,
    And all my flowers so fine."

. . . .

The sun was bright on hill and dale,
    The roses were in bloom;
White daisies starred the meadow vale,
And buttercups were thick as hail,—
    When, listless in her room,

I saw again the little maid,
    With damp curls dangling low.
"What matters now?" I gaily said.
"It is too hot! Just see my head!
    And see this stringy bow!"

                    —JANE L. PATTERSON.

Thursday Evening, August 5th.

THAT is the date, and on that evening, in the
Music Room, a gentleman of commanding
presence, possessed of a clear, resonant voice,
and who won national distinction at the Chicago convention in 1892, by an eloquent speech upon
the resolution of sympathy with our distinguished
fellow-citizen, the late Hon. James G. Blaine, will
appear, and present a subject which cannot fail to
interest every one here.

Mr. Edward C. Swett will deliver his lecture
on "Picturesque Maine," showing many beautiful
views, of which the following is clipped from the
Boston Transcript:

"Leaving the ocean and going inland, the
Poland Spring and its attractions next claimed
attention. The large hotel and spring house were
shown; then through avenues lined with birches,
oaks, and maples, all of which the spectators were
made to see, the lecturer proceeded to Shaker Hill
and Rumford Falls. After a flying visit to Bangor,
the screen showed, one after another, views of the
hunting grounds of the center of the state that
were enough to make even those who were not
sportsmen ambitious for a trip to the heart of the
pine forests, where few go except the sportsmen,
their guides, and the lumbermen. Caribou and
deer appeared on the screen, as well as a noble
specimen of the moose, which measured in life
seven feet from hoof to shoulder. Aroostook with
its potato fields; Camden, at the mouth of the
Penobscot, the Mecca of many yachtsmen every
summer; with all the various scenes of beauty
about Mt. Megunticook and Mt. Beattie were
described, as well as the points of attraction about
Mount Desert. The lecturer finished with views
of Dog's Head Rock and Eagle Lake."

Tid-Bits.

August.

Catalogues.

Golf is King.

Last of the summer months.

The Art Catalogues are ready.

Mrs. T. J. Little of Portland is at the Mansion House.

Bowling string on Thursday. Mr. Oaks, 259; Mr. Mitchell, 249.

The steam launch Poland now makes its regular trips through the lakes.

Mrs. G. F. Noyes and Miss Deering of Portland, are at the Mansion House.

Mr. E. C. Jordan of Portland has been spending a few days at Poland Spring.

Capt. J. A. Henriques and Mrs. Henriques of Portland are at the Mansion House.

Mr. and Mrs. Benjamin Green of Brunswick spent Sunday at the Poland Spring House.

Mr. S. J. Lanahan and Mr. Wallace Lanahan of Baltimore are at the Poland Spring House.

Rev. Father Sylvester Malone, regent of the University of New York, is at Poland Spring.

Hon. Joshua Holden of the Massachusetts Senate and Mrs. Holden were recently at Poland Spring.

Mr. and Mrs. W. B. Pratt and daughter of Elkhart, Indiana, are among the recent western arrivals.

Miss Whitman, at the Poland Spring House, is an experienced manicurist. She has been here several seasons.

Mr. John C. Black, the well-known Chicago banker, has rejoined his family, who were among the early June arrivals.

In looking over the field for a place to go this autumn or next spring, do not leave Haddon Hall out of your calculations.

Mr. G. H. Goodwin of Boston, well known at Poland in former years, has returned after an absence of several seasons.

Hon. Seth L. Larrabee, speaker of the Maine House, with Mrs. Larrabee and sons, spent Sunday at Poland Spring House.

Mr. George L. Osgood of Boston brought a fine string of fifteen bass from the lake, four of which weighed 3¾ pounds each.

Mr. A. Turner, President of the Franklin Savings Bank, New York, is accompanied by Mrs. Turner in their first visit to Poland.

Miss Katherine M. Ricker, the well-known contralto of Boston, is spending a few days at the Poland Spring House.

Mr. William Oskamp, a prominent resident of Cincinnati, Ohio, accompanied by his son, are making their first visit at Poland Spring.

Mr. H. F. Wood, purchasing agent of the West End Railroad, Boston, and Mrs. Wood, have joined their friends, Mr. and Mrs. Yeomans.

Mr. Eugene Hale, Jr., and Frederick Hale, sons of Senator Eugene Hale. are the guests of their grandmother, Mrs. Z. Chandler of Michigan.

Miss Helen Colburn and her friend Miss Morgan of San Francisco are at the Poland Spring House. Miss Colburn is a niece of General Draper.

Mr. and Mrs. N. E. Weeks spent Sunday at the Poland Spring House. Mr. Weeks is well known in transportation circles as publisher of the Pathfinder.

Miss Flora J. White's Home School for girls will open for the winter, October 1st, at Concord, N. H. Exceptional references can be given on application.

Mr. R. Massey, Jr., of Philadelphia, who during the summer is one of Bar Harbor's cottagers, has made a visit here this week to visit his daughter, Mrs. Hecksher.

Among the regular visitors who annually visit Poland, and who have recently arrived, are Colonel and Mrs. H. S. Osgood, Mr. and Mrs. W. A. Vose, Miss Vose, and George A. Vose

Guests who may not be aware of the fact are informed that Mrs. Robinson, a skillful masseuse, is regularly at the Poland Spring House every summer, and her services may be had at any time.

We are indebted to the Notman Photographic Co. for the very fine group photograph presented on the first page. It is a pleasure to visit their studio and see the remarkably fine work there on exhibition.

Khaldah, an Egyptian Mind Reader, gave an exhibition of his ability in the Music Room on Wednesday evening, which was in many respects astonishing. His experiments were clever and successful.

Mr. and Mrs. William V. Hester of Brooklyn are a charming addition to the circle of young people. Both are enthusiastic golfers, and Mr. Hester is well known from his connection with the Brooklyn Eagle.

Mr. and Mrs. F. H. Williams and Miss Williams of the Charlesgate, Boston, arrived on Friday, the 23d, at the Poland Spring House from Isle of Shoals. This is the third season that Mr. Williams and family have spent at Poland.

Conceit.

THE concert at the Poland Spring House, July 29th, by Miss Katherine M. Ricker and Mr. George Edmund Dwight, assisted by the Kuntz Orchestral Club and Mr. Hauser, pianist, met with pronounced success.

Miss Ricker, who is contralto at the Central Congregational Church of Boston, has a large dramatic voice of fine quality and sings with thorough musical and artistic feeling. She was heartily encored in all selections.

Mr. Dwight, who has recently returned from Milan, where he has acquired a pronounced Italian school and an extensive operatic *répertoire*, sang with brilliancy and finish his difficult numbers. His voice will surely be heard in the large cities, and his future is promising.

Mr. Kuntz' Orchestra, composed of Symphony men, sustained their high standard of work. Mr. Hauser was thoroughly at ease, and the accompaniments were played with a delicacy and assurance which was felt by the audience.

The programme was as follows:

1. Overture—Si j' etais roi.   .   .   . Adam.
   Orchestra.
2. Aria—Amor viens Aider.   .   .   Saint-Saens.
   Miss Katherine M. Ricker.
3. { a. Pur dicesti.   .   .   .   . Antoini Lotti.
   { b. Causene.   .   .   .   . Bononcini.
   Mr. George E. Dwight.
4. { a. Emer's Farewell to Cucullan.   . Stamford.
   { b. Battle Hymn.   .   .   .   . Stamford.
   Miss Ricker.
5. Aria—Ecco ridente in Cielo. .   .   . Rossini.
   Mr. Dwight.
6. Duet—La Favorita.   .   .   . Donizetti.
   Miss Ricker and Mr. Dwight.

The Hill=Top

IS PRINTED AT THE

Office of the Lewiston Journal.

If you wish work executed in like style, address

————— JOURNAL OFFICE, LEWISTON, ME.

George Edmund Dwight,

An American baritone, has recently returned from Milan, where he has passed the last three years, studying with Maestri, Blasco, Marino, Buzzi, Peccia, and others. Before leaving the United States he took a most beneficial course of training with Sig. Campanari, the famous baritone, at whose advice he went to Europe to finish his studies. Before his return he sang at Ancona, Valentine in "Faust," and Alphonso Il Re in "La Favorita," with success. He should meet with excellent opportunities in America, as he returns well equipped.

Mr. Dwight has the French and Italian, as well as local *répertoire*, has taken the best of what a foreign market affords, but chooses to keep his American name and associations free from prefixes or suffixes, that he may identify himself with American art and musicians, rather than cater to tradition, which is fast being dispelled by the concentrated rays of fact and reason. His present address will be at the Hardware Club, New York.
—*Musical Courier.*

Sunday Services.

Rev. B. S. Rideout of Norway, Me., preached on Sunday morning, July 25th, from the text, "Then spake Jesus again unto them, saying, I am the light of the world."—John 8 : 12. The subject of the discourse was, "Christ the Interpreter of the World's Needs and Wants."

Mass was held on Sunday morning, July 25th, at 6 A.M. Rev. Father Sylvester Malone, the Brooklyn regent of the University of New York, and Rev. Father T. J. Early of New York, officiated at the service.

An Episcopal clergyman's wife living in southern Texas sends to Mrs. Hiram Ricker a large quantity of Mexican drawn work. Mrs. Ricker will be glad to show it to all who will call at her cottage. It is charity work, and the prices are very reasonable.

FRANK CARLOS GRIFFITH. |
NETTIE M. RiCKER, } EDITORS.

PUBLISHED EVERY SUNDAY MORNING DURING THE MONTHS
OF JULY, AUGUST, AND SEPTEMBER, IN THE INTERESTS OF

POLAND SPRING AND ITS VISITORS.

All contributions relative to the guests of Poland Spring
will be thankfully received.

To insure publication, all communications should reach the
editors not later than Wednesday preceding day of issue.

All parties desiring rates for advertising in the HILL-TOP
should write the editors for same.

The subscription price of the HILL-TOP is $1.00 for the
season, post-paid. Single copies will be mailed at 10c. each.

Address,
EDITORS "HILL-TOP,"
Poland Spring House,
South Poland, Maine.

PRINTED AT JOURNAL OFFICE, LEWISTON.

Sunday, August 1, 1897.

Editorial.

CAN anything be more delightful to the senses than one of those perfect days after a period of cloud and mist? Wherever we may be, this is true, but a perfect Poland day reveals beauties of nature, such as the microscope reveals when placed above a delicate leaf or flower.

How distinct each field, fence, roadway, and farm-house becomes on the hill-side far away, and we behold, almost like a piece of cloth, the delicate texture, and wonder if it has been there all the time.

One can almost hear the tinkle of the cow-bells, as the cows graze in the hundreds of pastures which come within the range of our vision, and the air is fresh, and one feels the invigorating effect at once, and the weak become strong, and the well, stronger, as an immediate result.

Out-of-door sports are planned and executed without fatigue, and the wheel, the lofter, the racket, or the bat are brought into service with beneficial effect.

It is the duty of all to enjoy these things when they may, and the indulgence of out-door games gives a picturesqueness to the landscape, by its added moving figures in healthful and harmonious recreation.

It May Be of Interest to Know

That the dome of the Palais de Justice in Brussels is made of papier maché and weighs sixteen tons.

That a horse at full trot has all four feet off the ground at once.

That there are 90 islands in the City of Amsterdam and 300 bridges.

That the bottom of the Pacific Ocean between California and Hawaii is almost perfectly level.

That there are twice as many non-Christians in the world as Christians.

That a cat has been known to recover after two hours immersion in cold water.

That a machine made in Connecticut will count, wrap, and tie in packages of 25 each, 500,000 postal cards in ten hours.

That the sun never sets on Uncle Sam. When it is 6 P.M. at Attoo's Island, Alaska, it is 9.36 A.M. the following day at East port, Me.

That Texas could accommodate every person in the world with a piece of land 49½ by 100 feet.

That the largest gun made by Krupp is one of 119 tons, and fires a projectile of 2,028 pounds with a charge of 846 pounds of powder.

That the most magnificent state carriage in the world is at Trianon Versailles. It was built for Charles X. and cost $200,000.

That blindness is said to be decreasing.

That the top of the Washington Monument tips four inches to the north on a very hot day, returning at night.

That one contractor has a monopoly of funerals in Paris.

That Shakespeare makes no mention of tobacco.

New Books.

FROM HENRY B. BROWN.
The House by the Medlar Tree; by Giovanni Verga.
The Law of Civilization and Decay; by Brooks Adams.

FROM MRS. WILLARD A. VOSE.
The Mistress of Beech Knoll; by Clara Louise Burnham.
Veronica; by Louise Brooks.
Violetta; by Mrs. A. L. Wister.
Jack Hall; by Robert Grant.

FROM MRS. J. R. BATES.
Won Under Protest; by Celia E. Gardner.

FROM MRS. AMOS R. LITTLE.
The Sowers; by Henry Seton Merriman.

FROM MRS. C. I. TRAVELLI.
Soldiers of Fortune; by Richard Harding Davis.

"Looking Backward."

A pleasant surprise was given to the on-lookers at the hop, Saturday night, July 24th. At nine o'clock a party of eight young people filed into the Music Hall, accompanied by a march played by the Kuntz Orchestral Club. The four couples gave an amusing version of the lanciers "Looking Backward" with so much eclat that an encore was called for. The two-step followed the lanciers. The following young people participated in this retrospective dance, which was so much enjoyed by the other guests: Mrs. Blackford and Mrs. Johnston, Miss Smith and Mr. Olney, Miss Blackford and Miss Roseiheim, Miss Ada Blackford and Mr. Comstock.

Morning Concerts.

On and after Monday, August 2d, the morning concerts at the Poland Spring House will be given at 11.30 A.M. instead of 11 A.M.

A progressive euchre party was given at the Mansion House, Wednesday evening, July 28th. Mrs. Van Beil won the first ladies' prize, a lovely cup and saucer. Miss Conover cut for the first prize and won the second, a beautiful rose bowl. The third prize, a bottle of cologne, went to Miss Ricker. Mr. S. Ross Campbell gained the first gentlemen's prize, a bottle of violet water. Mrs. Wood won the second prize, a china pen tray. Mrs. Ernst won for the third prize a box of Huyler's cream bonbons. Mrs. Keene displayed good taste in selecting the prizes, and the euchre party was enjoyed by all.

Golf.

THE first golf tournament of the season was held Friday, July 23d. It was a handicap, nine holes, medal play. There were ten entries, and all finished except Mr. A. C. Judd and E. N. Huggins, who intended to play late in the afternoon, but the heavy shower kept them from doing so.

The winner was Mr. C. I. Travelli, who played a very steady game. He made the round in 49 strokes, which is 12 strokes better than his best previous round. He played from scratch and had to do better to win, as Mr. W. P. Comstock, who had a handicap of 12 strokes, was a close second. He made the round in 64, and his handicap of 12 gave him a net score of 52.

Mr. A. H. Fenn, who was 15 behind scratch, made the round in 49, same as Mr. Travelli, but had to add 15 to his score, which made his net score 64.

Robert Marsh won the prize for the largest number of actual strokes on the round.

The following are the scores in full:

	Gross.	Handicap.	Net.
C. I. Travelli,	49	— 0	= 49
W. P. Comstock,	64	— 12	= 52
F. L. Castner,	74	— 15	= 59
A. H. Fenn,	49	Plus 15	= 64
J. H. Maginnis,	80	— 15	= 65
E. W. Olney,	86	— 15	= 71
Austin Palmer,	109	— 20	= 89
Robert P. Marsh,	112	— 20	= 92

Monday, July 26th, handicap, hole play, foursome tournament.

Fenn and Vose. Scratch. Travelli and Corbin 18. Olney and Comstock 18. Maginnis and Howland 36.

First round. Travelli and Corbin beat Fenn and Vose, 3 up, 2 to play.

Olney and Comstock beat Maginnis and Howland, 6 up, 5 to play.

In the finals Olney and Comstock beat Travelli and Corbin, 2 up, 1 to play. Finals very close and not decided until the 17th hole.

Travelli and Corbin had Olney and Comstock 1 down at the end of the first nine holes. At the 15th hole they were all even. In playing for the 16th hole Travelli had hard luck in approaching the hole, striking a tree and landing his ball in the long grass, making it very difficult to play. Corbin failed to get it out on the next stroke, and Olney and Comstock won the hole, making them 1 up, 1 up. They also won the next hole, by good play, winning the match 2 up, 1 to play.

On Tuesday, July 27th, the ladies and gentlemen had a foursome tournament, lady and gentleman playing partners, Mr. Fenn and Miss Vose winning first prize. The players were Mr. Fenn and Miss Vose, Mr. Travelli and Mrs. Putnam, Mr. Maginnis and Miss Soria, Mr. Comstock and Mrs. Blackford, Mr. Vose and Miss Brown, Mr. Olney and Miss Blackford. The score:

	1st Round.	2d Round.	Gross.	Handicap.	Net.
Fenn and Vose,	69	79	148	0	148
Travelli and Putnam,	80	89	169	0	169
Maginnis and Soria,	111	98	209	36	173
Comstock and Blackford,	92	95	187	12	175
Vose and Brown,	103	96	199	18	181
Olney and Blackford,	117	96	213	18	195

Mention has been made in these columns of "sporty" golf links which were well-nigh unplayable. It is pleasant, therefore, to speak of golf links in the White Mountains which are "sporty," yet where it is a pleasure to play golf. Such are those of the Mt. Pleasant Golf Club at Mt. Pleasant, N. H., which are available for summer visitors at the hotel of that name. They are situated in the beautiful meadow in front of the house, looking toward the Presidential Range. The first drive, to the "Ammonoosuc" hole, is from in front of the hotel across the river from which the hole takes its name, to the meadow, 198 yards. The second hole, "Woodchuck," gives an opportunity for a good drive and brassey shot back toward Mt. Washington, 217 yards. The third drive is from a hill 35 feet high, across a swamp at its foot, a good drive being rewarded by a good lie. The distance to the hole—the "Range"—is 186 yards. The drive to the fourth hole, 258 yards, passes a windmill, which gives this hole the name of "The Windmill." From a small bluff which affords a fine view of Crawford Notch, a course of 175 yards takes one to "The Notch" hole. No. 6, "Trouble," is a short hole of 122 yards, but the drive must be carefully judged, as a small brook has to be crossed. The next hole is 251 yards, and is named "The Onion," after the Florida hotel with that title. "Setting Sun," the longest hole on the course, 336 yards, is due west, beside the Ammonoosuc River. The home drive, to a good dinner and a talk over the scorecards, is "Mt. Pleasant," 142 yards. There is considerable playing on the links at present, and the course is getting in excellent shape. Golf is being made a great feature at Mt. Pleasant, and the club promises to be the most active in the mountains this season.—*Boston Evening Transcript.*

Musical Programme.

SUNDAY, AUGUST 1, 1897.

1. Overture—Maritana	.	.	Wallace.
2. Flute Solo—Lugretia Borgia	.	.	Briccialdi.
3. Music of the Spheres	.	.	Rubenstein.
For String Quartette.			
4. { a. Melodie	.	.	Paderewski.
{ b. Menuette.			
5. 'Cello Solo { Romanza	.	.	Popper.
{ Spanish Song	.	.	Abel.
6. Selection—Si j' etais Roi	.	.	Adam.

Arrivals.

POLAND SPRING HOUSE.
FROM JULY 23 TO 29, 1897.

Atvood, Horace — Hampden
Allen, Mr. and Mrs. F. A. — Cambridge
Allen, Miss Annie E. — Cambridge
Alland, S. — Boston
Brovn, Mr. and Mrs. E. L. — Portland
Bartlett, Mr. and Mrs. T. L. — Boston
Bonney, Mrs. A. S. — Mechanic Falls
Boothby, W. A. R. — Waterville
Black, John C. — Chicago
Beardsley, A. H. — Elkhart
Burbank, Maurice A. — New Haven
Chandler, Henry — Manchester
Crovley, Miss M. — New York
Cox, H. P. — Portland
Chadbourn, E. R. — Lewiston
Colburn, Miss Helen — Hopedale
Day, Harry A. — New York
Dvight, George Edvard — Springfield
Darling, Mr. and Mrs. Charles P. — Boston
Darling, Esther Russell — Boston
Douglas, Miss — Pittsburg
Dunham, D. F. — Malden
Fair, A. W. — Boston
Ellis, Mrs. B. F. — Boston
Edvards, George C. — Providence
Eastman, Miss Laura — Littleton
Elliott, George H. — Wilmington, Del.
Echeverria, Mrs. Pio — New York
Greene, Mr. and Mrs. Benjamin — Brunswick
Goodale, Mr. and Mrs. E. S. — Syracuse
Gilligan, M. — Medford
Greenleaf, Mr. Charles — Profile House
Gutman, Mrs. F. — Lewiston
Gutman, Miss — Lewiston
Gutman, W. C. — Lewiston
Hill, James W. — Manchester
Holbore, Mr. and Mrs. T. Pearce — Germantown
Holden, Mr. and Mrs. Joshua B. — Boston
Hart, Miss Lisette — Louisville
Hersey, Dr. A. L. — Oxford
Hersey, Miss H. E. — Boston
Harris, A. H. — Montreal
Hall, Henry — Boston
Hale, Eugene, Jr. — Ellsworth
Hale, Frederick — Ellsworth
Havkes, Mrs. N. L. — Westbrook
Hester, Mr. and Mrs. William T. — Brooklyn
Hahn, Miss — Boston
Hochstadler, Mrs. — New York
Hochstadler, Miss May — New York
Hobart, Mrs. A. W. — Boston
Johnson, Miss — Ansonia
Jordan, Archer — Auburn
James, Fred S. — Chicago
Knovlton, J. S. W. — Boston
Keene, Mrs. William F. — Central Falls, R. I.
King, Miss Zayma — Quincy, Mass.
Khaldah — Boston
King, Mr. and Mrs. T. — Quincy
King, Delcevan — Quincy
Levis, Mrs. J., Jr. — Washington
Larrabee, Mr. and Mrs. Seth L. — Portland
Lounsbury, Edw. H. — Woburn
Lanahan, Mr. and Mrs. S. J. — Baltimore
Lanahan, Master Wallace — Baltimore
Lutmis, Benjamin A. — New York
McCarthy, J. J. — Boston
Moore, Dr. and Mrs. Ira L. — Boston
Malone, Rev. Sylvester — Brooklyn
Miller, A. Q. — Auburn
Moulton, B. P. — Rosemont, Pa.
Massey, R. J. — Bar Harbor

Moore, P. H. — Saco
Mover, George H. — Malden
Mover, Miss L. E. — Malden
McDonald, Mr. and Mrs. John B. — New York
McDonald, Miss Georgie — New York
Marston, James — Yarmouth
Morgan, Miss Eleanor — San Francisco
Nevton, Dr. and Mrs. — New York
Nichols, Mr. and Mrs. Thomas M. — New York
Nields, Mary Given — Penn.
Nichols, James — Hartford
Osgood, Mr. and Mrs. H. S. — Portland
Olney, Frank F. — Providence
Perkins, Mrs. J. — Mechanic Falls
Plummer, Miss — New York
Plummer, Miss M. G. — New York
Pinkham, J. W. — Portland
Pratt, Mr. and Mrs. W. B. — Elkhart
Pierce, Mrs. F. H. — Boston
Prescott, Mrs. Lizzie — Greenwich, Conn.
Phelan, Mr. and Mrs. C. C. — Westbrook
Page, R. C. — Saco
Rogers, Mr. and Mrs. Alphens G. — Portland
Ricker, Mr. and Mrs. J. S. — Portland
Ring, Mr. and Mrs. Constant Q. — Winthrop, Mass.
Robb, Miss M. A. — New York
Rideout, B. S. — Norway
Ricker, Katherine M. — Falmouth
Roeck, Mrs. C. — New York
Schindler, Mrs. Clarissa — Ansonia
Schindler, Miss — Ansonia
Schindler, Miss Bianca — Ansonia
Sevier, Mr. and Mrs. J. — Orange Co., N. Y.
Sykes, E. H. — Auburn
Scovell, Miss — Wakefield
Stoddard, F. H. — New York
Stoddard, Miss Lucy — New York
Staples, Charles, Jr. — Portland
Strong, Prof. Wm. C. — Lewiston
Savyer, Henry N. — Boston
Springer, Nathan A. — Woburn
Sveetser, Francis K. — Stoneham
Terry, Mr. and Mrs. John T. — Irvington, N. Y.
Tooker, Mr. and Mrs. G. W. — New York
Thayer, Charles H. — Manchester
Turner, Mr. and Mrs. A. — New York
Tovne, F. B — Holyoke
True, Mr. and Mrs. F. D. — Portland
Torsey, Mr. and Mrs. H. A. — Auburn
Thompson, Mr. and Mrs. D. W. — Bridgeport
Trull, S. Frankford — Woburn
Vose, Mr. and Mrs. Willard A. — Brookline
Vose, Miss — Brookline
Vose, George A. — Brookline
Vanderbilt, John — New York
Williams, Mr. and Mrs. F. H. — Boston
Williams, Miss L. A. — Boston
Weeks, Mr. and Mrs. N. E. — Brookline
Williams, Mr. and Mrs. Fred — W. Somerville
Wales, Mr. and Mrs. John — Brookline
Wales, Miss M. W. — New York
Williams. C. E., Jr. — Auburn
Wilson, Miss Georgie — Westbrook
Waitt, Lottie H. — Malden
Yeomans, A. H. — Brookline

MANSION HOUSE.

Deering, Miss — Portland
Dovnes, A. L. — Westfield
Henriques, Mr. and Mrs. J. A. — Portland
Henderson, Mr. and Mrs. James A. — New York
Jordan, E. C. — Portland
Kitchin, Mr. and Mrs. S. R. — Lawrence
Little, Mrs. T. J. — Portland
Marsh, Allyn T. — Springfield
Marsh, Mary J. — Springfield
Noyes, Mrs. G. F. — Portland
Piper, Mrs. F. R. — Boston

Mr. Allyn R. Marsh and his sister Miss Mary Marsh of Springfield, Mass., arrived at the Mansion House, July 28th.

The Sawyers made a fine catch of fish on Wednesday, returning at night, after a day spent on the brook, with one hundred and forty fine trout.

Mr. and Mrs. Theophilus King of Quincy, Mass., and Mr. D. King are at Poland. Mr. King is Vice-President of the National Bank of Redemption, Boston, and an enthusiastic golfer.

Mrs. Ripley and Mrs. Van Beil found in the Peterson woods, Tuesday morning, a small bush of ground hemlock with the fruit, a crimson waxen berry. It is unusual to find the hemlock with the fruit.

Monday, July 26th, Mr. and Mrs. F. R. Thomas gave a delightful brake ride around Sabbath-Day Lake and through the Peterson woods. The party included Mrs. Ireson, Miss Richards, Miss H. Blackford, Miss Kutz, Mr. Kutz, and Mr. George French.

Mr. and Mrs. John T. Terry, who are old patrons, but who were not with us last season, are here again. Mr. Terry is well known in New York business circles. He is a member of the firm E. D. Morgan & Co., and a director in many large financial institutions and companies.

Mrs. H. M. Kinsley of New York, and Miss Nias of Chicago, spent last Sunday at the Poland Spring House, and expressed themselves much pleased with the beauties of the place. Mrs. Kinsley is the widow of the famous hotel man, H. M. Kinsley of the Holland House, New York.

THE ALPS OF NEW ENGLAND.

The Hill Top

POLAND SPRINGS SO. POLAND, ME.

THE HILL·TOP·

Vol. IV.   SUNDAY MORNING, AUGUST 8, 1897.   No. 6.

Perfect Poland.

WE frequently read frantic and hurt cries in the papers to the effect that Mr. X. Y. Z. has visited some locality and returned to the metropolis, rushing into print with the declaration that "there are no fish" in such a lake, or the beach at such a place "is rocky," or the view from such a point is "not worth the expense," and a multitude of these complaints which the answering scribe refutes *in toto*.

To the Poland visitor such an outbreak would be a curiosity. Has any one ever seen or heard of such a person? We wot not. What is a disappointed visitor? We have never seen one. We will not say we should like to, for we should not; but, as we have a place for rare and curious things, under glass in the Maine State Building, we should at once be inclined to cage it there.

No; Poland guests go away with a sense of fullness, of the vision and of the flesh, and feel that their capacity, mental and otherwise, requires more than one visit to absorb all the

tion, and there are guests to-day who have been
coming here a score of years and more, and they
have not yet established a record for weariness of
Poland's delights.

We do not think the thing exists. It is a sort
of visionary "Mrs. 'Arris," which, like the sea-
serpent, may be sighted sometimes at remote
localities, but resolves itself into a sea-voced of
the imagination and never materializes.

Poland is—Poland. We have hills on all
sides, but from our ærie height we peep over and
beyond them until the vision is intercepted by the
grand Presidential Range and its retainers on
every side. The eye traverses a scene of hill-side
and lake, farms and farm-houses, forest and field,
and never wearies of the sight.

Our groves of fragrant pine touch our very
walls, and a liquid, living, nearly stream gushes
from the clover rock beneath our feet, while the
airs from heaven are laden with the odors of the
new-mown hay, the clover, and the ripening fruit.
Thus much for the artist and the poet.

Music, pictures, books—a rare and never-
wearying combination. Are you weary, and need
the soothing influences of melody, exquisitely
interpreted? The tuneful issue of the Masters of
the Muse is daily rendered by their faithful students. The ear is pleased, is gratified and calm ;
the eye seeks the artistic efforts of the artist's
brush. The art world is at your will. The sea,
the sky, the flowers, the fruit, the woods, the
shaded path, the thoughts of artists pictured on
the canvas,—all these are here in plenitude and
wealth.

The ear, the eye, has feasted to the full, and
now that inner sense—the mind—is not neglected,
for when fatiguing exercise gives way to calm
repose, the thoughts of others, crystallized in print,
bears us from ourselves and holds the magic
mirror to our face to show the comfort we enjoy,
while truth, in fiction, shows what right have
been.

' Dreams, books, are each a world; and books, we know,
Are a substantial world, both pure and good.
Round these, with tendrils strong as flesh and blood,
Our pastime and our happiness will grow.''

All these and more, much more, are Poland
Spring's to give; so how imagination, run riot as
it may, could form conception of a being not
content, is past the comprehension of the loyal
Poland guest.

An Episcopal clergyman's wife living in southern Texas sends to Mrs. Hiram Ricker a large
quantity of Mexican drawn work. Mrs. Ricker
will be glad to show it to all who will call at her
cottage. It is charity work, and the prices are
very reasonable.

How I Won Dorothy.

"I WILL wager you fifty guineas you cannot do
it, and beside, if you succeed, you are a
deuced sight smarter than I have given you
credit for being, and I will consent to your
attentions to my daughter." This statement was
made by a very grand, pompous-appearing, elderly
gentleman one evening at the Carlton Club in Pall
Mall to a rather inoffensive and modest-appearing
young man, who was lazily smoking a cigar.

"I'll go you on that," said the latter. "Here,
Charley," he called to a friend standing near.
"I want you to listen to this wager, and you shall
be the referee."

"Go on, Algie."

"Lord Shoughten wagers fifty guineas that I
cannot disguise myself in any manner and stand at
any place I please, between Piccadilly Circus and
Ludgate Hill, on the right-hand side of the way
going east, between the hours of one and five P.M.
on a certain day which shall be agreed upon, and
he not be able to detect me at once."

"I should say Lord Shoughten is very likely
to win fifty guineas," laughed Charley.

"That's all right, my boy. To-day is Monday.
Let the trial be set for to-day week. What do
you say?"

"Agreed,". replied his lordship, and agreed
it was.

We will now let Algernon relate the result
himself.

. . . .

"You see, my boy, I stood to win fifty guineas—
and the girl, or to lose fifty guineas. As it happened, I did not have fifty guineas to lose, so I
had to win.

"I had a friend who was acting manager of
one of the theatres, whose good services I immediately enlisted. He procured for me one of the best
ragged suits I ever saw, from one of those board-
men who patrol the streets, sausage fashion, with
posters front and back.

"This I had steamed and disinfected, and
under it I wore a complete suit of combination
silk fleshings, feeling quite safe from vermin or
contagion.

"I engaged Clarkson, in Wellington Street, to
make for me, on a fine piece of silk, the best
imitation of a stubby, two-weeks'-old, red beard
imaginable, and to come to my rooms and adjust it,
together with a perfect wig.

"One eye I covered with a black silk patch,
through which the eye was invisible, but which I
could see through quite distinctly. The other eye,
black naturally, I covered with a light-blue glass
eye, fastening it over the closed lid, and held it in
place with a pair of false lids, made of gutta-percha,

heated in hot water and moulded to suit. This made a very bulgy, but dissolute, bad eye, and when the face was made to conform to this, I should have desired the companionship of a revolver, had I been likely to meet myself alone at night.

"My right leg was doubled up at the knee, and strapped there, and a wooden stump took its place from the knee down, and my left arm was strapped inside my ragged shirt.

"With a very dilapidated broom and a crutch, I took my stand at the crossing, at the south-west corner of Waterloo Place and Pall Mall, and awaited the result.

"About two-thirty, when I had already taken in about three shillings in gratuities, I beheld his lordship and Dorothy strolling leisurely down Regent Street toward me. He had evidently intended to have her witness his cleverness and my disgrace.

"As he approached the sweeper on the opposite side, who crosses Waterloo Place at that point, he stopped and looked well at him, and then handing him a coin, crossed toward me. I had already gotten several feet away from the curbing when, becoming aware of their proximity, I stopped and touched my greasy cap.

"The glance bestowed upon me was but a momentary one, and a penny offered, which I took, and they passed on, much to my relief; but they had not passed the center of the Place before they stopped and his lordship looked back, while Dorothy evidently urged her father to continue his walk, but to no purpose.

"Of course I pretended not to notice any of this, and kept on with my occupation.

"'A—h, my man, where did you lose that leg?' was his inquiry.

"'Hi lost that 'ere leg, Guv'nor, hon the rilewye halong near Coventry, sir,' said I.

"'And the arm?' he continued.

"'Wery same hidenticle spot, sir.'

"'What's your name?'

"I saw that this catechism must be stopped, so I at once assumed a very free and familiar air, which could not but be repugnant to both.

"'Stephenson, sir, hit you please,' touching my cap respectfully, however, each time. 'Ye see, Guv'nor, me and Jim Smithen—'im ye know wots hauled for cracking that 'ere safe in Paddington on'y last Chewsday. Well, Guv'nor, one was a—'' but by this time Dorothy, the little darling, was so confused by this long harangue with a crossing sweeper that she pulled her papa's sleeve, until he, being evidently satisfied, I could not be the man, yielded to her persuasion, and tossing me a shilling, which I still possess, went on his way, much to my satisfaction once more.

"As he approached the man on the other side of the Place, by the United Service Club, he stopped short, gave him a sharp look over, and burst into a loud laugh, to the utter consternation of the mendicant.

"'So this is you, is it? You didn't deceive me, did you? Aha, my boy—' but the poor fellow, who was half frightened out of his wits, beckoned a policeman from across the way, by Strong-i-the-Arm's, and shouted:

"'Say, Bobby, 'ere's a hinsane chap agoin' hon horful. Clap the hirons on 'im, Bobby. Run 'im hin, hor 'e'll do somebody a mischief.'

"I could see that explanations were made, and the sweeper made richer by a tip, and his lordship, very much crestfallen, stalked on toward Trafalgar Square.

"To cut it as short as possible, at five o'clock sharp my friend the referee came along with Lord Shoughten and introduced me to him, announcing me as the winner.

"His surprise may be better imagined than described, and as we sat at dinner that evening, Lord Shoughten, Dorothy, my friend Charles, and myself, we had a merry time over his lordship's recital of his afternoon's adventures.

"I got my fifty guineas—and Dorothy, and there in that glass case is the entire suit, and the shilling I was not cut off with."

Were You Aware of the Fact?

That the heaviest creature that flies is the great bustard of southern Russia. It sometimes weighs forty pounds.

That the Lord Chancellor of England is not allowed to leave Great Britain during his term of office.

That a fast ocean steamship consumes 350 tons of coal a day.

That the dog is mentioned 33 times in the Bible.

That about 15,000 sovereigns pass over the counter of the Bank of England daily, about $225,000.

That Italy leads Europe in the number of murders.

That there are over 3,000 operators in the telegraph office in the General Post-Office, London.

That Gladstone wears a 7¾ hat; Beaconsfield wore only a 7; Charles Dickens a 7⅛; Dean Stanley 6¾.

That the Emperor of Germany stands twenty-first in the direct line of succession to the British throne.

That the horse-power developed in firing a 100-ton gun is 17,000,000.

That the smallest flying insect is the fairy fly, about one ninety-second of an inch in length.

Golf.

At the tournament on Saturday, July 31st, Mr. Harris of Montreal won first scratch. The following are the scores in full:

	1st Round.	2d Round.	Gross.	H'dicap.	Net.
Harris,	48	53	101	0	106
Vose,	69	57	126	18	108
Maginnis,	64	68	132	20	112
King, Sr.,	71	67	138	12	126
Olney,	80	75	155	25	130
King, Jr.,	79	84	163	22	141

There was great interest taken in the ladies' tournament which was held on Tuesday last. It was nine holes, medal play, handicap. Miss Hoeke with a handicap of 15 strokes, won first prize. Following are the scores of all the players:

	Gross.	Hanicap.	Net.
Miss Hoeke,	115	15	100
Miss Brown,	118	12	106
Mrs. Blackford,	118	10	108
Miss Peterson,	123	14	109
Miss Gale,	127	0	127
Miss May Peterson,	132	5	127
Miss Blackford,	152	18	134
Miss Vose,	174	22	152

On Wednesday the gentlemen held a handicap golf tournament, 18 holes, medal play. Mr. R. G. Lockwood won first prize. A. H. Fenn and H. Berri tied for second. The following are the scores in full:

	1st Round.	2d Round.	Gross.	Handicap.	Net.
R. G. Lockwood,	62	61	123	4	119
H. Berri,	65	73	138	16	122
A. H. Fenn,	48	51	99	plus 23	122
George A. Vose,	65	61	126	0	126
J. H. Maginnis,	65	75	140	12	128
E. W. Olney,	74	73	147	15	132
W. Berri,	71	72	143	8	135
J. W. Chick,	73	72	145	9	136
F. M. Sawtell,	88	83	171	25	146
W. C. Chick,	92	82	174	18	156

A. H. Fenn lowered the record for nine holes in a match with Mr. R. G. Lockwood on Thursday. His score was: 6-4-5-3-6-5-5-4-7—45.

The Library.

During the month of July, 1,008 books were taken out by guests, being an average of 32 1-2 a day. The average for each day in the week was, Fridays, 38; Saturdays, 37; Sundays, 35; Tuesdays, 31; Wednesdays, 31; Thursdays, 29; and Mondays, 25; showing Friday to have been the busiest day of the week, and Monday the least.

The average for the first seven days of July was 28, the second 30, the third 34, and the fourth 38, with the odd last three days averaging 33 per day.

This record shows Fridays, Saturdays, and Sundays to be above the average, and a handling of 2,016 books during the month.

The Drives of Mount Pleasant.

One would as soon think of visiting Poland without drinking at its famous fountain as to go into the White Mountains and not take its famous drives. For one going there for the first time it is desirable, in order to accomplish that end with the greatest comfort, to go at once to a central location. Of all the large houses in the mountains, none is so favorably located in relation to the drives as the Mount Pleasant House, excepting possibly Fabyans and Twin.

The drive to the summit of Mt. Willard is but five miles and a half; the drive through the famous "Crawford Notch" to the Willey House, the scene of the great avalanche of 1826, is but seven miles and a half; to the base of Mt. Washington, by the old "Mt. Washington Turnpike," passing the Upper Falls of the Ammonoosuc, is six and a half miles; to Jefferson, via Cherry Mountain, thirteen miles; the lovely drive through farming country to Whitefield, thirteen miles; to Maplewood, twelve miles; to Bethlehem, thirteen miles; while for long all-day drives the twenty-four mile drive around Cherry Mountain and the drives to Forest Hills Hotel in Franconia, to Sugar Hill, to Littleton, and to the Profile House, complete the list of daily trips which delight the lovers of mountain grandeur and beauty who rendezvous at that finest of White Mountain hostelries, the New Mount Pleasant House. The houses upon the outskirts of the mountains can take advantage of the drives in the section nearest them, but it is only from such a location as that described, in the very heart of the mountains, that they can all be reached in a one-day's trip.

HIS UNFORTUNATE SELECTION.

"He said that when he left college he would hitch his chariot to a star."

"He did so; but unfortunately he selected a fixed orb for the purpose."—*Truth.*

Thistles.

Jagson—"I tried to pay the new woman a compliment last night in my speech, but it didn't seem to be appreciated."

Bagson—"What did you say?"

Jagson—"I said the new woman would leave large footprints on the sands of time."—*Tid-Bits.*

WHAT STRUCK HER MOST IN VENICE.

"Did you visit Venice when you were in Europe, Mrs. Jenkins?"

"Oh, yes, indeed."

"It is a fascinating place, is it not?"

"Well, there's a good deal of water; but we were rowed all around by a chandelier in such a lovely costume!"—*New York Evening Post.*

FOUND ONE AT LAST.

Thompson—"I had a great surprise last evening."

Darrow—"How was that?"

Thompson—"My wife introduced me to a fellow who never was one of her old beaux."
—*Cleveland Leader.*

DECIDEDLY WRONG.

He—"Do you think it wrong for a man to kiss a girl he is not engaged to?"

She—"I think it would be wrong for him to be engaged to all the girls he kisses."—*New York Journal.*

WHAT A FOOLISH QUESTION.

"Oh, ah—pardon me, Miss Minnie, but at what age do you think women should marry? You know the newspapers are discussing the question."

"At about my age, I think, Mr. Timid," she replied, sweetly.—*Odds and Ends.*

ONE GOOD REASON.

Mrs. Warmheart—"My good man, why do you let your children go barefoot?"

Pat O'Hoolihan—"For the raison, ma'am, that I have in my family more feet than shoes."
—*Harper's Round Table.*

LOST HIS INFLUENCE.

Minister (approvingly)—"I notice that you don't sleep during my sermons any more."

Old Dozer (shaking his head)—"No; you are not the preacher you used to be."—*New York Journal.*

DIME WASTED.

Big sister—"Dick, I wish you would go and get Mr. Nicefellow a glass of water."

Mr. Nicefellow—"Yes, my boy, and here's a dime for you."

Little brother—"Thank you; I'll go pretty soon. Mamma said I shouldn't leave the parlor until she came back."—*New York Weekly.*

Minerals.

The Mineral Exhibit won instant recognition, as being of much beauty and value, and to those who know and appreciate the merit of the numerous specimens, they appeal very strongly, and many purchasers have been found among the guests. Mr. Chadbourne will be at the Maine State Building every Thursday, and give interested parties full information.

Children's Column.

If by your art you cannot please all, content the few. To please the multitude is bad.
— *Schiller.*

The Difficulty Regarding Hannah.

One summer Sunday afternoon, in her cottage by the sea, a mother gathered her little ones around her—as was her wont—to read and explain to them such verses from the Bible as she thought they could comprehend. That day she read:

"Rejoice with those who do rejoice, and weep with those who weep."

"H'm!" interrupted Harry, "How can you rejoice one minute and weep the next?"

"Well," replied the mother, "if a dear friend of yours had just been married, don't you think you could go and rejoice——" whereupon little six-years-old Willie piped up, and with a nasal drawl inquired, "But suppose you had intended Hannah for yourself?"

Afterward, when laughingly relating Willie's latest, his papa remembered that he, two or three weeks before, had read aloud an account of a wedding in a country church, while little Willie, apparently absorbed only by his playthings, had listened and understood.

The story said that all went smoothly on at the wedding until the officiating clergyman solemnly uttered the words, "If any one knoweth any impediment, let him now speak, or forever after hold his peace," when up from his seat sprang an elderly deacon, who, with flushed face and glittering eye, forbade the marriage.

"On what grounds, sir?" sternly asked the astonished minister.

And the disconsolate deacon nasally whined, "I *had* intended Hannah for myself!"

                      E. A. T.

An American lady, now in lovely Cornwall, England, not long ago was strolling across the fields with her little boy who felt twice his usual age and size that day, for it was his first day in trousers. Noticing that mamma held up her dress as they walked, little John looked down at his newly emancipated legs with great satisfaction and said: "Now I have on t'ousers *I* don't have any kilts to hold up. Modder, why don't *you* go into t'ousers?"

"What is an average?" asked the teacher. The class seemed to be posed, but a little girl held out her hand eagerly: "Please, it's what a hen lays her eggs on." Bewilderment followed, but the mite was justified by the lesson-book, in which was written: "The hen lays two hundred eggs a year on an average."—*Household Words.*

An Open Letter.

By Sally Backus Griggs, from Harper's Young People.

"Mary, Mary, quite contrary, how does your garden grow?
Silver bells, and cockle shells, and pretty maidens, all in a row."
               —*Mother Goose.*

Mary, Mary, quite contrary, hard I've tried, indeed,
To have a garden just like yours, but oh, I can't succeed,
Because I do not know the place to buy the things I need.
    I have a little plot of ground,
      And I've a silver bell,
    And on the ocean beach I found
      A tiny cockle-shell,
But where to get the pretty maid is what I cannot tell.
So please, dear Mary, quite contrary, whisper just the word
Of counsel that will help me most to any summer bird,
And swiftly he will fly this way, and sing me what he heard.

Survivors of the War.

TWO-THIRDS OF THEM ALREADY ON THE PENSION
ROLLS—THEIR EXPECTATION OF LIFE.

It is estimated that, excluding deserters, the Union survivors of the war now, 1897, number 1,095,628, and that not until the year 1945 will the last one of the veterans have disappeared. In 1945, 80 years will have elapsed since the close of the war, and if by any strange peradventure there still be a survivor at that remote date he must necessarily be at the least calculation 100 years old. The very youngest survivors, the drummer boys, are now 50 years old and upward.

One of Col. Ainsworth's tables shows the probable survivors of the war of the rebellion on June 30th of each stated year as follows:

Year.	Survivors.	Year.	Survivors.
1897	1,095,628	1908	705,197
1898	1,064,524	1909	665,832
1899	1,032,418	1910	626,231
1900	999,339	1915	429,727
1901	965,313	1920	251,727
1902	930,380	1925	116,073
1903	894,885	1930	37,033
1904	858,002	1935	6,296
1905	820,687	1940	340
1906	782,722	1945	0
1907	744,196		

            —*Boston Globe.*

Tid-Bits.

Sunsets.

More old friends.

Now some fine weather, please.

The hotels were never more full.

Picturesque Maine. Rightly named.

Mr. W. H. Hyde and Mrs. Hyde arrived August 3d.

Mrs. Franklin Smith and Miss Smith of Philadelphia are with us.

Mr. Rhodes G. Lockwood of Boston arrived Saturday, July 31st.

Mr. A. M. Mayo of Springfield, Mass., is visiting Poland Spring.

Haddon Hall is an all-the-year-round hotel and lovely at any season.

Mr. and Mrs. J. E. Spencer of New York have returned for the season.

Mr. Edward A. Filene of Boston arrived at the Mansion House, July 31st.

Mrs. Charles F. Everitt of New York City, N. Y., is at the Mansion House.

Mr. J. S. Martin and Mrs. Martin of New York are at the Poland Spring House.

Mrs. W. H. Hoeke and Miss Hoeke of Washington, D. C., are at the Poland Spring House.

Mr. E. F. Adams of Memphis, Tenn., registered at the Poland Spring House, Sunday, August 1st.

Among the welcome guests, Tuesday, August 3d, was Mrs. William C. Perkins of Burlington, Iowa.

Mr. D. Willis James, a prominent resident of New York, and Mrs. James, are at the Poland Spring House.

Mrs. S. Skaats, Mrs. N. E. Ten Broeck, and Miss E. A. Prall of New York, are at the Poland Spring House.

Among the welcome guests, Monday, August 2d, was Mrs. C. L. Holbrook of Boston.

Mr. Walter T. Almy and Mrs. Almy of New Bedford, Mass., are spending a few days at Poland. They came on their wheels.

Mr. C. J. Heppe and Mrs. Heppe, Miss Virginia and Miss Alverde Heppe of Philadelphia, are at the Poland Spring House.

Mrs. John C. Kerr of Brooklyn, daughter of Mr. Andrew R. Culver, was among the welcome arrivals on Saturday, July 31st.

The Waumbek, at Jefferson, accommodates three hundred and fifty guests, and has eight cottages connected with the hotel.

Mrs. E. M. Hammond of Boston has returned for the season. Mrs. Hammond always spends several weeks at the Mansion House.

It was a pleasure to welcome, July 30th, Rev. and Mrs. W. P. Lewis and Mr. and Mrs. Harry Zeigler and Miss C. F. Zeigler of Philadelphia.

Mrs. W. H. Newell, Mrs. James Cheever, and Miss M. E. Cheever of Boston registered at the Poland Spring House, Monday, August 2d.

Mr. and Mrs. George Brown of Boston are at the Mansion House. Mr. Brown is fond of sketching, and finds many charming places about Poland.

Mr. J. M. Wood of Chicago is at Poland Spring. Mr. Wood is the architect for the beautiful Portland Theatre which is in process of construction.

Mr. Samuel Olney and Mrs. Olney of Pawtucket, R. I., are with us. This is their first visit, and they are charmed with the beautiful scenery and high elevation of the place.

It is not to be wondered at that the great artist, William M. Hunt, when he sat upon the rock where the Poland Spring House now rests, remarked that they had no finer sunsets in Italy than he had seen right here, after the truly magnificent display of last Wednesday evening.

FRANK CARLOS GRIFFITH, | EDITORS.
NETTIE M. RICKER, |

PUBLISHED EVERY SUNDAY MORNING DURING THE MONTHS
OF JULY, AUGUST, AND SEPTEMBER, IN THE INTERESTS OF

POLAND SPRING AND ITS VISITORS.

All contributions relative to the guests of Poland Spring
will be thankfully received.

To insure publication, all communications should reach the
editors not later than Wednesday preceding day of issue.

All parties desiring rates for advertising in the HILL-TOP
should write the editors for same.

The subscription price of the HILL-TOP is $1.00 for the
season, post-paid. Single copies will be mailed at 10c. each.

Address,

EDITORS "HILL-TOP,"
Poland Spring House,
South Poland, Maine.

PRINTED AT JOURNAL OFFICE, LEWISTON.

Sunday, August 8, 1897.

Editorial.

TOWARD Paris the thoughts of all travellers
turn when planning their first trip across,
and each subsequent tour includes Paris as
one of its prominent features. Why? Is it
because of its people, or its size, or romantic and
picturesque location? Evidently not. It is because
the French people are thoroughly imbued with the
love of the beautiful, and carry that principle into
everything they do.

We build a bridge and call it useful, and look
upon it with satisfaction, and say that it is good
for *fifty years*. Yes; they build a bridge and
make it graceful, and artistic, and substantial, and
congratulate themselves upon the fact that it will
please the observer and last for all time.

It is for *all* the beauties of that city the traveller
from all parts of the globe journeys thither. Not
for the Arc de Triomphe, alone, or the Place de la
Concorde, but for its *ensemble*—its streets, which
reflect back the image of the passer even in dry
weather; its Column Vendome, its Louvre, its
Luxembourg, its Champs Elysee, and its myriads
of delightful objects.

Wealth pours into this great show city because
of these very things. How much would pour into
our cities for the same reason?

Six boys pool their pennies and produce something better, more artistic, than other boys, and
charge an admission fee to view it. Two boys
had the pennies; four boys the skill. The pennies
are still in the community. All the fees received
to view the objects go to enrich these six boys.
Two million people build a beautiful city, and the
wealth of the world turns toward its gates.

Cities should be made beautiful as well as
substantial; streets and roads should be made
permanent and kept in perfect condition. Admire
the beautiful, and make things beautiful that they
may be admired.

Sunday Services.

Rev. C. H. McClellan preached Sunday morning, August 1st, from the text, "And it came to
pass, when Jesus had ended these sayings, the
people were astonished at his doctrine, for he
taught them as one having authority and not as
the scribes."—Matthew 7 : 28, 29. A collection
was taken, and one hundred dollars given for
the benefit of the Children's Sea-Side Home at
Atlantic City.

Mass was held in the Poland Spring House,
Sunday, August 1st, by Rev. Father Sylvester
Malone, assisted by Rev. Father Gilligen.

Rev. Father Sylvester Malone preached Sun-
day evening, August 1st. The subject was :
"The Sacred Heart of Christ, the Saviour of all
Mankind."

Drag Ride.

Mr. Moses W. Richardson gave a delightful
drag ride, Monday morning, August 2d. The
party included Mrs. Augustus Richardson and her
daughters Miss Richardson and Miss M. A. Richardson, Mr. and Mrs. John Wales, Mr. and
Mrs. Thomas, Mrs. Lefavour, Mrs. Baines, Mrs.
Hobart, Miss Williams, Miss Englis, and Mr.
Gregory.

They went to Upper and Lower Gloucester,
and returning, visited Mr. Sanborn's, where they
saw his fine horses, Gemare, Lothair, and Tel-
maque. Mr. Sanborn then invited them to his
beautiful home, where they enjoyed a pleasant call.

The day being pleasant, all the participants
were full of enthusiasm, even including the horses,
and the seventeen miles were covered in high
spirits.

Progressive Euchre.

On Friday evening, July 30th, the guests gathered in the amusement room of the Poland Spring House for progressive euchre. The room was prettily decorated with ferns and flowers, and the ladies, with their exquisite gowns, made a charming picture.

Seventeen games were played, and the highest number, thirteen, was made by Mrs. Osgood, who won the first ladies' prize, a centre-piece; Miss Ray gained the second, a doily; Mrs. Griffin the third, a silver tape measure; the fourth, a Shaker duster, went to Mrs. Rogers.

Mr. Ivers won the first gentlemen's prize, a bouillon set; the second prize, a silver paper knife, went to Miss Richardson; Mrs. Beardsley gained the third, a silver bag tag; and Miss Elliott the fourth, a silver pen-holder.

The prizes were beautiful, and the party was one of the most enjoyable of the season.

The Notman Photographic Co.

If you have not already done so, you should not delay further making a visit to the studio and arranging for a sitting. Here, one can be and feel at their best, and leisurely carry out the arrangements, with the assurance that no better work is done by any photographic artists in America.

The Hill-Top in Lewiston.

Hereafter the HILL-TOP may be found in Lewiston, on Monday of each week, at N. D. Estes', 80 Lisbon Street. This is for the convenience of Lewiston people who may desire to see the paper.

Picturesque Maine.

" Blessings on thee. little man.
Barefoot boy, with cheek of tan !
With thy turned-up pantaloons,
And thy merry whistled tunes;
From my heart I give thee joy,—
I was once a barefoot boy !
O for boyhood's time of June,
Crowding years in one brief moon,
When all things I heard or saw,
Me, their master, waited for.
I was monarch, pomp and joy
Waited on the barefoot boy ! "

Mr. Edward C. Swett delivered his delightful lecture on " Picturesque Maine " on Thursday evening, and he was listened to with marked attention by a large audience, who followed the speaker and his interesting views thrown upon the screen with great pleasure. Mr. Swett's delivery is clear and distinct and his manner graceful, making a fine impression upon his audience. His views were particularly fine, and Maine owes him a debt of gratitude for presenting its beauties so forcibly and in such an attractive manner. Mr. Swett should be welcomed everywhere as a desirable addition to the list of platform orators.

The Art Store.

At the corner of the Poland Spring House will be found a room very fully supplied with art embroidery and work of all kinds—Bagdad curtains, Persian rugs, Mexican drawn work, and goods from many European countries, calculated for the decoration of the person and of the home.

Mr. A. L. Harris of Montreal, General Freight Agent of the Grand Trunk Railroad, is at Poland Spring. Mr. Harris plays a fine game of golf.

Tid-Bits.

Miss Belle Woodman of Springfield is at the Mansion House.

Mrs. F. Beck of Yardville, N. J., is at the Mansion House.

Mr. Walter Bliss of Hartford, Conn., is at the Poland Spring House.

Dr. and Mrs. Ira L. Moore of Boston are spending the season at Poland Spring.

Mr. John de Windt has joined his mother, Mrs. de Windt, at the Mansion House.

Miss Mary T. Van Vechten of Castleton, N. Y., has rejoined her friend, Mrs. Mortimer.

Mr. Frank A. Barnaby and Mrs. Barnaby of New York arrived Wednesday, August 4th.

Mrs. N. P. Merriam and Mrs. C. M. Bixby of Malden are registered at the Mansion House.

Mr. William M. Cole and Master Ford S. Cole of New York are at the Poland Spring House.

Mr. and Mrs. George Fred Winch and Mr. Joseph R. Winch of Brookline registered Aug. 4th.

Mrs. Jeannette Eastman of Boston is here. Mrs. Eastman has been for many years a patron of Poland.

Mrs. Thomas Smith of Brooklyn and her daughter, Mrs. C. W. Sheldon, are at the Poland Spring House.

Mr. Sawyer made a trip to Trip Lake on Thursday, and returned with one hundred and forty-three fine perch.

Mrs. T. A. Sawtell and Mr. F. M. Sawtell of Malden, have joined their friends, Mr. and Mrs. Nelson Bartlett, at Poland Spring.

Miss Flora J. White's Home School for girls will open for the winter, October 1st, at Concord, Mass. Exceptional references can be given on application.

Mr. John I. Pinkerton of West Chester, Pa., a noted lawyer, formerly of the firm of which Hon. Wayne MacVeigh was a partner, is again a welcome guest at Poland.

Mrs. F. A. Gilbert, Lester F. Gilbert, and Frieda H. Gilbert, of Brookline, arrived August 3d. Mrs. Gilbert is the wife of the President of the Boston Electric Light Co.

Mr. and Mrs. B. P. Moulton of Rosemont, Pa., have returned for the season. Mrs. Moulton's friends have been anxiously awaiting her return. She is a very fine whist player.

Miss Katharine M. Ricker wishes, through the columns of the HILL-TOP, to thank the guests at Poland Spring for the kind testimonial given to her, Saturday morning, July 31st.

If you desire anything in the nature of medicines, where reliability is a prime factor, and great care is exercised in compounding, read the advertisement of Schlotterbeck of Portland.

Mr. Fenety was again very fortunate in the display of his work in the card room on Wednesday. His pictures are the work of an accomplished artist, and it is a pleasure to know they find appreciation.

Mr. and Mrs. Dan C. Nugent of St. Louis, Mo., Miss Louise Nugent, D. Casey Nugent, and Morgan Nugent arrived Tuesday, August 3d. They are occupying the beautiful rooms at the Maine State Building.

Prof. R. H. Mohr, illusionist, ventriloquist, and charcoal artist, gave an entertainment in Music Hall, Tuesday evening, August 3d. Prof. Mohr is a very clever man, and the entertainment was an enjoyable one.

Mrs. Albert Douglas, Jr., and Miss Douglas of New York, arrived August 4th. Mrs. Douglas is the daughter of Mr. and Mrs. Franklin E. Taylor of Brooklyn, and is delighted to find her mother so much improved in health.

Mrs. Charles Greenlief and her friend, Miss Eastman of Littleton, have been spending a few days at the Poland Spring House. Mrs. Greenlief is the wife of Col. Greenlief, the well-known proprietor of the Vendome and Profile House.

Mr. T. P. McGowan, of the Portland *Board of Trade Journal*, was at the Poland Spring House during the week. Mr. McGowan claims to be the most extensive dealer in European steamship tickets of any concern in Maine, his headquarters being at 420 Congress Street, Portland.

Col. A. Loudon Snowdon of Philadelphia, minister to Greece under President Harrison and ex-Comptroller of the Mint, is again at Poland with Mrs. Snowdon. Col. Snowdon's eloquent speech in favor of sound money during last year's campaign will be long remembered.

A hotel contemporary, proud of its gentler sex, rises to remark, "Beat our ladies if you can." Is this a challenge or an onslaught with fists, clubs, or what? Perhaps they mean to intimate that they are sufficiently muscular to defend themselves against all comers. The announcement, however, is much in line with that of the furniture dealer who advertised that his "carpets can't be beat."

Don Quixote says that "in the night all cats are gray," but the catlette found by Mrs. Vose and presented to the office staff with her compliments and a new ribbon was black as Egypt's dark ages and brimming over with Mascot, for it had no sooner walked across the register than it began to fill up (the register, not the cat), and a full house has continued ever after.

Art Notes.

ADELAIDE PALMER is a native American artist, and her subjects are flowers and fruit. Her work is much appreciated at all the principal exhibitions, and she is a lady of fine natural instincts, modest in her pretensions, and paints with a strong yet delicate touch, which makes her pictures so successful. She has seven very excellent pictures in this season's exhibition, Nos. 83 to 88, all in Alcove B, and one of cherries not included in the catalogue. Her pictures find ready purchasers, and adorn many homes in all parts of the country.

William Stone has three very excellent pictures; notably so his "Cape Cod Cedars," No. 107 in Alcove E. Two others of his works here are 105 in Alcove A and 106 in Alcove C. Mr. Stone is an exhibitor of the Paris Salon, Boston Art Club, Jordan Gallery, Boston, Society of American Artists and National Academy, New York, Pennsylvania Institute, Philadelphia, and other prominent exhibitions.

Caroline A. Savary only sends one picture to this exhibition, 102 in Alcove A, but it is a very fine example of her work. Miss Savary is a pupil of Monson, Courtois, and other masters in Paris, and exhibits at the Boston Art Club and other galleries where acceptance depends upon merit.

Charles W. Sanderson submits some very superior water colors for the approval of visitors. Nos. 97, 98, and 99 will be found in Alcove F, and they show the skill of the artist in every feature. Mr. Sanderson was a pupil of Boulanger and Lefebvre, Paris, and Van Borselin of The Hague, and he received second prize at the New York Water Color Exhibition, and at Julien's, Paris.

Henry W. Rice is also a water-color artist, and his work is finding rapid appreciation among art lovers. He is an exhibitor of the Boston Art Club, the Jordan Gallery, etc. His pictures are 91 and 92 in Alcoves D and F.

Elmwood Farm.

Three miles from the Poland Spring House is Elmwood Farm, the home of Mr. J. S. Sanborn, the New England Coffee King. Here are raised some of the finest horses in America, and it is a pleasure to have Poland guests drive over there and inspect his magnificent animals. This is one of the features of Poland and should never be omitted by the admirer of the horse in all its perfection.

Thursday afternoon Mr. Sanborn brought the Mountain to Mahomet, and showed in magnificent style several of his special beauties, to the great admiration of all. Mr. Sanborn led the van, driving that superb specimen of horse flesh, Genmare, and following him were some six or seven other teams, all in perfect style and beauty. They drove around the course in front of the Poland Spring House several times, giving all an opportunity to note the fine points. Mr. Sanborn is to be congratulated on his valuable possessions.

Power of Prayer.

The little son of a wealthy lady was very ill, and given over by the physicians, but possessing quite a little store of personal savings, he gave it to the Sunday-school in advance of death. The superintendent asked all the scholars that day to pray for his recovery, which they did, and strange or not, as you please, shortly the little fellow's illness abated, and he recovered.

This little incident is related as fact by one of our most esteemed guests.

Tid-Bits.

Mrs. W. H. Baines of New York is at the Poland Spring House.

Mr. and Mrs. Robert Dornan of Philadelphia are at Poland Spring.

Mr. and Mrs. Eugene H. Smith of Boston are visiting Poland Spring.

Mrs. J. W. Lefavour of Beverly, Mass., is at the Poland Spring House.

Dr. and Mrs. D. Kaisner of Germantown, Penn., are at Poland Spring.

Mr. John Clark Ridpath of Boston is registered at the Poland Spring House.

Rev. W. H. Bolster of Dorchester, Mass., was a welcome guest Tuesday, August 3d.

Mrs. Christine Marburg and the Misses Marburg of Baltimore are visiting Poland Spring.

The Sawyers caught 153 trout, Monday, August 2d. Several weighed $\frac{1}{4}$ to $\frac{1}{2}$ lb. each.

If manicuring or chiropody is desired, Miss Whitman's services are at the call of the guests.

The many friends of Mrs. S. C. Dizer of Boston, were delighted to welcome her again in Poland.

Mr. Frank H. Brown and Mrs. Brown of Waltham, Mass., are at the Poland Spring House.

Mr. and Mrs. Eugene G. Blackford of Brooklyn have joined their family at the Poland Spring House.

The many friends of Dr. George H. Brett and Mrs. Brett were glad to welcome them again in Poland.

Mr. H. P. Gleason and Mrs. Gleason of Newark, N. J., were among the welcome guests Friday, July 30th.

Mr. and Mrs. George Wescott and their friends, Mr. Albert H. Moise and Mrs. Moise of Boston, are at Poland Spring.

Mr. and Mrs. F. H. Wyeth of Philadelphia and their friend, Miss E. M. Horner, are at the Poland Spring House.

Mr. and Mrs. L. P. Worthington and Miss Worthington of Doylestown, Penn., have returned for their second season.

Among the welcome guests on Saturday, July 31st, were Mrs. T. F. Jeremiah of New York City, and Miss C. M. Hertzel.

Mrs. Edmund Brush of Southampton, L. I., and Mrs. Kate H. Parker of New York, have registered for a two weeks' sojourn.

Mr. E. T. Williams, a prominent resident of St. Louis, Mo., accompanied by Mrs. Williams and their son, are visiting Poland Spring.

Mrs. William Berri and her sons, Messrs. Walter and Herbert Berri, were heartily welcomed by their friends at the Poland Spring House.

Mr. George W. Beyer and Mr. Henry G. Beyer of Portland, nephews of Mr. and Mrs. George Wescott, have been spending a few days here.

Mr. Franklin N. Gregory of Brooklyn has been cordially welcomed by the young people. Mr. Gregory's mother and sister, who are so pleasantly remembered by last season's guests, are this year in Europe.

Mr. H. H. Towle, General Baggage Agent of the Maine Central Railroad, and his friends, Mr. Dewey and Miss Dewey of Watertown, South Dakota, took dinner at the Poland Spring House, Sunday, August 1st.

Have you read the advertisement of Charles O. Bass of New York? It should interest you, and having secured a chart, the Genealogical Index in the library will tell you where to look for the information to fill it out if you do not already possess it.

Monday morning, August 2d, Mr. Campbell and Mr. Wampole played Mr. William Read and Mr. Allyn Marsh 6 sets of tennis. Each side won 3 sets and each side had 34 games. The sets stood 6-2, 1-6, 9-7, 6-3, 6-8, 6-8. Mr. Read and Mr. Marsh won the first set.

Mr. and Mrs. Walch of Brooklyn are spending a few weeks at the Poland Spring House. Rev. Father Sylvester Malone, who has been their guest, left Thursday for Boston, en route for Brooklyn, where he is to attend, August 15th, the laying of the corner-stone of the Henry McCaddin Hall. This hall is being built by Mrs. Walch, in memory of her brother, Mr. Henry McCaddin. It is a grand building, costing over one hundred thousand dollars. Rev. Father Sylvester Malone, Regent of the University of the State of New York, and Mrs. Walch agree as to the purpose of this building,—subserving the good of the community at large where no principle is compromised.

Mr. Maurice Augustus Burbank, who has been spending a few days at the Poland Spring House, made a fine run on his wheel from New Haven. On the first day he went from New Haven to Palmer, Mass, a distance of 93 miles. He was overtaken by the rain and obliged to take the train to Boston. The second run was made from Boston to Yarmouthville, Maine, a distance of 134 miles. Mr. Burbank left Boston at 4.30 A.M. and arrived at Yarmouthville at 8.30 P.M., spending one hour for rest at noon. The third run was from Yarmouthville to Poland Spring, a distance of 20 miles. On this last run he was joined by his friend, Mr. James R. Marston. The young men will return to Boston on their wheels.

Arrivals.

POLAND SPRING HOUSE.

FROM JULY 30 TO AUGUST 5, 1897.

Adams, E. T.	Memphis
Adams, Mr. and Mrs. A. H.	Haverhill
Athanasius, Fr.	Boston
Atherton, Mrs. W.	Boston
Allen, Mr. and Mrs. George O.	Scitnate, Mass.
Allen, Miss F. J.	Portland
Barnaby, Mr. and Mrs. Frank A.	Brooklyn
Belcher, Mrs. A. S.	Brockton
Bliss, Walter	Hartford
Bradley, M.	Haverhill
Baker, George F.	Hyannis
Belcher, Mr. and Mrs. J. White	Randolph, Mass.
Bertholf, Mrs. John C.	Rochester, N. Y.
Berri, Mrs. William	Brooklyn
Berri, Walter	Brooklyn
Berri, Herbert	Brooklyn
Billmyer, Mr. and Mrs. George S.	York, Pa.
Brush, Mrs. Edmund	Southampton, L. I.
Baines, Edward F.	Newton
Brown, Mr. and Mrs. F. H.	Waltham
Browne, Mrs. C. W.	Newark
Brett, Dr. and Mrs. George H.	Boston
Basset, Mr. and Mrs. W.	Boston
Barnes, Mrs. W. H.	New York
Blackford, Mr. and Mrs. Eugene G.	Brooklyn
Beyer, George W.	Portland
Beyer, Henry G.	Portland
Banks, S. S.	Bridgeport
Bolster, W. H.	Boston
Carpenter, F. W.	Providence
Carpenter, Miss S. T.	Providence
Carpenter, Miss Mary A.	Providence
Cole, William M.	New York
Cole, Fred S.	New York
Carman, Mr. and Mrs. Nelson G.	Brooklyn
Clarkson, Miss	Brooklyn
Chadbourn, Mr. and Mrs. E. R.	Lewiston
Cheever, Miss M. E.	Boston
Cheever, Mrs. James	Boston
Chick, Mrs. I. W.	Boston
Chick, Miss Mabel	Boston
Chick, Master William C.	Boston
Conway, Mrs. J. D.	Somerville
Conway, Miss Bessie	Somerville
Conway, H. A.	Somerville
Conyngham, Mrs. John N.	New York
Comstock, Mr. and Mrs. Arthur	Utica
Cook, Charles Sumner	Portland
Day, Mrs. A. S.	New Orleans
Davis, Charles C.	Pittsfield, Mass.
Davidson, Miss	Brooklyn
Douglass, Mrs. Albert, Jr.	New York
Douglass, Miss	New York
Dolnan, Mr. and Mrs. Robert	Philadelphia
Donald, J. W.	Boston
Du Puy, the Misses	New York
Dewey, Mr.	Portland
Dizer, Mrs. S. C.	Boston
Elliott, Mr. and Mrs. Alfred S.	Wilmington, Del.
Elliott, Miss Jessie L.	Wilmington, Del.
Ewell, Mrs. W. W.	Quincy
Elliot, Miss I. H. M.	New York
Evans, Miss	Brooklyn
Fall, Annie L.	Boston
Fillebrown, Miss Isabel	Boston
Fowler, A. B.	Boston
Fox, Mrs. Louis R.	Philadelphia
Fuller, B. B.	Auburn
Gifford, A. L.	New York
Gregory, Franklin H.	Brooklyn
Gibb, Miss	Brooklyn

Gattison, Mr. and Mrs. W. F.	Brooklyn
Gleason, Mr. and Mrs. H. P.	Newark
Gosholn, A. T.	Cincinnati
Gosholn, Miss A.	Cincinnati
Holbrook, Mrs. C. L.	Boston
Halvey, Mr. and Mrs. Huxley	Wilmington, Del.
Heitzel, Miss C. M.	New York
Hall, Daniel	New York
Hoeke, Mrs. W. H.	Washington
Hoeke, Miss	Washington
Horner, Miss E. M.	Philadelphia
Heppe, Mr. and Mrs. C. J.	Philadelphia
Heppe, Miss Virginia	Philadelphia
Heppe, Miss Alverda	Philadelphia
Inslee, Mrs. S.	New York
Jeremiah, Mrs. T. F.	New York
James, Mr. and Mrs. D. Willis	New York
Jordan, N. I.	Auburn
Knight, W. H.	New York
Knight, H. E.	New York
Kerr, Mrs. John C.	Brooklyn
Katsnel, Dr. and Mrs. D.	Germantown
Lewis, Rev. and Mrs. W. P.	Philadelphia
Lefavour, Mrs. J. W.	Beverly
Lea, Miss Alice M.	Wilmington, Del.
Lockwood, Rhodes G.	Boston
Lyford, Mr. and Mrs. C. D.	Boston
Marston, Gertrude M.	Lewiston
McGowan, T. P.	Portland
Matheson, S.	New York
Morse, Miss Florence W.	Brookline
Mitchell, Mr. and Mrs. J. G.	Toledo
Melcher, Arthur S.	Auburn
Marshall, Mrs. James	Newark
Mangel, Mr. and Mrs. G. A.	Camden, N. J.
Moulton, Mrs. Byron P.	Rosemont, Pa.
Morse, Mr. and Mrs. Albert H.	Boston
Meeks, Hamilton W.	Weehawken, N. J.
Martin, Mr. and Mrs. J. S.	New York
Marburg, Mrs. Christine	Baltimore
Marburg, the Misses	Baltimore
Mayo, A. N.	Springfield
Mohl, R. H.	Boston
Moore, Miss	New York
Mulqueen, Mr. and Mrs. M. J.	New York
Newell, Mrs. W. H.	Boston
Nugent, Mr. and Mrs. Dan. C.	St. Louis
Nugent, Louise	St. Louis
Nugent, D. Casey	St. Louis
Nugent, Morgan	St. Louis
Osgood, H. S.	Portland
O'Mara, Mrs. David	Newark
Perkins, Miss L. M.	Haverhill
Pearson, Miss	Harrisburg
Pearson, Miss M. H.	Harrisburg
Parker, Mrs. Kate H.	New York
Perkins, Mrs. William C.	Burlington, Ia.
Putnam, George J.	Brookline
Pinkerton, John I.	West Chester, Pa.
Prall, Miss E. A.	New York
Ridley, A. C.	Lewiston
Ridley, Albert S.	New York
Robertson, Miss J.	New York
Rixey, Dr. P. M.	Washington
Rollins, Miss L. M.	New York
Rollins, Miss E. V.	Washington
Rogers, A. G.	Portland
Kidrath, John Clark	Boston
Radcliffe, Miss	Boston
Salter, Thomas P.	New York
Skaats, Mrs. S.	New York
Skidmore, Mr. and Mrs. W. L.	New York
Skidmore, Miss	New York
Snowdon, Mr. and Mrs. A. Loudon	Philadelphia
Staples, E. L.	Portland
Sawtell, Mrs. T. A.	Malden
Sawtell, F. M.	Malden

Shaw, Mr. and Mrs. John	Quincy
Smith, Mr. and Mrs. Eugene H.	Boston
Spencer, Mr. and Mrs. J. E.	New York
Seavey, James F.	New York
Smith, Mrs. C. Thomas	Brooklyn
Sheldon, Mrs. C. W.	Brooklyn
Swett, Edward C.	Portland
Swett, Edward G.	Portland
Spencer, Mrs. M. K.	Brooklyn
Torsey, Archie V.	Auburn
Towel, Mr. and Mrs A. J.	Brookline
Towel, Miss Alice M.	Brookline
Towel, Miss Gertrude C.	Brookline
Tisdale, Mrs. Wilson	Quincy
Towle, Mr. and Mrs. H. H.	Portland
Ten Broeck, Mrs. N. E.	New York
Van Vechten, Miss Mary F.	Castleton, N. Y.
Vose, Mrs. E. F.	Portland
Winch, Joseph R.	Brookline
Winch, Mr. and Mrs. George Fred	Brookline
Wheelock, Mr. and Mrs. H. M.	Boston
Wright, Mrs. J. Hood	New York
Wight, Nellie A.	Lewiston
Wellington, Miss Grace	Orange, N. J.
Worthington, Mr. and Mrs. L. P.	Doylestown, Pa.
Worthington, Miss	Doylestown, Pa.
Williams, Mr. and Mrs. E. F.	St. Louis
Wescott, Mr. and Mrs. George P.	Portland
Whittaker, Benjamin	Brooklyn
Wight, Pearl	New Orleans
Welles, Fred J.	Brooklyn
Wood, J. M.	Chicago
Wyeth, Mr. and Mrs. F. H.	Philadelphia
Weiler, Mr. and Mrs. A.	Indianapolis
Young, Mr. and Mrs. F. W.	New York
Ziegler, Mr. and Mrs. Harry D.	Philadelphia
Ziegler, Miss C. F.	Philadelphia

MANSION HOUSE.

Beck, Mrs. F.	Yardville, N. J.
Bixby, Mrs. C. W.	Malden
Brown, Mr. and Mrs. George W	Boston
Chamberlain, Miss M. C.	Bahia, Brazil
De Windt, John	New York
Dean, Herbert	Taunton
Douglass, O. G.	Lewiston
Everitt, Mrs. Chas. F.	New York
Eastman, Mrs. Jeannette	Boston
Elsbree, Mr. and Mrs. T. D.	Valley Falls, R. I.
Filene, Edward A.	Boston
Gilbert, Mrs. F. A.	Brookline
Gilbert, Lester F.	Brookline
Gilbert, Frieda H.	Brookline
Hammond, Mrs. E. M.	Boston
Hyde, Mr. and Mrs. W. H.	Ridgway, Pa.
Hicks, Mr. and Mrs. J. Everett	Boston
Hughson, Mr. and Mrs. F.	New York
Hughson, Miss Annie J.	New York
Heath, C. E.	Taunton
Little, Thomas J.	Portland
Marshall, I. W.	Brooklyn
Millett, Mr. and Mrs. F. L.	South Paris
Morey, Frank A.	Lewiston
Merrill, C. E.	Freeport
Merriam, Mrs. N. P.	Malden
Olney, Mr. and Mrs. Samuel	Pawtucket
Olney, Mr. and Mrs. Walter T.	New Bedford
Smith, Mrs. Franklin	Philadelphia
Smith, Miss	Philadelphia
Sherman, Miss J. C.	Montclair, N. J.
Turner, R. H.	Portland
Woodman, Miss	Springfield

Tid-Bits.

"To what base uses may we not come," as the diamond quoted when turned into a ball field.

Sister Aurelia Mace will read selections from her new book, on Monday. See the notice in the office.

The Hampton students will appear in their characteristic entertainment in the Music Hall, on Tuesday evening.

Dr. P. M. Rixey of Washington, D. C., who has been spending a few days at the Poland Spring House, left August 2d.

Mr. and Mrs. W. L. Skidmore and Miss Skidmore, who spent July at Narragansett, have registered for the rest of the season at Poland Spring.

Mr. A. H. Adams and Mrs. Adams of Haverhill, Mass., have returned for the month of August. Mr. and Mrs. Adams always spend that month in Poland.

Mrs. Pio Echeverria, Mrs. C. Roeck, and Mr. Benjamin R. Lummis of New York, are at the Poland Spring House. They have just returned from Bar Harbor.

Mrs. E. J. Robinson, the skillful masseuse, now at the Poland Spring House, has found her services much in demand of late. There is nothing so refreshing as massage.

Mr. and Mrs. M. J. Mulqueen of New York, who are at the Poland Spring House, expect to be joined later by Mrs. Mulqueen's father and mother, Ex-Mayor and Mrs. Gilroy.

Mr. Campbell and Mr. Wampole played Mr. Read and Mr. Marsh eight sets of tennis Tuesday morning, August 3d. The score stood 6-2, 6-2, in favor of Mr. Read and Mr. Marsh.

Mrs. J. Hood Wright, Mrs. John N. Conyngham, and Miss Moore of New York, are now at Poland Spring, and occupying the north suite in the Maine State Building, and are thoroughly charming people. Mrs. Wright is the widow of Mr. J. Hood Wright, former partner of the well-known bankers, J. P. Morgan & Co.

It may be that you have not been down to see the Indians in their cool retreat near the Spring. If not, lose not a moment, but hie to the tent of Hiawatha, and purchase bows and arrows, lovely boxes made of sweet grass, and various things which the noble red man and his squaw know so well how to make. You will find the dweller in tents a most interesting person, although civilized.

Beauty and Grace.

THE hop at the Poland Spring House Saturday evening, July 31st, was a grand success. The ball-room with its delicate tints, the soft strains of music, and the ladies in their beautiful gowns, made a picture long to be remembered. Where so many were present we can mention only a few, but all were charming, attractive, and elegantly attired.

Mrs. Blackford was becomingly dressed in lavender silk, with white lace trimmings.

Miss Richardson, in gray silk, with corals.

Miss Soria, white organdie, with lace.

Miss Ada Blackford was charming in gray taffeta with white trimmings.

Miss Vose made a pretty picture in white figured silk, white chiffon and green ribbons.

Miss Eddy was daintily attired in a pink organdie.

Miss Blackford wore cerise taffeta with chiffon.

Miss Rosenheim was beautifully gowned in striped taffeta, pearl trimmings, and mousselaine de soie.

Mrs. Vose was charming in black, with green trimmings and diamonds.

Mrs. Corbin was elegantly gowned in lavender brocade silk, lace and jewels.

The Misses Peterson were daintily attired in white organdie with yellow ribbons.

Miss Olive Gale looked sweet in a figured organdie over pink.

Miss Carrol wore blue silk with chiffon.

Mrs. Palmer, a beautiful dress of white dotted Swiss muslin, over heliotrope silk with lace stripes.

Miss Conover was lovely in a figured blue taffeta with white chiffon.

Miss King wore white muslin over pink silk.

Mrs. Peterson, a black and white brocade silk, velvet ribbons, lace, and jewels.

Mrs. Spencer, gray silk, rich lace, and diamonds.

Mrs. Osgood, a combination of black and white silk with red velvet trimmings.

Mrs. Murray, a black silk skirt, and white chiffon waist.

Miss Englis was charming in yellow satin, white lace and velvet trimmings.

Mrs. Wescott, brocade silk, beautiful lace, and jewels.

Mrs. Conover, green silk, with velvet and white chiffon.

Mrs. Ripley, gray silk, trimmed with cherry silk and white lace.

Mrs. Eddy, black silk, lace, and diamonds.

Mrs. Ziegler, lavender silk striped with black, a beautiful lace.

Mrs. Carson, black skirt with pink bodice.

Mrs. Mathews, white silk with jewels.

Miss Underwood, heliotrope silk, trimmed with chiffon and violets.

Mrs. Little was charming in a figured grenadine over black silk, lace, and jewels.

Mrs. Thornton, white brocade silk with yellow trimmings.

Mrs. Griffin wore a beautiful gown of white brocade silk with black and white lace trimmings.

Mrs. Bartlett, gray silk, rare lace, and diamonds.

Mrs. Thomas, black silk with chiffon.

Mrs. Van Beil, cherry taffeta with black and white lace trimmings.

Mrs. Bright, black silk, beautiful lace and jewels.

Mrs. Oaks, white silk, striped with gray, and rich lace.

Miss Hobart was lovely in white mull over lavender.

Mrs. Mitchell, black silk with lace, and diamonds.

Mrs. Gleason, figured muslin with lavender trimmings.

Mrs. Berri, black brocade satin, with Persian bodice, and diamonds.

Mrs. George Osgood wore a beautiful gown of striped lavender silk, velvet trimmings with white chiffon.

Mrs. Keene, lavender silk, lace, and diamonds.

Mrs. Hoffman, black silk and beautiful jewels.

Mrs. Meeks, an exquisite gown of lavender and green striped satin, trimmed with lace and velvet, and beautiful jewels.

New Books.

FROM JOSHUA BENNETT HOLDEN.

Census of Massachusetts—1895.
Agriculture of Massachusetts—1896.
Board of Education, 1895-6.
Year-Book, Department of Agriculture, 1895.
Report of Boston Transit Company, 1896.
Memorial of Frederic Greenhalge.
A Legislative Souvenir (Massachusetts), 1897.
Highways of Massachusetts—1896.
Manual of the General Court (Massachusetts), 1897.
Boston, Illustrated. By George W. Englehardt.

FROM MRS. F. F. OLNEY.
Equality. By Edward Bellamy.

FROM MRS. J. P. BATES.
The Broom-Squire. By S. Baring-Gould.

FROM MRS. WILLARD A. VOSE.
Heidi. By Louise Brooks.

FROM MISS E. A. PRALL.
Hiram Golf's Religion; by George H. Hepworth.
They Met in Heaven; by George H. Hepworth.
Don Orsino; by F. Marion Crawford.

FROM MRS. N. E. TEN BROECK.
The One Who Looked On; by F. F. Montrésor.

Portland.

Have you ever been to Portland? If not you should not fail to do so, for it is a very beautiful and interesting city,—Munjoy Hill and its observatory, Western Promenade, the birthplace of Longfellow, and much more than we have space to mention. The Preble House is next door to the Longfellow Homestead, and not far from the very fine statue of the poet. The streets in the residential districts are beautifully shaded, and innumerable small steamers ply between the city and the beautiful islands in the harbor, which, by the way, is the only one which the Great Eastern could enter.

Longfellow's poem, "My Lost Youth," is in reference to his birth city, and how beautiful the lines—

"Often in thought I wander down
The pleasant streets of the dear old town,
And my youth comes back to me."

Mr. and Mrs. I. W. Chick and Miss Mabel Chick of Boston, are at the Poland Spring House for the month of August. Mr. Chick is of the firm of John H. Pray & Sons.

The Hill=Top

IS PRINTED AT THE

Office of the Lewiston Journal.

If you wish work executed in like style, address

⬗———— JOURNAL OFFICE, LEWISTON, ME.

THE ALPS OF NEW ENGLAND.

New Mount Pleasant House

WHITE MOUNTAINS.

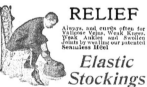

IT STANDS AT THE HEAD.

Unrivalled in Popularity!
Unsurpassed in Location!
Unapproached in Patronage!

THE

POLAND * SPRING * HOUSE

IS A SUPERB ILLUSTRATION OF

● ● ● SUCCESS ● ● ●

EMBRACING AS IT DOES

ALL THE DESIRABLE FEATURES

EXPECTED IN THIS

The Leading Resort of America,

WHILE THE

MAINE STATE BUILDING

WITH ITS

SUPERB ART FEATURES

IS UNEQUALLED BY ANY SIMILAR ENTERPRISE

IN THE WORLD.

●●●

HIRAM RICKER & SONS (Incorporated),

PROPRIETORS.

MAINE STATE BUILDING.

The Hill Top

POLAND SPRINGS, SO. POLAND, ME.

HARRY C. WILKINSON

THE HILL·TOP·

VOL. IV.   SUNDAY MORNING, AUGUST 15, 1897.   No. 7.

The Kuntz Orchestral Club.

MR. DANIEL KUNTZ, }
MR. AUGUST KUNTZ, } . . . . Violins.
MR. ARTHUR BROOKE, ... Flute.
MR. ADOLF CANNIS, ... Cornet.
MR. ERICH LOEFFLER, ... 'Cello.
MR. EMIL GOLDE, ... Bass.
MR. CARL HAUSER, ... Piano.

WE take great pride in the excellence of our
orchestra, and feeling that many of the
guests who have daily enjoyed the exquisite
music which they have provided, may feel
a further interest in knowing something of them,
and of seeing a complete reproduction of the Kuntz

Orchestral Club in the HILL-TOP, we present a brief sketch of each member.

Mr. D. Kuntz, the leader of the Kuntz Orchestral Club, is so well known to the guests of the hotel that he needs no introduction. He has been at the Poland Spring House for several seasons; in fact it would scarcely seem like the same hotel if Mr. Kuntz were absent from the Music Room. He was born in South Germany, but came to this country when a very young man. He studied music in his native city and also in Paris. He has been one of the first violins of the Boston Symphony Orchestra since its commencement. He is also first violin of the Boston Philharmonic Quartette, and has been a member of the leading quartettes of Boston; he was also a member of the Bairetith Festival Orchestra. His violin solos are always thoroughly enjoyed by the guests of the hotel. He is also a skillful canoeist, and may be seen any fine day on the lake with Mrs. Kuntz.

Mr. Auguste Kuntz, brother of the leader of the Kuntz Orchestral Club, is also a member of the Boston Symphony Orchestra, having been engaged by Mr. Paur last season. He is also quite a familiar figure at the Poland Spring House. He has played with most of the principal orchestras and organizations of this country; among others, Siedl's Orchestra and the Philharmonic Orchestra of New York. He was born in Germany, but, like his brother, came to this country when very young. He commenced the study of the violin at a very early age. He is the expert swimmer and oarsman of the club.

Mr. Erich Loeffler, whose beautiful 'cello solos are one of the features of the concerts, is one of the earliest members of the Boston Symphony Orchestra, having been with the orchestra since the second season of its organization. He is a native of Germany, and was a fellow-student with the celebrated Victor Herbert. He is always in the orchestras of the high-class concerts in and around Boston. He looks forward with pleasure each season to his visit to Poland Spring. Being an expert fisherman, he is on one of the lakes whenever the weather permits.

Mr. Emil Golde, the bass of the club, hails from Dresden, Saxony, but has lived in this country for a number of years. He has been a member of several of the finest organizations in various parts of the States, and has played with the Boston Symphony Orchestra for eight consecutive seasons. He is a familiar figure at all the concerts of the Handel and Haydn, St. Cecilia, and other high-class concerts in Boston. He is also a deep student of astronomy, and leader of philosophical works, but this does not prevent him being a fine swimmer and lover of aquatic sports generally.

Mr. Arthur Brooke is an Englishman and came to this country in 1888. He is, since the commencement of last season, a member of the Boston Symphony Orchestra. He comes of a musical family, being one of three brothers, also musicians; his father was one of seven brothers, all musicians. He has played in the principal orchestras and concerts of England, including DeJong's and Sir C. Halle's orchestras of Manchester, and the Leeds Festival Orchestra, under Sir Arthur Sullivan, and all the leading choral and philharmonic concerts of the North of England. He has toured several times through the United States, Canada, British Columbia, and Mexico, with the Emma Juch Grand Opera Company and other high-class organizations. This is his second season at the Poland Spring House. Mr. Brooke is an enthusiastic bicyclist, having ridden with Mr. Kuntz to Mechanic Falls without being thrown off above once.

Mr. Carl Hauser, the pianist of the club, is on his first visit to the hotel, where he is already a great favorite. He was born in San Francisco, Cal., but removed while quite young to Cincinnati, where he was later a professor at the Conservatory of Music. He studied in Leipsic. His home is in New York, where he is well known as pianist and violinist, playing with the leading orchestras and concerts of that city. We sincerely trust this will not be the last visit of Mr. Hauser to the Spring. He is a devotee of the piscatorial sport, and holds the record of having lost more lines in the lake than any fisherman in Poland.

Mr. A. Cannis, the cornet, comes from Saxony, a country noted for its brass instrument performers. He has lived in this country a number of years. He was a member of Theodore Thomas's celebrated orchestra, also of the Metropolitan Opera House orchestra of last season. He plays with the principal orchestras and military bands of New York City, where he makes his home.

The concerts are given daily at 11.30 A.M. except Sunday, when it takes place in the evening. The orchestra also provides the music for the evening hops, which are so favorite a feature of Poland Spring.

The very excellent photograph was taken by the Notman Photographic Company, and adds another to the gems which they constantly provide.

Musical Programme.

SUNDAY, AUGUST 15, 1897.

1. Overture—Zampa.		Herold.
2. Violin Solo—Legende.		Wieniawski.
	Mr. August Kuntz.	
3. Selection—Mignon.		Thomas.
4. 'Cello Solo—Berceuse.		Godard.
	Spanish Song.	Abel.
	Mr. E. Loeffler.	
5. Cujus Animum—From Stabat Mater.		Rossini.

Musical Progiamme.

SUNDAY EVENING, AUGUST 8, 1897.

Note.—The Managing Editoi wishes to apologize for the omission of the musical piogiamme last week. The copy was fuinished the Musical Editoi, who gave it piomptly to the City Editoi, but thiough some oveisight on the pait of the Night Editoi it was oveilooked. The Night Editoi haviug apologized to the City Editoi and the Musical Editoi, the Managing Editoi has decided, on matuie delibeiation, not to call in the Fighting Editoi, but to condone the offeuse. So heie it is, as a mattei of iecoid :

1. Maich.	Lachnei.
2. Violin Solo—Piize Song, fiom Meisteisingei.	Wagnei.
3. Selection—Der Freischütz. . . .	. Webei.
4. Piano Solo—	
a. Aufschwung.	Schumann.
b. Berceuse.	. Giieg.
c. Gavotte.	Sgambati.
5. Minuet—Fiom Oipheus.	. Gluck.
6. Hungaiian Rhapsodie.	. Liszt

Mrs. Cail Hausei assisted the oichestia. She is au excellent pianiste, and her solo numbeis weie admiiably iendeied. Iu assisting the oichestia in the Hungaiian Rhapsodie by Liszt, she showed she was a fine ensemble playei. Mrs. Hausei studied in the Cincinnati College of Music, and latei became one of the iustiuctois in that institution. She went to Beilin and became the pupil of the celebiated piano teachei, X. Schaiwenka.

It is Said to be True

That the ninth symphony is the gieatest woik that exists, for the piano.

That the biggest faim in the woild is in southwest Louisiana, and embiaces 1,500,000 acies.

That theie is a stained glass window in St. Cuthbeit's Chuich, Philbeach Gaidens, Kensington, in which St. Cuthbert is iepiesented playing golf.

That a lady was maiiied in Piovidence, R. I., in Decembei last, for the sixth time, to which ceiemony foui of her pievious husbands came.

That Napoleon was only twenty-seven when he commanded the aimy in Italy.

That moie cases of consumption aie found among needle makeis and tile makeis than in any othei class.

That the couit of Pope Leo XIII. compiises one thousand peisons.

That sixteen haiis make one baileycoin, and thiee baileycoins make au inch. Now we know what a haii-bieadth escape is.

That the whole woild's coinage of gold amounts to $3.582,605,000, and of silvei to $1.042,700,000.

That theie are twenty-two allusions to the east wind in the Bible, nineteen being uncomplimentary.

Art Notes.

CHARLES H. DAVIS, who contiibutes two veiy excellent pictuies to the Poland Spiing Exhibition, and who is one of the best aitists in Ameiica, was boin in Amesbuiy, Mass., and aftei study in Boston, began exhibiting at the age of 20, when he went to Paiis and studied undei Boulangei and Lefebvre. He ieceived the gold medal of the Ameiican Art Association, New Yoik, in 1886, also $2,000 piize, 1887 ; honoiable mention, Paiis Salon, 1887 ; silvei medal, Paiis Exposition, 1889 ; Palmei piize of $500, Chicago, 1890 ; gold medal, Massachusetts Chaiitable Mechanics' Association, 1890. His woiks hang in Metropolitan Museum of Art, New Yoik, Art Institute, Chicago, and Pennsylvania Academy of Fine Aits. His pictuies aie Nos. 23 and 24 in Alcoves C and E.

Haiiiette Wood Robinson is a Maine aitist of decided talent, her woik showing a maiked advance ovei pievious exhibits. She iesides in Aubuin, and is au enthusiastic woikei. Her "Strawbeiiies" iu Alcove E, No. 94, show excellent feeling and aie stiong in coloi. The one of "Oianges and Watei Bottle," No. 95 in the same alcove, is also a veiy excellent pictuie, which should add to her ieputation as an aitist.

Heniy W. Rice is a Boston aitist who has woiked his way to the fiont, and who for yeais has been doing good woik. His watei-colois are chaiacteiized by a iichness and waimth of coloi and a geneial pictuiesqueness which is found to be pleasing. His woiks are hung at the Boston Art Club, the Joidan Gallery, and othei notable galleiies.

Helen M. Knowlton piesents foui of her pleasing pictuies this season. Nos. 66 to 69, the lattei numbei in Alcove B being a paiticulaily well-modeled head, the subject being a favoiite one with aitists. No. 68 in the same alcove, "Algeiian Dancing Girl," is also a veiy attiactive woik. Miss Knowlton was a pupil of William Moiiis Hunt and Fiank Duveneck, and is an exhibitoi at the Boston Art Club, Tennessee Centennial, also the piincipal exhibitions in New Yoik, Philadelphia, Chicago, aud elsewheie.

Chambeilin-Lewis Conceit.

The enteitainment given Thuisday, by Ella M. Chambeilin, the whistling soloist, and Emma Tuttle James, was one of the most successful given this season. Both are aitists in theii paiticulai line, and Mrs. James's ieadings, or moie piopeily iecitations, showed the expeiience and tiaining of the tiue aitist which she is. They should be a most valuable addition to the list of enteitaineis at any of the iesoits.

Children's Sea-Shore House.

AFTER the service held on Sunday, August 1st, by Rev. C. H. McClellan, D.D., of Lakewood, N. J., a collection was taken for the benefit of the Children's Sea-Shore House of Atlantic City, N. J. It is with pleasure that we announce that one hundred dollars was raised for this object, which amount has been duly forwarded (and acknowledged in an interesting note). A few notes concerning this most worthy institution may be of interest here. It was the first of its kind in the United States, and was opened in a small cottage in 1872, being incorporated as the "Children's Sea-Shore House for Invalid Children." From a small beginning it grew steadily to its present size, until now it has accommodations for about one hundred and twenty-five children and thirty mothers. Its object is to maintain at the sea-shore an institution in which children of the poorer classes, suffering from non-contagious diseases, or debility incident to the hot weather and a crowded city, may have good nursing and medical care, without regard to creed, color, or nationality. Any boy under twelve years of age, and any girl under twenty, suffering in the ways described, can be received when properly certified, and have all the care and benefit of the institution. The house is under most admirable discipline. It has at its head Dr. William H. Bennett, one of the leading physicians of Philadelphia; it employs a number of skilled, trained nurses, and it receives its patients largely through the endorsement of physicians in charge of the city hospitals. From the statistics published annually, it is seen that a large percentage of the children are permanently cured, who without such care and the benefit of a stay in the invigorating air of the sea-shore, would remain crippled and feeble through a miserable life, since their poverty at home would deprive them of all chance of relief. The institution is entirely undenominational and depends for its support largely on voluntary contributions. Poland Spring has done its part generously, and we believe the donors of this purse of one hundred dollars will be none the less happy in their summer outing from thinking they have aided in giving a new lease of life to these little ones, for hath not the Master said, "Inasmuch as ye have done it unto one of the least of these my brethren, ye have done it unto me."

Progressive Whist.

One of the most delightful occasions of the season was the progressive whist party, given Wednesday evening, August 11th.

Mr. Carpenter gave a silver cup for the lady or gentleman taking the highest number of tricks during the evening. The game lasted two hours, and there were nineteen tables. At half-past ten the bell sounded, and a committee of five, Mr. Osgood, Mr. Ives, Mr. Mayo, Mr. Baker, and Mr. Danielson, was selected to count the number of tricks on each card and award the prizes.

The first to be considered was the silver cup, which was won by Miss E. Marburg, who had 182 tricks. The first ladies' prize, a sofa pillow, went to Mrs. Perkins, who had 180 tricks; the second prize, a table spread, to Mrs. C. G. Mitchell, who had 177 tricks. Mrs. Van Beil had 173 tricks and won the third ladies' prize, a silver pin-box. The consolation prize, a bon-bon spoon, went to Mrs. Holbrook.

The first gentlemen's prize, a Dresden ink well, was won by Mr. A. Gilbert, who had 181 tricks. Mr. Ives gained the second, a desk set, 180 tricks; Mr. Boyd, the third prize, a Dresden candle-stick, 176 tricks. Mrs. Williams won the consolation prize, an umbrella strap. The silver cup was beautiful, and the ladies who selected the prizes showed exquisite taste.

Moonlight Straw Ride.

Mr. and Mrs. S. Ross Campbell gave a straw ride Tuesday, August 10th. The party started at half-past eight, and by the sound of horns and bells one knew they were off for a jolly time. The party included Mr. and Mrs. Gallagher, Mr. and Mrs. Brown, Mr. and Mrs. Kuntz, Miss Woodman, Miss Mary Marsh, Mr. deWindt, Mr. Allyn Marsh, Mr. Harry Wampole, Mr. Robert Marsh, Master Albert Wampole, and Arthur Marsh. They went to Poland Corner and around the lower lake. Upon their return they were served with refreshments at Mr. and Mrs. Campbell's cottage. The cutting of a birthday cake belonging to Mr. Allyn Marsh added to the enjoyment of the occasion. The evening was beautiful, and every one pronounced the ride the best of the season.

Children's Column.

Tell (for you can) what it is to be wise.
'Tis but to know how little can be known;
To see all others' faults and feel our own.
—*Pope.*

"How did the Queen of Sheba travel when she went to see Solomon?" asked the teacher of her Sunday-school class of little girls. No one ventured an answer. "If you had studied your lesson, you could not have helped knowing," said their teacher. "Now look at the verses again. Could she have gone by the cars?" "Yes'm," said a little girl at the end of the class. "She went by steam-cars." "Did she, indeed? Well, Louise, we would like to know how you found that out." "In the second verse," responded the child, "it says 'she came with a very great train.'"

LITTLE LOUISE.

Little Louise, our three-year-old,
With eyes of hazel, and curls of gold,
And cheek with a cunning dimple dent,
And mouth like a Cupid's bow down-bent,
From her little couch at her father's side
Arose, in the flush of morning-tide;
And, "Mamma, papa, dood-morning, I say.
Papa, I was naughty yesterday,
But I'll tell you why" (with a positive nod
Of the curly head): "'Twas cause the dood Dod,
Who helps little children, went away
For a dreat long visit yesterday;
But now He's tome back again, and so
Louise will be dood to-day, you know."
Dear little one, in whose innocent heart
The demons of doubt and unrest have no part,
Who looks with unwavering trust above,
Nor questions the truth that "God is love."
May the good Lord never be farther away
From little Louise than yesterday!
—*Helen L. Churchill, in Harper's Young People.*

Little Edward, while driving with his mother, noticed the horses shaking their heads. He said: "Mamma! See! the horses are courtesying to each other."

Murray (surveying the new baby sister with a dissatisfied air, evidently not admiring the little red, puckered visage)—"Mamma, won't we be ashamed to take her out?"

An Episcopal clergyman's wife living in southern Texas sends to Mrs. Hiram Ricker a large quantity of Mexican drawn work. Mrs. Ricker will be glad to show it to all who will call at her cottage. It is charity work, and the prices are very reasonable.

New Books.

FROM MRS. J. REED WHIPPLE.
Flowers of Field, Hill, and Swamp. By Caroline A. Creevey.

FROM F. W. RICE.
America's Successful Men. By Henry Hall. 2 vols.

Sunday Service.

Rev. William H. Bolster of Dorchester, Mass., preached in the Music Hall, Sunday, August 8th, at 11 A.M. His text was from II. Corinthians, 11:3—"The simplicity that is in Christ." The sermon was excellent. The hall was well filled, as it always is when Mr. Bolster preaches.

Tid-Bits.

Mr. Henry C. Sears of Boston is with us.

Mr. G. D. Pratt of Elkhart, Indiana, is with us.

Mr. C. H. Colburn of Boston is at Poland Spring.

Mr. J. L. Putnam of Chicago arrived Monday, August 9th.

Miss Alice Putnam of Boston is registered at Poland Spring.

Mr. J. D. Conway of Boston is at the Poland Spring House.

Mr. W. Pearre of Cumberland, Md., is at Poland Spring.

Mrs. H. McCoy of Brooklyn is at the Poland Spring House.

Mr. and Mrs. J. W. Danielson of Providence, R. I., have returned.

Mr. D. J. Morrison of Savannah, Ga., is at the Mansion House.

Mr. B. F. Cole of Washington, D. C., arrived Saturday, August 7th.

Mr. J. F. Vaile of Denver, Col., arrived Saturday, August 7th.

Mr. H. S. Hale of Philadelphia is at the Poland Spring House.

Mr. and Mrs. H. C. Swain of New York are at the Poland Spring House.

Mrs. John C. Bertholf of Rochester, N. Y., is at the Poland Spring House.

Mr. H. P. Woodbury and Mrs. Woodbury of Beverly, Mass., are with us.

In two days the names of Hall, Hill, Hale, and Hull are found on the register.

Mr. James F. May and Mrs. May of Chicago, are at the Poland Spring House.

Mr. Thomas S. Kurtz of New York is registered at the Poland Spring House.

Miss Blanche C. Myers and Miss Juna V. Pyle of Jersey City are at Poland Spring.

Mr. Thomas P. Salter of New York has rejoined his brother at Poland Spring.

Mr. Nelson G. Carman and Mrs. Carman of Brooklyn, N. Y., are at Poland Spring.

Mr. Alpheus G. Rogers of Portland registered at the Poland Spring House, August 7th.

Mrs. Evans T. Walker and Miss Watson of New York are at the Poland Spring House.

Mr. and Mrs. Pearl Wight and Miss Wight of New Orleans arrived Saturday, August 7th.

Mr. John T. Underwood has rejoined his sister, Miss Underwood, at the Poland Spring House.

Mr. and Mrs. Charles R. Ruggles of Chicago are at Poland Spring.

Mr. G. C. Schleier and Mrs. Schleier of Denver, Col., arrived Monday, August 9th.

Among the welcome guests, Tuesday, August 10th, was Mr. Amos R. Little of Philadelphia.

Mr. T. Osborne Shepard of New York and Miss Shepard of Salem, are at the Poland Spring House.

Mr. William W. Smith and Mrs. Smith of Poughkeepsie, N. Y., are at the Poland Spring House.

Mr. George A. Calkin and Mr. George W. Roach of St. John, N. B., are at the Mansion House.

Mr. H. F. Jordan of Washington, D. C., registered at the Poland Spring House, Friday, August 6th.

Mr. Abram Atwood and Mrs. Atwood of Auburn, took dinner at the Mansion House, Sunday, August 8th.

Mr. E. H. Lawry and his son, George A. Lawry, of Rockland, Me., spent Saturday, August 7th, at the Poland Spring House.

Among the welcome guests August 7th were Col. and Mrs. Joseph A. Ingalls, Miss Claire Ingalls, and Horace Bright Ingalls.

Mr. Clarence Swan and Mr. Samuel Swan of Bridgeport, Conn., have joined Mr. and Mrs. James Swan at the Poland Spring House.

Mr. William A. Marburg of New York, a member of the well-known firm, Marburg Brothers of Baltimore, is at the Poland Spring House.

Miss Whitman is proficient in the art of manicuring and chiropody, and is at Poland every season, where her ability is constantly put to the test.

Mr. and Mrs. Charles Bong of Boston, Miss Edith E. Allen of Arlington, Mr. F. L. Wood and Mr. Lyman Gibbs of Boston, are spending a few weeks at Poland Spring.

Inquire of any one who has ever stopped at Haddon Hall, and they will tell you of its excellence, and of the superior qualities possessed by Messrs. Leeds & Lippincott as hosts.

Mr. and Mrs. C. H. Chappell and their friend, Mrs. B. A. Eckhert of Chicago, registered at the Poland Spring House, August 9th. Mr. Chappell is General Manager of the Chicago & Alton Railroad.

There are people who doubtless find elastic stockings, knee caps, or anklets, of value, and in that case the best are desirable. Curtis & Spindell of Lynn, whose advertisement appears on the cover, are to be highly recommended for quality and price.

SWAMPSCOTT, MASS., August 1, 1897.

To the Hill-Top:

DRIVING on the North Shore Road through the town of Swampscott, just after one passes Phillips Beach, one notices an inconspicuous entrance to a driveway leading down toward the shore, and if one is an old frequenter or of an investigating turn of mind you will turn in, follow down the driveway through an avenue of trees that gives you a delightful feeling of anticipation as to what is beyond, then down a little hill just right for coasting on your wheel, and there you are—in front of the famous Lincoln House.

You alight under the inviting *porte-cochere* and immediately walk around the porch to find the ocean, the salt breeze from which you already feel, and as you stand on the broad deck-like porch on the front of the house and think of the people in the hot city, you feel what a delightful place you have fallen into, or, to be more truthful, onto, as you are out on a point in the ocean, but a mild and gentle ocean, sheltered as it is by Nahant on one side and Gallaupe's Point on the other. The breeze is just as cool and invigorating, however, as if you were many miles out to sea. The view is superb, with the picturesque variety of the rocks which jut out into the water and make tiny, sandy beaches, where the bathing is both safe and delightful. In front of the house the water comes almost to the porch, and in a severe storm the spray dashes up almost to one's very doorstep.

On the east is a fine tennis court in the unusually fine grove of trees, and just back of that is a row of comfortable cottages, where one can be a little more secluded and yet enjoy the pleasures of the hotel.

Certainly the greatest attraction of the Lincoln House is its situation, but there are others which make it more popular than ever this season. This is shown by the fullness of the register and the numbers of disappointed people who cannot get accommodations. As one looks over the register it might almost be for bachelor apartments, the masculine names predominate to such an extent. The Lincoln House might trade off a few of these men for some of the charming young ladies of the Poland Spring House very advantageously on both sides. At the same time, these young men are another of the attractions, according to the summer girl.

Then, to speak of personal comforts, the sleeping rooms are so clean and comfortable, and the servants so pleasant and willing, that one is not troubled by the necessity of spending a part of each day in these same rooms. The circular says the dining-room is the finest on the coast, and if one is not a grumbling dyspeptic they can agree most decidedly with the circular. The view from each of the many windows is equally delightful, and to eat dinner gazing out on the sunset while the orchestra is playing is quite romantically charming. Then the table is so excellent and the service so good that one can truthfully compliment Mr. Ryder on his successful management, and you who read the HILL-TOP, if you decide to try the North Shore next season for a while, and stop at the Lincoln House, I am sure you will be welcomed so heartily and entertained so royally that you will not be disappointed and regret your decision; but remember one thing, to be sure and come directly from there back to dear old Poland Spring again for the rest of the season.

JULIA CARPENTER.

A PLAIN DIRECTION.

Canon Knox-Little told a good story once at a church congress. He said he remembered a lych gate in front of a beautiful church, which had been restored and made very nice. There was painted over the door, "This is the Gate of Heaven," and underneath was the large notice, "Go round the other way."—*Household Words.*

EVIDENCE OF EXTENSIVE TRAVELING.

"Berge must have traveled a great deal."

"Yes, he doesn't seem to know much about any one place."—*Chicago Journal.*

FRANK CARLOS GRIFFITH. | Editors.
NETTIE M. RiCKER, |

PUBLISHED EVERY SUNDAY MORNING DURING THE MONTHS
OF JULY, AUGUST, AND SEPTEMBER, IN THE INTERESTS OF

POLAND SPRING AND ITS ViSiTORS.

All contributions relative to the guests of Poland Spring
will be thankfully received.

To insure publication, all communications should reach the
editors not later than Wednesday preceding day of issue.

All parties desiring rates for advertising in the HILL-TOP
should write the editors for same.

The subscription price of the HILL-TOP is $1.00 for the
season, post-paid. Single copies will be mailed at 10c. each.

Address,

EDITORS "HiLL-TOP,"
Poland Spring House,
South Poland, Maine.

PRINTED AT JOURNAL OFFICE, LEWISTON.

Sunday, August 15, 1897.

Editorial.

"O Solitude! where are the charms
That sages have seen in thy face?"

THESE are the words Cowper puts into the
mouth of Alexander Selkirk, probably in the
supposition that he was getting too much of
a good thing; for a little solitude is good, but
solitude in large blocks is undesirable.

It is questionable, also, if the hermit, even,
does not feel, way down in his heart, with the poet
who sings—

"How sweet, how passing sweet, is solitude!
But grant me still a friend in my retreat,
Whom I may whisper, Solitude is sweet."

These thoughts were impressed upon us in
taking an early Sunday morning stroll to that
lovely point down by the lower lake, where the
lofty pines stand patient sentinels, and where
scarcely a sound, save that of a borer in a dead
trunk, was heard, and the gentle lapping of the
tiny waves upon the pebbly shore.

It was solitude, and it was sweet; but to be
left to the utter absence of sounds, never to hear
the voice of a friend, the bark of a dog, or the
mew of a cat, to become a hermit absolutely and
indefinitely, presents more horrors and dangers to
the mind than the temptations of a great city.

Some occupation, some social intercourse, some
noise, and some silence, is necessary, but, like
water, even be it never so pure and healthful, one
cannot live on one thing alone, and should recognize that fact, and also that possibly when your
period for noise may be on your calendar, that
may be the period for another's quiet, and frame
your acts to disconcert your neighbor as little
as you can.

Unlike a little learning, which is a dangerous
thing, a little solitude, Milton says, "is best society," but that depends very largely upon the individual, and the reasons for the sentence.

The Mineral Exhibit.

Few mineralogical specimens excite such exclamations of wonder as those of limpid quartz,
penetrated by tiny, needle-like crystals of rutile.
In some marvellous specimens from Brazil the long
golden-red rutile crystals are so thickly matted as
to give a decided and beautiful color to the mass.

The turquoise leads all American gems in the
value of the annual product, New Mexico having
yielded $50,000 worth in 1895. The turquoise in
its native rock may be seen in the Maine Building.

The beautiful green feldspar known as Amazon
stone was a very rare mineral until 1875, when a
new find was made on Pike's Peak. This locality
was forty miles from any village and seven miles
from a road, and so highly prized was the mineral
that a new road was constructed for the latter distance across lofty peaks solely to gain specimens
for the cabinets of collectors. Most of the supply
was secured by Dr. A. E. Foote. The quantity
was large enough to cause a fall to about a hun-
dredth of former prices, but we understand the
mineral is again becoming difficult to obtain, and
those who secure specimens now may soon find
reason to consider themselves fortunate. Attention
is called to the remarkably fine large specimen at
Poland. Mr. Chadbourne is here every Thursday,
all day.

The Art Store.

What this neat and attractive Poland feature
has not, it would be difficult to say; but gold dress
trimmings, bureau covers, sofa cushions, decorative
hangings, etc., are seen in profusion. Every
known fancy stitch is shown and taught, and the
Mexican drawn work is of an elegant nature.

Progressive Euchre.

The largest progressive euchre party of the season was given Friday evening, August 6th.

Eighty of the guests gathered in the amusement room, which had been prettily decorated by Mrs. Sherman, the house-keeper. On one mantel-piece in the center was a beautiful oil painting of nasturtiums by Mr. Fenety. Around this, Mrs. Sherman placed ferns, and at each end a bunch of nasturtiums peeped out from under the green. So perfect was the painting that it was difficult to tell which was nature and which was art. The opposite mantel was a combination of ferns and white flowers. The centre-table was graced by a handsome bouquet, and around this were clustered snowy white packages containing the prizes.

There were twenty tables. Sixteen games were played, and the highest number gained was twelve. Mrs. Munger won the first ladies' prize, a centre-piece; Miss Ziegler the second, a statuette; Mrs. Mulqueen the third, a jewel case. The fourth went to Mrs. Boyd, a Dresden case for jewels; and Mrs. Collins won the consolation prize, a pretty memorandum tablet.

Three cut for the first gentlemen's prize. Mrs. Perkins cut a nine spot, Mr. Mitchell an eight spot, Mr. Keene a seven. Mrs. Perkins won the first prize, a cut-glass vase; Mr. Mitchell the second, a mirror with silver mountings; Mr. Keene the third, a silver knife. Mr. Winch gained the fourth prize, a silver pen-holder; and the consolation prize went to Colonel Talbot, silver-mounted sleeve elastics.

The prizes were exquisite, and the ladies who selected them are to be congratulated upon their excellent taste.

It is a Curious Fact

That Wordsworth called Burns's "Scots wha hae wi' Wallace bled," trash, stuff, and miserable inanity.

That Horace Walpole considered Dante extravagant, absurd, and disgusting.

That the celebrated Downing Street, London, world-famous as the official residence of the First Lord of the Treasury, was named from a native American, George Downing of Boston, Mass.

There is no such term in heraldry as bar sinister.

That 10,283 words have been written with a pen, upon a postal card, perfectly legible with a microscope.

That the term "The Iron Duke" was originally applied to an iron steamboat named the Duke of Wellington, but so fitted the characteristics of the famed general, it was soon applied to him.

That Napoleon III. died at 10.45 A.M., precisely the hour the great clock of the Tuileries stopped, when the palace was burned by the Commune.

That William III., Queen Anne, George I., George II., George III., George IV., Victoria's mother, and the Prince Consort, all died on Saturday.

That the slang phrase, "come off," was used by Chaucer in exactly the modern sense—

"Come off!" they cryde, "alas! you will us shende!"

That Samuel Pepys called "Romeo and Juliet" the worst play that ever he heard; "Othello" also a mean thing; "Twelfth Night" a silly play, and "A Midsummer Night's Dream" the most insipid, ridiculous play that ever he saw.

Golf.

THE Poland Spring golf links, which are now in perfect order, are said to be the finest hotel links in the East. Mr. A. H. Fenn, who plays over them daily, says that he has visited most of the links at the different resorts and he thinks they are superior to them all. The grass on the fair green is kept down very close by the use of a horse lawn-mower, which is kept going on all pleasant days.

The first tee is located within twenty yards of the main entrance to the hotel, and fair drive of 125 yards will carry you over the main road to the hotel, where you will get a good lie for a brassie stroke to take you over a bunker which was formerly an old stonewall, but which has been taken away, and a raised bunker now stands. Once over the bunker it will take another brassie stroke or a long iron to reach the green. This hole is called the "Woods," and is the longest hole, 480 yards. The green is located on a gentle slope at the edge of the woods, from which it derives its name. The second tee is located near the first hole, under three birch trees. This hole is called "Trouble," and is 180 yards long. A very long drive will carry you over a bunker which is about 150 yards from the tee, but as it is up hill, very few players try to carry it on the drive. If you are unfortunate enough to get into it you will certainly have trouble, and that, I presume, is why it received its name, "Trouble." Once over it, and your troubles are ended for that hole.

The third tee is located only a short distance from the second hole ; a good drive will bring you over the main road to the hotel, then an iron stroke to the green, which is located near the famous Spring. This hole is 260 yards, and is called the "Spring." The green is on a natural slope of the hill and requires good judgment in approaching and putting to make the hole in four or five strokes. Here the players rest for a moment to get a refreshing drink of the world-renowned Poland water.

The fourth hole, called the "Hill," is 135 yards, and is the shortest and easiest hole of them all. As the drive is up hill it takes a very long cleek stroke to reach the green, and most players will use a driver on that account. A well-directed drive should bring you on the green or near it, so that the hole should be made in three strokes. This hole has been made in two strokes. The fifth hole is called "Lakeview," from the beautiful view one gets of the lakes, which are about half a mile distance from the green. This hole is 280 yards. A good drive brings you over a roadway, and a good iron stroke onto the green. The sixth hole is 275 yards, and named the "Poland." A good

drive takes you over the main road to the hotel, and a long iron stroke to the green, which is located near the hotel and first tee.

The seventh hole is called the "Grove," and is just 200 yards. From the tee one can see the flag in the hole, which is located in the edge of the oak grove. In driving from the tee one crosses the roadway immediately in front of the tee, then across the lawn, and, as there are no difficulties, the hole should be made in four strokes. The eighth hole you can see the flag in the distance from the tee, and a good drive carries you well over a roadway, then an iron shot over another road onto the Mansion House lawn, where the hole is located in the center of the lawn, making one of the finest of greens. This hole is called the "Mansion," and is 290 yards.

The ninth and home hole is called the "Maine State," and is 365 yards. A fair drive carries you over a roadway and a deep ditch, then a brassie stroke takes you over a road by the Maine State Building, where you can get a mashie stroke to the green, which is protected by another roadway, and located in the edge of the pine grove. After holing out the ninth hole, a short walk of 100 yards through this lovely grove brings you again to the first tee.

The whole length of the nine holes is 2,465 yards, and Col. Bogie's score is 5-4-4-3-4-4-4-5-5=38. The record is held by Mr. A. H. Fenn, who made the nine holes in 41 strokes.

—*Boston Herald.*

Saturday, August 7th, handicap tournament, 9 holes, medal play. Master William C. Chick won first prize, and his father, Mr. I. W. Chick, won second. Both played better than formerly, and this is the first time that the son had beaten the father's score. The scores:

	Gross.	Handicap.	Net.
William C. Chick	64	42	22
I. W. Chick	68	30	38
E. W. Olney	68	25	43
J. H. Maginnis	68	22	46
A. H. Fenn	46	0	46
R. G. Lockwood	59	10	49
H. Berri	74	25	49
B. P. Moulton	90	40	50
W. Berri	72	20	52
George A. Vose	72	17	55
F. M. Sawtell	90	32	58

There was a handicap tournament, 18 holes, medal play, held on Monday, August 9th. Mr. J. H. Maginnis won first prize, with a net score of 78 ; Walter Berri, second prize, with a net score of 87 ; and I. W. Chick third, with a net score of 93. The following are all the scores in full :

	1st Round.	2d Round.	Gross.	H'dicap.	Net.
J. H. Maginnis	61	55	116	38	78
Walter Berri	64	63	127	40	87
I. W. Chick	68	65	133	40	93
Herbert Berri	67	70	137	42	95

A. H. Fenn	47	48	95	0	95
George A. Vose . . .	60	68	128	32	96
R. G. Lockwood . . .	61	65	126	20	106
F. M. Sawtell	90	74	164	55	109
H. B. Ingalls	73	69	142	32	110
William C. Chick . .	90	71	161	35	126
S. F. Gilbert	91	102	193	50	143

On Tuesday, August 10th, the boys had a handicap tournament, 9 holes, medal play, for two prizes given by Mr. I. W. Chick. First prize, a golf club, won by W. H. Oskamp; and second prize, three golf balls, by W. C. Chick. Following are the scores:

	Gloss.	Handicap.	Net.
W. H. Oskamp	88	15	73
W. C. Chick	74	0	74
Lester Gilbert	90	15	75
Austin Palmer	84	6	78
Robert Marsh	90	10	80

There is a very noticeable improvement in the playing of most of the players, especially among the ladies. Miss Hoeke, in playing one round with Mr. Fenn on Tuesday afternoon, broke the ladies' record for 9 holes, making the round in 94 strokes. Mr. Fenn also broke the record for 9 holes on the same round, making the low score of 42 strokes, which is within four strokes of bogie, and this he again reduced Thursday to 41.

There was a handicap tournament held on Thursday, and three prizes were given by Robert Dornan of Philadelphia. There were 31 entries; 23 handed in cards. Miss Alice D. Colburn, Mr. F. M. Sawtell, and William C. Chick were tie for the lowest net score. Miss Colburn played a very steady game, and lowered the ladies' record in her last round 21 strokes, making the round in 73. The following are the scores in full:

	1st Round.	2d Round.	Gloss.	Handicap.	Net.
Miss D. Colburn	. 85	73	158	80	78
F. M. Sawtell	. 64	72	136	58	78
Wm. C. Chick	. 60	66	126	48	78
H. B. Ingalls	. 65	65	130	45	85
Walter Berri	. 60	62	122	36	86
G. Gilbert	. 82	78	160	73	87
J. H. Maginnis	. 64	56	120	30	90
G. A. Vose	. 62	58	120	30	90
A. H. Fenn	. 48	44	92	0	92
W. H. Oskamp	. 84	79	163	71	92
Miss L. Hoeke	. 100	94	194	100	94
R. P. Marsh	. 90	80	170	73	97
J. A. Collins	. 83	76	159	58	101
S. P. Holton	. 73	85	158	50	108
Miss Olive Gale	. 114	113	227	116	111
M. J. Mulqueen	. 96	88	184	70	114
H. Berri	. 76	77	153	38	115
Miss P. Vose	. 150	126	276	160	116
Mrs. T. Blackford	. 114	112	226	109	117
I. W. Chick	. 78	84	162	42	120
Wm. Berri	. 94	86	180	60	120
J. A. Ingalls	. 109	104	213	65	148
Miss T. Englis	. 164	115	279	130	149

There were eight others who did not hand in cards.

In the play-off on the ties, Friday forenoon, Miss Colburn wins first, reducing the ladies' record to 69; Mr. Sawtell, second; Mr. Chick, third.

Brake Rides.

A most enjoyable brake ride was given August 8th, by Mr. Olney. The party included Mrs. Blackford, Miss H. Blackford and Miss A. Blackford, Miss Sotia, Miss Vose, Mr. Maginnis, Mr. Vose, and Mr. Toppan.

The afternoon was perfect, and they drove to Lower Gloucester. Returning, they came over Bald Hill and passed Elmwood Farm.

Mr. and Mrs. F. R. Thomas gave a delightful brake ride, Saturday afternoon, August 8th. The party consisted of Mr. and Mrs. Darling, Miss Esther Darling, Mrs. Chase and Miss Florence Chase, and Mr. George B. French.

Mr. Underwood gave a most enjoyable brake ride Tuesday morning, August 10th. The party included Miss Underwood, Mrs. Palmer, Miss H. Blackford, Miss J. Englis, Miss A. B. Englis, Mr. W. F. Englis, and Mr. Gregory. They took the beautiful drive around Trip Lake, over Harris Hill and Bailey Hill.

Tid-Bits.

Mr. John C. Van Dyke of New Jersey is with us.

Miss Alice D. Colburn has joined her sister at Poland Spring.

Mr. James A. Collins of Cincinnati is with us.

Mr. Thomas Potts and Mrs. Potts of Brooklyn are at Poland Spring.

Mr. George A. Macdonald of New York City is at the Mansion House.

Mr. Allan Stevenson and Miss Isabella Stevenson of Brooklyn, N. Y., are with us.

Mr. W. G. Kimball and Mrs. Kimball of East Orange, N. J., arrived August 10th.

Captain Hall of the steamer John Englis, and Miss Hall, are at the Poland Spring House.

Mr. Henry U. Palmer of Brooklyn has rejoined Mrs. Palmer at the Poland Spring House.

Mr. John Englis and his friend, Mr. I. H. Emanuel, Jr., of Brooklyn, are at Poland Spring.

Mr. Fenety has been requested to exhibit a few of his beautiful paintings, in the amusement room, Tuesday, August 17th.

Mr. Horace H. Hall of Baldwinville, and Mr. Charles F. Hall of Boston, came on their bicycles from Portland, August 9th.

Dr. E. W. Pyle, a prominent physician of Jersey City, and his friend Mr. Frank Richardson, arrived at the Poland Spring House, August 11th.

The Notman Photographic Company furnish us another of their fine group photographs this week, a work which proves another evidence of their superiority.

Among the welcome guests on Tuesday, August 10th, was Mr. William Berri of Brooklyn, who has rejoined his family at the Poland Spring House.

Mr. and Mrs. O. L. Jones, Messrs. C. H. Jones, R. G. Jones, and A. E. Jones of New York, registered at the Poland Spring House, August 11th.

Mr. and Mrs. George C. Clausen of New York, Mrs. R. C. Luther of Pottsville, Pa., and Mrs. H. A. Maner of New York, are at the Poland Spring House.

Jones, McDuffee & Stratton Co., of Boston, furnish the crockery for the Poland Spring House, and their great establishment in Boston is a perfect treasure house of art ware.

Mr. H. B. Frissell, principal of the Hampton Normal and Agricultural Institute, Hampton, Va., registered at the Poland Spring House, Tuesday, August 10th.

Senator S. G. Hilborn of Oakland, California, finds Poland air and Poland water even more attractive than the glorious climate of California, for a time at least.

Mrs. Robinson reports a very high appreciation of her work as a masseuse, and that her services are in frequent demand. She can be found at any time by applying at the office.

Mr. N. Whitman and sister, Mrs. E. A. Knapp, arrived Tuesday, August 10th. Mr. Whitman and Mrs. Knapp have spent several seasons at Poland Spring.

Gen. A. T. Goshorn and Miss A. Goshorn of Cincinnati are at the Poland Spring House. General Goshorn was the Director General of the Centennial Exhibition at Philadelphia.

Among the welcome guests were Mrs. O. H. Taylor and her daughter, Miss Taylor, of Jersey City, N. J. Mrs. Taylor is the wife of the General Passenger Agent of the Fall River Line.

The condition of the dining-room at dinner time last Sunday, reminded one of the remark of the Hibernian at the concert, who said, "Indade, miss, I should be glad to give you a sate, but the impty ones are all full."

John Englis, Sr., who died in 1888, was the builder of the Drew, St. John, Dean Richmond, Newport, Old Colony, C. H. Northam, Tremont, Falmouth, Columbia, Saratoga, City of Troy, and many other famous boats.

The Oliver Ditson Company of Boston has recently published three songs, "Beneath the Stars," "Love's Dilemma," "Within that Holy City," composed by J. Howard Richardson of Boston. Mr. Richardson is well known at Poland Spring.

The kite flying by Austin and Chester Palmer, Tuesday, August 12th, was much enjoyed by all the guests. To the string of the kite was attached a flag, and 4,000 feet of string was used. It was a box or scientific kite, and the rush of air through it was distinctly audible on the other side of the lake.

The Waumbek and Laurel.

When seeking a pleasant and comfortable hotel, where all the adjuncts and surroundings are of a delightful nature, the air pure, and at a high elevation, turn your steps toward the Waumbek, in the summer or early autumn; but when the leaves begin to fall and the snow is seen to fly, then take the train for the Laurel, at Lakewood, where golf can be played nearly all winter, and comfort can be secured, when the summer houses are banked with snow.

Arrivals.

POLAND SPRING HOUSE.

FROM AUGUST 6 TO AUGUST 12, 1897.

Abbott, Mr. and Mrs. P. H.	New York
Allen, Miss Edith E.	Arlington
Alexander, Mrs. W. F.	East Somerville
Arundel, Mrs. Robert J.	Philadelphia
Atwood, Mrs. T.	Auburn
Atwood, Maud J.	Auburn
Austin, Mr. and Mrs. L. D.	Portland
Armstrong, E. D.	Auburn
Barton, Miss	New York
Bong, Mr. and Mrs. Charles M.	Boston
Brown, F. H.	Waltham
Brown, Mrs. Charles A. L.	Boston
Brown, Dr. Lucy Hall	Brooklyn
Browne. R. G.	Brooklyn
Berri, William	Brooklyn
Bolster, W. W.	Auburn
Bolster, Miss	Auburn
Burke, William, Jr.	Washington
Chadbourne, Mr. and Mrs. E. R.	Lewiston
Chamberlin. Ella M.	Cambridge
Clausen, Mr. and Mrs. George C.	New York
Colburn, Alice D.	Beverly Farms
Cox, Mr. and Mrs. F. W.	Portland
Cox, Mr. and Mrs. E. W.	Portland
Colburn, C. H.	Boston
Cole, B. F.	Washington
Conway, J. D.	Boston
Clark, A. W.	Boston
Clark, M. J.	Boston
Cook, Miss	Boston
Cox, Neal	Portland
Collins, James A.	Cincinnati
Crockett, Ralph W.	Lewiston
Crockett. Mr. and Mrs. E. A.	Lewiston
Chappell, C. H.	Chicago
Clark, Howard	Northampton
Conway, John A.	Washington
Danielson, Mr. and Mrs. J. W.	Providence
Dodge, Mrs. E. F.	Providence
Dotger, Mr. and Mrs. A. J.	South Orange, N. J.
Donald, J. W.	Boston
Dodworth, A. George	New York
Dawes, Frederick F.	New York
Eckhart, Mrs. B. A.	Chicago
Englis, John	Brooklyn
Emanuel, I. H.	Brooklyn
Fallon, William F.	Lewiston
Flissell, H. B.	Hampton, Va.
Faunce, E. P.	Oxford
Fowles, Mr. and Mrs. A. W.	Auburn
Gaston, Willard	New York
Gay, Mrs. W. N.	Boston
Gibbs, Lyman	Boston
Gross, E. W.	Auburn
Grafly, Mrs. M. C.	Philadelphia
Grafly, Miss	Philadelphia
Grafly, Mr. and Mrs. D. W.	Philadelphia
Higgins, Miss	Philadelphia
Heald, Gertrude	Cambridge
Holmes, Miss	New York
Hutchinson, Jonas	Chicago
Hutchinson, Helen	Chicago
Hull, Charles F.	Boston
Hull, Horace H.	Baldwinville
Hale, H. S.	Philadelphia
Hill, Warren E.	Brooklyn
Hill, Miss Ethel	Brooklyn
Hilborn, S. G.	Oakland, Cal.
Hall, Mr. and Mrs. V. C.	Brooklyn
Ingalls, Mr. and Mrs. Joseph A.	Boston
Ingalls, Claire	Boston
Ingalls, Horace Bright	Boston
James, Emma Tuttle	Boston
Jones, Mr. and Mrs. O. L.	New York
Jones, C. H.	New York
Jones, R. G.	New York
Jones, A. E.	New York
Jordan, H. T.	Washington
Jefferies, Miss	Brooklyn
Knapp, Mrs. E. A.	New York
Kimball, Mr. and Mrs. W. G.	East Orange, N. J.
Kilgore, Miss	Lewiston
Kurtz, Thomas S.	New York
Keith, Mrs. I. M.	Oxford
Langdon, Mr. and Mrs. Thomas P.	Baltimore
Luther, Mrs. R. C.	Pottsville, Pa.
Leybolt, Miss	Scranton, Pa.
Little, Amos R.	Philadelphia
Manser, Mrs. H. A.	New York
Matburg, William A.	New York
May, Mr. and Mrs. James F.	Chicago
Myers, Blanche C.	Jersey City
McCoy, Mrs. H.	Brooklyn
Mason, Miss	Auburn
Murphy, Miss H. L.	Philadelphia
Murphy, William H.	New York
Nele, Mr. and Mrs. Thomas O.	Baltimore
O'Connor, T. L.	Providence
Osgood, H. S.	Portland
Osgood, Mr. and Mrs. W. C.	Portland
Osgood, Henry F.	Portland
Oakes, Mr. and Mrs. Wallace K.	Auburn
Oakes, Hubert H.	Auburn
Peckham, Alice	Providence
Pennie, Mary	Auburn
Pearle, W.	Cumberland, Md.
Piatt, G. D.	Elkhart, Ind.
Pyle, Jane V.	Jersey City
Pyle, Dr. E. W.	Jersey City
Plumb, S. H.	New Haven
Putnam, J. L.	Chicago
Potts, Mr. and Mrs. Thomas	Brooklyn
Palmer, Henry U.	Brooklyn
Piatt, Mr. and Mrs.	Boston
Pease, Dr. Daniel P.	New York
Bailey, Miss	Lewiston
Richardson, Frank	Jersey City
Robbins, Mrs. E. J.	City of Mexico
Robertson, Miss	Brooklyn
Ruggles, Mr. and Mrs. Charles R.	Chicago
Russell, Charles H.	Brooklyn
Rich, Mr. and Mrs. H. W.	Portland
Rich, Elvin	Portland
Ricker, H. H.	Portland
Rogers, Alpheus G.	Portland
Shepard, Miss	Salem
Shepard. F. Osborne	New York
Smith, Mr. and Mrs. William W.	Poughkeepsie
Schleier, Mr. and Mrs. G. C.	Denver
Sterling. Miss	Peaks Island
Stevenson, Allan	Brooklyn
Stevenson, Isabella	Brooklyn
Stockbridge, Mrs. J. C.	Providence
Sullivan, Alice	Lewiston
Stabler, Mr. and Mrs. Jordan	Baltimore
Sterling, Miss Eva A.	Peaks Island
Smith, Mr. and Mrs. W. B.	New York
Slack, F. W., Jr.	Hillsdale, Mich.
Savory, E. H.	Rockland
Savory, George A.	Rockland
Swain, Mr. and Mrs. H. C.	New York
Sabin, F. C.	Lewiston
Sullivan, Mrs. M.	Hoboken
Sullivan, Miss	Hoboken
Swan, Clarence	Bridgeport
Swan, Samuel	Bridgeport
Thacher, Mr. and Mrs. W. H.	New York
Toppan, William J.	Boston
Tyler, Miss	Boston

Taylor, Miss O. H.	Jersey City
Underwood, John	New York
Van Dyke, John C.	New Jersey
Verrill, Mr. and Mrs. A. E.	Auburn
Ward, F. L.	Boston
Warren, Mr. and Mrs. C. M.	Portland
Walker, Mrs. Evan T.	New York
Watson, Miss	New York
Wight, Mr. and Mrs. Pearl	New Orleans
Woodbury, Mr. and Mrs. H. P.	Beverly
Wheelock, W. V.	Auburn
White, Miss Alice	Auburn
Wallace, Thomas H.	Lewiston
Wyman, Mrs. L. J.	E. Somerville
Whitman, N.	New York

MANSION HOUSE.

Atwood, Mr. and Mrs. Abram	Auburn
Calkin, George A.	St. John, N. B.
Carson, L. I.	Boston
Hasty, Mr. and Mrs. Charles D.	Windham, Me.
Jones, Mr. and Charles W.	Windham, Me.
Kellogg, Mr. and Mrs. A. A.	New Haven
Little, Mr. and Mrs. George O.	Washington.
Locke, George P.	Portland
Morrison, D. J.	Savannah
Macdonald, George A.	New York
Roach, Fred W.	St. John, N. B.
Reid, W. E.	Portland
Schleir, Mr. and G. C.	Denver
Sears, Henry C.	Boston
Stearns, Mr. and Mrs. George A.	Ridgewood, N. J.
Schaul, Mr. and Mrs. H. H.	Atlanta
Vaile, J. F.	Denver

Sister Aurelia's Reading.

Sister Aurelia Mace gave a reading in Music Hall, Monday evening, August 9th, from the manuscript of her new book, "Sketch of the Life and True Doctrine of Shakerism." The hall was well filled, and the guests were much interested in the subject.

After Sister Aurelia had finished, Mr. William Paul made a few remarks supporting Shakerism and the good they are trying to do. Mr. Paul spoke with much feeling and eloquence. He is an educated man, having been graduated from the University of Glasgow, Scotland. In 1876 he came to this country. While traveling through Maine he stopped at the Shakers', and in 1877 he was converted to Shakerism by the Poland Shakers. A year later the two societies, Poland and Gloucester Shakers, united. From 1878 to 1881 Mr. Paul conducted the public Shaker meetings at Gloucester. In 1881 he was called to Scotland to settle some property which he had inherited. For several years he studied and traveled, until he had made a trip around the world. In 1895 he became homesick for the Shakers, and so returned to them. The writer said: "I suppose you are happy or you would not remain." "I am perfectly happy here," was his reply.

On a fence between here and Lewiston is a sign, "The best drugs are none too good," at Blank's, onety-one Twoth Street, Auburn. Ambiguous?

Obey the Laws of Health.
[Contributed.]

It is customary for thousands of our people to visit the spas in Europe every year in the hope of being benefited for some real or fancied trouble. They consult a physician, who orders them to visit the springs, drink a glass or two of disagreeable water, walk a mile or two before breakfast, and they return home to sing the praises of the particular place which they have visited.

Here they remain in bed the most beautiful part of the day, come down in the elevator, and almost seem to regret the short distance which they have to walk to reach the breakfast room. The result is that they are troubled more or less with discomfort and indigestion.

Now we have here much better facilities for retaining or regaining our health, unless we are troubled with some chronic difficulty, than to take a European trip.

I have for some years during my visit here, risen early, walked to the Spring, taken one or two glasses of water, and then returned through the woods, making a distance of about a mile and a half. The result has been that the system is kept thereby in perfect order, and the appetite for breakfast is such as to make serious inroads into Messrs. Rickers' supplies. I advise all to test it, at least for a week.   A Guest.

Mount Pleasant House.

On Sunday evening next will be repeated at the Mount Pleasant House the combining of the two popular orchestras, the Mount Pleasant House and the Maplewood, for a grand concert. Both of these orchestras are organized by Mr. Wiley P. Swift, the one at Mount Pleasant being under the directorship of Felix Winternitz and the Maplewood being conducted by Louis G. Kapp. This promises to be the great musical event of the season in the White Mountains. The artists who will take part in this concert are as follows: Messrs. Felix Winternitz, Louis G. Kapp, William Caption, Charles Morenhaut, violins; William Howard, George Sauer, violas; Carl Hemman, 'cello; O. L. Southland, Max Kunze, contra basses; W. B. Mayberry, E. G. Blanchard, cornets; Charles Behr, trombone; Max Guetter, Walter M. Johnson, flutes; F. S. Coolidge, Wiley P. Swift, clarinets.

The Hampton Quartette of Hampton, Va., gave an entertainment at the Poland Spring House, Tuesday evening, August 10th. They sang plantation melodies, and some of the students gave an account of the life at Hampton. A collection of $175.80 was the result, a generous guest contributing fifty dollars.

Thistles.

THE LATEST IN FANS.

Mrs. Nucash—"I must get one of those sickle fans, like Mrs. Beeswinger's."

Mr. Nucash—"Sickle fans?"

"Yes; that's what she called it. I heard her say to Clara Uptodate that it was real fau de sickle, and she was fanning herself at the time."—*Cleveland Plain Dealer.*

A POSSIBILITY.

"How is it that your son's head seems to be drawn to one side? Only a year ago he was straight as an Indian." "I can only account for it through the fact that he did his courting on a tandem."—*Detroit Free Press.*

Boston Herald Witticisms.

CERBERUS.

Spacerayt—"While you were out a man left this manuscript. He said he wrote it to keep the wolf from the door."

Editor (after looking it over)—"Well, I think it might answer the purpose."

DEFINED.

"Papa, what is a reception?"

"A reception, my son, is a social function where you have a chance to speak to every one but your hostess."

GREAT SECURER.

Seedy individual (in editorial sanctum)—"Does the editor of this paper make any effort to secure poetic talent?"

Office Boy—"Does he? He chased th' last poek as far as th' river!"

A MARVEL.

Simplex (after an evening of Longbow's stories at the club)—"What a wonderful memory that fellow has!"

Cynicus—"Yes; he remembers more things that never happened, and in more different ways, than anybody I ever knew before."

HARD LUCK.

Reals—"Is Bagley head over heels in debt?"

Beals—"Yes, I hear so. He signed a contract with his tailor to pay two dollars a night for the hire of a dress-suit till he returned it. After the second night it was stolen!"

SURVIVAL OF THE FITTEST.

Bobbie—"On my way to school this morning I met the new boy who has moved in next door."

Mrs. Bingo—"Yes, and here's a note from the teacher saying you were late."

Bobbie—"That's nothing. The new boy didn't get there at all."

EVIDENCE.

Husband (in the early dawn)—"It must be time to get up."

Wife—"Why?"

Husband—"Baby has just fallen asleep."

Mrs. I. M. Keith of the Oxford Spring House spent Sunday, August 8th, at Poland Spring. It is one of the most delightful features of Poland life to drive over to Mrs. Keith's and dine, where guests will find a most excellent table, and return in the afternoon.

A complimentary brake ride was given on Thursday afternoon to the Kuntz Orchestral Club, by a guest of the Poland Spring House. The drive included Lower Gloucester, returning by Elmwood Farm, and the trip was highly enjoyed by all.

An Acrostic.

This is the Rest—and the Refreshing lies
Here in this fairy-land—to wondering eyes
Earth seems transformed—this must be Paradise!

Here from the rush, the turmoil, and the strife
Into a marvelous calm we glide—and Life
Looks radiant once again—Hope discrowning fear
Lightens our weariness, and soothes us with her cheer.

Too soon we part—yet oft in coming days
Our hearts to thee will turn—our voices we will raise,
Poland the Beautiful, forever in thy praise!

Peace be within thy walls—and may a kindly Fate
On thee e'er smile, good Fortune on thee wait.
Let fair Prosperity upon thee ever shine
And Heaven enrich thee with its gifts divine!
Ne'er may thy beauty fade, and with each passing year,
Dear as thou art to us—thou yet shalt glow more dear!

A. L. T.

Drag Ride.

Mr. and Mrs. George R. Wescott gave a delightful drag ride, August 8th, to Upper Gloucester and around Sabbath-Day Lake.

The party included Mr. and Mrs. Vose, Mr. and Mrs. A. G. Rogers, Mr. and Mrs. Pearl Wight, Mr. and Mrs. J. S. Martin, Mr. and Mrs. A. H. Morse, Miss Wight, and Mr. Thomas S. Kutz.

IT STANDS AT THE HEAD.

Unrivalled in Popularity!
Unsurpassed in Location!
Unapproached in Patronage!

THE

POLAND * SPRING * HOUSE

IS A SUPERB ILLUSTRATION OF

° ° ° SUCCESS ° ° °

EMBRACING AS IT DOES

ALL THE DESIRABLE FEATURES

EXPECTED IN THIS

The Leading Resort of America,

WHILE THE

MAINE STATE BUILDING

WITH ITS

SUPERB ART FEATURES

IS UNEQUALLED BY ANY SIMILAR ENTERPRISE

IN THE WORLD.

◄●●►

HIRAM RICKER & SONS (Incorporated),

PROPRIETORS.

MAINE STATE BUILDING.

The Hill-Top

POLAND SPRINGS, SO. POLAND, ME.

HARRY C. WILKINSON

Did you know that the majority of the large portraits hanging in the Maine Building were made
by THE SPRAGUE & HATHAWAY COMPANY of Somerville, Mass.? The World's Fair pictures were
also made by the same company.

Vol. IV.   SUNDAY MORNING, AUGUST 22, 1897.   No. 8.

Wet.

THERE is other water in Poland beside Poland Water, but it is not drinking water, only just boating water or fishing water, and of the 26,000 acres of land in Poland a considerable number of them is water. Now that is an irish

bull, but it was premeditated and perpetrated with malice aforethought.

Thompson's Pond contains eight square miles, Tripp Pond has one and one-fourth square miles, while the chain of ponds partially surrounding this hill have respectively : Upper, nearly one square mile ; Middle, a trifle over half a square mile ;

and the Lower, just a half square mile. The Middle and Upper are connected by a canal which admits of the passage of the steam launch when the water is at a normal height to enable it to pass under a bridge which spans it at one point. On the Middle Lake are numbers of boats, a steam launch which makes frequent trips, and sailing yachts.

One of the prime features of interest concerning these lakes is its fishing, for in the season when fish are foolish enough to bite at what is thrown to them, fine large black bass are taken out in large numbers and size—one at a time, remember.

The streams abound with trout as well, and as evidence of the truth of these remarks we give a summary of our separate record of the catches of the season thus far, and goodness knows how many big ones got away, or the account of catches which have never reached the HILL-TOP's ears :

Sawyer, Leeds, and Lippincott—23 bass; largest 3 pounds.
S. H. Howe—landlocked salmon, 2 1-2 pounds.
Masters Hartshorne and Wilson—6 bass.
Sawyer, Love, and Strong—12 bass, 18 pounds.
Cole and Davis—17 trout, each over 1 pound.
H. Ricker, Jr.—1 bass, 1 pound.
Master Winthrop Nay—1 bass.
Campbell and Reed—fine catch; 2 over 3 pounds.
Little and Yates—23 bass; largest 3 1-2 pounds.
George L. Osgood—13 bass, 31 pounds; largest 3 1-4 pounds.
Little and Yates—12 bass; largest 3 1-2 pounds.
A Party—12 bass; largest 4 pounds.
Master Nay—2 bass; largest 2 pounds.
Campbell and Simmons—several bass; largest 3 pounds.
A Party—9 bass; largest 3 pounds.
George L. Osgood—7 bass; largest 3 pounds.
Simmons and Wampole—9 bass, 31 3-4 pounds.
Simmons, Wampole, and Reid—12 bass; 7 over 3 pounds each.
George L. Osgood—15 bass; 4 weighed 3 3-4 pounds each.
The Sawyers—140 trout.
Mr. Sawyer—143 perch.
The Sawyers—153 trout.
George L. Osgood—7 bass; 15 pounds.

Now these are simply the catches reported to us, but they prove that the labors of the Fish Commissioners in stocking these ponds were not in vain.

Ricker Hill, which is no new hill, but which rose to eminence away back in prehistoric times, was placed here in graceful ease to watch over these ponds, and it is doing it now, and it does it very well, and it is more than probable that it will continue doing business at the same stand, affording the thousands of visitors its grand view of hill and dale, water and wood, to the end of time. So mote it be.

Picture Sales.

Several sales of Mr. Fenety's pictures were made on Tuesday, and on the previous day Nos. 72 and 74 of the exhibition, painted by Agnes Leavitt, were sold to Mr. Joseph Lathrop of St. Louis. The first of these two, "Birch Tree a Century Old," has been one of the most admired pictures in the whole collection. Both the purchasers and the artists are to be congratulated.

Art Notes.

A VERY largely increased interest has been noted of late in the Art Exhibition as its exceptional merit becomes more generally known. Here are scores of pictures by America's famous artists, men and women honored by the best critics and judges, and such an exhibition if thrown open at the usual art clubs would attract marked attention. Nearly every artist has won distinction, as will be seen by a glance at the catalogue, and even those who have not, richly deserve it, and will receive it at no distant day.

Weekly we have been able to call particular attention to some special artists, and this week we will add to those names the names of—

Edmund H. Garrett, who was a pupil of John B. Johnston, Boulanger, Lefebvie, and Jean Paul Laurens. He received a silver medal, Boston, in 1893. Exhibitor at the Boston Art Club, Jordan Gallery, and elsewhere. Painting purchased by Boston Art Club, which is in itself a mark of distinction. An excellent water-color by Garrett is that of "Bermuda," No. 34, at the head of the stairs, and there are two more in Alcove F, Nos. 35 and 36, which are works of rare excellence.

Martha A. Platt, who was a pupil of that excellent artist, Frederick D. Williams, shows two very excellent pictures, in Alcove B. They are numbers 89 and 90, two fruit pieces. It must be admitted that they possess unusual merit.

Ernest L. Ipsen is a young man who has a fine future, to judge him by his four pictures in the exhibition. Ipsen was a pupil of the Royal Academy of Fine Arts, Copenhagen, Denmark, receiving first prize in competition for figure painting. He is an exhibitor at the Boston Art Club, Jordan Gallery, etc., and is making rapid strides toward a front rank. His most ambitious work here is probably No. 63, a "New England Blacksmith Shop," in Alcove C. Other of his works are in the same department, and numbered 64 and 65, while yet another larger one is seen in A, No. 62, a very noticeable work.

With the upward tendency in prices, tariff on imported works of art, and other conditions at present and about to come, it would be well to make a selection before the full return of Prosperity, whom we are told is headed toward America.

The Art Store.

Persian Rugs which are a delight to the eye and a comfort to the feet ; Bagdad Curtains, Mexican and Persian Drawn Work, and scores of elegant articles, including all kinds of embroidery, with every known stitch, may be found at Mrs. Mallouf's, at the corner of the hotel.

Golf.

The handicap tournament held on Wednesday was won by W. H. Oskamp with a net score of 73; George A. Vose won second with net score of 78; William C. Chick and G. A. Munger tied for third prize with net score of 83. The prizes which were given by I. W. Chick of Boston was a Caddy bag with set of five golf-clubs for first prize, one dozen silvertown balls for second prize, and a Fenn driver for third prize. The following are the scores in full:

	1st Round.	2d Round.	Gross.	Handicap.	Net.
W. H. Oskamp	70	63	133	60	73
George A. Vose	53	57	110	32	78
William C. Chick	65	63	128	45	83
G. A. Munger	71	72	143	60	83
H. C. Swain	70	74	144	60	84
I. W. Chick	68	69	137	49	88
Walter Belli	59	59	118	30	88
A. H. Fenn	48	44	92	0	92
J. H. Maginnis	66	58	154	32	92
A. Collins	80	62	142	50	92
H. B. Ingalls	70	63	133	39	94
William Belli	73	72	145	50	95
F. W. Sawtell	66	77	143	45	98
Herbert Belli	73	67	140	42	98
J. A. Ingalls	84	76	160	60	100
Lester Gilbert	78	80	158	55	103
J. H. Lake	86	79	165	60	105
R. P. Marsh	82	92	174	60	114
N. G. Calman	87	88	175	60	115
M. J. Mulqueen	89	99	188	60	128

Mr. A. H. Findlay, of Wright & Ditson, Boston, who is one of the best Scotch golf-players in the country, had a very close and interesting match with Mr. A. H. Fenn on Wednesday. Mr. Fenn won by 3 up, 2 to play, lowering the record of the links to 88. The following is the score by holes:

	1	2	3	4	5	6	7	8	9	
Fenn	7	5	5	4	4	5	4	5	6	45
Findlay	8	4	5	4	5	4	5	5	6	46
Fenn	6	5	5	4	3	5	3	5	6	42
Findlay	7	5	4	4	5	5	4	4	5	43

On Thursday morning, Mr. Fenn and Mr. Findlay had another very close match, Mr. Findlay winning by 1 up, and lowering Mr. Fenn's record one stroke to 87, Mr. Fenn playing in his previous record of 88. Score by holes:

	1	2	3	4	5	6	7	8	9	
Findlay	5	4	4	4	5	4	4	6	6	42
Fenn	6	4	5	3	4	5	4	5	5	41
Findlay	6	5	5	4	5	5	5	5	5	45
Fenn	5	6	5	4	5	6	4	7	6	47

Total—Findlay 87, Fenn 88.

In the final match between A. H. Fenn and A. H. Findlay, A. H. Fenn won at the 18 hole by one stroke, making him one hole up. A large crowd followed the match throughout, and great interest was taken in each play. At the end of the first round the score was all even; at the 17th hole Mr. Fenn was one up, and the last hole was halved, leaving Mr. Fenn one up and the match. The following is the score in full:

	1	2	3	4	5	6	7	8	9	
A. H. Fenn	6	5	5	5	5	5	4	4	6	45
A. H. Findlay	5	3	5	4	5	5	5	7	5	44
Fenn	7	4	5	4	6	5	4	6	6	46
Findlay	7	4	6	4	4	5	5	5	6	46

Base-Ball.

At Poland Spring, Saturday, August 14th, the Athletics defeated the Norways as follows:

ATHLETICS.

	A.B.	R.	B.H.	P.O.	A.	E.
McCarty, c.,	6	2	3	4	1	0
Bridgham, 2b.,	6	3	2	6	2	1
Boardman, 3b.,	4	2	2	2	4	0
G. Dostie, r.f.,	5	1	2	0	0	0
Mynahan, l.f.,	5	0	0	5	0	0
Hegarty, 2b.,	2	1	1	0	0	1
Lowell, c.f., s.s.,	5	2	1	2	2	1
Peterson, 1b.,	5	2	3	7	1	1
Menihan, p.,	5	2	3	0	2	0
Curran, c.f.,	3	0	0	1	0	0
Totals,	53	15	17	27	9	4

NORWAYS.

	A.B.	R.	B.H.	P.O.	A.	E.
Rawson, s.s.,	3	3	2	3	5	0
H. Nevers, 1b.,	5	3	2	12	0	1
Cushman, c.,	6	3	4	10	1	1
Hastings, r.f.,	6	1	2	0	0	0
Wilson, l.f.,	5	1	1	1	0	0
P. Nevers, c.f.,	5	1	3	2	0	0
Spiller, 3b.,	5	1	3	1	3	2
Briggs, 2b.,	5	0	0	0	1	1
Shaw, p.,	5	1	2	0	5	0
Totals,	45	14	19	27	16	6

SCORE BY INNINGS.

	1	2	3	4	5	6	7	8	9	
Athletics,	1	0	0	5	3	2	0	2	2—	15
Norways,	2	0	0	0	9	0	1	0	2—	14

Two-base hits—McCarty 2, Dostie 2, Menihan, H. Nevers, Cushman, Shaw. Three-base hits—McCarty, Boardman. Home runs—Peterson, H. Nevers. Double plays—Lowell, Bridgham, and Peterson. Stolen bases—Athletics 9, Norway 4. Hit by pitched ball—Boardman. Base on balls—by Menihan 4, by Shaw 1. Struck out—by Menihan 4, by Shaw 5.

Mr. Mathews's Gift.

The library has received as a generous gift from Mr. George Mathews, of the Jones Brothers Publishing Co. of Cincinnati, a set of sixteen volumes of Ridpath's Library of Universal History, giving an account of the origin, primitive condition, and ethnic development of the great races of mankind, and of the principal events in the evolution and progress of civilized life among men and nations, from recent and authentic sources; containing over 6,000 pages, and illustrations, maps, race charts, etc., to the number of over 3,000. By John Clark Ridpath, LL.D.

The guests of Poland Spring will appreciate the value of this gift, and Mr. Mathews receives most sincere thanks.

The St. James, whose advertisement is on the last cover, is finely located at the corner of Franklin Square, next to the New England Conservatory of Music, Boston, and has two handsome corner suites for the winter, steam heat, and excellent plain cooking; is convenient to all points, and in a fine neighborhood.

Children's Column.

Never bear more than one trouble at a time. Some people bear three kinds—all they have ever had, all they have now, and all they expect to have.   —Edward Everett Hale.

Wanderer and the Black Cat.

On Saturday evening, Wanderer, the St. Bernard dog on the place, and "the black cat" met on the plank walk between the Poland Spring House and the Mansion House. Wanderer has his preference among cats, and this one is not a favorite. In fact, there is but one on the place that he really loves, and this belongs to Tim, the fireman at the Mansion House. Wanderer is devoted to Tim, and anything that Tim loves, Wanderer loves and protects. He will allow this kitten to jump on his back, pull his hair, and roll over him.

But he has no use for the black cat, and their meeting Saturday night was not agreeable. After exchanging a few words, there was nothing left for the cat to do but to scramble up the telegraph post and wait until Wanderer went home.

Wanderer enjoys the moonlight, and finding it a comfortable place to rest, he threw himself down on the grass at the foot of the telegraph post, and remained there three hours. People passing called him, but he raised his head, as much as to say, "No, I thank you, I am very comfortable where I am." Then he would look up at the cat to see that she had not escaped. It was not until the night watch found Wanderer and persuaded him to go on duty with him that he gave up his watch, and the black cat returned to her mother.

JOHNNIE'S REMEDY.

"This won't do," exclaimed Mrs. Box, excitedly, "there's thirteen at table."

"Never mind, ma," shouted little Johnnie, "I kin eat fur two."—*Pearson's Weekly*.

AN OBSERVANT YOUTH.

"Now, Bobbie," said the teacher, "spell pipe."

"P-i-p-e," said Bobbie.

"That's right. And now tell me something about pipes. What do people do with them?"

"Well," said Bobbie, thoughtfully, "boys blow bubbles with 'em; plumbers put 'em in; Scotchmen blow music out of 'em; and men like my pa smoke 'em. It all depends on the kind of pipes you want me to tell you about."

  —*Harper's Round Table*.

A Juvenile Tea.

One of the most delightful occasions of the season was an afternoon tea, given Thursday, August 19th, from 3 to 5, in Miss Pearl Wight's apartment. Miss Celeste Heckscher and Miss Louise Nugent assisted Miss Wight.

The room was artistically decorated with exquisite pink sweet peas and ferns. Here and there were lovely bunches of asters, tied with blue, white, and pink ribbon. On the center-table was a bowl of geraniums and ferns.

Miss Wight was daintily attired in a blue muslin; Miss Heckscher was charming in a combination of blue and white, and Miss Nugent was lovely in a pink muslin. It was one of the largest receptions of the season, and all were beautifully gowned.

Among the number were Miss Madeline Gilroy, Miss Dorothy Gilroy, Miss Estelle Mulqueen, Miss Mary Piatt, the Misses Marguerite and Janette Ricker, Miss Marion Ricker, Mrs. Nugent, Mrs. Pettee, Mrs. Skaats, Mrs. E. P. Ricker, Mr. and Mrs. Wight, Mrs. A. B. Ricker, Mrs. Ten Broeck, and Miss Piall.

Refreshments were furnished by a well-known caterer, and consisted of cake, candy, peaches, oranges: and Poland water was served instead of tea.

Mrs. John Greenwood, whose china painting is so much admired, is spending a few weeks at Lake View Cottage, Poland. Her salad set, now on exhibition at the Maine State Building, was painted from the designs of Leikoff, who is famous for his fish, shells, and sea-weeds. Mrs. Greenwood has many original designs that are beautiful.

Some Recollections.

AN interested reader asks if we can not "write up" a few of our early recollections, and is quite sure they will be enjoyed. Certainly.

We chance to recollect one of our "recollections" at the present moment, and it concerns a man by the name of Zype. Yes, Zype, and worse yet, Zebulon Zype. Phœbus, what a name! we hear you exclaim. That name was the bane of his existence. He was an ambitious man, and wanted to get on, but he was always missed in sending out cards of invitation; his name came so far down in the list, the number was always exhausted, or the writer was, one or both, before arriving at his name. When lovely booklets and samples of patent soaps or calendars were mailed from the local blue book, he wasn't "in it," for the appropriation was exhausted also, before Zype was arrived at.

He went to caucus, but when candidates were suggested from the check list, Zype was never reached, and Brown and Jones, his hated rivals, were always selected early in the proceedings, and they were not half as smart as Zype, so Zype thought.

Finally Zype struck a scheme. He applied to the legislature, and the first thing we knew Zebulon Zype was among the has beens, and a new name headed every list, and that name was Aaron Aar, and circulars, calendars, samples, invitations, honors, and office were shortly heaped upon the devoted head of the first man in the blue book. Brown and Jones took the inferior things in life after that, until one day a new man came to town, by the name of Aab, and lo! Ben Aab's name led all the rest.

What became of Aar? Mysterious disappearance. Turned up in Mexico, or somewhere later we heard. Never did know exactly. Crushed aspirations, you know.

Oh, yes—by the way, that recalls still another "recollection." This "recollection's" name was Onion—John Onion. Onion was a handsome man, and knew it, but his name was not as fascinating as he was. However, his good looks or his shape impressed a young lady by the name of Peach, to a sufficient extent to abandon being a Peach to become an Onion. Fancy that, now. They were happily married twenty years, when the Onion that was a Peach, departed, leaving the male Onion to mourn her loss, which he genuinely did.

John never liked his name of Onion, any more than Zype did his, but for different reasons, and after a couple of years fell in love with a buxom woman named Union, but she insisted upon his giving up his O for her U, or no trade. John did it, and the union was solemnized.

This union, however, did not prove to be as strong as the Onion union, and divorce cut it in twain in three years' time, and to add to Onion's misfortunes, the government which had been paying John Onion a pension, did not consider Union the same man, and in spite of protests, he was cut off the rolls, and in sheer despair, one day his "shape," which he had traveled on until it showed wheel ruts, suddenly became "remains," and he sleeps in the tombs of his fathers. Selah.

Earl Smith of Lowell, Mass., an *attaché* of the Poland Spring House, has received word from Brown University that he has won a scholarship of $150. This is the second scholarship that Mr. Smith has won. He is in the Class of 1900.

Tid-Bits.

Foie.

Circus.

Base-ball.

Great golf.

Now buy pictures.

Much fine weather.

1,792 books in the library.

Mr. J. Clark Morton of Brooklyn is at Poland Spring.

Mr. and Mrs. A. J. Secor of Toledo, Ohio, are with us.

Mr. William W. Merrill of Deering, Me., is at Poland Spring.

Mr. and Mrs. H. W. Eddy of Worcester, Mass., are with us.

Mr. J. A. Houston and Mrs. Houston of Boston, arrived August 18th.

Dr. W. H. Prescott, a well-known physician of Boston, is at Poland Spring.

Mr. J. C. Lovering and Mrs. Lovering of Brookline are at Poland Spring.

Mr. William H. Chappell and Miss Chappell of Chicago are at Poland Spring.

Mr. S. B. Hinckley, Jr., and Mrs. Hinckley of Boston are at the Mansion House.

Mrs. E. H. Durell and Miss Gebhard of Dover, N. H., are at the Poland Spring House.

Mr. Charles N. Judson and Mrs. Judson of Brooklyn, N. Y., arrived Tuesday, August 17th.

The HILL-TOP may be found each week on Monday at N. D. Estes's, 80 Lisbon Street, Lewiston.

Mr. W. L. Lawson and Mrs. Lawson of Philadelphia, Pa., arrived Tuesday, August 17th.

Mrs. J. A. Gahn of Boston has joined her sister-in-law, Mrs. Daniel Kuntz, at the Mansion House.

Mr. Samuel Ivers of New Bedford, Mass., was warmly welcomed by his friends, Tuesday, August 17th.

Mr. E. S. Converse, a prominent resident of Boston, and Mrs. Converse are at the Poland Spring House.

Mr. John I. Kenney and his friend, Mr. Henry P. Morrison of New Brighton, registered Wednesday, August 18th.

Mr. and Mrs. William I. Merrall and the Misses Merrall of New York are at the Poland Spring House. Mr. Merrall is of the well-known firm of Aker, Merrall & Condit.

Fine article on "Teneriffe Drawn Needle Work," illustrated, in September *Magazine of Art*, in the reading-room.

Mr. and Mrs. F. F. Robins of New York, and Miss Mitchell of Philadelphia, Pa., are at the Poland Spring House.

Mr. Franklin Taylor is receiving congratulations on having won the beautiful oil painting of nasturtiums by Fenety.

Senator Eugene Hale of Ellsworth, Me., made us an agreeable but brief call a few days since. It is to be hoped he may return.

Mr. Crosby S. Noyes, proprietor of the *Washington Star*, Washington, D. C., and Mrs. Noyes, are at the Poland Spring House.

Mr. C. C. Corbin of Webster, Mass., has rejoined Mrs. Corbin at the Poland Spring House. Mr. Corbin is a fine golf player.

Mr. F. J. Bartlett and Master Howard M. Bartlett of Boston, have joined Mr. and Mrs. Nelson Bartlett at the Poland Spring House.

Mr. and Mrs. A. F. Gault, Miss Gault, Miss Ethel Gault of Montreal, and Miss Harman of London, Eng., registered at the Poland Spring House, Tuesday, August 17th.

Mr. and Mrs. George W. Furbush, Miss Maud Furbush of Lewiston, Mrs. H. M. Webster and son of Braintree, Mass., took dinner at the Poland Spring House, Saturday, August 14th.

Sons, Daughters of the Revolution, Colonial Dames, and all interested in their ancestry, should read Charles O. Bass's advertisement in another column. Then consult the Genealogical Index in the library.

This time it is a bouquet of sweet peas instead of a robin's egg which is laid upon the editorial table by Johnny Chamberlain. Johnny is ambitious, and if his ascent to fame be through the newspaper, the Lord knows he may yet become the Lord Chamberlain.

The fire seen during the severe shower of last Sunday was caused by the burning of "The Long Barn" on the Hawkes Farm in West Minot, and it was struck by lightning. Forty tons of hay, several hogs, horses, calves, and sheep were consumed. It belonged to Harrison Dudley, and his loss is about $1,000, with no insurance.

The revival of Jefferson dates from 1888, when its principal hotel, The Waumbek, came under the control of the managers of the Laurel House of Lakewood, N. J. The system of improvements inaugurated and continued unremittingly since that date has worked such changes in the hotel and grounds that one who visited the place five years ago would in no wise recognize it.

Progressive Euchre.

Among the most popular things at the Poland Spring House are the progressive euchre parties which take place Friday evenings. The one on August 13th was very enjoyable. There were eighteen tables, and eighteen games were played. The highest number for the ladies was thirteen, and the highest for the gentlemen fifteen.

Mrs. Keene and Mrs. A. Gilbert cut for the first ladies' prize. The first time they both cut a seven-spot, and the second time Mrs. Keene cut a king, so won the first ladies' prize, a beautiful cut-glass pitcher with gold trimmings. The second prize, an exquisite vase, went to Mrs. A. Gilbert. Miss Peckham won the third prize, a dainty French mirror. Mrs. Baker cut for the third prize and won the fourth, a lovely bon-bon dish. The consolation prize, an ink-eraser and letter-opener, went to Mrs. Charles Mitchell.

Mr. Whitney won the first gentlemen's prize, a handsome clock; Mrs. Sawtell the second, a picture frame; Mr. Adams the third, silver whist counters; Miss Williams the fourth, a pocket-book; and Mrs. Hobart the consolation prize, a silver pencil.

Moonlight Ride on The Poland.

Archie Cole, foreman of the Bottling House, and Mrs. Cole of the Mansion House, gave a moonlight ride on The Poland, Friday, August 13th. The party included Misses Winslow, Shed, Mary Winslow, Edwards, Noble, Herrick, Crooker, Redding, Fahey, Mack, Broughton, Hayes, Norton, Hoey, and Mrs. Lane; Messrs. Crooker, Benson, Mitchell, Hellon, Strout, Stout, O'Lery, Wilkson, Frank, Boody, and Frazier.

They went through the middle and upper lakes. The night was perfect, and the party had a most enjoyable time.

The temptation for us to play golf has been great the past week, for we certainly have had big golfers.

Music at Mt. Pleasant.

The concert in the great music hall in the Mount Pleasant House on Sunday evening last by Swift's combined Mt. Pleasant House and Maplewood orchestras of sixteen pieces, was a most gratifying success. This massing of two of the leading orchestras of the White Mountains for a concert has become the most interesting musical event of the White Mountain season. The programme is given below :

Grand March, from the Queen of Sheba.	. . . Gounod.
Overture—Fingal's Cave.	. . . . . Mendelssohn.
Opera Selection—Lohengrin.	. . . . . . Wagner.
{ Le Dernier Sommeil de la Vierge.	. . . Massenet.
{ The Mill.	. . . . Gillet.
Song—Alalia.	. . . . Bizet.
	Miss Clifford Walker.
Opera Selection—Faust.	. . . . Gounod.
A Hunting Scene.	. . . . Bucallossi.

The morning dawns, heralded by the crowing of cocks. The bugle sounds. "A hunting we will go." The hounds take the scent. Horses' hoofs resound. The death.

An Interesting Visitor.

On Saturday, the 14th, Poland Spring extended a genuine, hearty welcome to its first "cure" who gave at the time (1860) a testimonial and affidavit as to the permanent nature of his recovery, and thirty-seven years after, he comes here, without ever having experienced a return of his trouble.

Mr. E. C. Jackson was a cattle driver, and has driven seventeen droves of cattle from Oxford County, some miles north of Poland, to Brighton, near Boston, and continued in the business until he was forced out by western competition.

It is twenty-five years since Mr. Jackson visited Poland, which is a long time to stay away—ask any old guest.

The book of testimonials on the counter at the office will show Mr. Jackson's testimonial and his unique signature. He now lives on a farm in Norway, working daily with his men, and is said to be very fond of horses.

FRANK CARLOS GRIFFITH. | Editors.
NETTIE M. RICKER, |

PUBLISHED EVERY SUNDAY MORNING DURING THE MONTHS
OF JULY, AUGUST, AND SEPTEMBER, IN THE INTERESTS OF

POLAND SPRING AND ITS VISITORS.

All contributions relative to the guests of Poland Spring
vill be thankfully received.

To insure publication, all communications should reach the
editors not later than Wednesday preceding day of issue.

All parties desiring rates for advertising in the HILL-TOP
should write the editors for same.

The subscription price of the HILL-TOP is $1.00 for the
season, post-paid. Single copies will be mailed at 10c. each.
Address,

EDITORS "HILL-TOP,"
Poland Spring House,
South Poland, Maine.

PRINTED AT JOURNAL OFFICE, LEWISTON.

Sunday, August 22, 1897.

Editorial.

YOU who were born and brought up in the
country, if any such there are, do you ever
think, as you drive past a hay-field, and see
the farmer and his boy busy doing what the adage
commands when the sun is shining, how you raked
after the cart when a boy, and how you disliked it,
but yet how happy you were and did not know it?

It is with but little effort we recall those days
spent during the summer with our country uncle,
whose name was not Isaac, but Nat, dear old
Uncle Nat, jolly, rotund, and hospitable; when
we rode one of the first horse rakes, a Hinds Rake,
the invention of the father of the Hinds so
famous as the chemist who prepares that delightful
concoction of the honey and the almond, and who
has made a fortune out of it and owns the finest
residence in Portland. Yes, we remember it well,
and clumsy but effective it was, and how we rode
on the cart and "stowed," having a snake so
and then cast up as a matter of variety, and then
rode to the old barn, where we clambered to the
great beams, and again assisted at the stowing, hot
almost to suffocation.

The other boys are grown up, and big fellows,
and one is an eminent physician and the surgeon-
general of the state; but the uncle, jolly old soul,
has been long with the majority, and the pleasant
old farm-house, where horrid nightmares possessed
our sleeping thoughts, of creeping dreadful things,
and caused our unconscious feet to toss in air, is
numbered among the things that were, and leaves
behind it but a cellar wall o'ergrown with vine and
bush, and dairy with gathering dews.

Then we recall the trips to the island in the
river hard by, in the old flat-bottomed boat, where
the old sailor lived in calm seclusion, with a wife
and a child, to say nothing of the dog, whom the
much-traveled tar had eccentrically christened,
"Pinkey-Fido-Funguntum-Tiddly-Addly-Up-a-fly-
Bark-Cuska-gee-Pera-Diablo," the purport of
which we could never understand, and no wonder.

Happy days, but we knew it not. Health,
happiness, comfort, of little value then, but how
priceless now. Bright days, with everything in
the future, no past, and a fleeting present.

Musical Programme.

SUNDAY EVENING, AUGUST 22, 1897.

1. Overture—Merry Wives of Windsor. . . . Nicolai.
2. Flute Solo—Babillard. . . . . Terschak.
    Mr. Brooke.
3. { Ases Death—From Peer Gynt Suite.
    { Anitras Dance. . . . . Grieg.
4. Piano Solo—
    { Prelude . . . . Chopin.
    { Warum . . . . Schumann.
    { Valse Caprice. . . . . Rubinstein.
    Mrs. Carl Hauser.
5. Nocturno. . . . . Doppler.
6. Selection from The Walküre. . . . . . . Wagner.

Sunday Services.

Mass was held in Music Hall, Sunday, August
15th, by Rev. Father John A: Conway of Washington, D. C.

Rev. W. P. Lewis of Philadelphia preached
in Music Hall, Sunday morning, August 15th.
His text was from 2 Peter, 2:9—"A Day of
Judgment."

Rev. Julius Gassauer was assisted Sunday
evening, August 15th, by Rev. Dr. Stone of
Chicago. The service was held in the dining-
hall, and was attended by guests as well as
employees. The text was John 14:27—"Peace
I leave with you; my peace I give unto you."
Dr. Stone's address was enjoyed by all. Mr. Merrill of Deering, Me., who has a beautiful tenor
voice, assisted in the singing.

What You Eat.

MANY requests have been sent in for a repetition of the "Food" article of previous seasons that we are pleased to comply, although we feared it might be a "chestnut;" but come to think of it chestnuts are food, and hence it is quite apropos.

Of course the amounts named for the busy season this year are about the same as last, there having been no addition to the room accommodations here, and the food supply includes all used under the direction of the Rickers on this hill.

Thus we find it takes 2,875 lbs. of beef, 2,260 lbs. of lamb, for one week's supply, the figures given in this article all being for seven days' consumption.

10,100 eggs are used, 2,700 lbs. of chicken, fowl, and turkey, and between 1,200 and 1,800 lbs. of fish.

860 lbs. of veal, bacon, and ham find their way to the table, and 80 bushels of potatoes. The squash supply is over 900 lbs., beans over 11 bushels, peas about 25 bushels.

Green corn requires over 3,000 ears to satisfy the craving, while of "greens" some 40 bushels are used.

Twenty barrels of flour are made into various articles of food, and of butter the demand is satisfied with 1,100 lbs. of the best.

200 lbs. of coffee, 53 lbs. of tea, and, only think of it, 555 quarts of cream.

In addition to all this, 2,775 quarts of milk are utterly consumed, and to add to the general sweetness of things, *one and a half tons* of sugar are weekly lost to sight, but to the purchaser dear.

The supply department of the great Poland Spring Resort is ably cared for by Mr. A. B. Ricker, who is less seldom seen than the other brothers, but the result of whose labors is highly appreciated by all who visit Poland. He is ably seconded by Mr. Dockham, the steward, and Mr. Sharron, the *chef*.

Another item which may be of interest, is the fact that the dining-room is 181 feet long and seats 430 people. The large glass at the end of the dining-room is 8 feet high and 14 feet wide.

Storm and Sunshine.

[Contributed.]

Oh, I love to stand in the midst of the gale
When the Storm King rules the land,
And lightning's flash and thunder's crash
Obeying his stern command.
When the whole world seems to be faint with fright,
And cries out in anguish again and again,
Till its agony throbs through the darkness of night
And the heart of Nature is torn with pain
In the clutch of the Storm King's hand.

And I love to lie on a summer's day
In the shade of a forest tree,
When all is still on meadow and hill
Save the lazy drone of the bee;
And the sunbeams reach through the leaves the while
To kiss into waking the slumbering flowers,
And the whole world basks in Nature's smile,
And sweet grace reigns through the sun-lit hours
O'er forest and meadow and lea.

Yet Nature in storm or in quietude
Is singing the self-same strain;
There's joy in sadness and pain in gladness,
Is the burden of each refrain.
The laughter we hear from the lips of youth
Is drowned in the anguish of boyhood's tears,
And little they differ, we find in truth,
When we're taught by the lessons of after years,
There's joy in anguish and pleasure in pain.

HADDON HALL, Atlantic City, N. J., U. S. A.

Located at a most delightful section of this famous beach.
Illustrated book mailed.

Open throughout the year.

LEEDS & LIPPINCOTT.

It is Nevertheless True

That it took 700 bullets to wound a man and 4,200 to kill one at the celebrated battle of Solferino.

That "By jingo" is profane, as jingo in the Basque language means God, and is a common form of adjuration. The English took it from Basque sailors.

That the briefest correspondence of note on record was between Victor Hugo and his publisher. Hugo wrote regarding the success of "Les Miserables":

"?"

The publisher's reply was equally brief:

"!"

That the shortest marriage service in the world is daily performed by Milwaukee justices: "Have him?" "Yes." "Have her?" "Yes." "Married. Two dollars."

That Spain has the most sunshine of any country in Europe, and Scotland the least.

That Washington has proportionately more bicyclists than any city in the world.

That in Iceland there are no prisons, and in one thousand years there have been but two cases of theft recorded.

That the library of 400,000 manuscripts collected by the Ptolemys, were burned during the siege of Alexandria, by Julius Cæsar.

That Scott's lines, "If thou wouldst view fair Melrose aright, go visit it by the pale moonlight," is but a paraphrase of Hazlitt's "He who would see old Hoghton aright, must view it by the pale moonlight."

That Scott told Moore he never saw Melrose by moonlight.

That the rhymes of "Thirty days hath September," etc., are traced back to Richard Grafton, 1590, but even he quoted them. The author deserves a monument, for no lines in the language are quoted as frequently.

SHE KEPT THE RING.

"Come, old man," said the kind friend, "cheer up. There are others."

"I don't mind her breaking the engagement so very much," said the despondent young man. "But to think that I have got to go on paying the installments for a year to come yet. That is what jars me."—*Indianapolis Journal.*

GREAT MEMORY.

School man, who had been telling the story of David, ended it with:

"And all this happened over 3,000 years ago."

A little cherub, his blue eyes wide open with wonder, said, after a moment's thought:

"Oh, my, what a memory you've got!"
—*San Antonio Express.*

New Books.

FROM HON. WILLIAM P. FRYE.

Messages and Papers of the Presidents. Vol. IV.

FROM H. D. LYMAN.

Education; by Herbert Spencer.

FROM F. H. WILLIAMS.

Mr. Isaacs; by F. Marion Crawford.

FROM A FRIEND.

The Orcutt Girls; by Charlotte M. Vaile.
Sue Orcutt; by Charlotte M. Vaile.
The Sign of the Four; by A. Conan Doyle. (Paper.)

FROM LAWRENCE W. BLACK.

Admiral J. of Spurwink; by James Otis.

FROM GEORGE MATHEWS.

Ridpath's Universal History; by John Clark Ridpath, LL.D. 16 vols.

FROM A FRIEND.

In Two Moods; by Stepniak and William Westall.

FROM GEORGE A. MACDONALD.

How Successful Lawyers were Educated; by George A. Macdonald.

FROM MRS. FRANKLIN E. TAYLOR.

Prisoners of Conscience; by Amelia E. Barr.
The Seats of the Mighty; by Gilbert Parker.
King Noanett; by F. J. Stimson.
Taquisara; by F. Marion Crawford. 2 vols.
The Wisdom of Fools; by Margaret Deland.

What Suits One, Can't Suit All.

Six little screech-owls all in a row,
Complaining about the weather;
   He-e! cried one,
   He-e! cried another,
He e-e! cried all together.

Six little bad girls all in a row,
Complaining about the weather;
   Oh-o! cried one,
   Oh-o! cried another, ·
Oh-o-o! cried all together.

Six little good girls all in a row,
Rejoicing in the weather;
   It rains! cried one,
   It snows! cried another,
Hurrah! cried all together.

Six little rabbits playing in the sun,
Leaping o'er one another.
   What suits one
   Can't suit another;
Jump! cried they all together.
   —*F. L. Ward, in the Independent.*

Miss Grace Hall of the Mansion House received congratulations, Friday, August 13th, on her birthday. Among her many gifts was a birthday cake from Mrs. Archie Cole. Dame Rumor says that there were no candles. Mrs. Cole is noted for her delicious birthday cakes, and this one was exceptionally good. It was a great surprise to Miss Hall.

Lawn Party at Lakeview.

MRS. WALKER gave a lawn party, Tuesday afternoon, Aug. 17th, at her Lakeview cottage, in honor of Master Elmer Walker's second birthday. The party included Rev. Dr. Baker of Philadelphia, Mrs. Samuel Bates, Miss Bates, Mrs. John Greenwood, Miss Greenwood, the Misses Clara and Cathaleen Greenwood, Miss Harshberger, Mrs. George Crofut, Miss Crofut, Messrs. Marguerite and Georgia Crofut, Mrs. A. S. Outhank, Miss Outhank, Mrs. Arthur Friend, the Misses Alice and Ruth Friend, Mrs. Pulsifer, Mrs. E. P. Ricker, Master E. P. Ricker, Jr., and little James Ricker, Mrs. A. B. Ricker and little Miss Marion Ricker, Mrs. Oliver Marsh, Messrs. Robert and Arthur Marsh, little Dexter Marsh, Mrs. Noble, and Mrs. Charles Brown.

Refreshments were served, and the table, which was set on the lawn, was artistically decorated with ferns and oranges.

Games were played, and the one that caused the most merriment was the pinning of a handkerchief on a tree. Several had tried, but failed; when Mrs. Samuel Bates, a lady of eighty-nine years, said that she would like to try. She was blindfolded, turned around twice, and with the handkerchief walked directly to the chosen tree and pinned it on.

They had dancing on the lawn, and the Virginia reel was a great success.

Brake Rides.

On Friday, August 13th, a delightful brake ride, to Lewiston, was taken by the following party: Mr. and Mrs. Skidmore, Miss Skidmore, Mrs. Wright, Mrs. Conyngham, Miss Moore, and Mr. Van Dyke.

At half-past nine Saturday morning, August 14th, a merry party, consisting of Mrs. Everett, Mrs. Keene, Miss Smith, Miss Woodman, Mr. Vaile, Mr. Sears, Mr. Macdonald, and Mr. de Windt started for a brake ride to Tenney Hill. The morning was clear and beautiful, and the view from Tenney Hill was grand. The party saw distinctly eleven lakes, and a sheet of water which was Portland Harbor. It was a delightful drive and one long to be remembered.

Tuesday morning, August 17th, the following party—Mrs. Blackford, Miss H. Blackford, Miss Vose, Miss Sorin, Mr. Maginnis, Mr. Sartell, Mr. Ingalls, and Mr. Vose—went to the circus at Lewiston, on the brake. A luncheon was put up for them at the hotel, and they were gone all day.

Wednesday morning, August 18th, Mr. and Mrs. Marburg, Dr. D. P. Pease, the Misses Marburg, Mrs. John B. Macdonald, Miss Georgie Macdonald, and Master Wallace Lanahan, went

to Lewiston. The party patronized our Lewiston stores and found them an excellent place for shopping.

Thursday morning, August 19th, the following party—Mrs. J. H. Wright, Miss Conyngham, Mr. and Mrs. Skidmore, Miss Skidmore, and Miss Moore—had a delightful brake ride.

Mr. Allen Swain of Dorchester, Mass., was happily surprised, August 14th, with a birthday cake. Mrs. H. W. Ricker, whom he has been visiting, presented him with the cake, surrounded by fourteen candles. It was a complete surprise, and there was much merriment over the cutting of it. Mr. Swain left for Dorchester on Tuesday morning, August 17th.

If very particular about a prescription, read Schlotterbeck's advertisement. They are reliable, and solicit the patronage of such of Poland's guests as are in need of superior skill and attention in the compounding of drugs.

Tid-Bits.

We bet on A. H. F. every time.

Mr. E. V. Collins of Boston is at the Mansion House.

Mr. and Mrs. George W. Palmer of Brooklyn are here.

Mr. E. N. Lawrence of New York arrived August 15th.

Mrs. McCauley of Washington, D. C., is at Poland Spring.

Mr. and Mrs. George E. Carter of Boston are at Poland Spring.

Mr. and Mrs. J. H. McKenney of Washington, D. C., are with us.

Mr. and Mrs. W. E. Whitney of Boston arrived August 13th.

Col. J. C. Reiff of New York is a guest at the Poland Spring House.

Mr. and Mrs. G. W. Bailey of Pittsfield are at the Poland Spring House.

Mr. Joseph W. Cone of Hartford, Conn., arrived Saturday, August 14th.

Mr. S. S. Clark and Mrs. Clark of New York are at the Poland Spring House.

Mr. Vincent King of Montreal registered at the Mansion House, August 16th.

Mr. George A. Burgess and Mrs. Burgess of Boston are at the Mansion House.

Mr. and Mrs. Edward Russell and Miss Gardiner of Brookline, Mass., are here.

Mr. and Mrs. Jordan Stabler of Baltimore are registered at the Poland Spring House.

Mrs. Phinehas Adams of Boston registered at the Poland Spring House, August 14th.

Mr. B. B. Thatcher and Mrs. Thatcher of Bangor are at the Poland Spring House.

Mr. L. I. Carson has been spending a few days with Mrs. Carson at the Mansion House.

Mr. G. W. Tooker of New York has joined Mrs. Tooker at the Poland Spring House.

Mr. James S. Stone and Miss V. E. Stone of Chicago are guests of Mrs. E. T. Watkins.

Mr. and Mrs. C. E. Mitchell of New York and their son, Mr. G. H. Mitchell, are with us.

Manicuring and chiropody by Miss Whitman, the regular attendant at the Poland Spring House.

Mr. David Thornton of Brooklyn, N. Y., has joined Mrs. Thornton at the Poland Spring House.

Among the welcome guests, August 12th, were Mr. and Mrs. Thomas P. Langdon of Baltimore.

Miss Alice Peckham of Providence, R. I., is at Poland Spring.

Mrs. M. Sullivan and Miss Sullivan of Hoboken, N. J., are with us.

Dr. C. H. Gray of Cambridge, Mass, and Miss Littlefield of Dorchester, registered August 14th.

Mrs. E. P. Stillman, Miss C. F. Stillman, and Miss B. G. Stillman of New York, are at Poland Spring.

Dr. Otis E. Hunt of Newtonville and Miss Ardelle H. Venno, arrived at the Poland Spring House, August 16th.

Mr. and Mrs. A. Anderson, Mr. and Mrs. L. W. Goldy, and Miss Goldy of Camden, N. J., are at Poland Spring.

The many friends of Mrs. John H. Maginnis of New Orleans, La., were glad to welcome her Saturday, August 14th.

Mr. James H. Lake of Boston is at Poland Spring. Mr. Lake is very fond of Poland, and always spends several weeks here.

Mrs. Henry K. Wampole, Miss Helen Wampole, and Miss Hattie Male of Philadelphia, registered at the Mansion House, August 13th.

Mr. George L. Osgood added to his record, on Monday the 16th, a fine catch of black bass, numbering seven, weighing in all fifteen pounds.

Among the welcome guests, August 13th, was Mr. S. B. Hubbard of Jacksonville, Fla., who has joined Mrs. Hubbard at the Poland Spring House.

Among the welcome guests, August 16th, were ex-Mayor Thomas F. Gilroy of New York and Mrs. Gilroy, Miss Madeline Gilroy, Miss Dorothy Gilroy.

Even though one may not want a photograph taken, yet they will find much to admire and interest them at the Notman Studio, and courteous attention.

Mr. Joseph Lathrop of St. Louis, Mo., spent Monday, August 16th, here. Mr. Lathrop is much interested in the art exhibition at the Maine State Building.

The services of an excellent masseuse may be secured by those desiring them, by sending for Mrs. E. J. Robinson, who is constantly at the Poland Spring House during every season.

Mr. George L. Blanchard of Cambridge, Mass., was a welcome guest on Monday, August 16th. Mr. Blanchard first came to Poland in 1865, but has not visited the place for sixteen years. He finds many changes, and as he expressed it yesterday, "I should think Aladdin with his lamp had passed over the place."

Arrivals.

POLAND SPRING HOUSE.

FROM AUGUST 13 TO 19, 1897.

Andrews, E.	Kennebunk
Adams, Mrs. Phinehas	Boston
Athanasius, Fr.	Boston
Andelson, Mr. and Mrs. A.	Camden, N. J.
Almeda, W, F.	Boston
Arnold, Mr. and Mrs. M.	Philadelphia
Atwood, Mr. and Mrs. I.	Germantown
Bartlett, F. J.	Boston
Bartlett, Howard M.	Boston
Boothby, Mr. and Mrs. F. E.	Portland
Benson, Mrs.	Chicago
Blackford, Eugene G.	Brooklyn
Baumgardner, Mr. and Mrs. L. S.	Toledo
Burns, H. E.	New York
Barnaby, Frank A.	Brooklyn
Browne, F. H.	Waltham
Brodie, Mr. and Mrs. James A.	Brooklyn
Bailey, Mr. and Mrs. G. W.	Pittsfield
Barker, C. I.	Lewiston
Barker, Mrs. R. H.	Lewiston
Barker, Mr. and Mrs. A. D.	Lewiston
Bartlett, M. F.	Waterville
Colwish, John B.	Boston
Chappell, William H.	Chicago
Chappell, Miss	Chicago
Converse, Mr. and Mrs. Charles N.	Boston
Carpenter, F. W.	Providence
Chadbourne, Mr. and Mrs. E. R.	Lewiston
Corbin, C. C.	Webster, Mass.
Cone, Joseph W.	Hartford
Carter, Mr. and Mrs. George E.	Boston
Cheney, William	Portland
Conant, F. A.	Lewiston
Clark, Mr. and Mrs. S. S.	New York
Dutell, Mrs. E. H.	Dover
Day, Mrs.	New York
Donnell, Mrs. R. L.	New York
Eddy, Mr. and Mrs. H. W.	Worcester
Furbush, Mr. and Mrs. George W	Lewiston
Furbush, Maud	Lewiston
Findlay, A. H.	Boston
Galacat, Charles E.	Springfield
Gault, Mr. and Mrs. A. F.	Montreal
Gault, Miss	Montreal
Gault, Miss Ethel	Montreal
Gebhard, Miss	Dover
Gale, Thomas M.	Washington
Goldy, Mr. and Mrs. L. W.	Camden, N. J.
Goldy, Miss	Camden, N. J.
Greenwood, Alma	West Newton
Gardiner, Miss	Brookline
Gray, C. H., M.D.	Cambridge
Gilroy, Mr. and Mrs. Thomas F.	New York
Gilroy, Miss Madeline	New York
Gilroy, Miss Dorothy	New York
Hubbard, S. B.	Jacksonville
Hodge, Dr. D. M.	Franklin, Mass.
Hale, Eugene	Ellsworth
Hilton, Mrs. L. H.	Sharon, Mass.
Hicks, M, F.	Portland
Hunt, Otis E., M.D.	Newtonville
Hatman, Miss	London, Eng.
Houston, Mr. and Mrs. J. A.	Boston
Hubbard, Mr. and Mrs. F. H.	Arlington
Hart, Miss Lizette	Louisville
Inman, Mrs. W. H.	New York
Ivers, Samuel	New Bedford
Ide, H. J.	Boston
Jackson, E. C.	Norway
Judson, Mr. and Mrs. Charles N.	Brooklyn
Knowles, James T.	Boston
Kennelf, John J.	New Brighton, N. J.
Knight, H. W.	New York
Knight, H. E.	New York
Lake, James H.	Boston
Lathrop, Joseph	St. Louis
Littlefield, Miss	Dorchester
Lawrence, E. N.	New York
Lawson, Mr. and Mrs. W. L.	Philadelphia
Loveling, Mr. and Mrs. J. C.	Brookline
Lawson, Harry	Philadelphia
Lawson, Mrs. L. M.	New York
Morton, J. Clark	Brooklyn
Milliken, Mrs. W, F	Portland
McCloskey, J. J. S.	Newburgh
McCloskey, Dr. John	New York
Morris, Miss A. C.	Toledo
Morris, John T.	Philadelphia
Morris, Miss L. T.	Philadelphia
Miller, Mr. and Mrs. A. A.	Auburn
Mitchell, Miss	Philadelphia
Marshall, W. D.	Cambridge
Merrall, Mr. and Mrs. William E.	New York
Merrall, Miss C. M.	New York
Merrall, Miss A. L.	New York
Merrall, Miss G. E.	New York
Morrison, Henry P.	New Brighton, N. J.
Marvin, Miss E.	New York
Merrill, William W.	Deering
McCauley, Miss	Washington
Maginnis, Mrs. J. H.	New Orleans
Mitchell, Mr. and Mrs. C. E.	New York
Mitchell, G. H.	New York
Maltby, W. Z.	Montreal
McKenney, Mr. and Mrs. J. H.	Washington
Nash, Emma B.	Whitman, Mass.
Norman, Mr. and Mrs. L.	Brookline
Norman, Master Aubrey	Brookline
Noyes, Mr. and Mrs. Crosby S.	Washington
Ould, Mr. and Mrs. M. H.	Baltimore
Osgood, H. S.	Portland
Outhank, Emma	Beaufort, S. C.
Parsons, P. H.	Brooklyn
Parsons, Mrs. F. A.	Brooklyn
Pierce, J. B.	Buffalo
Palmer, Mr. and Mrs. George W.	Brooklyn
Prescott, Mrs. D.	Boston
Payne, Mrs.	New York
Riddell, Miss	Cleveland
Ruggles, E. O.	Boston
Robins, Mr. and Mrs. F. F.	New York
Reed, Horace	Whitman, Mass.
Reiff, J C.	New York
Russell, Mr. and Mrs Edw.	Brookline
Rideout, Mr. and Mrs. E. E.	Boston
Secor, Mr. and Mrs. A. J.	Toledo
Stackpole, Richard	New York
Stackpole, Miss May	New York
Swindell, Miss Susie O.	Baltimore
Stone, James B.	Chicago
Stone, Miss V. E.	Chicago
Stillman, Mrs. E. P.	New York
Stillman, Miss C. F.	New York
Stillman, Miss B. G.	New York
Stock, F. W., Jr.	Lewiston
Treat, Mr. and Mrs. S. A.	Chicago
Thornton, David	Brooklyn
Tonkel, G. W.	New York
Thatcher, Mr. and Mrs. B. B.	Bangor
Venno, Miss Adelle H.	Newtonville
Walbridge, Mrs. F. E.	Brooklyn
Whitney, Mr. and Mrs. W. E.	Boston
West, Mrs. J. L.	New York
Walsh, A. S.	New York
Webster, H. M.	Braintree
Wurts, Mr.	Philadelphia
Wurts, Dundas	Philadelphia

Wood, Howard K.	New York
Wadleigh, Mrs. H. W.	Boston
Wade, Mr. and Mrs.	Cleveland
Wilson, Miss	Plainfield, N. J.

MANSION HOUSE.

Blanchard, George L.	Cambridge
Burgess, Mr. and Mrs. George A.	Boston
Borton, S.	Brooklyn
Crawford, Fred	Portland
Collins, E. V.	Boston
Gahn, Mrs. J. A.	Boston
Huston, L. P.	Portland
Hinckley, Mr. and Mrs. S. B., Jr.	Boston
Jones, Mr. and Mrs. George H.	Oxford
King, Vincent	Montreal
Little, Miss D. F.	Boston
McNamee, Mr. and Mrs. J. F.	Boston
Ross, Charlie	Portland
Shea, J. J.	U. S. S. New York
Wampole, Mrs. Henry K.	Philadelphia
Wampole, Miss Helen	Philadelphia
Wampole, Miss Hattie	Philadelphia
Wade, I. R.	Boston
Young, Thomas M.	Boston

A Smart Ladd.

95 Maple Street, Malden, Mass., }
August 11, 1897. }

Hiram Ricker & Sons, South Poland, Me. :

Dear Sirs—It gives me great pleasure to add my testimony in favor of the use of Poland Spring Water.

About twenty-two years ago I was very ill and a great sufferer. The physicians whom I consulted at that time pronounced my trouble Bright's disease, and they were positive in their opinion that I could live only a short time.

A friend recommended my trying Poland Spring Water, and I sent at once for a barrel and commenced drinking it regularly. Almost immediately it gave me relief, and I continued to improve in health.

I often say to my friends : " I owe my life to Poland Spring Water, and I think I could not live without it." I have drank it almost continuously for the past twenty-two years, and my health is now very good. On the seventh day of this month I celebrated the ninety-first anniversary of my birth.

Very sincerely yours,

Mrs. Abigail K. Ladd.

Dictated and signed by Mrs. A. K. Ladd.

I hereby certify to the correctness of the above testimonial.

Frank J. Bartlett,

Treasurer of the Boston Ice Company.

No. 66 State Street, Boston, Mass.,
August 12, 1897.

Hotel La Pintaresca.

The old Painter Hotel at Pasadena, Cal., which is now being enlarged to nearly twice its former capacity, has been rechristened " La Pintaresca," a Spanish word meaning " the picturesque." The building when complete will have a hundred large, pleasant, and elegantly-furnished rooms, more than half of them en suite with private bath-rooms and open fires. The public rooms will be exceedingly pleasant. The whole house is to be warmed throughout with steam, a new and elegant dining-room is to be added, with new kitchen, cold storage, etc. The old part of the house is to be remodeled, renewed, and refurnished, until the whole establishment will offer as fine accommodations as can be had on the Pacific Coast.

The house is located about one mile from the center of the city of Pasadena, on an eminence commanding one of the finest views of the entire San Gabriel valley to the south, east, and west that can be had, and to the north the majestic Sierra Madre Range of mountains, with their snowy peaks, within easy distance, while the whole surrounding valley and foot-hills are covered with green verdure, beautiful groves of orange, lemon, and citron trees, roses and flowers of all kinds in profusion.

General Wentworth is to manage this beautiful hotel the coming winter, and extends to all his old guests a cordial invitation to spend the winter with him. The hotel will be kept on the same high level of excellence which has characterized Wentworth Hall, and it is safe to say that there will not be a house on the Pacific Coast better equipped to take care of the best people who travel than will La Pintaresca.

Drag Ride.

A most enjoyable drag ride was taken Friday, August 13th. The party included Mr. and Mrs. Dornan, Mr. and Mrs. Little, Mr. and Mrs. Berri, Mr. and Mrs. Ziegler, Mr. and Mrs. Elliott, Miss Elliott, Miss Hoeke, Miss Ziegler, and Mr. Pinkerton.

They went to the Shakers' and Lower Gloucester, returning over Bald Hill and by Elmwood Farm.

Mr. Ralph Stout of Brooklyn, N. Y., who is an *attaché* of the Mansion House, is receiving congratulations on his splendid success at Harvard. Mr. Stout ranks among the first nine out of a class of almost four hundred. This means a scholarship for him. This is the third scholarship which Mr. Stout has won at Harvard. He is in the Class of 1898.

Thistles.

WHY, SHE COULDN'T USE THEM.

This is what was heard in a theatre the other night. They were in a private box, and she was both pretty and well dressed. But she was in a bad temper because she could not see the stage. "Why," said he, trying to mollify her, "did you not bring your opera glass?"

"I did, but I can't use it."

"Is it broken?"

"No, but I forgot to put on my bracelets."
— *Tid-Bits.*

HOW IT SEEMED TO WILLIE.

"I wish I was as strong as the man that lifted us up in this thing," said Willie, as he stepped out at the sixth floor on the occasion of his first ride in an elevator. "He gave one pull on the rope, and we didn't stop goin' till we got clear up!"
— *Chicago Tribune.*

LACK OF REALISM.

Mr. Wickwire—"What ridiculous, impossible things these fashion plates are."

Mrs. Wickwire—"I know they used to be, but most of them are engraved from photographs nowadays."

Mr. Wickwire—"This one can't be. Here are two women going in opposite directions, both with brand new gowns on, and neither looking back at the other."

THOSE LETTERS.

The husband (seeing his wife off)—"You must promise not to ask for money every time you write."

The wife—"But that would necessitate my writing so much oftener."—*Life.*

A LOGICAL DEDUCTION.

Bobby—"Mamma, do the streets of heaven flow with milk and honey?"

Mother—"So the Bible says, dear."

Bobby—"And is that why the angels have wings, 'cause the walking's so bad?"—*Puck.*

WORKED WRONG WAY.

Huston—"Hurrah! I've made a discovery that is going to be one of the greatest things that has ever happened for science and mankind."

Buxley—"What is it?"

Huston—"I've found that mosquitoes are full of microbes."

Buxley—"Humph! I don't see what good that's going to do us. What you want to do is to get the mosquitoes to believe that people are full of microbes. Then you'll have accomplished something worth crowing about."—*Cleveland News.*

WHY?

"Why does that Blodgett girl wear such a thick veil?"

"She thinks it increases her beauty."

"Then why doesn't she get behind a screen door?"—*Cleveland Plain Dealer.*

FRIENDLY TIP.

Smither—"Know any especially good places to fish, old man?"

Rinktums—"Well, no; but I will give you my experience. I have always caught the most fish where there have been signs conspicuously placed which, strange to say, most broadly proclaimed that there should be no fishing there."—*Judge.*

Boston Herald Witticisms.

"OH, SAY!"

Englishman—"I wouldn't want to hear more than the first line of 'The Star-Spangled Banner' to know that it was written by an American."

American—"Why so?"

Englishman—"The first two words tell me that."

GEOGRAPHICAL.

Miss Beacon Hill—"Dear me! Strange, but I cannot remember. Where is Dresden?"

Young Lakeside—"O, that's easy. In China. Saw the address in a show-window to-day."

CARRIED THE AIR AWAY.

"You have a very fine climate here," said the visitor to a resident. "Such a bracing air!"

"Yes," replied the resident, gloomily, but when there bicyclists come along and pump the air into their pneumatic tires and carry it off."

NATURAL THEOLOGY.

Bobby—"Say, mamma, was the baby sent down from heaven?"

Mamma—"Why, yes!"

Bobby—"Um! They likes to have it quiet up there, doesn't they?"

To Poland Spring.

[Continued.]

To breathe fresh air,
　And drink pure water,
　A place to rest,
　　Is what we're after.

O, Poland Spring,
　We come to thee;
Place of all places,
　From care free.

We view for miles
　The beauties round,
And wander through
　Thy spacious grounds.

Nature's done so much for thee,
　Fair Poland Spring;
And thou in turn dost much for me;
　We drink to thy prosperity.

A GUEST.

The Mineral Exhibit.

The vicinity of Joplin, Mo., is one of the most interesting of mineral localities. Lead is mined, the sulphide—galena or galenite, crystallizing in cubes and octahedrons—being the prevailing ore. Large calcite crystals in great variety are obtained, recent finds of golden yellow and other colors being especially handsome and showy. Pearl spar, a variety of dolomite, associated with tetrahedral crystals of chalcopyrite, is also found. The prettiest specimens of the variety of sphalerite, or zinc sulphide, known as ruby blende, are secured here, and the dark sphalerite crystals, called black jack, also occur. Fine specimens of these minerals are shown in the Maine State Building. Mr. Chadbourne will explain them every Thursday when he is here.

An Episcopal clergyman's wife living in southern Texas sends to Mrs. Hiram Ricker a large quantity of Mexican drawn work. Mrs. Ricker will be glad to show it to all who will call at her cottage. It is charity work, and the prices are very reasonable.

The Hill=Top

IS PRINTED AT THE

Office of the Lewiston Journal.

If you wish work executed in like style, address

◆━━━━ JOURNAL OFFICE, LEWISTON, ME.

THE ALPS OF NEW ENGLAND.

IT STANDS AT THE HEAD.

Unrivalled in Popularity!
Unsurpassed in Location!
Unapproached in Patronage!

THE

POLAND ✳ SPRING ✳ HOUSE

IS A SUPERB ILLUSTRATION OF

◦ ◦ SUCCESS ◦ ◦ ◦

EMBRACING AS IT DOES

ALL THE DESIRABLE FEATURES

EXPECTED IN THIS

The Leading Resort of America,

WHILE THE

MAINE STATE BUILDING

WITH ITS

SUPERB ART FEATURES

IS UNEQUALLED BY ANY SIMILAR ENTERPRISE

IN THE WORLD.

◦ ◦ ◦

HIRAM RICKER & SONS (Incorporated),
PROPRIETORS.

MAINE STATE BUILDING.

The Hill-Top

POLAND SPRINGS, SO. POLAND, ME.

HARRY C. WILKINSON

THE HILL·TOP·

Vol. IV.   SUNDAY MORNING, AUGUST 29, 1897.   No. 9.

Lewiston.

PROBABLY there are many people annually at
Poland who never get to Lewiston. This
should never be, for it is not only a pretty
drive, especially through Minot, but an interesting place to investigate. The falls of the Androscoggin, which are between Lewiston and Auburn,
are picturesque in the extreme, and the natural
descent of 38 feet is formed by a ledge of gneiss and
mica-schist, which crosses the river diagonally.
This rock is above water level on the eastern shore,
and on the western rises to a little hill, while in the
stream it forms two islands of over half an acre in
extent.

The stone dam increases the height of the fall to
50 feet, and crossing at a considerable height above
all is the bridge of the Maine Central Railroad.

Of course these falls have their interesting tradition connected with early colonial days, and it has been given very general belief. It is said that two scouts in search of a party of Indians who had carried a girl away captive, encountered at the falls, near night, an Indian who had just landed from a canoe, and was gathering material for a fire, at a point just above the falls, where it would serve as a beacon. They killed the Indian, and suspecting a large body of Indians to be coming down the river in canoes, they quickly retired to a hill below and in a line with the point where the Indian was preparing the beacon. There they kindled a fire, and the Indians were lured by its deceitful light beyond the point of safety, into the swift rapids they were unable to escape, and all went over the fall and perished.

Lewiston is particularly rich in mills, having six corporations engaged in the manufacture of cotton goods. The Continental Mills has the largest number of spindles, 70,000, but there are others, viz., the Lincoln, with 21,744; the Bates, with a capital stock of $1,000,000; the Hill, $1,000,000; also the Lewiston and Androscoggin.

This is not all that Lewiston possesses, for it is proud of the possession of Bates College, of many fine residences, of a fine City Hall, some pleasant residential streets, and of a pushing, enterprising population.

It is the residence of the Hon. William P. Frye, U. S. Senator, and of the Hon. Nelson Dingley, the author of the Dingley tariff, as chairman of the ways and means committee of Congress, and the proprietor of the *Lewiston Journal*.

The State Fair is held at Lewiston annually, and the coming week will witness its appearance, when a drive over, and across the new steel bridge, commanding a fine view of the falls, to the fair grounds, will well repay any in search of novelty and the picturesque.

There are many things in Lewiston which we have not the space to mention, and on the west side of the river you will drive through "sweet Auburn, loveliest village of the plain," which has more pleasant streets, and a gaol, which is not pleasant, and the wonderfully interesting Turner Center Creamery, with its great vats of cream, large enough to float a boat in, and where the whole establishment will be shown you with pleasure.

Returning, take in Mr. Sanborn's famous Elmwood Farm, and gaze upon the beautiful horses, a sight in itself worth the whole journey.

Finally, take a copy of the HILL-TOP with you, for it is a directory of Lewiston's best business houses; but do not miss the State Fair.

Among the welcome guests Saturday, August 21st, was Mr. Thomas J. Craven of Salem, N. J.

Mrs. Samuel Bates's Eighty-Ninth Birthday.

ON Tuesday afternoon, August 24th, several of Mrs. Samuel Bates's friends gathered at Mrs. Walker's, Lakeview Cottage, to celebrate her eighty-ninth birthday. The room in which Mrs. Bates and her daughter received was beautifully decorated with pond-lilies and sweet peas.

Mr. Daniel Kuntz and Mr. Carl Hauser played several choice selections, which were much enjoyed by Mrs. Bates, who is very fond of music.

The mantel-piece in the dining-room was banked with goldenrod and evergreen. On the center-table was a large bouquet of wild flowers, and four daisies peeped out from under the green, as if to say, " We lived to pay you homage."

Rev. Dr. Baker of Philadelphia, who is a nephew of Mrs. Bates, made a few remarks and read the following poem, which was composed by one of the guests at Lakeview:

To Mrs. Bates on Her Birthday, August 24, 1897.

Oh, happy day, when Mrs. Bates
Came a stranger to our gates.
Of Lakeview Cottage she's the queen,
As very quickly can be seen.
Her pleasant face, her sunny smile,
We'll ne'er forget, though many a mile
Erelong will stretch between us.
Glad greetings on her birthday, then.
Though eighty-nine, she seems but ten,
When swinging high up in the air—
Her heart still young, though gray her hair.
Oh, may she still live many a year
And make herself to others dear
As to her friends at Poland.

                    ANONYMOUS.

Refreshments were served, and a happy surprise to Mrs. Bates was a birthday cake. She received many gifts and beautiful flowers. Before separating, her friends gathered at the piano and sang "Auld Lang Syne," Mrs. Bates leading in the singing. She and Miss Bates will return to their home in Washington, D. C., in the early part of September.

Those present were: Mrs. John Greenwood, Miss Greenwood, Misses Clara and Cathaleen Greenwood, Miss Harshberger, Mrs. George Crofut, Miss Crofut, Misses Marguerite and Georgia Crofut, Mrs. S. Onthank, Miss Onthank, Mr. and Mrs. Arthur Friend, Misses Alice and Ruth Friend, Mr. and Mrs. Nelson Bartlett, Mr. and Mrs. Oakes, Mrs. Walker, Miss Edith Walker, Miss Lena Mullen and Master Elmer Walker, Mrs. E. P. Ricker and little Edward, Mrs. Kuntz, Mrs. A. B. Ricker and Miss Janette and little Marion, Mrs. Martha Pulsifer, Mrs. Oliver Marsh, and Miss N. M. Ricker.

Mr. Frank N. Nay, the well-known lawyer of Boston, registered Monday, August 23d. Mr. Nay has just returned from the Rangeley Lakes.

Art Notes.

THE increased interest in the Art Exhibition, mentioned in the last number, has continued, and picture talk has been a very common event as the time draws near for the departure of some, and the exceptional merit of the works becomes more generally known and appreciated.

Frederick D. Henwood is finely represented this year, first by an excellent portrait which has attracted universal attention and comment for its superiority, and again for a study head called "The Model," No. 60, in Alcove A. Mr. Henwood was born in Gloucestershire, England, and after his preliminary studies in London he passed ten years in study in Paris, with various continental trips at times. This was followed by two years in Algeria. He is a pupil of Bouguereau, Lefebvre, Carolus, Duran, and Boldini, five splendid masters; has exhibited, in the Paris Salon, portraits, figures, and landscape, and has painted many well-known people in Paris, London, New York, and Boston. The portrait of Mrs. William C. Ulman, No. 61, in Alcove D, is highly complimented by large numbers of visitors to the gallery.

Hendricks A. Hallett is an American artist, born in Charlestown, Mass., under the shadow of Bunker Hill Monument, and went to Antwerp in 1875 to study art, and to Paris the following year. His work has been purchased by the Boston Art Club, and has also received the distinction of a medal award at the Massachusetts Charitable Mechanics Exhibition. He is an exhibitor at all notable exhibitions. Nos. 41 and 42, "A Shady Nook" and "Winter," will be found at the head of the stairs, and 43 and 44, "Early Morning on the Bar" and "Morning, Boston Harbor," in Alcove F. Mr. Hallett's work will be found to possess exceptional merit, and ranks well in the world of art.

D. D. Coombs is one of Maine's most excellent artists and one who has received considerable distinction as a painter of cattle; a man modest in his pretensions, but whose work has been shown in several notable galleries. Two of his cattle pieces, Nos. 18 and 19, may be seen in Alcove E, where they have attracted the attention of all visitors.

Catalogues are free, and may be had at the Library, also a list of the prices of all the pictures.

Progressive Euchre.

On Friday evening, August 20th, the guests gathered in the Amusement Room of the Poland Spring House for their usual game of progressive euchre. There were twenty-two tables. Seventeen games were played. The highest number for the ladies was fourteen, and for the gentlemen thirteen.

Mrs. Van Bell, Mrs. Osgood, and Mrs. Soria cut for the first ladies' prize. Mrs. Van Bell won the first, an exquisite center-piece; Mrs. Osgood the second, a beautiful cut-glass bonbon dish; Mrs. Soria the third, a lovely bureau scarf. The fourth prize went to Mrs. Everett, a dainty lunch set; and the consolation to Mrs. E. P. Ricker, a lovely box of stationery.

Mr. Swain won the first gentlemen's prize, a statuette. Mr. Palmer and Mr. Munger cut for the second prize. Mr. Palmer won the second, a cut-glass bottle, and Mr. Munger the third, a pocket-book. Mr. Mulqueen gained the fourth, a picture frame; and the consolation prize went to Miss Ziegler, a silver paper-cutter.

It was the largest party of the season, and the prizes were beautiful.

Tuesday evening, August 24th, a small progressive euchre party was given at the Mansion House. There were seven tables. The highest number for the ladies was twenty-seven, and the highest for the gentlemen thirty-one.

Mrs. Stuart won the first ladies' prize, a lovely doily, of Mexican drawn work; Mrs. Shaw the second, a silver button-hook. The consolation prize went to Mrs. Kellogg, a miniature water-color head. Master Lester Gilbert won the first gentlemen's prize, a Dresden candle-stick; Mrs. Van Bell the second, an ink-well.

Mrs. Keene displayed excellent taste in her selection of prizes, and the evening passed very pleasantly.

Brake Rides.

The following party, Mr. Emanuel, Mr. Palmer, Mrs. Palmer, Mrs. Englis, Miss Englis, Miss Underwood, Miss Eddy, and Miss Anna B. Englis, had a delightful brake ride to White Oak Hill and Tripp Lake, August 20th.

Saturday, August 21st, an enjoyable brake ride was given to Tripp Lake. The party included Mr. and Mrs. Charles G. Mitchell, Mr. and Mrs. J. G. Mitchell, Mr. and Mrs. C. E. Mitchell, and Mr. and Mrs. E. J. Secor.

Mrs. J. Hood Wright, Mr. J. N. Conyngham, Mrs. Conyngham, Miss Moore, Miss Skidmore, and Mr. George B. North enjoyed a brake ride, August 22d.

Mr. and Mrs. Marburg, the Misses Marburg, Dr. Pease, Miss G. MacDonall, Mr. Wallace Lanahan, and Mr. J. MacDonall went to Oxford on the brake, Monday, August 23d.

An Episcopal clergyman's wife living in southern Texas sends to Mrs. Hiram Ricker a large quantity of Mexican drawn work. Mrs. Ricker will be glad to show it to all who will call at her cottage. It is charity work, and the prices are very reasonable.

Children's Column.

So many gods! So many creeds!
So many paths that wind and wind—
While just the art of being kind
Is all the sad world needs.
—*Ella Wheeler Wilcox, in Century.*

Favorite Dishes.

THE VIANDS PREFERRED BY SOME FAMOUS MEN
AND WOMEN.

Every day of the year Queen Margherita of Italy has a dish of strawberries served to her upon a gold plate. Indeed, the king and queen always dine from golden dishes, and the king's favorite viand is artichokes cooked with the livers and combs of chickens.

The Queen Regent of Spain has a weakness for gooseberry jelly. During the early days of her life in Spain she ate only one kind of bread, which was sent to her from Vienna, but of late she eats the bread of the country.

Ex-Queen Isabella always has rice served with her dinner.

The dowager Empress of Germany is especially fond of pastry.

The dowager empress of Russia is fond of the Danish black or rye bread, such as is baked for the soldiers. During Her Majesty's visits to her old home, Denmark, she always has this kind of bread, and when in Russia a loaf is sent to her every fifth day.

Her sister, the Princess of Wales, confesses that her favorite dish is Yorkshire pudding.

Sweden's queen loves, above all things, the meat pies that are served in Nice; next to that dainty she prefers the national dish of buried salmon, and beefsteak is an invariable part of each meal's bill of fare. She is also fond of eggs fried in milk and oil.

One of Queen Victoria's favorite dishes is smoked ham; another is baked potatoes; and after her dinner she always wants a few nuts. She likes tea, and it is always Couchong. Her usual dinner beverage is pale sherry, which she drinks from a beautiful gold cup, a relic of the time of Queen Anne.

A Rheims biscuit, dipped in a cup of milk, is the Pope's tid-bit. In Lent His Holiness lives on eggs, fish, and macaroni.

Mr. Gladstone is devoted to that plebeian dish, rice pudding, and as for tea he has a Johnsonian love for it, and never fails taking several cups at five o'clock every day.

The King of Greece prefers his viands cooked in the fashion of his native country, Denmark, and his queen insists upon her native Russian cooking.

The Emperor of Germany has a special fondness for ham and eggs *a l'Anglaise*, and he has muffins and crumpets sent him from England.

The Sultan of Turkey lives on rice and mutton and drinks only water.

The favorite dish of the Shah of Persia is lamb, a week old, roasted whole with the wool on, and stuffed with dates, chestnuts, and almonds.

—*Boston Globe.*

Sunday Services.

Mass was held in the Music Hall, Sunday, August 22d, by Rev. Father John A. Conway of Washington, D. C.

Rev. James S. Stone of Chicago preached in the Music Hall, Sunday morning, August 22d. His text was from II. Corinthians, 13th chapter, 14th verse: "The grace of the Lord Jesus Christ, and the love of God, and the communion of the Holy Ghost, be with you all."

Rev. W. P. Lewis of Philadelphia preached in the dining-room, Sunday evening, August 22d. His text was from St. Matthew, 6th chapter, 10th verse: "Thy will be done on earth as it is in heaven."

The Art Store.

Hand Embroideries, the work of the women of Constantinople, Damascus, Persia, and other eastern countries; Gold Dress Trimmings, Bed and Table Spreads, lovely Doilies, Mantel Draperies, and an innumerable variety of other articles, useful, curious, and interesting, are to be found at Mrs. Mallouf's, at the corner of the hotel.

Some Valuable Presents.

VERY recently the Maine State Building has been enriched by the addition of several valuable gifts from most generous and interested guests of Poland Spring. Mr. George G. Crowell, president of the Insurance Company of the State of Pennsylvania, and Mr. W. B. McClellan, special agent for the same, have forwarded a very beautiful Japanese vase, which Mr. Vautine, the art dealer of Broadway, New York, says "is one of the largest ever brought to this country," being over five feet in height and six feet two inches in circumference. "The decoration is considered very fine and the coloring exceedingly good." It is a valuable and beautiful gift, and will be an ornament to the rotunda, where it now is.

John C. Paige & Co., the firm which succeeded to the business of the late John C. Paige, Boston, have forwarded the twenty-five volumes which comprise the original Encyclopædia Britannica, being one of the best editions and of great value as reference books. These books are not of the commonly circulated reprints so much advertised, but are the latest edition of the genuine Britannica. It was a most generous and graceful act on the part of the new firm, to present this work to the library, which Mr. Paige had already enriched with his gifts.

Mr. D. W. Thompson of Bridgeport, Conn., a son-in-law of P. T. Barnum, who was recently a guest with Mrs. Thompson, has forwarded to the library an elegantly-bound copy of "The Struggles and Triumphs of P. T. Barnum," with a particularly fine photogravure portrait of the prince of showmen as a frontispiece. He also sends an elegant large photograph of Mr. Barnum, framed, with the autograph of Mr. Barnum affixed. So famous a personage and so fascinating a book will be welcome additions, thanks to the kindness of Mr. Thompson.

Mrs. M. B. Hoffman has presented to the Poland Spring Library the very sumptuous edition of "Modern Artists," published under the direction of F. G. Dumas, Leibrarie d' Art, Paris, and No. 755 of an Edition de Luxe, of which only twelve hundred copies were published. It is a very elegant work of 288 pages, elaborately illustrated with steel and wood engravings. In addition to this, Mrs. Hoffman has given an elegant copy of Moore's "Lalla Rookh," very profusely illustrated. Both these volumes will make permanent and valuable additions to a library destined to become one of the largest and finest in the state.

Mr. and Mrs. W. F. Rose and Miss E. W. Rose of Cambridge, arrived Monday, August 23d, and are at the Maine State Building.

The big slide that occurred on Mt. Clay during the recent storm is an object of interest to old guests who notice it as a new wrinkle that has appeared upon the face of the old mountain. It is nearly a mile long, extending from near the top of the ravine down into the depth of Clay gulf. It is probably the largest avalanche that took place in the White Mountains during the recent floods. Another large slide appears upon Mt. Washington, a little above Base station, and others can be seen on Mounts Pleasant and Clinton. All can be viewed with the naked eye from the verandah of the Mt. Pleasant House.

Tid-Bits.

Masque.

Come again.

All promenade.

Who wins the cup?

Mr. John Hoyt and Mrs. Hoyt of Boston are here.

Mr. F. H. Browne of Waltham is at Poland Spring.

Mr. Joseph Moore, Jr., of Philadelphia, is with us.

Dr. C. C. Schuyler of Plattsburgh is at Poland Spring.

Mr. and Mrs. T. Gilmour of Toronto are at Poland Spring.

Mrs. J. C. Nulsen of St. Louis is at the Mansion House.

Mr. E. S. Bryant of Providence, R. I., is at the Mansion House.

Mr. S. A. Treat and Mrs. Treat of Chicago are at Poland Spring.

Mr. Tenny Smith of New York arrived Monday, August 23d.

Miss Sarah F. Hardy of New York is at the Poland Spring House.

Mr. George Trott of Philadelphia registered Monday, August 23d.

Mr. C. C. Converse and Mrs. Converse of Boston have returned.

Mr. A. Gilbert of Plainfield, N. J., is at the Poland Spring House.

Mr. Charles M. Gay, Jr., of Boston, is at the Poland Spring House.

Mr. John T. Morris and Miss L. S. Morris of Philadelphia are here.

Mr. C. Edward French of Boston arrived Saturday, August 21st.

Mr. Talbot Lanston and Mrs. Lanston of Washington, D. C., are here.

Mr. A. R. Wright and Mrs. Wright of Philadelphia arrived August 23d.

Mr. and Mrs. L. Norman and Master A. Norman of Brookline, Mass., are with us.

Mr. W. F. Almeder of Boston, Mass., has joined Mrs. Almeder at Poland Spring.

August 23d, Mr. C. E. Mitchell caught several black bass, the largest weighing $3\frac{3}{4}$ lbs.

Mr. Eugene Tompkins of Boston has joined his mother at the Poland Spring House.

Mr. and Mrs. Arnold of Philadelphia, and Miss Wilson, Plainfield, N. J., are with us.

Mr. Eugene G. Blackford of Brooklyn, N. Y., has rejoined his family at the Poland Spring House.

Mr. and Mrs. Maxwell Wyeth and Master Francis M. Wyeth of New York arrived Aug. 21st.

Mr. F. T. Murray and Mrs. Murray of New York arrived at the Mansion House, August 23d.

Mr. and Mrs. W. H. Fletcher and family of New York City arrived Wednesday, August 25th.

Mr. S. P. Payne of Greenfield, Mass., registered at the Mansion House, Tuesday, August 24th.

Mrs. W. H. Inman, Mrs. Day, and Mrs. Payne of New York, are at the Poland Spring House.

Mr. and Mrs. Charles H. Richardson of Boston have joined their father, Mr. Moses W. Richardson.

Mrs. C. L. Wilson of Brookline, and Miss Martha Heaton of Quincy, Mass., are at the Mansion House.

Mr. and Mrs. Robert Bleakie, Mr. Eugene Bleakie of Hyde Park, Mass., and Mr. Bleakie of Sabattus, registered August 21st.

Prof. W. E. Sargent and Mrs. Sargent of Hebron, Me., Mr. H. D. Scribner and Mrs. D. A. Scribner of Brooklyn, spent Monday, August 23d, here.

Mr. W. L. Lawson has purchased the very much admired little picture, entitled "Chums," by Sid. Brackett, from the Art Exhibition. It is a charming little picture, and has received much attention.

Charles O. Bass, 132 Nassau Street, New York, will send you a genealogical chart for a few cents, by which one may easily make a record of their lineage, and they will be much assisted by the genealogical index in the library.

Mr. and Mrs. C. F. Linsey and Miss Linsey of Meriden, Conn., Mrs. Haley and Miss Haley of Brooklyn, N. Y., registered at the Poland Spring House, Monday, August 23d. They have been spending several weeks at the Oxford, Fryeburg, Me.

An October wedding just announced is that of Miss Louise Prescott Allen, daughter of Mr. and Mrs. Granville C. Allen of East Bridgewater, to Mr. Cleaveland Angier Chandler of Jamaica Plain, which will take place at the Unitarian Church, East Bridgewater, Tuesday afternoon, October 12th.

The hotels are so crowded that every available place is taken. A party arrived, and the only room to offer them was one at the stable. They accepted it and slept there. The next morning they were asked if they rested well. The reply was, "Yes, thank you; but we had hay fever and the nightmare; however, I presume we will feel our oats before we leave the hill."

It is a Melancholy Fact

That Maggie Tulliver, in "The Mill on the Floss," could not have been overwhelmed by the floating debris, this being a scientific impossibility.

That Rider Haggard, in "King Solomon's Mines," makes an eclipse of the moon take place at the new moon instead of the full, an astronomic impossibility.

That Walter Besant, in "Children of Gibeon," causes a new moon to rise in the east at 2 A.M.

That Dean Swift said in 1729 that Pennsylvania needed the shelter of mountains to prevent the north winds from Hudson's Bay destroying the plantations of trees.

That Amelia B. Edwards, in "Hand and Glove," compares her hero to an overseer on a Massachusetts cotton plantation.

That Thackeray causes Clive, in "The Newcomes," in a letter dated 183-, to ask why they have no picture of the Queen and Prince Consort, by Smee. Easily answered. There was no Prince Consort until 1840.

That Shakespeare talks of cannon in "King John," a century and a half too soon.

That Trollope makes "Andy Scott" come whistling up the street with a cigar in his mouth.

That Jules Verne causes his hero in "Round the World in Eighty Days" to enter the club in London just as all the clocks in London pealed forth ten minutes to ten. Where are those extraordinary clocks?

Drag Ride.

Mr. Moses W. Richardson of Boston gave a drag ride, Saturday, August 21st. The party included Hon. and Mrs. A. L. Snowden, Hon. and Mrs. E. S. Converse, Mr. and Mrs. I. W. Chick, Mr. and Mrs. C. H. Richardson, Mrs. L. R. Fox, Mrs. Phinehas Adams, Mrs. H. S. Osgood, Hon. C. C. Corbin, and Mr. J. I. Pinkerton. The day was perfect, and the party took the charming drive to Upper and Lower Gloucester, and over Bald Hill.

Tid-Bits.

Now for September days.

Mr. E. L. Peters of Boston has returned.

Mr. J. W. Langford of Boston is with us.

Mr. C. P. Thompson of Albany, N. Y., is here.

Mr. W. H. Abbott of Waterville, Me., is with us.

Mrs. Byron Sprague of Providence, R. I., is at Poland Spring.

Mrs. John L. Batchelder of Boston, arrived Tuesday, August 24th.

Mr. C. Dennett and Mrs. Dennett of New York, arrived August 25th.

Mr. and Mrs. R. H. Abbott of New York are at the Poland Spring House.

Miss A. D. Mills and Miss S. L. Mills of Boston, are at Poland Spring.

Mr. Charles Sayre and Mrs. Sayre of Brooklyn, N. Y., are at the Poland Spring House.

Mrs. Frederick J. Nott of New York, and Mrs. Frederick S. Fish, are at Poland Spring.

Mr. and Mrs. A. G. Coue and Mrs. W. S. Bond of Chicago, are at the Poland Spring House.

It was Mr. Ralph Stout who won the scholarship at Harvard, not Strout, as published in last week's HILL-TOP.

Mr. and Mrs. L. S. Baumgardner and Miss A. C. Miller of Toledo, Ohio ; Mr. and Mrs. Wade, Miss Riddle, Cleveland, registered at the Poland Spring House.

Mr. Thomas M. Gale of Washington, D. C., has rejoined his wife at the Poland Spring House. Mr. Gale is proprietor of "The Raleigh," Washington, D. C.

Curtis & Spindell make very superior elastic stockings and bandages, and all troubled with varicose veins, weak knees or ankles, will do well to consult their advertisement on the back cover.

FRANK CARLOS GRIFFITH. | Editors.
NETTIE M. RICKER, |

PUBLISHED EVERY SUNDAY MORNING DURING THE MONTHS
OF JULY, AUGUST, AND SEPTEMBER, IN THE INTERESTS OF

POLAND SPRING AND ITS VISITORS.

All contributions relative to the guests of Poland Spring
will be thankfully received.

To insure publication, all communications should reach the
editors not later than Wednesday preceding day of issue.

All parties desiring rates for advertising in the HILL-TOP
should write the editors for same.

The subscription price of the HILL-TOP is $1.00 for the
season, post-paid. Single copies will be mailed at 10c. each.

Address,

EDITORS "HILL-TOP,"

Poland Spring House,

South Poland, Maine.

PRINTED AT JOURNAL OFFICE, LEWISTON.

Sunday, August 29, 1897.

Editorial.

A VERY good illustration of typical American
humor is the following: "An Indiana man
bet ten dollars that he could ride the fly-
wheel in a saw-mill, and as his widow paid the
bet, she remarked, 'William was a kind husband,
but he didn't know much about fly-wheels.'"

Yet three thousand years ago a parallel to this
is found in II. Chronicles 16 : 12, 13—"And Asa
in the thirty and ninth year of his reign was dis-
eased in his feet, until his disease was exceeding
great; yet in his disease he sought not to the Lord,
but to the physicians. And Asa slept with his
fathers, and died in the one and fortieth year of
his reign."

The first one of these stories is a good indication of the result of attempting what one is utterly
unfamiliar with. It appears to be very simple to
the on-looker, when he witnesses the apparent ease
with which a great business is conducted, and
forthwith mayhap the aforesaid on-looker attempts
the same feat, thinking to start at the same point
he had witnessed the successful operation. But

there is a difference. A man may haul a very
heavy burden easily, if the road is smooth, hard,
and level, and the vehicle possesses pneumatic tires
and ball-bearings, which other and less favorable
conditions will defy a much greater power to move.
The road must be prepared, and ability and tact
and strength are required to pull up the hill to the
level of prosperity, and then only the guiding hand
is necessary.

The second story proves that there is nothing
new under the sun, and however small we may
think ourselves, the creative process has been going
on many ages, and there have been others, previous—too previous, perhaps. It further shows
that gout was an early cause of demise among
kings.

Musical Programme.

SUNDAY EVENING, AUGUST 29, 1897.

1. Priests' March . . . . . Mendelssohn
2. Violin Solo
   { a. Prize Song from Meistersinger   Wagner-Wilhelmj}
   { b. Vivace . . . . Ries}
3. Selection—Oberon . . . . . Weber
4. Menuet from Orpheus . . . . . Gluck
5. Hungarian Rhapsodie, No. 12 . . . . Liszt
6. Hymn.

The Sin of Omission.

[Contributed.]

It isn't the thing you do, dear,
It's the thing you leave undone
Which gives you a bit of a heartache
At the setting of the sun.
The tender word forgotten,
The letter you did not write,
The flower you might have sent, dear,
Are your haunting ghosts to-night.

The stone you might have lifted
Out of a brother's way,
The bit of heartsome counsel
You were hurried too much to say;
The loving touch of the hand, dear,
The gentle and winsome tone
That you had no time or thought for,
With troubles enough of your own.

For life is all too short, dear,
And sorrow is all too great,
To suffer our slow compassion
That tarries until too late.
And it's not the thing you do, dear,
It's the thing you leave undone,
Which gives you the bit of heartache
At the setting of the sun.   —Selected.

Miss Alice Luce of Auburn, Me., and Miss
Helen Sanborn were at Poland Spring, Thursday,
August 26th. Miss Luce is the first and only
woman in the United States to have the degree of
Ph.D. conferred upon her by the University of
Heidelberg. This was in 1895.

Mrs. O. Smith of Chicago is at Poland Spring.

Mr. and Mrs. W. R. Howe of New York are at the Poland Spring House.

Among the welcome guests Monday, August 23d, was Mrs. T. Smith of New Orleans.

Mrs. John C. Haynes, Miss E. M. Haynes, and Mrs. A. J. Simpson of Boston, are here.

Mr. J. B. Sawyer and Mr. Geo. L. Osgood went fishing Friday, August 20th. They brought home 50 trout, several weighing from 1-2 lb. to 3-4 lbs.

Booker T. Washington and the students of the Tuskegee Normal and Industrial Institute, added $114.71 to their fund by their appearance at the Poland Spring House on Tuesday evening.

Mrs. Robinson, the excellent masseuse at the Poland Spring House, is at all times prepared to attend any in want of such services. Massage is very generally recommended by physicians.

Miss Dingley, daughter of Congressman Dingley, Miss L. M. Ricker of Lewiston, Miss M. S. Dwight and Mr. M. C. Holden of Springfield, Mass., registered at the Poland Spring House, Tuesday, August 24th.

The Waumbek.

There must be a certain harmonious combination of altitude, soil, and location to produce perfect air, and an ideal combination is claimed at Jefferson. It lies on the south slope of the Pliny range, has a very porous soil, and is distant from any large body of water, which contributes in no small degree to the dryness of the air, while the altitude (1,500 feet) and latitude give its tonic quality. Such a location gives the Waumbek an advantage which has made it so justly popular.

Golf.

There is to be held, on the Poland Spring Links, a Golf Tournament, on Thursday, September 2d, when Hiram Ricker & Sons offer a handsome cup, to be played for under the following conditions : 36 Holes Handicap Medal Play, open to all amateurs. A special prize will also be offered for the lowest gross score. Entries will close on Wednesday, September 1st. Entrance free.

This should call out some fine players, and prove of especial interest in the golf world.

The gentlemen's handicap tournament which was postponed from Tuesday until Wednesday, on account of the rain, was won by W. Berri ; H. B. Ingalls was second. The prizes, which were given by Mr. Byron P. Moulton, were, first prize, caddy bag with four clubs ; second prize, dozen golf balls. The following are the scores in full :

	1st Round.	2d Round.	Gross.	Handicap.	Net.
W. Berri	54	47	101	30	71
H. B. Ingalls . .	64	58	122	41	81
Wm. C. Chick . .	62	62	124	41	83
H. Berri	67	61	128	44	84
I. W. Chick . . .	72	60	132	45	87
J. H. Maginnis . .	60	60	120	33	87
C. C. Converse . .	69	65	134	46	88
A. H. Fenn . . .	45	45	90	0	90
S. P. Holton . . .	71	65	136	44	92
F. M. Sawtelle . .	70	70	140	45	95
C. C. Schuyler . .	69	72	141	44	97
N. G. Carman . .	79	79	158	60	98
J. A. Ingalls . . .	44	72	156	55	101
Geo. A. Vose . .	67	66	133	30	103
Lester Gilbert . .	78	77	155	48	107
B. P. Moulton . .	87	85	172	60	112
H. C. Swain . .	89	75	164	50	114
F. F. Robbins . .	89	83	172	58	114
Geo. L. Osgood .	90	91	181	60	121
J. H. Lake . . .	105	95	200	60	140

The ladies' golf tournament was held on Wednesday, and Miss Mabel Chick won first prize and Mrs. I. W. Chick won second. Miss Hoeke, Miss Ingalls, and Miss Peterson, who played from scratch, did not do as well as they usually do in practice. The following are the scores in full :

	Gross.	Handicap.	Net.
Miss Mabel Chick	100	32	68
Mrs. I. W. Chick	111	28	83
Miss Harriet F. Blackford . .	117	32	85
Mrs. Wm. Berri	122	35	87
Miss Anna L. Hoeke	92	0	92
Miss Janette I. Englis	107	15	92
Miss E. W. Morgan	125	32	93
Mrs. Nugent	126	30	96
Mrs. McCauley	128	32	96
Miss A. B. Englis	112	16	96
Miss Olive Gale	112	15	97
Miss M. N. Skidmore	139	35	104
Miss May Peterson	111	0	111
Mrs. James Swan	148	35	113
Miss Claire Ingalls	115	0	115
Mrs. Geo. L. Osgood	150	28	122

There was a handicap tournament held on Thursday, 18 holes, medal play, for three prizes given by Mr. J. A. Ingalls of Boston. The first prize was a handsome silver cup; second prize, box of silvertown balls; third prize, golf club.

Mr. I. W. Chick and S. P. Holton were tied, with a net score of 84 for first and second prize. A. H. Fenn won third prize, lowering the 18-hole record to 85 strokes. In the play-off for first prize, Mr. Chick beat Mr. Holton 8 strokes, after a very close and exciting match. The following are the scores in full :

	1st Round.	2d Round.	Gross.	Handicap.	Net.
I. W. Chick . . .	68	49	117	33	84
S. P. Holton . . .	61	61	122	38	84
A. H. Fenn . . .	43	42	85	0	85
J. H. Maginnis . .	60	57	117	30	87
Geo. A. Vose . .	57	60	117	26	91
C. C. Schuyler . .	63	65	128	36	92
Herbert B. Berri .	63	66	129	36	93
R. P. Moulton . .	77	69	146	50	96
Wm. C. Chick . .	65	60	125	28	97
Lester Gilbert . .	75	72	147	50	97
H. C. Swain . .	78	69	147	50	97
Geo. L. Osgood .	78	69	147	50	97
W. Berri	60	54	114	16	98
H. B. Ingalls . .	68	58	126	28	98
C. C. Converse . .	73	64	137	38	99
A. Palmer . . .	84	68	152	50	102
B. F. Cole	77	77	154	47	107
J. A. Ingalls . . .	83	76	159	50	109
F. M. Sawtell . .	75	71	146	36	110
James H. Lake . .	89	91	180	50	130

The following was the score in playing off the tie for first and second prize :

	1st Round.	2d Round.	Gross.	Handicap.	Net.
I. W. Chick . . .	66	57	123	33	90
S. P. Holton . . .	66	70	136	38	98

New Books.

From John C. Paige & Co.
Encyclopædia Britannica. 25 vols.

From D. W. Thompson.
Struggles and Triumphs of P. T. Barnum.

From Mrs. A. Gracie.
Doctor Luttrell's First Patient; by Rosa Nouchette Carey.

From Mrs. John W. Danielson.
Mrs. Cliff's Yacht; by Frank R. Stockton.

From a Friend.
Marietta's Marriage; by W. E. Norris. (Paper.)
The Marriage of Elinor; by Mrs. Oliphant. (Paper.)

From Alpheus Collins.
Bob Covington; by Archibald Clavering Gunter. (Paper.)

From Mrs. M. B. Hoffman.
Modern Artists. (Edition de Luxe.)
Lalla Rookh; by Thomas Moore.

From John Page Woodbury.
Menticulture; by Horace Fletcher.
Patrins; by Louise Imogen Guiney.
Seven Dreamers; by Annie Trumbull Slosson.

From Mrs. A. R. Bradford.
Springhaven; by R. D. Blackmore. (Paper.)

From George Mathews.
The Comical Cure-All. (Paper.)

Professor L. Water, the magician and prestidigitateur, gave an entertainment in the Music Hall, Monday evening, August 23d. Professor Water is a clever man, and some of his tricks are remarkable. The hall was well filled, and he expressed himself as being much pleased with the collection.

ELMWOOD FARM

OF FRENCH COACHERS

IMPORTED STALLIONS

GEMARE, 134. LOTHAIR, 979. TELMAQUE, 515.

3 Miles from Poland Spring, Maine,

the Home of the Ideal Coach and Road Horse of America.   Half-Bred French Coach Carriage Horses for Sale.
Also, Young Registered French Coach Stallions. Size, Intelligence, Courage, Endurance, and Conformation Insured.
STOCK SHOWN DAILY.

J. S. SANBORN.

Reed & Barton

✳ Silversmiths ✳

Trade Mark

Sterling

Salesrooms

41 Union Square and
8 Maiden Lane N. Y.
103 State Street Chicago

Factory and Offices
Taunton Mass.

Also manufacturers of the Reed & Barton Silver-Plated Ware, so well known and in designs especially adapted for Hotel, Steamboat, and Dining-Car Service. Samples and estimates promptly furnished.

Arrivals.

POLAND SPRING HOUSE.

FROM AUGUST 20 TO 26, 1897.

Arents, Mr. and Mrs. Geo.	New York
Abbott, Mr. and Mrs. R. H.	New York
Abbott, W. H. L.	Waterville
Bline, Mrs. Ida	Chicago
Batcheldei, Mrs. John L.	Boston
Broadway. Jos.	Tuskegee, Ala.
Buzzell, Eugene	Worcester
Browne, F. H.	Waltham
Blakie, Mr. and Mrs. Robert	Hyde Park
Blakie, Eugene	Hyde Park
Barclay, Mr. and Mrs. A. Chas.	Philadelphia
Barclay, Miss Emily	Philadelphia
Bond, Mrs. W. S.	Chicago
Chase, Jonathan C.	Syracuse
Creed, Miss K. E.	Boston
Claik, Mr. and Mrs. G. A.	New York
Clark, Miss	New York
Claik, Mr. and Mrs. W. B.	Lowell
Crowell, Mr. and Mrs. J. L.	Providence
Connot, D. D.	Lewiston
Craven, Thos. J.	Salem, N. J.
Conyngham, John N.	Wilkesbarre
Covell, Mr. and Mrs. W. H.	Boston
Cooper. Miss	Pittston, Pa.
Converse, Mr. and Mrs. C. C.	Boston
Cone, Mr. and Mrs. A. G.	Chicago
Chadbourne, Mr. and Mrs. E. R.	Lewiston
Cross, Mrs. Mary	Brockton
Cook, Mr. and Mrs. Wm. G.	Trenton
Clawford, Mrs. Francis M.	Brooklyn
Clawford, Miss	Brooklyn
Clawford, Miss Leona	Brooklyn
Cody, John F.	Boston
Dingley, Miss	Lewiston
Dennett, Mr. and Mrs. C.	New York
Dolan, James W.	Boston
Dwight, M. L.	Springfield
Dingley, Miss Anna	Auburn
Dingley, Miss Florence	Auburn
Englis, John	Brooklyn
French, C. Edward	Boston
Foss, Mrs. J. O.	Auburn
Fish, Mrs. Frederick S.	New York
Guerin, Mr. and Mrs. Craig R.	New York
Gay, Chas. M.	Boston
Gilbert, A.	Plainfield, N. J.
Goodwin, Mr. and Mrs. Howard	Boston
Gordon, Dr. S. C.	Portland
Gardner, Mrs.	Portland
Gilmour, Mr. and Mrs. Thos.	New York
Gillespie, Annie	Boston
Glacknor, John	New York
Glacknor, Miss Violet	New York
Hauscom, O. M.	Boston
Howard, Mrs. Chas.	Brockton
Holden, M. C.	Springfield
Haynes, Mrs. John C.	Boston
Haynes, Miss E. W.	Boston
Harris, Chas. G.	Tuskegee, Ala.
Huntley. Robert	Lewiston
Haley, Mrs.	Brooklyn
Haley, Miss	Brooklyn
Hawes, Miss	Lewiston
Healey, Mr. and Mrs. J. F.	Brooklyn
Holmes, Mrs. G. F.	New Gloucester
Holmes, C. P.	New Gloucester
Hardy, Sarah F.	New York
Hoyt, Mr. and Mrs. John	Boston
Jordan, H. W.	Portland
Jackson, Mr. and Mrs. Thos.	New York
Jones, Miss Ellen F.	Somerville
Kincaide, Henry L.	Quincy
Kata. Miss Rosa	New York
Keith, Mr. and Mrs. Preston B.	Brockton
Keith, Miss	Brockton
Livesey, J. H.	Chicago
Livingston, Mrs. C. G.	Chicago
Little, Amos R.	Philadelphia
Lanston, Mr. and Mrs. Talbot	Washington
Littlefield, C. E.	Rockland
Langford, J. W.	Boston
Leybolt, Calvin	Scranton, Pa.
Leybolt, Miss	Scranton, Pa.
Leybolt, Louise	Scranton, Pa.
Leybolt, Romayne	Scranton, Pa.
Loud, Mr. and Mrs. O. M.	Portland
Little, Mr. and Mrs. S. H.	Morristown, N. J.
Lemann, Mr. and Mrs. M.	New Orleans
Lemann, Miss.Alice	New Orleans
Linsley, C. F.	Meriden, Conn.
Linsley, Mrs.	Meriden, Conn.
Linsley, Miss	Meriden, Conn.
McCahan, Mr. and Mrs. W. J.	Philadelphia
Mone, E. J.	Boston
Moore, Joseph, Jr.	Philadelphia
McLellan, W. B.	Boston
McLellan, C. S.	Boston
McDonald, John D.	Boston
Malbuig, T.	New York
Mason, Evelyn	Auburn
Matthews, W. S. B.	Chicago
Mills, Miss A. D.	Boston
Mills, Miss S. L.	Boston
Mora, Mr. and Mrs. Frank J.	New York
McKeever, Mr. and Mrs. A.	New York
Mergler, Marie J., M.D.	Chicago
Mowl, Mr. and Mrs. W. R.	New York
Moore, Mrs. Gordon G.	Chicago
Milick, Mrs. E. G.	New York
Milick, Miss	New York
Nott. Mrs. Frederick J.	New York
North, Geo. B.	New York
O'Donnell, J. V.	Chicago
Osgood, H. S.	Portland
Peters, E. D.	Boston
Prescott, W. H.	Boston
Ricket, L. M.	Lewiston
Ryan, Mr. and Mrs.	Orange, N. J.
Rawson, Miss Della	Chicago
Richardson, Mr. and Mrs. Chas. H.	Boston
Rose, Mr. and Mrs. W. F.	Camden, N. J.
Rose, Miss E. W.	Camden, N. J.
Soper, E. D.	Lowell
Skelley, J. R.	Grand Rapids
Schuyler, C. C.	Plattsburgh
Sturges, Mr. and Mrs. W. P.	Brooklyn
Smith, Mr. and Mrs. John B.	Lewiston
Sturgis, Mr. and Mrs. J. S.	New Gloucester
Smith, Tunny	New York
Sargent, Mr. and Mrs. W. E.	Hebron
Scribner, H. D.	Brooklyn
Scribner. Mrs. D. A.	Brooklyn
Smith, Mrs. T.	New Orleans
Simpson, Mrs. A. J.	Boston
Sprague, Mrs. Byron	Providence
Shull, Mr. and Mrs. J. F.	Wenonah, N. J.
Sayle, Mr. and Mrs. Chas. D.	Brooklyn
Smith, Mrs. Orson	Chicago
Sawyer, C. A.	Boston
Smith, Mr. and Mrs. J. L.	Auburn
Smith, Alice E.	Auburn
Smith, Master Richard I.	Auburn
Thomas, Mr. and Mrs. H. O.	Brockton
Thompson, C. P.	Albany
Tompkins, Eugene	Boston
Thompson, Miss Fannie	Auburn
True, Mr. and Mrs. F. D.	Portland
Tiott, Geo.	Philadelphia

Vogal, Mr. and Mrs. Wm.	Brooklyn
Van Valkenburg, Miss Susanne	Indianapolis
White, Mr. and Mrs. F. H.	Lewiston
Wyeth, Mr. and Mrs. Maxwell	New York
Wyeth, Master Francis M.	New York
Wheelock, Mr. and Mrs. H. M.	Boston
Wheelock, W. W.	Auburn
Wheelock, Miss	Auburn
Wright, Mr. and Mrs. A. R.	Philadelphia
Washington, Booker T.	Tuskegee, Ala.
Whitehead, H.	Tuskegee, Ala.
Whitefield, Mrs. E. A.	Chicago
Wilkinson, Harry C.	Lewiston
Whitman, Mrs. W. E.	Auburn
Wheeler, Mr. and Mrs. E. R.	Chicago
White, Marion	Gardiner
Young, Mr. and Mrs. Geo. W.	Boston

MANSION HOUSE.

Bryant, E. S.	Providence
Cochrane, F. A.	U. S. Navy
Fletcher, Mr. and Mrs. W. H.	New York
Gillander, Dr. G. H.	Boston
Hinckley, Freeman	Boston
Heaton, Miss Martha	Quincy
Hornet, Louis H.	Boston
Kingsley, Mr. and Mrs. E.	Yarmouth
Lowell, D. E.	Auburn
Lindsey, J. W.	Fall River
Leighton, C. E.	Cumberland
Melcher, Arthur S.	Auburn
Mulsen, Mrs. J. C.	St. Louis
Murray, Mr. and Mrs. F. T.	New York
Noyes, Geo. F.	Portland
Nay, Frank N.	Boston
Pierce, A. M.	Boston
Pope, Miss Margaret R.	Boston
Parrott, J. E.	Oxford
Parrott, C. S.	Lynn
Payne, S. R.	Greenfield
Smith, Mrs. Jas. B.	Springfield
Sturtevant, Mrs. Julia B.	Springfield
Wilson, Mrs. C. L.	Brookline

THE ALPS OF NEW ENGLAND.

IT STANDS AT THE HEAD.

Unrivalled in Popularity!
Unsurpassed in Location!
Unapproached in Patronage!

THE

POLAND ✳ SPRING ✳ HOUSE

IS A SUPERB ILLUSTRATION OF

◦ ◦ ◦ SUCCESS ◦ ◦ ◦

EMBRACING AS IT DOES

ALL THE DESIRABLE FEATURES

EXPECTED IN THIS

The Leading Resort of America,

WHILE THE

MAINE STATE BUILDING

WITH ITS

SUPERB ART FEATURES

IS UNEQUALLED BY ANY SIMILAR ENTERPRISE

IN THE WORLD.

◦—◦◦—◦

HIRAM RICKER & SONS (Incorporated),
PROPRIETORS.

MAINE STATE BUILDING.

The Hill-Top

POLAND SPRINGS, SO. POLAND, ME.

HARRY C. WILKINSON

THE HILL-TOP

Vol. IV.   SUNDAY MORNING, SEPTEMBER 5, 1897.   No. 10.

Seen From the Tower.

WE present as an illustration this week a view from a remarkably good photograph, taken by the Sprague & Hathaway Co. recently, from the tower of the Poland Spring House, and showing a portion of the golf links on a quiet day. In this picture the trees, even on the farther shore of the lake, are distinct and separate, while in the near-by woods they are remarkably so.

Golf has taken a tremendous hold upon the people all over the country, and Poland can boast of as good links as are to be found in the East; but, even excellent as they are, much improvement is likely to be found next season, for standing still is not one of the characteristics at Poland Spring.

We give herewith a record of the tournaments of the past week.

The ladies' handicap tournament of 9 holes medal play was played on Saturday, August 28th. The prizes were given by Mr. I. W. Chick of Boston, Mass. Great interest was taken in the playing of the ladies, by all the guests. A good many of the gentlemen carried clubs and did the scoring for their lady friends. Miss A. B. Englis won first prize; three golf clubs, with a net score of 67. Miss Grace Douglass and Mrs. McCauley, with a net score of 69, tied for second and third prizes. The second prize was two golf clubs, and third prize one golf club. The following are the scores in full:

	Gross.	Handicap.	Net.
Miss A. B. Englis	92	25	67
Miss Grace Douglass	99	30	69
Mrs. McCauley	109	40	69
Mrs. Wm. Berri	102	32	70
Mrs. D. C. Nugent	111	40	71
Miss Florence C. Peterson	107	35	72
Miss M. N. Skidmore	113	38	75
Miss Anna Louise Hoeke	87	10	77
Miss Mabel Chick	93	16	77
Mrs. C. C. Converse	122	45	77
Miss Olive Gale	104	25	79
Mrs. Joseph A. Ingalls	123	42	81
Miss Eleanor Wilcox Morgan	128	43	85
Miss B. W. Eddy	114	28	86
Miss Claire Ingalls	101	12	89
Mrs. C. N. Sheldon	124	35	89
Miss May Peterson	109	16	93
Miss A. Soria	129	35	94
Mrs. A. Peckham	133	38	95
Mrs. Geo. L. Osgood	141	45	96

On Monday afternoon Mr. A. H. Fenn lowered the record for nine holes to 37 strokes, which is one stroke lower than Bogie. This record will probably not be beaten this season. Mr. Fenn is playing very steady golf now and is practicing daily, expecting to leave Poland on September 7th for Chicago to play in the open tournament there for the amateur championship of the United States.

There was a gentlemen's handicap foursome held on Monday. Messrs. W. C. Chick and C. C. Converse won first prize, and B. F. Cole and T. Lanston won second prize. The following are the scores in full:

	Gross.	Handicap.	Net.
W. C. Chick and C. C. Converse	131	20	111
B. F. Cole and T. Lanston	147	35	112
H. B. Ingalls and J. H. Maginnis	127	10	117
E. W. Olney and W. P. Comstock	122	4	118
B. P. Moulton and C. C. Schuyler	151	28	123
H. Berri and W. Berri	123	0	123
A. H. Fenn and J. A. Ingalls	125	0	125
S. P. Holton and I. W. Chick	125	0	125

A ladies' handicap tournament was held on Monday, also—18 holes, medal play. There were three prizes, presented by Mr. C. C. Converse of Boston. The first prize was won by Miss Anna Louise Hoeke, who had the lowest handicap of any of the players. She played a very steady game throughout, and lowered her best record for the links. The second prize was won by Miss Olive Gale, and the third prize by Miss Eddy. The score:

	1st Round.	2d. Round.	Gross.	Handicap.	Net.
Miss Hoeke	76	80	156	20	136
Miss Gale	105	95	200	54	146
Miss Eddy	106	101	207	60	147
Mrs. Nugent	112	110	222	73	149
Mrs. Osgood	124	106	230	80	150
Miss Englis	97	96	193	40	153
Miss M. Peterson	103	92	195	36	159
Miss M. Chick	100	97	197	32	165
Miss C. Ingalls	102	92	194	27	167
Mrs. Berri	118	112	230	60	170
Miss McCauley	116	132	248	72	176
Mrs. Chick	120	98	218	40	178

On Tuesday there was a handicap tournament, 18 holes, medal play, for three prizes presented by Walter and Herbert Berri. A. H. Fenn won first prize from scratch. In doing so he lowered the record to 83 strokes, which is four strokes lower than Findlay, the Scotch player from Boston. The second prize was won by H. B. Ingalls, and the third prize by A. Palmer. The score:

	1st Round.	2d Round.	Gross.	Handicap.	Net.
A. H. Fenn	42	41	83	0	83
H. B. Ingalls	59	56	115	30	85
A. Palmer	65	68	133	45	88
J. H. Maginnis	65	52	117	28	89
E. W. Olney	64	57	121	32	89
Dr. Schuyler	67	60	127	38	89
W. P. Comstock	58	52	110	20	90
Walter Berri	57	54	111	20	91
S. P. Holton	61	63	124	30	94
B. P. Moulton	67	72	139	45	94
Miss Olive Gale	101	90	191	93	98
Daniel Kaisner	67	64	131	32	99
Herbert Berri	72	64	136	36	100
I. W. Chick	63	61	124	22	102
Miss Claire Ingalls	92	100	192	85	107
W. C. Chick	72	64	136	25	111
C. C. Converse	67	70	137	26	111
Miss Mabel Chick	102	94	196	85	111
Geo. L. Osgood	83	78	161	45	116
Mrs. Geo. L. Osgood	113	122	235	100	135
J. A. Ingalls	95	89	184	45	139

The open tournament for the handsome cup presented by the proprietors of Poland Spring was held on Thursday, it being 36 hole medal play. There were 25 entries, and 21 handed in cards. This tournament has been looked forward to with much interest, and the day was a fine one, with the exception of a shower for a few minutes in the afternoon. The cup bore the inscription: "Presented by the Proprietors Poland Spring House. Handicap Golf Tournament, September 2, 1897." It was a large silver cup, with two buck-horn handles, and was won by Dr. Daniel Kaisner of Philadelphia, his score being 235 gross, 40 handicap, 195 net. It was thought that Mr. Chick and Mr. Converse had tied for the prize, when Dr. Kaisner quietly handed in his card, and the result was greeted with loud applause. A pleasant feature of the tournament was held in reserve for the tied players, who found, on entering the dining-room, a huge table with covers for 26 placed

in front of the great window at the end of the dining-room. This table was a marvel of ingenuity and elaborate display. Covering the large central portion was a perfect reproduction in little, of the golf links, all the details being placed, with a ground of green baize for the links, the miniature teeing grounds correctly located, with the holes marked by neat little red flags bearing the name of its particular hole as found in the score card. There were small drivers, four in number, two crossed and placed at each end of the links, which were eight feet long and five feet wide. The golf balls were represented by marbles, and the bunkers were made of sweet peas. Around the edge was a profusion of sweet peas and green, while at each end of the links was a large mound of sweet peas. The tees and flags were nine in number, and each gentleman was provided with a boutonniere. This very ornate and charming composition was the work of Mr. Louis Warcham, and his skill and artistic labors deserve the highest praise, for it is seldom so charming a realization is presented to a party of banqueters, wherever it may be, and whatever may be the means at his command. This is twice during the week Mr. Warcham has covered himself with glory, but being a very modest man he bears his honors blushingly. Mr. A. H. Fenn had the distinguished honor of making the lowest gross score, but being plus 40 lost him the prize. Mr. Fenn's score, as will be seen, was 186. The following is the score in full :

	Gross.	Handicap.	Net.
Dr. Daniel Katsner	235	40	195
I. W. Chick	228	32	196
C. C. Converse	244	48	196
J. H. Maginnis	231	24	207
H. Betti	243	36	207
W. C. Chick	246	36	210
W. Berri	220	8	212
W. P. Comstock	220	8	212
S. R. Campbell	245	32	213
B. P. Moulton	278	60	218
A. Palmer	259	40	219
E. N. Olney	255	36	219
G. S. Ellis	231	12	219
C. Morton Sills	225	0	225
H. B. Ingalls	249	24	225
A. H. Fenn	186	Plus 40	226
W. C. Eaton	262	24	238
Allyn Marsh	276	32	244
George L. Osgood	331	60	271
H. P. Frank	313	40	273
W. C. Emerson	306	32	274

The Art Store.

Fine specimens of Mexican Drawn Work and Hand Embroideries of every kind may be found at Mrs. Mallouf's, at the corner of the hotel. Great quantities of other goods suitable for gifts, prizes, etc., are to be found in great profusion, and a visit to the store is like a visit to an eastern bazaar.

The Masquerade.

TUESDAY evening last, one who was fortunate enough to have been at the Poland Spring House, might have imagined himself suddenly transferred to Bangs's "House-Boat on the Styx," for Moses was hobnobbing with Columbus, and Charles II. found himself enjoying a tête-à-tête with the ebony Topsy.

All went merry as a marriage bell, and the annual masquerade ball of the Poland Spring employees passed into history as the most successful affair ever given here of a similar nature. The march began from the Dining-Room, and through the office to the Music Hall, around the Amusement Room, and after a variety of evolutions, the festivities of the evening began. The leaders of the march were Mr. Castner and Miss Elliot, in the bridal costumes of the time of Charles the Second; and Mr. Murphy and Miss Rice as the bride and groom of to-day, and the selections were well made in every instance, for all were elegant and blushingly interesting, the ladies looking too sweet, and the gentlemen handsome and contented with their respective partners.

Among the notable characters which followed, none attracted more interest and favorable comment than Mrs. Sawyer in a dress of Poland Water seals, 2,000 being used in the construction of the costume, and innumerable corks, which were strung upon strings and artistically draped.

Of course we feel a natural pride in our own representative for "THE HILL-TOP," Miss Murphy, who wore a costume of much attractiveness, composed of HILL-TOPS, and carried a satin banner with a superb fac-simile of the cover. This work was most successfully done by William Thresher, to whom much praise is due.

Mrs. Noble looked all that her name implies, in the costume of "The Goddess of Liberty," and was a continual feast.

Miss Ella Shea wore also a delightfully ingenious costume made up of Poland Water bottle labels, arranged in bottle form, and looked charming.

Miss Perry was most attractive also as the "Pine Tree State," a costume which attracted attention.

The "Mt. Pleasant House" had as its representative, Miss Connors, and it could not complain of its representation in any respect, for she was in every way an interesting figure, and among the best seen.

The "Lewiston Journal," too, was finely represented by Miss Buynor, her dress being characteristically composed of scores of Journal headings.

Miss Clancy commanded attention as the "Golfer," bearing a huge golf club; Miss Danahy also, as "Aunt Ophelia," was perfectly made up to represent that famous creation of Mrs. Stowe, while Miss Wedgwood whirled in the mazy, attired in Kennedy's famous biscuit. As long as the biscuit lasted, she need never go hungry.

The Misses Haskin and Beglin, as the "Girls of the Twentieth Century," showed some very artistic dancing, and were noticeable in some very mannish get-ups.

There were scores of other most charming and ingenious costumes displayed by the ladies, which there is not space to mention, but which were nevertheless noteworthy.

Among the gentlemen, one might instance Mr. Thresher as "Moses," with a Moses bottle, who was a noticeable figure, from his characteristic costume and manly and dignified bearing; also Mr. Frazier as the "Globe Man," with a rotundity of surpassing dimensions, which caused great merriment.

Mr. Archie Cole as a "Crow" deserves mention, as also Martin Neveus as "Lopez," which was a becoming and attractive costume.

Mr. Briton and Mr. Bird, as "Uncle Sam" and "Brother Jonathan," gave proof that Columbia's children were twins, whereas it had been popularly supposed that they were one and the same being.

There was a sprinkling of clowns, Chinamen, Indians, Monkeys, Harlequins, and Sailors, all neat and noticeable, but all together there were so many masks, it is not possible to name all.

The music was furnished by the Kuntz Orchestral Club, and was as ever superior.

A bounteous supper was served during the evening by the Messrs. Ricker, who also provided all the gentlemen's costumes, as well as much other material, and the innumerable accessories which were required to make the affair the success it was.

The Dining-Room was most elaborately and artistically decorated by Mr. Louis Wareham, and reflects great credit upon that always amiable person. Mr. Wareham also directed the decoration of the Music Hall and the Amusement Room, being successfully aided by Mrs. Sherman and Miss Annie Hanson. Mr. Wareham has several times shown his exceptional skill and fine artistic taste in this connection, but never before to better advantage, or with more interest in its success.

To Mrs. E. P. Ricker belongs much credit for her earnest and indefatigable labors in every direction to further the success of the undertaking.

To Mr. William Thresher belongs a vast amount of credit for his artistic efforts, which have been most earnest, and deserving of every recognition.

Mr. Murphy has also been untiring in his labors, and should not be forgotten, where praise is bestowed.

There are many others whose presence was not seen, but who aided behind the scenes, and should be remembered, as just as essential to its success as those who came under the eye of the spectator.

The order of dances was neatly gotten up by the Lewiston Journal Job Office, and serves as a neat souvenir of the occasion.

Much credit is due the following members of the committee: Miss Annie Danahy, Miss Lillian Haskin, Miss Sadie Haskin, Miss Delia Clancy, Miss Mabel Martin, Miss Katharine Beglin, Miss Katharine Murphy, Miss Helen Wescott, Miss Della Doyle, Miss Alice McCarthy.

We present a photograph of Miss Murphy as "THE HILL-TOP," furnished by the Notman Photographic Company, who made it possible, through the interested efforts of the Lakeside Press of Portland, to present it in this issue.

The guests of Poland Spring were enthusiastic in their praise, and universally pronounced it a huge success.

We append herewith a complete list of the participants who appeared in costume, but there were several others who did not provide any distinctive character, but who took part in the delightful affair.

Following is a list of the ladies and gentlemen and the characters they assumed.

Miss Elliott,	Bride of the time of Charles II.
Miss Rice,	Bride of To-Day
Mrs. Noble,	Goddess of Liberty
Miss Perry,	Pine Tree State
Miss Ella Shea,	Poland Water Labels
Miss Connols,	Mt. Pleasant House
Mrs. Sawyer,	Poland Water Neck Labels
Miss Buynor,	Lewiston Journal
Miss Murphy,	Hill-Top
Miss Clancy,	The Goltel
Miss Danahy,	Aunt Ophelia
Miss Martin,	Topsy
Mrs. J. Danahy,	The Summer Girl
Miss Sullivan,	Looking Backward
Miss Thomasine Sullivan,	Looking Backward
Miss Rohrfuchs,	Pop-Corn Girl
Miss Wilson,	Little Bo-Peep
Miss Savage,	Two Little Girls in Blue
Miss Adams,	Mistress Mary
Miss Clockett,	Blue Bell
Miss Leveque,	Night
Miss Edwards,	Morning
Miss Hanson,	Highland Lassie
Miss Rich,	Heliotrope
Miss Tierney,	Sweet Peas
Miss Wedgewood,	Cracker Girl
Miss Wescott,	Japanese Girl
Miss McBean,	Japanese Girl
Miss Stevens,	Spanish Tambourine Girl
Miss Kearns,	Spanish Tambouring Girl
Miss Baker,	Rainbow
Miss Briggs,	Aster
Miss Seniol,	Milkmaid
Miss Merrill,	Golden-Rod
Miss Jordan,	Snow-Ball
Miss Hackett,	Organ Grinder
Miss Mara,	
Miss McCarthy,	Chums
Miss Beglin,	
Miss Cutler,	School Girls
Miss Haskin,	Spanish Lady
Mrs. Lane,	Ferns
Miss Malcom,	Butterfly
Miss Fahey,	Yellow Chrysanthemum
Miss Nolton,	Symphony of the Rose
Miss Mack,	Maud Muller
Mrs. Archie Cole,	Violet
Miss Shea,	Poppy
Miss Lottie Hackett,	Pond Lily
Miss Mullay,	Italian Peasant
Miss Corbett,	Quakeless
Miss May Halligan,	Red Riding-Hood
Miss Jordan,	Dancing Girl
Miss O'Neil,	Fortune Teller
Miss Lillian Haskin,	
Miss Elizabeth Beglin,	Girls of the 20th Century
Miss Minahan,	Boot-Black
Miss Noble,	Calfs
Miss Gertrude Noble,	Artist
Miss Mary Adams,	Wild Flowers
Miss Toluian,	Chinese Woman
Miss Doyle,	Vanity
Miss Grove,	Dew-Drop
Miss Kerrigan,	The Yellow Kid
Miss Harper,	Apple Woman
Miss Casey,	Maid of Erin
Miss Katie Mara,	Early September
Miss Flarity,	
Miss Doyle,	Poland Waitresses
Miss Divel,	Lady in White
Miss Campbell,	Gipsy
Mr. Casuer,	Bridegroom of time of Charles II.
Mr. Murphy,	Bridegroom of To-Day
Mr. O'Brian,	De Mauprat
Mr. Theisbel,	Moses
Mr. Barbey,	Mephisto
Mr. King,	Montjoy
Mr. Emery Thomas,	Duc de Montmorency
Mr. Blown,	Sailor
Mr. Head,	Duke Frederick
Mr. Estes,	Hotspur
Mr. Shailor,	Columbus
Mr. Brijon,	Uncle Sam
Mr. Irving Hubbard,	Earl Salisbury
Mr. Bird,	Brother Jonathan
Mr. Binele,	De Bellingen
Mr. Martin,	Monkey
Mr. Lawrence,	Clown
Mr. Manchester,	Brigand
Mr. Benson,	Chinese Clown
Mr. Crooker,	Clown
Mr. Wilson,	Lopez
Mr. Martin Nevens,	Cowboy
Mr. J. H. Finzier,	Globe Man

Mr. McCann,	Brownie
Mr. McKnight,	Harlequin
Mr. Winslow,	Jockey
Mr. Archie Cole,	Clow
Mr. Petley Cole,	Indian
Mr. Helen,	Don Leonardo
Mr. Hodgman,	Indian
Mr. Cullis,	Charles II.
Harry Cripps,	Card Clown
Mr. Sawyer,	Chinaman
Mr. Fisher,	French Pierrot
Mr. Farley,	Indian
Mr. Bjett,	Clown
Mr. Hilton,	Humpty Dumpty

Following was the order of dances :

March and Circle.	Welcome
Plain Quadrille.	Our Proprietors
Waltz and Two-Step.	Our Orchestra
Lady of the Lake.	
Unmask at sound of cornet.	Look at us.
Waltz, Schottische, Two-Step.	Happy Days
Lanciers.	Ladies' Choice
Galop.	Our Girls
Portland Fancy.	Hill-Top
Waltz.	Success
Boston Fancy.	Au Revoir till '98

𝒯id=ℬits.

Take the Cup.

Did you go to the Fair?

Paper dresses are great things.

1,843 books in the library September 1st.

Mr. John C. Haynes arrived August 28th.

1,198 books taken out of the library in August.

Mr. C. J: Milne of Philadelphia arrived August 29th.

Mr. and Mrs. James M. Gifford of New York are with us.

Mr. Frank D. Hatfield and Mrs. Hatfield of New York are with us.

Mrs. S. B. Payne of Greenfield arrived Wednesday, September 1st.

Mr. Z. Jellison and Mrs. Jellison of Brooklyn are at the Mansion House.

Mr. John C. Kerr of Brooklyn has rejoined Mrs. Kerr at Poland Spring.

Mr. R. S. Marshall and Mrs. Marshall of Cincinnati, are at Poland Spring.

Mrs. Fred S. Salisbury and Miss Salisbury of New York are at Poland Spring.

Mr. Walter White and Mrs. White of Newton, Mass., are at the Mansion House.

Mr. J. L. Batchelder of Boston has joined Mrs. Batchelder at Poland Spring.

Mr. and Mrs. W. Francis and Miss Gladys Francis of Toronto arrived August 30th.

Mr. T. L. Vickens, Mrs. Vickens, and Miss Vickens of Brooklyn, N. Y., are here.

Mr. John B. Manning and John B. Manning, Jr., of New York, arrived August 28th.

Mrs. E. F. Leland and Miss E. A. Leland of Boston are at the Poland Spring House.

Mr. John Blackie and Mrs. Blackie of Denver, Col., are at the Poland Spring House.

Mr. E. W. Olney and Mr. William P. Comstock of Providence, R. I., have returned.

Mr. and Mrs. H. H. Longstreet and Master Harry Longstreet of New Jersey are with us.

Mrs. E. P. Stillman and the Misses Stillman of New York are at the Poland Spring House.

Mr. R. H. Greenleaf of New Mexico registered at the Poland Spring House, August 28th.

Mr. and Mrs. Benjamin Lapham, Mr. and Mrs. A. Harkness of Providence, R. I., are here.

Mr. W. I. Woodman and Mrs. Woodman of St. Augustine, Florida, arrived Monday, August 30th.

Mr. E. H. Bright of Cambridge, Mass., has joined his father and mother at the Poland Spring House.

Mrs. Louis R. Cassaid and Miss Sarah E. Brown of Baltimore, arrived at the Mansion House September 1st.

Mr. and Mrs. E. M. Fainsworth and Mrs. Charles C. Hoyt of Brookline are at the Poland Spring House.

Among the welcome guests were Mrs. M. E. Hildreth, Miss Hildreth, and Mr. Henry A. Hildreth, of Boston.

Mr. John H. Shortridge, Miss T. E. Shortridge, and Miss F. A. Shortridge of Philadelphia, arrived August 27th.

Friday, August 27th, Mr. C. E. Mitchell returned from a day's fishing, bringing twenty speckled beauties with him.

Among the welcome guests Wednesday, September 1st, were Mrs. Henry P. Sondheim and Mrs. Joseph Gibson of New York.

Miss S. N. Farrington of Ashtabula, Ohio, Miss Emily Williams and Miss A. H. Williams of Worcester, Mass., are at the Mansion House.

Mr. and Mrs. Gale, Miss Olive Gale, Mrs. Berri, Mrs. Swan, and Messrs. Herbert and Walter Berri, enjoyed the Maine State Fair on Wednesday, September 1st.

Mr. and Mrs. N. A. Chapman, Miss Chapman, and Miss Whitcomb, of Bangor, Me., arrived Saturday, August 28th. Mr. Chapman is one of the proprietors of the Bangor House.

Miss N. G. Holland of 7 Temple Place, Boston, is prepared at all times to do manicuring and chiropody for ladies and gentlemen. She is at No. 73 of the Poland Spring House.

Mr. J. W. Bowers of Portland, Mrs. J. M. Hughes of Westfield, N. Y., and Mr. Isaac M. Daggett of New York City, registered at the Poland Spring House, Saturday, August 28th.

Miss Alice B. Ricker of Falmouth, Me., is spending a few days at Poland Spring. Miss Ricker is a sister of the noted contralto singer of Boston, and is in the class of '98, Smith College.

Mr. and Mrs. S. A. Sweetland of Natick, Mass., and Mr. and Mrs. Henry W. True of Lewiston, spent Saturday, August 28th, here. Mr. True is manager of the Lewiston and Auburn Electric Road.

On Wednesday, September 1st, the following party, Mr. and Mrs. Doman, Mr. and Mrs. Brooks, Mrs. J. B. Sawyer, Miss Murphy, Mr. and Mrs. Treat, enjoyed a brake ride to the Oxford Spring House, Oxford, Maine, where they were served an excellent dinner.

Art Notes.

A. S. MONKS was born at Cold Spring on the Hudson, N. Y. He was first a wood engraver and then an etcher, and finally, becoming more ambitious, he became a pupil of Inness, making the painting of sheep a special study of his life. He has made sheep a study from Maine to Florida, and from Scotland to southern Italy. He is a member of the Salmagundi Club of New York, the Etching Club, and Boston Art Club. His picture, "Under the Apple Trees," No. 75 in Alcove E, is one of unusual merit, and has received high praise from Boston art critics. His other works in the Poland Spring Gallery are 76 at the head of the stairs. No. 78 in Alcove C, and a design for a frieze, very artistic, in Alcove D, No. 77.

Henry Sandham has one picture here, No. 101 in Alcove B, called "The Summer Girl," a very excellent picture. By an error, No. 100 was attributed to Mr. Sandham, but is really the work of his daughter. It is in Alcove F and called "Hydrangeas." Mr. Sandham was a pupil of V. O. R. Jacobi and John A. Frass; is a Royal Canadian Academician, and ex-vice-president of the Boston Art Club; is an exhibitor at many of the principal galleries of America and Europe; has received medals from London, Boston, etc. His works are hung in the National Gallery and Senate Chamber, Ottawa, National Gallery, Washington, D. C., and other places of note. Mr. Sandham was the illustrator of "King Noanett," "Lalla Rookh," and other excellent works.

Abbott Graves sends only one picture, also, and that a very good one as usual—No. 40 in Alcove A, called "Fisherman's Daughter." Mr. Graves's work has met with very marked approval, and each new picture from his studio has tended to advance his position in the art world. Mr. Graves was a pupil of Georges, Jeannin, and Cormon, Paris; was an exhibitor in the Paris Salon, 1888 and 1889. and all the principal American exhibitions; received medals in 1887, 1890, and two in 1892; and is a member of numerous art societies.

Musical Programme.

SUNDAY EVENING, SEPTEMBER 5, 1897.
1. Cujus Auimum, from Stabat Mater . . . . . . Rossini
2. Flute Solo—Andante and Rondo . . . . Popp
Mr. A. Brooke.
3. { Nachtgesang . . . . Voigt
    { Liebeseiedchen . . . . Taubert
    For Strings.
4. Piano Solo.
    ⸤a. Caprice . . . . Schutt
     b. Concert Etude . . . . Glasse
     c. Fire charm from the Walküre   Wagner-Brassin
    Mrs. C. Hauser.
5. Selection—I. Pagliacci . . . . Leoncavallo
6. Hallelujah Chorus from the Messiah . . . . Handel

Sunday Services.

Mass was held Sunday, August 29th, by Rev. Father John A. Conway of Washington, D. C.

Rev. Henry R. Rose of Auburn, Me., held divine service in the Music Hall, Sunday, Aug. 29th.

FRANK CARLOS GRIFFITH,) Editors.
NETTIE M. RICKER,   )

PUBLISHED EVERY SUNDAY MORNING DURING THE MONTHS
OF JULY, AUGUST, AND SEPTEMBER, IN THE INTERESTS OF

POLAND SPRING AND ITS VISITORS.

All contributions relative to the guests of Poland Spring
will be thankfully received.
To insure publication, all communications should reach the
editors not later than Wednesday preceding day of issue.
All parties desiring rates for advertising in the HILL-TOP
should write the editors for same.
The subscription price of the HILL-TOP is $1.00 for the
season, post-paid. Single copies will be mailed at 10c. each.
Address,
EDITORS "HILL-TOP,"
Poland Spring House,
South Poland, Maine.

PRINTED AT JOURNAL OFFICE, LEWISTON.

Sunday, September 5, 1897.

Editorial.

BOOKS are in reality food for the mind, but, like other food, all books do not fatten. There are people, the more they read, the less they know, the result being to make a sort of brain mixture, like a certain Scotch broth, so made up of everything, that it is neither the one thing nor the other.

Certain books become standards, and to digest them is to broaden and enlarge, and those books have been epoch-marking works. In this respect no book is more full of meat than "Les Miserables," every chapter of which is a feast. It must make one better, it cannot have any other effect.

There are scores on scores of popular books of the day which are poured into the seemingly bottomless hopper of the brain, which never leave a shred to remember them by, but they become amalgamated in the process and leave no flavor of their own.

Scott, Shakespeare, Dickens, Hugo, Thackeray, and a great number of others, have written lines which will reverberate down the avenues of time in loud, emphatic tones, or echo a merriment which never becomes stale. It is not the amount we read, but what we read. Many readers cannot tell ten days after a book is finished a single atom of its plot or purpose, if it ever had any, and many of the much discussed, deep, and knotty questions, involved in the popular book of the day, are not worth a thought to-morrow, and do not receive it, either.

A writer says he reads scarcely a modern book of fiction, but keeps abreast of the time in the passing events, and that to read other than this chronicle of the progress in science, art, and kindred subjects is only to confuse the mind and not furnish it a new idea of any value.

This may or may not be true, but the lightest of bright reading is better than a barren waste of attempted wisdom embodied in the so-called social or "problem" works of the day.

We recall an experience, after crossing the Irish Sea from Dublin to Holyhead, then taking train and riding for an hour or two through Wales, our being asked by a *seemingly* well-educated and bright young *English* lady, mind you, if we were still in Ireland. This same intelligent (?) reader of books, on being informed regarding a set of Burns's poems published in Edinburgh about 1840, exclaimed: "Oh, I have such a lovely set of Burns, published in sixteen something or other." We told her that if she possessed such a remarkable copy of Burns as that she need never work.

By this we see that mere reading is not always educating.

New Books.

FROM MRS. JOHN C. BLACK.

The Descendant; by Ellen Glasgow.
Book and Heart; by T. W. Higginson.
The Children; by Alice Maynell.
The Pomp of the Lavilettes; by Gilbert Parker.
For the Cause; by Stanley J. Weyman.
Mr. Peters; by Riccardo Stephens.
Nature in a City Yard; by Charles M. Skinner.
A Woman's Part in a Revolution; by Mrs. John Hays
Hammond.
A Wedding Trip; by Amelia Pardo Bazan. (Paper.)
A Comedy of Masks; by Ernest Dawson and Arthur
Moore. (Paper.)
The Story of Antony Grace; by George Manville Fenn.
(Paper.)
The Career of Candida; by George Paston. (Paper.)
Fidelis; by Ada Cambridge. (Paper.)

FROM JOSEPH A. INGALLS.

The Columbian Almanac for 100 years.

Another "Recollection."

HAVE we any more "recollections" in stock? A few slightly shop-worn, which we will dispose of at a bargain. One relates to a number of gentlemen who were residents of my early residential small city, and the new minister.

The former pastor had died, and the church had been trying a lot of new applicants, and on this particular Sunday, after his "premier" in the morning, he noticed as he left the edifice a small knot of sad-looking men in dismal conversation, whereupon he approached, and proceeded to open a conversation.

Were they all members of his congregation and the church? They were, to a man. They appeared sad, downcast; why not be cheerful and hopeful? They could not, for times were dull, and scarce enough dollars came to them to keep the wolf in the backwoods.

Ah, that was sad, but hope on, hope ever, and things would take a turn. What was the first gentleman's name? Smith. The second? Brown. The third? Jones. The fourth? White. He would try and help them.

The afternoon service came, and the pastor *pro tem.* was eloquent, and during the service at one point he offered the most fervent and eloquent appeal for each of our quartette in turn. Might prosperous times come to brother Smith; might brother Brown be constantly in demand; might brother Jones be so overwhelmed with the duties of his trade that he might be obliged to work even into the night; and brother White become a busy and cheerful citizen once again.

The congregation sat aghast. A hum, a buzz, a smile, a groan, came from all over the church; and presently, when the service ended, all hurried to put as much distance as possible between themselves and the preacher, who found himself soon alone, excepting the presence of the aged sexton.

The explanation of the strange action of the congregation was soon given. Brother Smith was a doctor, brother Brown was an undertaker, brother Jones a grave-digger, and brother White the marble cutter.

Our Recent Visitors.

Poland has many visitors of national fame during each season, and always welcomes them with open arms; but on Saturday, the 28th, for the first time, our Maine statesman, Thomas B. Reed, ascended the hill and gazed upon the beauties of Poland.

All the features were shown to Mr. Reed and the party who accompanied him; and especial praise was bestowed upon the Maine State Building and all that it illustrates of the advancement on Poland Hill.

Accompanying Mr. Reed were Mr. George F. Evans, the General Manager of the Maine Central Railroad; Mr. R. R. Cable, President of the Chicago, Rock Island & Pacific Railroad; and Mr. R. A. Waller, Comptroller of the city of Chicago.

They arrived at and departed from Danville Junction in Mr. Cable's private car, and the day was one of pleasure to all concerned. As they drove away from the Poland Spring House, the leading men from the East, South, and West gave vent to cheers for Mr. Reed.

Children's Column.

Bishop Ames says that the responsibility of talking should never be forgotten.

Marbles Made in Germany.

Most of the stone marbles used by boys are made in Germany. The refuse only of the marble and agate quarries is employed, and this is treated in such a way that there is practically no waste. Men and boys are employed to break the refuse stone into small cubes, and with their hammers they acquire a marvelous dexterity. The little cubes are then thrown into a mill, consisting of a grooved bed-stone and a revolving tunnel. Water is fed to the mill and the tunnel is rapidly revolved, while the friction does the rest. In half an hour the mill is stopped, and a bushel or so of perfectly-rounded marbles taken out.

A Pie-ous Question.

"Cast your bread upon the water, brethren," exorted the minister, as the deacons were "waiting upon the congregation."

"Say, ma," inquired the four-year-old in a stage whisper, "what makes him ask for bread and send the pie-plate?"—*Texas Siftings*.

"What time is it, my lad," asked an American traveller of a small Irish boy who was driving a couple of cows home from the fields.

"About 12 o'clock, sir," replied the boy.

"I thought it was more."

"It's never any more here," returned the lad in surprise. "It just begins at 1 again."

Little Edward, our four-year-old baby, seemed much disturbed while driving, and kept moving his legs and looking under the blanket. Presently he said, "Mamma, there are splinters in your dress and they are sticking into me."

"No, sweetheart, there are no splinters in mamma's dress."

Upon investigation, Edward's splinters proved to be the hair-cloth in mamma's gown.

It is Rather Odd

That monosyllables were sufficiently expressive for Shakespeare to use four lines in "King John," Act III., Scene 3, and again in "King Lear," Act IV., Scene 6, without a single word of more than one syllable. Here are the former:

"Good friend, thou hast no cause to say so yet;
But thou shalt have; and creep time ne'er so slow,
Yet it shall come, for me to do thee good.
I had a thing to say;—but let it go."

That the "Monroe Doctrine" originated in the message of President Monroe, December 2, 1823.

That Virginia was the birthplace of seven Presidents—Washington, Jefferson, Madison, Monroe, Harrison, Tyler, and Taylor.

That Henry M. Stanley was originally John Rowlands; Bayard Taylor was James B. Taylor; Whitelaw Reid was Jacob W. Reid; and Henry Irving was John H. Brodribb.

That "In no single instance down to the end of the reign of Anne have I noticed any person bearing more than one Christian name," says H. A. Hamilton, in his "Quarter Sessions from Queen Elizabeth."

That there should be no less than 12,000 windmills in Holland, many with sails exceeding sixty feet in length.

That in London all applicants for a cab driver's license have to drive a critical police inspector through several crowded streets and to out-of-the-way places which he may name.

That Queen Victoria travels under the name of the Countess of Balmoral, the Prince of Wales as the Count of Chester, the ex-Empress Eugenie as the Countess of Pierrefonds, and the King of Belgium as the Count of Ravenstein.

As a mistress of the art of massage, Mrs. Robinson, the masseuse of the Poland Spring House, will be found equal to the requirements in that direction. Any needing such services can secure them by applying at the office.

A Mount Pleasant Caravan Journey Over the Mountains to Franconia Inn.

On Tuesday a large party drove over from the Mount Pleasant House to witness the ball game and to dine at Franconia Inn. This was one of the most notable expeditions ever organized in the White Mountains. The six-horse Poland wagon, two five-passenger surreys, and a carryall carrying thirty people started from the Mt. Pleasant House at half-past nine, reaching Franconia Inn shortly before one. The 21-mile drive was made via Fabyan House, Twin Mountain House, Maplewood, Sinclair, and the line of little hotels and boarding-houses along Bethlehem Street. Over Mt. Agassiz were obtained magnificent views of Mt. Lafayette and Franconia Notch. At Forest Hills Hotel the party stopped to get the incomparable view from the front veranda, and then went on down through the little village of Franconia in the valley below, and then up the long slope of Sugar Hill to Franconia Inn, before which is spread one of not only the grandest, but most beautiful views in all the White Mountains. Several of the guests came by rail with the ball team, so there were 43 in all assembled from the Mt. Pleasant House for dinner at the Inn.

The superb view from Sugar Hill, the fine dinner at the Inn, and the hospitable reception by Mr. and Mrs. Peckett and their guests made the visit one of great pleasure and interest. Leaving at 4.30, the party drove 11 miles to Bethlehem Junction, arriving at sunset, and there took the train from New York, arriving at the Mt. Pleasant House at 7.35.

Progressive Euchre.

A most enjoyable progressive euchre party was given Friday evening, August 27th. There were fourteen tables; eighteen games were played. The highest number for the ladies was fourteen, and for the gentlemen thirteen.

Mrs. Nugent won the first ladies' prize, an exquisite center-piece; Mrs. Adams the second, a cut-glass bonbon dish with gold trimmings; Mrs. Snowden the third, a jet bag; and the consolation prize, a pair of scissors, went to Miss Shortridge.

Mr. Cook won the first gentlemen's prize, a beautiful clock; Colonel Talbot the second, a hat brush with silver mountings; Mr. Gilbert the third, a cigar receiver; Mr. French the consolation prize, a silver key ring.

After the prizes were distributed, Mr. Mathews proposed that a vote of thanks be given Mrs. Griffin, who has been most kind in selecting the prizes and arranging for the progressive euchre parties this season. This was followed by hearty applause.

Notman.

We wish to recall to the attention of the guests the excellence of the photographs which we have used this season which have come from the studio of the Notman Photographic Company. Without exception their work has been of a high class, which will bear the most favorable comparison with any known, and an opportunity like the one presented here should not be allowed to pass unimproved.

Concert.

The Shaker Quartette of East Canterbury, N. H., will give a concert for the benefit of the Children's Mission, in Music Hall, Tuesday evening, September 7, 1897. Exercises will open at 8 o'clock sharp. The Sisters will take up a collection.

Tid-Bits.

Mr. James Dater of New York is here.

Mr. Roger C. Eastman of Boston is here.

Mr. Walter Crane Emerson of Portland is here.

Miss Bayley of Boston is at the Mansion House.

Mr. and Mrs. F. W. Mead of Portland are with us.

Mr. William Neely of New Haven arrived August 29th.

Mr. and Mrs. William H. Brooks of Philadelphia are here.

Mr. and Mrs. G. A. Powers of Brooklyn, N. Y., are here.

Mr. Charles Goold Stevens of Cambridge, Mass., is with us.

Mr. John C. Kerr of Brooklyn has joined Mrs. Kerr, at Poland.

Mr. D. W. Entyne of Montreal arrived Wednesday, September 1st.

Mr. William Brenton Phillips of Philadelphia is at Poland Spring.

Mr. E. B. Levy and Miss Levy of New York are at Poland Spring.

Mr. and Mrs. F. W. Carpenter of Providence, R. I., have returned.

Dr. Charles E. N. Phillips and Mrs. Phillips are at Poland Spring.

Miss E. R. Clark and Miss F. J. Parsons of Yonkers, N. Y., are here.

Mrs. F. C. Wood and Mrs. John McCargo of St. Louis, arrived September 1st.

Mrs. J. H. Swett and Mrs. J. H. Smyser of Brookline, Mass., are at Poland Spring.

Mr. Louis C. Norris and Mrs. Norris of Philadelphia are at the Poland Spring House.

Mr. Samuel Cutler and Mr. S. Weston Cutler of Somerville, Mass., arrived August 31st.

Mrs. Yeutzer Derr and Mrs. Florence Seully of Chicago are at the Poland Spring House.

Dr. John Kurtz and Mrs. Kurtz of Washington, D. C., are at the Poland Spring House.

Mr. S. A. Roberts, Mr. S. N. Robert, and Miss Langley of Milton, Mass., are with us.

Mrs. W. L. Maltby and Miss Emma Maltby of Montreal, are at the Poland Spring House.

Mr. R. S. Hoxie of the U. S. Army and Mrs. Hoxie registered at the Poland Spring House.

Mrs. Helen R. Prince and Master James Prince of Portland, registered Tuesday, August 31st.

Mrs. M. T. Hoffman of New York has returned. Mrs. Hoffman has been spending a week at Newport.

Miss Bessie McCargo, Miss Blanche Rees, and Miss Clementine Rees of Pittsburgh, are at Poland Spring.

Mr. C. G. Allen and Mr. Henry P. Frank of Portland, are here. Mr. Frank plays a good game of golf.

Miss Gertrude E. D. Jenkins and Miss Agnes J. Force of Montclair, N. J., are at the Poland Spring House.

Mrs. Matier and Miss Matier of Providence, R. I., and Mr. Clarence Fahrestore of New York, are with us.

Mr. and Mrs. H. Martin Brown, Miss Brown, and Miss Marion Brown of Providence, R. I., are at Poland Spring.

Mr. Charles Main of San Francisco, Cal., and Mr. E. H. Winchester of Portsmouth, N. H., are at Poland Spring.

Mr. and Mrs. C. J. Bonaparte of Baltimore, and Miss S. G. Haydock of Philadelphia, are at the Poland Spring House.

Mr. and Mrs. William C. Eaton, Mr. E. M. Sills, and Mr. G. S. Ellis of Portland, arrived Thursday, September 2d.

Mr. Amos Little of Philadelphia, is to be congratulated on having won the beautiful plates painted by Mrs. John Greenwood.

Among the welcome guests Tuesday, August 31st, were Miss M. F. Bishop of Bridgeport, Conn., and Miss S. S. Clark of Boston.

Mr. N. Whitman of New York is receiving congratulations on having won the violin made by Mr. Joseph Schillinger of South Poland.

Rev. Edward C. Moore, pastor of the Central Congregational Church, Providence, R. I., is the guest of Mr. and Mrs. F. W. Carpenter at the Poland Spring House.

Miss Helen M. Bartlett of Boston was a welcome guest Tuesday, August 31st. Miss Bartlett has joined her grandfather and grandmother, Mr. and Mrs. Nelson Bartlett, at the Poland Spring House.

Dr. Schuyler recently exhibited in the office some mushrooms, twenty-five on one bunch, belonging to the armillaria family, and another of a handsome dark orange color, belonging to the chantarelli family.

Mr. and Mrs. R. S. Thomas of Smithfield, Va., are at the Poland Spring House. They have been spending several weeks at the White Mountains and Bar Harbor. Mr. and Mrs. Thomas express themselves as much pleased with Poland.

Arrivals.

POLAND SPRING HOUSE.

FROM AUGUST 27 TO SEPTEMBER 2, 1897.

Ashman, Mr. and Mrs. S. A.	Philadelphia
Atwood, Mr. and Mrs. Tascus	Auburn
Atwood, W. P.	Auburn
Allen, C. G.	Portland
Abercrombie, Mr. and Mrs.	New York
Bond, C. E.	Haverhill
Bowers, Mrs. J. W.	Philadelphia
Bayne, C. H.	Harrisburg
Blackie, Mr. and Mrs. John	Denver
Blight, E. H.	Cambridge
Batchelder, J. L.	Boston
Bryant, Mr. and Mrs. Geo. W.	Somerville
Breed, Miss	Boston
Burrill, John W.	Auburn
Bonaparte, Mr. and Mrs. C. J.	Baltimore
Brown, Mr. and Mrs. H. Martin	Providence
Brown, Miss A. Helen	Providence
Brown, Miss Marion N.	Providence
Rowly, Samuel	Baltimore
Brooks, Mr. and Mrs. Wm. H.	Philadelphia
Bishop, Miss	Bridgeport
Bartlett, Miss Helen M.	Boston
Comstock, Wm. P.	Providence
Cable, R. R.	Chicago
Chapman, Mr. and Mrs. H. A.	Bangor
Chapman, Miss	Bangor
Carpenter, Mrs. F. W.	Providence
Crowther, P. E.	Boston
Clark, Miss E. R.	Yonkers, N. Y.
Cross, Dr. and Mrs. H. B.	Jamaica Plain
Cross, Miss S. S.	Boston
Carpenter, F. W.	Providence
Cutler, Samuel	Somerville
Cutler, S. Newton	Somerville
Chandon, Miss	New York
Chase, M. Fowler	Cincinnati
Durrell, Mr. and Mrs. Chas. W.	Cincinnati
Daggett, Isaac M.	New York
Dater, James	New York
Dell, Mrs. Yeutzer	Chicago
Dibblee, Miss	New York
Duhme, Mr. and Mrs. C. H.	Cincinnati
Dickinson, Charles	New York
Dickinson, Mrs. John	New York
Evans, Geo. F.	Portland
Entyne, D. W.	Montreal
Emerson, Walter Crane	Portland
Eaton, Mr. and Mrs. William C.	Portland
Ellis, G. S.	Portland
Eastman, Roger C.	Boston
Farnsworth, Mr. and Mrs. E. M.	Brookline
Foss, Mr. and Mrs. W. H.	Newton
Foss, Mr. and Mrs. W. O.	Auburn
Ferguson, Mr. and Mrs. T. W.	Boston
Frank, Henry P.	Portland
Fahnestock, Clarence	New York
Force, Miss Agnes J.	Montclair, N. J.
Greenleaf, R. H.	Albuquerque, N. M.
Gove, Mrs. O. M.	Waltham
Gross, E. W.	Auburn
Gutmann, Mr. and Mrs. F.	Lewiston
Gutmann, Miss	Lewiston
Gutmann, Walter U.	Lewiston
Gifford, Mr. and Mrs. James M.	New York
Hilliard, J. C.	Boston
Haydock, Miss S. G.	Philadelphia
Haynes, George H.	Portland
Holland, Miss N. G.	Boston
Harkness, Mr. and Mrs. A.	Providence
Haynes, John C.	Boston
Hildreth, Mrs. M. E.	Boston
Hildreth, Miss	Boston
Hildreth, Henry A.	Boston
Hughes, Mrs. J. M.	Westfield, N. Y.
Hoyt, Mrs. Chas. C.	Brookline
Hatfield, Mr. and Mrs. Frank D.	New York
Hayden, Mrs. J. H.	Raymond
Helsey, R. W.	Portland
Hutchinson, Miss	Boston
Hoffman, Mrs. M. T.	New York
Hoxie, Mr. and Mrs. R. L.	U. S. Army
Hayden, George E.	Boston
Jones, Miss	New York
Jenkins, Miss Gertrude E. D.	Montclair, N. J.
Johnson, Mrs. Mary T. W.	Roselle, N. J.
Johnston, Wm. F.	Boston
Kerr, John C.	Brooklyn
Kurtz, Dr. and Mrs. John	Washington
Longstreet, H. H.	Matawan, N. J.
Lawrence, Miss	South Gardiner
Langley, Miss	Milton
Libbey, Mrs. B. E.	New York
Leland, Mrs. E. F.	Boston
Leland, Mrs. E. A.	Boston
Longstreet, Mr. and Mrs. H. H.	Matawan, N. J.
Longstreet, Master Harry	Matawan, N. J.
Lapham, Mr. and Mrs. Benj. N.	Providence
Leonard, J. M.	Fall River
Lee, Mrs. C. E.	Los Angeles
Libby, A. O.	New York
Low, Lydia H.	New York
Low, Juliet W.	New York
Leader, Miss J. Francis	Lewiston
Levy, R. B.	New York
Levy, Miss R.	New York
Marshall, Mr. and Mrs. R. S.	Cincinnati
Moorhouse, Mr. and Mrs. W. H.	Chicago
Moorhouse, Miss F. S.	Chicago
Merrick, Miss Zelka	Chicago
Manning, John B.	New York
Manning, John B., Jr.	New York
Mackenzie, Thos.	Boston
Mackenzie, Miss Octavia	Boston
Moore, John D.	Lewiston
Moore, Edw. G.	Springfield
Moore, Miss	Springfield
Metcalf, Miss	Lewiston
MacDonald, Chas. M.	Portland
McCargo, Mrs. John	St. Louis
Mead, Mr. and Mrs. F. W.	Portland
Main, Charles	San Francisco
Maltby, Mrs. W. L.	Montreal
Maltby, Miss Emma	Montreal
Moore, Edward C.	Providence
McCargo, Miss Bessie	Pittsburgh
Milne, Caleb J.	Philadelphia
Matier, Mrs.	Providence
Matier, Miss	Providence
Murphy, Charles	Skowhegan
Nason, J. L.	Boston
Nason, Miss Ella G.	Boston
Nugent, Frank S.	Winnipeg, Manitoba
Neely, William	New Haven
Norris, Mr. and Mrs. Lewis C.	Philadelphia
Osgood, Miss E. A.	New York
Olney, E. W.	Providence
Page, Kilby	Boston
Page, Miss K. M.	Boston
Page, Mr. and Mrs. Geo. R.	Auburn
Packard, Mr. and Mrs. H. M.	Auburn
Phillips, William Bunton	Philadelphia
Parsons, Miss F. J.	Yonkers, N. Y.
Phillips, Dr. and Mrs. Charles E. H.	New York
Prince, Mrs.	Portland
Powers, Mr. and Mrs. G. A.	Brooklyn
Roberts, L. H.	Milton
Roberts, L. N.	Milton
Rees, Miss Blanche	Pittsburgh
Rees, Miss Clementine	Pittsburgh
Robbins, F. F.	New York
Reed, Thomas B.	Portland
Rodgers, Capt. Frederick	U. S. Navy

Rodgers, Capt. Robert M.   Fort Preble, Me.
Rose, Mr. and Mrs. Henry R.   Auburn
Skillings, Mrs. I. D.   Bath
Skillings, Miss   Bath
Steven, Charles Goold   Cambridge
Swett, Mrs. J. H.   Brookline
Smysel, Mrs. J. H.   Brookline
Scully, Mrs. Florence   Chicago
Sills, C. M.   Portland
Small, Mr. and Mrs. S. R.   Portland
Shortlidge, John H.   Philadelphia
Shortlidge, Miss D. E.   Philadelphia
Shortlidge, Miss F. A.   Philadelphia
Stillman, Mrs. E. P.   New York
Stillman, Miss C. F.   New York
Stillman, Miss B. G.   New York
Sweetland, Mr. and Mrs. S. A.   Natick
Salisbury, Mrs. Fred S.   New York
Salisbury, Miss   New York
Tappan, Miss M. A.   Haverhill
Torrance, Mrs. Daniel S.   New York
Thomas, Mr. and Mrs. R. S.   Smithfield, Va.
True, Mr. and Mrs. Henry W.   Lewiston
Townsend, Col. Chas. H.   Philadelphia
Vickers, Mr. and Mrs. T. L.   Brooklyn
Vickers, Miss Lou G.   Brooklyn
Vinelle, Miss   Boston
Vickers, S. R.   Baltimore
Vanderhoef, Mr. and Mrs. N. J. W.   New York
Wood, Mrs. F. C.   St. Louis
Winchester, E. H.   Portsmouth
White, Mrs. G. W.   New York
Wing, Henry A.   Lewiston
Wallel, R. A.   Chicago
Whitcomb, Miss W.   Chicago
Williams, Mr. and Mrs. S. W.   Roselle, N. J.
Williams, Miss   Roselle, N. J.
Wescott, Miss J. S.   Brookline
White, Miss A. L.   Auburn
Woodward, Arthur   Chicago
Woodman, Mr. and Mrs. W. I.   St. Augustine
Woodward, Mr. and Mrs. F. F.   New York

MANSION HOUSE.

Adams, J. H.   Boston
Boss, Rev. and Mrs. Nelson R.   Brooklyn
Brown, Mrs. Sarah E.   Baltimore
Bayley, Miss   Boston
Cassald. Mrs. Louis R.   Baltimore
Clasto, Rev. Edwin N.   Madison, N. J.
Dana, Mr. and Mrs. G. W.   Somerville
Francis, Mr. and Mrs. W.   Toronto
Francis, Gladys   Toronto
Gibson, Mrs. Joseph W.   New York
Hathaway, A. M.   Boston
Jellison, Mr. and Mrs. Z.   Brooklyn
LeGrow, Maud L.   North Windham
Maxcy, Mr. and Mrs. W. G.   Oshkosh
Newcomb, Mr. and Mrs. G. W.   Bridgton
Neilsen, John C.   St. Louis
Payne, Mrs. S. B.   Greenfield
Rickel, Miss Alice B.   Falmouth
Scull, Miss Anna   Haddenfield, N. J.
Shaw, Mrs. Thomas   Portland
Shaw, Miss H. C.   Portland
Scott, B., Jr.   New York
Sondheim, Mrs. H. P.   New York
Taylor, Miss Grace   Boston
Thompson, Mrs. F. H.   Deering
Thompson, F. M.   Deering
Williams, Miss A. H.   Worcester
Williams, Miss Emily   Worcester
White, Mr. and Mrs. Walter   Newton
Warren, E. B.   Boston
Yarrington, Miss S. N.   Ashtabula

Mr. Sawyer's fishing trip on Monday, resulted in removing one hundred and twenty-five trout from the brook to the basket of Mr. Sawyer.

An Old Lady's Riddle.

Many years ago a prominent merchant promised an old lady a prize, if, taking her subject from the Bible, she could compose a riddle which he could not guess. She won the prize by the following :

> Adam, God made out of the dust,
> But thought it best to make me first;
> So I was made before the man,
> To answer God's most holy plan.
> My body God did make complete,
> But without arms or legs or feet.
> My ways and acts he did control,
> Yet to my body gave no soul.
> A living being I became,
> And Adam gave to me my name;
> From his presence I withdrew,
> And more of Adam never knew.
> I did my Maker's law obey,
> And from it never went astray.
> Thousands of miles I go in fear,
> But seldom on the earth appear;
> For purpose wise which God did see,
> He put a living soul in me.
> A soul from me my God did claim,
> And took from me that soul again;
> Yet when from me that soul had fled,
> I was the same as when first made.
> And without hands or feet or soul,
> I travel on from pole to pole.
> I labor hard by day and night,
> To fallen man I give great delight.
> Thousands of people, young and old,
> Will, by my death, great light behold.
> No light or wrong can I conceive,
> The scriptures I cannot believe;
> They are to me an empty sound.
> No fear of death doth trouble me,
> Real happiness I ne'er shall see.
> To heaven I shall never go,
> Nor to the grave nor hell below.
> Now, when these lines you slowly read,
> Go search your Bible with all speed,
> For that my name's recorded there
> I solemnly to you declare."

Answer in our next.

Brake Ride.

On August 27th the following party enjoyed a brake ride : Mrs. C. E. Mitchell, Mr. and Mrs. J. G. Mitchell, Mrs. Chappell, Mr. and Mrs. C. G. Mitchell, and Mr. Secor. They went to Oak Hill and around the Middle Lake.

A little girl has an uncle who taught her to open and shut his crush hat. One evening, however, he appeared with an ordinary silk hat, which he left in the hall. Presently he saw the child coming with his new hat crushed into accordion pleats. "Oh, uncle," she cried, "this one is very hard. I've had to sit on it, but I can't get it more than half shut."—*Household Words.*

An Episcopal clergyman's wife living in southern Texas sends to Mrs. Hiram Ricker a large quantity of Mexican drawn work. Mrs. Ricker will be glad to show it to all who will call at her cottage. It is charity work, and the prices are very reasonable.

Thistles.

IN CUPID'S COURT.

"He who hesitates is lost,"
  Thus the ancient saying ran.
Wandering far or tempest-tossed,
  Men have learned it to their cost
  Ever since the world began.

In the Court of Cupid, though,
  Be it light of moon or sun,
Be the future weal or woe,
While Sir Plume is bending low,
  She who hesitates is won.   —*Truth.*

HOW TO POINT.

She—"How would you punctuate the following: 'Bank of England notes of various values were blown along the street by the wind?'"

He—"I think I would make a dash after the notes."—*Household Words.*

THE DECISIVE TEST.

Giles—"I'm in love with both girls, and can't for the life of me make up my mind which is the prettier."

Merritt—"Take them into a crowded car some day and see which gets a seat first."—*Life.*

CAPITAL BADLY NEEDED.

He—"They say she's worth half a million."

She—"Well, she needs it in her business."

He—"What's that?"

She—"Looking for a husband."
    —*Odds and Ends.*

HIGH-HANDED.

"I don't like a friend to domineer over me," said the young man with the patient disposition.

"Who has been doing that?"

"My room-mate. He borrowed my evening clothes."

"That's a good deal of liberty."

"I didn't mind it. But when he asked for my umbrella, I told him I might want to use it myself. But he got it just the same."

"How?"

"He simply stood on his dignity and said: 'All right; have your own way about it. They're your clothes that I'm trying to keep from getting spoiled, not mine."—*Washington Star.*

TO ORDER.

"My task in life," said the pastor, complacently, "consists in saving young men."

"Ah," replied the maiden, with a soulful longing, "save a nice-looking one for me."
    —*Dublin World.*

HER NATURAL REMARK.

"What did the woman say when the life-saving crew pulled her out?"

She said, 'Goodness! How do I look?'"
    —*Chicago Record.*

JUST WHAT THE REASON WAS.

Jinks (at a party)—"I don't see what's the matter with that pretty woman over there. She was awfully flirty a little while ago, and now she won't have anything to do with me."

Stranger—"I've just come in. She's my wife."
    —*Odds and Ends.*

APT TITLE.

"Briggsdon intends to start a paper 'devoted to new journalism.'"

"What is he going to call it?"

"The Avalanche."

"What is his idea in giving it that name?"

"Everything goes."—*Chicago Tribune.*

HER QUESTION.

A little Somerville girl going to church with her mother last Sunday saw some men working on the street car tracks.

"See those men breaking the Sabbath," said her mother, thinking to suggest a moral lesson.

The little girl watched them gravely. Then she looked up in her mother's face and said:

"And can't God mend it?"
    —*Somerville Journal.*

THE WISDOM OF YOUTH.

Small sister—"How do you s'pose peoples way up Norf keep warm in de winter, Bobby?"

Small brother (scornfully)—"Why, what does you s'pose de fur-twees is for, 'toopid?"
    —*Cincinnati Commercial-Gazette.*

On Wednesday, the following party, Mr. and Mrs. Bartlett, Mr. and Mrs. C. G. Mitchell, Mr. and Mrs. Griffin, Miss Hildreth, and Mrs. Hildreth enjoyed a trip to Lewiston, and visited the Maine State Fair.

Among the welcome guests Wednesday, September 1st, were Mr. & Mrs. G. W. Davis of Somerville, Mass., and Miss Grace Taylor of Boston. Miss Taylor is the daughter of General Taylor of the *Boston Globe.*

The selection, "Conceit Etude," which Mrs. Carl Hauser will play this evening, was composed by Edwin Grasse of New York. He is thirteen years old and plays the violin beautifully, and the piano equally as well. He speaks German, French, and English fluently. Ysaye and Sauret, two of the most celebrated violin players of the present day, have heard him play, and consider him a boy of great promise. Although bereft of his sight, he has been endowed with this wonderful gift for music and the languages.

About 300 organ-grinders arrive in London every June from Italy, and leave again about October.

English, Certainly.

One cannot fail to be astonished on noting for the first time the variety of Nature's showiest minerals yielded by a small area in Cumberland and adjoining shires. The chief ores are those of tin, copper, zinc, and iron, and with these are associated some of the most beautiful cabinet specimens the world produces. Hematite, or iron oxide, occurs in botyroidal masses, having a bright, shining surface, this variety being commonly known as kidney ore. With the kidney ore, and sometimes covering it, is the dusy specular iron, which consists of brilliant black crystals set on edge, and often thrown into pleasing contrast with crystals of clear quartz scattered among them. Barite, or heavy spar, is found in many forms and colors. Odd as well as pretty are the golden-shadow barites, a new variety, and blue barite, with calcite, is exceedingly attractive. Of the marvels in form and color of the calcites and fluorites pages could be written, the twin crystals being not the least interesting of the forms. These minerals are well represented at Poland, where Mr. E. R. Chadbourne will be each Thursday at the Maine State Building to explain and offer specimens for sale.

Haviland China "Tarascon,"
Stock pattern, always readily matched.

The Hill=Top IS PRINTED AT THE

Office of the Lewiston Journal.

If you wish work executed in like style, address

JOURNAL OFFICE, LEWISTON, ME.

English, Certainly.

One cannot fail to be astonished on noting for the first time the variety of Nature's showiest minerals yielded by a small area in Cumberland and adjoining shires. The chief ores are those of tin, copper, zinc, and iron, and with these are associated some of the most beautiful cabinet specimens the world produces. Hematite, or iron oxide, occurs in botyroidal masses, having a bright, shining surface, this variety being commonly known as kidney ore. With the kidney ore, and sometimes covering it, is the dusy specular iron, which consists of brilliant black crystals set on edge, and often thrown into pleasing contrast with crystals of clear quartz scattered among them. Barite, or heavy spar, is found in many forms and colors. Odd as well as pretty are the golden-shadow barites, a new variety, and blue barite, with calcite, is exceedingly attractive. Of the marvels in form and color of the calcites and fluorites pages could be written, the twin crystals being not the least interesting of the forms. These minerals are well represented at Poland, where Mr. E. R. Chadbourne will be each Thursday at the Maine State Building to explain and offer specimens for sale.

IT STANDS AT THE HEAD.

Unrivalled in Popularity!
Unsurpassed in Location!
Unapproached in Patronage!

THE

POLAND * SPRING * HOUSE

IS A SUPERB ILLUSTRATION OF

° ° ° SUCCESS ° ° °

EMBRACING AS IT DOES

ALL THE DESIRABLE FEATURES

EXPECTED IN THIS

The Leading Resort of America,

WHILE THE

MAINE STATE BUILDING

WITH ITS

SUPERB ART FEATURES

IS UNEQUALLED BY ANY SIMILAR ENTERPRISE

IN THE WORLD.

HIRAM RICKER & SONS (Incorporated),
PROPRIETORS.

MAINE STATE BUILDING.

The Hill Top

POLAND SPRINGS, SO. POLAND, ME.

HARRY C. WILKINSON

THE HILL-TOP

VOL. IV. SUNDAY MORNING, SEPTEMBER 12, 1897. No. 11.

Portland.

IT is not possible within the scope of an article such as we have space to publish, to give anything of the history of a city of the importance of Portland, but a mere fragmentary ing guests to the attractions of that lovely city, the birthplace and home of America's greatest poet.

Its location is beautiful in the extreme, covering as it does a gentle rise of land, which overlooks a charming harbor and bay, everywhere dotted with islands.

clms, and its parks, or promenades, present a pleasant outlook, on the one side to the sea, and on the other to the majestic Presidential Range.

BIRTHPLACE OF LONGFELLOW.

It was here the poet Longfellow was born, at the corner of Fore and Hancock Streets, and it was of this delightful city he wrote in later years :

"Often I think of the beautiful town
    That is seated by the sea;
Often in thought, go up and down
The pleasant streets of that dear old town,
    And my youth comes back to me."

And as if to typify the thought of Longfellow it is at a prominent point, at the junction of Congress and State Streets, we find the artistic and graceful statue of the bard.

THE LONGFELLOW MONUMENT.

A short distance off Congress Street is the home of "Tom" Reed, Maine's famous son.

Next the Preble House (which, by the way, was the former mansion of Commodore Preble, the hero of our early victory over the Bey of Algiers) is the old red brick mansion, "slightly aback from the village street," where Longfellow passed the early years of his life. This was the first brick house erected in Portland, and of which we present a picture on the first page, as it appears at the present time.

Passing to the right, down Middle Street, we soon pass the post-office on the left, and the Fal-

MIDDLE STREET.

mouth House on the right, following on past the building of the Lakeside Press, which furnishes the cuts for the HILL-TOP, to the Custom House, the wharves, and the Grand Trunk Railway Depot.

Portland has many public buildings of note, the City Hall being a fine building, as also is the new Jefferson Opera House, just completed, and of which Portland is justly proud.

Near the Longfellow Monument will be seen the very fine Public Library Building, which was

THE PUBLIC LIBRARY.

presented by the mayor of the city, and built of rough freestone, in the Romanesque design.

The Union Depot is one of the finest and best located of any in the county, with a magnificent open plaza of extensive proportions at its side.

Days might be advantageously spent here, and in its vicinity, with drives to Cape Elizabeth and Deering Park; boats to the islands; or cars to Songo River and Bridgton, the home of Artemus Ward, and back in seven hours.

Altogether, Portland is a lovely and interesting city, and while there take a drive through Deering's Woods, for—

"Deering's Woods are fresh and fair,
And with joy that is almost pain
My heart goes back to wander there,
And among the dreams of the days that were
I find my lost youth again."

Progressive Euchre.

On Friday evening, September 3d, the guests gathered in the Amusement Room, which was prettily decorated with ferns and flowers, for their usual game of progressive euchre. There were twelve tables; sixteen games were played. The highest number for the ladies was fourteen, and the same for the gentlemen. Mrs. C. G. Mitchell and Miss Myers cut for the first ladies' prize. Mrs. Mitchell won the first prize, a lovely glass bonbon dish with gold trimmings; Miss Myers the second, a pocket-book and card-case combined; Mrs. Keene won the third prize, a brass candlestick; Mrs. E. P. Ricker the consolation prize, a bottle of cologne water. The gentlemen's first prize went to Mrs. Moulton, a beautiful plate decorated with violets; Mrs. P. Adams won the second gentlemen's prize, a statuette; Mr. Knowles the third, a Dresden clock; and Miss Mitchell the consolation, a bottle of cologne water. The ladies showed excellent taste in their selection of the prizes, and the evening was one of the most enjoyable of the season.

New Books.

Hill's Manual of Social and Business Forms; by Thomas E. Hill.

FROM CAPT. A. J. FARRAR.

Through the Wilds; by Capt. A. J. Farrar. 2 copies.
How Plants Grow; by Asa Gray.
Field, Forest, and Garden Botany; by Asa Gray.
Manual of Botany; by Asa Gray.

FROM MRS. SARAH C. WORTHINGTON.

Stephen Grellet; by William Guest.
Present Tenses; by F. B. Meyer.
Love Made Perfect; by Rev. Andrew Murray.
The Christian's Secret; by Hannah Whitall Smith.
A Retrospect; by J. Hudson Taylor.
Pleasure and Profit; by D. L. Moody.
Where Kitty Found Her Soul; by Mrs. J. H. Walworth.

FROM MRS. S. W. KEENE.

The Birth of a Soul; by Mrs. A. Phillips.

Just Figures.

October 15, 1895, the Library contained 854 books. September 10, 1896, 1,435 books, a gain of 581 during its second season. September 2, 1897, 1,843 books, a gain of 408 during its third season thus far.

The record for the highest number of books taken out in a single day is still held by Monday, August 24, 1896, for 72 books. The next highest is Sunday, August 29, 1897, for 56 books. The fourth week of August, 1897, holds the record for the highest daily average, it being 43, while the second week of September, 1896, was the highest in that year, being 40 daily average.

In August, 1896, 1,107 books were taken out, and in August, 1897, 1,198 was the number, being an excess of 91 over the same month of last year.

The August record in full for 1897 is as follows: Books taken out, 1,198, an average of 39 daily. The average for each day in the week was Sundays, 45; Thursdays, 42; Fridays, 41; Mondays, 40; Saturdays, 39; Wednesdays, 32; and Tuesdays, 31, showing Sunday to have been the busiest day of the week, and Tuesday the least. The average for the first seven days of August was 34, the second 38, the third 39, and the fourth 43, with the odd last three days averaging 39 per day.

This record shows Sundays, Thursdays, Fridays, and Mondays to be above the average, Saturday an average day, and Wednesdays and Tuesdays below the average, and a handling of 2,396 books during the month.

The Art Store.

Have you made any purchases at Mrs. Mallouf's, at the hotel corner? If not, just step inside and see the multitude of rare and costly goods displayed. It is like an Oriental bazaar, filled with finery, and will certainly suggest some souvenir to take away with you when you go, October 15th.

Children's Column.

The individual who gets on in the world most honorably is he who makes a study of his own nature instead of the nature of other people. He will find close at hand both good and bad qualities, and the study of man should be himself.

The following story was told by Mr. Long-fellow to a friend who related it to the writer:

How Evangeline Came to be Written.

Longfellow, Hawthorne, and a noted lawyer were dining together. The lawyer turned to Hawthorne and said, "Why don't you write a story of Acadia? There is so much material that is interesting in the Provinces." Hawthorne tossed his head and said: "I can't write anything about it." A few days after this, Longfellow was talking with Hawthorne and asked him if he intended to write on the subject of Acadia. Hawthorne said "No," and then Longfellow told him that he would take the subject and write a poem. And the beautiful story of Evangeline was written.

Little Edward Pulsifer, four years old, was tired of looking at the rain and wanted to go out to play. Presently he said—"Mamma, turn off the faucet, I want to go out and play." Mamma explained that she could regulate the bath-tub, but not the weather.

The Castle Builder.

A gentle boy, with soft and silken locks,
A dreamy boy, with brown and tender eyes,
A castle-builder, with his wooden blocks,
And towers that touch imaginary skies.

A fearless rider on his father's knee,
An eager listener unto stories told
At the Round Table of the nursery,
Of heroes and adventures manifold.

There will be other towers for thee to build;
There will be other steeds for thee to ride;
There will be other legends, and all filled
With greater marvels, and more glorified.

Build on, and make thy castles high and fair,
Rising and reaching upward to the skies;
Listen to voices in the upper air,
Nor lose thy simple faith in mysteries.
—*Henry W. Longfellow.*

"Well, Teddy, have you been a good boy to-day?" asked his mother upon her return home late in the afternoon.

"No, ma'am," replied the truthful Ted.

"I hope you have not been a bad boy?"

"No, ma'am; not a very bad boy and not a very good boy—just comfortable!"
—*Harper's Round Table.*

"What were the Dark Ages?" asked the governess at the morning lessons.

"That must have been before spectacles were invented," guessed May.

"Oh, no!" interrupted Cedric; "I know why they were called the Dark Ages, because there were more knights then."—*Harper's Round Table.*

Golf.

The Poland Spring House and the Portland Golf Club played a team match on Friday, September 3d, 18 holes, match play. The Poland Spring team won, 20 to 6. The following are the names of the players and the ones they were matched against:

W. P. Comstock	. . . 3	Rev. C. Morton Sells .	0
W. Berri	 0	G. S. Ellis	 6
I. W. Chick	 7	W. C. Eaton	 0
J. H. Maginnis	. . . 4	W. C. Emerson	 0
H. Berri	 6	H. P. Frank	 0
Total	. . 20		6

A. H. Findlay and A. H. Fenn on Saturday, September 4th, played 18 holes match. Mr. Findlay won 2 up. In the afternoon they played another match and Mr. Fenn won 2 up. On Monday, September 6th, they played two matches and Mr. Findlay won in the morning 3 up, and in the afternoon Mr. Fenn won 7 up. They have now played 144 holes and Mr. Fenn is 5 holes up, which shows remarkably close golf, probably the closest that has been played in this country.

On Monday there was a handicap tournament, 18 holes medal play, for three prizes given by Dr. Daniel Kaisner of Philadelphia. First prize was won by Allyn Marsh; second prize, A. J. Secor; and third prize, F. L. Castner. The following are the scores in full:

	1st Round.	2d Round.	Gross.	Handicap.	Net.
Allyn Marsh	. . . 56	52	108	24	84
A. J. Secor	. . . 68	65	133	40	93
F. L. Castner	. . 57	55	112	16	96
H. P. Frank	. . . 62	63	125	28	97
B. P. Moulton	. . 70	68	138	38	100
F. M. Thompson	. 69	72	141	38	103
A. Palmer	. . . 57	64	121	16	105
J. H. Maginnis	. . 58	57	115	10	105
D. C. Nugent	. . 65	71	136	30	106
Miss Olive Gale	. 93	103	196	90	106
S. Ross Campbell	. 58	56	114	6	108
H. Berri	. . . 66	67	133	24	109
Walter Berri	. . 53	58	111	0	111
E. W. Olney	. . 54	71	125	14	111
W. P. Comstock	. 52	64	116	0	116
Geo. L. Osgood	. 71	79	150	34	116
Mrs. Geo. L. Osgood	110	107	217	100	117
S. P. Holton	. . . 64	70	134	16	118
Mrs. D. C. Nugent	112	113	225	100	125

Several did not hand in cards.

are No. 52, owned by Hiram Ricker & Sons, and Nos. 53, 54, 55, and 56.

Frank W. Cowles is a teacher of art in Boston and the head of the Cowles Art School. He is a member of the Boston Art Club and an exhibitor in many prominent galleries.

His picture, No. 22 in Alcove D, "In the Twilight," is an excellent illustration of his style in figure painting.

Among the welcome guests Tuesday, September 7th, were Mrs. E. M. Knight and Miss Knight of Boston. Mrs. Knight and Miss Knight always spend September at the Mansion House.

MARCUS WATERMAN.

Art Notes.

MARCUS WATERMAN, A. N. A., was born in Providence, R. I., and was educated at Brown University. He first worked in New York at his profession, and later opened a studio in Boston in 1874. In 1878 a collection of his works was sold in Boston, just previous to his European trip. At the Centennial Exhibition in 1876 his "Gulliver in Lilliput" attracted attention. He is an associate of the National Academy and a member of the Artists' Fund and American Water Color Societies.

No. 130, in Alcove A, is his only picture here, and was painted especially for this exhibition. It is called "In the Rue Annibas, Algiers," and is a very superior work, strong and beautiful in color, for which this artist is so justly famous.

Joseph H. Hatfield is so well known to visitors to the Poland Spring Exhibitions that an introduction seems hardly necessary. However, he was a pupil of Constant, Doucet, and Lefebvre, Paris, an exhibitor at all principal exhibitions in America, at the Paris Salon, and he received a silver medal at the Massachusetts Charitable Mechanics' Association, and second Hallgarten prize, New York, 1896. His pictures have been purchased by the Boston Art Club and other art galleries, public and private. At Poland, this season, his works

Tid-Bits.

Mr. J. C. Whitman of Boston is with us.

Mr. Charles S. Rea of Salem, Mass., is with us.

Buy pictures before it is "good-bye, pictures."

Mr. and Mrs. Henry H. Melville of Boston are here.

Mr. W. H. Amerman, Jr., of New York, is here.

Mr. H. C. Sears of Boston is at the Mansion House.

Mr. and Mrs. Winthrop Burr of New York are here.

The answer to the riddle in the last edition, is *a whale.*

Mr. I. W. Marshall of Yorklyn, Del., has returned.

Mr. R. I. Cox and Mrs. Cox of Chicago are with us.

Mr. and Mrs. Blackie of Denver, Col., have returned.

Mr. H. O. Seixas of New Orleans arrived September 4th.

Mr. C. C. Corbin has joined Mrs. Corbin at Poland Spring.

Mr. and Mrs. F. A. Sterling of Cleveland are at Poland Spring.

Mr. and Mrs. Ross and Miss A. M. Ross of Ipswich are here.

Mr. and Mrs. T. D. Covel of Fall River, Mass., are with us.

Mr. John K. Cilley and Miss A. L. Cilley of New York are here.

Mr. and Mrs. F. F. Cutter of Brookline, Mass., are at Poland Spring.

Mrs. A. H. Fenn has been a few days at the Poland Spring House.

Mr. A. B. Ivins and Mrs. Ivins of Philadelphia, Pa., are with us.

Mr. George Waymouth and Mrs. Waymouth of Cambridge are here.

Mrs. Raymond, *née* Annie Louise Cary, is at the Mt. Pleasant House.

Dr. and Mrs. Charles Wirgman of Philadelphia are at Poland Spring.

Among the welcome guests was Master Nelson F. Bartlett of Malden, Mass.

Mrs. H. O. Thomas of Brockton, Mass., arrived Tuesday, September 7th.

Mr. J. H. Mann and Mrs. Mann of Boston, arrived Monday, September 6th.

Mr. C. E. Buzby of Philadelphia arrived Thursday, September 9th.

Mr. Jeremiah J. Boyle of Cambridge, Mass., registered at the Mansion House.

Mr. F. Edward Long and Mrs. Long of New York are at the Mansion House.

Mr. and Mrs. I. H. Selma of New York registered Saturday, September 4th.

Dr. W. F. Carolin of Lowell, Mass., registered at the Poland Spring House.

Miss Hattie Reiley of Jamaica Plain is spending a few days at the Mansion House.

Mr. and Mrs. E. H. Whitney and Miss Lillian B. Whitney of Cambridge are with us.

Hon. E. B. Mallet, Jr., of Freeport, was a welcome guest Saturday, September 4th.

Mrs. C. A. Richards and Miss A. L. Richards of Boston, arrived Tuesday, September 7th.

After playing golf there is nothing so refreshing as Hinds' Honey and Almond Cream. Fact.

Mrs. George A. Hearn and Mrs. J. G. Brown of New York are at the Poland Spring House.

Miss Francis A. Stetson and Miss Jenny Roberts of Bangor are at the Mansion House.

Mrs. William Scott and Mr. Charles H. Scott of New York are at the Poland Spring House.

Miss Inez E. Hill of Augusta, Me., registered at the Mansion House, Saturday, September 4th.

I. De. L. Burckhalter, M.D., of Aiken, South Carolina, registered at the Poland Spring House.

Mrs. G. H. Leonard and Miss Gwendolen Leonard of Boston are at the Poland Spring House.

Mrs. Preston B. Keith and Miss Keith of Campello, Mass., are at the Poland Spring House.

Mr. W. G. Tobey and Mrs. G. W. Tobey of Portland, registered at the Poland Spring House.

Mr. J. Craven and Miss Craven of Jersey City were welcome guests on Monday, September 6th.

Mrs. G. W. Chauncey, Miss A. Chauncey, and Master W. Chauncey of Brooklyn, are at the Poland Spring House.

Mr. and Mrs. Hugh Porter, Miss Maud Porter, and Miss Madge Porter of New York City are at Poland Spring.

Mr. H. Kimball of New York and his sister, Mrs. W. L. Gage of Hartford, Conn., are at the Mansion House.

The Mt. Pleasant House reports every room in the house full Saturday night, September 4th, and that, without an excursion.

Miss Anna Pulsifer of Rochester, N. Y., was a welcome guest, Monday, September 6th. Miss Pulsifer is a daughter of Mrs. Martha Pulsifer.

It Appears Remarkable

That accidental death on the railways of Holland only average one a year.

That the Norwegian lives longer on an average than any other people.

That lobsters can smell.

That the greatest chain ever forged was made at Tipton Green Iron Works, and consists of oval links forged of 3½-inch rods, each link 20 inches long and 13 inches wide.

That "Big Ben," the great clock on the Parliament Buildings in London, did once actually strike thirteen.

That Louis XIV. of France reigned 72 years.

That greyhounds are found sculptured on Egyptian monuments, 5,000 years ago.

That C. H. McGurrin, official stenographer of the ninth judicial district of Michigan, holds the record of 208 words a minute on a type-writer. It was a memorized sentence repeated.

That the height of the tallest living woman is 9 feet. Her name is Ella Ewing, 24 years of age, and weighing 290 pounds.

That Imperial Tokay wine is unpurchasable. Not a gallon is ever disposed of, but it is all reserved for the Austrian imperial cellars.

New Pictures.

Miss Agnes Leavitt has replaced the two pictures of hers which were recently sold, by two others. The large picture is replaced by "Birch Trees in Autumn," No. 72, and the smaller one by a "Clump of Young Birches," which are conspicuous figures on the Poland Golf Links, down in front of the Poland Spring House. Both these pictures will well repay a visit to the Gallery. Miss Leavitt is stopping at Mrs. Colly's cottage, near the hotel, where other of her pictures may be seen.

Miss Leavitt will give another private exhibition of her work at Mrs. Colly's cottage, next below Mr. Nevens's, on the road to the lake, directly in front of the Poland Spring House, on Tuesday next, from 10 to 1 and 2 to 5.30, and all interested in excellent water-colors will be well repaid for the few minutes the trip will occupy.

Frank S. Nugent of Winnipeg, Manitoba, has been making a visit to his brother, Mr. Dan. C Nugent. Mr. Nugent is returning from a professional trip to London, where he represented the colony at the Queen's Jubilee, and comes back laden with interesting souvenirs.

FRANK CARLOS GRIFFITH, } EDITORS.
NETTIE M. RICKER.   }

PUBLISHED EVERY SUNDAY MORNING DURING THE MONTHS
OF JULY, AUGUST, AND SEPTEMBER, IN THE INTERESTS OF

POLAND SPRING AND ITS VISITORS.

All contributions relative to the guests of Poland Spring
will be thankfully received.

To insure publication, all communications should reach the
editors not later than Wednesday preceding day of issue.

All parties desiring rates for advertising in the HILL-TOP
should write the editors for same.

The subscription price of the HILL-TOP is $1.00 for the
season, post-paid. Single copies will be mailed at 10c. each.

Address,

EDITORS "HILL-TOP,"
Poland Spring House,
South Poland, Maine.

PRINTED AT JOURNAL OFFICE, LEWISTON.

Sunday, September 12, 1897.

Editorial.

THERE is an end to all things excepting circles
and expeditions in search of the North Pole,—
hence the HILL-TOP season, which has run a
full cycle, ceases with the present number.

There are things which remind us of the dying
man who smelled the cooking of ham, and, remarking that it had an agreeable smell, requested some,
to which his faithful spouse replied, that he could
not have that, for that was for the funeral.

There are events in the calendar which the
HILL-TOP would like to witness and chronicle;
there are tournaments and jousts and evoluting
euchres, hops, and concerts, and the coming of old
friends yet to arrive whom the HILL-TOP will not
be here to greet. "There will come a time,
Audrey," and that time will come soon again, when
the little perennially-green sheet will bloom and
blossom like a June rose and start in fresh to note
the pleasures of the throng.

Our Arithmetical Editor reports that our circulation is good and that it is a great pity we should
be obliged to expire under the statute of limita-
tions, but, as good old Mrs. Partington might
reply, we do not know but what that is as good a
place to select as Cæsar chose, under the statue of
Pompey.

However, in these brief parting remarks of
'97 we may say we have endeavored to do our
duty faithfully and fearlessly ; and in a few well-
chosen words, which it is unfortunate for our reputation for originality Abraham Lincoln uttered
first, we will add, "with malice towards none,
with charity for all."

In a few more days all that we are may be
consulted between two green cloth covers in a glass
case in the Poland Spring Library, and we know
no better place to repose during the winter than in
that delightful spot. And now

"Farewell! a word that must be,—and hath been,—
A sound that makes us linger; yet—farewell."

Sunday Services.

Mass was held in the Music Hall, Sunday,
September 5th, by Rev. Father Chase.

Rev. Edward C. Moore of Providence, R. I.,
preached in the Music Hall at 11 A.M., Sunday,
September 5th. His text was from St. Mark,
15 : 21—"And they compel one Simon, a Cyrenian,
who passed by, coming out of the country, the
father of Alexander and Rufus to bear his cross."

Rev. Edward C. Moore addressed the Sunday
evening congregation in the dining-room. His
text was from St. Luke, 5 : 5. There were many
guests present as well as employees.

Mt. Pleasant House Concert.

ARTISTS.

Mr. Felix Winternitz, } Mr. W. H. Caplon, }	. . . . Violins
Mr. Wm. Howard,	. . . . Viola Accompanist
Mr. Carl Behr,	. . . .
Mr. O. L. Southland,	. . . . 'Cello
Mr. Max Guetter,	. . . . Flute
Mr. F. H. Coolidge,	. . . . Clarinet
Mr. W. B. Mayberry,	. . . . Cornet

SUNDAY EVENING, SEPTEMBER 5, 1897,
AT 8.30 O'CLOCK.
Mrs. Marian Van Duyn, Contralto.

1. Overture—Nabucodnosor . . . . Verdi
2. Intermezzo—From Naila . . . . Delibes
3. Selection—From Traviata . . . . Verdi
4. Flirtation . . . . Steck
     String Orchestra.
5. { Song—To the Evening Star—From Tannhauser.
   { Pilgrim's Chorus—From Tannhauser . . Wagner
5. March—From Symphonie Leonore . . . . . Raff

Mr. and Mrs. Herman Adler and Master George
Adler of New York were welcome guests at the
Mansion House on Saturday, September 4th.

Just Like Live Teeth.

A recent improvement in artificial teeth, and perhaps the most important one made within half a century, consists in placing a little pink nerve in each tooth precisely similar to the pulp, or what is commonly called the nerve, in the natural organ. This small, but important portion, previously overlooked in the manufacture of artificial dentures, explains why, under certain lights and shades, they have been so conspicuously false.
—*Boston Herald.*

Bell Telephone, Calumet and Hecla, Air Brakes, or Kloudike Gold Mines are not in it with the fortune in store for this inventor. Already we behold a pile of discarded, pale, porcelain, uncanny looking objects, as large as the pyramids of Cheops, when it becomes generally known that "live teeth," with nerves that are proof against pain, can be had just as easily as the weird ones, and it is not a second-hand tooth either, but made to order, and correct measure taken.

Why, bless us, the next thing we know, live legs and arms will be imitated, with nerves, veins, arteries, and muscles, and soon we shall hear of some overdaring but impecunious Johnny being ejected from the home of his sweetheart by an irate parent, immediately in front of a real live natural false leg.

But the little pink nerve which hereafter must be in all teeth, will enable us to exclaim truthfully, "With all thy false, I love thee still."

Among the welcome guests Friday, September 3d, were Mrs. B. F. Sturtevant of Jamaica Plain, Mass., and Mr. and Mrs. S. P. Hibbard of Boston.

The Laurel House.

"The fame of Lakewood has traveled too widely to make necessary any extended mention of the place. It is to-day, without doubt, the most popular winter resort of the middle east. Its climate is remarkably equable and mild, permitting outdoor sports throughout the winter, and its location is within nine miles of the Atlantic, in the midst of the Jersey pine land. Within about fifty miles of the two great cities, New York and Philadelphia, it is within easy reach of all New England, as well as the central portion of the country, and with a temperature which affords easy escape from the rigors of a northern winter, the early fall months are particularly delightful to throngs of those interested in golfing, cross-country riding, and other outdoor sports." The Laurel House opens October 1st; in the meantime, the Waumbek, under the same management, is still open.

Concert by the Shakers.

On Tuesday evening last a very fine concert was given in the Music Room by the E. Canterbury Shakers. The quartettes were especially well given, and in "Massa's in the Cold, Cold Ground," the imitation of the banjo accompaniment was particularly well rendered. The selections were well made, and the quiet, demure character of the entertainers gave it a very pleasing effect. The collection taken up amounted to $77.45.

Mr. and Mrs. John G. Noyes, Mr. and Mrs. Charles R. Knowles, Miss Myers, and Miss Young of Albany, N. Y., are at the Poland Spring House.

HADDON HALL, Atlantic City, N. J., U. S. A.

Tid=Bits.

Miss McCarty of Brooklyn is here.

Mr. C. A. Campbell of Boston is here.

Miss Leland of New York has returned.

Mrs. J. A. Swan of Newport, R. I., is here.

Mr. and Mrs. George A. Miner of Boston are here.

Mr. and Mrs. F. A. Gaskill of Worcester are here.

Mr. and Mrs. Charles E. Jones of Brookline are here.

Mr. C. W. Shaw of Boston arrived Thursday, September 9th.

Mr. and Mrs. Charles Morton of Boston, are at Poland Spring.

Mr. Charles W. Haskell of Rockford, Ill., is at Poland Spring.

Mrs. H. Randall and sister of Lewiston spent Thursday here.

Mr. W. P. Knapp of New York arrived Thursday, September 9th.

Mr. and Mrs. John B. Morgan of Philadelphia are at Poland Spring.

Mrs. George M. Parsons of Columbus, Ohio, is at Poland Spring.

Mr. B. F. Morgan and Mrs. Morgan of Wilkesbarre, Pa., are here.

Mrs. George Buckham and Miss McNulty of New York are here.

Mr. A. H. Findlay of Boston registered at the Poland Spring House.

Mr. Arthur Sias and Mrs. Sias of New York, arrived September 8th.

Mr. Arthur H. Dakin of Boston, arrived Wednesday, September 8th.

Mr. and Mrs. J. S. Piatt of Auburn were with us Thursday, September 8th.

Mrs. H. M. Kent and Miss M. E. Simonds of Boston are at Poland Spring.

Mr. W. H. C. Follansby and Mrs. Follansby of Exeter, N. H., are here.

Mr. Alfred S. Malcomson and Miss Malcomson of New York, are with us.

Mr. K. C. Elliott and the Misses Elliott of Philadelphia are at Poland Spring.

Mrs. A. Battin and Miss E. Iuslee of New York arrived Thursday, September 9th.

Mr. and Mrs. D. E. Conklin of Baltimore, and Miss Mary A. Crane of Boston, are here.

Mr. and Mrs. J. B. Lawrence, Jr., and Miss M. N. Lawrence of New York are with us.

Mr. and Mrs. A. Marburg and Master W. A. Marburg of New York are at Poland Spring.

Mr. William S. Clough and Mrs. M. P. Clough of Lynn, arrived Wednesday, September 8th.

Mrs. Charles D. Hammer and Miss Hammer of Brookline are at the Poland Spring House.

Mr. Preston B. Keith of Brockton, Mass., has joined Mrs. Keith at the Poland Spring House.

Mr. Joseph Chadbourn and Mrs. Chadbourn of Wilmington, N. C., are at the Poland Spring House.

Mr. and Mrs. Charles S. Leete and Miss Ida L. Leete of New Haven, are at the Poland Spring House.

Mr. and Mrs. Elias Thomas, Miss Helen B. Thomas, and Mr. W. W. Thomas, 2d, of Portland, have returned.

Mr. E. H. Dyer of Pittsburg and Mr. C. P. Mattocks of Portland, registered at the Poland Spring House.

Mr. Samuel W. Parker and Mrs. Parker of Chicago arrived at the Poland Spring House on September 7th.

Mr. and Mrs. Theodore Marburg of Baltimore, and Mr. William A. Marburg of New York, are at Poland Spring.

Mr. and Mrs. E. Hayes Trowbridge of New Haven, Conn., registered at the Poland Spring House, September 9th.

Mrs. N. E. C. Smith, wife of the Rev. Mr. Smith of Dorchester, and Mrs. C. G. Beeke are at the Poland Spring House.

Among the welcome guests on Wednesday, September 8th, were Mr. and Mrs. Curtis Guild and Miss Guild of Boston.

Among the welcome guests, Tuesday, September 7th, were Mr. Albert E. Carroll and Miss Julia S. Carpenter of Providence.

Col. Charles H. Greenleaf and Mr. C. F. Eastman of Littleton, N. H., were welcome guests on Thursday, September 9th.

Rev. and Mrs. Kirkland Husk of New York, the Misses Hewlett, and Mr. George Hewlett, registered at the Poland Spring House.

Congressman Dingley and Mrs. Dingley, Mr. and Mrs. E. N. Dingley of Lewiston, were welcome guests on Thursday, September 9th.

Mr. and Mrs. W. W. Thomas, Jr., of Portland, were recently at the Poland Spring House. Mr. Thomas was formerly U. S. Minister to Sweden.

Still Another Recollection.

SPEAKING of people with odd names, we recollect another in the little city of our youth—one I. William Knott. His father's name was Canby Knott, and being always annoyed at being called "Can-not," he meant that his son should reverse the negative implied by his name and be forever called "I. Will" (Chicago papers please notice). He forgot until it was too late that the surname continued the negative again another generation, and of late years, he being still living, he is frequently called by the very wicked small boy, "Nit."

Knott was born lucky, all the same, as was another Knott from Kentucky who protruded from the same genealogical tree, and made himself famous by a speech on Duluth, "the zenith city of the unsalted sea."

Knott became famous first by the singular result of a singular trial. He had traded for a piece of land with a man named Willing, and gave two hundred dollars down, and a horse, and a mortgage back for a couple hundred more. In the blank form of the mortgage used, where it says "I, ——, agree to," etc., his name was inserted by an ignorant or careless party, not a lawyer (to save expense), "Will. Not," just as he phonetically was called, and no one discovered the peculiarity (except Knott) until the payment became due, when Knott made no move in that direction. A letter came—another and another—but no notice was taken, until a lawyer was called in and wrote, also, but with the same result.

To make a long matter short, Knott was sued, and Knott won, on the defense that he never intended to pay any more for the land, and that the mortgage purposely stated that fact—"I will not agree," etc. Furthermore, Knott said it was all a joke, anyway, and Willing agreed to it at the time as a blind to his wife. At one time Knott was willing, but Willing was not willing, to accept a compromise; then Knott fought to a finish, thinking that even if he lost the case the advertisement was worth the expense. Technicalities and the longest purse gave the case to Knott, who henceforth was world-famous.

Knott was always doing extraordinary and wild things, and so, instead of sending warming-pans to the West Indies, as Lord Timothy Dexter did once upon a time, he shipped—what? Not ice to Greenland, but ice-cream freezers to Norway. How about that? He sent a silver-plated one to the royal household, with a recipe for making the delicious food, and it "caught on" great, and every soul in Norway must *frappé* his cream at once, and Knott's fortune grew amazingly.

Knott was not smart, or even bright, but he was always blundering into these things, as he did into the one which gave him his greatest lift. An early chum had worked hard all his life, and at last developed a wonderful patent which cost thousands of dollars to manufacture, and got it all into working order, when another fellow invented an improvement and reaped all the benefit. Knott was grunting over the fastening of his shoe one day, and presently he made a new fastening which can be made for fifty cents a thousand, and revolutionized the business, and his royalties at one cent a shoe became enormous.

Luck is a great thing, and some people, like Will Knott, have it thrown at them in perfect avalanches.

———

Professor W. E. Sargent and Mrs. Sargent of Hebron, Me., Mrs. V. A. Scribner and the Misses Scribner of Brooklyn, were the guests of Mrs. B. F. Sturtevant at the Poland Spring House, Tuesday, September 7th.

Another Noted Visitor.

ON Thursday last, Poland Spring was favored with a call from Congressman and Mrs. Dingley and Mr. and Mrs. E. N. Dingley. This is the first visit our Maine statesman has made to Poland the present year, and he was delighted to find so much that was new and interesting.

After an inspection of the Maine State Building and its Art Gallery, he remarked to the curator that he was delighted to find so superior a collection of paintings, and furthermore that he was surprised at the ability to procure such fine specimens of the best artists' work to be sent down into Maine for so long a time.

He found occasion to compliment all the fine additions to the building, its decoration and its library, and in reference to its collection of portraits of Maine's prominent sons, which adorn the walls, a little incident was related to him of a former visitor who inquired of the librarian if Mr. Reed had ever been to Washington.

This elicited a similar anecdote from Mr. Dingley to this effect : His daughter, Miss Dingley, was recently visiting in New York, and in conversation with a young lady with whom she became acquainted, she (Miss Dingley) was asked if her father was in Congress. On being informed that he was, the conversation eventually drifted on to the tariff, whereon Miss Dingley was seriously asked if her father *was interested in the tariff*.

Mr. Dingley's call was productive of much pleasure to all who had the good fortune to meet our distinguished neighbor, and the wish is father to the thought that he may find time to make a more prolonged visit.

The Woodstock Inn.

It is never too late to do good, and if, even now in our last issue, we call attention to that delightful resort, which is open the year around, we shall be doing a good deed. See the cut in another column. They have fine golf links, and the advantages of a public library; and in the winter, all the seasonable sports. The hotel is located in a lovely New England village on the Ottanquechee River, and the cycling is said to be fine. Carriage and bicycle livery are connected with the hotel. Passenger elevator and all modern requirements. Their advertisement may be seen elsewhere.

Miss Ella M. Chamberlin, whose whistling was so much enjoyed a few weeks ago, has composed two pieces of music, "Love is All," and "O Wake, My Love." Oliver Ditson Company are the publishers.

Brake Rides.

Mrs. James Swan gave a delightful brake ride on Friday, September 3d. The party included Mrs. Robert Dornan, Mrs. W. H. Brooks, Mrs. William Bersi, Mrs. Thomas Gale, Mrs. Samuel Treat, Mrs. J. C. Chappell, and Miss Murphy. They took the charming drive around Sabbath-Day Lake and through Peterson Woods.

On Saturday, September 4th, the following party, Mr. and Mrs. Treat, Mr. and Mrs. Dornan, Mr. and Mrs. Brooks, Mrs. Swan, and Miss Murphy, enjoyed a brake ride over Harris Hill.

Business.

At the time of writing, the business at Poland Spring is simply phenomenal. With this great hotel *full;* arrivals, sent outside to the "emergency" rooms, at Mr. Hiram Ricker's cottage, the extra and unusual quarters, where guests are sent at the high tide of August business, and the register showing pages of new arrivals daily to take the place of those departing, the proprietors may lay the flattering unction to their souls, that they have a very popular resort, and made so by their untiring efforts to please. With this number THE HILL-TOP expires, with the battle raging thick about it. *Au revoir.*

Musical Programme.

SUNDAY EVENING, SEPTEMBER 12, 1897.

1. March . . . . Lachner
2. Cello Solo.
   - { a. Romanza . . . . Popper
   - { b. La Cinquantaine . . . . Marie
   Mr. E. Loeffler.
3. { a. Remembrance . . . Mrs. Henry Carmichael
   { b. Impromptu
4. Flute Solo.
   Fantasia . . . . Briccialdi
   Mr. A. Brooke.
5. { a. Chanson D'Amour . . . . Jonas
   { b. Fly Minuet . . . . Czibulka
6. Selection—Cavalleria Rusticana . . . . Mascagni

Miss Mabelle Carroll of Boston has joined Mr. and Mrs. Carpenter at the Poland Spring House.

Captain and Mrs. Charles Deering, and Miss Crane of Boston, registered at the Poland Spring House. Captain Deering is of the steamer Portland, running between Portland and Boston.

Mrs. Henry Carmichael of Malden, Mass., is the composer of several choice selections which have been given at various times by the orchestra at the Poland Spring House. Her compositions have been much enjoyed, and two, "Remembrance" and "Impromptu," will be given by the orchestra Sunday evening. "Remembrance" was played by the Boston Symphony Orchestra at the promenade concerts last spring.

Arrivals.

POLAND SPRING HOUSE.

FROM SEPTEMBER 3 TO 9, 1897.

Ametman, W. H., Jr.	New York
Atherton, L. B.	Lewiston
Buckham, Mrs. George	New York
Buzby, C. E.	Philadelphia
Battin, Mrs. A.	New York
Beck, Mrs. C. G.	Boston
Boyce, A. P.	Sharon, Mass.
Boyce, A. Parks	Sharon, Mass.
Bleed, F. W.	Mass.
Blanchard, Mr. and Mrs. Denman	Lynn
Blettell, Mrs. W. H.	New York
Bartlett, Nelson F.	Malden
Beel, Mr. and Mrs. Winthrop	New York
Bain, William H.	Boston
Bartlett, Miss	Lewiston
Burckhatten, I. de S., M.D.	Aiken, S. C.
Blann, Lee	Lewiston
Blackie, Mr. and Mrs. J.	Denver
Biggs, M. M.	Lewiston
Brown, Mrs. J. G.	New York
Chadbourne, Mr. and Mrs. E. R.	Lewiston
Chadbourn, Mr. and Mrs. James H.	Wilmington, N. C.
Conklin, Mr. and Mrs. D. E.	Baltimore
Crane, Miss Mary A.	Boston
Clough, Micajah P.	Lynn
Clough, Wm. S.	Lynn
Cushing, Mr. and Mrs. C. B.	New York
Cushing, Miss	New York
Carroll, Miss Mabelle	Boston
Cilley, Miss Alice L.	New York
Craven, J.	Jersey City
Craven, Miss	Jersey City
Carroll, Albert E.	Boston
Carpenter, Julia S.	Providence
Cummings, E. S.	Lewiston
Colby, Frederick W.	Boston
Catolin, Dr. William F.	Lowell
Corbin, C. C.	Webster
Cutler, Mr. and Mrs. F. F.	Brookline
Cox, Mr. and Mrs. R. I.	Chicago
Campbell, C. A.	Boston
Cunningham, Mrs. F.	Boston
Cilley, John K.	New York
Chauncey, Mrs. George W.	Brooklyn
Chauncey, Miss Adelaide	Brooklyn
Chauncey, Master Wallace	Brooklyn
Clark, Mr. and Mrs. John N.	New York
Covel, Mr. and Mrs. T. D.	Fall River
Coombs, G. M.	Lewiston
Dyer, E. H.	Pittsburg
Dingley, Mr. and Mrs. Nelson	Lewiston
Dingley, Mr. and Mrs. E. N.	Lewiston
Deering, Mr. and Mrs. Chas.	Boston
Dakin, Arthur H.	Boston
Denny, Mr. and Mrs. Charles A.	Leicester
Dennett, O.	New York
Daly, Frank A.	Lowell
Eastman, C. F.	Littleton
Elliott, the Misses	Philadelphia
Elliott, A. H.	Philadelphia
Ellis, Mrs. B. F.	Boston
Findlay, A. H.	Boston
Greenleaf, C. H.	Franconia
Guild, Mr. and Mrs. Curtis	Boston
Gaskill, Mr. and Mrs. F. A.	Worcester
Guild, Miss	Boston
Gilmaine, C. Gerome	Washington
Green, Mrs. Martha	Somerville
Griffin, Mr. and Mrs. H. M.	Onset
Gordon, Mr. and Mrs. F. A.	Boston
Gray, W. H.	Portland
Hammer, Mrs. Charles D.	Brookline
Hammer, Miss	Brookline

Hood, Alice	Lewiston
Hearn, Mrs. George A.	New York
Hotchkiss, Miss S. V.	New Haven
Hanscom, H. C.	New York
Hatt, Miss Mary A.	Brooklyn
Hibbard, Mr. and Mrs. S. P.	Boston
Haskell, Charles W.	Rockford, Ill.
Harding, Mr. and Mrs. H. M.	New York
Harding, Marion	New York
Husk, Rev. and Mrs. Kirkland	New York
Hewlett, Miss	New York
Hewlett, Miss Josephine	New York
Hewlett, P. W.	New York
Inslee, Miss E.	New York
Ivins, Mr. and Mrs. A. B.	Philadelphia
Jones, Mr. and Mrs. Charles E.	Brookline
Jensen, Miss L. M.	New York
Knapp, W. P.	New York
Kent, Mrs. H. M.	Boston
Keith, Mr. and Mrs. Preston B.	Campello
Keith, Miss	Campello
Keep, Mrs. Charles T. B.	Orange, N. J.
Knowles, Mr. and Mrs. Charles B.	Albany
Knighton, Mr. and Mrs. E.	Boston
Leland, Miss	New York
Lawrence, Mr. and Mrs. John B., Jr.	New York
Lawrence, Miss M. N.	New York
Lete, Mr. and Mrs. Chas. G.	New Haven
Lete, Miss Ida L.	New Haven
Lombard, M. L.	Everett, Mass.
Lee, Mr. and Mrs. Stephen	Lewiston
LeMassena, A., Jr.	Newark
Lawrence, Miss J.	Boston
Leonard, Mrs. G. H.	Boston
Leonard, Miss Gwendolin	Boston
Livingstone, Miss	New York
Liscomb, Mr. and Mrs. J. F.	Portland
Liscomb, Miss M.	Portland
Lynch, T. J.	Beverly
Mattocks, C. P.	Portland
McNulty, Miss	New York
Morgan, Mr. and Mrs. John B	Philadelphia
Marburg, Mr. and Mrs. A.	New York
Marburg, Master W. A.	New York
Minel, Mr. and Mrs. Geo. A.	Columbus
Marburg, W. A.	New York
Marburg, Mr. and Mrs. Theodore	Baltimore
Malcomson, Alfred S.	New York
Malcomson, Miss	New York
McCarty, Miss	Brooklyn
Morton, Mr. and Mrs. Charles	Boston
Morgan, Mr. and Mrs. B. F.	Wilkesbarre
Mann, Mr. and Mrs. Jonathan B.	Boston
Melville, Mr. and Mrs. Henry H.	Boston
Morton, Katie	Grand Rapids
McCormick, Jessie	Providence
Millet, Miss	Brooklyn
Marsh, Mrs. H.	Boston
Myers, Mr. and Mrs. John G.	Albany
Myers, Miss	Albany
Mallett, E. B., Jr.	Freeport
Millet, W. R.	Lewiston
O'Donnell, Queen	Lewiston
O'Donnell, Theresa	Lewiston
O'Donnell, Winnie	Lewiston
O'Shea, Mr. and Mrs. Thomas E.	New York
Platt, Mr. and Mrs. J. S.	Auburn
Parsons, Mrs. Geo. M.	Columbus
Perkins, Mrs. Mary A.	Mechanic Falls
Plummer, E.	Lisbon Falls
Parker, Mr. and Mrs. Samuel W.	Chicago
Pearce, Henry C.	New York
Porter, Mr. and Mrs. Hugh	New York
Porter, Miss Maud	New York
Porter, Miss Madge	New York
Randall, Mrs. H.	Lewiston
Ridley, Alice	Lewiston
Richards, Mrs. C. A.	Boston
Richards, Miss A. L.	Boston
Rea, Charles S.	Salem
Robertson, Miss	New Haven

Rice, John O.	Portland
Ross, Mr. and Mrs. J.	Ipswich
Ross, Miss A. W.	Ipswich
Rowland, William	New York
Riordan, P. M.	Beverly
Simonds, Miss M. E. J.	Boston
Shaw, C. W.	Boston
Smith, Mrs. W. E. C.	Boston
Swan, Mrs. J. A.	Newport
Sias, Mr. and Mrs. Arthur W.	New York
Stevens, George D.	Malden
Smith, Payson	Portland
Saboutin, T.	Lewiston
Sanborn, Miss Mabel	Boston
Sargent, Mr. and Mrs. W. E.	Hebron
Scribner, Mrs. V. A.	Brooklyn
Scribner, Ella V.	Brooklyn
Scribner, Mary J.	Brooklyn
Staples, S. O	Boston
Scott, Mrs. William	New York
Scott, Charles H.	New York
Sturtevant, Mrs. B. F.	Jamaica Plain
Selina, Mr. and Mrs. J. H.	New York
Seixas, H. O.	New Orleans
Stelling, Mr. and Mrs. F. A.	Cleveland
Shortell, J. F.	Salem
Sanborn, Miss Helen J.	Somerville
Scott, Mr. and Mrs. Charles W.	Springfield
Trowbridge, Mr. and Mrs. E. Hayes	New Haven
Tobey, Mr. and Mrs. W. G.	Portland
Title, J. H.	Portland
Townshend, Mrs. C. H.	New Haven
Thomas, Mrs. H. O.	Brockton
Thomas, Mr. and Mrs. Elias	Portland
Thomas, Miss Helen B.	Portland
Thomas, W. W., 2d	Portland
Thomas, Mr. and Mrs. W. W., Jr.	Portland
Thomas, Elias, Jr.	Portland
Townsend, R. H. L.	New York
Welsh, Willard	Malden
Willard, Mrs. Sarah S.	Worcester
Wirgman, Dr. and Mrs. Charles	Philadelphia
Waid, Mrs. E. R.	New Haven
Weymouth, Mr. and Mrs. George	Cambridge
Weed, Mr. and Mrs. George E.	New York
Wales, Mr. and Mrs. Joseph H.	Boston
Whitney, Mr. and Mrs. E. H.	Cambridge
Whitney, Miss Lillian B.	Cambridge
Wentworth, W. G.	Canton, Mass
Wilkinson, Harry C.	Lewiston
Walker, Mr. and Mrs. C. T.	Lewiston
Walker, Miss J.	Portland
Young, Miss	Albany
Zanoni	New York

MANSION HOUSE.

Adler, Mr. and Mrs. Herman	New York
Adler, George Herman	New York
Adams, S. L.	West Gray
Beacham, Mr. and Mrs. R. H.	Portsmouth
Buzby, Miss Annie K.	Rosemont, Pa.
Buzby, G. P.	Rosemont, Pa.
Bayle, J. J.	Cambridge
Conway, Mrs. Charles H.	Lynn
Conway, Master Ned	Lynn
Cross, Dr. and Mrs. H. B.	Boston
Durant, Mrs. F. M.	Rosemont, Pa.
Donald, E. P.	Portland
Evans, Miss L. B.	Boston
Follansby, Mr. and Mrs. W. H. C.	Exeter
Felt, Mrs. William H.	Lynn
Graves, Miss M. E.	Rosemont, Pa.
Graves, Horace Curtel	New York
Gage, Mrs. W. L.	Hartford
Hait, Mrs. W. R.	Rosemont, Pa.
Hait, Dorothy	Rosemont, Pa.
Hoyt, Mrs. L. E.	Rosemont, Pa.
Hill, Miss Inez E.	Augusta, Me.
Ibelin, Miss	. Toronto
Knight, Mrs. E. M.	Boston
Knight, Miss	Boston
Klaus, Mr. and Mrs. Harry	New York
Klaus, Miss Maude R.	New York

Klaus, Master William, Jr.	New York
Marshall, I. W.	Yorklyn, Del.
Ryan, C. E., Jr.	Landenburg, Pa.
Roberts, Miss Jenny	Bangor
Reiley, Hattie S.	Jamaica Plain
Reid, Mrs. E. A.	New York
Reid, Miss	New York
Seals, H. C.	Boston
Small, S. W.	Portland
Stearns, W. H.	Portland
Stetson, Miss Frances A.	Bangor
Wardrop, Mrs.	Toronto
Wardrop, Miss	Toronto
Whitman, J. C.	Boston
Yorks, Dr. John R.	Philadelphia

Tid-Bits.

The small cuts used in the article on Portland were kindly loaned by the Passenger Department of the Maine Central Railroad, to which we are greatly indebted.

Among the welcome guests Tuesday, September 7th, were Mrs. C. H. Townshend and Miss S. V. Hotchkiss, Mrs. E. R. Waid and Miss Robertson of New Haven.

Should massage treatments be desired, remember that a thoroughly skilled masseuse is constantly in attendance at the Poland Spring House. Inquire at the office for Mrs. Robinson.

Mr. and Mrs. George E. Weed, Mr. and Mrs. Thomas E. O'Shea, Mr. William Rowland, and Miss Livingston of New York, registered at the Poland Spring House, September 4th.

Do you want a drive? Order a team from the livery. The drives about here abound in pleasant places, and there are outlying towns of pleasant and romantic interest to visit.

The Maine State Building and the Library are open from 9 A.M. to 9 P.M., excepting Sundays, when it is from 10 A.M. to 8.30 P.M. Books are free to guests, one to each person, to be retained one week. There are no fees whatever. Catalogues to the Art Exhibition are free, and are to be obtained in the Library.

Down by the spring is an encampment of Indians. Did you know it? They make bows and arrows as did their ancestors centuries ago, and who killed the flying Mudjokivis, or some-think of that sort, as he flew from limb to limb. Go thou and purchase a bow and emulate the aboriginal archers, and kill Mudjokivii.

En Passant.

Before closing a season, full of delightful experiences, let us mention the drive to Elmwood Farm, where Mr. Sanborn has such a number of the finest horses. It is worth a day's journey any time to see a fine animal, and there are scores. It is but a short drive, and you will be royally welcomed by this most genial gentleman.

Thistles.

TO DO THE LIFTING.

There was a crowd in the street, and the old farmer was naturally interested.

"What's that there gal been doin'?" he asked.

"O, she's a shoplifter," answered a city man in the crowd, "and has just been arrested."

"A what?" demanded the old farmer in astonishment.

"A shoplifter," repeated the city man.

"Does she use a derrick?"—*Chicago Post.*

A NATURAL QUESTION.

Pat—"Faith, it's meself has sot four or foive times, and dommed if Oi kin get a natural fortygraph at all."

Mike—"Shure, mon dear, kin yez expict a natural fortygraph when yez niver been naturalized yit?"—*Texas Siftings.*

LOOKED THAT WAY.

Mrs. Brown—"Does Mrs. Dorcas belong to the sewing circle?"

Brown—"I think so. I've noticed that her husband fastens his suspenders with a string."

—*New York Journal.*

Some of the vineyard owners in New York state are fattening hogs with their grapes. Perhaps we shall see advertisements of "champagne hams" next spring.

COMFORT FOR HER.

"Sometimes I think I shall never marry," said Miss Elder, in a burst of confidence.

"O, don't despair," replied Miss Flip; "we read in the Bible that Naomi was 580 years old when she married."—*Harlem Life.*

OVER THE ALMONDS.

"Do you know, Miss Barker, I'm mighty thankful."

"And what, Mr. Jones, are you thankful for?"

"That all my meals are not eaten in your company."

"Dear me! Not very complimentary, are you?"

"Indeed I am. I should starve to death just gazing at you."—*Harper's Bazaar.*

JUST LIKE THE OTHERS.

"Now don't try to tell me anything about honeymoons," said Mrs. Sprightly to her sentimental husband.

"And why not, pray?"

"Because I've basked in four of them, and you talk just like any novice."—*Detroit Free Press.*

Last Look Around.

If you get your gun and go a-hunting in the fall, take the Bangor & Aroostook Railroad to the happy hunting grounds away in the Aroostook county, where the moose and caribou are so plentiful you almost have to push them apart to get through the open. It is a great hunting and fishing country, and one cannot fail to come back with a bag full of game.

If "furthest north" be your object, Quebec has attractions which should not be overlooked, and Renfrew will fit you out with sealskins and the furs of other animals as you may desire.

Should your hunting experience cause you an injury to limb, there is the Curtis & Spindell Co. of Lynn, to provide elastic stockings, for sprained ankles or injured knees.

The HILL-TOP points the way to all the requirements of man, so never be without a copy, and subscribe now for another season.

The Mineral Exhibit.

The large meteorite recently discovered in the Sacramento Mountains, New Mexico, continues to attract much attention from scientific men throughout the world. The original weight was about 520 pounds, and analysis shows a composition of 91.39 per cent. of iron, 7.86 per cent. of nickel, and about half of one per cent. of cobalt. It is supposed that this meteor was seen to fall in 1876. Mr. Warren M. Foote, who published the first description last January, has sent a large slice of the iron to Poland Spring, and this and the fragments of the Cañon Diablo meteorite may be recorded as Poland's first guests from any other world than our own. The Sacramento Mountains specimen is a grand prize for some collector, the etched surface showing beautifully the Widmann-stätten figures distinctive of meteoric iron.

An Episcopal clergyman's wife living in southern Texas sends to Mrs. Hiram Ricker a large quantity of Mexican drawn work. Mrs. Ricker will be glad to show it to all who will call at her cottage. It is charity work, and the prices are very reasonable.

IT STANDS AT THE HEAD.

Unrivalled in Popularity!
Unsurpassed in Location!
Unapproached in Patronage!

THE

POLAND * SPRING * HOUSE

IS A SUPERB ILLUSTRATION OF

⊙ ⊙ ⊙ SUCCESS ⊙ ⊙ ⊙

EMBRACING AS IT DOES

ALL THE DESIRABLE FEATURES

EXPECTED IN THIS

The Leading Resort of America,

WHILE THE

MAINE STATE BUILDING

WITH ITS

SUPERB ART FEATURES

IS UNEQUALLED BY ANY SIMILAR ENTERPRISE

IN THE WORLD.

⊸ ⊙ ⊶

HIRAM RICKER & SONS (Incorporated),

PROPRIETORS.

MAINE STATE BUILDING.